Learning C# Programming
with Unity 3D

Learning C# Programming with Unity 3D

Second Edition

Alex Okita

CRC Press
Taylor & Francis Group
Boca Raton London New York

CRC Press is an imprint of the
Taylor & Francis Group, an **informa** business

AN A K PETERS BOOK

CRC Press
Taylor & Francis Group
6000 Broken Sound Parkway NW, Suite 300
Boca Raton, FL 33487-2742

International Standard Book Number-13: 978-1-138-33681-0 (paperback)
978-1-138-33682-7 (hardback)

Library of Congress Cataloging-in-Publication Data

Names: Okita, Alex, author.
Title: Learning C# programming with Unity 3D / Alex Okita.
Description: Second edition. | Boca Raton, FL : CRC Press/Taylor & Francis
Group, 2019.
Identifiers: LCCN 2019010020 | ISBN 9781138336810 (pbk. : acid-free paper) |
ISBN 9781138336827 (hardback : acid-free paper)
Subjects: LCSH: Computer games--Programming. | C# (Computer program language)
| Unity (Electronic resource) | Three-dimensional display systems.
Classification: LCC QA76.76.C672 O43 2019 | DDC 794.8/1526--dc23
LC record available at https://lccn.loc.gov/2019010020

Visit the Taylor & Francis Web site at
http://www.taylorandfrancis.com

and the CRC Press Web site at
http://www.crcpress.com

Contents

1. Introduction: What This Book Is About 1
  1.1   Why Read a Book: Why This Book May or May Not Be for You 1
        1.1.1   Do I Need to Know Math? 2
        1.1.2   Programming as a Form of Expression 2
        1.1.3   Games as a Stage with Lights 2
  1.2   Personal Information 2
  1.3   A Brief History of Computer Programming: How Programming Came to Be 3
        1.3.1   Mechanical Computers 3
        1.3.2   Logic 3
        1.3.3   Computer Science 3
        1.3.4   The Origin of Software 4
        1.3.5   Modern Computer Language 4
        1.3.6   The Future of Computer Languages 4
  1.4   C#: A Flexible Programming Language 4
        1.4.1   C# Paradigm 5
        1.4.2   Unity 3D: A Brief History of Game Engines 5
        1.4.3   Why Use Unity 3D to Learn? 6
        1.4.4   How Does Unity 3D Use C#? 6
                1.4.4.1   How to Tell Unity 3D What to Do 7
  1.5   What Is Programming? 7
        1.5.1   What Does C# Look Like? 8
        1.5.2   Learning to Copy and Paste 9
        1.5.3   Iteration 9
  1.6   Compiling: Turning Words into Computer Instruction 9
  1.7   What We've Learned 10
  1.8   Leveling Up: The Path Ahead 10

2. Before You Begin 11
  2.1   What Will Be Covered in This Chapter 11
  2.2   Unity 3D Installation 13
        2.2.1   Visual Studio Installation 15
        2.2.2   Unity Version Numbering 16
  2.3   Git SCM Installation 17
        2.3.1   Git-SCM.com Git Software (Optional) 17
        2.3.2   GitHub.com Sign Up! (Also Optional) 18
        2.3.3   Git: The Basics 20
        2.3.4   Your First Repo 22
        2.3.5   Before Moving On 25
  2.4   Unity General Overview 26
        2.4.1   The Main Window 27
                2.4.1.1   Toolbar 27
                2.4.1.2   Scene, Game View, and Asset Store 28
                2.4.1.3   Hierarchy Panel 28

                        2.4.1.4   Inspector Panel 29
                        2.4.1.5   Project and Console Panel 29
                        2.4.1.6   Assets Directory 31
                        2.4.1.7   Project Settings Directory 32
                        2.4.1.8   Packages Directory... 32
              2.4.2   Git Ignore 32
              2.4.3   What We've Learned 32
     2.5   Sample Code 33
              2.5.1   Code Fragments 33
              2.5.2   Are Errors Bad?.. 34
                        2.5.2.1   Compile-Time and Run-Time Errors..................................... 34
              2.5.3   How to Follow Along.. 35
              2.5.4   Comments: A First Look 36
              2.5.5   What We've Learned 37
     2.6   Working with C#: Game Engines... 37
              2.6.1   Creating and Assigning a New C# File: Now It's Your Turn 40
              2.6.2   Naming Your New File.. 42
              2.6.3   Using Your New File... 43
              2.6.4   Additional Unity 3D Tools... 48
              2.6.5   Working in a Live Scene 50
              2.6.6   Saving a Scene 50
              2.6.7   Opening a Scene 50
              2.6.8   What We've Learned 51
     2.7   Leveling Up: The Journey Has Just Begun... 51

3. **First Steps: Just Getting Started** 53
     3.1   What Will Be Covered in This Chapter 53
     3.2   Review.. 54
              3.2.1   Submitting Changes to Git... 54
     3.3   Let's Build a Game—Part 1 56
              3.3.1   Movement Experiments 57
              3.3.2   Reading Programmer Documentation 58
     3.4   Tokens 61
              3.4.1   Writing C#.. 62
              3.4.2   Comments a First Look.. 63
              3.4.3   Separator Tokens.. 64
              3.4.4   Operator Tokens... 65
              3.4.5   Literals 66
              3.4.6   Transitive and Non-Transitive Operations 67
              3.4.7   Putting It All Together 67
              3.4.8   What We've Learned 69
     3.5   Statements and Expressions.. 69
              3.5.1   Expressions 70
              3.5.2   How Unity 3D Executes Your Code 70
              3.5.3   Thinking in Algorithms.. 70
                        3.5.3.1   Wash, Rinse, Repeat.. 73
              3.5.4   What We've Learned 73
     3.6   Keywords 73
              3.6.1   The Class Keyword... 74
              3.6.2   What We've Learned 76
     3.7   White Space 76
              3.7.1   Code Style 78
              3.7.2   What We've Learned 79

3.8	Code Blocks		79
	3.8.1	What We've Learned	81
3.9	Classes: A First Look		81
	3.9.1	Objects	82
	3.9.2	What We've Learned	86
3.10	Variables		86
	3.10.1	Identifiers	87
	3.10.2	Data	88
	3.10.3	Variable Manipulation	89
		3.10.3.1 Declaration Placement Examples	90
	3.10.4	Dynamic Initialization	90
	3.10.5	What We've Learned	91
3.11	Variable Names		91
	3.11.1	Useful Variables in Unity 3D	94
	3.11.2	Variable Assignment	96
	3.11.3	Putting It Together: Using the Variables	98
	3.11.4	What We've Learned	100
3.12	Types: A First Look		100
	3.12.1	Value and Reference Types	100
	3.12.2	What We've Learned	101
3.13	Strong Typing		102
	3.13.1	Dynamic Typing	102
	3.13.2	What We've Learned	103
3.14	Type Casting, Numbers		103
	3.14.1	Explicit versus Implicit Casting	104
		3.14.1.1 A Basic Example	105
	3.14.2	What We've Learned	107
3.15	Comments		108
	3.15.1	Line Numbers	111
	3.15.2	Code Folding	111
	3.15.3	Summary Comments	113
	3.15.4	Navigating in Code	114
	3.15.5	What We've Learned	115
3.16	Leveling Up: Moving on to Basics		115
	3.16.1	Git Revision History	115
4. Basics: The Building Blocks of Code			**117**
4.1	What Will Be Covered in This Chapter		117
4.2	Review		117
4.3	Building a Game—Part 1		118
	4.3.1	Mouse Point	119
	4.3.2	Move to Point	120
	4.3.3	What We've Learned	121
4.4	Class Construction		121
	4.4.1	Class Declaration	123
		4.4.1.1 A Basic Example	123
		4.4.1.2 Value and Reference Types	124
	4.4.2	Adding Data Fields	125
	4.4.3	Access Modifiers and the Dot Operator	125
	4.4.4	Class Scope	127
	4.4.5	Class Members	128
	4.4.6	What We've Learned	128

4.5	Directives	129
	4.5.1 Libraries	130
	4.5.2 Ambiguous NameSpaces	133
	4.5.3 What We've Learned	134
4.6	Functions	134
	4.6.1 What Are Functions?	135
	4.6.2 Unity 3D Entry Points	136
	4.6.3 Writing a Function	137
	4.6.4 More on White Space and Tabs	139
	4.6.5 What We've Learned	140
4.7	Order of Operation: What Is Calculated and When	140
	4.7.1 Evaluating Numbers	141
	4.7.1.1 Math	141
	4.7.1.2 Operator Evaluation	144
	4.7.2 What We've Learned	145
4.8	Scope: A First Look	146
	4.8.1 Class Scope	146
	4.8.2 Function Scope	149
	4.8.3 Blank Scope	151
	4.8.4 What We've Learned	152
4.9	This	152
	4.9.1 A Basic Example	152
	4.9.2 When This Is Necessary	153
	4.9.3 What We've Learned	154
4.10	Building a Game—Part 2	155
	4.10.1 Additional Components	155
	4.10.2 The Projectile	158
	4.10.3 The Target	160
	4.10.4 What We've Learned	161
4.11	Logic and Operators	162
	4.11.1 Booleans	162
	4.11.2 Equality Operators	163
	4.11.3 Logical Not!	165
	4.11.4 Greater and Less than Operators	166
	4.11.5 Logical And and Or Operators	168
	4.11.6 If and Branching	169
	4.11.7 What We've Learned	173
4.12	Loops	173
	4.12.1 Unary Operators	173
	4.12.2 While	174
	4.12.3 For	175
	4.12.4 Do-While	177
	4.12.5 Postfix and Prefix Notation	178
	4.12.6 Using Loops	179
	4.12.7 Loops within Loops	182
	4.12.8 Runaway Loops	183
	4.12.9 Breakpoints: A First Look	185
	4.12.10 What We've Learned	186
4.13	ScopeAgain	187
	4.13.1 Visibility or Accessibility	187
	4.13.1.1 A Basic Example	187
	4.13.2 Global Scope	188
	4.13.3 What We've Learned	190

4.14   Warnings versus Errors 190
    4.14.1   Warnings 190
    4.14.2   Errors 191
    4.14.3   Understanding the Debugger 192
    4.14.4   What We've Learned 194
4.15   Leveling Up: Fundamentals 194
    4.15.1   Style Guides 194

5. Fundamentals: Building a Foundation 195
5.1   What Will Be Covered in This Chapter 195
5.2   Review 196
    5.2.1   Modular Code 199
5.3   Inheritance: A First Look 202
    5.3.1   Class Members 204
        5.3.1.1   Inheriting Members 205
        5.3.1.2   Is-A and Has-A 206
    5.3.2   Instancing 206
    5.3.3   Parent Child 208
    5.3.4   Object 209
        5.3.4.1   A Type Is Not an Object 212
    5.3.5   != null 213
    5.3.6   What We've Learned 214
5.4   Instancing 214
    5.4.1   Class Initialization 215
    5.4.2   New 215
    5.4.3   Constructors 216
    5.4.4   What We've Learned 219
5.5   Static 220
    5.5.1   A Basic Example 220
    5.5.2   Static Variables 222
        5.5.2.1   A Basic Example 222
    5.5.3   Static Functions 224
    5.5.4   Putting It All Together 225
    5.5.5   What We've Learned 228
5.6   Building A Game—Part 3 228
    5.6.1   The Player 228
    5.6.2   The Mover 229
    5.6.3   The Shooter 230
    5.6.4   Physics Settings.. 232
    5.6.5   What We've Learned 233
5.7   Jump Statements and Return 233
    5.7.1   Return.. 234
        5.7.1.1   A Basic Example.................................... 235
    5.7.2   Returning Objects 235
    5.7.3   A Class Is a Type 236
    5.7.4   Tuples 238
    5.7.5   Null Is Not Void 240
    5.7.6   What We've Learned 240
5.8   Arrays: A First Look.. 241
    5.8.1   Fixed-Sized Arrays 241
        5.8.1.1   A Basic Example.................................... 241
    5.8.2   Foreach.. 246
        5.8.2.1   A Basic Example.................................... 246

	5.8.3	Dynamic Initialization	246
	5.8.4	Using the While Loop with Arrays	247
		5.8.4.1 Setting Array Values	247
		5.8.4.2 Getting Array Values	248
	5.8.5	What We've Learned	248

5.9 Jump Statements: Break and Continue 248
    5.9.1 A Basic Example 249
        5.9.1.1 Continue 249
    5.9.2 ZombieData 249
    5.9.3 Foreach Again 251
    5.9.4 What We've Learned 252
5.10 Multidimensional Arrays 252
    5.10.1 Columns and Rows 253
        5.10.1.1 A Basic Example 254
    5.10.2 A Puzzle Board 255
    5.10.3 Camera and Screen Setup 257
    5.10.4 Checking Range 259
    5.10.5 What We've Learned 261
5.11 Array List 262
    5.11.1 A Basic Example 263
    5.11.2 `ArrayList.Contains()` 265
    5.11.3 Remove 266
    5.11.4 Sort and Reverse 267
    5.11.5 What We've Learned 268
5.12 Strings 268
    5.12.1 Declaring a String 268
        5.12.1.1 A Basic Example 269
    5.12.2 Escape Sequences 270
    5.12.3 Verbatim Strings: @ 271
    5.12.4 What We've Learned 272
5.13 Combining What We've Learned 272
    5.13.1 Timers 273
    5.13.2 What We've Learned 278
5.14 Leveling Up: On to the Cool Stuff 278

6. Intermediate: The Tricks of the Trade 281
6.1 What Will Be Covered in This Chapter 281
6.2 Review 281
    6.2.1 Class Members 282
        6.2.1.1 A Basic Example 282
        6.2.1.2 Thinking Like a Programmer 283
    6.2.2 Return 286
        6.2.2.1 A Basic Example 286
    6.2.3 Arguments aka "Args" (Not Related to Pirates) 287
        6.2.3.1 The Basic Example 287
        6.2.3.2 Multiple Args 288
        6.2.3.3 Using Args 290
    6.2.4 Assignment Operators 292
        6.2.4.1 A Basic Example 292
    6.2.5 What We've Learned 294

6.3		Building a Game—Part 4	294
	6.3.1	ChaseCamera	294
	6.3.2	Tile Floor Generator	295
	6.3.3	What We've Learned	297
6.4		Class Constructors	298
	6.4.1	A Basic Example	299
	6.4.2	What We've Learned	301
6.5		Arrays Revisited	302
	6.5.1	Using Arrays in Unity 3D	302
		6.5.1.1 Starting with 0	304
		6.5.1.2 Mathf	306
		6.5.1.3 Time	307
	6.5.2	Instancing with `AddComponent();`	307
	6.5.3	Type Casting Unity 3D Objects	309
	6.5.4	What We've Learned	311
6.6		Enums	311
	6.6.1	Using Enums	312
	6.6.2	Combining What We've Learned	315
	6.6.3	What We've Learned	317
6.7		Switch	317
	6.7.1	A Basic Example	318
	6.7.2	Default	319
	6.7.3	More On Cases	322
	6.7.4	Fall Through	326
	6.7.5	goto Case	327
	6.7.6	Finite State Machine	328
	6.7.7	What We've Learned	330
6.8		Structs	330
	6.8.1	Building a Struct	331
	6.8.2	Struct versus Class	332
	6.8.3	Without Structs	334
	6.8.4	Handling Structs	335
	6.8.5	Accessing Structs	336
	6.8.6	Global Access	337
	6.8.7	What We've Learned	337
6.9		Class Data	338
	6.9.1	Character Base Class	339
	6.9.2	Const	340
	6.9.3	Readonly	341
	6.9.4	What We've Learned	342
6.10		Namespaces	342
	6.10.1	A Basic Example	342
	6.10.2	Directives in Namespaces	344
	6.10.3	Ambiguous References	345
	6.10.4	Alias Directives	345
	6.10.5	What We've Learned	346
6.11		Functions Again	346
	6.11.1	Parameter Lists	346
	6.11.2	Side Effects	347
	6.11.3	Multiple Arguments	348

6.11.4 Useful Parameters...348
  6.11.4.1 The Rule of Three 349
6.11.5 Foreach versus For..350
6.11.6 What We've Learned 351
6.12 Unity 3D Execution Order...351
6.12.1 A Basic Example...353
6.12.2 Component Execution Order 356
6.12.3 What We've Learned 358
6.13 Inheritance Again 358
6.13.1 Function Overrides 359
  6.13.1.1 A Basic Example 359
6.13.2 Class Inheritance..362
  6.13.2.1 Sharing Common Attributes..............................362
6.13.3 Object 364
6.13.4 What We've Learned 367
6.14 Type Casting Again 368
6.14.1 (<Type>) versus "as" 368
6.14.2 User-Defined Type Conversion 370
6.14.3 Implicit versus Explicit Type Conversion 372
6.14.4 What We've Learned 373
6.15 Working with Vectors...374
6.15.1 Vectors Are Objects..374
6.15.2 Stepping through MonsterGenerator 375
6.15.3 Gizmos 377
  6.15.3.1 A Basic Example 377
  6.15.3.2 DrawRay..379
6.15.4 Using Gizmos..380
6.15.5 What We've Learned 381
6.16 goto Labels...381
6.16.1 Skipping Down 383
6.16.2 Zombie State Machine 383
6.16.3 This as a Reference to Yourself 386
6.16.4 Just for Zombies 386
6.16.5 What We've Learned 388
6.17 More on Arrays...389
6.17.1 Length and Count..389
  6.17.1.1 A Basic Example 389
6.17.2 Foreach: A Reminder..390
6.17.3 Discovery 393
6.17.4 Putting It Together 394
  6.17.4.1 Breakpoint, Observing Inheritance 395
6.17.5 What We've Learned 399
6.18 Out Parameter..399
6.18.1 A Basic Example...401
6.18.2 Simple Sort (Bubble Sort) 403
6.18.3 Simple Sort Proof...405
6.18.4 What We've Learned 406
6.19 Ref Parameter 407
6.19.1 A Basic Example...407
6.19.2 Code Portability Side Effects...408
6.19.3 What We've Learned 410

6.20		Type Casting Numbers	411
	6.20.1	Number Types	413
	6.20.2	Integers	413
		6.20.2.1 Signed Numbers	414
	6.20.3	Floating Point	414
	6.20.4	What We've Learned	415
6.21		Types and Operators	415
	6.21.1	GetType()	416
	6.21.2	More Type Casting	417
	6.21.3	Type Aliasing	420
	6.21.4	Boxing and Unboxing	420
6.22		Operator Overloading	422
	6.22.1	A Basic Example	423
	6.22.2	Overloading*	424
	6.22.3	Overloading < and >	426
	6.22.4	What We've Learned	427
6.23		Controlling Inheritance	427
	6.23.1	Sealed	428
		6.23.1.1 A Basic Example	428
	6.23.2	Extension Functions	429
	6.23.3	Abstract	430
		6.23.3.1 A Basic Example	430
	6.23.4	Abstract: Abstract	432
	6.23.5	Putting This to Use	434
	6.23.6	What We've Learned	435
6.24		Building A Game—Part 5	436
	6.24.1	Generating Rooms	436
	6.24.2	What We've Learned	439
6.25		Leveling Up	440
7. Advanced			**441**
7.1		What Will Be Covered in This Chapter	441
7.2		Review	442
	7.2.1	Moving Forward	442
7.3		Visual Studio	442
	7.3.1	The Debugger	443
	7.3.2	Mono History	443
7.4		Function Overloading	444
	7.4.1	A Closer Look at Functions	444
		7.4.1.1 A Basic Example	445
	7.4.2	Function Signature	446
	7.4.3	Different Signatures	447
	7.4.4	Putting It Together	448
	7.4.5	Not Quite Recursion	449
	7.4.6	DrawWords	450
	7.4.7	What We've Learned	453
7.5		Accessors (or Properties)	453
	7.5.1	Value	454
		7.5.1.1 A Basic Example	455
	7.5.2	Set Event	455
	7.5.3	Read-Only Accessor	457
	7.5.4	Simplification	458
	7.5.5	What We've Learned	459

7.6   Base Classes: Another Look 459
        7.6.1   Generalization—Base Classes 459
        7.6.2   Specialization 461
        7.6.3   Base 461
        7.6.4   Partial 463
        7.6.5   Protected, Private, and Public 466
        7.6.6   What We've Learned 467
7.7   Optional Parameters 467
        7.7.1   Using Optionals 468
                 7.7.1.1   A Basic Example 469
        7.7.2   Optional Arguments 470
        7.7.3   Named Parameters 471
                 7.7.3.1   A Basic Example 472
        7.7.4   Combining What We've Learned 473
        7.7.5   What We've Learned 474
7.8   Delegate Functions 474
        7.8.1   Delegates 474
                 7.8.1.1   A Basic Example 474
        7.8.2   Delegate Signatures 476
        7.8.3   Stacking Delegates 476
        7.8.4   Using Delegates 477
        7.8.5   Updating Delegates 478
        7.8.6   What We've Learned 480
7.9   Interface 480
        7.9.1   Early Planning 480
                 7.9.1.1   A Basic Example 481
                 7.9.1.2   Using Accessors 483
        7.9.2   Multiple Interfaces 486
        7.9.3   IComparer 488
        7.9.4   Using IComparer 490
        7.9.5   What We've Learned 491
7.10   Class Constructors Revisited 491
        7.10.1   A Basic Example 492
        7.10.2   When to Create a New Class 495
        7.10.3   What We've Learned 498
7.11   Preprocessor Directives 498
        7.11.1   A Basic Example 499
        7.11.2   UNITY_EDITOR 500
        7.11.3   Mobile Development 502
        7.11.4   Warning 504
        7.11.5   Organizing 505
        7.11.6   What We've Learned 506
7.12   Try Catch Finally 506
        7.12.1   A Basic Example 506
        7.12.2   Exception Messages 508
        7.12.3   Custom Exceptions 510
        7.12.4   Finally 512
        7.12.5   Try-Catch and Finally in Use 513
        7.12.6   What We've Learned 513
7.13   IEnumerator 514
        7.13.1   Enumeration 515
                 7.13.1.1   A Basic Example 515
                 7.13.1.2   What Doesn't Work 517

	7.13.2	Implementing IEnumerator	517
	7.13.3	What We've Learned	521
7.14	Generics		521
	7.14.1	Generic Functions	522
		7.14.1.1 A Basic Example	522
		7.14.1.2 Why T?	523
	7.14.2	Making Use of Generic Functions	523
	7.14.3	Generic Types	526
	7.14.4	Var	527
	7.14.5	Multiple Generic Values	529
	7.14.6	Anonymous Objects	530
	7.14.7	What We've Learned	533
7.15	Events		533
	7.15.1	A Basic Example	534
	7.15.2	A Proper Event	536
	7.15.3	EventArgs	537
	7.15.4	Generic EventArgs	539
	7.15.5	What We've Learned	540
7.16	Extension Functions		540
	7.16.1	Extensions	541
	7.16.2	A Basic Example	541
	7.16.3	Overloading with Extensions	543
	7.16.4	Magic Mirror	544
	7.16.5	What We've Learned	546
7.17	Destructors		546
	7.17.1	A Basic Example	547
	7.17.2	Clearing Events or Delegates	549
	7.17.3	OnDestroy	550
	7.17.4	The Ugly Truth	552
	7.17.5	What We've Learned	554
7.18	Concurrency or Co-Routines		555
	7.18.1	Yield	555
		7.18.1.1 A Basic Example	557
	7.18.2	Setting Up Timers	558
	7.18.3	Arrays of Delegates	561
	7.18.4	Stopping a Co-Routine	562
	7.18.5	What We've Learned	565
7.19	Dictionary, Stacks, and Queues		565
	7.19.1	A Basic Example	565
	7.19.2	ContainsKey	567
	7.19.3	Stacks	568
		7.19.3.1 A Basic Example	568
	7.19.4	Movement Stack	569
	7.19.5	Queues	571
	7.19.6	What We've Learned	573
7.20	Lambda Expressions		573
	7.20.1	Anonymous Expressions	574
		7.20.1.1 A Basic Example—Action Func and Expression	575
	7.20.2	Lambda Expressions	577
	7.20.3	A Queue of Lambdas	577
	7.20.4	What We've Learned	578
7.21	Leveling Up		578

8. Extended... 579
   8.1   What We'll Be Covering in This Chapter 579
   8.2   Review 579
   8.3   Readability.. 581
        8.3.1   ?: Notation 581
        8.3.2   If 582
        8.3.3   Smell 583
               8.3.3.1   Comments.. 583
               8.3.3.2   One Responsibility Rule........................... 583
               8.3.3.3   Duplicated Code 584
               8.3.3.4   Naming 584
        8.3.4   What We've Learned 584
   8.4   Git Revisited 584
        8.4.1   Git Branch and Merge.. 585
        8.4.2   Merge Conflicts... 588
        8.4.3   What We've Learned 591
   8.5   Recursion 591
        8.5.1   A Basic Example... 593
        8.5.2   Understanding Recursion.. 593
        8.5.3   In Practice 594
        8.5.4   What We've Learned 601
   8.6   LINQ.. 601
        8.6.1   Lambdas and Arrays.. 601
                8.6.1.1   A Basic Example 601
        8.6.2   Var.. 602
        8.6.3   LINQ From 603
        8.6.4   Strange Behaviors in LINQ 604
        8.6.5   LINQ on Lists 605
        8.6.6   Monsters Linq 608
        8.6.7   What We've Learned 611
   8.7   Reflection 613
        8.7.1   A Basic Example... 615
        8.7.2   Reflection MethodInfo... 615
        8.7.3   What We've Learned 618
   8.8   Dynamic.. 620
        8.8.1   ExpandoObject.. 621
        8.8.2   Expando Reader 622
        8.8.3   What We've Learned 623
   8.9   Bitwise Operators 624
        8.9.1   Big Endian and Little Endian 624
        8.9.2   Signed or Unsigned 625
        8.9.3   Bitwise Or | 627
        8.9.4   Enums and Numbers.. 627
        8.9.5   Bitwise And & 628
        8.9.6   Bitwise Exclusive Or ^ (xor) 629
        8.9.7   Setting Bitwise Flags 630
        8.9.8   Bitwise Shortcuts | = and ^ = ... 631
        8.9.9   Bits in Numbers 632
        8.9.10 Bit Shifting >> and << 632
        8.9.11 What We've Learned 634
   8.10   Attributes 635
        8.10.1 A Basic Example... 635
        8.10.2 Custom Attributes... 639

8.10.3   Custom Attributes for Default Values 639
8.10.4   Multiple Attributes 641
8.10.5   Putting Attributes to Work 642
8.10.6   Attribute Flags 644
8.10.7   What We've Learned 645
8.11   Bitwise Math 646
8.11.1   Two's Complement Unary Operator ~ 647
8.11.2   Bitwise Addition and Subtraction 648
8.11.3   Bitwise Multiplication 650
8.11.4   Bitwise Tricks 651
8.11.5   What We've Learned 652
8.12   Architectures and Organization 653
8.12.1   Planning Structure: Namespaces and Directories 653
8.12.2   Divide and Conquer 654
8.12.3   Refactoring 655
8.12.4   What We've Learned 656
8.13   Design Patterns 656
8.13.1   Creational Design Patterns 657
         8.13.1.1   Singleton Pattern 657
8.13.2   Structural Design Patterns 657
8.13.3   Behavioral Design Patterns 658
8.13.4   What We've Learned 658
8.14   Continuing on Your Own 658

9. Stuff We Couldn't Cover 661
9.1   The Extern Keyword 661

10. Good Luck 663

Index 665

1

Introduction: What This Book Is About

This book was written as an answer for anyone to pick up a modern programming language and be productive. You will be able to start a simple game in Unity 3D from scratch. By the end of this book, you will have the basic skills to eventually become a capable unity game programmer, or at least know what is involved with how to read and write some code.

You should have general computer skills before you get started. Come prepared; you'll need a modern Windows or OSX computer capable of running modern software with an internet connection. After this book, you should be armed with the knowledge required to feel confident in learning more.

Each chapter has example code organized by chapter and section. We'll try to make a fun project starting with the basic functions of a typical game and we'll see how the basic game can be expanded upon and we'll learn a bit about what's involved with a larger project.

1.1 Why Read a Book: Why This Book May or May Not Be for You

You could go online and find videos and tutorials to learn; however, there is a disadvantage when it comes to learning things in order and in one place. Most internet video or tutorial websites may gloss over or dwell on a subject. You could skip ahead, but then what are you paying for?

Online content is often brief and doesn't go into much depth on any given topic. It is incomplete or still a work in progress. You'll often find yourself waiting weeks for another video or tutorial to come out.

Just so you know, you should find the act of learning exciting. If not, then you'll have a hard time continuing through to the end of this book. To learn any new skill, a lot of patience is required.

I remember asking an expert programmer how I'd learn to program. He told me to write a compiler. At that time, it seemed rather unfair, but now I understand why he said that. It is like telling someone who wants to learn how to drive Formula 1 cars to go compete in a race. In both cases, the "learning" part was left out of the process.

It is very difficult to tell someone who wants to learn to write code where to begin. However, it all really does start with your preparedness to learn. Your motivation must extend beyond the content of this book.

You may also have some preconceived notions about what programming is. I can't change that, but you should be willing to change your thoughts on the topic if you make discoveries contrary to your knowledge. Keep an open mind.

As a game developer, you should find the act of making a game, or simply learning how to make a game, is just as fun as playing a game. If your primary goal is only to make that game that you've had in your head for years, then you might have a problem. You may find this book a tedious chore if learning C# is just something in the way of making your game.

Computer artists often believe that programming is a technical subject that is incompatible with art. I find the contrary to be true. Programming is an art, much as literature and design are an art. Programming just has a lot of obscure rules that need to be understood for anything to work.

No, programming is not too hard to learn. Writing a massive multiplayer online role-playing game is quite hard. Learning how to write a simple behavior isn't hard; like drawing, you start off with the basics drawing spheres and cubes. After plenty of practice, you'll be able to create a real work of art. This applies to writing code, that is, you start off with basic calculations and then move on to the logic that drives a complex game.

1.1.1 Do I Need to Know Math?

With complex rules in mind, does programming require the knowledge of complex mathematics? Unless you are writing mathematical software, only a bit of geometry is required. Most of the examples here use only a tiny bit of math to accomplish their purpose. Mathematics and programming do overlap quite a lot in their methodology.

Math taught in schools provides a "best" solution. Programming results tend to behave a bit like a math proof, but the proof isn't just another bit of math. Rather, the proof of your code means that your zombies chase after humans. A considerable amount of math required has been done for you by the computer. It is just up to you to know what math to use, and then plug in the right variables.

1.1.2 Programming as a Form of Expression

There is a deeper connection between words and meaning in programming. This connection is more mechanical, but flexible at the same time. In relation to a programming language, programmers like to call this "expressiveness."

When you write words in literature, you infer most if not all of the meaning. When programming inference isn't implied, then you're free to define your own meanings for words and invent words freely.

One common merging of art and code appears within a video game. Anytime characters can react to each other and react to user interaction conveys a greater experience. An artist, an animator, or an environment designer should have some ability to convey a richer experience to the audience. A character artist can show a monster to his or her audience; but to really experience the creature, the monster should glare, grunt, and attack in reaction to the audience.

1.1.3 Games as a Stage with Lights

To do this, we're going to use Unity 3D, a game engine. If you were to write a play, you would not have to build the auditorium for your performance. Building lights and generating electricity to run them would distract you from writing your play. Playwrights don't often build lights and auditoriums from scratch, and there are plenty of venues you could use as your stage, which is where game engines come in.

Game engines such as Unity 3D, Unreal Engine, Crytek, and even Game Maker, or Godot have a lot of the basic game and math-related functions built for you. They are ready-built stages that allow you to focus on making your game. The necessary code for rendering and physics have been done for you.

1.2 Personal Information

I started in the 1990s cleaning up sprites for Atari. Back then the job qualifications were basically having Photoshop and a Wacom tablet. Oh, how times have changed!

I've worked for many different game studios, in both 2D and 3D, as an artist. I was exposed to many different software packages including Strata 3D on the Mac and Alias (PowerAnimator) on the SGI (Silicon Graphics International), among many others. I loved learning new 3D modeling, rendering, and animation applications. During my work as an artist, I used Maya, a popular 3D modeling package. While using Maya, I was introduced to the Maya Embedded Language (MEL) script. Today I use Modo with Python.

After working as a character rigger and technical artist, I learned many programming languages including MAXScript, MEL, and Python, which helped me to write tools for my fellow artists to use for speeding up production.

I eventually moved into the job of programmer as my primary job function. I wrote prototypes for Microsoft in Unreal using UnrealScript, a programming language much like JavaScript. This game studio was run by John Gaeta and Peter Oberdorfer, who are award-winning movie special effects directors.

I began my career path as an artist, then became a technical artist, and finally a programmer. This seems to be a common trend among a small variety of 3D artists like myself. I know quite a few folks who have followed the same career path.

During my transition from artist to programmer, I found that there was very little by way of help, documentation, web pages, or similar to complete the transition from an artist to a programmer. Many people assumed that you were either a programmer to begin with, or not interested in making that transition. After a long discussion, with my then girlfriend—now wife, about what a variable is, I decided it was time to write a book.

1.3 A Brief History of Computer Programming: How Programming Came to Be

Basic insight into the inner workings of your computer may help understand why and how some text gets converted into computer instruction. The words that make up C#, or any other programming language get converted into what is called byte code.

Skilled programmers tend to know more about the inner workings of their computer. Like any trade or learned skill, the more you know about how your tools work, the better understanding of the entire process you'll have.

To understand why programming tools work as they now do stems from knowing how they used to work. To understand how the current tools came about means knowing a bit of computer history and how computers used to work.

1.3.1 Mechanical Computers

The first programmable computer is arguably the Babbage machine built by Charles Babbage in the 1820s. Made of tens of thousands of moving parts and weighing several tons, it was a gigantic mechanical calculator that could display a 31-digit number. It was called the Difference Engine. in 1824 Babbage won a gold medal from the British Astronomical Society, by using his gigantic calculator, for correcting a set of tables used to chart the movement of planets through the sky.

In 1833, a countess named Augusta Ada King of Lovelace, commonly known as Ada Lovelace, met Babbage at a party where she was introduced to the Difference Engine. Several years later, it became evident that she understood the machine better than Charles himself. Despite being a housewife to the Earl of Lovelace, she wrote several documents on the operation of the Difference Engine as well as its upgraded version, the Analytical Engine. She is often considered to be the first computer programmer for her work with the Difference Engine and its documentation.

1.3.2 Logic

In 1848, George Boole gave us Boolean logic. It would take nearly a century between the Difference Engine and the first general programmable computer to make its appearance. Thanks to George, today our computers count in binary (1s and 0s), and our software thinks in terms of true or false.

In 1887, Dorr Eugene Felt built a computing machine with buttons; thanks to him, our computers have keyboards. In the 1890s, a tabulating machine used paper with holes punched in it representing 1s and 0s to record the US census. Back then it saved US$2 million and 6 years of work.

There was a moment in time where a trinary computer existed. In 1840, Thomas Fowler created a competing mechanical computer which worked with −1, 0, and +1. Even as late as 1958 an electronic version was created in the Soviet Union, but its usefulness lost out to binary which was easier to build and used less power.

In the 1900s, between Nicola Tesla and Alexander Graham Bell, modern computers were imminent with the invention of the transistor. In 1936, Konrad Zuse made the Z1 computer, another mechanical computer like that of Babbage, but this time it used a tape with holes punched in it like the tabulating machine. He'd later move on to make the Z3 in 1941.

1.3.3 Computer Science

In the 1940s, Alan Turing, a British computer scientist, designed and built an encrypted message decoder called the Bombe that used electromechanical switches for helping the Allied forces during World War II.

Between the 1930s and the 1950s, Turing informed the computer scientists that computers can, in theory, solve anything calculable, calling this concept *Turing completeness*. All of these components were leading toward our modern computer.

In the mid-1940s, John Von Neumann demonstrated, with the help of his theory, that the computer can be built using simple components. In this way, the software that controls the hardware can add the complex behavior. Thanks to Tesla and Bell, the Z3 was made completely of electronic parts. It included the first use of logic while doing calculations, making it the first complete Turing-complete computer. In 1954, Gordon Teal at Texas Instruments introduced the silicon-based transistor, a key component for building solid-state electronics that are used today in every computer.

1.3.4 The Origin of Software

The Z3 was programmed using Plankalkül, the first high-level programming language, invented by Zuse shortly after he finished building the machine. In 1952, Grace Hopper created the first compiler software that could translate human-readable words into machine operations. For the first time, the programmer didn't need to know how the transistors operated in the hardware to build software for the computer to run. This opened computer programming to a whole new audience.

Between the 1950s and 1970s, computers and computer languages were growing in terms of complexity and capability. In 1958, John McCarthy invented LISP (for LISt Processor) at the Massachusetts Institute of Technology (MIT). Object-oriented programming appeared in Simula 67 in 1967. Imperative and procedural programming made its appearance in Pascal in 1970.

1.3.5 Modern Computer Language

Bell Labs, started by Bell in the 1920s, hired Dennis Ritchie in 1967. In 1974, Ritchie published the C programming language that has become the most popular computer programming language. In 1983, Bjarne Stroustrup introduced C++ as "C with Classes."

In 2001, Microsoft released C#, a combination of several programming language paradigms taking the concepts from C, C++, LISP, Haskell, and others, and incorporating the ideas and concepts into a single language. Today, C# is in its seventh major revision, whereas C++ is in its seventeenth revision. C# is an evolving language having new features and concepts. Each revision makes the language more flexible and most important, more expressive.

1.3.6 The Future of Computer Languages

The International Business Machines Corporation (IBM), a US company founded in the 1920s, is currently engineering new technology using particle physics discovered nearly a century ago. Modern spintronics derived from the work of German physicists in the late 1920s.

Without particle physics and physicists such as Friedrich Hermann Hund, we wouldn't understand quantum tunneling, and the solid-state storage or universal serial bus (USB) thumb drive wouldn't exist. After the discovery and confirmation of the Higgs boson, you might ask "Why bother?" This question might not get a good answer for another hundred years, but it'll be worth it.

C# is not the last computer language; many others have been introduced just recently. Google has introduced Kotlin specifically for developing apps for Android and Apple has introduced Swift for their iOS platform. Microsoft, not to be outdone, introduced Q# for the future of quantum computing.

Using Q# for game development isn't likely, at least for now. Programming languages have advantages and disadvantages in different disciplines. The purpose of programming languages is to allow human readable text to be converted into instructions that run on a computer's CPU.

1.4 C#: A Flexible Programming Language

There are plenty of programming languages and each language was created to fulfill different roles. Modern programming languages in use today are often described by their paradigms. A paradigm can be explained as a sort of writing style; each style follows a different set of rules.

1.4.1 C# Paradigm

In poetry, a haiku follows a 5-7-5 syllable tempo. A sonnet follows an iambic pentameter with 10 syllables per line and rhymes in a specific pattern. Not all prose needs to end in rhyme like haiku, but many do. Rhyming and tempo are paradigms used in poetry.

Modern programming paradigms include object oriented, functional, imperative, and logic programming. Some programming languages use one or more of these paradigms together. For instance, F# is an imperative, object oriented, and functional language. However, Haskell is purely functional.

C# (pronounced "see sharp") is a combination of many different paradigms. As the name infers, C# is a C-style language and primarily expressed using the object-oriented paradigm. How C# expresses its different paradigms, and how you choose to write with it, is greatly up to you. Due to this flexibility, C# offers a variety of uses reaching far beyond game development.

You may have heard of C++, another multiparadigm language. It is often used by programmers who need detailed control over memory management and many other aspects of their final product. This attention to detail and design is required to produce a refined final product.

C# is an imperative language, that is to say, it carries out operations in order. It is also object oriented, so each object is allowed to do things on its own. Finally, it is also memory managed, aka garbage collected, so your computer's memory is organized for you. However, it does provide the flexibility to manage memory if you require that level of control. Just as well, C++ has recently added garbage collection features to match C#.

1.4.2 Unity 3D: A Brief History of Game Engines

A game engine is basically software that provides many of the basic functions that are commonly used to build a video game. Most game engines allow for rendering either 2D or 3D shapes by importing files generated in a third-party software such as Blender, or 3D Studio Max or Maya, if you can afford them. Another function often found in a game engine is the ability to write software for the game engine to run. Unity 3D allows you to write software to run your game in C#.

3D game engines have a relatively short history in general computing. Their evolution has been hot and fast. Starting around the 1990s, the 486 processor finally made its way into the general populace as a processor fast enough to allow for everyone to play 3D games. Or at least pseudo-3D, 2D images drawn in the shape of three-dimensional geometry. The technology for true 3D polygons would take a few more years to make it onto the average person's desktop.

Pseudo-3D was used to describe skewing and scaling flat sprites or 2D images to appear as though they were in 3D space. True vertex transformation wouldn't appear in popular video game engines on the PC with games such as Quake 1 until 1995. This was greatly with the help of faster and enhanced graphics processors. The modding community took Quake 1 and created many new additions and full conversions.

When powerful graphics processing units (GPUs) were introduced, it opened the floodgates for many more 3D games to make their appearance. At first, these games functioned only on million-dollar computers, but thanks to 3dfx, nVidia, Maxtrox, and ATi in the late 1990s, the GPU quickly took over being a requirement for any 3D game. At that time, id Software, run by John Carmack, quickly came to the forefront of the 3D gaming engine technologies that introduced many concepts such as spline surfaces, complex shadows, and lighting with Quake 2.

Around 1998, Epic Games' Unreal Engine and Valve Software's Source Engine took off with the launch of Unreal Tournament and Half-Life. More modding and conversions exploded onto the scene. Many successful game modifications including Counter-Strike would go on to be one of the most played online multiplayer games Valve Software would publish for years to come.

Before the availability of dedicated GPU and cheap RAM, computers didn't have enough free resources to support a game engine with editing tools. Often the game itself required so much of the computer that there was little room left for any extras, such as particle editors or just-in-time compiling.

The modding community influenced business, making Unreal 2 and Source more modder friendly. Garry's Mod and Unreal Editor changed how game engines were made by adding tons of user-friendly tools. Many users bought games specifically to "mod," or modify, and create new games.

It's no surprise that at this time many game engines would show up on the scene to cater to the modding community and the independent game developer. The large game engines found themselves top heavy by focusing on large publishers. Companies such as RenderWare and Gamebryo found themselves poorly positioned to compete against newcomers who focused on the independent developers such as Unity 3D.

With the independent game developer in mind, many game engines focused on affordability and cross-platform development. Tools such as Game Maker, Unreal Engine, and of course Unity 3D allowed for many more people to learn and build games without the multimillion-dollar investment formerly required for game production.

1.4.3 Why Use Unity 3D to Learn?

Making a game is more fun than making accounting software.

Having fun learning is more important as getting high test scores. After a test, you pretty much forget the anguish of studying all night and what it was for. So there is no reason to make learning menial work because studying should not be boring.

Once learning becomes entertainment, the lessons become something you want to remember. As a fun experience, you remember the experience longer. I've found that learning how to write game artificial intelligence (AI) and behavior is the best way to retain programming experience.

Programming lessons are often taught using stiff diagrams and simple math problems with little or no immediate or obvious applicable use. How often have you actually needed to know where trains would meet leaving two different cities at two different speeds? Experience shows that readers lose interest in any example involving grade-point averages or a train leaving from New York.

Unity 3D offers examples by blowing things up. Calculus and vector examples are usually explained using grids and lines. These concepts are lost by abstract pictures that lack meaning or application. In this case, we'll use math to solve for where a bad guy needs to throw a grenade in order to hit a moving target.

Finally, we'll end up with both the knowledge that will help build a game and the skills needed to write software outside of Unity 3D. With any luck, we'll also have fun while learning. Some of these examples may even help with your math classes.

Unity 3D also provides us with a complete set of tools we can use in our code quickly and easily. These tools are a part of the Unity 3D application programming interface (API). The Unity 3D API is filled with useful things such as commonly used routines, data structures, and classes. These parts of the API are often called a library. We'll learn what all that means in the remaining chapters.

1.4.4 How Does Unity 3D Use C#?

Not that long ago, Unity 3D supported three programming languages. First there was Boo, which was given an accompaniment with JavaScript followed by C#. As of the latest version of Unity 3D, C# is considered the primary, or first-class programming language. Both JavaScript and Boo have been phased out.

In general, C# is gaining more support across many open source projects and has a growing user base. The Dot Net Foundation which maintains .NET Core, is an open source project supported on multiple platforms.

You might be surprised to learn that programming languages have version numbers. With each new version of a language comes new features. As of the writing of this book, Unity 2018 and newer supports. NET 4.7 which is C# version 7.0. What does that mean? It's not so simple, actually. Microsoft created .NET (dot net): a framework or a standardized environment in which code can accomplish common tasks with fewer commands. Using software without a framework often means reinventing code that's been written many times. The framework is also intended to be easily extended. Unity 3D includes many game-related additions to help make building games easier.

The progression looks something like this table:

January 2002	C# 1.0	.NET 1.0	
April 2003	C# 1.2	.NET 1.1	
November 2005	C# 2.0	.NET 2.0	Unity 3D 4.1
November 2007	C# 3.0	.NET 3.5	
April 2010	C# 4.0	.NET 4.0	Unity 3D 5.6
August 2012	C# 5.0	.NET 4.5	
July 2015	C# 6.0	.NET 4.6	Unity 3D 2017.1
March 2017	C# 7.0	.NET 4.7	Unity 3D 2018.1
August 2017	C# 7.1	.NET 4.7.1	

As new versions of .NET were introduced, the language that went along with it was also upgraded, though with different version numbers. Confusing? Yes. Unfortunately, to add to the confusion there's also three versions of .NET that include .NET Standard, .NET Framework, and .NET Core. The differences between these have no effect on what we'll be learning in this book, so I'll leave that research up to you to do on your own. For now, we're not so concerned with the version of either so long as the features we learn about the C# language work within the context of Unity.

C# is used by a large community of general application programmers, not just game engineers. Unity 3D is also a cross-platform game engine, and a developer working on either OSX or Windows can both share and use files for Unity 3D. C# is the same on both Mac and PC as well as Android and iOS for mobile, so there is no concern over what operating system you're going to use.

1.4.4.1 How to Tell Unity 3D What to Do

Unity 3D and Microsoft Visual Studio are going to be our integrated development environment (IDE). IDEs come in many different forms. Many professional Windows programmers use Visual Studio, and Apple developers usually use Xcode in OSX. Microsoft has also made Visual Studio available for OSX. An IDE provides many tools that make programming easier by highlighting the lines of code and automatically completing many commonly repeated tasks.

When it comes to learning about the nuts and bolts of programming, you're basically learning about how your computer thinks, or in more general terms, how your computer does what it is told. Somewhere along the way you'll realize how unintelligent your computer is and how smart good programmers are.

Programming is basically writing detailed instructions on what to do and when. In short, get data then do something with the data. A big part of programming is figuring out where to get information; we'll call this data management. Then you use logic to determine what to do with the data once you have it. Programming logic is organized into algorithms found in statements organized into functions.

Unity 3D provides tools to move characters and objects with your code. These assets all live in the project directory as separate files or entities that you can control through code. Unity 3D provides scenes to give structure to your assets—3D models particle systems for explosions, fire, and other special effects—and tools to create and edit all these things. It is largely up to you to learn these different systems on your own, but this book covers the code part of things.

Unity doesn't provide a set of 3D modeling or 2D image editing tools. For this you'll want to find something like Blender 3D which is free or use another 3D modeling and texturing tools set. You'll also want to look into Gimp or Dogwaffle to paint 2D images to import into Unity.

1.5 What Is Programming?

It's all about writing code.

Programming is a process in which we organize data and use logic to do something with the data. The data is everything a computer can store; they can range from numbers to zombie characters in a video game. You do this by writing text into many files called source code. Source code written into text files replaces punch cards used by the computing machines half a century ago.

When data is combined with logic and then written into a single file, it's called a class. Classes are also data and, as such, can be managed with more logic. Classes are used to create objects in the computer's memory and can be duplicated to have a life of their own.

Classes are used to build objects. Each piece of data within the class becomes a part of that object. Different chunks of data inside of a class are called class members. Class members can also be chunks of logic called functions or methods. If that is not clear right now, don't worry we'll go into detail on that in Chapter 2.

Objects created from a class are called instances. In a game with a horde of zombies, each zombie is duplicated or instanced from a zombie class. Each zombie has unique values for each attribute or data element in the class. This means hit points and positions are unique for each duplicate zombie object.

Similar to families, objects can inherit properties from one another. The child, sometimes called a subclass, inherits attributes from its parent. For instance, the child created from a zombie may inherit the parent's hunger for brains. To be useful, the child zombie can also add new objects and change the objects it inherited from its parent class. As a result, now the child zombie might have tentacles that the parent didn't have.

Objects talk to each other through events and messages. Shooting at zombies can create an event, or in programmer terms, it "raises" an event. The bullet impact event tells the zombie class to then take necessary steps when hit by a bullet. Events command the class to take actions on its data, which is where functions come in.

Functions, also known as methods, are sections of logic that act on data. They allow your class to create additional events and talk to yet more objects. As the player presses the trigger and moves the joystick around, yet more events can be raised and messages can be sent. Events and messages allow the player to interact with your world; logic events and objects together build your game.

1.5.1 What Does C# Look Like?

A game in Unity 3D is made up of many different C# files. Each file can be referred to as a "class" and ends with the .cs file extension (which stands for C Sharp). This isn't a class like those that are taught. It is more akin to biology in which classes are categories that define different groups of organisms.

Controller.cs
Visual C# Source file
268 KB

Explosion.cs
Visual C# Source file
33.7 KB

Monster.cs
Visual C# Source file
100 KB

Player.cs
Visual C# Source file
67.2 KB

Projectile.cs
Visual C# Source file
33.8 KB

Weapon.cs
Visual C# Source file
67.1 KB

A basic game might have several different classes, each one named according to its purpose. Each one of these classes contains the text that is your actual C# code. Just so you know, by default Windows will hide the extensions of your files. As a result, if classes appear as simply Weapon or Monster and there is no extension.cs, then you should go into the Tools menu, select Folder Options/View, and enable file extensions.

As an exercise, we'll be building a simple game involving monsters and shooting. We'll start with a basic skeleton with simple object classes and simple movement behaviors. From this we'll build on some basic events when the player presses keys, moves the mouse, and shoots at targets.

1.5.2 Learning to Copy and Paste

>   A good artist creates, a great artist steals.

Code examples exist for you to copy and paste into your project. The content for this book and all downloadable content are no different. You'll have to understand what the code does and fit it to your needs.

Every programmer copies code habitually. Whether it is from code written in a previous project, or code found on the internet. Programmers copy code to learn. Of course, it's still important to know how to write new code from scratch; most programming classes in school will prefer that you do this for all your assignments. With practice, being able to recognize what to copy and where to paste is something you'll only know from writing code to begin with.

Programming is a constant learning process. It is a language to command computers. Anytime you learn a new language, there will be plenty of words which you'll have to look up. Add to this the fact that every programmer gets to make up new words, and you've got a language that always needs a dictionary.

This is one reason why programmers are usually fast typists. This is also cause for programmers to be picky about what keyboard they prefer.

In most cases, the projects in this book will be in some state where you can read text that is already in place. Most of the projects are in a more complete state where you'll be able to run them and see an intended result.

As a programmer, I've gotten used to searching the internet for example code. Once I've discovered something that looks useful, I copy that code and paste it into a simple test case. After I've wrapped my head around what the code is doing, I rewrite it in a form that is more suited for my specific case.

Even if the code involves some fun trick, I'll learn from that code. As I learn new tricks, I grow as a programmer. The only way to learn new tricks is finding the necessity to solve a new problem for which I haven't already figured out a solution. Finding solutions to problems is a fundamental part of being a programmer.

1.5.3 Iteration

Programming is an iterative process. It's irregular to write an entire class or function without testing it many times. The general flow is to write a part of a function, test it, add a bit more, test again, and repeat until the function accomplishes its goal. Even then, many functions often work together in sequence. Often, you'll write a function, verify that it's working, write another function, and verify some more. Then you'll have them work with one another and test again, all the while you'll be changing and re-arranging your code to fix mistakes.

Most of the time you'll start off with a bunch of placeholders until you get around to finishing your code. As you're adding features and finishing code, you'll have chunks of work that aren't finished. This is a part of game development and a part of learning as well.

1.6 Compiling: Turning Words into Computer Instruction

To test and use your code, it is time to compile. Compiling is the process of taking all of your source files and building bytecode. Unity 3D uses .NET, as it is a compiler to generate the bytecode, but Unity 3D does this automatically. Mono is an open-source compiler that runs on many different processors and operating systems.

The combination of the central processing unit (CPU) and operating system is often called a platform. Each platform requires a unique native machine code to execute or run. Building code for each platform is called a target. Unity 3D converts the bytecode into a native machine code and can target Mac, PC, Android, and iOS.

Native machine code is the set of instructions that directly talk to the CPU and operating system (think of the holes punched into a card and fed to a machine). Unity 3D is a simple way to generate the complex set of instructions for your computer to run. Code that talks directly to the hardware is referred to as "low-level" programming.

There are layers of software between you and the computer's hardware. When writing C# for games using Unity 3D, your code is compiled by .NET. Unity 3D then takes the bytecode from .NET and compiles a target platform into a native machine code.

Both Unity 3D and .NET are the layers underneath your code and the computer's hardware, putting you on a higher level. This is often referred to as a computer layer abstraction. That is why C# is usually considered a high-level programming language.

Programming at a lower level requires much more knowledge of memory management and a wide variety of other APIs that might include graphic cards, physics, sound, and everything else that runs a game. Writing for a layer involves an in-depth knowledge of both the layers below and above the one you're writing for.

The computer hardware, such as CPU, graphics card, memory, and storage, live on the lowest level. Above them is the basic input/output system (BIOS) and software that starts the hardware when you press the Power button. Above that is your computer's operating system and drivers that talk to the hardware. Finally, Unity 3D lives above the operating system and your code lives above Unity 3D.

That is why we're going to use Unity 3D to write games and not start from scratch in raw C++. Otherwise, we'll have to spend a few years learning about physics, rendering, and assembly language or the instruction set that your CPU uses to operate.

1.7 What We've Learned

We should have an idea of what C# is, and what is required of you to learn it. If you haven't done so already, download and install the required software.

Unity 3D is free; there are no fees or royalties that need to be paid to the Unity 3D developers so long as you're not building any commercial product. Git is also free to use and you'll need that to follow the chapters on Git.

You're even allowed to deploy your projects on anything Unity can target. Until you're ready for a commercial launch, the free license is all you'll need for learning and sharing your game with your peers on your computer.

Optionally, you may also want to setup an account on the Unity 3D site if you want to download and use any of the assets from their Asset Store. A Visual Studio Community account and a GitHub account may also come in useful later.

1.8 Leveling Up: The Path Ahead

The computer systems in place today have evolved from machines with moving parts. Telling these machines what to do involved setting knobs and switches. Today, we use text organized into statements and logic.

It is difficult to imagine a time when computers were so slow that simple calculations involved waiting for clattering switches to finish moving around to produce an answer. Today, computers complete many billions of calculations in a single second. All too often, we take for granted that computers rely on the same concepts and systems engineered nearly a century ago.

Understanding how computers work puts into context how we write software. It is possible to write software without this understanding, but it is harder to appreciate how it works.

2

Before You Begin

This book focuses on learning C# and the fundamentals involved with programming a computer language. This book does not necessarily focus on the use of Unity 3D to complete a specific game. You're not required to make any purchases, since this book assumes that you're using the free version of Unity 3D and other software.

You will need an internet connection to download software. There are also some cases where you'll want to create an account for some websites. This is optional and not required. The services suggested are free and popular among game developers, so it's probably something a new game developer should learn how to use regardless.

Throughout the tutorials in the book are useful building blocks of code for game development. By no means will the final product be a finished game; at least one that's ready to ship. Access to free assets are included with this book. You're free to use them for any project you have in mind.

Along with Unity 3D you'll need to work with Git SCM, commonly known simply as "Git." Git is a source code manager, sometimes referred to as a Version Control System. This means you'll be able to store different versions of your project with revisions kept in history. Changes to files need to be organized to prevent the loss of effort. To coordinate, developers use git merged changes and track the history of every source file in a project.

As a new software developer, you'll be happy to have learned to use Git. Many millions of software developers rely on sites like GitHub.com or BitBucket.org to manage and share their code with both their team members and the rest of the world. Even as a solo developer, you'll see the benefits of source control indispensable.

2.1 What Will Be Covered in This Chapter

Before we get to know C#, we're going to need to make sure that you're ready with Unity Git and Visual Studio; otherwise you're not going to be able to follow along with the content of the rest of this book.

If you are already familiar with Unity and Git, then this chapter might be a review. If you think you already understand how a scene works and how to attach scripts to objects, then you can skip ahead to the next chapter. To ensure you've installed everything necessary, let's preview what we'll be covering in this chapter:

- Installing the Unity Editor
- What Git SCM aka "Git" is, and how it is used for this book
- Getting around in Unity Editor
- How to read C#
- GitHub and how to save code
- How to make use of C# within Unity 3D

The chapters that discuss Unity 3D will remain focused on how the code works and interacts with software that usually involves C#. There are plenty of books that focus on Unity 3D's game development tools for effects and art. It is recommended that you also obtain some reading materials to help you learn the rest of the Unity 3D tool set.

Microsoft Visual Studio is installed along with Unity 3D. Both the free and professional versions of Unity 3D use the same version. Visual Studio is commonly referred to as an integrated development environment, or IDE. You could use another text editor such as Notepad; examples found in later chapters will require Visual Studio for a complete experience.

Most of the elements of the Unity 3D tools such as particle systems, animation systems, and other components, such as lighting and sound, are not covered in this book. However, this book enables you to add any interactivity with those systems in the engine. By the time you finish this book, you should be able to intuitively know how to look up what's involved with playing a sound when the player clicks buttons and fires weapons.

We will be looking at a lot of source code. Source code is the term given to the text that is entered into a file by programmers. Fragments of source code, and in many cases a complete source, are provided as a part of completing the Git SCM tutorials. A sample of source code will look like the following:

```
1   using System.Collections;
2   using System.Collections.Generic;
3   using UnityEngine;
4
5   public class NewBehaviourScript : MonoBehaviour {
6
7       // Use this for initialization
8       void Start () {
9
10      }
11
12      // Update is called once per frame
13      void Update () {
14
15      }
16  }
```

If the sample makes no sense at all, don't worry; after just a few chapters you'll be more comfortable looking at the new punctuation and formatting. Each character, space, color, and words have a special meaning. To programmers, this formatting of characters is called *syntax*. If you've written something like HTML or even JavaScript, some of this might be familiar.

Unity calls the source code a script. Much like an actor in a play follows a script, the objects in Unity follow a script assigned to them. Web programmers write in JavaScript; before Unreal Engine 4, Unreal Engine used UnrealScript. Unity simply uses C# as its scripting language.

Don't make the mistake that C# is merely a scripting language and not a programming language. C# is used to write plenty of desktop and mobile apps from scratch. Unity calls C# a scripting language but it doesn't mean you're not programming.

It is important that you take care to notice the syntax—the placement of words and punctuation. Each curly brace, colon, and period is important. Forgetting a single period or a semicolon will stop all code from working.

The syntax is colored by Visual Studio with what is called syntax highlighting. The colors are chosen automatically based on the context in which the word or special character is used. The colors can also be customized to your personal preferences with settings found in Visual Studio. So, if you prefer a dark theme, that option can be found in the preferences.

We will spend a lot of time writing code and inspecting each line to understand what is going on. More importantly, we'll be thinking about why the code works and the alternate methods of accomplishing the same task. One important topic we'll also be looking at is how a line of code can break and how to fix it. There are many common mistakes all programmers make, which we may also get used to them early on.

Just as important, we'll look at how the code misbehaves and what common mistakes can take place. Error messages are not a problem, they are clues that inform where you need to fix your code. You can expect a lot of errors when you first get started; in many cases, a single line may have more than one error, so there might be multiple fixes before you're able to move on.

Alternate methods are important, you know that each task you approach isn't solved with a single solution. Approaching a problem is more important than memorizing and regurgitating the same solution when you see a similar problem again. In the real world, no two situations will be exactly alike. Each time you need to solve a problem, you'll need to invent a unique solution.

Programming is a creative process that allows for any number of different methods to accomplish a single task. Each variation of code has pros and cons. Each line of code may vary depending on the programmer; in this case, you may feel differently about what code to use and why you prefer it. Always use the version which you find easier to read and understand.

No doubt, if you're really going to get into making games with Unity 3D, you'll want to get an additional book that focuses on building assets, scenes, and effects. If you don't already know your way around Unity 3D, we should have a brief introduction to the Unity 3D interface that we're most concerned about when it comes to writing scripts.

2.2 Unity 3D Installation

There's a lot of software to install, so hopefully this won't take too long. Sometimes there are a lot of options, so it's best to double check with the book to make sure you don't miss something.

If you haven't already, download Unity 3D from https://store.unity.com/

This will present a menu of options. Pick the free version on the following page then select the Download button, Unity Hub, for your operating system.

Unity Hub is a helper app that lists the latest builds of Unity. The list includes beta releases as well as different versions of Unity. Depending on your download speed, this might take a while to finish downloading. It is worth getting the latest version, as many features and options are always added with every new update.

Once the Unity Hub has finished installing, it's time to install Unity from the Unity Hub. When the Hub opens it will ask if you would like to sign into an existing account or if you'd like to create a new Unity ID. A third option exists if you're not connected to the internet. Follow any steps necessary to log into the Unity Hub. There's no fee required to install Unity, just a valid email address.

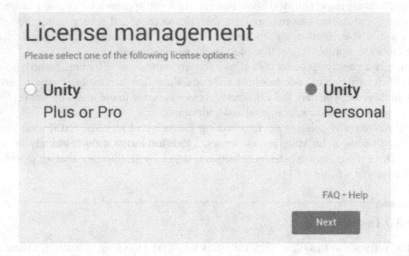

The License management panel will ask what version of Unity you will be using; select Unity Personal unless you've purchased a license. You'll be prompted with a dialog where you'll need to promise you are not using Unity in a professional capacity. You're allowed to download Unity once the personal license is activated. Under the Installs tab, you'll see options for "On My Machine," "Official Releases," and "Beta Releases."

Teams often settle on a specific version of Unity for compatibility. Some custom tools or plug-ins are targeted to a specific version of the Editor. So, upgrading the Editor may also mean upgrading plug-ins and fixing bugs between versions. To avoid forcing users to upgrade, Unity continues to support past versions of the Editor for developers who can't upgrade easily.

As a newcomer, you'll want all the latest features and that means picking the most recent version from the list of official releases. Aside from the Editor itself, you'll want to install the Dev tools: Microsoft Visual Studio Community as well as the official documentation. Be patient, we're just getting started.

If you're on OSX you'll see the following:

To continue, allow the various installation pop-ups and agree to additional license agreements. Eventually, you'll see a progress bar replace the download button and the Unity Installation is officially underway. After the installation of the Unity Editor, the Visual Studio Install will automatically launch.

2.2.1 Visual Studio Installation

Visual Studio Installer opens on its own. When it's complete, the Unity 3D installer pops back to the front. With Visual Studio Community you'll also be able to write and build applications outside of Unity 3D! Visual Studio is not just an editor for Unity 3D alone. You'll be able to create practically any app from scratch for Windows, Android, and much more!

If your machine has problems with the installation, you'll be able to select one of the installations from the Hub and try again. There's also an "Add Component" option to try re-installing Visual Studio from the Hub as well.

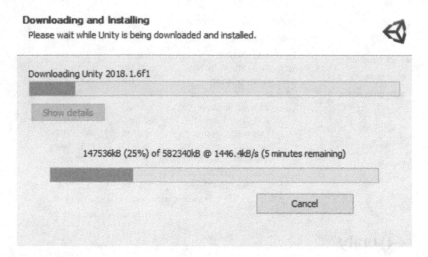

Once the installation is complete, start Unity 3D. If your splash screen looks different from the one below it's only because a newer version has been released and they updated the splash screen image. Don't worry, it's just cosmetic.

2.2.2 Unity Version Numbering

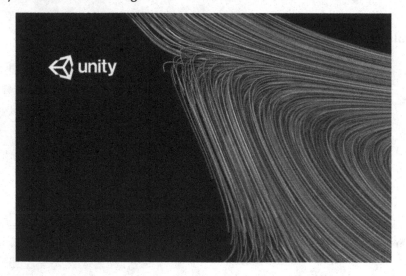

You might be wondering why there are so many different versions of Unity to download. The company keeps past versions around for various reasons. The latest version of Unity in the Official Releases list is going to be the recommended version. Older versions don't all support the same version of C# and the .NET framework, so some example code shown in this book might not work in older versions of Unity.

The Unity versions are numbered by year followed by a major and minor update version. You'll also see either a letter "a," "b," or "f" in the last part of the minor version number. This represents either an alpha, beta, or final release. Some versions are suffixed as LTS for Long Term Support; these are versions that are known to be the most stable.

Major updates often include engine changes that could interfere with custom plugins or may require some C# code changes between major versions. Minor updates usually don't include engine changes, but fix behaviors that might not have been working as expected by some users.

Alpha releases mean that the version is a work in progress or feature incomplete. Not all Alpha releases are available through the Hub. Unity often releases previews in their forums. Beta releases mean that the features require more testing before final release. Unity relies testing by their users to fully vet the functionality of their Editor before final release.

Final release updates mean bug fixes have been integrated, but no new features have been added. A new LTS version is released when most of the known bugs have been fixed. Of course, nothing is perfect, so as new bugs are found and fixed a new LTS version will be updated and released.

For the best experience it's a good idea to use the latest LTS version from the Official Releases list. Though for the most current features the newest final release in the Official Releases list is also safe. For all the coolest bleeding-edge tech, go for the Beta Releases. Upgrade notes and release notes accompany each release. In some cases, old features are removed as new ones take their place. In 2018, the MonoDevelop tool that used to be included is no longer supported as well as old programming features like Javascript and Boo support.

2.3 Git SCM Installation

For clarity, it's not necessary to download and install Git. Git is a stand-alone source code manager and it's great. GitHub, not to be confused with Git, is a free web service that facilitates sharing and storing a Git code repository. Signing up for a GitHub account is also not required. Both the Git software and the GitHub.com web service are fantastic resources and you're welcome to try them out, but neither are necessary.

Eventually, you will need to know your way around Git as a programmer. To the detriment of the curriculum, source code management is rarely, if ever, taught in a classroom setting. It's impossible to say how often source code management has saved a project. You will want Git if you write code.

Given a chance, I hope you'll follow along and learn a little Git. Some form of code management is used in every setting where programmers work together. At least some exposure to Git will help. Both personal and cooperative projects can leverage the power of Git.

If you want to skip out on Git, simply go to the "BookContents" URL and download the Zip file.

https://github.com/CSharpWithUnity/BookContents

Click the "Clone or Download" button, and then select Download ZIP from the following pop-up. This contains the Content, Unity projects and assets for each Chapter in this book. Unzip to somewhere on your computer and carry on.

2.3.1 Git-SCM.com Git Software (Optional)

If you're interested in joining the millions of programmers who do use Git, download the Git SCM software. Navigate to:

https://git-scm.com/downloads

Download and install the software. No account is necessary to download and install the software. Just a few dialogs during the installation need to be clicked through with default settings and you're done.

Git changes how you'll want to save files. Without Git you'll often resort to saving a file as Character1.cs followed by Character2.cs and eventually Character2Final_Final_Final2.cs, hardly optimal. Also consider that the contents of the file can interfere with one another. Using Git you'll leave the file's name unchanged, but Git will retain the content history of each file. At any time, you'll be able to retrieve any version of any file.

2.3.2 GitHub.com Sign Up! (Also Optional)

To fully leverage the power of Git you'll want to start your own GitHub.com account. If for some reason you don't need GitHub, then you can skip to the next section and just get into the basics of the Git software.

GitHub is an independent service that integrates with Git. It's an on-line storage system that makes source code available on the internet and can act as a back-up for your projects. It's also a resource used by many programmers to share example code and open-source projects with the world. You'll find tens of thousands of Unity and C# projects on GitHub, the contents of this book are just some of them.

Visit https://github.com/ and fill in the new account form.

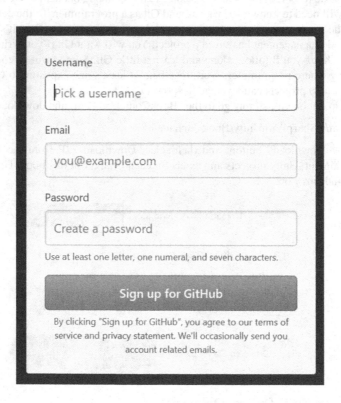

Make sure to write down your information since we'll need to match this up with the Git software we just installed in the previous chapter.

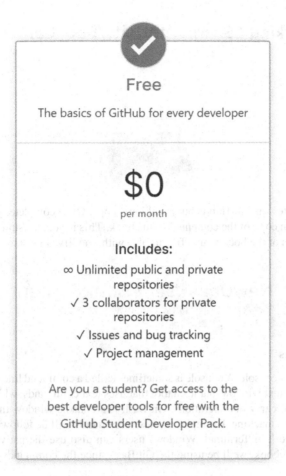

To start, select the Free option; this will give you unlimited private repos. Then, select Continue. You may need to wait for an email from GitHub to verify your humanity. After doing this, you'll be able to make a clone of the book contents to your own GitHub account.

Fill in the questionnaire with any response you feel comfortable with. These aren't going to change your interaction with the software, so the step is optional.

Next, you'll want to find the repo for this book. While you're logged in your new GitHub account, visit https://github.com/CSharpWithUnity/BookContents to find the contents for this book. On that page you'll have several options; the one we're looking for is called fork.

Clicking on this button will tell GitHub that you want to make a personal copy of the BookContents on the GitHub site. This means you'll have your own version, which you'll be able to edit and make changes to without disturbing the original.

Forking CSharpWithUnity/BookContents

It should only take a few seconds.

The above image indicates that GitHub is busy making a copy. Once complete, you'll have a new URL which points to your own copy of the contents for this book. This is your version; a completely independent copy of the contents of the book you're free to play with, modify, and share.

⅄ NewUnityUser / **BookContents**
forked from CSharpWithUnity/BookContents

2.3.3 Git: The Basics

Git runs in what's called a console. A console is sometimes called a command line or, in OSX, a Terminal. The console looks like a text window, but it's a tool that uses text commands, which are usually referred to as shell commands, to carry out operations. Git Bash is a console window that uses Unix-like shell commands on a Windows machine. Examples of these commands will be following soon.

Mac users have the built-in Terminal. Windows users can also use the native Windows console or the Power Shell. For this book, we'll be using the Git Bash since the commands are the same in OSX's Terminal software.

A new window should pop up once Git has finished installing. There should also be a shortcut to Git Bash located either in your start menu, or desktop. This new window is a shell, or sometimes folks refer to it as a Terminal. The "$" symbol is called a "Prompt" and indicates the shell is ready for a shell command to execute. Our first command will be asking Git what version is running.

In the window type the following:

```
git --version
```

The start of the line "`git`" calls on the Git software. The double dash or perhaps minus-minus indicates the start of a command for Git to run. The enter key at the end tells Git to execute the command. When run, Git should reply with something like the following:

```
git version 2.18.0.windows.1
```

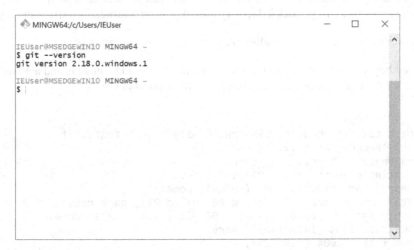

Git should reply with whatever version was installed. No doubt a newer version has come out since the writing of this chapter. Git gets updated often so expect a higher number than shown here.

Simply entering the following:

```
git
```

starts the Git software without any commands. Git replies with a list of commands it's able to run. In this list is "`clone`," which we will use to make a copy of the contents of the book.

Enter the shell command:

```
git clone
```

This will reveal the help text for the Git clone command. The first line is "`fatal: You must specify a repository to clone.`" Don't worry, nothing died; "fatal" is just a dramatic word Git uses when it stops doing something unexpectedly. From here you should also type in:

```
pwd
```

The "`pwd`" command is a regular shell command used to print out in what directory you're currently performing operations. When you want to know where you are in your computer the "`pwd`" command will tell you. For me I get "`/c/Users/alexokita`" indicating I'm in my user home directory. If you open your file browser, you can also find the same directory. Next, move into our Documents directory by using this command:

```
cd Documents
```

The letters "`cd`" is another regular Unix shell command that means "change directory" the following word is the directory you want to change to. This command also changes the prompt we've been seeing above the command prompt. You'll see your user name @ computer name followed by "~/Documents" this tells you that you're now running commands in your Documents directory. To get a list of what is in the Documents directory use the shell command:

```
ls
```

This will print out in text the names of the directories and files visible in the Documents directory. If there's nothing named BookContents then we'll make a clone of the Contents for the book here. If you have somewhere else that you'd prefer the "BookContents" go, then you can navigate there using the cd or change directory command. To go back a directory use cd.. or cd followed by a space and two dots.

```
git clone https://github.com/CSharpWithUnity/BookContents.git
```

This command begins downloading the repository to a directory in Documents and automatically creates a directory called "BookContents" named after the repo from Git.

```
alexokita@Buggy MINGW64
$ git clone https://github.com/CSharpWithUnity/BookContents.git
Cloning into 'BookContents'...
remote: Enumerating objects: 91, done.
remote: Counting objects: 100% (91/91), done.
remote: Compressing objects: 100% (66/66), done.
remote: Total 2267 (delta 42), reused 60 (delta 22), pack-reused 2176
Receiving objects: 100% (2267/2267), 4.80 MiB | 1.45 MiB/s, done.
Resolving deltas: 100% (1403/1403), done.
Checking out files: 100% (725/725), done.
```

Your results might look a bit different, but you'll get the contents so long as you're connected to the internet and can reach GitHub.

2.3.4 Your First Repo

On your GitHub account with the book contents repo open, look for the Clone or Download button located to the right of the contents. This is how Git will locate the online version of your code. If you didn't create your own account and skipped creating a fork, you can clone directly from this URL instead: https://github.com/CSharpWithUnity/BookContents.

Copy the URL that's in the pop-up box. This works the same from your own fork as it does from the original repo you may have forked. You can do this by clicking on the clipboard icon on the right.

Now back to that Git Bash window.

If you're not in your ~/Documents directory, cd back to it. This is where we will create a clone of the contents for this book. This directory is the same as if you were to open your Documents folder in the Windows file explorer. If you're familiar with using the command line, then you're free to clone your GitHub repo to another directory if you like using the cd command.

When we copy the URL from the pop-up dialog, we can't use CTRL+V to paste that into Git Bash; instead we use the mouse middle click. This may seem unusual, yes, but that's just how Git Bash works.

Enter the command in the bash window:

git clone followed by the middle click which should look a bit like the following:

```
git clone https://github.com/NewUnityUser/BookContents.git
```

The NewUnityUser should be replaced with your own user name on GitHub.

This will make a copy of the data from the remote data source on GitHub from your fork to your Documents directory. A new folder called BookContents stores all the files and project directories you'll need for this book. With your own GitHub account, you'll also be able to save your work on GitHub. If you've already cloned BookContents you should delete it before cloning your own repo.

The Git Bash is going to be our interface into GitHub. There are a lot of new useful GUI versions of Git and they all have their pros and cons. The command-line tool is the only version that's consistent and doesn't have different names and icons for each possible button. For consistency, we'll stick to the command-line version of Git.

That's enough for now; done with all the setup!

A fork is a copy of the contents that has split away from the original content. You've created a unique and original version of the original contents of the book. You're free to make changes and modify the code in any way. None of the changes you make will accidentally get made to the original source of your fork.

This also means that if the original source gets updated, you'll need to "pull" those changes into your version to get the latest updates. Use the following command:

```
git add remote add upstream http://github.com/CSharpWithUnity/BookContents
```

This makes a connection from your fork of your repo to the original source that you originally split off from. As the command implies, there's a remote repo, something distant from your repo. You're adding something that's upstream of it. Upstream means that the remote source has updates that you may need to catch up with. The URL you're adding to is the source you want to make a remote connection.

To see if the remote has make progress, you use the following command:

```
git fetch upstream
```

This tells Git to collect the data that might be updated on the remote repository. This doesn't yet combine or update your local data to the remote version. This saves a local hidden preview of what's updated. To match your local data to the remote version use:

```
git merge upstream/master
```

This merges the data that's been updated on the remote repository into your local copy. If there have been a lot of updates, you might have a new text window pop open asking if you want to make a comment on what's been merged. Save and close the window, and the merge will proceed.

If all goes well, then your local stream has caught up to the upstream repo. Your local copy on your computer has updated, but your fork on Github is still behind. To update your fork on GitHub use the following:

```
git push
```

This sends your local data up to GitHub for safe keeping. Now, you've updated your repo!

2.3.5 Before Moving On

Visual Studio, like Unity and Git, sees regular updates. Like the Unity Hub, the Visual Studio Installer is a stand-alone app that checks for updates. In addition, when Visual Studio is open there's a little flag on the top right.

If you ever see the flag light up, it's time to upgrade or at least look at what upgrades are available by clicking on it. Built into Visual Studio is a list of updates and changes that are available.

Before getting too far ahead we should review what we have installed. We should also write down the user names and passwords for the new accounts we created. Here's a checklist of where you should be at before moving on:

- Unity 3D has been installed
- Visual Studio Community was installed with Unity 3D
- Git SCM with the Git-Bash shell has been installed (Optional)
- Your Github.com account has been created (Optional)
- You've obtained the BookContents by either:
- A fork of https://github.com/CSharpWithUnity/BookContents to your Github account (Optional)
- Cloned your fork of the BookContents to your local Documents directory
- Or you downloaded the Zip and decompressed it to BookContents

With a copy of the contents of the book source code and all the examples on your disk, and Unity 3D and Visual Studio installed, you're ready to continue. There's still a bunch of stuff to learn about Git, but we'll save that for later.

In case you wanted somewhere handy to keep this information, here's a place for you to write your information.

Unity 3D Account Info
User Name: _____
Password: _____
GitHub Account Info (Optional)
User Name: _____
Password: _____
Visual Studio Account Info (Optional)
User Name: _____
Password: _____

2.4 Unity General Overview

Let's start with a brief overview of the user interface (UI) for the Unity Editor. For each chapter there's a prepared Unity Project with C# files and scenes named after each chapter. The personal and professional versions of Unity interact with C# in the same way.

When you're starting the Unity Hub for the first time, you may be asked to sign in with your Unity User account. If you got through the previous chapter, then you should already have your login and password. Hopefully you wrote down your login information.

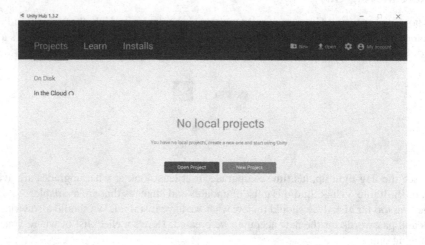

Across the top you'll see the menu tabs Projects, Learn, and Installs. These are the major tabs; on the right you'll also find New, Open, a gears icon, and an account icon. The Projects icon shows you a list of any local project, or if you're using the Unity Cloud project service, you'll see the projects listed there. The Learn tab will show some of the official Unity tutorials instructing you on how to use different tools that have been added to the Unity Editor. The Installs tab shows installers for different versions of Unity.

To get started Click on the Open Project icon and navigate to BookContents/Chapters/Chapter2 and select the folder.

Upon opening a project, you may be asked if you want to upgrade. Specify the latest version of Unity and use the Current Build Target. Press Open and upgrade the project to the newer version of Unity. Unity updates the project and generates a few new directories with temp files used to build the game. Assets like textures, meshes, and sounds are all prepared for building a game. Once this is complete the main Editor view opens.

2.4.1 The Main Window

The default Unity Editor interface is divided into five major parts: (1) toolbar, (2) Hierarchy panel, (3) Scene and Game view, (4) Inspector panel, and (5) Project and Console panel.

The tabs for any view can be dragged out and re-arranged in the Editor. Pulling a tab off detaches it from the main UI. The free tabs can remain a separate window, or they can be re-attached or grouped with other tabs. To restore the default layout, select Windows→Layouts→Default.

2.4.1.1 Toolbar

Label 1 in figure shows us the toolbar. The icons to the left are the navigation and manipulation tools. Toward the center of the tool bar are the Play, Pause, and Step Forward buttons. We will be using the Play-in-Editor button to test our code. On the right are various logins and view filters to help identify specific objects in the scene.

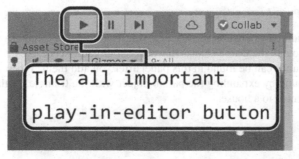

When the Play-in-Editor button is pressed, the Game view panel automatically comes to the front. Scripts attached to game objects in the open scene are executed and output is written to the Console panel. The contents of this book depend on opening a scene, examining code in the scene, and pressing the Play button to see what the code does. This pattern persists throughout the content of this book.

2.4.1.2 Scene, Game View, and Asset Store

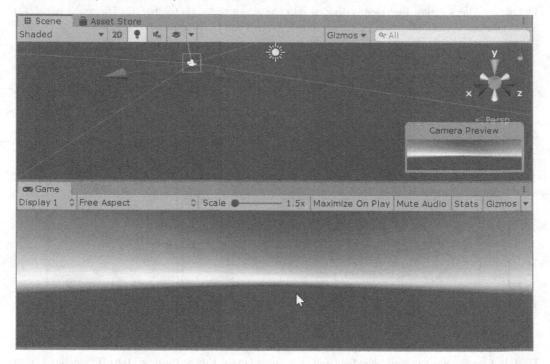

Label 2 shows us the Scene and Game view just mentioned. As the scene updates, the view from the Main Camera is shown through the Game view. The Scene tab falls to the background when the Game view comes forward. Clicking on the Scene tab allows us to see what's going on behind the scenes as the game updates. You're also able to move Game objects around using tools in the toolbar while the game is running. There are some exercises in this book which may require you to move game objects around as the game is being played.

The scene is more like a construction view of the game. The Game panel is the view of the game through the Main Camera. The difference here is that the Scene panel cannot be seen by the player, only you as the creator of the game can access the Scene view. With this view, you'll be able to arrange any object, light, or zombie the way you want.

2.4.1.3 Hierarchy Panel

Label 3 shows us the Hierarchy panel. In a new scene, you'll have a Main Camera and a Directional Light. The Hierarchy shows you all the Game objects that make your game scene. Any zombies, environments, cameras, lights, and sounds can be found in this panel after you add them. When any object is parented to another, it can be found by expanding the parent object with the triangle. In the following example, you'll find a piggy parented to a house.

The hierarchy of the scene contains the Game objects in the currently open scene.

2.4.1.4 Inspector Panel

Label 4 shows us the Inspector panel. By selecting an object in either the Hierarchy or the Scene view, you'll be able to look at their various properties such as a Transform, which shows the object's position, rotation, and scale in the scene. Objects in the scene are updated with the Inspector.

Take note of the Add Component button in this panel. This is one of the many ways in which we can assign a C# file to an object in the scene. If this seems a bit confusing, don't worry, we'll get back to what Components and Game objects are in a moment.

2.4.1.5 Project and Console Panel

Finally, label 5 shows us the Project and Console panels. The Project view shows us all the assets in the project. When we save a scene, it then turns into an asset for us to open from the Project view. As new C# files are added, they are shown here. To read the names of the files in the Project window use the slider located to the lower right of the window. Move the slider to the left to make the file names clearly readable.

The last but most important part is the Console panel. By clicking on the Console tab, the Console view will be brought forward. This view displays the output text that is created by the C# code we write. Any problems, warnings, and errors will also be presented in the Console panel.

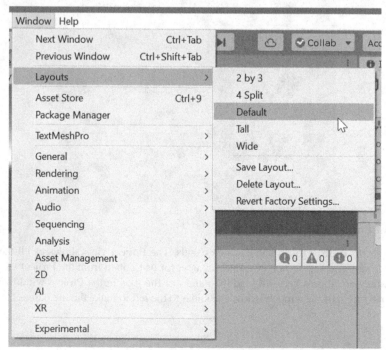

The Unity 3D installer also installed Visual Studio Community, the IDE used to edit code. We haven't written any C# yet, so we haven't gotten to Visual Studio, but that will come soon enough. Before that, we'll want to make sure that we're not too surprised by what we're about to get into.

2.4.1.6 Assets Directory

A Unity Project is a collection of many files and directories that store settings and assets used to build a game. Programming projects are made of many small text files called source files. In addition to these files, Unity includes 3D models, textures, sounds, and other resources used to build a game.

The primary location for all your C# files and assets is in the Assets directory. If you add a file outside this directory, your game will not be able to access it. When a project gets bigger, subdirectories in the Assets directory help keep your game organized. How you organize is up to you and your team; however, when you move or rename files it's best to do that from inside Unity 3D.

Living next to every file in the Assets directory is a .meta file. This meta file helps Unity 3D identify the file, as well as keep track of any settings related to that file. For instance, the SampleScene.unity generated with a new Unity Project has a neighboring .meta file that looks like the following:

Open that meta file in Visual Studio and you'll see something like the following:

```
SampleScene.unity.meta    ⊣  ✕
     1    fileFormatVersion: 2
     2    guid: 99c9720ab356a0642a771bea13969a05
     3    DefaultImporter:
     4      externalObjects: {}
     5      userData:
     6      assetBundleName:
     7      assetBundleVariant:
     8
```

You should never need to directly edit a meta file, but it's important to know why it's there. When you share your game project, you'll want to include all the generated .meta files. Otherwise, your settings for each object in the scene might get lost!

When starting your own projects double check that the Editor has the Visible Meta Files mode selected for Version Control in the Project Settings dialog. This will ensure that the files maintain their links between scenes and assets.

2.4.1.7 Project Settings Directory

The Editor itself has a lot of settings stored to prepare the environment to build to different platforms, Windows versus Android for instance. Global settings like those used by plugins, editor extensions, licenses, etc. are all stored in the Project Settings directory. Since many things like quality settings should be shared with your team, you should include the Project Settings directory when sharing your project.

2.4.1.8 Packages Directory

Next to the Assets directory in the computer's file browser is the Library directory. This contains the glue which Unity 3D uses to tie assets and logic together behind the scenes. Your editor preferences, platform settings, and many bits that game engines need are placed here. It is very rare any user will need to go in here to make any modifications, so it is best to avoid messing with the contents of this directory.

2.4.2 Git Ignore

Several directories are created when Unity opens a project. When using Git, the generated files need to be left out when checking for changes to add. Git uses a text file called .gitignore as a template to filter out files to ignore.

The file uses patterns in text, if a file name or directory matches a pattern in the .gitignore file then it'll skip the file when searching for changes. If the .gitignore file contains log.txt then all files, anywhere, which the repo named log.txt will be ignored.

Thankfully, there are plenty of Unity users who also use Git and .gitignore examples are readily available. A quick search on the internet reveals something on GitHub called the Unity.gitignore. With a couple dozen contributors, it's promising, and it's also what I've included in the Git repo for the BookContents.

To inspect the .gitignore file use a text editor—Visual Studio would be good—and navigate to the root of the BookContents directory. Open the .gitignore and you'll see about 40 lines of text.

2.4.3 What We've Learned

Unity 3D has a diverse set of tools, all of which are useful once you've decided to go ahead and build a game. The engine has been used to create everything from 2D side-scrolling games to 3D first-person shooters. Fantasy role-playing games and top-down strategy games have all been produced and published using the Unity 3D game engine.

It is best for you to look around online for additional information on the Editor itself. There's plenty of cool stuff you can do once you follow some of the online tutorials that cover the basics of the Editor.

Topics on materials, particles, and animation will not be covered in this book. It's a good idea to get into the different aspects of the Editor to understand the most out of Unity 3D, once you've gotten through a portion of this book.

The Unity Project is a directory. In this directory are a few subdirectories generated by Unity when it's launched. Only the Assets, Project Settings, and Packages ever need to be backed up. New directories generated by Visual Studio and Unity when launched may include a hidden ".vs" directory, ".obj", and various other files, but they're updated when Unity or Visual Studio are launched, and these don't need to be backed up.

To be an independent game developer, you'll have to cover the breadth of skills that are usually taken on by different team members in a larger game production cycle. As a "lone-wolf" game developer, you must take on a variety of tasks, not just the code.

If you're an artist looking to add programming on top of your current skill list, then the rest of the Editor's functions will come more easily. It is still a good idea to know your way around Unity 3D if you're new to this game engine.

2.5 Sample Code

Throughout this book, samples of code will be shown in what is called a code fragment. Fragments, as the word infers, are small parts of a whole code sample. Complete code samples will be given when it is necessary to show how a completed source file will look like. If only one or two lines change in a complete file, only the changed lines will be shown as a code fragment. Here's an example of a complete source file:

```
Example.cs  ✛ ✕
Assembly-CSharp                                    ▾    Example
 1      using System.Collections;
 2      using System.Collections.Generic;
 3      using UnityEngine;
 4
 5      public class Example : MonoBehaviour {
 6
 7          // Use this for initialization
 8          void Start () {
 9
10          }
11
12          // Update is called once per frame
13          void Update () {
14
15          }
16      }
17
```

The above example shows a new C# file generated by Unity 3D. We'll observe how it is created in a moment. What's important is that you could copy the text carefully into a new file named Example.cs and use it as is. First, let's see what a fragment will look like and then we'll go into how this is done.

2.5.1 Code Fragments

The following example shows a fragment of code taken from the completed source file:

```
16          // Update is called once per frame
17          void Update()
18          {
19
20          }
```

You should be able to identify where the code was taken from, line numbers seen to the left of the code should help indicate where in the file to look. After identifying where its original is, you should be able to see what's changed or added. This means you should make the same changes in your version of the source code.

A fragment is intended to showcase smaller, more important components of a complete code sample. Rather than reading through the completed source file and looking for the change, a fragment will help you find the important differences when a new concept is shown.

Not all examples in the book will start with a complete source file. Often, the code fragment will require only one line to represent the concept being explained. The context of the code sample and your ability to understand the context should be sufficient by the time you begin to see those examples.

Most of the programming fragments will not make a visual impact in the scene inside of Unity 3D. There isn't a single command to make monsters appear or dragons breathe fire. Programming is the manipulation of data with logic, not magic.

If the changes are added correctly, your version will function the same way as described by the tutorial you're reading. A code fragment cannot function on its own. The rest of the code is required by Unity 3D to run without errors.

Once a concept has been introduced, you'll be required to remember how it is used. Later lessons will again reinforce the concept that learning how to program is a skill-building process. To program a complete game, you need to combine the different ideas taught here and write your own code. Building upon your own skill will not only expand your understanding of C#, but once concepts have been learned, you'll be able to apply them to other programming languages.

Occasionally, I'll refer to how C# differs from other programming languages. I'll leave it up to you to investigate what the other languages look like on your own. This provides a context as to why C# looks or acts in a particular way and how other programming languages solve the same problem. In most cases, you may find that many programming languages look and behave quite similar.

2.5.2 Are Errors Bad?

No, errors and warnings are there to help you. Don't be afraid to make mistakes. The code you write cannot break Unity 3D or your computer. At least nothing you'll learn from this book will enable you to do so.

As a matter of fact, it is often good to produce errors. The errors tell us what we can and cannot do. Programmers often ask themselves, "Will the compiler let me do this?," which may produce an error. If not, then the programmer will continue his thought with "Huh, I guess it will, so that means I can ...."

Creating and fixing errors tells us what the code expects from us. It is a sort of a conversation between the programmer and the computer; for example, the programmer asking questions in the form of a code statement and the computer replying with an error to the programmer who asks for things the computer can't do.

Many years ago, programming magazines used to share code in print. This meant that you'd have to copy word for word what was written in an article to get a program to run. Back then the compiler wouldn't tell you where the error was.

Hidden in your code could be a 1 (one) in place of an l (lower case L) and you'd have to find it yourself *after* typing in a few hundred lines of text. Be thankful for the modern IDE that tells you not only that there's an error, but often where the error is.

2.5.2.1 Compile-Time and Run-Time Errors

There are two general cases of errors: compile-time and run-time errors. Compile-time errors often include syntactical errors that are usually found right away by Unity 3D before the code is even run. These are shown in the Console panel which we saw in a previous chapter.

An error where specific words may be misspelled, or an incorrect character is placed in the code will result in an error in the syntax in your code.

There are many cases in which compile-time errors can pop up, far too many to list here. However, compile-time errors (sometimes called parsers) occur when the code itself is written incorrectly.

Run-time errors happen while the game is running and the code is executed. These errors are usually created by a misunderstanding of what the code can do. When Unity 3D comes across a statement that contains unexpected data or tries to do something mathematically impossible, for example, divide by zero, we get a run-time error. Such errors are usually a bit harder to fix as they only show up when there are specific conditions in the game. For these, we can mark the statement in Visual Studio and tell Unity 3D to stop when it gets there. Once that happens, we can inspect every bit of data and its value. This will help find and fix any problems that exist.

Errors simply stop Unity 3D from running your code. Some properly written code may follow correct syntax, but might require you to force Unity 3D to close using the task manager. However, this is rare and often easy to fix. Read the code samples carefully as you enter them into Visual Studio.

To fix the error, you find what character was mistyped and replace it with a correction. To test if the error is fixed, go back to Unity 3D from Visual Studio. If no errors or warnings are produced, then your code is clear of syntactical errors.

2.5.3 How to Follow Along

Many examples will require that you use both Visual Studio and read Unity 3D's console window. We'll be switching back and forth often for each section. When working in Unity 3D, you might need to have the Editor take up a lot of screen space to have access to all the different parts of the Unity 3D interface. Primarily we'll need to see both the Console and the Inspector panels. This is often why programmers like having multiple monitors. One monitor with their code and the other monitor with an editor open, showing them the resulting behaviors.

Each section may have a corresponding Unity 3D scene. Open the Unity Hub to open the different chapter exercises.

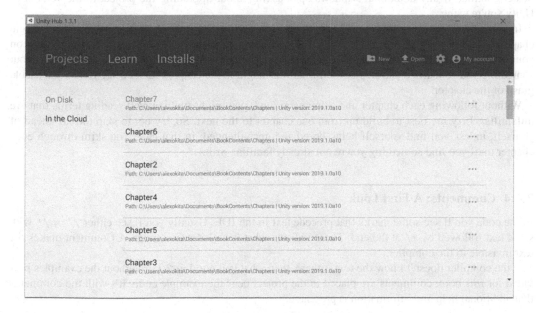

The Hub is a separate app from the Unity 3D Editor. It's used to install new and beta releases of Unity as well as create and open projects. From here, select the Open icon to the top right of the Hub app.

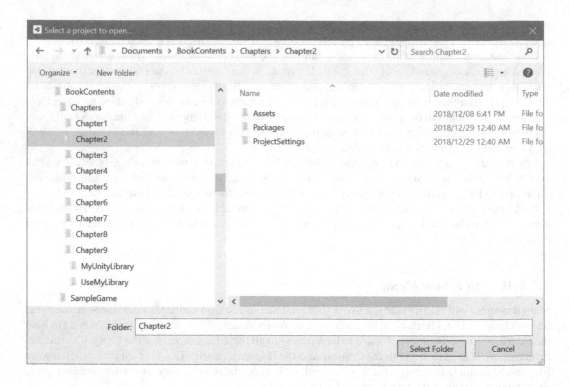

Select the directory of the chapter you're currently reading about and click on Select Folder. An additional window may open asking which version of Unity to use; select the latest version and continue. Select continue if any additional windows open asking about upgrading the project to the version of Unity you're using.

In each project for each chapter are Unity Scenes, each named by section. I'd suggest taking in a single chapter at a time and then letting the information sink in a bit. You should also conduct experiments on your own to gain a better understanding of what you just learned. If you can make assumptions about something you've learned and step beyond what was taught in the chapter, then I'd say you have a usable grasp of the chapter.

Without following each chapter and skipping around, you might find yourself reading terms that are unfamiliar. I try my best to build up from one chapter to the next. So, try not to skip too far ahead of yourself, unless you find yourself being bored and unchallenged; in that case, you skim through each chapter until you find something you're not already familiar with.

2.5.4 Comments: A First Look

In the code you'll see some marks that precede text in the IDE. Usually you'll see either // or /* with some text followed by */ at the end. These indicate what is called a Comment. A Comment makes the text invisible to the compiler.

If the compiler doesn't know the text is there, then what is it good for? Throughout the examples provided for this book comments are placed in the project near the example code. It's with the comments that additional help and information is presented.

```
7        // Use this for initialization
8    ⊟   void Start () {
9            Debug.Log("Everything is working!");
10       }
```

Even the engineers at Unity leave helpful breadcrumbs in the code hinting at what the code in the file does. The image above shows the comment "// Use this for initialization" to indicate what the following code is used for. Comments are useful, and you should remember to use them to keep notes for yourself as you learn.

Comments are used like breadcrumbs in a deep forest. Comments help leave behind some of the thought process in why your code is written the way it is.

2.5.5 What We've Learned

We're going to have to do a lot of reading and writing. Sorry, that's just the case when it comes to code. If this doesn't detract from the experience of learning, then great! Otherwise you're going to have to just get over the fact that programming involves a lot of typing and thinking at the same time. If you're used to doing that sort of thing, then great!

2.6 Working with C#: Game Engines

Unity 3D is a game engine. You will be writing code that runs inside of this game engine. So, you're writing software that's run inside of another piece of software. What this means is that your code operates a layer further from your computer's hardware resources.

NOTE: What do I mean by further from the computer hardware resources? This is where the term "high-level programming" comes from. At the lowest level is the actual computer hardware. Programmers at this level are building silicon chips.

```
/* * * * * * * * * * * * * * * * * * * * * * * * * * * * *
 *                                                        *
 *             ┌─────────────────────────────────────┐   *
 *             │ Art Assets          Node Based       │   *
 *             │ Sounds and Music    Game Behaviour   │   *
 *             │ UI construction                      │   *
 *             │                                      │   *
 *  high level │ C# Game Behaviour                    │   *
 *      ↑      │ Implementation                       │   *
 *             │                                      │   *
 *             │ 3rd Party Libraries and DLLs         │   *
 *             │ Usually specific for each target OS  │   *
 *             │                                      │   *
 *             │ Unity 3D Engine C#                   │   *
 *             │ Platform Independence                │   *
 *             │ Layer                                │   *
 *             │                                      │   *
 *             │ Unity 3D Engine                      │   *
 *             │ Math Rendering Effects               │   *
 *             │ File Management                      │   *
 *             │ Physics (All the hard stuff)         │   *
 *             │                                      │   *
 *             │ Operating System                     │   *
 *             │ Windows/OsX/Android/iOS/Linux        │   *
 *             │ etc...                               │   *
 *             │                                      │   *
 *             │ Hardware Software Interface          │   *
 *             │ Drivers Specific Application         │   *
 *             │ Programming Interfaces               │   *
 *      ↑      │                                      │   *
 *  Low Level  │ Hardware Chips Controllers           │   *
 *             └─────────────────────────────────────┘   *
 * * * * * * * * * * * * * * * * * * * * * * * * * * * * */
```

At one level above the silicon are things such as bus and motherboard where everything is either plugged into or soldered on. At another level above those are components that tell the motherboard what to do when power is turned on, how to look for data storage to launch operating systems, and just about everything else that happens when the computer is turned on.

Once this level finds an operating system, it hands over the tasks to the lowest level of your computer operating system where drivers and other hardware-to-software interfaces come into play to get your computer running. Once the computer gets booted and your operating system is properly talking to all the hardware components, it is ready for software applications to start running. At this level your software is usually not talking to any computer hardware directly, but it is talking to the software that runs the operating system.

Unity 3D is a software that talks to the operating system. When you write your game software your code usually talks directly to Unity 3D, but not to the operating system or computer hardware. Your code is being run with many other layers of software between you and the hardware. Similar to so many mattresses between you and the floor, there is more padding between you and any of the complexities that run your computer.

When your code is compiled, it turns into a machine language. The details here are simplified as there's a bit more going on under the hood than what we can explain here. The game code is made up of many different objects called classes. Classes are composed of data (also known as variables), logic (also known as functions or methods), and a name (also known as an identifier).

Functions and data work together inside of Unity 3D to make your game experience come to life. This coordinated effort can be packaged and turned into a new program that you can publish to any number of computer platforms including browsers, game consoles, and mobile devices.

C# has a few simple parts that we'll be studying later in this chapter. As a part of an exercise, we'll have to learn how to read a bit of code. Open the LineNumbers.cs class by double clicking on it in the Assets directory of the BookContents/Chapters/Chapter2 project.

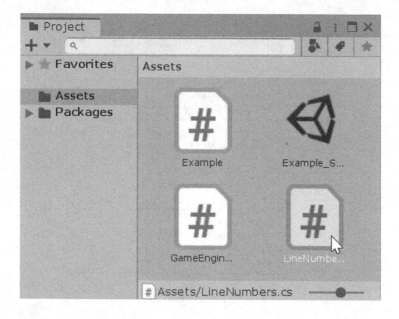

An underappreciated part of reading code is the line number. These numbers are found to the left of the code.

```
1    using System.Collections;
2    using System.Collections.Generic;
3    using UnityEngine;
4
5    public class LineNumbers : MonoBehaviour
6    {
7        public int SomeInt = 1;
8        public int OtherInt = 7;
9
10       // Use this for initialization
11       void Start () {
12           print(MyFunction(SomeInt, OtherInt));
13       }
14
15       // Update is called once per frame
16       void Update () {
17
18       }
19
20       int MyFunction(int a, int b)
21       {
22           return a + b;
23       }
24   }
25
```

Each line of code is numbered starting with 1 at the top and ascending as you scroll down. Here we can see that lines 1–3 of the code are required to access libraries or software that has already been written by many engineers to empower your code with a vast wealth of software.

At line 5, you'll find what is called a class declaration. This serves as a good overview of what to expect in the remaining chapters, so don't worry if this seems like a lot of unfamiliar information.

Continuing down you'll find some public variables at lines 7 and 8. At line 10, you'll find a comment describing the use of void Start(), which is the first line of code declaring a function. Inside the function at line 12, you'll find a statement that will be executed when the Start() function is called.

At lines 16–18, you'll find another function named Update() that doesn't do anything right now, and at line 20, you'll find another function named MyFunction(). At line 24, you'll find the closing curly brace that closes the LineNumbers class.

When Visual Studio comes across an error, the error list indicates both the type and the line the error appears. Place a random letter in the code and Visual Studio will be quick to indicate something is out of place.

```
29       int MyFunction(int a, int b)
30       {
31           return a + b; :D
32       }
33   }
```

	Code	Description	Project	File	Line	Suppr
❌	CS1513	} expected	Assembly-CSharp	LineNumbers.cs	31	Active
❌	CS1002	; expected	Assembly-CSharp	LineNumbers.cs	31	Active
❌	CS0103	The name 'D' does not exist in the current context	Assembly-CSharp	LineNumbers.cs	31	Active

2.6.1 Creating and Assigning a New C# File: Now It's Your Turn

Let's start with the BookContents/Chapters/Chapter2 project we've been working with.

C# files are basic text files. It is possible to open Notepad or any other simple text editor and create a new file from scratch, but it is better to have Unity 3D create a clean, error-free starting file to work from. Right click on the Project panel and select Create→C# Script from the pop-up menu.

This will create a new C# file in the Assets directory in your project. We'll go into organizing these files with a bit more logic later, but for now we'll just leave it in the Assets directory. Alternatively, you can use the menu and select Assets→Create→C# Script to create a script in the Assets directory.

NOTE: You can resize the file display with the slider on the lower right. This will make longer file names easier to read.

This will create a file called `NewBehaviourScript`, which needs to be renamed as `MyScript` to follow along. If you unselect the file, it'll be created as `NewBehaviourScript`. This means you'll need to change the file name both in the Assets directory and in the class once it is opened in Visual Studio. We will cover how this is done in a moment. It's not necessary to add the .cs at the end of the file name when using the Asset Panel in Unity 3D; the Editor will keep track of the file types and add the correct file extensions.

To the right in the Inspector panel, you'll notice some code shown in the panel. This is a preview of the content in your new file. Selecting different objects both in the Assets panel and in the game scene will prompt different options to appear in the Inspector panel.

The Inspector panel will be useful for many different things, so we'll be using this quite a lot.

Don't bother trying to edit your code in the Inspector panel. This only serves as a preview to your code, so you might get a clue as to what the code is for. Editing the code is best done in an IDE which we'll jump into next.

Double click on the C# Example file in the Project panel to open Visual Studio.

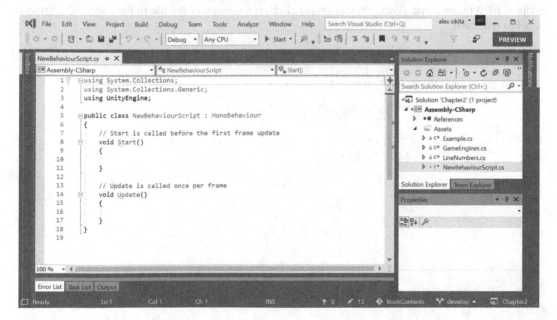

This is where we will be spending most of our time. An IDE is a software made specifically for editing code. Visual Studio is a popular IDE that has many modern features such as *automatic code completion* and *syntax highlighting*, and most importantly, the *debugger*. We'll get to know how to use these features as we read on.

2.6.2 Naming Your New File

Just to make sure we're off to a good start, the name of the C# file should match the name of the class. For example, if the file name was called PeanutButter.cs, you need to make sure that the class name matches.

Observe the line that reads as "public class Chocolate : MonoBehaviour {." When I mean the file name, I do mean the actual file located on the disk in your operating system. To get to these files, right click on the object in Unity 3D's Project panel to get to additional options. In Windows, select Show in Explorer from the right-click window.

If the name of the file doesn't match the name of the class, you'll get a class definition error when the script is used in the game. Also, you can simply click on the name of the file in the Unity 3D's Project panel to rename it.

```
using System.Collections;
using System.Collections.Generic;
using UnityEngine;

public class Chocolate : MonoBehaviour
{
    // Start is called before the first frame update
    void Start()
    {

    }
```

If the name of the file matches the name of the class, we're in a good position to get started. Keep this file around as we're going to be using it in Chapter 3. Once the class name and the file name match up, you can move on. If the file is named NewMonoBehaviour, change its name to match the class name.

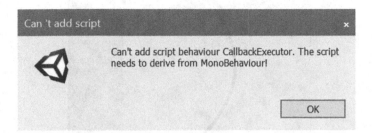

2.6.3 Using Your New File

To assign the C# file to an object in the scene, you can drag it from the Project panel onto an object in the scene. This seems to be simple, but the object might not be in view, or it might be too small to easily select.

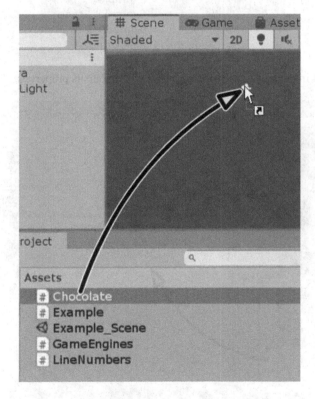

You can also drop it on an object in the Hierarchy panel. Everything in the scene is found in the Hierarchy panel.

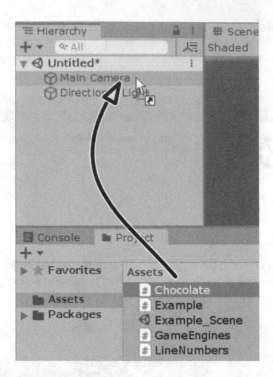

With a selected object in the scene, the Inspector panel will update its properties.

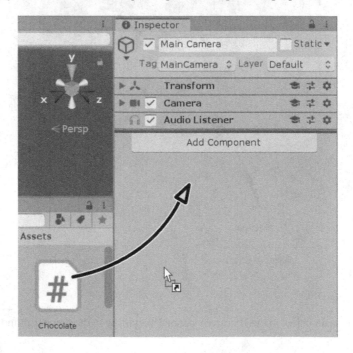

Dropping the Chocolate.cs file anywhere under the other properties in the Inspector panel will also add it to the selected object. If that's not enough, then you can press the Add Component button on a selected object in the scene and pick Scripts to select any scripts available in your project.

Using the Add Component button, you can even create, name, and add a script all at once! This has become my preferred system of creating and adding scripts to objects in a scene. It does everything all at once. After this it is just a matter of moving the script from the root of the Assets directory into a more organized directory.

There are plenty of ways to use the Editor, but any one of the methods of assigning a script to an object in the scene will work just fine. The end result is that our script will be attached to an object in the scene. As soon as the Start Game button is pressed, your code will go live.

Press the button again to stop the game and your code from running.

After a script has been added to an object in the scene, it becomes a component of that object. All of the components of the object appear as additional rollouts in the Inspector panel. To edit a script component added to the object in the scene, you can double click on the component.

As an alternative you can click on the gear icon and select Edit Script from the pop-up menu.

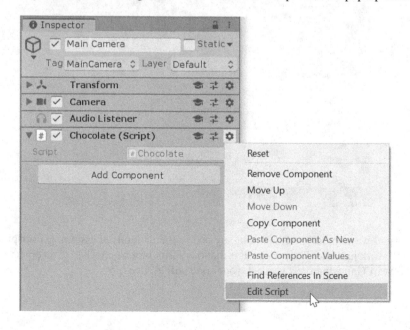

And finally, by clicking on the script attached to the component, the file in the Assets directory will highlight pointing out where the script lives in the project.

If a script becomes detached from a script component, the script can be replaced or changed by clicking on the little circle to the right of the script name.

Clicking on this little interface widget will open the following dialog showing you all of the available scripts in the project.

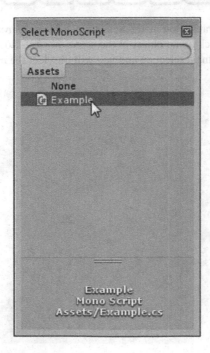

Selecting a script in the panel by double clicking will assign the script to the missing slot in the Inspector panel. To remove an unwanted script or script component, right click on the title of the component and select Remove Component.

2.6.4 Additional Unity 3D Tools

To get an idea of what to expect in the remaining chapters, we can drop in a few simple shapes into the scene. Select GameObject→Create Other→Cube to drop a cube into the scene viewport. To pan around in the scene, press the Q button. Use the left mouse button in the scene viewport to pan around. The mouse wheel zooms the cube, and the right mouse button enables common "first person shooter style" navigation with WASD keyboard keys and mouse-look mode.

The W key enables the object translation mode. Select any tool aside from the View tool and you'll be able to box select or directly click on an object in the scene. Shift + Box select adds to your selection. Press the CTRL key while making a selection and you will unselect the next selected item.

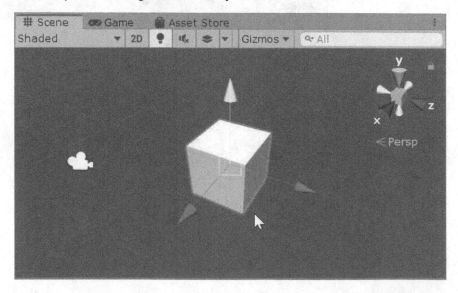

The Transform tool allows you to pick and drag the object around in the scene. Dragging left and right on a property in the Inspector will change the individual value.

You can watch the Position values change under the Transform tab in the Inspector panel as you manipulate the cube. The numbers can also be entered directly into the X, Y, and Z fields of the Inspector panel if you want to have a precise control over an object's placement.

The E key will turn on the Rotation tool. Like the Transform tool, you can watch the object's rotation update in the Inspector panel as you manipulate the object in the scene.

The R key activates the Scale tool and you can change the size of an object or enter the values in the Inspector panel. All three of these tools allow you to pick and drag on various parts of the Manipulation tool in the scene. This changes the manipulation's behavior by constraining the action to one or two axes of freedom.

On the top right of the Scene viewport is a little widget that allows you to switch between various views of your scene. Top, front, and side views can be accessed quickly by clicking on one of the cones on the widget's cube. To change between a perspective and a parallel camera view, click on the Persp/Iso icon to toggle how the scene is rendered.

2.6.5 Working in a Live Scene

While the game is running, you're allowed to reach into the game through the Scene panel. You can select and move objects while the code is being updated. You can also use the Inspector panel to manipulate a selected object's parameters and variables.

Once you stop the game, any changes you made to anything in the scene are immediately reverted to whatever settings they had just before you started the game. This might mean losing some settings which you have tuned while playing the game.

If the settings were saved every time you stopped the scene, then testing a scene would be more troublesome. Going through a level shooting all of the zombies means that the next time you start the level again, everything would already be dead.

2.6.6 Saving a Scene

All the changes we've been doing have been created and applied to objects in a scene. After adding objects to a scene such as lights, cameras, and other objects, it is time to save the scene. The standard Save dialog instructs you to save and name the scene. The default location for a scene is the Assets directory in the project. It is possible to create a sub-directory in the Assets directory called Scenes or something similar; however, for our use, we'll save the scene in the Assets directory of the project.

2.6.7 Opening a Scene

While working with each and every tutorial of this book, there's always going to be a scene file named Scene. Throughout the book, the tutorials will begin with the Scene file found in the downloaded project. To open the scene simply double click on the scene icon located in the Project panel under the Assets directory. You can also select File→Open Scene to open any scene in the project.

2.6.8 What We've Learned

Creating and assigning a new C# file to an object doesn't require so much work. There are plenty of ways to do this within the Unity 3D Editor. Once we add some code to the new C# file we're just a button press away from seeing our code in action. With some of the tutorials in this book, you'll be expected to create a new project, create new scripts, and assign the scripts to an object in a scene. With some of the more detailed tutorials, a completed version of the scene will be provided for you.

Amazingly enough, other professional tools for building things for Windows, Linux, or OSX all involve a similar process for creating desktop software. There's generally a lot more footwork involved with getting started. Templates, frameworks, and other IDE setup processes are required before even being able to get something to print out to a Console panel.

Learning C# with Unity 3D is one of the shortest routes from typing to execution that I can think of that has the most interactive results. The Editor itself allows you to interact with variables and values in real time. Selecting an object in the Scene editor and changing numbers in the Inspector panel allow you to have a direct connection to your code and see the changes in behavior in real time. This kind of interaction is only possible in the real-time nature of a game engine.

So far, we've gotten to do a bit of setup and preparation. Getting Unity 3D up and running is necessary, and if you've gotten stuck somewhere, make sure that you check the internet for any solutions. Naming files and classes correctly is also necessary to get your code to work. A single spelling error can break your code and nothing will work. Also remember that the upper- and lowercase letters matter a great deal. Naming your file the same as the contained class is also important, as a mismatch will also break your code and produce errors.

Programming is a highly rewarding endeavor. Don't let a small hitch bring you down. As you accumulate knowledge, writing code will only get easier. After you've learned one programming language, it is much easier to learn another.

I hope that after you've managed to wrap your head around C#, you'll be able to take the knowledge earned here, look at other programming languages, and feel a need to learn more. If you're an artist, adding the cool tricks that programming can offer to your palette of skills will only make you richer. And I mean richer in more than just the depth of skill.

2.7 Leveling Up: The Journey Has Just Begun

Get ready for some new concepts. Telling computers what to do and how to do it takes a lot of work. Computers aren't very bright; they're actually downright dumb. They do exactly what you tell them to do. If you get unexpected behaviors, it is up to you to make yourself clearer.

Of course, this all involves talking to a computer in its language, something that we should be able to do part way into this book. Once we've gone through the basics, we should be able to tell the computer simple commands and get expected results.

If you feel that you've gotten to a saturation point while reading this book, put this book aside for a bit and practice some of the concepts you've just learned. If you feel that you've explored all you can on your own, it is time to come back and pick up where you left off.

3

First Steps: Just Getting Started

This section will cover many basic terms and some of the basic ideas behind writing code. C# is among the many programming languages which share words and concepts to convey instructions to the computer. Once we get through the first few chapters you'll be introduced to some more of the basics which are directly related to reading and writing code.

Before we can get to that, we'll need to cover some terms and concepts that hold true for many different programming languages, not just C#. The methods and systems that allow converting words into executable code require strict rules.

When writing English or chatting online we tend to ignore formatting and punctuation. The brevity allows for faster communication; though only because we as humans have learned many new words and can use context to better interpret the contractions and acronyms in the written form of English used online or in text messages. Computers aren't so smart as to be able to interpret intent precisely.

Unity 3D is a 3D game engine. By 3D we mean three dimensions, which means we have an x, y, and z coordinate space. 2D or two-dimensional game engines like Game Maker only use x and y. This is the difference between a cube and a square. One has depth to each shape and the other does not.

Later, we will be working with three-dimensional vectors. Unity 3D uses Euclidian vectors to describe where objects are positioned in a 3D scene. When a position is described in terms of $x = 1$, $y = 2$, and $z = 3$, you should understand that this describes a position in 3D space. Unity 3D isn't limited to 3D space. Plenty of games use the x and y coordinates to make plenty of 2D games, but Unity 3D is by default a 3D game engine.

3.1 What Will Be Covered in This Chapter

We'll go over the specifics of the most basic concepts behind the C# programming language. C# has a great deal in common with other programming languages, so much of the knowledge here is transferable to many other programming languages. To get started on our journey toward an understading of C#, we'll investigate the following:

- Tokens, the smallest elements of C#
- How statements, give tokens meaning
- Keywords in C# with specific meaning
- How to use white space and proper formatting
- How statements are grouped together into a code block
- How classes are organized and what they're used for
- What a variable is and how it's used
- Types and how they behave when converted between one another
- Commenting on code and leaving messages to yourself and others within the code

Each section of this chapter will cover each new term in detail with some examples. There is a lot of vocabulary to learn. If you speak to a programmer, it may sound like they're speaking in a different language. The words they use have specific meaning in relation to programming. To continue through the rest of the book you'll need to learn what these new words mean in relation to writing code.

3.2 Review

In Chapter 2 we looked at what code looks like. Before going too much further, we want to make sure that we are able to open each of the different projects in Unity 3D to follow along.

Near the start of Chapter 2 you may have created a new GitHub account. In GitHub a fork of the book's repo was created to your account. From the fork the contents were pulled to your computer.

Your fork of the repo is visible to the public. You're the only one with access rights to make changes to your fork. If you discover a typo or any errors or "bugs," feel free to post a comment on the original repo.

If you didn't create a GitHub account and just downloaded a zip of the contents, that's fine too. Just be aware that there are a few chapters covering Git which you should still look at, since Git is indispensable even if you're not using it right now.

Before continuing you should be able to run Unity 3D, create and open C# files, and attach and remove the C# files to an object in a scene. You should also have the BookContents repo on your computer. Once all of this is done, you should be able to open a project from any of the chapters, then open a scene from the project. Finally, test the scene with the Play-in-Editor button and read the output in the Console window.

Double check by opening the BookContents/Chapters/Chapter2 project. Open the Sample Scene and press the Play-In-Editor button to make sure you've got everything working by looking for the output in the Console window.

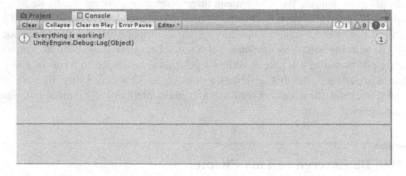

If any of this seems unfamiliar, go back and review Chapter 2; we'll be doing quite a lot here which depends on your being able to move objects and create and edit C# files. It's time to get into what code is, so keep calm and carry on!

3.2.1 Submitting Changes to Git

To make the most of Git you'll want to make some changes to files and submit them for safe keeping. At the root of BookContents is a README.md or markdown file. This is basically a text file with some clever formatting. Open this with Visual Studio and add in some information.

```
README.md    ⊞ ✕
  1  # This is My version of the README
  2  Make sure to personalize it with your own welcome message!
  3
```

In the first line I've added the above two lines. Make sure you're more original than I am with your welcome message. Once you're done with your welcome message open Git Bash. Enter the following command:

```
git status
```

```
alexokita@Buggy MINGW64 ~/Documents/BookContents (master)
$ git status
On branch master
Your branch is up to date with 'origin/master'.

Changes not staged for commit:
  (use "git add <file>..." to update what will be committed)
  (use "git checkout -- <file>..." to discard changes in working directory)

        modified:   README.md

no changes added to commit (use "git add" and/or "git commit -a")

alexokita@Buggy MINGW64 ~/Documents/BookContents (master)
$
```

The status command asks Git to show you what's changed. The changes shown reflect any file modified throughout all the content in the BookContent repo. The line "Changes not staged for commit" show you which files have been modified, added, or deleted.

In the changes you'll see modified : README.md as well as instruction to discard changes if you would like to reset the file. To keep the changes, enter the command:

```
git add README.md
```

```
alexokita@Buggy MINGW64 ~/Documents/BookContents (master)
$ git add README.md
```

This adds the README.md to a list of files that will be included with a checkpoint of changes. In git terms this "stages" the file for commit. Think of this as a save point in a game. You can load your game from a checkpoint and start over if you mess up. Git grants your code with the same ability. To save the checkpoint we need to commit the changes with the following command:

```
git commit -m "adding changes to readme"
```

```
alexokita@Buggy MINGW64 ~/Documents/BookContents (master)
$ git commit -m "Adding changes to README.md"
[master 58a4fb7] Adding changes to README.md
 1 file changed, 5 insertions(+), 2 deletions(-)
```

The git commit command has two parts: the -m which indicates we'll add a note to our save point and the "Adding changes to README.md," which is the message to identify what the commit was created for.

This turns into a save point which we can come back to. You'll also notice the section that says [master 58a4fb7]; this is the code name for the save point. This is how Git remembers everything you've added to the repo. These numbers and letters are called hash codes. Your commit will have a different hash, so don't worry if it looks different. Every commit will be unique.

GitHub comes into play once you want to save your changes on your GitHub account. To upload the commit, use the command:

```
git push
```

alexokita@Buggy MINGW64 ~/Documents/BookContents (master)
$ git push
Enumerating objects: 5, done.
Counting objects: 100% (5/5), done.
Delta compression using up to 4 threads
Compressing objects: 100% (3/3), done.
Writing objects: 100% (3/3), 402 bytes | 402.00 KiB/s, done.
Total 3 (delta 2), reused 0 (delta 0)
remote: Resolving deltas: 100% (2/2), completed with 2 local objects.
To https://github.com/CSharpWithUnity/BookContents.git
   f016455..707a2f4 master -> master

alexokita@Buggy MINGW64 ~/Documents/BookContents (master)
$

Depending on how you've set your security settings you may need to enter a user name and password. Once that's done your commit will be pushed into GitHub. This means that even if your computer gets eaten by zombies, your work is safe on GitHub.

The pattern that we repeat is Add Commit Push. Every time you want to create a save point for your work, remember "Add, Commit, Push" to create a checkpoint.

To inspect your work, go to your GitHub page in a web browser.

The changes you've made to your README.md will appear in your fork of the repo.

3.3 Let's Build a Game—Part 1

An additional resource for you is a Unity "SampleGame" found in the SampleGame directory in the BookContents Git repo. A small set of free to use assets are ready for you to use in your own projects. This project also contains many helper objects that will show you how games are built.

Often, small game studios store their art assets in the Git repo along with the source code for the game. I've stored some asset files in the Art Assets directory next to the Unity Project. Feel free to inspect the 3D models in Blender and the 2D assets in Gimp. Both Blender and Git are open source and free to use for noncommercial use.

In the Unity Project directory called Unity-SampleGame you'll find that Assets has various directories to keep the Assets directory relatively organized. All the assets used specifically for the sample game are under the SampleGame sub-directory. In there, you'll find that Meshes, Prefabs, Materials, Textures, Scripts, and others have their own homes. Starting many projects in Unity 3D has formed a habit of organization. Your projects don't need to follow the same pattern, but anything similar will help in the future.

When an asset from the Unity asset store is downloaded, you'll usually find that it will live in its own directory, not unlike the one created for SampleGame. This convention of creating a directory in Assets for your own work is standard and should be followed to avoid conflicting files.

To get started with a new Unity 3D project you'll want to look at a checklist of a few settings before using source control. First are the meta files. Unity 3D creates additional text files that help link different assets to one another. To remember these associations in Git, you'll want to make them visible. Meta files allow the editor to restore the associations when a project is opened. Select Edit → Project Settings → Editor and find the drop-down menu with the Version Control section and set the Mode to Visible Meta Files.

A game development cycle starts with a game design document. This includes what the player does and concept art as to what the game looks like as the player experiences your game. Often game designs also include some story and a world description. Assuming all of that is done, the engineering begins.

Programmers begin with the Unity Project and sometimes start some sort of technical document. A large game would often involve specific programming goals like database management for inventory, automatic loot box generation, or a multi-player match-making strategy. Before all of that comes prototyping and experimentation.

It's common for the experimentation to change the game design. Through experimentation unexpected game play experiences can emerge. New game play elements appear as code is written and unexpected results often appear either by accident or inspiration. Experimentation in Unity 3D means reading what Unity 3D has in its tool kit. Documentation available online often gives a general description of each Unity 3D function, but that hardly has meaning without seeing how the function works or what it does.

3.3.1 Movement Experiments

In the SampleGame Unity Project open the Assets/SampleGame/Scenes/Chapter3 Unity scene. A strange little object made of colored arrows should sit in the middle of the scene. This was created with a box collider and a rigid body attached. This gives the object physics properties that will make it fall and land on the ground under it without falling over.

This object has been named TransformPrimitive to denote that we're going to use this to show us how to use the `Transform` Component of the Game Object. This little object has arrows pointing in each coordinate direction with a + sign pointing in the positive direction of that axis. Attached to this object is a script called MovementExperiment.cs which we'll open in Visual Studio to inspect. This can be found in the `Assets/SampleGame/Scripts` directory in the project.

The Start function contains a single line:

```
// Use this for initialization
void Start () {
    gameObject.transform.position = new Vector3(0, 0, 1);|
}
```

This line tells the object to set the GameObject's `transform.position` to a new `Vector3` with the values for *x* and *y* set to 0 and *z* set to 1. As a hint, since we're new to Unity 3D most objects in a scene hierarchy are GameObjects. The GameObject is the fundamental type of "thing" that makes up the different elements that can interact within the game's scene. This is discovered by reading the Unity Documentation.

3.3.2 Reading Programmer Documentation

Programming documentation has become roughly standardized, to some extent programmers have come to use a similar format when it comes to sharing how their code is used. Unfortunately, it's still written by programmers, so for the uninitiated, definitions are obtuse.

Most of the time there's some type of outline with entries describing everything available in the API, or Application Program Interface. You can open the web page directly from Unity with the Help → Scripting Reference menu selection.

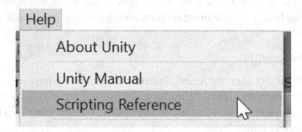

The following page is the Unity Scripting Reference. A column on the left shows you everything that the Unity 3D engineers have written anticipating what you might want to do in your game. This assumes you know what to do with the information.

Under the UnityEngine are most of the different systems that you'll eventually find useful for your game. In UnityEngine/Classes/GameObject you'll find an entry describing the GameObject.

After the description you'll see the different things accessible inside of the object, or the object's members. Each one of the members is something that you can access, read, or ask the object to do. The members are separated as Properties, Constructors, Public Methods, etc.

Clicking on a member of the object will usually show you a similar page with the name of the function, sometimes followed by some example for using the member in question. The documentation for `GameObject` tells us that `Transform` is always added to a `GameObject` when created.

In addition to online documentation, Visual Studio has useful information built-in. Open the SampleGame/Chapter3/Scripts/MovementExperiment.cs script and Right click on the word `position` in Visual Studio and select `Peek Definition Alt+F12` from the pop-up menu. In Visual Studio for Mac you'll select `Go To Declaration ⌘D` to see a similar description.

```
gameObject.transform.position = new Vector3(0, 0, 1);
```

In Visual Studio for Mac

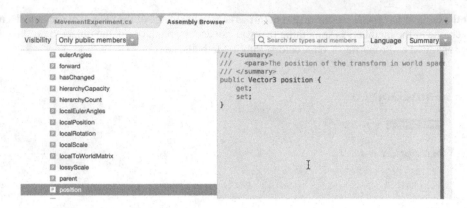

A new window, or part of a window appears beneath the line of code we're looking at. This window allows us to scroll through different members of the Transform class that position shares a relation with. As you scroll through the different listings you'll see a `get;` and a `set;` by some of the members and just `get;` listed under others. The members with `set;` mean this is a property you can change, ones with just `get;` you're only able to read.

Scrolling down even further you'll see some listings which end with `();` some of these have additional code in the parenthesis, these are called function members. Clicking on the small box with the + sign in the left margin expands a comment left by the programmer with a summary of what the function or property member is used for.

```
//
// Summary:
//      The position of the transform in world space.
public Vector3 position
```

Expanding the comment next to Position reveals the summary: `The position of the transform in world space`. The name of the member is preceded by `Vector3` indicating the type the property represents. With this you have the start of how to navigate around in Visual Studio just enough to begin experimenting. Press Escape to close the window or click on the close icon on the top right of the tab.

If we wanted to experiment with rotation, we might look at `localEulerAngles` see if we can change the transform primitive's rotation when the game starts. Pressing Play shows the transform primitive tipped up for a moment before falling. As we learn more vocabulary, the different sections in the documentation will have more meaning. The headings Static Methods, Inherited Members, and some others may not mean much right now, but as you read on they will.

The scripts you create for your game should live together in their own directory. When you download additional Unity Packages from the Asset store they will usually also live in their own respective project directories. Assets like your Materials, Prefabs, Scenes etc. should all live in their own directories to stay organized.

Unity 3D also has included a few of their own built-in packages for in-app purchases and analytics which live in their own sub-directories in the Packages directory in your projects next to the Assets directory.

When you feel more confident, continue some experiments on your own. If you can't get things working immediately don't let that put you off. As you learn more about C# you'll also have more knowledge to experiment with. As you feel more comfortable with the language, you'll also learn to read and understand what the comments left by the Unity 3D programmers mean.

For now, at least, we have a project setup in which we'll be able to construct our sample game.

3.4 Tokens

To get started open the BookContents/Chapters/Chapter3 Unity Project. To see the example code, look in the Assets and open the C# files named after each section. To follow along with this chapter you should open the Tokens.cs file in Visual Studio to see what the code looks like.

In written English the smallest elements of the language are letters, numbers, and punctuation. Individually, most letters and numbers lack specific meaning. The next larger element after the letter is the word. Each word has more meaning, but complex thoughts are difficult to convey in a single word.

To communicate a thought, we use sentences. The words in a sentence each have a specific contribution to the intent, as seen in the diagram below. To convey a concept, we use a collection of sentences grouped into a paragraph. And to convey a story we use a collection of many paragraphs organized into chapters and integrated into a book.

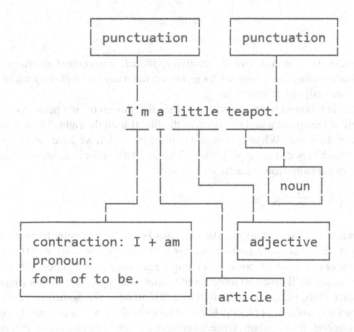

Programming has similar organizational mechanisms. The smallest meaningful element is a token, followed by statements, code blocks, and functions, followed by classes and namespaces, and eventually a program, or in our case the program is a game. Every file created in the process of writing C# is called a Compilation Unit, or source file.

We will begin with the smallest element and work our way up to writing our own classes. However, it's important to know the very smallest element to understand how all the parts fit together before we start writing complex code.

3.4.1 Writing C#

C# is an English-based programming language; like any other C-like programming language, it can be broken into tokens, the smallest meaningful fragment of text that the computer can understand. In a mechanical way of thinking, writing a story is the process of arranging words to convey meaning. In much the same way, writing code is arranging tokens to instruct the computer to carry out a process.

A token is made of a single character or a series of characters. For instance, in a simple statement like the following there are five tokens.

Tokens can be categorized as a *keyword, identifier, literal, assignment operator*, and *separator*. The above statement contains five tokens with spacing between each provided by white space. Together these tokens create an assignment statement.

The keyword `int` is followed by the identifier `i`. This is followed by an operator `=` which assigns the identifier on the left of the operator and the value of the literal `0` on the right. The last token `;` is a separator which ends the statement. White spaces and comments, which we have yet to cover, are not considered tokens, although they can act as separators. This is a lot to take in at once, but each one of these words will be further explained as we continue.

```
int j = 0; int k = 1;
```

The code shown above is two statements, the separator keeps the computer from misreading the code as a single statement. However, there are humans involved with writing code, and thus code needs to be readable by humans, or any other life form which might read your code. Proper code means following a specific formatting style. We'll dive into more about proper code style later in this chapter.

Each group of characters, or text, is converted by a *lexical analyzer*, sometimes called a *lexer*, in the computer and turned a *symbol*. This process is called *tokenization*, or as a computer scientist would say, a lexer tokenizes your code into symbols. Once tokenized, the symbols are *parsed*; this process organizes the tokens into instructions for the computer to follow. This unique vocabulary does frame programmers as a strange group of alien beings with a language all to themselves; I promise, however, conversations about lexical analyzers don't come up very often when talking with most programmers.

This may seem like a great deal of work and we are jumping ahead into more complex computer science topics, but all of this happens behind the scenes, so you don't need to see any of this taking place. It's important to understand what a compiler does and how it works, so you can write code in a way that the computer can understand. Therefore, a simple typo will stop the lexer from building code.

A computer can't interpret or guess at what it is you're trying to do. Therefore, if you mistype `int i = 0:` and not `int i = 0;` the last token cannot be converted by the lexer into a proper symbol, and thus this statement will not be parsed at all. This code results in an error before the code is even compiled.

3.4.2 Comments a First Look

In the Assets directory open the Comments script. One of the first types of tokens we'll want to investigate is the comment. Each section in the code will have a corresponding comment like the one below.

```
/* * * * * * * * * * * * * * * * * * * *
 * Section 3.15 Comments a first look        *
 * * * * * * * * * * * * * * * * * * * * */
```

We'll go into more detail on various types of comments and how they're used in Section 3.14, but it's important to know what they look like before moving on. In each C# source file, you'll see various with `//` at the beginning of the line. This tells the lexical analyzer to ignore anything appearing after the `//` on that line.

```
//This is a single line comment.

// ← the two forward slashes make
// any line invisible to the lexer
```

Comments allow the author of the C# script to inform other readers of any information not included in the code itself. In addition to the `//` comment is the `/*` comment `*/` where anything between the start of the `/*` comment and the ending `*/` will also be invisible from the lexical analyzer.

```
/*
 ↑
 └ This is a multiline comment.
   everything between the opening
   token slash star stays hidden
   until you get to the closing
 ┌ slash star
 ↓
*/
```

Both types of comments are used extensively through all the code samples provided with each chapter.

```
/*          not hidden           */
/*              ↓                 */
/*hidden*/ int i = 0; /*hidden*/
```

In some cases, working code will be hiding behind a comment. To see how the code works, delete the `//` at the start of the line of code to reveal the statement to the lexical analyzer for compiling. To hide the code, simply put the `//` back at the beginning of the line. Programmers often leave code they're working on in comments to keep work in progress knowing that the code isn't fully functioning.

```
/* uncomment one of the three someInt lines
 * below by deleting the //
 * then make sure that only one
 * is visible to the lexer by commenting
 * the others out.
 */
int someInt = 0;//I print 0 through 10
//int someInt = 3; //starts at 3
//int someInt = 11; //this won't print
while (someInt < 10)
{
    System.Console.WriteLine(someInt);
    someInt++;
}
```

Single line comments that use // are used extensively throughout the code with the intent for you to uncomment them to see how code works. Uncommenting one line and commenting out another is a common strategy to test out various ways to solve a problem.

In a clean code base the code itself will speak clearly as to what it's doing. Comments would be kept to a minimum. If a function requires comments to explain how it works, then the function could be re-written to be easier to understand.

3.4.3 Separator Tokens

The most common separator is the semicolon (;). This mark of punctuation is used to end a code statement. Other separator tokens come in pairs. Curly braces are used in pairs to separate groups of code statements. The opening curly brace is the { with the pointy end pointed to the outside of the group; this is paired with the } which closes the curly brace pair.

```
/* ┌ Opening                     *
 * |                  Closing ┐ *
 * ↓                          ↓ *
 * { Curly braces           } *
 * [ Square Brackets        ] *
 * ( Parenthesis            ) *
 * < Angle Brackets         > */
```

Parentheses start with the (and end with the) while square brackets start with [and end with]. The different opening and closing braces, brackets, and parentheses have specific purposes that are used to help identify what they are being used for. There are angle brackets < and > as well; these are used to surround data types. And don't forget both single quotes ' and double quotes ", which are used in pairs as well to surround symbols called strings.

NOTE: In many word processors a beginning and an ending quote (" and ") are often used. The lexical analyzer doesn't recognize these smart quotes, so the text editor for programming uses straight quote marks (") instead. These subtle changes aren't so subtle once you realize that letters, numbers, and every other character used in programming are all parsed as American Standard Code for Information Interchange (ASCII) or unicode transformation format (UTF)-8, -16, or -32. Both ASCII and UTF are names given to the database of characters that the computer uses to read text. Computers don't use eyes to read. Rather, they use a database of numbers to look up each character being used. Therefore, to a computer " looks more like 0×201C and " like 0×0022 (the expected quotation mark), if we were using UTF-16.

Curly braces are used in code to separate statements. Parentheses are usually used to accept data. Square brackets are often used to help identify arrays. We'll get into arrays later; imagine something like a spreadsheet or a graph paper until we get to their explanation.

```
int[] arrayOfNumbers = { 1, (int)3.0, 9000 };
```

The above statement assigns three numbers to an array. The curly braces contain a pair of statements separated by a comma. The second statement in the curly braces is converting a number with a dot (.) into a number without a dot in it. This will take a bit of explanation, but it's good to get used to seeing this sort of thing. We'll get to what an array is soon enough, as well as a dot operator.

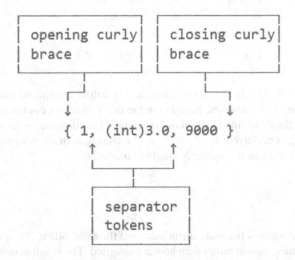

Often, when learning to program you'll see many strange tokens which might not seem to have any meaning. It's up to you to observe every token you come across and try to understand what it does. If none of the statements makes sense that's fine. At this point you're not expected to know what all this means yet, but you soon will.

3.4.4 Operator Tokens

Operators are like keywords but use only a few non-word characters. The colon or semi-colon is an operator; unlike keywords, operators change what they do based on where they appear, or how they are used. This behavior shifting is called operator overloading, and it's a complex subject that we'll get into later. It's also important to know that you can make up your own operators when you need to.

Commas in C# have a different meaning. A comma is used to separate different data values. Another special operator token is the semi-colon.

```
/*              semicolon operator    */
/*                    ↓               */
public class Example : MonoBehaviour
{
}
```

Here, the : was used following the name of the class to inform the compiler we're going to be adding to a pre-existing class called MonoBehaviour. In this case, : will tell our class to add new behaviors to MonoBehaviour. This means to build upon a class which already exists. We're creating a new child object related to MonoBehaviour; this is a class that was created by the developers at Unity 3D.

Here's a list of the various math related operators you can expect to find in C#.

=	Assignment Operator
+	Addition Operator
-	Subtraction Operatorr
*	Multiply Operator
/	Divide Operator
%	Remainder Operator

Operators provide our basic ability to do math in code. Operators are special characters that take care of specific operations between variables. Notation or the order in which operators and variables appear is normally taught with the following notation or mathematic grammar: a + b = c. However, in programming the following is preferred: c = a + b; the change is made because the = operator in C# works differently from its function commonly taught in math class.

```
result = operation
    c = a + b;
```

The left side of the = operator is the assignment side, and the right side is the operation side. This puts the emphasis on the value assigned rather than how it's assigned. The result is more important than how the problem is solved since the computer is doing the math. In programming the above example should be read as "c is assigned a plus b."

3.4.5 Literals

Literals are values which come in many different forms. Literals are things you assign to variables, or compare variables to. Literals can be considered tokens used in a literal manner. Numbers can be called numeric literals. Words like "This is a string" is also considered a literal.

Numbers are literals as well. The int or integer is a hole number like 1 or 100. We are used to seeing large numbers like 10,000 or ten thousand with a comma separating every thousand. However, commas have a different meaning in C#. To the compiler, 10,000 is a value 10 followed by a different value 000, a second number. This causes problems so large numbers need to be written without the comma. So, ten thousand in C# needs to be written as 10000 without the comma.

```
Vector3 vector = new Vector3()
{
    /* commas separate terms    */
    /*    ↓         ↓            */
    x = 1, y = 2, z = 3
};


/*        commas separate terms   */
/*             ↓              ↓  */
for (int i = 0, j = 1; ; i++, j++)
{
}
```

When assigning values to variables we often use literals to set a value for something specific. For example, if we wanted to convert radians to degrees we use the equation `degrees = (radians × π) / 180` to get an answer. In C# that would look like the following:

```
float degrees;
float radians = 3.14159f;

degrees = (radians * Mathf.PI) / 180;
Debug.Log("Degrees from 3.14
```

⊞ (constant) float Mathf.PI = 3.14159274
The infamous 3.14159265358979... value (Read Only).

The example shows `float radians = 3.14159f;` where `3.14159f` is the literal assigned to `radians`. Later `Mathf.PI` is not a literal but a different type of number called a const; more on that later. `radians` which is a variable that was assigned a literal. Then we divide that by `180` which is a literal.

When values like `180` are used in code directly it's sometimes called a "hard-coded" value. In cases where the math isn't going to change, like in the radian to degree conversion, this isn't a bad practice. However, in some cases like screen resolution a hard-coded value might work against you.

If you wanted to check where a mouse pointer was in relation to the center of a screen you might use half the screen width and half the screen height to get the center of the screen. Assuming you're on a computer with a 1920 pixel wide screen that's 1080 pixels tall you might use $x = 960$ $y = 540$ as the center of the screen. This would be wrong if the screen resolution were to change. You can't change a hard-coded value once you've built your project into a game to distribute.

When something is put into quotes, as in "I'm a literal," you are writing a string literal. Literals are common throughout nearly all programming languages and form the base of C#'s data types. Right now, we're dealing with only a few different types of literals, but there are many more we will be aware of soon.

3.4.6 Transitive and Non-Transitive Operations

In math class it's sometimes taught how some operations are transitive and others not. For instance, $2 + 3 + 4$ and $4 + 3 + 2$ result in the same values. Where each number appears between the operators doesn't matter, so the + operator is considered transitive. This concept holds true in C#. Results change when we start to mix operators.

```
int a = 1 + 2 - 4 + 7;
int b = 7 + 4 - 2 + 1;
int c = (7 + 4) - (2 + 1);
int d = (1 + 2) - (4 + 7);
```

This code fragment shows two different results using the same operators but with different number placement. We'll see how to overcome these problems later when we start using them in our game. Operator order is something to be aware of, and it's important to test each step as we build up our calculations to make sure our results end up with values we expect.

To ensure that the operations happen as you expect, either you can use parentheses to contain operands or you can do each calculation. We'll dive further into more detail with a second look at operators later, but this will have to wait until we have a much better understanding of the basics of C#.

3.4.7 Putting It All Together

The Unity 3D engineers have prepared many data types, functions, objects, and classes tailored specifically for game development. Classes often work together to share and manipulate data. There are exceptions to this rule, but C# allows for many different writing styles and paradigms.

Creating data produces components of an object. In general, you've created something that can be reused many times. Once you have created a zombie by adding brain-seeking logic and how many bullets are required to stop him, it's only a matter of duplicating that zombie to create a mob to terrorize your player.

As we proceed we'll become more familiar with what it means to use classes as objects; the tutorials will be aimed at making sure that this is all clear.

```
303    public void Start()
304    {
305        int i = 0;
306        while (i < 10)
307        {
308            Debug.Log(i);
309            i++;
310        }
311    }
```

In the Assets directory for Chapter 3 you'll find a Tokens_Scene Unity scene. Open this and press the Play-in-Editor button. Open the Console window and you'll see the following output.

Let's break this code sample down. The first word is `public`, which is a keyword followed by `void` another keyword token. `Start()` is an identifier. A Tokens game object in the Unity scene has the Tokens.cs script attached and Unity executes the `Start()` function when the game begins.

The parentheses after the Start are operators used when we need parameters for our function. The parameters are discussed in Section 3.3.2. For now, take in the fact that both opening (and closing) parentheses are necessary after function identifiers. They're useful; trust me.

To begin the contents of the function we start with curly braces, the opening { and closing } curly braces. Everything that the function will do must be contained between the two braces. Any text appearing outside of them will not be part of the `Start()` function. The code contained in the curly braces becomes the function block of code, or code block.

The first statement in the function's code block is int i = 0; this is an assignment statement, where we declare int i and then use the = to assign i a literal value of 0. This is then separated from the next statement with the ; operator.

The assignment statement is followed by while (i < 10), which is called a looping condition. We'll read more on looping conditions later in Section 4.12. This looping statement is followed by an opening { curly brace. This indicates a code block specifically written for the while loop.

The code block contains the statement Debug.Log(i);, which is a function call using i as a parameter or argument. After the print function call is i++;, which applies the post-increment operator ++ to the variable i. This code block is ended with the closing } curly brace.

The while code block and the int = 0; are both within the Start() code block. To make the code more readable, tabs are added to indicate a separation between each section of code. Now bask in the knowledge that we've got words to describe everything presented in the above code sample. We may not understand everything that has been written, but we've got some vocabulary where we can get started.

3.4.8 What We've Learned

Programmers are meticulous about syntax. They have to be. The following two statements are very different: int myint0 = -1; and Int my 0int = - 1:. The first one will compile; the second one has at least five errors. You may not be able to spot the problems in the second statement, but by the end of the next section you will.

Internet forums are a great source for getting help when learning how to write code. When asking programmers for help it's best to limit your subject and consider your words carefully. Asking "How would I write a video game where you shoot zombies with a flame thrower" involves so many different concepts it's impossible for anyone to tell you where to start. At best you might get a link to a book on Amazon. In a single post, you're asking for too much.

If you formulate a smaller question like, "How do I attach flames to a zombie after it's been hit by a projectile?" you're more likely to get an answer. When talking to a programmer, using proper syntax, and providing context as to what you're code looks like and asking why it doesn't work, you are more likely you'll get the answer you were looking for.

3.5 Statements and Expressions

To continue, open the StatementsAndExpressions.cs file to follow along. When reading a book or story, you extract meaning from an ordered chain of words. In a similar way, computers extract commands from a chain of ordered instructions. In English we call this a sentence; programmers call this a *statement*. A statement is considered to be any chunk of code which accomplishes some sort of task separated by a semicolon.

At the center of any given task is the *algorithm*, not to be confused with a logarithm. An algorithm is a systematic process that accomplishes a task. In many ways you can think of it as a recipe, or rather a recipe is an algorithm for making food.

It could take one or two statements to accomplish a task, or it could take many hundreds of statements. This all depends on the difficulty of a given task. Each individual statement is a step toward a goal. This is the difference between spending a few minutes frying an egg, or spending an hour baking a soufflé. Each individual step is usually fairly simple; it's the final result that matters.

Like sentences, statements have different forms. Statements can declare and assign values to variables. These are called *declaration* and *assignment* statements. These statements are used to set up various types of data and give them names.

3.5.1 Expressions

The subjects of your statements are called *identifiers*. An *assignment statement* is used to give an identifier a value. When you read "The menu has kale for lunch and broccoli for dinner." The C# version might look a bit like the following:

```
private enum Food
{
    kale,
    broccoli
}
Food lunch = Food.kale;
Food dinner = Food.broccoli;
```

Assignment statements often incorporate some sort of operation. These are called *expressive statements*. Different from expressing an emotion, expressions in code look more like "x + y." Expressions process data. After processing, the result of an *expression* can be assigned to a variable. We'll learn more about variables and assignments in Section 3.10.2. Literals can also be used in an expression, for example myInt = x + 1; where 1 is a literal, but x may be a variable assigned before this expression. Together, x + 1; is an expressive statement, but x and 1 alone are not.

A collection of statements is called a *code block*, like a building block, something that's used to build. When writing a story, we call a collection of sentences a paragraph. The statements in a block of code work with each other to accomplish a task. An expression can also ask a block of code to execute. This is called an *invocation expression* or an expression that invokes a method.

3.5.2 How Unity 3D Executes Your Code

When a class is created, the contained instructions are not carried out at the same time. As it's been explained, each collection of parts in a class is made up of lines of text called *statements*. Each statement is carried out in order. Where the computer starts is usually dependent on which collection of statements it's told to start with. You're in charge of how the code is started.

Unity 3D provides us with a function called Start(), which we'll go into later. However, this is the preferred place to begin our code using Unity 3D. Once Start() is called, the computer goes to the first line in Start() and begins to carry out the instructions written there. As the computer gets to each statement the computer starts on the left of the statement and works its way to the right. Basically, a computer reads code like you're reading this sentence. In our examples we'll add code to the Start() method provided by Unity to run code when a scene is first started. If we want to repeat our code with every frame then we'll use the Update() method.

This is different from other development environments which often use Main() as their first place to begin running the code. When you start writing software in other environments you'll most likely start with Main(). We don't have to get into that right now, but it's good to know once you're done with this book.

3.5.3 Thinking in Algorithms

An algorithm is a step-by-step process. This lends itself to being written in an imperative programming language like C#, which executes operations one at a time and in order. Algorithms are written with statements starting at a beginning statement and finishing that statement before moving on to the next.

Just because we know what an algorithm is doesn't mean it's any easier to create one. Therefore, how do we go about writing the all-important algorithm? The first thing should be how you might accomplish any given task by hand.

As an example, say we're a computer surrounded by a mob of zombies. Thankfully, computers are very fast so we can do a lot before the zombies can get to us. With this in mind, we're going to want to focus on the zombie closest to us. Unfortunately, computers are also very dumb, so there's nothing which allows us to just guess at which one is the closest.

First, we're going to need to know how far away every zombie is from our point of view. Therefore, the computer would probably start with measuring the distance from itself to every zombie available to make a measurement to. After that we're going to have to compare zombies and distances, so we'll start with the first zombie we found and compare its distance to the next zombie we found.

If the next zombie is closer, we'll have to remember that one as being the closest one we've come across. Otherwise, if the next one is farther away, then we can forget about him and move on to the next zombie and compare numbers again. Once we've gone through all the zombies, we should have identified the zombie who is the closest one to us.

The process which we just thought through is an algorithm for finding the zombie closest to us. It's not complex, but we had to do a few steps to get to it. First, we needed to get a list of all the zombies we needed to sort through. After that it was an iterative process, by which we needed to remember one zombie as the closest one, then compare others against him to decide whether he would retain the status of being the zombie nearest to us. We'll be going over many of these problem-solving thought processes as we learn how to program.

This algorithm would look something like the following code block:

```
void Update()
{
    // Gather Data
    float closestDistance = Mathf.Infinity;
    GameObject closestGameObject = null;
    GameObject[] allGameObjects = FindObjectsOfType<GameObject>();

    // Process Data
    foreach(GameObject g in allGameObjects)
    {
        // Gather Data
        bool notMe = g != this.gameObject;

        // Process Data
        if (notMe)
        {
            // Gather Data
            Vector3 otherPosition = g.transform.position;
            Vector3 mPosition = transform.position;
            Vector3 difference = otherPosition - mPosition;
            float distance = difference.magnitude;

            // Process Data
            if(distance < closestDistance)
            {
                closestDistance = distance;
                closestGameObject = g;
            }
        }
    }

    // Gather Data
    Vector3 myPosition = transform.position;
    Vector3 closestPosition = closestGameObject.transform.position;
    Color red = Color.red;

    // Process Data
    Debug.DrawLine(myPosition, closestPosition , red);
}
```

We won't cover the entirety of how this code works, as we are yet to discuss the bulk of what's going on here, but in short, we gather data, then process data. We repeat the pattern of gathering data, then processing it. At the beginning, we gather data; a starting distance, a close game object and all the game objects in the scene. Then we process it with `foreach(GameObject g in allGameObjects)`. This happens again once in the foreach loop. You can see the pattern in this example, but this pattern exists throughout most programming tasks. Gather the data you need, then process it.

Just for a proof of concept we draw a line from the object. Because the script is attached to the object, we draw a line from the object the script is attached to toward the object selected as the closest. The scene will look something like this:

To view this open the `StatementsAndExpression_Scene` in the Editor and press the Play-in-Editor button, then switch over to the Scene panel. The `Debug.DrawLine` is not visible in the Game view and is only visible in the Scene editor. You can move some of the objects around the sphere to see the red line switch to different objects as they change distances. We put the code in the `Update()` method to make sure that the line is always visible, and the closest object can change if you move the objects around.

Programming is a lot more about a thought process than it is about processing. In other words, programming is less about how to do multiplication as it is about what to do with the result of a multiplication. In your everyday life we take for granted the everyday things we do on a regular basis. However, take a moment and really consider the complexity involved with something as simple as breathing.

Your diaphragm is receiving signals from your autonomic nervous system, causing several chemical reactions in the diaphragms muscle tissue, which then pull proteins toward one another causing it to contract. This in turn creates a lowered air pressure in your lungs, which pulls in air. A number of chemical processes allow the oxygen in the atmosphere to enter your blood stream. Thankfully, all of this happens without our thinking of it because of chemistry and physics. In programming, nothing is so automatic.

3.5.3.1 Wash, Rinse, Repeat

In our everyday life we see instructions written everywhere. However, if we follow instructions too closely we'd run into problems. If you interpreted, for example, the instructions on most shampoo labels like a computer we'd run out of shampoo the first time we used it.

To interpret the "wash, rinse, repeat" instructions like a computer we'd wash our hair, rinse it, then wash our hair, then rinse it, then wash our hair, then rinse it, ...; you get the picture. You'd continue the process until you run out of shampoo. Because there are no further instructions, once the shampoo has run out, a computer would send out an error of some kind. There wasn't a number given for how many times the instructions should be followed; there was no way to *terminate* the process, as a programmer would say. A computer would need to have the "shampooing" process killed to stop washing its hair. Simply put, computers lack common sense.

Here's a simple scenario: A spouse tells the programmer to go to the grocery store and says "Get some bacon, if there's milk get three." The programmer comes home with three packs of bacon, and no milk. If this makes sense, then you're thinking like a programmer. There are conditions to tell the programmer to get three packs of bacon if milk was available; just the fact that there was milk meant bringing home 3 × bacon.

3.5.4 What We've Learned

Programmers are often a group of literal thinkers. A programmer uses a different thought process from the artist. In terms of order of operation, programmers take things one step at a time. An artist tends to start with a broad picture, then refines detail where necessary. This process in programming terms is an imperative procedure, a step-by-step process where operations are carried out in a linear fashion.

As an artist or newcomer to programming, this imperative process can be a bit out of the ordinary. With some time and practice, however, this paradigm of thinking will become second nature. The approaches a programmer and an artist would take to solve a problem often diverge.

To learn how to write code is to learn how to think like a programmer. This may sound a bit awkward, but perhaps after some work, you'll understand why some programmers seem to think differently than everyone else.

3.6 Keywords

Keywords are special words, or symbols, that tell the compiler to do specific things. For instance, the keyword class at the beginning of a line tells the compiler you are creating a class. A *class declaration* is the line of code that tells the compiler you're about to create a new class.

```
class ClassName
{
}
```

The order in which words appear is important. English requires sentences and grammar to properly convey our thoughts to the reader. In code, C# or otherwise, programming requires statements and syntax to properly convey instructions to the computer.

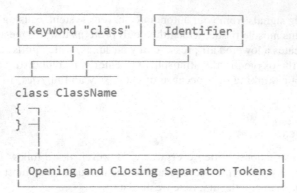

```
class ClassName
{ ┐
} ┤
```

This creates a new class object called "ClassName"
Note: class needs to be all lower case.

Every class needs a name; in the above example we named our class ClassName, although we could have easily named the class Charles. When a new class is named the name becomes a new *identifier*. This also holds true for every variable's name, though *scope* limits how long and where the variable's identifier exists. We'll learn more about variables and scope soon.

You can't use keywords for anything other than what C# expects them to be used for. These are called reserved keywords. Some keywords are only used in context with other keywords. There are exceptions, but in general, keywords inform the lexical analyzer of specific commands. Because keywords are reserved for a specific reason, you can't use them for anything other than the intended purpose. Altogether in C# there are roughly 80 keywords you should be aware of. We don't need to go over all of them now, so instead we'll learn them as we come across them.

```
int abstract = 0;
```

Because the word abstract is a reserved keyword, you can't use it as a variable name. The above class contains an error informing you on proper use of the abstract keyword.

3.6.1 The Class Keyword

To create a class named Charles we used the keyword class. The keyword commands C# to expect a word to identify the new class. The following word becomes a new identifier for the class. In this case Charles is used to name the class. Keywords often precede a word, and the computer uses the word following as its identifier.

The contents of Charles are defined between curly braces. After the class definition, the opening curly brace { is followed by any statements that Charles needs to be a proper Charles. When you're finished defining the contents of Charles, you use the closing curly brace } to indicate you're done with defining the Charles class.

```
class Charles { }
```

It's important to note that keywords start with lowercase letters. C# is a case-sensitive programming language, and as such, Class and class are two different things. In C# there is no keyword Class; only class starting with a lowercase c can be used. The same goes for every keyword in C#.

However, programming works this way: class Charles {} begins with the start of the class indicated with the open curly brace { and the end of the class indicated by the closing curly brace }, after which we go back and add the body later. Not everything works in this way, and it takes a bit of getting used to before you understand the flow. Certainly, however, this will come naturally after some practice.

Now we have a new class called Charles, which has no data and does nothing. This is to be expected since we haven't added any data or functions yet. You can also use the terminology this class is identified as Charles.

This class can't be used directly by Unity 3D. It lacks some of the necessary additions needed by the Unity 3D game engine to directly interact with this class. To be specific, this class doesn't have enough information to allow Unity 3D to know what to do with it. However, there are methods which make a minimal class, such as `Charles`, quite useful inside of Unity 3D, but we need to cover a great deal of ground before we can do that.

In Section 2.4 we looked at a complete source file, `Example.cs`, which is ready for use in Unity 3D. However, it's important to know what creates a minimal class before adding all the rest of the keywords and declarations which make it do anything in Unity 3D, our game engine.

Keep in mind, no two classes can share the same name. We'll go further into detail about class names and what's called a namespace later. The contents of the class are contained in the following pair of curly braces. All of the variables and functions that live between the opening curly brace { and the closing brace } become the contents of the class object.

Other keywords that we'll come across in this chapter include those that indicate a variables type. Some variable keywords which will be covered in the next few chapters are as follows:

```
int
```

```
float
```

```
string
```

These keywords indicate a type of variable. There are many more, but we're just going to look at these as an example. An int variable looks something like the following:

```
int i = 0;
```

A float looks like this:

```
float f = 3.14159f;
```

A string is used to store words like this:

```
string s = "some words in quotes";
```

If `int` and `float` seem similar, it's because they both deal with numbers, but as we will see, numbers behave quite differently when computers use them. Keywords are used quite often and they are case sensitive. Therefore, `int` and `Int` are different things, and thus using `Int i = 0;` will not work. Only `int` is recognized as a keyword, and there has been no definition written to tell C# what `Int` is. Keywords are also used to indicate special changes in code behavior. The keyword `if` is what is used to control code execution based on a conditional statement.

```
if ( i < 10 )
{
        // Code goes here.
}
```

As you are introduced to more and more keywords, you'll be expanding your ability to create new code as well. Keywords make up the complex vocabulary that is required to use C#.

3.6.2 What We've Learned

This was a short section, but it covered a fundamental component of a C# construct. Classes are both construction instructions and rules for objects to obey. Writing a complex class takes a step-by-step approach.

Keywords are an important component of any programming language. Some languages have very few keywords. LISP has a mere 18 keywords, C# has about 76, and COBOL has over 400 words reserved for special purposes.

Most programming languages use the same keywords for similar purposes. The `var` keyword is often used to indicate that a variable is being declared. Because of the similarities between programming languages, once you've learned one language, it's often easy to pick up and learn new languages.

3.7 White Space

Open the WhiteSpace.cs script found in the Assets of the Chapter3 Unity Project. White Space refers to the spaces between words and lines. When typewriters were still in fashion, new lines were entered by pushing on a lever which pushed the roller that held onto the paper to reposition the hammers with letters on them back to the beginning of the next line. This is the origin of the term "Carriage return character" where the mechanism holding the paper was referred to as the carriage. Now, these are called line feed character, next line character line separator, or paragraph separator. It's also interesting to note that these are unique Unicode characters. On Windows you'll find the option under Edit → Advanced → View White Space

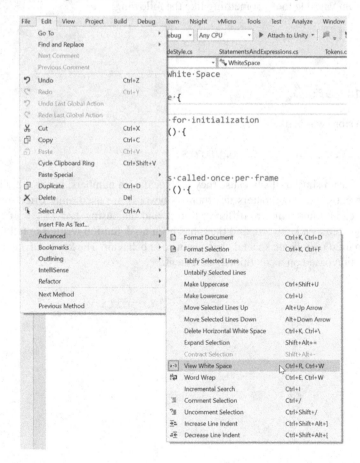

In OSX with Visual Studio Community you'll find the option in the Preferences → Markers and Rulers → Show Invisible characters: and select Always

Like letters and numbers, white spaces are also characters entered in your code. In the editor you'll see faint dots arrows and on OSX you'll see \n marks spaced throughout your code.

```
1      //·Chapter·3.6·White·Space
2
3    ⊟class·WhiteSpace·{
4
5       →  //·Use·this·for·initialization
6    ⊟  →  void·Start·()·{
7       →    →
8       →  }
9       →
10      →  //·Update·is·called·once·per·frame
11   ⊟  →  void·Update·()·{
12      →    →
13      →  }
14   └ }
15      □
```

In many cases the new lines and spaces and tabs are there only to help make the code more readable. And depending on what a programmer was taught, the white spaces will be used differently. For instance, adding white space after a function declaration is unnecessary, and the location of the curly braces can pretty much be moved anywhere before or after the contents of the function itself. Leaving the white spaces showing isn't necessary, but it's good to know what white space means when talking to a programmer. If none of this makes sense right now, it will later.

The placement of curly braces is easy to change; these decisions often lead to debates on standards among programmers. There's little difference either way. However, keeping your own code consistent helps you read your code and find errors faster.

It's important to remember that if you're going to be working with more classically trained programmers, they might get a headache when reading poorly formatted code. It's best to copy your programmer friends' style before coming up with your own way to format your classes and functions. No doubt, before the end of this book you will have formed opinions of your own when it comes to the use of white space and formatting your own code.

Normally, code might look a bit like the following:

```
void MyFunction()
{
    int i = 0;
    while (i < 10)
    {
        System.Console.Write(i);
        i++;
    }
}
```

This looks like a readable collection of statements. However, the compiler could care less about how you use white space. Therefore, here is what would this code sample look like without the unnecessary white space:

There are still some necessary white space characters used to separate the different tokens in the function. There is the space between `void` and `MyOtherFunction`, and the space between `int` and `i`. In any case the white space is required after the use of a keyword. Keywords are unique words reserved for C#. If we used `voidMyFunction()` then there would be an error stating something about not knowing what a `voidMyFunction()` is. White space is also used to make code more readable. Without the white space the code becomes more difficult to interpret.

`imagineforamomentwhatenglishwouldlooklikewithoutanyspacesorpunctuation`

White space should also be used as needed. I once worked with a programmer who would put a few pages of white space between different functions. He said it made it easier to focus on what he was looking at when there was only one line of code on the screen at a time. Of course, this drove other programmers nuts. It's hardly a common practice.

Although he had a point, being able to focus on one code block at a time is important, but there's a thing called code folding that we'll learn about later on to help make your code more easy to organize.

3.7.1 Code Style

Between programmers there's often a discussion of code style. Many heated debates might flare up based on the use of white space. The differences are entirely based on style and in most cases have no effect on the efficacy of the code. In the following fragments the { is placed in different places.

```
void SomeFunction() {
    // Some Code here...
}

void SomeOtherFunction()
{
    // Some Other Code here...
}
```

The execution of the two functions will perform equally, but the placement of the first curly brace { can make the code more or less readable depending on what you're comfortable with. Unity's developers offer us the first version, but for clarity we'll stick to the second version.

The finer points on where variables appear in a statement or how many statements can appear on a single line are usually dictated by how a programmer has learned to write code. Old school programmers prefer no line of code extending beyond 80 characters. This limit formed in 1928, when IBM punch cards had only 80 columns to poke holes in the paper. Though it's unlikely you'll have to work with an old curmudgeon, at least now you know why they might be grumpy.

Today, there's no physical limit other than what would make a statement difficult to read. If a single line of code spans several widths of your screen it's probably unreadable. In these cases it's better to break apart your statement into a few smaller statements. This will help keep the code more readable. Within the confines of this book we're somewhat more limited by space, so we too will be limiting the length of our statements based on the width of the margins of the book.

Likewise, if you've got a lovely 4k monitor you might be comfortable reading mile-long lines, but if you're stuck on a low-res laptop then you might hate having to scroll left and right just to read a single statement. Consider the fact that not everyone has a giant monitor.

Interpreting your own code several days or weeks after you've written it is just as important as handing your code off to someone else, with that person being able to read it. There are many times when I've come back to a project written several weeks ago and needed to spend a few minutes trying to figure out what I was thinking when I wrote the code. Sometimes, it takes only a few days for me to forget about the code I've written. Worse yet, if I write the code half asleep then I might forget what I was doing before I've even reached the end of a statement.

In the end it's up to you to pick what you'll stick to. However, it's considered rude to pick through someone else's code and reformat it. Code can sometimes become quite personal, and reformatting code might end up feeling like someone sneaking into your bedroom and reorganizing your sock drawer.

Another common debate rises between the use of tabs or spaces. In your IDE (integrated development environment) you can tell the editor how many spaces a tab is to represent, usually this number is either 4 or 2 spaces. Style guides often bring this up, and in large corporate environments some preference is usually enforced. This isn't something you need to immediately concern yourself with, but it's good to be aware that there are programmers out there with a strong opinion on what works best.

3.7.2 What We've Learned

White space and formatting are important to creating a clean easy-to-read class. Every large company will have a set of rules for their programmers to follow. These coding standards, as they are called, are usually maintained by a lead programmer and can vary from company to company.

Smaller teams of engineers can have a less restrictive set of rules, but this often leads to some confusion and large bodies of unreadable code. Everyone has his or her own coding style and preferences. If there is an established set of coding standards, then it's best to follow it.

So far as this book is concerned, it's best that you learn how to make your code work before concerning yourself with strict coding rules. Code formatting and style are important. How you express yourself through code is up to you, so long as it works. Getting your code to work is a big enough challenge; style and proper formatting will come naturally with time as you see the benefits of different code styles, and how they contribute to your code's readability.

3.8 Code Blocks

To follow along, open the CodeBlocks.cs file in the Chapter3 Unity Project. Code blocks, or a "block of code," are collections of statements grouped together. The block, or chunk is separated by a starting curly brace { then ended with a closing curly brace }. C# programmers often use tabs to indent the contents of a code block.

This makes the different blocks more readable. This becomes more apparent when we have blocks within blocks. Some languages like python rely on the tabs to indicate separate blocks of code. Code blocks help organize statements together in a continuous set of steps.

Getting used to how spacing is essential for writing readable code. Next, we'll use a logic control statement followed by a block of code. The block for this `if` statement is indented to the right to indicate it's confined within the logic control statement.

```
// im outside of the block of code below
if (true)
{
    // code goes here
    // im also in this block of code
}
// im outside of the block of code above
```

If we take a look at a more complex section of code we can see why it's important to differentiate code by using tabs. When looking at code it might not be apparent, but programmers are very fastidious about text layout. Each programmer has a preferred style, but it's safe to say that most, if not all, programmers hate seeing badly formatted code.

```
int i = 7;
int j = 13;
if (i < j){
j = 7;}
```

In the above example we can clearly see `int j` being set twice. What isn't obvious is why it's declared twice. All the lines start at the same position and look crowded. Programming tools offer many text layout options, so white space is used to separate different blocks of code.

```
int k = 8;
int l = 9;


if (k < l)
{
    l = 8;
}
```

By adding in some white space, we can make the `if` statement more visible. Adding white space around our blocks of code is important to maintain readability. There are also blocks of code that can live within another block of code. In general, it's all related to the same block. Blocks inside of a block are called nested code blocks. White space is used to separate the nested code from the block it's found in.

```
if (true)
{
    //code here
    if (true)
    {
        //another block of code.
    }

}
```

The block of code following the second if statement is considered to be nested inside of the first block of code. This is because of the placement of the first opening curly brace { and the related closing curly brace }. You form hierarchies by placing the different curly braces within one another.

```
if (true)
{//code here
if (true)
{//another block of code.
}
}
```

Poorly indented curly braces make for confusing code; the above code is still valid, but it's less readable compared to the previous version. Most code-editing tools will automatically add in the proper number of indents for you. It's something you'll have to get used to when writing your own code.

We'll go into further detail as to what this all means later. Just gather from this discussion that a bunch of statements appearing between a pair of curly braces is considered a block of code.

3.8.1 What We've Learned

Much of programming involves proper use of style and a great deal of white space to accomplish that style. So far we've just been covering vocabulary; yet, without that vocabulary we can't have a proper conversation about programming. This includes talking to other programmer friends, who will have a hard time understanding you if you can't speak their language.

3.9 Classes: A First Look

To follow along open the Classes.cs file found in the Chapter3 Unity Project. The most important part of any C# program is the class. Classes here are not the sort that students go to; rather, they are classes in terms of classification. Classes in C# appear in several different forms. Some are called partial classes, and some classes can even appear inside of another class; these classes are called nested classes.

A class is a collection of data and instructions. The instructions can be referred to as functions methods or, sometimes, procedures. The data in a class is called a field or property. Everything in a class together are members of the class. All the naming aside, what's important is what classes do and how they're used.

```
/* Class Stuff has Things,  */
/* and can Do A Thing.      */
class Stuff
{
    int Things;       /* ← Data member     */
    void DoAThing() /* ← Function member */
    {
        //Do the thing!
    }
}
```

Classes are flexible and easily changed, but this flexibility is not without some complexity. As we've seen before, the class declaration can contain a lot more than the following example. However, much of the complexity comes later in this book, when needed.

When you approach a game or any sort of programming task first gather data; then figure use of the data; last, act on the data. In most programming paradigms it's best to start off with variables at the beginning of your new class. For instance, in this pseudo code we might want to know what day it is before going out:

```
bool PartyTonight = false;/* ← Collect your */
void DoParty()/*                ┌───── data.        */
{   /*                      ❶↓                   */
    DateTime today = DateTime.Now;
    /*       test your data                    */
    /*                    ❷↓                   */
    if (today.DayOfWeek == DayOfWeek.Friday)
    {   /* act on your data                    */
        /*                  ❸↓                   */
        PartyTonight = true;
    }
}
```

We start off with getting a day, and then deciding what to do tonight based on the day. We should refrain from partying based on what the day is, unless we want to show up for work late. Almost every operation follows that pattern, get data, check data, set data. We'll go into more detail on this topic later, after we've learned about how to use a variable in a class properly.

3.9.1 Objects

Object oriented programming (OOP) was invented to associate data and logic into nicely packaged bundles of code. When you write a class in C# you're creating blueprints and instructions for a new object. Any number of objects can then be constructed based on your blueprints. Programmers use the term *instantiate* when talking about creating an object from the class blueprint.

Each instantiated object is an *instance* of the class from which it was constructed. The class is not itself one of the instances created by it. The newly created object contains all the functions and data written into the class.

```
        /*   ┌─────────────────┐ */
class Zombie/* ←─┤This is the plan │*/
{        /*   │to build a zombie│*/
}        /*   └─────────────────┘*/
          /*   ┌─────────────┐   */
          /*   │this is an   │   */
void MakeZombie()/* │instance of  │   */
{   /*       ┌──┤a zombie     │   */
    /*       ↓  └─────────────┘   */
    Zombie zombie = new Zombie();
}
```

To make this clear, a class in of itself is not an object, just a plan for making objects. We start with a C# class which contains instructions to build an instance of itself. Unity 3D hides a bit of this instantiation from you when you've attached a script to an object in the scene. A script attached to a GameObject in the scene tells Unity to instantiate the class at the start of the game.

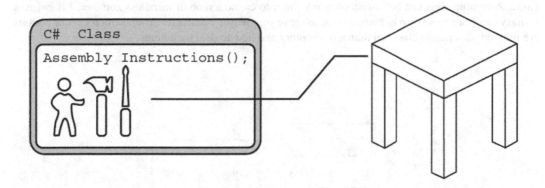

A class might be nothing more than a container for some data. As an example, our zombie shooter could have a hypothetical ammunition pick-up class. In the ammunition pick-up, we could store a type of ammo, along with how many rounds are stored in it. When a player discovers a stock-pile of ammunition, the variety and count can be randomized for any number of pick-ups.

```
class Ammunition
{
    AmmoType ammoType;
    int ammoCount = 10;
}
```

On the other hand, a class can also contain behaviors for a complex boss who plans to crash a comet into the earth, or any other instruction for world domination. The contents of which are a bit out of reach for this book.

Just as important, a class can create more than one instance of an object. This process is called *instancing*. Each instance is created from the same blueprint and thus behaves the same as all the other instances of the same class. Each instance can have unique values. In Unity 3D, each instance of an object can have unique positions in 3D space.

OOP is particularly useful for video games. Individual classes can address different aspects of your game. A zombie class can be instanced many times to create a mob of mindless zombies. Likewise, a solitary class can be written to manage how to move your player's character around when keys or buttons are pressed. A separate class can manage inventory and how to deal with items.

Monsters, bullets, cameras, and lights all have classes from which they are created. Almost every object you see in any level in Unity 3D can be instanced from a class. An instance of an object communicates to another object through *messages* and *events*.

When people in the real-world deal with household items they are rarely concerned with how they function. Knowing how a toaster works has little effect on the toaster's performance. We put bread in a toaster, push down on a button, and wait for a delicious toast.

A toaster, however, is more than a button and a receptacle for bread. It's a collection of wires, heating elements, transformers, and other electrical components which are hidden under a shiny cover. We interact with an *abstraction* of a toaster, never dealing with the insides ourselves.

Abstraction presents only the parts we need to accomplish a given task and hides the rest. To make toast we need a place to put bread and a button to start the machine. The toaster does its work and toast happens, or at least it should.

Messing with the insides of the toaster class isn't recommended; that's why there are labels telling us to keep forks out of the toaster. To protect a human class from fumbling around with the insides of a toaster class the toaster is protected by *encapsulation*.

Encapsulation is the term used to define to how classes hide data and functions from the outside world. To interact with the toaster we must use the toaster's *interface*, but there are other objects in the kitchen which have buttons, and the human class is very good at pushing buttons.

When you put bread into a blender and press a button you will get a very different result from the toaster, but they are both kitchen appliances and use the same power outlet. They're both made of metal and run on the same electricity, but they do different things.

When and where it's possible, a programmer will reuse as much code as possible. A blender and a toaster could share similar components, only the operation carried out on a slice of bread is different when they are used. The capability to change the contents of an operation is described as *polymorphism*.

A generic kitchen appliance would be a place to put food and a button to press to process food. Each version of a kitchen appliance does different things to food. A wise programmer would make sure that all the appliances inherit from the generic kitchen appliance.

Inheritance allows many classes to share common attributes and behaviors. If you wanted a toaster with more than one slot and a knob to adjust the darkness of your toast you would want to inherit the original toaster's functions first. This means that the base of both toaster and blender is a kitchen appliance. A dual slot toaster inherits from toaster, which inherits from kitchen appliance. This in turn means that if any changes are made to kitchen appliance that change or addition is inherited by all of the subclasses inheriting from kitchen appliance.

This would mean inheriting the original toaster's electronic systems, casing, and original button. All of these components may also be made from other classes. This would mean only changing one electronic part to adapt a toaster for sale, say, in Europe.

Aggregating many different classes into a single class allows another layer of flexibility. By aggregating many separate components or classes into a single useful toaster or blender means you can more easily swap individual parts for new behaviors. A toaster is the aggregate total of many smaller parts.

You may find yourself writing code for a zombie or a toaster and see some similarities between those things and other objects in your game. When your player attacks a zombie or a toaster, they may both break apart. Both the zombie and toaster can share functions related to getting attacked.

As far as your code may be concerned, one object chases after you trying to eat your brains, and the other object turns bread into delicious toast. Keep this in mind when you start writing your own code. Even though some things may seem unrelated, maybe even humans and zombies can both enjoy toast.

3.9.2 What We've Learned

I'll let this sink in a little bit. Being new to programming is usually a very intimidating experience. Having to learn any new language is a daunting task. Because much of programming is taught in English we've got a slight advantage. At least the mentioned 80 keywords aren't written in a foreign language.

The main take away from this chapter is the fact that OOP is the process of building objects, instancing them, and then using them. Using objects involves reading data, using logic on the data, and then carrying out tasks based on the logic.

As we move on, feel free to jump back between chapters to refresh your memory if there are concepts which you might have forgotten. It's important to proceed at your own pace; jumping ahead before you're clear on a topic leads to confusion, then frustration, and leading to quitting altogether.

We're here to learn and have fun while learning. Building a game for modern gaming platforms is easy once you've got your head wrapped around this whole C# thing, so stick to it and you'll reap the rewards. Not only will you be able to write your own games from scratch, you'll also be able to write plenty of other apps using other development tools which use C#.

We've also come across a great deal of vocabulary related to classes. If you're not completely clear as to what these words mean we'll be covering chapters dedicated to these more complex concepts. When you're ready, it's time to continue learning and getting ready to make some games.

3.10 Variables

To follow along open the Variables.cs script from the Chapter3 Unity Project. Programming is only able to accomplish a task once it's able to read, manipulate and create data. Variables are the little bits of data or information which make up the game world. Everything you see in a game scene, and even things that are implicitly assumed, like gravity, can be interpreted as data that can be stored into a variable. Logic behavior can be controlled by comparing values stored in variables.

The concept of a variable is something we might take for granted in day-to-day life. When you save a contact in your phone you've assigned values to a name; you added "Mom" with a phone number to your address book.

A variable can be either something that's constantly changing or something you've set once and shouldn't change. For instance, an object's location should be updating if it's falling or getting pushed on by other forces in the world. This object's location is a variable, which the programmers at Unity have named transform.position. The Position value has three parts, an *x*, *y*, and *z* component.

Various numbers used in common math operations have been named with easy to remember identifiers. A value like PI, which doesn't need to change, lives in Unity 3D's API. It can be found as UnityEngine. Mathf.PI.

3.10.1 Identifiers

Identifiers, which are considered symbols or tokens, are words that you invent and then assign a meaning. Identifiers can be as simple as the letter i or as complex as @OhHAICanIHasIdentifier01. We'll get into properly creating names later, but *identifier* is the word that's used to name any function, variable, or type of data you create. From the address book example above, the entry "Mom" is the identifier and its value is the phone number you assigned.

With a GameObject or a Camera in a Unity Scene, a collection of variables can be seen in the Inspector panel. The Camera has a Transform Component, the Transform has a Position, Rotation, and Scale. Inside of each of these are X, Y and Z variables. The Camera component has a longer list of variables starting with Clear Flags and ending with Target Display. Each of the Identifiers name a different type of data you're able to modify and save in the scene.

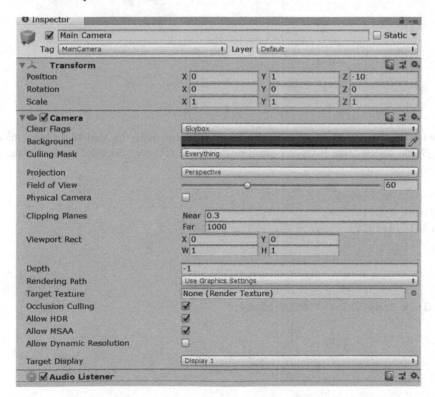

3.10.2 Data

Data, in a general sense, is sort of like a noun. Like nouns, data can be a person, place, or thing. Programmers refer to these nouns as objects, and these objects are stored in memory as variables. The word *variable* infers something that might change, but this isn't always the case. It's better to think of a variable as a space in your computer's memory to put information.

When you play word games like MadLibs you might ask for someone's name, an object, an adverb, and a place. Your result could turn out like "*Garth* ate a *jacket*, and *studiously* played at the *laundrymat*." In this case the name, object, adverb, and place are variable types. The data is the word you use to assign the variable with.

Programmers use the word *type* to denote what kind of data is going to be stored. Computers aren't fluent in English and don't usually know the difference between the English types noun and adjective, but they do know the difference between letters and a whole variety of numbers. There are many predefined types that Unity 3D is aware of. If you add that to the ability to create new types of data, the kinds of data we can store is practically unlimited.

The C# built-in types are sometimes called POD, or plain old data. The term *POD* came from the original C++ standard which finds its origin dating back to 1979. POD types have not fundamentally changed from their original implementation.

Programmers define the word *type* to describe the variety of data to be stored. Variables are created using declarations. Declaration is defined as a formal statement or announcement.

Each set of words a programmer writes is called a statement. In English we'd use the word *sentence*, but programmers like to use their own vocabulary. Declaration statements for variables define both the type and the identifier for a variable.

The Unity Inspector panel allows us to see variables in action. With the Variables GameObject in the Variables_Scene selected, the Inspector panel reveals three variables declared as seen in the example code below.

```
public float MultiplyBy;/*→─┐   ①              */
public float InputValue;/*→┐ │ values are */
public float Result;/*←┐  │ │ assigned  */
void Update()        /* │  │ │           */
{    /*    ┌─────────────┘  │ │           */
     /* │       ┌───────────┘ │           */
     /* ↑       ↓             ↓           */
    Result = InputValue * MultiplyBy;
     /* ↑       ↓      ┌───┐ ↓           */
     /* │result is└───┤ * ├─┘            */
     /* ③updated      └───┘② operation   */
     /* └──────────────────┘ is performed */
}
```

The Three identifiers `InputValue`, `MultiplyBy`, and `Result` are declared and made visible to the Editor. In the `Update()` function we assign `Result` by multiplying `InputValue` by `MultiplyBy`. If you change either `InputValue` or `MultiplyBy` you'll see the `Result` automatically Update the value seen to the right of the Identifier.

You may have noticed the keyword `public` before the `float`; we'll explain that later in Chapter 4 where we discuss access modifiers. In this case, this tells Unity 3D to show that variable in the Inspector panel with the attached script. By placing the `Result` calculation in the `Update()` function we ensure that the calculation is updated every frame.

3.10.3 Variable Manipulation

Declaring a variable creates space in the computer's memory for a value. The manifestation of this can be seen by the box to the right of the declared identifier in the Inspector panel in Unity 3D. In the previous example, we made space for three values. Unity 3D took the first two values and modified the value stored for `Result`.

Now that we know what parts are required to make a variable declaration, what can we do with them? Once a variable has been declared and assigned it can be reassigned at any time.

```
int i = 0;
System.Console.Write(i);
// i has been assigned 0

i = 1;
System.Console.Write(i);
// i reasssigned to 1
```

On the second line the variable `i` is no longer `0`; it's `1` now. If we check what value is being stored at `i` we'd find a `1`. So long as `i` is not assigned again, `i` will retain its value.

```
int i = 1;|
```

> 💡 ▾   [⚙] (local variable) int i
>
> A local variable or function named 'i' is already defined in this scope
>
> The variable 'i' is assigned but its value is never used
>
> Show potential fixes (Alt+Enter or Ctrl+.)

To create another declaration of i in the same block of code will produce an error as we're trying to create a declaration for i twice. A declaration for i has already been made the identifier cannot be declared more than once.

3.10.3.1 Declaration Placement Examples

A valid variable declaration can only appear in a few places in your code. Some of the conditions for valid placement of a variable declaration are related to something called scope which will be covered in further detail in Chapter 4. To ease into variable declaration, we'll confine our attention to declaring a variable to a single class. A declaration for someInt should appear between the opening and closing curly braces of a class.

```
int outterInt;
```

> 💡 ▾   🔧 (field) int <invalid-global-code>.outterInt
>
> A namespace cannot directly contain members such as fields or methods
>
> Show potential fixes (Alt+Enter or Ctrl+.)

```
class SomeClass
{
    int innerInt;
}
```

The code above shows a problem with the first outterInt declaration happening above the definition of class SomeClass. The declaration of int innerInt inside of SomeClass is allowed, as we have seen demonstrated before.

One common mistake many new and old programmers make is forgetting to add the semicolon to the end of a statement. Visual Studio helps a great deal with pop-ups like the one above. The red squiggle lines underline problems and highlight errors which keep Unity from running your code.

We've now completed two important tasks. We created a variable identifier giving the variable a way to access the contents of the variable. C# under the hood gave that variable some space in your computer's memory to put an integer. The int variable is now defined as SomeNumber, an object we can fill with a number with practically any int value.

When variables are declared for the first time, or initialized, in C# they are usually immediately given a value. This is not true with all types of variables, but number values are assigned 0 when they are created. For more complex data types their default value is null when they are initialized. This initialization behavior will become useful later when we start inspecting the values of variables.

3.10.4 Dynamic Initialization

When we both define and assign a variable we use the term *dynamic initialization*. Some data types automatically give themselves a default value when they are initialized without an assignment. For instance, a Boolean automatically assumes it's false when it's created.

```
bool SomeBool;
bool AnotherBool = false;
```

In this case, if we were to use `SomeBool` before assigning it then the result would act as though it were initialized false. In the above example both `SomeBool` and `AnotherBool` have the same value. Likewise, most numbers are initialized to 0 (zero).

```
int SomeInt;
int AnotherInt = 0;
```

So in this case both `SomeInt` and `AnotherInt` have the same value. However, this changes when we dynamically assign a value to a variable when initializing.

```
int OtherInt = 7;
int LastInt = 11;
```

When we assign a value to an `int` when it's initialized we skip the default initialization, and the value assumes its assignment when it's created.

3.10.5 What We've Learned

Variables are stored in your computer's memory. By defining a variable by its type, you instruct the computer to set aside a block of memory in the computer's RAM (Random Access Memory) to store data. To access the data you give it a name, or an identifier.

Once the identifier has been defined you can assign or read the data stored in memory through its identifier. In many cases the identifier needs to be unique. Depending on when it was created an identifier might have the same name as one created before it.

When this happens you get an error telling you that a variable has already been defined with that identifier. Changing one or the other's name solves the problem. When creating identifiers we need to consider what they're used for and how to name them.

Some code standards place rules on how an identifier should be named. For instance, a bool might always start with is to indicate how it's used. Therefore, a zombie might have `isWalking` or `isRunning`, indicating what it's doing. Other standards might use a prefix b for bools, so `bWalking` or `bRunning` could be used to indicate the same thing. How you decide to name variables is up to you, but it's good to know what we're about to get into so far as naming variables, which we'll be covering next.

3.11 Variable Names

Continuing in the Variables_Scene open the VariableNames.cs script in the Assets directory of the Chapter3 Unity 3D Project. It's important to know that variable identifiers and class identifiers can be pretty much anything. There are some rules to naming anything when programming. Here are some guidelines to help. Long names are more prone to typos, so keep identifiers short. A naming convention for variables should consider the following points:

- Short and easy to remember
- Succinct and to the point
- Meaningful but not long
- Unique
- Avoid special characters
- Describes what it's used for

The variable name should indicate what it's used for, or at least what you're going to do with it. This should be obvious, but a variable name shouldn't be misleading. Or rather, if you're using a variable named radius, you shouldn't be using it as a character's velocity. It's also helpful if you can pronounce the variable's name; otherwise, you're likely to have issues when trying to explain your code to another programmer.

```
public int SomeLongComplexHardToRememberVariableName;
```

If you were to use a long complex hard to remember variable name, Unity 3D wouldn't be able to show you the entire name in the Inspector panel.

There is an advantage to keeping names as short as possible, but still quite clear. Your computer screen, and most computers for that matter, can only fit so many characters on a single line. You could make the font smaller, but then you run into readability issues when letters get too small.

Consider the following function, which requires more than one variable to work.

```
SomeCleverFunction(TopLeftCorner - SomeThickness + OffsetFromSomePosition,
BottomRightCorner - SomeThickness + OffsetFromSomePosition);
```

The code above uses many long variable names. Because of the length of each variable, the statement takes up multiple lines making a single statement harder to read. We could shorten the variable names, but it's easy to shorten them too much.

```
CleverFunc(TL-Thk+Ofst, LR-Thk+Ofst);
```

Variable names should be descriptive, so you know what you're going to be using them for; too short and they might lose their meaning.

```
int a;
```

While short and easy to remember, it's hard for anyone else coming in to read your code and know what you're using the variable a for. This becomes especially difficult when working with other programmers. Variable naming isn't completely without rules.

```
int 8;
```

A variable name can't be a number. This is bad; numbers have a special place in programming as much of it has other uses for them. MonoDevelop will try to help you spot problems. A squiggly red line will appear under any problems it spots. And speaking of variable names with numbers, you can use a number as part of a variable name.

```
int varNumber2;
```

The above name is perfectly valid, and can be useful, but conversely consider the following.

```
int 13thInt;
```

Variable names can't start with any numbers. To be perfectly honest, I'm not sure why this case breaks the compiler, but it does seem to be related to why numbers alone can't be used as variable names.

```
int $;
int this-that;
int (^_^);
```

Most special characters also have meanings, and are reserved for other uses. For instance, in C# the minus or dash character (-) is used for subtraction; in this case C# may think you're trying to subtract that from this. Keywords, you should remember, are also invalid variable names as they already have a special meaning for C#. In MonoDevelop, you might notice that the word this is highlighted, indicating that it's a keyword. Spaces in the middle of a variable are also invalid.

```
int spaces are bad;
```

Most likely, adding characters that aren't letters will break the compiler. Only the underscore and letters can be used for identifier names. As fun as it might be to use emoticons for a variable, it would be quite difficult to read when in use with the rest of the code.

```
int ADifferenceInCase;
int adifferenceincase;
```

The two variables here are different. Case-sensitive languages like C# do pay attention to the case of a character; this goes for everything else when calling things by name. Considering this: A is different from a.

NOTE: Trained programmers are often taught a variation of naming conventions, which yields easier-to-read code. Much of this is dependent on scope, which we will discuss in Section 4.4.4. There are also conventions which always prefix variable names with an indication of what sort of data is stored by that variable.

As a programmer, you need to consider what a variable should be named. It must be clear to you and anyone else with whom you'll be sharing your work with. You'll also be typing your variable name many times, so they should be short and easy to remember and type.

The last character we discuss here is the little strange @ or at. The @ can be used only if it's the first character in a variable's name.

```
int @home;
int noone@home;
int nobodyhome@;
```

In the second variable declared here we'll get an error. Some of these less regular characters are easy to spot in your code. When you have a long list of variables it's sometimes best to make them stand out visually. Some classically trained programmers like to use an underscore to indicate a class scope variable. The underscore is omitted in variables which exist only within a function.

You would find the reason for the odd rule regarding @ when you use int, which is reserved as a keyword. You're allowed to use int @int, after which you can assign @int any integer value. However, many programmers tend to use MyInt, mint, or _int instead of @int based on their programming upbringing.

Good programmers will spend a great deal of time coming up with useful names for their variables and functions. Coming up with short descriptive names takes some getting used to, but here are some useful tips. Variables are often named using nouns or adjectives as they describe an attribute related to what they're used for.

A human character can often have a health attribute. Naming this `HealthPoints` or `NumberOfHealthPoints` is sometimes considered too wordy, or even redundant. However, if you and your friends are accustomed to paper role-playing games, then perhaps HitPoints would be preferred.

In the end, once you start using the name of the variable throughout the rest of your code, it becomes harder to change it as it will need to be changed everywhere it's used. Making a global change like this is known as refactoring. Visual Studio can help change the name of a class, variable, or function throughout a project by refactoring your code.

NOTE: You may also notice the pattern in which uppercase and lowercase letters are used. This is referred to as either BumpyCase or CamelCase. Sometimes, the leading letter is lowercase, in which case it will look like headlessCamelCase rather than NormalCamelCase.

Many long debates arise between programmers as to which is correct, but in the end either one will do. Because C# is case sensitive, you and anyone helping you should agree whether or not to use a leading uppercase letter.

These differences usually come from where a person learned how to write software or who taught that person. The use of intermixed uppercase and lowercase is a part of programming style. Style also includes how white space is used.

When you name variables in Unity 3D the use of CamelCase or BumpyCase will automatically separate the different words indicated by an uppercase letter in the Inspector panel. This doesn't actually affect how the declaration was written. This will only change how your variable's name appears in the Unity 3D Editor.

3.11.1 Useful Variables in Unity 3D

Open the UsefulVariables_Scene in Chapter3/Assets. Open the UsefulVariables.cs script attached to the game object of the same name in the scene.

Unity 3D is a great way to demonstrate what variables look like and how they act. When variables of different types are added to a script the Inspector represents the data type in various different ways.

```
public bool MyBool;
public int MyInt;
public int MyOtherInt = 700;
public float MyFloat;
public string MyString;
public Vector3 MyVector3;
```

Adding the keyword `public` before the type and the identifier informs the Unity 3D Editor to expose the variable to the Inspector panel. The different types change how the variable is represented in the Inspector. You may also notice that `MyBool` has a space added to show "My Bool" next to the checkbox. Unity 3D formats bumpy text into different words for readability, but it doesn't actually change the text in your code.

By setting values in the Inspector panel, we tell the script what values to start with when the script is run. The Int and Float we declared are by default initialized to 0 when they appear in the Inspector.

Dragging on the My Float item left and right adjusts the value stored on the object in the scene. Many variable types are initialized with a default value if nothing is provided when they are declared.

Initialization is the process by which variables and other chunks of data are created and stored for the first time in a class object. Initialization can be either automatically declared, like MyInt or MyFloat, or declared as variables are initialized. Or they can be dynamically assigned like MyOtherInt where we assigned 700. The default values will be overwritten when they are edited in the Inspector panel.

If you make changes to the default values and save the scene, the changes will be saved to the scene where the script is used. To bring the defaults back, right click on the script's component title bar and select Reset to revert the values to those declared in the script.

Integers or int are whole numbers. Numbers which have a decimal in them are not integer values. Such numbers, having values with fractions, have several different names, for example, float, or double. We'll go into some more depth as to what number types mean in Chapter 4. You'll notice you're not able to change `MyInt` to `0.1` or any number with a decimal point in it. The fields provided for each parameter is limited to the type of value that's allowed to be entered. We'll study why this is in the next chapter.

3.11.2 Variable Assignment

We stepped through some basic guidelines regarding assignment of variables, but what happens when we change the assignment? The variables' assignment happens one line at a time. The computer starts at the top of the code and works its way down one line at a time. What this means is, the value of a variable shows its changes only after the assignment is made.

For instance, in the following code sample we'll start off with one variable and change its assignment several times and print the results.

```
/* int declares a new thing       */
/* assignment operator = assigns   */
/* the new int thing a value       */
/*                                 */
/*          ┌───┐                  */
/*        ┌─┤ = ├─┐                */
/*        ↓ └───┘ ↑                */
int MyVariable = 7;
/*        ↓                        */
/*        └──────┐                 */
/*               ↓                 */
Debug.Log(MyVariable);
/* Debug.Log prints to the console */
/* what is in it's argument list () */
// 7
/*       ┌───────┐ MyVariable      */
/*       ↓       ↑ gets a new value */
MyVariable = 13;
Debug.Log(MyVariable);
// 13
/* the new value is printed        */

MyVariable = 3;
Debug.Log(MyVariable);
// 3
MyVariable = 73;
Debug.Log(MyVariable);
// 73
```

With the code included in a new C# script named Variables assigned to the GameObject in the scene of the same name, we'll get the following output in the Console panel.

Using the same variable named MyVariable and after assigning it different values, we get different numbers printed to the Console panel. This is because the identifier MyVariable is nothing more than its value; it's just a number. In other words, we could use the following code fragment and get the same result from both print outputs.

```
int MyVariable = 7;
/* terms are                    then the */
/* evaluated    ① ( 7 + 7 ) result is*/
/* first        ②=( 14 )     printed   */
Debug.Log(MyVariable + MyVariable);
// 14              ③ 14 appears in the console
/* this is functionally the same as */
Debug.Log(7 + 7);/* this              */
// 14
```

If we want to mix variables together, we can do that too. Because MyVariable is an integer value, we can treat it like any other integer, or whole number. This can be demonstrated best with another int variable.

```
int MyVariable = 7;
int MyOtherVariable = 3;


/*  terms are    ( 7 * 3 )            */
Debug.Log(MyVariable * MyOtherVariable);
// 21
/* the same as   ( 7 * 3)             */
Debug.Log(MyVariable * 3);
// 21
```

Here we'll get an expected 21 printed out to the Console panel from both Debug.Log functions. To be clear, MyVariable * MyOtherVariable and MyVariable * 3 are equivalent. Next, let's consider what happens when we assign a variable to another variable:

```
int MyVariable = 7;
int MyOtherVariable = 3;
Debug.Log(MyVariable * MyOtherVariable);
// 21
/*      ┌──←=(3)┐ MyVariable              */
/*  ↓          ↑ gets a new value         */
MyVariable = MyOtherVariable;

/*  terms are    ( 3 * 3 )                */
Debug.Log(MyVariable * MyOtherVariable);
// 9
```

Now we have `MyVariable` being assigned the value that is `MyOtherVariable`. Therefore, let's think through this logic. `MyOtherVariable` is assigned a value of 3, so if we assign `MyVariable` a value of 3 the second print function will return `MyVariable` * `MyOtherVariable`. This means it's actually just 3 * 3, which means 9 will be printed out to the Console panel.

3.11.3 Putting It Together: Using the Variables

We've named variables and given them assignments. It's about time we start to consider how to apply these new concepts to something useful in Unity 3D. Open the UsingTheVariables_Scene in the Chapter3 Unity Project.

We'll start off with a basic scene with a handy TransformPrimitive; we'll be seeing this gizmo quite often. Next, open the `UsingTheVariables` script attached to the TransformPrimitive in Visual Studio. To start with, we're going to add in a `public` variable at the class level. We will be getting to what this all means in Section 4.4.3, but for now what we're doing is making this variable available to the rest of the functions as well as the Editor.

```
public float RotationSpeed;
public float Rotation;
```

Your code should look like the one above. Now, hopping back into Unity 3D you should see both `RotationSpeed` and `Rotation` in the Inspector panel.

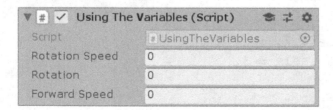

This little thing has a 0 in it; that's what we want. We'll be making use of this variable in the `Update()` function found in the class. Let's add the following code to the `Update()` function and see how it works.

```
Rotation += RotationSpeed * Time.deltaTime;
```

The `Time.deltaTime` object is a useful value. The calculation of the value comes from the amount of time that passes between updates. The `Update()` method is run once per frame. Slow computers struggle to update as often as faster computers.

More time passes between updates on a slow machine. If you want a value to update at the same speed on both slow and fast machines `Time.deltaTime` is a good way to regulate how much a value is changed when it's updated. As an example, if you have a machine that runs at 100 frames per second then 1/100th of a second passes between `Update()` calls. On a machine that runs at 10 frames per second 1/10th of a second passes between frames. You can't rely on `Update()` to increment a value at the same speed in both situations.

When the Play-in-Editor button is pressed we see the `Rotation` value increment up based on `Rotation Speed` values.

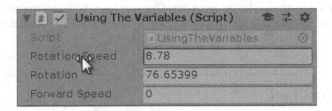

With this we can plug the `Rotation` value into the object's rotation with the following code:

```
transform.localEulerAngles = new Vector3(0, Rotation, 0);
```

Small values in `RotationSpeed` will rotate the object very slowly. In the Inspector you can watch the `Y` of the `Rotation` in the `Transform` component update with the same value as seen in `Rotation`. Also try assigning negative values to rotate the transform primitive the other way.

Play with this for a little bit; just make sure `RotationSpeed` is a value other than 0.

To make this more interesting, we'll add `public float ForwardSpeed;` after the `Rotation Speed` and the `Rotation` variables.

```
public float RotationSpeed;
public float Rotation;
public float ForwardSpeed;
```

With this we could modify the position of the Transform primitive object.

```
transform.position += transform.forward * (ForwardSpeed * Time.deltaTime);
```

The line above should appear after the `transform.localEulerAngles` are updated. With three lines of code and two inputs, a `ForwardSpeed` and a `RotationSpeed` variable we've created a small sort of steerable object.

We haven't quite created a driving simulator, but we've only written three lines of code to move around a funny looking colored arrow mesh. Altogether, there is actually quite a lot of interesting things to play with here.

3.11.4 What We've Learned

We're taking very small steps to start off. There's a great deal of new concepts for you to absorb and many questions to be asked. If there is anything unclear then take a moment to go back and review.

So far, we've mostly covered terms related to writing C#. Learning about programming is somewhat about learning new vocabulary, and we've covered keywords and a few operators and variables. We just wrote variables to a C# class object and added it to an object in our Unity 3D scene.

C# is an OOP paradigm. Every class is an object. Once we learn how to write our own objects, we'll learn how to read other objects and possibly even begin to understand the complexity laid out in Unity 3D's library.

3.12 Types: A First Look

For this chapter we'll look at the Types script found in Chapter3 Project Assets directory. When we assign a variable a value such as `int i = 1;` we're making an interesting assumption. We assume using `1` automatically infers a value type that matches the variable type. Computers use a wide variety of different types of data for storing numbers.

We've been seeing the keyword `int` being thrown around as though you know what an `int` is. In our everyday lives we hardly think there's any difference between numbers `1` and `1.0` or even the word *one*. As humans we can easily conceptualize numbers as units of measure and converting between them. The conversion between the word *one* and the number 1 isn't so easy for a computer.

The keyword `int` is short for integer. Integers are whole number values. The integer is a C# built-in type, as mentioned before it's considered plain old data. Basically, this means that integers are a fundamental part of C#. Other built-in types include `float`, `double`, `string`, `bool`, and `object`. Less commonly used built-in types are `char`, `short`, and `byte`. Altogether, there are 15 different built-in types. All of these, except `object` and `string`, are value types.

Every type of data you're able to build must be based on built-in types. The system which creates `floats`, `doubles`, and `bools` is rooted in the origin of computing. Remember the punch tapes and pieces of paper with holes in them? Those were records of 1s and 0s which were fed into computers for storing in the form of mechanical switches, either on or off. The patterns represented numbers or instructions and logic.

Today, we still use the same system of 1s and 0s, or binary, only we don't need to punch holes in paper to tell the computer what to do. The methods of creating and storing the instructions have become many times more complex, but nonetheless the principle of the `1` and `0` are the same. These are called bits; one possible origin for that name is the little bits of paper that were left over from punching holes in the paper cards.

3.12.1 Value and Reference Types

The `int`, `float`, `double`, and `bool` are commonly used value types. The basics of this usage pattern relate to the system that stores and organizes the computer's memory. When you talk about computer storage you use the word *megabyte* or *gigabyte*. Value types are stored with a very specific purpose in mind: to keep track of a numeric value.

NOTE: The word *mega* refers to how many millions of bytes a component in your computer can store. *Giga* indicates how every many billions of bytes are being stored. Have you ever thought about what a byte actually is?

A byte is what's called an 8-bit unsigned integer, or a system of using 8 bits to form a number. What this means is, it's a whole number like 0, 7, or 32,767. The word *unsigned* indicates that the number cannot be negative, like –512.

A 1 or 0 in computer terms is called a bit. We won't go into detail on how computers use bits to count, and it's a rather fun thing to learn on your own. However, it's important to know that a byte has a limited range, from 0 to 255. I'll just leave you with the idea that you could count up to 1023 on your 10 fingers if you used binary rather than decimal. Your fingers can be used to represent a 10-bit unsigned integer. The computer's calculation capabilities used to be far more limited than they are today. An 8-bit game console made in the 1980s had a limited number of colors, 256 to be exact. This limitation was based on the number of bits that the processor could handle. The processor had a limited number of transistors which could be used at any one time. Shortly after, floating point co-processors were introduced, which had a much larger numeric range allowed, by having closer to 32 bits to work with.

In all of these cases, when you use a value type, that number is actually stored as 1s and 0s in your computer's RAM. This should be considered remarkable. In the past you'd have to go through flaming hoops to store a value. Now you just type in `float f = 3.1415926535;` and you can measure the circumference of the galaxy accurately to within the width of a single atom.

What all these types have in common is that they are stored as a single element. Large values like `double gigawatts = 1210000000.0` and `double mint = 2.0` use the same amount of memory.

Your computer doesn't assign one double or the other more space in memory. These types are referred to as *primitive types*. The only difference between an `int` and a `float` is the number of bits they use at a time, 8 and 32 respectively; `doubles` use 64 bits.

The `string` and `object` types differ a bit in how they are stored. These types are a composite of any number smaller elements. The bigger a string or object the bigger chunk of memory the computer opens to place that object or string. These are called *reference types* or sometimes called *nullable types* because C# doesn't look to a single element in memory to get data from it.

We will explain nullable types in Section 4.4.1.2, but in short, a nullable type is a space in memory which is reserved for data that has yet to be fulfilled. Primitive or value types are commonly reserved and assigned at the same time. There are systems which allow this to be changed, but we're getting ahead of ourselves for now.

In Unity 3D, a commonly used type is the Vector3. Vectors, in the math world, are directions in *x*, *y*, and *z* with a length. Unity 3D uses vectors to keep track of a position in 3D space. The `Vector3` type is a composite of three `float` variables. This means that a Vector3 is made up of different components. From this, we may infer that a `Vector3` is a *nullable* type. Each float is labeled x, y, and z. However, unlike the primitive types the `Vector3` needs to be instanced. This means that you can't simply use the following syntax.

```
int i = 0;//a valid initialization of an int.
Vector3 v1 = (x = 0, y = 0, z = 0);//not valid initialization.
Vector3 v2 = new Vector3();//this is how it's done.
```

Nullable types need to be initialized; that is, they need some form of initial value. We'll go into further detail on this later. It's important to remember there are differences between types when they are being initialized. Later on, as you begin to create and use objects and variables it'll be important to remember how to initialize the different variable types.

3.12.2 What We've Learned

There are many different forms which data can take. Each form is called a type. The different forms depend on how they are organized and how they are initialized. Reference or nullable types require some form of initial parameters before they can be used. Value or primitive types usually have an initial value when they are created.

When variables are declared, they are assigned a type. The type changes how the variable behaves and what values it's allowed to store. As we move forward, remembering how types behave is important. C#, and many other C-like programming languages, has specific rules with how to deal with data of differing types.

3.13 Strong Typing

Continue with the same Types script from the previous chapter. Strong typing has nothing to do with how hard you type on the keyboard! C# sees a difference between numbers in how they are written. A whole number like 1 is different from 1.0, even though we can think of them as having the same value. Some of these differences can be added by adding a letter. Therefore, `1.0` and `1.0f` are different numbers as well.

C# is a *strongly* typed programming language. When a programming language uses strong types, you're expected to keep the different types separated. This means that a `1 + 1.0f` can create a problem. Because the two numbers are actually different types of numbers we must convert one of them to match the other before the operation can take place.

To convert from one type to another we must tell C# that we intend to make that conversion from a `1` to a `1.0` by using what's called a *cast operator*. Thus, `1 + 1.0` will either become `1 + 1` or `1.0 + 1.0` depending on what operation you choose. Aside from changing how memory is used, types also limit any problems which might come about when working in a team of programmers.

If one programmer is new to your game and has made assumptions about hit points being in floating point values, he'd quickly find out as soon as he looked that you're using integer values and change how he intends to use those numbers. Value types not only store a value assigned to them but also provide a great deal of information to be inferred by the programmer reading the code.

```
Vector3 vec = new Vector3(1.0, 1.0, 1.0);
```

In Unity, the statement `Vector3 vec = new Vector3(1.0, 1.0, 1.0)` will throw an error. The number `1.0` is called a `double`, which uses 64 bits, whereas `1.0f`, which is a `float`, uses 32 bits. The difference means float `1.0f` is half the size of the double `1.0` in memory. A `Vector3` is made up of three `float` values, not three `doubles`.

```
float f = 1.0f;
double d = 1.0;
```

Therefore, in terms of declaring a variable and assigning it `float f = 1.0f` and `double d = 1.0;` the same type problems exist as with assigning a `Vector3 ()`, which is made of three different float values. To properly tell C# you mean a 32-bit version of 1.0 would be to add an `f` after the number: `1.0f` means you want to use the 32-bit version of 1.0 and not the 64-bit version of 1.0. Therefore, to declare `Vector3 vec = new Vector3 (1.0f, 1.0f, 1.0f);` is the correct way to assign a proper `Vector3()`.

Confused? I'd imagine so; we'll clear things up in a bit. Just hang in there.

For our purposes of learning how to code, knowing anything about bits may not mean a lot. However, if you ever talk to a programmer it'll be very important that you know the difference. Before getting too far ahead we should know that Unity 3D uses `floats` and `ints` quite often. There is also a difference between the different data types in that they cannot be simply used interchangeably without consequence.

3.13.1 Dynamic Typing

Not all programming languages are so strict with types, but it's a good idea to get used to working with strict types before learning more lazily typed programming languages, like Lua (http://www.lua.org/). These are sometimes called "Duck"-typed languages; this refers to the proverb "if it looks like a duck and it sounds like a duck, it's probably a duck." Type conversion is important for learning more complex languages like C, or C++. These languages offer a wider number of platforms and a more detailed level of control.

With dynamically typed languages like Lua or UnrealScript, you can run into strange hard-to-track-down bugs. However, when it comes to a type we might see something like this:

```
var i = 1; // int?
if(i) // bool?
{
    Console.WriteLine("is " + i + "i true or a 1?"); // int string or a bool?
    i = i * 0.1; // now is i a double?
}
```

In the above it's not clear what the variable i is supposed to be, is it a bool or an int or a double? When var above starts off as an integer, but we use it as a bool and then multiply it by a floating point value, what is i? What have we turned it into if we want to use it as something else, or how do we turn it back?

As we will see in Section 7.14.4, we are allowed to make some exceptions to the type of a variable. The keywords var and dynamic do mean you're expecting an unexpected type to be coming, but once it's there, you had better know what to do with it.

3.13.2 What We've Learned

We have glossed over the specifics of how numbers work in the computer's memory, but we'll get into that in Section 6.20.2. Superficially, we should know that not all numbers are the same. A byte is 8 bits, a nibble is 4. An int is 32 bits, and an int64 is 64 bits, but that's not all. A float is also 32 bits and a double is 64 bits, but these can't hold the same values as an int or int64.

The float and double use some of their bits called a mantissa to hold the numbers after the decimal. Therefore, 1.01 requires some of the bits to represent the 1, and these are called the significant digits. The mantissa uses some bits to represent the other 1 in the number. Then there are more bits set aside to tell C# where the dot (.) goes in the number, and these bits are called the exponent. Therefore, with 1.02, the exponent tells the mantissa 2 to move an extra zero after the dot, so 1.02 is the final result.

We take for granted the work going on under the hood to store a simple number. All of this happens thanks to many computer scientists who have worked in the last several decades. Konrad Zuse and John von Neumann introduced a system of floating point representation to computing in the 1940s, with the Z1 and later the Z3. Their system is roughly the same system in use today.

3.14 Type Casting, Numbers

Continue with the Types script from the previous chapter. Data in C# comes in various forms. Not just number type, but a class or any object for that matter becomes a new type of data. At least, numbers can be thought of as having comparable value. Casting is a tricky topic which we'll come back to a few more times.

The following is a simple exercise, but an important one nonetheless. When you start to deal with keeping score, or recording injuries to a monster, it's important that behaviors are predictable. Many problems begin to show up if the math you're using involves mixing numbers with decimal values like floats or doubles, or with integers which have no fractional value.

```
int hundredInt = 100;
```

Decimals are not allowed on an int value. In this case, 100.2 is not an int data type.

```
float hundredFloat = 100.0f;
double hundredDouble = 100.0;
```

Decimals are allowed for both float and double. The only caveat is that a float requires an f post fixed to the number when it's assigned.

Converting types between one another is simple when you need to deal with numbers. When we start creating our own classes the task of casting becomes a bit more detailed, but not necessarily more difficult; there's just a bit more work involved. We'll get to that soon enough.

When we go between number types or the built-in value types (POD), we work with things which seem to come with C#. So far we've seen things like `int` and `float`. Integer values like 1, 7, and 19 are useful for counting. We use these for counting numbers of items in an array, or how many zombies are in a scene, for instance. Integers are whole numbers, even though we might be counting zombies whole or not.

Once we start needing numbers with fractions we need to use float values. To get an object's speed or *x*, *y*, and *z* coordinates in space we need to use values like `12.612f`, or `x = 13.33f`, to accurately place an object in space. If not, objects would move around in a scene as though they were chess pieces locked to a grid.

When a float value exists as `0.9f` we lose some values after the decimal when converting the floating point value to an integer.

```
float a = 0.9f;
int b = (int)a;
Debug.Log(b);
```

If we observe the above code in the Types_Scene in Unity 3D running by pressing the Play-in-Editor button, we'll see the following output in the Console panel.

Without the cast operator int b = a; we get an error telling us we need to cast the value before assigning it.

```
Assets/Types.cs(75,17): error CS0266: Cannot implicitly convert type `float'
to `int'. An explicit conversion exists (are you missing a cast?)
```

The first part of the error message says "`Cannot implicitly convert type`," which has a very specific meaning that we'll get to before the end of this chapter, but first let's cover explicit type casting.

3.14.1 Explicit versus Implicit Casting

As we have seen, in the `Start ()` function where we declared `float a = 0.9f`; a was converted to 0. Even though we were only `0.1f` away from `1f` to `0.9f` away from 0 we're left with a 0 instead assigned to `int b`. To do these conversions we use the explicit casting method, as shown with `(int) a`;, which explicitly tells C# to convert the value stored at a to a float value. When we are required to use an explicit cast, we're also warned that there may be some data lost in the conversion.

Casting is a process by which C# changes the type of a variable to another type. This may or may not involve a loss of information. In some cases, the conversion doesn't require the explicit cast operator. The following code casts an `int` to a `float`.

```
int c = 3;

float d = c;

Debug.Log(d);
```

With the above code we get a 3 printed out to the Console panel. We didn't need to use an explicit casting operator. This is because when we cast from an `int`, in this case 3, there would be no data loss when it's cast to a float. This is possible through an implicit cast. Implicit casts are allowed only when there is no data lost in the process of converting from one type to another.

There are no integer values which will result in a loss of any value when it's converted to a float. Technically, there are more float numbers between 0 and 1 than there are integer numbers between 0 and 1, or any other sequence of two numbers for that matter.

3.14.1.1 A Basic Example

Continuing on with the Types script we've been using for the last few chapters.

```
int mInt = 1;
double mDub= 0.9;
int c = mInt * mDub;
```

If we look at what is going on here we'll want to think for a moment about what it means. The integer `mInt` is assigned 1 and `double mDub` has 0.9 assigned. We should assume that 0.9 will be assigned to c after the multiplication, but this assignment is stopped by a type conversion error. C# usually gives us pretty clear reasons for its errors. In this case we know there's a cast missing between an `int` and a `double`. We get the "Cannot implicitly convert type 'double' to 'int'." error.

The error states we can't implicitly convert a `double` to an `int`. Why not? 1 certainly looks like 1.0, or so it seems. However, 0.9 can't be turned into an integer. There's no integer between 0 and 1. Even though 0.9 is very close to being 1, it's not.

```
int c = mInt * (int)mDub;
```

We use type conversion to tell C# to explicitly change b from a `double` to an `int` by preceding the b with `(int)`. What value is going to be assigned to c if it can't be 0.9? The `(int)` operator is an explicit cast. Casting with the explicit operator works by using the destined type surrounded by the () operators.

If we read the cast value for `(int)mDub` is 0, which means we've lost data going from the double value to an integer value. Even though 0.9 is almost a 1, the first `int` value is 0, followed by values that are cut off by the type conversion. Now we see why type conversion matters.

In a simple case, observe the type double 1.0 preceded by the (float) operator. The type assigned to the operator matches the destination float f. We will find other casts which look like this in Sections 6.14 and 6.20, but we're introducing the concept early on as it's a very common problem to come across. The syntax (int) turns a number following this operator into an int. Likewise int i = 0; double d = (double) i; is a way to cast an int into a double. However, this isn't always necessary.

Some conversions take place automatically as an implicit cast. In the above example we can use the following code without any problems.

```
int anotherInt = 1;
double anotherDouble = 0.9;
int yetAnotherInt = anotherInt * (int)anotherDouble;
Debug.Log("yetAnotherInt: " + yetAnotherInt);
double yetAnotherDouble = yetAnotherInt;

// this doesn't need a cast
Debug.Log("yetAnotherDouble: " + yetAnotherDouble);
```

Here we assign double d = a; where a is int 1, which we know isn't a double. This produces no errors. The same goes if we add another line float f = a;. In this case f is a float. These are called implicit casts. An integer value doesn't have a mantissa or an exponent. Both the double and float do have these two possibly large and important values. These two terms were explained at the end of Chapter 2.

When mashing a double into an int we lose the mantissa and exponent. By using an explicit cast, we tell C# that we don't mind losing the data. This doesn't mean that an implicit cast will not lose any data either. An int can hold more significant values than a float. We can observe this with the following lines of code added to the Start () function.

```
int largeInt = 2147483647;
Debug.Log("largeInt: " + largeInt);
float largeFloat = largeInt;
Debug.Log("largeFloat: " + largeFloat);
int backAgain = (int)largeFloat;
Debug.Log("backAgain: " + backAgain);
```

This code produces the following console output, after a bit of cleaning up:

> (!) **largeInt: 2147483647**
>   UnityEngine.Debug:Log(Object)
>
> (!) **largeFloat: 2.147484E+09**
>   UnityEngine.Debug:Log(Object)
>
> (!) **backAgain: -2147483648**
>   UnityEngine.Debug:Log(Object)

When we start with the value 2147483647 assigned to int we're at one extreme of the integer value. This is the biggest number the int can hold, for reasons discussed in Section 3.11.1, but in short, it's because it's using only 32 bits to store this number.

If we cast this into largeFloat we can use an implicit cast, which converts the value from int to float. In this case, we see only 2.147484 followed by the exponent E+09, which tells us that the dot (.) is actually nine places over to the right.

When we convert the float back into an int with an explicit cast we get a −2147483648, which is certainly not what we started with. This tells that there's some significant information lost in the conversion from float to int, but there were also numbers lost in the implicit cast from int to float.

This still happens if we remove a digit from the end.

```
int largeIntAgain = 214748361;
Debug.Log("largeIntAgain: " + largeIntAgain);
float largeFloatAgain = largeIntAgain;
Debug.Log("largeFloatAgain: " + largeFloatAgain);
int backAgainAgain = (int)largeFloatAgain;
Debug.Log("backAgainAgain: " + backAgainAgain);
```

This sends the following numbers to the Console:

> ⓘ largeIntAgain: 214748361
> UnityEngine.Debug:Log(Object)
>
> ⓘ largeFloatAgain: 2.147484E+08
> UnityEngine.Debug:Log(Object)
>
> ⓘ backAgainAgain: 214748368
> UnityEngine.Debug:Log(Object)

The last digit is changed from 1 to 8. The 8 is coming from some strange conversion when we go from int into float. Even if we look at the numbers being stored in the float value we can tell that there's already a change in value. This tells us that in general, we need to be very careful when converting from one type into another.

Logically, another difficult problem is converting from a string to a number value. When you use string s = "1"; you're not able to use (int)s to convert from a string to an int. The types of data are very different since strings can also contain letters and symbols. The conversion of (int) "five" has no meaning to the computer. There's no dictionary which is built into C# to make this conversion. This doesn't mean that there are no options.

```
string s = "1";
int fromString = int.Parse(s);
Debug.Log("fromString: " + fromString);
```

The code added to the Start () function will produce the following number:

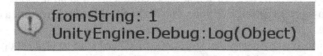

> ⓘ fromString: 1
> UnityEngine.Debug:Log(Object)

There are plenty of options when faced with dealing with significantly different types. The int.Parse() function is an option that we can use to convert one value into another. Again, we might be getting a bit ahead of ourselves, but it's important to see that there are different ways to convert between different types.

3.14.2 What We've Learned

In this chapter we used some syntax which has not been formerly introduced. For the sake of seeing what happens to numbers between casting we needed to do this. In Section 6.20, we will cover the details of what happened in this chapter, so don't worry. Everything in this chapter will be explained in detail soon enough.

We've still got a lot to cover about types. It's a bit early to see how they relate to one another and why there is a difference. Once we move into evaluating numbers we'll start to see how the different types interact. Accuracy is one place where we begin to see the effects of type conversion. A float with the value of 0.9 turns into 0 when it's converted to an int.

This chapter is just a cursory look at types. There's a lot more to conversion than just losing some numbers. Later on we'll see what happens when we need to convert between different game play characters like zombies and humans. Many attributes need to have specific conversions but then they're both bipedal creatures.

3.15 Comments

We've already been seeing plenty of comments in the code. All of the text between /* and */ are comments as well as text following // are comments. Comments are left as breadcrumbs to help keep notes in your code. Once a new line is started the // no longer applies and the next line is becomes visible to the lexical analyzer.

```
//these are not the lines you are looking for...
```

Programmers use comments for many reasons. Mostly, comments are used to describe what a function is used for. Quite often, comments are left as notes for both the person who wrote the code and for others. Sometimes, when a function is confusing, or isn't always working, a comment can be left as a "to do" list.

To facilitate the programmer, Visual Studio even has a window that reads comments and looks for the notation //TODO: and adds them to a list of tasks. You can find this in the View → Task List window. Where you might see the following:

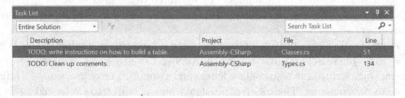

If you check in the window, you'll be able to jump to the line in the highlighted file by double clicking on the Task List item. Whatever text appears on that line will show up in the Task List.

Once we start writing our own functions, we'll want to leave comments to help remember what we were thinking when we wrote them. Sometimes, if we need help, we can indicate to our friends our intentions. You can leave comments like //I'm still working on this, I'll get back to it tomorrow... if you're still working on some code.

Or you can ask for help: //help, I can't figure out how to rotate the player, can someone else do this?! is a simple short comment. Even professional programmers leave comments for their co-workers, letting everyone who may be looking at their work a clue as to what was going on in their code.

In more than one case, the comments in a large code base needed to be cleaned up before releasing to the public. The engineers responsible needed to remove foul language from the comments to avoid any public ridicule. In some instances, the comments in the code were also defaming competing game engines.

When a comment requires more than a single line, use the following notation:

```
/* this is a multiline comment
   which can carry on to other lines
   you can keep on writing anything
   until you get to the following */
```

There are various styles which you can follow with multi-line comments.

```
/* this is also a multiline comment
 * but we have little * at the start
 * of each line and we finish this
 * with the closing comment on it's
 * own line
 */
```

Anything between the /* and the */ will be ignored by the C# compiler. It's often a good habit for a programmer to introduce a class by leaving a comment at the top of the file. For instance, it's common to see the following in a class written for other people to edit.

```
/* Player class written by Alex Okita
 * This class manages the player's data and logic
 */
```

The use of comments isn't limited to simple statements. They are often decorated by extra elements to help them stand out.

```
/*****************************************
 * This comment was written by Alex Okita *
 *****************************************/
```

Comments have several other uses which will come in handy; for instance, when testing code you can comment a section of code that you know works and test out new code next to the code commented out. If your test doesn't work you can always clear it out and un-comment the code that does work. We'll play with this idea later in this chapter.

Using comments on the same line of code is also a regular practice.

```
void MyFunction()
{
    int someInt = 0; // declaring some regular int as 0
}
```

We can inform anyone reading our code what a specific statement is doing. Although we want to be smart with how our comments are written, if we add too many comments in our code the actual statements that matter get lost between a bunch of words that don't matter.

Comments are also useful for testing different collections of code. When you're learning about how different behaviors affect the results of your functions it's often useful to keep different versions of your code around. This is often the case when trying to debug a problem and eliminate lines of code without having to completely get rid of them.

```
void MyOtherFunction()
{
    int someInt = 0;//I print 0 through 10
    //int someInt = 3; //starts at 3
    //int someInt = 11; //this won't print
    while (someInt < 10)
    {
        System.Console.WriteLine(someInt);
        someInt++;
    }
}
```

It's possible to test out various test cases using comments to allow you to pick and choose between different statements. In the above code fragment, we've got someInt declared three different ways. Depending on which line is left un-commented we can choose between different values.

We can leave another comment on the line after the statement, reminding us what the result was. For covering an entire section of code it's easier to use the /* */ form of commenting.

```
void AnotherFunction()
{
    int someInt = 0;//I print 0 through 10
                    //int someInt = 3;//starts at 3
                    //int someInt = 11;//this won't work, so leave me out.
                    //trying out new code here
    for (int i = 0; i < someInt; i++)
    {
        System.Console.WriteLine(someInt);
    }

    //the code below will do the same thing.
    /*
    while(someInt < 10) {
    System.Console.WriteLine(someInt);
    someInt++;
    }
    */
}
```

In the above code, we've commented out the while loop following the for loop which accomplishes the same task. In this way we can easily switch between the two different loops by switching which loop is commented out. Programmers often leave sections of code in their functions commented out so they verify the validity of the new code they've added in.

The /* */ notation for comments can also be used in smaller places. Anytime the // notation appears everything on the same line is commented out. Using the /* */ notation we can hide a segment of a line of code.

```
void InLineComment()
{
    int someInt = 0;

    while (someInt </*10*/100)
    {
        System.Console.WriteLine(someInt);
        someInt++;
    }
}
```

For instance, we can hide the 10 in the while loop and replace it with another number altogether. The /*10*/ is hidden from the computer so the 100 is the only part of the condition that's seen by the computer. This can easily get a bit uglier as a single statement can begin to stretch out and become unreadable.

```
Vector3(/* this is the x variable */1.0f,
    2.0f/* <- that was the Y variable*/,
    /* the z */3.0f/*variable is here*/);
```

Although the above code is perfectly valid, it's not recommended that something like this appear in your code. When mixing in too many comments a simple declaration can get ugly.

3.15.1 Line Numbers

Each line of code in Visual Studio is indicated in the margin of the Editor to the left. When Unity 3D or Visual Studio comes across a typo or some unexpected character it's indicated in the Console panel or the Visual Studio Error List.

The Error List in Visual Studio tells us where an error may have occurred in our code. There's an expected } at line 95. Right after the line with the red squiggle you'll see a lonely ? in the middle of the function. Unity shows us a similar error.

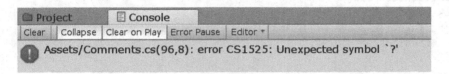

The error tells us: `Comments.cs(96,8): error CS1525: Unexpected symbol '?'`. The (96,8) tells us the position where the error is occurring. The first number is the line number. In the source code mentioned, we added in the ? on the 96th line. The 8 tells us that the character is on column 8, or the 8th character position from the left. If you were to count the number of spaces from the left you'd reach 8 and find the ?, which Unity 3D is erroring on.

This is a more precise example of an error, but we may not always be so fortunate. In general, the line number indicated is more or less a starting place where to start looking for an error. It's difficult to say when and how various errors take place in code, but in general, syntax errors tend to be fairly easy to fix. Difficulties arise when the code itself is using proper syntax but the result is erroneous or deviates from expected behavior.

When this happens we'll have to use other techniques to track down the bugs. We'll save those techniques for when we're ready for them. For now we'll just stick to learning proper syntax and comments.

3.15.2 Code Folding

When you add in a long comment using the /* */ notation, MonoDevelop recognizes your comment.

Clicking on the little box in the number column will collapse the comment into a single line. This feature comes in most of the modern IDEs meant for writing in C#. This feature is also handy when you're rewriting large segments of code, in that it reduces any distractions.

```
void FunctionsCanFold()
{
    int someInt = 0;
    while( someInt < /*10*/ 100)
    {
        someInt++;
    }
}
```

We can collapse many blocks of code into a single line. If you look at the line numbering following the Update () function you'll see the numbers jump from 79 to 93. This process of collapsing has hidden three lines of code; moreover, this feature will be particularly handy when you need to see two different functions which might have a great deal of code between them.

```
void FunctionsCanFold()...
/* clickint on the [+] in the left margin next
 * to the function above will turn the function into
 * void FunctionsCanFold()[...]
 */
```

This also works for any instance where the opening curly brace { is followed by the closing curly brace }. This folds the for statement into a more compact form, so we don't have to look at what it's doing. This allows us to focus on the code block we're most interested in focusing on.

A special type of comment is the region. This uses the # character followed by the word region to create a foldable area of text. The words following the start of a region indicate a starting point of a foldable area of text.

```
#region Special Area of Interest
void SomeFunction()
{
    // doing things in area of interest
}
int SomeInt = 0;
class SomeClass
{
    int SomeClassesInt = 1;
}
#endregion
```

The end of the region is indicated by #endregion to close off the foldable text area. When the region is folded the first line of text remains visible to identify the folded region's content.

```
Special Area of Interest
```

Regions can also have other regions within them. Visual Studio will help highlight hierarchies of regions when you leave the cursor on one of the beginnings or ends of the region.

```csharp
#region Special Area of Interest
void SomeFunction()
{
    // doing things in area of interest
}
int SomeInt = 0;
#region Sub Section in the area
class SomeClass
{
    int SomeClassesInt = 1;
}
#endregion
#endregion
```

A large C# file can be made a bit easier to navigate by adding regions. These are intended to help collapse groups of functions or variables to make other parts of the same file easier to read. To focus on a smaller section of code it's often useful to create regions to hide away sections you're less interested in.

```csharp
#region Special Area of Interest
void SomeFunction()
{
    // doing things in area of interest
}
int SomeInt = 0;
Sub Section in the area
#endregion
```

Often regions are setup around parts of a class that serve a specific function. This affords the engineer a clever and elegant way to help organize code. In a way, the fussy organizational skills of a good programmer are expressed through comments, regions and function grouping.

The code examples for this book have regions to delineate sections of code for each chapter.

3.15.3 Summary Comments

```csharp
/// <summary>
/// A Vector3 function of my own!
/// </summary>
/// <param name="v1"></param>
/// <param name="v2"></param>
/// <param name="v3"></param>
private void Vector3(float v1, float v2, float v3)
{
    //?
    /* uncomment the ? above to see the error
     * produced in the book.
     */
}
```

If you type in three slashes (/s) over a function, Visual Studio will automatically add in a summary comment. Like the other comments the summary comments are also collapsible. Visual Studio also recognizes many different forms of comment tags.

When you add in a < the above automatic code completion pop-up dialog appears. You can add in description examples and other tags. This feature of Visual Studio demonstrates how important comments are in a well-written source file. Comments and comment tags have many different options. To avoid writing the rest of this book about comments I'll leave experimenting with the comment tags to you. They are important, but not essential, to learning how C# works.

3.15.4 Navigating in Code

There are also clever ways to get around in a source file. Up at the top of the panel in Visual Studio is a handy drop-down menu which has a list item for every function in the class. You'll also notice an icon next to each listing.

Add in a `public` keyword before the `void MyPublicMethod()` function and the lock icon goes away. This indicates that the `CleverComments()` function is `public`. Selecting the item jumps the cursor to the beginning of the function. This comes in particularly handy when dealing with large source files which might have many different functions in them.

3.15.5 What We've Learned

Comments are a necessary part of any good source file. Available online tools will parse your source files, find summary comments, and generate an entire website documenting your code. Organized code and comments are parts of your code style. The more organized your code is the more readable it becomes.

```
public class Comments
{
        Chapter 3.15 Comments

        Chapter 3.15.1 LineNumbers

        Chapter 3.15.2 Code Folding

        Chapter 3.15.3 Summary Comments

        Chapter 3.15.4 Navigating in Code
}
```

When you've written several dozen different C# files you'll find that code written months ago might look alien. I often find myself thinking to myself "What was I thinking when I wrote this?" when I open a file from many months before.

In these cases, I hope I wrote in detailed comments, leaving myself at least some clue as to what was going on to lead to the code that has been written;. Usually, however, I haven't and I need to read through the rest of my code to come up with an understanding of what was going on.

It's time to get back to Unity 3D and start writing something more interesting than comments. We spent a great deal of time in this chapter writing things that are ignored by the computer. It's time to get to writing code that matters.

3.16 Leveling Up: Moving on to Basics

At this point we've looked at the components that make up C#. We should be able to look at code and identify the different tokens and roughly what they do. The ; is a separator token which ends a code statement. Likewise, we should understand that a : and a ; have different roles in code and cannot be used interchangeably.

Variables have a type, and this type determines how the variable can be used. We should also know that different types cannot interact without explicit conversions between them. Converting between different types can result in loss of data, and thus we should be mindful when doing so.

When we look at a statement, we should be able to identify the different tokens which the statement is composed of. In a statement like int a = 6; we should be able to see that we're using five different tokens.

What the different tokens are used for may not be clear, but that information will be presented as we continue. Learning a programming language is just as involved as learning any other language. Just like any language has grammar and vocabulary, C# has syntax, keywords, and structure.

3.16.1 Git Revision History

Using Git to save the history of a file is its main strength. With every commit and push you create a new checkpoint for the files updated with the commit. The changes don't need to include every file affected in the commit.

With the Git Bash open you can browse the history of each file. The revisions for the README.md file can be seen with

```
git log README.md
```

The command prints out a commit followed by a long hash value followed by the author, date, and comment from the commit. If there are a lot of commits then using:

```
git log --oneline README.md
```

will produce an easier to read history of the file. The shorter hash also makes it easier to pick a version of the file.

```
git checkout 38cd1c9 README.md
```

This will revert the README.md to its initial commit version. Open the file in a text file to confirm.

```
git status
```

alexokita@Buggy MINGW64 ~/Documents/BookContents (master)
$ git status
On branch master
Your branch is up to date with 'origin/master'.

Changes to be committed:
  (use "git reset HEAD <file>..." to unstage)

        modified: README.md

alexokita@Buggy MINGW64 ~/Documents/BookContents (master)
$ █

This will show the status of the README.md as modified. To get the latest version of the README.md file again use:

```
git checkout HEAD README.md
```

The file will be back to the latest version checked in. Git log and checkout are simple commands to remember. With the add commit and push commands you'll be able to keep track of your files and see what's changed between revisions. Git is great!

4

Basics: The Building Blocks of Code

After covering the small parts that make up code, it's time to start learning how all the parts come together to create a behavior. Creating data is easy; keeping the data organized is harder. Adding logic to do something with the data is harder still. That said, it's not impossible; otherwise, no one would write code.

This chapter covers how a statement of code works and where the power that drives the code originates. Programming is much less enigmatic when you understand the mechanisms that drive it. To understand why code behaves the way it does, it's important to know your way around the language.

4.1 What Will Be Covered in This Chapter

This chapter is about getting past the simple details and going into the structure of code. This process is somewhat comparable to learning the grammar of the C# programming language. We'll cover the basics about the different types of logic statements and looping statements.

Logic allows you to pick different actions based on the result of a calculation. If you want to tell a human to run away from a zombie or run to a human for help, you'll need logic, to control that human's behavior. Logic takes data, makes a comparison, and chooses which section of code to execute.

Looping statements can read and react to more than one data set. If you're in a room with any number of zombies, you'll want to take them into account all at once. Looping statements are an integral part of any programming language. We'll see why they're so useful in this chapter, in which we discuss the following topics:

- Building a game starting with input
- Creating a new class
- Directives: The keyword `using`
- Functions
- Order of operation
- Scope
- Keyword `This`
- Logic and operators
- Loops
- Warnings and errors

4.2 Review

Before getting ahead of yourself, it's important to remember some of what we just covered. We will be learning many new tokens in this chapter. A token, as we know, is the smallest element that makes up a statement.

Statements are tokens organized to accomplish a task. Tokens can be keywords, or words reserved by C# for special purposes. Some tokens are used to separate statements, and others are used to assign values to variables.

A keyword cannot be used for anything other than what it has been reserved for. Some keywords can be used only in a specific context. Several keywords are used only if you've defined a specific library, where they have been defined; we'll discuss some of these topics later in this chapter.

When you create a variable, you've created a new token. Some variables exist only in the context they were created in; the control of this existence is called scope, something which is coming up in this section as well. As a reminder, when you invent a word to identify a variable that word becomes a new token.

Once created, the token can be used in many ways; you can apply an operation to a token and use it to assign values to other variables. These operations all happen in a very specific order. Create a variable, execute an operation or an expression, assign the value. This is what makes C# an imperative language.

4.3 Building a Game—Part 1

Building an entire game is a large undertaking, to say the least. Creating a core game play mechanic is something that should be prototyped in different forms. In short when you're learning, it's better to make many simple small games or test cases that explore a single mechanic. Then the classes you write for Input, navigation, inventory, score etc. It's best to write code that can be copied to a larger project.

Designing a complete game with backstory, character development can be done in parallel with the core functionality of what the player does from moment to moment. Often, what you're able to accomplish as an engineer influences the kind of story you're able to convey. A vast open world with many different stories would take hundreds of hours to build content. Narrowing the scope of your project is important.

At the beginning of almost every game development project, the input. It's also quite interesting since Unity 3D has a lot of options on how to deal with getting Input. Keyboards, Game Controllers, the Mouse, Touch Screens, and any number of alternative systems count as "Input" in a broad sense. But let's just get something simple working first.

In the Unity-SampleGame project, open the Scenes/Section 4.3 unity scene. In the hierarchy, find the game object called TransformPrimitive with a DirectMousePosition script attached. Open the DirectMousePosition.cs in Visual Studio to follow along. This is about as simple as it can get.

```
// Update is called once per frame
void Update () {
    gameObject.transform.position = Input.mousePosition;
}
```

This may not be the most useful of input systems, but it's useful to see what `Input.mousePosition` is doing. After pressing the Play-In-Editor button you might be able to observe the TransformPrimitive in the unity scene moving around rather quickly as the mouse moves around over the Game window. Select the game object and take a look at the Inspector panel's transform values. The x and y values increase as the mouse gets further away from the lower left corner of the game window.

The lower left of the Game window puts lower numbers into the Transform of the GameObject, the top right puts larger numbers in there. If the game camera is only looking at what is near the center of the world, then you'll rarely see the TransformPrimitive in view unless your mouse is near the lower left of the game view; truly not a useful input system.

We learned something, you can move an object with the mouse, though erratically. Mouse X and Y turn into game object X and Y. The game view's origin or x = 0 y = 0 coordinate is at the lower left and the maximum values are at the top right.

The above image shows some values assigned to the Transform of the TransformPrimitive in the Inspector. The cursor moved toward the middle of the view of the game while being played in the editor shows values in the hundreds taken from the mouse coordinates. As to be expected, the X and Y values change as the mouse moves around on the game view. The Z is left at 0 since the screen is a 2D image.

4.3.1 Mouse Point

To make better use of the input values we'll want to use the mousePosition data. Open the Section 4.3.1 unity scene to observe a better way to use the mouse position. Selecting objects, pointing at a position, and drawing lines need mouse positions translated into world coordinates to work. Many common tasks have starting points built into Unity 3D.

Our Unity scene to follow has a MousePointController object with MousePoint.cs script attached. To start, the code gets the camera used to see the game. One quick way is to use the Main Camera, or in this case the code myCamera = Camera.main; does this for us. To move the transform primitive to where the mouse cursor is pointing, we use myTransformObject = GameObject.Find("TransformPrimitive"); to find the object in the scene.

```
myCamera = Camera.main;
myTransformObject = GameObject.Find("TransformPrimitive");
```

Now that we have a reference to the two objects being updated in each frame; we'll start to use them in the Update() function provided by Unity. In the Update() function we'll use what's called a ray, a mathematic type that is basically a starting point in 3D space with a direction. That ray will start with the Main Camera in the scene, and point at the mouse point in the screen to the world.

Once the ray is cast, Unity provides a physics system that takes the ray and checks if it collides with anything in the world. That method is called Physics.RayCast(); and that updates what is called a RaycastHit with the outcome from the Physics.RayCast();. Physics uses the mousePosition to create a line from the center of the game camera through the mousePosition on the screen and into the game world. If Physics tells is we've intersected with something, then we put the TransformPrimitive at the location where the hit occurs.

```
Ray ray = myCamera.ScreenPointToRay(Input.mousePosition, Camera.MonoOrStereoscopicEye.Mono);
RaycastHit hit;
if (Physics.Raycast(ray, out hit))
{
    myTransformObject.transform.position = hit.point;
}
```

The position of the transform primitive is assigned to the hit.point when updated by Physics. Raycast();. This happens on every frame; when we run the game at this point we'll see the transform primitive act like a cursor under the mouse as it's move around in the Game view.

Games don't usually move a character around in the scene as quickly as you can move a mouse. But the world position is important. If we want a character to move to the cursor we will need to know where in the world the mouse is pointed.

4.3.2 Move to Point

The Unity scene Section 4.3.2 has the same setup as the previous section with the addition of a little character with a MoveToPoint.cs script attached. This will point the little robot to the point in the world where the transform primitive is. When we click the left mouse button the robot will move to the transform primitive's position.

First we'll need a Vector3 that represents the direction that we need to point the robot in. This is done by subtracting the position of the robot from the position of the transform primitive.

```
Vector3 lookTarget = myTransformObject.transform.position - transform.position;
```

With this Vector3 we need to get a rotation value. Rotations in Unity are stored as Quaternion, a type of math that stores angles of directions. Quaternions can be tricky, but the engineers at Unity have provided us with a way to calculate the proper quaternion values with Quaternion.LookRotation();. This is calculated with the look target's position and the upward angle of the robot. The upward direction comes from transform.up so we know what axis to rotate the robot around and the lookTarget gives us what direction to rotate to.

To use the direction value we want to rotate the robot with Quaternion.Slerp() which means Smooth Linear-interpolate. Interpolation means we'll use time to step with small values from one value, the transform.rotation of the robot to a goal rotation, in this case the direction we got from the LookRotation() function.

```
Quaternion direction = Quaternion.LookRotation(lookTarget, transform.up);
transform.rotation = Quaternion.Slerp(transform.rotation, direction, Time.deltaTime * 5f);
```

This rotation is updated on every frame by virtue of being in the Update() function. Now we'll use the Input. GetMouseButton(0) to let us know when the left mouse button is pressed. GetMouseButton(1) would be the right mouse button. With use of an if() statement to update the movement target called moveToPosition.

When the left mouse button is down we set the value of the moveToPosition to the position of the transform primitive with myTransformObject.transform.position; as seen in the code.

```
if (Input.GetMouseButton(0))
{
    moveToPosition = myTransformObject.transform.position;
}
```

This now updates so long as the left mouse button is down. To get the robot to actually move to that position we'll assign the robots `transform.position` to the result of another interpolation position with `Vecter3.Lerp()` where we use the current position and the target position as values.

Now when we run the game we'll have a robot that faces the position of the mouse in the world and will move to it so long as the left mouse button is pressed.

This counts as a very simple system of navigation for a character to move in a scene. This acts as our starting point. As we come across new systems we'll be able to understand more about the functions we just used and add new systems to make the robot navigate a more complex environment.

4.3.3 What We've Learned

We're just getting started. Our road toward zombie destruction needs a great deal of footwork and studying. Some of what we're about to get into might seem a bit mundane, but it's only the beginning.

We're learning a new language with new words and concepts. With the help of Unity 3D we're going to have a foundation on which pretty much any game can be built. Stick to it and you'll be writing lots of code in no time.

The intent of the direct input experiment is to discover how data is presented to you. In a similar fashion, systems like touch and gyro from mobile devices may present data in an unexpected format. You can't necessarily change how data is given to you, but you can change how to use the data.

4.4 Class Construction

The class object is the focus as a new Unity C# engineer. In the previous chapter we saw a `MousePoint` and `MoveToPoint` class, but how were these classes created? As a Unity 3D engineer all of work goes into building the contents of a class. This was mentioned in Section 3.8, but we didn't look at what's involved with writing a new class. To see the creation of a class in action, The ClassConstruction_Scene and the ClassConstruction script in the scene on the object of the same name.

To get our heads around what a class is, we're going to write a class declaration inside of a class. This is what is called a nested class. To write a class you start with a *class declaration*.

A class declaration is basically the keyword `class` followed by an identifier. As a reminder, an identifier is simply a word you use to name any data you've created. Once a class has been declared, it's a matter of filling it with all the useful things that classes can do.

```
/*
 * A nested class can appear down below this comment.
 *
 *
 *    ┌──────────┐   ┌────────────┐
 *    │ keyword  │   │ Identifier │
 *    └──────────┘   └────────────┘
 *       │              │
 *       └──┐     ┌──────┘
 *          │     │
 * class MyNewClass
 * {
 * }
 * ↑
 * │
 * └──┐
 *    │
 *    ┌────────────┐
 *    │ separators │
 *    └────────────┘
 *
 * Don't forget the { and } separators following the class declaration.
 *
 */
```

Where did ClassConstruction.cs come from? Much of this work is done for you by the Unity 3D Editor when you have Unity create a C# script for you. Alternatively, you can have Visual Studio create a script for you.

The right-click popup from the Assembly-CSharp item in the Solution Explorer window will bring up a menu to select Add→Class… item. This opens the following Dialog:

From here you can select a new CSharp MonoBehaviour or Editor script to build new scripts on. By default a file is called NewBehaviourScript.cs. In here, Unity 3D wrote some directives, declares a class called NewBehaviourScript, then adds in some base functions to get started. We'll go through the same steps to understand why the file is written like it is. And we'll start with the class declaration. Compare the NewBehaviourScript with the ClassConstruction script to see what the differences are.

```
Debug.Log(dataOne.myNumber);
// 1
Debug.Log(dataTwo.myNumber);
// 7
Debug.Log(dataThree.myNumber);
// 11
```

4.4.1 Class Declaration

A "class declaration" makes an announcement to tell Unity 3D that your object exists. In the preceding example we the `MyNewClass` object with the keyword `class` followed by the identifier `MyNewClass`. Together the `class MyNewClass{}` declared to your entire project that there's an object called `MyNewClass`. This declaration also means that `MyNewClass` as an identifier is special, and if you were to reuse the name for another object you'll create an error.

```
class MyNewClass
{
}
```

Classes are objects that could contain more objects called members, or *class members*. Often words like attributes, fields, properties, and components can also be used to describe a member of a class. In all cases each member of the class is given identifiers as well.

When you add a contact to your phone, you add a name, number, and email address into empty boxes; programmers often refer to these as fields. They are open spaces in your computer's memory into which you put data.

The sections of a class that contain logic and code statements are called *function members*. These are also accessed by their identifiers. Depending on what a function does for the class, it can be categorized as a *method, constructor, destructor, indexer, operator, property,* or *event*. How these functions differ from one another will be discussed in Sections 4.7.1.1, 5.4.3, 7.5, 7.13, and 7.15.

Classes need to talk to one another for any number of reasons. Zombies need to know where humans are, and bullets need to take chunks out of zombies. Suppose a zombie has several chunks left before slain, and the human has a position in the world where the zombie needs to chase him; this information needs to be shared. The availability of the information is called *accessibility*.

Data and function members can be made accessible to each other using the *public* keyword. We'll observe how this works in a moment. In a class that inherits from `MonoBehaviour`, making a variable `public` makes an identifier visible to the Inspector panel in the Editor. Inheritance is something coming in Section 5.3, so there's a bit to cover until then. However, it's important to know that accessibility has various effects with how classes interact with one another.

4.4.1.1 A Basic Example

Consider the class declaration shown for `MyNewClass()`. This is a nested class inside of the ClassConstruction class. A nested class encapsulates the purpose of the declaration for a specific purpose within its parent class. A Zombie and a Player class may have independent nested inventory classes. This would allow the inventory in each to behave differently.

Look just below that and you'll find a line that has the statement void Start(); this statement creates a function that is a member of the Example class. To create an instance of this class we add MyNewClass mClass = new MyNewClass(); to the Start() function.

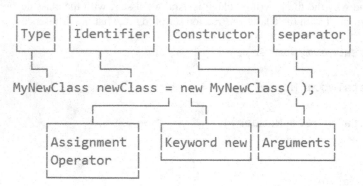

Let's examine the first two words, or tokens. The first token MyNewClass indicates the type of object we intend to create. The class we created is now a new type of data. Once MyNewClass has been declared as a class, it becomes an instruction to create a new type of data known by its identifier.

We know a variable is declared by a keyword followed by an identifier like int i; a class variable is declared in a similar way: MyNewClass mClass. However, unlike an int a class *cannot* be assigned with plain old data.

What differentiates an int from a class is how the type is created and then assigned. We'll have to go into detail a bit later when we would have a deeper understanding about data types, but for now, we'll consider an int as a fundamental type.

In practice, nearly every new behavior you create will begin with a new class. At the start of your project you'll likely create a unique classes for each game item, character, effect, etc. That's not to say you'll create a different class for similar items. For instance, a blue key and a red key might act in a similar way with their only distinction being color. In cases like this your class can contain options to be any color required.

4.4.1.2 Value and Reference Types

Although we declared class MyNewClass we have yet to give it anything to do. For now, there's nothing written in MyNewClass. Once we start adding features to MyNewClass the task of assigning a value to the class becomes ambiguous. In context:

What would that mean if MyNewClass was a zombie? Is the 1 his name? How many hit points does he have? or what is his armor rating? Because C# can't be sure, the computer has no hope of making a guess.

This differentiates a *value type*, like an int, over a *reference type*, such as MyClass. However, before we go into a chapter about types we need to know more about classes, so we'll get back to the topic at hand.

Therefore, when creating a new instance of a reference type we need to use the form new MyNewClass(); to assign a variable of type MyNewClass. Thus, MyNewClass newClass = new MyNewClass(); is used to create a variable for MyNewClass and assign the variable newClass a new instance of the correct class.

To make things clear, `int i` can be assigned in the exact same way we assign `newClass`.

```
int i = new System.Int32();
```

We can use the above statement if we want to make our int declarations look the same as our class declarations. This is unorthodox and unnecessary, but it's possible. It's important to know that things like this do exist and that C# is flexible enough to allow us to do this.

4.4.2 Adding Data Fields

A data field is any type of information that lives inside of a class. We'll cover what data type really means in Section 6.5.3 but for now we'll assume that data can be pretty much anything, including a number. When a class has data fields added to it, we're giving the class a place that holds onto information and allows the class to remember, or store, some data. For instance, were we to write a zombie for a game we'd need the zombie to know, or store, how many brains it has eaten, or how many whacks it has taken from the player.

```
class DataFields
{
    int myNumbers;
}
```

To add a data field to a `DataFields` class we use the same declaration as we would for any other variable. This should be obvious, but since we're writing a class inside of a class this might be a bit confusing. However, when this is declared as `int myNumbers;` we're not allowed to use it yet.

4.4.3 Access Modifiers and the Dot Operator

To see to members of a class we use the *dot operator* (.) to tell C# we want to access a member of a class. When a new data field is added to a class it's assigned a type and an identifier. The identifier turns into the word we use after the dot to request access to that data or function.

```
class DataFields
{
    int myNumber;
}

void TestAccess()
{
    DataFields data = new DataFields();
    data.
```
```
    ♥ Equals
    ♥ GetHashCode
    ♥ GetType
    ♥ ToString
```

If we try to find the `myNumber` data field when using Visual Studio we won't see the `myNumber` data field in the list of members. To make the `int myNumber` accessible we need the `public` keyword. The `public` keyword is like several other keywords that change the accessibility of a variable within a class; such keywords are called *access modifiers*. There are several access modifiers we'll come to use, but for now we'll just get familiar with the `public` access modifier.

```
void TestAccess()
{
    DataFields data = new DataFields();
    data.
```

```
        Equals
        GetHashCode
        GetType
        myNumber
        PrintMyNumber
        ToString
```

Adding the keyword `public` before the `int myNumber` changes the accessibility to the classes outside of `DataFields` and allow for other objects to see the data field. The data fields that can be changed this way are called *instance variables* that are unique to each instance of the class.

An instance is a unique version, or object, based on the class from which it was created from. Each instance stands on its own as a new object created from the class it's based on. All the class members are unique to each instance. There are systems that circumvent this behavior, but we'll get to that in Section 5.5.

To observe this point, we'll create a few instances of the class and set the data fields to different values.

```
DataFields dataOne = new DataFields();
dataOne.myNumber = 1;
DataFields dataTwo = new DataFields();
dataTwo.myNumber = 7;
DataFields dataThree = new DataFields();
dataThree.myNumber = 11;
```

Here, we created three instances of `DataFields`. Each one has its own `myNumber` data field and each one can be assigned a unique value. To check this, we use A Unity `Debug.Log` to print out the value of each instance of `DataFields myNumbers` field.

```
Debug.Log(dataOne.myNumber);
// 1
Debug.Log(dataTwo.myNumber);
// 7
Debug.Log(dataThree.myNumber);
// 11
```

Add in these three lines after `dataThree.myNumber` is assigned. We could do something useful by adding a function into the class that does this for us. Class members can include more than variables. Functions as members are accessible through the dot operator.

```
class DataFields
{
    public int myNumber;

    public void PrintMyNumber()
    {
        Debug.Log(myNumber);
    }
}
```

A function to print with `Debug.Log(myNumber);` added into the `PrintMyNymber()` function, is made `public` in the same way as `myNumber`. We'll get a better look at functions in Chapter 5, but this example serves as a quick and dirty introduction come back to a simple function nonetheless.

The `PrintMyNymber` function and the `myNumber` field both live together in the `DataFields` class and share the same scope. The dot operator is only necessary to access members inside of an object. The members of `DataFields` are next to one another inside of the class.

```
DataFields firstData = new DataFields();
firstData.myNumber = 3;
firstData.PrintMyNumber();
// 3
```

The instance of `firstData`, in the example above *contains* the `myNumber` and `PrintMyNumber()` members. To access the members inside of `firstData` you do need the dot operator. The dot operator allows you to use the specific member of a specific object. Each instance of the object is unique. This allows you to specify what happens to each unique instance of a `DataFields` object.

4.4.4 Class Scope

Members of a class may appear in any order within the class definition. The arrangement of data and function depends on style and practice. One practice might be to keep data fields next to the functions that use them.

```
class DataFunctionPairGrouping
{
    public int MyCounter;
    public void UseMyCounter()
    {
        MyCounter += 1;
        Debug.Log(MyCounter);
    }

    public float MyFloat;
    public void UseMyFloat()
    {
        MyFloat += 1.0f;
        Debug.Log(MyFloat);
    }
}
```

With the above example we can see that `MyCounter` lives next to `UseMyCounter()`, and likewise for `MyFloat` and `UseMyFloat()`. Here we see the data and function are grouped together.

```csharp
class DefineVariablesFirst
{
    public int FirstInt;
    public int SecondInt;
    public int ThirdInt;

    public void UseFirstInt()
    {
        Debug.Log(FirstInt);
    }
    public void UseSecondInt()
    {
        Debug.Log(SecondInt);
    }
    public void UseThirdInt()
    {
        Debug.Log(ThirdInt);
    }
}
```

C# allows for functions and variables to appear in any order within the class definition. C# ignores how the different members are arranged. This doesn't always hold true, especially once we get into how code itself is executed, but at the class level, or at the class scope, as programmers like to say, the ordering isn't as important.

Not all programming languages will allow this. UnrealScript, for example, enforces all variables live at the beginning of a function. Declaring them anywhere else raises an error. C# understands that formatting is less important than clarity. Declaring variables close to where they are used, however, is important for readability.

4.4.5 Class Members

As we add functions and variables to a class, we're adding *members* to the class. In the previous example, num is a member of `MyClass`. So too are `PrintNum()` and any other functions or variables included in the class. We can refer to some of the members as public, which means that other classes can access them, while the inaccessible members are private.

In most cases, if public is not used then you can assume the member belongs to private. Private members cannot be accessed from outside of the class, at least not directly. However, functions on the inside or local to the class can modify them freely.

4.4.6 What We've Learned

We just covered some of the very basic concepts of what makes up a class. There are plenty of other keywords and some complex concepts that we have yet to touch on. Later, we'll get into some additional clever tricks that classes allow for.

On your own, you should practice creating different data fields and add more functions to your class to get a feel for how they work. As you learn how to use more keywords, you should add them to your own classes to check that you understand how the keywords work.

In this chapter, we created `MyNewClass` as well as a few others inside of the `ClassConstruction` class. `MyNewClass` is an example of a nested class, or a class inside of a class. Multiple nested classes are allowed in C#, and nested classes are allowed inside of nested classes, should you really want to go there.

Using the dot operator we gain access to fields and functions inside of a class. C# relies on the features of classes and class members. We'll see how to access the many functions available to us in Chapter 5.

We've been working in a nested class all this time. To show how this works in another class, we can go back to Unity 3D and create a new class next to ClassConstruction.cs called DifferentClass.cs.

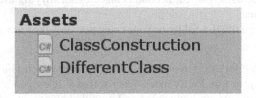

The above class is the automatically visible to `ClassConstruction` in Visual Studio. The `AccessOtherClass()` function in the `ClassConstruction` script sees the `DifferentClass` and can access it just like a nested class.

```
void AccessOtherClass()
{
    DifferentClass someOther = new DifferentClass();
    someOther.myInt = 1;
}
```

With these basic concepts we'll want to explore the different classes which Unity 3D and Microsoft have created to allow us to access the various abilities that are contained in the Unity 3D game engine. Accessing the classes and fields which Unity 3D has provided is quite simple, as we will see in Chapter 5.

4.5 Directives

Let's open the Directives.cs script in the Chapter 4 project. When you start writing code in Unity 3D, or any other programming environment, you consider the tools you must have to begin with. For instance, with the .NET (read as "dot net") framework we get things like `int`, `bool`, `float`, and `double`. These tools are given to us by adding `using System;` to our code.

We also have been taking for granted the use of `using UnityEngine;` this function gives us another massive set of tools to work with including a ton of work that allows us to use functions and events that are triggered by the Unity 3D game engine itself.

All these classes, functions, and events are stored in the `library` software. Basically, this is code that has been written to enable your code to communicate with Unity 3D. These resources provide a gigantic foundation to build your game on. Much of the difficult math and data management functions in relation to Unity 3D has been written for you.

Knowing what they are and how they are used is important. It's like knowing what tools you have in your toolbox. In Chapter 5, we'll go over their basic use and how to find out more about what they offer.

Directives provide the connection between your class and a selected library. Many hundreds of classes, written by the programmers who created Unity 3D, allow you to communicate between the player, the characters, and every other object in the game. In short, a library is software for your software. When we have Unity 3D create a new C# class the generated file has several blocks of code.

```
1    using System.Collections;
2    using System.Collections.Generic;
3    using UnityEngine;
```

In the first three lines of the class we had Unity 3D prepare for us are the directives we needed to get started. The connection between Unity 3D and your code is made, in part, by using directives. A directive makes a connection to outside or external resources called libraries.

Directives are required to appear at the beginning of a file before the class they're to be used in. This is different from how a variable can be used inside the scope of a class. Though there are some ways to bend the rules a little bit, but we'll leave that for Section 6.10 where we cover namespaces in a bit more detail.

The libraries that the directives call upon are connected to compiled code. Unity 3D is also connected to the libraries that your code uses. The connection is made by identifying the name of the library after the keyword `using` is entered.

Libraries live in paths, like a file in a folder on your computer, only they are compiled into a few tightly bundled binary files.

NOTE: The initialism *DLL* refers to *dynamically linked library*, which is a complete set of software compiled ahead of time for your use. Pretty much every software released these days include many different DLLs that allow the software to be updated and modified by only updating the DLLs they come with. Often some DLLs are located in your computer's operating system's directory, but depending on the software involved it too will bring along its own DLLs.

The first line, `using UnityEngine;`, pulls all of the resources that deal with specific Unity 3D function calls. For instance, moving an object, playing sounds, and activating particle systems are found inside of the `UnityEngine` library. The functions necessary for making bullets and magic spells work are built into `UnityEngine`.

As the resources that make up your game are imported into Unity 3D, they're made available to your code. The libraries provided by Unity 3D expose all the imported assets in such a way that they can be found like files on your computer.

The programmers at Unity 3D have taken on the bulk of these complex tasks for you so you don't have to deal with all the physics and PhD-level science of rendering 3D graphics. The keyword `using` is how we tell C# that we're going to ask for a specific library to access.

Many other programming languages do the same thing; for instance, Python uses the statement `import module` to do the same thing; JavaScript is more wordy, by requiring a path like `src = "otherScripts/externalLibrary.js"` to access external code.

C++ and C both do the same as C# with the keyword `using` to access external libraries. In the end, your code can work with pre-existing code stored in nicely packaged libraries. For Unity 3D, this is pretty much necessary.

4.5.1 Libraries

Libraries are collections of classes and data that have been bundled into a convenient package with Unity 3D. You can consider them to be like a compiled application. A library contains classes that are all accessible through the dot operator, like the classes we wrote in Chapter 3. Inside of Visual Studio you can look at some of the other libraries we can use.

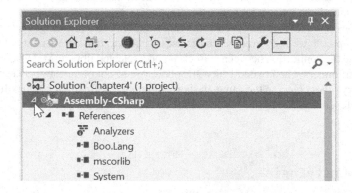

Inside of MonoDevelop, expand the References icon in the Solution Explorer. In case the Solution Explorer panel isn't open, then use the following menu to show the panel: View → Solution Explorer.

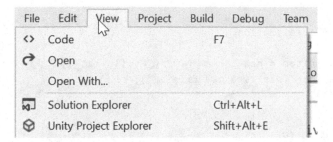

Scroll through the list to read the numerous entries listed. These are the tools written into Unity 3D at your disposal. In the Directives.cs class, entering the using UnityEngine. will prompt a pop-up. The pop-up window shows you the many different libraries available to Unity 3D.

We won't go too far into how to use these other functions. We are just now getting to know the functions we already have. Between both UnityEngine and System.Collections we've got quite a large set of tools already. Later, we'll be able to create our own libraries. Within our own libraries, we'll be able to write useful functions that can be used like anything found in UnityEngine.

In our Directives.cs class, we'll use the Start() function and look for a StreamWriter function. A StreamWriter is a class that will help us write some text to a new text file. However, the auto-complete pop-up shows "No Completions Found" as we start to enter the class we're looking for.

```
// Use this for initialization
void Start () {
    StreamWriter
}           ⊙ ▾    The name 'StreamWriter' does not exist in the current context
// Update is     Show potential fixes (Alt+Enter or Ctrl+.)
void Update () {
```

Click on the helper icon to the left will expand some options to fix the problem. Select the second option where we have Visual Studio write System.IO.StreamWriter in place of StreamWriter.

Optionally we can have Visual Studio add the using Stream.IO; at the beginning of our class definition.

```
14    public class Directives : MonoBehaviour {
15
16        // Use this for initialization
17        void Start () {
18  ⊙ ▾        StreamWriter
19   using System.IO;
20   System.IO.StreamWriter
21   Generate property 'Directives.StreamWriter'
22   Generate field 'Directives.StreamWriter'
23   Generate read-only field 'Directives.StreamWriter'
24   Generate local 'StreamWriter'
25
```
⊗ CS0103 The name 'StreamWriter' does not exist in the current context
...
using System.Collections.Generic;
using System.IO;
using UnityEngine;
...
Preview changes

Adding using SystemIO; to our class provides us with a connection to all of the contents of the System.IO libraries. StreamWriter is used to write to a text file.

```csharp
// Use this for initialization
void Start () {
    StreamWriter writer = new StreamWriter("MyFile.txt");
    writer.WriteLine("This is a new file...");
    writer.Flush();
}
```

Using the StreamWriter we create a new object called writer. When the StreamWriter is instanced we pass a parameter with a string used for the file name; in this case, "MyFile.txt" is given to the new writer object.

With the object instanced as writer, we use the object and call upon the WriteLine member function and give it some text to write into the new file. The text "This is a new file..." will appear in the MyFile.txt file that Unity 3D will write for us. After that we need to use the Flush(); call to tell the writer to finish its work.

Press the Play button with Directives_Scene open to execute the Start() function in the C# class. To find the file, right click on the Assets directory in the Project view and select Show in Explorer from the pop-up menu.

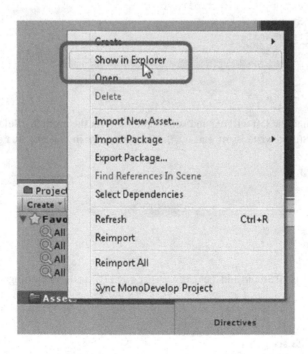

This action should bring up the directory where the new MyFile.txt has been written.

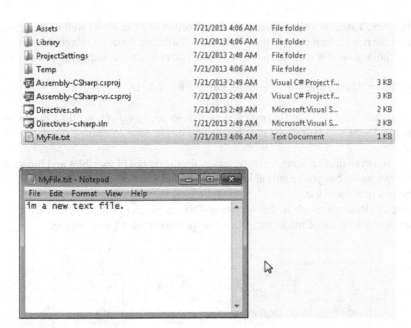

Opening the `MyFile.txt` will open the file in your usual text editor; in my case, it was Notepad. You could imagine writing various bits of information in this, or even begin to read from a text file into your game! This might make writing dialog for an RPG (role-playing game) game a bit easier. You wouldn't have to write all of the text into each object or even code in your game. Reading from a text file would make more sense.

Of course, we'll have to do more work to get the most out of reading and writing to text files, but this is just the beginning. We'll move on to more sophisticated tricks later on. This is just a glimpse into what we can do by accessing the different parts of the libraries available to us.

4.5.2 Ambiguous NameSpaces

The names of functions from libraries, should have unique names for each function. However, what happens if Unity 3D and System used the same name?

One of the many tools is a simple random number generator. The `Random.Range()`; function was written by the Unity 3D programmers and requires a minimum and a maximum number. There's also a Random provided inside of System written by Microsoft which does a similar thing.

```
using UnityEngine;
using System;
```

However, if we add `using System;` to the list of directives, as in the above code sample, we'll get an error telling is there's an ambiguous reference between `UnityEngine.Random` and `System.Random`.

```
int rand = Random.Range(0, 10);
```

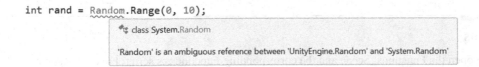

This means that there's an identically named `Random` function in `System` as well as `UnityEngine`. To resolve this error, we need to be more specific when we use `Random`. Since we might need to use other parts of the `System;` library, we'll want to keep this included; otherwise, we wouldn't have this problem at all.

```
int randUnity = UnityEngine.Random.Range(0, 10);
```

If we change `Random.Range()` to `UnityEngine.Random.Range()`, we'll fix the problem of conflicting functions. There will be many times where you might have to change the names of a specific library as well.

A Namespace is a system of creating reserved spaces for the names of variables and functions. The system doesn't always work, but you're still able to work around conflicting names by writing out the full path to a name you're want to use.

By expanding the References tab in the Assembly-CSharp project in the Solution Explorer in Visual Studio you can read a long list of namespaces that are included with a Unity Project.

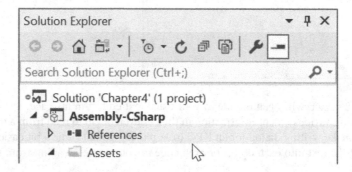

Only a few of these are ever included with a new MonoBehaviour script generated by Unity. Dozens of tools ranging from networking to file systems, diagnostics to security are included in the .NET framework alone. Unity also includes tools from Sprites path finding and terrain to vehicle physics lighting and particles.

Keeping a class specified to a single purpose means to use digression when picking what tools to use to accomplish a task. The available tools are separated into different categories to avoid including unrelated code.

4.5.3 What We've Learned

Knowing where to look for these functions is something that can be done only by having an investigative hunch. Usually, a quick search on the Internet can drum up a few clues as to what function you need to search for to get a specific task done.

Different libraries provide us with systems which help us add additional functionality to our classes. By default, we're given a rich set of tools to build into our game. It's also possible to write your own DLLs creating libraries for your game. This might allow you to add in platform-specific functions to accelerate various aspects of the game outside of the abilities of the built-in Unity 3D tools or engine.

The .NET frameworks as a whole have a number of namespaces that section off different sets of tools.

4.6 Functions

To follow along open the Functions_Scene and the corresponding Functions.cs script. Functions, sometimes called methods, contain statements which can process data. The statements can or cannot process data. Methods can be accessed by other statements. This action is referred to as *calling a function* or *making a function call*. In this chapter we touch on the `Start()`, but we've yet to figure out why the `Start()` functions work.

So far we've created a class and we gave the class some places to store data. We've even used some of those variables in Unity 3D. Then we exposed some variables to the editor to update when manipulated in the Inspector panel. We also wrote a simple function to print a number, but we really didn't get into how that worked or why the syntax looked the way it did.

To add useful behavior to our game, we'll need to add in logic. The logic needs to process data for anything in the game to happen. To coordinate this merging of data and logic, we'll need to write some functions.

4.6.1 What Are Functions?

In Chapter 3, we talked about the process of shampooing. A second look at the idea of a function is to comprehend the words *wash*, *rinse*, and *repeat* in more depth. If you've never heard of the word *wash* before then you're probably dirty, or a computer. Computers need every word defined for them before they understand it.

```
void Wash()
{
}
void Rinse()
{
}
void Repeat()
{
}
```

On a superficial level, we've used the above code to define the three words used to shampoo hair. However, none of the definitions contains any actions. They define the words or identifiers, but when they're used nothing will happen. However, the computer will be able to Wash(); Rinse(); Repeat(); without any problems now.

In the previous chapter we wrote in DataFields:

```
public void PrintMyNumber()
{
    Debug.Log(myNumber);
}
```

PrintMyNumber() which is a simple function. Now that we can write some functions for use in Unity 3D let's get to some real coding.

NOTE: Functions may look different in different programming languages, but the way they work is mostly the same. The usual pattern is taking in data and using logic to manipulate that data. Functions may also be referred to by other names, for example, methods.

The major differences come from the different ways the languages use syntax. Syntax is basically the use of spaces or tabs, operators, or keywords. In the end, all you're doing is telling the compiler how to convert your instructions into computer-interpreted commands.

Variables and functions make up the bulk of programming. Any bit of data you want to remember is stored in a variable. Variables are manipulated by your functions. In general, when you group variables and functions together in one place, you call that a class.

In Chapter 3, we discussed a bit about writing a class starting with a declaration and the opening and closing curly braces that make up the body. Functions are written in a similar fashion.

We start with the declaration `void MyFunction;` then we add in both parentheses `()` and the curly braces `{}`, indicating to ourselves that we may or may not fill this in later. The first pair of parentheses `()`, doesn't necessarily always require anything to be added. However, the curly braces `{}`, or the body of the function, do need code added for the function to have any purpose.

When writing a new function, it's good practice to fill in the entirety of the function's layout before continuing to another task. This puts the compiler at ease; leaving a function in the form `void MyFunction` and then moving on to another function leaves the compiler confused as to what you're planning on doing.

The integrated development environment, in this case Visual Studio, is constantly reading and interpreting what you are writing, somewhat like a spell checker in a word processor. When it comes across a statement that has no conclusive form, like a variable, function, or class definition, its interpretation of the code you're writing will raise a warning or an error. Visual Studio might seem a bit fussy, but it's doing its best to help.

4.6.2 Unity 3D Entry Points

The Unity 3D developers provided us with MonoBehaviour which is a class that grants our C# classes to have direct access to the inner workings of the Unity 3D game scene. The `MonoBehaviour` class is a collection of every function and data type available to Unity 3D. We'll learn how to use these parts of Unity 3D in the following tutorials.

NOTE: It's also important to know that when learning the specifics of Unity 3D, you should be aware that these Unity 3D-specific lessons can be applied to other development environments. When you use C# with Windows or OSX, you'll be able to write applications for other operating systems for software other than Unity 3D.

Think of `MonoBehaviour` as a set of tools for talking to Unity 3D. Other systems have different sets of tools for making apps for other purposes. Learning how to use the other systems should be much easier after reading this book and learning how to talk to Unity 3D.

When dealing with most other C# applications, you'll need to use `Main()` as the starting point for your C# application. This is like many other development environments using C++ and C.

When Unity 3D creates a class it automatically added in `void Start()` and `void Update()` to the body of the class. These two functions are called *entry points*. Basically, the base `MonoBehaviour` class has several functions, that include `Start()` and `Update()`, which are called based on events that happen when your game is running.

There are other functions that are also automatically called when `MonoBehaviour` is used: `Awake()`, `OnEnable()`, `Start()`, `OnApplicationPause()`, `Update()`, `FixedUpdate()`, and `LateUpdate()`; these functions are commonly called when the object is created and your game is running. When the object is destroyed, `OnDestroy()` is called. There are also various rendering functions that can be called, but we don't need to go over them here.

To better understand what happens during each frame of the game it's best to imagine the game operating a bit like a movie. At the very beginning of the game, when the player presses Start, every actor in the scene with a script based on `MonoBehaviour` has its `Start()` function called.

Calling a function basically executes the lines of code that live inside of the curly braces that follow the function's declaration. Before the end of the first frame, the `Update()` functions of each script in the scene are called in no particular order.

At the beginning of the next frame, if there are no new scripts in the scene, the `Start()` functions are not called. Only `Update()` functions are called from that point on. Only if new scripts are introduced to the scene are `Start()` functions called on scripts new to the scene. If there is no code in the `Start()` function or if there is no `Start()` function in the script, then nothing happens.

To benefit from anything happening on each frame you'll need to put code into the `Update()` function. When a class is first introduced into the game world you need to add code into the `Start()` function. There are several other entry points that we'll be working with. And you'll be able to make use of them all as you see fit. It's important to know that without these entry points your class will be functioning on its own.

Functions all have specific names or identifiers. So far we've seen `Start()` and `Update()`, but there are many more functions which we'll make use of throughout this book. The first function we'll make use of the `Log();`, which is a function found inside of the `Debug` class. We'll return in a moment to how this function is used, but first we'll demonstrate how it's used.

If `Debug` is a class, this means that `Log()` is a member of `Debug`. The dot operator allows us to access the `Log()` function found in the `Debug` class.

```
Debug.Log("Start");
```

Inside of the `Start()` function add in `Debug.Log("Start");`, as seen in the example above. When the game is started, the class will execute the code found inside of the `Start()` function. This means that the `Debug.Log("Start");` statement is executed.

Continuing in the Functions_Scene, click on the Play button and then click on the Console panel to bring it to the top. You should see the following lines of text in the Console panel.

The first line says `Start`, followed by `UnityEngine.Debug:Log(Object)`, which is the expected result. If not, then double check a few different things. First check that the line of code you wrote ends with a semicolon (`;`) and is not left empty. Next, make sure that you're using quotes around the word: `"Start."`

Then, check that your spelling and case are correct: `Debug` and `Log`. Also make sure you didn't forget the dot operator (.) between `Debug` and `Log`. The punctuation matters a great deal. Missing any one of these changes the outcome of the code. Syntax is important for programming. Missing one detail breaks everything.

There are a few important things happening here, though many details left out for now. By the end of this chapter everything should be clear.

4.6.3 Writing a Function

A function consists of a declaration and a body. Some programmers like to call these *methods,* but semantics aside, a function is basically a container for a collection of statements. Let's continue with the Functions.cs script in the Chapter 4 Assets directory.

```
/*  ┌─────────────────────┐  ┌──────────────┐  */
/*  │function declaration │  │parameters    │  */
/*  └─────────────────────┘  └──────────────┘  */
/*                                             */
/*                                             */
void MyFunction()
{
    // Function Body
}
```

Here is a basic function called `MyFunction`. We can add in additional keywords to modify the function's visibility. One common modifier we'll be seeing soon is `public`. We'll get further into the `public` keyword in Section 4.13 on accessibility.

```
public void MyPublicFunction()
{
}
```

The `public` keyword needs to appear before the return type of the function. In this case, it's `void`, which means that the function doesn't return anything. Return types are something else that we'll get into in Section 6.3.3, but functions can act as a value in a few different ways. For reference, a function that returns an `int` would look like this. A `return` statement of some kind must always be present in a function that has a return type.

```
public int MyIntFunction()
{
    return 1;
}
```

The `public` modifier isn't always necessary, unless you need to make this function available to other classes. If this point doesn't make sense, it will soon. The last part of the function that is always required is the parameter list. It's valid to leave it empty, but to get a feeling for what an arg, or argument in the parameter list, looks like, move on to the next example.

```
public void MyArgFunction(int i)
{
}
```

For the moment, we'll hold off on using the parameter list, but it's important to know what you're looking at later so it doesn't come as a surprise. Parameter lists are used to pass information from outside of the function to the inside of the function. This is how classes can pass information between one another.

We've been passing an argument for a while now using the `Debug` class. The Log member function of the Debug class takes a single argument. In `Debug.Log("start");` the `"start"` is an argument we've been passing to the `Log` function. The `Debug` class is in the `UnityEngine` library and made available because of the `using UnityEngine;` statement.

We'll see how all these different parts of a function work as we get to them. Functions are versatile but require to be set up. Luckily, code is easy to build up one line at a time. It's good to know that very few people are capable of writing more than a few lines of code at a time before testing them.

To use a function, you simply enter the identifier followed by its argument list.

```
void SimpleFunction()
{
    Debug.Log("Simple function called.");
}

// Update is called once per frame
void Update ()
{
    SimpleFunction();
}
```

The placement of `SimpleFunction()` in the class has no effect on how it's called. For the sake of argument we can use `SimpleFunction()` anywhere in the class as long as it's been declared at the class scope.

For a function to work, we need to give it some instructions. If we declare an `int` a and set it to 0, we'll have some data to start with. In a function called `SetAtoThree()`, we set a to 3. If we call `CheckOnA()` a in the `Start()` function we'll get 0, the value which a was set to in the beginning. Then the function `SetAtoThree()` is called, which sets a to 3, so when a is logged again its new output is 3.

4.6.4 More on White Space and Tabs

Tabs are used to delineate the contents of a function. So far, we've been seeing each function written with its contents tabbed to the right with a single tab.

```
120      void MoreTabs()
121      {
122          //tabbed over once!
123          int i = 0;
124          //while statement tabbed over as well
125          while (i < 10)
126          {
127              //tabbed over even more
128              Debug.Log(i);
129              i++;
130          }
131      }
```

The contents of the function are tabbed over once. The contents of the `while` statement inside of the function are tabbed over twice, as indicated by more spaces. This presentation helps to clarify that the contents of the `while` statement are executed differently from the rest of the function.

To help understand how the previous code fragment is read by the computer, we will step through the code one line at a time. This emulates how the function is run when it's called upon. Of course, a computer does this very quickly, but it's necessary for us to understand what the computer is doing many millions, if not billions, of times faster than we can comprehend.

NOTE: For a moment imagine your central processing unit (CPU) was made of gears spinning more than 2 billion times per second. The 2.4 GHz means 2,400,000,000 cps. A cycle is an update of every transistor in the silicon on the chip: over 2 billion pulses of electrons running through the silicon, every second turning on and off various transistors based on your instructions. Of course, not all the updates are dedicated to your game; many of the cycles are taken up by the operating system running Unity 3D, so performance isn't always what it should be.

The first line void `MoreTabs()` is identified by the computer and is used to locate the code to execute. Once the function is started the contents of the code begin at the first statement. In this case we reach `//tabbed over once!`, which is a comment and ignored.

Next we reach `int i = 0;`, which is a declaration and assignment of a variable that is identified as i, an identifier commonly used for integers. This declaration tells the computer to create a small place in memory for an integer value and it's told that we're going to use i to locate that data.

Following the variable declaration, we get to another comment that is also ignored by the computer. The `while (i < 10)` line of code follows the comment and this opens another space in memory for some operations. This also creates a connection to the i variable to check if the while statement will execute. If i is a value less than 10 then the statements in the following {curly braces} will be executed; otherwise, the contents of the while statement are ignored.

Another important character the computer finds is the opening curly brace ({) that tells it to recognize a new context for execution. The computer will read and execute each line in the while statement till it finds a closing curly brace (}). In this new context we'll return to the first curly brace until the while statement's condition is false.

Because i is less than 10, the while statement's condition is true, so we will proceed to the first line of the while statement. In this case, it's a comment that is ignored. This is followed by a Debug.Log() function, which also has a connection to the i variable. Therefore, this line prints to the console the value which is being stored at i. Once the value has been printed to the console the computer moves to the next line down.

The i++; statement tells the computer to look at the contents of i, add 1 to that value, and assign that new value back to i. This means that the new value for i is 1 since we started at 0. Once the computer reaches the closing curly brace, we jump back to the top of the while statement.

The contents of the curly braces are repeated until the value for i reaches 10; once the iteration returns 11, the condition of the while statement changes from *true* to *false*. Because 11 is not less than 10, the statements found between the curly braces will not be read. Therefore, the code in the while statement will be skipped. Once the computer reaches the closing curly brace of MoreTabs(), the computer stops running the function.

Computers do exactly what they're told and nothing more. The compiler runs using very explicit rules which it adheres to adamantly. Because of this, any strange behavior, which you might attribute to a bug, should point to how you've written your code. In many cases, small syntactical errors lead to errors which the computer will not be able to interpret.

It's greatly up to you to ensure that all of your code adheres to a format the computer can understand. When you write in English, a great deal of the sentiment and thought you put into words can be interpreted by each reader differently. For a computer there's only one way to interpret your code, so either it works or it doesn't.

4.6.5 What We've Learned

Function declaration is a bit like class declaration. Functions are the meat of where logic is done to handle variables. How variables make their way into and out of a function is covered in Section 6.18. There are many different ways to handle this, but we'll have to handle them one at a time.

On your own experiment with functions like the following:

```
void ATimesA()
{
    a = a * a;
}
```

You might want to set int a to a value other than 0 or 1 to get anything interesting out of this. Later, we'll be able to see how logic and loops can be used to make functions more powerful.

4.7 Order of Operation: What Is Calculated and When

Variables and functions work together to make your class operate as a part of your game. As an example, we're going to move an object through space using some simple math. To use numbers correctly, we need to be very specific. Remember, computers do exactly what they're told and nothing more.

Code is executed only when the function the code lives in is called. If the function is never called then nothing in the function will run. Once a function is called, the operation starts with evaluating the code at the top and works its way down to the end of the function one line at a time.

```
int a = 1;
Debug.Log(a); // 1
a = a + 3;
Debug.Log(a); // 4
a = a * 7;
Debug.Log(a); // 28
```

The first order which we've been working with so far is by line number. When code is evaluated each line is processed starting at the top; then it works its way down. In the following example, we start off with an integer variable and perform simple math operations and print the result.

As you might expect the first line prints 1, followed by 4, and then by 28. This is a rather long-handed method to get to a final result. However, things get a bit strange if we try to shorten this to a single line, as math operators work in a different order than we just used them.

```
int b = 1 + 3 * 7;
Debug.Log(b); // 22
```

After shortening the code to a single line like in this example, we get a different result, 22, which means 3 and 7 were multiplied before the 1 was added. Math operators have a priority when being evaluated, which follows the order of precedence. The multiply and divide operators have a higher precedence than add and subtract.

When evaluating int a, C# looked at the math operators first, and then did the math in the following order. Because the * is more important than the +; 3 * 7 was computed, turning the line into 1 + 21; then, the remaining numbers around + were evaluated, resulting a being assigned to 22, and then ultimately printing that to the Console output.

We'll observe the other behaviors and learn to control how math is evaluated. This section might not be so exciting, but it's worth the while to have this section as a reference. When your calculations begin to have unexpected results, it's usually because of order of operation coming into play and evaluating numbers differently from what you expected.

4.7.1 Evaluating Numbers

Calculation of variables is called *evaluation*. As we had mentioned before, each object added to the scene in Unity 3D's Editor has several components automatically added when it's first created. To make use of these components, you simply use their name in your code. The first component we'll be using is transform attribute. Transform contains the position rotation and scale of the object. You can see how these are changed when you select the object in the scene and move it around.

You can also enter numbers using the Inspector panel, or even click on the variable name and drag left and right as a slider to modify the data in the field. Moving objects around with code works in a similar manner as entering values in the Inspector panel. The position of the object is stored as three float values called a `Vector3`.

Operators in C# are the tools that do all of the work in your code. The first set of operators we'll discuss is arithmetic operators.

4.7.1.1 Math

+ −/* and %

The + and − do pretty much what you might expect them to: 1 + 3 = 4 and 1 − 3 = −2; this doesn't come as a surprise. Divide uses the /, putting the first number over the second number. However, the number *type* is important to sort out before we get too much further.

```
Debug.Log(10 / 3);
Debug.Log(10f / 3f);
Debug.Log(10.0 / 3.0);
```

The first line above is a 10/3, which might not return what you would expect. Writing a number without any decimal tells the compiler you're using integers, which will give you an integer result. Therefore, the result is simply 3, with the remaining one-third cut off since it's rounded down. The second line has an f after the number, indicating we want a float value. The third line without the f indicates a double value. This has twice the number of digits as a float.

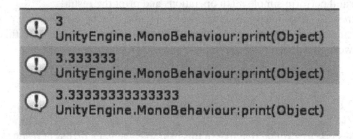

The result here shows the different number of trailing 3s after the decimal. We mentioned in Section 4.4.1.2 that there are different types of numbers. Here is an example of what that really means. An integer is a whole number without any decimal values. A float is a decimal type with only 7 digits in the number; a double is quite a lot bigger, having a total of 15 digits in the number.

```
28         // Use this for initialization
29  ⊟      void Start ()
30         {
31             Debug.Log (10 / 3);
32             Debug.Log (10f / 3f);
33             Debug.Log (10.0 / 3.0);
34             Debug.Log (10000000.0f / 3.0f);
35             Debug.Log (1000000000000000.0 / 3.0);
36  ─      }
```

Doing this experiment again with larger numbers exposes how our numbers have some limitations.

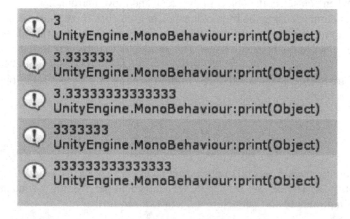

Like the integer, the large doubles and floats only have so many places where the decimal can appear. The number for the double is huge to begin with, but we should have more 3s after the number than are shown with a decimal. Where did they go? Keep in mind there *should* be an indefinite number of trailing 3s, but computers aren't good with indefinite numbers.

NOTE: Computers without special software can't deal with numbers with an unlimited number of digits. To show bigger numbers, computers use scientific notation like E+15 to indicate where significant numbers begin from the decimal point. Games, in particular, rarely ever need to deal with such large numbers. And to keep processes running fast, numbers are limited.

Software applications designed to deal with particularly huge numbers tend to work more slowly as they need to run with the same limitations, but instead perform operations on the first part of a number and then another operation on the second half of a number. This process can be repeated as many times as necessary if the number is even bigger. Scientific computing often does this and they have special number types to compensate. There are some additional number types, as well as other data types that aren't numbers. We'll leave the other data types for later (Section 5.3.4). The operators we're dealing with here are mainly for numbers.

Next up is the multiply operator (*). All the limitations that apply to the divide operator apply to the multiply operator as well. One important thing to consider here is that multiplication is technically faster than division. Therefore, in cases where you want to do 1000/4, the computer is going to be faster if you use 1000 * 0.25 instead.

This difference is a result of how the computer's hardware was designed. To be honest, modern CPUs are so much faster than they used to be, so using a / versus a * will usually make no noticeable difference. Old school programmers will beg to differ, but today we're not going to need to worry about this technicality, though I feel every classically trained programmer wants to scratch out my eyes right now.

Last up is the %, which in programming is called modulo, not percent as you might have guessed. This operator is used in what is sometimes called clock math. An analog clock has 12 hours around it. Therefore, a clock's hours can be considered %12, or modulo twelve, as a programmer might say.

To use this operator, consider what happens when you count 13 hours on a 12-hour clock and want to know where the hour hand will be on the 13th hour. This can be calculated by using the following term: 13%12; this operation produces the value 1 when calculated. Modulo is far easier to observe in operation than it is to describe.

The output from the code below here repeats from 0 to 11 repeatedly. Clocks don't start at 0, but computers do. Therefore, even though i is not being reset and continues to increase in value. On each update i is not being reset to 0, instead it continues to increment until you stop the game. A programmer would say "int i mod twelve" to describe i%12 shown here.

```
// Update is called once per frame
int mod = 1;
void Update ()
{
    int mod12 = mod % 12;
    Debug.Log(mod + " mod 12 = " + mod12);
    mod++;
}
```

Programmers are particular about their vocabulary and syntax, so it's best to understand how to think and talk like one. Programmers will usually assume you already know something like this, but it is worthwhile elaborating on the topic. Compilers, however, don't all think in the same way. Therefore, if you're curious and feel like learning other programming languages in the future, you might find that other languages will behave differently.

4.7.1.2 Operator Evaluation

As we saw before with 1 + 3 * 7 you may end up with different results, depending on the order in which you evaluated your numbers. To prevent any human misinterpretation of a calculation you can reduce the preceding numbers to 4 * 7 or 1 + 21. To make our intent clear we can use parentheses.

To gain control, we use the open and close parentheses to change the order of evaluation. For example, we can do this: 1 – 2 – (3 + 4), which turns into 1 – 2 – 7; a whole different result: –1 – 7 yields –8. A simple change in the order of operation can result in a completely different number when evaluated. This sort of thing becomes more important once we start shooting at zombies and dealing out damage. Some monsters might have thicker skin, and you'll want to reduce the damage done by a specific amount based on where he was shot.

4.7.1.2.1 A Basic Example

As we saw before, 1 + 3 * 7 will result in 22. We could use the long-winded version and start with a, then add 1 to it, then add 3 to that, and then multiply that by 7 to get 24. There's an easier way.

```
int c = (1 + 3) * 7;
Debug.Log(c);
```

By surrounding a pair of numbers with parentheses, we can tell the compiler to evaluate the pair within the parentheses before the multiplication. This results in 28, like the long-handed version of the same math. To elaborate we can add in another step to our math to see more interesting results.

```
int d = 1 + 3 * 7 + 9;
Debug.Log(d);
```

The code above results in 31 printed to the Console panel. We can change the result to 49 by surrounding the 7 + 9 with parentheses, like in the following.

```
int e = 1 + 3 * (7 + 9);
Debug.Log(e);
```

The complier computes the 7 + 9 before the rest of the math is computed. Parentheses take precedence over multiplication, regardless of where they appear. It doesn't matter where the parentheses appear, either at the beginning or at the end of the numbers: The parentheses are computed first.

Adding another set of parentheses can change the order of computation as well. Parentheses within parentheses tell the computer to start with the innermost pair before moving on. For instance (11 * ((9 * 3) * 2)) starts with 9 * 3; this turns into (11 * ((27) * 2), which then yields 27 * 2, which turns into (11 * (54)); 11 * 54 turns into 594. This can be switched round by shifting the placements of the parentheses to a different number. Try it out!

```
int f = (11 * ((9 * 3) * 2));
Debug.Log(f);
```

At this point, you will need to be very careful about the placement of the parentheses. For each opening parenthesis, there needs to be a corresponding closing parenthesis. If you're missing one, then Unity 3D will let you know. It's important to have a sense of what sort of math to use and when to use it.

In this case, where the parentheses encapsulate the entire expression their presence is redundant. Taking out the first and last parentheses will have no effect on the final result. This is true for most operations, but for clarity it's useful to know that they are indeed optional. To be clear about this, we can add any number of extra parentheses to the operation and there will be no other effect to the result, though it may look a bit strange.

```
int g = ((((11 * ((9 * 3) * 2)))));
Debug.Log(g);
```

To make things clearer, we can rearrange this expression to be a lot more readable by setting up different variables. For each set of operations, we can create a new variable. The operations begin with the first variable; then, after the value is stored, the value is carried to the next time it's used. Just remember, a variable cannot be used until it's been created.

```
int h = 9 * 3;
int i = h * 2;
int j = i * 11;
Debug.Log(j);
```

In this example, we've created a different variable for each part of the math operation. First, we created a 9 * 3 variable assigned to h. After that we multiplied h by 2 and assigned that to i. Finally, we multiplied i by 11 and assigned that result to j. To view the result, we printed out j to get 594, the same result as the long, fairly obscure operation we started with. This example shows a simple use of variables to make your code more readable.

This seems like we're back to where we started with, at the beginning of this section. To be honest, both methods are perfectly valid. The decision to choose one system over another is completely dependent on which you find easier to understand.

What we should take away from this is the order in which the lines are read. The operations start at the top and work their way line by line to the bottom of the function. As variables are assigned new values, they are kept until they are reassigned.

It's important to note that by creating more than one variable, you're asking the computer to use more space in your computer's memory. At this point we're talking about very small amounts of memory. A classically trained programmer might want to fix this code upon reading it, and then convert it to a single line. To be honest, it does take up more space and not only visually.

When starting a new set of operations, it's sometimes helpful to use a more drawn-out set of instructions, using more variables. When you're more comfortable that your code is doing what you expect it to, you can take the time to reduce the number of lines required and do a bit of optimization. There's nothing wrong with making things work first and cleaning them up later.

4.7.2 What We've Learned

Therefore, you've been introduced to variables and you've learned about functions, two big components of programming needed to make a game. Directives will allow your code to talk with Unity 3D and put meaning behind your variables and functions.

We're using C# and .NET, which is an object-oriented programming environment. We just learned objects are all the little bits of information that make up your different C# classes. When we're done with writing some code, Unity 3D will automatically interpret your code for your game.

At this point, we've got a pretty strong grasp of the basics of what code looks like and the different parts of how code is written. We've yet to make use of any logic in our functions, but we should be able to read code and know what is and isn't in a function.

It would be a good idea, by way of review, to make a few other classes and get used to the process of starting new projects, creating classes, and adding them to objects in a Unity 3D Scene. Once you're comfortable with creating and using new classes in Unity 3D you'll be ready to move on.

4.8 Scope: A First Look

Encapsulation is the term given to where data can be accessed from. The amount of accessibility is called scope. The visibility of a variable to your logic changes depending on where it appears.

Encapsulation can hide, or change the accessibility of data between statements, functions, and classes. Another way to think about it is keeping data on a need-to-know basis. This invisibility is intended for several reasons. One reason is to reduce the chances of reusing variable names.

```
// Use this for initialization
void Start ()
{
    for (int i = 0; i < 10; i++)
    {
        Debug.Log(i);
    }
}
```

4.8.1 Class Scope

To get a better look at how scope and encapsulation work together, Open the Scope_Scene in the Chapter 4 Unity Project. Attached to the Scope GameObject is the Scope script. When the scene is run, the code attached to the Scope GameObject will run as normal.

```
// Use this for initialization
void Start ()
{
    for (int i = 0; i < 10; i++)
    {
        Debug.Log(i);
    }
}
```

The MyInt variable exists at the class scope level. MyInt can be used in any function that lives in the class scope. The example code you're looking at will produce the following Console output:

Both Start() and Update() live in the class scope so both can see the MyInt variable. Therefore, the following code will send a 1 to the console. Both Start() and the Update() functions will keep sending 1s to the Console window.

```
int myInt = 1;

void Start ()
{
    Debug.Log(myInt);
}

void Update ()
{
    Debug.Log(myInt);
}
```

Placement of a variable at the class scope has little effect on where it's used. The code above can be rearranged easily. The code below will behave the same as the code above.

```
void Start ()
{
    Debug.Log(myInt);
}

void Update ()
{
    Debug.Log(myInt);
}

int myInt = 1;
```

The functions and variables act in the same way, irrespective of where they appear in the class. However, class scope is easy to override with other variables of the same name. This is called *variable collision*, the effects of which you should be aware of, as discussed in Section 7.4.

```
int myInt = 2;|
Debug.Log(myInt);
```

[✋] (local variable) int myInt

If we declare a variable of the same name in more than one place then it will be overridden by the newest version of our variable. If you were to run this script in your scene, you'd have the Console printout 2 because of the line that preceded the print function call.

There are problems with how variables can collide with one another. And the best way to avoid this problem would be to come up with good names for your variables. What happens if we try to use both versions of myInt?

```
Debug.Log(myInt);
int myInt = 2; // stomps on class scoped myInt
Debug.Log(myInt);
```

The scope in which the new myInt declaration appears wipes out the existence of myInt defined at the class scope. The result of such a declaration will be an error: "A local variable myInt cannot be used before it is declared." You may have expected the first print function to print out the class scope version of myInt, but this isn't the case.

Variables named at the class scope still exist even if you reuse the name with new variables named in a function. The word "this" is a keyword. If "this" preceeds a variable, C# understands to use the variable named in the class scope and not the variable named in the function scope.

```
Debug.Log(this.myInt);
int myInt = 2; // stomps on class scoped myInt
Debug.Log(myInt);
```

By creating an int myInt inside of the Start() function in your class you have effectively hidden the class scoped myInt from the function. Although it can be accessed as this.myInt, the function scoped version of myInt in the function takes precedent.

This example should also highlight that a variable can be used only after it's been initialized. This is a situation best avoided, so it's good to remember what variable names you've used so you don't use them again.

To elaborate, a function starts from the first curly brace ({) and computes one line at a time, working its way from the top, moving toward the bottom until it hits the closing curly brace (}). An error occurs if a variable is used in a statement before the variable is declared.

```
int myInt = 1;
float myInt = 1; //nope.
```

Something that might be obvious but should be mentioned is the fact that you can't reuse a variable name. Even if the second variable is a different type, we'll get the following error in MonoDevelop explaining our error.

Another effect of creating a variable inside of a function is the fact that another function can't see what's going on. In the following code we declare a StartInt in the Start() function. After that we try to use it again in the Update() function, which results in an error.

```
void Start ()
{
    int declaredInStart = 1;
    Debug.Log(declaredInStart);
}


void Update ()
{
    Debug.Log(declaredInStart);
}
```

C# is telling us that we can't use a variable before it's declared. Of course, we did declare it once, but that was in a different function. The Update() function can't see inside of the Start() function to find the declatedInStart variable declared in the Start() function.

You'll have to keep this in mind once you start writing your own functions. There are two common ways to work with declaring variables. The first is to place all your variables at the top of the function.

This way you ensure that everything you may need to use is already declared before you need them. The second method is to declare the variable just before it's needed.

```
int firstInt = 100;
int secondInt = 200;
Debug.Log(firstInt);
Debug.Log(secondInt);
```

In this case, we're being very clear inside of this function about what variables we may use. For short functions this can sometimes be a lot easier to deal with. You can easily sort your variables and change their values in one place. It's also easier to check if you're accidentally reusing a variable's name.

```
int thirdInt = 300;
Debug.Log(thirdInt);
int fourthInt = 400;
Debug.Log(fourthInt);
```

In this second case, we're using the variable only after it's created. When writing long functions you may find the second method a bit more clear as you can group your variables together near the logic and functions that will be using them.

This is a small example of code style. When reading someone else's code, you'll have to figure out how they think. In some cases, it's best to try to match the style of existing code. However, when you're writing everything on your own, it's best to keep to your own style and decide how you want to arrange your code.

If we declare a variable at the class scope, all functions inside of the class can see, and access, that variable. Once inside of a function, any new variables that are declared are visible only to that function. Some statements can declare variables as well, and those variables are visible only inside of the statement they are declared. Once we get to know about more statements, we'll see how they work, but we'll need to keep scope in mind when we get there.

4.8.2 Function Scope

Variables often live an ephemeral life. Some variables exist only over a few lines of code. Variables may come into existence only for the moment a function starts and then disappear when the function is done. Variables in the class scope exist for as long as the class exists. The life of the variable depends on where it's created.

In a previous exercise, we focused on declaring variables and showing them in the Unity 3D's Inspector panel. Then we observed when variables need to be declared to be used without any errors. The placement and `public` keywords were necessary to expose the variables to the Unity 3D editor.

The `public` keyword can be used only at the class scope. This is called class scope as the variable is visible to all of the functions found within the class. Making the variable `public` means that any other class that can see this class can then also have access to the variable as well. We'll go into more detail on what this means and how it's used in a bit.

```
void SomeFunction()
{
    public int fifthInt;
}
```

Adding the `public int` within the a function will produce an error. You're not allowed to elevate a variable to the class scope from inside of a function. Visual Studio will not give you the most informative error message, but Unity will have a different message for you. Unexpected symbol "public"; the reason is that variables within a function cannot be made accessible outside of the function.

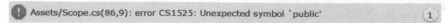

Assets/Scope.cs(86,9): error CS1525: Unexpected symbol `public'　　　　　　①

There are systems in C# to make data within a function accessible, but using the keyword public is not it. We'll look into how that's done in Section 6.1. A variable declared inside of a function exists only as the function is used. The functions declared in the class are also a part of the class scope, and at the same level as the variables declared at the class scope level. If a function in a class is preceded by the public keyword, it's accessible by name, just like a variable. Without the public keyword the function will remain hidden. We'll make use of public functions in Section 6.3.2, but it's important to know that a function can be made publicly available, like variables.

Referring to the Scope script created for this chapter, we're going to make use of the functions given to us by the programmers at Unity 3D. The location of a variable in code changes where it can be seen from and how it can be used.

As noted, limiting accessibility of any variable is called encapsulation. The curly braces, {}, and parentheses, (), have a specific context. This context can keep their contents hidden from other sections of code. This means that Start() can have one value for myInt, and if you a different myInt in Update(), it will not be affected by the myInt in Start().

If we look at the above figure we can visualize how scope is divided. The outer box represents who can see ClassInt. Within the Start() function we have a StartInt that only exists within the Start() function. The same is repeated for the UpdateInt, found only in the Update() function. This means that Start() can use both ClassInt and StartInt but not UpdateInt. Likewise, Update() can see ClassInt and UpdateInt but not StartInt.

In the diagram below the boxes represent different levels of scope.

```
class Scope
{
    int ClassInt;
    void Start()
    {
        int myInt;          ↓
        while(myInt < ClassInt)
        {
            Debug.Log(myInt);
            myInt++;
        }
    }
    void Update()
    {
        int myInt;
    }
}
```

Within the `Start()` function is a while loop. The `while()` loop can use both `ClassInt` and `myInt`. The following `Update()` function can see `ClassInt` but not `myInt`, which exists in the `Start()` function. The variable `ClassInt` was declared in the class scope, whereas the `myInt` variable was only declared inside of the `Start()` function's scope and isn't accessible outside of the `Start()` function.

4.8.3 Blank Scope

Blank Scope is obscure and not often used, but worth mentioning. Curly braces are used to encapsulate code, we've observed plenty of how that works with classes and functions. However, a pair of curly braces can encapsulate code without a specific reason.

```
void BlankScope()
{
    int a = 0;
    {
        int b;
        Debug.Log(a);
    }
    Debug.Log(b);
}
```

The name 'b' does not exist in the current context

Show potential fixes (Alt+Enter or Ctrl+.)

In the code above, we have a function named `BlankScope` but there's also a pair of curly braces where `int b;` has been declared. This is called a *blank scope*. The `Debug.Log(b);` cannot see `int b` outside of the blank scope. This does help in cases where working on a particularly tricky code might require some isolation.

```
{
    int b = 0;
    Debug.Log(b);
}
{
    int b = 1;
    Debug.Log(b);
}
```

With blank scope you can declare variables with identifiers that were already used elsewhere in the code. If you were testing out different algorithms you might want to use blank scope to isolate different ideas.

If you're using blank scope you're also able to fold code bracketed by the curly braces.

```
{
    Debug.Log("blank scope...");
}// put a label of what the code is doing here.
```

One clever trick is to put a comment at the bottom of the curly braces.

```
⊞     ...// put a label of what the code is doing here.
```

With the comment at the bottom, when your code is folded it will have a title so you can identify what the code does. Organizing your code is something that comes after quite a lot of practice. Eventually you'll end up coming up with schemes of your own to help keep your code organized. No suggestions on *how* to organize code have been made. Tools and systems have been introduced, but no style has been recommended. I'll leave the specific style up to you to make your own decisions on.

4.8.4 What We've Learned

Encapsulation describes a system by which a variable's scope is defined. Depending on where a variable is declared, the scope of the variable changes. Encapsulation prevents variables from overlapping when they're used. Encapsulation, therefore, allows one function to operate independently from another function without our needing to worry about a variable's name being reused.

We'll cover more situations where scope becomes a useful tool to help classes message one another. Encapsulation and scope define a major principle of object oriented programming, and understanding this concept is important to learning how to write C#.

4.9 This

What happens when a class needs to refer to objects in itself? In most cases, a class can use its own properties and fields and not get confused what variable is being referred to. For instance, we can take a look at a basic class that has the following.

```
int someInt = 0;
void AssignInt(int i)
{
    someInt = i;
}
```

Here, we have someInt defined at the class scope. We've have a function that assigns the someInt to i. There are no problems with this setup. On the other hand, should the AssignInt be modified to look like the following:

4.9.1 A Basic Example

In the KeywordThis_Scene open the KeywordThis script found on the KeywordThis object. Looking at the AssignInt function, there's no confusion with the assignment of someInt. The situation changes when the parameter name in AssignInt changes to someInt.

```
void AssignSomeInt(int someInt)
{
    someInt = someInt;
}
```

The AssignSomeInt(int someInt) function has no errors, and the project builds. The expectation is that someInt will be assigned the value that was coming into the function through the parameter. However, we get a different result.

```
private void Start()
{
    Debug.Log(someInt); // 0
    AssignSomeInt(3);
    Debug.Log(someInt); // still 0?
}
```

If we use this to assign someInt in the Start() function we get the Log output of 0 both before and after using the function. Hover over the assignment in the AssignSomeInt function and you'll observe the message "Assignment made to same variable; did you mean to assign something else?" To solve this problem, we'll look at the simple solution.

```
void AssignThisSomeInt(int someInt)
{
    this.someInt = someInt;
}
```

This assigns the class scoped someInt the value of the incoming parameter someInt. This is because in the function AssignThisSomeInt, where we assign the parameter someInt variable this. someInt. Without the keyword this, the local scope of the function overrides the class scope use of someInt.

4.9.2 When This Is Necessary

With the addition of the keyword this to the function above, we can specify which version of the someInt variable we're talking about. It's easy to avoid the requirement of the this keyword. Simply use unique parameter names from the class's variables and you won't need to use the this keyword.

There is no unexpected behavior if we superfluously use the this keyword anytime we want to.

```
void AssignThisInt(int i)
{
    this.someInt = i;
}
```

The use of this can help make the code more readable. In a complex class where we have many different variables and functions, it sometimes helps to clarify if the variable being assigned is something local to the function we're reading or if the variable is a class scoped variable. Using this we can be sure that the variable is assigned to a class variable, and not something only in the function.

Getting into something somewhat obscure, but worth mentioning is self-referencing. In some cases, an object may need to look to itself as a variable. To do this you'd have an object store itself as a variable.

```csharp
class ThisThing
{
    ThisThing myThing;
    public void AssignThing()
    {
        myThing = this;
    }
}


void AssignAThingToItself()
{
    ThisThing thing = new ThisThing();
    thing.AssignThing();
}
```

The example above shows a class called ThisThing. Inside of it there's a variable declaration called myThing that's the same type as itself. To assign the class itself to the myThing variable there's a function called AssignThing() where the contents of that function assigns this to myThing.

The function AssignAThingToItself() executes the code and creates a thing and has it assign itself to the myThing variable. With some data types where objects need to reference to both themselves and similar components you'll create what's called a linked list. One of the components of a linked list is being able to reference itself among other objects it might be linked to.

We may be jumping ahead into some complex data structures, so we'll hold off more complex subjects for now. It's not too common for an object needing to reference itself in this way, but C# lets you do it.

4.9.3 What We've Learned

In general, this is a somewhat awkward keyword. The necessity of using the keyword this arises in very few use cases.

When naming variables and functions, it's best to keep to a consistent pattern. In general, many people use longer names at the class scope. For instance, the following code uses a pattern of shorter and shorter variable names depending on the variable's scope:

```csharp
class MyClass
{

    int MyInt;
    void MyFunction(int mInt)
    {
        int m = mInt;
        MyInt = m;
    }
}
```

At the scope of the entire class the `int` is `MyInt`. Within the function `MyFunction` in `MyClass` a local variable visible to `MyFunction` in the argument list is called `mInt`. The variable defined inside of the function is simply m.

There are obvious limitations to using a convention like shortening variable names. It's very easy to run out of letters and end up with unclear variable names, but it's a simple place to get started.

This isn't a common practice convention by any means; it's one that I've personally become used to using. These sorts of personal conventions are something that everyone needs to invent for his or her individual use. I'd expect you to find your own convention for naming variables.

The flexibility of C# allows everyone to have a personal style of writing code. Identifiers aren't the only place where one can find self-expression through code. Another way to express one's self through code is deciding to use a `for-while` or `do-while` loop. Both can be used for the very similar tasks, but the decision is ultimately left to the programmer writing the code.

For any reason should you feel like you prefer one method over another you should follow your own intuition and write how you like to. Programming is a creative process and writing expressive code is a process just like any other form of art.

4.10 Building a Game—Part 2

Previously we worked to get at a little robot character moving with a point and click system. Unity 3D allows us to attach more than one script to a GameObject in a scene. The additional components attached to the game object append additional behaviors.

An entity with behaviors is a conceptual relationship or Entity Component Model. Programmers, like scientists, use categorization to classify work. Words like Domain Driven Design (DDD), or Model-View-ViewModel (MVVM), or Component Object Model (COM) are techniques. Design patterns are intended to help organize what classes contain what functions and where to store data.

Most game engines, Unity 3D included, follow the Entity Component Model where an object in the scene has various components attached to it. The components include sounds, particle effects, 3d models, and so forth. Each component can in turn, also have more components attached to them. Weapons can have sounds effects and models which are then attached to a character. Where the division of work splits a component into multiple parts is dependent on the engineer coming up with the systems that drive the game. Split things up too small and you've got numerous classes with different interfaces and functions that can be confusing. Too few components and classes can grow into large masses of complex code.

Decisions like when to split a class into multiple components only comes with experience. After writing a few different games, the natural lines of delineation between components becomes more apparent. We have yet to write one game, though, so let's get back to that.

If we want to add some shooting behavior to our character, we should use the right mouse button. The previous exercise used the left mouse button to tell the character to move toward the mouse position. Lots of projectiles are more fun than one so right click down should start spraying a bunch of projectiles at the mouse point and when we release the shooting stops.

We should also have some targets to shoot at, so we'll also want to have a system to pop up something to shoot at. When the targets take enough hits, we'll have them explode and go away. This means we'll need to build some sort of target damage system.

4.10.1 Additional Components

Layers of behaviors added to an entity in a scene makes creating complex behavior easier. The alternative is to create a single script that manages every entity in the scene at once. Let's avoid that and write a system to allow our little guy some target practice.

Continuing with the Unity-SampleGame, open the Section 4.10 scene to review what's going on.

The process begins with needing to fire projectiles from the character. Projectiles will originate from the Robo character, so the script should start there.

Following the logic we'll want a way to determine how and when the projectiles should be created. Weapons in games often have a rate of fire, or how many projectiles are created per minute.

```
// convert RPM to tenthsOfSeconds
float NextShot(float rpm)
{
    // 600 rounds per minute
    //÷ 60 minute
    //———
    //= 10 rounds per second
    float perSecond = rpm / 60;

    // tents of a second
    // between each round
    //
    //   1 second
    //÷ 10 rounds per second
    //———
    //=0.1 seconds

    float tenths = 1 / perSecond;
    return tenths;
}
```

To use this in Unity we need to convert rounds per minute into tenths of seconds. The conversion in the example takes a supposed 600 rpm and converts that into 0.1f seconds with some basic math.

```
if (Input.GetMouseButton(1) && Time.time > NextTime)
{
    // calculate how soon we can fire the next shot
    NextTime = Time.time + NextShot(RateOfFire);
```

In the Update function we check for GetMouseButton(1) for the right mouse button. We use the NextShot function to set NextTime to regulate how often the weapon will fire. To give ourselves a bullet to create we use GameObject ProjectileObject and assign a Prefab of a projectile to the Robo in the scene. Prefabs are assemblies of game objects that have been stored in the Assets directory. These are GameObjects that have components added so they can function on their own.

```
public GameObject ProjectileObject;
public GameObject ProjectileStart;
public AudioClip BlasterShotClip;
```

The projectiles need to have a transform to be instantiated with. An instantiated object without a position and orientation to start with will appear at the origin of the scene. To provide the projectile with a position in front of Robo, an empty GameObject named "ProjectileStart" has been added. This gets assigned to the ProjectileWeapon script. Last is a SoundClip that will play when the weapon is fired. To play the audio, the Robo has an AudioSource component attached, so the audio clip has a something to play from.

Now the rest of the `Update()` function can be filled in.

```
// get the position of the "barrel" of the weapon
Vector3 pos = ProjectileStart.transform.position;
// get the rotation of the "barrel" of the weapon
Quaternion rot = ProjectileStart.transform.rotation;

// create a new projectile with the barrel position
// and rotation.
Instantiate(ProjectileObject, pos, rot);

// make a pew! noise
GetComponent<AudioSource>().PlayOneShot(BlasterShotClip);
```

We get a `Vector3` and a `Quaternion` from the `ProjectileStart` object and assign it to the Instantiate function that uses the "Original" as a template to create a new projectile. Once the object is created we play a "Pew!" sound. So what is the projectile?

4.10.2 The Projectile

The projectile has three features. First, it has a travel speed; second, it's got a life time; and last, it's got a damage value. To ensure that the world doesn't get populated with too many bullets that never hit anything we assign a number to terminate a projectile after a time limit.

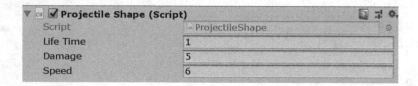

In the `Start()` function we use the Life Time's value to both Get and Set a time limit.

```
LifeTime = Time.time + LifeTime;
```

Here, imagine that if time was 3, it's just assigned 3 + the Current Time which might be 21 seconds into the game. With that math, Life Time of 3 becomes Current Time 21 + Life Time 3. This sets the end of life to 24. So in Update we check the following:

```
if (Time.time >= LifeTime)
{
    Destroy(this.gameObject);
}
```

When the current time is past the Life Time of the Projectile GameObject, the projectile destroys itself. The speed value is used to set its initial Velocity when it's created.

```
GetComponent<Rigidbody>().velocity = transform.forward * Speed;
```

When the projectile is instantiated, it's given a position and orientation to start with. Velocity of `transform.forward` multiplied by its `speed` will simply shove the projectile forward. Making the physics in Unity a bit easier to work with, we turn off gravity on the rigid body attached to the Projectile GameObject.

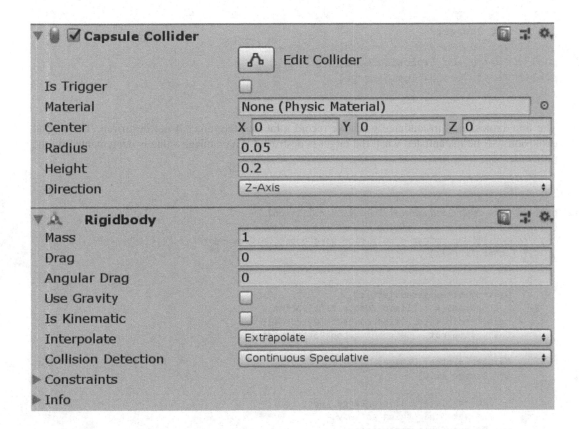

Features like Interpolate and Collision Detection are set to Extrapolate and Continuous Speculative, as recommended by the Unity documentation for fast moving projectiles. This ensures that the projectile doesn't pass through stationary objects without collision detection. If an object is moving fast enough the `Update()` function might miss a collision. Our projectile also has a colorful contrail attached to it for added visual effect.

4.10.3 The Target

We need something to shoot at. The large red boxes populating the scene have a DamageSystem script attached. This has three values as well, a damage number, and Two GameObjects that are spawned when it's hit with a projectile.

```csharp
public int Damage;
// Prefabs to instantiate when a hit is recorded
public GameObject ExplosionSmall;
public GameObject ExplosionLarge;
```

The first explosion is instantiated when we record a hit, but the target is not destroyed. The second explosion will be instantiated when the target is destroyed. The damage value is decremented by the projectile.

```csharp
private void OnCollisionEnter(Collision collision)
{
    ProjectileShape other = collision.gameObject.GetComponent<ProjectileShape>();
    if (other != null)
    {
        // make the projectile go away.
        Destroy(other.gameObject);
        Vector3 pos = collision.contacts[0].point;
        Vector3 dir = collision.contacts[0].normal;
        Quaternion rot = Quaternion.LookRotation(dir);

        Damage -= other.Damage;
        if (Damage <= 0)
        {
            Instantiate(ExplosionLarge, pos, rot);
            // make this thing go away.
            Destroy(this.gameObject);
        }
        else
        {
            Instantiate(ExplosionSmall, pos, rot);
        }
    }
}
```

To record collision events we use the MonoBehaviour OnCollisionEnter event delegate. To check what collided with the target we use ProjectileShape other. Everything that touches the target will trigger the OnCollisionEnter delegate. By using GetComponent() on anything touching the target, we can check if the colliding object is a projectile. The statement if (other != null) is true when the collision occurs with an object that has the ProjectileShape script attached.

We reduce the target damage by the projectile's damage value and check if the value is less than or equal to 0. If we are not at or below 0, we create a small explosion, otherwise we create a large explosion and destroy the target game object. The large and small explosions are particle systems with the sound source attached to them to play the explosion sound. When the particle system is finished, the object is set to destroy itself.

You might ask why the target doesn't play the sound. The audio source component needs to be in the scene for the audio to be heard. If the target destroys itself, it takes the audio source away with it. An audio clip never gets played on an object that doesn't exist.

4.10.4 What We've Learned

Here's where we get a tad philosophical. With the idea in mind that the explosion object plays the explosion sound, does that mean that the projectiles should play the blaster shot sound? The current setup has the weapon playing the blaster shot sound, but we could easily change the responsibility of the audio source. To change things completely, we could have a third object in the scene that plays all the sounds. A sound management object could be marked to not be destroyed, so this ensures that all the sounds will be played when objects are destroyed.

Quite a lot has been accomplished with very simple behaviors. We rely on events and options Unity 3D has built. Unity 3D is a game engine after all, so we should leverage all the features prepared for making games.

We've invested some time in seeing how to pool together simple language features to make complex behavior, so let's continue to see how C# works to understand more about what we just looked at in this chapter.

4.11 Logic and Operators

Logic allows you to control what part of a function is evaluated based on changes to variables. Using logic, you'll be able to change which statements in your code will run. Simply put, everything you write must cover each situation you plan to cover. Logic is controlled through a few simple systems, primarily the if keyword and variations of "if."

4.11.1 Booleans

Open the LogicAndOperators.cs script in Visual Studio along with the LogicAndOpetarors_Scene in the Unity Editor. Using George Boole's logic is a basic tool in nearly every programming paradigm. This is a rather detailed section, since there's a lot to cover. So let's dig in!

In programming booleans, or bools for short, are values that represent either true or false, in some cases 1 or 0. It's easiest to think of these as switches in either on or off position. To declare a variable as a bool, you use something like the following.

```
public class LogicAndOperators : MonoBehaviour
{
    /* This value appears in the Inspector */
    /* panel.                            */
    public bool someBool;
```

By using public you'll expose the boolean variable to Unity 3D's Editor. This declaration will make the variable appear in the Inspector panel. The boolean needs to appear here to be seen by the rest of the class in Unity 3D. We'll learn why this is so in Section 4.13 on scope, but we'll digress for now.

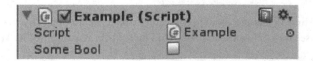

The value for `Some Bool` appears in the Inspector as an empty check box. This means that you can set the `bool` as either true or false by checking it on or off, checked or unchecked. Your code can also set your `public` variables by running the game.

```
void Start()
{
    someBool = (1 == 1);
}
```

NOTE: C# does a pretty good job of automatically initializing many of its built-in types. Number values are always initialized to 0 when they are not given a value. Bools are initialized as false when not given a value. This is handy to know since not all languages do this.

For instance, Lua, another commonly used game programming language, assumes nothing about the value until it's given one. Therefore, when any variable is first declared, it's initialized as nil, which is like C#'s behavior when creating a variable of a more complex data type. Though C# calls this uninitialized state `null`, this means the same as nothing. For good measure, UnrealScript uses the keyword none to mean the same as `null`.

Changes made before the game is run will be saved on that object. For making a game, for example, you can place treasure chests throughout a dungeon and set the amount of gold in each one. This is great since you will not need to make a different script for each treasure chest.

```
public int Gold;
```

For instance, setting a number for gold in the treasure chest will allow you to change the gold in each instance placed in a scene.

4.11.2 Equality Operators

Equality operators create boolean conditions. There are many ways to set a boolean variable. For instance, comparisons between values are a useful means to set variables. The most basic method to determine equality is using the following operator: ==.

There's a difference between use of a single and a double equal symbol. = is used to assign a value, whereas == is used to compare values. Another way to read the == is to say the left value "is equivalent to" the right value.

When you need to compare two values you can use the following concept. You'll need to remember that these operators are called equality operators, if you need to talk to a programmer. The syntax here may look a bit confusing at first, but there are ways around that.

```
/*
 * value 1 compared to value 1
 * 1 == 1 is true
 */
someBool = (1 == 1);
```

There are other operators to be aware of. You will be introduced to the other logical operators later in the chapter. In this case, we are asking if two number values are the same. When the game is started, you'll be able to watch the `someBool` check itself to `true` if not then the operator returns `false`. This is the same as the following.

```
someBool = true;
someBool = false;
```

To explain how this works, we'll need to look at the order of operation that just happened. First, the right side of the first single = was calculated. `1 == 1` is a simple comparison, asking if `1` is the same as `1`, which results with a `true` value. Test this out and check for the result in Unity 3D.

To make this a clearer, we can break out the code into more lines. Now, we're looking at a versus b. Clearly, they don't look the same; they are different letters after all. However, they do contain the same integer value, and that's what's really being compared here.

```
/* values in a and b are compared    */
/* ❶ a is assigned 1                  */
/* ❷ b is assigned 1                  */
int a = 1;/*1 == 1 is true            */
int b = 1;/*↓      ↓ ❸                */
someBool = (a == b);
/*    ↑           true                */
/*    └─────❹─────┘                   */
/*   someBool is assigned             */
/*   true                             */
```

Evaluations have a left and a right side. The single equal to operator (=) separates the different sides. The left side of the = is calculated and looks to the value to the right to get its *assignment*. Because `1 == 1`, that is to say, `1` is equivalent to `1`, the final result of the statement is that `someBool` is `true`. The check box is turned on and the evaluated statement is done.

```
/* values in a and b are compared    */
/* ❶ a is assigned 1                  */
/* ❷ b is assigned 3                  */
int a = 1;/*1 == 3 is false           */
int b = 3;/*↓      ↓ ❸                */
someBool = (a == b);
/*    ↑           false               */
/*    └─────❹─────┘                   */
/*   someBool is assigned             */
/*   false                            */
```

As you might expect, changing the value in one of the variables will change the outcome of this equality test. `someBool` will be clicked off because the statement is no longer `true`. Or in plain language, Is a equal to b? The answer is no, or as far as `someBool` is concerned, `false`.

4.11.3 Logical Not!

If we compare values that are equal, we get a value that's `true`. If we need a value that's `false` the ! symbol flips the result. As we saw with the above statement, 1 is 3 is `false`, we can also use 1 is not 3 to be `true`.

```
bool a_IsNot_b;
/* values in a and b are compared     */
/* ❶ a is assigned 1                  */
/* ❷ b is assigned 3                  */
int a = 1;/* 1 != 3 is true           */
int b = 3;/* ↓       ↓ ❷             */
a_IsNot_b = (a != b);
/*  ↑             true                */
/*  └─────❸─────┘                    */
/*   a_IsNot_b is assigned            */
/*   true                             */
Debug.Log("a_IsNot_b:" + a_IsNot_b);
// a_IsNot_b:true
```

The operator `!=` means not equal. In the `(1 != 3)`, we get true since 1 is not equal to 3. Logically this also means that `1 != 1` is `false`. It is not `true` that 1 is not equal to 1.

```
/* values in a and b are compared     */
/* ❶ a is assigned 1                  */
/* ❷ b is assigned 1                  */
bool a_IsNot_b;
int a = 1;/* 1 != 1 is false          */
int b = 1;/* ↓       ↓ ❷             */
a_IsNot_b = (a != b);
/*  ↑           false                 */
/*  └─────❹─────┘                    */
/*   a_IsNot_b is assigned            */
/*   false                            */
Debug.Log("a_IsNot_b:" + a_IsNot_b);
// a_IsNot_b:False
```

The not operator ! can also be assigned to a value after it's been calculated. After an evaluation comes in as either `true` or `false`, the ! can be applied to the value to flip the result from `true` to `false`.

```
bool not_a_is_b;
int a = 1;/*   1 == 1 is true         */
int b = 1;/*   ↓     ↓                */
not_a_is_b = !(a == b);
/* ❷↑         ↑  true                 */
/*  └─────❶─────┘                    */
/*   ❷ not true                       */
/*   ❸ false is assigned              */
Debug.Log("not_a_is_b:" + not_a_is_b);
// not_a_is_b:false
```

In the above, the 1 == 1 value returns true. Before it's assigned to not_a_isNot_b the ! is applied to the true resulting in not_a_isNot_b set to false. This can be applied to any other value as well.

```
bool not_a_isNot_b;
int a = 1;/*        1 != 1 is false       */
int b = 1;/*          ↓    ↓              */
not_a_isNot_b = !(a != b);
/* ❶↑              ↑  false               */
/*  └───────────────❶──┘                  */
/*  ❶ not false                           */
/*  ❷ true is assigned                    */
Debug.Log("not_a_isNot_b:" + not_a_isNot_b);
// not_a_isNot_b:true
```

The logic of 1 is not 1 evaluates as false, then not is applied so false becomes true. Applying the not ! operator to a not equals operation makes the statement hard to read. It's important to simplify how and when the operators are used. The fewer operators you can use the better.

4.11.4 Greater and Less than Operators

To further empower the comparisons, we can use the > and < operators. These are the greater than and less than operators. This operator compares values. In the statement (3 > 0) we ask if 3 is greater than 0 which evaluates true.

```
/* this compares the values of numbers  */
/* -5 -4 -3 -2 -1 ±0 +1 +2 +3 +4 +5      */
/*├──────────────┼──────┼───────┤        */
/*               0      3                */
bool greaterThan = (3 > 0);
Debug.Log("greaterThan:" + greaterThan);
// greaterThan:true
```

The order around the operator is important and evaluates as you would expect. If you reverse the terms of the operation where we ask if (0 > 3) zero is greater than 3, we get false.

```
/* this compares the values of numbers  */
/* -5 -4 -3 -2 -1 ±0 +1 +2 +3 +4 +5      */
/*├──────────────┼──────┼───────┤        */
/*               0      3                */
bool greaterThan = (0 > 3);
Debug.Log("greaterThan:" + greaterThan);
// greaterThan:false
```

This can be modified by the ! not operator as with the previous == operations. This does the same thing to the operation as before.

```
bool greaterThan = !(0 > 3);
/*                  ↑ not operator        */
Debug.Log("greaterThan:" + greaterThan);
// greaterThan:true
```

In contrast we can also use the < operator to see if the left operand is less than the right operand.

```
bool lessThan = (0 < 3);
Debug.Log("lessThan:" + lessThan);
// lessThan:true
```

As with the greater than operator the less than functions in the same way with the left value compared to the right value. What may be less expected is if the values are the same.

```
/* -5 -4 -3 -2 -1 ±0 +1 +2 +3 +4 +5       */
/*├─────────────────────────┼──────┤      */
/*                          3 vs 3 ?      */
bool lessThan = (3 < 3);
Debug.Log("lessThan:" + lessThan);
// lessThan:false
bool greaterThan = (3 > 3);
Debug.Log("greaterThan:" + greaterThan);
// greaterThan:false
```

Both (3 < 3) and (3 > 3) are false. The result of the evaluations only checks if the values are greater or less than when making a comparison. If the values are equal, then the value of the operation is false. To check for greater than or equal to or for less than and equal to we use the >= and <= operators.

```
bool lessThanOrEqual = (3 <= 3);
Debug.Log("lessThanOrEqual:" + lessThanOrEqual);
// lessThanOrEqual:true
bool greaterThanOrEqual = (3 >= 3);
Debug.Log("greaterThanOrEqual:" + greaterThanOrEqual);
// greaterThanOrEqual:true
```

By changing the < and > to <= and >= the same check of 3 versus 3 returns true since the value evaluates as equal to. The <= and >= operators combine the > or < and the == operators into a single operator. There are operators that enable further logical combinations.

4.11.5 Logical And and Or Operators

When we use the $<=$ and the $>=$ operators we are asking is less than or equal to. This is an abbreviation of using a $<$ || == where || is the logical "or" operator. This can also be read as "double bar" but, "or operator" is preferable.

```
bool lessThanOrEqual = (3 < 3 || 3 == 3);
Debug.Log("lessThanOrEqual:" + lessThanOrEqual);
// lessThanOrEqual:true
bool greaterThanOrEqual = (3 > 3 || 3 == 3);
Debug.Log("greaterThanOrEqual:" + greaterThanOrEqual);
// greaterThanOrEqual:true
```

The logical or operator returns true if any one of the operands returns true. The above shows that the left $3 > 3$ is false, but the $3 == 3$ is true. The assignment of lessThanOrEqual is true since the right side of the || operator is true. This is clearer if we use a combination of true false statements.

```
/* logical || or operator                 */
bool logicalOr = (false || true);
Debug.Log("logicalOr:" + logicalOr);
// logicalOr:True
bool logicalOrs = (false || false || false || true);
Debug.Log("logicalOrs:" + logicalOrs);
// logicalOr:True
bool oneFalse = (false || true || true || true);
Debug.Log("oneFalse:" + oneFalse);
// oneFalse:True
```

The evaluation of a logical or requires at least one true value in the statement to return a true evaluation. In the second statement shown you can see four different values where only the far right one is true, but the logicalOrs value is assigned true. Any number of || operators can be used in a statement.

```
/* logical && and operator                */
bool falseTrue = (false && true);
Debug.Log("falseTrue:" + falseTrue);
// falseTrue:False
bool falseFalse = (false && false);
Debug.Log("falseFalse:" + falseFalse);
// falseFalse:False
bool trueTrue = (true && true);
Debug.Log("trueTrue:" + trueTrue);
// trueTrue:True
bool notTrueEnough = (false && true && true && true);
Debug.Log("notTrueEnough:" + notTrueEnough);
// notTrueEnough:False
```

The logical && and operator requires all values of a statement to be true to return true. If any one value in the statement is false then the final evaluation is false. Using the logical operators in practice is usually for comparing a range of values.

```
/* this compares the values of numbers  */
/* -5 -4 -3 -2 -1 ±0 +1 +2 +3 +4 +5      */
/*├──────────┼──────────┼──────────┤      */
/*           ├──────────┼──────────┤      */
/*          -3 < x          x < 3         */
int x = -5;
while(x < 5)
{
    bool inRange = (-3 < x && x < 3);
    Debug.Log(x + " inRange:" + inRange);
    x++;
}
/* -5 inRange:False
 * -4 inRange:False
 * -3 inRange:False
 * -2 inRange:True
 * -1 inRange:True
 *  0 inRange:True
 *  1 inRange:True
 *  2 inRange:True
 *  3 inRange:False
 *  4 inRange:False
 */
```

Using a statement like "–3 is less than x and x is less than 3" we can create a range from –2 to 2 to return true and every other number to return false. The while loop also uses the < operator to control the termination of the statement. We'll get into loop statements in more detail in the next chapter. In any case, there's no restriction on how the values can be checked.

```
bool ranges = (x < 3 && -3 < x) &&
              (x > -3 && 3 > x) &&
              (x > -3 && x < 3) &&
              (x < 3 && x > -3);
```

The above statement returns the same values as the previous form. The range is a bit harder to read, but the same result comes out. Each one of the variations on checking the range between –2 and 2 as True.

4.11.6 If and Branching

The boolean values allow functions to make decisions based on a true false condition. The "if" statement controls when a block of code is invoked based on the contained condition.

```
if(true)
{
    Debug.Log("Do the thing!");
}

if(false)
{
    // unreachable code.
    Debug.Log("Won't do a thing.");
}
```

The condition in the parameter for the "if" statement controls whether the code following the statement is invoked. This also shows us that unreachable code can result if a statement is never true. To use what we had just seen in action we'll generate a grid of cubes. Then we'll use an "if" statement to set the color of each cube based on its distance from the LogicAndOperators game object.

```
// change the color with the if statement
if (2 < distance && distance < 4)
{
    mat.color = Color.red;
}
else
{
    mat.color = Color.white;
}
```

The above statement uses an "if" statement to set the color of the cube to red when the distance to the cube is more than 2 and less than 4. The else statement changes the color to white where the "if" statement isn't true.

The if-else statement is used often. The else case occurs where the if statement is not true. We can expand this to include additional "if" statements. Checking the position of the cube's x value against the LogicAndOperators.position.x we set the color to blue.

```
if(cubePos.x > myPos.x)
{
    mat.color = Color.blue;
}
```

If the cube's x value is greater than myPos.x then the cube is blue, otherwise the previous statements values are left alone.

As the game object orbits around the center of the world, the blue divide can be seen traveling across the white cube objects. The else statement cannot stand alone, it can only appear after a valid if statement. Adding if-else-if after the blue creates another pattern.

```
if(cubePos.x > myPos.x)
{
    mat.color = Color.blue;
}

if(cubePos.z > myPos.z)
{
    mat.color = Color.green;
}
else if(cubePos.x < myPos.x)
{
    mat.color = Color.yellow;
}
```

The above changes the coloring of the cubes to yet another pattern:

Experimenting with different values in the "if" statements dramatically changes the colors of the cube array. Unreachable code can easily creep into nested if-else statements.

```
if (2 < distance && distance < 4)
{
    mat.color = Color.red;
}
else
{
    mat.color = Color.white;
    if (cubePos.x > myPos.x)
    {
        mat.color = Color.blue;
        if (cubePos.z > myPos.z)
        {
            mat.color = Color.green;
        }
        else if (cubePos.x < myPos.x)
        {
            mat.color = Color.yellow;
        }
    }
}
```

If you look closely, in the second "else" statement we have a condition if(cubePos.x > myPos.x) where we also ask inside of that else if(cubePos.x < myPos.x). The second statement will never be true. The second statement is excluded by the first. Unfortunately, this isn't caught by Visual Studio, and isn't flagged as unreachable code.

Playing with different combinations of the `if-else` statements for the colored cubes can be fun and interesting. The results turn into color patterns revolving around the LogicAndOperators game object. An interesting challenge would be to split the colors into red blue green and white with the red circle. Think that's something you can do?

4.11.7 What We've Learned

Thinking through logic is one of the most difficult parts of programming in general. For now, the logic has been straightforward, but logic can get quickly very fast. Once things get more difficult, it may be easier to set and calculate values ahead of when they're used. Rather than chain long if-else statements it's sometimes easier to use one at a time and layer the effects rather than multiple embedded if-else statements.

4.12 Loops

To follow along, we'll be using the Loops script found on the object of the same name in the Loops_ Scene in the Chapter 4 Unity Project.

This section is something you may need to return to several times for reference. Learning these different loops is all very different. Most of them accomplish the same thing, but with subtle differences. In general, the `for(;;)` loop is the easiest to use, and sometimes the fastest.

The `Update()` function is run once every frame. Within that function, our logic is evaluated, starting at the top moving toward the bottom. Once the function is complete, the next frame begins, and the `Update()` function is called again to restart the evaluation at the top. This process is then repeated for every frame while the game is running.

To further understand how this process affects our code, we should be able to count the number of frames and thus the number of times the `Update()` function has been called. To do this, we'll simply create a `public int` to count the number of times the `Update()` function has been called.

4.12.1 Unary Operators

The term *unary operator* means there's only one operation required. In C#, and many other programming languages, unary operators work only on integers. Integers are best at counting whole values. In this case, we're going to keep track of how many times the `Update()` function has been called.

Integers are whole numbers, like `1`, `2`, and `1234`. Unlike how numbers are commonly used in written English, in code, no commas are used: "1,234," for example, should be written "1234." Commas are special characters in C#, so the computer will look at 1,234 as a `1` followed by a different number `234`. We'll go further into the differences between numbers, but we need to know a bit about integers before proceeding. In a new project in Unity 3D start with the Loops project.

```
// Update is called once per frame
void Update () {
    counter = counter + 1;
}
```

To start, we should look at how the process looks like in long hand. Adding `counter` = `counter` + `1` means we're going to take the previous value of `counter` and add `1` to it. Some programming languages require this counting method. Lua, for example, needs to increment variables in this manner.

More complex languages like C# can shorten this to a single statement with the use of a unary operator.

```
counter++;
```

The unary operator ++ works the same as the long-hand version from the previous statement. When you run the game you can watch the counter value update in the Inspector panel in Unity 3D. After only a few seconds, you can see the counter running up very quickly. Each time the Update() function is called, the counter is incremented by 1.

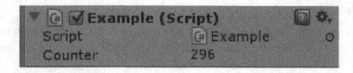

Another unary operator is the --, which decrements a value rather than increments. Replace ++ with -- and you can watch the counter running down into negative numbers. Each one of these has important uses.

4.12.2 While

If we want to run a specific statement more than once in a loop, we need another method. To do this, C# comes with another couple of keywords, while and for. The while() statement is somewhat easier to use. It needs only one bool argument to determine if it should continue to execute.

This statement is somewhat like the if() statement, only that Unity 3D returns to the start of the while() statement checks if the contained statement is true and repeats the code block again.

```
void Update ()
{
    while (counter < 10)
    {
        Debug.Log(counter);
        counter++;
    }
}
```

We start again with public int counter. The while() loop checks if the counter is less than 10. While the counter is less than 10, then we run the contents of the while statement that increments the counter. Once the counter is larger than 10, the while statement doesn't evaluate its contents. As a programmer might say, the while loop's code block will not be executed.

There is one danger using while statements. If the while statement remains true, it will not stop. In this case, it means that the Update() function will not finish and the game will freeze on the frame until while(false). This also means that any input into Unity 3D will respond very slowly as it's still waiting for the Update() function to end. We'll observe how runaway loops behave later in this chapter.

One important observation to make is that counter++ lives inside the while with the above code sample. This means that the Update() no longer increments the counter value. The while loop increments the value.

```
void Update ()
{
    counter++;
    int i = 0;
    while (i < 10)
    {
        Debug.Log(i);
        i++;
    }
    Debug.Log(counter);
}
```

The form above creates an int i = 0; just before the while() statement. Inside of the while() statement the value of i is incremented as before. After the loop the counter value is printed to the Unity Console. The output for the above sends a string of numbers 0 to 9, then a number from counter. This means that counter is incremented with the start of the Update() function, the while() loop executes 10 times, then the counter is incremented.

4.12.3 For

To gain a bit more control over the execution of a loop, we have another option. The for() loop requires three different statements to operate. The first statement is called an initialization, the second is a condition, and the third is an operation.

```
for( initialization ; condition ; operation )
{
    code goes here...
}
```

The first argument allows us to set up an integer. After that, we need to have some sort of boolean condition to inform the for loop when to stop. The last argument is something that operates on the initialized variable from the first statement in the for loop. The following code block is a typical example of the for() loop statement.

```
for (int i = 0; i < 10; i++)
{
    Debug.Log(i);
}
```

Inside of the Update() loop, the for() statement contains int i = 0; restricted to its own scope. The three arguments, are separated by a semicolon (;). The first part, int i = 0, is the initialization. The condition checks if i < 10 to return true or false. The operation of the for() loop uses a unary operator and increments the value for i.

```
for (int i = 0; i < 10; i++)
{
    Debug.Log(i);
}
Debug.Log(i);
```

The variable i we wrote into the for loop is gone once you leave the for loop. The attempt to Debug. Log(i); after the for() statement fails since i no longer exists outside of the context of the for() statement.

At the same time, you're not going to want to declare an int i before using one in the for loop.

```
int i = 0;
for (int i = 0; i < 10; i++)
{

}
```

The second part of the for loop is i < 10, the condition letting the for loop know when to stop running. This is similar to the while loop we just took a look at. The for loop offers alternative uses of its arguments, some uses may seem awkward. This is unorthodox, but you can leave out the initialization section if an int value has been declared before the loop.

```
int i = 0;
for (; i < 10; i++)
{
    Debug.Log(i);
}
```

There's not much of a reason for this but it's not going to break anything. The last argument of the for loop is an operation which runs after the first two arguments are evaluated. If the second part of the for loop is true, then the contents of the curly braces are evaluated. The last part of the expression is i++ that can also be moved around.

```
int i = 0;
for (; i < 10;)
{
    Debug.Log(i);
    i++;
}
```

Unlike the while loop that relies on an external variable, the for loop contains everything it needs to operate, although, as we've just seen, we can still move the parts of the for loop around. If only the condition argument of the for loop is used then the for loop acts the same as a while loop. Although rearranging the parts of a for loop like this is not recommended, this does serve as a way to show how flexible C# can be.

```
int i = 0;
bool loop = true;
for (; loop;)
{
    Debug.Log(i);
    i++;
    if (i > 10)
        loop = false;
}
```

Just so you know, a classically trained programmer might have a migraine after looking at this for() statement, so give him or her a break and just do things normally.

The while loop runs only once after the counter reaches 10 after the first time it's evaluated. Each time the Update() function is called, the for loop starts over again. We can use a slight variation of this using float values, though this isn't any different from using integers. Again, it's best to use integer values in a for loop, and this is only to show how C# can be changed around freely.

```
for (float f = 0; f < 10f; f = f + 1.0f)
{
    Debug.Log("float: " + f);
}
```

Try not to be too clever with your loops. Yes, you can do quite a lot and C# is very lenient and will let you get away with the code above. I would never recommend you use float values in a for() statement. However, I will not tell you to *never* use a float in a for() loop. I would just be curious as to why.

4.12.4 Do-While

Do-while is another loop to add to our toolbox. We saw the for() and the while() looping statements in Section 4.12.3. The for() and while() loops are the most common and the simple to use. There are, however, variations on the same theme that might come in handy.

The great majority of the tasks can be handled by the simple for() loop. However, variations in looping statements are created either to support different programming styles or to conform to changing requirements in different programming styles or to allow for different conditions to terminate the loop.

The while() and the for() loops both check various conditions within their parameter list before executing the contents of the loop. If we need to check after the loop's execution, then we need to reverse how the loop operates.

```
int i = 0;
do
{
    Debug.Log(i);
    i++;
} while (i < 10);
```

The do-while loop has some subtle differences. For most programmers, the syntax change has little meaning and, for the most part, do-while can be rewritten as a simple while loop.

It's worth noting that most programming languages use the same keywords for the same sort of task. Lua, for instance, uses for in a similar fashion:

```
for int i = 1, 10 do
    print(i)
end
```

However, Lua likes to shorten the conditions of the for loop by assuming a few different things in the condition and the operation of i. Other languages like Java, or JavaScript, use for and while more like C#. Things get really strange only if you look at something like F#:

```
for I = 1 to 10 do
printfn "%d" i
```

Syntax aside, once you know one version of the for loop, it's easier to figure out how another language does the same thing. The more basic concepts like booleans and operators also behave the same across languages. Therefore, you won't have to relearn how to use operators now that you know how they're used in C#.

4.12.5 Postfix and Prefix Notation

The placement of a unary operator influences when the operation takes place. Placement, therefore, has an important effect on how the operator is best used. This is a difficult concept to explain without seeing in use, so we'll skip right to some sample code.

```
int i = 0;
Debug.Log(i);        // 0
while (i < 1)
{
    Debug.Log(i++); // 0
    Debug.Log(i);    // 1
}
```

For various reasons, the i++ is the more standard use of the unary operator. When this code is executed, the first Debug.Log(i);, before the while() loop, will produce a 0, just as when i was first initialized. The first time the Debug.Log(i++); inside of the while loop is called, another 0 is produced in the Unity 3D Console panel. Where things become interesting is at the third Debug.Log(i); statement, where we have a different number.

The statement where i++ appears will use the value which i held before it was incremented. After the statement where i++ appears, the value of i will have been incremented. This is the difference between postfix and prefix, where i++ is a postfix notation and ++i is prefix notation. To illustrate this difference, observe the change when we use a prefix notation:

```
int i = 0;
Debug.Log(i);           // 0
while (i < 1)
{
    Debug.Log(++i); // 1
    Debug.Log(i);    // 1
}
```

The first version, with postfix notation, produces two 0s and a single 1 before the while loop terminates. The second version produces one 0 and two 1s before the while loop terminates. The choice of which notation to use depends mostly on what value you need i to take when you use it. The syntax difference is subtle, but once it's understood, the effects can be controlled. To make the difference more drastic, we can move the placement of where the unary operation occurs.

```
int i = 0;
Debug.Log(i);
while (++i < 1)
{
    Debug.Log(i); //unreachable code
}
```

The above statement will produce a single 0 in the Unity 3D's Console panel. The condition to execute the while loop begins as false, where the value for i is not less than 1, thus the Debug.Log() statement is never called. However, if we change things around, we'll get a 0 and a 1 printed to the Console panel.

```
int i = 0;
Debug.Log(i);
while (i++ < 1)
{
    Debug.Log(i); // 1
}
```

This code block means that the while loop started off true, since the value of i was 0 when evaluated, and only after the evaluation was complete was i incremented. Using the while loop in this way is unconventional, and it might be best avoided even though it's clever.

4.12.6 Using Loops

To continue to follow along, we'll open the UsingLoops_Scene In the Chapter 4 Unity Project. In the scene open the UsingLoops script. Loops are used to complete repetitive tasks. In the following use of the while loop, we count up the number of cubes. To see results from the while loop, we'll create a new cube for each execution of the while loop. To do this, we'll create a new GameObject named box.

To initialize the box, we start with GameObject.CreatePrimitive(PrimitiveType.Cube). This initialization has a couple of new concepts. The first is the GameObject.CreatePrimitive() function. CreatePrimitive()is a function found inside of the GameObject class.

To let `CreatePrimitive` know what to make, we're using the `PrimitiveType.Cube`, which is of `PrimitiveType`; technically, it's an enum, but more on that later. Then, as we've seen before in the `while` loop, we're incrementing the `numCubes` variable to make sure that the `while` loop doesn't run uncontrolled.

```
public class UsingLoops : MonoBehaviour
{
    int numCubes = 0;
    private void Start()
    {
        while (numCubes < 10)
        {
            GameObject box = GameObject.CreatePrimitive(PrimitiveType.Cube);
            box.transform.position = new Vector3(numCubes * 2.0f, 0, 0);
            numCubes++;
        }
    }
}
```

To tell where each cube is created, we move each cube to a new position by setting the box to new `Vector3`. In `Vector3()`, we'll take the value of `numCubes` and multiply it by `2.0f`, making sure that each cube is moved to a different x location. Logically, each iteration of `numCubes` will increment by 1. Therefore, on the first execution, we'll have `0 * 2.0f` that ends with 0. Then, the second time through the `while` loop, the result will be `1 * 2.0f`, then `2 * 2.0f`, and so on, until `numCubes` is larger than 10.

Each time the `while` loop is evaluated, the `box` points to a new instance of a cube primitive. The previous iteration of the `while` loop forgets about the previous instance of the `box`, which instance box is referencing becomes very important as we don't necessarily want to deal with every instance of the box game object we're thinking about.

Running the code in the scene results in a long chain of 10 cubes.

An inquisitive person should be asking, "Where did `CreatePrimitive` come from?" The answer to that is found inside of the `UnityEngine.dll.GameObject` is going to be the primary focus of creating any object in the game, as the name might suggest. Peek at the definition by right clicking on the `GameObject` found inside of the Solution Explorer in Visual Studio, we find a promising `CreatePrimitive()` function. This is related to how we found `Vector3()` in an earlier section.

```
        GameObject box = GameObject.CreatePrimitive(PrimitiveType.Cube);
                                                      GameObject [from metad

269         // Parameters:
270         //   type:
271         //     The type of primitive object to create.
272         [FreeFunction("GameObjectBindings::CreatePrimitive")]
273         public static GameObject CreatePrimitive(PrimitiveType type);
274         //
```

The `CreatePrimitive()` function expects a `PrimitiveType` as an argument. Clicking on the `PrimitiveType` found in the Assembly Browser window, you are presented with the following set of code.

```
        GameObject box = GameObject.CreatePrimitive(PrimitiveType.Cube);
                                                      PrimitiveType [from meta

7       //
8       // Summary:
9       //     The various primitives that can be created using the GameObje
10      //     function.
11      public enum PrimitiveType
12      {
13          //
14          // Summary:
15          //     A sphere primitive.
16          Sphere = 0,
17          //
18          // Summary:
19          //     A capsule primitive.
20          Capsule = 1,
21          //
22          //  Summary:
```

Here is an enum called `PrimitiveType`. Inside this is `Sphere`, `Capsule`, `Cylinder`, `Cube`, and `Plane`. Each one is a value inside of the `PrimitiveType`. Enums are another generic type that C# makes extensive use of, which we'll introduce in Section 6.6.1. The `CreatePrimitive` function inside of the `GameObject` class is followed by: `GameObject`. This means that it's creating a `GameObject` for you to access. We'll learn about this once we start writing our own classes and functions with return types.

NOTE: Looking things up on the internet is also a huge help. There are many people asking the same questions as you. If you don't find what you're looking for, then you might just be asking the wrong question, or phrasing it in an obscure way. To find information on CreatePrimitive, search Google using "CreatePrimitive Unity" to get some quick possible answers.

In most cases, the answers are going to be brief and obscure, but they at least serve as an example for what you might need to look for in your own code to complete the task you're trying to complete.

This discussion might be a bit much to swallow right now, so we'll stick with the small bite we started with and get back to the deeper picture later. For now, let's get back to figuring out more on loops.

4.12.7 Loops within Loops

We've created a line of cubes, but how would we go about making a grid of cubes?

We'll write two `for` loops, one within the other. The first `for` loop will use `int i = 0` and the second will use `int j = 0` as their initialization arguments. Then we'll leave the numCubes as a `public int` we can change in the editor. If we set the `numCubes` in the inspector to 10, then each `for` loop will iterate 10 times.

```
public int numCubes = 10;
private void Start()
{
    [...]
    {
        for (int i = 0; i < numCubes; i++)
        {
            for (int j = 0; j < numCubes; j++)
            {
                GameObject box = GameObject.CreatePrimitive(PrimitiveType.Cube);
                box.transform.position = new Vector3(i * 2.0f, j * 2.0f, 0);
            }
        }
    }
}
```

Only in the second `for` loop do we need to create a box; then, in the x and y values of the `Vector3`, we will do some of the same math we did before. This time we'll use the int i variable for x and j for y to create a grid. This declaration creates a row and column relation between the two `for` loops. As one iterates through the row, the other inside of the row fills in the column with cubes.

Hop to the Scene panel in the Unity 3D Editor to look at the grid of cubes that was produced when you pressed the Play button. When the first `for` loop begins, it gets to the second `for` loop inside of it. Only after the second `for` loop is done with its statements of creating 10 boxes will it go back to the first `for` loop that moves on to the next iteration. Also since we changed numBoxes to 10, the first `while()` loop we wrote will get skipped run since numCubes is not less than 10. Also worth noting, the numCubes++ that appears in the `while()` loop isn't in the `for()` loop. The line in the `for()` loop would create a runaway loop since the condition for loop termination would never be met.

4.12.8 Runaway Loops

Loops can often lead to runaway functions. A `while` loop without any condition to stop it will make Unity 3D freeze. The following shows some conditions that will immediately make Unity 3D stop on the line and never finish the frame. Adding any of these will halt Unity 3D, and you'll have to kill the Unity 3D app though the Task Manager.

```
while (true)
{
}


for (; ; )
{
}
```

In some cases, these conditions are used by some programmers for specific reasons, but they always have some way to break out of the function. Using either `return` or `break` can stop the loop from running on forever. These keywords are referred to as Jump Statements. It's worth mentioning that the keyword `return` is usually used to send data to another function. If there isn't a function waiting for data, it's better to use `break`.

```
while (true)
{
    return;
}

for (; ; )
{
    break;
}
```

There is a specific behavioral difference between `return` and `break`. With `return` you're stopping the entire function. With `break` you're stopping only the block of code the `break` is in.

```
Debug.Log("Starting");
for (; ; )
{
    Debug.Log("before break");
    break;
    Debug.Log("after the break");
}
Debug.Log("Ending");
```

First of all, we'd get a couple of warnings informing us of some unreachable code. However, that doesn't keep us from testing out the results printed on the Console panel.

> ⓘ Starting
> UnityEngine.Debug:Log(Object)
>
> ⓘ before break
> UnityEngine.Debug:Log(Object)
>
> ⓘ Ending
> UnityEngine.Debug:Log(Object)

We do get the first line of the just before the `for()` loop function as well as the line before the `break` command. However, the line following `break` is not reached. This behavior changes if we replace `break` with `return`.

```csharp
Debug.Log("Starting");
for (; ; )
{
    Debug.Log("before break");
    //break;
    return;
    Debug.Log("after the break");
}
Debug.Log("Ending");
```

We get only one warning of unreachable code, but we do get a third line printed to the Console window.

> ⓘ Starting
> UnityEngine.Debug:Log(Object)
>
> ⓘ before break
> UnityEngine.Debug:Log(Object)

We do not to see "Ending" printed to the Console. We'll go into more detail on the specifics of how these functions are used later, which provides a very short example for break; For instance, we can use the following code to see how a `while (true)` can be stopped with a specific instruction.

```csharp
int counter = 0;
while (true)
{
    counter++;
    if (counter > 10)
    {
        Debug.Log("Break!");
        break;
    }
}
```

The `counter` builds up while we're trapped in the while loop. Once the counter is above 10, we break out of the `while` loop with the break keyword.

4.12.9 Breakpoints: A First Look

To have a better understanding on what we're seeing here, we're going to use a very important feature of an IDE. With the code we just entered in the previous `Update()` function, we have a `while (true)` and a `counter++` incrementing away inside of it.

```
74      while (true)
75      {
76          counter++;
77          if (counter > 10)
78          {
79              Debug.Log("Break!");
80              break;
81          }
82      }
```

There's a narrow margin to the left of the numbers. The margin is for adding breakpoints. Breakpoints are small bookmarks that help you see exactly what's going on inside of your code. Click in the margin on the line with the `counter++;` and you'll see the line highlight.

In Visual Studio select Debug→Attach Unity Debugger. This action will open a dialog box with a list of Unity 3D game engines you might have open. In most cases, you would have only one.

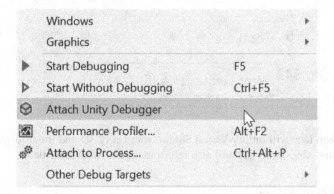

	Windows	▶
	Graphics	▶
▶	Start Debugging	F5
▷	Start Without Debugging	Ctrl+F5
◈	Attach Unity Debugger	
🖼	Performance Profiler...	Alt+F2
⚙	Attach to Process...	Ctrl+Alt+P
	Other Debug Targets	▶

Select Unity in the following dialog and click on OK. Back in Unity press the Play-in-Editor button and wait for Visual Studio to hit the breakpoint.

```
74      while (true)
75      {
76          counter++;
77      ▶| if (counter > 10)
78          {
79              Debug.Log("Break!");
80              break;
81          }
82      }
```

You'll see that the line in Visual Studio is now highlighted, and a new set of windows has appeared at the bottom of the panel. Select the Locals panel and take a look at the `counter`. There are three columns: Name, Value, and Type, which tell you the `counter` is at 0, which will tell you the value for `counter` and that it's an `int`.

Press F5 to release the `break` and you'll see the `count` increment by 1. As soon as the code gets back to the breakpoint, it will stop again. What you're looking at is your code being updated only when you press the F11 key. This is called *stepping through code*. And it's a very important reason why Visual Studio is to be used with Unity 3D, and not something like Notepad.

By tapping F11 a few times you can watch the code execute one line at a time. You can hover over each value with the cursor and watch their values change.

Debugging code is a major part of observing how your code is actually working. Breakpoints, and debugging tools like this and tools like the Locals tab are indispensable when it comes to writing complex code.

To stop debugging the code, and let Unity 3D go about its normal work, press the Stop button.

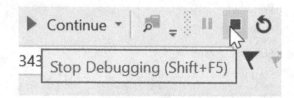

Pressing the little Stop icon will unlink Visual Studio from Unity 3D and the information that we were watching will stop updating. Unity 3D will also return to regular working order.

4.12.10 What We've Learned

The `for` loop is a tight self-contained method to iterate using a number. The `while` loop may be shorter, and use fewer parameters, but its simplicity requires more external variables to control. When faced with different programming tasks, it can be difficult to choose between the two loops.

In the end, each loop can be used to do the same thing using various techniques we have yet to be introduced to. Don't worry; we'll get to them soon enough. At this point, though, we have learned enough to start thinking about what we've learned in a different way.

The last major concept we learned was the breakpoint, used to inspect what's going on inside of a loop. Breakpoints can be set anywhere and bits of information can be picked out and inspected while your code is running.

Debugging code is a part of the day-to-day routine of the programmer. Using a debugger that allows you to step through your code's execution allows for a greater understanding of what your code's activity involves. The debugger shows you what your code is actually doing.

4.13 ScopeAgain

Scope was explored for a bit in Section 4.8, but there is some explaining left to do. We know that some variables exist only for the scope they were declared in. Other variables end up being shown in the Unity 3D Properties editor. This point doesn't explain how one class can talk to another class through a variable, or even whether this was even possible.

4.13.1 Visibility or Accessibility

Normally, variables and class definitions are considered private. This is usually implied and if you don't tell C# otherwise, it will assume you mean every variable to be private information.

```
private
public
protected
internal
```

There are only four keywords used to change the accessibility of a variable. Each one has a specific use and reason for being. For now, we'll examine the first two keywords in more depth. The keywords private and public are the two most-simple-to-understand ways to change a variable's accessibility.

We've used public before when we wanted a bool to show up in the Inspector panel in Unity 3D.

```
public bool SomeBool;
private void Start()
{
    SomeBool = true;
}
```

We have a public bool SomeBool; declared at the beginning of this ScopeAgain script. Because private is assumed, we can hide this by simply removing the public keyword. At the same time, we can be very explicit about hiding this bool by adding the private keyword.

```
private bool hiddenBool;
bool alsoHidden;
```

To the editor, there's no real difference between hiddenBool and alsoHidden. The differences will come in later when we look at *inheritance*. It's important to know about the other keywords that can precede both class and variable statements.

4.13.1.1 A Basic Example

For a better observation of a variable's scope, we're going to want to start with a scope project different from before. This time, we'll start with the MoreScope project. In this project, we have a scene file where our Main Camera has the MoreScope component added. On a cube in the same scene, we have another script component added called OtherScope.

Here's where things get interesting. From the camera, we're able to see the OtherScope class. This is indicated by MonoDevelop allowing us to access the OtherScope class as we type.

As we begin to type `Other`, the class `OtherScope` appears in the Autocomplete pop-up. This tells us that there are accessible objects, which we can access from class to class. This is referred to as the global scope.

4.13.2 Global Scope

When each class is created in Unity 3D, C# is used to make additions to the global scope of the project. This means that throughout the project, each class will be able to see every other class. This also means we can't have two class files with the same name. If we manage to create two scripts with the same name, we'll get the following error.

```
Assets/OtherScripts/OtherScope.cs(4,14): error CS0101: The namespace
"global::" already contains a definition for "OtherScope"
```

By creating two classes with the same name each class is added to the global namespace. This would happen should we define two variables with the same name in a class. Changing the name of one of the classes resolves the problem. There are other work arounds involving namespace, but we'll get to that later in Section 6.10.

Going back to the ScopeAgain script form the beginning of the tutorial we added an `OtherScope other;` variable. Next we want to assign a variable within other a value. In the game scene assign the `OtherScope.cs` class to a new `Cube GameObject` before running the game. In the `MoreScope's Start()` function, use the following statement.

```
OtherScope other;
private void Start()
{
    SomeBool = true;
    other = (OtherScope)GameObject.FindObjectOfType(typeof(OtherScope));
    Debug.Log(other.gameObject.name);
}
```

Unity's `GameObject` class has a function called `FindObjectOfType()` that will search the scene for any object of the type we're requesting. The statement following the assignment to other is `Debug.Log(other.gameObject.name);`, which prints the name of the `gameObject` that the component is attached to in the Console panel. When the game is run, we get the following output.

> ⓘ **ArrowCube**
> UnityEngine.Debug:Log(Object)

This output indicates that we've correctly found and assigned the variable `other` to the component attached to the `cube` object in the scene. Now let's add some meaningful variables to `OtherScope`.

```
public float Size;
Vector3 mScale;
```

In the OtherScope class, we'll create two variables, one public float named Size and a Vector3 called mScale. The "m" notation is commonly used by programmers as a short version of "my." Thus "mScale" refers to "MyScale." In the Update() function of the OtherScope class, we'll add the following statements:

```
private void Update()
{
    mScale = new Vector3(Size, Size, Size);
    transform.localScale = mScale;
}
```

This will set the size of the cube object's transform.localScale to the public Size variable on the *x*, *y*, and *z* axes. In the a new public variable called otherScale is used to update the size in.

```
public float otherScale;
private void Update()
{
    other.Size = otherScale;
}
```

Because the size variable in the OtherScope class was made public, it's now accessible through the dot operator. When the scene is run, the size of the cube is controlled by the otherScale variable assigned to ScopeAgain class in the Inspector panel.

You can click-drag on the otherScale variable that has been exposed to the Inspector panel with the ScopeAgain game object selected. This action directly affects the size of the cube in the scene. Even though there's no visible connection between the two objects, their variables have been connected to one another through a global connection.

Accessing a variable is not the only way a class can manipulate another class. Functions can also be accessed by another class, if they've been made public.

The importance here is that ScopeAgain can see properties in OtherScope. Once they can see each other, the variables inside one another are accessible if they're made public. Could it be possible to declare variables that are accessible globally?

We could try to put a variable outside of a class. This might make it visible to any class that might want to access it. This, unfortunately, won't work. However, it doesn't mean that there are no systems that can make a variable globally accessible. However, we'll have to leave off here for now. The systems that allow for globally accessible variables require some steps along the way to fully understand, so we'll get to that stuff soon enough.

4.13.3 What We've Learned

Defining public variables allows for interobject communication, which is one of the principles behind object-oriented programming. This enables objects to communicate to one another in many unique ways.

Scope and object-oriented programming are related. Variable scope is related to object-oriented programming. By defining and maintaining scope, you're better able to control how other objects can communicate.

When working with a team of programmers, it's important to inform all on how your code behaves. You should communicate which variables in your class can be modified by how they are defined. Making variables public informs everyone that these are the variables allowed to be altered.

By protecting them, you're able to tell others which variables they are not allowed to touch. Much of the time, it's simple to leave things public while testing and making decisions on what needs to be made public. Once you've isolated what can and cannot be altered, it's best to hide variables that shouldn't be changed by outside objects.

4.14 Warnings versus Errors

There are two basic events that we will encounter early on in C#. The first are errors, and then we will get to the many warnings. Compile-time errors will stop all your classes from compiling. Because one class can look at and interact with another class, we need to make sure that every class is free from errors before our code can be compiled.

Most of these compile-time errors occurs from typos or trying to do something with the code that can't be interpreted by the lexer. Most of these errors deal with syntax or type-casting errors, which will prevent the rest of the code from working, so it's best to fix these errors before moving on.

At the same time, we'll get many warnings. Some of these warnings can be considered somewhat harmless. If you declare a variable and don't do anything to either assign something to it or use it in any way, then the lexer will decide that you're wasting resources on the variable. This produces a simple unused variable warning.

In some cases, code can still be compiled, but there will be some minor warnings. Warnings usually inform us that we've either written unused code, or perhaps we've done something unexpected. Code with a few warnings will not stop the compilation process, but it will let us know we've done something that might not necessarily work with Unity 3D.

4.14.1 Warnings

Open up the Warnings_Scene and find the Warnings script attached to the Warnings GameObject in the scene. The most common warning is an alert bringing to your attention a variable declaration without any use. This is something you may have been seeing from the previous projects. The Visual Studio IDE is quite good at reading your code and interpreting how it's used. A function like the following will produce a warning:

```
10
11     public class Warnings : MonoBehaviour
12     {
13         void Function()
14         {
15             int i = 0;
16
17
18
```

Remove unused variable ▸ | ⚠ CS0219 The variable 'i' is assigned but its value is never used

Suppress CS0219 ▸

```
...
{
    int i = 0;
}
...
```

Preview changes

Fix all occurrences in: Document | Project | Solution

Visual Studio even gives you a helper to remove the unused variables. This simply states that i is unused, which is true. Nothing is doing anything with it, so is it necessary? Often, while you code, you'll be gathering and preparing data for later use. When we do this, we might forget that we created some data that might have been useful but never did anything with it.

In this case, we might do something with it later, so it's sometimes useful to comment it out.

```
void MyFunction()
{
    //int j = 0;
}
```

This leaves the variable around in case we need to use it, but it also clears out the warning. Most warnings don't lead to any serious problems.

4.14.2 Errors

One most common error occurs when we are dealing with missing variables or incorrect types. These errors show up often when we first start off writing our own functions and aren't used to working with different data types or know how they interact.

```
float f = 1.0;
```

This is a commonly written statement that produces the following error:

> ❌ CS0664   Literal of type double cannot be implicitly converted to type 'float'; use an 'F' suffix to create a literal of this type

The fix for the error is included in the error message. The message includes "Add suffix 'f' to create a literal of this type," which means we need to do the following.

```
float f = 1.0f;
```

This fixes the error. Many of the error messages give a clue as to what's going on and how to fix the error. Many of these errors show up before the game is run. These are called compile-time errors. Errors that show up while the game is running are called run-time errors.

Run-time errors are harder to track down. Often, this requires a debugging session to figure out where and why an error is happening.

4.14.3 Understanding the Debugger

Writing code that works is hard enough. To make sure that the code works, it's often easier to make it readable. To understand how the code works, we often need to add in additional statements to make it easier to debug as well.

We haven't covered declaration of multiple variables in one line; this is because it's bad form, but it's not illegal. We can declare both a and b in one statement. In the above, a remains unassigned, and b is now storing 0.

```
int a, b = 0;
Debug.Log(a);
```

This now produces an error, where a is used before it's assigned; however, the error might not be clear because in the line there certainly is a declaration and an assignment. The assignment is harder to read since it's all happening on one line.

```
int a = 0, b = 0;
Debug.Log(a + b);
```

This is also valid, but we've done nothing for readability or debugging.

```
52                       1
53          int a = 0, b = 0;
54          Debug.Log(a + b);
55                       1
```

Setting a breakpoint on this line highlights both the first variable, but doesn't help if we want to highlight the second declaration on the same line. This creates a problem if we're trying to find a problem with just one of the variables. This also highlights why we need to change our writing style to help debug our code.

```
61          int a = 0;
62          int b = 0;
63          Debug.Log(a + b);
```

Breaking up the declaration across multiple lines allows for setting a breakpoint on a specific statement rather than a multiple declaration statement. Likewise, debugging a statement like the following is no better.

```
int c = a; int d = b;
```

This line has two statements, but does not have a line break between them. This creates the problem of both readability and debuggability. When you're trying to isolate a problem, it's important to keep each statement on its own line so a breakpoint can be applied to it.

If we continue this exercise, we can take a look at an `ArrayList` that contains different types of data.

```
ArrayList list = new ArrayList();
list.Add(1);
list.Add(1.0f);
list.Add(1.0);
list.Add("1");
/* Lists can have pretty much anything
 * added to them. The foreach loop
 * doesn't know what is in the list.
 */
foreach (int i in list)
{
    Debug.Log(i);
}
```

In the list, we have an `int` of `1`, a string `this`, a float `1.0f`, and a double `1.0` and a `string` `"1"`. The `foreach` loop assumes `int` and this works fine with the first iteration. Setting a breakpoint here shows in the Locals panel an `int` `i` with a value of `1`. So far so good. When we step through the code by pressing F11 to get to the next item in the list, we get an error.

> ⚠ InvalidCastException: Cannot cast from source type to destination type.
> Warnings.Start () (at Assets/Warnings.cs:93)

`InvalidCastException` shows up in the Unity Console panel. Since `float` this isn't `int`, we get an error telling us what error was raised and in what line the error occurred on. This sort of debugging is only a contrived example setup to fail in a known location.

In most instances, problems like this aren't so easy to spot. The warnings and errors are often described with a line number, but it's not always easy to know why the exception was raised. Stepping into the code and checking out values is the only tool we really have to search for problems. To make things easier on yourself, it's sometimes better to break things out even more.

```
  92
➡ 93    ⊟        ▶| foreach (int i in list)
  94               {                          ● i (⇥
  95                   Debug.Log(i);
  96               }
```

To get a better look at each variable in play, highlight the `i` in the `foreach` loop. This "pins" the variable to the window. If we step into each step of the code Visual Studio will open the following pop-up.

We can see that i is storing the value this that cannot be cast to an int. Stepping through code in the debugger should be a regular practice. Anytime anything remotely confusing comes up your first move past re-reading your code should be to start the debugger.

4.14.4 What We've Learned

Working through problems takes a step-by-step approach. Setting your code up for debugging requires some formatting changes to your code to help the debugger do its work. Once the code has been laid out for debugging, it's sometimes easier to read but our code can lose some efficiency.

It's always a good idea to keep your code clean and readable, but it's just as important to help your debugger do its work as well. Seeing the debugger step through your code also helps you understand how your own functions do their work.

When you have a chance to observe your code in operation, it's sometimes easier to see where code can be optimized—for example, when you see the same data being used over and over again. Passing values between variables in a visual sense can help reveal patterns. Once the patterns are seen, it can be easier to produce code that creates and reuses the same value less often.

4.15 Leveling Up: Fundamentals

At this point, I can say that you've gained enough of the basic skills to feel confident in your ability to read code and begin to ask the right questions. Just as important, the basics we've covered are shared among most programming languages.

Coming up with clever systems to control data is only a part of the task of programming. A great deal of work is coming up. It's also important to think of clear and concise names for variables. One thing is for sure: There have been plenty of pages written by people trying to wrangle in rampant names for identifiers.

At worst, you might have a situation where humans use health points, zombies hit points, vampires blood units, werewolves silver damage, and each one is simply a record of how many times they take damage before going down. It would be unfortunate for you to have to write functions for each human to shoot at every other type of monster and vice versa.

If someone offers help with your game, looks at your code, and you never hear back from that person again, it's surely due to the confused mess of code he or she got to look at. Some simple guidelines to help with naming have been outlined a number of times by various groups.

4.15.1 Style Guides

When faced with the fact that your code will have to eventually be seen by other programmers, it's best to try to avoid some of the embarrassment of explaining every identifier you've written. Furthermore, as a beginner, it's important that you gain some insight into the common practices that classically trained programmers have used throughout their careers. With any luck, books will help you keep up.

A style guide is a reference that often involves preferences involving everything from the placement of white space to naming conventions of identifiers. Official Microsoft style guides for C# provide details on how to name every different type of identifier. This enables us to tell identifiers apart from one another based on their use for variables, functions, or any other construct that C# uses.

As we learn about the different things that identifiers are used for, we'll also want to know how to best name the construct we're creating. A simple internet search for "C# style guide" will bring up various links, for example, coding standards, guidelines, and coding guidelines.

Once you start working with any number of programmers, it's best to come to some agreement on the practices you'll choose to follow. Everyone learned slightly different methods and ideologies when he or she was introduced to a programming language, even if C# wasn't the first programming language that person learned. This leads to many different styles and conventions.

5

Fundamentals: Building a Foundation

We've covered many of the basic concepts and terms that are commonly taught to new programmers. It's time to learn some of the fundamental concepts that are required for functioning code. By now, you should know what code looks like; now it's time to start writing it.

It is important that you compare C# to other programming languages. This comparison helps to contrast C# against languages that might do a similar task in a slightly different way. With such comparison results in mind, we're better able to understand why C# looks the way it does, and we'll be better prepared to understand a concept if we look something up on the Internet exemplified in a different language. Examples found on the Internet may be in another language. Armed with a bit of knowledge, you'll have a better chance of translating the discovery into C#.

A few assets available on the Unity 3D Asset Store are might still be written in JavaScript. This might be a good indication that it's not seen an update in a long time. When necessary, you might want to read the code to understand how to use one of the downloaded assets. If you've never seen JavaScript before, you might notice how some of the code will seem familiar, but you might also find much of it to be quite alien.

The internet provides us example code in many languages. A search for "how do I sort a list" would show examples in many programming languages. It's not a bad idea to be able to read all sorts of programming languages, get the gist of what it's trying to do and then translate that into C# for your own use.

5.1 What Will Be Covered in This Chapter

Learning how to add complexity to your code takes time. We'll cover how to make classes communicate with one another on a more global scope. Then we'll learn how to control the flow of our data in more comprehensive ways. Finally, we'll want to understand one of the more useful constructs in C#, the array, and all its related forms. To make use of the concepts we've learned so far, we'll want to investigate the following points:

- Review of classes
- Class inheritance
- The keyword *static*
- Jump statements, return, continue, break
- Conditional operators
- Arrays of various types, array lists, jagged arrays, dictionaries
- Strings

Some of the specifics in this chapter will require using the latest version of the .NET set up in Unity. To avoid compatibility issues with built-in packages, the player settings and packages directories are not included with each chapter. When a project is opened for the first time the Unity Editor creates new directories. When Visual Studio is launched after that, even more directories are created. To change the .NET version in Unity, open the Player Settings panel found in Edit -> Project Settings.

In here change API (application programming interface) Compatibility Level to .NET 4.x to enable the use of the latest features of the C# programming language. If there are errors in a project this may be one of the causes. Just make sure to double check this before continuing in each chapter.

It's likely that support for older versions of .NET will be phased out and this won't be an issue. Unity will eventually deprecate or exclude the option all together. Until then, you'll need to check on the Project Settings option to make sure you're using the correct version of the .NET API.

5.2 Review

For review open the Chapter 5 Unity Project, find the Review script in the Review_Scene attached to the Review game object. The topics covered thus far have a lot in common with programming languages like JavaScript, UnrealScript, Lua, and Java, to name a few. Some of the syntax might look different, but the basic operation of how variables are created and assigned mechanically works the same. For instance, in C#, we understand assigning a variable to look like the following statement.

```
int a = 10;
```

In Lua, another commonly used game programming language, you might see something more like

```
local a = 10
```

In JavaScript, we might see something like the following:

```
var a = 10;
```

A language might not use some of the tokens we're used to seeing in C#, but use of a keyword, an identifier, and an assignment operator with a value is the same. This rule also goes for something like a for loop. In C#, and many other C-style languages, we're used to using the following:

```
for (int i = 0; i < 10; i++)
{
    // Code Here
}
```

Javascript changes the above statement, using var in place of int, but the rest remains the same. However, in Lua, again, we would see something more like the following:

```
for i = 0, 10, i++
do
    // Code Here
end
```

Some programming languages like Lua tend to omit many of the tokens used to help show how code statements are encapsulated; some prefer the brevity of the language. For a C-style language, the use of curly braces helps visually separate the statements more clearly.

Often, getting to this point is a difficult and unforgiving task. I hope you had some classmates, coworkers, friends, or family members to help you work out some of the exercises. If you're still a bit foggy on some of the concepts, you may want to go back and review. We've covered many cool things so far. For instance, you should be able to identify what the following code is. To follow along with this section open the SomeNewClass script attached to the SomeNewClass GameObject in the Review_Scene.

```
class SomeNewClass
{

}
```

If you understood this to be a class declaration for SomeNewClass, then you'd be right. We should also know that for a class to be useful to Unity 3D, we need to add some directives that will look like the following. To add in directives, we start before the class declaration. We use the keyword using followed by a library path and add in both UnityEngine and System.Collections.

```
using UnityEngine;
using System.Collections;
class SomeNewClass
{

}
```

Directives allow our class to have access to the tools that .NET has to offer. For an app to have access to data storage on disk, you need to use similar directives. If you wanted to open an internet connection to a server and ask for a web page, you would include System.Net.Sockets. Once you get some data if you wanted to save it to a file on disk you'd add System.IO.

```
using System.IO;
using System.Net.Sockets;
```

We're still a couple keywords away from a usable class in Unity 3D, though. First, we need to make this class visible to the rest of Unity 3D. To change a class's visibility, we need to add some accessibility keywords.

```
using UnityEngine;
using System.Collections;
using System.IO;
using System.Net.Sockets;
public class SomeNewClass
{

}
```

We're almost there, and now we get to a part that might be confusing.

```
using UnityEngine;
using System.Collections;
using System.IO;
using System.Net.Sockets;
public class SomeNewClass : MonoBehaviour
{

}
```

What is this: MonoBehaviour stuff that's coming in after our class identifier? You should be asking questions like this. We'll get around to answering this in mode depth in Chapter 6. MonoBehaviour is another class that the programmers at Unity 3D have written. SomeNewClass is now inheriting from the class MonoBehaviour; we'll dive into what this all means in Chapter 6.

A class is the fundamental system for C#. You're allowed to write classes with nothing in them; for instance, class NothingClass{} is a complete class structure. You can add a single type of data in a class and give it an identifier. In this case, class MyData{int SomeNumber;} is an entire object with one integer value called SomeNumber in it. On the other hand, a file without anything other than int NothingInParticular; is meaningless.

A class can also be a complex monster, with many different behaviors. It's not uncommon for a class to contain several hundred or even a few thousand lines of code. The general practice is for a class to be as small as possible. Once a class grows past a few hundred lines, it's often time to consider breaking the class into several smaller classes of reusable code.

The intent is to reduce the amount of code that could cause an error. Complex code means difficult code to debug.

What all of this means in relation to Unity 3D is that we need to write several short classes and add them to the same GameObject. The same goes for any other programming project. The more modular your code is, the easier it is to create complex behavior by creating different combinations of code.

A search on Microsoft's .NET Framework API Reference will help you look for functionality you would like to add to a class. The using UnityEngine; directive gives you access to Unity specific functions. The using System.IO; gives you access to reading and writing data to local storage. The online reference will show you many hundreds of namespaces you can include in your Unity project. The API Browser is located at:

https://docs.microsoft.com/en-us/dotnet/api/

You'll want to navigate to the latest .NET Framework to see what tools are available, it's a long list!

5.2.1 Modular Code

Many different game types use a game controller to move around a character on the screen. You might want to re-use some of that code to move around the player's foes. A more modular approach provides a chance to reduce the amount of code you need to re-write.

The same goes for functions. Rather than having a long algorithm operating in the Update() function, it's better to modularize the algorithm itself. First, you might have some sort of initialization where you obtain the character's mesh and animation system. This should be done in a separate function call rather than being repeated at the beginning of every frame. We'll look at a better way to do this later in Section 7.18.

For now, we're reviewing all the different things we've learned. Next, we are going to want to add in the an entry point created by the Unity 3D programmers called Start() and to do this, we'll simply add them into the class code block.

```
public class SomeNewClass : MonoBehaviour
{
    private void Start()
    {
    }
}
```

The `UnityEngine` library has within it an `EventSystem` that is a part of the `MonoBehaviour` class you're inheriting from. That `EventSystem` then sends messages at appropriate times to every class instance of `MonoBehavior` to invoke various methods, so long as they are named correctly. In this case, `Start()` is the method we can rely on being invoked as a child of `MonoBehaviour`.

To review our understanding of the functions that will be called by the `MonoBehaviour` `EventSystem`, let's look at what `void Start()` `{}` means. The keyword `void` implies that the function returns no values when it is done being invoked. You should note that the `Start()` begins with an upper case letter, the letter case matters as C# is case sensitive thus `start` and `Start` are different. The `()` open and closed parenthesis mean that `Start()` requires no arguments to be provided to be invoked.

```
private void Start()
{
    Debug.Log(MyFunction(7));
}


int MyFunction(int inPut)
{
    return inPut;
}
```

If we examine the function we added, we would find we created a new function called `MyFunction`. This function returns an `int`, and accepts an `arg` or argument with type `int`. In our `Start()` function, we're using a `Debug.Log()` function that comes from the `Debug` class in the `UnityEngine` library. The `Start()` function then passes an `int` 7 to `MyFunction()` argument list. The `MyFunction` returns a value `inPut`, which is then sent back up to the `Debug.Log()`, which sends 7 to the Console panel in Unity 3D.

If any of the return and argument list information is confusing we'll be going into further detail on that in Section 5.7.

Before moving on, we'll add in one last for loop. If you can guess that this code will print out a 0 through 10 in the Console output panel in Unity 3D, then you're doing great. If you were able to follow along with this example, then you've come quite a long way in understanding the basics behind C#.

```
void MyLoopFunction(int loops)
{
    for (int i = 0; i < loops; i++)
    {
        Debug.Log(i);
    }
}
```

Now that we've got most of the basics under our belt, it's time to move onto more interesting things that make C# a powerful language. What differentiates C# from older programming paradigms is the fact that it's an object oriented programming language. Objects make programming powerful, and—if you're not fully informed—confusing.

Modularity refers to the ability of code to be reused, or shared between objects. This means that you could have a generalized helper class where functions exist that you intend to use elsewhere. Going back to the Review script we can use the from there as well.

```
private void Start()
{
    SomeNewClass newClass = (SomeNewClass)FindObjectOfType(typeof(SomeNewClass));
    Debug.Log(newClass.MyFunction(11));
}
```

There are a few strategies to make this modularity more formal, but we've just got started with the basics. Each MonoBehaviour could also take on a more direct approach to modularity.

```
public class RotateX : MonoBehaviour
{
    void Update ()
    {
        transform.Rotate(new Vector3(1f * Time.deltaTime, 0, 0));
    }
}
```

```
public class RotateY : MonoBehaviour
{
    void Update ()
    {
        transform.Rotate(new Vector3(0, 1f * Time.deltaTime, 0));
    }
}
```

```
public class RotateZ : MonoBehaviour
{
    void Update ()
    {
        transform.Rotate(new Vector3(0, 0, 1f * Time.deltaTime));
    }
}
```

The three scripts above, attached to the same object, would effect the rotation of an object each in their own way.

The object would tumble as though all three were applied in one script. This means you can layer multiple effects with multiple scripts. Each one can make modifications to the same GameObject in the scene.

From here on out, you're going to get into the more interesting capabilities behind C#. The basics we've covered have similar utility in most programming languages. Declaring functions and variables will look the same in many different languages. Order of operation and logic both behave similarly in most modern programming languages.

Try not to limit yourself to learning a single programming language. The science of computers is always changing. New languages are being written, and new business models rely on people who know about the latest developments.

5.3 Inheritance: A First Look

Once we've written a new class, we should be thinking toward generalizing what a class can do. When we started our class declarations, we always had the following ": MonoBehaviour" added after the class name. This means that our class is inheriting from another class named MonoBehaviour.

A pop-up with some interesting options appears over the word. Selecting "Go To Definition," opens the MonoBehavior assembly file. The word declaration is used here with the same meaning as when we use a declaration statement to create a new identifier. A declaration statement is used to assign a variable a new identifier.

```
⊞using ...

☐namespace UnityEngine
 {
⊞     ...public class MonoBehaviour : Behaviour
      {
          public MonoBehaviour();

⊞         ...public bool useGUILayout { get; set; }
⊞         ...public bool runInEditMode { get; set; }

⊞         ...public static void print(object message);
⊞         ...public void CancelInvoke(string methodName);
⊞         ...public void CancelInvoke();
⊞         ...public void Invoke(string methodName, float time);
⊞         ...public void InvokeRepeating(string methodName, float time, float repeatRate);
⊞         ...public bool IsInvoking(string methodName);
⊞         ...public bool IsInvoking();
⊞         ...public Coroutine StartCoroutine(string methodName);
⊞         ...public Coroutine StartCoroutine(IEnumerator routine);
⊞         ...public Coroutine StartCoroutine(string methodName, [DefaultValue("null")] object value);
⊞         ...public Coroutine StartCoroutine_Auto(IEnumerator routine);
⊞         ...public void StopAllCoroutines();
⊞         ...public void StopCoroutine(IEnumerator routine);
⊞         ...public void StopCoroutine(Coroutine routine);
⊞         ...public void StopCoroutine(string methodName);
      }
 }
```

This indicates that MonoBehaviour is a class that programmers at Unity 3D wrote for us to use. A closer look into MonoBehavior you'll see it inherits from Behavior. We can dive even deeper.

```
⊞using ...

☐namespace UnityEngine
 {
⊞     ...public class Behaviour : Component
      {
          public Behaviour();

⊞         ...public bool enabled { get; set; }
⊞         ...public bool isActiveAndEnabled { get; }
      }
 }
```

Seeing Behavior we can see that it too is inheriting from another object called Component. Component then inherits from Object. And Object doesn't inherit anything. Programmers like to call classes who form the foundation for many other classes a base class.

You'll also see that in each class there are functions described in each one. For instance, in Behavior, you'll see two functions called enabled and `isActiveAndEnabled`. These are things that `Behaviour` does that `Component` doesn't.

This might be a bit too much information right now, but this is showing you all the public members that you can access within the class `MonoBehaviour`. More interestingly, everything that `Behavior`, `Component`, and `Object` do `MonoBehaviour` also has. Each new child class inherits the important functions of its parent, this includes all of its ancestors.

`MonoBehaviour` is a class that is tucked away in a DLL (dynamically linked library). A DLL is a container of referenceable code shared between Unity 3D and you. In this case, the code was written by the engineers at Unity.

The keyword `using` allows us access to the contents of the library where MonoDevelop is living inside of. To allow us to inherit from MonoBehaviour, we need to add in the UnityEngine library with the statement `using UnityEngine;`.

In Visual Studio open the Solution Explorer under View -> Solution Explorer.

Then expand the References hierarchy, and select UnityEngine by double clicking it. An Object Viewer panel opens with a long list of objects living in the UnityEngine library. Change to the NameSpaces view of the object viewer by right clicking on the UnityEngine object and expand the UnityEngine object to reveal all of the different object types contained in UnityEngine.

To summarize, UnityEngine is a library written by Unity's programmers. This library contains `MonoBehaviour`, a class that is required for our C# code to communicate with Unity's game object related functions. To use the `MonoBehaviour` functions, we tell our class to inherit from it.

The `gameObject` with your behavior will then connect to the rest of Unity through the code in the `MonoBehaviour` class.

5.3.1 Class Members

To see how classes and inheritance works together to make something useful, we'll look at building a simple character class. One important reason to create a base class for a character is to reduce the necessity of writing redundant code. If all characters will have a name, then it's certainly useful for all characters to use the same string variable to store their names.

To use programmer nomenclature, start with a "BaseCharacter.cs" to store attributes common among all the characters in the game. You'll find this in the Assets directory of the Chapter 5 Unity Project.

```
public class BaseCharacter : MonoBehaviour
{
}
```

This BaseCharacter.cs is now an object. When you declare a class, its identifier is an important name to identify the class by. The keyword class tells the computer to hold onto the following word as a new type of data. Each class's identifier basically becomes a new reserved word, much like a keyword, with special meaning.

In addition to the name of the class, all contained variables and functions should be considered special components of that new object. Encapsulation and accessibility determine how easily these contained objects can be used.

One interesting system that is offered by Visual Studio is in the Project view. You can display the members of the class you are writing.

Members of a class are not restricted to its functions. Any public variable or function becomes an accessible member of that class. To see how all of this works, we'll need to write some really simple classes in Visual Studio. We'll come back to this in a moment.

5.3.1.1 Inheriting Members

To begin open the InheritingMembers script in the Chapter5 Unity Project.

```
public class InheritingMembers : MonoBehaviour
{
    public class Cat
    {
    }

    public class PianoCat : Cat
    {
    }

}
```

The PianoCat class that inherits from Cat. In programming terms, PianoCat inherits from the base class Cat. So far, nothing interesting is happening, at least anything worthy of posting to the Internet.

To see what it means to inherit properties, we need to add some properties to Cat. Let's give our base Cat the ability to meow. Start with Debug.Log("Meow"); in our Cat class. Since this is happening as a nested class in InheritingMembers class Cat and PianoCat are both able to reference the libraries that are declared at the beginning of this file.

```
public class Cat
{
    int paws = 4;
    public void Meow()
    {
        Debug.Log("Meow");
    }
}

public class PianoCat : Cat
{
    public void PlayPiano()
    {
        Meow(); // inherited from Cat
    }
}
```

So while PianoCat plays piano in a new function, he can also meow Meow();, which is a function inherited from Cat. Both PianoCat and any other class inheriting from Cat are Cats. PianoCat is a Cat.

The terms "is-a" and "has-a" relate to component model and inheritance model object-oriented programming. The PianoCat object "is-a" Cat. In Unity you can observe a game object in the scene has a "Transform" component. So you can say a GameObject "has-a" Transform component.

The PianoCat objects can do things that Cat can do like Meow().

5.3.1.2 Is-A and Has-A

In the creation of a class you create a new Object. Objects can inherit from another object. An object can have any number members. Each member counts as something the Class has, but they do not count as something the class is.

```
public class LaptopComponent : Component
{
}


/* ComputerCat Is-A Cat       */
public class ComputerCat : Cat
{
    /* ComputerCat Has-A LaptopComponent */
    LaptopComponent Laptop;
}
```

The is keyword allows you to check if a PianoCat is a Cat.

```
Cat cat = new Cat();
PianoCat pianoCat = new PianoCat();
ComputerCat computerCat = new ComputerCat();

bool pianoCatIsCat = pianoCat is Cat;
Debug.Log("PianoCat is a Cat?" + (pianoCatIsCat ? "True" : "False"));
// PianoCat is a Cat? True

bool pianoCatIsComputerCat = pianoCat is ComputerCat;
Debug.Log("PianoCat is a ComputerCat?" + (pianoCatIsComputerCat ? "True" : "False"));
// PianoCat is a ComputerCat False
```

The above shows that bool can be set by checking if an instance of a `pianoCat is Cat`. This doesn't mean that a PianoCat object is a ComputerCat which returns false. Visual Studio also flags this knowing that a pianoCat will never be a ComputerCat.

Checking if a Cat has various properties is possible, but we'll need to wait for a chapter on reflection to comb through the members of a class.

5.3.2 Instancing

To make use of these two classes, we're going to need to do something useful with them. In the first part of our IneritingMembers.cs class, we've still got our void `Start()` that we can begin to add code to. When we start to enter PianoCat, the auto complete pop-up provides us with a PianoCat option.

```
private void Start()
{
    PianoCat famousCat = new PianoCat();
    famousCat.PlayPiano();
}
```

To make use of a class, we need to create an instantiation of the class. Instancing a class means to construct it from a blueprint. Each instance is a new object created from the class; any changes you do to the instanced version is unique to that instance.

We've created a famousCat with the properties of a PianoCat. To make this new cat (famousCat) play piano, we call on the member function found in the PianoCat class. famousCat.

`PlayPiano();` is easily added through the handy pop-ups that Visual Studio gives us. As soon as we add in the dot operator after `famousCat`, we're given several options, one of which is `PlayPiano`, but we also get `Meow()` function which originated in `Cat`.

```
PianoCat famousCat = new PianoCat();
famousCat.PlayPiano();
famousCat.Meow();
```

The `Meow()` is a member function of `PianoCat` because `PianoCat` inherited from `Cat`. Likewise, if we made a `NyanCat` or `HipsterCat` based on Cat, they would also inherit the `Meow()` function from `Cat`. Running the code in Unity 3D returns an expected meow in the Console panel.

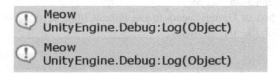

We also had a number of paws on Cat; we can access that value through `famousCat`. In our `Start()` function, in the first class we started with, we can use `Debug.Log()` to show how many paws the `famousCat` inherited from `Cat`. However, we forgot to add something.

Change the accessibility of the paws value in `Cat` to `public`. And the `Debug.Log` will be able to access the paws value from the `Start()` function in the `IneritingMembers` script.

```
public int paws = 4;
```

In our `Start()` function, in the `InheritingMembers` class we started with, we can use `Debug.Log()` to show how many paws the `famousCat` inherited from `Cat`.

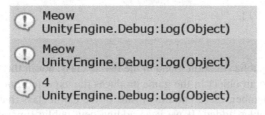

When any class you create has the notation `: MonoBehaviour` added to the class declaration you inherit a great number of functions and properties. This inheritance works in the same way `PianoCat` inherited paws and `Meow()` from `Cat` with the `:Cat` notation.

We've gotten to a point where we'd like to search the entire scene for a specific object. In this case, we should look for every player in the scene. Useful functions definitions are found in the GameObject class.

We can find an object using its name or tag. If we want to find any object that happens to have a player. cs component, we need to know which GameObject it's attached to first. It's hard to know the name of the object we're looking for if we only know one thing about it. However, there is a more general way to find things.

Of course, we could just use Unity 3D's Editor and assign tags, but we wouldn't learn how to do things with code alone. In a more realistic situation, we could just have our game designers assign tags to everything, use the `FindWithTag()` function, and be done with it.

To give ourselves a better understanding of objects and types, we should go through this process without tags. This way, we will gain a bit more understanding as to what defines objects and types, and how to use null. The null keyword basically means "nothing"; we'll see how that's used in a moment.

5.3.3 Parent Child

To see an example of how object types work, we'll inspect two classes. The first is ObjectParent.cs and the second is ObjectChild.cs. Both of these are in the Assets directory of the Chapter5 Unity Project and found together in the ParentChild_Scene.

Both scripts are attached to GameObjects in the ParentChild_Scene. The class declaration in the ObjectChild.cs should look like the following.

```
public class ObjectChild : ObjectParent
{

}
```

Observe that the usual `MonoBehaviour` following the colon (:) is replaced with `ObjectParent`. Now to prove that the Child inherits the functions found in its Parent, we should add a function for the Child to use. This code appears in the Parent class.

```
public void ParentAbility()
{
    Debug.Log("inheritable function.");
}
```

To see that the function can be used by Child.cs, we'll use it in the `Start ()` function in the ObjectChild.cs, as follows.

```
private void Start()
{
    ParentAbility();
}
```

`ParentAbility()` is a public function found in the Parent class, not in the Child class. Running this script when it's attached to an object in the game produces the expected *inheritable function* printout in the Console panel. Remember, there's nothing inside of the Child class that has yet to have any new member functions or variables added. If we keep adding new public functions to Parent, Child will always be able to use them.

To confirm this, the ObjectChild class has the following.

```
public void ChildAbility()
{
    Debug.Log("My parent doesn't get me.");
}
```

Then, check if the Parent class can use that function. The `ChildAbility()` function in the ObjectParent's `Start()` function produces an error.

```
private void Start()
{
    ChildAbility();
}
```

As it turns out, parent's can't inherit from their children. The ChildAbility does not exist in the current context.

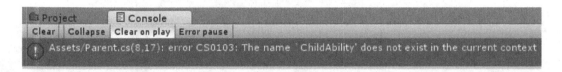

Even though the function is public, the parent doesn't have access to the functions that the Child class has. This is an important difference. The other main takeaway from this tutorial is to remember that Parent inherited from MonoBehaviour, as did all the other scripts we've been working with to this point.

The significance behind this discussion is that Child.cs has all of the functions found not only in Parent.cs but also in MonoBehaviour. One more thing should be noted:

public int ParentInt;

Adding a public int to the Parent class will also allow the Child class to use the ParentInt variable. This includes what is visible to the Inspector Panel in the Editor.

ParentInt is available as though it were declared as a part of Child, because it is. It's important to know that changing anything in the Child class will never affect the Parent class. Inheritance only works one way: The children of a parent can never change the functions in a parent. Such an occurrence rarely happens in real life as well as in C#.

5.3.4 Object

`GameObject`, is a class that inherits from `Object`. Then `GameObject` adds new functions to on top of anything that already existed in `Object`. As we have just observed from our simple inheritance example, if we find a function in `Object`, we can use it in `GameObject`.

What this means to us is that we may use any interesting functions inside of the Object in the Assembly Browser in Object as well. To view all the different classes available to you in Visual Studio, select View→Object Browser Ctrl + Alt J. Then in the Options select NameSpaces. In the left column are all sorts of items. In there is an entry for UnityEngine, expanding that opens hundreds more objects. In that list is the `Object`, or rather `UnityEngine.Object`. Selecting the `Object` found under `UnityEngine` you'll see the right panel populate with the members found in `Object`.

The members of Object are also numerous and many seem to do similar things with slight differences in how they are used. In the list is a group of `FindObjectsOfType` members.

Highlighting that populates the panel below with some additional information. The text here was generated by the comments the original programmer left in their code as they wrote the function.

public static **UnityEngine.Object[]** **FindObjectsOfType**(**System.Type** *type*)
  Member of **UnityEngine.Object**

Summary:
Returns a list of all active loaded objects of Type type.

Parameters:
type: The type of object to find.

Returns:
The array of objects found matching the type specified.

It's important to get used to searching through the libraries for useful functions. Very often you'll find some solution hidden in the vast resources of Unity 3D. Many common game related tasks have code already in place waiting for you to use in your project.

Stepping through that thought process, we begin with "I'd like to find an object in the scene, but I might not know what it's called." From that, I would likely look for something called FindObjects. The objects I need to find are going to be GameObjects, so that does narrow things down a bit. Inside of `Object`, we find a function called `FindObjectsOfType()`, which is probably what we're looking for. The summary for that reads "returns a list of all active loaded object of Type." This continues with some parameters and returns.

Parameters are arguments that go into the parenthesis `()`. The returns mean the function can be assigned to a variable. We haven't covered everything necessary to completely understand what all that means yet, but we'll show how the function is used assuming you'll come up to speed soon enough.

Continuing with the ParentChild_Scene from the previous chapter, open the `ObjectFinder` script attached to the ObjectFinder GameObject in the scene. In the Start() function, we need to set up an array for every Object in the scene. Use `Object[]`; the square brackets tell the variable it's an array. We'll cover arrays in more depth in Section 5.9. Then we name it something short, like objects. Then we can have Object run its FindObjectsOfType function to fill in our array with every Object in the scene.

```
void Start ()
{
    Object[] objects = FindObjectsOfType(typeof(Object));
    foreach (Object o in objects)
    {
        Debug.Log(o);
    }
}
```

`FindObjectsOfType()` works just as `Object.FindGameObjectsOfType()`, which should be interesting. Inheritance in C# makes things complex and clever. Keep this behavior in mind in the following example. Unfortunately, System includes type `object` which is different from the UnityEngine type `Object` with an upper case `O`. Keyword `typeof()` informs the parameter with the type of Object, rather than Object itself. This part is a bit confusing, but we'll cover this in more detail again in Section 6.5.3.

The function assigns the objects variable an array of all the objects in the scene. The foreach. To do this, we're going to reuse the foreach loop prints out everything it finds, which is quite a lot.

Altogether over 30 Objects have been found in the scene. This includes each component of each GameObject in the scene. The Camera, light, transform components, etc are all listed. So how do we find a specific Object like a Parent or Child?

```
ObjectParent parent = o as ObjectParent;
if (parent != null)
{
    Debug.Log("FoundParent:" + parent);
}
```

The addition to the loop will now look for all Parents in the scene. This oddly includes the ObjectChild since it inherited from ObjectParent, so it's counted as a ParentType. The first line `Object parent = o as ObjectParent;` is what is called a cast. We'll learn more about that in Section 6.5.3 again, but it's important to know how Object is the base class for all Unity Objects, and Parent is the base from which Child inherits.

> ① FoundParent:ObjectParent (ObjectParent)
>   UnityEngine.Debug:Log(Object)
>
> ① FoundParent:ObjectChild (ObjectChild)
>   UnityEngine.Debug:Log(Object)

NOTE: You could enter `Component.FindObjectsOfType()`, and this will work the same as though it were called from `Object` or `GameObject`. Inheritance is a complex topic, and right now, we're only observing how functions can be shared from the parent to children, but there's a problem when children try to share. We've used `GameObject.CreatePrimitive()` to make cubes and spheres. And we know Object has FindObjectsOfType, which both GameObject and Component can use because of inheritance. Therefore, does that mean Object.CreatePrimitive will work?

Actually, no; Object doesn't inherit functions of variables from its children. In programming, parents don't learn from their kids. Suppose `GameObject.CreatePrimitive()` is a function found in GameObject, and GameObject and Component both inherit from Object; does that mean `Component.CreatePrimitive()` will work? Again, no; in C#, children don't like to share. C# is a pretty tough family, but rules are rules.

Now we have a handle on getting an `ObjectChild` or `ObjectParent` if they're in the scene. So for instance, we could add in a `ParentObject parent;` and when we find one in the scene we assign the `Object o` to the `parent`.

5.3.4.1 A Type Is Not an Object

Type, as we've mentioned, is the name given to a class of an object. Like a vowel, or noun, type refers to the classification of a thing, not the actual thing itself. Semantics is important when dealing with programming, and it's very easy to miss the meanings behind how words are used. For instance, if we need to tell a function the type of a class, we can't simply use the class's name.

```
FindObjectsOfType(Object);
```

If the function expected the type Object and not the object of Object, you'd get an error. There's a subtle difference here. The type of an object is not the object itself. However, it's difficult to say "this is the type Child" and not the "Child" class object. The two things use the same word, so it's easy to confuse.

There is a function that will get the type of an object and satisfy functions that need types and not objects. And that's where `typeof(Object)` comes in. If we have the object Object `typeof(Object)`, we can put `Object` into the `typeof()` function and use that function as the type of an `Object` and not the class `Object`.

Give the `FindObjectsOfType()` function a `typeof(Object)` and it returns an array with every instance of Object in the scene. We can give the ObjectFinder.cs a Player to chase after. Just so we don't get confused what version of the word Player we're looking for, we should make it tremendously clear what we're looking for.

5.3.5 != null

To look for a GameObject with the ObjectChild script Add in a GameObject variable for the `ObjectFinder` at the class scope. The not null check is important. We'll find out why in Section 5.7.4, but for now we'll just observe how it's used.

```
GameObject foundObject;
void Update ()
{
    if (foundObject == null)
    {

    }
}
```

When the game is started `foundObject` starts off without anything assigned. Since it's not POD or Plain Old Data, the initialization of the GameObject is `null`. This is important since we'll check on this assignment in the `Update()` function in the `ObjectFinder` script.

```
if (foundObject == null)
{
    Object[] objects = FindObjectsOfType(typeof(GameObject));
    // a list of all game objects in the scene

    foreach (GameObject o in objects)
    {
        Debug.Log(o);
        ObjectChild child = o.GetComponent(typeof(ObjectChild)) as ObjectChild;
        if (child != null)
        {
            foundObject = o;
        }
    }
}
```

Like the previous code, we use `FindObjectsOfType`, but we use the `GameObject` as the type. We follow that with the same foreach, but we use `GameObject o` to list each object in the array. Then we use `ObjectChild child = o.GetComponent(typeof(ObjectChild)) as ObjectChild` to find individual components attached to the GameObject o.

Last and most important we use `if(child != null)` to assign the `foundObject` to the o in the foreach loop. The `child != null` statement is true if child is assigned. When a GameObject doesn't have a component that matches the `GetComponent` statement child is assigned `null`, or rather the child remains `null`.

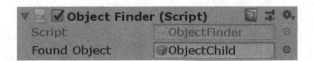

We can run the game, and check the foundObject variable. We'll see that it's ObjectChild, the gameObject in the scene Hierarchy.

The statement (thing != null) is commonly used to know when something has been found. When the something is not empty, you've found what it is you're looking for. This is a useful trick to apply for many different purposes. The statement (null != thing) can also be used. In some languages this might execute faster, but it's not as commonly used so it might look awkward.

5.3.6 What We've Learned

Using data to find data is a commonplace task in programming. With Unity 3D, we have plenty of functions available which make finding objects in a scene quite easy. When monsters go chasing after players, we need to have a simple system for allowing them to find one another.

Computers don't use senses like we do. They have another view of the game that can't be compared to how we, as players, perceive the world. By searching through data, and using algorithms, the computer-controlled characters require a different set of parameters to operate.

In one sense, the computer has complete knowledge over the game world. How that world is perceived by the computer requires our instruction. A monster's ability to understand its environment depends on our code.

5.4 Instancing

In the Instancing_Scene open the Instancing script attached to the game object of the same name. An important feature of C# and many C-like programming paradigms is the use of a class as a variable. When we use a class as a variable, it's created as a new object. Some of these classes are values, which means that the function itself can be used to assign to variables, and many classes are used as values. Using a class as an object which is itself a value is at the heart of object-oriented programming.

To make use of a class, or object, we often need to create a new instance of the class. Instancing is basically creating space in memory for a class of a more complex data type. We do this in the same way we create a variable for a simple data type. However, when assigning a value to the variable of this sort, we need to change things up a bit.

The Vector3 class is located in the guts of the UnityEngine library. Open the Object Browser. Inside there, and change the option to view namespaces and find the Vector3 object.

```
⊕ Angle(UnityEngine.Vector3, UnityEngine.Vector3)
⊕ AngleBetween(UnityEngine.Vector3, UnityEngine.Vector3)
⊕ ClampMagnitude(UnityEngine.Vector3, float)
⊕ Cross(UnityEngine.Vector3, UnityEngine.Vector3)
⊕ Distance(UnityEngine.Vector3, UnityEngine.Vector3)
⊕ Dot(UnityEngine.Vector3, UnityEngine.Vector3)
⊕ Equals(object)
⊕ Equals(UnityEngine.Vector3)
⊕ Exclude(UnityEngine.Vector3, UnityEngine.Vector3)
⊕ GetHashCode()
⊕ Lerp(UnityEngine.Vector3, UnityEngine.Vector3, float)
⊕ LerpUnclamped(UnityEngine.Vector3, UnityEngine.Vector3, float)
```

Selecting the `Vector3` object you will find that the contents are arranged alphabetically to make things easier to find.

Don't let this cacophony of information bewilder you. We only need to deal with a small portion of these objects to get started. Later, we'll be able to browse the classes in each one of these DLLs and look for classes we can include in our code.

5.4.1 Class Initialization

The reason why we don't need to create an instance for an int or a bool is that they are built-in types found in the system library. We also create our own types every time we write a new class. for our own game. Yes, we get to invent new types of data. For instance, you'll need a player type and a monster type.

For these new types, we'll want to store the status of their health and possibly their ammunition. These bits of information can be any value; however, they are usually ints or floats. Of course, to store a player's location in the world, we'll want to include a Vector3, inferring that a type can contain many other non-primitive types. Eventually, everything in the game will have a class and a type of its own.

In C#, the built-in types do not need a constructor. We'll get into constructors when we start instancing objects later in this chapter. Plain old data types (PODs) include not only the built-in types but structures and arrays as well. The term came from the C++ standards committee, and was used to describe data types that were similar between C and C++. This term can be extended to C# that shares the same POD types.

5.4.2 New

The new keyword is used to create a new instance of an object. Some data types that are assigned to a variable, do not need the new keyword. For example, when you declare an int, you simply need to set it to a number, as in `int i = 7;`. This declaration creates space in memory for an int named `i`, and then sets the value for `i` to 7. However, for more complex data types, like a Vector3, you may need to give three different float values. Unity 3D calls a 3D vector a Vector3, because there are three values stored in it: `x`, `y`, and `z`.

```
// creates new int i assigns 7
int i = 7;

/* creates new int j and assigns  *
 * a new int, but it's not given   *
 * any value.                     */
int j = new int();
```

The MonoBehaviour acts a bit differently. There are several constructs that are constructed with the new keyword within the MonoBehaviour, but MonoBehaviours are components that are added with a different method.

A MonoBehaviour related script is something attached to a gameObject in the scene. The Instancing. cs script attached to the gameObject in the Instancing_Scene is attached to a game object. The following attaches an example to the same game object the Instancing script is already attached to:

```
/* creates and assigns      *
 * Thing t to a new Thing    */
Thing t = new Thing();

/* creates and assigns                      *
 * Example e to new Example : MonoBejaviour  */
Example e = gameObject.AddComponent<Example>();
```

The notation seen is not regular usage of C# scripting conventions for instancing an object, but that's okay. C# allows for a lot of flexibility and the Unity conventions use this to its advantage. The explanation for the above will have to wait until a few other concepts have been discussed. It's important to understand that there's more than one system to create an instance of a class.

NOTE: Unity 3D also has a Vector2 and a Vector4 type. These are instanced in the same way as a Vector3, but have more specific uses. Vector2 only has an x and y value; Vector4 has an additional vector, w, after x, y, and z.

Normally, in 3D space, you'd need only a Vector3, but when dealing with something called quaternions, you'll need the extra fourth number in a vector; we'll get into this a bit later on.

Remember, declaring a variable starts with the type followed by the name we're assigning to the variable. Normally, you'd start with something like Vector3 SomeVector;. The difference comes in when assigning a value to the variable. To do this, we start with the new keyword, followed by the Vector3's initialization.

5.4.3 Constructors

Constructors add an extra, but necessary, step when using a variable type that's derived from an object class. With many classes, there are different ways in which they can be initialized with a constructor. Most initializations can be done without any parameters, as in the following example.

```
void Start()
{
    Vector3 vector = new Vector3();
    Debug.Log(vector);
}
```

The use of a pair of parentheses after the type refers to a constructor, or a set of parameters that can be used to build the instance when it's created. Peek at the Vector3 object and you'll see some definitions called public Vector3(float x, float y); and public Vector3(float x, float y, float z); in the opened window.

```
Vector3 vector = new Vector3(1.0f, 1.0f);
```

```
                                                    Vector3 [from metadata] ⓐ ▾ ✕
        // Parameters:                                                        ▲
        //   x:
        //
        //   y:
        public Vector3(float x, float y);
    ...  public Vector3(float x, float y, float z);
```

Constructors are named the same as the class. There's always going to be an assumed () version, with no parameters for construction. There can be any number of alternative constructors. In this case, there are two additional constructors created for Vector3().

We should also note that float is another name for single, as seen in the Assembly Browser. The word *double*, which we've mentioned in Section 4.5, has twice the amount of space in memory to store a value than a single; a single is a 32-bit floating point, and a double is a 64-bit floating point value.

We can add information, or parameters, when initializing a new Vector3 type variable. Parameters, also known as arguments, the values added to the parenthesis of a function. The different parameters are setting variables within the class we're instancing. Inside of a Vector3, there is an x, y, and z variable. Like the variables we've been using. When using parameters, we can get some guides from our integrated development environment (IDE).

Hover over the Vector3() as you type in Visual Studio you'll see the following helper dialog.

Vector3()

> ⬡ Vector3.Vector3() (+ 2 overloads)

The pop-up indicates alternative constructors for the Vector3 are available. To use the vector we created, we'll assign the object in Unity's Transform, in the Position component, to the vector variable we just assigned. This assignment will move the object to the assigned Vector3 position. We'll go into further detail on how to know what a component expects when assigning a variable when we start to explore the classes that Unity 3D has written for us.

```
Vector3 vector = new Vector3(1.0f, 2.0f, 3.0f);
transform.position = vector;
```

When this class is attached to the Main Camera in the scene and the Play-in-Editor button is pressed, we will see the following in Unity 3D. Notice entries for Position in Transform roll out in Inspector.

The declaration and initialization of a new vector requires an extra step. For instance, this situation can be translated into English as follows: "I'm making a new Vector3, and I'm naming it to vector. Then I'm assigning the x, y, and z to 1.0f, 2.0f, and 3.0f. Then, I'm setting the position in the Transform component to vector." Likewise, the shorter version could simply be "I'm setting the Position in the Transform component to a Vector3, with x, y, and z set to 1.0f, 2.0f, and 3.0f."

NOTE: Natural language programming, like the English translation above, has been tried before. However, the compiler's job would be to both interpret and translate English into byte code, and this has proven to be quite tricky. Interpretation of English is part intuition and part assumption. Neither of these abilities can be easily programmed into software to work consistently and perfectly predictably.

Various ways to program computers using different formatting options to make code more humanly readable have been tried many times. In the end, the formatting almost always ends up using more and more keywords, which restrains the programmer by taking away the options and freedoms that are allowed when fewer rules are applied.

You can also use an initialized vector without assigning it to a variable name first. This is perfectly valid; when Position in the object's Transform component is set, it's automatically assigned a Vector3 that's created just for the position.

```
transform.position = new Vector3(1.0f, 2.0f, 3.0f);
```

Once a new class has been initialized, you can modify the individual variables found inside of the Vector3 class. A variable found in a class is referred to as a member variable of the class. We'll go into more detail in Section 6.3.2 about what sort of variables and functions can be found in a class that Unity 3D has written for your benefit. To change one of these variables inside of a class, you simply need to assign it a value like any other variable.

```
Vector3 vector = new Vector3(1.0f, 2.0f, 3.0f);
vector.x = 3.0f;
transform.position = vector;
```

There's an interesting difference here. An f has been used: the 3.0f is assigned to the x member of vector. This informs the compiler that we're assigning a float type number to vector.x and not a double. By default, any number with a decimal with no special designation is assumed to be a double number type.

Some parameters for constructors could be expanded into their own scope. For some clarity, you're able to add a scope for the constructor of the Vector3() instantiation. In the scope live the parameter names that are used in the object being instanced.

```
Vector3 vector = new Vector3()
{
    x = 1.0f,
    y = 2.0f,
    z = 3.0f
};
transform.position = vector;
```

To tell Unity 3D we're assigning a float to the x member of vector, we need to add the suffix f after the number. This changes the number's type to float. This is related to type casting, which we will cover in Section 6.5.3. It's also worth noting that you're allowed to omit some initializations using this notation. In this form, x and y are left at 0.

```
Vector3 vector = new Vector3()
{
    z = 3.0f
};
transform.position = vector;
```

We can also assign POD as an object.

```
int i = new int();
Debug.Log("new int(): " + i); //new int(): 0
```

Adding this after the previous code block, we'll get 0 sent to the Unity 3D Console panel. We don't need to do things like this for all data types, but it's interesting to see that it's possible. Most data types can be initialized in this way. There are some tricky constructors, like string, which need some additional work for us, to understand the parameter list. The details here will have to wait till Section 6.4 in the book.

5.4.4 What We've Learned

The examples in this section created Vector3s in various ways. Setting variables in an object is controlled by how that object was written. The visibility of the variables in the Vector3 class is determined in the same fashion as we have declared variables in the objects that we have been writing. We can make changes to the x, y, and z float variables in the Vector3 class because of their public declaration.

Each nuance and use of the C# language takes some time to get used to. When certain tasks are shortened into easier-to-write code, the code ends up being harder to read. However, most of the harder tasks often have a commonly used format. These shorthand formats are sometimes called idioms.

Idioms in English do not often make the most sense when logically analyzed, but they do have specific meanings. Much like in English, programming idioms might not make sense when you look at them, but they do have a specific meaning when in use. As we make further progress, you'll be introduced to some of the more commonly used idioms in C#.

Complex objects like MonoBehaviours require several steps for the Editor and Game to come together. For this reason, MonoBehaviours do several things behind the scenes that take care of special case constructors. When you drag a script onto a game object in the scene it's not simply calling on a Constructor to attach the script. Updating the UI (user interface), creating meta files, and the like also need to take place. None of this is required of the scripts you're going to be writing, but it's important to know why we don't use new when instancing a MonoBehaviour derived class.

5.5 Static

Open the Chapter5 Unity Project's Static_Scene and open the Static script on the game object of the same name. The static keyword is a keyword that ties all instances of a class together. This allows all instances of a class to share a common variable or function. When you see static next to a function, this means you don't need to make a new instance of the class to use it. Because static functions and variables are class-wide, we access them in a slightly different way than an instance of a variable or function.

There is a static function found inside of Input called `GetKey()`, which we will use. The last keyword is bool, after public and static. We've seen bool before, but this is used as a return type. When we write our own functions, we'll also include our own return type, but just so you know, return types are not limited to bool. Functions can return any data type, and now we'll take a look at how this all works.

5.5.1 A Basic Example

Let's start with the Static_Scene in Chapter 5 Unity Project and open the Static script attached to the Static Game Object in the scene. The code here will send the following to the Console panel in Unity 3D.

```
void Update()
{
    bool aKey = Input.GetKey(KeyCode.A);
    if (aKey)
    {
        Debug.Log("aKey");
    }
}
```

The KeyCode object has a public variable for each key on your computer's keyboard. The `Input.GetKey()` function returns the `bool` value based on which the key is checked in the `KeyCode` object. We assign the bool `aKey` to the returned value from the `Input.GetKey(KeyCode.A)` function.

The statement for if (aKey) executes the `Debug.Log("aKey");` which then prints out "aKey" to the Unity Console window. The `GetKey()` function is a member of the Input class and is accessed by using the dot operator (.). Now that we're reading libraries we need to know how to get to the members of the classes we're looking at. Peek at the definition and you'll see other static accessible members in the Input class.

```
public static bool GetKey(KeyCode key);
...public static bool GetKeyDown(KeyCode key);
...public static bool GetKeyDown(string name);
...public static bool GetKeyUp(KeyCode key);
...public static bool GetKeyUp(string name);
...public static bool GetMouseButton(int button);
...public static bool GetMouseButtonDown(int button);
...public static bool GetMouseButtonUp(int button);
...public static Touch GetTouch(int index);
...public static bool IsJoystickPreconfigured(string joystickName);
...public static void ResetInputAxes();
```

We're shown `public static bool GetKey(KeyCode key)` as the function's definition. You'll notice that we never made an instance of Input. To use the Input class, we didn't need to create an Instance of the Input object first. The static members of a class don't need to be initialized before they're used.

This process provides us with the beginnings of a player controller script. Filling in the rest of the WASD keys on the keyboard will allow you to log the rest of the most common movement keys on your keyboard. The Input class is found in UnityEngine that was included in this class with the using UnityEngine directive at the top of the class.

From previous chapter lessons, you might imagine that we'd need to create an instance of Input to make use of its member functions or fields. This might look like the following:

```
Input input = new Input();
bool aKey = input.GetKey(KeyCode.A);
```

> [◆] (local variable) Input input
>
> Member 'Input.GetKey(KeyCode)' cannot be accessed with an instance reference; qualify it with a type name instead

While this syntactically makes sense, and the practice so far has been to make an instance to use its members. The `GetKey()` function is static, so we get an error when we try to use a static function. This will make more sense once we write our own static function later in this chapter.

```
Input input = new Input();
bool aKey = input.
```

> bool object.Equals(object obj)   ◈ Equals
> Note: Tab twice to insert the 'Equals' snippet.   ◈ GetHashCode
>   ◈ GetType
> }   ◈ ToString

When we check for any functions in the input object after it's been instanced, we won't find much. The only things available are universal among all things inheriting from the object class.

The lack of functions or variables is because all the functions and variables have been marked as static, so they're inaccessible through an *instance* of Input. Statically marked functions and variables become inaccessible through an instance. This inaccessibility is related to an object's interface and encapsulation. This doesn't mean that they are completely inaccessible, however; but to see them, we'll need to write our own class with our own functions and variables.

5.5.2 Static Variables

Let's start off with a simple concept: a static variable. Using our previous analogy of toasters, each new toaster built in a factory has a unique identity. Each unit built would have a different serial number. Once in someone's house, the number of times the toasters have been used, when they are turned on and begin to toast, and their location in the world are all unique to each toaster. What they all share is the total number of toasters that exist.

The static keyword means that the function or variable is global to the class it's declared in. Let's make this clear; by declaring a variable as static, as in static `int i;`, you're indicating that you want to use the int i without needing to make an instance of the class that the variable is found in. Variables that are unique to each instance of a class are called *instance variables*. All instances of the class will share the static variable's value regardless of their instanced values.

If we create a mob of zombies, we might find it important to maintain a certain number of zombies. Too many and the computer will have problems keeping up. Too few and the player will go around with nothing to shoot at. To give ourselves an easier time, we can give each zombie a *telepathic* connection with all other zombies. A programmer would call this a *static variable* or a *static function*.

As we've seen, variables usually live a short and isolated life. For instance, the variable used in the ever-powerful for loop exists only within the for loop's code block. Once the loop is done, the variable in the for loop is no longer used and can't be accessed outside of the loop.

```
for (int i = 0; i < 10; i++)
{
    Debug.Log(i); // prints 1 to 10
}
// i no longer exists.
Debug.Log(i); //i is undefined.
```

Now that we're creating objects based on classes, we need to make those classes interact with one another in a more convenient way. To keep track of the number of undead zombies in a scene, we could have the player keep track; as each zombie is created or destroyed, a message could be sent to the player.

The Player class keeping track of important zombie data is awkward. Zombie-related data should remain in the zombie class, unrelated classes should not depend on one another in this way. The more spread out your code gets, the more problems you'll have debugging the code. Creating self-contained classes is important, and prevents a web of interdependent code, sometimes referred to as spaghetti code.

Remember that when an object is created it's instanced from a single original blueprint, which can include some variables that are shared between each instance of the class. With static variables instanced cases can talk to the blueprint for a common connection between any new instances made from it.

5.5.2.1 A Basic Example

```
public class Zombie : MonoBehaviour
{
    public static int numZombies;
    void Start ()
    {
        numZombies++;
    }
}
```

Here, in a pretty simple-looking zombie class, we've got a `static` keyword placed before an `int` identified as numZombies. This statement turns `int numZombies`, which would normally be confined to this class alone, to an int that's shared among all zombies. As Unity 3D creates more zombies, each zombie has its `Start()` function called once the class has been instanced: numZombies increments by 1.

With the above code attached to a collection of different capsules, we'll be better able to see how many zombies there are in the scene through code. Just be sure that each capsule has the zombie script attached.

```
void Start ()
{
    numZombies++;
    Debug.Log(numZombies);
}
```

The `Debug.Log()` function in each Zombie's `Start()` function prints out the numZombies value. Each new instance of a Zombie increments the same numZombies variable.

By knowing how many zombies are around, you can change a zombie's behavior, making them more aggressive, perhaps. Maybe only after five zombies have been spawned, they'll join one another and perform a dance routine. Having a shared property makes keeping track of a similar variable much easier.

When the same code is run without static before the numZombies variable, the following output is the result:

The numZombies value is independent to each instance of the zombie class. When each new Zombie instance is created it's numZombies int is initialized independently to 0. When the Start () function is called in each zombie instance the numZombies value is incremented independently from 0 to 1. Therefore when white, rob and stubbs call their own Start () function their own instance of the numZombies int is incremented, numZombies doesn't get incremented for all zombies because it's not static.

This is an interesting concept here. Up to this point, we've been thinking of classes as encapsulated independent entities. With the static keyword, there's a way to keep the separated objects connected to one another through a variable. This raises the question: Can this be done with functions?

5.5.3 Static Functions

Static functions act on behalf of all instances of the class they are a member of. They work only with static variables of the class. If we extend our zombie class with a new static function, we can use the zombie class to call a static function that can read static variables. To make the static function accessible to other classes we need to make the static function public as well.

```
public static void CountZombies()
{
    Debug.Log(numZombies);
}
```

Then we'll add a call to Zombie.CountZombies(); to find out how many zombies have been created in the Update() function of the static class, by adding it to the if (AKey) code block.

```
bool aKey = Input.GetKey(KeyCode.A);
if (aKey)
{
    Zombie.CountZombies();
}
```

Now when the A key on the keyboard is pressed, we'll get a count printed to the Console panel indicating the number of zombies in the scene along with the `Debug.Log("aKey");` Console log.

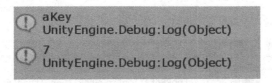

The number being printed out comes from the `public static void CountZombies();` function call being made to Zombie, not from any of the instances of the zombie class attached to the capsules in the scene.

To call static functions, you use the class name, not the name of an instanced object made from the zombie class. As you can see, there's more than one way the class identifier is used. Up to this point, we've been using the class name mostly to create an instance of that class. With a static function or variable, the class identifier is used to access that static member of the class.

5.5.4 Putting It All Together

To build a simple example with our Zombie we'll want him to chase after a player in the scene. To do that we'll open the Zombie_Scene in the Chapter5 project and add to the zombie script we've been working with. Attached to the Robo character in the scene is a Player script. To find the player we'll use the same technique as before where we use `FindObjectsOfType()`.

```
public Player player;
private void Update()
{
    if (player == null)
    {
        /* Find the player */
        player = FindObjectOfType(typeof(Player)) as Player;
    }
}
```

Once we have a handle on the script attached to the Player GameObject we can now add in a method to Move our Zombie to the player. To make use of the MoveToPlayer function we'll add the following to the `Update()`.

```
if (player != null)
{
    MoveToPlayer();
}
```

By checking that the player is not null we make sure that the reference to the player object is there and not null. And to start, our MoveToPlayer will look like the following:

```
void MoveToPlayer()
{
}
```

If you remember the system we used for the MoveToPoint script, we'll do the same again here.

```
void MoveToPlayer()
{
    Vector3 playerPos = player.gameObject.transform.position;

    Vector3 towardPlayer = playerPos - transform.position;
    transform.position = Vector3.Lerp(transform.position, playerPos, Time.deltaTime);

    Quaternion direction = Quaternion.LookRotation(towardPlayer, transform.up);
    transform.rotation = Quaternion.Slerp(transform.rotation, direction, Time.deltaTime * 5f);
}
```

At this point pressing the Play-in-Editor button should have a group of zombies marching at the player.

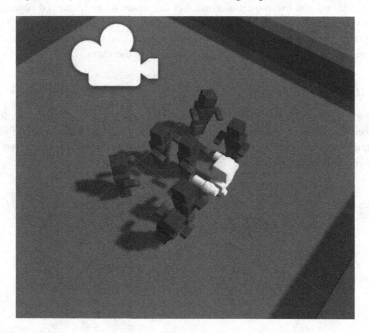

Now that the zombies are moving, it's time to get the player moving. For this we'll use a simple WASD to move the robot around.

```
public class Player : MonoBehaviour
{
    void Update()
    {
        bool w = Input.GetKey(KeyCode.W);
        bool a = Input.GetKey(KeyCode.A);
        bool s = Input.GetKey(KeyCode.S);
        bool d = Input.GetKey(KeyCode.D);
    }
}
```

Next, we a value is created for the *x* and *y* axis of input. These are used to add to the position of the character.

```
float xAxis = 0;
float yAxis = 0;
```

Next we'll use the Booleans we created for the input and use them to add or subtract from each axis.

```
if (w)
{
    yAxis += 1;
}
if (a)
{
    xAxis -= 1;
}
if (s)
{
    yAxis -= 1;
}
if (d)
{
    xAxis += 1;
}
```

Then finally we apply the new values to the direction we want to move in. The transform component has a forward value as well as a right value. Multiply these values by either +1 or −1 when a key is down. If no keys are down then we multiply the forward or right value by 0, which means we add no new value to the current direction.

```
Vector3 direction = transform.position;
direction += transform.forward * yAxis;
direction += transform.right * xAxis;
```

Once we have a vector which represents where we want to go, we can apply it to where we are.

```
transform.position = Vector3.Lerp(transform.position, direction, Time.deltaTime * 5f);
```

Next, to get the robot to rotate using Q and E:

```
bool q = Input.GetKey(KeyCode.Q);
bool e = Input.GetKey(KeyCode.E);
float rot = 0;
if (q)
{
    rot -= 10;
}
if (e)
{
    rot += 10;
}
transform.Rotate(new Vector3(0, rot, 0));
```

We handle the rotation much like we handled the positioning.

5.5.5 What We've Learned

Using static functions certainly layers a distinctive level of complexity on an already complex understanding of what a class is. Not only do classes have functions talking to one another, they can also share information.

You should use a static variable only if all the classes of the same type need to share a common parameter. This goes the same for a static function. We'll go further into how static functions can help in Section 6.11, when we get back to some of the more complex behaviors, but for now, we'll leave off here.

Moving forward, we'll want to keep in mind that C# has static variables and functions for a specific reason. There are efficiency and optimization considerations to keep in mind as well. For instance, the player's `transform.position` is the same for each zombie. Each zombie doesn't need to have its own instance variable for the player. We could have easily converted the `Vector3 position;` in the player class to a static value.

```
public static Vector3 position;
```

The `static Vector3 position;` variable could then be used by the zombies in the following manner.

```
Vector3 direction = (Player.position - transform.position).normalized;
float distance = (Player.position - transform.position).magnitude;
```

This certainly works, and it might be considered easier to read. This would even make the `GameObject player;` obsolete since `Player.position` is a static value, and you don't need to use `GameObject.Find()` to begin with. This type of optimization should be thought of as you look at your code and discover new ways to make it more efficient and easier to read.

5.6 Building A Game—Part 3

In the previous game-building chapter, we first looked at moving around a character Section 4.3. Then we looked at shooting projectiles in Section 4.10. Immobile red blocks don't stand a chance against a rapid-fire missile launcher. To add challenge, the targets should move and shoot back.

To start off we'll want a system for our bad guys to be able to find the player. We just covered static which is a great way to store a variable for anyone to access.

5.6.1 The Player

```
public class Player : MonoBehaviour
{
    public static GameObject ThePlayer;
    /*                              ↑         */
    private void Start()/*          |         */
    {   /*      ┌───────────────────┘         */
        /*      ↑                             */
        ThePlayer = this.gameObject;
        /*      ↑                  ↓          */
        /*      └──────────────────┘          */
        /*      assign the static            */
        /*      to this gameObject           */
    }
}
```

The static variables become accessible to any other object. This works to enable the bad guys to find the player. The Start() functions in the scene finishes before the first Update() is called by any other object in the scene.

5.6.2 The Mover

```
private GameObject _Target;
protected GameObject Target
{
    get
    {
        if (_Target == null)
        {
            // find the player, keep
            // a reference to it.
            _Target = Player.ThePlayer;
        }
        return _Target;
    }
}
```

In the Mover.cs script we'll use the Player.ThePlayer variable and keep it around as a local variable. To limit problems, an accessor is used where the set statement is excluded.

```
protected virtual void Update()
{
    if (Target == null)
        return;
    Vector3 TargetDirection = GetDirection(Target);
    MoveTo(TargetDirection);
    LookAt(TargetDirection);
}
```

To stop pursuing a Target after the player is gone, or is null, we stop our Update() with a null check. So long as the Target isn't null we get a TargetDirection, then MoveTo() and LookAt() the TargetDirection.

```
private Vector3 GetDirection(GameObject target)
{
    Vector3 myPosition = transform.position;
    Vector3 otherPosition = target.transform.position;
    return otherPosition - myPosition;
}
```

The GetDirection() function returns the Vector3 pointing at a given GameObject. This value is used by the following MoveTo() and LookAt() functions. The direction is likely to change during each update, so it's refreshed at the start of the Update() function.

```
private void MoveTo(Vector3 targetDirection)
{
    Rigidbody rb = GetComponent<Rigidbody>();
    rb.AddForce(targetDirection, ForceMode.Force);
}
```

The MoveTo() function applies a force in the direction of the target. Get the rigid body component attached to the player and give it a push in that direction. The rigid body has a few settings to look at to make sure that this works out well.

The Capsule Collider and the RigidBody work together. The collider gives the rigid body a shape, then the rigid body gives the Collider physical properties like mass and drag. Here the drag has been set to 1 to make sure that the bad guy doesn't skate around like it's on ice.

```
private void LookAt(Vector3 targetDirection)
{
    Quaternion look = Quaternion.LookRotation(targetDirection);
    transform.rotation = Quaternion.RotateTowards(transform.rotation, look, 15f);
}
```

The last thing we do is turn the bad guy around so he's looking at the player. The LookRotation() function in Quaternion gives us a rotation value. We then plug the look direction into the RotateTowards() function. The result is assigned to the bad guy's rotation value.

5.6.3 The Shooter

Inheritance means we don't need to copy too much code. Though we can see where some cross over can come into place between very similar classes. The ProjectileWeapon class isn't very complex. But we should still observe some optimizations.

```
public class Shooter : Mover
{
    public GameObject ProjectileObject;
    public GameObject ProjectileStart;
    public AudioClip BlasterShotClip;
    private float NextTime;
    public float RateOfFire;
```

The Shooter inherits from Mover. We also see a few members that look like they were copied out of the ProjectileWeapon class. That's because they were. Regardless, we inherit from Mover for a more specific reason.

```
protected override void Update()
{
    base.Update();
    ShootAt();
}
```

In Mover, the Update() function a protected virtual function. This doesn't change the fact that it's called by MonoBehaviour during the Update() cycle of the game. We take advantage of this by using the base.Update() from the Mover. Shooter inherits the MoveTo() and LookAt() functions. After the base.Update() is called we then call the ShootAt() function.

```
private void ShootAt()
{
    if (Time.time > NextTime)
    {
        NextTime = Time.time + NextShot(RateOfFire);
        Vector3 pos = ProjectileStart.transform.position;
        Quaternion rot = ProjectileStart.transform.rotation;
        Instantiate(ProjectileObject, pos, rot);
        GetComponent<AudioSource>().PlayOneShot(BlasterShotClip);
    }
}
```

A minor change here includes the ShootAt() has the same setup as the Update() loop from the ProjectileWeapon class. We exclude the critical Input.GetMouseButton() check to see if the right mouse button is being pressed.

The Shooter's script component has a greatly reduced Rate Of Fire. Once there is more than one weapon in the scene the game comes to an end much faster. This is especially true if all the projectiles are aimed at the player.

5.6.4 Physics Settings

To keep things all in check on the physics, the colliders that are on both the Bad Guys and the Player are set to the Target tag. The projectiles are set to the Projectile tag. Tags allow a filter to enable the physics certain leeway to enable specific objects to pass through some colliders and hit others. In the grid above the Projectile/Target box is checked. This means that the projectiles can only contact a target. The Target/Target checkbox is also checked to prevent the characters from passing through one another.

The start point is placed away from the character. This is to ensure that the projectile doesn't contact the BadGuy or the Player as the projectile is instantiated. The z axis (the blue arrow) indicates the forward direction of the starting point.

Once there are more than a few shooters in the scene we get a lot of friendly fire. We could add a few more physics filters to prevent this, but it's better to enjoy the crazy explosions for a few moments before the player is also obliterated.

5.6.5 What We've Learned

Physics layers, inheritance, and simple small classes are the key to quickly building a fun game. It may be worthwhile to make `ProjectileWeapon` more modular and reusable, but code is easily copied and pasted between classes anyway.

Monolithic classes which handle a multitude of responsibilities are cumbersome. Making small classes with few responsibilities allows us to attach multiple behaviors to GameObjects. Small classes make adding new layers of behavior much easier.

We saw a lot of terminology here that's yet to be covered more formally. It's important to understand how the code works in more situations than what we've seen here. This project only serves as one example of infinite possibilities.

5.7 Jump Statements and Return

Follow along with the JumpStatements_Scene Unity 3D scene in the Chapter5 Unity Project. Then open the JumpStatements script found in the scene on the JumpStatements game object. Suppose you're in the process of looking for a specific color of crayon in a large assortment of art tools. After grabbing handfuls of different pencils and pens, you find the crayon you want and stop looking through the rest of your bin. You've just used a jump statement and returned to your work with the colored crayon of your desire.

The keywords `break` and `continue` come in particularly handy when sorting through a list of objects. Like `return`, these keywords stop the function from further execution or they jump to a different part of the same function. return has the additional feature of coming out of a function with a value. We have looked at these keywords briefly before, but it's important to get a better understanding of break, continue, and return in use.

The keyword `continue` restarts a loop from the top and then continues the function again, whereas break stops the block of code it's in altogether.

5.7.1 Return

We need to love the `return` keyword. This keyword turns a function into data. There are a couple of conditions that need to be met before this will work. So far, we've been using the keyword `void` to declare the return type of a function. This looks like the following code fragment.

```
void Function()
{
}
```

In this case, using return will be simple.

```
void MyFunction()
{
    // code here...
    return;
}
```

This function returns `void`. This statement has a deeper meaning. Returning a value makes a lot more sense when a real value, something other than a `void`, is actually returned. Let's look at a function that has more meaning.

The keyword `void` at the beginning of the function declaration means that this function does not have a return type. If we change the declaration, we need to ensure that there is a returned value that matches the declaration. This can be as simple as the following code fragment.

```
int MyIntFunction()
{
    //return 1.0f;
    return 1; // 1 is an int
}
```

This function returns int 1. Declaring a function with a return value requires that the return type and the declaration match. When the function is used, it should be treated like a data type that matches the function's return type.

5.7.1.1 A Basic Example

Here is a quick review class that has a function declared as `int MyNumber()` in the `Start()` function.

```
int MyNumber()
{
    return 7;
}
void Start()
{
    int a = MyNumber();
    Debug.Log(a);
}
```

When this code block is executed in the scene, 7 is printed to the Console panel. The function `MyNumber()` returned 7 when it was called. When we add some parameters to the function, we can make the return statement much more useful.

```
int MyAdd(int a, int b)
{
    return a + b;
}
```

```
void Start()
{
    int add = MyAdd(6, 7);
    Debug.Log(add);
}
```

In this fragment, we have `int MyAdd(int a, int b)`, which we then assign to int a in the `Start()` function. This prints 13 to the Console when run. We can skip a step to make the code a bit shorter.

```
Debug.Log(MyAdd(11, 12));
```

This code produces the same 13 being printed to the Console panel and should make it clear that the function can easily be used as a value.

5.7.2 Returning Objects

We can get something more interesting out of a function once it begins to return something more substantial than a simple number—this would be a more significant uses of return.

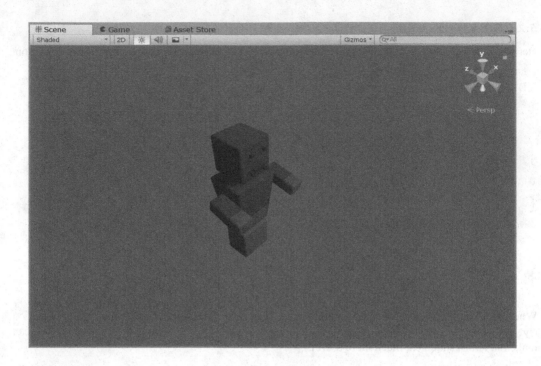

In the JumpStatements_Scene in the Chapter5 Unity Project we have a single Zombie. In the JumpStatements script on the JumpStatements game object we'll add a function that returns type Zombie.

```
Zombie GetZombie()
{
    return (Zombie)FindObjectOfType(typeof(Zombie));
}
```

Adding a `Debug.Log(GetZombie());` to the `Start()` function and we'll have the following text sent to the Console panel in Unity 3D.

5.7.3 A Class Is a Type

Our function that returns a Zombie, is at the end of our Unity 3D C# default template. We've called our function `GetZombie()`, and we're using a simple function provided in `GameObject` called `FindObjectOfType();`, which requires a *type* to return. The different classes we create become a new type. Much as an int is a type, a `Zombie` is now a type that we created in a new class called `Zombie`. This goes the same for every class we've created, which are all types.

To inform the `FindObjectOfType()` function of the type, we use the function `typeof(Zombie)`, which tells the function that we're looking for a type `Zombie`, not an actual zombie. There's a subtle difference between telling someone we'd like a thing that is a kind of zombie, not a specific zombie. We'll get into the specifics of types in Section 6.5.3 that focuses on dealing with types, but we're more interested in return, so we'll get back to that.

```
public Zombie myZombie;
Zombie GetZombie()
{
    return (Zombie)FindObjectOfType(typeof(Zombie));
}

void Update()
{
    Debug.DrawLine(transform.position, myZombie.transform.position);
}
```

We'll leave a variable in the class for myZombie, and in the Update() we'll draw a line from the transform.position to the myZombie.transform.position. Debug.DrawLine() starts at one position and goes to another position. The second position is a function's transform.position.

```
myZombie = GetZombie();
Debug.Log(myZombie);
```

In the Start() function the GetZombie() function assigns the myZombie variable. When the scene is played in the editor look into the Scene panel, you'll see a white line being drawn between the push pin and the Zombie Primitive with the Zombie component added to it.

Another possible method to use would be to inquire how many zombies exist in the scene. If there are zombies then get one to draw a line. With the following method we use the static numZombies to count how many zombies are in the scene. Then we use GetZombie() as an object to draw a line to the position of the Zombie it returns.

```
if (Zombie.numZombies > 0)
{
    Debug.DrawLine(transform.position, GetZombie().transform.position);
}
```

This remarkably means that the `GetZombie().transform.position` is returning the value as though the function is the `Zombie` itself, which has some interesting consequences. Having classes, or rather objects, communicate between one another is a particularly important feature of any programming language. Accessing members of another class through a function is just one way our objects can talk to one another.

This reliance on the function breaks if there are no zombies in the scene. What would happen if we were to deactivate the Zombie by checking it off in the Inspector panel while the code is running?

Unchecking here while the game is running will immediately bring up an error.

> NullReferenceException: Object reference not set to an instance of an object
> JumpStatements.Update () (at Assets/JumpStatements.cs:103)

A Null Reference Exception is caused when the return type of the function has nothing to return. Errors aren't good for performance and we should handle the problem more effectively. We need to make our use of the function more robust. Likewise, if you delete the ZombiePrimitive while the game is playing we'll get this error.

> MissingReferenceException: The object of type 'Zombie' has been destroyed but you are still trying to access it.
> Your script should either check if it is null or you should not destroy the object.

If we need to add a check to see if Zombie is null, doing so will avoid giving the `Debug.DrawLine()` function nonexistent data. We could hold onto a Zombie variable, and check each frame if the variable is not null. Better yet, we can add the following code to the Zombie script.

```
private void OnDestroy()
{
    numZombies--;
}
```

The code above decrements the `numZombies` static value. This means that a check to see if the number of zombies is greater than 0 will be false and we'll stop drawing lines when the last zombie is gone.

5.7.4 Tuples

Various languages like Lua allowed for more than one thing to be returned from a function. For C# to return a zombie and a number you'd need to create a struct which contained a zombie and a number.

```
struct ZombieNumber
{
    public Zombie Zombie;
    public int SomeNumber;
}

ZombieNumber RetrunsZombieAndNumber()
{
    ZombieNumber zombieNumber = new ZombieNumber();
    zombieNumber.Zombie = (Zombie)FindObjectOfType(typeof(Zombie));
    zombieNumber.SomeNumber = 1;
    return zombieNumber;
}
```

To create a struct and populate it every time a variety of information was required to come from a function would be cumbersome. The eventual population of numerous structs would get messy; each struct becomes a new type. The above does return the desired result:

```
ZombieNumber zn = RetrunsZombieAndNumber();
Debug.Log("Zombie: " + zn.Zombie + " Num:" + zn.SomeNumber);
// Zombie: ZombiePrimitive (Zombie) Num:1
```

The extra structs required for returning more than one value can be avoided using a tuple or "too-ple." A tuple is a system to organize data with names much like a struct. The return value of the function changes quite a lot when returning a tuple.

```
(Zombie zombie, int number) ReturnsTuple()
{
    Zombie z = (Zombie)FindObjectOfType(typeof(Zombie));
    int n = 1;
    var zombieNumber = (zombie: z, number: n);
    return zombieNumber;
}
```

Rather than void or a type, the tuple value looks a lot like a parameter signature for the function. The syntax works the same with a type followed by an identifier. The tuple above is a (Zombie zombie, int number) which means a Zombie and an int will be returned when the function is called.

```
var zn = ReturnsTuple();
Debug.Log("Zombie:" + zn.zombie + " Num:" + zn.number);
// Zombie: ZombiePrimitive (Zombie) Num:1
```

When the function is invoked the data is stored as a var. The var type is a just-in-time type, so var can accept practically any type value. Once it's assigned, its type becomes set. In the case var zn = ReturnsTuple(); the var zn is now a type that contains the zombie and number from the ReturnsTuple() function.

```
(string outString, int outInt, float outFloat ) ReturnsStringIntFloat()
{
    return (outString: "SomeString", outInt: 1, outFloat: 1f);
}
```

Visual studio will help fill in the tuple as you type it out.

```
return (outString:inString, )
```
    (string outString, **int outInt**, float outFloat)

The tuple requires you to fill in the output labels with the colon. These act a bit like optional arguments, something that will be covered in a later chapter. The value stored in a tuple can be decomposed from the var, but the data contained is recognized when printed as the following:

```
Debug.Log(ReturnsStringIntFloat());
// (SomeString, 1, 1)
```

Tuples have a variety of uses by combining data into an impromptu type. The simple return value use of the tuple is just one of the several uses of a tuple. We'll have to come back to that once we get into Linq in Section 8.8 since complex tricks are involved.

5.7.5 Null Is Not Void

There is conceptual difference between void, which is *nothing,* and null, which is more like *not something.* The word *void* means there is no intention of anything to be presented, whereas *null* implies that there can be something. We may add if (target != null) and can say that target can be empty or it can be Zombie. When target isn't a zombie, target is null; when it is there, it's Zombie.

```
Zombie target = GetZombie();
if (target != null)
    Debug.Log(target);
```

We may add if(target != null)—in more readable English, "if the target is not null"—and then conditionally execute the following code block. In the case where we have a target, we can draw a line from the camera's transform.position to the target's transform.position. This code alleviates the error, and thus we don't have to worry about sending Draw.DebugLine an error-inducing null reference.

5.7.6 What We've Learned

Functions that return class objects are quite useful. The properties that are associated with the class are accessible through the function that returns it. There are various jump statements that have different results.

The return statement has a clear purpose when it comes to jumping out of a function. Not all return jump statements need to be followed by a value. If the function is declared as void MyFunction(), the return statement only needs to be return; without any value following it.

We'll cover more jump statements in a following chapter.

5.8 Arrays: A First Look

Open the ArraysAFirstLoop_Scene and open the ArraysAFirstLoop script in the scene. Arrays are nicely organized lists of data. Think of a numbered list that starts at zero and extends one line every time you add something to the list. Arrays are useful for any number of situations because they're treated as a single hunk of data.

For instance, if you wanted to store a bunch of high scores, you'd want to do that with an array. Initially, you might want to have a list of 10 items. You could in theory use the following code to store each score.

```
int score1;
int score2;
int score3;
int score4;
int score5;
int score6;
int score7;
int score8;
int score9;
int score10;
/* if you've guess there's a much better way
 * to store lots of data like that then
 * you'd be correct.
 */
```

To make matters worse, if you needed to process each value, you'd need to create a set of code that deals with each variable by name. To check if `score2` is higher than `score1`, you'd need to write a function specifically to check those two variables before switching them. Thank goodness for arrays.

5.8.1 Fixed-Sized Arrays

An array can be initialized as a fixed-sized array, or an array can be created to be a resizable; we'll get to these types of arrays in Section 5.12. A fixed-sized array is easier to create, so we'll cover that first. Dynamic arrays require a more interesting step, where an array object is instantiated before it's used.

Arrays are a fundamental part of computer programming, in general. Without arrays, computers wouldn't be able to do what they're best at: repeating a simple task quickly and consistently. We'll be covering a few different types of arrays in Sections 5.11 and 5.12, and we'll be starting with the simplest type of array: the fixed-sized array.

5.8.1.1 A Basic Example

Let's start with the Arrays project and open the scene. The concept is simple in theory, but it's so much easier to see what's going on if you use the following code and check out what's going on in the Unity 3D Inspector panel. Attach this script to the Main Camera in an empty scene, and then take a look at what shows up.

```
public class ArraysAFirstLook : MonoBehaviour
{
    public int[] scores = new int[10];
}
```

The inclusion of the square brackets tells the compiler you're creating an array of ints and naming it scores. Because we're working with a built-in type of an int, each value stored in the array is initialized to 0. A new int[] array needs to be created before it's assigned to the scores array.

The best part is that the scores array is handled as a single object; we'll get into what that means in a moment. Rather than write a function to process one number value at a time we can write a function to deal with the array and process all the number values at once. We'll look at a simple sorting method in Section 7.9.4.

Assigning scores to int[10] creates an array with 10 items. As you might imagine, you can make larger or smaller arrays by changing the number in the square brackets. There aren't any limitations to the size you can assign to an array. Some common sense should apply, however; an array with many trillions of values might not be so useful.

Each chunk of data in the array is located by what is called an *index*. The index number is an integer value since it's not useful to ask for a value between the first and second entry in the array. Arrays can be created from something other than ints as well.

```
public string[] strings = new string[10];
public float[] floats = new float[10];
```

Both these statements create valid types of arrays. You are also allowed to create new data types and make arrays of those as well. An array can be created for any type, not just numbers and strings. This isn't necessarily a requirement. We can use any valid identifier to use for an array.

It's important to notice the difference between types. Floats, ints, and numbers in general will have 0 as the default value in the array when they are created. Strings, on the other hand, are initialized with nothing in the array; they are *null,* or, rather, they have no value assigned. You'll need to remember that an array can contain only a single type across all its entries. Therefore, an array of strings can contain only strings, an array of ints can contain only ints, and so on.

```
public string[] TopScoreList = new string[10];
```

The convention of using a plural does make for a more easily read variable name, but by no means is it necessary for identifying an array. Again, it's up to you to come up with readable variable names, and it's nice to use plurals for identifying an array.

```
public class MyClass
{
}
public MyClass[] MyClasses = new MyClass[10];
```

This creates a new class called MyClass, which for this example is a class of nothing. It's important that both sides of the MyClasses statement match. In the example above an array was created for the `MyClass` type. Unfortunately, because Unity isn't aware of what to do with MyClass, the array doesn't show up in the Inspector panel. Later, we'll figure out some ways to make this sort of information show up in Unity.

What makes an array in Unity more interesting is when we do not assign a number to set the size of the array. We can add the following statement to the list of other variables we've already added.

```
public GameObject[] GameObjects;
```

If we simply leave an array unassigned, we're free to set the size afterward. Select the Main Camera and click on the lock icon at the top right of the Inspector panel. This will prevent the Inspector from changing when you select something else in the scene. Then, select the other objects in the scene and drag them down to the `GameObjects` variable in the Inspector.

This action sets the size of the array once objects have been dragged into the array. However, this doesn't mean that the code is aware of the size of the array. The size of an array cannot easily be changed once it's been created. Therefore, how do we know how many objects are in an array? This can be accessed by the `.Length` property of the array type.

In the `Start()` function, we can use the following statement:

```
void Start()
{
    Debug.Log(GameObjects.Length);
}
```

Click the play icon and observe the Console panel. The `Debug.Log()` command will print out how many objects had been dragged into the array.

The number should reflect what is being observed in the Inspector panel, where we dragged objects into the array.

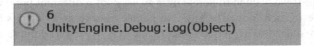

So far so good, but how do we use this? Now that we have an array of game objects from the scene, we're able to manipulate them in a for loop.

```
for (int i = 0; i < GameObjects.Length; i++)
{
    GameObjects[i].name = i.ToString();
}
```

This code changes the names of the game objects in the array to a number. The property of the array .Length returns an integer value which we can use for a few different reasons, the most practical use being to set the number of iterations in a for loop.

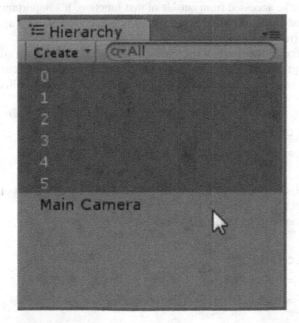

5.8.2 Foreach

This loop also happens to reflect how the objects are organized in the array. As we had experimented before with loops, we can use the array in a multitude of ways. We can also iterate over an array using the foreach loop. Once we've changed the names of each object, we can tell one from the other by its name.

5.8.2.1 A Basic Example

```
foreach (GameObject go in GameObjects)
{
    Debug.Log(go.name);
}
```

The foreach statement is dependent on the type of data found on the inside of the array. Therefore, we use `GameObject go` to set up a place to hold each member of the `GameObjects` array while in the `foreach` loop. If we wanted to iterate over an array of a different type, we'd have to change the parameters of the foreach loop. Therefore, to iterate over an array of ints which was declared `int[] MyInts;`, we'd need to use `foreach(int i in MyInts)` to iterate over each member of that array.

Of course, the variable's name can be anything, but it's easier to keep it short. To use `foreach(int anIntegerMemberFromAnArray in MyInts)`, for example, would be a bit of work to key in if we wanted to do a number of operations on each int found in the array. Then again, there's nothing preventing us from spending time being verbose. We'll cover the foreach loop in more detail in Section 6.11.5.

5.8.3 Dynamic Initialization

```
float[] dynamicFloats = new float[10];
```

We can also initialize a new array in a function. This means that the array exists only while in the scope of the function and can't be accessed from outside of that function. It's important to know that the size of an array is determined ahead of its use. When the array is declared in this way, the size or rather the number of objects the array can contain is set.

Here, we split the initialization into two statements. The first line tells C# we are creating a `float[]` variable identified as `dynamicFloats`. Then, we need to populate this floats array with a new array. The array floats is then assigned a new float array of 10 indices. We cannot switch this assignment to a different type.

```
float[] dynamicFloats;
dynamicFloats = new float[10];
```

Changing the type creates an error, which we'll have to fix. There are clever ways to avoid this, but we'll get into that in Section 6.14.

We can also use a variable to set the length of the array.

```
float[] dynamicFloats;
int numFloats = 10;
dynamicFloats = new float[numFloats];
```

This code sets the length of the dynamically defined array. This can be helpful once we need to make our code more flexible to change for various game design settings. On the other hand, we can populate an array with predetermined information.

```
public int[] primes = new int[] { 1, 3, 5, 7, 11, 13, 17 };
```

The above statement declares and sets an array that has seven members and assigns each number to a low prime number value. These even show up in the Inspector panel in Unity 3D.

▼ Primes	
Size	7
Element 0	1
Element 1	3
Element 2	5
Element 3	7
Element 4	11
Element 5	13
Element 6	17

5.8.4 Using the While Loop with Arrays

Iterating through our array is pretty simple. We've covered some basic loops that handle arrays quite well. If we use a simple while loop, we can process each value stored in a fixed array.

```
int[] scores = new int[10];
int i = 0;
while (i < 10)
{
    Debug.Log(scores[i]);
    i++;
}
```

At this point, all of the values are indeed zero, so we get 10 zeros printed to our Console panel. However, there are a few interesting things to point out here. First of all, int i is initialized to 0 ahead of the while loop. We'll get into what this means later on, but remember for now that arrays start at zero. The next interesting thing is how the numbers stored in scores[] are accessed.

5.8.4.1 Setting Array Values

```
scores[0] = 10;
```

We can set the value of each index of scores to a specific value by accessing the scores by their index. When the scores array was initialized as int[10], scores now has 10 different int number spaces. To access each value, we use a number 0 through 9 in square brackets to get and set each value. The while loop starts at 0 because we started with an int i = 0; before entering the while loop.

```
int[] scores = new int[10];
int i = 0;
while (i < 10)
{
    scores[i] = UnityEngine.Random.Range(0, 100);
    Debug.Log(scores[i]);
    i++;
}
```

With this code, we're using a function called Random and using its member function Range, which we're setting to a value between 0 and 100. The index is picked by using the i that was set to 0 before the loop started. The loop starts with scores[0] being set to a random number between 0 and 100.

At the end of the while block, the i is incremented by 1 and the while loop begins again. The next time, though, we are setting scores[1] to a random number between 0 and 100.

5.8.4.2 Getting Array Values

Each time, we're getting the value from scores[i] to print. We can make this a bit more clear with the following example.

```
int[] scores = new int[10];
scores[0] = 10;
int i = 0;
while (i < 10)
{
    scores[i] = UnityEngine.Random.Range(0, 100);
    int score = scores[i];
    Debug.Log(score);
    i++;
}
```

If we add in the line int score = scores[i];, we'll get the score to the value found in scores[i]. Each value remains independent of the other values stored in the array. Because we're able to use the entirety of scores[] as a single object with index values, we're able to accomplish a great deal of work with fewer lines of code.

Arrays are simple objects with lots of uses. We'll get into a pretty interesting use in Section 5.11.3, but for now, we'll have to settle on playing with some numbers in the array.

5.8.5 What We've Learned

Arrays are useful for more than just storing scores. Arrays for every monster in the scene will make it easier to find the closest one to the player. Rather than dealing with many separate variables, it's easier to group them together. Arrays are used so often as to have special loops that make dealing with arrays very simple.

5.9 Jump Statements: Break and Continue

Open the JumpStatementsBreakAndContinue_Scene and open the corresponding script in the scene. Loops are often used to iterate through a series of matching data. In many cases, we're looking for specific patterns in the data, and we'll change what we want to do depending on the data we're sifting through. In most cases, a regular if statement is the easiest to use. When our logic gets more detailed and we need to add more complex behaviors to our code, we need to start adding in special keywords.

When we come across the one thing we're looking for, or maybe the first thing we're looking for, we might want to stop the for loop that might change our result. In this case we use the break; keyword.

5.9.1 A Basic Example

The following code added to the BreakAndContinue() function in the script demonstrates a basic effect of the break keyword.

```
for (int i = 0; i < 100; i++)
{
    Debug.Log(i);
    if (i > 10)
    {
        break;
    }
}
```

When we run this code, we'll get a printout from 1 to 11, and since 11 is greater than 10, the for loop will stop. In the for loop's second argument, we've got i < 100, because we assume that the Debug. Log(i); would work till we hit 99 before the for loop exits normally. However, since we have the if statement that breaks us out of the for loop before i reaches 100, we only get 1–11 printed to the console. Of course, there are reasons for using break other than cutting for loops short.

5.9.1.1 Continue

```
for (int i = 0; i < 100; i++)
{
    Debug.Log(i);
    if (i > 10)
    {
        Debug.Log("i is greater than 10!");
        continue;
    }
}
```

The keyword continue changes when a loop begins on it's next iteration. Where the break terminates a loop the continue keyword tells the loop to skip the rest of the code and continue as normal. In the loop above the Debug.Log("Got Past Continue."); only appears for the first 10 iterations of the loop. Once i is greater than 10, the continue keyword interupts the loop execution and skips the rest of the code in the for loop.

The continue allows the for loop to finish iterating, break escapes the for loop before it's finished iterating.

5.9.2 ZombieData

The keyword break is often used to stop a process. Often, when we go through a group of data, we might be looking for something specific; when we find it, we would need to process it. If we create an array of zombies, we'll need to assign them some specific zombie behaviors. Therefore, we might create a new ZombieData.cs class that could include some zombie information.

```csharp
using UnityEngine;
public class Zombie : MonoBehaviour
{
    public int HitPoints;
}
```

Here's a very simple zombie class that has nothing more than some HitPoints. I'll leave the rest up to your game design to fill in. Then, in a new JumpStatementsBreakAndContinue.cs script in the UseZombieData() function, gameObjects are created and placed. Some of them have Zombie data, some don't.

```csharp
gameObjects = new GameObject[10];
for (int i = 0; i < 10; i++)
{
    //make a game object
    GameObject go = GameObject.CreatePrimitive(PrimitiveType.Cube);

    //find a random place for it
    Vector3 position = new Vector3();
    position.x = UnityEngine.Random.Range(-10, 10);
    position.z = UnityEngine.Random.Range(-10, 10);
    go.transform.position = position;

    //name it something unique
    go.name = i.ToString();
    if (i % 2 == 0)
    {
        // pick every other one to be a zombie
        Zombie z = go.AddComponent(typeof(Zombie)) as Zombie;

        // assign a random value to the hit points
        z.hitPoints = UnityEngine.Random.Range(1, 20);
    }

    //add the game object to the array
    gameObjects[i] = go;
}
```

The for loop in Start() creates 10 new game objects temporarily stored as go. This is done with GameObject go = GameObject.CreatePrimitive(PrimitiveType.Cube); we're creating 10 cube primitives. Then, we create a new Vector3() with Vector3 position = new Vector3();. Once position is created, we give x and z a new value between −10 and 10 using Random. Range (-10, 10); and then assign the position to the new game object go with go. transform.position = position. For clarity, we give each go a new name after its iterative number from the for loop by using go.name = i.ToString();. Once the new game object go is created, we assign it to an array at the class level called gameObjects.

Then, we get to if(i % 2 == 0) {go.AddComponent(typeof(Zombie));, which assigns a new Zombie object to each go if i % 2 is 0. The i%2 is a clever way to check if a number is even or odd. Therefore, in this case, if the number is even, then we assign a new Zombie; otherwise, no Zombie is assigned. This means half of the cubes are not zombies. After creating a zombie we assign it a random value for hitPoints.

5.9.3 Foreach Again

In a normal game setting, you might have many different types of objects in a scene. Some objects might be zombies, whereas others might be innocent humans running away from the zombies. We're creating a number of game objects to simulate a more normal game setting.

```
foreach (GameObject go in gameObjects)
{
    Zombie z = (Zombie)go.GetComponent(typeof(Zombie));
    if (z == null)
    {
        /* if we don't find a zombie skip
         * the game object and move on to
         * the next one in the array.
         */
        continue;
    }

    if (z.hitPoints > 10)
    {
        Debug.Log("This has more than 10 hit points: " + z.name);
        break;
    }
}
```

Now, just for the sake of using both continue and break in some logical fashion, we use the array to check through our list of game objects using foreach (GameObject go in gameobjects). The first line, `Zombie z = (Zombie)go.GetComponent(typeof(Zombie));`, assigns a Zombie to the variable z. The next line does something interesting.

Here, null is useful; in this case, if the object in the array has no Zombie, then z will not be assigned anything. When z is not assigned anything, its data remains null. Therefore, in this case, if there's no zombie data assigned to the object in the array, we're looking at *then continue,* or in this case, *go back to the top of the loop, and move on to the next item in the array.* Continue means stay in the loop, but skip to the next item in the array.

If `Zombie z` exists, then we move to the next line down and we don't hit continue. Therefore, we can check if z.hitpoints is greater than 10; if it is, then we'll stop the loop altogether. This lets us know there's at least one Zombie that's got more than 10 hit points.

The result of this loop prints out the even-numbered named game objects and stops naming them if it comes across one that's got more than 10 hit points.

For an AI (artificial intelligence) character, it would be useful to know what objects in the scene are zombies. And your zombies should know what objects in the scenes are players. In your zombie behavior code, you might use something like the following.

```
foreach (Player p in players)
{
    if (p == null)
    {
        continue;
    }
}
```

This code is used to skip on to the next object in the scene, which might be a player. Likewise, you could do the following with null.

```
if (p != null)
{

    AttackPlayer();
}
```

This statement would be just as useful. Likewise, you can do things before using continue. If your zombie needed a list of characters in the scene, you would want to add them to an array list, which is different from an array, and you would want to add them to an array first.

```
foreach (GameObject go in gameObjects)
{
    Player player = go.GetComponent(typeof(Player)) as Player;
    if (player != null)
    {
        players.Add(player);
        continue;
    }
}
```

In the above example, we'd check the go if it's got a Player component. If it does, add it to an array list called players, and then continue; to the next object in the list.

5.9.4 What We've Learned

The previous section was a simple use of break and continue. As more complex situations arise, then using jump statements come in handy. The jump statements are often used while searching through an array of many kinds of objects.

When reading through other people's code, it's often useful to do a search for various keywords when you're interested in seeing how they are used. By searching for continue; or break;, you might find several different uses that might have not come to your mind immediately.

Discovering the different ways code can be used comes with experience, and it is something that cannot be taught in a single volume of text. The process of learning different programming features is like looking at a tool box and knowing what a screw driver looks like. It's an entirely different process to understand how it's best used.

5.10 Multidimensional Arrays

```
int[,] TwoDimensionalArray;
```

Open the MultidimensionalArrays_Scene and the corresponding MultidimensionalArrays script found in the scene. An array is a single list of objects. Each entry is identified in the array by an index. By adding an additional index, we're allowed to create an additional depth to the array. When working with a single-dimensional array, we can get several simple attributes about the contents of that array.

```
Object[] objects = new Object[10];
for (int i = 0; i < objects.Length; i++)
{
    Debug.Log(objects[i]);
}
```

With the above statement, we get 10 objects printed to the Console panel in Unity 3D. Using oneDimension.Length, we get a value representing the number of items in the array. At the moment, though, we have not added anything to the contents of each index. This situation is altered with the following change to the array's declaration.

```
Object[,] objects = new Object[2, 3];
for (int i = 0; i < objects.Length; i++)
{
    Debug.Log(i);
    /* how do we address
     * two parameters in
     * a multi dimensional
     * array?
     */
}
```

```
GameObject a = new GameObject("a");
GameObject b = new GameObject("b");
GameObject c = new GameObject("c");
GameObject d = new GameObject("d");
GameObject e = new GameObject("e");
GameObject f = new GameObject("f");
GameObject[,] twoDimensions = new GameObject[2,3] { { a, b, c }, { d, e, f } };
```

With the above statement, we get 0–5 printed to the Console panel in Unity 3D. The Array.Length parameter simply returns the total number of items in the array, but we're not able to get any specific information on how the indices are arranged. To get a better feel for the contents of the array, we might consider the TwoDimensionalArray; a grid of two columns by three rows.

5.10.1 Columns and Rows

As shown in the below image, we have a 2 by 3 grid as a representation of the GameObject[2, 3] array. Each box holds onto a GameObject. A multidimensional array has its place in programming, though it is rare, and the coding is usually better handled using a couple of single-dimensional arrays. However, it's more convenient to pass a single multidimensional array to a function than it is to pass two different single-dimensional arrays.

To utilize this array, we'll want to populate the array with some GameObjects.

5.10.1.1 A Basic Example

Let's begin with the MultiDimensionalArray project in Unity 3D and open the scene.

```
GameObject a = new GameObject("a");
GameObject b = new GameObject("b");
GameObject c = new GameObject("c");
GameObject d = new GameObject("d");
GameObject e = new GameObject("e");
GameObject f = new GameObject("f");
GameObject[,] twoDimensions = new GameObject[2,3] { { a, b, c }, { d, e, f } };
```

Notice how the array is assigned. There are two sets of curly braces, a pair of curly braces in a set of curly braces. We group three items into two subgroups, and assign them to the 2D array. The notation {{}, {}} is used to assign a 2 by 3 array with 6 GameObjects.

Next, we'll add a function to sift through the 2D array.

```
void InspectArray(GameObject[,] gameObjects)
{
    int columns = gameObjects.GetLength(0);
    Debug.Log("columns:" + columns);
    int rows = gameObjects.GetLength(1);
    Debug.Log("rows:" + rows);
    for (int column = 0; column < columns; column++)
    {
        for (int row = 0; row < rows; row++)
        {
            Debug.Log(gameObjects[column, row].name);
        }
    }
}
```

With this code, we'll get an idea of what types of loops will work best with a 2D array. First off, we have a function with one argument. The function `InspectArray(GameObject[,] gameObjects)` takes in a 2D array of any size. Therefore, a GameObject[37,41] would fit just as well as the GameObject[2, 3] that we are using for this tutorial.

We're then using GameObjects (gos).GetLength(0); to assign our columns count. The `GetLength()` array function takes a look at the dimensions of the array. At index 0 in [2, 3], we have 2, which is assigned to columns. Next, we use GetLength(1); to get the number of rows in the 2D array.

Using two for loops, one inside of the other, we're able to iterate through each one of the objects in the 2D array in a more orderly manner. Without a system like this, we're in a more difficult situation, not knowing where in the array we are.

```
InspectArray(twoDimensions);
```

At the end of the `Start()` function, we can make use of the `InspectArray()` function and get a log of the items in each position in the 2D array.

```
!  columns:2
   UnityEngine.Debug:Log(Object)

!  rows:3
   UnityEngine.Debug:Log(Object)

!  a
   UnityEngine.Debug:Log(Object)

!  b
   UnityEngine.Debug:Log(Object)

!  c
   UnityEngine.Debug:Log(Object)

!  d
   UnityEngine.Debug:Log(Object)

!  e
   UnityEngine.Debug:Log(Object)

!  f
   UnityEngine.Debug:Log(Object)
```

5.10.2 A Puzzle Board

In the same MultiDimensionalArrays_Scene is a Grid2D game object in the Hierarchy. Attached is the Grid2D script to follow along with. Puzzle games often require a great deal of 2D array manipulation. To start a project, we can use the Grid2D project. The code in the Grid2D.cs class will begin with the following:

```
public int Width;
public int Height;
public GameObject PuzzlePiece;
public GameObject[,] Grid;
```

A few public variables that will allow us to make changes in the editor. We can make various sizes for the grid and we'll also be able to change the puzzle piece that's used in the puzzle.

```
void Start()
{
    Grid = new GameObject[Width, Height];
    for (int x = 0; x < Width; x++)
    {
        for (int y = 0; y < Height; y++)
        {
            Vector3 position = new Vector3(x, y, 0);
            GameObject go = new GameObject("x:" + x + "y:" + y);
            go.transform.position = position;
            Grid[x, y] = go;
        }
    }
}
```

The PuzzlePiece on the script will need an object assigned to it. This means you'll have to drag the puzzle piece object in the Project under the Meshes directory to the Puzzle Piece variable in the Inspector panel.

In the Grid2D.cs class, the first variables we're going to look at is the public int Width and public int Height. These two variables are made visible to the Inspector in the Unity 3D Editor. I've set both of these to 8 in the Inspector panel. This is followed by a GameObject, which we'll fill the grid with. The last variable is a 2D array, which we will fill with the GameObject PuzzlePiece.

In the Start() function, we'll add an initialization for the grid with Grid = new GameObject[Width, Height]; to set up the 2D array so we can use it. Every fixed-sized array, whether 1D, like a GameObject[], or 2D, which looks like the above GameObject[,], needs to be initialized before it's used. Before being initialized, the array is null, which means it's lacking any size or any place for us to put anything into the array.

To fill in the array, we use the following code block added to the Start() function.

```
Vector3 position = new Vector3(x, y, 0);
GameObject go = GameObject.Instantiate(PuzzlePiece) as GameObject;
go.transform.position = position;
Grid[x, y] = go;
```

This code has two functions; the first for loop iterates through each position along the x; inside of each x position, we make a column for y with another for loop. At each position, we create a new GameObject.Instantiate(PuzzlePiece) as GameObject; to assign to GameObject go. When GameObject.Instantiate() is used, an object of type object is created. To be used as a GameObject type it must be cast. Without the cast, you'll get the following warning in the Unity 3D Console panel:

Assets/Grid2D.cs(14,28): error CS0266: Cannot implicitly convert type

"UnityEngine.Object" to "UnityEngine.GameObject." An explicit conversion exists (are you missing a cast?)

This error is telling us we need to cast from Object to GameObject, quite a simple fix even if you forget to do this ahead of time.

After making a new instance, we need to use the x and y to create a new Vector3 to set the position of each puzzle piece. Use Vector3 position = new Vector3(x, y, 0); to create a new

Vector3 for each position. Once the new Vector3 position has been created and assigned, we can tell the GameObject go where it should be in the world. This is done with the statement that follows: go.transform.position = position;.

Once the GameObject has been created and positioned, we can assign it to the GameObject[,] array with Grid[x, y] = go;, where we use x and y to pick which index in the 2D array the GameObject is to be assigned to. Once this is done, we can use the Grid[x, y] to get a reference to the puzzle piece.

5.10.3 Camera and Screen Setup

To pick a puzzle piece with the mouse, we're going to need to modify the camera's settings.

Three changes are required; the first is Projection, which we'll change from Perspective to Orthographic. This will mean that lines will not converge to a point in space. *Orthographic* projection means that the line where the mouse appears over the game will be parallel with what the camera is looking at. We'll also want to resize the camera to match the grid.

```
Camera.main.orthographic = true;
Camera.main.orthographicSize = Width/2;
Camera.main.farClipPlane = 20;
```

Then the position of the camera is set to match the center of the puzzle grid. We use half the width for *x* and half the height for *y*. Then a half a unit is taken off of each to position the camera to look at the middle of a puzzle piece rather than the top right corner of a grid square.

```
float xPos = (Width * 0.5f) - 0.5f;
float yPos = (Height * 0.5f) - 0.5f;
Camera.main.transform.position = new Vector3(xPos, yPos, -5);
```

To catch the mouse pointer position in the world a collider of some kind needs to be added to the grid as well. This will allow us to find where the mouse is hovering over when the game is playing.

```
GameObject collider = GameObject.CreatePrimitive(PrimitiveType.Plane);
collider.transform.localScale = new Vector3(Width * 0.1f, 1, Height * 0.1f);
collider.transform.eulerAngles = new Vector3(-90, 0, 0);
collider.transform.position = new Vector3(xPos, yPos, 0);
```

The Plane primitive is 10 units wide and 10 units deep. To modify it to match our grid size we use `Width` and `Height` multiplied by `0.1f` to change its size. Then it's rotated up to match the grid orientation and then we move its center to match the center of the grid reusing `xPos` and `yPos`.

In the `Update()` function on the Grid2D.cs class, we can use the same ray cast to the mouse position we did in the Sample Game.

```
Ray ray = Camera.main.ScreenPointToRay(Input.mousePosition);
RaycastHit hit;
if (Physics.Raycast(ray, out hit))
{
    mousePosition = hit.point;
}
```

This gives us an *x* and *y* coordinate that will roughly match up to a puzzle piece. To get a better match, we'll need to convert the position from a float value into an int value, but we'll need to remember that values are rounded to 0 even if the value is above 0.5.

```
public int xGrid;
public int yGrid;
void PickPuzzlePiece(Vector3 position)
{
    int x = (int)(position.x + 0.5f);
    int y = (int)(position.y + 0.5f);
    if (x >= 0 && x < Width)
    {
        xGrid = x;
    }
    if (y >= 0 && y < Height)
    {
        yGrid = y;
    }
}
```

With a rough evaluation we can check that the x and y are within the bounds of the width and height values used to build the grid. To store the values an xGrid and yGrid are created to help us visualize what the values are being set to.

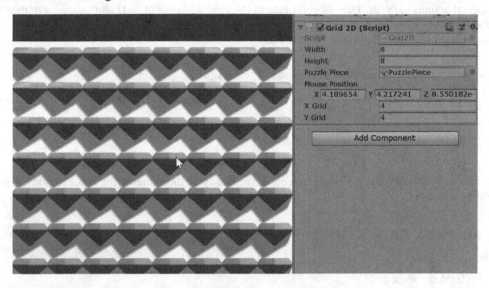

With the float value of *x* and *y* converted to an int that corresponds to a grid value, we can change the color of the puzzle piece in the grid based on where the mouse is positioned.

```
GameObject go = Grid[xGrid, yGrid];
Renderer renderer = go.GetComponent(typeof(Renderer)) as Renderer;
renderer.material.color = Color.red;
```

GameObject go = Grid[x, y]; works, but only when the cursor is over a puzzle piece. When the cursor is over a puzzle piece, we turn its material color to red. When the cursor is no longer over a puzzle piece, we get a bunch of warnings informing us we're selecting an index that is out of range.

5.10.4 Checking Range

```
IndexOutOfRangeException: Array index is out of range.
Grid2D.Update () (at Assets/Grid2D.cs:27)
```

This is true when the cursor is at −4, 7; there is no assigned object to the Grid[−4,7]; we've only assigned from 0 to 6 on the *x* and 0 to 6 on the *y*. These errors should be resolved before we move on. This can be done with an if statement or two.

```
if (x >= 0)
{
    if (x < Width)
    {
        if (y >= 0)
        {
            if (y < Height)
            {
                GameObject gameObject = Grid[x, y];
            }
        }
    }
}
```

This code checks first that x is at least 0, and then does the same for y. After that, we check that x is less than the width we chose initially, and do the same for y. However, this is a messy bit of code. It works but we can clean this up. There's nothing happening if only x < = 0; none of the if statements require any special actions to occur. They all contribute to the same assignment and color change statements at the end. That's how we know they can be reduced to one if statement.

The reduced statement looks like the following:

```
if (x >= 0 && x < Width && y >= 0 && y < Height)
{
    xGrid = x;
    yGrid = y;
}
```

However, with so many && in a single statement, the clarity of the values being checked and assigned should be separated.

```
if (x >= 0 && x < Width)
{
    xGrid = x;
}
if (y >= 0 && y < Height)
{
    yGrid = y;
}
```

Much better. Therefore, this code works to highlight every game object we touch, but the objects remain colored red. The puzzle piece should return to white when the mouse is no longer hovering over them; How would we do that? The logic isn't so simple. We could pick every other object and set it to white, but that's impractical. Strangely, the solution is to set all of the objects to white, and then color the current object red.

```
// set all of the game objects to white
for (int w = 0; w < Width; w++)
{
    for (int h = 0; h < Height; h++)
    {
        GameObject go = Grid[w, h];
        Renderer renderer = go.GetComponent(typeof(Renderer)) as Renderer;
        renderer.material.color = Color.white;
    }
}
```

Iterate through all of the game objects in a similar way to how we instantiated them. Because this code is sharing a function with x and y, where we converted the float to an int, we need to make new versions of x and y for this function; therefore, we'll use _x and _y to create a new variable for the for loops. With this, we set them all to white. After resetting all of the puzzle pieces to white, we move to the next function that sets them to red.

We're not so interested in what our scene looks like in the middle of the Update() function, just how the scene looks like at the end. None of the intermediate steps appears in the scene, until the Update() function has finished. This means we can do all sorts of unintuitive actions during the course of the Update() function, so long as the final result looks like what we need.

```
//set the one that the mouse is near to red
GameObject go = Grid[xGrid, yGrid];
Renderer renderer = go.GetComponent(typeof(Renderer)) as Renderer;
renderer.material.color = Color.red;
```

Now, we have a very simple way to detect and pick which puzzle piece is selected in a grid of objects using a 2D array and a Vector3. Of course, the strategy used here may not fit all situations. In addition, applying various offsets for changing the spacing between each object might be useful to make differently proportioned grids. Later on, you will want to add in additional systems to check for color to determine matches, but that will have to wait for Section 5.11.4.

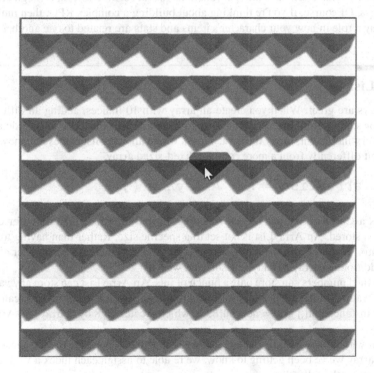

With the code moved into its own function, our Update() loop is easier to read. We're very specific about what is required to update the picked piece. We just need to remember to rename mousePosition to a position inside of the new function. We can also extend the new function to return the piece that has been picked. By breaking apart a long string of code into smaller, more simplified functions, we're able to gain more flexibility and allow for changes more easily.

5.10.5 What We've Learned

Back in the MultidimensionalArrays script arrays can be a bit of a pain to work with, but after some practice, the logic becomes more intuitive. Puzzle games that use a grid of colored objects to match up often use a 2D array to check for patterns.

We could expand the concept to more than two dimensions as well. Using the previously defined GameObjects, we could make a 3D array that looks like the following:

```
GameObject[,,] threeDimensions = new GameObject[4, 3, 2]
{
    { {a, b}, { c, d}, { e, f} },
    { {a, b}, { c, d}, { e, f} },
    { {a, b}, { c, d}, { e, f} },
    { {a, b}, { c, d}, { e, f} }
};
```

Something like this is easier to produce using code to fill in each value, but it's important to be able to visualize what a [4,3,2] array actually looks like. Though a bit impractical, these sorts of data structures are important to computing, in general. Outside of video game development, multidimensional arrays become more important to data analysis.

Large database systems often have internal functions that accelerate sorting through arrays of data in more logical ways. Of course, if you're thinking about building a complex RPG, then multidimensional arrays might play a role in how your character's items and stats are related to one another.

5.11 Array List

Fixed-sized arrays are great. When you create an array with 10 indices, adding an 11th score or more will be cause for some rethinking. You'd have to go back and fix your code to include another index. This would be very inefficient, to say the least. This is where an array list comes in handy. An ArrayList is initialized a bit differently from a more common fixed-sized array.

```
ArrayList arrayList = new ArrayList();
```

An ArrayList is a C# class that has special functions for building lists that allow for changes in the number of values stored. An ArrayList is not set to a specific size. Rather than having to pick an index to put a value into, we merely use the ArrayList function Add(); to increase the number of objects in the ArrayList. In addition, an array has a type associated with it.

An array like int[] numbers can store only a bunch of ints. An ArrayList can store any variety of object types. Another feature which we'll find out later is that an array, not an ArrayList, can have multiple dimensions, for instance, int[,] grid = new int[8,8];, which creates an 8 by 8 array. An ArrayList cannot be used like this.

The drawback with an ArrayList is the fact that we're not able to populate the list ahead of time. With the fixed-sized array we've been getting to know, we're able to assign each index a value ahead of time; for instance, consider the following:

```
int[] primeNumbers = new int[] { 1, 3, 5, 7, 11, 13, 17 };
```

We know that this statement will appear in the Inspector panel with seven numbers in a nice UI roll-out. An array list doesn't allow for this behavior, as it needs to be created and then populated after its creation. The reason why Unity 3D allows us to assign values to objects in a scene is the scene file. The scene itself has had special data or metadata added to the scene. The scene now has specific bindings created to tie the data you've created to the class attached to an object.

To simulate this in a more common Windows app, you'd have to create a secondary file that stores specific settings. When the app is started, the settings need to be read in and then assigned to the classes as they are instanced into the scene. Unity 3D has done much of the specific bindings for you, which allows your game to have scenes with arranged objects and unique settings for each object.

```
int i = 3;
arrayList.Add(i);
```

The identifier inherits the ArrayList member methods. The Add method is used to append a value to the end of the ArrayList object. The arrayList from the above code fragment is now an ArrayList type with one item. With this, we're able to use the arrayList as an object.

```
Debug.Log(arrayList[0]);
```

This statement will send 3 to the Console panel, as you might expect. In practice, the ArrayList type is often used to collect an unknown number of objects into something more manageable. Once we've gathered the objects we're looking for, it's easier to deal with the multitude of objects. Therefore, if there are between 0 and 100 zombies in a room, we can have different behaviors based on the number of zombies found. If we want to convert the ArrayList into a regular array, we'd need to do some copying from the ArrayList to the array.

In addition to allowing for any number of objects, we can also consume any variety of types in the array.

5.11.1 A Basic Example

To observe how an ArrayList is used, it's best to see it all in action; therefore, we'll start with the ArrayLists project in Unity 3D. In the scene, we can have any number of cube game objects. Should the number of objects be something that can't be predetermined, we'd want to use an ArrayList to store a list of them.

```
ArrayList arrayList = new ArrayList();
Object[] allObjects = FindObjectsOfType(typeof(Object));
foreach (Object o in allObjects)
{
    GameObject go = o as GameObject;
    if (go != null)
    {
        arrayList.Add(go);
    }
}
//initialize GameObjects Array
GameObject[] gameObjects = new GameObject[arrayList.Count];
arrayList.CopyTo(gameObjects);
foreach (GameObject go in gameObjects)
{
    Debug.Log(go.name);
}
```

The code above is attached to the ArrayLists game object. This behavior adds everything in the scene to an array. If it's an object, then we add it to the array. Afterward, we iterate through the array using foreach(Object o in AllObjects), which allows us to check if the object in the allObjects array is a GameObject. This check is done using GameObject go = o as GameObject;, and the following line checks if the cast is valid. If the cast is valid, then we add the object to our array list arrayList. This is done using the same arrayList.Add(go) function we used before.

After the iteration through the list, we end up with a final pair of steps. The first is to initialize a regular GameObject array to the size of the ArrayList. Then, we need to copy the arrayList to the freshly initialized GameObject array with arrayList.CopyTo().

The final result is an ArrayList of each game object in the scene. If we skip the cast checking of whether Object o is a GameObject, then we get an invalid cast error. This happens only when we try to copy the arrayList to the GameObject array. We can do the following in the iteration to populate the arrayList without any problems.

```
foreach (Object o in allObjects)
{
    arrayList.Add(o);
}
```

This code simply adds everything that FindObjectsOfType() finds to the arrayList. This tells us that arrayList ignores the type that it's being filled with. To see what this foreach loop is doing, we can use the following modification:

```
foreach (Object o in allObjects)
{
    Debug.Log(o);
    arrayList.Add(o);
}
```

Here, we log each o to the console. We get many more objects than you might have guessed. In the scene I've created, there are 76 different lines printed to the Console panel. The list includes the game objects as well as dozens of other objects that are added to the ArrayList; too many to spell out in this case. A regular array can accommodate only one type at a time. And a GameObject[] array can have only GameObjects assigned to each index.

Since we might not necessarily know how many GameObjects reside in the final list, we need to dynamically add each one to the ArrayList, and wait till we stop finding new GameObjects to add. Once the list is done with iteration, we can then use the final count of the arrayList, using `arrayList.Count`, to initialize the GameObject array. The ArrayList has a function called CopyTo, which is designed to copy its contents to a fixed-sized array; therefore, we use it to do just that, with the last two statements:

```
gameObjects = new GameObject[arrayList.Count];
// copy the list to the array
arrayList.CopyTo(gameObjects);
```

5.11.2 ArrayList.Contains()

`ArrayList.Contains()` is a static function of ArrayList. The ArrayList type has several useful functions aside from just copying to an array. Say, we add a public GameObject SpecificObject; to the ArrayLists class. Then we can drag one of the cubes in the scene to the variable in the Inspector panel.

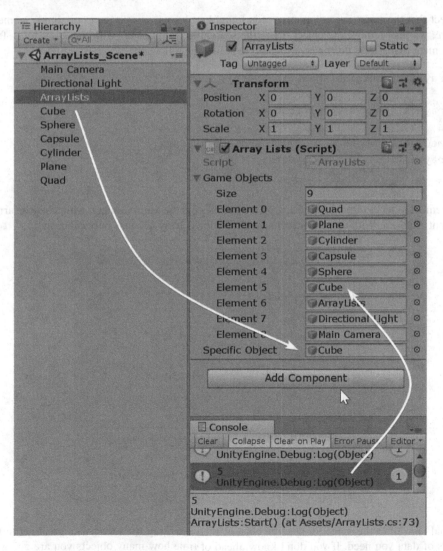

Now, we have an object and a populated array list. This allows us to search the array list for the object.

```
if (arrayList.Contains(specificObject))
{
    Debug.Log("SpecificObject:");
    Debug.Log(specificObject);
    Debug.Log("is in arrayList at index ");
    Debug.Log(arrayList.IndexOf(specificObject));
}
```

We can use two different array list functions. The first is `Contains()` and the second is `IndexOf()`. The `Contains()` function searches through the array list and returns true if it finds the object and false if the object isn't in the list. The `IndexOf()` function returns the index where the `SpecificObject` is found. Therefore, if the array list has the `specificObject` at index 5, the `Debug.Log` above returns 5.

5.11.3 Remove

The object that the script is a component of is found by `this.gameObject`, or simply, gameObject. Therefore, we may remove the object doing the searching from the list with the `Remove()` function. The statement that effects this behavior would look like the following:

```
if (arrayList.Contains(specificObject))
{
    arrayList.Remove(specificObject);
    //now update the list in the inspector panel
    gameObjects = new GameObject[arrayList.Count];
    arrayList.CopyTo(gameObjects);
}
```

This statement reduces the size of the array list and takes out the Main Camera, which has the array list's component attached. With the camera removed, the copied array now has only cubes in it.

If the goal is to filter the scene for specific objects, then the array list serves as a great net to fill with the types of data you need. If you don't know ahead of time how many objects you are going to find, then an array list is a useful utility class that allows for some interesting tricks. Therefore, we've looked at removing and finding an object in an array list, but we don't need to stop there.

5.11.4 Sort and Reverse

▼ Messy Ints	
Size	8
Element 0	12
Element 1	14
Element 2	6
Element 3	1
Element 4	0
Element 5	123
Element 6	92
Element 7	8

Let's add public int[] messyInts = {12,14,6,1,0,123,92,8}; to the class scope. This should appear in the Inspector panel, where we can see that messyInts is indeed a collection of messy ints. To copy the messyInts into a new ArrayList, we use AddRange().

```
ArrayList sorted = new ArrayList();
sorted.AddRange(messyInts);
sorted.Sort();
sorted.CopyTo(messyInts);
```

With the above code added to the Start() function, we get the following result once the game is run.

▼ Messy Ints	
Size	8
Element 0	0
Element 1	1
Element 2	6
Element 3	8
Element 4	12
Element 5	14
Element 6	92
Element 7	123

The elements of the array have been sorted, starting at the lowest and ending with the highest. The sort function is a nicely optimized sort function. You might expect this from the experienced computer scientists working on the C# library we've been using. If we want to reverse the order in which the numbers are sorted, then we can use the sorted Reverse(); function.

```
sorted.Reverse();
sorted.CopyTo(messyInts);
```

Having some numbers rearranged is great, but there's little inherent value to the numbers if there are no associated objects in the scene that relate to the numeric values. The `Sort()` function is good for simple matters where the data that's sorted has no association with anything in particular outside of the array. However, should we want to compare GameObjects in the scene, we might need to do something more useful.

5.11.5 What We've Learned

Making a custom sorting system requires some new concepts, which we have yet to get to. A specific type of class called an interface is required to create our own system of sorting. We could use this class in many different ways and take advantage of the power behind C#'s library.

A performance issue comes up with array lists. We may add objects to an ArrayList by simply using `MyArrayList.Add(someObject);`, which is easy. When we need to see what's in that array list, we begin to have a few problems.

As this was mentioned at the beginning of this chapter we didn't find out what happens if we use the following.

```
ArrayList arrayList = new ArrayList();
arrayList.Add(123);
arrayList.Add("strings");
```

We have an issue with the above code fragment. If we assumed the ArrayList would only contain numbers; multiplying 123 by "strings" would result in an error. Of course we can't multiply these two very different types. We'd need to do a few tricks to check if we're allowed to multiply two objects from the ArrayList. First, we'd check if both are indeed numbers, if they are then we can proceed with a multiplication statement. If not, then we'd have to find another two objects which are numbers or we'd get an error.

This process takes time, and if the array list is big, then we'd be spending a great deal of time on checking object types. If we use a regular array, we can be sure that each object in the array is the same type, or possibly null. Checking against null for each object in the list is an extra step in the process. Reducing the number of steps your function need to work will speed up your functions and code will run faster.

When dealing with arrays, we might need to stuff an array into an array. Each array inside of an array can be of a different size. Imagine array A to be 10 items long. At A[0], you can create another array B that is, for example, 3 items long. If each index of A is of a different size, you've created what is called a jagged array.

5.12 Strings

Strings are collections of letters. C# has no concept of what words are, so a string is nothing more than a collection of meaningless letters. When you use a string, it's important to remember that the data stored in it is not like words.

5.12.1 Declaring a String

Basically, strings are presented to the computer by using the " or ' operator. Strings act somewhat like an array, so we've held off until after we looked at arrays before getting to strings. Later on, strings will become a bit more useful, once we start naming GameObjects.

Strings can be used as user names and will be useful if you wanted to use them for dialog windows when talking to characters in a role-playing game. Being able to process strings is a useful skill to have for many general purpose programming tasks.

5.12.1.1 A Basic Example

Let's start with the Strings_Scene in the Chapter5 Unity Project. And open the Strings.cs script attached to the Strings game object in the scene.

```
string s = "Something in quotes.";
```

This statement creates a string with the identifier s and then assigns Something in quotes to s. Strings have several additional functions that are important. Be careful to not use smart quotes, which word processors like to use. Quotes that have directions are not the same as the quotes a compiler is expecting. Words in special quotes ("words") actually use different characters when written in a word processor.

The compiler expects a different character. The character set that most word processors use is different from what C# uses to compile. For instance, if you hold down the ALT key and enter four numbers on the number pad, you'll get a special character.

```
string s = "Something in quotes.";
Debug.Log(s);
```

Printing the s results in a predictable output to the Console panel.

> ! Something in quotes.
> UnityEngine.Debug:Log(Object)

There's not a whole lot unexpected happening here. However, we can do something with strings that might unexpected.

```
s += "more words.";
```

We can add this statement just before the print (s); and get a different result. When we run the game, we get the following Console output:

> ! Something in quotes.more words.
> UnityEngine.Debug:Log(Object)

We forgot to add in a space before the *more* in "more words," so it ran into the word quotes. White space is important to how we use strings. There's no logic to what's happening when we add more words to a string. To correct this, we need to add a space before *more* and we'll get a more expected result: "more words."

Strings do have some tricks that make them very useful. The string class has many member functions we can use, like Contains.

```
bool hasSomething = s.Contains("Something");
Debug.Log(hasSomething);
```

This returns `true`; the word `"Something"` is contained in the string stored in s. Use any other set of letters which doesn't appear in our string and the console will print `false`.

We can also do the following.

```
s = "First Word " + "Second Word";
Debug.Log(s);
```

The reassignment of s prints out what you might expect.

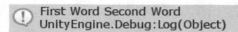

> ⓘ First Word Second Word
>   UnityEngine.Debug:Log(Object)

For argument's sake, we'll try another operator in the string declaration.

```
s = "First Word " - "Second Word";
```

Here, we're going to try to subtract "Second word" from the first. Of course, this doesn't work and we get the following error.

> ⚠ Assets/Strings.cs(29,17): error CS0019: Operator `-' cannot be applied to operands of type `string' and `string'

So why does the + work and not the − in our declaration? The answer is operator overloading. Operators change their meaning depending on the context in which they appear. When the + is placed between two strings, we get a different result than when we put the + between two numbers. However, strings are rather particular. It's rather difficult to say for sure what it would mean to subtract one word from another. Computers are horrible at guessing.

5.12.2 Escape Sequences

Strings in C# need to be handled very differently from a regular word processor. Formatting strings can be somewhat confusing if you treat C# like any other text format.

```
string s = "test a
    line return";
```

If you want to add in a line return, you might end up with a mess as in the above image. Sometimes called line feeds, or carriage returns, these line returns tend to break C# in unexpected ways. To add in line feeds into the string, you'll have to use a special character instead.

```
string s = "First line. \n Second Line";
Debug.Log(s);
```

Escape sequences work to convert two regular text characters into more specialized characters without needing to mess up your code's formatting. The `\n` creates a "new line" where it appears in the string. A `\t` adds a tab wherever it appears.

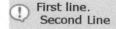

> ⓘ First line.
>   Second Line

Unity 3D diverges a bit from most C# libraries as it doesn't implement all of the different escape sequences that are generally included. For instance, \r is carriage return, as is \f that are generally included in other common .NET development environments. The \n, which creates new line sequence, is more commonly known.

In old mechanical type writers, a carriage return is a lever that would both push a roll of paper and add in a new line at the same time; hardly something you see around today, unless you're a street poet. Not all these escape characters work, but there are several others which you'll find useful.

```
Debug.Log("\"I Want Quotes!\"");
```

So, if you want quotes:

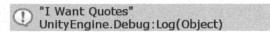

```
"I Want Quotes"
UnityEngine.Debug:Log(Object)
```

You get quotes. To get double quotes to print in your console, you'll use the \" escape sequence. Here's a list of regular escape sequences.

```
\a  (beep)
\b  Backspace
\f  Formfeed
\n  New line
\r  Carriage return
\t  Tab
\v  Vertical tab
\'  Single quote
\"  Double quote
\\  Backslash
\?  Literal question mark
```

In addition to these escape sequences, we have an additional three types that are used less often but are just as important. C# and Unity 3D will recognize some hexadecimal characters that are accessed with \x followed by two hexadecimal values. We'll find out more about these hex values and other escape sequences in a later chapter. Using hexadecimals is another way to get the more particular characters often found in other languages.

5.12.3 Verbatim Strings: @

In some cases, it's useful to use the @ operator before a string. This tells C# that we're really not interested in formatting or not being able to make modifications to our string, like string s = "This\nThat";, as opposed to the @ operator string s = @"This\nThat";

```
s = "This\nThat";
Debug.Log(s);
s = @"This\nThat";
Debug.Log(s);
```

This code produces the following:

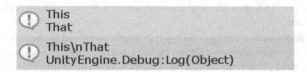

This also means something as strange looking as:

```
        Debug.Log(s);
        s = @"this
that and
the other";
        Debug.Log(s);
```

prints to the console

> this
> that and
> the other
> UnityEngine.Debug:Log(Object)
> Strings:Start() (at Assets/Strings.cs:57)

Notice that the console output includes exactly what was used in Visual Studio. If the words lined up using the indents, the white space would be included in the verbatim string. This is allowed because of the verbatim operator. When using `Debug.Log()`, the verbatim operator can be used to format your strings to include new lines wherever you may need them.

Strings that contain information can easily be created; it's often the case when trying to track the behavior of a creature in the scene.

5.12.4 What We've Learned

We're not going to be building any word-processing software within Unity 3D. It's not something that sounds all that fun, and there are better environments for doing that. As far as strings are concerned, we're better off using them as seldom as possible.

Very few game engines dwell on their text-editing features, Unity 3D included. If you're planning on having your player do a great deal of writing and formatting to play your game, then you might have a tough time. For most purposes, like entering character names or setting up a clan name, the string class provided will have you covered.

5.13 Combining What We've Learned

We just covered some basic uses of loops. The for and the while loop have similar uses, but the for loop has some additional parameters that can make it more versatile. We also covered some relational, unary, and conditional operators.

Together with if, else if, and else, we've got enough parts together to do some interesting logic tests. We can start to give some interesting behavior to our statements. For instance, we could build a cityscape using cubes that grows over time.

5.13.1 Timers

In the Timers_Scene project in the Chapter5 Unity Project, we'll start with the Timers.cs script attached to the Timers game object in the scene. Let's say we want to create a number of towers, but we want to create them one at a time. To do this, we should use a timer; therefore, we should start with that first.

```
void Update()
{
    Debug.Log(Time.fixedTime);
}
```

If we start with `Time.fixedTime`, we should see how that behaves by itself. We get a printout to the console starting with 0, which then counts up at one unit per second. Therefore, if we want some sort of action 3 seconds later, we can set a timer to 3 seconds from 0.

```
if (Time.fixedTime > 3)
{
    Debug.Log("Times Up");
}
```

If `Time.fixedTime` is greater than 3, "Times Up" is repeatedly printed to the console. However, we want that to print only once, since we want only one thing to happen when our if statement is executed. To do this, we should add in some way to increment the number we're comparing `Time.fixedTime` to.

```
if (Time.fixedTime > NextTime)
{
    NextTime = Time.fixedTime + 3;
    Debug.Log("Times Up");
}
```

With a class scoped variable called `NextTime`, we can store our next "Times Up" time and update it when it is reached. Running this code prints "Times Up" once the game starts. If `NextTime` was declared to 3, then we'd have to wait 3 seconds before the first Times Up is printed to the console.

```
public float NextTime;
public int Counter = 10;
```

Therefore, now, we have a timer. We should next add some sort of counter, so we know how many times the if statement was executed.

```csharp
if (Counter > 0)
{
    if (Time.fixedTime > NextTime)
    {
        NextTime = Time.fixedTime + 3;
        Counter--;
        Debug.Log("Times Up");
    }
}
```

First, add in int Counter = 10 to store how many times we want to run our if statement. If the Counter is greater than 0, then we need to check our Time.fixedTime if statement. Once the timer is reset, we need to decrement our Counter by 1. Once the counter is no longer greater than 0, we stop. There's a cleaner way to do this.

```csharp
if (Time.fixedTime > NextTime)
{
    NextTime = Time.fixedTime + 3;
    Counter--;
    Debug.Log("Times Up");
}
```

We can reduce the extra if statement checking the counter value. To merge if statements, use the && conditional operator. If either side of the && is false, then the if statement is not evaluated. Because there's no code in the if statement checking the counter, there's no reason why it can't be combined with the if statement it's containing.

Now, we have a timer and a counter. We can make this more useful by exposing some of the variables to the editor.

```csharp
if (Counter > 0 && Time.fixedTime > NextTime)
{
    NextTime = Time.fixedTime + Delay;
    Counter--;
    Debug.Log("Times Up");
}
```

Add in public before some of the existing variables, and for good measure, let's get rid of the 3 that we're adding to Time.fixedTime and make that into a variable as well. This is common practice; use some numbers to test a feature, and then once the feature roughly works, change some of the numbers into editable parameters that may be handed off to designers.

Now we can replace print ("Time Up"); with a more useful function. Once we've got the chops, we'll start replacing boxes with building pieces, but we'll leave that to the artists, the code below serves as a good example for now.

```
GameObject box = GameObject.CreatePrimitive(PrimitiveType.Cube);
box.transform.position = new Vector3(Counter * 2f, 0, 0);
NextTime = Time.fixedTime + Delay;
Counter--;
Debug.Log("Times Up");
```

This little block of code will slowly pop a new cube into existence around the scene origin. We're using Counter to multiply against 2 so each box object will appear in a different place along the *x* coordinate.

You can speed up the process by lowering the Delay value we just added. What if we wanted to have more than one box created at each counter interval? This objective can be accomplished using either a while or a for statement being run inside the if statement.

```
public float NextTime;
public float Delay = 0.5f;
public int Counter = 10;
```

Adding in the for loop is the easiest way to do this. UnityEngine.Random.Range(); is a new function that returns a number between the first argument and the second argument. We're just testing this so we can use any number to start with.

Okay, looks like everything is working as we might have expected. We should take out the numbers we're using in the `Random.Range()` and make them into more public parameters for use in the editor.

```
public float NextTime;
public float Delay = 0.5f;
public int Counter = 10;
public int MinimumHeight = 1;
public int MaximumHeight = 10;
public float XSpacing = 0.5f;
public float YSpacing = 0.5f;
```

Adding more variables to control spacing will also make this more interesting.

By tweaking some of the parameters, you can build something that looks like this with code alone! The reason why we should be exposing so many of these variables to the editor is to allow for creative freedom. The more parametric we make any system, the more exploration we can do with what the numbers mean.

```
if (Counter > 0 && Time.fixedTime > NextTime)
{
    int vertical = UnityEngine.Random.Range(MinimumHeight, MaximumHeight);
    for (int i = 0; i < vertical; i++)
    {
        GameObject box = GameObject.CreatePrimitive(PrimitiveType.Cube);
        box.transform.position = new Vector3(Counter * XSpacing, i * YSpacing, 0);
    }
    NextTime = Time.fixedTime + Delay;
    Counter--;
    Debug.Log("Times Up");
}
```

If you feel adventurous, then you can add in a second dimension to the stack of cubes.

Look at that. What started off as some cube-generating system turned into some 3D pixel art city generator.

```
if (Counter > 0 && Time.fixedTime > NextTime)
{
    for (int i = 0; i < 10 ; i++)
    {
        int vertical = UnityEngine.Random.Range(MinimumHeight, MaximumHeight);
        for (int j = 0; j < vertical; j++)
        {
            GameObject box = GameObject.CreatePrimitive(PrimitiveType.Cube);
            Vector3 position = new Vector3()
            {
                x = Counter * XSpacing,
                y = j * YSpacing,
                z = i * ZSpacing
            };
            box.transform.position = position;
        }
    }
    NextTime = Time.fixedTime + Delay;
    Counter--;
    Debug.Log("Times Up");
}
```

If we spend more time on this, then we can even start to add little cubes onto the big cubes by setting scale and position around each of the cubes as they are generated. We won't go into that right now; I'll leave that on to you to play with.

5.13.2 What We've Learned

We're starting to build more complex systems. Adding functions to classes and using them in for loops is a fairly flexible and reusable setup. What's important here is to understand a bit of the thought process of writing a complex system. We started off with one line, made sure that the line of code worked, then added another line or two. After several iterations we went from a simple timer to a small cube shaped pixel like city scape.

We should be a bit more comfortable reading complex algorithms in the functions we read on forums and in downloaded assets. If we come across something new, then we should be able to come up with some search terms to find out what we're looking at.

5.14 Leveling Up: On to the Cool Stuff

We've come further along than most people who set out to learn how to program. By now, you should be able to read through some code and get some idea of how it's working. We've gotten through some of the tough beginnings of learning how to write in C#, but things are just about to get more interesting.

The clever tricks that programmers use to save time are about to start to come into play. If you take the time, you should review Chapters 1 through 4 to strengthen your grasp of the core concepts we've been studying.

There's an interesting topic that hasn't found a place in any chapters yet. If you open the MagicComponent project in Unity 3D, you'll be able to see some interesting behavior. Say we have an object in the scene with a component attached. We'll look at something called FirstComponent.cs attached to a cube.

If the Main Camera has a component attached that has a couple of variables that are set for FirstComponent and SecondComponent, how do we add the GameObject's component to that slot in the Inspector panel? We drag it, of course!

Therefore, even though the variable isn't GameObject, you can still drag the object from the scene into the Inspector panel. Unity 3D is clever enough to find a component of the same type as the slot in the Inspector.

This feature also means that any variable changed on the object in the scene will have a direct connection to the Magic.cs class that is holding onto the variable. This means a couple of strange things. First, the objects in the scene are instances, but they are acting in a rather weird limbo. Second, the connection between variables is stored in some magic data stored in the scene file.

The weird limbo infers that when you drag a class onto an object in the editor, it is immediately instanced. This behavior is unusual in that this only happens in the Unity 3D Editor, your player and the finished game never has any behavior like this. The class instances an object and attaches it to the `GameObject` in the scene, as though you used `GameObject.Instance()` or even new `FirstComponent();`, or perhaps `Component.Add();`, and added it to the `GameObject` in the scene.

The fact that the `Start()` and `Update()` functions aren't called means that the game isn't running. However, the class is still an instanced object created by the .cs file in the Assets directory. There are editor scripts that do run while the game might not be playing. Editor scripts are often used to help game designers.

Editor scripts can be used to create tools and other fun interfaces specifically for the Unity 3D Editor. These are often not running while the game is playing. We shouldn't venture too far into Unity 3D-specific tricks as this distracts us from learning more about C#, but it's fun to know what to look for if we want to build our own C# tools for Unity 3D.

The strange fact that the variable in Magic.cs has a handle on an object in the scene without having to run `GameObject.Find();` or `Transform.Find();` means that there's a lot going on in the scene file. All of this is actually stored in the meta files that seem to be appearing as you work with others on Unity 3D projects.

These meta files are required for these magic data connections between objects in a Unity 3D Scene file. Of course, other file settings and project settings are also stored in these meta files. If you open one, you'll find many things called GUIDs, which stands for globally unique identifiers, and they're used in meta files to find a specific object in the scene and apply settings to them.

It wasn't long ago when game engines referenced everything in the scene by their GUID alone. Today, they're at least hidden from view, but they still affect our lives as game programmers. We can't reference a specific object by name alone. If you've got several objects named GameObject, then you're going to have a rough time remembering which one actually has the data you're looking for. Because of this, everything is assigned a GUID and that's just the way it's gotta be.

6

Intermediate: The Tricks of the Trade

The coming chapters are big, dense, and exciting. Getting into a programming language means discovering many cool tricks. The basics of most programming languages have already been covered.

From here on out, you'll be learning some of the more clever systems that make the C# language elegant and concise. Rather than having long chains of if-else statements, you can use a switch statement. Rather than having a large uncontrolled nest of different variables, you can group them together in a struct.

Don't worry about not making rapid progress; learning is more about the journey than it is about the goal. Of course, if you do have a goal of making a featured mobile game, then by all means, speed forth toward your goal. Just try not to skip around too much; there's much stuff that is explained for a reason.

6.1 What Will Be Covered in This Chapter

The long journey begins. We're going to cover some important concepts here, including the following:

- Classes as objects
- Class constructors
- Arrays
- Enums
- Switch statement
- Structures
- Namespaces
- More on functions
- More on inheritance
- More on type casting
- Some work on vectors
- Goto
- Out parameter
- Ref parameter
- Operator overloading

This chapter discusses a few concepts more than once, or rather, we look at different aspects of type casting, for instance, but we divide the concept over more than one chapter. In between the chapters, we cover a few other concepts that do relate back to the topic. Learning a single concept can mean taking in a few separate concepts before coming back to the original topic.

6.2 Review

By now you've been equipped with quite a vocabulary of terms and a useful set of tools to take care of nearly any basic task. Moving forward, you'll only extend your ability and come to grips that you've still got a long way to go. Even after years of engineering software, there's always more to learn. Even once you think you've covered a programming language, a new version is released then you need to learn more features.

Aside from learning one language, most companies will eventually toss in a task that involves learning another programming language. In a modern setting, it's likely you'll need to learn some of the programming languages while on the job. This might involve knowing something like Scala or PHP, yet another programming language you'll have to learn.

Learning additional programming languages isn't as daunting as you might think. Once you know one language, it's far easier to learn another. The keyword var is used in many other programming languages in the exact same context. It's a keyword used to store a variable. In C#, we see `var v = "things";`, which is similar to JavaScript where `var v = "things";`.

So far, the principles that have been covered in this book are general enough such that almost every other programming language has similar concepts. Nearly all languages have conditions and operators. Most languages use tokens and white space in the same way as well.

6.2.1 Class Members

Classes provided by Unity 3D become accessible when you add using UnityEngine at the top of your C# code. All the classes found inside of that library have names which you can use directly in your own code. This includes Input, and all the members of Input are imported into your code.

6.2.1.1 A Basic Example

Follow along with the ClassMembers_Scene and the ClassMembers script found in the Chapter 6 Unity 3D project. Let's start off with a new class that will have some functions in it. We've done this before by creating a new C# class in the Project panel.

```
public class Members
{
    public void FirstFunction()
    {
        Debug.Log("FirstFunction");
    }
}
```

Create a new class called Members.cs because we're going to use members of the Members class. Then we'll add public `void FirstFunction()` with `Debug.Log("First Function");` to print to the Console panel when it's invoked.

There are two classifications for the stuff that classes are made of: data members and function members. As you might imagine, function members are the lines of code that execute and run logic on data. Data members are the variables that are accessible within the class.

In our Example class we've been abusing a lot, we'll add in the following line to the `Start()` function:

```
void Start()
{
    Members m = new Members();
}
```

This creates what's called an instance. We're assigning the identifier m to being a new copy or instance of the Members class. The keyword new is used to create new instances. `Members();` is used to tell the new keyword what class we're using. It seems like we're using the class as a function, and to a limited extent we are, but we'll have to leave those details for Section 6.3.3.1.

The m variable that is an instance of the Members class is now a thing we can use in the function. When we use m, we can access its members.

```
28        void Start()
29        {
30            Members m = new Members();
31            m.|
32        }            Equals
     void Members.FirstFunction()   FirstFunction
34            GetHashCode
35            GetType
             ToString
```

Type "m." and a new pop-up will appear in Visual Studio showing a list of things that m can do. FirstFunction, as well as a few other items, is in the list. These other items were things that Object was able to do. Accessing the different functions within a class is a simple matter of using the dot operator.

```
void Start()
{
    Members m = new Members();
    m.FirstFunction();
}
```

Finish off the m. by adding `FirstFunction();`. Running the script when it's attached to a cube or something in the scene will produce the following Console output. Objects and its members have many uses; though, this might not be clear from this one example.

6.2.1.2 Thinking Like a Programmer

A peek into a programmer's thinking process reveals a step-by-step process of evaluating a situation and finding a solution for each step. The plan begins with an overall goal but finding the small incremental steps to reach the goal are just as important.

Gathering data and then doing something with the data follows. Then logic takes the front seat in this case, as the programmer needs to not only investigate each function, he or she must use but also clean up the thinking process as he or she writes code.

Intuition and deduction are a huge part of programming. The programmer needs to guess what sort of functions he or she should be looking for. With each new development environment, the programmer needs to learn the software's application programming interface, the interface between you (the programmer) and the application you're working with, in this case, Unity 3D.

At this point, we have some basic tools to do something interesting with our game scene. However, to make a game, we're going to read input from the keyboard, mouse, and any other input device that the player might want to use. An appropriate place to start would be looking up the word "input" in the Solution Explorer in Visual Studio.

Dig into the UnityEngine.dll and expand the UnityEngine library. You should find an Input class that looks very promising. From here, we can start hunting for a function inside of input that might be useful for us. At this point, I should mention that programmers all seem to use a unique vocabulary.

The words "Get," and "Set" are often used by programmers for getting and setting values. For getting a keyboard command, we should look for a function that gets things for us. We can find "GetKey" in the numerous functions found in Input.

```
public static bool GetKey (string name)...
public static bool GetKey (KeyCode key)...
public static bool GetKeyDown (string name)...
public static bool GetKeyDown (KeyCode key)...
public static bool GetKeyUp (string name)...
public static bool GetKeyUp (KeyCode key)...
```

There seems to be a string name and KeyCode key for each one of the functions. We did mention that reusing names for things means erasing a previously used name. However, this doesn't always hold true. In the case of functions, when you duplicate a name, you're allowed to share the name, as long as you do something different with the arguments found in parentheses. This is called overriding, and we'll learn more about that in Section 6.13.1. It's just good to know what you're looking at so you don't get too lost.

So now that we've found something that looks useful, how do we use it? The "GetKey" function looks like its public function, which is good. Functions with the keyword public are functions that we're allowed to use.

The context when using the dot operator in numbers changes an int to a double or float if you add in an f at the end of the number. When you add the dot operator after the name of a class found in UnityEngine, you're asking to gain access to a class member. In this case, we found GetKey inside of Input, so to talk to that function we use the dot operator after Input to get to that function.

There were two GetKey functions: The first had "KeyCode key" and the second had "string name" written in the arguments for the function. This means we have two options we can use.

When you add the first parenthesis, MonoDevelop pops up some helpers.

These help you fill in the blanks. There are many KeyCode options to choose from. You can see them all by scrolling through the pop-up. I picked the KeyCode.A to test this out. I'm guessing that pressing the A key on the keyboard is going to change something. In the Example.cs file, add in the following:

```
bool AKey = Input.GetKey(KeyCode.A);
Debug.Log(AKey);
```

We're setting the bool AKey to this function; why a bool and why even do this? Remember that the function was designated as a public static bool. The last word is the reason why we're using a bool AKey. The variable type we're setting matches the return type of the function.

Finally, we're printing out the value of AKey. Run the game and press the A key on your keyboard and read the Console output from Unity 3D.

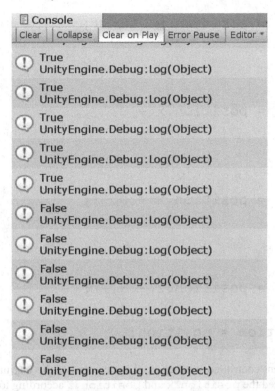

When the A key is down, we get True; when it's not down, we get False. It looks like our hunch was correct. Our AKey bool is now being controlled by the Input class' member function GetKey. We know the return type of GetKey because of the bool that was written just before the name of the function. We also know how to access the function inside of Input through the dot operator.

Let's keep this going. Make a bool for WKey, SKey, and DKey. This will allow us to use the classic WASD keyboard input found in many different games. Then we'll make them set to the different GetKeys that we're going to use from Input.

Now we're going to make our cube move around, so we're going to look at the Transform class. To move our cube around, we're going to keep track of our current position. To do this, we're going to make a Vector 3 called pos as a class scoped variable.

```
position = transform.position;
```

The first thing we want to do is set the pos to the object's current position when the game starts. This means we can place the cube anywhere in the scene at the beginning of the game and the pos will know where we're starting.

```
bool AKey = Input.GetKey(KeyCode.A);
bool WKey = Input.GetKey(KeyCode.W);
bool SKey = Input.GetKey(KeyCode.S);
bool DKey = Input.GetKey(KeyCode.D);
```

In the function named Update(), we're going to set the transform.position of the cube to pos in each frame. This means that if we change the x, y, or z of the pos Vector3 variable, the cube will go to that Vector3. Now all we need to do is change the position.x and position.z when we press one of the keys.

```
if (AKey)
{
    position.x = position.x - 0.1f;
}
if (DKey)
{
    position.x = position.x + 0.1f;
}
if (WKey)
{
    position.z = position.z + 0.1f;
}
if (SKey)
{
    position.z = position.z - 0.1f;
}
transform.position = position;
```

I've added an if statement controlled by each bool we created at the beginning of the `Update()` function. Then we changed the `position.x` and `position.z` according to the direction I wanted the cube to move in by adding or subtracting a small value. Try this out and experiment with some different values.

This is not the only solution, nor is it the best. This is a simple solution and rather restricted. The speed is constant, and the rotation of the cube is also fixed. If we want to improve on this solution, we're going to need a better way to deal with many variables.

A big part of programming is starting with something basic and then refining it later. You start with the things you know and add to it stuff you figure out. Once you learn more, you go back and make changes. It's a process that never ends. As programmers learn more and figure out more clever tricks, their new code gets written with more clever tricks.

6.2.2 Return

The `return` keyword is powerful and it's a very clever trick. It's used in a couple of different ways, but certainly the most useful is turning a function into data. If a function doesn't give out data, it's given the return type void. For instance, we've been using `void Start()` and `void Update()`.

void indicates that the function doesn't need to return any data; using the keyword return in a function like this returns a void or a nothing. Any keywords that precede the return type modify how the function operates; for instance, if we wanted to make a function available to other classes, we need to precede the return type with the keyword public.

6.2.2.1 A Basic Example

Using the return keyword gives a function a value. You're allowed to use the function name as though it were the function's return value.

```
int ImANumber()
{
    return 3;
}
```

In the `Start()` function the following sends 3 to the console.

```
Debug.Log(ImANumber());
```

When you run this basic example, you'll see a 3 printed out in the Console panel. To prove that `ImANumber()` is just a 3, you can even perform math with the function. In the following example, you'll get many 6 s being printed out to the Console panel.

```
Debug.Log(ImANumber() + ImANumber());
```

Most often when we want to reduce complexity within a single function, we need to separate our code into other smaller functions. Doing so makes our work less cluttered and easier to manage. Once the code has been separated into different smaller functions, they become individual commands that can contain their own complexity.

We're going to reduce the number of lines required in the Update loop. To do this, we'll write our own function with a return type Vector3. Reducing the number of lines of code you have to muddle through is sometimes the goal of clean code.

`ImANumber()` isn't a variable; it's a function; more so, it's a function that returns a value. In other words, you will not be able to assign something to `ImANumber()` as in the following example:

```
ImANumber() = 7;
```

There are ways to do something like this. We'll need to use the contents in parentheses to assign `ImANumber()` a value for it to return.

6.2.3 Arguments aka "Args" (Not Related to Pirates)

We've seen the use of arguments (also known as args) earlier when we initialized a "Vector3 (x, y, z);" with three parameters. Review with a function that's very simple and takes one arg.

6.2.3.1 *The Basic Example*

This function takes a number and returns it.

```
int INeedANumber(int number)
{
    return number;
}
```

The function `int INeedANumber (int number)` is used in our `Start()` function. The argument field is populated with `int number`, indicating two things. First is the type that we expect to be in our function's argument list as well as a name or an identifier for the int argument. The identifier number from the argument list exists throughout the scope of the function.

```
Debug.Log(INeedANumber(1));

int val = INeedANumber(3) + INeedANumber(7);
Debug.Log(val);
```

In this second example, we use the INeedANumber() function as a number. It just so happens to be the same number we're using in its argument list. When we print out val from this, we get 10 printed to the Console panel. However, this doesn't have to be the case.

```
Debug.Log(INeedANumber(1));

int val = INeedANumber(3) + INeedANumber(7);
Debug.Log(val);
```

If we were to modify the return value to number +1 and run the previous example, we'd have 12 printed out to the Console panel. This would be the same as adding 4 and 8, or what is happening inside of the function 3 + 1 and 7 + 1.

6.2.3.2 Multiple Args

When you see functions without anything in parentheses, programmers say that the function takes no args. Or rather, the function doesn't need any arguments to do its work. We can expand upon this by adding another argument to our function. To tell C# what your two arguments are, you separate them with a comma and follow the same convention of type followed by identifier.

```
int INeedTwoNumbers(int a, int b)
{
    return a + b;
}
```

This is used in the Start() function which looks like the following:

```
Debug.Log(INeedTwoNumbers(7, 10));
```

The function takes two arguments, adds them together, and then prints out the result to the Unity 3D's Console panel. Just for the sake of clarity, you're allowed to use any variety of types for your args. The only condition is that the final result needs to match the same type as the return value. In more simple terms, when the function is declared, its return type is set by the keyword used when it's declared.

This also includes data types which you've written. We'll take a look at that in a bit, but for now we'll use some data types we've already seen.

```
int INeedTwoNumbersOfDifferentTypes(int a, float b)
{
    return a + (int)b;
}
```

Mixing different types together can create some interesting effects, some of which might not be expected. We'll study the consequences of mixing types later on as we start to learn about type casting, but for now just observe how this behaves on your own and take some notes. To convert a float value to an int value, you precede the float with the number type you want to convert it to with (ToType) DifferentType, but we'll get into type conversions again later.

So far we've been returning the same data types going into the function; this doesn't have to be the case. A function that returns a boolean value doesn't need to accept booleans in its argument list.

```
bool NumbersAreTheSame(int a, int b)
{
    bool returnValue;
    if (a == b)
    {
        returnValue = true;
    }
    else
    {
        returnValue = false;
    }
    return returnValue;
}
```

In this case, if both a and b are the same number, then the function returns true. If the two numbers are different, then the function returns false. This works well, but we can also shorten this code by a couple of lines if we use more than one return.

```
bool NumbersAreTheSameSimple(int a, int b)
{
    if (a == b)
    {
        return true;
    }
    else
    {
        return false;
    }
}
```

The return keyword can appear in more than one place. However, this can cause some problems. If we return a value based on only a limited case, then the compiler will catch this problem.

```
bool NumbersAreTheSameSimple(int a, int b)
{
    if (a == b)
    {
        return true;
    }
    // else
    // {
    //     return false;
    // }
}
```

This example will cause an error stating the following:

```
Assets/Example.cs(16,6): error CS0161: "Example. NumbersAreTheSame(int,
int)": not all code paths return a value
```

The most simple form of the above returns on a single line.

```
bool NumbersAreTheSameMostSimple(int a, int b)
{
    return a == b;
}
```

The rest of the possibilities need to have a return value. In terms of what Unity 3D expects, all paths of the code need to return a valid bool. The return value always needs to be fulfilled, otherwise the code will not compile.

6.2.3.3 Using Args

Doing these little changes repeatedly becomes troublesome, so they leave some things up to other people to change until they like the results. Each function in the Input class returns a unique value. We can observe these by looking at the results of Input.GetKey().

```
Debug.Log(Input.GetKey(KeyCode.A));
```

Once you type in Input, a pop-up with the members of the Input class is shown. Among them is GetKey. Once you enter GetKey and add in the first parenthesis, another pop-up with a list of various inputs is shown. Choose the KeyCode.A. Many other input options are available, so feel free to experiment with them on your own.

To test this code out, run the game and watch the output in the Console panel. Hold down the "a" key on the keyboard and watch the false printout replaced with true when the key is down. Using the print() function to test things out one at a time is a simple way to check out what various functions do. Test out the various other keys found in the Input.GetKey() function.

```
Vector3 Movement(float dist)
{
    Vector3 vector = Vector3.zero;
    if (Input.GetKey(KeyCode.A))
    {
        vector.x -= dist;
    }
    if (Input.GetKey(KeyCode.D))
    {
        vector.x += dist;
    }
    if (Input.GetKey(KeyCode.W))
    {
        vector.z += dist;
    }
    if (Input.GetKey(KeyCode.S))
    {
        vector.z -= dist;
    }
    return vector;
}
```

We should add an argument to the `Movement()` function. With this we'll add in a simple way to change a variable inside of the `Movement()` function and maintain the function's portability. Replace the 0.1f value with the name of the argument. This means that anything put into the function's argument list will be duplicated across each statement that uses it.

This means we need to pass in a parameter to the argument list in the `Movement()` function. We can test by entering a simple float, which is what the `Movement()` argument list expects.

```
transform.position += Movement(0.2f);
```

This means we're just reducing the number of places a number is being typed. We want to make this number easier to edit and something that can be modified in the editor.

public float Speed;

Add in a public float so that the Inspector panel can see it. Then add the variable to the `Movement()`'s parameter list.

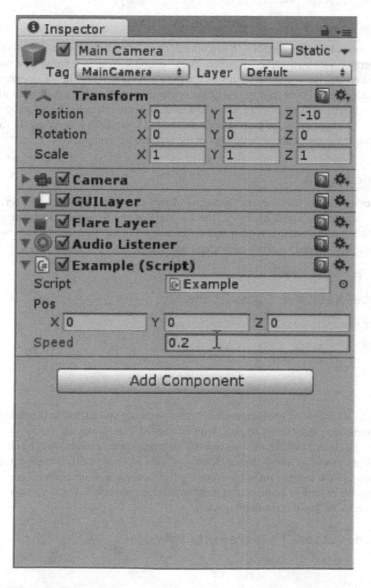

Change the value for Delta in the Inspector panel and run the game. Now the WASD keys will move the cube around at a different speed, thanks to the use of a public variable. There are a few different ways to do the same thing. For instance, we could have ignored using the arguments and used Delta in place of Dist. However, this means that the function would rely on a line of code outside of the function to work. Everywhere you want to use the function, you'd have to write in a public float Delta statement at the class level.

6.2.4 Assignment Operators

Operators that fill variables with data are called assignment operators. We've been using = to assign a variable a value in the previous chapters. There are different types of assignment operators that have added functionality.

```
void UpdateAssignmentOperators()
{
    transform.position += new Vector3(0.1f, 0, 0);
}
```

Introduce the += operator to the Vector3. When operators are used in pairs there are no spaces between them. The + operator adds two values together. The = operator assigns a value to a variable. If there was white space between the + and the =, this would raise a syntax error. The += operator allows you to add two vectors together without having to use the original variable name again. This also works with single numbers. An int MyInt += 1; works just as well. Rather than having to use position.z = position.z + 0.1f, you can use position.z += 0.1f, which is less typing. If you run the code up above, then you'll see your cube scooting off in the positive *x* direction.

6.2.4.1 A Basic Example

The example uses a function called in the Update() function in the ClassMembers script. As we have seen with the ++ and the -- unary operators, the += operator and its negative version, the -=, work in a similar way. One important and easy-to-forget difference is the fact that the ++ and -- works only on integer data types. The += and -= work on both integer and floating point data types.

```
float f = 0;
void UpdateAssignmentOperators()
{
    f += 0.25f;
    Debug.Log(f);
}
```

In this example, the f variable will be incremented 0.25f with each update call. In the code fragment above, this increase is something that cannot be done with an integer. This is like using f = f + 0.25f; though the += is a bit cleaner looking, or "less verbose" as a programmer might say. The change is primarily aesthetic, and programmers are a fussy bunch, so the += is the preferred method to increment values.

A part of learning how to program is by decoding the meaning behind cryptic operators, and this is just one example. We're sure to come across more mysterious operators, but if you take them in slowly and practice using them, you'll learn them quickly.

```
transform.position += Movement(Speed);
```

Rather than using a new `Vector3` to add to the transform.position, we want to use a function. To make this work, the function has to have a `Vector3` return type. For a function to return the type, we need to include the keyword return in the function.

```
void UpdateAssignmentOperators()
{
    transform.position += Offset();
}

Vector3 Offset()
{
    return new Vector3(0.1f, 0.2f, 0.3f);
}
```

This function is now a `Vector3` value. Based on any external changes, the value returned can also change. This makes our function very flexible and much more practical. Again, the cube will scoot off to the *x* if you run this code. This and the previous examples are doing the exact same thing. Don't forget that C# is case sensitive, so make sure the vector is named the same throughout the function.

```
Vector3 vector = Vector3.zero;
if (Input.GetKey(KeyCode.A))
{
    vector.x -= dist;
}
if (Input.GetKey(KeyCode.D))
{
    vector.x += dist;
}
if (Input.GetKey(KeyCode.W))
{
    vector.z += dist;
}
if (Input.GetKey(KeyCode.S))
{
    vector.z -= dist;
}
return vector;
```

If += works to add a number to a value, then -= subtracts a value from the number. There are some more variations on this, but they're going to have to wait for Section 8.9.

The `Movement()` function is portable. If you copy the function into another class, you have made reusable code. As any programmer will tell you, you should always write reusable code. The function operates mostly on its own. It relies on very few lines of code outside of the function. There are no class scoped variables it's depending on, so you need to only copy the lines of code existing in the function.

This function is not completely without any external dependencies. The `Input.GetKey` function does rely on the UnityEngine library, but there are ways to reduce this even further. To figure out other ways to reduce complexity and dependencies, we need to learn more tricks.

Wherever you need to read input and return a `Vector3` to move something, you can use this function. Copy and paste the function in any class, and then add the `transform.position += Movement ();` into the `Update()` function of that object, and it will move when you press the WASD keys.

6.2.5 What We've Learned

The earlier discussion was an introduction to arguments and return values. We started to learn a bit about how to use members of classes and how to find them. There's still a lot more to learn, but I think we have a pretty good start and enough of a foundation to build on by playing with things in the game engine.

It's time to start having functions talk to other functions, and to do this, we're going to start writing some more classes that can talk to one another. Accessing other classes is going to require some more interesting tricks, and with everything we learn, we expand the tools that we can build with.

6.3 Building a Game—Part 4

What the player sees while playing is an important part of how the game is played. Camera control is just as important as Player control. We created a simple input system to move and shoot for the player. Adding some basic camera behavior should follow.

6.3.1 ChaseCamera

If the goal is to simply have the camera follow the player we can do this with a simple script that uses the player's x and z coordinates and adds that to the camera. There are a few tricks that we need to look at to get something that works as we expect. To start we'll begin with a script that looks like the Mover script from Chapter 5.

```csharp
public class ChaseCamera : MonoBehaviour
{
    private GameObject _Target;
    private GameObject Target[...]

    private void Update()
    {
        if (Target == null)
            return;
    }
}
```

A camera that follows the player should keep its relative position away from the Player. The difference between the target position between frames can be used to move the camera.

```
private Vector3 Offset;
private void Update()
{
    if (Target == null)
        return;
    // Calculate the difference between previous position
    // and the new position.
    Vector3 diff = Target.transform.position - Offset;
    // Move the camera that difference.
    transform.position += diff;
    // update the Offset value.
    Offset = Target.transform.position;
}
```

As the player moves and updates are called, we calculate that movement by maintaining a `Vector3` `Offset`. As the Player object moves around the `Target.transform.position` changes. We track that difference as the player's position - `Offset`. Once calculated we add that to the camera's position. After the camera's position is updated, the `Offset` is updated with the current position of the `Target`.

6.3.2 Tile Floor Generator

So that was a simple example of a camera following system. But what about the environment? Running around on a plain white floor isn't exciting. A procedurally generated floor plane might be more interesting.

```
[ExecuteInEditMode]
public class FloorGenerator : MonoBehaviour
{
    // Trigger in the Inspector Panel to
    // generate tiles
    public bool GenerateTiles;
    // Original prefab objects to make
    // a tile floor from
    public GameObject[] TileOriginals;
    // a List of tiles to store if
    // we want to make new tiles
    public GameObject[,] TileObjects;
    // How many tiles to make
    public int Width;
    public int Depth;
    private List<GameObject> TileObjectList;
```

Various systems in the script can be updated in the Editor before the game begins. These are added with what is called an Attribute. The Attribute called `[ExecuteInEditMode]` can be added to a script to enable it's execution before the game has started. We'll cover this in more detail in Section 8.10. The short story is that this specific Attribute allows the Update() to be computed while we are setting up the Scene.

```
if (GenerateTiles)
{
    GenerateTiles = false;
```

To control how often we generate the tiles we use a bool `GenerateTiles`. This keeps the `Update()` from generating new tiles every frame. An array is used to keep a reference to a couple of prefabs that we'll use to generate the tile floor from. In this case we have a light and a dark tile. A `List<GameObject>` named `TileObjectList` is used to store the generated tiles. With this we can store the tiles that are generated. This is used to remember the generated tiles, so we can clear them before generating new ones. The list is used to iterate through all the generated tile objects.

```
//clear any tiles that might already be there
foreach (GameObject tile in TileObjectList)
{
    DestroyImmediate(tile);
}
TileObjectList = new List<GameObject>();
```

`Width` and `Depth` parameters are used to store the `TileObjects` in a 2D array. A simple system to alternate through the different tiles is used to pick which original tile to make an instance of.

```
TileObjects = new GameObject[Width, Depth];
for (int x = 0; x < Width; x++)
{
    for (int z = 0; z < Depth; z++)
    {
        int o = (z + x) % TileOriginals.Length;
        TileObjects[x, z] = GameObject.Instantiate(TileOriginals[o], transform);
        TileObjects[x, z].transform.position = new Vector3()
        {
            x = x - (Width / 2),
            z = z - (Depth / 2)
        };
        // keep track of what to delete when we
        // need to make a new set of tiles.
        TileObjectList.Add(TileObjects[x, z]);
    }
}
```

The value `int o = (z + x) % TileOriginals.Length;` will increment with each object. This then returns a value that's incremented up through each tile. The value is limited to the number of tiles in the originals list. The position of each tile instance is then positioned with x -(Width/2) and z - (Depth/2). This makes the tiles generated around the origin. Without this, the tiles begin at the origin but only expand in the positive quadrant away from the origin. As the tiles are created they're added to the List to easily delete them when the size is changed and a new set of tiles is created.

Once the tiles are generated, a list copies them to the `TileObjects` array so we can delete them before making a new set.

Now a small array or a large array of tiles can be generated. Change the `Width` and `Depth` parameters and click on the `GenerateTiles` bool check box to change the size of the grid.

Using a script to generate results in the editing of a Scene is useful. When the generated data is saved in the scene it's not generated again unless the editor is run. Manually duplicating and placing tiles would be tedius. It's better to spend time coming up with new game play elements rather than placing tiles.

There are some considerations when it comes to using a system to generate tiles. The first is that we need to keep a list of things that were created. When a checkbox triggers the creation of many objects, we should delete the ones that are already in the scene.

6.3.3 What We've Learned

Plenty of new syntax was seen in this chapter. Your familiarity with how the keywords and variable types are created and used will catch up to what was just seen in the coming chapters. This project should serve as a starting point to dismantle and experiment with.

The code here is purposely written in small easily digested chunks. Each class has a clear and focused purpose. In practice, code should be written in small easily separated components. This makes editing and changing how each component works easier. Keep that in mind when you begin work on your own project.

6.4 Class Constructors

Follow along with the ClassConstructors script found in the ClassConstructors_Scene on the ClassConstructors object in the Chapter6 Unity 3D project. In the script is written the following example:

```
class Zombie
{
}
```

We start off with very little information. As we assign member fields and member functions, we create places for the class to store data and provide the class with capability.

```
class Zombie
{
    public string Name;
    public int BrainsEaten;
    public int HitPoints;
}
```

The use of these parameters is inferred by their name and use. When we create a new `Zombie()` in the game, we could spend the next few lines initializing his parameters. Of course, we can add as many parameters as needed, but for this example, we're going to limit ourselves to just a few different objects.

```
void Start()
{
    Zombie rob = new Zombie();
    rob.Name = "Zombie";
    rob.HitPoints = 10;
    rob.BrainsEaten = 0;
}
```

One simple method provided in C# is to add the parameters of the classes in a set of curly braces. Each field in Zombie is accessible through this method. Each one is separated by a comma, not a semicolon.

```
Zombie rob = new Zombie()
{
    Name = "Zombie",
    HitPoints = 10,
    BrainsEaten = 0
};
```

Note the trailing ";" after the closing curly brace. This system doesn't do much to shorten the amount of work involved. With each public data field provided in the `Zombie` class, we need to use the name of the field and assign it. Doing this for every new zombie might seem like a bit of extra work.

While building prototypes and quickly jamming code together, shortcuts like these can inform how we intend to use the class object. Rather than coming up with all possibilities and attempting to predict how a class is going to be used, it's usually better to use a class, try things out, and then make changes later.

6.4.1 A Basic Example

A class constructor would save a bit of extra work. You might have noticed that the statement `Zombie rob = new Zombie()` has a pair of parentheses after the class it's instancing. When a class `Zombie()` is instanced, we could provide additional information to this line. To enable this, we need to add in a constructor to the `Zombie()`'s class. This looks like the following:

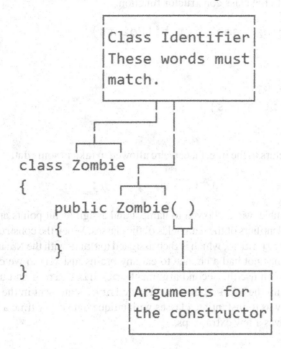

To give this example more meaning, we'll use the following code:

```
class Zombie
{
    public string Name;
    public int BrainsEaten;
    public int HitPoints;
    /* ... */
    public Zombie()
    {
        Name = "Zombie";
        BrainsEaten = 0;
        HitPoints = 10;
    }
}
```

After the data fields, we create a new function named after the class. This function is called a class constructor. The function public `Zombie()` contains assignment statements that do the same thing as the previous class instantiation code we were using.

```
Zombie rob = new Zombie();
```

This statement `Zombie rob = new Zombie();` invokes the `Zombie()` constructor function in the Zombie class. When the Constructor function is called, `Name`, `BrainsEaten`, and `HitPoints` are all assigned at the same time. However, this will assume that every zombie is named "Zombie," has eaten no brains, and has `10 HitPoints`. This is not likely the case with all zombies. Therefore, we'd want to provide some parameters to the class constructor function.

```
public Zombie(string name, int hitPoints)
{
    Name = name;
    BrainsEaten = 0;
    HitPoints = hitPoints;
}
```

By adding in a few parameters to the interface, we're allowed to take in some data as the class is instanced.

```
Zombie rob = new Zombie("Rob", 10);
```

When we create a new zombie, we're allowed to name it and assign its hit points at the same time without needing to remember the identifiers of the data fields of the classes. When the constructor is invoked, the first field corresponds to a `string name`, which is then assigned to `Name` with the `Name = name;` statement.

Assume a new zombie has not had a chance to eat any brains just yet, so we can assign it to 0 when it's instanced. Finally, we can use the second argument `int hitPoints` and use that to assign to the instance's `HitPoints` with the `HitPoints = hitPoints;` statement in the constructor.

Class constructors allow us to instantiate classes with unique data every time a new class is instanced. Putting this into use involves a few extra steps.

```
float height;
GameObject gameObject;
public Zombie(string name, int hitPoints, Vector3 startPosition)
{
    Name = name;
    BrainsEaten = 0;
    HitPoints = hitPoints;

    // find the zombie from the Resources folder.
    gameObject = Resources.Load("ZombiePrimitive") as GameObject;
    // add the resource to the scene.
    Instantiate(gameObject);

    gameObject.name = Name;
    gameObject.transform.position = startPosition;
    height = Random.Range(1f, 3f);
    gameObject.transform.localScale = new Vector3()
    {
        x = 1,
        y = height, // give him a random height
        z = 1
    };
}
```

By adding a mesh to each zombie, we can more directly observe the instantiation of a new zombie in a scene. To make this more clear, we create a vector with a random *x* and a random *z* position so that they can appear in different places.

```
string[] names = new string[] { "Stubbs", "Rob", "White" };
for (int i = 0; i < names.Length; i++)
{
    Vector3 startPosition = new Vector3(i, 0, 0);
    Zombie z = new Zombie(names[i], Random.Range(5, 10), startPosition);
}
```

To make use of the different parameters, we create a new list of zombie names. Then in a for loop, we create a new zombie for each name in the list. For good measure, we assign a random number of hit points for each one with `Random.Range(10, 15)` which assigns a random number to each zombie between 10 and 15.

6.4.2 What We've Learned

A class constructor is very useful and should almost always be created when you create a new class. We are also allowed to create multiple systems to use a constructor. We'll get around to covering that in Section 6.13.1 on function overrides, but we'll have to leave off here for now.

When building a class, it's important to think in terms of what might change between each object. This turns into options that can be built into the constructor. Giving each object the ability to be created with different options allows for more variations in game play and appearance. Setting initial colors, behaviors, and starting variables is easier with a constructor. The alternative would be to create the new object and then change its values after the object is already in the scene.

6.5 Arrays Revisited

By now, we're familiar with the bits of knowledge that we'll need to start writing code. In Chapter 7, we'll become more familiar with the integrated development environment known as Visual Studio, and we'll go deeper into variables and functions.

Let's start off with a task. Programmers usually need something specific to do, so to stretch our knowledge and to force ourselves to learn more, we're going to do something simple that requires some new tricks to accomplish. If we're going to make a game with a bunch of characters, we're going to make and keep track of many different bits of information such as location, size, and type.

6.5.1 Using Arrays in Unity 3D

To follow along open the Chapter 6 Unity Project and open the ArraysRevisited_Scene and open the ArraysRevisited script attached to the game object of the same name.

So far, we've dealt with variables that hold a single value. For instance, `int i = 0;` in which the variable i holds only a single value. This works out fine when dealing with one thing at a time. However, if we want a whole number of objects to work together, we're going to have them grouped together in memory.

If we needed to, we could have a single variable for each box `GameObject` that would look like the following:

```
public GameObject box1;
public GameObject box2;
public GameObject box3;
public GameObject box4;
public GameObject box5;
public GameObject box6;
public GameObject box7;
public GameObject box8;
public GameObject box9;
public GameObject box10;
```

While this does work, this will give a programmer a headache in about 3 seconds, not to mention if you want to do something to one box, you'd have to repeat your code for every other box. This is horrible, and programming is supposed to make things easier, not harder on you. This is where arrays come to the rescue.

```
public GameObject[] boxes;
```

Ah yes, much better, 10 lines turn into one. There's one very important difference here. There's a pair of square brackets after the GameObject to indicate that we're making an array of game objects. Square brackets are used to tell a variable that we're making the singular form of a variable into a plural form of the variable. This works the same for any other type of data.

```
//a single int
int MyInt;
// an array of ints
int[] MyInts;
// a single object
object MyObject;
//an array of objects
object[] MyObjects;
```

To tell the boxes variable how many it's going to be holding, we need to initialize the array with its size before we start stuffing it full of data. This will look a bit like the Vector 3 we initialized in Section 3.10.2. We have a couple of options. We can right out tell the boxes how many it's going to be holding.

```
public GameObject[] TenGameObjects = new GameObject[10];
```

Or we can initialize the number of boxes using the Start() function and a public int variable.

```
public int numBoxes = 10;
public GameObject[] SomeBoxes;
private void Start()
{
    SomeBoxes = new GameObject[numBoxes];
}
```

In the above code, we're going to add a numBoxes variable and then move the initialization of the boxes variable to the Start() function using the numBoxes to satisfy the array size. In the Unity Inspector panel you'll see a field "Num Boxes" appear rather than numBoxes. Unity automatically changes variable names to be more human readable, but it's the same variable.

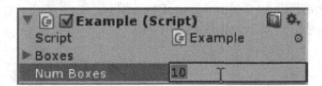

In the editor, we can pick any number of boxes we need without needing to change any code. Game designers like this sort of stuff. Once you run the game, the boxes array is initialized. To see what is contained in the array, you can expand the boxes variable in the Inspector panel and get the following:

We've got an array filled with a great deal of nothing, sure. However, it's the right number of nothing. Since we haven't put anything into the array of GameObjects we shouldn't be surprised. So far everything is going as planned. Testing as we write is important. With nearly every statement we write, we should confirm that it's doing what we think it should be doing. Next, we should put a new cube primitive into each one of the parts of this array.

6.5.1.1 Starting with 0

Zeroth. Some older programming languages start with 1. This is a carryover from FORTRAN that was created in 1957. Some programming languages mimic this behavior. Lua, for example, is a more modern programming language that starts with 1. C# is not like these older languages. Here we start with 0 and then count to 1; we do not start at 1. Thus, an array of 10 items is numbered 0 through 9.

Now we have an empty array, and we know how many things need to be in it. This is perfect for using a for loop. Numbering in C# may seem a bit strange, but a part of numbering in programming is the fact that 0 is usually the first number when counting.

We get accustomed to counting starting at 1, but in many programming paradigms, counting starts with the first number, 0. You might just consider the fact that 0 was there before you even started counting. Therefore, the first item in the boxes array is the 0th or *zeroth* item, not the first. It's important to notice that when dealing with arrays, you use square brackets.

```
SomeBoxes = new GameObject[numBoxes];
for (int i = 0; i < numBoxes; i++)
{
}
```

Right after we initialize the boxes array, we should write the for loop. Then we'll create a new box game object and assign it to the boxes.

```
SomeBoxes = new GameObject[numBoxes];
for (int i = 0; i < numBoxes; i++)
{
    GameObject box = GameObject.CreatePrimitive(PrimitiveType.Cube);
    SomeBoxes[i] = box;
}
```

Notice the notation being used for boxes. The SomeBoxes[i] indicates the slot in the array we're assigning the box we just made. When the i = 0, we're putting a box into SomeBoxes[0]; when i = 1, we're assigning the box to SomeBoxes[1] and so on.

Items in the array are accessed by using an int value in the square brackets. To check that we're doing everything right, let's run the code and check if the array is populated with a bunch of cube primitives just as we asked. Therefore, if you want to get some information on the fourth cube, you should use SomeBoxes[3]; again the 0th, pronounced "zeroth," item makes it easy to forget the index in the array we're referring to.

So far this is promising. We created an array called boxes with 10 items. Then we wrote a for loop that creates a box on every iteration and then adds that box into a numbered slot in the boxes array. This is working well. Arrays lend themselves very well for iterating through.

We need to match the variable type with the type that's inside of the array. Because the array boxes[] is filled with type GameObject, we need to use GameObject on the left of the in keyword. To the right of the in keyword is the array we're going to iterate through.

We're accessing all of the array, not just a single item in it, so we don't need to use something like foreach(GameObject g in boxes[0]) which would infer that at index 0 of boxes, there's an array for us to iterate through. Though arrays of arrays are possible, it's not our goal here.

Iterating through arrays with the foreach doesn't give us the benefit of a counter like in the for loop, so we need to do the same thing as if we were using a while loop or a heavily rearranged for loop by setting up a counter ahead of time.

Let's check our Console panel in the editor to make sure that this is working. It looks like the loop is repeating like one would expect. At the beginning of the Update() function, int i is set to 0; then while the foreach loop is iterating, it's incrementing the value up by 1 until each item in boxes has been iterated through.

Put the i to some use within the foreach() loop statement by multiplying the x of the vector by
i * 1.0f to move each cube to a different x location. Note that multiplying any number against 1 is
all that interesting, but this is just a simple part of this demonstration. Again, check in the editor to make
sure that each cube is getting put in a different x location by running the game.

```
int i = 0;
foreach (GameObject go in SomeBoxes)
{
    go.transform.position = new Vector3(i * 1.0f, 0, 0);
    i++;
    Debug.Log("Box: " + i);
}
```

So far everything should be working well. You can change the offset by changing the value that the i is
being multiplied by. Or, better yet, we should create a public variable to multiply the i variable by.

```
public float Spacing;
```

If you create a new public float spacing in the class scope, you can use it in your foreach loop.

```
go.transform.position = new Vector3(i * Spacing, 0, 0);
```

By adding this here, you can now edit spacing and watch the cubes spread apart in real time. This is starting to get more interesting! Next let's play with some math, or more specifically Mathf.

6.5.1.2 Mathf

The Mathf class is filled with many commonly used math helpers. Mathf contains many functions
such as abs for absolute value, and Sin and Cos for sine and cosine. To start with, we're going to create
a float called wave and we'll assign that to Mathf.Sin(i); which produces a sine wave when we put
wave in place of y in the Vector3.

To make this animated, we can use another useful trick from the `Time` class. Let's take a moment to thank all the busy programmers who know how to implement the math functions we're using here. There's more to these functions than just knowing the mathematics behind the simple concept of something like `Sin`. There's also a great deal of optimization that went into making the function work. This sort of optimization comes only from years of computer science experience and lots of know-how and practice. The mechanics behind this stuff is far beyond the scope of this book, so we'll just take advantage of their knowledge by using `Mathf`.

```
int i = 0;
foreach (GameObject go in SomeBoxes)
{
    float wave = Mathf.Sin(Time.fixedTime + i);
    go.transform.position = new Vector3(i * Spacing, wave, 0);
    i++;
}
```

6.5.1.3 Time

`Time.fixedTime` is a clock that starts running at the beginning of the game. All it's doing is counting up. Check what it's doing by printing it out using `Debug.Log(Time.fixedTime);` and you'll just see a timer counting seconds. The seconds will be the same for all of the cubes, but by adding int i to each cube's version of wave, each one will have a different value for the wave.

We could have had a public double `1.0` and incremented this with a small value, 0.01, for instance. This will have a similar effect to Time.fixedTime. The difference here is that `fixedTime` is tied to the computer's clock. Any slowdowns or frame rate issues will result in your Sin function slowing down as well.

What you should have is a slowly undulating row of cubes. This is also a pretty cool example of some basic math principles in action. We could continue to add more and more behaviors to each cube in the array using this method of extending the foreach statement, but this will only get us so far.

Once we want each cube to have its own individual sets of logic to control itself, it's time to start a new class. With the new class, it's important that we can communicate with it properly. Eventually, these other cubes will end up being zombies attacking the player, so we're on the right track.

6.5.2 Instancing with `AddComponent();`

The project contains a script named `Monster` which is added to the array using the `AddComponent()` function found in the `GameObject` class. The `GameObject` is a class written to handle everything related to how Unity 3D manages characters, items, and environments in a scene. Should you leave this comfortable game development tool and move on to some other application development, you will have to most likely use a different function to perform a similar task.

When you have a `GameObject` selected in the game editor, you have an option to add component near the bottom of the Inspector panel. We used this to add the ArraysRevisited script to our first cube. This should lead you to thinking that you can also add component with code. Looking into `GameObject`, you can find an `AddComponent()` function with a few different options.

```
MonsterBoxes = new GameObject[numBoxes];
for (int i = 0; i < numBoxes; i++)
{
    GameObject box = GameObject.CreatePrimitive(PrimitiveType.Cube);
    box.AddComponent(typeof(Monster));
    MonsterBoxes[i] = box;
}
```

You can use `box.AddComponent(typeof(Monster));` to tell the box to add in the script of the same name. If there wasn't a Monster script you get an error but Visual Studio can fix the problem by generating a class.

After generating a class add `using UnityEngine` and `: MonoBehaviour;` change `internal` to `public` and you've converted the generic class to a Unity 3D component for use in the scene.

```
using UnityEngine;
public class Monster : MonoBehaviour
{

}
```

To prove that the script is behaving correctly, add in a print function to the `Start()` function of the Monster.cs file.

```
void Start()
{
    Debug.Log("Im Alive!");
}
```

When the game starts, the ArraysRevisited.cs will create a bunch of new instances of the Monster.cs attached to each cube. When the script is instanced, ArraysRevisited executes the `Start()` function. The Console should reflect the fact that the `Start()` function was called when the `Monster` script was instanced.

This reduces the amount of work a single script needs to do. Each object should manage its own movement. To do this, each object will need its own script. In the Monster.cs file, we need to replicate some of the variables that we created in the ArraysRevisited.cs file.

```
public int ID;
public float Spacing = 1.1f;
```

Remember that we need to make these public, otherwise another script cannot find them. MonoDevelop is already aware of these variables.

After the box is created, we need to add in the "Monster" class to it. However, that's just half of the task necessary to get our script up and running. We added an ID and a spacing value to Monster.cs, but we have yet to initialize them. We need to get a connection to the component we just added to the box object. To do this, we need to use GetComponent(), but there's a bit more than just that.

6.5.3 Type Casting Unity 3D Objects

GetComponent() returns a component type, but it's unaware of the specific type we're looking for. We use some type casting to convert one type to another. Remember from before, we can turn an int 1 to a float 1.0f through type casting.

When type casting between objects or reference types, things get tricky. A component is about as general as Unity 3D will get. However, we want a type Monster when we get that component back. Therefore, we need to say, "I want this component from the box as a type monster." To do this, C# has the keyword as for some basic type casting.

```
MonsterBoxes = new GameObject[numBoxes];
for (int i = 0; i < numBoxes; i++)
{
    GameObject box = GameObject.CreatePrimitive(PrimitiveType.Cube);
    box.AddComponent(typeof(Monster));
    Monster m = box.GetComponent(typeof(Monster)) as Monster;
    MonsterBoxes[i] = box;
}
```

After adding the component, we need to get access to it. Therefore, we create a Monster variable named m. Then we use the GetComponent(); function to get a type of Monster, and we ask that we get it as a type Monster by adding as Monster after we ask for it.

This cast is necessary because GetComponent() doesn't necessarily know what it's getting; other than it's some component type, you have to tell it what it's getting. Monster and typeof Monster appear in different places. This is the difference between the word "Monster" and the actual class object called Monster. The object is what is used after the as keyword because we're referring to the type, not what it's called. This might be a little bit confusing, but GetComponent() is expecting a type and not an object for an argument.

When you enter the m., a dialog box pops up in Visual Studio. This is a handy helper that shows you all members in the object. This also shows you any of the public variables you may have added to the class. Now that we have a connection to the Monster script that's attached to the box, we can set a couple of parameters.

```
Monster m = box.GetComponent(typeof(Monster)) as Monster;
m.ID = i;
```

We use the dot notation to access the members of the Monster class found in m. Therefore, m.ID is i that increments with each new box made. Then the spacing will be the spacing we set in the Example. cs file.

```
13      // Update is called once per frame
14      void Update () {
15          float wave = Mathf.Sin( Time.fixedTime + ID);
16          transform.position = new Vector3(ID * spacing, wave, 0.0f);
17      }
```

Add a very similar line of code to the Update() in the Monster.cs file and then remove it from the Update() in the ArraysRevisited.cs file. The spacing was only set once when the object was created, which you can't update it by sliding on the ArraysRevisited.cs file. However, each object is acting on its own, running its own script.

There are a few different ways to use GetComponent(), but we'll look at those in Section 6.14 when we need to do more type casting. Not all casting operations work the same. We're going to change a few other things we're doing to make the movement behavior more interesting as well, but we will need to learn a few more tricks before we get to that.

Alternatively, we can assign and get the `Monster` m variable at the same time with the following notation:

```
Monster m = box.AddComponent(typeof(Monster)) as Monster;
```

This automatically assigns m as it's assigned to the box component. The component assignment and the variable assignment save a step.

6.5.4 What We've Learned

This was a pretty heavy chapter. The new array type was used to store a bunch of game objects, but it could have easily been used to store a bunch of numbers, or anything for that matter. We learned about a foreach loop that is handy for dealing with arrays.

In this chapter, we also made use of some math and found a nice timer function in the `Time` class. Afterthat, we figured out how to attach script components through code, and then we were able to gain access to that component by `GetComponent()` and a type cast to make sure it wasn't just a generic component.

There are still a few different data types we need to study. Now that we're dealing with so many types, we're going to learn more about type casting as well.

6.6 Enums

Start with the Chapter6 Unity Project's Enum_Scene and open the Enum script on the object of the same name. We've got two classes, an Example.cs and a Monster.cs, we've got the Example.cs creating and assigning objects, effectively spawning a Monster. We could take the older version of the Example.cs we wrote and turn it into Player.cs, which would give us a total of three objects.

```
public class Player : MonoBehaviour
{
    public float Speed = 1;

    // Update is called once per frame
    void Update()
    {
        gameObject.transform.position += Movement(Speed);
    }

    Vector3 Movement(float dist)
    {
        Vector3 vec = Vector3.zero;
        if (Input.GetKey(KeyCode.A))
        {
            vec.x -= dist;
        }
        if (Input.GetKey(KeyCode.D))
        {
            vec.x += dist;
        }
        if (Input.GetKey(KeyCode.W))
        {
            vec.z += dist;
        }
        if (Input.GetKey(KeyCode.S))
        {
            vec.z -= dist;
        }
        return vec;
    }
}
```

Therefore, here's the Player.cs I'm using for this chapter; we're going to use this to move the little box around in the scene. We'll pretend that the box is a pretty cool-looking monster hunter armed with a sword, shotgun, or double-barreled shotgun.

We may want to rename the Example.cs to something like MonsterSpawner.cs or MonsterGenerator.cs, but I'll leave that up to you. Just remember to rename the class declaration to match the file name. This will spill out monsters to chase the player around. Then the Monster.cs attached to each of the objects that the MonsterSpawner creates will then seek out the player and chase him around. At least that's the plan.

NOTE: Prototyping game play using primitive shapes is a regular part of game development. This is somewhat related to what has become to be known as "programmer art." Changes to code often mean changes to art. It's difficult to build a game keeping art and code parallel. Often a simple change in code means days of changes to art. It's quite often easier to prototype a game making no requests of an artist. Most of the time, the programmer doesn't even know himself what to ask of an artist.

6.6.1 Using Enums

The keyword "enum" is short for enumeration. A programmer might say that an enum is a list of named constants. The meaning may seem obtuse. Translated, an enumeration is a list of words that you pick. For our Monster to have a better set of functions for its behavior, we're going to create a new enum type called MonsterState.

We've already interacted with the PrimitiveType enum.

```
namespace UnityEngine
{
    public enum PrimitiveType
    {
        Sphere = 0,
        Capsule = 1,
        Cylinder = 2,
        Cube = 3,
        Plane = 4,
        Quad = 5
    }
}
```

An enum replaces an ambiguous value with a human readable value. You technically don't need to use an enum to compare values to control logical statements.

```
enum YesOrNo
{
    yes,
    no
};
YesOrNo yesOrNoEnum;
```

An enum with two values is not necessarily more clear than `bool yesNoBool` since both only have two values. In practice you'd look at something like

```
if (yesOrNoEnum == YesOrNo.yes)
{
    Debug.Log("yes");
}

bool yesOrNoBool = true;
if (yesOrNoBool == true)
{
    Debug.Log("yes");
}
```

And if you saw `if(primitiveInt == 0){Debug.Log("Sphere");}` you'd be able to react in a similar way only using integer values, but you'd have to remember what each value was supposed to represent. This ends up being prone to error if you thought `primitiveInt == 2` might be Capsule.

```
int primitiveInt = 0;
/* 0 = Sphere,    *
 * 1 = Capsule,   *
 * 2 = Cylinder,  *
 * 3 = Cube,      *
 * 4 = Plane,     *
 * 5 = Quad       */

if (primitiveInt == 0)
{
    Debug.Log("Sphere");
}
```

Conversely an enum with many hundreds of values is also not necessarily clearer than something more usable like a string as a name. Though we have seen that enums can store many different names. For instance, the InputType enum had a different enumeration for every key on the keyboard and each input for your mouse or trackpad and controller.

Enumerating through a long list of defined objects is to help name every possibility with something more useful than a simple numeric index. It's important to remember that enumerations don't need to follow any pattern. It's up to you to decide on any organization to keep your enums organized.

At the top of the Enums class there's a `public PrimitiveType MyPrimitiveType;`

```
public PrimitiveType MyPrimitiveType;
/* Right Click on PrimitiveType to go to the   *
 * definition and see what the enum looks like. */
```

In the editor, you'll see the availability of a new pop-up of the different PrimitiveTypes. In the `Start()` function, we use the CreatePrimitive member function in GameObject to create a new object of the selected type.

We can extend this more to get a better feel of how enums work for us by creating our own enums. A new enum is a new type of data. New data types are easy to create, especially for enums.

```
public enum MyColors
{
    red,
    blue,
    green
};
```

In this case, we use the `public` keyword followed by `enum` to tell the compiler we're creating a new enum which can be made accessible to other classes. We follow the declaration with a name. In this case, `MyColors` is the name of our new enum. Following the name of the enum, we need to start a new code block with any number of words separated by commas. Just don't add a comma after the last word in the list.

```
/* also valid                                          *
 * public enum MyColors {red, blue, green }; */
public MyColors MyColor;
```

To be clear, declaring an enum doesn't require the line breaks between each word. White space has no effect on how an enum, or practically any variable for that matter, is declared. After the new data type is created, we need to create a variable that uses that data type.

A `public MyColors` with the name `MyColor` follows the declaration of the enum. In the editor, we'll be able to pick the enum we want from our new list of words we added to the enum `MyColors`.

To make use of the enum, we can use several different methods. The system we might already be familiar with is using a bunch of different if statements.

```
gameObject = GameObject.CreatePrimitive(MyPrimitiveType);
MeshRenderer meshRenderer = gameObject.GetComponent(typeof(MeshRenderer)) as MeshRenderer;
Material material = meshRenderer.material;
if (MyColor == MyColors.red)
{
    material.color = Color.red;
}
if (MyColor == MyColors.blue)
{
    material.color = Color.blue;
}
if (MyColor == MyColors.green)
{
    material.color = Color.green;
}
```

This setup is clumsy; after the object is created, we check for what word `MyColor` is set to. Compare it against the MyColors's options and act when you've got a match. A slightly cleaner solution is to use a `switch()` statement.

Just as a note, if you look at the scene and all you see is a black sphere, you might need to add in a directional light. Without any lights, every object in the scene will appear dark since there's no light to illuminate them. You can add in a light by selecting GameObject → Create Other → Directional Light. This will drop in a light that will lighten up any objects in your scene.

6.6.2 Combining What We've Learned

We've been using `PrimitiveType.Cube` to generate our example monsters. We could just as easily change that to a sphere or anything else in the PrimitiveType enum. As we've seen, the PrimitiveType has some words that reflect what type of Primitive we can choose from. Likewise, we're going to make a list of states for the monster to pick.

```
public enum MonsterStates
{
    standing,
    wandering,
    chasing,
    attacking
}
public MonsterStates MonsterState;
```

Enums are declared at the class scope level of visibility. `MonsterState` is now another new data type. When setting up enum names, it's really important to come up with a convention that's easy to remember.

If you make both the enum MonsterState and mState public, you'll be able to pick the state using a menu in the Unity's Inspector panel. You should consider using enums for setting various things such as weapon pickup types or selecting types of traps.

Then, just as we define any other variable, we declare a variable type and give type a name. This is done with the line `MonsterState mState;` which gives us mState to use throughout the rest of the `Monster` class. mState is a variable with type MonsterState. In some instances, we may need to ignore what was set in the editor. To set an enum in code rather than a pop-up, we can use the following code. To use the mState, we need to set it when the Monster.cs is started.

```
void Start()
{
    Debug.Log("Im Alive!");
    MonsterState = MonsterStates.standing;
}
```

mState is set to `MonsterStates.standing;` this allows us to use mState in the `Update()` function to determine what actions we should take. Like before, we could use a series of `if` statements to pick the actions we could take. For instance, we could execute the following code:

```
if (MonsterState == MonsterStates.standing)
{
    Debug.Log("Standing monster is standing...");
}
if (MonsterState == MonsterStates.wandering)
{
    Debug.Log("Wandering monster is wandering...");
}
if (MonsterState == MonsterStates.chasing)
{
    Debug.Log("Chasing monster is chasing...");
}
if (MonsterState == MonsterStates.attacking)
{
    Debug.Log("Attacking monster is attacking...");
}
```

This will work just fine, but it's rather messy. If we add more enums to the MonsterState, we will need more `if` statements. However, there's an easier way to deal with an enum, so it's time to learn a new trick.

6.6.3 What We've Learned

So far enums have been made to make a list of options. Normally, enumerations are limited to a single option, but this doesn't always have to be the case. Enums are capable of multiple options, which has been discussed throughout this section.

Using an enum means to take action based on a selection. An enum is actually based on a number. You can cast from an enum to an `int` and get a usable value. When this is done, the first name in an enum is 0 and anything following is an increment up in value based on its position in the list of enumerations.

Therefore, based on the following code, the logged value is 3 since the first state is 0 and the fourth state is 3.

```
int number = (int)MonsterState;
Debug.Log(number);
```

There are other ways in which the enum can be manipulated, but to understand how and why this works, we'll want to cover a few other topics before getting to that.

6.7 Switch

To follow along open the Switch_Scene and begin with the Switch script attached to the switch game object. The switch comes into play often once we have reached more than one condition at a time. For instance, we could come across a situation where we are looking at a lengthy ladder of `if-else` statements.

```
public int intValue;
void IfElseLadder()
{
    if (intValue == 0)
    {
        Debug.Log("int is Zero");
    }
    else if (intValue == 1)
    {
        Debug.Log("int is One");
    }
    else if (intValue == 2)
    {
        Debug.Log("int is Two");
    }
    else if (intValue == 3)
    {
        Debug.Log("int is Three");
    }
    else if (intValue == 4)
    {
        Debug.Log("int is Four");
    }
    else
    {
        Debug.Log("int is greater than 4 or less than 0");
    }
}
```

There should be something awkward about this block of code. There is in fact a system in place called a switch statement that was made to alleviate the awkwardness of this long chain of `if-else` statements. The switch starts with the keyword switch followed by a parameter `()` that controls a block of code encapsulated by a pair of curly braces `{}`.

```csharp
void SwitchStructure()
{
    switch (someVariable)
    {
    }
}
```

The contents of the switch statement use the keyword case. Each case is fulfilled by an expected option that matches the argument in the switch parameter.

6.7.1 A Basic Example

A switch can be used with any number of types in the parameter. The awkward if-else ladder we saw just before can be replaced with a much more simple `switch()` statement.

```csharp
void SwitchStatement()
{
    switch (intValue)
    {
        case 0:
            Debug.Log("int is Zero");
            break;
        case 1:
            Debug.Log("int is One");
            break;
        case 2:
            Debug.Log("int is Two");
            break;
        case 3:
            Debug.Log("int is Three");
            break;
        case 4:
            Debug.Log("int is Four");
            break;
        default:
            Debug.Log("int is greater than 4 or less than 0");
            break;
    }
}
```

This is a basic switch with a case. The case is followed by 1 or 2 ending with a colon. Before another case, there's a couple of statements, with the last statement being `break;` that ends the `case:` statement. The first `case 1:` is executed because i == 1; or in more plain English, i *is* 1 that fulfills the condition to execute the code following the case. The `break;` following the statements jumps the computer out of the switch statement and stops any further execution from happening inside of the `switch` statement.

```
switch (intValue)
{
    case 0: Debug.Log("int is Zero"); break;
    case 1: Debug.Log("int is One"); break;
}
```

When you deal with short case statements, it's sometimes easier to remove the extra white space and use something a bit more compact. Each case is called a *label*; we can use labels outside of a switch statement, but we will have to find out more about that in Section 6.7.5.

The switch statement is a much better way to manage a set of different situations. Upon looking at the switch statement for the first time, it might be a bit confusing. There are a few new things going on here. The general case of the switch is basically taking in a variable, pretty much of any type of POD (Plain Old Data). The code then picks the case statement to start. The main condition is that all of the cases must use the type that is used in the switch() argument. For instance, if the switch statement sees an enum argument, you can't use a case where the enum is compared to an int.

The advantage of switch may not be obvious when looking at the block of code that was written here. The important reason why switch is useful is speed. To step through many different if statements, the contents of each argument needs to be computed.

Having a dozen "if" statements means that each one needs to be tested even though the contents of the statement are to be skipped. When using a switch, the statement needs to have only one test before evaluating the contents of the case.

The switch statement can use a few different data types, specifically integral types. Integral types, or data that can be converted into an integer, include booleans or bools, chars, strings, and enums. In a simple boolean example, we can use the following:

```
bool someBool = true;
switch (someBool)
{
    case true: Debug.Log("true"); break;
    case false: Debug.Log("false"); break;
}
```

With integers where int i = 1; switch(i) {} is used to pick the case which will be used. Using integers allows for a long list of cases when using a switch statement.

With a switch statement, if the argument matches the case then code is executed until break; jumps out of the switch. Each appearance of the keyword case is called a case label. Cases are built by using the keyword case followed by the value we are looking for from the variable used in the switch. After the case label is declared, any number of statements can be added. The code following the colon after the case statement is evaluated until the break; statement that stops the switch. The break statement must appear before another case label is added.

6.7.2 Default

What if there's a case that's not included in the switch statement? It would be difficult to cover every case for an integer. You'd have to write a case for every and any number. That's where the default: case comes in. When dealing with any of the switch statements, a default condition can be added when a case appears that isn't handled.

```
int i = 3;
switch (i)
{
    case 0:
        Debug.Log("i is Zero");
        break;
    case 1:
        Debug.Log("i is One");
        break;
    case 2:
        Debug.Log("i is Two");
        break;
    default:
        Debug.Log("Every other number");
        break;
}
```

With the default added, any conditions that aren't taken care of can be handled. If the default isn't added, then any unhandled case will be ignored and the switch will skip any code from any of the cases. The default case is an optional condition when working with the switch statement.

```
public enum Cases
{
    First,
    Second,
    Third,
    Fourth,
    Fifth,
    Sixth,
    Seventh
}
public Cases MyCase;
```

Of course, a switch statement seems to be most at home when in use with an enum. A slightly different variation on the appearance of the enum itself is that we need to use the dot operator to compare the incoming value against one of the enum values.

Here we have an elaborate array of cases, each one falling in order based on the enum values for Cases. Writing all of the cases might feel tedius, so Visual Studio has some short cuts for you. Highlight the `MyCase` in the switch statement and click on the lightbulb waiting in the left margin. From here you can select adding just the missing cases, a default case or both.

```
switch (MyCase)
{
    case Cases.First:
        break;
    case Cases.Second:
        break;
    case Cases.Third:
        break;
    case Cases.Fourth:
        break;
    case Cases.Fifth:
        break;
    case Cases.Sixth:
        break;
    case Cases.Seventh:
        break;
    default:
        break;
}
```

Select the "Add both" option from the popup to fill in the switch case cases with all possible case labels for the enum automatically. From here it's just a matter of filling in what happens in each case. Inside of the Unity 3D Editor, the C# class provides a useful roll-out in the Inspector panel when assigned to a GameObject.

This conveniently gives us the opportunity to pick an enum and watch the `Debug.Log()` send different strings to the Console panel. It's important that you note what variable is being used in the switch statement's argument. It's often mistaken to use `switch(Cases)` with the type in the argument. This of course doesn't work as expected. Here we get the following error:

Assets/SwitchStatements.cs(21,25): error CS0119: Expression denotes a "type," where a "variable," "value" or "method group" was expected

Each case statement must have a `break;` statement before the next case appears. You can have any number of statements between case and break, but you must break at the end. This prevents each case from flowing into one another. If you forget to add break after the first case statement, then you get the following warning:

Assets/SwitchStatements.cs(21,17): error CS0163: Control cannot fall through from one case label to another

It's easy to forget to add these breaks, but at least we are informed that we're missing one. However, we're directed to the beginning of the switch statement. It's up to you to make sure that there's a break statement at the end of each case. It's also required after the default case.

Normally, the default label is the last case at the end of the series of case labels. However, this isn't a requirement. You can write the default label anywhere in the switch statement. Style guides usually require that you put the default at the very end of the switch. Not doing so might invoke some harsh words from a fellow programmer if he or she finds a misplaced default label.

As a convenience, C# can decode each case as a string. This may seem like an obvious feature, but it's something that has yet to come to older more established languages like C++.

```
case Cases.First:
    Debug.Log(MyCase);
    break;
```

The case above will simply print the following to the Console window:

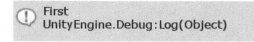

6.7.3 More On Cases

Switch statements are a common combination. Each label is clear and the parameter for the switch is also quite clear. We know what we're expecting and its obvious what conditions each case needs to be written for.

```
enum MoreCases
{
    FirstCase,
    SecondCase,
    ThirdCase
}
```

The above enum might be quite contrived, but we know how many labels we need if we use this case in a switch. It should be obvious that our first case label should look like case cases.firstCase: and we should fill in the rest of the case statements in order.

switch statements are limited to a select different types of data.

```
float f = 2.0f;
switch (f)
{
    case f < 1.0f:
        Debug.Log("less than 1");
        break;
}
```

The above code might look valid, but we'll get the following error:

```
Assets/Test.cs(15,1): error CS0151: A switch expression of type "float"
cannot be converted to an integral type, bool, char, string, enum or nullable
type
```

A switch is only allowed "integral, bool, char, string, enum, or nullable" types of data. We have yet to cover some of these different data types, but at least we know what a data type is. We do know that we can use ints and enums. In most cases, this should be enough. Switch statements should be used when one and only one thing needs to happen based on a single parameter.

```
int a = 0;
int b = 1;
switch (a)
{
    case 0:
        switch (b)
        {
            case 1:
                Debug.Log("might be more confusing...");
                break;
        }
    break;
}
```

Having a switch statement nested in one of the cases of another switch statement isn't common. There's nothing really stopping you from being able to do this, but it's probably better to look for a more elegant solution.

```
int c = 0;
switch (c)
{
    case 0:
        ZerothFunction();
        break;
    case 1:
        FirstFunction();
        break;
}
```

Each case can simply call on a more complex function.

```
void FirstFunction()
{
    Debug.Log("First Case");
}

void ZerothFunction()
{
    Debug.Log("ZerothCase");
}
```

Using a function in each case is a simple way to keep things tidy, though it's not always clear what's going on. Anyone reading the code will be forced to jump back and forth between the switch and the different functions. However, this does mean that you might be able to make more switch cases within each function in the switch statement.

```
int a = 0;
switch (a)
{
    case 0:
        a = 1;
        FirstFunction(a);
        break;
    case 1:
        Secondfunction();
        break;
}
```

Once a case is entered, the switch() statement is finished. The parameter in the case of the switch statement is no longer evaluated once in a case. This also means that the parameter can be manipulated before it's used in the case.

```
                        ┌─────────────────────────────┐
                    ┌───┤ ① variable set to 0         │
int a = 0;──────────┘   └─────────────────────────────┘
switch(a)───────────────┤ ② value 0 enters switch     │
{                       └─────────────────────────────┘
                              ┌───────────────────────────────────────────────┐
    case 0:───────────────────┤ ③ case 0: is evalueated                       │
        a = 1;────────────────┤ ④ variable a is assigned a new value          │
        FirstFunction(a);─────┤ ⑤ new value 1 is entered into FirstFunction   │
        break;────────────────┤ ⑥ case closed.                                │
    case 1:                   └───────────────────────────────────────────────┘
        SecondFunction();
        break;
}
        ┌──────────────────────────────────────────────────┐
        │ ⑦ After the break; we start again down here.     │
        └──────────────────────────────────────────────────┘
```

When we enter the case 0: we set the value that entered into the case to 1. This means that the data going into the function after that change gets a new value for a.

```
void FirstFunction(int i)
{
    switch (i)
    {
        case 0:
            Debug.Log("I won't get called.");
            break;
        case 1:
            Debug.Log("incoming case is 1");
            break;
    }
}
```

Because a = 1; appears after we've entered the case and is followed by a break;, case 1: is not triggered, and we don't skip to the second case. The logic might seem cloudy, but it's important that we really understand what's going on here.

Inside of the switch statement, the switch cannot change our destination once we've arrived at a label. After we've got to the label, we can change the data that got us there. Once we get to the break; at the end of the case, we leave the switch and move to any statements that follow the switch statement code block.

```
switch (a)
{
    case 0:
        FirstFunction(a);
        continue;
}
```

No enclosing loop out of which to break or continue

A switch is not a loop, so we can't go back to the beginning of the switch by using continue; actually this is just an error telling you that there's no loop to continue to. A switch statement isn't meant to be looped; there are systems that allow this, but in general, these sorts of statements are one-way logic controls. A switch can work only with a single argument.

Something like switch (a, b) could make sense, but this isn't the case. Keeping things simple is not only your goal, but you're also limited by what is allowed. In some cases, the language can force simplicity. In practice, it's best to keep things as simple as possible if only for the sake of anyone else having to understand your work.

6.7.4 Fall Through

Using the break; statement jumps us out of the switch. Therefore, something like the following will execute one or the other statements after the condition and jump out of the switch.

```
switch(condition)
{
    case firstCondition:
        //Do things
        break;
    case secondCondition:
        //Do something else
        break;
}
```

If we want to, a case can be left empty, and without a break; included, anything in the case will "fall through" to the next case until the code is executed and a break; statement is found.

```
switch(condition)
{
    case firstCondition:
    case secondCondition:
        //Do something else
        break;
}
```

In the above example, if we get to case first condition:, we'll simply find the next case afterward and run the code there until we hit the next break; statement. It's rare to use this in practice as the conditions included act the same; in this case, both the first and second conditions do the same thing. However, things get a bit more awkward if we need to do something like the following:

```
switch(condition)
{
    case firstCondition:
    case secondCondition:
        //Do something else
        break;
    case thirdCondition:
    case fourthCondition:
    case fifthCondition:
        //Do another thing
        break;
}
```

Here we have two different behaviors based on five different conditions. The first two and the next three cases can result in two different behaviors. Although you might not use this behavior immediately, it's important to know what you're looking at if you see it. There are some catches to how this can be used.

```
switch(condition)
{
    case firstCondition:
        //Do Something ————| not allowed without
    case secondCondition:   | break; after.
        //Do something else  ————
        break;
    case thirdCondition:
        //Do another thing
        break;
}
```

In the above example, our first condition might have some added code before the second condition. This might visually make sense; go to the first condition, execute some instructions, fall through to the next case, do more instructions, and break. However, this behavior isn't allowed in C#.

In order to accomplish what was described, we need to be more explicit.

6.7.5 goto Case

```
Cases someCases = Cases.First;
switch (someCases)
{
    case Cases.First:
        FirstFunction();
        goto case Cases.Second; // Jumps to next case
    case Cases.Second:
        SecondFunction();
        break;
}
```

Using the goto keyword allows us to hop from one case in the switch statement to another. This allows for an expected fall through-like behavior, but also gives us an added functionality of going to any other case once inside of the switch statement.

```
switch (someCases)
{
    case Cases.First:
        FirstFunction();
        goto case Cases.Third;
    case Cases.Second:
        SecondFunction();
        break;
    case Cases.Third:
        ThirdFunction();
        goto case Cases.Second;
}
```

The utility of the above statement is questionable. Although the statement is valid, it's hardly something that any programmer would want to read. Bad habits aside, should you see this in someone else's code, it's most likely written as a work-around by someone unfamiliar with the original case.

Aside from being awkward and strange looking, it's important that the switch case finally lead to a break, otherwise we're caught in the switch statement indefinitely. Debugging a situation like this is difficult, so it's best to avoid getting caught in a switch statement longer than necessary.

Strange and unusual code practices when working inside of a switch statement aren't common, as the regular use of a switch statement is quite simple. If you need to do something more clever, it's better to have a switch statement that points toward a function with additional logic to handle a more specific set of conditions.

6.7.6 Finite State Machine

A finite state machine is a system used to control the flow of processes in a complex system. In some ways, Unity has provided us with various ways to control when and how objects are started and updated with the `Start()` and `Update()` methods in MonoBehaviour. Enums will help keep track of specific character update states "Updateing Idle" "Updating walk" etc. A lot of this might sounds familiar if you've used Unity 3D's animation system.

A simple system to manage transitions between states is the FiniteStateMachine script attached to the object of the same name in the Switch_Scene. Each step of a process, or state of mind for a character, can be represented as a "state" to enter and exit. The character or object can only be in one state at a time. This is where finite state comes from. The machine infers there's some mechanism that's controlling the state transitions.

For our cylinder the finite states are waiting, changing colors, picking colors, and color changed. These are represented in an enum:

```
public enum ChangingStates
{
    Waiting,
    PickingColor,
    ChangingColor,
    ColorChanged
}
public ChangingStates MyState;
```

The variable is stored as `MyState` which is public so it's visible in the Inspector panel in the editor. We also have setup some additional variables to store colors and time.

```
private float ColorTime;
private Color MyColor, NextColor;
private Material MyMaterial;

// Start is called before the first frame update
void Start()
{
    MyMaterial = GetComponent<MeshRenderer>().material;
    ColorTime = Time.time + 1;
}
```

These are setup at and used while the states are updated. To change color we set the `NextColor` by picking random values for a color to transition to. The `PickColor()` function creates a new color and stores the value in the `NextColor` variable.

```
private void PickColor()
{
    float r = Random.Range(0f, 1f);
    float b = Random.Range(0f, 1f);
    float g = Random.Range(0f, 1f);
    NextColor = new Color(r, g, b);
    ColorTime = Time.time + 3;
}
```

This is called once the state decides it's time to pick a color, then the finite state changes to a color changing state where we use a `ChangeColor()` function to smoothly change from the previous color to the next color:

```
private void ChangeColor()
{
    MyColor = Color.Lerp(MyColor, NextColor, Time.deltaTime);
    MyMaterial.color = MyColor;
}
```

After the color blend has finished we set a moment of time to admire the selected color in an idle state called Waiting:

```
private void ColorChanged()
{
    ColorTime = Time.time + 1;
}
```

The states can be seen updated in the `Update()` function with a switch statement:

```
switch (MyState)
{
    // Hold onto color here for a second
    // then pick a color
    case ChangingStates.Waiting:
        WaitForColor();
        if (Time.time > ColorTime)
        {
            Debug.Log("Finished Waiting...");
            MyState = ChangingStates.PickingColor;
        }
        break;
    // pick a random color, then go to changing color.
    case ChangingStates.PickingColor:
        PickColor();
        Debug.Log("Color Picked...");
        MyState = ChangingStates.ChangingColor;
        break;
    // allow some time to lerp between colors
    case ChangingStates.ChangingColor:
        ChangeColor();
        if (Time.time > ColorTime)
        {
            Debug.Log("Color Changed...");
            MyState = ChangingStates.ColorChanged;
        }
        break;
    // finish color change
    case ChangingStates.ColorChanged:
        ColorChanged();
        Debug.Log("Finished Color Change.");
        MyState = ChangingStates.Waiting;
        break;
    default:
        break;
}
```

The different states Waiting, PickingColor, ChangingColor and ColorChanged are called sequentially. When the switch statement enters a case, settings are updated, and the MyState is set to the next state to enter. This pattern works for many different situations. Characters talking, walking, stopping and running can all have similar finite states to enter and leave.

This is a simple form of a finite state machine and works linearly. A common variation is to store a "previous" state. This allows us to react to the state we're entering knowing what state we left. For characters to enter an Idle state from a hit reaction means we can pick a different animation to blend between the two states. A simple but powerful design pattern.

6.7.7 What We've Learned

The switch statement is powerful and flexible. Using special case conditions where we use either the fall-through behavior or goto case statement, we're able to find additional utility within the switch statement.

Just because we can doesn't mean we should use fall-through or goto case. Often, this leads to confusing and difficult-to-read code. The bizarre and incomprehensible fall-through or goto case should be reserved for only the most bizarre and incomprehensible conditions. To avoid bad habits from forming, it might be better to forget that you even saw the goto case statement.

Now that warnings have been issued, experimenting and playing with code is still fun. Finding and solving problems with unique parameters is a part of the skill of programming. Using weird and strange-looking structures helps in many ways. If we're able to comprehend a strange set of code, we're better equipped to deal with more regular syntax.

switch statements can be used with any number of different parameters. Strings, ints, and other types are easily used in a switch statement.

```
string s = "Some Condition";
switch (s)
{
    case "Some Condition":
        // Do things
        break;
    case "Other Condition":
        // Do something else
        break;
}
```

6.8 Structs

Data structures specific and concise organization of information. By themselves floats, ints, and Vector3 are useful. However, copying and moving around each variable individually can look rather ugly. This lack of organization leaves more opportunity for errors.

```
float X;
float Y;
float Z;
void SetX(float x)
{
    X = x;
}
void SetY(float y)
{
    Y = y;
}
void SetZ(float z)
{
    Z = z;
}

void SetValues()
{
    SetX(1.0f);
    SetY(1.0f);
    SetZ(1.0f);
}
```

When having to deal with a complex character or monster type, collections of data should be organized together. The best way to do this is by using a struct, or structure. A Vector3 is a basic collection of three similar data types: a float for X, Y, and Z. This is by no means the limitation of what a structure can do.

```
Vector3 Vector;
void SetVector()
{
    Vector = new Vector3(1, 1, 1);
}
```

6.8.1 Building a Struct

Begin with the Structs_Scene in the Chapter6 Unity Project. In the scene open, the Structs script on the Structs game object in the scene. Structures for a player character could include the location, health points, ammunition, weapon in hand, and weapons in inventory and armor, and other related things that should be included in the player.cs, not excluded. To build a struct, you use the keyword struct followed by an identifier. This is very similar to how an enum is declared. What makes a structure different is that we can declare each variable in the struct to different data types.

After a structure is built to access any of the public components of the structure, you use dot notation. For example, `playerDataStruct.HitPoints` allows you to access the int value stored in the structure for `HitPoints`. PlayerData now contains the vital values that relate to the player.

```
public struct PlayerDataStruct
{
    public Vector3 Position;
    public int HitPoints;
    public int Ammunition;
    public float RunSpeed;
    public float WalkSpeed;
}
PlayerDataStruct playerDataStruct;
```

When you first look at declaring and using a struct, there might seem a few redundant items. First, there's a public struct PlayerData, then declare a PlayerData to be called playerData, and notice the lowercase lettering on the identifier versus the type. The first time PlayerData appears, you're creating a new type of data and writing its description.

6.8.2 Struct versus Class

At the same time, the struct may look a lot like a class and in many ways it is. The principal differences between the struct and the class is where in the computer's memory they live and how they are created. We'll discuss more on this in a moment.

You fill in some variables inside of the new data type and name the data inside of the new type. This new data type needs to have a name assigned so we know how to recognize the new form of packaged data. Therefore, `PlayerDataStruct` is the name we've given to this new form of data. This is the same as with a class.

The second appearance of the word `PlayerDataStruct` is required if we want to use our newly written form of data. To use the data, we write a statement for a variable like any other variable statement. Start with the data type—in this case, `PlayerDataStruct` is our type—then give a name, or identifier, to call a variable of the stated type. In this case, we're using `playerDataStruct` with a lowercase p to hold a variable of type `PlayerDataStruct`.

A struct is a data type with various types of data within it. It's convenient to packaging up all kinds of information into a single object. This means that when using the struct, you're able to pass along and get a breadth of information with a single parameter. This matters most when having to pass this information around.

This system of using a struct as data means that a struct is a value type, whereas a class is a reference type. You might ask what the difference between a value type and a reference type is. In short, when you create a struct and assign a value to it, a new copy is made of that struct. For instance, consider the following:

```
PlayerDataStruct otherPlayerStruct = playerStruct;
```

In this case, `otherPlayerStruct` is a new struct, where we make another version of `playerStruct` and copy the contents into `otherPlayerStruct`. Therefore, if we make `PlayerDataStruct` pd2 and assign `playerStruct` to it, or even `otherPlayerStruct`, we'll have yet another copy of that same data in a new variable. Each variable `otherPlayerStruct`, pd2, and `playerDataStruct` now all have unique versions of the data.

However, should we change struct to class, we'd have a different arrangement.

```
public class PlayerDataClass
{
    public Vector3 Position;
    public int HitPoints;
    public int Ammunition;
    public float RunSpeed;
    public float WalkSpeed;
}
PlayerDataClass playerDataClass;
```

The only change to the above code is changing struct to class. This is still a perfectly valid C# class and appears to be the same as a struct, but the similarities cease once a variable is assigned. The differences can be seen in the following simple example.

```
void Start()
{
    PlayerDataStruct playerStruct = new PlayerDataStruct();
    PlayerDataClass playerClass = new PlayerDataClass();
    playerStruct.HitPoints = 1;
    playerClass.HitPoints = 1;

    PlayerDataStruct otherPlayerStruct = playerStruct;
    otherPlayerStruct.HitPoints = 3;
    Debug.Log(playerStruct.HitPoints + " and " + otherPlayerStruct.HitPoints);
    // 1 and 3
    PlayerDataClass otherPlayerClass = playerClass;
    otherPlayerClass.HitPoints = 3;
    Debug.Log(playerClass.HitPoints + " and " + otherPlayerClass.HitPoints);
    // 3 and 3
}
```

In the above code, we use both the PlayerDataStruct and PlayerDataClass. Both have a public field called int HitPoints; once in the Start() function a new PlayerDataStruct() and a new PlayerDataClass() are created. As soon as these classes are created, we assign 1 to the .HitPoints fields in both the struct and the class.

After this, we have an interesting change. Using the PlayerDataStruct otherPlayer-Struct = playerStruct, we create a copy of the PlayerDataStruct from playerStruct and assign that copy to otherPlayerStruct. Doing the same thing to PlayerDataClass otherPlayerClass, we assign playerClass to otherPlayerClass. If we check the value of playerClass.HitPoints and otherPlayerClass.HitPoints, we get 1 and 3, respectively.

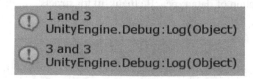

Doing the same thing to `playerClass.HitPoints` and `otherPlayerClass.HitPoints`, we get 3 and 3, respectively. How did this happen and why is mc.a changing the value of mClass.a? When a class is assigned to a variable, only a *reference* to the class is assigned. A new copy is not made and assigned to the variable mc.

In the statement `PlayerDataClass otherPlayerClass = playerClass;`, we assign `other-PlayerClass` a reference to `playerClass`. This contrasts to `PlayerDataStruct otherPlayerStruct = playerStruct`, where ms gets a copy of the value stored in `playerStruct`. After a struct is assigned, it becomes an independent copy of the struct that was assigned to it. To break the reference, we cannot use mc = mClass, otherwise a reference will be created.

```
PlayerDataClass anotherPlayerClass = new PlayerDataClass();
anotherPlayerClass.HitPoints = playerClass.HitPoints;
anotherPlayerClass.HitPoints = 7;
Debug.Log(playerClass.HitPoints + ":" +
          otherPlayerClass.HitPoints + ":" +
          anotherPlayerClass.HitPoints);
// 3:3:7
```

By making a new instance of `PlayerDataClass` called `anotherPlayerClass`, we can assign the value from `playerClass.HitPoints` to `anotherPlayerClass.HitPoints`, which will avoid a reference from being created between `anotherPlayerClass` and `playerClass`. The above code prints out the following output:

Even though we assigned the `.HitPoints` field of `anotherPlayerClass` to `playerClass. HitPoints`, we lose the reference between `anotherPlayerClass` and `playerClass`. When we change `anotherPlayerClass.HitPoints` to 7, it has no effect on `otherPlayerClass. HitPoints` and `playerClass.HitPoints`. The differences between the struct and the class is subtle but distinct.

The values of structs are copied when assigned in the `otherPlayerStruct = playerStruct` fashion. To accomplish the same behavior with a class, we need to assign each field separately with `anotherPlayerClass.HitPoints = playerClass.HitPoints;`. Only in this fashion can we actually a copy of the value to `anotherPlayerClass.HitPoints` from `playerClass.HitPoints`, not a reference.

6.8.3 Without Structs

The alternative to the struct is to use another form of data containment like the array. Each object in the array can hold a different data type, but it must be addressed by its index number in the array. It would be up to you to remember if the walk speed was at index 4 or 3 in the array. Organizational issues make this far too easy to mess up and forget which index holds what data.

Once you start adding new types of data to this method of record keeping, chances are you'll forget something and your code will break. There are languages out there that don't have structs, and this is the only way to manage a collection of data types. Be thankful for structs.

```
object[] playerDataArray = new object[5]
{
    new Vector3(),   // Position
    10,              // HitPoints
    13,              // Ammunition
    6.5f,            // Run Speed
    1.2f             // Walk Speed
};
object[] copyOfPlayerDataArray = playerDataArray;
Debug.Log(playerDataArray[1]);
// 10
copyOfPlayerDataArray[1] = 1;
Debug.Log(playerDataArray[1] + ":" + copyOfPlayerDataArray[1]);
// 1:1
```

An array of objects allows for different types of data to be mixed together. In the case where we copy one array into another, we get a reference. So in the above we check `playerDataArray[1]` and get 10 reflecting how the array was initialized. When we make a new array and set `copyOfPlayerDataArray` to `playerDataArray` and change the copy's second value to 1, this changes the original as well.

When another creature contacts the player, it should be given a copy of the entire PlayerData stored. This confines all the data into a single object and reduces the need for making separate operations to carry over different data. To do the same to a class, we'd have to use the same idea of copying each parameter one at a time because of the earlier mentioned behavior between a class and struct assignment.

6.8.4 Handling Structs

Structs are best used to contain a collection of data for an object. If we wanted to make a simple set of parameters for a box, we might use the following struct:

```
struct BoxParams
{
    public float width;
    public float height;
    public float depth;
    public Color color;
}
```

With this added to a new class attached to a box in the scene in Unity 3D, we have a system of storing and moving a collection of data using a single object. Within this object, we've assigned public variables for width, height, depth, and color.

To make use of this, we can adjust each one of the parameters individually within the structure using the dot operator.

```
BoxParams box = new BoxParams();
box.width = 2;
box.height = 3;
box.depth = 4;
box.color = Color.red;
```

We can access the box variables and assign them values. Once usable values are assigned to the BoxParams box, we can use them as a variable passed to a function.

```
void CreateCube(BoxParams b)
{
    GameObject go = GameObject.CreatePrimitive(PrimitiveType.Cube);
    go.transform.localScale = new Vector3(b.width, b.height, b.depth);
    go.GetComponent<MeshRenderer>().material.color = b.color;
}
```

The function can access the BoxParams passed to it using the same dot accessor and expose values that were assigned to it; the dot is an operator, and not exclusive to just accessors, but properties, functions, and all struct and class members. The first statement creates a new Vector 3 size. The size is then assigned a new Vector3(), where we extract the width, height, and depth and assign those values to the Vector3's x, y, and z parameters.

Once the Vector3() is created, we assign the values to the gameObject.transform.localScale. After this, we're also able to change the gameObject material's color by assigning the renderer.material.color to the b.color from the BoxParams values.

6.8.5 Accessing Structs

If a structure is limited to the class where it was created, then it becomes less useful to other classes that might need to see it. By creating another class to control the camera, we can better understand why other classes need access to the cube's BoxParams.

```
public class OtherClass
{
    //BoxParams Not accesible
}
```

By moving the struct outside of the class, we break out of the encapsulation of the classes.

```
// not inside of the Structs script
public struct PublicBoxParams
{
    public float width;
    public float height;
    public float depth;
    public Color color;
}
public class OtherClass
{
    //BoxParams Not accesible
    PublicBoxParams box;
    //Public Box Params is visible!
}
```

A new struct called `PublicBoxParams` lives outside of the Structs class scope. This changes the `PublicBoxParams` into a globally accessible struct.

When a class is made, its contents are encapsulated within curly braces. The variables or functions created inside of the class contents are members of that class. Should any new enum or struct be moved outside of that class, it becomes a globally declared object.

6.8.6 Global Access

In practice, it's a good idea to have a more central location for your globally accessible structs and enums. The term global just means to be accessible to the entire project. An additional class in the project called Globals.cs can contain the following code:

```csharp
using System.Collections;
using System.Collections.Generic;
using UnityEngine;
/* ... */
public struct BoxParameters
{
    public float width;
    public float height;
    public float depth;
    public Color color;
}
```

With something as simple as this, we're able to create a central location for all globally accessible information. Starting with simple things such as public struct `BoxParameters`, we can then continually add more and more useful information to our globally accessible data. Each C# script file need not declare a class. Although it's common, it's not restrictively enforced that a C# script file contains a class. Utility files like a Globals.cs are handy and can provide a clean system in which each programmer on a team can find handy structures that can be shared between different objects in the scene.

6.8.7 What We've Learned

In Section 6.8.6, we talked about global access. This concept is not that new. When you write a class, in this case Structs, it's accessible by any other class. Therefore, when we assigned Structs to the Struct game object in the scene, it's able to use the global version of `BoxParameters`.

```csharp
public class OtherClass
{
    //BoxParams Not accesible
    PublicBoxParams box;
    //Public Box Params is visible!

    BoxParameters globalBox;
    // Found in Global.cs
}
```

6.9 Class Data

Open the ClassData_Scene find the ClassData script in the hierarchy attached to the ClassData game object to follow along. Using a struct is preferred over a class due to how the computer manages memory. Without going into detail, one type of memory is called the heap and the other is the stack. In general, the stack is a smaller, more organized, faster part of the memory allocated to your game. The heap is usually larger and can take longer to access than the stack.

Values can be allocated to the stack, and a struct is a value type; thus, a stack can be accessed faster than a class. Though often structs and other value types are used in ways that disallow their allocation to the stack, they go into the heap instead. Classes and other reference data types end up in the heap regardless.

In a simple function call, the variables that appear in it are all pushed into the stack. As soon as the function is complete, any of the temporary values created and used inside of the function are immediately destroyed once the function is done executing.

```
void DoThings()
{
    int[] arrayOfInts = new int[100];
    for (int i = 0; i < 100; i++)
    {
        arrayOfInts[i] = i;
    }
}
```

The DoThings() function does pretty much nothing, but makes an array of ints that are added to the stack. As soon as this function is done, the array of ints is cleared out. In general, the stack grows and shrinks very fast. The second object that's added to the stack is the int i, which is being used inside the for loop.

The primary advantage a class has over a struct is the addition of a constructor and class inheritance. Aside from that, you're able to add assignments to each variable in a class as it's created.

```
struct MyStruct
{
    public int a = 0;
    public MyStruct()
    {
    }
}
```

MyStruct.MyStruct()

Structs cannot contain explicit parameterless constructors

A struct cannot have a parameterless constructor. Also, a struct cannot have variables initialized as they are declared.

```
struct MyStruct
{
    public int a = 0;
}
```

(field) int MyStruct.a

'MyStruct': cannot have instance property or field initializers in structs

On the other hand, as we've seen before, a class does allow this.

```
class MyClass
{
    public int a = 0;
    public MyClass()
    {
    }
}
```

In a struct, you're not allowed to assign values to the fields. Therefore, `public a = 0;` is allowed only in a class. Default values are allowed only in classes. Likewise, the constructor `public MyStruct()` isn't allowed, but it is in a class. In addition we're structs cannot inherit properties from another struct.

```
struct AddingToMyStruct : MyStruct
{
}
```

> 🔧 struct MyStruct
>
> Type 'MyStruct' in interface list is not an interface

We could easily declare a class that has nothing more than data in it; this will look much like any struct.

```
class PlayerData
{
    public Vector3 Position;
    public int HitPoints;
    public int Ammo;
    public float RunSpeed;
    public float WalkSpeed;
}
```

This would do the same things as a struct of the same complexity is concerned. However, a struct has the chance to be a bit faster than a class to access. A struct is also a step up from an enum. The declaration might look somewhat similar, but an enum doesn't allow any values to be assigned to its constituent declarations.

6.9.1 Character Base Class

For all the monsters and players to have an equal understanding of one another, they need to share a common base class. This means that simply they all need to share the same parent class that holds data structures, which all of them are aware of. This concept is called inheritance, and it's something that only a class can do.

```
public class BaseMonster
{
}
```

```
public class Zombie : BaseMonster
{
}
```

The Zombie uses the : BaseMonster statement to tell C# that the Zombie is inheriting from BaseMonster. We will go into this again in Sections 6.13 and 6.23, but it's important that we're used to seeing this notation and what it's for.

Once each type of character shares the same parent class, it can use the same data. This is important so that zombies can understand what data makes up a human, and vampires can know to avoid zombie blood. To do this, the zombies need to know how to deal with the player's data structure and the player needs to know how to deal with zombies and vampires.

When we start our game, we're going to have a starting point for the player and for each monster. Classes are a clean way to store data when a game is started. Starting data can include basic chunks of information that don't change, such as minimum and maximum values.

Structs don't allow you to declare values for variables when they are created. Classes, on the other hand, do allow you to assign values. More important, we can make them unchangeable.

6.9.2 Const

The const keyword is used to tell anyone reading the class that the value assigned cannot change during the game. The keyword is short for constant, and it means that you shouldn't try to change it either. There are a few different ways which you can assign a value to behave the same as a const, but just by looking at the code, you should know that the following code has a value that shouldn't be changed while playing.

```
public class BaseMonster
{
    /*  ... */
    const int MaxHitPoints = 10;
}
```

If a value is declared to be const, then you should keep in mind how it's used. These are good for comparisons, if a value is greater than MaxHitPoints, then you have a very clear reason for why this value is set.

When you've declared a class and set several const values, this gives the class purposeful location to store all kinds of "set in stone" numbers. One problem with giving a class const values is that they cannot be changed after they have been set. So make sure that these values shouldn't need to change once the game is running.

This allows you to create a constant value for the class. To make the value accessible, we need to change the declaration. In addition, a const value must be initialized. This means const int MaxHitPoints; isn't valid. Visual Studio will warn:

```
public const int MaxHitPoints;// = 10;
```

> 🔲 (constant) int BaseMonster.MaxHitPoints
>
> A const field requires a value to be provided

The proper declaration will look like the following:

```
public const int MaxHitPoints = 10;
```

> 🔲 (constant) int BaseMonster.MaxHitPoints = 10

The accessor must come before the readability of the variable. Likewise, this can also be made private const int MaxHitPoints =10;. This allows you to set the value when writing the code for the classes. However, if you want to make a variable have a limited availability to set, then we can use a different declaration.

6.9.3 Readonly

The readonly declaration allows you to change the variable only when a class is declared or as it's written when it was initialized.

```
public readonly int MaxMagicPoints = 10;
public void SetMaxMagicPoints(int mp)
{
    MaxMagicPoints = mp;
}
```

> (field) int BaseMonster.MaxMagicPoints
>
> A readonly field cannot be assigned to (except in a constructor or a variable initializer)

This means that a readonly variable can only be set in a variable, an initializer, or a constructor. This means that the only way to set `MaxHitPoints` can be with the following code:

```
public BaseMonster(int maxMP)
{
    MaxMagicPoints = maxMP;
    // this is valid
}
```

By using a constructor, we can set the `MaxMagicPoints` once, or we can use the value when the variable is declared. Therefore, the first way `MaxMagicPoints` can be set is when we use the initialization line public `readonly int MaxMagicPoints = 10;` where we set `MaxMagicPoints` to 10, or in the constructor where we set the value to the `(int maxMP)` in the argument list. This differs from the const keyword, where we can use the initializer only to set the value of the variable `MaxMagicPoints`.

When you add in constructors to a base class, or a class that you're expecting other classes to inherit from, it's important to remember that each child class needs to build corresponding inheriting functions.

```
Zombie : BaseMonster
```

> class Zombie
>
> There is no argument given that corresponds to the required formal parameter 'maxMP' of 'BaseMonster.BaseMonster(int)'

A quick fix for this is to allow Visual Studio to write the required functions for you.

```
public class Zombie : BaseMonster
```

> Generate overrides...
> Generate constructor 'Zombie(maxMP)' ▶
> Move type to Zombie.cs

```
...
{
    public Zombie(int maxMP) : base(maxMP)
    {
    }
}
...
```

> Preview changes

You'll notice a very similar use of: `base(maxMP)` following the `Zombie()` constructor.

```
public class Zombie : BaseMonster
{
    public Zombie(int maxMP) : base(maxMP)
    {
    }
}
```

There are other consequences to the inheriting from different classes. There will be more in-depth study of these effects in a later chapter when we look at functions again in Section 6.11.

These are only simple uses of the `const` and `readonly` variable declarators. Once you begin reading other programmer's code you've downloaded online or observed from team members, you'll get a better idea of the various reasons for using these keywords. It's impossible to cover every context in a single chapter.

The primary reason for these keywords is to prevent misunderstanding between engineers. If you have a good reason for setting a value that should never change then you'll use `const`. If you have a reason to make a value only change when an object is first created, then you'll use `readonly`. If you write code that depends on the value and assumes it's never going to change then it's good to prevent anyone from changing it.

6.9.4 What We've Learned

Using these keywords is quite simple, and it makes quite clear what you're allowed to do with them. Understanding what keywords mean to the accessibility of the variable, you'll gain insight into how the value is intended to be used.

Keywords `const` and `readonly` mean that the variable cannot be changed either outside of an initial declaration or as the code is written. This means that the value needs to remain unchanged for a reason. Of course, knowing that reason requires a great deal of context, so it's impossible to lay out every reason here. However, it's safe to assume someone added the declaratory keyword for a reason.

6.10 Namespaces

Follow along with the Namespaces_Scene and open the NameSpaces script on the game object of the same name. Classes are organized by their namespace. A namespace is a system used to sort classes and their contained functions into named groups. This helps isolate classes with the same name which would conflict without a namespace.

```
/* Section namespaces protect the contents of this section      *
 * from interfering with the contents of another section        */
namespace Chapter6_10_1
{
```

It will be problematic if programmers in the world come up with unique names for their classes and functions. Namespaces are used to control scope. By encapsulating functions and variables within a namespace, you're allowed to use names within the namespace that might already be in use in other namespaces.

6.10.1 A Basic Example

A namespace is basically an identifier for a group of classes and everything contained in the classes. The same rules as variable naming applies to namespace identifiers. Within that namespace, we can declare any number of classes. Starting in the Chapter6 Unity Project, we'll look at the NameSpaces_Scene and the NameSpaces.cs class in the scene on the object of the same name.

```
namespace MyNamespace
{
}
```

A namespace is declared as seen above. This assigns the identifier following the keyword to a new namespace. A namespace gives us a way to group objects under a unique identifier. In this case, `MyNamespace`.

A namespace doesn't collide with another namespace in the same scope. Instead, the contents of a namespace can collide with one another. A namespace only expands the scope of an exsisting namespace. Inside of a second `MyNamespace`, we can add in a new class with its own functions. However, to make the class available to anyone who wants to use the class in the namespace, we need to make it public.

```
namespace MyNamespace
{
    public class SomeClass
    {
    }
}
```

The using directives haven't been added to any of the namespaces in the file. In the above MyNamespace SomeClass exists without access to `UnityEngine` functions like `Debug.Log()`. To enable this a directive needs to be added to the namespace.

```
namespace MyNamespace
{
    /* Adds the UnityEngine library  *
     * to this scope of MyNamespace  */
    using UnityEngine;
    public class MyClass
    {
        public void MyFunction()
        {
            //Debug.Log() comes from UnityEngine
            Debug.Log("MyClass says Hello from MyNamespace");
        }
    }
}
```

The directives can exist at the beginning of any namespace. The scope of each directive added to a namespace is limited to the scope where it was declared. In this case, MyClass has access to `Debug.Log` where as the previous SomeClass does not.

As was said in an earlier chapter, we can slightly bend the rules for directives always appearing at the top of a file. The objects written in a file exists in a global unnamed namespace. The class and directives appear in the unnamed namespace and can be access globally without a directive.

```
namespace MyNamespace
{
    public class AnotherClass
    {
        void SomeFunction()
        {
            global::UnityEngine.Debug.Log("Using Global");
        }
    }
}
```

NOTE: Not that this is commonly used, but global:: can be prefixed ahead of a function or type in a declaration. This only really matters if you want to use a namespace that's already in use in a library like System, for instance. This means that if you create your own namespace System, to use libraries in the .NET system then you'd need to prefix global:: to access them.

6.10.2 Directives in Namespaces

As a namespace is created the contents become accessible through directives. The previous chapter created a namespace called MyNamespace inside of a Chapter6_10_1 namespace. To access the objects in that namespace the using MyNamespace can be added to any other namespace like adding using UnityEngine.

```
namespace SecondNamespace
{
    using UnityEngine;
    using Chapter6_10_1.MyNamespace;
    public class UniqueClass
    {
        private Chapter6_10_1.MyNamespace.MyClass myClass;
        public void UseOtherNamespace()
        {
            myClass = new MyClass();
            myClass.MyFunction();
        }
    }
}
```

In the Chapter6_10_2 namespace we use a SecondNamespace to declare a new scope. This allows UniqueClass to access the directives present in the SecondNamespace. Here, both UnityEngine and the previous chapter's MyNamespace are accessible.

The UseOtherNamespace() function in UniqueClass is allowed to instantiate a new MyClass from the Chapter6_10_1.MyNamespace scope. It should also be noted that the lighter shading of some of the directives indicate that they are not necessary. Visual Studio knows where MyClass comes from and indicates the use of unnecessary keywords by shading them lighter.

```
namespace SecondNamespace
{
    using UnityEngine;
    /* Unity finds the only MonoBehaviour that matches the file name   *
     * and uses this as the component to attach to the gameObject      *
     * in the scene.                                                   */
    public class NameSpaces : MonoBehaviour
    {
        private void Start()
        {
            UniqueClass uniqueClass = new UniqueClass();
            uniqueClass.UseOtherNamespace();
        }
    }
}
```

By wrapping the NameSpaces: MonoBehaviour in the SecondNamespace the UniqueClass() is accessible without adding a directive. Within a namespace the objects are accessible without adding any directives.

This shows where the function was called and what namespace the function originated in. In most cases, you'll create a new namespace for the classes in your new game. This becomes particularly important when you need to use third-party libraries. You might have a function called `Random()`, but another library might also have a function with the same name.

6.10.3 Ambiguous References

Coming up with unique names for every variable, class, or function can be difficult. Another class might already use commonly used words like speed, radius, or vector. Namespaces offer a system to help separate your class member names from another class that might already be using the same names. In the same Namespaces_Scene open the AmbiguousNamespaces.cs script on the NameSpaces game object.

```
using UnityEngine;
using Chapter6_10_2.SecondNamespace; // has UniqueClass
using AnotherNamespace;              // has UniqueClass
```

This will involve duplicates for the UniqueClass, which is cause for some problems. Then Unity 3D will show you the following error:

```
// which UniqueClass to use?
UniqueClass uniqueClass = new AnotherNamespace.UniqueClass();
```

class Chapter6_10_3.AnotherNamespace.UniqueClass

'UniqueClass' is an ambiguous reference between 'Chapter6_10_3.AnotherNamespace.UniqueClass' and 'Chapter6_10_2.SecondNamespace.UniqueClass'

Show potential fixes (Alt+Enter or Ctrl+.)

Ambiguous references become a common problem when we include many different namespaces. We could possibly fix this by changing the name of the classes in one of the functions, but that wouldn't be possible if the reference came from a dynamic linking library (DLL) or another author's code. We could also change namespaces which we're using, but again, that would be a work around and not a solution.

If we hover over the class with the cursor in Visual Studio, we'll get a pop-up telling us which version is currently being used. Of course, this is just a guess, and a bad one at that. This can be resolved by expanding the declaration using the Namespace dot operator and picking the to uniquely identify the `UniqueClass` we want from the other namespace.

```
/* this is more specific */
AnotherNamespace.UniqueClass uniqueClass = new AnotherNamespace.UniqueClass();
Chapter6_10_2.SecondNamespace.UniqueClass secondUniqueClass = new Chapter6_10_2.SecondNamespace.UniqueClass();
```

Of course, it's not the most pretty, but this is the most correct method to fix the namespace we're requesting a `UniqueClass()` object from. Things can get too long if we need to nest more namespaces inside of a namespace.

Long namespaces represent a little bit of a style problem. It's cleaner to use short statements. So how would we avoid needing to use dot operators to access directives with shorter names?

6.10.4 Alias Directives

Attached to the same NameSpaces game object is also a script called `UsingAliasDirectives`. Open this to follow along. Sometimes namespaces can get quite long. Often when you need to refer to a namespace directly you may want to shorten the name into something easier to type. Alias directives make this easier.

```
using UnityEngine;
/* This allows you to shorten the name of a   *
 * namespace to something easier to use.      */
using Sub = Chapter6_10_3.AnotherNamespace.SubSpace;
```

A directive is aliased using the syntax using x = UnityEngine; for instance. When we have a namespace nested in another namespace, we can assign that to an identifier as well. To shorten AnotherNamespace.SubSpace to Sub, we use a statement that looks like using Sub = AnotherNamespace.SubSpace; to reduce how much typing we need to use to express which namespace we're using.

```
/* uses Sub rather than                              *
 * Chapter6_10_3.AnotherNamespace.SubSpace          */
Sub.SubSpaceClass subClass = new Sub.SubSpaceClass();
subClass.UseSubSpaceFunction();
```

Now we can reduce the declaration to a shorter statement. Of course, unless we have an ambiguous name to worry about, there's no need for being so explicit with the function we're specifically trying to call. With descriptive function and variable names, we can avoid directive aliases.

6.10.5 What We've Learned

This is a simple way to allow multiple classes to work together by sharing a class through a namespace. Decisions around how you organize the code for your game should include how to separate classes by namespace. In a practical sense, namespaces follow function. A Utilities namespace would include classes you use as tools for your game. A game title is a good root namespace.

A Utilities namespace for your game would be a member of the game namespace. The namespace should also contain common structs that every class will need to make use of. So a game.dataTypes namespace would help organize where those are stored. These are just some example of the sorts of namespaces that would be useful to help organize your game.

6.11 Functions Again

So far, we've been working in either the Start() function or the Update() function because they are entry points. Because of this, they are automatically called by the engine. In a non-Unity 3D Engine program, the default entry point would be something like public static void Main().

6.11.1 Parameter Lists

When a function is called, its identifier followed by its parameter list is added to code. Parameters are like little mail slots on the front door of a house. There might be a slot for integers, floats, and arrays. Each slot on the door, or argument in the parameter list, is a type followed by an identifier.

If we look at a basic example, we'll see how all this works.

```
public class FunctionsAgain : MonoBehaviour
{
    int a = 0;
    void SetA(int i)
    {
        a = i;
    }
}
```

The function declaration `void SetA (int i)` takes in one parameter of type `int`. This is a simple example of a value parameter; there are other types of parameters which we'll go into next. The value parameter declares the type and an identifier whose scope is limited to the contents of the function it's declared with.

```
void Start()
{
    Debug.Log("a:" + a); //0
    SetA(3);
    Debug.Log("a:" + a); //3
}
```

To use our function, add in the preceding lines of code to the `Start()` function in Unity 3D. When you start the game, you'll see a 0 followed by a 3. We can do this any number of times, and each time we're allowed to change what value we set A to. Of course, it's easier to use a = 3 in the `Start()` function, but then we wouldn't be learning anything.

6.11.2 Side Effects

When a function directly sets a variable in the class the function lives in, programmers like to call this a side effect. Side effects are usually things that programmers try to avoid, but it's not always practical. Writing functions with side effects tend to prevent the function from being useful in other classes. We'll find other systems that allow us to avoid using side effects, but in some cases, it's necessary.

```
int b;
void SetBtoFive()
{
    b = 5;
}
```

The above `SetBtoFive()` function sets `int b` to 5. The `SetBtoFive()` function does have a clear purpose, setting b to 5, but there's nothing in the function that indicates where the variable it's setting lives. If the variable lived in another class which `FunctionsAgain` inherited from, then you wouldn't even see the variable in this class.

Once the complexity in a class grows, where and when a variable gets changed or read becomes more obscure. If a function remains self-contained, testing and fixing that function becomes far easier. Reading what a function does should not involve jumping around to find what variable it's making changes to. This brings us back to the topic of scope. Limiting the scope or reach of a function helps limit the number of places where things can go wrong.

```
int b;
void SetBtoFive()
{
    b = 5;
}
public void SetBAgain()
{
    b = new int();
}
```

The more functions that have a side effect, the more strange behaviors might occur. If an `Update()` function is expecting one value but gets something else entirely, you can start to get unexpected behaviors. Worse yet, if `SetBAgain()` is called from another class and you were expecting a to be 5, you're going to run into more strange behaviors.

6.11.3 Multiple Arguments

There aren't any limits to the number of parameters that a function can accept. Some languages limit you to no more than 16 arguments, which seems acceptable. If your logic requires more than 16 parameters, it's probably going to be easier to separate your function into different parts. However, if we're going to be doing something simple, we might want to use more than one parameter anyway.

```
int c = 0;
void SetCtoLeftPlusRight(int left, int right)
{
    c = left + right;
}
```

We can add a second parameter to `SetCtoLeftPlusRight()`. A comma token tells the function to accept another variable in the parameter list. For this example, we're using two ints to add to one another and assign a value to c. There isn't anything limiting the types we're allowed to use in the parameter list.

```
void SetAtoLeftBtoRight(int left, int right)
{
    a = left;
    b = right;
}
```

The function with multiple parameters can do more. Value parameters are helpful ways to get data into a function to accomplish some sort of simple task. We'll elaborate more on this by creating something useful in Unity 3D.

6.11.4 Useful Parameters

Often, we need to test things out before using them. Let's say we want to create a new primitive cube in the scene, give it a useful name, and then set its position. This is a simple task, and our code might look like the following:

```
GameObject go = GameObject.CreatePrimitive(PrimitiveType.Cube);
go.name = "MrCube";
go.transform.position = new Vector3(0, 1, 0);
```

Our cube is given a name, and it's assigned a place in the world. Next, let's say we want to make a bunch of different cubes in the same way. We could do something like the following:

```
GameObject go = GameObject.CreatePrimitive(PrimitiveType.Cube);
go.name = "MrCube";
go.transform.position = new Vector3(0, 1, 0);
GameObject go1 = GameObject.CreatePrimitive(PrimitiveType.Cube);
go.name = "MrsCube";
go.transform.position = new Vector3(0, 2, 0);
GameObject go2 = GameObject.CreatePrimitive(PrimitiveType.Cube);
go.name = "MissCube";
go.transform.position = new Vector3(0, 3, 0);
GameObject go3 = GameObject.CreatePrimitive(PrimitiveType.Cube);
go.name = "CubeJr";
go.transform.position = new Vector3(0, 4, 0);
```

If this code looks horrible, then you're learning. It's accomplishing a task properly, but in terms of programming, it's horrible. When you intend to do a simple task more than a few times, it's a good idea to turn it into a function. This is sometimes referred to as the "Rule of Three," a term coined in an early programming book on refactoring code.

6.11.4.1 The Rule of Three

The Rule of Three is a simple idea that any time you need to do any given task more than three times manually, it would be better served by creating a new single procedure to accomplish the task. This reduces the chance of error in writing the same code more than three times. This also means that changing the procedure can be done in one place.

```csharp
void CreateANamedObject(PrimitiveType pType, string name, Vector3 pos)
{
    GameObject go = GameObject.CreatePrimitive(pType);
    go.name = name;
    go.transform.position = pos;
}
```

We take the code that's repeated and move it into a function. We then take the values that change between each iteration and change it into a parameter. In general, it's best to put the parameters in the same order in which they're used. This isn't required, but it looks more acceptable to a programmer's eyes.

```csharp
CreateANamedObject(PrimitiveType.Cube, "MrCube", new Vector3(0, 1, 0));
```

We then test the function at least once before writing any more code than we need to. If this works out, then we're free to duplicate the line of code to accomplish what we started off doing.

```csharp
CreateANamedObject(PrimitiveType.Cube, "MrCube", new Vector3(0, 1, 0));
CreateANamedObject(PrimitiveType.Cube, "MrsCube", new Vector3(0, 2, 0));
CreateANamedObject(PrimitiveType.Cube, "MissCube", new Vector3(0, 3, 0));
CreateANamedObject(PrimitiveType.Cube, "CubeJr", new Vector3(0, 4, 0));
```

Again, though, we're seeing a great deal of duplicated work. We've used arrays earlier, and this is as good a time as any to use them. By observation, the main thing that is changing here is the name. Therefore, we'll need to add each name to an array.

```csharp
string[] names = new string[]
{
    "MrCube",
    "MrsCube",
    "MissCube",
    "CubeJr"
};
```

The variable declaration needs to change a little bit for an array. First of all, rather than using type identifier;, a pair of square brackets are used after the type. The statement starts with `string[]` rather than string. This is followed by the usual identifier we're going to use to store the array of strings.

Unlike an integer type, there's no default value that can be added in for this array of strings. To complete the statement, we need to add in the data before the end of the statement. The new keyword is used to indicate that a new array is going to be used. The array is a special class that is built into C#. Therefore, it has some special abilities that we'll get into later.

Now that we've declared an array of names, we'll need to use them.

6.11.5 Foreach versus For

The foreach loop is often our goto loop for iterating through any number of objects.

```
foreach (string s in names)
{
    Debug.Log(s);
}
```

The parameters for the foreach also introduce the keyword in that tells the foreach iterator what array to look into. The first parameter before the in keyword indicates what we're expecting to find inside of the array. Therefore, for this use of the foreach iterator, we get the output in the following page.

As expected, we get a list of the names found in the array we added. As we add in new functions and variables, it's important to test them out one at a time. This helps make sure that you're headed in the right direction one step at a time. Now we can switch out the print function for the clever function we wrote now.

```
foreach (string s in names)
{
    CreateANamedObject(PrimitiveType.Cube, s, new Vector3(0, 1, 0));
}
```

The foreach loop in some respects operates in the same way as a while loop.

```
float y = 1.0f;
foreach (string s in names)
{
    CreateANamedObject(PrimitiveType.Cube, s, new Vector3(0, y, 0));
    y += 1.0f;
}
```

It's simple to add in a variable outside of the loop that can be incremented within the loop.

It's time to admire our clever function. The foreach means we can add in any number of names to the array and the tower of cubes will get taller with named boxes.

6.11.6 What We've Learned

The foreach loop is useful in many ways, but it's also somewhat limited. If we had more than one array to iterate through at the same time, we'd have some difficulties. In some cases, it's easier to use a regular for loop. Arrays are lists of objects, but they're also numbered.

Arrays are used everywhere. On your own, experiment by adding more parameters to the function and more names to the list. We'll look at how to use other loops with multidimensional arrays and even jagged arrays in Chapter 7.

6.12 Unity 3D Execution Order

C# is an imperative language, which means that operations are executed in order, first one thing and then another. When Unity 3D makes an instance of a new gameObject with MonoBehaviour components, each component will have at least five functions called on it before the end of the frame where it was created. Additional rendering calls can be called as well.

Specifically, the `Start()` and `Update()` functions in Unity 3D are called in each MonoBehaviour in a specific order. Several other functions are also used by Unity 3D, and they each have specific moments when they are called. In Visual Studio the key-combo: CTRL+Shift+M will open the Implement Unity Messages dialog box:

Implement Unity Messages   ✕

Select methods to create:

Filter...

- ☐ Awake()
- ☐ FixedUpdate()
- ☐ LateUpdate()
- ☐ OnAnimatorIK(int)
- ☐ OnAnimatorMove()
- ☐ OnApplicationFocus(bool)
- ☐ OnApplicationPause(bool)
- ☐ OnApplicationQuit()
- ☐ OnAudioFilterRead(float[], int)
- ☐ OnBecameInvisible()
- ☐ OnBecameVisible()
- ☐ OnBeforeTransformParentChanged()
- ☐ OnCanvasGroupChanged()
- ☐ OnCollisionEnter(Collision)
- ☐ OnCollisionEnter2D(Collision2D)
- ☐ OnCollisionExit(Collision)

Insertion point: API version:

At cursor   ▾   Latest   ▾

☐ Generate method comments

0 of 69 selected (0 already implemented)   [OK   ]   [Cancel]

Of the 69 messages that all MonoBehaviours will receive in game, here are 8 used most often:

```
Awake()
OnEnable()
Start()
FixedUpdate()
Update()
LateUpdate()
OnDisable()
OnDestroy()
```

The order of this should make sense, considering that C# will execute statements in order. However, what happens when another class is instanced in the `Awake()` function and it too will have its own `Awake()`, `OnEnable()`, and `Start()` functions?

6.12.1 A Basic Example

Begin by examining the ExecutionOrder project; the ExecutionOrderFirst.cs class will look a bit like the following:

```
public class ExecutionOrderFirst : MonoBehaviour
{

    void Awake()
    {
        Debug.Log("First Awake");
    }

    void OnEnable()
    {
        Debug.Log("First OnEnable");
    }

    void Start()
    {
        Debug.Log("First Start");
    }

    void FixedUpdate()
    {
        Debug.Log("First FixedUpdate");
    }

    void Update()
    {
        Debug.Log("First Update");
    }

    private void LateUpdate()
    {
        Debug.Log("First LateUpdate");
        Destroy(this);
    }

    private void OnDisable()
    {
        Debug.Log("First OnDisable");
    }

    private void OnDestroy()
    {
        Debug.Log("First OnDistroy");
    }
}
```

This prints out the following:

The Console shows that the code is executed in the same order in which we laid them out in the class. When the `LateUpdate()` function is called, we use `Destroy(this);` to begin deleting the class from the scene. When the class begins to delete itself, it's first disabled and then deleted.

When a new instance of a MonoBehaviour is created, it will also call its `Awake()`, `OnEnabled()`, and `Start()` functions. Intuitively, it would make sense if you create an object in the `Awake()` function; the new object might wait till the end of `Awake()` before it begins its `Awake()` function. However, this isn't always the case.

```
void Awake()
{
    Debug.Log("Awake Start");
    this.gameObject.AddComponent(typeof(Second));
    Debug.Log("Awake Done");
}
```

Say we create a new class called Second.cs and have it log its `Awake()` and `Start()` functions as well. Then, in the Second.cs class we have the following code:

```
void Awake()
{
    Debug.Log("Second Awake");
}

void OnEnable()
{
    Debug.Log("Second OnEnable");
}
```

This produces the following output:

> (!) First Awake
> UnityEngine.Debug:Log(Object)
>
> (!) First Awake Start
> UnityEngine.Debug:Log(Object)
>
> (!) Second Awake
> UnityEngine.Debug:Log(Object)
>
> (!) Second OnEnable
> UnityEngine.Debug:Log(Object)
>
> (!) First Awake Done
> UnityEngine.Debug:Log(Object)
>
> (!) First OnEnable
> UnityEngine.Debug:Log(Object)
>
> (!) First Start
> UnityEngine.Debug:Log(Object)
>
> (!) Second Start
> UnityEngine.Debug:Log(Object)

Before the First class was created, the Second was able to get its Awake() done and move on to OnEnable() without interruption. First waited for Second to finish its Awake() and OnEnable() functions before First finished its own Awake() function. Afterward, OnEnable() of the First was finally called, even if Second took its own time to finish its Awake() function.

```
Debug.Log("Second Awake Start");
for(int i = 0; i < 1000; i++)
{
    Debug.Log("Wait!");
}
Debug.Log("Second Awake Done.");
```

The ExecutionOrderFirst.cs class finishes its `Awake()` function, then the ExecutionOrderSecond.cs class finishes its `Awake()` function and starts its `OnEnable()`. After, ExecutionOrderFirst finishes its `Awake()` and starts its `OnEnable()` function. The First and Second being their Start() function. Notice that "First Awake Done" doesn't appear until after "Second OnEnable." The "Second OnEnable" is only printed once the "Second Awake Done" is printed, indicating that the for loop was able to finish.

　　When more objects are being created, the order in which these functions are called becomes more difficult to sort out. If you created several different objects, some of them might take even longer or shorter to finish their `Awake()`, `OnEnable()`, and `Start()` functions. Figuring all of this out takes a bit of thinking things through.

6.12.2　Component Execution Order

The execution of classes becomes a bit more confusing when they're attached to a gameObject as a prefab. In the scene, adding Second and Third classes to the Main Camera will show us some unexpected results.

Once all three MonoBehaviours have been attached to the Main Camera, we can observe the execution order of the functions found in each class.

The `Third Awake()` and `OnEnable()` are called before the Second and the First even though the components look like they've been reordered in the opposite order on the game object they are attached to. However, this isn't always the case.

In the above screenshot, we swapped the First component with the Second. Even after changing the order in which they appear in the components list, we get no change in the Console's log output. This tells us that there's no specific order in which the objects are created and how they are ordered in the gameObject's components list. However, there is a simple system in which we can change the execution order manually.

Select the ExecutionOrderFirst.cs file in the Project Assets directory. To the top right is a button labeled Execution Order...

After your classes have been added to the list, you can make any changes by altering the number in the box to the right. Clicking on the—icon removes them from the list. Press Apply once you've added all your classes to the list.

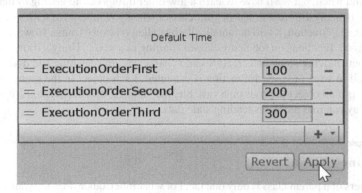

Once the scripts have been added to this list, they are guaranteed to be called in this order, ignoring how they are ordered in the components list on the gameObject they've been added to. Playing the scene with the components attached to the Main Camera in any order will always result in the following output:

After the scripts order is set, the Console panel shows us a more expected result. You could use a single GameController.cs class that operates as a central dispatch of updates. This would be a monolithic update system which every other class waits for an update from.

For now it's important that we observe how the functions operate and how to best use these behaviors to our advantage. From observation, we know that we can maintain when each function is called.

6.12.3 What We've Learned

In this chapter, we looked at how to manage execution order between multiple classes. For simple projects, this execution ordering system should suffice. However, when you're not inheriting from MonoBehaviour, this management system will no longer work.

Once we get into more complex systems that do not inherit from MonoBehaviour, we'll build our own system for managing the execution order. There are systems that allow you to better control what functions are called and when, but we'll have to learn a few other things before getting to that.

Unity 3D expects many different things of your classes when you inherit from MonoBehaviour. If you include an `Update()` function, it will automatically be called on every frame. However, when there are too many `Update()` functions on too many classes running in a scene, Unity's frame rate can suffer.

Once a game gets moving along and creatures and characters are spawning and dying, it's impossible to know when and in what order each function is executed. Each object in the scene should be able to operate on its own. If an object depends on a variable, the value of which needs to be updated before it's used, then you may run into problems reading stale data.

6.13 Inheritance Again

Inheriting members of a parent class is only one facet of what inheritance does for your code. The behaviors of the functions also carry on in the child classes. If the parent has functions that it uses to find objects in the world, then so do the children. If the parent can change its behavior based on its proximity to other objects, then so do the children.

The key difference is that the children can decide what happens based on those behaviors. The data that is collected can be used in any way. A child class inherits the functions of its parent class. When the child's function is executed, it operates the same way as its parent. It can be more interesting to have the child's function behave differently from the inherited version of the function.

6.13.1 Function Overrides

The override keyword following the public keyword in a function declaration tells the child version of the function to clear out the old behavior and implement a new version. We've seen how member functions work when they're used by another class. Now we're going to see how to effect the operation of inherited functions.

6.13.1.1 A Basic Example

Revisiting the Parent–Child relation again in the Chapter 6 Unity Project in the InheritanceAgain_Scene. We find the following code to the ParentClass:

```
public class ParentClass
{
    public void ParentFunction()
    {
        Debug.Log("Parent Says Hello.");
        FunctionA();
        FunctionB();
    }

    public void FunctionA()
    {
        Debug.Log("Parent Function A Says Hello.");
    }

    public void FunctionB()
    {
        Debug.Log("Parent Function B Says Hello.");
    }
}
```

When the ParentFunction() is called in the Start() function of the InheritanceAgain script in the InheritanceAgain_Scene, this will produce the expected "Parent says Hello." followed by "Parent Function A says Hello." and then "Parent Function B says Hello." in the Console panel.

ChildClass is based on ParentClass, and we have an opportunity to make modifications by adding layers of code. To make see this modification, we need to reuse the code from the ParentClass class in the ChildClass. The ParentFunction() is called from the ChildFunction() of the Child class.

```
public class ChildClass : ParentClass
{
    public void ChildFunction()
    {
        ParentFunction();
    }
}
```

Running this will produce the same output to the Console panel as the Parent class. Right now, there is no function overriding going on. If we intend to inherit a function and add modifications to it, we should make the Parent class allow for functions to be overridden by adding the virtual keyword to the function we plan to override.

```
public virtual void FunctionA()
{
    Debug.Log("Parent Function A Says Hello.");
}
```

Adding the `virtual` keyword after the `public` declaration and before the return data type, we can tell the function it's allowed to be overridden by any class inheriting its functions. Back in the ChildClass, we have the option to override the virtual function.

```
public override void FunctionA()
{
    base.FunctionA();
    Debug.Log("Child's Addition to Function A.");
}
```

This has an added instruction for `FunctionA()`. As you might expect, the output to the Console panel has a new addition. The Child class will send new data to the Console that should read:

> ⓘ Parent Says Hello.
>   UnityEngine.Debug:Log(Object)
>
> ⓘ Parent Function A Says Hello.
>   UnityEngine.Debug:Log(Object)
>
> ⓘ Child's Addition to Function A.
>   UnityEngine.Debug:Log(Object)

Without the keywords override and virtual, we get the following warning:

```
public void FunctionB()
{
}
```

> ⚙ void ChildClass.FunctionB()
>
> 'ChildClass.FunctionB()' hides inherited member 'ParentClass.FunctionB()'. Use the new keyword if hiding was intended.
>
> Show potential fixes (Alt+Enter or Ctrl+.)

We can see this in the ChildClass `FunctionB()` and watch the resulting output. In the ChildClass, we'll add in the new keyword. However, the output will remain the same as though the Parent class' version of `FunctionB()` was being used. This is because the `FunctionB()` living in the ChildClass is a new one, and not the one being used by the `ParentFunction()`.

```
public new void FunctionB()
{
    Debug.Log("Child's New FunctionB? I'm too new and not called from anywhere.");
}
```

To explain a bit more about what happened when `ParentFunction()` is called.

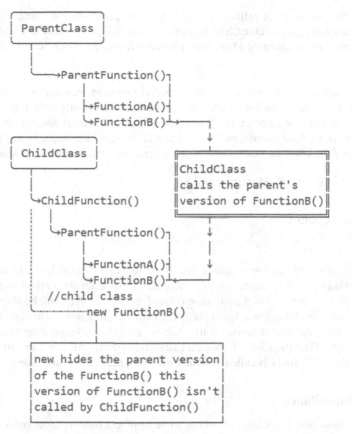

The ChildClass has a new FunctionB() this breaks the relation with the ParentClass version of FunctionB(). So when ParentFunction is called, the Parent's version of FunctionA and FunctionB are called. By using the override on a virtual function we add new behaviors to the FunctionA that's called in the ParentClass.

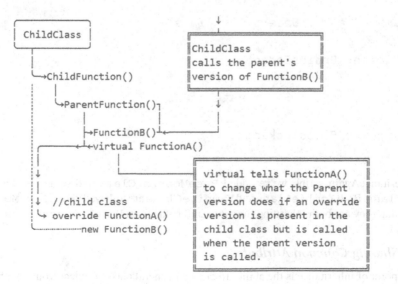

So when `ChildFunction()` is calling on `ParentFunction()` to run `FunctionA()` we get the added behavior that was created in the `ChildClass` version of `FunctionA()`. The difference between `override` and `new` when inheriting a function or variable from a parent create very different behaviors.

6.13.1.1.1 Base

The Child class' version of the `FunctionB` hides the inherited member from its `ParentClass`. Hiding means that the parent version of `FunctionB` cannot be directly called by the `ChildClass`. When the child calls the new `FunctionB()`, only the `ChildClass` version is visible.

On the other hand, we have overridden `FunctionA()` from the `ParentClass`. To use the original version, we can add the keyword `base` version in `FunctionA` which was overridden.

```
public override void FunctionA()
{
    base.FunctionA();
    //"Parent Function A Says Hello."
```

This produces the expected "`Parent Says Hello.`" to be printed out in the Console panel. For the `ChildClass` to take over the `FunctionA()` and create its own version of the function, omit the base `FunctionA()` and the contents of the parent version of `FunctionA()` will be skipped.

Therefore, when the InheritanceAgain script `Start()` function calls on the ParentClasses `ParentFunction()`, the ParentClass version of `FunctionA()` is called printing "`Parent Function A Says Hello.`" When the ChildClasses `ChildFunction()` calls on `ParentFunction()` the overridden `FunctionA()` is called, but the new `FunctionB()` isn't called.

6.13.2 Class Inheritance

We've seen a bit about how a function can inherit some members from a parent version of a class. To see how this works lets investigate some nested classes for some new Monsters.

```
class BaseMonsterClass
{
    public int HitPoints;
}
class ZombieClass : BaseMonsterClass
{
    public int BrainsEaten;
}
class VampireClass : BaseMonsterClass
{
    public int BloodSucked;
}
```

In the InheritanceAgain script, we've added `BaseMonsterClass` and `ZombieClass` as well as `VampireClass`. Both `ZombieClass` and `VampireClass` are followed with: `BaseMonsterClass` to indicate that they are both inheriting functions and fields from `BaseMonsterClass`.

6.13.2.1 Sharing Common Attributes

The whole point of inheritance is the ability to create a general class of object from which child objects can inherit the same properties. If all the characters in a game are going to share a system for taking damage, then they should all use the same system. Games use "mechanics" as a generalized term for game rules. Often used like "this game's mechanics are fun." Recovering health, taking damage, and interacting with objects should all be added to what is called a *base class*.

Consider building base classes for things such as destructible objects and monsters. Base classes allow for the multitude of objects in your game to have a shared attribute for something obvious like hitpoints and share the ability of the player to interact with them. Breaking down a door and basting away a zombie shouldn't require a different set of code to accomplish the same thing.

By adding `public int HitPoints` to BaseMonsterClass, we've given both Zombie and Vampire a `HitPoints` variable. This is a main strength of why we need to use inheritance. Objects that share common attributes should be able to share that data. We need to make this public so that when the class is used, you can access the `HitPoints` variable from outside of the class. To demonstrate, we'll need to make some instances of both the zombie and the vampire.

```
ZombieClass zombie = new ZombieClass();
VampireClass vampire = new VampireClass();
zombie.HitPoints = 10;
vampire.HitPoints = 10;
/* Assignment of HitPoints = 10
 * every time might be redundant.
 */
```

Now Vampires and Zombies have HitPoints. In the `Start()` function, we'll create a new Zombie and a new Vampire. Then we'll give them some starting `HitPoints` by using the identifier and adding `.HitPoints = 10;` to make the assignment.

However, if we add in a constructor, we can put the `HitPoints = 10;` into the constructor for the Monster instead! While we're at it, extend the Monster by adding a capsule to its presence. We'll also make him announce himself when he's created.

```
public int HitPoints;
public GameObject gameObject;
public BaseMonsterClass()
{
    HitPoints = 10;
    gameObject = GameObject.CreatePrimitive(PrimitiveType.Capsule);
    Debug.Log("A New Monster Rises!");
}
```

To make use of the `HitPoints` variable, we will create a function that will deal with damage done to the Monster. Adding in a new public function that returns an `int` called `TakeDamage` will be a good start.

```
public virtual int TakeDamage(int damage)
{
    return HitPoints - damage;
}
```

In the `TakeDamage()` argument list is `(int damage)` that will return the `HitPoints - damage` to let us know how many HitPoints the monster has after taking damage. Now both the Zombie and the Vampire can take damage. To allow the Zombie and Vampire to reuse the function and override its behavior, we add in virtual after the public keyword.

```
class VampireClass : BaseMonsterClass
{
    public int BloodSucked;
    public override int TakeDamage(int damage)
    {
        return HitPoints - (damage / 2);
    }
}
```

Perhaps we've decided vampires are more durable than zombies, we'll make the vampire take half the damage that is dealt to him. Using `public override` tells the function to take over the original use of the `Monster.TakeDamage()` function. This allows us to reuse the same function call on both zombies and vampires. For the Zombie, we'll return the default result of the `Monster.TakeDamage()` function by using return base. `TakeDamage(damage);`. Remember, the keyword base allows us to refer the original implementation of the code. The following appears in the Zombie:

```
public override int TakeDamage(int damage)
{
    return base.TakeDamage(damage);
}
```

In the `Start()` function, we'll make the following uses of zombie and vampire. The following code produces 5 and 8:

```
Debug.Log(zombie.TakeDamage(5));
Debug.Log(vampire.TakeDamage(5));
```

This looks useful, though remember that we're dealing with int values and not float. When we divide int 5 by int 2, we get 3, not 2.5. When building new objects, the goal is to reuse as much code as possible. Likewise, we can leave the `TakeDamage()` out of the zombie altogether if we don't need to make any changes.

However, it's sometimes unclear what's going on and might end up being less obvious when damage is dealt to the two monsters. In the end though, it's up to you to choose how to set up any functions that are inherited from your base monster class.

This should serve as a fair example as to what objects and classes are created in the way they are. When functions and variables are separated in classes, they allow you to compartmentalize for very specific purposes. When you design your classes, it's important to keep object-oriented concepts in mind.

6.13.3 Object

Changing behaviors of previously implemented functions is fundamental to object-oriented programming (OOP). The base class from which all classes in Unity 3D inherit is object. The .Net Framework provides object as a foundation for any other class being created. This allows every new object a common ground to communicate between one another.

In Visual Studio the Solution Explorer panel is a regular fixture in the default layout. From here the a class diagram can be created from a each file in the solution. Selecting View Class Diagram shows a view which allows you to further edit your work in a more visual manner.

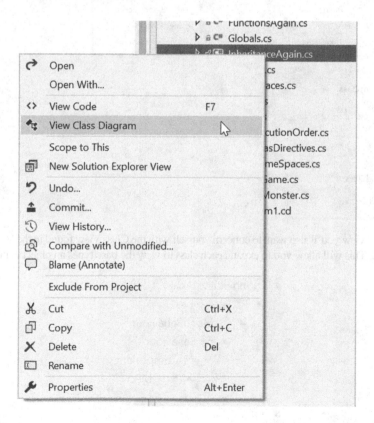

There have been many attempts to make a more visual system to build code. Viewing the class diagram for the InheritanceAgain.cs class you get a view similar to the following: Clicking on the icon on the top right of each box expands the object showing its contents. Using this view you're able to add new functions, aka methods, properties, fields, events, constructors, destructors, and constants. Further in the Class Details panel you're able to add type, parameters, and more to each added feature. It's a fun feature, and something which might help quickly build a useful start for your next game object.

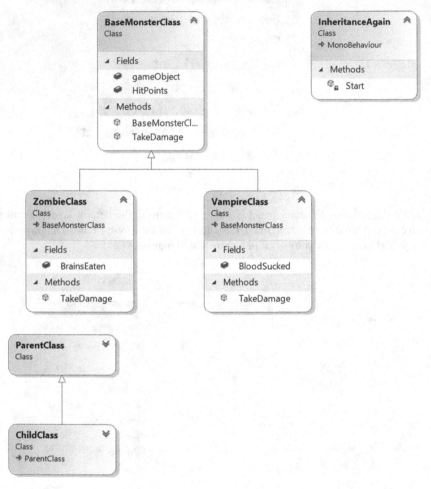

In addition to this view you'll also want to concern yourself with the Class View found in the View→Class View CTRL+Shift+C. This will allow you to expand each class to view the base types an object is inheriting from.

From here you can double click on the lowest class which InheritanceAgain is based on. The following Object Browser view is opened to reveal public class Object Member of System.

Object reveals several functions available to every class inheriting from it. The function `ToString()` is used every time we use values which are not strings in the `Debug.Log()` function in Unity 3D. In the ZombieClass we could add an override for `ToString()` with a custom value.

```
public override string ToString()
{
    return "I'm a Zombie!";
}
```

Using the override we get to see the following printed out to the Unity Editor's console panel:

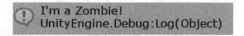

In your own project you may want to add more useful information to the `ToString()` override, but this should work as a starting point.

It's useful to find functions that are already in use and update them to fit our current class. The object class was created with `ToString()`, which provides every object in C# to have some sort of `ToString()` behavior. This also means that we can override `ToString()` with pretty much any class we create.

6.13.4 What We've Learned

At this point, we've got a great deal of the basics down. We can write classes and we know how the basics of inheritance work. This is important, as we proceed to use inheriting properties and methods more and more. We've studied a bit of flow control systems using if and switch, which are indispensable statements.

We've created several classes already, but we've yet to really use classes as objects. In Chapters 7 and 8, we're going to learn the core of what OOP is all about.

6.14 Type Casting Again

Type casting is the process of converting one data type into another. To follow along open the Chapter 6 Unity Project's CastingAgain_Scene and open the CastingAgain script on the CastingAgain game object in the scene. When programmers use the word *integral type*, they mean things that can be numbered.

```
enum SimpleEnums
{
    FirstValue,
    SecondValue,
    ThirdValue
}

void Start()
{
    SimpleEnums simpleEnum = SimpleEnums.SecondValue;
    int convertedEnum = simpleEnum as int;
}
```

As we can see, we've written an enum with three options. With simpleEnums.SecondValue we try to change it into an `int`.

As we try to cast `simpleEnum as int;` we get an error!

> ⓘ Assets/CastingAgain.cs(26,40): error CS0077: The `as` operator cannot be used with a non-nullable value type `int`

The as operator can't be used for this because an int is not actually an enum. Therefore, we get a conflict here. We're trying to use the enum as though it were already an int, which it's not. There is a way to convert different types from one to another.

```
void Start()
{
    SimpleEnums simpleEnum = SimpleEnums.SecondValue;
    int convertedEnum = (int)simpleEnum;
    Debug.Log("convertedEnum: " + convertedEnum);
    // convertedEnum: 1
}
```

The line `int convertedEnum = (int)simpleEnum;` uses the explicit cast `(int)` to convert the `SimpleEnums` value into an int value. This isn't always possible, but in some cases, this will work when an explicit cast has been defined. Explicit casting requires the type's destination to have been expected. When the programmer creates a new data type, they may expect a conversion to another type. In this case, enum to int, the C# developers created a definition to enable that type conversion explicitly. Thus the naming: explicit type cast operator.

So why is "`convertedEnum: 1`" in the Console when we run the game? Remember that numbering lists in C# starts at `0`, so the second item in a list will be indexed at `1`. Of course, not all explicit conversions work. For instance, you can't turn a Monster GameObject into a float value. Zombies aren't just numbers!

6.14.1 (<Type>) versus "as"

We're starting to see the difference in type casting methods. The difference between (`<Type>`) cast and the `as` cast can come up during an interview process if you're trying to get a job as a programmer.

We should also note that some casting is also going on when we use float f = 1; where 1 is an int value, but it's accepted into a float f without any question. This is an implicit cast, or rather this is a cast that is accepted without any explicit cast operation. This also works for a double d = 1.0f; where 1.0f is a float value and d is a double.

The two different methods we can use are called *prefix casting* and *as casting*. Prefix casting is what the (int) syntax is called; this is also referred to as an explicit cast operator. The as operator works a bit differently than the explicit cast operator.

```
class Humanoid
{
}


class Zombie : Humanoid
{
}


class Person : Humanoid
{
}
```

Here we have three classes: Humanoid, Zombie, and Person. The Zombie and Person inherit from the Humanoid class. Discovering the differences with as and (Type) is significant only once we start getting into the nitty-gritty of doing something with the results of the type casting.

```
void CastingHumanoids()
{
    Humanoid h = new Humanoid();
    Zombie z = h as Zombie;
    Debug.Log(z);
    //"Null"
}
```

In the CastingAgain script the Start() function calls CastngHumanoids() where we perform the cast as seen above using the as-casting method. A new Humanoid h, instantiates a new Humanoid type object identified as h. Then a Zombie identified as z is assigned h as Zombie. This assumes that the Humanoid is a Zombie type convertable. When we use Debug.Log(z), we get Null.

> ⚠ Null
> UnityEngine.Debug:Log(Object)

Compare this result to the following explicit cast operator. If we use the prefix system as in the following example code:

```
Zombie x = (Zombie)h;
Debug.Log(x);
```

We get a different result, this time an error:

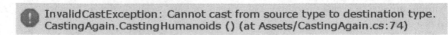

This tells us that a type Humanoid cannot be converted to a type Zombie. This doesn't change when converting between a Person and a Zombie. To create an explicit cast, we need to implement a function to allow the cast to work.

```
Person p = new Person();
Zombie zombieFromPerson = p as Zombie;
```

As before, we get a similar error.

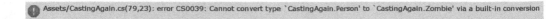

The last part of the error indicates some built-in conversion. We need to add some lines of code to allow us to build in a cast between Zombie and Person.

You can imagine that this would happen quite a lot when playing a zombie game. C# is trying to make changes to the data to conform it so that it matches the type we're asking for it to be converted to. In some cases, the as operator is more appropriate than the prefix operator. A Null is much easier to deal with than an error. This conversion makes sense only when the types are incompatible if there is no conversion possible.

We can cast between ints and floats, no problem aside from losing numbers after a decimal. There are conversions available through C#, but no effort has been made to convert a Humanoid to a Zombie. A method should be made available to do so. The conversion work has been written for the built-in data types. The work has not yet been done to convert between a Person and a Zombie, so we shall do this.

6.14.2 User-Defined Type Conversion

Continuing, observe the code for the CastableHumanoid, which has some HitPoints.

```
class CastableHumanoid
{
    public int HitPoints;
}
```

This way we can have some significant meaning for converting between a Person and a Zombie. For this example, assume zombies use negative hitpoints and a person has a positive number for hitpoints. Thanks to inheritance, we can safely assume that both the Person and the Zombie will have a HitPoints property when they derive from the CastableHumanoid class.

Now we'll create a new function in the CastablePerson, so we can convert him into a CastableZombie.

```
class CastablePerson : CastableHumanoid
{
    static public implicit operator CastableZombie(CastablePerson person)
    {
        CastableZombie castable = new CastableZombie();
        castable.HitPoints = person.HitPoints * -1;
        return castable;
    }
}
```

With this we can see that we'll need to add a few new keywords. The keywords `implicit` and `operator` work together to allow us to use the `CastableZombie` cast when working with a `CastablePerson` type object. Now we can check what the hitpoints of a Person is if it was to be treated as a Zombie type object.

```
void CastingCastableHumanoids()
{
    CastablePerson p = new CastablePerson();
    p.HitPoints = 10;
    CastableZombie z = p as CastablePerson;
    Debug.Log("Cast Zombie: " + z.HitPoints);
    //"Cast Zombie: -10"
}
```

Through the `implicit` keyword, we can quite nicely assign the Zombie z to the Person type. We're also allowed to do something very simple like the following code sample:

```
CastableZombie personZombie = new CastablePerson();
Debug.Log(personZombie);
```

This automatically assigns `personZombie` a new `CastablePerson()` that is then implicitly converted to a `CastableZombie` upon assignment. Likewise, we can use a prefix conversion and get the same result by using an as operator.

```
CastablePerson p = new CastablePerson();
p.HitPoints = 10;
CastableZombie z = (CastableZombie)p;
Debug.Log(z + " " + z.HitPoints);
// CastableAgain+CastableZombie -10
```

Should you want to get the average health in a scene—zombies, vampires, mummies, and humans together—you'd want to iterate through a single data type. Get all gameObjects in the scene, then cast every component to humanoid. You'll have a humanoid for every zombie, vampire, mummy, and human in the scene. If you can't cast it to a humanoid, you'll get a null object. Null objects can be ignored and skipped. All that's left to do is calculate the average health.

6.14.3 Implicit versus Explicit Type Conversion

Explicit casts are used if there is a conversion that might end with some loss of data. Implicit casts assume that no data is lost while converting from one type to another. Explicit implies you understand that the conversion isn't going to be perfect.

For instance, if a zombie has a regeneration ability, the functions for that will be lost when you've cast a zombie to humanoid through the explicit type cast. You can cast a humanoid to as a zombie since it's assumed all attributes of a humanoid are still present in the zombie. Consider the following:

```
CastableHumanoid[] humanoids = new CastableHumanoid[]
{
    new CastableZombie(),
    new CastablePerson(),
    new CastableHumanoid(),
    new CastableZombie(),
    new CastablePerson()
};


foreach (CastableHumanoid humanoid in humanoids)
{
    Debug.Log(humanoid + " is a humanoid");
}
```

An array of humanoids is populated with zombies humanoids and persons. Each one of these is indeed a type of `CastableHumanoid`. They all share the same attributes as a `CastableHumanoid`. Adding a public bool `isZombie;` to the zombie makes the `CastableZombie` unique from the `CastablePerson`.

```
class CastableZombie : CastableHumanoid
{
    public bool isZombie;
    static public implicit operator CastablePerson(CastableZombie zombie)
    {
        CastablePerson castable = new CastablePerson();
        castable.HitPoints = 1;
        // imply you've revived someone
        // and they're barely alive.
        return castable;
    }
}
```

A variable which appears in a derived class but not in its base class is new data. This addition isn't something that the `CastableHumanoid` has available. Thus if you were to try to access the `CastableZombie`'s `isZombie` bool from the `CastableHumanoid` type you'll get an error:

```
foreach (CastableHumanoid humanoid in humanoids)
{
    Debug.Log(humanoid + " is a humanoid");
    Debug.Log("humanoid has: " + humanoid.HitPoints + "HP");

    if (humanoid.isZombie)//variable could not be found!
    {
        Debug.Log("humanoid is a zombie?");
    }

}
```

The variable `isZombie` could not be found in `CastableHumanoid`. The process of going up and down in the relationship between base classes and derived classes is called Upcasting and Downcasting. The fancy view class diagram could reveal that both `CastablePerson` and `CastableZombie` can be "Upcast" to a `CastableHuman` and a `CastableHuman` can be "Downcast" to either a `CastablePerson` or a `CastableZombie`.

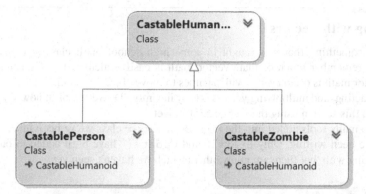

This upcasting and downcasting can also be seen when casting an int to a float. The int value 1 is the same as a float value 1.0, an implicit cast infers that nothing is lost. In some edge cases, there can be data lost, so implicit casts are not perfect, though they are generally reliable.

It also just so happens that all of this is the effect of what is called "Polymorphism"; a programming term that covers the topic of casting between types and type conversion. The roots of the word "Poly" is Greek for "many"; the second root is "morph" or "shape."

6.14.4 What We've Learned

Using the explicit and implicit type casts requires a bit of thought. When dealing with a large number of different types, we need to keep in mind what we're trying to accomplish by casting between types. In many cases, we should avoid unnecessary cast operations.

If data needs to be shared between different classes, it's better to create a parent class, or base class from which child classes inherit. Rather than requiring specific casts between people and zombies, a new version should be instanced between the two without using a cast.

Most casts should only be between specific data types. It should also be noted that casting is allowed between structs.

```
struct A
{
    public static explicit operator B(A a)
    {
        return new B();
    }
}


struct B
{
    static public explicit operator A(B b)
    {
        return new A();
    }
}
```

Here we can make an explicit cast from a to b and back again. Though there's nothing really going on here, a struct is somewhat different from a class, but offers many of the same functionality. Defining explicit cast operators is one of the shared abilities between a class and a struct.

6.15 Working with Vectors

Vector math is something that was taught in some high school math classes. Don't worry, you're not expected to remember much of that. Vector math is easily calculated in C# using the Unity 3D libraries, as vector math is often used in video games to move objects around.

Adding, subtracting, and multiplying vectors is easy in Unity 3D. We'll look at how simple vector math is in Unity 3D in this section using the Vector3() object.

There are also many tools added into the MonoBehaviour class we've been inheriting for most of the classes we've been writing. Only Start() and Update() have been added to our prebuilt class we've been starting with, but there are many others which we haven't seen yet.

6.15.1 Vectors Are Objects

Start with the WorkingWithVectors script attached to the game object of the same name in the WorkingWithVectors_Scene in the Chapter6 Unity Project. From this same Chapter 6 project in Section 6.5 Arrays Revisited, we worked on a Monster: MonoBehaviour where we made some simple floating cubes.

```
public int numMonsters;
//Use this for initialization
void Start()
{
    for (int i = 0; i < numMonsters; i++)
    {
        GameObject sphere = GameObject.CreatePrimitive(PrimitiveType.Sphere);
        sphere.AddComponent<Monster>();
        Vector3 pos = new Vector3()
        {
            x = Random.Range(-10, 10),
            z = Random.Range(-10, 10)
        };
        sphere.transform.position = pos;
    }
}
```

Random.Range(); is a new function. Random is an class located in the UnityEngine namespace. We use this to give us a number between -10 and 10. The two arguments are separated by a comma. The first argument is the minimum value and the second number is the maximum value we want. Then Random sets the x and z to a number between these two values.

Assuming that NumMonsters is set to 10 or so, play the game and `MonsterGenerator` creates a field of sphere monsters placed randomly in the x and z directions. As an alternative, we could have put the positioning information inside of the monster himself using the `Start()` function.

6.15.2 Stepping through MonsterGenerator

We introduced breakpoints in Section 4.12.9, but this is a good point to come back to how breakpoints are used to see how your code is working. Why does each monster appear at a different place? Let's add in a breakpoint near the first line within the "for" statement.

Here, I have the breakpoint added on line where the Monster component is added. Press the Run button and attach Visual Studio to Unity 3D.

In MonoDevelop, select Run → Start Debugging and then select Unity 3D in the following pop-up panel. Go back to the Unity 3D editor and press the Play button. You may notice not much happening in Unity 3D, which means that MonoDevelop grabbed Unity 3D's thread and is holding it at the breakpoint.

Start stepping through the code. Pressing the F10 key on the keyboard will push the arrow one line at a time through the "for" statement. After pressing it once, you'll notice that the highlighted line will begin to move over your code. Also notice the data populating the Callstack and the Locals windows that open below the code.

Click on the word "sphere." Each instance of the word will highlight and a new dialog box will open up with specifics on the new sphere object. Hover the cursor over "sphere" to invoke a pop-up with information on the sphere object.

```
for (int i = 0; i < numMonsters; i++)
{
    GameObject sphere = GameObject.CreatePrimitive(PrimitiveType.Sphere);
    sphere.AddComponent<Monster>();
    Vecto ▶ ● sphere  "Sphere (UnityEngine.GameObject)" ▭
    {
        x = Random.Range(-10, 10),
        z = Random.Range(-10, 10)
    };
    sphere.transform.position = pos;
```

Step again and we'll get details on the new Vector3 called pos, which I'm using as an abbreviation of "position." Press F10 to *step over* once to move to the next line.

```
    sphere.AddComponent<Monster>();
    Vector3 pos = new Vector3()
    {                   ▶ ● pos  "(0.0, 0.0, 0.0)" ▭
        x = Random.Range(-10, 10),
        z = Random.Range(-10, 10)
    };
    sphere.transform.position = pos;
```

It's important to understand that data isn't fulfilled on the line it's created on. Only after stepping one more line with F10 does the data become fulfilled.

```
    sphere.AddComponent<Monster>();
    Vector3 pos = new Vector3()
    {                   ● pos  "(-9.0, 0.0, 0.0)" ▭
        x = Random        ▶ 🔧 magnitude        9
        z = Random           🔧 normalized       "(-1.0, 0.0, 0.0)"
    };                        🔧 sqrMagnitude     81
    sphere.transfo            ● x                -9
                              ● y                0
                              ● z                0
                           ▶ ● Static members
```

Step through a few more times, and allow a few monsters to be created. With each iteration the values for pos will have changed to different values.

Keep on pressing F10 and you'll be able to follow the flow of the code as each line highlights again. Each time the line is executed, the values coming from the `Random.Range()` function will be different. Therefore, the code will scatter the monsters around the `MonsterGenerator`.

Unity and Visual Studio are rather locked together. Unity is stuck in debug mode and Visual Studio is holding onto Unity's activity. To release Unity from Visual Studio's hold, press the "stop debugging" button.

This releases Unity from Visual Studio's debugger and the two apps will act independently again. Connecting Visual Studio to Unity allows you to thoroughly inspect how your code is updated as the game is played, a powerful tool for finding bugs and figuring out where they originate from.

The option of where to set the initial position of an object is up to the programmer. It's up to you to decide who and where the position of a new object is set. This flexibility allows you to decide how and when code is executed.

6.15.3 Gizmos

While stepping through code helps a great deal with understanding how our code is being executed, visualizing things as they move can be more helpful. That's where Unity 3D has provided us with a great deal of tools for doing just that.

Unity 3D calls its helper objects "Gizmos." Visualizing data is carried out by using Gizmos to draw lines and shapes in the scene. In other game engines, this may be called DrawDebugLine or DrawDebugBox. In Unity 3D, the engineers added the Gizmos class. The members of this class include DrawLine and DrawBox.

Colored lines, boxes, spheres, and other things can be constructed from the code. If we want to draw a line from the monster to a target, we might use a line between the two, so we know that the monster can "see" its next meal. It's difficult to mentally visualize what the vectors are doing. Having Unity 3D display them in the scene makes the vector math easier to understand.

6.15.3.1 A Basic Example

Open the Gizmo script attached to the game object of the same name in the in the Working With Vectors_Scene. project is the `DrawLine();` function that requires two arguments or parameters. The first argument is a start vector followed by an end vector. In the Gizmo script is the `OnDrawGizmos()` after the `Start()` and `Update()` functions. The `OnDrawGizmos()` can be placed before or after the `Start()` or `Update()` function, but to keep organized we'll add it after the preconstructed functions.

```
public class Gizmos : MonoBehaviour
{
    // Start is called before the first frame update
    void Start()
    {

    }

    // Update is called once per frame
    void Update()
    {

    }

    private void OnDrawGizmos()
    {
        |
    }
}
```

To see what's going on, create a new Sphere GameObject Object using the GameObject → Create Other → Sphere menu, and then add the Gizmos.cs component in the Inspector panel.

To draw a Gizmo, we'll need to pick the Gizmo we want to use.

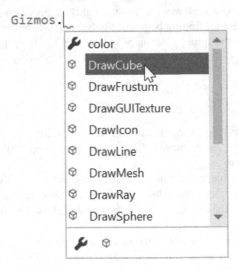

When we start with "Gizmos." we are presented with quite a list of things we can try out. Thanks to MonoDevelop, it's quite easy to figure out how these are used. Each function has some pretty clear clues as to what data types are used and what they are for.

```
Gizmos.DrawCube()
```
void Gizmos.DrawCube(**Vector3 center**, Vector3 size)
Draw a solid box with center and size.

Starting with "DrawCube," we'll be prompted with a Vector3 for the cube's center and another Vector3 for the cube's size. To fulfill the DrawCube member function in Gizmos, enter the following arguments:

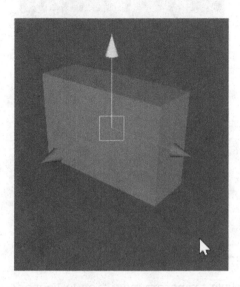

The Gizmo will be drawn with the center point at `Vector3.zero` which is the scene's origin, and the size will be `Vector3 (1, 2, 3)`, making the object 1 unit wide, 2 units tall, and 3 units deep. Gizmos are interesting as they represent some very useful debugging tools. Gizmos do not draw in the game, they're only visible in the Scene view in the editor.

6.15.3.2 DrawRay

Some of the other Gizmo functions require data types we haven't encountered yet, such as rectangles and rays. With a little bit of detection, we can figure out how these work. Let's start off with a DrawRay we're presented with (Ray r) as its argument. We can start with a new Ray (and we'll be given a (Vector3 origin, Vector3 direction)).

We can fulfill this with `Gizmos.DrawRay(new Ray(new Vector3 (0, 0, 0), new Vector3 (0, 1, 0)));`. This might seem like a bit of a convoluted line to read, so we can make this more easy to read by breaking out one of the arguments.

```
Ray ray = new Ray();
ray.origin = Vector3.zero;
ray.direction = Vector3.up;
Gizmos.DrawRay(ray);
```

This code will produce a simple white line that starts at the origin and points up in the *y*-axis 1 unit. Rays are useful tools that show an object's direction or angle of movement. We'll take a closer look once we get more used to how Gizmos are used. Assuming the object with the script applied is a cube at the origin of the scene, you'll have a similar effect to the following figure:

6.15.4 Using Gizmos

```
Gizmos.DrawLine(transform.position, Vector3.zero);
```

The `Gizmos DrawLine()` from `transform.position` to `Vector3.zero` traces a line from the object's center to the scene origin. The appearance of the `Gizmos` class cannot function outside of the `OnDrawGizmos()` function. Using the `Gizmos` class in an `Update()` function will not produce any results.

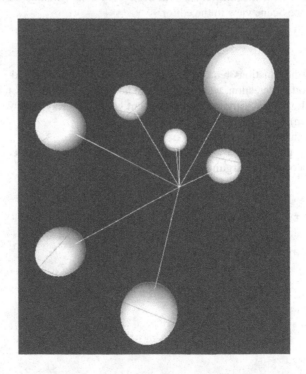

Now we're drawing a bunch of white lines from the center of the Gizmo game objects to the center of the world. To make use of this we can attach a Player class to an object in the scene and have the spheres draw a line to it

Gizmos are intended to help debug a scene and provide various visual aids to the game designer to help setup a scene.

6.15.5 What We've Learned

Unity 3D has many tools built in for doing vector math functions. It's a good idea to figure out how they're used. We'll explore as many different uses of these tools as we can, but we're going to be hard pressed to see all of them.

A Gizmo is a handy tool to help see what your code is trying to do. Gizmos draw lines, boxes, and other shapes. You can even have text printed into your 3D scene for debugging purposes. Again, we'll try to use as many of the different Gizmos as we can.

The sort of optimization we did here is in the reduction of lines of code only. There was no actual change to the speed at which the code here was executed. There are some cases in which a line or two should be added to speed things up.

For now, we're going to focus on keeping our code clear and readable. Later, we'll learn some basic programming idioms. Programming idioms are little tricks that programmers often use to reduce complex tasks to just a line or two. They're sometimes rather cryptic, but once you understand them, they're quite useful.

6.16 goto Labels

We've gone through several of the usually employed logical controls in Section 4.11.3. This time we have the goto keyword. It is a commonly misused control statement, and it's about time we learned about how it's used.

The goto keyword allows you to jump around in a statement. The non-linear behavior is one of the reasons why most programmers would tell you to avoid using goto if it's unnecessary. When using many goto statements, you end up making your code difficult to read as you need to jump around to follow the flow. It's still important to understand how goto works if you come across it so lets go ahead and learn how goto works.

A goto statement is the keyword `goto` followed by an identifier, which is referred to as a *label*. This looks like `goto MyLabel;` which tells C# which label to go to, in this case as `MyLabel;` which is the identifier followed by a colon.

To follow along, open the GotoLabels_Scene in the Chapter6 Unity Project, then open the GotoLabels script found on the GotoLabels game object in the scene. A goto statement should be encapsulated by some sort of logical statement. It's very easy to get caught in a loop with a goto statement. This has a similar behavior to `for(;;)` and `while (true)` which will hold Unity 3D in an endless loop forcing you to kill the process from the Task Manager.

```
StartOver:
goto StartOver;
```

Using a label and a goto in this way will create an infinite loop that will require you to kill Unity 3D from the Task Manager.

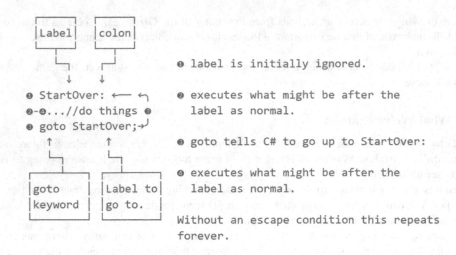

The statement `StartOver:` acts as bookmark. Initially the bookmark has no effect on how code is executed. Anything after the identified label is executed as normal. When the `goto` is reached execution jumps to the bookmark and continues executing code from that point on. There's nothing wrong with the above statemen syntactically, and it's just not very useful. The flow of execution can be controlled by other means between the label and the `goto` statement.

```
int num = 0;

StartOver:

num++;
if (num > 3)
{
    goto Stop;
}

Debug.Log("Looping: " + num + " times.");
goto StartOver;

Stop:

Debug.Log("Stopped.");
```

This code runs until `num` has incremented to more than 3. Then the `goto Stop:` is reached and we skip over the `Debug.Log();` and `goto StartOver;` statements and continue after the `Stop:` label. The console in Unity 3D has the following output. In this case the `goto Stop;` acts as our escape from the repeating loop.

> (!) Looping: 1 times.
> UnityEngine.Debug:Log(Object)
>
> (!) Looping: 2 times.
> UnityEngine.Debug:Log(Object)
>
> (!) Looping: 3 times.
> UnityEngine.Debug:Log(Object)
>
> (!) Stopped.
> UnityEngine.Debug:Log(Object)

This is the same as `for(int i = 0; i < 3; i++);` only some might find it a bit harder to read. Of course, it's up to you to choose when to use a goto statement, but there are some useful cases. Finding a good reason to use the goto statement comes with experience in spotting when it might be useful. Because they're tricky to use and to read, most programmers shy away from using them at all. We're learning as much as we can in this book, so we may also learn how it's used.

6.16.1 Skipping Down

In a very simple form a goto label can be used to skip code based on a condition.

```
int num = 0;/*  setting this to 1          */
if (num > 0)/*  will jump our code          */
{                         /*                 */
    goto FirstLabel;   /* from here⌐        */
}                         /*   ↓             */
Debug.Log("Before FirstLabel:"); /*  | skipped */
FirstLabel:                /*   ↓             */
Debug.Log("After FirstLabel:"); /*⌐ to here */
```

By adding in a public int num to the class, we're able to pick the goto label we're using. If we set num to 0, then both print statements will be executed. If the number is greater than 0, then only the second "After FirstLabel:" print function will be executed.

When we started off with the switch statement, we looked at the keyword case. The case keyword set up conditions which the statement would skip through till a case fits the statement. It then executed the code that followed the case.

switch and goto statements share the colon (:) notation for labels. However, goto lets you set up labels anywhere in a code block, whereas the switch statement allows labels only within the switch statement. When goto is used, it sends the software to the line following the label it was told to jump to.

6.16.2 Zombie State Machine

In the GoToLabels_Scene are some ZombieWithStates game objects. On these is a ZombieWithStates script. The script has an enum MovementStates where we've defined an Idleing, Wandering, Looking, Chasing, and Feeding.

For this project we'll create a zombie which stands around for a moment. After some time, the zombie may decide to look for a meal or just wander before standing around again. If the zombie encounters a meal they'll pursue for a moment, then eat or give up and go back to standing around.

```csharp
public enum MovementStates
{
    Idleing,
    Wandering,
    Looking,
    Chasing,
    Feeding
}
public MovementStates MovementState;
public float StateTimer;
```

Labels can allow us to group statements together in a single function. The intent would be to allow us to quickly prototype different behaviors. After a state change check we use a switch statement to jump our execution to different labels later in the same function. This acts as a hub to determine where in the function to go to.

```csharp
switch (MovementState)
{
    case MovementStates.Idleing: goto Idle;
    case MovementStates.Wandering: goto Wander;
    case MovementStates.Looking: goto Look;
    case MovementStates.Chasing: goto Chase;
    case MovementStates.Feeding: goto Feed;
}
```

The labels live at the bottom of the Update() function waiting to be filled in with their behaviors. For now, we've just added a Debug.Log() in place to update which state the Zombie is in.

```csharp
Idle:
Debug.Log("Idle");
goto UpdateTimer;

Look:
Debug.Log("Look");
...
goto UpdateTimer;

Wander:
Debug.Log("Wander");
...
goto Look;

Chase:
Debug.Log("Chase");
...
goto UpdateTimer;

Feed:
Debug.Log("Feed");
...
goto UpdateTimer;
```

After spending time in each mode, the statement jumps to an `UpdateTimer:` label. Under the `UpdateTimer` label of the same function we're checking the `StateTimer`. Once the game time has past the `StateTimer`, we pick a new length of time for the `StateTimer` and pick a new `MovementState`.

```
UpdateTimer:
if (Time.time > StateTimer)
{
    StateTimer = Time.time + Random.Range(3.0f, 7.0f);
    switch (MovementState)
    {
        case MovementStates.Idleing:
            switch (Random.Range(0, 3))
            {
                case 0:
                    MovementState = MovementStates.Idleing;
                    break;
                case 1:
                    MovementState = MovementStates.Looking;
                    break;
                case 2:
                    MovementState = MovementStates.Wandering;
                    break;
            }
            break;
        case MovementStates.Wandering:
        case MovementStates.Looking:
        case MovementStates.Chasing:
        case MovementStates.Feeding:
            MovementState = MovementStates.Idleing;
            break;
    }
}
// escape from Update()
return;
```

In the `UpdateTimer:` label we decide that if zombie is in Idle, then we're able to pick a different state, either continue to `Idle`, change to `Looking`, or change to `Wandering`. This provides us with some opportunity for variations in behavior.

After the game time has run past the `StateTimer` we return to `Idle`. The first label to inspect is the `Look:` label. This is a basic function that we'll want to use to update what direction the zombie is facing.

```
// update rotation
transform.rotation = Quaternion.RotateTowards(transform.rotation, targetRotation, 5f);
```

To rotate the character, we create a targetRotation value. The direction of we want to face the character. To smoothly rotate the character toward the targetRotation we call `RotateTowards()`.

To check when `RotateTowards()` is finished rotating the character, we check the angle between the character's current facing and the target using `Quaternion.Angle()`. Once the angle is less than a fraction of a degree we pick a new targetRotation value.

```
// checking if we're facing our target direction
float angle = Quaternion.Angle(transform.rotation, targetRotation);
if (angle < 0.1f || angle == 180)
{
    Vector3 dir = new Vector3()
    {
        x = Random.Range(-1f, 1f),
        y = 0,
        z = Random.Range(-1f, 1f)
    };
    targetRotation = Quaternion.LookRotation(dir, transform.up);
}
```

If we then look at the `Wander:` label we see the Zombie move in its forward direction. Then the code jumps back to the `Look:` label to continue picking new directions to look in.

```
Wander:
transform.position += transform.forward * 0.01f;
goto Look;
```

By adding a single line of code and jumping back into the `Look:` label we're able to add a new layer of behavior quickly and easily. Without too much effort we're able to add additional layers of behavior with simple jump statements using `goto`. The jump statements can also be used within loops.

If we come across a human, the zombie should chase after him. To accomplish this there are `HumanWithStates` scripts attached to the Human objects in the scene. The HumanWithStates script is based on the `ZombieWithStates` class. This means that it will inherit the `Update()` function with the chase and feed behaviors as well.

6.16.3 This as a Reference to Yourself

This can be skipped by checking if the class is a `HumanWithStates`, jumping out of the update look, and going to the `UpdateTimer` label early.

```
if (this.GetType() == typeof(HumanWithStates))
    goto UpdateTimer;
```

The above does two things. The first part of the statement is this. `GetType()` the type of data were it to be a `ZombieWithStates` would return the type ZombieWithStates. Then it compares it to a `typeof(HumanWithStates)`. The inherited version of the script is `HumanWithStates` and the if statement returns true, the zombie does not.

When true, the goto jumps the execution of the script to the `UpdateTimer` label. The zombie will continue to execute past the jump statement and continue to update its behavior for seeking out humans to prey on.

The this keyword behaves as though it's the class it's in. In many ways the keyword is redundant, but it does serve as a visual reminder to the programmer as to what we're checking on. The statement could have easily been `GetType() == typeof(HumanWithStates)`. By using the this keyword ahead of `GetType()` we make it more clear as to what object we're getting the type of.

6.16.4 Just for Zombies

With a type check we can block the human from accessing Zombie actions. For the zombie to do zombie like things we should sort through the scene, find humans, and chase after the closest one in range.

```
HumanWithStates closestHuman = null;
GameObject[] allGameObjects = GameObject.FindObjectsOfType<GameObject>();
float closest = Mathf.Infinity;
Vector3 direction = Vector3.zero;
foreach (GameObject go in allGameObjects)
{
    HumanWithStates human = go.GetComponent<HumanWithStates>();
    if (human != null)
    {
        float distance = (go.transform.position - transform.position).magnitude;
        //check if it's a zombie
        if (distance < closest)
        {
            closestHuman = human;
            direction = go.transform.position - transform.position;
            closest = distance;
        }
    }
}
```

At the first block of code at the start of each Update() loop, we populate a list with all-GameObjects. To check only humans in the scene we use GetComponent<HumansWithStates>() to check if the object has a human script attached. If the object is a human, then we calculate the distance to it.

By storing the closest distance, we can check if there's a closer human than the previous human checked. As we update the values we keep a record of the shortest distance the closest human, and the direction that human is in.

```
if (closest < 5)
{
    targetRotation = Quaternion.LookRotation(direction, transform.up);
    transform.rotation = Quaternion.RotateTowards(transform.rotation, targetRotation, 5f);
    MovementState = MovementStates.Chasing;
}
```

In the section of the code the Zombie is allowed access, we check if any humans are within 5 units away. If there are then we use the stored direction and update the targetRotation toward the human. Once we've taken aim at a human, we change to MovementState.Chasing.

Once we jump down to the Chase: label we check if the closest human is within feeding range. If not, we continue to move toward the target.

```
if (closest < 0.25f)
{
    MovementState = MovementStates.Feeding;
}
transform.position += transform.forward * 0.01f;
```

Once we're in range to feed we take care that there's a human to eat with a null check. Finally, we swap in a ZombieWithStates component as well as the character mesh.

```
if (closestHuman != null && closest < 0.25f)
{
    // convert human to zombie
    Transform zombiePrimitive = transform.Find("ZombiePrimitive");
    if (zombiePrimitive == null)
        return;
    Destroy(closestHuman.transform.Find("HumanPrimitive").gameObject);
    GameObject newZombie = GameObject.Instantiate(zombiePrimitive.gameObject);
    newZombie.transform.parent = closestHuman.gameObject.transform;
    newZombie.transform.localPosition = Vector3.zero;
    newZombie.transform.localRotation = Quaternion.identity;
    closestHuman.gameObject.AddComponent<ZombieWithStates>();
    Destroy(closestHuman);
    return;
}
```

6.16.5 What We've Learned

Goto labels don't have to be cumbersome to be useful. As a simple divider to a long `Update()` function, they can work for you and remain clear so long as the mechanism that switches between labels is clear and contained in one place such as a switch statement.

You can easily make an argument to leave all the logic within the switch statement and avoid the labels altogether, but this can easily make the switch statement larger and bulkier than necessary as well. In the end, the only difference is readability. If by using labels you make your code easier to follow, then using labels is fine. If your switch statement begins to overflow with different cases, then you might want to try another system outside of the switch, and labels might be a nice option.

On your own it's a good idea to see what this code would look like by adding different states. Perhaps when a zombie gets close enough to a human, that human could turn into a zombie. When a pair of humans gets close to a zombie, then the zombie might turn into a human. Simple mechanics like this can quickly add a very unpredictable level of behavior and emerge into a game mechanic simply through experimentation with the code itself.

6.17 More on Arrays

In the previous chapter we generated an array by using the FindAllObjectsOfType() function. This returned an array filled with everything in the scene, cameras and lights included. To iterate through the array we used the foreach() function and searched every game object for a human component. Using that array we were also able to find the closest human to the zombie.

Arrays have a few different descriptions. Your standard array is called a single-dimensional array. The Array of game objects from the previous example is a single dimensional array. Other array types include multidimensional and jagged. Arrays can store any data type; this includes other arrays.

6.17.1 Length and Count

Declaring an array is simple and uses a different operator than a class or function to contain its data. The square brackets [and] are used to tell the compiler that your identifier is going to be used for an array. The following statement declares an array of integers:

```
int i;
/* a single int value */
int[] ints;
/* array of ints without any values */
Debug.Log(i + ints[0]);
/* Cannot use i or ints without values */
```

We can dynamically declare an array of ints using the following notation. Use curly braces { } to contain the contents of the array assigned to primes.

```
int[] primes = new int[] { 1, 3, 5, 7, 11, 13, 17, 23, 27, 31 };
/*  ↑                   ↑            */
/*  ┌───────────────────┴─────┐     */
/*  │ brackets tell lexer to  │     */
/*  │ create array for given type│  */
/*  └─────────────────────────┘     */
```

Arrays have several functions associated with them, which we can use with different loops. To get the number of items in an array, we use the Length property of the array.

6.17.1.1 A Basic Example

In the MoreOnArrays scene start with the MoreOnArrays.cs script attached to the MoreOnArrays game object in the scene.

```
int[] primes = new int[] { 1, 3, 5, 7, 11, 13, 17, 23, 27, 31};
int primeLength = primes.Length;
```

In this example, we assign primeLength to the Length of the primes array. We'll see why this is more useful than creating an array of a set length ahead of time in a moment. To use this in a for loop, we use the following syntax shown in the following code fragment added to the Start() function:

```
for (int i = 0; i < primesLength; i++)
{
    Debug.Log(primes[i]);
}
```

This code prints out a new line for each number stored in the array. Each time the for loop iterates, the int i moves to the next item in the array starting with the zeroth index. Once the end of the list is reached, the for loop exits. We could also use a while loop to do the same thing.

```
int j = 0;
while (j < primesLength)
{
    Debug.Log(primes[j++]);
}
```

This produces the same output with the brevity of the while syntax, but the counter j required for the while loop needs to live outside of the while statement's code block. Something to consider for why we'd store the Length property is performance.

Consider the Length property of an array needs to be looked up may take several nano seconds. Each iteration of a for loop and a while loop would need ask the array for the Length property. By storing an arrayLength by request the Length property once you've shaved off a few nano seconds of compute time.

```
/*                                                       */
/*       ┌─────────────────────────┐                     */
/*       │  Length needs to be     │                     */
/*       │  requested every loop   │                     */
/*       └─────────────────────────┘                     */
/*                      ↓                                 */
for (int i = 0; i < primes.Length; i++)
{
    Debug.Log(primes[i]);
}
```

Yet another option, and one that's slightly tailored for an array, is foreach.

6.17.2 Foreach: A Reminder

With an array of ints in our primes variable, we can use the following syntax to print out each item in the array:

```
int[] primes = new int[] { 1, 3, 5, 7, 11, 13, 17, 23, 27, 31 };
foreach (int p in primes)
{
    Debug.Log(p);
}
```

This syntax is quite short, simple, and easy to use. The keyword in assigns the int p variable to each element in the primes array it's given. Using a foreach loop we lose a counter to keep track of the number of iterations we've looped through the statement.

Which form you use is up to you, but it's important to know that you have more than one option. Of course, you can use any identifier for counting indexes; int j could just as easily be int index or anything else that makes sense. Though the common convention is to use the for (int i = 0; i < items; i++) form for iterating through an array, the int i variable initialized in the parameter list of the for loop can be used for various things related to the element we're stepping through in the array. We often need to know where we are in the array. If this information isn't necessary, then it's easier to stick to the foreach iterator when using an array.

We can declare arrays of different lengths by using different bits of data. Each one is of a different length. Using the Length property of each array, it's easier for us to print out each array without knowing how many items are stored in each one.

```
int[] primes = { 1, 3, 5, 7, 11, 13, 17, 23, 27, 31 };
int[] fibonacci = { 0, 1, 1, 2, 3, 5, 8, 13, 21, 34, 55, 89, 144 };
int[] powersOfTwo = { 1, 2, 4, 8, 16, 32, 64, 128, 255, 512, 1024 };
```

Of course, these aren't complete sets of numbers, but that's not the point. They are different lengths, and we don't need to keep track of how many items are stored in each array to print out their contents.

```
int[] primes = { 1, 3, 5, 7, 11, 13, 17, 23, 27, 31 };
int[] fibonacci = { 0, 1, 1, 2, 3, 5, 8, 13, 21, 34, 55, 89, 144 };
int[] powersOfTwo = { 1, 2, 4, 8, 16, 32, 64, 128, 255, 512, 1024 };
ArrayList numbers = new ArrayList{ primes, fibonacci, powersOfTwo};
int numArrays = numbers.Count; /* ArrayList uses .Count, not .Length */
for (int i = 0; i < numArrays; i++)
{
    int[] nums = numbers[i] as int[];
    int items = nums.Length;
    for (int j = 0; j < items; j++)
    {
        Debug.Log(nums[j]);
    }
}
```

In the above code fragment, we've added in three different arrays of integers. After that we declare a new `ArrayList` called numbers fulfilled with a new `ArrayList` {primes, fibonacci, powersOfTwo};. This fills the new `ArrayList` with the three different int[] arrays, where each int[] has a different `Length` property.

ArrayLists differ from a regular array in that its `Length` property is called `Count`. Therefore, to get the number of items stored in the `ArrayList`, we use numbers.Count rather than `Length`. This is assigned to an int numArrays for use in a for loop.

To learn about the difference, we could post on a forum, "How do I get the size of an ArrayList?" Alternatively, we could right click on the `ArrayList` type and select Go To Definition F12 from the following pop-up:

```
int[] powersOfTwo = { 1, 2, 4, 8, 16, 32, 64, 128, 255,
ArrayList numbers = new ArrayList{ primes, fibonacci, p
int nu │ 💡   Quick Actions and Refactorings...    Ctrl+.        ht
for (i │ 🔲   Rename...                             Ctrl+R, Ctrl+R
{      │      Remove and Sort Usings                Ctrl+R, Ctrl+G
    in │ 🔍   Peek Definition                       Alt+F12
    in │ ➡   Go To Definition  🖱                   F12
    fo │      Go To Implementation                  Ctrl+F12
    {
```

This brings us to the declaration of classes and all of the things that the `ArrayList` allows us to do. Scroll through the options till we find something we can use.

```
public virtual int Count
{
    get;
}
```

In the Assembly Browser, we'll find a Count property that sounds reasonably usable. It's possible to do many different things with the other options found in the `ArrayList` class, so we'll experiment with them next.

It's important to remember the Go To Definition function in Visual Studio to be a self-sufficient programmer. If it's late at night and you have a final or dead-line due in the morning, you may not have enough time to wait for an answer on a forum.

Unfortunately, there aren't so many options with the `int[]` as this brings you to only what an int32 is defined as. Luckily, most of the questions have been asked about how to deal with an array in C#. There is, however, a class definition for Array. This can be found by using the Search field in the Assembly Browser.

From here, you can find all the functions and properties available to use with the Array type. The ArrayList's count can be used as a condition to stop the for loop. Once we have the ArrayList's count, it's used in the following for loop as the condition to stop the loop.

```
int numArrays = numbers.Count;
for (int i = 0; i < numArrays; i++)
{

}
```

This code will allow us to iterate through each array stored in the numbers array list. Next, we need to get the `int[]` array stored at the current index of the array list. This is done by using the for loop's initializer's int i variable and a cast. `ArrayList` stores each item as a generic `object` type. This means that the item at `numbers[i]` is an undeclared type of `object`. In this case, the `object` stored at the index is an `int[]` type.

```
int[] nums = numbers[i] as int[];
```

Casting the object to an `int[]` is as simple as `numbers[i] as int[];`. Without this cast, we get the following error:

| ❌ CS0266 | Cannot implicitly convert type 'object' to 'int[]'. An explicit conversion exists (are you missing a cast?) | Assembly-CSharp | MoreOnArrays.cs | 97 | Active |

This assumes that an `object` is trying to be used as an `int[]`, as indicated by the declaration `int[]` nums, and to do so, we need to use the as `int[]` cast. Once nums is an `int[]` array, we can use it as a regular array. This means we can get the `nums.Length` to start another for loop.

```
/* ❶ nums assumes the type array of ints          */
/*   ┌──────────────────────────────┐         */
/*   ↓                              │  ┌─────────┐ */
int[] nums = numbers[i] as int[];/* ├─┤ ❷ this allows │*/
int items = nums.Length;/* ←───────┘ │  the use of  │*/
                  /*                  │   .Length   │*/
                  /*                  └─────────────┘*/
```

This loop will begin the next loop printing out each item stored in the nums `integer array`. As we did earlier, we use the following fragment:

```
for (int j = 0; j < items; j++)
{
    Debug.Log(nums[j]);
}
```

This fragment is inside of the first for loop. Using this, we'll get each item of each array stored at each index of the numbers array list. This seems like a great deal of work, but in truth it's all necessary and this will become second nature once you're used to the steps involved in dealing with arrays.

`ArrayLists` allow you to store any variety of object. To store an array of arrays, you need to use an `ArrayList`. What might seem correct to start off with might be something like the following:

```
int notAvailable = numbers.Length;
```

In fact, this is syntactically correct, and intuition might tell you that there's no problem with this. However, the Array type isn't defined as it is without any type assigned to it. However, we can use the following:

```
object[] obj_numbers = { primes, fibonacci, powersOfTwo };
```

This turns each `int[]` into an object, and numbers is now an array of objects. To an effect we've created the same thing as before with the `ArrayList`; only we've defined the length of the Numbers array by entering three elements between the curly braces.

For clarification, we can use the foreach iterator with both the `ArrayList` and the `int []` array.

```
object[] obj_numbers = { primes, fibonacci, powersOfTwo };
foreach (int[] nums in obj_numbers)
{
    foreach (int n in nums)
    {
        Debug.Log(n);
    }
}
```

This produces the same output to the Console panel in Unity 3D as the previous version; only it's a lot shorter. It's important to recognize the first foreach statement contains `int [] nums in obj_numbers` as each element in the `obj_numbers` array is an `int []` array type.

6.17.3 Discovery

Learning what a class has to offer involves a great deal testing. For instance, we saw many other functions in `ArrayList` which we didn't use. We saw Count that returned an integer value. This was indicated when the listing showed us Count: int in the Assembly Browser.

However, it's good to learn about the other functions found in `ArrayList`. Let's pick the `ToArray(): object[]` function; this sounds useful, but what does it do? More important, how do we find out? The steps here begin with testing various features one at a time.

The return type indicates that it's giving us an object, so let's start there.

```
ArrayList numbers = new ArrayList { primes, fibonacci, powersOfTwo };
object thing = numbers.ToArray();
Debug.Log("thing is: " + thing);
```

This sends the following output to the Console panel:

```
thing is: System.Object[]
UnityEngine.Debug:Log(Object)
```

The thing is apparently a System.object[] that was sent to the Console output panel. From this, we learned that thing is, indeed, an object[], or rather it's an array of objects. What can we do with this? Let's change this to match what we've observed.

```
object[] anotherThing = numbers.ToArray() as object[];
Debug.Log("anotherThing Length: " + anotherThing.Length);
```

Now that we know it's an array, let's cast it to being a proper array by adding in a cast. Now the thing returns a length. We get 3 sent to the Console panel of Unity 3D when we press the Play game button. But what's going on here? Remember that earlier we had to use numbers.Count to get the size of the ArrayList. Now we're dealing with a regular Array, not an ArrayList. Therefore, should we need to use an Array and not an ArrayList, this function could come in handy! Good to know.

This little exercise is important; a part of learning any new language is testing the code that you discover when browsing through a class' functions. Anything listed in the Assembly Browser is there for a reason. At some point, somebody thought the function was necessary, so he or she added it.

6.17.4 Putting It Together

Arrays are used for storing many objects and commanding them in a coordinated manner. We did this earlier by making a line of undulating cubes. However, what if we want to keep track of a multitude of monsters approaching the player?

You're likely to have a situation where a designer makes a feature request: A weapon to shoot the zombies with; a self-operated gun turret. The turret has two features. First it should only shoot at the nearest zombie. Second, it will only shoot zombies not near any humans as to not accidentally hit the human with a projectile.

This project begins in the MoreOnArrays _ Continued _ Scene in the Chapter6 Unity Projects. In this scene is a new GunTurret game object. On this is a GunTurretController and a GunTurretLogic script. The logic used to pick targets is what we're going to focus on, so we'll open the GunTurretLogic script and see how arrays are used there.

The first thing we'd need to do is figure out how to find the zombies and humans. We'll start with a couple of arrays.

```
GameObject[] allObjects = FindObjectsOfType<GameObject>();
ArrayList zombies = new ArrayList();
ArrayList humans = new ArrayList();
```

These three arrays are arranged so we have allObjects which finds all GameObjects in the scene. After this we have an empty ArrayList setup for zombies and another for humans. As you might expect we will need to search through the allObjects array to find humans and zombies.

```
foreach (GameObject go in allObjects)
{
    HumanWithStates aHuman = go.GetComponent<HumanWithStates>();
    ZombieWithStates aZombie = go.GetComponent<ZombieWithStates>();
    bool isHuman = aHuman != null;
    bool isZombie = aZombie != null;
    {
        if (isHuman)
        {
            humans.Add(go);
        }
        if (isZombie)
        {
            zombies.Add(go);
        }
    }
}
```

With our first block of code we'll use a check to see if there is a human or a zombie component attached to the game object in the `allObjects` array. To confirm the component, use a `null` check for `isHuman` and `isZombie`. We've used this method to find specific game objects before where we had zombies searching for humans. However, we have to check how they are different, yet actually quite similar.

6.17.4.1 Breakpoint, Observing Inheritance

To observe how class inheritance and casting behaves add a breakpoint. To look at what was added to the zombies `ArrayList` we'll have to add a break point to the point after it's been filled. The importance of learning how to use breakpoints to debug code is difficult to fully express. Hours can be wasted searching for a bug that could easily be found by stepping through code.

To observe something easily overlooked, we'll add the breakpoint to where zombie array list is used. For the debugger in Visual Studio to work, have Unity up and running in the background where Scene has the script with the added breakpoint.

Click the Attach to Unity button and wait for Visual Studio to make the connection to Unity. After a moment, Visual Studio will build the source code and indicate it's ready for the Scene to start playing in editor. In the Unity Editor, press the Pause button before pressing the Play button. Starting the game paused will ensure that we catch the first update loop of the scene. If we haven't hit the breakpoint, then Unity will wait for the step button to be pressed.

The third button will step Unity a single update cycle at a time. Visual Studio's debugger should catch the update of the `zombie ArrayList`.

```
                                        ▾ | ⚙ GunTurretLogic                              ▾ | ⚙ Upd
       if (isHuman)                                  ▸ ● [0]  "ZombieWithStates (10) (UnityEngine.GameObject)"
       {                                             ▸ ● [1]  "ZombieWithStates (3) (UnityEngine.GameObject)"
           humans.Add(go);                           ▸ ● [2]  "ZombieWithStates (UnityEngine.GameObject)"
       }                                             ▸ ● [3]  "ZombieWithStates (4) (UnityEngine.GameObject)"
       if (isZombie)                                 ▸ ● [4]  "HumanWithStates (8) (UnityEngine.GameObject)"
       {                                             ▸ ● [5]  "ZombieWithStates (8) (UnityEngine.GameObject)"
           zombies.Add(go);                          ▸ ● [6]  "ZombieWithStates (6) (UnityEngine.GameObject)"
       }                                             ▸ ● [7]  "HumanWithStates (1) (UnityEngine.GameObject)"
   }                                                 ▸ ● [8]  "ZombieWithStates (1) (UnityEngine.GameObject)"
}                                                    ▸ ● [9]  "ZombieWithStates (9) (UnityEngine.GameObject)"
                                                     ▸ ● [10] "HumanWithStates (3) (UnityEngine.GameObject)"
GameObject[] theZombies = new GameObject [zombies.C ▸ ● [11] "ZombieWithStates (2) (UnityEngine.GameObject)"
zombies.CopyTo(theZombies);                          ▸ ● [12] "ZombieWithStates (5) (UnityEngine.GameObject)"
foreach (GameObject z in theZombies)                 ▸ ● [13] "HumanWithStates (10) (UnityEngine.GameObject)"
{                                                    ▸ ● [14] "HumanWithStates (7) (UnityEngine.GameObject)"
    //check distance from zombie to all humans
    foreach (GameObject h in humans)
    {
```

In the array list you'll notice Humans were added. The gate catching isZombie must be true for the humans to be added to the zombie list. The HumansWithStates class inherited from ZombieWithStates, so in a sense, they are zombies with added or modified features. In the statements where humans and zombies get their components from the game object both prove true with humans. A cast from zombie to human gets inferred so isZombie is always true.

The isHuman is only true when the component is a Human since it's an evolution of the Zombie. If you were to use object instead of ZombieWithStates then you'd add every type of component and object in the scene, transforms, lights, cameras, etc. The object class is the base class of every construct in the scene. The HumanWithStates class is based on ZombieWithStates so the isZombie gate adds humans to the zombies ArrayList. So, after the first update, you get an array of 22 objects on the first Update with both humans and zombies.

```
if (isHuman)
{
    humans.Add(go);
    continue; // added to skip the zombies.Add(go); statement.
}
```

To avoid that you can add a continue; jump statement to finish the loop early and skip any following statements in the foreach loop. As an alternative you could also use the following condition to add the game object to the zombies ArrayList.

```
if (!isHuman && isZombie)
{
    zombies.Add(go);
}
```

The statement can be read as: if value isHuman is false and value isZombie is true; add go to the zombies list. Running the code again in the debugger will need a re-build of the code.

Press Stop Debugging (Shift+F5) to release the breakpoint. Make your code changes, press Attach to Unity again to check your changes press Play in Unity. This time around rather than all humans and zombies, the zombies ArrayList should only contain 11 objects exclusively of zombies. The Autos view in Visual Studio will also show you the variables involved with BreakPoint.

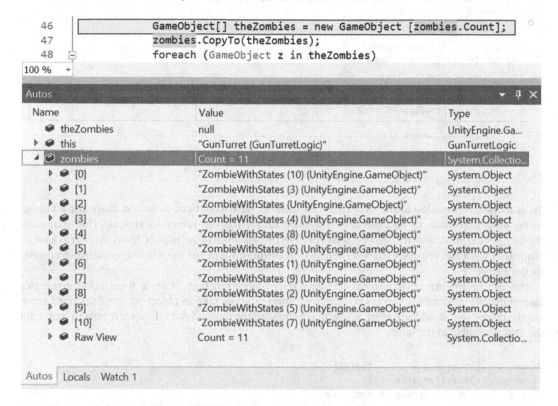

Once you're satisfied with the results of the debugging session, you can delete the breakpoint by selecting the highlighted line and from the right-click menu select Delete Breakpoint.

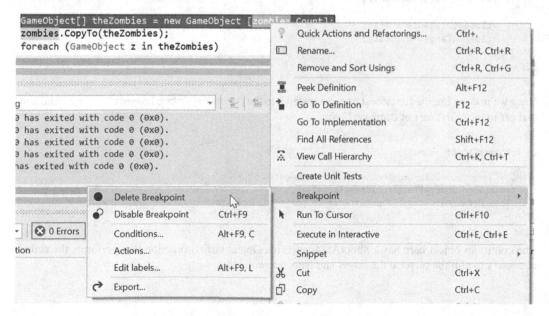

Now that we have a clean list of zombies, we're able to parse through them and check each zombie's proximity to the humans.

```
GameObject[] theZombies = new GameObject [zombies.Count];
zombies.CopyTo(theZombies);
foreach (GameObject z in theZombies)
{
    //check distance from zombie to all humans
    foreach (GameObject h in humans)
    {
        float dist = (z.transform.position - h.transform.position).magnitude;
        float tooCloseToZombie = 1.0f;
        if (dist < tooCloseToZombie)
        {
            zombies.Remove(z);
        }
    }
}
```

To start, we've decided arbitrarily that 1.0f units is what we'll consider too close for a human to be near a zombie to be considered a valid target for the turret to aim at. The statement `dist < tooCloseToZombie` will remove the zombie game object from the ArrayList of zombies. With the reduced list we then search through them for the closest remaining zombie to the turret.

The use of the ArrayList affords the Remove() object function. With a fixed sized array like GameObject[] theZombies, there is no Remove feature. You can take an object out of a fixes sized array, but the empty spot would still exist as a null. Finally with the reduced ArrayList we're able to search for the closest zombie to the turret.

```
float closestDistance = Mathf.Infinity;
GameObject closestTarget = null;
foreach (GameObject zombie in zombies)
{
    float dist = (zombie.transform.position - transform.position).magnitude;
    if (dist < closestDistance)
    {
        closestDistance = dist;
        closestTarget = zombie;
    }
}
```

Once we're done finding the closest one, we assign it to the GameObject `closestTarget`. And hand that off to the `GunTurretController`.

```
if (closestTarget != null)
{
    GunTurretController controller = GetComponent<GunTurretController>();
    controller.ShootAtTarget(closestTarget);
    Debug.DrawLine(closestTarget.transform.position, transform.position, Color.red);
}
```

The controller object here has a ShootAtTarget(GameObject target) function that performs the actions necessary to aim the turret at the target and launch a projectile.

After completing the features requested by the designer it may seem unfortunate that the zombies standing next to humans are not targeted. Perhaps this is something that should be brought to the attention of the designer.

6.17.5 What We've Learned

We'll leave off here for now and move on to a different topic next. Arrays are a fundamental part of programming in general. A database is not much more than a complex array of different types of data. The principal difference is that a database has some relational connections between one element and another. Arrays without this relational data mean you'll have to keep track of the different relations.

Sorting through objects is an important part of general computing that many algorithms do nothing more than sort and organize values. Computer scientists spend years trying to speed up these sorting processes. We can't necessarily spend too much time on comparing these different methods of sorting in this book, as the field of study has filled countless volumes of text. If it were not for this importance, companies wouldn't base their entire business on storing, sorting, and organizing data.

You could imagine dealing with a few dozen monster types; each one with different sets of data, stats, and members can quickly become cumbersome to deal with. There are ways to maintain some control; that's where data structures come into play.

6.18 Out Parameter

We have been thinking that functions return a single value. Another method to get more than one value from a function is to use the out keyword in the parameters. The out keyword is usable in most situations even if you need only one return value though its use is different from how return is used.

```
int GetSeven()
{
    return 7;
}
```

The above is a function that simply returns 7. In use, you might see something like the following code fragment:

```
void GettingSeven()
{
    int Seven = GetSeven();
}
```

What limits us is the ability to return multiple values. What we'd like to be able to do is something like Lua that looks like the following:

```
function ReturnsSevenAndEleven()
    return 7, 11
end
local seven, eleven = ReturnsSevenAndEleven()
```

Lua has some clever tricks like returning multiple values. With some extra work in C# we can simulate various work arounds, or a tuple as we have seen in Section 5.7.4. This is not elegant to say the least, and this does not mention the performance issues that will creep up if something like this is used too often.

```
ArrayList GetSevenEleven()
{
    ArrayList list = new ArrayList();
    list.Add(7);
    list.Add(11);
    list.Add("Eleven");//not an int?
    return list;
}

void GettingSevenEleven()
{
    ArrayList list = GetSevenEleven();
    int seven = (int)list[0];
    int eleven = (int)list[1];
}
```

From the above example, we created a function called GetSevenEleven() that returned a 7. return which is used to provide a system to turn the function into some sort of value, which can be an array, but then we start to lose what sort of data is inside of the array. Because of this, we will run into type safety issues. For instance, we could modify the statement in sevenEleven() to look like the following:

```
ArrayList GetSevenEleven()
{
    ArrayList list = new ArrayList();
    list.Add(7);
    list.Add("Eleven");//not an int?
    return list;
}
```

The parser will not catch the error, until the game starts running and the `GetSevenEleven()` function is called and the int eleven tries to get data from the array. You will get this printed out to the Console panel.

> InvalidCastException: Specified cast is not valid.
> OutParameter.GettingSevenEleven () (at Assets/OutParameter.cs:36)

This type of error is not something we'd like to track down when you're using an array for use with numbers. Vague errors are rarely fun to figure out. It's best to avoid using anything like the code mentioned above.

The advantage of the tuple is knowing the parameters that went into the return value. However, tuples can often add to the complexity of a function's signature. Ultimately, the reason for using any one system over another is readability. The out parameter flows nicely, the value goes into the function and can be used immediately. Tuples need to get assigned to a var and then the var's members can be used after.

6.18.1 A Basic Example

In the OutParameter script, The parameter seven is defined in the argument in the `GetSevenOut()` function. In the body of the function the int 7 is assigned to the seven parameter which is then sent to the out parameter. Values used for the out parameter need to be created in the body of the function. Incoming values are ignored and new values are assigned to the variable. The out parameter works in one direction—out.

```
void GetSevenOut(out int seven)
{/*                         ↑           */
    seven = 7; /*           |           */
}/*   └→❶──────────────────┘           */
 /* ❶ variable given to seven          */
 /*   gets assigned 7                  */
```

When the function is used you'll see something like the following:

```
int i = 0;/* int i goes in as 0    */
/*   └❶→──────────┐  i = 0         */
GetSevenOut(out i);
/*          ┌←❷───┘  i = 7         */
Debug.Log(i);/* comes out as 7     */
```

You need to do a couple of things before the out keyword is used. First, you need to create a new variable to assign to the function. Then to use the function, you need to put that variable into the parameters list preceded by the same out keyword. When the function is executed, it looks at the variable's value inside of it and sends it back up to the parameters list with its new value. Of course, we can add more than one out value.

```
void GetThreeValuesOut(out int first, out int second, out int third)
{/*                           ↑              ↑             ↑  */
    first = 1;/* assigned 1   |              |             |  */
 /*   └→❶──────────────────────┘             |             |  */
 /*                                          |             |  */
    second = 2;/* assigned 2                 |             |  */
 /*   └→❷───────────────────────────────────┘             |  */
 /*                                                        |  */
    third = 3;/*   assigned 3                              |  */
 /*   └→❸──────────────────────────────────────────────────┘  */
}
```

Using more than one out parameter allows you to create multiple values.

```
/* this works with multiple values           */
int i, j, k;
/*  |   |   └●→                               */
/*  |   └●→                                   */
/*  └●→                      i = 0 |j = 0 |k = 0     */
GetThreeValuesOut(out i, out j, out k);
/*                   ┌──┘i = 1 |j = 2 |k = 3     */
/*                   |      └─┐      └───┐     */
/*                   ●        ●          ●     */
/*                   ↓        ↓          ↓     */
Debug.Log("i: " + i + " j: " + j + " k: " + k);
```

The above code produces the following in the Console:

> ⚠ i: 1 j: 2 k: 3
> UnityEngine.Debug:Log(Object)

Using the function in this way allows you to produce many useful operations on incoming values as well. The additional benefit is the fact that the function can act as a pure function. This means that as long as none of the variables inside of the function rely on anything at the class level, the code can be copied and pasted or moved to any other class quite easily.

```
void GoingInAndOut(int inValue, out int outValue)
{/*           ┌←●─────┘              ↑    */
    outValue = inValue * 2;/*        |    */
/*       └→●────────────────────────┘    */
}/*  outValue is set to inValue multiplied by 2 */
```

The outValue can be based on incoming parameters.

```
int i = 0;
/*  └●→─────────────┐   i = 0              */
GoingInAndOut(6, out i);
/*           ┌←●─────┘   i = 12            */
Debug.Log(i);/* comes out as 12           */
```

This example shows an incoming parameter that is multiplied by 2 before it's assigned to the `outValue` parameter. The `out` keyword is handy and allows for more tidy functions. A simple function in Unity is called the `Physics.Raycast();` function.

```
Ray ray = new Ray(transform.position, transform.forward);
RaycastHit raycastHit;
/*          └●→───────────┐                                     */
if(Physics.Raycast( ray, out raycastHit))
{/*       ↓               |   hit value has a point            */
 /* conditional statement |   in the world where it hit something...  */
 /* if there's anything   |           ●            ●  and orientation of */
 /* actually hit by the ray └──────────────────────┐  the surface it hit */
    AimPoint.transform.position = raycastHit.point;/*   ↓ */
    Quaternion normal = Quaternion.LookRotation(raycastHit.normal, AimPoint.transform.up);
    AimPoint.transform.rotation = normal;
}
```

The function returns a bool, true if the raycast hits something, and false if it doesn't. In the scene, the OutParameters object is aimed at a lower area of a sphere.

When we play the scene the AimPoint object jumps to the point on the sphere where the ray intersects with a physics object.

Compare the out parameter with how a tuple works. The readability doesn't indicate what values are contained in `var abc`. The values are masked, and you'd need to have the function close by to read what's hidden in the `abc` variable before it's assigned.

```
(int a, int b, int c) GetThreeValuesOut()
{
    return (a: 1, b: 2, c: 3);
}
/*                                                     */
/*   ┌─●─┐ a var gets assigned the tuple               */
var abc = GetThreeValuesOut();
/*   │        one value contains all three members     */
/*   └─●─────────────────────────────────┐             */
/*            ↓               ↓           ↓             */
Debug.Log("a: " + abc.a + " b: " + abc.b + " c: " + abc.c);
```

This shouldn't diminish the usability of a tuple by any means, it's just something to keep in mind when choosing between out parameters or a tuple return value. The tuple requires unboxing from a var, out is explicit.

6.18.2 Simple Sort (Bubble Sort)

In the scene are plenty more Spheres to deal with. Lists of monsters and values make for an important part of any list of data when making decisions on what to do in an environment.

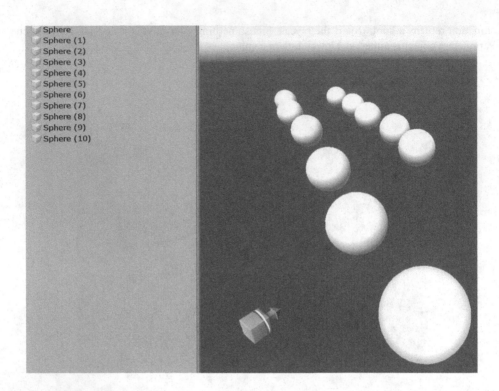

Around our OutParameter object we have several other game objects duplicated from the sphere where we cast a ray. We're going to create a simple ArrayList that will have all the objects in the scene added to it. Then we're going to create a new GameObject[] array that will be sorted based on the distance to the capsule.

Sorting algorithms have a long history in computer programming. Many thesis papers have been written on the topic. However, we're going to make use of a simple sort algorithm to order an array of game objects from the shortest distance to the longest distance.

We'll start with a simple system to get an ArrayList of objects in the scene.

```
GameObject[] allObjects = FindObjectsOfType<GameObject>();
ArrayList sphereList = new ArrayList();
foreach(GameObject go in allObjects)
{
    bool isSphere = go.name.Contains("Sphere");
    if(isSphere)
    {
        sphereList.Add(go);
    }
}
```

The allObjects GameObject[] array gathers all of the GameObjects in the scene. Then an ArrayList called sphereList is created to store any object with "sphere" in its name.

After the sphereList is populated, a new GameObject[] array is created to store the unsorted sphereList.

```
/* now we have some objects to sort*/
GameObject[] spheres = new GameObject[sphereList.Count];
/* copy the list to the array */
sphereList.CopyTo(spheres);
```

Now we're ready to sort through the sphereList based on distance by plugging in the target gameObject, the unsorted array and the sorted array into the SortDistanceFromObject function.

```
bool SortDistanceFromObject(GameObject target, GameObject[] unsorted, out GameObject[] sorted)
{
    int len = unsorted.Length;
    for (int i = 0; i < len; i++)
    {
        /* start at the beginning of the array */
        for (int j = 0; j < len - i - 1; j++)
        {
            /* then compare everyone against every other one */
            /* get positions of an object in the array  */
            /* and the following one.                   */
            Vector3 posA = unsorted[j].transform.position;
            Vector3 posB = unsorted[j + 1].transform.position;

            /* get the distance of each object from the target */
            float distA = (posA - target.transform.position).magnitude;
            float distB = (posB - target.transform.position).magnitude;

            /* compare distances */
            if(distA > distB)
            {
                /* if B is further than A then swap them */
                GameObject temp = unsorted[j];
                unsorted[j] = unsorted[j + 1];
                unsorted[j + 1] = temp;
            }
        }
    }
    sorted = unsorted;
    return sorted.Length > 0;
}
```

The first outer loop for(int i = 0; i < len; i++) starts with the first object in the unsorted list. The inner loop for(int j = 0; j < len - i - 1; j++) iterates through the rest of the array.

To clarify, assume we might have an array with 4 items. The outer loop starts with item 1, then the inner loop compares the first item against the second. The second to the third, and the third item to the fourth. The outer loop counts up 1, then the inner loop compares first to second, and second to third. Then the last iteration compares the first and second again. Each time swapping the lower value toward the first value in the array.

The unsorted array is now sorted so we can assign the array to the out parameter's sorted GameObject[] array.

```
sorted = unsorted;
return sorted.Length > 0;
```

6.18.3 Simple Sort Proof

To test our sort, we'll use a for loop. Each higher value in the array will hold onto a different model. The furthest model will be the last in the array and thus have the highest index in the array. The closest object will be at GameObjectArray[0], and the furthest one will be at the end of the array. Therefore, if there are 10 objects in the scene, the furthest object will be at GameObjectArray[9]. Remember that arrays start at 0, not 1.

```
/* now send the unsorted array to the function, then get a sorted array out */
if(SortDistanceFromObject(gameObject, spheres, out spheres))
{
    int lineHeight = 1;
    foreach(GameObject go in spheres)
    {
        Vector3 up = new Vector3(){ y = lineHeight++ * 0.5f};
        Debug.DrawRay(go.transform.position, up, Color.red);
    }
}
```

To help visualize how the objects are arranged in the array we'll draw a longer line based on the position the object is in the array. The first item will have a short red line, and the last item will have the longest line drawn up from the game object.

As you move the OutParameter game object around in the scene, you'll notice the length of the lines changing based on the distance away from the capsule. This means that you can use this sort algorithm to place a priority on which object is closest and which is the furthest away based on its index in the array.

6.18.4 What We've Learned

We should leave off here for now; sorting is a very deep topic that leads into the very messy guts of computer science. The algorithm isn't complete and lacks any efficiency. It's effective, but only superficially. The only reason why this works at all is the fact that `Update()` is called many times per second.

Bubble sorting is slow. For just the hand full of items we have in the scene, it's performance will not hinder your computers frame rate. However with many more objects the performance will get worse.

Most of the commonly used sorting algorithms have names such as bubble sort, heap sort, or quick sort. This means we looked at the first two elements in the array, and if one had some greater value than the other, we swap them.

For games such as tower defense, or anything where a character needs to shoot at the closest target and then move on to the next closest, we can use sorting to help provide the character with some more interesting behaviors. Perhaps he can target more than one object with different weapons at the same time. Maybe the character can simply shoot at the closest three objects. The great thing about writing your own game is that you can explore behaviors like this freely, but only once you understand how to use the code you're writing.

In the end, we're required to keep our code as simple as possible. The out keyword is best used when we can't return a single value. In the case with a single return value, the later version of sortObjects where we simply return the sorted array is more readable.

6.19 Ref Parameter

The ref keyword, which is short for *reference,* works with variables in a slightly less intuitive way than we have experienced to this point. This is related to how we've been thinking about variables. In the usual case, we use the statement int x = 1;, and now when we use x, we can assume we're dealing with the value it's storing.

The difference with ref enters when we start to manipulate the data stored under an identifier. If we use a statement like x = 1; y = x;, we aren't actually taking x and putting it into y. What's really going on is that y is looking at the value that x is holding onto and changes its own value to match what x is storing.

```
int x = 1; /* Initial assignment of the value 1 is put into x  */
/*   └─1→┐     the value of x is 1                              */
int y = x; /* the value 1 in x is copied into y                */
/*   └←1─┘     y is assigned 1, the value from x               */
/* no link to x has been made.                                 */
   y = 3; /* y is assigned 3, x is still 1                      */
/*   └←3─┘                                                      */
Debug.Log("x: " + x); // "x: 1"
Debug.Log("y: " + y); // "y: 3"
```

In memory, y is storing a 1 and x is storing a different 1. However, functions can use the ref in its parameter list. This maintains a link to the original variable.

This may seem hard to understand, and to be honest, it is. This concept is one that takes a while to get used to and that is why some programming languages are more difficult to learn than others. However, the concept becomes more apparent when we see the code in action.

6.19.1 A Basic Example

The ref keyword acts somewhat like the out keyword. In practice we'll see how they differ with the following example code fragment.

```
void UseRefManipulateValue()
{
    int x = 3;/* ─────────────┐               */
    int y = 3;/*              ‖               */
          /*                  ‖               */
    RefManipulateValue(ref x, y);
          /*            ‖──────────────┐      */
    Debug.Log("UsingRefManipulation: x:" + x + " y:" + y);
    /* "UsingRefManipulation: x: 4 y: 3               */
}
void RefManipulateValue(ref int refValue, int notRefValue)
{              /* linked to x    ‖           │       */
    refValue++;/*o ──────────────‖ just value │      */
    notRefValue++;/*← ───────────────────────┘       */
}
```

The code above takes in the ref of x which is assigned in by the parameters of the function. The in argument now has a direct connection to the contents of x. When refValue++; is executed, the value that x was holding is incremented. A link to the original value is maintained. After the function is completed, the value of the original x has been modified.

The y value on the other hand, is handled like a regular variable in the `RefManipulateValue()` function. The `notRefValue++;` is run, but the increment doesn't change the value stored in y. Without the `ref` keyword, the link to the original variable isn't maintained.

The difference between ref and out can become obvious when you see them together. When using ref you can assume that the value is already initialized before being used in the function. Using the out keyword, it's necessary to initialize a value within the body of the function before assigning the value for the out parameter.

```
void UseRefAndOut()
{
    int x = 3;
    int y = 3;
    RefAndOut(ref x, out y);
    Debug.Log("UsingRefAndOut: x:" + x + " y:" + y);
    /* "UsingRefAndOut: x: 4 y: 1                    */


}
void RefAndOut(ref int refValue, out int outValue)
{/*                         ↓ ↑              ↑      */
 /*      ┌──────────────────────┐  │        │      */
 /*      ↓                      │  │        │      */
    refValue++;/*              │  │        │      */
 /*      ↓                      │  │        │      */
 /*      └──────────────────────┘  │        │      */
    outValue = 0;/* new value created  │     */
    outValue++;  /*────────────────────┘     */
}
```

To get a similar effect with ref using out you'd need to provide an in as well. The following example shows the first `refValue` incremented, the second `value` is then manipulated in the body of the function before being assigned to the `outValue`.

```
void UseRefAndInAndOut()
{
    int x = 1;
    int y = 1;
    int z = 1;
    RefAndInAndOut(ref x, y, out z);
    Debug.Log("UsingRefAndInAndOut: x:" + x + " y:" + y + " z:" + z );
    /*"UsingRefAndInAndOut x: 2 y: 1 z: 2"                   */
}
void RefAndInAndOut(ref int refValue, int value, out int outValue)
{/*                               ↕           ↓          ↑ */
 /*      ┌──────────────────────────┐         │          │ */
    refValue++;/*                   │         │          │ */
 /*      ┌────────────────────────────────────┘          │ */
    outValue = value + 1;/*                              │ */
}/*      └─────────────────────────────────────────────┘ */
```

6.19.2 Code Portability Side Effects

A side effect is the result of a function manipulating values that are not directly within the scope of the function.

```
public int publicX;/*←┐                        */
void IncrementX()  /* | directly manipulate    */
{                  /* | class wide variable.    */
    publicX += 1;  /*←┘                         */
}
```

When the `IncrementX()` function is used, the `publicX` variable in the class scope is incremented.

```
Debug.Log(publicX); // "0"
IncrementX();
Debug.Log(publicX); // "1"
```

There is no problem with using a function like this. The fact that the Increment function works only on the `publicX` variable means that you know exactly what it's allowed to do, and what it's limited to.

Reusing code can help speed along your own development. Often, you'll find simple tricks that help with various tasks. When we talk of reusing code, we need to think about how a function interacts with its input and output to consider portability. If a function relies on the class it was written in, then it becomes less portable. When a function can operate on its own, it becomes more utilitarian and more portable.

Consider the `SortDistanceFromObject` code from the previous chapter. We replaced the in and out parameters with ref. This reduces the amount of work going into the parameters.

```
bool SortDistanceFromObject(GameObject target, ref GameObject[] sortableObjects)
{
    int len = sortableObjects.Length;
    for (int i = 0; i < len; i++)
    {
        int restLen = len - i - 1;
        /* start at the beginning of the array */
        for (int j = 0; j < restLen; j++)
        {
            /* then compare everyone against every other one */
            /* get positions of an object in the array  */
            /* and the following one.                   */
            Vector3 posA = sortableObjects[j].transform.position;
            Vector3 posB = sortableObjects[j + 1].transform.position;

            /* get the distance of each object from the target */
            float distA = (posA - target.transform.position).magnitude;
            float distB = (posB - target.transform.position).magnitude;

            /* compare distances */
            if(distA > distB)
            {
                /* if B is further than A then swap them */
                GameObject temp = sortableObjects[j];
                sortableObjects[j] = sortableObjects[j + 1];
                sortableObjects[j + 1] = temp;
            }
        }
    }
    return sortableObjects.Length > 0;
}
```

This version is considerably more portable; you only need to give it a gameObject to sort distances from and an array of game objects to sort. To copy and paste code from place to place is much easier than re-typing. Most programming tools even come with built-in code snippet management tools. Visual Studio has it's code snippets manager under Tools→Code Snippets Manager…

6.19.3 What We've Learned

In Section 6.18, we covered the `out` keyword, and here we learned the `ref` keyword. Values coming in to a parameter using the `out` keyword are not initialized with any value.

```
void OutFunction(out int outValue)
{
    outValue++;
    /* the above doesn't work since */
    /* it assumes outValue already  */
    /* has a value.                 */
}
```

In much the same way you're not able to increment an int that has no assigned value.

```
int noValue;
noValue++;
/* works the same way, you can't     */
/* increment an int that has no value */
/* assigned yet.                     */
/*                                   */
```

With no value to increment in the `int`, you're not able to add 1 to nothing. That being the case though you're able to assign a value to the outValue and pass that along to the variable given to that parameter. Assuming of course that the types match.

```
void OutFunction(out int outValue)
{
    outValue = 7;
}
void UsingOutFunction()
{
    int localInt;
    /*        └──────────┐           */
    /*                   ↓ unassigned int */
    OutFunction(out localInt);
    /*        └────────┐            */
    /*        assigned value 7 ↓    */
    Debug.Log("localInt: " + localInt);
}
```

The `ref` keyword on the other hand assumes that the incoming data has already been initialized.

```
void RefFunction(ref int refValue)
{
    refValue++;
}
void UsingRefFunction()
{
    int localInt;
    RefFunction(ref localInt);
    Debug.Log("UsingRefFunction: " + localInt);
}
```

If the variable given to a ref has no value, then you'll get the same error of using an unassigned local variable. The difference here is that the error occurs before getting to the body of the `RefFunction()`. To allow either of these to work, the variable in use needs to have a value before it's used.

```
int localInt = 0;
RefFunction(ref localInt);
Debug.Log("UsingRefFunction: " + localInt);
```

There are plenty of options and each has a purpose. It's important to know how to accomplish a task using different methods. Readable, easy to understand code should always be the goal.

Ultimately, your skill dictates how complex your own code will be. Your ability to read your own code may even help others who encounter your work. You express your ideas and methods through code. Different programming languages have different levels of expressiveness or expressivity. Basically, some languages are stricter, while others allow for more than one way to carry out any given task.

The expressivity of C# is high, allowing you to try out many different methods to do the same thing. There are more commonly used systems, but by no means should you feel limited to a commonly used syntax. If you feel that a less commonly used syntax is more helpful, use it.

6.20 Type Casting Numbers

We need to know more about a variety of different data types and how they're used before we can begin to understand how and why type casting is important. At this point, we need more casting from one type of data into another. Now that we've had a chance to use a wide variety of different data types, it's time we started learning why converting from one type to another is necessary.

From the array exercises we used cast from object to float, but why is this required? C# is a *type-safe* programming language. What this means is that your code is checked for mixed types before it's compiled into machine-readable code. This is done to prevent any errors that show up while the code is running. When converting between types that are similar, we don't usually see too many errors. In the following code sample, we demonstrate why we don't want to use an integer for setting an object's position or rotation.

```
FloatRotationY += Time.deltaTime;
/*      ↑                        ↓ The amount of time that's passed between Updates */
/*      └────────────────────┘ slowly increases FloatRotationY                      */
/*          ┌──────────────┐                  */
/*          │cast to int│                    */
/*          └──────┬───────┘                  */
/*                 ↓                          */
IntRotationY = (int)FloatRotationY;
/*    ↑                        ↓ only the whole digit of float gets carried through */
/*    └─( X.000...000)────┘ the cast from float to int                              */
/*          ↑                    */
/*  only numbers past the decimal  */
/*  are carried over               */
```

```
IntPointer.transform.localEulerAngles = new Vector3(0, IntRotationY, 0);
FloatPointer.transform.localEulerAngles = new Vector3(0, FloatRotationY, 0);
```

In the TypeCastingNumbers_Scene is a rotation indication game object. The script in control is attached to the TypeCastingNumbers game object. The white pointer has its rotation controlled with a float value that's incremented with Time.deltaTime. The red pointer is controlled with an int value that's cast from the value driving the white pointer.

As time passes, the white pointer smoothly rotates, the red pointer ticks, skipping directly to the next degree marker on the rotation indicator.

Simply put, an integer is a whole number such as 1, 2, and 3. A fraction can have a value between 1 and 2, for example, 1.5625. Therefore, if we change from an int to a float, we'll get a smooth movement. This becomes more apparent when we look at the values in the Inspector panel in the editor.

Going in the other direction, from int to float, we don't need to use a cast operator. This is because there are no values being lost.

```
float FloatFromInt = IntRotationY;
/*              ↑              ↓ going from int to float doesn't require a cast */
/*           └─( X.??? )──┘ since we don't lose any values in the cast        */
```

A cast from int to float is still being done, it's just an implicit cast operation.

6.20.1 Number Types

This leads us to numbers having a size. In fact, so far we've used int and float, and there was even mention of a double. However, why do these have a size related to them and how is an int smaller than a float? This is a computer science question, and to explain this, we need to remember how computers count.

In the old days, when computers had moving parts, instructions were fed to them using a flat piece of physical media with holes punched into it. Each hole in the media represented either a 0 or a 1, which was then converted back into decimal numbers which we use in our everyday life. The primary limitation in these old computers was size, and to hold big numbers, computers needed to be physically bigger.

Each number was stored in a series of switches. In 1946, the Electronic Numerical Integrator and Computer (ENIAC) used flip-flop switches to store a number; imagine a light switch, with *on* being a 1 and *off* being a 0. Each group of switches was called an accumulator and it could store a single 10-digit number for use in a calculation. Altogether with 18,000 vacuum tubes and weighing over 25 tons, the ENIAC could store a maximum of 20 numbers at a time.

Because programming languages have such a deep-rooted history with limited data space, numbers today still have similar limitations. On your PC, you might have the memory to store many hundreds of billions of numbers, but this doesn't hold true for every device. Every year new smaller, more portable devices show up on the market, so it's good to be aware that forming bad habits of wasting data space will limit the platforms you can write software for.

6.20.2 Integers

It's important to know how computers convert 1s and 0s into decimal numbers. To explain, let's start with a 4-bit number. This would be a series of four 1s or 0s. A zero would be as simple as 0000. Each place in the number is a different value. The first place is either a 1 or a 0, the second 2 or 0, the third 4 or 0, and the fourth 8 or 0. Each whole number between 0 and 15 can be represented with these 4 bits.

To demonstrate 0101 means 2 + 8 or 10. An interesting change is to shift both 1s to the left to get 1010 that translates to 1 + 4 or 5. This is called a bit shift, or in this case a shift left. The number 15 looks like 1111. It just so happens that a 4-bit number is called a *nibble*. A nibble also happens to easily represent a single hex number.

Hex numbers are used often when dealing with assigning colors on a web page. Hex numbers range from 0 to 9 and include an additional A through F to fill in the last six digits. A color is denoted by three

8-bit numbers for red, blue, and green. An 8-bit number is called a *byte*. Each color gets a range from 0 to 255. This turns into a two-digit hex number. Therefore, 0 is 00 and 255 is FF in hex.

6.20.2.1 Signed Numbers

Today C# uses numbers starting with the *sbyte* up to the decimal. The sbyte is a number from –127 to 127, and the byte is a number from 0 to 255. The s in the sbyte is an abbreviation of the word *signed*. Therefore, you can actually call an sbyte a *signed byte*.

This is an important difference: Signing a number means it can be either positive or negative. However, you lose half the maximum range of the number since one of the 1s and 0s is used to tell the computer if the number is positive or negative. If we use the first bit to represent the signedness of a number in terms of our nibble, this turns 0100 into positive 1, while 1100 turns into negative 1. Negative 3 is 1110 and negative 7 is 1111, or "negative + 1 + 2 + 4."

sbyte	8 bits	−128 ↔ 127
Byte	8 bits	0 ↔ 255
Short	16 bits	−32,768 ↔ 32,767
Unsigned short	16 bits	0 ↔ 65,535
Int	32 bits	−2,147,483,648 ↔ 2,147,483,647
Unsigned int	32 bits	0 ↔ 4,294,967,295
Long	64 bits	−9,223,372,036,854,775,808 ↔ 9,223,372,036,854,775,807
Unsigned long	64 bits	0 ↔ 18,446,744,073,709,551,615

The above table represents most of the useful varieties of integer numbers. None of these have a decimal point in them to represent a fraction. Numbers that do have a decimal are called floating point numbers. We've used float and double as well; only that it hasn't been so obvious.

6.20.3 Floating Point

Floating point numbers have been a focus of computers for many years. Gaining floating point accuracy was the goal of many early computer scientists. Because there are an infinite possibilities of how many numbers can follow a decimal point, it's impossible to truly represent any fraction completely using binary computing.

A common example is π, which we call pi. It's assumed that there are an endless number of digits following 3.14. Even today computers are set loose to calculate the hundreds of billions of digits beyond the decimal point. Computers set aside some of the bits of a floating point number aside to represent where the decimal appears in the number, but even this is limited.

The first bit is usually the sign bit, setting the negative or positive range of the number. The following 8 bits is the exponent for the number called a mantissa. The remaining bits are the rest of the number appearing around the decimal point. A float value can move the decimal 38 digits in either direction, but it's limited to the values it's able to store.

We will go further into how numbers are actually stored in terms of 1s and 0s in Section 8.9. For now just understand that numbers can represent only a limited number of digits. Without special considerations, computers are not able to handle arbitrarily large numbers.

To cast a float into an int, you need to be more explicit. That's why C# requires you to use the cast and you need to add the (int) in `int IntYRotation = (int)FloatYRotation;`. The `(int)` is a cast operator; or rather `(type)` acts as a converter from the type on the right to the type needed on the left.

6.20.4 What We've Learned

There's still a bit left to go over with numbers, but we'll leave off here for now. A CPU is a collection of transistors. The computer interprets the signal coming from each transistor as a switch which is either on or off.

Computers collect these transistors into groups to accomplish common tasks. A floating point unit (FPU) is a collection of transistors grouped together to assist in floating point number processing. A graphics processing unit (GPU) is a variety of different groups of transistors specifically used to compute computer graphics.

These groups of transistors are built with highly complex designs. Their organization was designed by software to accomplish their task quickly. Software was used to build the hardware designed to run more software. It all sounds a bit of catch-22, but at least we have some historic reference where all of this comes from.

6.21 Types and Operators

Most of the operators we've been using compare equally. This works just fine when dealing with numbers. However, we can use operators on types that are not numbers, but which comparative operators can we use?

For number types, we can use relational operators. This affords us the ability to set booleans by using greater than >, less than <, greater than or equal to ≥, and less than or equal to ≤. All of these operators produce a boolean result.

```
float a = 1.0f;
float b = 3.0f;
bool c = a > b;// false
bool d = a < b;// true


Debug.Log("c:" + c + " d:" + d);
```

As you might imagine, math operators such as add +, subtract –, multiply X, divide /, and modulo % work on any number type data. However, we can also use the + on the string type.

```
string a = "hello, ";
string b = "world.";
string c = a + b;


Debug.Log("c: " + c);
```

In the fragment shown string c is assigned a + b. When sent to the Unity console we get "hello, world." Printed from the Debug.Log() function. Some other things we can do with strings are comparisons.

```
string a = "hello, ";
string b = "world.";
bool c = a == b; // false
bool d = a == "world."; // true
bool e = a == "hello, "; // false
bool f = a != b; // true
string g = a + b; // hello, world.
```

where c is assigned (a == b), we get `false`. Likewise, we can use numbers and compare their values as well. We can also use the not equal != operator on strings in the assignment for f. The comparative operator !=, or not equal operator, works on strings as well as numbers. Knowing which operators takes a bit of intuition, but it's important to experiment and learn how types interact with one another.

Another system in which a string could be used is in a switch statement.

```
string a = "hello";
switch (a)
{
    case "hello":
        Debug.Log("a was hello");
        break;
    case "world":
        Debug.Log("a was world");
        break;
    default:
        break;
}
```

In a switch statement the input value is compared against each case. In the code fragment before we used d = a == "hello,"; where d was assigned true. In a switch statement the value that proves true will get executed. In the switch statement here we'll get `Debug.Log("a was hello");` to execute.

6.21.1 `GetType()`

We can also compare data types. This becomes more important later when we start creating our own data types. To know how this works, we can use the data types that are already available in C#.

```
int a = 7;
string b = "hello";
bool c = a.GetType() == b.GetType();
Debug.Log("a and b are the same type? " + c);
// "a and b are the same type? False"
```

The built-in types in C# have a function called `GetType()` which allows us to check against what type of data each variable is. In this case, int a is a `System.Int32` which is not the same as a `System.String`.

```
int a = 7;
string b = "7";
bool c = a.ToString() == b;
Debug.Log("a as a string is the same as b? " + c);
// "a as a string is the same as b? True"
```

Even though we have two different types here, we can convert an int to a string by using the `ToString()` function in the `Int32` data class. Here we've got an int 7 and we're comparing it to the string "7"; when the int is converted to a string, the comparison results in `True`.

```
int a = 7;
float b = 7.0f;
bool c = a == b;
Debug.Log("int a == float b? " + c);
// "int a == float b? True"
```

Dissimilar numeric values can also be compared so long as there's no imprecision of the value with a decimal point. An `int` 7 and a `float` 7.0f are still equal.

6.21.2 More Type Casting

We can compare ints and floats without conversion. This works because C# will convert the int to a float implicitly before the comparison is made. However, C# does know that they are different types.

```
int a = 7;
float b = 7.9f;
bool c = a == b; // false
/*   ↑   ↓     ↓                        */
/*   |   |     L───┐                    */
/*   |   |         |                    */
/*   |  ┌─┐    ┌────┐                   */
/*   |  | 7 | == |7.9f|                 */
/*   |  └─┘  ↓ └────┘                   */
/*   |                                  */
/*   |  ┌──────┐                        */
/*   L──┤ False |                       */
/*      └──────┘                        */
bool d = a == (int)b;
/*   ↑   ↓     ↓    ↓                    */
/*   |   |     |    |                    */
/*   |   |     |  ┌────┐                 */
/*   |   |     |  |7.9f|                 */
/*   |   |     |  └────┘                 */
/*   |   |     L→(int) cast to int */
/*   |   |          ↓                    */
/*   |   |     ┌────┐                    */
/*   |  ┌─┐    ┌────┐                    */
/*   |  | 7 | == | 7  |                  */
/*   |  └─┘  ↓ └────┘                    */
/*   |                                   */
/*   |  ┌──────┐                         */
/*   L──┤ True |                         */
/*      └──────┘                         */
```

```
Debug.Log("c: " + c + " d: " + d);
// c: False d: True
```

We can force the cast using the `(int)` on b that was assigned 7.9f, which we know is clearly greater than 7. However, when we cast `float` 7.9f to an int, we lose the numbers following the decimal. This makes the cast version of the comparison true.

Can we cast a string to a number data type?

```
int a = 7;
string b = "7";
bool c = a == (int)b;
// Cannot convert type 'string' to 'int'
```

No, there's no built-in method to allow us to change a string data type into an int or any other number type. Therefore, type conversion has limitations. However, don't let this get in your way. Comparing values should used with like types to begin with. What else can we compare?

```
GameObject a = GameObject.CreatePrimitive(PrimitiveType.Capsule);
GameObject b = GameObject.CreatePrimitive(PrimitiveType.Capsule);
bool c = a == b;
Debug.Log("GameObjects a == b? " + c);
// GameObjects a == b? False
```

What is being compared here? Well, these are two different objects in the scene. Even though they share a good number of attributes, they are not the same object. A clear way to compare two instances of a game object is to use the following fragment:

```
int a_InstanceID = a.GetInstanceID();
int b_InstanceID = b.GetInstanceID();
Debug.Log("a_InstanceID: " + a_InstanceID);
// a_InstanceID: -2500
// though the number itself will change every time you run the game
Debug.Log("b_InstanceID: " + b_InstanceID);
// b_InstanceID: -2510
// though the number itself will change every time you run the game
Debug.Log("GameObjects a_InstanceID == b_InstanceID? " + c);
// GameObjects a_InstanceID == b_InstanceID? False
```

Here we're being more specific as to what we're comparing. If every object in the scene has a unique instance ID, then we're going to more clearly debug and test what's being compared when we need to check objects in the scene for matches. When we compare objects in the scene, which don't have a clear comparison, there's usually a method to allow us to make a more readable difference between objects.

```
GameObject a = GameObject.CreatePrimitive(PrimitiveType.Capsule);
GameObject b;
b = a;
bool c = a == b;
Debug.Log("GameObject a == b? " + c);
// GameObject a == b? True
```

In this case, yes, they are the same object, so the behavior is correct. However, again we should do the following to ensure that we're comparing something more easily debugged.

```
GameObject gameObject = GameObject.CreatePrimitive(PrimitiveType.Capsule);
int a = gameObject.GetInstanceID();
int b;
b = a;
bool c = a == b;
Debug.Log("InstanceIDs a == b? " + c);
// InstanceIDs a == b? True
```

It's always important to understand what our code is doing. Comparing types between one another is useful for a multitude of situations. Checking for projectile types on targets, puzzle pieces types, or specific environment props.

In the case where we are looking to see if they are GameObjects, we'd need to check for type. This means that we can make sure that we're looking for GameObjects. To do this, we need to check if one object's type matches another object's type.

```
GameObject a = GameObject.CreatePrimitive(PrimitiveType.Capsule);
GameObject b = GameObject.CreatePrimitive(PrimitiveType.Capsule);
Type aType = a.GetType();
Type bType = b.GetType();
bool c = aType == bType;
Debug.Log("aType: " + aType + " bType: " + bType + " aType == bType? " + c);
// aType: UnityEngine.GameObject bType: UnityEngine.GameObject aType == bType? True
```

There is a very important difference here. We're starting with two GameObjects. This allows us many more options than an int type. GameObjects may have many components or scripts attached for more specific comparisons.

```
GameObject a = GameObject.CreatePrimitive(PrimitiveType.Capsule);
a.AddComponent<ZombieComponent>();
// check if the GameObject a is a zombie by looking for the attached zombie component
ZombieComponent component = a.GetComponent<ZombieComponent>();
Type b = component.GetType();
Type c = typeof(ZombieComponent);
bool d = b == c;
Debug.Log("b type: " + b + "c type: " + c + "b == c?" + d);
```

Using `AddComponent()` we attach a `ZombieComponent`: `Monobehaviour` to the instance of a GameObject when the game is started. To follow up we then ask the GameObject if it has a ZombieComponent attached using the `GetComponent()` function. Then we check the type of the component and compare it to the `typeof(ZombieComponent)` and we get `True`.

In Unity 3D when collisions occur between game objects that have physics components attached, the `OnCollisionEnter()` event will provide the GameObjects that are involved in the collision. To discover what hit the GameObject you use the same `GetComponent()` and take action based on the presence of specific attached scripts. The significant take-away here is the fact that the type of data in memory has a type, rather, a form or shape that each data has in the computer's memory.

We've come to expect the names of some objects are what we have written them as. When we write the type of an int to the console with `Debug`.

```
System.Int32 a = 1;
int b = 3;
bool c = a.GetType() == b.GetType();
Debug.Log("a == b? " + c);
// "a == b? True

System.Single d = 1.0f;
float e = 3.0f;
bool f = d.GetType() == e.GetType();
Debug.Log("d == e? " + f);
// "d == e? True
```

The fragment is showing that the `System.Int32` and `int` are equivalent types. So too are the `System.Single` and the float. These certainly act the same, but how are they being created with different names to define the same type?

6.21.3 Type Aliasing

We could use the above code in place of float, but float is the naming convention that started with C#. Therefore, we'll give in to convention and use float rather than System.Single, even though both are acceptable by C#. The word float came from someone early on in C# who decided to add a type alias. We can add our own type aliases with a using statement.

```
using MyOwnType = System.Int16;
/*    new name for an old type */
```

Along with the directives at the top of the TypesAndOperatives.cs file, we can add in another using directive. Adding using MyOwnType, we can assign it to System.Int16; which turns our identifier MyOwnType into a System.Int16.

```
MyOwnType a = 1;
Debug.Log("a is a: " + a.GetType());
// "a is a: System.Int16"
```

Using the above fragment tells us that the type of a is a System.Int16.

Therefore, the float was assigned to System.Single somewhere in the depths of Unity 3D. It's unlikely that we're going to find out where the convention of using float is a Single, but it's important to know how the keyword was assigned. The fact is that the float keyword, even though it has become superfluous in programming, is still just the alias given to a System.Single.

Likewise, int or double, and some other keywords we commonly use are just aliases to simplify our code. Other systems have aliased the system types with words such as bigint, smallint, and tinyint as mappings to different numbers of bytes held for the integer value.

Therefore, now that we know a bit where types come from and how to convert one type into another, it's time to put this to some use.

6.21.4 Boxing and Unboxing

Boxing is the term that programmers use when a generic container is used to assign a multitude of types. Once it's discovered what has been "put in a box," we can decide what to do next. When the data is pulled from the variable, you "unbox" the data once you know what it is and what to do with it.

Back when we created the HumanWithStates we had it inherit from the ZombieWithStates. It's possible to describe the HumanWithStates as a ZombieWithStates with new features. Because of this we can assign any child of a type to its parent.

```
GameObject a = GameObject.CreatePrimitive(PrimitiveType.Capsule);
// remember, HumanWithStates : ZombieWithStates?
ZombieWithStates b = a.AddComponent<HumanWithStates>();
/*         ↑                                    ↑         */
/*         └──────────────────────────┬─────────┘         */
/*                            │                           */
/*                    ┌───────┴──────────┐                */
/*                    │types don't match │                */
/*                    │but HumanWithStates│               */
/*                    │inherits from     │                */
/*                    │ZombieWithStates  │                */
/*                    └──────────────────┘                */
```

Like the `HumanWithStates` inherited from `ZombieWithStates`, the `ZombieWithStates` inherited from `MonoBehaviour`. And so, a `ZombieWithStates` can be assigned to a `MonoBehaviour` type object.

```
GameObject c = GameObject.CreatePrimitive(PrimitiveType.Capsule);
MonoBehaviour d = c.AddComponent<ZombieWithStates>();
/*         ↑                                    ↑         */
/*         └────────────────────────────────────┘         */
/*                            │                            */
/*              ┌─────────────────────────┐               */
/*              │types don't match        │               */
/*              │either but               │               */
/*              │ZombieWithStates         │               */
/*              │inherits from            │               */
/*              │MonoBehaviour            │               */
/*              └─────────────────────────┘               */
```

This also means that since everything we've been seeing so far inherit from object, we can assign anything to an object.

```
object e = GameObject.CreatePrimitive(PrimitiveType.Capsule);
/* ↑          ↑                                       */
/* └──────────┘                                       */
/*      │                                             */
/* ┌─────────────────────┐                            */
/* │GameObject inherits  │                            */
/* │from object          │                            */
/* │but every class in   │                            */
/* │C# inherits from     │                            */
/* │object!              │                            */
/* └─────────────────────┘                            */
object f = 1;
object g = 1.0f;
object h = new object[] {1, 1.0f, e, d, c, b, a};
```

In this case we have e d c b and a being the objects we've been using in the previous two code fragments as well as an int 1 and a float 1.0f. Notice the last line. We've assigned object h to an array object[]. If we think carefully about what's going on here object[] and object should be different types.

```
object h = new object[] {1, 1.0f, e, d, c, b, a};
Debug.Log("what is h really? " + h);
// what is h really? System.Object[]
```

The `Debug.Log` tells us that object h is actually a `System.Object[]`, so it is indeed an array "boxed" in object. To unbox the array from object we use the as `object[]` operator.

```
object[] objArray = h as object[];
foreach(object o in objArray)
{
    Debug.Log("got object from objArray: " + o);
}
```

To discover the type hidden in the box we need to check the type assigned as an object.

```
foreach(object o in objArray)
{
    if(o is GameObject)
    {
        Debug.Log("got a GameObject!");
    }
}
// got a GameObject!
// got a GameObject!
// got a GameObject!
```

The use of the `is` operator can be used to compare the type of object. In the case here we check if object o in the objArray is `GameObject`. If the statement is true then we print "got a GameObject!" and we get that printed to the console three times. Since e c and a are GameObjects, this is correct. Something that might surprise you are the things in the Scene you might not know about.

```
UnityEngine.Object[] allObjectsInTheScene = FindObjectsOfType<UnityEngine.Object>();
foreach(UnityEngine.Object o in allObjectsInTheScene)
{
    Debug.Log("Object: " + o);
}
```

The fragment above exposes the hidden objects lurking in the scene. Objects like the NavMeshSettings, LightMapSettings, RenderSettings, StreamingManager, and ResourceManagers are all working in the shadows of your scene. It's also important to note that object and Object are not the same thing. `System.object` and `UnityEngine.Object` do conflict on some level. The UnityEngine version has more to do with the actual game engine itself.

The system version has more to do with data types that even `UnityEngine.Object` inherit from. Unfortunately, the function `FindObjectsOfType()` comes from the UnityEngine. Because of this it's a feature that doesn't exist in `System.object`. The features you're allowed to do with boxing are limited to the eldest parent.

6.22 Operator Overloading

With all of the work we did discovering types and seeing how they can be interchanged it's important to see how they can be used a bit more definitively. In cases like ints floats and the like, we can apply math operators. Both int and float are types that inherit from object.

What happens if you'd like to do something specific when you add one zombie to another? Operators, like anything else it seems in C#, can have additional functionality added to them. When it comes to dealing with new classes, we need to manage data using methods which we feel fit. In most cases, operator overloading should be considered a bit like voodoo.

```
Zombie a = new Zombie();
Zombie b = new Zombie();
Zombie c = a + b;
// Operator + cannot be applied to operands of type 'Zombie' and 'Zombie'
```

In a more practical sense, a puzzle game could have a special class used to handle each puzzle piece. To facilitate how the puzzle combines points and position, the class could store an x and y position as well as a point value.

```
public class Puzzle
{
    public int x;
    public int y;
    public int points;
}
```

Operator overloading of a non-numerical value can result in a loss of readability. For purposes of learning how to do this, we'll ignore this. In most cases math operations should be deployed on the number values in a class. When it makes sense, math operations can be used on a new class with a reasonable outcome.

6.22.1 A Basic Example

With the Operator Over loading script in the Operator Over loading_Scene from the Operator Over loading Game Object, lets skip down to the public class Puzzle. In the class we have a new function signature.

```
/*                                                                    */
/* |Accessibility|static means    |return type  |indicates we |the operator|*/
/* |             |the function is |the addition |will override|to be       |*/
/* |             |available to all|of a puzzle  |an operator  |over-ridden |*/
/* |             |objects of this |to a puzzle  |             |            |*/
/* |             |type            |is another   |             |            |*/
/* |             |                |puzzle       |             |            |*/
/* |             |                |             |             |            |*/
/* |             |                |             |             |            |*/
/* |             |                |             |             |            |*/
/* |             |                |             |             |            |*/
/* |             |                |             |             |            |*/
/*       ↓            ↓              ↓            ↓           ↓             */
        public static Puzzle operator + (Puzzle a, Puzzle b)
        {
            Puzzle p = new Puzzle()
            {
                x = a.x + b.x,
                y = a.y + b.y,
                points = a.points + b.points
            };
            return p;
        }
```

In the class structure, a new function to add Puzzle pieces together requires a new syntax. The important new parts is the operator + section of the function. The function parameters are the operands to be added. The keywords public and static relate to the accessibility of the function and the Puzzle keyword indicates the return type of the function.

To create a `Puzzle` object to return we add the members of each parameter argument together to create the new `Puzzle` object.

```
Puzzle a = new Puzzle()
{
    x = 1,
    y = 2,
    points = 1
};
Puzzle b = new Puzzle()
{
    x = 0,
    y = 1,
    points = 3
};
Puzzle c = a + b;
Debug.Log("c.x: " + c.x + " c.y: " + c.y + " c.points: " + c.points);
// c.x: 1 c.y: 3 c.points: 4
```

When we add Puzzle a to Puzzle b we get Puzzle c, the result as indicated by the operation when Puzzle p was created in the operator override function. Conceptually there are now three Puzzle objects in existence, one for each operand, a and b, and one for the result of the addition, c. After they're used and the addition is finished, unless you store the result, all three are deleted once the function they are used in is complete.

By including a + override we should also include the – override as well. Just because a + was created for the class doesn't necessarily dictate that a – override should exist. The string class has a + but no – because it's not as obvious as what to do when you subtract a string from another string.

```
public static Puzzle operator -(Puzzle a, Puzzle b)
{
    Puzzle p = new Puzzle()
    {
        x = a.x - b.x,
        y = a.y - b.y,
        points = a.points - b.points
    };
    return p;
}
```

6.22.2 Overloading*

We're not restricted to overloading a class by a class. We can overload our Puzzle operator * with a number. To double a Puzzle piece we could conceptually use the following:

```
public static Puzzle operator *(Puzzle a, int b)
{
    Puzzle p = new Puzzle()
    {
        x = a.x * b,
        y = a.y * b,
        points = a.points * b
    };
    return p;
}
```

In the above example, we take `Puzzle` a and multiply it by `int` b. To make use of the new operator, our code would have to look something like the following:

```
Puzzle a = new Puzzle() { x = 1, y = 2, points = 3 };
int b = 3;
Puzzle c = a * b;
Debug.Log("c.x: " + c.x + " c.y: " + c.y + " c.points: " + c.points);
// c.x: 3 c.y: 6 c.points: 9
```

In this case, `c = a * b;` takes the original and then multiplies it by 3 and assigns the new value to `c`. Another effect of using the `*` with an int in the override is the ability to use the `*=` operator.

```
c *= 3;
Debug.Log("c.x: " + c.x + " c.y: " + c.y + " c.points: " + c.points);
// c.x: 9 c.y: 18 c.points: 27
```

This might bring up the question, can we use `+=` as well?

```
public static Puzzle operator +(Puzzle a, int b)
{
    Puzzle p = new Puzzle()
    {
        x = a.x + b,
        y = a.y + b,
        points = a.points + b
    };
    return p;
}
```

Using a different set of parameters we can add the ability to add an int to the values of the `Puzzle`.

```
c += 1;
Debug.Log("c.x: " + c.x + " c.y: " + c.y + " c.points: " + c.points);
// c.x: 10 c.y: 19 c.points: 28
```

The result of adding 1 to all the values in the Puzzle has the effect you might guess when used. The utility of adding 1 to all three members of Puzzle might be questionable, but certainly it could be used for only the points. The problem with this becomes more apparent once we start using them. If we assumed `c += 1` was only to be used to add value to the points we could do such a thing. We could also assume that adding puzzle `c += a` Vector2Int could just modify two of the parameters in the Puzzle object.

```
public static Puzzle operator +(Puzzle a, Vector2Int b)
{
    Puzzle p = new Puzzle()
    {
        x = a.x + b.x,
        y = a.y + b.y,
        points = a.points
    };
    return p;
}
```

We can omit adding a value to a.points, but we do need to include a.points in new Puzzle p before returning it. Otherwise the new value after the + operation will have 0 points. A revised version of the + overload should look like the following as well.

```
public static Puzzle operator +(Puzzle a, int b)
{
    Puzzle p = new Puzzle()
    {
        //x = a.x + b,
        //y = a.y + b,
        x = a.x,
        y = a.y,
        points = a.points + b
    };
    return p;
}
```

With the modifications to the code, we're now able to move puzzle objects around with a Vector2Int and adjust the values with a single int. Conceptually keeping track of what's going on can be difficult. Adding, multiplying, and incrementing in different ways with different values is confusing. This means that we've lost some readability; not always the best option. However, in light of this, does this mean we should never use operator overloading? The readability of the code is the only thing we need to question.

Up until recently there wasn't a Vector2Int object available in Unity 3D, there was only Vector2 which uses float values for x and y. Puzzle game authors often created their own version of Vector2Int to help facilitate keeping objects in a grid. This meant replicating the available operator overrides in Vector2 for their own integer version of the same function. Perhaps if you were to require a specific type for your own game it's important to understand how to write operator overrides.

In addition to the previous examples using + and *, we can also overload the true and false keywords. For operators such as > and <, we can test if one puzzle object is more valuable than another.

6.22.3 Overloading < and >

Rather than returning a new Puzzle, operators return a bool value. The operators < and > can be overridden to return a true or false value. The code fragment that accomplishes this is as follows:

```
public static bool operator <(Puzzle a, Puzzle b)
{
    return a.points < b.points;
}
```

Before we can use this, Unity 3D will likely remind us that we're forgetting something with the following error message: "The operator 'OperatorOverloading.Puzzle.operator <(OperatorOverloading.Puzzle, OperatorOverloading.Puzzle)' requires a matching operator '>' to also be defined."

```
public static bool operator >(Puzzle a, Puzzle b)
{
    return a.points > b.points;
}
```

To comply, we'll add in the opposite version of the less than < operator overload. A quick copy/paste and a replacement of less than < to greater than > is all it takes to allow us to use the less than < and greater than > overload.

To continue with our example, we can use the following few statements to check if our overload is working.

```
Puzzle a = new Puzzle() { points = 1 };
Puzzle b = new Puzzle() { points = 7 };
bool c = a > b;
Debug.Log("a > b? " + c);
// a > b? False

bool d = a < b;
Debug.Log("a < b? " + d);
// a < b? True
```

The initialization of the Puzzle sets points for a to 1 and b to 7. Then Puzzle object a does indeed have fewer points than Puzzle b. In this if statement, we do get a is not greater than b, and a is less than b.

However, you decide to use overloaded operators is left to how you've decided to work with your classes. In many cases, if you find yourself comparing a few variables between two objects of the same class to execute some block of code, then you should consider using an operator overload. Likewise, if you find yourself adding multiple things together using the + for multiple attributes, then that's another candidate for an overload.

6.22.4 What We've Learned

With all of what we just learned, you should be able to see how overriding less than < and greater than > can be useful in terms of sorting. You'd be able to make a sort based on specific properties between classes. Comparing distances and threat levels can be a very interesting behavior.

Some of what we're doing here is a bit awkward and mostly contrived. In general, greater than > and less than < should be used to compare more numeric values. In the above code, comparing two zombies directly is misleading. Are we comparing size, armor, and number of brains eaten? It's impossible to know with the operator alone. In this case, a.armor > b.armor would make far more sense.

It's important to always leave the code in a readable state. Simply comparing two classes against one another makes it impossible to know exactly what it is we're comparing. This also goes for any other math operator. In general, math operations are best suited for numbers, not zombies.

6.23 Controlling Inheritance

Understanding the details of inheritance is key to using any object-oriented programming (OOP). Polymorphism, specialization, and encapsulation are considered the three pillars of OOP. Polymorphism is related to how classes inherit traits from one another. To be fair, some consider inheritance as a pillar on its own.

If someone needs to add behaviors to a class, but you require something like movement to remain consistent between all characters in your game, then you'll have to implement various systems to keep people from breaking your code. A sealed class, often referred to as a final class, cannot be inherited from. This sort of data ends the line as far as inheritance is concerned. This class is used when you want to finalize a class and prevent any further inheritance.

The common metaphor used to describe inheritance is a family tree; however, what more closely describes class inheritance is biological classification or scientific taxonomy. This is a system to organize and categorize organisms into groups such as species, family, and class. Each category is a taxonomic rank.

To biologists the species *Agaricus bisporus,* the average button mushroom, belongs to the genus *Agaricus* of the family Agaricaceae of the order Agaricales in the phylum Basidiomycota in the kingdom Fungi. That's quite a mouthful, even if you don't like them on pizza.

In a very similar way, when you create a Zombie: MonoBehaviour, you are creating a class Zombie based on MonoBehaviour, Behaviour, Component, Object, and object. Notice that Object with an upper-case O is based on object with a lowercase o.

In this ranking and categorizing of mushrooms and zombies, the hierarchy that is formed means there are common traits shared among objects. A death cap mushroom is a fungus like a button mushroom. Both share common traits, reproduce by spreading spores, and have similar structures made of chitin. One of these makes pizza deadly, and the other just makes pizza yummy.

In a similar way, all of the classes we've written based on MonoBehaviour share common features, for example, `Start()` and `Update()`. From Behavior, they are inherit enabled. From Component, they inherit various messaging and component properties. `UnityEngine.Object` gives them the ability to instantiate or destroy themselves and find one another. Finally, System.object gives them all `ToString()`.

Nature might take eons to create a new class of life. For a programmer, a new class in Unity 3D just takes a few mouse clicks. Programmers also have the ability to override how inherited functions behave. However, unexpected behaviors usually result in bugs. To control this, it's best to put preventative measures around inherited functions through encapsulation and special controls.

6.23.1 Sealed

The sealed prefix to a function is one of the systems that allows you to control how a function is inherited. Once you've written a well-constructed class, it's a good idea to go back and prevent anyone from breaking it. The sealed keyword prevents a class member from being misused by a child inheriting the member.

One commonly written class is a timer. The timer should have some features such as setting the length of time for the timer, asking for how much time is left, pausing and restarting the timer, and events for when the timer ends and starts.

If you want all of the timers to behave exactly the same, then you'll have to prevent anyone from making any unnecessary modifications to the timer class. This is why they need to be sealed. A sealed class is meant to prevent any further modifications from the point where it has been sealed.

6.23.1.1 A Basic Example

Adding in the sealed keyword before the class keyword does the trick. Once this is added, no class can inherit from the class. In the ControllingInheritance_Scene open the ControllingInheritance script on the appropriately named game object.

```
sealed class FinalizedObject
{
}

class InheritFromSealed : FinalizedObject
{
}
/* cannot derive from sealed type 'ControllingInheritance.FinalizedObject' */
```

Once in place, you can create another class in an attempt to inherit from it. The following class tries to inherit from the sealed class. It would be easy to remove the sealed keyword from the class and open it up for basing more classes on it. However, this does inform you that you are indeed making a change that isn't intended. This behavior is meant to limit the amount of tampering of a class written to do something specific. Usually, classes written with sealed are for very basic and very widely available functions that shouldn't require any other class to inherit from it.

We do have one option open to us in order to add additional functionality to a sealed class.

6.23.2 Extension Functions

An Extension is a secondary class that contains a function that we intend to use to add to a sealed class.

```
static class FinalizedObjectExtension
{
    public static void ExtensionFunction(this FinalizedObject finalObj)
    {
        Debug.Log("Extending the finalizedObject.");
    }
}
```

A static class means that the class members are available globally. This is required such that the ExtensionFunction is available to any FinalizedObject. The first argument to the ExtensionFunction is this FinalizedObject finalObj where this indicates that the function relates to the FinalizedObject identified as finalObj. To use the ExtensionFunction as a member of the sealed class use the regular dot operator as though it were a member of the FinalizedObject.

```
void UsingControllingInheritance()
{
    FinalizedObject finalizedObject = new FinalizedObject();
                                          /*               |      */
    finalizedObject.ExtensionFunction();/*←───────────┘      */
    /*                          ↑                            */
}   /*                          |                            */
    /*           ┌──────────────────────────────┐           */
    /*           |function not actually written in|          */
    /*           |the FinalizedObject class.       |          */
    /*           └──────────────────────────────┘           */
```

The instance of the FinalizedObject identified as finalizedObject has access to the new ExtensionFunction() which was written in the static class FinalizedObjectExtension. To add parameters to the function you'd add them after the first argument.

```
public static void AnotherExtension(this FinalizedObject finalObj, int someArg)
{
    Debug.Log("AnotherExtension: " + someArg);
}
```

In the above, someArg takes an int and adds it to the end of the Debug.Log output. To make things more interesting, it's possible to add extensions to other classes in the same FinalizedObjectExtension static class.

```
sealed class AnotherSealedClass
{
    public void SealedFunction(int sealedArg)
    {
        Debug.Log("SealedFunctions's sealedArg:" + sealedArg);
    }
}
```

With the addition of AnotherSealedClass, we've also added a function which prints out an input argument. An extension can access the members of the class in the body of the extended function.

```
public static void AnotherExtension(this FinalizedObject finalObj, int someArg)
{
    Debug.Log("AnotherExtension: " + someArg);
}

public static void AnotherExtension(this AnotherSealedClass anotherClass, int anotherArg)
{
    anotherClass.SealedFunction(anotherArg);
}
```

The second version of `AnotherExtension` just changes the type for the first argument. In technical terms it's the same function with a different signature, this is allowed since it's now a regular function override.

```
finalizedObject.AnotherExtension(7);
// AnotherExtension: 7

AnotherSealedClass another = new AnotherSealedClass();
another.AnotherExtension(3);
//SealedFunctions's sealedArg:3
```

In the same `FinalizedObjectExtension` static class the `ExtendingAnotherSealedClass` function uses a different signature. This allows for both the first example of the finalized object and the `anotherSealedClass` to have access to a similarly named `AnotherExtension()` extension function.

    The key notion is that a class that is widely available should be stable and unchanging. Reliability is key for preventing too many bugs from creeping into your code. The different accessibility modifications such as sealed are intended to help prevent unexpected behavior. Of course, this doesn't by any stretch of the imagination mean that it prevents bugs completely.

6.23.3 Abstract

If a sealed class means it's not intended to be extended upon, an abstract is the opposite. An abstract is a class which is required to be extended. The abstract keyword is used to tell inheriting classes that there's a function they need to implement. If you forget to implement a function that was marked as abstract, Unity 3D will remind you and throw an error.

6.23.3.1 A Basic Example

To inform another programmer or yourself that you need to implement a specific function, the abstract keyword is used. Setting up a class to inherit from helps you plan your classes and how the classes are intended to be used.

```
abstract class BaseCounter
{/*     ↑                                    */
  /*     └──────────────────────┐ ┌──────────┐ */
    public int Counter;/*  ├─┤abstract  │ */
    /*         ┌──────────────┤ │declaration│ */
    /*         │              │ └──────────┘ */
    /*         ↓                              */
    public abstract void IncrementCounter();
}
```

An `abstract` `BaseCounter` class has a defined abstract void `IncrementCounter();` created. As a class implements the `BaseCoutner`, Visual Studio immediately warns you to Implement Abstract Class.

```
class ImplementsCounter : BaseCounter
{

}
```

The implementation uses override to indicate it's implementing the abstract function. If you add a body to the abstract function another error comes up to tell you a body for an abstract function is not allowed.

```
public abstract void IncrementCounter()
{
}
```

void BaseCounter.IncrementCounter()

'ControllingInheritance.BaseCounter.IncrementCounter()' cannot declare a body because it is marked abstract

The `abstract` keyword implies that the function declared is to be implemented by its inheriting class. The programmer implementing from the `BaseClass` there are important functions which must be filled in. The implementation, however, is left up to the author of the inheriting class.

This only means to inform you that you cannot implement an abstract function. You must rely on a child class making the implementation. The intent here is to provide a clear and specific structure for all classes inheriting from the `BaseClass`. This assumes there is a common structure between all the classes using the abstract class.

To continue, we should make a sibling class similar to ChildClass with a different implementation of the `IncrementCounter()` call.

```
public override void IncrementCounter()
{
    Counter++;
    Debug.Log("Counter: " + Counter);
}
```

With this we increment `Counter` by 1 each time the function is called. The `UseCounter()` function is called in `Start()`, and we get some numbers going up.

```csharp
void UseCounter()
{
    ImplementsCounter counter = new ImplementsCounter();
    counter.IncrementCounter();
    counter.IncrementCounter();
    counter.IncrementCounter();
    counter.IncrementCounter();
    counter.IncrementCounter();
}
```

This results in the following Console output:

```
Counter: 1
UnityEngine.Debug:Log(Object)

Counter: 2
UnityEngine.Debug:Log(Object)

Counter: 3
UnityEngine.Debug:Log(Object)

Counter: 4
UnityEngine.Debug:Log(Object)

Counter: 5
UnityEngine.Debug:Log(Object)
```

If the classes are considered final, they can be sealed.

```csharp
sealed class ImplementsCounter : BaseCounter
{
    public override void IncrementCounter()
    {
        Counter++;
        Debug.Log("Counter: " + Counter);
    }
}
```

This means that the IncrementsCounter can no longer be derived from. However, this doesn't apply any sibling that hasn't been sealed. A sibling is considered a branch from BaseClass. C# is informing us that it cannot create an instance of the abstract class or interface BaseClass. An interface works in a similar way to an abstract class, but with a few more restrictions. All these mechanisms are there to prevent problematic issues that have come up with different languages. We'll get into the hows and whys of the interface in Section 7.6.4.

6.23.4 Abstract: Abstract

The Abstract topic should be expanded to look at additional abstract classes inheriting from abstract classes. These can be used to add more diversity to a simple base class. By creating a branch that is also abstract, you can add more data fields and functions to provide a variation on the first idea.

```
abstract class BaseLimitCounter : BaseCounter
{
    public int Limit;
    public abstract bool AtLimit();
    public abstract void SetLimit(int 1);
    public override void IncrementCounter()
    {
        Counter++;
        Debug.Log("Counter: " + Counter);
    }
}
class LimitCounter : BaseLimitCounter
{
    public override bool AtLimit()
    {
        return Counter >= Limit;
    }

    public override void SetLimit(int 1)
    {
        Limit = 1;
    }
}
```

The key function behind using abstract classes is to create a commonality between all the deriving classes. They'll all use the same `IncrementCounter()` function. `BaseLimitCounter` implements the `IncrementCounter()` function the same as any other class based on the `BaseCounter` abstract class.

Organizationally, `LimitCounter` only has two new functions. A check to see if we're at the limit and a function to set the limit. By breaking up the classes into separate files we've kept the amount of code contained in each class to a minimum. This prevents a single class from becoming overly complex and allows for focus of purpose. In a team of programmers, separating files also provides a means of isolating work. When multiple people are working on a single file work changes can collide, and work can be lost.

Additional fields and functions are added in the abstract class BaseLimitCounter that is based on the abstract class `BaseCounter`. This avoids making modifications to the BaseCounter, as there might be other classes relying on its stability. Keeping code in use intact is necessary to avoid conflict. Modifications to a base could cause problems to ripple through the rest of the project.

The implementation the abstract member `AtLimit();` and `SetLimit(int)` means that we get to keep our current implementation of `IncrementCounter()` and we need to add only the missing functions.

```
void UseLimitCounter()
{
    LimitCounter limitCounter = new LimitCounter();
    limitCounter.SetLimit(3);
    Debug.Log("at limit: " + limitCounter.AtLimit());
    // "at limit: False"
    limitCounter.IncrementCounter();//already implemented in BaseLimitCounter
    // "Counter: 1"
    limitCounter.IncrementCounter();
    // "Counter: 2"
    limitCounter.IncrementCounter();
    // "Counter: 3"
    Debug.Log("at limit: " + limitCounter.AtLimit());
    // "at limit: True"
}
```

6.23.5 Putting This to Use

We'll start with a construct that's used often for many different game systems.

```
abstract class BaseTimer
{
    public float EndTime;
    public float Timer;
    public abstract void SetTime(float time);
    public abstract void BeginTimer();
    public abstract bool Ended();
}
```

An `abstract` `BaseTimer` gives us a few abstract members to work with. The three functions will set when the timer will end, when it begins and whether or not it's ended. Also in the `BaseTimer` class is a float variable for the `Timer` and the `EndTime` values.

The implementation of this abstract class is called `GameTimer`, in which we can set a number of seconds and check for the `Ended()` boolean to become true.

```
class GameTimer : BaseTimer
{
    public override void SetTime(float time)
    {
        throw new System.NotImplementedException();
    }

    public override void BeginTimer()
    {
        throw new System.NotImplementedException();
    }

    public override bool Ended()
    {
        throw new System.NotImplementedException();
    }
}
```

The `GameTimer` can make use of Visual Studio's handy auto complete tools which create the appropriate overrides.

```
class GameTimer : BaseTimer
{
    public override void SetTime(float time)
    {
        Timer = time;
        Debug.Log("GameTimer set for: " + Timer + " seconds.");
    }

    public override void BeginTimer()
    {
        EndTime = Time.fixedTime + Timer;
        Debug.Log("GameTimer EndTime: " + EndTime);
    }

    public override bool Ended()
    {
        return Time.fixedTime >= EndTime;
    }
}
```

Each function requires thought as to how best implement each function. The intent of each function can be interpreted by the engineer. What's important is that the class works as expected, not necessarily how it works.

The SetTime assigns the argument time to the Timer value. This value doesn't change unless SetTime is used again to change the Timer's value. The BeginTimer function sets the EndTime to the current time with the addition of the Timer's value. So if the Timer was set to 3 seconds the EndTime becomes now + three seconds, or Three seconds from now. Finally the Ended() function checks if the current time is equal or exceeded the EndTime value. The function returns false so long as the current time is less than the EndTime value.

To use the new class it's instanced when the game begins using a Start() in a MonoBehaviour script in the scene. A gameTimer object is stored in the script and is assigned a new instance of the GameTimer class.

```
GameTimer gameTimer;
void UseGameTimer()
{
    gameTimer = new GameTimer();
    gameTimer.SetTime(3);
    gameTimer.BeginTimer();
}
```

The Update() then checks on every frame for the timer's Ended() function. By opting to not inherit from MonoBehaviour, GameTimer class doesn't need to rely on its own Update() function. As the class it's used in checks with an Update() the GameTimer ultimately gets updated every frame.

```
void Update()
{
    if (gameTimer.Ended())
    {
        Debug.Log("GameTimer Ended.");
    }
}
```

Once the gameTime.Ended() returns true we log "GameTimer Ended." Running the scene will instance the GameTimer as soon as the scene starts. Three seconds later the GameTimer Ended will repeat in the Console window.

6.23.6 What We've Learned

We can continue to make variations on the BaseTimer class easily. We could make an implementation which returns true until the timer has ended. All we'd have to do is switch one operator in the Ended().

```
class NotGameTimer : GameTimer
{
    public override bool Ended()
    {
        return !(Time.fixedTime >= EndTime);
    }
}
```

The only function that we need to override in NotGameTimer is the Ended() function. When NotGameTimer inherits from GameTimer, both the BeginTimer and SetTime functions are already in place.

```
notGameTimer = new NotGameTimer();
notGameTimer.SetTime(3);
notGameTimer.BeginTimer();
```

The Update() function in the script in use in the scene checks with a very similar if statement.

```
if (notGameTimer.Ended())
{
    Debug.Log("NotGameTimer has not Ended");
}
```

As soon as the BeginTimer() function is called, the notGameTimer.Ended() is true until the time ends. Making minor changes to a class built around inheriting functions makes testing and creating new behaviors much easier. Any individual change on a base can have wide-reaching problems if unchecked. C# in general is built to allow for these sorts of behaviors, for better or worse.

6.24 Building A Game—Part 5

As we layer more and more behaviors onto the environment or characters in the scene we can begin to see a game take shape. Adding the Damage System to a wall tile makes for instant doors. Monsters can still get in, but it takes longer. Finding what makes a game fun is in part the job of the designer. As a programmer you're integral to finding something interesting and making it into something fun.

6.24.1 Generating Rooms

After building a system to generate a floor it's time to setup a system to build rooms with walls. The floor tile 2D array gives us a grid in which we can cut out rooms. Various systems to build a dungeon level exist, and many examples are available in C#. As a starting point we'll go into some of the basic steps to build a set of room walls.

```
[ExecuteInEditMode]
public class RoomGenerator : MonoBehaviour
{
    public bool GenerateRooms;
    public GameObject WallObject;
    public int RoomCount = 5;
    // minimum is 5.
    public int MaxRoomWidth = 7;
    public int MaxRoomDepth = 7;
    private List<GameObject> WallObjectList;
```

We start with the [ExecuteInEditMode] tag. This allows us to build the rooms and save them in the scene. Tags like this will enable faster testing of the code as well, since we don't need to wait for the game to play to test out the code. Having the editor open while we edit code narrows the iteration time.

```
// Update is called once per frame
void Update()
{
    if (GenerateRooms)
    {
        GenerateRooms = false;

        // clear any walls
        if (WallObjectList != null)
        {
            foreach (GameObject wall in WallObjectList)
            {
                DestroyImmediate(wall);
            }
        }
        // create list to remember objects to clear
        WallObjectList = new List<GameObject>();
```

In the Update() loop a similar bool is used to prevent continuous iterations. We're also creating a list of wall objects that need to be cleared when the generation is redone. DestroyImmediate() is a editor specific function that's used outside of the game play cycle. This skips over the objects OnDestroy() function that might play a particle effect when the object is destroyed. After the objects are cleared, we create a fresh list to populate later in the function.

```
/*        14-6 = 8                             */
/*          × ┌────────┐ ××××                  */
/*        12345678901234                       */
/*      ×1┌──────────────                 Width = 14   */
/*     ┌2│①────┐ ■■■□□□□│          Height = 13   */
/*     │3│ ∘∘∘ │ ■■■□□□□│   ① is the first valid point  */
/*     │4│ ∘∘∘ │ ■■■□□□□│        to start a room.   */
/* 13│5│ ∘∘∘ │ ■■■□□□□│                   */
/* -6│6│ └────┘ ■■■□□□□│                  */
/* ──│7│ ■■■■■■■■■□□□□│   if MaxRoomWidth/Depth = 5   */
/* 7└8│ ■■■■■■■②────┐   ② Last point in the area that  */
/*    ×9│ □□□□□□□│ ∘∘∘ │        can fit a 5x5 room  */
/*    ×0│ □□□□□□□│ ∘∘∘ │                  */
/*    ×1│ □□□□□□□│ ∘∘∘ │                  */
/*    ×2│ □□□□□□□ └────┘                  */
/*    ×3└──────────────                  */
/*                                        */
/* if a room is going to be a                 */
/* maximum size of 5x5 then the               */
/* last point we can select in                */
/* each row is 5 away from the                */
/* edge.                                      */
```

A bit of the logic to picking where to create rooms is diagrammed in the code in the form of a comment. We want to have a max width provided for the room so Something like 7×7 is easy to work with. Next, we'll want to know that each room is started at the same corner. In the diagram it's the top left. This means that we'll want to acknowledge that there's a safe space in which we can create a room.

```
// get some data for floor size
FloorGenerator generator = GetComponent<FloorGenerator>();
// get safe area
int maxW = 1 + generator.Width - MaxRoomWidth;
int maxD = 1 + generator.Depth - MaxRoomDepth;
```

Collect the data required to calculate the safe area. The generator object is the FloorGenerator used in the last chapter to create the floor tiles. This provides us with our maximum size minus the maximum size for a room.

```
for (int i = 0; i < RoomCount; i++)
{
    // a point somewhere in the safe zone
    int x = Random.Range(1, maxW);
    int z = Random.Range(1, maxD);
    MakeRoom(x, z, generator);
}
```

Using the maximum sizes we can populate the scene with the number of rooms requested. The function MakeRoom takes a random position in the safe area and creates a random position in the safe area.

```
void MakeRoom(int x, int z, FloorGenerator generator)
{
    // make a room size startPoint + width/height
    int sizeX = x + Random.Range(5, MaxRoomWidth);
    int sizeZ = z + Random.Range(5, MaxRoomDepth);
```

The MakeRoom function takes the starting point and generates a randomly sized room with a minimum of 5 to the maximum specified in the editor. The size value is then used in an imbedded for loop. The logic starts with the following:

```
// generate walls for the room
for (int sX = x; sX < sizeX; sX++)
{
    for (int sZ = z; sZ < sizeZ; sZ++)
    {
```

A for loop to iterate across and for each step across we step down the Z axis. A check for either the north south edge or the east west edge is made to generate a wall.

```
bool isEdge = sX == x || sX == sizeX - 1 || sZ == z || sZ == sizeZ - 1;
if (isEdge)
{
    GameObject wall = Instantiate(WallObject, transform);
    WallObjectList.Add(wall);
    wall.transform.position = new Vector3()
    {
        x = sX - (generator.Width / 2),
        z = sZ - (generator.Depth / 2)
    };
}
```

The logic for this appears in a long chain of ‖ statements. We check if x is the starting edge or the ending edge. This can also be read as "is left or is top or is bottom or is right"; create wall.

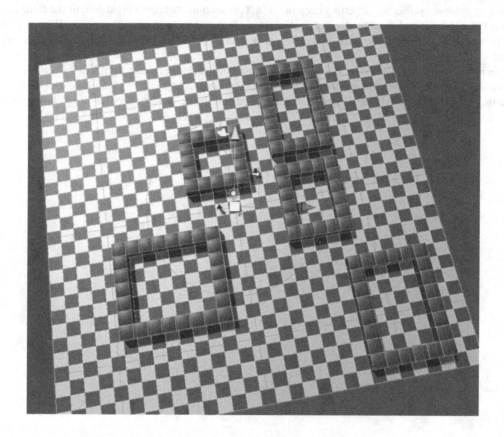

Clicking on the GenerateRooms check box a few times will create overlapping rooms. Fairly often though a random set of rooms that aren't touching can be generated.

More sophisticated systems that do this overlap check can also be created. A system can look at each corner and compare them to other corners to check that the rooms aren't covering the same space. I'll leave that up to you to experiment with.

6.24.2 What We've Learned

Rogue like dungeon generators have plenty of code resources available. Generating rooms with walls is one of the first steps toward a complete dungeon. Next comes adding hallways and doors. Starting with a center point of each room then drawing a line from room to room creates an array for a hallway to be generated from.

The logic required for figure out where to place the walls can be worked out on paper first. The diagrams here are intended to help visualize what the code is going to do. Truth be told, the code here started off as a diagram as what needed to be done before the logic was created to carry out the steps necessary to create the rooms.

6.25 Leveling Up

Building up some skills. We're getting deep into C#. This section contains a great deal of the things that make C# powerful and flexible. A great deal of the code we've learned up to this point allow us to get functional and get some basic work done. Even some of the more complex tasks can be completed with what we already know.

We had a short introduction to the more interesting constructs that make up C#. It's about time we had a short review of constructors, namespaces, and inheritance. We'll also look at more uses of arrays, enums, and goto labels. All these systems make up a part of the skills that every C# programmer uses.

7

Advanced

Chapter 6 was complex and covered many interesting topics. No doubt if you've gotten this far you're willing to find out more about what C# can do. With the content of Chapters 1 through 5, you would be capable of quite a lot. Continue to learn more clever tricks.

Most game logic and control systems need only the fundamentals that have been provided in Chapters 3 through 6. Once the behaviors need more coordinated events and simultaneous actions, you'll need to learn a few more tricks.

To make your work more predictable and to prevent bugs, you'll need practice; there are also some features that make C# more precise. This is to say that you would be able to enforce your own structure to how you allow others to work with your code in the ways you intended.

Since programming is just reading and writing text, there are many things that can go wrong. A simple misspelling or misplaced dot operator can break everything. There are many systems which you can use to help your fellow programmers follow your instructions through how they interact with what you've written.

7.1 What Will Be Covered in This Chapter

Many layers of simple code with layers of basic logic create a complex behavior. C# allows for different ways to keep your code contained in simple classes and functions. Simple classes and functions are easier to write and debug. Complex behaviors required for game interactions come about when you combine many simple behaviors with interesting logic.

We'll look at the following features in this chapter:

- Visual Studio's user interface (UI) and navigation of some of their interface widgets
- Further exploration into comments
- More function overloading
- More on base classes
- Optional parameters in functions' argument lists
- Delegate functions and events
- Class interfaces
- Class constructors again
- Basic preprocessor directives
- Exceptions
- Generics
- Events
- Unity 3D-friendly classes
- Destructors
- Concurrency and coroutines and even threads!
- Dictionary, stack, and queue types
- Callbacks
- Lambda expressions
- Accessors or properties

7.2 Review

In the previous chapter, we looked at some interesting material. We were able to overload the regular + and − with some new functionality. We looked at a few new ways to use the argument list in a function and write a loop.

There are some additional concepts worth mentioning. There are several online articles on the allocation of objects to either the stack or the heap. The heap is built up in order, but isn't rearranged too often.

When objects are added to the heap, the size of the heap grows. When objects are destroyed, they leave holes in the heap. This leaves gaps between the objects that were not deleted. Suppose we have 100 spaces in memory and object A takes up addresses from 1 to 20, B takes up from 21 to 40, and C takes up from 40 to 60. When object B is removed, spaces 21 to 40 are empty, between A and C. If a new object D is only a bit bigger than 20 spaces, say 22, it needs to find the next biggest place at the end, so D uses 61 to 82. If another object D is created, we're out of luck and the game stops running due to lack of memory.

The stack, however, is more organized based on how your code is executed. When a for loop is started, the int i = 0; parameter is always tossed into the top of the stack; as soon as it's no longer needed, it's chopped off, leaving room for the next object to be added to the stack.

In the end, memory management is a result of how you've arranged your data. So long as you use structs to move around large amounts of complex data, you'll most likely be allocating them to the stack. By instancing too many classes, you're leaving yourself to the heap that can eventually lead to memory problems. There is a problem if a stack is passed around in a class, in which case you're still working in the heap.

7.2.1 Moving Forward

We don't want to limit our experiences to the lessons we've just managed to get through. There's still plenty left to learn when it comes to the interesting parts of C#. In this chapter, we'll learn how to make C# bend to our will. Or at the very least, we'll come to understand what some of the more complex concepts look like.

We'll find out more about how functions can have different numbers of arguments. We'll even learn how a variable can be a function. Interfaces are special chunks of classes that serve as a template for other classes to follow. Then we'll look at some more interesting uses of those interfaces.

Later, we'll explore some more possibilities of how arrays can be handled and some simple tricks to make those arrays more manageable. Interfaces come into play again when dealing with arrays. After all, much of what computers are good at is iterating through long lists of data.

Speaking of data, because not all data is the same, we'll need to learn how to make functions more accepting of different types of data and still do what we expect them to. We can generalize functions to operate on practically any type of data.

After this, we'll finish some of the functionality of how C# works and then move on to how to use C# to its fullest. Many of the lessons in the following chapters are transferable to other languages. Modern features such as delegates and lambda functions are common among many other languages. Learning the principles of how modern programming features work in C# is useful in any other modern programming language.

Programming languages are as much about communicating to the computer as they are about conveying your thought process to another programmer reading your code.

7.3 Visual Studio

Visual Studio Community is a free version of the Visual Studio Software which has been in development by Microsoft for a few decades. Previous versions of Unity 3D were bundled with MonoDevelop, which is still an option if you'd like to try it out.

The Visual Studio the Installation app helps install plugins and components. One of the components is the Game development with Unity add-on. In addition to Unity, plenty of other add-ons are available.

Individual components enable development with C++, Python, and F#. This enables web, machine learning, and database software development as well.

Visual Studio has the advantage of being a wide audience and allows you to create software for much more than Unity 3D. Another option is Visual Studio Code, a light weight version of Visual Studio intended initially for Web Development. It's possible to have several integrated development environments (IDEs) installed side-by-side on your computer. To select which IDE is launched from Unity open the Preferences panel:

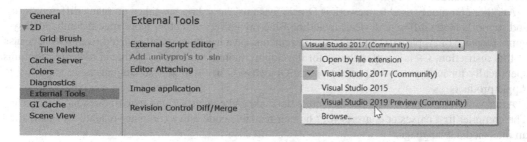

From here select the editor installed, if it's not in the list then you'll need to Select Browse and find the app you intend on using for editing scripts.

The main advantage of using an IDE software like Visual Studio over a plain text editor is a feature called the debugger. Aside from that are other features like syntax highlighting, auto completion, and syntax error checking. The debugger allows you to watch variables update with live values from the game and walk, line at a time, through your code to watch for errors as they happen.

In the coming chapters we'll cover some of the more useful features of your IDE as it's an important part of becoming a skilled game developer. The debugger is also very helpful to learn what your code is doing in a more visual manner.

7.3.1 The Debugger

When your code compiles, your game runs in the editor and you still get unexpected results; what are you to do? The debugger is there to let you see your code in action. Visual Studio has the ability to connect directly to the Unity 3D Editor while your game is running and pause your game as it executes each line of code you've written.

Let's look at how this works.

7.3.2 Mono History

Mono is open-source, free-to-use software. Mono is an implementation of the .NET Framework. Microsoft based their .NET Framework for C# language on the European Association for Standardizing Information and Communication Systems (ECMA). Like many European acronyms, because of language translation, the letters are unrelated to the words in the acronym.

The parts that come together to help build games in Unity are the C# language version and the .NET run time version. Both the language and .NET have different update schedules and version numbers. As of October 2018, .NET was up to version 4.7.2, thus Unity supports version 4.x keeping up with the latest features. C# at the same time saw a release on May 2018, bringing it up to version 7.3 to match features supported in the latest .NET.

As confusing as this might seem, the engineers at Unity are now trying to keep their version of the Unity.NET run-time up to date. Before 2017, this wasn't the case. Unity was using the Mono Runtime, which was behind the official standard, so for several years Unity was stuck on .NET version 2 and many features of the programming language were left out. Thankfully, this is no longer the case.

The Mono compiler was first developed by Miguel de Icaza, Ravi Pratap, Martin Baulig, and Raja Harinath. The compiler had many other contributors that helped improve and standardize how the internals work. Many improvements are continuously added every year.

Unity uses its own .NET run time. The latest version of Unity is compatible with the latest features of the C# language. There are a few things to keep in mind when looking at compatibility across different platforms. Now that you're learning C#, you'll be able to use your new language skills to build apps for practically every modern platform, with caviots.

In an effort to maintain cross-platform compatibility, Unity 3D utilizes Mono 4.x, though this is a recent addition. It's this broad platform compatibility that enables Unity 3D to support practically every form of distribution, including browsers, phones, and the most common PC operating systems.

Another commonly used framework is Oracle Systems' Java. Java has taken on many different forms and supports many different devices, including Blue-ray players and other more specific embedded systems. Because of Apple's strict platform requirements, Java has been greatly barred from iOS. Because of this restriction, C# is a better choice for developing mobile games. If you intend to write programs specifically for iOS, you would need to learn Objective-C or Swift. These languages are exclusive to Apple products.

After you write code, a compiler interprets the code and converts it into machine-readable language. The compiler first parses or converts your human-readable code into a computer-readable format called an intermediate language.

When your code is parsed, it's scanned for errors and syntax. Once this passes, various optimizations are applied. Extraneous comments, unreachable code, and unused variables are omitted during this conversion. Finally, the intermediate language is generated, which is then converted into machine code specific to the central processing unit (CPU) and operating system.

In the case with Unity 3D, the C# compiler eventually builds a file that is compiled just before the game begins. This library works similar to the libraries that you include in your own C# code. Because the code written for Unity 3D is based on MonoBehaviour, Unity 3D is able to make its connections into your code.

You may have become used to the fact that one operating system cannot normally run an application built for another operating system. For instance, you can't natively run an application built for Android on your PC. Even more difficult is emulating another CPU architecture altogether. This is because the binary executable that is produced by a compiler needs to know what to convert your language into ahead of time.

7.4 Function Overloading

Overloading, in the programming sense, means use of the same function name with different parameter values. Functions, so far, have had a single purpose once they're written. This most directly relates to the parameters which we give them. For example, consider the following.

7.4.1 A Closer Look at Functions

Open the FunctionOverloading_Scene and find the script attached to the FunctionOverloading Game Object. If we consider the following code for a moment, it looks like we're trying to write a function that returns half the value of a number fed into the parameter.

```
void UseDifferentFunctions()
{
    int a = 8;
    float b = 7f;
    int halfA = HalfInt(a);
    float halfB = HalfFloat(b);
    Debug.Log("halfA: " + halfA + " halfB: " + halfB);
    // halfA: 4 halfB: 3.5
}

int HalfInt(int a)
{
    return a / 2;
}

float HalfFloat(float a)
{
    return a / 2;
}
```

The function `HalfInt()` accepts an int and returns that int value divided by 2. `HalfFloat()` accepts a float value and returns a float that's half the value fed into its parameter.

What if we wanted to use the same function name for both? This would certainly make remembering the function's name a lot easier. The function name `HalfValue()` would be a lot easier than remembering `HalfInt()`, `HalfFloat()`, `HalfDouble()`, and anything else we might want to divide into two. We're actually allowed to do this quite easily using function overloading.

7.4.1.1 A Basic Example

```
void UseFunctionOverloading()
{
    int a = 8;
    float b = 7f;
    int halfA = HalfValue(a);/* ┌──────────────────┐    */
    float halfB = HalfValue(b);/* ┌─────────────────┐ │   */
    Debug.Log("halfA: " + halfA + " halfB: " + halfB);/* │ │  */
    // halfA: 4 halfB: 3.5                              │
}/*           ┌────────────────────────────────────────┘   */
 /*           ↓  a is an int so it uses this version │   */
int HalfValue(int i)//                                  │   */
{                   //                                   │   */
    return i / 2;   //                                   │   */
}/*           ┌─────────────────────────────────────────┘   */
 /*           ↓ b is a float, so it uses this version    */
float HalfValue(float f)
{
    return f / 2f;
}
```

This code might seem a bit awkward, given in our learning that once an identifier has been used, it can't be used again for a different purpose. In C# we're allowed to do this with functions. This is one of the few places this is allowed. In many cases the return value would be the same as to avoid unexpected return types from a similarly named function.

```
/* Both return int, but use different parameters  */
/*             uses a float                         */
/*                  ↓                               */
int HalfToInt(float f)
{
    return (int)f / 2;
}
/*             uses an int                          */
/*                  ↓                               */
int HalfToInt(int i)
{
    return i / 2;
}
```

In this case the two functions match both input parameters and return values. The only difference is how the value is calculated. In this case, C# will complain that there is no difference between the two functions.

```
int HalfFull(int i)
{
    return i / 2;
}

int HalfFull(int i)
{
    return i * 0.5f;
}
```

7.4.2 Function Signature

Here, we have the same function written twice, but we get an error this time that the function is already defined! And, as a matter of fact, yes, it has already been defined once before. A function is defined by not only its identifier but also its parameters. The function name and its parameter list together are called a *signature*.

The return type is not a part of a function's signature. What this means is best illustrated by the following code fragment.

```
int ReturnValue()
{
    return 1;
}
// return value doesn't count
// as a part of the signature
float ReturnValue()
{
    return 1f;
}
```

Unfortunately, C# isn't smart enough to understand that we're asking for one of two different functions here. Because the return type is not included when looking at a function signature, the two functions look the same to C#. The code fragment above results in an error.

7.4.3 Different Signatures

So far, we've used a single parameter for the above examples. This doesn't need to be the case. We're allowed to use as many different parameters as we require.

```
public static int Overloaded()
{
    return 1;
}
public static int Overloaded(int a)
{
    return a + 1;
}
public static float Overloaded(int a, float b)
{
    return a / b;
}
public void UseOverloads()
{
    int a = Overloaded();
    int b = Overloaded(1);
    float c = Overloaded(1, 3f);
    Debug.Log("a: " + a + " b: " + b + " c: " + c);
}
```

The above code uses no parameters in the first version of the function Overloaded(); this is followed by a single int, and then we're using an int and a float. However, all three of these have return values. Can we do the same with the ref and out as well? Let's add the following code to the versions of the above-mentioned functions and see what happens next.

```
public static void Overloaded(int a, ref float b)
{
    b = (float)a / 3;
}
```

It's important to remember that there are two Overloaded functions that start with int and use a float.

```
float d = 7;            /* initialized to 7                           */
Overloaded(3, d);       /* doesn't use ref in signature               */
Debug.Log("d: " + d);   /* doesn't change from initialized version    */
// d: 7                 /* prints 7 since it didn't get changed       */
Overloaded(3, ref d);   /* this one uses ref which is a different signature */
Debug.Log("d: " + d);   /* d has been modified by ref                 */
// d: 1                 /* prints 1 since it's been modified 3/3      */
```

An int followed by a float will use a different version of the Overloaded function than an int and a ref float.

```
public static double staticDouble;
public static void Overloaded(double d)
{
    staticDouble = d;
}
```

Again, it's important to remember that the use of a 9.0 without the f means a double 9.0 not float 9.0f. So when you use the following:

```
Debug.Log("staticDouble: " + staticDouble);
// staticDouble: 0
Overloaded(9.0);
Debug.Log("staticDouble: " + staticDouble);
// staticDouble: 9
```

We get an expected result of a function that's overloaded to use a double and not a float. A function's signature is a function name and a list of parameters. For a function overload to work, we can use the same function name, but overloads require that each function have the same name but a different parameter list.

Why is this so important; wouldn't using the same name with different results end up being confusing? If the intent remains the same, this is easy to reconcile; we'll see how this works before the end of the chapter.

7.4.4 Putting It Together

By creating functions with overloads, we're allowed to give ourselves some options when using the same function name. Making our code more flexible without adding complexity is possible with very few changes to the function.

```
GameObject CreateObject()
{
    GameObject g = GameObject.CreatePrimitive(PrimitiveType.Cube);
    return g;
}
GameObject CreateObject(PrimitiveType primitive)
{
    GameObject g = GameObject.CreatePrimitive(primitive);
    return g;
}
GameObject CreateObject(PrimitiveType primitive, Vector3 position)
{
    GameObject g = GameObject.CreatePrimitive(primitive);
    g.transform.position = position;
    return g;
}
void UseCreateObject()
{
    GameObject a = CreateObject();
    // makes a cube
    GameObject b = CreateObject(PrimitiveType.Capsule);
    // makes a capsule
    Vector3 position = new Vector3(0, 0, 1f);
    GameObject c = CreateObject(PrimitiveType.Sphere, position);
    // makes a sphere at x:0, y:0, z:1
}
```

This code sample was created for an Example.cs assigned to an object in the scene. I assigned it to the Main Camera in an empty new scene in the Unity 3D editor. There are three versions of `CreateObject()`, each one having a different signature. In the `UseCreateObject()` function, each version is used to demonstrate going from no parameters to two parameters. Of course, you can add as many parameters as you think are manageable.

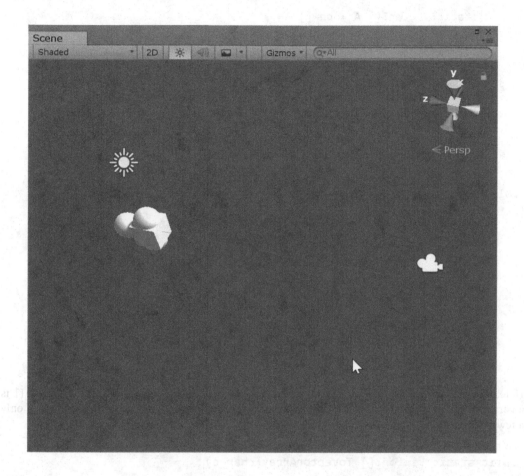

The objects in the image above would be made in the scene based on the three functions we just wrote. We have access to the three objects assigned as a, b, and c in the `Start()` function, so we can make additional changes to them in the `Start()` function.

7.4.5 Not Quite Recursion

Where function overloading becomes interesting is when a function refers to an overloaded version of itself. The logic here is that a function can be accessed in one of two different forms without needing to write another function. The scenario arises when you have a simple function, say, drawing a word to the screen with some debug lines.

The task starts off with drawing a letter, so first we'll want to build a system for storing letters. We'll also want to create some system to give the collection of array points of a letter to whoever is asking for it. We'll start off with two letters; I'll let you figure out the rest on your own.

7.4.6 DrawWords

This DrawWord project example is available with the full alphabet available in the Unity 3D projects downloaded from GitHub along with the rest of the content for this book, but here we'll look at a shorter fragments of the code taken from the DrawWords C# class.

```csharp
public static Vector3[] A = new[]
{
    new Vector3(-1, -1, 0),
    new Vector3(-1, 0, 0),
    new Vector3(0, 1, 0),
    new Vector3(1, 0, 0),
    new Vector3(-1, 0, 0),
    new Vector3(1, 0, 0),
    new Vector3(1, -1, 0)
};

public static Vector3[] B = new[]
{
    new Vector3(-1, -1, 0),
    new Vector3(-1, 1, 0),
    new Vector3(0, 1, 0),
    new Vector3(1, 0, 0),
    new Vector3(-1, 0, 0),
    new Vector3(1, 0, 0),
    new Vector3(1, -1, 0),
    new Vector3(-1, -1, 0)
};
```

Here, we are looking at two letters A and B stored in the form of 3D points in space. The Vector3[] is an array of Vector3s and the A or B identifies the array. They are rather boxy since they're made of only a few points each.

```csharp
public static Vector3[] ToVectorArray(char c)
{
    switch (c)
    {
        case 'A':
            return A;
        case 'B':
            return B;
        OtherLetters
    }
}
```

In the same class is the ToVectorArray returns which set of points based on an incoming type char. We'll look at what a char is in a moment.

```
public static void DrawWord(char c, float scale, Vector3 position, Color color)
{
    Vector3[] lines = ToVectorArray(c);
    for (int i = 1; i < lines.Length; i++)
    {
        Vector3 start = (lines[i - 1] * scale);
        start.x *= spacing;
        Vector3 end = (lines[i] * scale);
        end.x *= spacing;
        Debug.DrawLine(start + position, end + position, color);
    }
}
```

In the above code, the function DrawWord() accepts a char c, as well as a scale, position, and color. This then asks for the lines to draw using the ToVectorArray function. Once the vectors are assigned to the array called lines, the for() loop iterates through each line segment.

The char type is short for character. A char is a single character in a string. Rather, a string is an array of chars. Chars can be only letters, numbers, or symbols; when we use "hello," we are assembling chars to make a word.

For readability, we create a start and an end Vector3 in the for loop. This takes the previous Vector3 and assigns that to start. An important, yet somewhat not-so-obvious, step here is to start the for loop with int i = 1; rather than 0. The start of the line begins with lines [i-1] that means that if the loop begins with i = 0;, the first line point will be lines [-1] that would give us an index out of range error. Remember that an array always starts at 0.

This function isn't only meant to draw a single letter. Instead, we'll write another version of the exact same function with the following code:

```
public static void DrawWord(string word, float scale, Vector3 position, Color color)
{
    //convert to uppercase first
    string uLetters = word.ToUpper();
    char[] letters = uLetters.ToCharArray();
    if (letters.Length > 0)
    {
        for (int i = 0; i < letters.Length; i++)
        {
            float offset = (i * scale);
            Vector3 offsetPosition = new Vector3()
            {
                x = position.x + offset,
                y = position.y,
                z = position.z
            };

            DrawWord(letters[i], scale, offsetPosition, color);
        }
    }
}
```

This version of the same function does a couple of things. First, we change the function's signature, which means that rather than char c as the first parameter, we use string word instead. This changes the signature in such a way that this DrawWord() function is now an overloaded version of the first DrawWord() function. We should convert string word into upper case. This conversion to upper case is necessary to convert any lower case letters to allow the `ToVectorArray()` function to convert each letter to an array of vectors. Once we have the string converted from something like "abba" to "ABBA" by using string `uLetters = word.ToUpper();`, we're ready for the next step.

To convert this string to an array of chars, we use the statement `char[] letters = uLetters. ToCharArray();`, where the `ToCharArray()` function in string returns an array of uppercase chars. So long as the array comes back with at least one result, we continue to the next for loop.

In this for loop, we start at the beginning of the char array. To keep the letters from piling up on top of one another, we create an offset, so each letter can start at a new location. This is done with `float offset = (i * scale);`, which we then use to create a new `offsetPosition Vector3`. The `x` of the `offsetPosition` is the only place where we need this `offset + position.x;` the `y` and `z` will just use the parameter at the beginning of the function.

When we use the overloaded version of the function in the function, we use the char parameter `DrawWord(letters [i], scale, offsetPosition, color);`, where letters `[i]` is passing a char to the function rather than a string. The overloaded version is automatically used.

To see our code in action, add the DrawWords.cs class as a component to the Main Camera in a new scene in the Unity Editor.

```
void UseDrawWords()
{
    DrawWords.DrawWord("Words Are Being Drawn", 1, Vector3.zero, Color.red);
}

private void Update()
{
    UseDrawWords();
}
```

In the `Update()` function we call `UseDrawWords()`. In that function we call `DrawWord()` word at the origin by using `Vector3.zero`, with scale of `1`, `Color.red;`, so they're easier to see.

The `Letters` class is added after the `DrawWords` class in the same file. Make sure that the Gizmos button on the top right of the Game view port is turned on; otherwise, the `Debug.DrawLines()` function will not be visible in the `Game` view panel.

7.4.7 What We've Learned

The above discussion also works as an interesting example of code portability. The `Letters` class is self-contained and doesn't depend on anything other than `UnityEngine` for the `Vector3` data type and the `Debug.DrawLine()` function. Overloading a function should come naturally when you want to use the same function in different ways. This also means that you can simply use `DrawWord('A', 1.0f, new Vector3.zero, Color.red);` to draw a single character.

7.5 Accessors (or Properties)

Encapsulation is an important property of any class. Keeping a class protected from misuse is critical if you want to keep your sanity when the time to debug anything comes. Consider the following class:

```
class MyNumberProperty
{
    public int PositiveNumbersOnly;
}
```

The `public int PositiveNumbersOnly` is open to anyone who wants to make changes. For the most part, this is just fine. Any objects can go in and make changes to the `PositiveNumbersOnly` value stored in the `MyNumberProperty` class anytime. This includes changing the positive number to a negative one. If having a positive number is critical for any of MyNumberProperty's functions, we might start to run into problems. To protect this number, you could have the access to the following:

```
class MyReadOnlyProperty
{
    public readonly int PositiveNumbersOnly;
}
```

This statement changes the read/write ability of `PositiveNumbersOnly` to read only. This also means that the class where the value lives in cannot freely change that value. Changing the value isn't allowed from outside of the class either. The only time this value can be set is on creation in the constructor.

```
class MySetOnceNumbers
{
    public readonly int ReadOnlyOne = 1;//set on initialization
    public readonly int SetByParamOnCreation;
    public readonly int SetOnCreation;

    /* Constructor */
    MySetOnceNumbers(int numberParameter)
    {
        /* Set once by parameter */
        SetByParamOnCreation = numberParameter;
        /* Set by assignment in constructor */
        SetOnCreation = 7;
    }
}
```

This example shows the three ways in which a `readonly` value can be set. The first is `ReadOnlyOne` which is assigned in its initialization. This becomes a hardcoded value, something that's not allowed to change after it's written in code. The second value `SetByParamOnCreation` is set by a value in the parameter when you instance the class. Once the class is instanced, that value cannot be changed. The last is `SetOnCreation`, which is assigned in the constructor as a hardcoded value. This cannot be changed again once it's assigned.

Should we want to protect a value internally, we should make it private, and then make a publiclly available version which has some checks to block values we don't want.

```
class MyPositiveAccessor
{
    /*                              */
    /* | This value isn't visible | */
    /* | outside of this class    | */
    /* | this is internal to this | */
    /* | class alone.             | */
    /*                              */
    /*              ↓               */
    private int privatePositiveNumber;

    /*                              */
    /* | This value is visible    | */
    /* | outside of the class.    | */
    /*                              */
    /*              ↓               */
    public int publicPositiveNumber
    {
        get
        {
            return privatePositiveNumber;
        }
        set
        {
            if (value >= 0)
            {
                privatePositiveNumber = value;
            }
            else
            {
                privatePositiveNumber = 0;
            }
        }
    }
}
```

Here we have a private value called `privatePositiveNumber` and a public value called `public-PositiveNumber`. We'll plan on using one of them inside of the class, whereas we'll make the other publiclly available. Presume the value for a positive number should never be negative. To prevent the `privatePositiveNumber` from ever getting incorrectly set to a negative number, accessors allow logic in the set parameter for `publicPositiveNumber` to keep valid values.

7.5.1 Value

The placement of `privatePositiveNumber = value;` in our code is important. The `value` keyword is the input where `privatePositiveNumber` gets assigned. Where we use the `get{}` `set{}` notation, `value` is a catcher's mitt to snag incoming data. This accounts for any value entering the variable. This could be a struct, a string, or anything at all, so long as the type matches up.

7.5.1.1 A Basic Example

In its most simple form, the `get;set;` notation can be as simple as follows:

```
class GetSet
{
    public int MyInt{get;set;}
}

void UseGetSet()
{
    GetSet getset = new GetSet();
    getset.MyInt = 10;
    Debug.Log("getset.MyInt: " + getset.MyInt);
    // "getset.MyInt: 10"
}
```

At this point, there's no difference between `public in myInt;` and `public int myInt{get;set;};` the two operate essentially the same. What we're starting to produce here is a simple system where we're allowed to add in some logic to how a value is assigned.

To make full use of the accessor, we need to have two versions of a variable: the public accessor and a value that remains private within the confines of the class. This ensures a certain level of encapsulation that defines what object-oriented programming is all about.

```
class GetSetWithValues
{
    private int privateInt;
    public int publicInt
    {
        get
        {
            return privateInt;
        }
        set
        {
            privateInt = value;
        }
    }
}
```

The above code has a `private int privateInt` and `public int publicInt` with an accessor. This is a standard notation that should be used to define a variable for a cleanly encapsulated class. This too operates the same as the previous `{get;set;}`, only with the idea that it's redirecting an incoming data `value` from a public variable to a private variable hidden inside of the class.

7.5.2 Set Event

One of the advantages of an accessor is the ability to add logic to how a number is set. In addition to logic is the ability to raise an event. As in Section 7.5.1 from before, we'll want to add the delegate and the event to the GetSet class. Inside of the set element of the accessor, we'll make a check to see if there are functions delegated to the handler and then raise an event.

```
class GetSetWithEvent
{
    private int privateInt;
    public int publicInt
    {
        get
        {
            return privateInt;
        }
        set
        {
            if (value <= 0)
            {
                privateInt = 0;
            }
            else
            {
                privateInt = value;
            }
            if (IntSetEvent != null)
            {
                IntSetEvent(privateInt);
            }
        }
    }
    public delegate void SetIntEventHandler(int i);
    public event SetIntEventHandler IntSetEvent;
}

void UseGetSetWithEvent()
{
    GetSetWithEvent getset = new GetSetWithEvent();
    getset.IntSetEvent += OnIntSet;
    getset.publicInt = 7;
    getset.publicInt = -13;
}

void OnIntSet(int i)
{
    Debug.Log("OnIntSet Called: " + i);
}
```

The above code instances the new class and then adds the OnIntSet() function to the getset. IntSetEvent inside of the GetSetWithEvent class. Once the value is set on the following line, we get the following output from the Console:

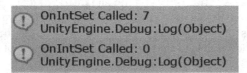

This is a very useful result of setting a value. Looking closer at how the event is raised brings us some ideas about what this event can be used for.

```
if (IntSetEvent != null)
{
    IntSetEvent(privateInt);
}
```

When the event is raised, we're passing in the value of the `privateInt`. This means that anytime privateInt is set, we're passing the new value to the event. Therefore, if `privateInt` is set to 7, the event is raised knowing the new value 7. If the value is set to a negative value, then the event is raised again with a value of 0. Once a proper accessor to a protected variable has been created, we're able to do a few more tricks with our new setup.

7.5.3 Read-Only Accessor

When writing a class, it's often a good idea to prevent some values from getting set inadvertently. It's not possible to set a variable if its value has been calculated by a function. In these cases, we need to make that variable a read only accessor.

```
class GetSetReadOnly
{
    public int Int;
    // Read only value
    public int doubleInt
    {
        get
        {
            return Int * 2;
        }
    }
}
```

The above code in the `GetSetReadOnly` class has a simple system to get a value that's two times the `Int` value. Notice too that there's no set; included in the accessor. If we try to set `doubleInt` with something like `doubleInt = 2;`, we get the following error:

```
getset.doubleInt = 2;
```

> 🔧 int GetSetReadOnly.doubleInt { get; }
>
> Property or indexer 'Accessors.GetSetReadOnly.doubleInt' cannot be assigned to -- it is read only

By omitting `set`, we've turned `doubleInt` into a read-only variable. This has a similar effect to the variable as the `readonly` accessor. The difference is that the class can still make changes internally to the value after the class has been initialized.

```
GetSetReadOnly getset = new GetSetReadOnly();
getset.Int = 7;
Debug.Log("getset.doubleInt: " + getset.doubleInt);
```

This set of code produces the following output:

> (!) getset.doubleInt: 14
> UnityEngine.Debug:Log(Object)

These examples with `get;set;` should expand to quite a variety of useful tricks. We can guard the internal value from bad values. We can raise events when a value is changed. And we can make the value read-only by omitting set; from the accessor.

7.5.4 Simplification

We have several options for getting information from a class. With accessors, we are spared the use of parentheses when we ask for a value from a class or struct.

```
struct AccessorStruct
{
    private int privateInt;
    public int publicInt
    {
        get
        {
            return privateInt;
        }
        set
        {
            privateInt = value;
        }
    }
    public int GetInt()
    {
        return privateInt;
    }
    public void SetInt(int i)
    {
        privateInt = i;
    }
}
```

We have a couple of options here with the above struct. We can set the value of the `privateInt` variable in the struct by the accessor or a pair of functions. We can set the value of `privateInt` to 3 with `SetInt(3);` or `publicInt = 3`.

How does this look in practice?

```
AccessorStruct accessorStruct = new AccessorStruct();
accessorStruct.publicInt = 3;
Debug.Log("accessorStruct.publicInt: " + accessorStruct.publicInt);
// accessorStruct.publicInt: 3
accessorStruct.SetInt(7);
Debug.Log("accessorStruct.GetInt(): " + accessorStruct.GetInt());
// accessorStruct.GetInt(): 7
```

The simplicity of `publicInt = 3;` means quite a lot. It's a notation that we're used to seeing; however, by the nature of the accessor, we have a great deal of control over what can be done in the accessor's logic.

7.5.5 What We've Learned

Accessors are useful for so many reasons. They provide functionality that has already been covered quite a lot, though in a simpler system. There are many powers which the accessor provides us. We'll be exploring some of the other tricks that make coding easier.

Many tricks in C# are made to make your work easier. Convenience offers more than just simplicity. If a trick makes things easier, then you're allowed to make more important decisions. Rather than dwelling on function names and parameters, you're allowed to focus on game play. After all, if you're making a game, the last thing you want to do is spend all your time rewriting code.

7.6 Base Classes: Another Look

When we begin to use inheritance and add keywords such as `virtual` and `override` onto functions, we begin to add many new layers of complexity onto the use of a class. How we write these class members greatly depends on how we want them to be used.

Depending on who you work with, you might find yourself seeing your code being used in unexpected ways. Often this is the case when you've written functions that have similar-sounding identifiers. Perhaps even misleading function names can be the cause for a great deal of confusion.

It's up to you to keep your code organized to begin with; however, given tight deadlines and poor sleeping habits, this can't always be the case. You can add descriptive comments, but these are all too often ignored. Your best option is to just disallow other code from seeing the variables and functions at all and prevent bugs from sneaking in.

This topic brings into question why any of these techniques is necessary. Inheritance is a system in which you can write a base class and have variations of that class extend functionality. The intent is to make a system that allows for a common set of base-level functions sharable. Based on what's been written, you make additions to, or variations of, that functionality.

To begin we'll look at building up some classes not derived or based on MonoBehaviour. This makes them regular C# classes outside of the influence of the normal `Update()` and `Start()` behaviors which we commonly see in most C# classes in Unity 3D.

The Unity 3D `MonoBehaviour` is not an abstract class, which means that we cannot make an abstract class based on it. An abstract class determines the necessary collections of data that every derived class will need to implement and use. To see how a base class can be used to do some work for us, we'll look at the BaseClassesAnotherLook script in the BaseClassesAnotherLook_Scene attached to the game object of the same name.

7.6.1 Generalization—Base Classes

Generalization allows us to make some wide-use cases for a class and then allow for more specific cases later. In general, if you were working on a game with a compendium of monsters there would still be plenty of shared attributes. If our behavior was nothing more than moving forward and turning left or right, we can add some variables that allow for this and name them appropriately.

A good base class will include some primitive variables, but at the same time provide a system for building up the types of behaviors we'll want. This is almost like writing code before it's written, but at least you can jump between classes and make changes when necessary. For our next behavior, we want some generic shapes driven by two numbers: a forward speed and a turn speed. Aside from that, the objects should have a very minimal set of instructions to prevent any unnecessary meddling in their activity.

```csharp
public abstract class BaseClass
{
    BaseProperties
    BaseFunctions
}
```

The BaseClassesAnotherLook.cs script is a detailed class. This data was necessary since we didn't have the usual objects inherited from MonoBehaviour. You can see its completion in the source code, collapsed here. Since we had to generate a great deal of this information from scratch, we needed to add in some accessors and other protections around the different data members to ensure that nothing unexpected might happen.

```csharp
public virtual void Speak()
{
    Debug.Log("Base Hello.");
}
```

As an abstract class, nothing has been implemented. We have one function called `Speak()`, which says `"Base Hello."` Everything else has been stubbed in to ensure that any class inheriting from BaseClass will have a great deal of work to do. The first region has been set up for many protected and private variables.

In the above class, we use the `abstract` keyword as well as `virtual`. In many cases, we might add many variables in anticipation of what we might need. These can be declared as we need or we might just leave in a bunch of place holders, thinking that we might need them later. Often, it's far better to create them as they are needed and decide if it's specific to a child class and move them into a parent class afterward. However, in this example, it's good to see that any number of variables can be added to this class for later use even if they're not necessary for all child classes to use them.

By making accessors for these variables, we've created a barrier between how the variables are set and who can set them. The protected variables are accessible only to siblings of the class. Other classes that might be trying to change these classes' movement patterns have to go through functions to change these variables. They won't be able to access them directly through a dot operator.

Following the base class, we have a ChildA class that inherits from the base class. Shown here in brief:

```csharp
public class ChildA : BaseClass
{
    #region ChildA_Properties
    protected GameObject Me;
    protected Mesh m_Mesh;
    protected MeshRenderer m_MeshRenderer;

    public override bool Equals(object obj)...
    public override int GetHashCode()...
    #endregion
    public override void Initialize(MeshFilter meshFilter, Material material)...
    public override void MoveForward(float speed, float turn)...
    public override void Speak()...
    public override string ToString()...
    public override void UpdateChild()...
}
```

This class has two important functions: `MoveForward()` and `ChildUpdate()`. Since we have bypassed the `MonoBehaviour` class, we don't get to have either of these. Just as important, we have the `Initialize()` function that replaces the `Start()` functionality.

7.6.2 Specialization

```
public override void Initialize(MeshFilter meshFilter, Material material)
{
    MeshFilter = meshFilter;
    Material = material;
    Me = new GameObject(this.ToString());
    Mesh = meshFilter.mesh;
    MeshRenderer = Me.AddComponent<MeshRenderer>();
    MeshRenderer.material = Material;
    MeshFilter = Me.AddComponent<MeshFilter>();
    MeshFilter.mesh = Mesh;
}
```

The `Initialize()` function has two arguments: `meshFilter` and `material`. These are then applied to a new `GameObject` Me. Here is where the `ChildA` starts to add layers of specialization on top of the BaseClass. The term *specialization* comes in whenever we add new properties or behaviors that were not present in the base class. The base class should be as generalized as possible. In our case, our base class is called `BaseClass`, just so we don't forget.

When we add additional behavior to a second `ChildB`, we have another opportunity to add another layer of specialization. In the following case, we add a color to the `Material` property.

```
public class ChildB : ChildA
{
    #region ChildB_properties
    private Color mColor;
    public Color MyColor
    {
        get { return mColor; }
        set { mColor = value; }
    }
    #endregion

    public override void Initialize(MeshFilter meshFilter, Material material)
    {
        base.Initialize(meshFilter, material);
        this.MyColor = new Color(1, 0, 0, 1);
        m_MeshRenderer.material.color = this.MyColor;
    }
}
```

7.6.3 Base

As new classes derive from each other, they require only smaller and smaller adjustments to gain added functionality. The specialization adds only thin layers of additional code on top of the base class and any class below. There are some important changes that need to be noted when deriving from a class that has some important functions already in place.

```
public override void Initialize(MeshFilter meshFilter, Material material)
{
    base.Initialize(meshFilter, material);
    this.MyColor = new Color(1, 0, 0, 1);
    m_MeshRenderer.material.color = this.MyColor;
}
```

The first line in the override void Initialize() function is base.Initialize(mesh, material);. Here we have some important new tricks to inspect. When the keyword base is invoked within a function, it's an indication that we're informing C# that we want to do what's already been done in the previous layer of that code. We can explore what the code looks like with what base. Initialize() is doing.

The base keyword tells C# to execute the parent classes' version of the function after the dot operator. The above code is what the function would look like to Unity 3D. Thanks to the base. Initialize, we've done the equivalent of this work without having to worry about any typos. Without invoking base. Initialize() we'd lose the mesh material and gameObject creation and setup process.

ChildB is based on ChildA and ChildA is based on BaseClass. This means that both ChildB and ChildA are related to one another because they both are also derived from BaseClass. This means that we can address them both as BaseClass objects. If we look at the ManageChildren.cs class, we'll have the following code:

```csharp
public MeshFilter ChildMesh;
public Material ChildMaterial;
BaseClass[] children;

public void Initialize()
{
    children = new BaseClass[2];
    children[0] = new ChildA();
    children[0].Initialize(ChildMesh, ChildMaterial);
    children[1] = new ChildB();
    children[1].Initialize(ChildMesh, ChildMaterial);
}
//Update is called once per frame
private void Update()
{
    for (int i = 0; i < children.Length; i++)
    {
        children[i].MoveForward(i * 0.1f + 0.1f, i * 3.0f + 1.5f);
        children[i].UpdateChild();
        children[i].Speak();
    }
}
```

This class is derived from MonoBehavior and we have the benefit of the Start() and Update() functions to use. It's worth noting that this is the only class based on MonoBehavior active in the scene in which we've added any code to. In ManageChildren class, we have a BaseClass[] array and an identifier children. This means that the array can accept any number of BaseClass type objects.

In the Start() function, we instantiate ChildA() and ChildB() and assign both of them to the BaseClass[] array. This is valid since they both derive BaseClass. Because BaseClass had the abstract functions MoveForward() and ChildUpdate(), they can be called in the Update() function in the Manager. This for loop provides some motivation to make the two little guys move around.

This also provides a system for them to speak. What's important here is how both the ChildA() and ChildB() classes are locked down. Only the exposed functions are available to outside classes.

Inside the Manager, they have just a few exposed functions or variables. Aside from `Child-Update()`, `Initialize()`, `MoveForward()`, and `Speak()`, the rest of the functions derive from the object. This is great for a few different reasons. The first is the fact that once the code starts working, it's hard to break.

Code turns into spaghetti when variables are accessed by many too many objects. Because options are now limited, your code must make changes to the internals of a class and therefore it's less likely your code will fall apart. Should we not have a BaseClass for the two child objects, we'd have to write our code more like the following:

```
if (FirstChild != null)
{
    FirstChild.MoveForward(0.1f, 3.0f);
    FirstChild.UpdateChild();
    FirstChild.Speak();
}

if (SecondChild != null)
{
    SecondChild.MoveForward(0.05f, -3.0f);
    SecondChild.UpdateChild();
    SecondChild.Speak();
}
```

Each one would have to be initialized and updated separately. This defeats the purpose of the base class entirely. There are still clever and dangerous tricks that we can use to add functionality to ChildA without needing to expand how much bigger that class might want to be.

7.6.4 Partial

If we're expanding on a class enough that our functions begin to feel crowded, we can split the work into different partial classes. One possible reason is to store all the accessors and properties in one partial class. Another partial class can store protected functions. Yet another could store the

Unity specific functions. Each partial class can live in a different .cs script. When working with a team, complex code merges can cause minor problems. One way to avoid this is splitting the work across multiple files.

```csharp
public partial class ChildC : ChildA
{

}
public partial class ChildC : ChildA
{

}
```

In the `ChildC` class, we could go in and extend `ChildA: BaseClass` with the prefix `partial` before `class` so that we have public partial class `ChildA: BaseClass`. This gives us the ability to tack on last-minute functionality to the `ChildA` class.

```csharp
// ChildCProperties.cs
public partial class ChildC : ChildA
{
    private float _scale;
    protected float Scale
    {
        get { return _scale; }
        set { _scale = value; }
    }
}
```

```csharp
// ChildCFunctions.cs
public partial class ChildC : ChildA
{
    protected void SetScale(float scale)
    {
        Scale = scale;
        Me.transform.localScale = Vector3.one * Scale;
    }
    public override void Initialize(MeshFilter meshFilter, Material material)
    {
        base.Initialize(meshFilter, material);
        SetScale(2.0f);
    }
}
```

Therefore, say we needed a system for ChildB to set its scale to some arbitrary new size, we can do that by adding the code locally to ChildB, or we can make sure that anything else deriving from ChildA will also have this ability. This also means that ChildA has that new ability as well.

The result of using partial classes like this tends to scatter code all over the place. This quickly leads to angry nights debugging code. Although there are some cases in which this can be quite helpful, it's best to start with the best use case for partial in mind.

```
// ShapeProperties.cs
public abstract partial class BaseShape
{
    public enum Shapes
    {
        Cube,
        Sphere
    };
    Shapes Shape;
}
```

```
// ShapeFunctions.cs
public abstract partial class BaseShape
{
    public abstract void SetShape(Shapes shape);
}
```

To facilitate separation of duty the BaseShape has been split into different partial classes. The concept here would be to store properties in one abstract class and the abstract functions in another class. When the partial classes are implemented the separation is invisible to the class inheriting from the abstract partial class.

```
public class SomeShape : BaseShape
{
    public GameObject Me;
    public override void SetShape(Shapes shape)
    {
        switch(shape)
        {
            case Shapes.Cube:
                Me = GameObject.CreatePrimitive(PrimitiveType.Cube);
                break;
            case Shapes.Sphere:
                Me = GameObject.CreatePrimitive(PrimitiveType.Sphere);
                break;
        }
    }
}
```

Setting up both the base class and the immediate child at the same time reduces the number of places you might have to go in order to find any problem areas in the code. This still isn't the best use case; however, when implementing various interfaces, you can have a different class as a helper for each interface being implemented. This certainly helps separate the different tasks. Suppose, for instance, that the BaseClass looked something like the following:

```
// ShapeICollection.cs
public abstract partial class BaseShape : System.Collections.ICollection
{
    public void CopyTo(Array array, int index)[...]

    public int Count => throw new NotImplementedException();

    public bool IsSynchronized => throw new NotImplementedException();

    public object SyncRoot => throw new NotImplementedException();

    public IEnumerator GetEnumerator()
    {
        throw new NotImplementedException();
    }
}
```

Both the IEnumerator and the ICollection interfaces are rather complicated. Having ShapeIEnumerator.cs and ShapeICollection.cs would help. Each one would start the same as Shape, but the contents of each would be related to the interface they are implementing. Thanks to Visual Studio, we have a quick way to generate the code we need.

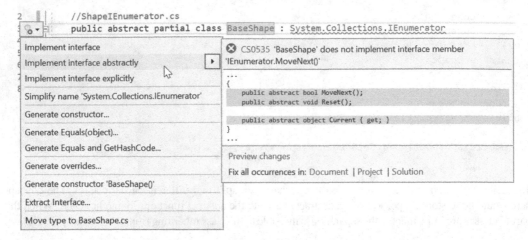

To the left of the function in the margins is a little lightbulb icon, this is a code helper where we can select various menu options to write in the required placeholders or abstract functions required to fulfill the interface.

By adding the different partial classes to each one of these different files, the Shape is already getting to be quite big. However, the original file has not increased in complexity. Each partial addition has only added complexity to its own portion of the class. The new behaviors we've been adding are all being inherited by ChildA and ChildB. This is a remarkable amount of work that can be done with less effort, thanks to our simplifying how classes can be merged as needed.

Normally, Unity 3D would complain that the class name doesn't match the file name. This exception is made for classes not deriving from MonoBehaviour. By avoiding MonoBehaviour, we're more able to take some liberties with the C# language. The partial, abstract, and virtual functions and classes offer a great deal of flexibility not allowed when deriving from MonoBehaviour.

7.6.5 Protected, Private, and Public

The accessibility keywords include protected to help shield your code from influence from other classes. The only classes allowed to see a protected member are related classes. Below we show a Base class that has a private protected and public string. The Child class inheriting from Base can only see the protected and public string,

```
class Base : System.Object
{
    private string MyPrivateString;
    protected string MyProtectedString;
    public string MyPublicString;
}
class Child : Base
{
    void VisibleProperties()
    {
        My
    }
}
```

For a class to hide any properties from any other class the private keyword is used to shield a member from outside influence. The `protected` accessibility attribute ensures that only inheriting members can see the variable. Once a property is made `public` anyone can see the variable.

```
partial class Half : System.Object
{
    private string MyPrivateString;
}

partial class Half : System.Object
{
    void SeesPrivates()
    {
        MyPrivateString = "";
    }
}
```

A `partial` class can see `private` members of the other portions of themselves. A partial class is still the same class, so `private` members are members of all parts of a partial class. The `private public` and `protected` accessor attributes can be applied to variables and functions of a class.

7.6.6 What We've Learned

It's difficult to set strict rules for breaking a class apart into base and child members. The reasons for this design behavior are three-fold. The first is to enable faster development by reducing the necessity for rewriting code. The second is for maintenance. If you fix code in one place you've fixed it for everyone inheriting the fix. The third is for reusing code. Working code should be used everywhere.

If you find a situation where multiple classes are looking for a specific object, make a base class that finds the object, then every child of that base class will inherit that code. Splitting a class into multiple parts can take a while as you'll re-write several functions to suit multiple specializations. Each class may need to inherit code differently.

This is often painful, but it's worth it. The second time, though, is almost always faster than the first time. Organizing everything into a clean simple group and branching with more reliable behaviors always comes once you've got a better understanding of what you wanted to do to begin with.

7.7 Optional Parameters

We've been putting a great deal of thought into how functions work and how we can make them more flexible through inheritance and overrides. The different features are not to add complications; they are meant to add flexibility. Once you get used to how the features work, you're allowed to do more things with less work. It's just a matter of understanding how the features work.

Hopefully, you're able to keep up with the break-neck speed at which we've been adding these features. If not, then it's time to practice what you know before going on. This is a pretty simple chapter that adds a pretty simple feature to our C# toolbox. Adding optional features is a pretty simple trick to our functions that often comes up. Normally, when we declare a function, we use syntax like the following:

```
void MyFunction()
{
    // some code here...
}
```

Therefore, we've used a few different variations on how to manipulate the argument list of a function to get a few different uses out of a single function. We're allowed to use a few other tricks that can help make things a bit easier to deal with when making many changes. When the process of writing code gets to a fevered pitch, you're going to be needing to write a great deal of code fast and finding yourself going back to fix things quite a lot.

Say for a moment that you've written a function that appears in many different places but you want to change it. This would mean spending the time to fix it everywhere it's used, and this can be a boring time-consuming chore.

Therefore, you wrote a function that might look something like the following:

```
GameObject CreateACube(string name, Vector3 position)
{
    GameObject cube = GameObject.CreatePrimitive(PrimitiveType.Cube);
    cube.name = name;
    cube.transform.position = position;
    return cube;
}
```

In use you might do something like this to use the function:

```
GameObject bobCube = CreateACube("bob", new Vector3(10, 0, 0));
Debug.Log("Created a cube named + " + bobCube.name + "At:" + bobCube.transform.position);
// "Created a cube named + bobAt:(10.0, 0.0, 0.0)"
```

For a moment, let's pretend that the function making use of `CreateACube()` is far too much work to change and we are incredibly lazy. What happens when we need to make some changes to the argument list, but we don't feel like making many changes everywhere the function appears? For a moment, we want all of the current uses of the function to use the same code, which means that an override will not work.

Suppose there is a request to make a fundamental change to the `CreateACube()` function, which tells us that we need to make a third parameter set the scale of the cube; we have a few options that we've been introduced to. The simple option is to simply make a new function with a new name. We're missing the point of using C#'s features if we do that.

The better option is to make a second version of the `CreateACube()` function with a different signature that might look like the following:

```
GameObject CreateACube(string name, Vector3 position, float scale)
{
    GameObject cube = GameObject.CreatePrimitive(PrimitiveType.Cube);
    cube.name = name;
    cube.transform.position = position;
    cube.transform.localScale = new Vector3(scale, scale, scale);
    return cube;
}
```

This would mean that we have two different versions of the same function, only the second one has some additional statements, to take care of the third parameter. This should bring up the question, Isn't there a cleaner way to take care of any additional parameters without making more than one version of the same function? The answer is an optional parameter.

7.7.1 Using Optionals

When a function is used the parameter list allows for default values. There are some simple rules to follow if you want to make some of the arguments in the parameter list optional.

```
GameObject CreateACubeWithOptions(string name = "bob", Vector3 position = new Vector3(), float scale = 1.0f)
{
    GameObject cube = GameObject.CreatePrimitive(PrimitiveType.Cube);
    cube.name = name;
    cube.transform.position = position;
    cube.transform.localScale = new Vector3(scale, scale, scale);
    return cube;
}
```

The third parameter is float scale = 1.0f. The addition of the = 1.0f predefines the incoming value unless it's overridden by a third parameter's value. In short, if there's no third parameter given, then the float scale parameter is defaulted at 1.0f, and fulfilling all three parameters is not necessary. The same goes for the first and second parameter so long as they have a default assignment set in the parameter list.

Without any modifications to the Start() function's use of CreateACube, we've added a simple override that handles both cases with little additional work. There are, however, some restrictions to how optional parameters are used.

Setting variables in case they're not used in the argument list is an easy way to skip writing several versions of the same function; in case there are different ways, you intend the function to be used. Even with one loss with a predefined parameter, they will retain their order and value types.

```
void ParamUsage(int i)
{
    Debug.Log("using an int " + i);
    // "using an int 5"
}


void ParamUsage(string words)
{
    Debug.Log("using a string " + words);
    // "using a string not a number"
}
```

For instance, we should remember that using two different signatures altogether can be used without any additional fuss.

This would result with two different types being used with predictable results. This works for situations in which this was expected and different types were used from the beginning since there was a predefined reason for the behavior of function's differences. However, does this mean we can add an optional parameter to either of these functions?

7.7.1.1 A Basic Example

Let's start with the OptionalParameters scene in the Chapter7 Unity Project and look at the OptionalParameters script of the game object with the same name.

```
void MoreParamUsage(int i)
{
    Debug.Log("using int i, " + i + " no optional floats here.");
}

void MoreParamUsage(int i, float optionalFloat = 1f)
{
    Debug.Log("using an int " + i + " and a float " + optionalFloat);
}
```

The option exists only because the parameter has an assignment in the parameter list. This does not mean that we cannot use regular overrides along with the regular use of the function. You're not actually required to write an override of any kind to begin with, though we're adding one just to show that it is possible to do so without any adverse or unexpected results.

The two functions above show a behavior which comes with the use of the optionalFloat parameter being given the default value. The override will never be called.

```
MoreParamUsage(7);
// using int i, 7 no optional floats here.
MoreParamUsage(5, Mathf.PI);
// using an int 5 and a float 3.141593
```

The function without the second parameter will be preferred over the override with the optional parameter. The most suitable version will take priority. In all cases where the second parameter is given a value, the default value for the optionalFloat will never be used.

7.7.2 Optional Arguments

We should check to see if the optional parameter can be made unoptional in a different version of the same function; this would look something like the following:

```
void MoreParamUsage(int i, float requiredFloat)
{
    Debug.Log("using an int " + i + " and a float " + requiredFloat);
}
```

Unity 3D gives us the following error:

❌ CS0111 Type 'OptionalParameters' already defines a member called 'MoreParamUsage' with the same parameter types

The signature combination for the function (int, float) is the same with both versions of the function. Therefore, no, we are not allowed to redefine the function with one using an optional parameter and another using a required parameter of the same type. This should make sense: When you're using the function, the appearance of the use would look the same. Why stop with just one optional parameter?

```
void UsingOptionals(int i = 1, float f = 1f)
{
    Debug.Log("using an int " + i + " using a float " + f);
}
```

We can set all of the parameters in a version of the function with defined values, which means that we're allowed to do the following in the Start() function:

```
void UsingUsingOptionals()
{
    UsingOptionals();
    // "using an int 1 using a float 1"
    UsingOptionals(7);
    // "using an int 7 using a float 1"
    UsingOptionals(9, 13f);
    // "using an int 9 using a float 13"

    /* the following are not valid uses */
    /* of optionals                     */
    UsingOptionals(23f);
    UsingOptionals(,31f);
}
```

The first use has no arguments, the second has an int for the first int, the third has an int and a float. The last two uses of the function are not valid. There is no version of the `UsingOptionals()` function that has one float argument. The empty int space followed by a float is also invalid since all parameter fields require some form of input before the list is usable.

To prevent further complication, use of the prefixes *ref* and *out* as we've used before in a parameter are also disallowed when assigning a default value to a parameter. The behavior of requiring a value in each parameter from left to right also means default values can only be assigned after required values are assigned.

```
void UsingOptionals(int i = 1, int j)
{
    Debug.Log("using an int " + i + "
}
```

Optional parameters must appear after all required parameters

7.7.3 Named Parameters

Naming the arguments can be an easy way to make the parameters easier to read. In the case of CreateACube (string name, vector3 position), it's pretty clear what the two parameters are for. And thanks to helpful pop-ups in MonoDevelop, we can get useful reminders telling us what each parameter is for.

```
CreateACube()
```

▲ 2 of 2 ▼ GameObject OptionalParameters.CreateACube(**string name**, Vector3 position, float scale)

A less commonly used feature which gives us additional flexibility is the named parameter. If we consider a function that might have several different parameters, some of which might be optional, it's easy to forget the order in which they are expected. Furthermore, if you want to use only one of the optional parameters but don't necessarily want to override any of the others, then we'd have a problem trying to express this.

Consider the following function's signature:

```
void LotsOfParams(int a = 0, int b = 1, int c = 2, int d = 3)
{
    Debug.Log("a: " + a + " b: " + b + " c: " + c + " d: " + d);
}

void UseLotsOfParams()
{
    LotsOfParams();
    //"a: 0 b: 1 c: 2 d: 3"
}
```

All the parameters are optional, and not using any of them prints the following line of output to the Console.

> ⚠ **a: 0 b: 1 c: 2 d: 3**
> UnityEngine.Debug:Log(Object)

This should be expected, but if we simply want b to be 99 and leave the rest of the parameters set to the provided default value, what then?

```
LotsOfParams(0, 99);
//"a: 0 b: 99 c: 2 d: 3"
```

From this result, we infer that a isn't an optional argument. Unfortunately, LotsOfParams(null,99); isn't even an option. We are missing out by not using named parameters. If the parameters from LotsOfParams had names, in this case a, b, c, and d, we can use them in the following manner.

7.7.3.1 A Basic Example

Named parameters follow a bit of a different look. Once there are a great deal of parameters, it's easy to forget which is which. By using a named parameter, it's more clear what the value is for and what the assignment is.

```
LotsOfParams(b:99)
```
> void OptionalParameters.LotsOfParams([int a = 0], **[int b = 1]**, [int c = 2], [int d = 3])

Just use the name of the argument you want to assign a value to followed by a: and the value you want to assign to it. The order is also ignored so long as the identifiers are used.

```
LotsOfParams(b: 99, a: 88, d: 777, c: 1234);
//"a: 88 b: 99 c: 1234 d: 777"
```

The b followed by a and then d before c should look rather confusing, and in practice, it's not the best form to mix arguments so badly. However, there's nothing preventing you from confusing anyone else when reading your code. From the previous CreateACube example, we're allowed to do the following:

```
CreateACube(scale: 6.0f, name: "Henry", position: new Vector3(2f, z: 0, y: 1));
```

Furthermore, the named parameters also work in the Unity 3D's own data types like Vector3 where we name z and y out of order.

Starting off with named parameters, we're going to have to use the rest of the names. They can be in any order, but once we start off with naming parameters before assigning them, we're stuck with naming all of them before finishing the function. Once the order is messed up, we're unable to tell the function our intent for the data going into the different slots in the argument list. For instance, consider the following three statements:

```
CreateACube("Bob", new Vector3(3f, 0, 0));
CreateACube("Henry", position: new Vector3(4f, 0, 0));
CreateACube(position: new Vector3(5f, 0, 0), "Jack");
```

> [●] (parameter) Vector3 position
>
> Named argument 'position' is used out-of-position but is followed by an unnamed argument

We created a cube named Bob in the first statement, as we have before; we didn't use the name in the second parameter. When we created Henry, we didn't use a name in the first parameter where the string is expected.

This works fine since the order has been retained. However, if we use position: as the first parameter but then use "Jack" to assign the string to an out-of-order position, we get the following error:

> ❌ CS8323 Named argument 'position' is used out-of-position but is followed by an unnamed argument

Basically, the position or order of the unnamed arguments must line up with the function's signature. After that names can be used for any remaining arguments in the list.

7.7.4 Combining What We've Learned

We've looked at the out and ref parameters, and now we've covered both optional and named parameters in relation to the arguments and functions. We should know a bit about how they should be used together.

If we write a strange combination of out, ref, and some optional parameters, we might come up with something like the following:

```
void Variations(ref float a, out float b, float c = 10.0f, float d = 11.0f)
{
    b = c / a;
    a = c / d;
}
```

There are a couple of important notes about this: First is the fact that ref cannot have a default value. It might look something like the following:

```
void Bad(ref int a = 1)
{

}
```

The logic that results in this error is simple. The ref keyword is reserved to tell the parameter that it's going to assume the place of another variable that already exists. This means that the value that's in the argument list can't be defined as the ref tells the value that it must be modifying something that exists outside of the function.

> ❌ CS1741 A ref or out parameter cannot have a default value

7.7.5 What We've Learned

We've got many options. At this point, there are very few things which you might come across in a function's parameter list that will come as a surprise. Keeping your code under control is largely dependent on your discretion and your team's decision making. Coming up with standards may or may not include using named or optional arguments, which are not too common.

Optional arguments are certainly clever, and when used properly, they're readable and easy to understand. Life can continue with or without these types of parameters appearing in your code. There's certainly nothing you can't do without them.

Optional parameters alleviate the necessity of writing additional overloaded functions, which saves some time. This is possibly best suited for a longer function that spans a heavy number of lines of code. In these cases, a repeated block of code is more likely to have errors.

Any time you need to write code again is another chance for a bug to creep in. Overloaded functions, in which one version works and another version doesn't, can lead to long nights searching for which version is being called and why it's broken.

Even in bug fixing, we learn how to write better code. Often having others check your work is a good practice to keep you in line with the rest of the team. Code reviews are a common practice among large companies, especially on high-profile projects in which a small bug can cause big problems.

7.8 Delegate Functions

A delegate acts like a data type; just like how both int and double are number types, a delegate is a type of function. The idea of a delegate is a bit weird. So far we've been thinking of functions as a construct that processes data.

A delegate allows us to use a function in a variable. If you're able to assign a variable to a function, you can use it like data. This means passing it between functions, structs, or classes through a parameter or assignment.

7.8.1 Delegates

A clever trick that C# has the ability to do is to store a function into a variable just like it was data. There are a few rules for doing this. The first important step is to ensure that the signature of the variable you're storing a function in and the function you're about to delegate match.

7.8.1.1 A Basic Example

Starting with the Delegates project, we'll look at the DelegateFunctions.cs class. First we need to write a new delegate function, which is a sort of a template signature for any function that is to be delegated. This is easier to see in code than to explain. At the class level, add in the following code statement:

```
delegate void MyDelegate();
```

We've defined a delegate, which is pretty simple; but if you look at the signature, there's not a whole lot going on. We defined the MyDelegate() with return type void and assigned no arguments in the parentheses. However, we'll go with this as a basic example and look at more complex delegates in a moment.

Now that we have a defined delegate, we need to make some functions that match the signature.

```
void FirstDelegate()
{
    Debug.Log("First Delegate Called.");
}

void SecondDelegate()
{
    Debug.Log("Second Delegate Called.");
}
```

It's important that any functions that are going to be used with MyDelegate() have matching signatures. If not, then you'll get an error before the code compiles. To make use of a delegate, you need to make an instance of the function like you would if it were a class object.

```
void UseDelegates()
{
    MyDelegate myDelegate = new MyDelegate(FirstDelegate);
}
```

Looking at the statement added to UseDelegates(), you should notice a couple of things. MyDelegate() is the name of the delegate we defined at the class scope. This defines not only the signature we're going to be matching but also the identifier of the delegate we're going to be using. To make an instance of that delegate, we use it's defined name.

This is followed by an identifier that is defined like any other variable. In this we're using a short identifier *del* to identify the MyDelegate function. This is then followed by an assignment. We use the new keyword to create an instance of the delegate function MyDelegate(), but then we add in a parameter to a set of parentheses.

We wrote two functions with matching signatures: FirstDelegate() and SecondDelegate(). Choose FirstDelegate() and add its name to the delegate parameter. This is a bit weird, but it's an overloaded use of parentheses for delegates. After the assignment, del is now a FirstDelegate(). To use it, simply add the following statement:

```
//call on function assigned to delegate
myDelegate();
// "First Delegate Called."
```

When the computer runs myDelegate();, we get "First Delegate Called." printed to our Console. Now here comes the interesting part.

```
// reassign who is assigned to myDelegate
myDelegate = SecondDelegate;

// call on function assigned to delegate
myDelegate();
// "Second Delegate Called."
```

We can give myDelegate a new assignment. To do this, we add myDelegate = SecondDelegate; to change what function has been assigned to the delegate myDelegate. When myDelegate(); is used again, we'll get "Second Delegate Called." printed to the Console of Unity 3D.

7.8.2 Delegate Signatures

Now for a more interesting example, let's add a delegate with a more interesting signature.

```
delegate int OtherDelegate(int a, int b);

public int ThirdDelegate(int a, int b)
{
    return a + b;
}

public int FourthDelegate(int a, int b)
{
    return a - b;
}
```

Here we have assigned a return value and two arguments to the delegate `MyDelegate()`. To make use of this signature, we wrote two different functions using the same signature: The first function returns a + b and the second function returns a − b, as you might expect.

```
OtherDelegate myDelegate = new OtherDelegate(ThirdDelegate);
int added = myDelegate(1, 2);
Debug.Log("added: " + added);
// "added: 3"

myDelegate = FourthDelegate;
int subtracted = myDelegate(5, 6);
Debug.Log("subtracted: " + subtracted);
// "subtracted: -1"
```

When del is assigned the duty of being the delegate to a function, it should be treated like a function. The clever trick is that now we're allowed to change which function `myDelegate` is delegating. There's a more important underlying use for delegates, but it's important to understand the basic setup and use of a delegate first.

The use of delegates involves first matching up all the signatures to ensure type safety. Once this is done, you're allowed some leeway to make changes, but only under some strict rules. We'll come back to that in a later chapter. We've got plenty to work with before we get there.

So far we've used del = SecondDelegate to assign a delegate that was created within the `Start()` function. There's a much more interesting way to assign and use a delegate function.

7.8.3 Stacking Delegates

When the delegate is first declared, it's useful to add a variable to store it in at the class scope. This allows other objects in the scene to have access to the delegate.

```
delegate void StackedDelegates(int i);
StackedDelegates stacked;

void FifthDelegate(int i)
{
    Debug.Log("FifthDelegate: " + i);
}
```

The default initialization of a delegate is null. The first assignment can be done as we have before with stacked = FifthDelegate; syntax. You can use the += notation to assign more than one function to the delegate. When the stack is called, the assigned functions are called. As we write more functions that fit the delegates' signature, we can chain more functions for del to execute when called.

```
void SixthDelegate(int i)
{
    Debug.Log("SixthDelegate: " + i);
}

void UseStackedDelegates()
{
    stacked = FifthDelegate;
    stacked += FifthDelegate;
    stacked(5);
    // "FifthDelegate: 5"
    // "FifthDelegate: 5"
    stacked += SixthDelegate;
    stacked += SixthDelegate;
    stacked(6);
    // "FifthDelegate: 6"
    // "FifthDelegate: 6"
    // "FifthDelegate: 6"
    // "FifthDelegate: 6"
}
```

This code stacks more functions onto our delegate. When this code is run, we get FifthDelegate: 5 followed by FifthDelegate: 6 twice then SixthDelegate twice printed to the Console panel in Unity 3D. The feature sounds cool, but when is it used? More importantly, how does this feature make C# more useful?

Once we get into events and event management, we'll get a clearer picture of what delegate functions are really used for, but it's important to understand how to create and assign delegates before we get to events. Events are basically functions that call other functions when something specific is triggered. Usually collision events and input events need to trigger user-defined events.

This is where delegates become important. The event that was initially written by the Unity 3D programmers doesn't have a specific task, because they don't know what you have in mind when a key is pressed or a collision occurs on a game object. They leave the definition of what to do on the event up to you to define in your own function. To use the event, we need to match the signature of the event with our own function. Then we assign the function we wrote to the event written by the Unity 3D programmers.

7.8.4 Using Delegates

A delegate is basically a type, like any other int or float. The functions GetSeven and GetThree do different things, but they both match the signature provided with IntDelegate(); as both return an integer value with no parameters.

```
delegate int IntDelegate();
int GetSeven()
{
    return 7;
}
int GetThree()
{
    return 3;
}
```

This also means we're allowed to pass them to functions as though they were variables as well. UseDelegate ignores the contents of the IntDelegate so long as they return an int.

```
void UseDelegate(IntDelegate intDelegate)
{
    IntDelegate intFromDelegate = intDelegate;
    int i = intFromDelegate();
    Debug.Log("int from intDelegate: " + i);
}
```

When GetSeven or GetThree are passed into UseDelegate they return a value and it's printed out.

```
void UseIntDelegates()
{
    UseDelegate(GetSeven);
    UseDelegate(GetThree);
}
```

The log produces the following results:

```
(!) int from intDelegate: 7
    UnityEngine.Debug:Log(Object)
(!) int from intDelegate: 3
    UnityEngine.Debug:Log(Object)
```

7.8.5 Updating Delegates

Delegates are often used to update multiple objects from a central function. In a basic form a Counter class would get an update from a single function. Given a class Counter as in the following:

```
class Counter
{
    private int Count;
    private int Limit;
    public Counter(int countLimit)
    {
        Limit = countLimit;
    }

    public void UpdateCount()
    {
        if(Count < Limit)
            Count++;
        if (Count >= Limit)
            ReportCount();
    }

    void ReportCount()
    {
        Debug.Log("Counts: " + Count + " Limit: " + Limit);
    }
}
```

We have a function called UpdateCount() where we increment the internal Count value and check if it's reached a limit, then we report that the limit has been reached. Without a delegate function we could use the following notation to call the update on a number of counters.

```
foreach (Counter c in Counters)
{
    c.UpdateCount();
}
```

Delegates give us an option to update them with a single call to a delegate of the function:

```
bool CountersInitalized = false;
Counter[] Counters = new Counter[10];
delegate void UpdateCounters();
UpdateCounters CounterUpdate;
void CreateAndUpdateCounters()
{
    if (!CountersInitalized)
    {
        for (int i = 0; i < 10; i++)
        {
            Counters[i] = new Counter(Random.Range(10, 30));
            CounterUpdate += Counters[i].UpdateCount;
        }
        CountersInitalized = true;
    }
    CounterUpdate();
}
```

After the Counter is created with a random number to count up to, we assign the Counter's `UpdateCount()` function to a `CounterUpdate()` delegate. Then when the `CounterUpdate()` delegate is called every assigned `Counter.UpdateCount()` function is called at once.

The function `CreateAndUpdateCounters()` is called in the script's `Update()` method called once per frame. This effectively becomes a system where we get a `Debug.Log()`; called after a random count has been reached.

7.8.6 What We've Learned

In Unity 3D, delegates are often used to update the state of an object that has been created in the scene. Unity 3D as a framework often leads to MonoBehaviour objects, getting `Start()` and `Update()` called in a non-specified order.

This means you can't rely on a specific function before or after another function as you might expect. To be more specific, you could check on a value during an update and make decisions that will effect the game on the following update. You can't ensure you can check a value at the start of an update and expect to effect the scene before the end of the update.

This is best done via events. We'll find out more about that in a few chapters. I'll leave you to play with some delegates for now; using events is going to take up a chapter, so we'll leave that for later.

7.9 Interface

An interface is a promise that your new class will implement a function from its base class. The implementation of an interface can be made for any method, event, or delegate. Anything that has a signature with an identifier and argument list can be turned into an interface for a base class. This promise of a new class implementing an interface is not unlike that of a class implementing an abstract class.

```
abstract class ThisClass
{
    public abstract void DoAThing();
}

abstract class ThatClass
{
    public abstract void DoAThing();
}
```

C# does not support multiple inheritance to avoid confusion with how behaviors may overlap. Consider the above two classes, if you were to implement both at the same time then which version of `DoAThing()` would be inherited?

The structure of your code depends on having a plan. With every new function and every new data structure, you're adding to the overall complexity of your game or software. The more people you collaborate with, the more complex it will get, necessitating some way to stay organized and maintain some sort of consistency. Your game's chance of success is based on your code remaining consistent and stable.

An interface provides a framework for derived classes to implement. An interface is an organizational tool that helps us when sweeping changes are made. Say you decide that all your zombies now need to have a new feature, for example, their arms needing to be cut off; it will help out in the end if you made an interface for building the body of the zombie when you started.

7.9.1 Early Planning

Using an interface could be considered early on. Creating them after many classes have already been written can turn into a nightmare if your different monsters took on a wide variety of implementations, but therein lies the strength of the interface.

An interface is a construct that helps other programmers understand what you've written. These tools are intended to provide a basis for understanding without needing to hover around the rest of your team to explain what your code does. Interfaces provide a system for constructing a class that implements your code.

When we consider why object-oriented programming helps us rather than hinders us, we need to remember a few things. First, we need to think of each new class as a progressive evolutionary process to a previous class. Every fundamental change we make to our game has to be reflected on as wide a scale as possible. Second, we need to remember that every object should share as much data as possible. Finally, we need to make sure that all our objects interact with one another as closely as possible.

To communicate this interaction and to solidify this unity between characters and properties in our game world, you need to set up some base rules. These rules are best communicated by using an interface. For an interface to make sense, we should create a class that the rest of the objects in our game should follow as their base, a common foundation for all objects in our game to share. Once we begin with some basic design patterns, we'll really understand why interfaces are important, but for now, we'll just look at a basic implementation.

7.9.1.1 A Basic Example

We'll start with the Interface_scene, in which we have an Interfaces.cs attached to the similarly named game object. Unlike many other classes, an interface isn't directly used in Unity 3D. The naming convention always starts with an I to indicate that the class is an interface and not necessarily an object for use in the game.

```
interface IThis
{
    string ThisName
    {
        get;
        set;
    }

    void ThisFunction();
}
```

As a common practice, we prefix the interface with an uppercase I, though it's not necessary. Inside our interface we added an arbitrary string called ThisName as well as a function ThisFunction. Everything needs a name, doesn't it? Of course, you can use any type inside the interface as an example, but a string is something easy to test, so we'll start with string ThisName in our example.

The new syntax we're seeing is called an *interface property,* and the format we're seeing is how a property is created in an interface. Interface properties are consistent identifiers, which all classes that implement the interface will have. Often you might see this done with the following style:

```
string ThisName { get; set; }
```

This looks cleaner, so we should get used to seeing the get; set; syntax, as in the above statement. The interface property is used as a system to allow each implementation of the interface to change how the property is used. We can change how the get and set work, depending on the goal for each implementation. Interface implementations need to be made public.

Until we fully implement the IThis interface, Unity 3D will be telling us that there are some errors because it doesn't implement all of IThing. This is corrected by adding in members of the interface.

```
50
51  ⌖ ▾      class ImplementsThis : IThis
52
53    Implement interface                          ▸   ⊗ CS0535 'Interfaces.ImplementsThis' does not implement interface
54                                                       member 'Interfaces.IThis.ThisName'
      Implement interface explicitly
55                                                   ...
      Generate overrides...                          {
                                                          public string ThisName
      Generate constructor 'ImplementsThis()'         {
                                                              get => throw new System.NotImplementedException();
      Move type to ImplementsThis.cs                          set => throw new System.NotImplementedException();
                                                          }
      Move type to Interfaces.ImplementsThis.cs
                                                          public void ThisFunction()
      Add accessibility modifiers                       {
                                                              throw new System.NotImplementedException();
                                                          }
                                                      }
                                                      ...

                                                   Preview changes

                                                   Fix all occurrences in: Document | Project | Solution
```

This can automatically be stubbed out by using the helper icon in VisualStudio. Selecting Implement interface will generate the following code:

```
class ImplementsThis : IThis
{
    public string ThisName
    {
        get => throw new System.NotImplementedException();
        set => throw new System.NotImplementedException();
    }

    public void ThisFunction()
    {
        throw new System.NotImplementedException();
    }
}
```

This shouldn't be the final code, but it's telling us what we need to provide to complete the implementation.

```
class ImplementsThis : IThis
{
    private string thisName;
    public string ThisName
    {
        get
        {
            return thisName;
        }
        set
        {
            thisName = value;
        }
    }

    public void ThisFunction()
    {
        Debug.Log("Hello, my name is " + thisName);
    }
}
```

We need a private local variable specific to the class to store in the class that holds onto string `ThisName`, which was supplied in the interface. In this case, we use `thisName` in the Toaster class. This isolates the local data, but uses the interface property for the variable `ThisName` that was created in the `IThis` interface.

How do we know what `ThisFunction()` is supposed to do? In most cases the naming of the function should be more clear. In many cases the name can't describe enough what the intent of the function is. In most cases a base implementation is provided as an example as to what is expected from the interface. With the class `ImplementsThis`, we could consider this to be an example of how `IThis` is to be implemented.

7.9.1.2 Using Accessors

The keyword value is used in the `get; set; {}` function to access the interface's variable. The `get; set;` statement is called an accessor statement and is used for interface implementation. The appearance of `get; set;` in a class implementing the interface now requires code to be complete. Finally, we can use an interface of the object in the `Start()` function of the Interfaces.cs script in the Interfaces scene.

```
void UseToaster()
{
    Toaster toaster = new Toaster();
    toaster.ThisName = "Talkie";
    toaster.ThisFunction();
    // Howdy, my name is Talkie
}
```

As an example, we create a new Toaster T, assign its name to "Talkie," and then print out the name to double check that the accessor is correctly implemented. Notice that we're not using ToasterName that was made private in the Toaster class. The use of This Name and not ToasterName is the key reason for why interfaces are important. For every class that implements the IThis interface, we must have a system to set a ThisName.

If you have programmers adding new monsters, they should be instructed to implement the IThis interface. With this rule, their code will not work unless their monster has a ThisName. If you make a rule to never check-in code that's broken, you should always confirm your code works before checking it in. Needing to implement an interface to every new object ensures that every object has a ThisName. Therefore, if we were to create a new zombie with the same interface, we'd need to do something like in the following example:

```
class Zombie : MonoBehaviour, IThis
{
    private string ZombieName;
    public string ThisName
    {
        get { return ZombieName; }
        set { ZombieName = value; }
    }

    public void ThisFunction()
    {
    }
}
```

This is a new zombie class that is based on `MonoBehaviour`. This means that we're creating a new ZombieGame object since we're inheriting from `MonoBehaviour`. We've also implemented the name accessor to follow the IThis interface. Without `public string ThisName{get;set;}` defined, we get the following error:

```
class Zombie : MonoBehaviour, IThis
{
    private string ZombieName;
    //public string ThisName
    //{
    //      get { return ZombieName
    //      set { ZombieName = value;
    //}
```

interface Chapter7_9.Interfaces.IThis

'Interfaces.Zombie' does not implement interface member 'Interfaces.IThis.ThisName'

Show potential fixes (Alt+Enter or Ctrl+.)

A programmer needs to know quickly when an error has occurred. I've heard people say "fail fast and fail often" to describe rapid development in small game studios. There are many reasons for this, and finding bugs in your code is one of them. Interfaces ensure that new game objects follow the proper setup you might want to use in your game. We should be careful when instancing a class that is based on `MonoBehaviour`. Using the following code fragment will give us an error:

```
void UseZombie()
{
    Zombie zombie = new Zombie();
}
```

The error looks like the following:

⚠ **You are trying to create a MonoBehaviour using the 'new' keyword.**
UnityEngine.MonoBehaviour:.ctor()

```
UnityEngine.MonoBehaviour:.ctor()
Zombie:.ctor()
Example:Start () (at Assets/Example.cs:11)
```

To remedy the error that this produces, we'll have to use gameObject.AddComponent();. Therefore, the code should look a bit more like the following:

```
void UseZombie()
{
    //Zombie zombie = new Zombie();
    Zombie zombie = gameObject.AddComponent<Zombie>();
}
```

Now with the Zombie MonoBehaviour added to the gameObject, we can also fill in the Zombie's ThisFunction()."

```
public void ThisFunction()
{
    Debug.Log("mmmmuh name is " + ZombieName);
}
```

Now we've created a gameObject that uses the IThis interface. Both Toaster and Zombie implement the same interface. Therefore, we can assign both a name and get that name to print. If you check the Unity attribute editor while running the code, you'll notice that a new component has been added to the Interfaces game object.

7.9.2 Multiple Interfaces

In C# we do not have the ability to inherit from multiple classes. We can however implement more than one interface.

```csharp
interface FirstInterface
{
    string FirstString { get;set; }
    void FirstFunction();
    void SameFunction();
}

interface SecondInterface
{
    string SecondString { get; set; }
    void SecondFunction();
    void SameFunction();
}
```

A special case appears when multiple interfaces use a function with the same name. Both interfaces suggest a SameFunction() needs to be implemented, but how to we tell which is which?

```csharp
class ImplementsFirstAndSecond : FirstInterface, SecondInterface
{
    private string firstString;
    public string FirstString
    {
        get { return firstString; }
        set { firstString = value; }
    }

    public void FirstFunction()
    {
        Debug.Log("First Function Called");
    }
    private string secondString;
    public string SecondString
    {
        get { return secondString; }
        set { secondString = value; }
    }

    public void SecondFunction()
    {
        Debug.Log("Second Function Called");
    }

    public void SameFunction()
    {
        Debug.Log("Which version is Called?");
    }
}
```

The explicit declaration of the interface is required to inform the class which of the two interface you're implementing.

```
void FirstInterface.SameFunction()
{
    Debug.Log("First SameFunction Called.");
}
void SecondInterface.SameFunction()
{
    Debug.Log("Second SameFunction Called.");
}
```

The explicit declaration is used by the interface name followed by the dot operator and the function name in the function declaration. To follow this up, each interface function needs to be called.

```
public virtual void SameFunction()
{
    Debug.Log("Which version is Called?");
    ((FirstInterface)this).SameFunction();
    ((SecondInterface)this).SameFunction();
}
```

The non-explicit implementation needs to call the explicit forms of the function call by casting to the interface within the class implementing them. The reference to the class itself is done with the `this` keyword. A cast from the class itself is done to the specific interface using the `(FirstInterface)` or `(SecondInterface)` syntax. This provides the connection to the specific interface in the class implementing that interface. The dot operator is used to call the function from the specific interface after the cast.

```
((SecondInterface)this).SameFunction();
/*          ↑          ↑          ↑           */
/*          |          |          |           */
/*          |    _____|_____    |           */
/*          |   |             |   |           */
/*          |   |reference    |   |           */
/*          |   |to this class|   |           */
/*          |   |which implements|  |         */
/*          |   |the interfaces|  |           */
/*          |   |_____|   |           */
/*   _____|_____    _____|_____    */
/*  |the interface to|     |the function in |  */
/*  |cast into from  |     |the interface   |  */
/*  |this class      |     |to call         |  */
/*  |_____|     |_____|  */
```

When the implementing class marks the `SameFunction()` as `virtual`, any implementing class will then call all three versions of the function.

```
class ImplementsBoth : ImplementsFirstAndSecond
{
    public override void SameFunction()
    {
        base.SameFunction();
    }
}
```

The `ImplementsBoth` class inherits from `ImplementsFirstAndSecond`. This becomes a class which brings the two interfaces into a single implementation.

```
void UsingMultipleInterfaces()
{
    ImplementsBoth fromBoth = new ImplementsBoth();
    fromBoth.SameFunction();
}
```

Calling on the `SameFunction()` from the class which implements the two interfaces which were called in the `SameFunction()` from the previous class produces the following output in the Unity 3D Console:

> ⚠ **Which version is Called?**
> UnityEngine.Debug:Log(Object)
>
> ⚠ **First SameFunction Called.**
> UnityEngine.Debug:Log(Object)
>
> ⚠ **Second SameFunction Called.**
> UnityEngine.Debug:Log(Object)

We call every version of the `SameFunction()` when we inherit from a class which implements the `SameFunction()` and then references two more functions, one from each interface. It's uncommon, but it's an edge case you should be aware of.

Most interfaces are written as a system to comply with various systems already implemented. Often an interface can be used to allow commonly used C# constructs to work with your custom script classes.

7.9.3 IComparer

Building a collection of interfaces makes sense so long as the interfaces provide necessary functionality. The interfaces provided by C# offer more interesting possibilities in that they can be customized for any suited purpose.

The System.Collections library built into C# has a class called the `ArrayList`. Starting with a list populated with int values ranging from 0 to 1000.

```
ArrayList numberList = new ArrayList();
for (int i = 0; i < 100; i++)
{
    numberList.Add(UnityEngine.Random.Range(0, 1000));
}
```

To show this list we simply read them out one at a time to the Unity 3D Console with a `Debug.Log()` command.

```
Debug.Log("Unsorted list.");
foreach (int i in numberList)
{
    // show list as generated by
    // a random number generator
    Debug.Log(i);
}
```

The fragment here prints out a hundred random numbers between 0 and 1000. The `ArrayList` has a function to rearrange the values stored in it called `Sort()`. After the `Sort()` function is used in the `ArrayList`, the values are rearranged from lowest to highest.

```
numberList.Sort();
Debug.Log("Sorted list.");
foreach (int i in numberList)
{
    // show list sorted
    Debug.Log(i);
}
```

The `ArrayList` isn't complete without having our own object to sort. The sort requires a customized version of the `IComparer` interface. The ArrayList has a built in comparison to sort the integer type. To enable sorting of a new type we need to create one.

```
class CompareDistance : IComparer
{
    public int Compare(object x, object y)
    {
        throw new System.NotImplementedException();
    }
}
```

In this interface, the public int `Compare()` function takes two objects.

We can extend this `CompareDistance` class with another object to compare against. We've added a third term called Target. This can be assigned after the `DistanceComparer` has been instanced. Therefore, after `DistanceComparer` dc; has been created with the new keyword, we assign the `Target` to another `GameObject` in the scene.

```
class DistanceComparer : IComparer
{
    public object Target;
    public int Compare(object x, object y)
    {
        GameObject xObj = (GameObject)x;
        GameObject yObj = (GameObject)y;
        GameObject target = (GameObject)Target;
        Vector3 tPos = target.transform.position;
        Vector3 xPos = xObj.transform.position;
        Vector3 yPos = yObj.transform.position;
        float distanceX = (tPos - xPos).magnitude;
        float distanceY = (tPos - yPos).magnitude;
        if (distanceX > distanceY)
        {
            return 1;
        }
        else
        {
            return -1;
        }
    }
}
```

The above code has the added Target GameObject and some math to check the distance from object x to the Target and the distance to object y. Once these two values are found, we compare them. If the distance to the first object is greater, then we return 1; if the value is less, we return −1. If neither of these two cases is fulfilled, then we return 0, inferring that x and y are equal.

The ArrayList.Sort() function uses the different 1, −1, and 0 values to move the objects it's comparing. 1 means to move the x object up one in the array, −1 down one in the array, and finally 0 means don't move any objects. Depending on the length of the list, the Sort() uses what is often referred to as a *quicksort* algorithm.

7.9.4 Using IComparer

In the scene we have several cubes placed around our game object with the Interfaces script. The first fragment of code collects an array and adds them to an ArrayList.

```
GameObject[] allObjects = FindObjectsOfType<GameObject>();
//get all game objects in the scene

ArrayList objectList = new ArrayList();
//make an arrayList to copy all of the game objects to

foreach (GameObject go in allObjects)
{
    objectList.Add(go);
}
```

This is followed by creating an instance of the DistanceComparer class which implements the IComparer interface.

```
DistanceComparer comparer = new DistanceComparer();
// create a distance comparer

comparer.Target = this.gameObject;
// assign the comparer a target

objectList.Sort(comparer);
// sort the list with the comparer
```

We then copy the sorted list to a public GameObject array we can observe in the editor.

```
SortedByDistance = new GameObject[objectList.Count];
objectList.CopyTo(SortedByDistance, 0);
// copy to Array we can observe in the Editor.
```

By adding the code to the Update() in the Interfaces script we can watch the SortedByDistance array change as we move the GameObject with the script attached.

The SortedByDistance array is now rearranged not by the order in the scene but by distance! Very quick and easy.

7.9.5 What We've Learned

There has already been a great deal of material in this chapter. Interfaces are sort of like promises to reuse both the same identifier and the same signature that were created in the interface.

This ensures that you always get the same implementation for each class that uses the same interface. It would be a good idea to have as few interfaces as necessary. You shouldn't implement a IMedPack interface and an IShieldPowerup interface. What should be implemented is an IPickup interface. An IPickup would cover anything that your player could pick up. An interface should be less specific, not more specific.

Likewise, an IWeapon would be fine to cover anything that shoots, needs to hold ammo, and does anything that a weapon is used for. The IPickup could hold information for incrementing ammo, health, armor, or anything else. Classes implementing the IPickup interface could decide which they are incrementing, allowing for one or all of the stats to be adjusted when the item is picked up.

We'll get into a few common-looking setups later on when we look at game design patterns. For now try to think on your own what sort of interfaces you'll be implementing.

7.10 Class Constructors Revisited

Interfaces provide a system to ensure that a class is talked to in a specific way. When we start building more complex classes, we need to use an apparatus to ensure a consistent creation of the class. When starting a game where zombies are spawned and chase after the player, we might begin with a single zombie type. Later, we'd want to change this up for more variety. Modifying the amount of damage to destroy a zombie or change its size, shape, and model would all need to be modified according to specific parameters.

When working with a team, you're going to be needing to make sure that the class you're writing is created consistently. If you allow one programmer to directly set the hit points and another one to modify its armor instead, then you might get some unexpected behavior between the two monsters. This could be mitigated by enforcing a specific interface. You set up a specific set of parameters that must be used to properly modify a zombie.

A class *constructor* is used to set up an initial set of parameters required to instance a new object. The constructor can include several parameters, including references to the object creating them.

7.10.1 A Basic Example

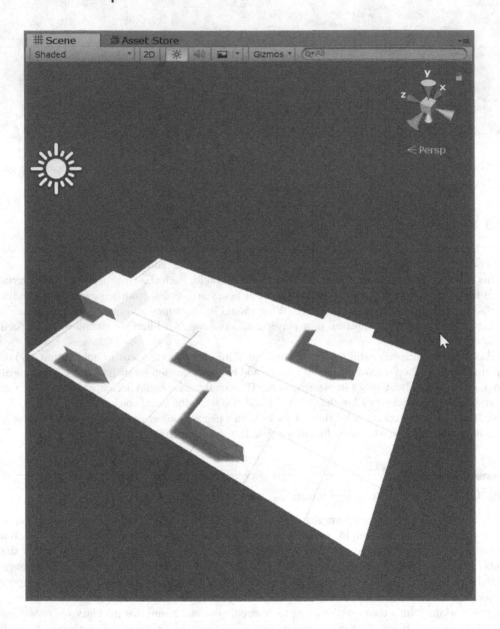

In the following code sample in the ClassConstructors_Scene in the Chapter 7 Unity Project, find the class ClassConstructors script on the game object of the same name. Within the ClassConstructor class is a nested class used to create a treadmill; a system useful for an endless runner style game.

```
class TreadmillSegment
{
    static int Segments;
    private float Speed;
    private int StepSize;
    private int Step;
    private GameObject Segment;

    public TreadmillSegment(float speed, ObstacleType obstacle, ref TreadmillUpdate treadmillUpdater)
    {
        Speed = speed;
        Segment = Instantiate(Resources.Load(obstacle.ToString()) as GameObject);
        treadmillUpdater += TreadmillUpdated;

        StepSize = (int)(1 / Speed);
        Step = Segments * StepSize;
        Segments++;
    }

    void TreadmillUpdated()
    {
        int totalSteps = Segments * StepSize;
        Segment.transform.position = new Vector3()
        {
            z = -(float)(Step++ % totalSteps) * Speed
        };
    }
}
```

The `TreadmillSegment` constructor takes three parameters. The first is a `float` used to designate how quickly the treadmill moves. The second is an enum to pick which shape the treadmill will use, and the last is a reference to a delegate.

```
enum ObstacleType
{
    Treadmill_Empty,
    Treadmill_Center,
    Treadmill_Left,
    Treadmill_Right
}
```

A Closer look at the `ObstacleType` enum shows four options. These coincide with the names of four prefabs found in the Resources directory of the Unity 3D project. Objects found in the Resources directory can be loaded by Unity 3D at run-time. This means after the game has started, a file located on disk can be loaded into the scene through script.

The last parameter is the reference to the `TreadmillUpdate` delegate. The delegate lives in the MonoBehaviour script that gets the `Update()` function called on every frame.

```csharp
private delegate void TreadmillUpdate();
private TreadmillUpdate UpdateTreadmill;
```

This is used to ensure that classes, like the `TreadmillSegment` will be able to receive an `Update()` call even though they are not inheriting from MonoBehaviour.

```csharp
int numSegments = 7;
for (int i = 0; i < numSegments; i++)
{
    ObstacleType obstacle = (ObstacleType)(i%4);
    new TreadmillSegment(0.015f, obstacle, ref UpdateTreadmill);
}
```

To use the `TreadmillSegment` class we create an arbitrary number of segments, in this case 7. This value could be anything. An `ObstacleType` is necessary to assign to the `TreadMillSegment` in the constructor. Using the `i` from the for loop cast from `int` to the `ObstacleType` enum. This approach is used to create a simple pattern quickly. More interesting logic aside, the cast from int to enum is possible since C# understands that an enum is a clever use of an int. Modulo 4 is used since there are only 4 values in the ObstacleType. The last `ref` `UpdateTreadmill` makes a reference to the delegate. The ref is necessary so the value of the delegate going in can retain an assignment.

```csharp
public TreadmillSegment(float speed, ObstacleType obstacle, ref TreadmillUpdate treadmillUpdater)
{
    Speed = speed;
    Segment = Instantiate(Resources.Load(obstacle.ToString()) as GameObject);
    treadmillUpdater += TreadmillUpdated;

    StepSize = (int)(1 / Speed);
    Step = Segments * StepSize;
    Segments++;
}
```

A closer look at the constructor of the `TreadmillSegment` shows we store the `Speed` value. The enum is converted to a string. The `string` is then used to load a resource from disk with the same name as the enum's value. We cast from an `int` to enum to `string` to load a file from disk. Then the incoming `ref` to the delegate `TreadmillUpdate` is assigned `TreadmillUpdated` function found inside of the `TreadmillSegment` class. After that we make and store a calculation for how much the segment will move on each update, where the treadmill starts, and how many treadmill segments there are in total.

```csharp
void TreadmillUpdated()
{
    int totalSteps = Segments * StepSize;
    Segment.transform.position = new Vector3()
    {
        z = -(float)(Step++ % totalSteps) * Speed
    };
}
```

The update function that gets assigned to the `ClassConstructors` delegate looks at how many steps there are in total. This is calculated by how many segments there are by how far they move per update. The `Step` value is incremented with every call. The position is reset to 0 by `Step` modulo `totalSteps` value. An integer value is used to keep track of the position since floating point values can begin to multiply small rounding errors over time.

```
void Update()
{
    if (UpdateTreadmill != null)
    {
        UpdateTreadmill();
    }
}
```

The last thing to do to update the segments is call the `UpdateTreadmill()` delegate in the `Update()` function of the `ClassConstuctors` class. There are only points in code in contact with the TreadmillSegment. The only contact with the `TreadmillSegment` is made through the constructor.

7.10.2 When to Create a New Class

Now that we've been working with classes for a few chapters, you might begin to wonder how often you'll need to write a new class. It's a good idea to separate groups of related functions into separate class. The pattern in which the treadmill appears should be something we can have more control over. Comment out the use of the first Treadmill system and uncomment the `UseTreadmillManager()` function.

```
void Start()
{
    //UseTreadmillSegments();

    UseTreadmillManger();
}
```

This deactivates the first test of the treadmill setup to allow us to inspect how a file can be used to store the pattern of our treadmill. We start at the beginning of the `TreadmillManager` class.

```
public readonly static string ProjectPath = System.IO.Directory.GetCurrentDirectory();
```

A `readonly static string` with the `ProjectPath` ensures that we cannot change this value once the game has started. The static keyword here also allows us to access the value more globally.

```
public static void WritePatternExample()
{
    string filePath = ProjectPath + "\\pattern.txt";
    // filePath = C:\Users\[user name]\Documents\BookContents\Chapters\Chapter7\pattern.txt

    StreamWriter writer = new StreamWriter(filePath);
    string defaultPattern =
        "Treadmill_Left\n" +
        "Treadmill_Center\n" +
        "Treadmill_Right\n" +
        "Treadmill_Right\n" +
        "Treadmill_Center\n" +
        "Treadmill_Left";
    // easier to read than a really long string.

    writer.Write(defaultPattern);
    writer.Close();
}
```

Also included in the header of this class is using System.IO, one of the many useful C# libraries that have been included with .NET giving Unity 3D plenty of tools to work with. This provides us with StreamWriter, a file utility that can write a file to disk so long as it's got a file path. In this case we used ProjectPath and added a file name. The ProjectPath leads to the directory where the Project is stored on your computer so your path may differ from the one indicated in the comment.

We then take a long string with '\n' between each value. This will allow us to break the string into usable parts later. Then we give the StringWriter the defaultPattern string to write to disk. The writer needs to be closed to finish writing the file.

```
public static string ReadPattern()
{
    string filePath = ProjectPath + "\\pattern.txt";
    // filePath = C:\Users\[user name]\Documents\BookContents\Chapters\Chapter7\pattern.txt

    StreamReader reader = new StreamReader(filePath);
    string readPattern = reader.ReadToEnd();
    /* reads something like "Treadmill_Left\nTreadmill_Center\nTreadmill_Right\n */
    /* until it reaches the end of the file.                                  */
    reader.Close();
    return readPattern;
}
```

We see a very similar pattern with reading that file. A StreamReader is given the same path. Then ReadToEnd() is used to consume the contents of the file into a string. Once that's done then we close the reader before returning the string.

```
public static string[] PatternToArray(string pattern)
{
    //remove trailing '\n'
    pattern.TrimEnd(new char[] { '\n' });
    /* if there was a "Treadmill_Center\n" at the end this will */
    /* cut it off.                                              */

    string[] patternArray = pattern.Split('\n');
    /* breaks this into string[]{ "Treadmill_Center", "Treadmill_Left"} */
    /* an array with each string part between the \n chars.            */

    return patternArray;
}
```

To break the string into an array we look for the "\n" characters to break the string into smaller parts. This does a few things at once. First we have a bunch of smaller strings to work with, each object in the string[] array is one of the values written in the string. Second we know how many segments were written to the string.

```
string pattern = TreadmillManager.ReadPattern();
// gets the pattern of segments from disk

string[] obstacleArray = TreadmillManager.PatternToArray(pattern);
// gets the converted string to string[]{ "Treadmill_Left", "Treadmill_Center" } etc...

int numSegments = obstacleArray.Length;
// get the number of segments in the array

for (int i = 0; i < numSegments; i++)
{
    switch (obstacleArray[i])
    {
        case "Treadmill_Empty":
            new TreadmillSegment(0.015f, ObstacleType.Treadmill_Empty, ref UpdateTreadmill);
            break;
        case "Treadmill_Center":
            new TreadmillSegment(0.015f, ObstacleType.Treadmill_Center, ref UpdateTreadmill);
            break;
        case "Treadmill_Left":
            new TreadmillSegment(0.015f, ObstacleType.Treadmill_Left, ref UpdateTreadmill);
            break;
        case "Treadmill_Right":
            new TreadmillSegment(0.015f, ObstacleType.Treadmill_Right, ref UpdateTreadmill);
            break;
    }
}
```

To use this we read the pattern from the `TreadmillManager.ReadPattern()` which returns the contents of the pattern.txt file. Then we convert that into an array with `TreadmillManager.PatternToArray()` which returns a `string[]` array. We know how many segments to create so a for loop using the num-Segments value allows us to check each object in the array for a string. The switch statement uses case "Treadmill_Empty," "Treadmill_Center," "Treadmill_Left" and "Treadmill_Right" to supply the `TreadmillSegment()` constructor with its proper `ObstacleType`.

```
public static void AppendPattern(ObstacleType obstacle)
{
    string previousPattern = ReadPattern();
    /* previous string might be like "Treadmill_Center" since we    */
    /* trim the trailing \n                                         */

    string newPattern = previousPattern + "\n" + obstacle.ToString();
    /* this adds a new "Treadmill_Left + "\nTreadmill_Center"        */
    /* to the end of the previous string                            */

    string filePath = ProjectPath + "\\pattern.txt";
    // filePath = C:\Users\[user name]\Documents\BookContents\Chapters\Chapter7\pattern.txt
    StreamWriter writer = new StreamWriter(filePath);
    writer.Write(newPattern);
    writer.Close();
}
```

To make things more interesting, we can add additional functions to the `TreadmillManager` like a system to append more obstacles to the text file. Here we convert the `ObstacleType` into a string preceded by a `'\n'` character to create each appended object on a new line.

When we use the `TreadmillManager` in the following manner:

```
TreadmillManager.WritePatternExample();

TreadmillManager.AppendPattern(ObstacleType.Treadmill_Center);
TreadmillManager.AppendPattern(ObstacleType.Treadmill_Center);
TreadmillManager.AppendPattern(ObstacleType.Treadmill_Center);
TreadmillManager.AppendPattern(ObstacleType.Treadmill_Empty);
TreadmillManager.AppendPattern(ObstacleType.Treadmill_Empty);
TreadmillManager.AppendPattern(ObstacleType.Treadmill_Empty);
```

The text file generated appears as such:

```
 1  Treadmill_Left
 2  Treadmill_Center
 3  Treadmill_Right
 4  Treadmill_Right
 5  Treadmill_Center
 6  Treadmill_Left
 7  Treadmill_Center
 8  Treadmill_Center
 9  Treadmill_Center
10  Treadmill_Empty
11  Treadmill_Empty
12  Treadmill_Empty|
```

Tools that allow you to read and write to disk will need to use some additional tricks to avoid interrupting your game while it's playing. Large files can cause your game to stall or glitch and you'll lose a frame or two. We'll learn a few tricks in Section 7.18 when we cover a system where your game can continue to run with new tasks running in the background.

7.10.3 What We've Learned

As we add new tricks to our bag, we need to consider how to use them. Even though the tricks are no more than organizational or even for practice, it's important that we use them. Practice is the only way we will get better at the craft of code. With each new tool we learn we should use it.

This might not always work out for the better. In many cases, inappropriate uses of some of these tricks can cause problems for other programmers when they come across your use of some interesting new programming trick. Only after some experience will you be more able to deploy these tricks in an appropriate manner. Until then, use them often until you find a case where you're in need of using a different trick.

7.11 Preprocessor Directives

We live in a computer-diverse age where PCs and mobile devices share code. More important to our everyday lives as a game developer, we must consider the differences between the Unity 3D Editor and the game that the editor produces on Windows, OSX, iOS and Android. To further complicate the development process, each platform may include many differences with how to address local storage or graphics.

The system in place to enable or disable blocks of code is called a *preprocessor directive*, which acts somewhat like a comment that can use logic to bypass or enable blocks of code. Many directives are already defined by the Unity 3D Editor; these include directives that are enabled specifically when targeting specific platforms like mobile or console.

7.11.1 A Basic Example

To follow along use the Chapter 7 unity Project, open the PreprocessorDirectives_Scene and find the PreprocessorDirectives script attached to the like-named game object. Preprocessors are placed above the usual header of the file. PreprocessorDirectives are created by using the hash tag define (#define) followed by an identifier.

The definition of the directive comes before the using UnityEngine and other usings that are included in your new C# file. This also provides the use of the preprocessor directives to define whether or not usings are included in the file.

```
#if TESTING
)using DOTNET = System.Diagnostics;
#endif
using UnityEngine;
```

This means we could include a diagnostics library from the dot net libraries just for testing. To keep specific blocks of code limited to specific tasks or scope the definition of TESTING is used by #if and #endif to create a scope of enabled code where TESTING allows. To make things a bit more simple to use, System.Diagnostics is renamed DOTNET to

```
    void Start()
    {
        Debug.Log("UNITY DEBUG TEST");
#if TESTING
        DOTNET.Debug.WriteLine("DOT NET TEST");
#endif
    }
```

Looking further down, we see the #if TESTING in the Start() function followed by the DOTNET. Debug.Log("DOT NET TEST");, which is followed by #endif to end the statements scoped by the directive. The result of this code allows us to easily pick chunks of code to switch on and off. In Visual Studio click on the Attach to Unity button, or go into the Debug menu and select Start Debugging. Then go back to Unity to start the game.

> UNITY DEBUG TEST
> UnityEngine.Debug:Log(Object)

We see the above output in the Unity Console. In the Visual Studio Output we get the following output:

```
DOT NET TEST
```

The `System.Diagnostics` version of `Debug` will send output exclusively to the Visual Studio output window and the Unity's version of `Debug` will send output to the Unity Console window.

The above code is enabled with #define TESTING located at the top of the class. If we comment out `//#define TESTING` and leave the rest of the code alone, The Visual Studio output is excluded.

```
#if !TESTING
        Debug.Log("Not using TESTING");
#endif
```

When the code is run, the second "Not using TESTING" log will not be sent to the console as TESTING is defined. Once TESTING is commented out, the directive `#if !TESTING` or "if not testing" enables the `Debug.Log()` with `Not using TESTING` and we'll get Unity's output with the second log. Preprocessors like this can be used to completely omit code from compiling, depending on whether or not the code it's around is needed. This is why it's called a preprocessor directive. Based on how the directives are set up, you can have entire sections of code omitted from various versions of the code. It's worth noting that you have to put all of your #define directive statements before any other token appears in the class, so all of the #define statements must appear at the top of the class file.

Using the #if preprocessor is a clever way to manage what code gets executed based on the programmer adding in or taking out various #define directives. In Unity 3D, however, we get a very useful predefined set of directives.

7.11.2 UNITY_EDITOR

Continuing in PreprocessorDirectives.cs file, take a look at the line where #if UNITY_EDITOR appears.

```
    void EditorOnly()
    {
#if UNITY_EDITOR
        Debug.Log("im an only editor message");
#endif
    }
```

The `UNITY_EDITOR` directive is defined only when the code is being run in the editor. A complete listing of the different symbols that have been defined can be found on the Unity 3D website. The other defined symbols include Unity 3D version number and the platform that the game is running on.

```
    public int Health;
    /* define not allowed in body of   */
    /* the class                       */
#define START_LOW_HEALTH
```

It's important to remember that you cannot define a new directive in the body of the code.

When the game is run in stand-alone mode or on a mobile device, the UNITY_EDITOR directive doesn't exist, so any code inside of any `#if UNITY_EDITOR` preprocessor directives will skip being compiled into the game. It's often useful to have specific behaviors when running in the editor. This can speed up testing if you find yourself changing numbers while testing in the editor.

```
    public int Health = 10;
    void EditorCheats()
    {
#if UNITY_EDITOR
        Health = 1000;
#endif


    }
```

With something like this, we can easily just skip over changing the numbers every time we start the game in the editor. This also prevents us from accidentally checking in code that might affect the final release of the game. We can add on some layers of complexity onto the use of directives.

```
#if UNITY_EDITOR && START_LOW_HEALTH
        Health = 1;
#elif UNITY_EDITOR
        Health = 1000;
#endif
```

Here we can comment in and out the directive definition at the top and switch between Low_Health and Unity_Editor testing. The first preprocessor statement `#if UNITY_EDITOR && START_LOW_HEALTH` only sets when we're running in the editor and we've uncommented out the `//#define LOWHEALTH` directive at the beginning of the class. The `&&` operator works the same as though we were using it in an if statement.

To make things more clear, we can use parentheses around the preprocessor's condition `#if (UNITY_EDITOR && START_LOW_HEALTH)`, which will produce the same result. This isn't required; however, programming style might dictate that you use parentheses anyway. To switch between the two statements, we use `#elif`, which is a preprocessor version of else if normally found in the rest of your code.

The difference comes from an old habit that originated from an older less integrated system. An external text editing software went through each file and deleted text before it was compiled. Each # command had to be one word for the macro to work properly. The macro has been incorporated into the parser now, but the formatting hasn't changed. We're also looking at `#endif` rather than a closing parenthesis or curly brace.

It's a whole different language, and to that there are some benefits. It's much more obvious that there's a secondary set of actions taking place on the code. Rather than using something that looks like the following:

```
public bool unityEditor = false;
public bool startLowHealth = false;

void UsingBools()
{
    if (unityEditor && startLowHealth)
    {
        Health = 1;
    }
    else if (unityEditor)
    {
        Health = 1000;
    }
}
```

Here it's not so clear if these are directives. The real problem here is that this code will be compiled into the shipping game and it's more likely someone might accidentally leave a check box turned on before checking in. Of course, the real issue is the fact that there is extra code being checked into the shipping version of the game that doesn't need to be there.

```
public bool unityEditor = false;
```

Of course, we could actually leave these check boxes on or off based on how they are being used. However, the automation provided by simply adding #if UNITY_EDITOR is preferable, and also less prone to mistakes. Before moving on, it should be mentioned that along with #define there's also #undef.

```
#undef UNITY_EDITOR
/* hides the UNITY_EDITOR define from this file */
```

This immediately undefines the UNITY_EDITOR directive and anything relying on this will deactivate.

7.11.3 Mobile Development

In a previous exercise we wrote a file to the project directory. In the code a StreamWriter was used to create and write text to a file.

```
// something like this doesn't work for Android!?
string filePath = System.IO.Directory.GetCurrentDirectory();
filePath += "\\fileData.txt";
string contents = "Editor File Data.";
```

We use the System.IO.Directory.GetCurrentDirectory() function to find where the Assets directory is located that Unity is currently using. With this the Unity 3D Editor is able to locate and write to the file, in this case we're writing "Editor File Data." However, if we used this in a mobile device we'd run into a few problems.

Unfortunately, iOS requires several hurdles to jump to become a developer and some of them are financial. Android doesn't offer as many blockades to development, so if you are an Android phone user, you'll be able to try this out yourself.

If you don't have access to an Android device don't worry, we'll cover the most important parts, which include how directives work in a mobile platform.

If you're not an Android developer, follow the link below to switch your phone over to enable developer options. Every phone is a bit different, so it's best to get the how to from the creators of Android—Google.

https://developer.android.com/studio/debug/dev-options#enable

Android is included in the different target platforms that Unity can produce a build. In short you'll need to do the following:

1. Open Settings
2. Scroll down to System, (Android 8 or newer)
3. Scroll down to Build number and tap on it 7 times.
4. Go back one screen and you'll see the Developer Options
5. Select that and enable USB Debugging.

Now you're officially an Android Developer. Plug your phone into your computer's USB port and allow your computer to talk to your phone.

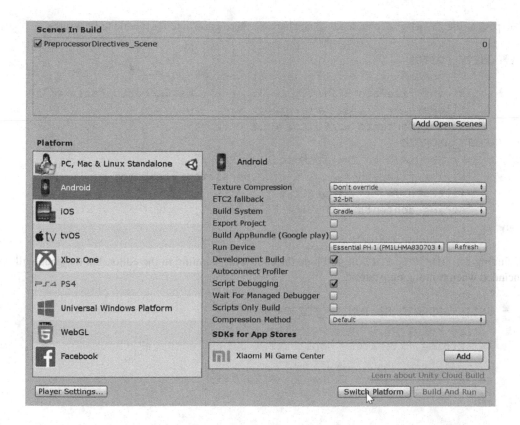

The list for building projects is extensive. Android, iOS, Xbox and web browsers are all targets for Unity 3D. Selecting Android and pressing the Switching Platform button changes which directives are enabled.

Once switched the preprocessor logic changes which blocks of code are enabled. Simply adding `#if UNITY_ANDROID` will not be enough to include code for that platform.

Running this code on an Android device will not work. Running the Android development tools and peeking at the log from the Console will show that `GetCurrentDirectory()` function doesn't do what we'd expect.

```
        Debug.Log(filePath);

// /\fileData.txt
// UnityEngine.DebugLogHandler:Internal_Log(LogType, String, Object)
// UnityEngine.DebugLogHandler:LogFormat(LogType, Object, String, Object[])
// UnityEngine.Logger:Log(LogType, Object)
// UnityEngine.Debug:Log(Object)
// PreprocessorDirectives: WriteToDevice()
// PreprocessorDirectives: Start()
```

The debug outout from the device looks a bit like the above. The file path looks like `"/\fileData.txt"` and lacks any directory structure. To get the proper directory path we need to use a different approach. This is followed by the StreamWriter running into problems as well.

```
UnauthorizedAccessException: Access to the path "/\fileData.txt" is denied.
  at System.IO.FileStream..ctor (System.String path, System.IO.FileMode mode,
```

The path to the `fileData.txt` leads to nowhere, so there's nowhere for the file to be written.

```
#if UNITY_EDITOR
        // something like this doesn't work for Android!?
        string filePath = System.IO.Directory.GetCurrentDirectory();
        filePath += "\\fileData.txt";
        string contents = "Editor File Data.";
#if UNITY_ANDROID
        // Required or the path looks like "/"
        string filePath = Application.persistentDataPath;
        filePath += "/fileData.txt";
        string contents = "Device File Data.";
#endif
```

Including `&& !UNITY_EDITOR` will hide the code when running in the editor, but the code will be included when running on Android.

```
#if UNITY_ANDROID && !UNITY_EDITOR
        // Required or the path looks like "/"
        string filePath = Application.persistentDataPath;
        filePath += "/fileData.txt";
        string contents = "Device File Data.";
#endif
```

Once the proper directives separate the editor's version of the function from the Android version of the function, both can operate as expected.

```
/storage/emulated/0/Android/data/com.CSharp.Project/files/fileData.txt
UnityEngine.DebugLogHandler:Internal_Log(LogType, String, Object)
UnityEngine.DebugLogHandler:LogFormat(LogType, Object, String, Object[])
UnityEngine.Logger:Log(LogType, Object)
UnityEngine.Debug:Log(Object)
PreprocessorDirectives:ReadbackPath() (at C:\Users\alexokita\Documents\BookContents\Chapters\Chapter7\Assets\PreprocessorDirectives.cs:68)
PreprocessorDirectives:Start() (at C:\Users\alexokita\Documents\BookContents\Chapters\Chapter7\Assets\PreprocessorDirectives.cs:79)
```

On Android the path assigned using `Application.persistentDataPath` looks quite different. The same path assignment works in the editor, but leads to a hidden directory in your user's folder, far less convenient than the project directory.

In some ways, the preprocessor directives means supporting multiple codebases. A block of code working in the editor, and another for your target platform. Imagine for a moment having to support multiple code projects, one in Objective-C or Swift, which is what iOS natively runs in XCode, another project written in Kotlin in Android Studio, and possibly something like C++ for Windows, etc. The list can go on and on for every platform.

Using preprocessor directives in Unity 3D can certainly add some complexity. Without preprocessor directives, you would use if else statements in your code for each operating system you might target. Preprocessor directives are a preferable alternative.

7.11.4 Warning

When using `#define` for debug purposes, it's often important to remind yourself that some directives are enabled. It's useful to add a reminder that a directive is active. In Unity the UNITY_EDITOR directive is useful; however, if you find it necessary it's possible to hide it in the class you're working in.

As a self-serving reminder, #warning can be added after an #if as a reminder in Unity 3D that there are modifications going on with your directives.

```
    void UseWarning()
    {
#if UNITY_EDITOR && TESTING
#warning TESTING MODE ACTIVE
#endif
    }
```

After adding this to the code, you'll get a warning once the script has been interpreted by Unity 3D that 'TESTING MODE ACTIVE':

⚠ Assets\PreprocessorDirectives.cs(130,10): warning CS1030: #warning: 'TESTING MODE ACTIVE'

This text can be anything you like, so long as the warning message you're giving to yourself makes sense. The warning message has no special formatting. Whatever appears on the line after the `#warning` is what will appear in the Unity 3D Console.

So your messages need to stay on the line where the `#warning` appears. The same goes for the rest of the `#define` preprocessor directives. As a rule of thumb, these should be short and in all caps. The all caps notation isn't enforced, although it is common practice. This helps point out where any of these special case definitions are happening in the code.

7.11.5 Organizing

Organization is a constant struggle. In a Visual Studio, you have little boxes for folding code. #region NAME is a useful directive that is used to help keep your development environment sane.

```
#region FirstSection
void FirstFunctionInFirstSection()
{
    //Do things here
}
void InFirstSection()
{
    //Do other things here
}
#endregion
```

Adding regions to your code can help collapse sections of code. Adding too many different #ifdef and #region tags might work against you. Having more hash tags in your code than actual functions defeats the purpose of why these are used to begin with.

Though used wisely in a long class, a few regions can help. A #region can be nested inside of another region. Once inside of a region you're able to collapse sections of a long function to help you observe relations between variables that might be far apart.

7.11.6 What We've Learned

We will be coming back to some of the preprocessor directives again once we've covered some error handling concepts. In general, preprocessors work on the code in a manner closer to how comments work. Because of this, we can use preprocessor directives to manage different chunks of code based on a single #define at the beginning of a class.

Directives are used for many different things: One of the most common is to manage work with multiple platforms. Using preprocessor directives, you can set different settings for screen resolutions based on make or model.

7.12 Try Catch Finally

Working with a few warnings such as unused variables is simple enough; having too many of these can create situations where an important warning might be missed. In general, it's best to keep your warnings to an absolute minimum, or at least, no unexpected warnings at all.

There are situations where we might want to get specific warnings. In situations where we try to read a uniform resource locator (URL) from a web page and the server is down, we don't want our game to simply crash or freeze.

There are also situations where you might expect some values to be incorrect. When dealing with a user, you might expect a numeric value and get a letter instead. Rather than freeze and crash the game, you can ignore the input until a correction is made.

7.12.1 A Basic Example

Starting in the TryCatchFinally_Scene in the Chapter 7 Unity Project, open the TryCatchFinally script on the like-named game object. In the function `DontUseTryCatch()`, `int.Parse()` is used to read a string and extract an integer value.

```
void DontUseTryCatch()
{
    int i = 0;
    i = int.Parse("1");
    // this does work, and we get 1
    Debug.Log("i is " + i);

    int j = 0;
    j = int.Parse("One");
    //throws an error

    Debug.Log("j is " + j);
    // never gets called, the game stopped.
}
```

In the first block of code we parse a string containing "1" and the `int i` is assigned an `int 1`. In the second block of code we parse the string "One" and Unity, or rather C# errors and the game stops.

Your game, mobile or otherwise, would have crashed. To keep Unity 3D from crashing, using the try-catch pattern will help prevent bad input from crashing the game.

```
void UseTryCatch()
{
    int i = 0;
    try
    {
        i = int.Parse("One");
    }
    catch
    {
        i = 1;
    }
    Debug.Log("i is " + i);
}
```

With the above we get "i is 1" printed to the Console. The attempt to parse the string "One" to a 1 failed, but we didn't error, and the game didn't stop. The code assigned 1 to i using the catch which only executes if the try block fails. How do we know it failed? There wasn't any warning, debug log, or any indication that the Parse("One") failed.

```
void UseTryCatchWithException()
{
    int i = 0;
    try
    {
        i = int.Parse("One");
    }
    catch (Exception e)
    {
        Debug.Log(e.Message);
        i = 1;
    }
    Debug.Log("i is " + i);
}
```

Adding (Exception e) to the catch block leaves an input variable for try to assign an exception. The Exception type comes from using System, a core .NET library. The output from e.Message can inform us as to what didn't work with the Parse function when reading the string.

> Input string was not in a correct format.
> UnityEngine.Debug:Log(Object)

The try{} statement makes an attempt to process to the input value. If it succeeds i is assigned a valid number. If it fails the catch{} statement picks up what failed. From here you can make a decision as to how to work around the error.

```
void UseCheckExceptions()
{
    object[] objs = new object[] { 7.0, "23", null, "Seventeen"};
    Debug.Log("Check for Exception.");
    foreach (object o in objs)
    {
        CheckException(o);
    }
}

void CheckException(object o)
{
    int i = 0;
    try
    {
        i = (int)o;
        Debug.Log("I guess it wasn't an int.");
    }
    catch (Exception e)
    {
        Debug.Log(e.Message);
    }
}
```

From a given object we can try to cast to int to unbox a value. In the above we have four objects, none of which are int, and each one may or may not be able to be converted to an int by C#. We can give ourselves more information about what is going wrong with some parameters going into the catch{}. To start, we'll want to add a new directive at the beginning of the class. This means that we know not only that try{} failed, but why it failed. We can create a specific response to the failure. When the failure occurs for different reasons, we can create different catches for each situation.

7.12.2 Exception Messages

The Exception is a generic catch all for all varieties of exception types. The more specific NullReferenceException and InvalidCastException are the two that are brought up with the above example.

```
void CheckExceptionType(object o)
{
    int i = 0;
    try
    {
        Debug.Log("Got: " + o);
        i = (int)o;
    }
    catch (NullReferenceException e)
    {
        Debug.Log("NullReferenceException " + e.Message);
    }
    catch (InvalidCastException e)
    {
        Debug.Log("InvalidCastException " + e.Message);
    }
    catch (Exception e)
    {
        Debug.Log("Unexpected Exception "  + e.Message);
    }
}
```

The `CheckExceptionType()` function can check for different types of input problems from object. When casting the different types to an int we usually get an `InvalidCastException`. In the case where we catch the `null` in the array we get the `NullReferenceException`. In all the cases, the cast doesn't halt the game as it usually would. This provides a bit of a safety net if we're dealing with an unreliable data source. Something like a text input field to be filled in by the player or calling a web URL could return an unexpected data type. Because we were able to catch this problem and make a decision on how to handle it, we can save our game from an execution error. In the Scene an InputText field sits centered in the Game view.

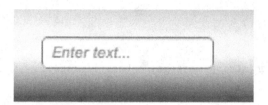

The field is connected to a function called `TextInputChanged()` where the field's text is sent to the functions parameter for evaluation. The text is then sent to a function to parse into an int value.

```
void ConvertFromStringToInt(string input)
{
    int i = 0;
    try
    {
        i = int.Parse(input);
        Debug.Log("int parse successful, got " + i);
    }
    catch (Exception e)
    {
        Debug.Log(e);
        try
        {
            i = (int)float.Parse(input);
            Debug.Log("float parse successful, got " + i);
        }
        catch{
            Debug.Log("input wasn't a float or an int.");
        }
    }
}
```

The first `try{}` block uses `int.Parse()` to check the string for an integer value. If that fails then we try to look for a float value, something like `1.0`. The nested try catch try catch will give us two ways to convert the string to an integer value.

Even if the input isn't a numeric value we'll get an exception not a crash. We could simply ask the player to try to provide a numeric input if that's what we're expecting. Rather than using Debug.Log, we could open an information pop-up and ask for a different input and have the player try again.

7.12.3 Custom Exceptions

Working with many different conditions complicates debugging. Finding and dealing with a specific error condition is best dealt with by using custom exception code.

```
public class MyException : Exception
{
    public MyException()
    {
    }
    public MyException(string message) : base(message)
    {
    }
    public MyException(string message, Exception innerException)
    : base(message, innerException)
    {
    }
}
```

Classes like int and float have a Parse() function. This function tries to read a string and interpret the characters in the string as a number value. If this fails, it creates a new exception and throws it. In a simple range example we'll do the following to check an array of numbers for integer values between 0 and 100 with a ValidateRange() function.

```
void ValidateRange(int i)
{
    if (i > 100)
    {
        MyException e = new MyException(i + " is above range.");
        e.Number = 100;
        throw e;
    }
    else if (i < 0)
    {
        MyException e = new MyException(i + " is below range.");
        e.Number = 0;
        throw e;
    }
}
```

The above function checks the incoming value for a number higher than 100 or a value below 0. If either case is true a new MyException is created and the keyword throw is followed by the created MyException. Visually, there's no connection between the ValidateRange() function and the catch{} block.

```
try
{
    ValidateRange(i);
    Debug.Log("input: " + i + " is in range.");
    /* this works a little bit like this    */
    /*      MyException e;                   */
    /*          └──────→─┐                   */
    /*      ValidateRange(i, out e);         */
} /*              ┌──────────←─┘             */
catch (MyException e)
{
    Debug.Log(e.Message + "value bypassed:" + e.Number);
}
```

In some of the C# syntax we've seen before we might expect that the Exception needs to go into a function before it comes out. When we use throw, the Exception appears without any visible variable to acknowledge its presence before it's used in the catch parameter. In addition, the only catch block that will execute is the one with the matching Exception type.

```
void UseCustomExceptions()
{
    int[] inputs = new int[] { 0, 1, -10, 50, 100, 3000 };
    foreach (int i in inputs)
    {
        try
        {
            ValidateRange(i);
            Debug.Log("input: " + i + " is in range.");
        }
        catch (MyException e)
        {
            Debug.Log(e.Message + "value bypassed:" + e.Number);
        }
    }
}
```

If the value throws an exception then the try{} block exits and we jump to the catch{} block. Once in the catch{} block we read back the message and the value that was passed by the input value. If the ValidateRange doesn't throw any Exceptions, then we get the Debug.Log() in the try block indicating that the input value passes the validation.

> (!) input: 0 is in range.
>   UnityEngine.Debug:Log(Object)
>
> (!) input: 1 is in range.
>   UnityEngine.Debug:Log(Object)
>
> (!) -10 is below range.value bypassed:0
>   UnityEngine.Debug:Log(Object)
>
> (!) input: 50 is in range.
>   UnityEngine.Debug:Log(Object)
>
> (!) input: 100 is in range.
>   UnityEngine.Debug:Log(Object)
>
> (!) 3000 is above range.value bypassed:100
>   UnityEngine.Debug:Log(Object)

We could add any number of possible catches to an Exception. However we can throw different types of Exceptions, not just MyException. For validating scene objects we could throw a `NullReferenceException` if an object provided isn't a gameObject.

Now once the Exception is caught, we can check what situation threw the message, and then react appropriately. In cases where we can't possibly come up with every imaginable situation, we have one last keyword to help us.

7.12.4 Finally

To complete our `try{}-catch{}` statement, we can add a `finally{}` statement. Since we're not doing anything complex here, all we need is the following:

```csharp
void UseFinally()
{
    try
    {
        ValidateRange(101);
    }
    catch (MyException e)
    {
        Debug.Log(e.Message);
    }
    finally
    {
        Debug.Log("Done.");
    }
}
```

In this situation, the `finally{}` statement is unnecessary. Where finally comes in handy is with functions that require some clean up afterward. After parsing player input we might want to clear lock the input field, or perhaps switch UI (user interface) panels to a new screen. The `finally{}` block only runs once try and catch have finished their tasks.

7.12.5 Try-Catch and Finally in Use

When working with System.IO and the StreamWriter function we often get a few UnauthorizedAccessExceptions. This is often because we've got the path wrong.

```
void UseWriteToFile()
{
    string path = System.IO.Directory.GetCurrentDirectory();
    FileStream file = null;
    FileInfo info = null;
    try
    {
        info = new FileInfo(path + "//FinalFile.txt");
        file = info.OpenWrite();
        for (int i = 0; i < 255; i++)
        {
            file.WriteByte((byte)i);
        }
    }
    catch (FileNotFoundException e)
    {
        Debug.Log(e.Message);
    }
    catch (UnauthorizedAccessException e)
    {
        Debug.Log(e.Message);
    }
    finally
    {
        if (file != null)
        {
            file.Close();
        }
    }
}
```

With this in mind, we use the try{} to create a new file called FinalFile.txt in our project directory. Once it's created, we open it for writing, and then add in a bunch of characters with file.WriteByte(). If we're not allowed to write to this directory, we catch that problem with UnauthorizedAccessException and have Unity 3D let us know if there was a problem. If the file has been written, it's closed with the finally{} block.

7.12.6 What We've Learned

The notation used here creates a clean and tidy way to create a file, check for problems, and finish the file writing process. The blocks are clear and the proper procedures are followed. We also get an interesting look at all of the different characters in a font.

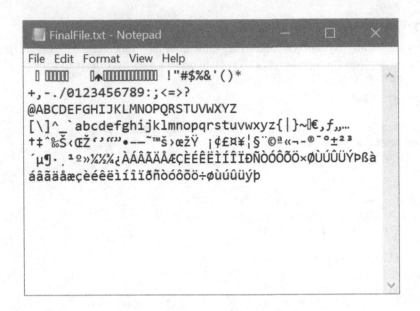

In the file.txt, we get many weird characters before we start to see letters and numbers. Aside from unusual characters, it's important to know how the try-catch-finally process works for using network connections.

When setting up a connection through hypertext transfer protocol (HTTP) to get an image from the internet or models from a web server, we'll want to make sure that the connection didn't disconnect halfway through. Possibly a user name or password was incorrect. All of these situations will need to be caught before we reach a `finally{}` block and pretend that everything went as expected.

After the file.txt was written, you can get properties on the file and change it to read only. This will throw the exception and you'll get the following error:

Access to the path "C:\file.txt" is denied.

UnityEngine. Debug:LogWarning(Object)

Warnings:Start () (at Assets/Warnings.cs:26)

This means that the `try{}` block failed and the `catch{}` block was activated. When the `finally{}` block is reached, the file is null and doesn't need to be closed.

There are many different types of exceptions that Unity 3D will often be throwing. It's likely that you might need to move an object and want to catch if a number gets out of hand or you suspect a divide by zero exception might be thrown. These situations are easier to work with if you use `try{}` and `catch{}`.

7.13 IEnumerator

C# has several built-in interfaces, IEnumerator is just one of them. We used the IComparer interface to sort through distances to gameObjects. The utility of an interface is a means to reduce work. Any task coming up more than a few times should lead toward simplification of work.

An enumerator is a system that is used to iterate through an array. The prefixed letter is an I, so it's an interface, but what does that even mean? An IEnumerator is something that we use on an array of an object with an enumerator interface.

The problem begins as a long list of items. The usual `for(int i = 0; i < array.Length; i++)` works fine for most situations, and in fact you can get by with just that. There are cases in which some data is not presented as an array but as an IEnumerator. Extended markup language, which looks a lot like a web page for data, doesn't always present its data to you in the form of an array. We'll find out more about that in a later chapter about reading and writing data.

With cases like this, we are forced to use either a foreach or a while loop. However, the way these loops are used aren't as simple as you might expect. Once you understand how it works, you will find that a large array is really easy to iterate through.

7.13.1 Enumeration

Before we make our own enumerator, it's easier to see how it's used. The IEnumerator is an interface with one property and two methods. The only property is called Current, and the two methods we can use are called Reset and MoveNext.

7.13.1.1 A Basic Example

Let's find the Enums class in the Assets directory of the Enums project.

```
int[] intArray = new int[] { 10, 20, 30, 40, 50, 60, 70, 80, 90, 100 };
void UseIntEnumerator()
{
    IEnumerator intEnumerator = intArray.GetEnumerator();
    while (intEnumerator.MoveNext())
    {
        Debug.Log("Current int: " + intEnumerator.Current);
    }
    // Current int: 10
    // Current int: 20
    // Current int: 30
    // Current int: 40
    // Current int: 50
    // Current int: 60
    // Current int: 70
    // Current int: 80
    // Current int: 90
    // Current int: 100
}
```

This is a pretty short example of what an IEnumerator does. First we get an array of integers, though the array can be of anything. We're calling the array `intArray`, just to keep things simple. Arrays have a method called `GetEnumerator()` that returns a type `IEnumerator`. To use this we can assign a variable, in this case o as a type `IEnumerator` to `intArray.GetEnumerator();`.

The variable `intEnumerator` is an `IEnumerator`, has a few simple functions. Peeking at the IEnumerator in Visual Studio will reveal the following:

```
namespace System.Collections
{
    public interface IEnumerator
    {
        object Current
        {
            get;
        }

        bool MoveNext();
        void Reset();
    }
}
```

It's important to note that the IEnumerator intEnumerator is an object. To use it for something else, we'll need to cast it to whatever it is we're expecting. We will need to remember this later on. We can use the IEnumerator o outside of a while loop.

```
void UseWithoutLoop()
{
    IEnumerator intEnumerator = intArray.GetEnumerator();

    intEnumerator.MoveNext();
    Debug.Log("Current int: " + intEnumerator.Current);
    // Current int: 10

    intEnumerator.MoveNext();
    Debug.Log("Current int: " + intEnumerator.Current);
    // Current int: 20

    intEnumerator.MoveNext();
    Debug.Log("Current int: " + intEnumerator.Current);
    // Current int: 30

    intEnumerator.MoveNext();
    Debug.Log("Current int: " + intEnumerator.Current);
    // Current int: 40
}
```

This might not be the most efficient way to use an IEnumerator, but this is a good approximation of what's happening inside of the while loop. The intEnumerator.MoveNext(); function call tells intEnumerator to change the value of intEnumerator.Current. To make this more clear, we'll add in why the while loop works.

```
void UseIfToIterate()
{
    int[] someInts = new int[] { 1, 3, 7 };
    IEnumerator intEnumerator = someInts.GetEnumerator();
    if (intEnumerator.MoveNext())
    {
        Debug.Log("Current int: " + intEnumerator.Current);
    }
    if (intEnumerator.MoveNext())
    {
        Debug.Log("Current int: " + intEnumerator.Current);
    }
    if (intEnumerator.MoveNext())
    {
        Debug.Log("Current int: " + intEnumerator.Current);
    }
    if (intEnumerator.MoveNext())
    {
        Debug.Log("I won't get called.");
    }
}
```

After shortening the array of ints to only three items, we'll see what happens if we use if intEnumerator.MoveNext() past the length of the array. Does intEnumerator.Current have a value? The array is three items long, so the fourth if statement returns false, and a fourth Current value won't be printed. The IEnumerator function of an array returns a useful little trick to use for tasks involving arrays.

7.13.1.2 What Doesn't Work

For many of the basic tasks involving arrays, you might use the foreach statement. The following code fragment could work on its own if you didn't use a foreach statement.

```
void UseStringArray()
{
    string[] strings = new string[] { "A", "B", "C" };
    IEnumerator strEnumerator = strings.GetEnumerator();
    foreach (string s in strEnumerator)
    {
        Debug.Log(s);
    }
}
```

With a foreach statement, we might expect the IEstring to contain something useful as though it were a simple array. However, this is not the case. The IEumerator type doesn't actually give access to its contents without providing it though Current. Just as interestingly enough, if you were to ask for IEString. Current, the first value found has nothing in it.

```
string[] strings = new string[] { "A", "B", "C" };
IEnumerator strEnumerator = strings.GetEnumerator();
Debug.Log(strEnumerator.Current);
```

Try doing the above code sample and you'll get a run-time error message:

> InvalidOperationException: Enumeration has not started. Call MoveNext.
> System.Array+ArrayEnumerator.get_Current () (at <ac823e2bb42b41bda67924a45a0173c3>:0)

The enumeration process has not started, it seems. This requires at least one use of MoveNext() before the IEnumerator variable's. Current object has a value of some kind. As we've seen, there are various ways to use MoveNext() to get a value from the Current property in the IEnumerable data type.

Take a moment to think about what's going on. The IEnumerator is an interface class written by C# programmers. It was created to provide you, the programmer, a method to make a consistent interface that can be incorporated into your code smoothly. Once implemented, other programmers can use your class as they would use any other IEnumerator. You can think of it as adding a handy feature to your class. However, to fully implement the feature and make sure that it does what you want it to, you'll need to understand how it's expected to work.

7.13.2 Implementing IEnumerator

The implementation of an enumerator comes in two new additions to your starting class. This means you can take any existing class and add an enumerator to it. So you could take any zombie, and make an array of that zombie enumerable. In this example we'll look at AZombie class which is simply a wrapper for a zombie's name.

To enumerate through the AZombie class we'll need the two additional classes. A ZombieEnumerator which inherits from the IEnumerator and an interfacing class that inherits from IEnumerable. The IEnumerable provides the GetEnumerator() function through an array of AZombie objects.

We're starting in the ZombieEnumerator class that implements the IEnumerator interface. This is an interface that is found in the System.Collections .NET library. We store two things in the ZombieEnumerator: a reference to the array that's going to be enumerated and an int that keeps track of where we are in the array.

```
class ZombieEnumerator : IEnumerator
{
    private AZombie[] AZombieArray;
    private int index;
```

To instantiate the IEnumerator object we assign it an array.

```
/* constructor saves the incoming array    */
public ZombieEnumerator(AZombie[] zombieArray)
{
    AZombieArray = zombieArray;
}
```

The locally stored array is assigned in the constructor. This is followed by the three functions that are required in the IEnumerator interface. The MoveNext(), Reset(), and the Current accessor.

```
/* MoveNext increments the locally stored  */
/* index of the array and returns true     */
/* so long as the index doesn't exceed     */
/* the length of the stored array          */
public bool MoveNext()
{
    index++;
    return index >= AZombieArray.Length;
}
```

```
/* put the array index back ahead of 0     */
public void Reset()
{
    index = -1;
}
```

```
/* return the object from the array at the */
/* index                                   */
object IEnumerator.Current
{
    get
    {
        return AZombieArray[index];
    }
}
```

The `MoveNext()` increments the `index` value and returns true so long as the `index` is either less than or equal to the length of the stored array of enumerable objects. The `Reset()` function simply sets the `index` value to −1 so when `MoveNext()` is called after a reset it returns the 0th, or zeroth, object in the stored array. The `object IEnumerable.Current` explicitly implements the IEnumerable's interface for the `Current` value. This only provides `get{}` since we don't want anything to change what is stored in the array.

When implementing an interface or any class inheriting from another class, you can use an explicit declarator. We will see this again when implementing the IEnumerable interface.

```
/* you then make an IEnumerable object where    */
/* an array of the enumerated object lives.     */
class Zombies : IEnumerable
{
    // the array to iterate through.
    private AZombie[] AZombieArray;

    // constructor to assign to the new Enumerator
    public Zombies(AZombie[] zombieArray)
    {
        AZombieArray = zombieArray;
    }

    // the explicit method which returns the IEnumerator
    // object to start enumeration
    IEnumerator IEnumerable.GetEnumerator()
    {
        return (IEnumerator)GetEnumerator();
    }

    // the actual Enumerator that's returned
    public ZombieEnumerator GetEnumerator()
    {
        return new ZombieEnumerator(AZombieArray);
    }
}
```

The `Zombies` class acts as the generator to the `ZombieEnumerator` class we just looked at. The `IEnumerator IEnumerable.GetEnumerator()` is the explicit declaration to fulfill the IEnumerable interface. The class stores an array of AZombie so it can assign it to the created ZombieEnumerator.

```
// the explicit method which returns the IEnumerator
// object to start enumeration
IEnumerator IEnumerable.GetEnumerator() /*→┐❶    */
{                                        /*  │    */
    return (IEnumerator)GetEnumerator();/*←┘❷   */
}                            /*           │     */
                             /*           ↓❸    */
public ZombieEnumerator GetEnumerator()
{
    return new ZombieEnumerator(AZombieArray);
}                            /*←❸ returned        */
                             /* after initalized  */
```

To more clearly see how the chain of calls is made to GetEnumerator(), we start with the first interface version of IEnumerator IEnumerable.GetEnumerator(). This is how the first call is made; this then looks for the local GetEnumerator, which is a public ZombieEnumerator GetEnumerator(). The second function returns the populated ZombieEnumerator().

To use the new Enumerator, an array of different AZombie objects is created and a new IEnumerator is made from the array.

```
AZombie Stubbs = new AZombie("Stubbs");
AZombie Bob = new AZombie("Bob");
AZombie Rob = new AZombie("Rob");
AZombie Freddy = new AZombie("Freddy");
AZombie Jason = new AZombie("Jason");
AZombie[] zombies = new AZombie[] { Stubbs, Bob, Rob, Freddy, Jason };
IEnumerator zombieEnumerator = zombies.GetEnumerator();
```

The new IEnumerator works as we created from the array of strings or ints. To enumerate through the zombieEnumerator we use the same syntax with the while loop.

```
while (zombieEnumerator.MoveNext())
{
    Debug.Log(zombieEnumerator.Current);
}
// Enumerations+AZombie
// Enumerations+AZombie
// Enumerations+AZombie
// Enumerations+AZombie
// Enumerations+AZombie
// Enumerations+AZombie
```

The catch here is that we need to cast or unbox the contained object in the Current value.

```
// reset the enumerator after you've used it
zombieEnumerator.Reset();

while (zombieEnumerator.MoveNext())
{
    // don't forget to cast!
    AZombie z = (AZombie)zombieEnumerator.Current;
    Debug.Log(z.Name);
}
// Stubbs
// Bob
// Rob
// Freddy
// Jason
```

Before using the zombieEnumerator again we need to Reset() the object. This sets the Current value of the Enumerator to −1 so the next time we see MoveNext() in a while loop there will be an object to assign to Current.

Take care to notice how Enumerator and Enumerable are used. It's easy to get mixed up between the two interfaces.

7.13.3 What We've Learned

This has been a pretty heavy chapter about implementing the IEnumerator and IEnumerable interface. It's great practice and it's important to know how to go about implementing an interface from the C# library.

There are many cool tricks that can be added to your classes to make them more feature complete. This does require more thought and time, but in the end your classes will be more useful to the rest of the team of programmers you might be working with.

When to decide to implement one of these programming features is up to you and your team. Sometimes adding a feature might make a simple class too complex. If you're fine with using simple code to avoid the complexity, then you're free to do so. Thankfully, C# allows you to do pretty much anything that's allowed within the language. There aren't any hard and fast rules in the language that limit how it's used.

Interfaces not only tell you what is expected out of your class but also how to get it done. You're allowed to provide the data in any way you feel fit, but it's important to not provide something to start testing with.

On your own you should figure out how to add and remove items in a dynamic array in the IZombieEnumerator. You've implemented the required functions and properties to make the IEnumerator interface happy, but there's nothing limiting you from adding more features to the class beyond the IEnumerator interface.

7.14 Generics

When you create a new data structure, you're creating a strict organization and naming of your new data. This begins to run into problems when you need to make small modifications to that structure to suit multiple tasks. As your project gets more complex, your data will become more complex as well.

Thankfully as of C# version 2.0, generics were included to make data flow a bit more easily. In Unity 3D, we get used to doing casts with the following syntax where (float) takes the int 1 and converts it into the expected type to assign to f.

```
void UseCastTypes()
{
    float f = (float)1.0d;
    Debug.Log(f);
    // 1
}
```

Of course, this can be avoided if we start off with the correct type to assign by using 1.0f to indicate that we're using 1.0d as a float and not a double. Although many conversions are automatic between int and float, for example, not all conversions can be done for you.

When faced with making different data structures for different needs, you'll end up with more and more new data types. This leads to more and more mismatching of data. New data types diminish your object's ability to inherit from other objects; therefore, we lose the power of an object oriented programming language.

All forms of data we create are based on the Object class, and as such we're able to use Object as a common ground to cast them from. However, we run into problems when casting incorrectly or not knowing what to cast a value to. This is the problem with type-safe programming languages; using an object is an unfortunate work-around to which we should have a better method, to ensure that we don't run into mismatching data.

There is a way to make your data more flexible, and to do this we need generic types.

7.14.1 Generic Functions

Generics finally make sense now that we've looked at and used delegates and lambda expressions. Generics allow a function to adhere to the type-safe nature of C# but also allow you to pretend that it matters a little less. In the case of building a game involving a variety of monsters, we could quite readily use a system to organize various items we're using in our game. If we were to think in a world without generics, we'd have to make a few different systems for storing and categorizing items and monsters.

Generics are indicated by a function followed by an identifier to be used to indicate the type expected in the function.

7.14.1.1 A Basic Example

The following code produces a debug output of what was put into it.

```
/*   ┌─────────────────────┐   */
/*   │ the "generic"       │   */
/*   │ type is indicated   │   */
/*   │ starting with <T>   │   */
/*   │ which is used again │   */
/*   │ in the parameter    │   */
/*   └─────────────────────┘   */
/*            │                */
/*          ┌─┴─┐              */
/*          ↓   ↓              */
void Log<T>(T thing)
{
    string s = "thing is: " + thing.ToString();
    s += " type: " + thing.GetType().ToString();
    Debug.Log(s);
}
```

To indicate the use of a generic, the <T> follows the identifier for the function where T is used again in the parameter list. With this we are able to use an int a GameObject or Vector3 in the log<T> function. Rather, we can use any object that has a ToString() function and a type. The function log<T> (T thing), where T indicates a placeholder for a type, accepts both ints and GameObjects. Without the <T>, how would this work for various other data types? Let's look at a simple alteration that would instantly create a great deal of additional work.

```
void LogInt(int i)
{
    string s = "int is: " + i.ToString();
    Debug.Log(s);
}

void UseLogInt()
{
    LogInt(13);
    LogInt(new GameObject("Zombie"));
    LogInt((int)new GameObject("Zombie"));
}
```

Suppose we wrote a `LogInt` for the `int` type; it might look something like the above code. The function won't work even if we cast `GameObject` to `int` first. Zombies aren't just numbers after all.

Okay, so `LogInt` doesn't like `GameObjects` mixed in with its ints; that's fair enough. We should know not to mix types by now. Without generics we'd have to write a different function for every type that can be converted to a string and logged to the Console panel. To attempt this would be a huge waste of time, impractical at best. Thanks to `<T>` we don't need to.

7.14.1.2 Why *T*?

We use the identifier `T` to denote a use of the type expected to be reused elsewhere in the function. This is just a convention and not a strict rule. We could break the convention and traditionally trained programmers' brains by writing the same function again with another type identifier.

```
void LogCat<LOL>(LOL cat)
{
    Debug.Log("I can has " + cat.GetType().ToString());
}

 void UseLogCat()
{
    LogCat(new GameObject("GameObject"));
    // I can has UnityEngine.GameObject
}
```

This works just fine, but it's hardly appropriate. The `T` is purely a convention that has stuck around since it was first implemented. This is somewhat like how the for loop is always taught with `for (int i; i < 10; i++)`; in this case, `int i` just seemed appropriate. My best guess is `i` is either from integer or possibly index, which can be defined as a list of items.

Therefore, in this case, generic type `T` seemed to match well. Unlike so much of mathematics, the letters we use in programming have much less intrinsic meaning. If this were not the case, then we'd need a whole lot more letters. Therefore, in the end, sticking to the convention `T` will make any other programmer more easily understand what you're trying to do.

The applied cases often require specific reasons in which no other solution could be found. Creating and assigning delegates like this are often avoided due to the uncommon nature of needing to write specific code for the same function call. However, that is the entire reason for the anonymous expressions for being in use.

On occasion, when you have several classes inheriting behaviors from one another, you'll want one class to react differently than other classes when a function is called. Shoving a wooden stake through the heart of a vampire has a very different effect on a zombie. Calling the same `OnStakedThroughHeart()` function on both should result in different code being executed.

Normally, you'd just want to have both zombie and vampire use an interface which includes an `OnStakedThroughHeart` event; however, your player's character might not necessarily care into what monster he's pushing the pointy end of the stake, through. This is where the problem begins.

The code running the player will probably not want to check for each type and decide what to do based on the different types encountered.

7.14.2 Making Use of Generic Functions

One benefit of a generic type is the fact that you can write your own types of data, vampires or zombies, to use as generic types. To begin with a simple example, we'll build a simple zombie class. After that we'll look at using a generic function to swap data between two variables. What should be a simple task will prove to be an interesting use of what we've learned so far. We'll start with the generic function and then observe how it can be used for more than one type of data.

```
void Swap<T>(ref T first, ref T second)
{
    T temp = second;
    second = first;
    first = temp;
}
```

Create a simple generic function in your code that looks like the above. We have a function called Swap<T>, where T can be any sort of data. We use the ref T to indicate that we're making a reference to the data stored in the variable that's being used in the argument list directly, rather than making a copy of it. Then we make a T temp that holds onto the value of second. After that we tell second to take on the value stored at first. Then we tell first to take on the value that was stored locally in temp. Here's what the function looks like when in use.

```
void UseSwap()
{
    int[] ints = new int[] { 7, 13 };
    foreach (int i in ints)
        Log(i);
    //thing is: 7 type: System.Int32
    //thing is: 13 type: System.Int32
    Swap(ref ints[0], ref ints[1]);
    foreach (int i in ints)
        Log(i);
    //thing is: 13 type: System.Int32
    //thing is: 7 type: System.Int32

    string[] strings = new string[] { "First", "Second" };
    foreach (string s in strings)
        Log(s);
    //thing is: First type: System.String
    //thing is: Second type: System.String
    Swap(ref strings[0], ref strings[1]);
    foreach (string s in strings)
        Log(s);
    //thing is: Second type: System.String
    //thing is: First type: System.String
}
```

This prints out 7 and 13, followed by 13 and then 7 after the swap has been applied. Then we apply Swap(ref first, ref second); that swaps the values stored in the array. Without making any additional changes to the swap generic function, we're allowed to pass in an array of strings. This sends First and Second followed by Second and First in the Console, as you might expect. To make this more interesting, we'll create our own form of data.

```
class GenericHumanoid
{
    public string Name;
    public GenericHumanoid(string name)
    {
        Name = name;
    }
}


class GenericZombie : GenericHumanoid
{
    public GenericZombie(string name) : base(name)
    {
    }

    public override string ToString()
    {
        return "A Zombie named " + Name;
    }
}
class GenericVampire : GenericHumanoid
{
    public GenericVampire(string name) : base(name)
    {
    }

    public override string ToString()
    {
        return "A Vampire named " + Name;
    }
}
```

Using a GenericHumanoid class that stores a Name variable we'll want a constructor with a string argument to accept a name. Then, to make the class return a more useful value when it's translated to a string, the ToString() function is overridden to return A Zombie or Vampire named Name.

```
void UseSwapGenerics()
{
    GenericHumanoid[] humanoids = new GenericHumanoid[2];
    humanoids[0] = new GenericZombie("Stubbs");
    humanoids[1] = new GenericVampire("D");
    Swap(ref humanoids[0], ref humanoids[1]);
    foreach (GenericHumanoid humanoid in humanoids)
        Debug.Log(humanoid);
    // A Vampire named D
    // A Zombie named Stubbs
}
```

The UseSwapGenerics() function, as in the above code, will print out A Vampire named D and A Zombie named Stubbs. This brings up a few questions about how the <T> works. What happens when we mix data types?

```
GenericZombie first = new GenericZombie("Rob");
string second = "Jackson";
Debug.Log(first + " " + second);
Swap(ref first, ref second);
// Error CS0411
// The type arguments for method 'Generics.Swap<T>(ref T, ref T)'
// cannot be inferred from the usage.
// Try specifying the type arguments explicitly.Assembly
```

For instance, if we try to use the above code with a string and a `GenericZombie`, we'll get an error. The type arguments for method 'Generics.Swap<T>(ref T, ref T)' cannot be inferred from the usage. Try specifying the type arguments explicitly.

When we try to mix different types, we won't be able to infer what we want to happen. When we tell a zombie that it's now a word, it's not likely to turn into anything comprehensible. This is very important for a C# to be able to parse your code. In the end there's no simple way to convert between different types that have very little in common. It's up to you to keep things organized in such a ways you won't have to worry about swapping types that don't match.

7.14.3 Generic Types

Speaking of types, a generic type can be created. You can make a data type that has no specific type to start off with. In particular, these come in handy when we want to organize data in a particular fashion. For instance, if we wanted to create a short list of three zombies, we might want to create new data, that is, three zombies, but why restrict this data type to just zombies?

```
class ThreeThings<T>
{
    public T FirstThing;
    public T SecondThing;
    public T ThirdThing;
    public ThreeThings(T first, T second, T third)
    {
        FirstThing = first;
        SecondThing = second;
        ThirdThing = third;
    }
    public override string ToString()
    {
        return "1:" + FirstThing + " 2:" + SecondThing + " 3:" + ThirdThing;
    }
}
```

Start off with a new class with a constructor for holding onto three different things of the same type. The declaration of `ThreeThings<T>` infers that we're going to have an object that has objects of a single generic type. We'll be able to create a new class `ThreeThings` to hold three ints, `floats`, `strings`, or even `GenericZombies`.

Next we'll want to create a new ThreeThings object in our `Start()` function and assign three different zombies to it using its constructor.

```
ThreeThings things = new ThreeThings(
//Using the generic type 'Generics.ThreeThings<T>' requires 1 type arguments
```

But wait; we're getting an error! So using the class constructor for a generic type involves a type argument. What does this mean? A `<GenericsZombie>` is required to declare the type of generic. This means that when we deal with generic types, we need to inform ThreeThings what it's going to be. Therefore, to fix this, we need to tell <T> what it is.

```
ThreeThings<GenericZombie> things = new ThreeThings<GenericZombie>(
new GenericZombie("Bob"),
new GenericZombie("Rob"),
new GenericZombie("White"));
Debug.Log(things.ToString());
// 1:A Zombie named Bob 2:A Zombie named Rob 3:A Zombie named White
```

We need to tell ThreeThings that it's going to be dealing with <GenericZombie> as the generic type. However, there's a more clever trick to dealing with generic types.

7.14.4 Var

Normally, when we use types, we'd create a type by assigning it explicitly. For instance, zombie `first-Zombie = new zombie("stubbs")` is an explicit type. It's a zombie and we knew that as it was created because it's a zombie class object. This is the same `int a = 10;`, which means that a is an int and it's assigned 10 as a value. This changes when the type can be anything and we don't necessarily know what it's going to be ahead of time.

To the computer, it's saying "The thing that SomeThings might turn into is going to be a generic of what ThreeThings is about to be assigned." We have to remind ourselves that computers aren't clever enough to figure this out. However, we can work with generics in a more straightforward way with the var keyword.

```
GenericZombie first = new GenericZombie("Stubbs");
GenericZombie second = new GenericZombie("Frankenstein");
GenericZombie third = new GenericZombie("Michael");
/*                                          */
/*  ┌─┤ Assumes the type after assigned │   */
/*↓ └─────────────────────────────────┘    */
var someThings = new ThreeThings<GenericZombie>(first, second, third);
Debug.Log(someThings);
// 1:A Zombie named Stubbs 2:A Zombie named Frankenstein 3:A Zombie named Michael
```

Here we use var someThings to tell the computer to expect any data type to store into someThings. That's right, *any* data type. There are some limitations, as one might expect with anything to do with computers, but var is a very open keyword. The var keyword means to implicitly get a type once it's been assigned. Only after the actual object is created and assigned to the identifier that was created with var will the identifier turn into a type. For instance, we can test this with a simple integer.

```
var whatAmI = 1;
Debug.Log(whatAmI.GetType());
// System.Int32
```

Every object has a `GetType()` function that returns the data type of the variable in question. Therefore, when we create var whatAmI and assign it 1, which is an integer, we get the following output to the Unity's Console panel:

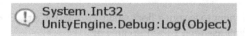

As it turns out, `System.Int32` is the integer that we've been using all this time. What happens when we do the same with `someThings`?

```
Debug.Log(someThings.GetType());
// Generics+ThreeThings`1[Generics+GenericZombie]
```

Well, it's a bit less clear, but we do know that it involves a Generics class, ThreeThings, and a 1, which indicates how many different types are involved along with a Zombie. Quite informative. Therefore, if var allows us to deal with any different type, why don't we use it more often? To be honest, the best reason is not because of code efficiency. The main reason why we don't want to use var so often is because of clarity. For instance, we can use the following code and give horrible nightmares to any programmer trying to follow our code.

```
int TellMeLies(float f)
{
    return (int)f;
}

void UseTellMeLies()
{
    var imAFloat = TellMeLies(11.8f);
    Debug.Log(imAFloat);
    // 11
}
```

This sends 11 to the Console panel; 11.8f is certainly not 11, and as such the var imAFloat is indeed telling lies. Were we to tell the truth from the beginning and use int imAFloat, we might have a clue right away that something is amiss with the naming of the integer imAFloat. This should prompt a meeting with the programmer concerned about naming variables clearly.

This can get a bit murky with generic classes, which don't have a specific constructor, but luckily the compiler will catch things for us.

```
class Stuff<T>
{
    T thing;
    public void AssignThing(T something)
    {
        thing = something;
    }
}
```

Here we can start with a generic class called Stuff<T>, that holds onto T thing. Then we make an available function afterward to assign T thing after the class has been instanced.

```
var what = new Stuff<int>();
what.AssignThing(1.0f);
// cannot convert from 'float' to 'int'
```

If we try the following assignment to assign a float value 1.0f to the Stuff<int>, we get an appropriate error telling us that we can't assign a float to an int.

> ⓘ Assets\Generics.cs(256,26): error CS1503: Argument 1: cannot convert from 'float' to 'int'

This is a good thing as we'd be losing any numbers when converting a float to an int value. Therefore, there are some limitations indeed when it comes to dealing with generic types. They start off being generic, but once assigned they change into the assigned type and must be used accordingly. When Stuff or any generic class is created, it's referred to as an open type. Once it's been assigned with <type>, it's then considered a closed type. Once a generic has been assigned, it can't be reassigned.

7.14.5 Multiple Generic Values

This is all fine and dandy, but what if we have more than one type that might be assigned later on?

```
class TwoThings<T, U>
{
    public T FirstThing;
    public U SecondThing;
    public void AssignThings(T first, U second)
    {
        FirstThing = first;
        SecondThing = second;
    }
}
```

As a good programmer, flexibility and forethought should anticipate using more than a single type in a generic class. The above code uses <T, U> to assign the first and second types. You might consider a zombie followed by its rank in the zombie army or a glass of water and its percentage of fullness. These tasks can be completed in any way you feel needed.

```
var twoThings = new TwoThings<int, double>();
twoThings.AssignThings(3, 30.0);
var differetThings = new TwoThings<GenericZombie, float>();
differetThings.AssignThings(new GenericZombie("Stubbs"), 1.0f);
```

Once one instance of TwoThings has been assigned; you're able to assign the next instance of TwoThings to two different types. Each one stands on its own, but after they have been assigned, they can't necessarily interact with one another in any expected way. This feature should not detract from the overall usefulness of a generic type or function.

This works in a similar way for a generic function.

```
void LogTwoThings<T, U>(T firstThing, U secondThing)
{
    string log = "FirstThing is a " + firstThing.GetType();
    log += " SecondThing is a " + secondThing.GetType();
    Debug.Log(log);
}
```

The function shown simply takes two of any time and then prints them out to the Console log.

```
void UseLogTwoThings()
{
    LogTwoThings(3, new GenericVampire("Vlad"));
    // FirstThing is a System.Int32 SecondThing is a Generics+GenericVampire
}
```

The first argument takes on the type of T and the second is assigned to the type of U. We can combine the examples in this chapter to fully demonstrate how generics can avoid type confusion.

```
class GetTwoThings<T, U> : TwoThings<T, U>
{
    public T GetFirstThing()
    {
        return FirstThing;
    }

    public U GetSecondThing()
    {
        return SecondThing;
    }
}
```

Here we use T and U as return values for the GetTwoThings<T, U> class. We can also see that inheriting from TwoThings we need to include the <T, U> type declarations. The public T GetFirstThing() returns the FirstThing, and public U GetSecondThing() returns the value stored in SecondThing. We can use LogTwoThings<T, U> to log the types of the objects that were used in the GetTwoThings class.

```
var gotTwoThings = new GetTwoThings<GenericZombie, float>();
gotTwoThings.AssignThings(new GenericZombie("White"), 3.0f);
LogTwoThings(gotTwoThings.GetFirstThing(), gotTwoThings.GetSecondThing());
// FirstThing is a Generics+GenericZombie SecondThing is a System.Single
```

We should get used to where the T appears throughout the function or class in which it makes its appearance. Once the type for T is assigned in the declaration of the class or function, T becomes whatever type it was assigned.

It might be tempting to use var as a return type. The convenience of being inspecific when passing data around could be used to get data from a function. However, C# has other mechanisms in place that allow for this and var isn't one of them.

```
var ReturnAVar()
{
    The contextual keyword 'var' may only appear within a local variable declaration or in script code
}
```

7.14.6 Anonymous Objects

In a practical sense, you should always know the data types you're working with. When bundling data to pass between objects it's sometimes easier to skip the work of writing a struct or class and use something more convenient.

```
var things = new { someInt = 3, someClass = this };
Debug.Log("What is things?" + things);
// What is things?{ someInt = 3, someClass = Generics (Chapter7_14.Generics) }
```

An anonymous object can be assigned to a var with the notation new   {}; syntax. Objects in the var are named with identifiers without a type. From the example seen above someInt = 3 skips it's type declaration.

```
var moreThings = new
{
    someIntArray = new int[] { 1, 2, 3 },
    someZombie = new GenericZombie("Stubbs"),
    someQueue = new System.Collections.Queue()
};
Debug.Log("MoreThings: " + moreThings);
// MoreThings: { someIntArray = System.Int32[],
// someZombie = A Zombie named Stubbs,
// someQueue = System.Collections.Queue }
```

Any sort of data can be packed into an anonymous object. This includes other anonymous objects.

```
void acceptAThing(object thing)
{
    Debug.Log(thing);
}

acceptAThing(new { things, moreThings });

/* formatted for readability:
 *
 * { things = {
 *    someInt = 3,
 *    someClass = Generics(Chapter7_14.Generics)
 *  },
 *  moreThings = {
 *    someIntArray = System.Int32[],
 *    someZombie = A Zombie named Stubbs,
 *    someQueue = System.Collections.Queue
 *  }
 * }
 */
```

The anonymous object can be passed to a function through a system.object type. Not knowing what each type in the anonymous object can lead to errors when unboxing the data. Aside from the name, it's easy to handle the anonymous data with functions that don't necessarily know what the variable is. Using a function in this way is unrecommended and may lead to bad habits, but it's interesting to know.

```
object returnsAThing()
{
    return new { things, moreThings };
}

Debug.Log("Can't use var, so lets try object:" + returnsAThing());
/* formatted for readability:
 * "Can't use var, so lets try object:"
 * { things = {
 *     someInt = 3,
 *     someClass = Generics(Chapter7_14.Generics)
 *   },
 *   moreThings = {
 *     someIntArray = System.Int32[],
 *     someZombie = A Zombie named Stubbs,
 *     someQueue = System.Collections.Queue
 *   }
 * }
 */
```

This may lead you to think that you can use object as a return type. This is possible and there isn't anything that disallows this abuse of object. In practice this should be avoided; strong typing is one of the strengths of C# and abusing object acts as a work around. It's preferable to avoid awkward code like the above, but again, it's interesting to know it's possible.

```
things.someInt++;
// properties of the anonymous object are
// read only.
```

The anonymous object might seem to have a lot of flexibility, however the properties in the anonymous object are read-only and cannot be changed once the object has been created. Not all properties in the anonymous object are read-only.

```
moreThings.someQueue.Enqueue(30);
moreThings.someQueue.Enqueue(20);
moreThings.someQueue.Enqueue(10);
Debug.Log(moreThings.someQueue.Peek());
// 30
moreThings.someQueue.Dequeue();
Debug.Log(moreThings.someQueue.Peek());
// 20
moreThings.someQueue.Dequeue();
Debug.Log(moreThings.someQueue.Peek());
// 10
```

The queue can be used as usual. Only POD (plain old data) types become read-only. Reference type objects are usable as expected.

```
things.someClass.LogInt(10);
// int is: 10
```

```
var readOnlyThings = new { floatThing = 1.0f, intThing = 1 };
readOnlyThings.floatThing = 10f;
readOnlyThings.intThing = 10;
```

The float and int type values cannot be modified once assigned. Anonymous objects have a place in very limited situations where a declared type may be cumbersome. When a multitude of data needs to be passed between two functions near one another an anonymous object may prove to be more convenient. Just make sure to leave clear comments when using one to enlighten others as to why the object was necessary.

7.14.7 What We've Learned

This chapter has covered a great deal about generics. In short, "generic" is the term given to a type that can be assigned once the function or the class it appears in is used.

```
void LogTwoThings<T, U>(T firstThing, U secondThing)
```

We can change the order in the signature from the declaration of the generic identifiers. Of course, this leads to confusion, so it's best to use them in order, although technically there are no adverse behaviors. The var keyword is handy, but mainly when dealing with generic types. It's important to try to use explicitly typed variables where possible. Generics should only be used when there are no other alternatives. It's good to know that you have options available to you when you find yourself cornered by your own data types.

Making collections of data by writing classes for each type is inefficient and excludes the ability to reuse code. When you need to make different functions for different situations that seem to behave in practically the same way, it's a good opportunity to look at a generic method to take care of the task at hand.

The main drawback of the generic methods is that once you start using them, it's difficult to break the habit. If your code begins with too many generic types, you'll end up writing code that depends on var and <T> in a myriad of different places.

This leads to type conflicts that are hard to track down. Debugging code with many generic classes and methods is difficult and can lead to a great deal of wasted time. In short, use them only when you have to.

Unity's GameObject describes a function as GetComponent<T>();, where <T> is a generic type.

```
var t = GetComponent<Transform>();
if (t is Transform)
{
    t.localPosition = new Vector3(1, 0, 0);
}
```

We might use the GetComponent function in a script to get a component in the game object our script is attached to. After we get the Transform component, it can be set. The alternative use is GetComponent(typeof (Transform));, which is a bit more verbose, but does the same thing.

7.15 Events

For many simple tasks, Unity 3D has provided some useful functions that update objects and execute when the object is first created in a world. There are event handlers in place ready for any mouse clicks which take place in the UI.

When an object receives a condition to act upon, any actions are usually limited to that object. With the tools we already know, we can probably find some way to spread out a message pretty easily, but they'd be awkward and use various static functions. This leads to spaghetti code: interdependent function calls leading to difficult debugging and long nights wondering why everything is broken.

Having a single large set of code that acts as the central switching board for the entire game becomes very cumbersome very quickly.

Delegates allow for many different cool tricks. Delegates with generic types allow for even more cool things, most notably, the event. An event acts as a container or a handy place to put any number of functions. When the event is called, all of the functions assigned to it are then called. It's a great system to notify another function that something has occurred that you were waiting for.

We identify a function using a declaration such as `public void functionName() {//code statements}`, something we've been doing already. Delegates are declared using `delegate void delegateName();` depending on what you're trying to accomplish. First we'll start with the minimal parts to explain what's required, and then we'll go into an example of why it's useful.

7.15.1 A Basic Example

Starting the Events_Scene in unity, locate the Events script on the like-named game object.

Normally the EventHandler is named based on what sort of event it will be handling. We'll decide on better names after we know how they're used.

```csharp
class Dispatcher
{
    /*   indicates type of method */
    /*   we are declaring         */
    /*           ↓                */
    public delegate void Handler();
    /*                    ↓       */
    /*          ┌──────────┘      */
    /*      Handler is the type   */
    /*          ┌┘                */
    /*          ↓                 */
    public Handler HandleDelegate;
    public event Handler HandleEvent;

    public void CallHandlers()
    {
        /*   check if handle delegate */
        /*   has an assignment        */
        /*           ↓                */
        if (HandleDelegate != null)
        {
            /* call function assigned */
            /* to the delegate handler */
            HandleDelegate();
        }

        /*   check if handle delegate */
        /*   has an assignment        */
        /*           ↓                */
        if (HandleEvent != null)
        {
            /* call function assigned */
            /* to the event handler   */
            HandleEvent();
        }
    }
}
```

The statement public delegate void Handler(); is a type declaration. After creating the type, the variable HandleDelegate is created. To wait for the delegate to be handled we'll create a new Listener class that has a function that will be assigned to the HandleDelegate variable. The event is declared using similar syntax to the delegate with the addition of the event keyword.

In many cases we assumed we can only assign data to a variable. Delegates have functions assigned to them. When the delegate is called, the functions assigned are called. The assignment comes with one condition: the signatures must match. Both the delegate's declaration and the function assigned to the delegate must have matching signatures. Let's create another new class called Listener, which should look like the following:

```
class Listener
{
    private string Name;

    public Listener(string name)
    {
        Name = name;
    }

    public void OnDelegateHandled()
    {
        Debug.Log(Name + "'s Delegate Was Handled");
    }
}
```

When Listener is created, we assign the OnDelegateHandled() event to the Dispatcher's HandleDelegate and HandleEvent variables.

```
/* attach the dispatcher to ourself. */
Dispatcher dispatcher = new Dispatcher();
/* make a couple of listeners to wait for the delegate or event */
Listener sigmond = new Listener("Sigmund");
Listener frasier = new Listener("Frasier");

dispatcher.HandleDelegate += sigmond.OnDelegateHandled;
dispatcher.HandleDelegate = new Dispatcher.Handler(frasier.OnDelegateHandled);
```

Once the dispatcher and the listeners are created, we can assign delegates in one of two ways. The first is using the += operator, the other is with a new Dispatcher.Handler() function initializer. However, something interesting happens with the second assignment.

```
dispatcher.CallHandlers();
// Frasier's Delegate Was Handled
```

Only Frasier's Delegate Was Handled, Sigmond didn't have his OnDelegateHandled function called when the dispatcher has its CallHandlers() function invoked. The HandleDelegate lost any previous assignments when new Dispatcher.Handler() was called. Clearing out a delegate is something allowed.

```
dispatcher.HandleDelegate = null;
dispatcher.CallHandlers();
// nothing is called.
```

We can assign null to the HandleDelegate handler, and when CallHandlers() is invoked, nothing happens. The HandleDelegate has been cleared of any functions to call. By marking the HandleEvent handler with the event keyword we prevent misuse of the HandleEvent variable.

```
dispatcher.HandleEvent = new Dispatcher.Handler(sigmond.OnDelegateHandled);
// The event 'Events.Dispatcher.HandleEvent' can only appear on the
// left hand side of += or -= (except when used from within the type 'Events.Dispatcher')
```

The error tells us we can only use the += or -= operators when making assignments to an event. So the event keyword is more like a special case accessor keyword for delegates. We see the same error when trying to set the HandleEvent to null.

```
dispatcher.HandleEvent = null;
```

The event protected delegate can only have += or -= used to assign functions.

```
dispatcher.HandleEvent += sigmond.OnDelegateHandled;
dispatcher.HandleEvent += new Dispatcher.Handler(frasier.OnDelegateHandled);
dispatcher.CallHandlers();
// Sigmund's Delegate Was Handled
// Frasier's Delegate Was Handled
```

This protects the variable from mishandling or accidentally clearing anything already assigned to the event handler. To remove a function from the handler, the -= operator is used.

```
dispatcher.HandleEvent -= frasier.OnDelegateHandled;
dispatcher.CallHandlers();
// Sigmund's Delegate Was Handled
```

By removing Frasier.OnDelegateHandled from the HandleEvent with -=, only Sigmund's delegate handler is called. Delegates and events operate in essentially the same way. The main difference is related to the protection level at which delegates and events are allowed.

7.15.2 A Proper Event

The .NET Framework has many conformant procedures to which your code needs to comply. Microsoft has described many different best practices that cover everything from variable names to events. Therefore, it's somewhat necessitated by Microsoft that we look at how we should be writing our events should we want to comply with proper code procedures.

```
public delegate void ProperEventHandler(object sender, EventArgs args);

class ProperDispatcher
{
    public delegate void ProperEventHandler(object sender, EventArgs args);
    public event ProperEventHandler ProperEvent;
    public void CallProperEvent()
    {
        ProperEvent?.Invoke(this, new EventArgs());
    }
}
```

Let's add the above delegate to our EventDispatcher class just after the old EventHandler. This has the addition of object sender and EventArgs args. We'll get into what these are in a moment.

After the delegate has been declared outside of the class scope, add in a handler for the delegate in the scope of the class.

```
class ProperListener
{
    private string Name;

    public ProperListener(string name)
    {
        Name = name;
    }

    public void OnProperEvent(object sender, EventArgs args)
    {
        Debug.Log(Name + "'s event from " + sender + " " + args);
    }
}
```

```
public event ProperEventHandler ProperEvent;
```

The above code should follow our MyEvent; just for sake of consistency. Next we'll want to make our event more useful by adding EventArgs, or rather Event Arguments, so our new event can have some additional functionality. EventArgs are used to pass parameters to anyone listening to the event. Before we can create a custom EventArg, we need to add in a new directive.

```
ProperDispatcher dispatcher = new ProperDispatcher();
ProperListener listener = new ProperListener("Sigmund");
dispatcher.ProperEvent += listener.OnProperEvent;
dispatcher.CallProperEvent();
// Sigmund's event from Events+ProperDispatcher System.EventArgs
```

The arguments object and EventArgs are a part of a conformant .NET event, but what are we supposed to do with them?

7.15.3 EventArgs

The system directive gives us access to a new class called an EventArg.

```
using System;
using UnityEngine;
```

The EventArg type comes from System, so to make a class based in it, we need to add the using System; at the class scope. Once this is done, we'll want to create a new class at the global scope of the EventDispatcher.

```
class MessageEventArgs : EventArgs
{
    public string Message;

    public MessageEventArgs(string message)
    {
        Message = message;
    }
}
```

This is a pretty simple class. Once the new `MessageEventArgs` class is created or instanced, we should assign string message in the constructor. It's important to note here is that the customized event arguments allow for specific event information to be passed to anyone who is listening for the event.

To dispatch an event with the new `MessageEventArgs` object we change the delegate signature to emit the `MessageEventArgs` type.

```
class ProperEventArgDispatcher
{
    public delegate void ProperEventHandler(object sender, MessageEventArgs args);
    public event ProperEventHandler ProperEvent;
    public void CallProperEvent()
    {
        ProperEvent?.Invoke(this, new MessageEventArgs("Listen to me."));
    }
}
```

Inside of the `ProperEventArgListener` class, the `OnProperEvent` function called by the event must match the signature of the `ProperEventHandler`.

```
class ProperEventArgListener
{
    private string Name;

    public ProperEventArgListener(string name)
    {
        Name = name;
    }

    public void OnProperEvent(object sender, MessageEventArgs args)
    {
        Debug.Log(Name + "'s event from " + sender + " said: " + args.Message);
    }
}
```

Now dispatcher has MyEvent calling the EventListeners CallMeMaybe function and ProperEvent calls the CallMePlease function. Finally, in the EventDispatcher, we need to add the ProperEvent to the if statement that makes calls.

```
ProperEventArgDispatcher dispatcher = new ProperEventArgDispatcher();
ProperEventArgListener listener = new ProperEventArgListener("Frasier");
dispatcher.ProperEvent += listener.OnProperEvent;
dispatcher.CallProperEvent();
// Frasier's event from Events+ProperEventArgDispatcher said: Listen to me.
```

The `MessageEventArgs()` object is a class, so it needs to be instanced with new before it's used. In the `ProperEvent` argument list, we use this as the sender and new `MessageEventArgs()` as the second argument. These two values are passed to the listener.

We've got some interesting concepts here that we can use. The best situation is to have a clean event-driven game. Rather than wait for conditions to be met and perform some sort of task, it's better to do nothing until an event happens. This approach ensures we avoid having too many scripts updating all at once. On a PC this might not be an issue; however, you'll have a much lower processor ceiling once you want to put your game on a mobile device.

7.15.4 Generic EventArgs

We can have multiple events derive from the single delegate type. To do this we need to use a generic type to declare the delegate.

```
public delegate void EventHandler<TEventArgs>(object sender, TEventArgs args);
public event EventHandler<MessageEventArgs> MessageEvent;
public event EventHandler<NumerEventArgs> NumberEvent;
```

Once the EventHandler delegate is created with <TEventArgs> in the description we use the generic type in place of a strong type for the arguments list. This means a MessageEvent and a NumberEvent can both derive from the delegate EventHandler. Each one replaces the TEventArgs with its own specific EventArg type. But why stop there?

```
public event EventHandler<GenericEventArgs<string>> StringEvent;
public event EventHandler<GenericEventArgs<int>> IntEvent;
public class GenericEventArgs<T> : EventArgs
{
    public T Value;
    public GenericEventArgs(T arg)
    {
        Value = arg;
    }
}
```

Using a generic value in the GenericEventArgs allows us to interface with the delegate EventHandler with a GenericEventArg. A type does need to be specified when the event is created. The matching type must also be included when creating the argument.

```
public void CallGenericString()
{
    StringEvent?.Invoke(this, new GenericEventArgs<string>("Generic generic arg!"));
}

public void CallGenericInt()
{
    IntEvent?.Invoke(this, new GenericEventArgs<int>(42));
}
```

Likewise, the listener for the generic types must also include event listeners with matching signatures.

```
public void OnGenericMessage(object sender, MessageEventArgs message)
{
    Debug.Log(Name + " got message " + message.Message + " from " + sender);
}

public void OnGenericNumber(object sender, GenericEventDispatcher.NumerEventArgs number)
{
    Debug.Log(Name + " got number " + number.Number + " from " + sender);
}

public void OnGenericEvent(object sender, GenericEventDispatcher.GenericEventArgs<string> args)
{
    Debug.Log(Name + " got value " + args.Value + " from " + sender);
}

public void OnGenericEvent(object sender, GenericEventDispatcher.GenericEventArgs<int> args)
{
    Debug.Log(Name + " got value " + args.Value + " from " + sender);
}
```

When using the events we get quite a lot of flexibility from just a few type definitions.

```
GenericEventDispatcher dispatcher = new GenericEventDispatcher();
GenericListener sigmund = new GenericListener("Sigmund");
dispatcher.MessageEvent += sigmund.OnGenericMessage;
dispatcher.NumberEvent += sigmund.OnGenericNumber;
dispatcher.IntEvent += sigmund.OnGenericEvent;
dispatcher.StringEvent += sigmund.OnGenericEvent;

dispatcher.CallMessageEvent();
// Sigmund got message Generic Message from Events+GenericEventDispatcher

dispatcher.CallNumberEvent();
// Sigmund got number 3 from Events+GenericEventDispatcher

dispatcher.CallGenericInt();
// Sigmund got value 42 from Events+GenericEventDispatcher

dispatcher.CallGenericString();
// Sigmund got value Generic generic arg! from Events+GenericEventDispatcher
```

The `sigmund.OnGenericEvent` is assigned to both `IntEvent` and `StringEvent`. Proper over-loaded functions are provided for each. The `GenericEventArgs<int>` and `GenericEventArgs<string>` allow the assignment to find which function is invoked when the different events are called.

7.15.5 What We've Learned

It's important to use events in an intuitive manner. Generics add flexibility when we create an event based on a flexible delegate declaration. The use of the event over a delegate is two main reasons. First events add a level of protection, the second is to allow multiple derivatives from a single delegate type.

7.16 Extension Functions

When writing new classes, a classic programmer's mentality would be to write a single monolithic class that handles many different tasks in a single complex algorithm. As a programmer, you might approach many different problems with a single complex solution. The better, more Unity-friendly approach is quite the opposite.

When we think about building a solution for a complex problem, it's sometimes easier to start with a generalized solution. For instance, should we want to build a complex behavior for managing a group of zombies and humans chasing and eating one another, the first thought might be to write a crowd man-ager class that keeps track of each zombie and human, and then moves each one around based on a set of parameters.

This approach leads to what might be a single solution, since we know everything about everyone in a scene. Writing this might be a difficult task, but getting it right would be quite an accomplishment; unfortunately, there are a few drawbacks. First off, now you have a single complex algorithm to debug, should small problems arise.

Next you run into an inflexibility problem. Rewriting anything to gain different behaviors turns into adding additional layers of complexity. Additional layers in an already complex class easily introduces more bugs and makes fixing those bugs more and more difficult.

The worst part of the monolithic approach comes when someone else needs to open your class and interpret what's going on. The more complex your code is, the more difficult it is to explain. What makes things worse, the longer your algorithm, the more the explanation that is required. Usually nobody likes to read every little comment, even if you wrote detailed comments throughout your code.

7.16.1 Extensions

When we're working with the built-in Unity 3D types such as GameObject, we're unable to extend those classes. If we try to use the following code, we'll get an interesting error:

```
public class MyGameObject : GameObject
{
}
```

class MyGameObject

'MyGameObject': cannot derive from sealed type 'GameObject'

This produces the following output: `'MyGameObject'`: cannot derive from sealed type `'GameObject'`

A `sealed` class means that its final, and no one is allowed to extend or make further modifications to the `GameObject` class. However, it doesn't mean that we can't give the GameObject new functions. For instance, if we wanted `gameObject.NewTrick();`, we're able to do this through Extensions methods.

7.16.2 A Basic Example

Let's start with the ExtensionFunctions_Scene and open the ExtensionFunctions.cs script on the object of the same name class.

At the top we add `using Tricks;` to enable the `ExtensionFunctions:` MonoBehaviour class to use the contents of the namespace tacked to the bottom of this class. In a more regular case, you should put the namespace into another file, but for clarity we're just going to merge these two objects together in this file.

In the namespace, we need to add a new class where we're going to be making use of our GameObject class.

```
namespace Tricks
{
    using UnityEngine;
    public static class GameObjectExtensions
    {
        public static void NewTrick(this GameObject gameObject)
        { /*                                              ↓  */
          /*                 reference this gameObject┘     */
          /*          ↓                                     */
            Debug.Log(gameObject.name + " has a new trick!");
        }
    }
}
```

Here we use `static class GameObjectExtensions`, but this could be anything. So long as the name is descriptive as to what it's going to be doing. The `namespace Tricks` indicates a new group of functions or objects. The .NET library contains many namespaces already: `System`, `System.Collections`, and Unity 3D's `UnityEngine` namespace. Inside of the static `GameObjectExtensions` class, we add a new `static` function that will extend the sealed `GameObject` class.

The public static void NewTrick() is our extension function. To extend the GameObject, we use the argument this GameObject gameObject where the this keyword informs C# that we're writing an extension method. In the argument list, we use the identifier gameObject that appears in the function as gameObject.name. This NewTrick() simply prints the name of the gameObject and "has a new trick!" to the Console.

```
GameObject go = new GameObject("Penn");
go.NewTrick();
// Penn has a new trick!
```

Back in the MonoBehaviour attached to the ExtensionFunctions game object in the ExtensionFunctions_Scene we are shown (Extension) void NewTrick() in the list of functions available to the gameObject type. Perhaps NewTrick() is not the most exciting trick for gameObject to have, but it is a good beginning. Selecting the NewTrick(); and running the game prints "Penn has a new trick!" to the Console.

Any additional arguments must come after the argument where the keyword this is used. Depending on the type that follows this in the first argument, you can change the function to extend a different sealed class.

```
public static void Move(this GameObject gameObject, Vector3 position)
{
    gameObject.transform.position = position;
}
```

Adding Vector3 position as a second parameter and then using gameObject.transform. position = position; will tell the gameObject to update its position. In use, we can use the following code to move gameObject to Vector3(0, 1, 0); when the Move() extension function is used. Even though the first parameter is the gameObject itself, it doesn't show up when it's used. The syntax using the first parameter referring to the object changes the function into an extension function for the object following the keyword this in the first parameter of the function.

```
go.Move(new Vector3(0, 1, 0));
// changes position to 0, 1, 0
```

Extension functions can be applied to any sealed class. When working with third-party libraries, it's often useful to add your own functions to classes which you don't have source code for.

The static keyword is necessary to make the function appear in any context. The same goes for the class in which the Extension function appears. The static class that the function is written in is a side effect of a function not being able live on its own. A function is always a member of a class, even though it might not be related to the class in which it's written in.

An extension function can technically be written into any static class, though it would be confusing if they appeared in an unrelated class. Clear naming practices are just as important as ever, when naming functions unrelated to the class they exist in.

Because of extensions, it's easy to keep adding to a sealed class. Often if you're able to do, it's far better to add the functions to the class itself. This sidesteps the necessity of writing any number of extension functions. This doesn't just have to work on a gameObject.

```
public static void Reset(this Transform transform)
{
    transform.position = Vector3.zero;
    transform.rotation = Quaternion.identity;
    transform.localScale = Vector3.one;
}
```

In the above example, we can use `gameObject.transform.Reset();` to move the gameObject or any other object in the scene that has a transform to the origin as well as reset it's rotation and scale. However, this does highlight the fact that `Reset()` should probably appear in a different class called `TransformExtensions`, or should it?

Functions can be overloaded, so we can have more than one `Reset()` extension function in the class.

```
public static void Reset(this GameObject gameObject)
{
    gameObject.transform.position = Vector3.zero;
    gameObject.transform.rotation = Quaternion.identity;
    gameObject.transform.localScale = Vector3.one;
}
```

Here we have a `Reset()` function that works on both the `GameObject` and the `Transform` types. Perhaps we should rename `GameObjectExtension` to something more like `GameExtensions`. Naming classes and functions is such a big part of writing code. Going back into your code only to rename a class or function is called refactoring.

7.16.3 Overloading with Extensions

In addition to adding new functions to the Transform or gameObject through extensions, you're also able to create new overloads to functions already in place. When the new `Reset()` extension is invoked, the gameObject moves to the origin of the scene. This includes if it's parented to an object that's moved away from the origin.

```
public static void SetParent(this Transform child, Transform parent, bool resetToWorldPosition = true)
{
    child.SetParent(parent);
    if (resetToWorldPosition)
    {
        child.Reset();
    }
}
```

The Transform object has a `SetParent()` function which has a few overloads in place. The first option sets the parent, but retains the child's local position rotation and scale. The second set parent retains the world position after parenting. The function shown above sets the child to the origin of the scene after the parent is set.

```
GameObject go = new GameObject("Child");
Debug.Log(go.transform.localPosition);
// (0.0, 0.0, 0.0)
go.transform.position = Vector3.one;
Debug.Log(go.transform.localPosition);
// (1.0, 1.0, 1.0)
GameObject parent = new GameObject("Parent");
parent.transform.position = new Vector3(0,0,1);
go.transform.SetParent(parent.transform, resetToWorldPosition: true);
Debug.Log(go.transform.localPosition);
// (0.0, 0.0, -1.0)
```

The code fragment above shows a new Child gameObject created at the origin. After it's created, it's repositioned to 1.0 1.0 1.0. Now the object is no longer at the scene's origin. A "Parent" object is created then moved to 0,0,1, a single unit above the origin. When we set the parent we use our overloaded version of SetParent on the Transform and write out resetToWorldPosition: true as the second parameter. When we check the local position of the child it reports 0.0 0.0 −1.0, which is −1 from the position of the parent putting the child back at the origin of the scene.

```csharp
parent.transform.position = new Vector3(0,0,1);
//go.transform.SetParent(parent.transform, resetToWorldPosition: true);
go.transform.SetParent(parent.transform, true);
Debug.Log(go.transform.localPosition);
// (1.0, 1.0, 0.0)
```

There are two overloads that use the signature (Transform, bool) pattern. The built-in version uses the bool to indicate whether or not the child will retain its relative world position. Using that option will report 1.0, 1.0, 0.0 for its localPosition after parenting. By writing out the name of the bool parameter name resetToWorldPosition:true we tell C# that we want to use our extension function instead of the built-in version.

7.16.4 Magic Mirror

A lot of what programmers do is write code to write less code. Seems paradoxical, but most programming time is spent writing large functions that are called by short functions. In the ultimate goal of reduced complexity, complexity is unavoidable.

```csharp
GameObject original = GameObject.Instantiate(Resources.Load<GameObject>("TransformPrimitive"));
original.Mirror(new Vector3(-1, 1, 1));
```

Here we use an extension function on GameObject that's called Mirror, which takes a Vector3 value to give it an axis of mirroring. In this case, we're reflecting the x axis.

```csharp
public static GameObject Mirror(this GameObject original, Vector3 reflection)
{
    GameObject mirror = GameObject.Instantiate(original, original.transform.position, original.transform.rotation);
    Vector3 reflected = new Vector3()
    {
        x = original.transform.localScale.x * reflection.x,
        y = original.transform.localScale.y * reflection.y,
        z = original.transform.localScale.z * reflection.z
    };
    mirror.transform.localScale = reflected;
    mirror.name = original.name + "_Mirrored";
    UpdateReflection reflector = new UpdateReflection(original, mirror, reflection);
    return mirror;
}
```

The Mirror function takes the original object and creates a clone. The clone is then set to the size and position of the original. A mirrored scale is calculated and then it's applied to the mirrored object. Then a system to update the mirrored object is created which is assigned the original object, the mirrored object and the reflection value used to create the mirror.

```
public class UpdateReflection
{
    GameObject Mirror;
    Vector3 Reflection;

    public UpdateReflection(GameObject original, GameObject mirror, Vector3 reflection)
    {
        UpdatesReflected reflector = original.AddComponent<UpdatesReflected>();
        reflector.ReflectionUpdateEvent += OnReflectionUpdated;
        Mirror = mirror;
        Reflection = reflection;
    }

    public void OnReflectionUpdated(Transform t)
    {
        // update the mirrored position
        Vector3 reflectedPosition = new Vector3()
        {
            x = t.position.x * Reflection.x,
            y = t.position.y * Reflection.y,
            z = t.position.z * Reflection.z
        };
        Mirror.transform.position = reflectedPosition;

        // now update the mirrored rotation
        Vector3 reflectedRotation = new Vector3()
        {
            x = t.localEulerAngles.x * -Reflection.x,
            y = t.localEulerAngles.y * -Reflection.y,
            z = t.localEulerAngles.z * -Reflection.z
        };
        Mirror.transform.localEulerAngles = reflectedRotation;
    }
}
```

The UpdateReflection class keeps track of two things, the mirrored object and the reflection vector. When it's created it adds a component called UpdatesReflected to the original object. The UpdatesReflected object has an update event which calls on the OnReflectionUpdated function. The updates set the mirrored object's position and rotation based on the reflection axis value.

```
public class UpdatesReflected : MonoBehaviour
{
    public delegate void UpdateReflected(Transform transform);
    public event UpdateReflected ReflectionUpdateEvent;
    private void Update()
    {
        ReflectionUpdateEvent?.Invoke(transform);
    }
}
```

The original object gets the MonoBehaviour UpdatesReflected attached to it where the Reflection-UpdateEvent calls the OnReflectionUpdated function in the UpdateReflection class. The event sends along the originals transform so the mirrored object can know what the original's transforms have updated to.

As update events are sent to the Mirror object through the `UpdateReflection` class, we get an object that mirrors the originals position and rotation.

A simplified `gameObject.Mirror()` function call performs quite a lot of steps behind the scene to create what seems like a simple task. The reality of this means that what might seem like a simple task hides a large scope of complexity.

7.16.5 What We've Learned

Other interesting tricks that often come up in a small C# class in Unity 3D is limiting how much of a library is used. When you add directives such as using `System;`, you're including a heavy amount of memory that needs to be accessed. This memory isn't necessarily used when you're running the game; however, this is used when your code is compiled.

For ease of use, it's a simple matter to have a simple case like the following:

```
using Vect3 = UnityEngine.Vector3;
```

This shortens `Vector3` into `Vect3`. Doing so helps to reduce namespace conflicts as well as speeds up picking names in the Autocomplete feature in MonoDevelop. The normal behavior always has Vector2 above Vector3 in the pop-up list. After a while, this behavior can easily be replaced if you get used to using Vect3 instead.

The usual practice is to use the regular name, in case the rest of the library is needed. However, it's good to know that tricks like this are possible, in case you come across something strange. Working in Unity 3D places specific constraints around what code will and will not work when it comes to the full feature set that the .NET Foundation has to offer.

The developers at Unity 3D are hard set on supporting many different platforms, and the lowest common denominator sets the height of the bar. Getting to know a language with a focus is great; this is why Unity 3D is a great stage for learning C#. Once you've gotten into how the language works, it's a good idea to explore other development environments where you can make games with the full .NET Framework. Never limit yourself.

7.17 Destructors

While you're busy creating objects, Unity 3D is busy cleaning them up. If you clean them up quickly, you limit how often and how long it takes Unity 3D to do this for you.

We've looked at the constructor in Chapters 5 and 6. Destructors are the opposite construct from the constructor. C# is a garbage-collected language, so in most instances, you're not in need of a specific cleanup of your own data when your object is no longer referenced. However, when you begin to use unsafe code, some cleanup might be more necessary.

Unity 3D provides the OnDestroy() event after any object based on MonoBehaviour has been destroyed. If you want to destroy an object that isn't based on MonoBehaviour, you don't have an OnDestroy() event. Therefore, what else is there to do?

7.17.1 A Basic Example

In the Destructors project, open the Example.cs component attached to the Main Camera and also open the DestroyMe.cs file. The DestroyMe has both a constructor and a destructor.

```
public class SelfDestructor : Object
{
    string Name;

    // Constructor
    public SelfDestructor(string name)
    {
        Name = name;
        Debug.Log(Name + " says hello.");
    }

    // Destructor
    ~SelfDestructor()
    {
        Debug.Log(Name + " says goodbye.");
    }
}
```

The destructor can be identified by the ~, or tilde, preceding the class identifier. Somewhat like a very simple-looking constructor, the destructor is called any time the object is garbage collected. C# is a garbage-collected environment. Specific destructors aren't specifically written into the language. If several seconds pass and there's nothing going on in the class and there's nothing accessing the class, the unused class is destroyed automatically.

```
void UseSelfDestructor()
{
    SelfDestructor bomb = new SelfDestructor("Bob-omb");
    // Bob-omb says hello.
    // after ~5 seconds
    // Bob-omb says goodbye.
}
```

In the Destructors.cs attached to the Destructors game object in the Destructors_Scene, we create an instance of the SelfDestructor() class. When we create a new SelfDestructor we give it a name so we can know what is being cleaned out and when. If we run the game scene, we see "Bob-omb says hello." printed to the Console when the game starts.

Several seconds later we see "Bob-omb says goodbye." There are other ways to destroy objects.

```
private UnityEngine.Object Bomber;
void UseDestroyBomber()
{
    Bomber = new SelfDestructor("Bomber");
    do
    {
        Bomber = null;
        GC.Collect(GC.MaxGeneration, GCCollectionMode.Forced, true);
    }
    while (Bomber != null);
}
```

In this code function we assign and destroy the SelfDestructor Bomber. The log shows the hello and goodbye immediately.

Bomber inherits from Object, so we can store a variable Bomber as UnityEngine.Object. A strange side effect of creating class wide variables is that they are sometimes created while the editor is running. This can be observed when the Bomber variable is changed to a SelfDestructor type.

A mysterious "says goodbye." appears in the first line and again after the "Bomber says hello." lines. The general practice with Unity is to let Unity, or rather .NET, run its own garbage-collection (GC) cycles in the background untouched.

In general, GC in C# works automatically. For objects such as a struct, GC should be done very quickly. Only when you need to work with many class objects do you need to pay close attention to the number of objects that are being created.

The automatic GC is done in random intervals. Usually there is little consequence of the GC on a PC. The memory and CPU are running so fast that it's imperceptible when the GC takes place.

On a mobile device, the GC can lead to a sudden loss in frame rate once every few seconds. The interval between GC cycles can be longer or shorter depending on how often objects are created. Because of this, it's important to build some sort of scheme to track and destroy objects on your own. Forcing garbage collection is generally shunned upon. In the above log, does this mean we had three SelfDestructor objects in memory? It's hard to say for sure, but it certainly seems that way. Because of these weird behaviors in the editor, it's difficult to say exactly how things will react when garbage collection is forced.

For reasons of unpredictability, it's better to create an object pool, this avoids the issue with creating and destroying many dozens or even hundreds of objects in the scene.

7.17.2 Clearing Events or Delegates

One important function the destructor does have a purpose for when being cleared is to clear an event or a delegate. With a simple delegate and event dispatcher we'll add in a couple of Debug.Log functions to announce when the dispatcher class is created and destroyed.

```
class EventDispatcher
{
    public EventDispatcher()
    {
        Debug.Log("Hello! from dispatcher");
    }

    public delegate void SomeDelegate();
    public event SomeDelegate SomeEvent;
    public void CallSomeEvent()
    {
        SomeEvent?.Invoke();
    }

    ~EventDispatcher()
    {
        Debug.Log("Goodbye from dispatcher");
    }
}
```

Then to make use of the function, we'll create a class which accepts the dispatcher as an argument in its constructor.

```
class SelfCleaning
{
    public int CountDown = 3;
    private EventDispatcher Dispatcher;
    public SelfCleaning(EventDispatcher dispatcher)
    {
        Dispatcher = dispatcher;
        Dispatcher.SomeEvent += OnSomeEvent;
        Debug.Log("Hello!, connecting to dispatcher");
    }

    public void OnSomeEvent()
    {
        Debug.Log("I should be destroyed in " + CountDown--);
    }

    ~SelfCleaning()
    {
        Dispatcher.SomeEvent -= OnSomeEvent;
        Debug.Log("Goodbye!, cleaning up dispatcher");
    }
}
```

In this class, the dispatcher's event gets assigned in the constructor, in the destructor we use the −= operator to remove the reference from the `SelfCleaning` class to the event dispatcher.

```csharp
SelfCleaning Cleaner;
void UseDispatcherAndSelfCleaner()
{
    EventDispatcher dispatcher = new EventDispatcher();
    Cleaner = new SelfCleaning(dispatcher);
    while (Cleaner.CountDown > 0)
    {
        dispatcher.CallSomeEvent();
    }
    Cleaner = null;
}
```

The `Cleaner` class is updated for a count of three, then the variable is set to `null`. The dispatcher runs the event till the Cleaner's `CountDown` value reaches 0, so we've called the event which connects both the cleaner and the dispatcher.

In the log we see the dispatcher is created followed by the cleaner being created and connecting itself to the dispatcher. We see the CountDown decrement, and then the logging stops for a moment. A few seconds later, the cleaner says Goodbye where it also removes its function from the dispatcher's event. After that, we see the dispatcher say Goodbye as well.

So this works well with very simple classes, but how do we handle GameObjects and MonoBehaviours?

7.17.3 OnDestroy

Classes which derive from `MonoBehaviour` use a slightly different function to destroy themselves. With a similar setup to a class which doesn't derive from `MonoBehaviour`, a class which does uses void `OnDestroy()` and not `~ClassName()` to clean its own memory.

In a very simple example, we'll have the `OnDestroy()` function in the MonoBehaviour derived class.

```
class DestroyMe : MonoBehaviour
{
    private void OnDestroy()
    {
        Debug.Log("I've been destroyed.");
    }
}

void DestroyDestroyMe()
{
    DestroyMe destroyMe = gameObject.AddComponent<DestroyMe>();
    Destroy(destroyMe);
}
```

As soon as the MonoBehaviour is destroyed the OnDestroy() function is called and "I've been destroyed." is printed to the Console. With a similar setup as before, we store a variable for the event dispatcher. Instead of a constructor assigning the dispatcher's event to a function, we use a separate function where we assign the event dispatcher.

```
class UsesOnDestroy : MonoBehaviour
{
    DestroyEventDispatcher Dispatcher;
    private int CountDown = 3;
    public void AssignListenerUpdater(DestroyEventDispatcher dispatcher)
    {
        Dispatcher = dispatcher;
        Dispatcher.UpdateListenerEvent += OnUpdateListener;
    }

    public void OnUpdateListener()
    {
        Debug.Log("Got Updated");
        gameObject.transform.localScale = Vector3.one * CountDown;
        if (CountDown-- < 0)
        {
            Debug.Log("CountDown less than 0");
            Destroy(this);
        }
    }

    // One of the built-in MonoBehaviour functions
    private void OnDestroy()
    {
        Debug.Log("OnDestroy Called.");
        // similar to ~Destroy() function.
        Dispatcher.UpdateListenerEvent -= OnUpdateListener;
    }
}
```

When we call the event dispatcher's event we send the listeners events until they are ready to destroy themselves.

```
class DestroyEventDispatcher
{
    public delegate void UpdateListeners();
    public event UpdateListeners UpdateListenerEvent;

    public void CallUpdateListenerEvent()
    {
        int count = 0;
        while(count++ < 5)
        {
            UpdateListenerEvent?.Invoke();
        }
    }
}
```

The class that sends the MonoBehaviour holds, calls the event a few times to make the MonoBehaviour decrement the CountDown value.

```
// cube primitive is created.
GameObject gameCube = GameObject.CreatePrimitive(PrimitiveType.Cube);
// the MonoBehaviour that scales the cube when the event is called
// then destroys itself once countdown is less than 0
UsesOnDestroy monoDestroyer = gameCube.AddComponent<UsesOnDestroy>();

// dispatcher will call the event that the self destroying MonoBehaviour
// is listening to.
DestroyEventDispatcher destroyDispatcher = new DestroyEventDispatcher();
// the event dispatcher is assigned to the MonoBehaviour
monoDestroyer.AssignListenerUpdater(destroyDispatcher);

// there will be a cube for a moment after start
// but it's destroyed almost right away.
destroyDispatcher.CallUpdateListenerEvent();
```

A cube primitive is created and the MonoBehaviour is attached to the cube gameObject. Following the creation of the class, an event dispatcher is created. The MonoBehaviour derived class gets the assignment to the dispatcher where it assigns the event listener to the dispatcher's event.

We call the dispatcher's event which then raises the event enough times to trigger the UsesOnDestroy self destruction call Destroy(this). The final product is a scene with a cube with scale of −1 on the *x*, *y*, and *z* axis without any scripts attached to it. The only evidence that there was a script attached is the scale and the "OnDestroy Called." printed to the Console.

7.17.4 The Ugly Truth

The unfortunate, or maybe fortunate truth to how garbage collection really works is a bit murky.

```
void UseDestroyTooMuch()
{
    GameObject gameCube = GameObject.CreatePrimitive(PrimitiveType.Cube);
    UsesOnDestroy monoDestroyer = gameCube.AddComponent<UsesOnDestroy>();
    DestroyEventDispatcher destroyDispatcher = new DestroyEventDispatcher();
    monoDestroyer.AssignListenerUpdater(destroyDispatcher);

    // Calling the event 100 times.
    destroyDispatcher.CallUpdateListenerEventTooManyTimes();
    // it should be gone, but it's still listening?
    destroyDispatcher.UpdateListenerEvent -= monoDestroyer.OnUpdateListener;
    // lets disconnect the event listener.

    Debug.Log("Calling event again");
    // Calling the event 100 times.
    destroyDispatcher.CallUpdateListenerEventTooManyTimes();

    Debug.Log("When will the UseOnDestroy script actually destroy itself?");
}
```

So with a different system to call the event the `UsesOnDestroy` class we call it 100 times.

```
public void CallUpdateListenerEventTooManyTimes()
{
    int count = 0;
    while (count++ < 100)
    {
        Debug.Log("Calling Update Event.");
        UpdateListenerEvent?.Invoke();
    }
}
```

In theory, this should not actually get a response from the object listening to it, after the `CountDown` is less than 0 the object should destroy itself.

⚠ Calling Update Event. UnityEngine.Debug:Log(Object)	100
⚠ Got Updated UnityEngine.Debug:Log(Object)	100
⚠ CountDown less than 0 UnityEngine.Debug:Log(Object)	96
⚠ Calling event again UnityEngine.Debug:Log(Object)	1
⚠ Calling Update Event. UnityEngine.Debug:Log(Object)	100
⚠ When will the UseOnDestroy script actually destroy itself? UnityEngine.Debug:Log(Object)	1
⚠ OnDestroy Called. UnityEngine.Debug:Log(Object)	1

The `UsesOnDestroy` gets the call to destroy itself 96 more times after it should have destroyed itself. Then we call the event again after removing it from the dispatcher. So it doesn't get any additional calls.

So disconnecting the listener from the dispatcher is working, but the script hasn't destroyed itself. It's not until after the function is finished that the OnDestroy is called.

It's important to be aware that garbage collection is lazy. Objects are usually still resident in memory for a few seconds after they've been destroyed. For this reason, after many objects are instanced it's unclear as to when memory will freed up. Once it does, it's usually all at once, and quite often causes a frame or two to be lost.

7.17.5 What We've Learned

Destructors are used when manual clean up of a class is needed. When using classes based on any of the Unity 3D class objects, it's not recommended you use the OnDetroy() function to clear any extra data created by the class. It's recommended that any class not based on a Unity 3D class use a destructor, though it's not a common practice to create classes not based on Unity 3D.

When classes add a delegate to an event, the destructor can be used to remove the delegate. Unfortunately, we can't use the -= operator to remove the reference to the event listener. This still leaves behind some traces to the created class in the memory and prevents GC from cleaning out the object.

Garbage collection happens in regular intervals, usually about a second between each pass through the heap. The heap is a pile of memory that can become disorganized. When an object is removed, it leaves behind a gap. After many hundreds of objects are created and destroyed, the heap can become a cube of Swiss cheese of usable and unusable spaces. Garbage collection tries to mitigate and clean the heap as often as it can. If the heap were processed any more, then performance in maintaining clean memory would take over your CPU cycles.

The balance between performance and memory management isn't always to your benefit. As improvements are made, there may be speed gains, but it's up to you to keep your use of memory as slim as possible to allow for quick GC passes.

This is one of the reasons why a struct is preferable over a class. Structs are allocated to a different section of memory for your game and, thus, don't need to be garbage collected at all. This isn't true if a struct is stored as a part of a class. A struct doesn't have a ~Destroy() function, so any clean-up needs to be done before clearing a struct.

```csharp
struct SomeStruct
{
    public int MyInt;
    public SomeStruct(int myInt)
    {
        MyInt = myInt;
    }
}


void UseSomeStruct()
{
    SomeStruct[] LotsOfStructs = new SomeStruct[1000000];
    //allocates a bunch of memory.
    for(int i = 0; i < 1000000; i++)
    {
        LotsOfStructs[i] = new SomeStruct(i);
    }
    //as soon as we exit this function they're all gone.
}
```

In the end, C# allows for so many different ways to use the language; the benefit far outreaches the limitation of memory management. Your task of creating a game shouldn't be hindered by the nitty-gritty of poking holes in memory and trying to fill them in manually. This sort of stuff isn't fun and should be left to the folks writing C# to figure out for you.

7.18 Concurrency or Co-Routines

So far, everything that has been talked about has been for writing code that is executed in order. As the code is executed, each statement must wait until the preceding statement has completed its task. For the most part, this is done exceedingly fast.

7.18.1 Yield

We've gone over the use of IEnumerator earlier; it's a handy interface for more than one reason. The IEnumerator type is notable for iterating over an array; in addition, in Unity 3D it also allows the use of yield. The primary reason for the yield keyword was to allow a computer to continue with a function and allow something like our Update() loop to come back to the function using the yield statement.

For instance, if we had a task that might take more than a single update frame to complete, we could use a function with a yield; this works only with a function that is an IEnumerator. This means that the function starts when it's called, but then allows us to come back to it again and check on how it's doing.

For instance, a really slow function, which fills the scene with 40,000 randomly placed cubes, might take a long time to complete.

```csharp
private bool UsedFillupObjects;
void FillUpObjects()
{
    if (!UsedFillupObjects)
    {
        UsedFillupObjects = true;
        int numObjects = 50000;
        GameObject[] lotsOfObjects = new GameObject[numObjects];
        for (int i = 0; i < numObjects; i++)
        {
            GameObject g = GameObject.CreatePrimitive(PrimitiveType.Cube);
            g.name = i.ToString() + "_Cube";
            g.transform.position = new Vector3()
            {
                x = Random.Range(-1000, 1000),
                y = Random.Range(-1000, 1000),
                z = Random.Range(-1000, 1000)
            };
            g.transform.localScale = new Vector3()
            {
                x = Random.Range(1, 10),
                y = Random.Range(1, 10),
                z = Random.Range(1, 10)
            };
            lotsOfObjects[i] = g;
        }
        Debug.Log("Finished at:" + Time.fixedUnscaledTime);
    }
}
```

Unity 3D will lock up for a few seconds waiting for this function to finish before the game begins. To measure the time passed, we'll have a log in the script's Start and we'll run another log once the function finishes in the first `Update()` loop.

```csharp
private void Start()
{
    Debug.Log("Started at:" + Time.fixedUnscaledTime);
}

void Update()
{
    FillUpObjects();
}
```

Depending on the speed of your computer, the time elapsed from the Start() of the script to the end of the FillUpObjects script will be different.

```
Started at:0
UnityEngine.Debug:Log(Object)

Finished at:2.337143
UnityEngine.Debug:Log(Object)
```

One way to get around this is to use a co-routine. In the System.Collections library is the IEnumerator. This is the same sort of class that enables the foreach(thing in stuff) enumerator type.

```csharp
private bool UsedFillWithYield;
IEnumerator FillWithYield()
{
    if (!UsedFillWithYield)
    {
        UsedFillWithYield = true;
        int numObjects = 1000;
        GameObject[] lotsOfObjects = new GameObject[numObjects];
        for (int i = 0; i < numObjects; i++)
        {
            GameObject g = GameObject.CreatePrimitive(PrimitiveType.Cube);
            g.name = i.ToString() + "_Cube";
            g.transform.position = new Vector3()
            {
                x = Random.Range(-1000, 1000),
                y = Random.Range(-1000, 1000),
                z = Random.Range(-1000, 1000)
            };
            g.transform.localScale = new Vector3()
            {
                x = Random.Range(1, 10),
                y = Random.Range(1, 10),
                z = Random.Range(1, 10)
            };
            lotsOfObjects[i] = g;
            /* Yield goes after an interation  */
            /* through the for loop.          */
            yield return null;
        }
        Debug.Log("Finished at:" + Time.fixedUnscaledTime);
    }
}
```

Rather than void, IEnumerator is used, then at the end of the for loop, and add yield return null; so that the IEnumerator interface has something to return. The new sort function is called differently from a regular function as we see in the following call:

```
StartCoroutine(FillWithYield());
```

StartCoroutine() calls the IEnumerator as a co-routine. When the game is started, we don't experience a lock, but we do get to watch cubes fill in the world. This is a simple example on how a co-routine is usually used. It's a great method to start an unusually long function and not have to wait for its completion before the rest of some code is executed. There's one drawback to using this method. To generate merely 1000 objects it takes considerably longer to create the field of cubes.

```
Started at:0
UnityEngine.Debug:Log(Object)

Finished at:35.91381
UnityEngine.Debug:Log(Object)
```

When using a co-routine, the Update() loop continues to run.

```
int count;
void Update()
{
    /*
     * Section 7.18.1 Yield
     */
    //FillUpObjects();
    StartCoroutine(FillWithYield());
    Debug.Log(count++);
}
```

The Debug.Log(count++); after the start of the co-routine continues to print out numbers even with the FillWithYield() running. Contrast this with the same function without using a coroutine. You'd simply wait until the function is finished before the Debug.Log() gets called.

7.18.1.1 A Basic Example

In terms of a usable function in a game, there are more interesting uses for the co-routine. To see how this works, we'll start a Unity 3D Scene with a new script called Concurrent attached to the Main Camera.

```
void UseDelayAStatement()
{
    StartCoroutine(DelayAStatement());
}                /*              ↑               */
                 /*    ┌─────────┴──────────────────┐  */
                 /*    │the function and parameter list│ */
                 /*    │is added as a parameter to the │ */
                 /*    │StartCoroutine function        │ */
                 /*    └─────────┬──────────────────┘  */
                 /*              ↑               */
IEnumerator DelayAStatement()
{
    Debug.Log("DelayAStatement Started at:" + Time.fixedTime);
    yield return new WaitForSeconds(3.0f);
    Debug.Log("DelayAStatement Finished at:" + Time.fixedTime);
}
```

With the above, we can see the statement `StartCoroutine(DelayAStatement());`. This starts the `IEnumerator` function. Functions defined with the `IEnumerator` return type and is identified must have a `yield return` somewhere in the body of the function.

In the DelayAStatement code block, we see that it starts with `Debug.Log("Started at:"` `+ Time.fixedTime);` followed by the `yield` statement.

The `yield` statement `return new WaitForSeconds();` creates a concurrent task that then pauses the DelayAStatement code block at the yield. Once the yield is done, it releases the function's operation and allows it to move to the next statement. It's also worth looking at starting multiple Concurrent co-routines.

```
void UseMultipleDelayAStatements()
{
    for (int i = 0; i < 3; i++)
    {
        StartCoroutine(MultiDelayAStatement(i));
    }
}


IEnumerator MultiDelayAStatement(int i)
{
    Debug.Log(i + ") DelayAStatement Started at:" + Time.fixedTime);
    yield return new WaitForSeconds(3.0f);
    Debug.Log(i + ") DelayAStatement Finished at:" + Time.fixedTime);
}
```

With the above code, we have the following output. Note that we're changing the `Debug.Log()` to include an index to identify each of the `MultiDelayAStatement()` functions as they are executed.

> ① 0) DelayAStatement Started at:0
> UnityEngine.Debug:Log(Object)
>
> ① 1) DelayAStatement Started at:0
> UnityEngine.Debug:Log(Object)
>
> ① 2) DelayAStatement Started at:0
> UnityEngine.Debug:Log(Object)
>
> ① 0) DelayAStatement Finished at:3
> UnityEngine.Debug:Log(Object)
>
> ① 1) DelayAStatement Finished at:3
> UnityEngine.Debug:Log(Object)
>
> ① 2) DelayAStatement Finished at:3
> UnityEngine.Debug:Log(Object)

The three concurrent tasks 0, 1, and 2 started in order. After their WaitForSeconds(), they finish in the same order. Concurrent co-routines are useful for a good number of tasks including setup with events and timings.

7.18.2 Setting Up Timers

So as a game play engineer, you're going to write a lot of code. Writing a timing function should be something you do once. With that in mind, you'll want it to be flexible; what you write should be easy to reuse. A good timing function should be something you can use to time explosions in a game, separate waves of monsters, or even just count down some numbers on screen. What each of these have in common, is a flexible amount of time, so we'll use a float for that. And some sort of action when the time has run out.

```
void TheAction()                    /*  ┌─────────────┐    */
{                                   /*  │this function│    */
    Debug.Log("Doing the thing!");/* │gets assigned│    */
}                                   /*  │as a variable│    */
                                    /*  └─────────────┘    */
void UseTimedAction()               /*         │           */
{                                   /*         ↓           */
    StartCoroutine(TimedAction(3f, TheAction));/*          */
}                                   /*         ↓           */
                                    /*         └─────────┐ */
private IEnumerator TimedAction(float time, Action action)
{                                         /*            ↓ */
    yield return new WaitForSeconds(time);/*            │ */
    action?.Invoke();/* ←──────────────────────────────┘ */
}                    /* then gets called here after wait */
```

The `UseTimedAction()` is called in the `Start()` of the script in the scene. A function named `TheAction()` which does a thing, is assigned as a variable to the `TimedAction()` function in the Coroutine. The `Action` type comes from `System`, as do many useful base types. In this case TheAction just prints out "Doing the thing!" to the Unity 3D debug Console. However, this could just as easy call on a script to set off an explosion, start a race, or let loose a horde of zombies.

```
/*
 * we have two parts here, a delegate
 * and the IEnumerator ValueUpdater
 */
delegate void UpdateValue(float value);

IEnumerator ValueUpdater(float start, float finish, float time, UpdateValue valueUpdated)
{
    /* starting at 0      */
    /* we increment this */
    /* toward 1           */
    float t = 0;
    while (t < 1)
    {
        /* Lerp goes from start value to  */
        /* the finish value using a range */
        /* from 0 to 1                     */
        float v = Mathf.Lerp(start, finish, t);

        /* increment the t value from     */
        /* 0 to 1                         */
        t += Time.deltaTime / time;

        /* call the event assigned        */
        valueUpdated?.Invoke(v);

        /* wait till the end of the frame */
        /* before starting the while loop */
        /* again.                         */
        yield return new WaitForEndOfFrame();
    }
}
```

We can make our timers more useful by adding a repeated event to a loop within the coroutine. A Mathf. Lerp takes two values and interprets a value between them using a value from 0 to 1. For instance, you can use the function to quickly get the value half way between 6 and 9 and see it's 7.5.

```
Debug.Log(Mathf.Lerp(6f, 9f, 0.5f));
// 7.5
```

We call our `lerp` co-routine using the same `StartCoroutine()` function calling the value updater.

```
/* starting at a value of 3, we go to 7 in 3 seconds */
StartCoroutine(ValueUpdater(6f, 9f, 3f, GetUpdatedValue));
```

The `GetUpdateValue` function starts with 6 and increments toward 9 in 3 seconds. A linear interpolation, or `Lerp`, isn't the only option. There's also `LerpAngle`, `SmoothStep`, and `LerpUnclamped` available in the `Mathf` library. These share similar parameters with `Lerp` and can be interchanged quite easily.

Containing a timer within a single function keeps the work contained. A co-routine encapsulates the work in a single function. With the following code, you can have a repeating timer that uses a co-routine instead:

```
float delayTime = 2.0f;
int repeatCount = 5;

StartCoroutine(RepeatTimer(delayTime, repeatCount));

IEnumerator RepeatTimer(float delay, int repeats)
{
    while (repeats > 0)
    {
        Debug.Log("Starting timer");
        yield return new WaitForSeconds(delay);
        Debug.Log("Restarting Timer");
        repeats--;
    }
}
```

This uses a while loop in `IEnumerator RepeatTimer()`. The `WaitForSeconds()` uses an incoming parameter `delay` to give us some flexibility to decide how long to wait till the `RepeatTimer()` restarts. When this while loop is restarted, the first statement `Debug.Log("Starting timer");` is executed immediately.

Any code found before the `yield return new WaitForSeconds();` statement will be executed normally. This means that you can set up new GameObjects, add components, and build any number of systems before the yield. Once the `WaitForSeconds()` statement is finished, all the following lines are then executed normally. Therefore, anything that needs to happen before the timer is reset should happen here.

A Coroutine can control another co-routine as well. A variable visible to both can be setup as a kill switch. A co-routine checks if the live bool is true to continue executing the while loop. Another co-routine is set to set that bool to false.

```
bool live = true;

StartCoroutine(KillCoRoutineIn(5f));
StartCoroutine(RepeatTimer(0.2f));

IEnumerator KillCoRoutineIn(float delay)
{
    Debug.Log("Kill Switch To hit in " + delay + " seconds");
    yield return new WaitForSeconds(delay);
    live = false;
    Debug.Log("Coroutine killed.");
}

IEnumerator RepeatTimer(float delay)
{
    while (live)
    {
        Debug.Log("Repeating...");
        yield return new WaitForSeconds(delay);
    }
}
```

7.18.3 Arrays of Delegates

Timers that call a function when they're finished are useful in many ways. We could make a modification to the co-routine to accept an array of delegates. In addition, the delegates can also have a return type to change the behavior of the coroutine.

```
delegate float ThingsToDo(string thing);
IEnumerator DoingTheThings(ThingsToDo[] things)
{
    Debug.Log("Doing the things:" + Time.fixedTime);

    foreach (ThingsToDo thing in things)
    {
        float nextTime = thing.Invoke("Doing the thing.");
        yield return new WaitForSeconds(nextTime);
    }

    Debug.Log("Things done:" + Time.fixedTime);
}
```

In this `IEnumerator` called `DoingTheThings()` we have a parameter which is an array of `ThingsToDo`. As we've seen before, delegate functions can be useful in many different situations. For this we'll use them to some very basic tasks. A delegate is simply a redirection of a function as a variable.

```
float FirstThing(string thing)
{
    Debug.Log("First thing is:" + thing + " at " + Time.fixedTime);
    return 3f;
}

float SecondThing(string thing)
{
    Debug.Log("Second thing is:" + thing + " at " + Time.fixedTime);
    return 3f;
}
```

We could have more variations, but in this case two different functions that match the signature of the ThingsToDo delegate are FirstThing and SecondThing. The functions themselves are not very complex, but this doesn't mean your functions couldn't do much more.

```
void UseThingsToDo()
{
    ThingsToDo[] someThings = new ThingsToDo[2] { FirstThing, SecondThing };
    StartCoroutine(DoingTheThings(someThings));
}
```

The delegate ThingsToDo as a type can be used as an array. In this example we're populating the some-Things variable with the two functions matching the delegate signature. Then we start the co-routine DoingTheThings with the ThingsToDo array.

> ⊕ Things Started:0
> UnityEngine.Debug:Log(Object)
>
> ⊕ First thing is:Do the thing. at 0
> UnityEngine.Debug:Log(Object)
>
> ⊕ Second thing is:Do the thing. at 3
> UnityEngine.Debug:Log(Object)
>
> ⊕ Things Finished:6.04
> UnityEngine.Debug:Log(Object)

When the co-routine is started we get the FirstThing and SecondThing functions are invoked by the same co-routine. The functions are invoked in the order they were added to the delegate array. Each returns a float value which is used to delay calling any following delegate. The system here allows you to set up a queue of actions. Each action can provide its own time before the next function is called.

7.18.4 Stopping a Co-Routine

To terminate all co-routines, the StopAllCoroutines(); function will terminate any co-routine in process. In some cases where co-routines aren't used often, stopping anything in process might not have any unexpected side effects.

```
void UseStopAllCoroutines()
{
    StartCoroutine(GetsInterrupted());
    StartCoroutine(StopsAllCoRoutines());
}


IEnumerator GetsInterrupted()
{
    Debug.Log("Started");
    yield return new WaitForSeconds(10f);

    Debug.Log("Stopped.");
    // never gets called.
}


IEnumerator StopsAllCoRoutines()
{
    yield return new WaitForSeconds(2f);
    Debug.Log("Stopping all coroutines");
    StopAllCoroutines();
}
```

With the above example, we start a co-routine which will log "Stopped." after 10 seconds. Before that is printed we start another co-routine that uses the StopAllCoroutines() function after 2 seconds. When the co-routine is interrupted "Stopped." is never printed to the Console.

```
void UseStopCoroutine()
{
    IEnumerator counter = Counter();
    /*              ↓              create and        */
    /*              └─┐            store the Counter() */
    /*              ↓              as a variable and pass */
    StartCoroutine(counter);/* the variable to be   */
    /*              ↓              used to stop it   */
    /*              └──────────┐                      */
    /*                         ↓                      */
    StartCoroutine(StopCounter(counter));
}
```

We can also pass an IEnumerator variable to start and stop a specific co-routine. The Counter() function is used to print a number to the Console every second.

```
IEnumerator Counter()
{
    int i = 0;
    while (true)
    {
        yield return new WaitForSeconds(1);
        Debug.Log("Counting:" + i++);
    }
}
```

This co-routine will continue to count so long as StopAllCoroutines() is not called. To stop this specific co-routine without stopping any others, we need to pass the IEnumerator counter to the StopCoroutine() function. The second co-routine started in the above example calls on the following:

```
IEnumerator StopCounter(IEnumerator counter)
{
    yield return new WaitForSeconds(3f);
    Debug.Log("Stopping Coroutine Counter()");
    StopCoroutine(counter);
}
```

This stops the counter after 3 seconds. The StopCoroutine can stop a specific co-routine given it's able to access as a variable. In some cases, it's not always convenient to stop a co-routine with this method. In some cases, it's easier for a co-routine to check a variable to see if it should continue to execute.

```
bool ContinueToDoTheThing = true;
IEnumerator ChecksToKeepGoing()
{
    Debug.Log("Starting to do the thing.");
    int i = 0;
    while (ContinueToDoTheThing)
    {
        yield return new WaitForSeconds(1f);
        Debug.Log("Continuing to do the thing " + i++ + " times.");
    }
    Debug.Log("Finished the things.");
}
```

A simple bool can be used in the co-routine to allow it to continue to execute. The condition to allow a co-routine to continue is checked before any yield return values are calculated.

```
IEnumerator StopDoingTheThing()
{
    yield return new WaitForSeconds(5f);
    Debug.Log("Setting ContinueToDoTheThing to false");
    ContinueToDoTheThing = false;
}

void UseExternalInterrupt()
{
    StartCoroutine(ChecksToKeepGoing());
    StartCoroutine(StopDoingTheThing());
}
```

To use the co-routine we start both co-routines at the same time. The first one checks a bool value to continue. If the value is true it waits for a second before printing out how many times it's run. The second co-routine sets the bool value the first co-routine used to continue to false.

If you read the log carefully you'll see there was a 4th log printed to the Console after the dependent bool was set to false. In the ChecksToKeepGoing co-routine notice that the while loop only checks at the beginning to see if it should keep going. The co-routine continues through the while statements until the while loop checks the bool again to repeat.

7.18.5 What We've Learned

Co-routines are useful in games to manage various aspects of timing. Complex behaviors often involve movement, logic, and awareness. Creatures in general do not continuously move without pause. It's possible to use regular Update ()–style timers, but this gets cumbersome.

With co-routines, we're free to make interesting combinations of behaviors with interesting decisions. The co-routines we looked at earlier could execute maneuvers and strategic behaviors. A co-routine can also call other functions, so it doesn't have to contain all of the logic in one block.

It's also possible for an IEnumerator to start its own co-routine. This can create overlapping behaviors, each one with its own timing. Combined with event handlers, you could trigger functions when a co-routine is started and when it is complete. If the event is raised before or after the yield, you can trigger an event when the co-routine begins or ends.

7.19 Dictionary, Stacks, and Queues

A dictionary type is an interesting version of an array. One basic use is setting up a list of items, say, zombies, vampires, and werewolves. Then we can give each one a value: 10 zombies, 13 vampires, and 7 werewolves. If we want to know the number of zombies, we can ask the dictionary what "Zombies?" and we'll get the value stored at "Zombies" as 10.

The system works in a fairly similar way to an ArrayList, only we'll want to assign some specific types. The Dictionary data type is found under `System.Collections.Generic;`. We'll start a new Dictionary project. We'll assign a simple Dictionaries.cs component to the Main Camera in the scene.

7.19.1 A Basic Example

This example starts with the DictionariesStacksAndQueues scene and the corresponding script in the scene.

```
Dictionary<string, int> MyDictionary = new Dictionary<string, int>();
MyDictionary.Add("Zombies", 10);
Debug.Log(MyDictionary["Zombies"]);
// 10

int[] UnnamedInts = new int[1] { 10 };
Debug.Log(UnnamedInts[0]);
// 10
```

The directive named Systems.Collections.Generic has the Dictionary data type in it. We can use it any number of ways, but one of the most common is the Dictionary<string,int> combination. This allows us to use a string to find a value in the dictionary. Similar to an array of int[], you can recall a value in the array by its index in the array. Rather than using a number to recall a stored value, you use a string as a name for the value. Dictionaries are organized as Key and Value. The string "Zombie" is the key, it's value is 10 as assigned in the example above.

The structure of the declaration of a Dictionary is <first type, second type>, where the first type you use is called a key and the second type is the value that is associated with that key. The key, or the first value, must all be unique throughout the dictionary.

```
MyDictionary.Add("Zombies", 7);
// ArgumentException: An item with the same key has already been added. Key: Zombies
```

If we try to use the above code, we'll get an error that the same key has already been added.

When a dictionary is used, the key is the value that is used to find the association to the second type. Therefore, in the above code, if you asked for "Zombies," the dictionary would not be able to tell you 10 or 7.

To add dictionary entries to the dictionary, we use the MyDictionary.Add("Zombies",10); to push strings with associated values into the variable. To retrieve them, we use what looks like addressing an array.

MyDictionary["Zombies"] acts as though it were the value assigned when using the .Add() statement. We can use different types in the dictionary as well.

```
Dictionary<int, Object> intObjectPair = new Dictionary<int, Object>();
Object[] allObjects = FindObjectsOfType<Object>();
for (int i = 0; i < allObjects.Length; i++)
{
    intObjectPair.Add(i, allObjects[i]);
}

foreach (int i in intObjectPair.Keys)
{
    Debug.Log("Number:" + i + " is " + intObjectPair[i]);
}
// finds 22 objects in the scene.
```

The above code will print out every Object found in the scene. The specific line obs[i] is all it takes to extract an object found in the scene by using an int. To make this a bit more clear, we can use the following three statements:

```
Debug.Log(intObjectPair[0]);
// NavMeshSettings (UnityEngine.NavMeshSettings)
Debug.Log(intObjectPair[8]);
// DictionariesStacksAndQueues (DictionariesStacksAndQueues)
Debug.Log(intObjectPair[13]);
// Directional Light (UnityEngine.GameObject)
```

Using an <int, object> key value pair isn't very different from using a regular array. Dictionaries use generics to help make any combination of types to map from one type to another, not just referencing objects by a number. These can be used for any number of data systems. Usually, when addressing a number of similar associations, we can use dictionaries to a great degree.

With this sort of data structure, we're allowed to ask how many zombies there are in the scene, with int numZombies = MyDictionary["zombies"];. Using a dictionary in this way adds a simple interface for storing an arbitrary number of values and things in the scene.

7.19.2 ContainsKey

To put a Dictionary to some use, we'll count how many GameObjects have the same name in the scene.

```
Dictionary<string, int> objectIntPair = new Dictionary<string, int>();
GameObject[] allObjects = FindObjectsOfType<GameObject>();
for (int i = 0; i < allObjects.Length; i++)
{
    // get the name of the object
    string name = allObjects[i].name;

    // check if we have a key with matching name
    if (objectIntPair.ContainsKey(name))
    {
        // found another, add 1
        objectIntPair[name]++;
    }
    else
    {
        // found at least 1
        objectIntPair.Add(name, 1);
    }
}
```

A dictionary called objectIntPair stores a string for the name of an object and an int to count how many objects have that name. Then we get an array of all the GameObjects in the scene called allObjects.

A foreach loop iterates through each object in the allObjects array. A check is made with ContainsKey() on the objectIntPair. The ContainsKey() function checks the dictionary if the string passed to it has already been added to the dictionary.

The if-else statement uses objectIntPair.Add(name, 1); to both add a new key to the dictionary and increment the value for that key to 1. If the name is already in use the value store there is incremented.

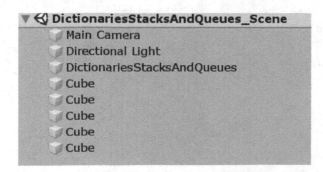

The scene reveals that there are 5 cubes in the scene and one Main Camera, one Directional Light and one DictionariesStacksAndQueues object.

7.19.3 Stacks

A stack is basically an array with some added features. You get a `Push()`, a `Pop()`, and a `Peek()` function when you use a stack. The names of the functions might not mean a lot, but they can act as a clue as to what they do.

A stack is basically an array which you can mentally imagine as an actual stack of books. The top of the stack is where all of the functions perform their operations. Pushing an object onto the stack loads another book on the top of the stack. Peeking at it means to look at the contents of the book on the top of the stack. Popping the stack means to take the top item on the stack off, not that popping a book makes all that much sense.

7.19.3.1 A Basic Example

A stack is an array with a specific order. To maintain the order of the stack you're only able to use three commands to access the contents of the stack. The first function is `Push()` which adds a new object to the top of the stack. To see what's on the top of the stack you use `Peek()`. To take the top object from the stack you use `Pop()`.

```
Stack stack = new Stack();
stack.Push("First"); /* "First"┐                  ┌──────────────┐   */
stack.Push("Second");/*          [↓]               |pushes "First"|   */
stack.Push("Third"); /*      ❶["First"]←❶─────┤into the top  |   */
                     /*                            |of the stack  |   */
                     /*                            └──────────────┘   */
                     /*"Second"┐                  ┌──────────────┐   */
                     /*          [↓]               |"Second" pushes|  */
                     /*      ❶["Second"]←❷─┤"First" down  |   */
                     /*      ❷["First"]            |into the Stack|   */
                     /*                            └──────────────┘   */
                     /* "Third"┐                  ┌──────────────┐   */
                     /*          [↓]               |"Third" pushes|   */
                     /*  ┌──❶["Third"]←❸─┤"Second" down |   */
                     /*  |   ❷["Second"]            |into the Stack|   */
                     /*  |   ❸["First"]             └──────────────┘   */
                     /*  ↓                                             */
object peeked = stack.Peek();/* ┌──────────────┐                      */
/*      ↑ ┌──────────┐    ↓      |Peek returns  |                      */
/*      └┤"Third"├←──────────┤what is on top|                      */
/*        └──────────┘            |of the stack  |                      */
Debug.Log(peeked);/*             └──────────────┘                      */
// Third
```

`Push()` makes the size of the stack longer. Objects down in the stack are not accessible using `Peek()` or `Pop()`. This enforces the fact that the Stack is meant to be accessed in a specific manner. This behavior is called "Last in first out" ordering. `Peek()` will return the value of the object on the top of the stack, but will not remove it.

```
object popped = stack.Pop();
/*       ↑  ┌──────────┐  ↓  ┌──────────────────┐              */
/*        └─┤ "Third"  ├◄────┤Pop() pulls the   │              */
/*          └──────────┘     │top off of the    │              */
/*          [↑]              │the Stack         │              */
/*       ●["Second"]→─┐      └──────────────────┘              */
/*       ●["First"]   │                                         */
/*                    ├──┐ ┌──────────────────┐                */
Debug.Log(popped);/*   │ │"Second" is now    │                */
// Third        /*   ↓ │top of the stack  │                */
                                └──────────────────┘
object secondPeek = stack.Peek();
Debug.Log(secondPeek);
// Second
```

To get the value of the object at the top of the stack and remove it use `Pop()`. By popping the stack you shorten the stack and the item before the top is promoted.

7.19.4 Movement Stack

Movement systems are often best managed by abstracting how something moves from asking it to move. This is best illustrated with the following:

```
public enum Moves
{
    None,
    Left,
    Right,
    Forward,
    Backward
}
```

You should limit your tasks to basic parameters. Let complex behavior do its work on its own. With a short set of Moves in the enum above we could move an object around with a short set of commands using a stack.

```csharp
public void Move()
{
    if (Movements.Count > 0)
    {
        StartCoroutine(Movements.Pop());
    }
}

private IEnumerator MoveTo(Vector3 direction)
{
    Vector3 start = transform.position;
    Vector3 finish = transform.position + direction;
    float t = 0;
    while (t < 1)
    {
        transform.position = Vector3.Lerp(start, finish, t);
        t += Time.deltaTime;
        yield return new WaitForEndOfFrame();
    }
    Move();
}
```

A MonoBehaviour called MoveStack has the above two statements. The public function Move() simply looks at a stack of IEnumerators called Movements and Starts the co-routine at the top of the stack. The Movement stack has a property called Count which is greater than 0 so long as there's something to Pop from the top of the stack.

The MoveTo co-routine it starts is the same sort of co-routine we saw in the previous chapter. At the end of the co-routine we call on Move again to check if there's another object in the stack to execute.

```csharp
private Stack<IEnumerator> Movements;

public void AddMove(Moves move)
{
    if (Movements == null)
        Movements = new Stack<IEnumerator>();

    switch (move)
    {
        case Moves.None:
            Movements.Push(MoveTo(Vector3.zero));
            break;
        case Moves.Left:
            Movements.Push(MoveTo(Vector3.left));
            break;
        case Moves.Right:
            Movements.Push(MoveTo(Vector3.right));
            break;
        case Moves.Forward:
            Movements.Push(MoveTo(Vector3.forward));
            break;
        case Moves.Backward:
            Movements.Push(MoveTo(Vector3.back));
            break;
    }
}
```

To add movements to the MonoBehaviour MoveStack, we have the AddMove() function which accepts the Moves enum. The switch statement pushes the IEnumerator MoveTo() with different Vector3 values based on the incoming Moves enum into the Movements stack.

```
GameObject capsule = GameObject.CreatePrimitive(PrimitiveType.Capsule);
MoveStack mover = capsule.AddComponent<MoveStack>();
mover.AddMove(Moves.None);
mover.AddMove(Moves.Forward);
mover.AddMove(Moves.None);
mover.AddMove(Moves.None);
mover.AddMove(Moves.Right);
mover.AddMove(Moves.None);
mover.AddMove(Moves.Right);
mover.Move();
```

This simplifies moving around a game object. Simply AddMove() and then tell the script to Move(). In the scene a capsule appears and begins moving around based on the stack of Movement commands.

Stacks aren't as intuitive since the ordering is "last in first out." The last command you add to the stack is the first command to be executed. An undo list is often a stack, since you want to keep the most recent command at the top of the stack. To have a better sense of execution order a Queue is more often used.

7.19.5 Queues

A Queue is first in first out. So by adding objects at the start of the queue, they're the first go come back out of a queue. So in the code fragment below we add first second and third in that order to the queue.

```
Queue queue = new Queue();
queue.Enqueue("First");
queue.Enqueue("Second");
queue.Enqueue("Third");
Debug.Log(queue.Peek());
// First
Debug.Log(queue.Dequeue());
// First
Debug.Log(queue.Dequeue());
// Second
Debug.Log(queue.Dequeue());
// Third
```

When we dequeue we get first second and third in the same order we added them. Rather than Push() and Pop() to add and remove from a stack we use Enqueue() and Dequeue() to add and remove from the Queue type. The Peek() function remains the same between the Stack and Queue types.

A modification to the MoveStack MonoBehaviour to a MoveQueue MonoBehaviour swaps the Stack for a Queue. Likewise, the commands in the AddMove() function change from Push() to Enqueue().

```csharp
private Queue<IEnumerator> Movements;

public void AddMove(Moves move)
{
    if (Movements == null)
        Movements = new Queue<IEnumerator>();

    switch (move)
    {
        case Moves.None:
            Movements.Enqueue(MoveTo(Vector3.zero));
            break;
        case Moves.Left:
            Movements.Enqueue(MoveTo(Vector3.left));
            break;
        case Moves.Right:
            Movements.Enqueue(MoveTo(Vector3.right));
            break;
        case Moves.Forward:
            Movements.Enqueue(MoveTo(Vector3.forward));
            break;
        case Moves.Backward:
            Movements.Enqueue(MoveTo(Vector3.back));
            break;
    }
}
```

The co-routine is also changed from Pop() to Dequeue() to execute the IEnumerator co-routine from the queue of Movements.

```csharp
public void Move()
{
    if (Movements.Count > 0)
    {
        StartCoroutine(Movements.Dequeue());
    }
}
```

The Movements.Count works the same on both the Queue and Stack.

The MoveQueue can be used in the same way as the MoveStack, only we might have a better idea on how it will move using a Queue rather than a Stack.

```csharp
GameObject capsule = GameObject.CreatePrimitive(PrimitiveType.Capsule);
MoveQueue mover = capsule.AddComponent<MoveQueue>();
mover.AddMove(Moves.None);
mover.AddMove(Moves.Forward);
mover.AddMove(Moves.None);
mover.AddMove(Moves.Left);
mover.AddMove(Moves.Right);
mover.AddMove(Moves.None);
mover.AddMove(Moves.Backward);
mover.Move();
```

7.19.6 What We've Learned

Organizing and referencing data is an important part of programming. Therefore, much of programming is collecting, organizing, and reorganizing data; there are already many mechanisms in place for use in your own code.

Learning every system in C# isn't our goal. What is important is remembering that there is a system that might be useful for many different situations. As you begin to remember them, you can look them up later to see how they're used.

The most important part of learning any language is the fact that there are words such as queue, stack, and dictionary, which all manage data differently. When you come across something that looks like a list of things that need to be handled, then you should look up what system might best suit your needs at the time.

It's impossible to learn everything at once. It's difficult to remember even half of the features that any programming language has. What's not difficult is looking things up on the Internet and remembering how they're used by reading some examples.

The best thing to do is observing how these constructs have been used here. When you're working on your own and come across something that seems familiar, it's a good idea to go looking around and try to remember what you learned here as a refresher. Then apply the discovery to your current task.

7.20 Lambda Expressions

Now that we're iterating through arrays, it's time to put those arrays to some work for you. Lambda expressions are relatively new to C#. The concept finds its origin in lambda calculus, an invention of the 1930s. The calculus form uses arrows with notation that looks a bit like the following:

$$(x) \rightarrow x \cdot x$$

Unity 3D now updates with the latest version of C#. Lambda expressions were first introduced with C# 3.5. Lambda expressions were an upgrade from what is called an anonymous function. Anonymous functions were basically clips of code that could be stored as a variable. This sounds a bit like a delegate, and in some ways it is.

To clarify, we've made some uses of delegates with some basic uses in previous chapters. When we create a delegate, we need to do a bit of setup ahead of time to use them. We can use a delegate only if it's been created and a variable defined to hold onto the delegated tasks. Lambda expressions allow for creating and using a delegate in a single line.

The major difference is that an anonymous function can appear in the middle of your `Start()` or `Update()` function. Then be set to a variable before being used. After the anonymous function is declared, its arguments are assigned in the same statement where it's used. Because anonymous expressions still work in C#, it's good to know how they work and why lambdas replaced them.

One strange syntactical situation that needs to be seen is the fact you can declare a function inside of a function.

```
void UseFunctionInAFunction()
{
    /* this function is hidden outside  */
    /* of this function.                */
    void FunctionInAFunction()
    {
        Debug.Log("Im a function in a function.");
    };
    FunctionInAFunction();
    // Im a function in a function.
}
```

The immediate utility of something like this might not be readily apparent, but when it comes to keeping code portable this might come into play. A complex situation where you're able to protect and hide the inner workings of a function might benefit from using a complex function as a base for abstract classes to inherit.

Where these weird situations do come up are where delegates and events might require a special case.

7.20.1 Anonymous Expressions

Anonymous expressions are basically short functions that can appear in the middle of a function. This seems a bit weird, but this will make more sense once we see what the code looks like.

```
delegate void SomeDelegate();
void NamedExpression()
{
    Debug.Log("Named Expression called.");
}
void UseAnonymousExpression()
{
    // un named function assigned to SomeDelegate();
    SomeDelegate del = () => Debug.Log("Anonymous Expression called.");
    del += NamedExpression;
    del.Invoke();
    // Anonymous Expression called.
    // Named Expression called.
}
```

In most cases you'll declare a delegate as a template to follow. In this case a very simple delegate called `SomeDelegate()` returns void and has no parameters. As delegates can accept more than one function assigned to them, the above code shows del being assigned a `Debug.Log()` call as assigned through the `= () => Debug.Log();` syntax. This is followed by the more common `+= NamedExpression()` syntax as we've seen before. When the `Invoke()` function is called on the delegate both the anonymous assignment and the named function are called in the order in which they were assigned.

```
delegate int Multiply(int a, int b);
void UseAnotherAnonymousExpression()
{
    Multiply m = (a, b) => a * b;
    Debug.Log("m = " + m.Invoke(5, 6));
    // m = 30

}
```

Depending on the complexity of the delegate definition, the anonymous expression would look different. The above delegate returns an int value and accepts two parameters. In the body of the function we assign m the values `(a, b) => a * b;` where the debut prints out the result of the math. This of course doesn't mean we must follow any rules when making the assignment.

```
m = (a, b) => a / b;
Debug.Log("m = " + m.Invoke(50, 5));
// m = 10
```

The name of the delegate is Multiply, but we can fib, and assign any use of the delegate we want. This allows quite a lot of flexibility, though we should keep in mind what's expected from a delegate named Multiply to do what it says.

```
/*                         ┌─────────────────┐    */
/*                         │ input parameters│    */
/*                         └─────────────────┘    */
/*                              ┌─┐               */
SomeDelegate del = ( ) => { };
/*                              └─┘               */
/*                    ┌──────────────────────┐   */
/*                    │ lambda expression    │   */
/*                    └──────────────────────┘   */


/*                    ┌──────────────────────┐   */
/*                    │ input parameters     │   */
/*                    └──────────────────────┘   */
/*                       ┌─────┐                 */
Multiply mult = (a, b) => a + b;
/*                          └─────┘              */
/*                    ┌──────────────────────┐   */
/*                    │ lambda expression    │   */
/*                    └──────────────────────┘   */
```

The syntax involves two main parts, a set of input parameters indicated with () the => operator followed by an expression. The expression can be encapsulated with a set of curly braces, or if it's simple enough the expression can appear in the same line with the => operator. Lambda expressions are intended to be short quick statements so in most cases a single line is often used without curly braces.

These are called anonymous expressions since the expression section of the assignment has no name. With a delegate assigned to a function we use a name pointing at a function. Something like void SomeDelegatedTask() can be assigned to a delegate. When using an anonymous expression there's no named function assigned, it's just the code without a named function around it.

7.20.1.1 A Basic Example—Action Func and Expression

Functions are meant to be reused. In many cases, writing a delegate type that's used once can feel a bit verbose. In the same way, functions written to assign to a delegate that's called once may also feel over-written. To avoid unnecessary code being written lambda functions can reduce the amount of excess code to accomplish a complex behavior.

```
void UseAction()
{
    IEnumerator delayedCall(Action del)
    {
        Debug.Log("Delayed Call Started.");
        yield return new WaitForSeconds(3f);
        Debug.Log("Delayed Call Finished.");
        del.DynamicInvoke();
    }
    StartCoroutine(delayedCall(() => Debug.Log("A Basic Action.")));
    // Delayed Call Started.
    // (3 seconds)
    // Delayed Call Finished.
    // A Basic Action.
}
```

The unusual use of an inner function can also be used to create an IEnumerator function to use as a co-routine. This can allow this one function to remain self contained. In previous examples the functions used in a coroutine were all separate functions.

The parameter of the delayedCall is an Action which is a type of Delegate. To start the coroutine, we assign a lambda function in the delayedCall parameter in the StartCoroutine() function. An Action is a type of Delegate. Remember that we normally have to define a delegates signature before we can use it. An Action is basically a collection of predefined delegate functions.

```csharp
void UseMoreActions()
{
    int delay = 0;
    IEnumerator delayedCall(Action<int, int> action, int a, int b, float delayTime)
    {
        yield return new WaitForSeconds(delayTime);
        action.DynamicInvoke(a, b);
    }
    Action<int, int> mult = (a, b) =>
    {
        Debug.Log("a * b = " + (a * b));
    };
    Action<int, int> add = (a, b) =>
    {
        Debug.Log("a + b = " + (a + b));
    };
    Action<int, int> sub = (a, b) =>
    {
        Debug.Log("a - b = " + (a - b));
    };

    StartCoroutine(delayedCall((a, b) => Debug.Log("a:" + a + " b:" + b), 2, 3, delay++));
    // a: 2 b: 3
    StartCoroutine(delayedCall(mult, 3, 5, delay++));
    // a * b = 15
    StartCoroutine(delayedCall(add, 7, 13, delay++));
    // a + b = 20
    StartCoroutine(delayedCall(sub, 23, 7, delay++));
    // a - b = 16
}
```

Some of the fun here is the reusing of code inside of a function. Three specific Actions are used in the above example: a mult, add, and sub. These print out a result after a delay provided by a co-routine. Without writing any additional code the above could continue to print many more lines of math once a second.

The Action has many pre-defined variations for incomint parameters. Func is another type of delegate that has a return value. The Func is an Action with a return value. When defining a Func you may notice that the auto-complete provided by Visual Studio has some additional notation.

```
Func<int, >

▲ 2 of 17 ▼  Func<in T, out TResult>
```

One of the options includes out TResult as one of the many provided overrides.

```csharp
Func<int, int> intOutFunc = (x) => x * x;
int result = intOutFunc(3);
Debug.Log(result);
// 9
```

Assigning the Func the above code returns the value to `int result` after processing 3. The Func uses generic types for both input and output. Generics allow for a great deal of flexibility.

7.20.2 Lambda Expressions

Lambda expressions are best recognized by the => operator. This is sometimes called either the *becomes* or the *points to* operator. This wording is used because the left side becomes the expression to the right side of the => operator. This works the same as the assignment operator =, only we're assigning a variable the result of an expression. The following code sample simply takes out some of the extra syntax used by the anonymous expression.

7.20.3 A Queue of Lambdas

Lambdas expand your ability to create different uses for events from within your code. Without writing many dozens of class functions you're able to assign unique behaviors to an object without needing to write hard-coded functions.

In a previous exercise we wrote a function that would start a co-routine based on a Movement enum. We'd then push different vectors into a queue to move an object around in the scene. Rather than a queue of co-routines, we can also create a queue of Lambdas expressions.

```
class DoesThings : MonoBehaviour
{
    // stored list of Delegates
    public Queue<Delegate> ThingsToDo;

    /* a single function to start      */
    /* and execute the generate        */
    /* task list.                      */
    public void StartDoingThings()
    {
        IEnumerator DoSomeThings()
        {
            int thing = 0;
            while (ThingsToDo.Count > 0)
            {
                yield return new WaitForSeconds(1);
                ThingsToDo.Dequeue().DynamicInvoke(thing++);
            }
            Debug.Log("Done doing things.");
        }
        StartCoroutine(DoSomeThings());
    }
}
```

In the function where we start doing the things we include an inner function. The innerfunction is a simple IEnumerator that's called immediately after it's defined. The `ThingsToDo` Queue is a collection of delegates where we use `DynamicInvoke()` to call the code contained in the Queue.

```
GameObject capsule = GameObject.CreatePrimitive(PrimitiveType.Capsule);
DoesThings doerOfThings = capsule.AddComponent<DoesThings>();

// assign procedural task list
doerOfThings.ThingsToDo = new Queue<Delegate>();
for (int i = 0; i < 7; i++)
{
    // Delegate functions generated
    Action<int> action = (x) =>
    {
        Debug.Log("doing #" + x);
    };
    // assign them to the MonoBehaviour
    doerOfThings.ThingsToDo.Enqueue(action);
}
// start the task list
doerOfThings.StartDoingThings();
```

The Action<int> is added to the ThingsToDo Queue. The Lambda here is static, but it's possible to pick different Lambda functions to assign to the queue in the MonoBehaviour attached to the capsule. Running the code above will execute doing #1 to #6 as the functions in the queue are invoked.

7.20.4 What We've Learned

Lambda expressions are more useful than simply printing to the Console; they're often used to sort through arrays of data. The same goes for anonymous expressions, but it's more important that we use a lambda expression to do this.

7.21 Leveling Up

We've reached the end of a very difficult chapter. One of the most important topics that have been covered more than once is inheritance. We looked at several different systems about controlling the inheritance of a class. Special classes such as the abstract class and the interface control how inheritance is managed.

We've been working to become a functional programmer, or at least being able to talk to one. At this point, it should be plausible that you would be able to build some interesting behaviors and write something compelling.

When talking about special programming tricks and learning new idioms and patterns, a great deal of work can be done by reading code. Finding interesting projects on GitHub or any other open-source code sharing site is a good place to start.

Studying code is more than trying to just understand what each statement is trying to do. The hard part is to interpret what an entire function is doing, determine how it works, and check if it's doing something you haven't seen before.

If the code contains a new trick, learn how it works. If the structure looks interesting, try to understand why it was built in that way. If there is new syntax, look it up and figure out how it works. The more code you read, the more you'll learn.

In Chapter 8, we'll look at some more interesting tricks and some common patterns, and syntax that is often used by more skilled programmers. Of course, not everything will be covered in as much depth as it deserves, but it's a starting point.

8

Extended

8.1 What We'll Be Covering in This Chapter

If we've got this far together, we're in a good position to learn some of the more interesting aspects of the C# language. Not everything in this chapter is common in everyday programming, but it's all good to know, or at least know about.

We'll cover a few new tricks that include some style, some interesting syntax with LINQ, and more obscure number of tricks. A few design patterns and structure ideas will also be introduced. It's easy to get carried away with the new tricks and use them everywhere. It's important to remember when these tricks are useful and to use them in moderation.

- Readability
- Source control, revisited
- Debugging techniques
- Recursion
- Reflection
- LINQ
- Bitwise operations
- Attributes
- Architectures
- Design patterns

This chapter is relatively short in comparison to the Chapters 2 through 7. At this point, it should only act as a launch pad to start you on your own into further study. Many of the basic concepts that will be covered have a wider scope into themselves than can be covered in this book.

Concepts like architecture and their related systems often cover entire volumes of text that dive deep into topics about optimizations and use cases. In this chapter, we'll cover the topics only in a very superficial way.

There are some important tricks here: Bitwise operations are useful for enums and dealing with what are called flags. We'll also be covering some of the trickier topics of attributes and reflection. We'll also cover the last looping system called recursion in which a function calls itself.

8.2 Review

Previously we looked over the topics of events and some interfaces. There are hundreds of other common interfaces, but thanks to implementing a few of them and making our own interfaces, we should be able to understand what interfaces are and how they're used.

Delegate functions and anonymous functions are useful abbreviations of a named function. When you need to deal with delays and call backs, delegates and concurrent functions work together to wait for data without holding up your other functions.

Accessors, also known as properties, are also very useful to catch bugs early on. As a creative engineer you can decide how your code communicates. You decide to use `MyClass.property = data;` or `MyClass.SetProperty(data);`. Because properties can be so flexible, it's good to know a bit about how to best think about them.

```csharp
public class Review : MonoBehaviour
{
    void UseHasProperties()
    {
        CanIHasProperties hasProperties = new CanIHasProperties();
        hasProperties.IHasFloat = 5f;
        Debug.Log(hasProperties.IHasFloat);
        // 5
        Debug.Log(hasProperties.IHasHalfFloat);
        // 2.5
        hasProperties.IHasHalfFloat = 9f;
        Debug.Log(hasProperties.IHasFloat);
        // 18
    }
}


class CanIHasProperties
{
    protected float hasFloat;
    public float IHasFloat
    {
        get { return hasFloat; }
        set { hasFloat = value; }
    }
    public float IHasHalfFloat
    {
        get { return hasFloat * 0.5f; }
        set { hasFloat = value * 2; }
    }
}
```

In the above code, we have a `IHasFloat` and `IHasHalfFloat` exposed to the public. We can get and set either one and get predictable values set by using either one. The `Debug.Log()` files return half and can set them at half. Whether or not these values make sense is determined by how you intend them to be used. Should setting `IHasHalfFloat` mean that you are giving a half value or giving it a value to be halved?

Like so many things, how the accessors are implemented is up to you; they're flexible in that you're allowed to write any form of logic into them. This power also opens the opportunity for problems. Expecting one thing and getting another means only a miscommunication or a bug in the code.

Like so many things, writing code that makes sense means communication not only by your code to the reader but also between engineers. When you are working on your projects alone at home, you might be moving between different side projects. The systems you write should be portable and usable between your projects.

If you write a useful character controller, it's a shame to have to write another one for a different project that has a similar behavior. Any time you can reuse good code, you're saving time and effort and making advancements in your game's progress. Make enough parts for a game; eventually you'll be able to assemble an entire game by copying and pasting code from your other projects!

8.3 Readability

Reducing complexity and keeping the notation short is a simple way to make your code easier to read. Some of these notations follow specific patterns. For example, the `foreach()` loop is a more simple version of the `for(;;)` loop without an internally scoped int. There are other optimizations that you can use to make your code more brief, but in some cases the code becomes a bit less clear.

Some of these optimizations have become common enough to be called idioms, or commonly used programming patterns. C# idioms have been inherited from other programming languages like C and C++, which have had a longer history and more time to develop common patterns.

8.3.1 ?: Notation

A simple system to change a value based on a single comparison is the ?: notation.

```
var result = condition ? true: false;
```

The above notation is a truncation of the following code:

```
string result;
bool condition = true;
if (condition)
{
    result = "True";
}
else
{
    result = "False";
}
Debug.Log("Result of condition = " + result);
// Result of condition = True
```

The first notation might be confusing the first time you see it; however, its compactness is its advantage. There are many cases where keeping a simple "if true do this, else do that" to a single line makes sense.

```
bool condition = true;
/*            ┌──────────┐                      */
/*            │          ↓                      */
string result = condition ? "True" : "False";
/*        ↑              ①──┬─── ②──┬──         */
/*        │              ┌──────────────────┐   */
/*        │              │first statement returned│ */
/*        └──────────────┤if condition is true else│ */
/*                       │second statement is returned│ */
/*                       └──────────────────┘   */
Debug.Log("Result of condition = " + result);
// Result of condition = True
```

The ternary is made of three parts a condition followed by a true statement then a false statement. In practice a ternary is usually used for short statements.

```
int greaterThan(int a, int b)
{
    return a > b ? a : b;
}
Debug.Log("Greater:" + greaterThan(5, 7));
// Greater:7
```

The above code simply returns the value of which int is greater than the other; it's simple and has only one line of code. If a is greater than b, return a; otherwise return b. The code is very simple and elegant and, more important, very hard to break. The above notation becomes less clear if you nest conditions.

```
int greaterThan(int a, int b, int c)
{
    return (a > b) ? ((a > c) ? a : c) : ((b > c) ? b : c);
}
Debug.Log("Greater:" + greaterThan(5, 7, 11));
// Greater:11
```

The above code compares all three values and returns the greatest, though from looking at the code it's not clear that this will do. The parentheses help, but they're not necessary. The above code could look like the following:

```
int greaterThan(int a, int b, int c)
{
    return a > b ? a > c ? a : c : b > c ? b : c;
}
Debug.Log("Greater:" + greaterThan(5, 7, 11));
// Greater:11
```

Even though the above code is perfectly valid, it's less readable.

8.3.2 If

Another common strategy to keep code clean is to ignore curly braces {} when an if statement controls only one line of code.

```
if (true)
    Debug.Log("No curly braces needed");
else
    Debug.Log("Doesn't do much for me.");
Debug.Log("done with if.");
```

The above code uses only tabs to determine the execution of each line. You're allowed to omit curly braces {} if each statement is only one line long. This works for a single if statement as well.

```
int i = 0;
while (i < 3)
    Debug.Log("No curly braces needed: " + i++);
Debug.Log("while done.");


int i = 0;
do
    Debug.Log("No curly braces here either:" + i++);
while (i < 3);
Debug.Log("do done.");


for (int i = 0; i < 3; i++)
    Debug.Log("still no curly braces:" + i);
Debug.Log("for done.");
```

The above code shows other statements without the regular curly braces. The readability of each form changes with the exclusion of the formatting afforded by the curly brace placements.

8.3.3 Smell

Programming style is sometimes referred to as either flavor or smell. As such there are good smells and bad smells. A bad smell doesn't necessarily mean that the code is broken and buggy. However, bad smelling code usually leads to problems later.

This programming style is categorized into several groups.

8.3.3.1 Comments

Comments are descriptive but useless. They make up a part of your code as much as functions and variables. They're used to inform fellow programmers as to what a function or code block is used for. Poorly commented code smells bad, and such bad smells cause many headaches.

The real problems begin once any major overhaul of the code is required. Poorly formatted or organized code can become more problematic when finding and replacing field names or function names. Code that conforms to an expected formatting can more quickly and easily be updated, whereas bad smelling code will often result in botched renaming and replacing in a process called refactoring that will be covered in Section 8.12.5.

8.3.3.2 One Responsibility Rule

Long extremely complex functions often exude a certain bad smell. When a function gets too long, it's often a source for many different problems. Here, bad smell means that finding a problem in the function can take a long time to fix. Short functions are easier to debug as there are only fewer lines of code to fix.

The problem usually comes about when a single function tries to do too many different tasks. In other words, a function should have enough statements to complete a specific task and nothing more. Once a function completes more than necessary, it's time to split the function into two or more different functions.

A function should ever take care of only a single task. If there's a repeated task that needs to happen, then another new function should be written to take on that responsibility. This means that many different functions can also make use of a function that has that one task.

8.3.3.3 Duplicated Code

Long functions often have many repeated sections of code, leading to more problems. If one block of code needs a fix, the same fix will need to be applied to every other block that looks and acts in a similar fashion. Repeated code means repeated effort in fixing bugs.

Long functions often use too many parameters; more than two or three arguments in a function's list can also lead to bad smelling code. Often these long parameter lists can feed into longer logical chains.

A long ladder of if-else statements can become very difficult to decode and interpret. Too many conditions in a single if statement also lead to bad smelling code. In some cases, they're difficult to avoid, but they will leave a bad smell even if the code works.

There are always more simple and clever ways to solve problems like too many arguments and conditions. Clever solutions come once you've accumulated experience. To gain this experience, you need to expose yourself to a lot of clever code and read and understand how it all works.

We're not seeing many clever examples in this book, only pragmatic examples to explain basic concepts. There are programmers who are quite clever and willing to share their wisdom on the internet. Forums are a great way to seek clever solutions to complex problems.

8.3.3.4 Naming

Both variables and functions should follow a simple naming convention. When a name becomes too long and cumbersome, it's difficult to read statements that use long identifiers. Programming shouldn't feel like a restrictive set of rules that confine what you're allowed to do. However, there are some general concepts that help keep code readable and easy to understand.

For true false data types like bools, it's often useful to prefix the variable with "is" such as bool isActive; or bool isEnabled. If the prefixing is consistent throughout your own code, you'll be able to identify a variable as a bool simply by its name.

Classes and structs should be named as nouns. A Zombie class is a perfect example. A classZombie is a horrible name for a Zombie class. If it's a noun, you already know it's a class object, and having a type in the name of the variable is redundant.

Classes that inherit from certain interfaces should start with an uppercase I, so, for example, a Graveyard which inherits from IEnumerable should be an IGraveyard. In most cases, a naming standard should be followed. Usually, when you join a company or group of programmers, you'll want to come to agree on a shared set of coding standards.

8.3.4 What We've Learned

Coding standards are commonly thought about and shared, so there are many references on the internet. General concepts can easily be followed to avoid bad smelling code and inconsistent identifier names. It's important to discover on your own why these rules have been written. This comes about only through practice and reading code on your own.

8.4 Git Revisited

Working in a team means more than one person might modify a file. When changes overlap, picking how the changes come together is called merging. In the best case your change will modify code in a different part of a file from someone else's change.

In the general case when you get started at the beginning of your day, you start with coffee, maybe a doughnut, boot up your computer and open Unity. However, if you're working with a team you missed a step. The first thing before opening Unity is Git. Since Git serves as a repository for everyone's work the first thing is to catch up with the work anyone else has contributed.

8.4.1 Git Branch and Merge

In the Git Bash shell start by creating what's called a branch. A Branch in Git is a system to isolate changes you're about to make. When a branch is created you've created a special save point. This can be better visualized with a graph created in the Git Bash console. Open the Git Bash and enter the command:

```
git log
```

This displays in text the last several check-ins with the most recent at the top. You can scroll through the log with the up and down arrow keys. The Q key quits the log view and you're free to type commands again.

```
commit 6d822783ef4adac0cac8b0ddb2f300e624a71703 (HEAD -> AddingReadMe, origin/develop, develop)
Merge: 64ce5bc e34f565
Author:       Alex Okita <            @        >
Date:   Tue Dec 11 22:17:20 2018 -0800

    Merge remote-tracking branch 'origin/master' into develop

commit e34f5654931beb37d15a4deb41ed1e267640d253 (origin/master, origin/HEAD)
Author: alexokita <            @        >
Date:   Tue Dec 11 22:16:59 2018 -0800

    Update README.md
```

Another way to check out what's going on is with the following command:

```
git log --graph
```

That's two dashes followed by "graph."

```
* commit 6d822783ef4adac0cac8b0ddb2f300e624a71703 (HEAD -> AddingReadMe, origin/develop, develop)
|\ Merge: 64ce5bc e34f565
| | Author:       \Alex Okita <          @          >
| | Date:   Tue Dec 11 22:17:20 2018 -0800
| |
| |     Merge remote-tracking branch 'origin/master' into develop
| |
| * commit e34f5654931beb37d15a4deb41ed1e267640d253 (origin/master, origin/HEAD)
| | Author: alexokita <          @          >
| | Date:   Tue Dec 11 22:16:59 2018 -0800
| |
| |     Update README.md
```

This shows the most detail for the `log` command. The string of numbers and letters after the commit is a unique hash creating an identifier for the check-in. To the right of the hash is the branch on which the check-in was made. The comment, date, and the author are also included with the check-in information. Another way to more clearly see the dots and lines is to hide the added information leaving only the comments with:

```
git log --graph --oneline
```

The above is git log space, followed by dash dash graph space, dash dash oneline.

```
*   6d82278 (HEAD -> AddingReadMe, origin/develop, develop) Merge remote-tracking branch 'origin/master
' into develop
|\
| * e34f565 (origin/master, origin/HEAD) Update README.md
* | 64ce5bc Merge branch 'master' into develop
|\ \
| |/
| * 2ff49d5 (master) Create README.md
* | 8c55836 added some more stuff to chapter 8
* | ac4c636 more stuff for chapter 7
* | f008904 adding some more stuff to ch7
* | 57f32f5 more last minute additions
:█
```

The `--oneline` command tells the graph to hide extra information making the dots and lines more visible. Each dot in the vertical time line is a check-in of changes. Not to a single file, but to everything that was committed and pushed. Each vertical line is a branch, imagine the branches as timelines with unique events. When branches come back together, they merge combining the changes from each timeline. When starting out you'll be working in the master branch. To observe how branches work, we'll make one with the command:

```
git branch NewReadme
```

This creates a branch called `NewReadme`. After this we'll need to jump to the branch we made. This is done with the command:

```
git checkout NewReadme
```

nothing to commit, working tree clean

alexokita@Buggy MINGW64 ~/Documents/BookContents/Chapters/Chapter8
(master)
$ git branch NewReadme

alexokita@Buggy MINGW64 ~/Documents/BookContents/Chapters/Chapter8
(master)
$ git checkout NewReadme
Switched to branch 'NewReadme'

alexokita@Buggy MINGW64 ~/Documents/BookContents/Chapters/Chapter8
(NewReadme)
$ ▌

The name of the branch you're in is indicated at the end of the line in the parenthesis (`NewReadme`) changes, based on the branch you're working in. Now the changes we make will take place in the `NewReadme` branch. The changes we make here are now in a new timeline. So when we add the following to a README.md text file in Chapter 8 we only effect the `NewReadme` timeline.

#Chapter8
- - -
Welcome to the Chapter8 project▌

A regular text file called README.md is added with the text seen above. The command:
  `git status` shows the following:

(NewReadme)
$ git status
On branch NewReadme
Untracked files:
** (use "git add <file>..." to include in what will be committed)**

**   README.md**

nothing added to commit but untracked files present (use "git add"
to track)

alexokita@Buggy MINGW64 ~/Documents/BookContents/Chapters/Chapter8
(NewReadme)
$ ▌

With the new README.md file created we should check it. As we had done before we add

```
$ git checkout master
Switched to branch 'master'
Your branch is up to date with 'origin/master'.
```

```
$ git push
fatal: The current branch NewReadme has no upstream branch.
To push the current branch and set the remote as upstream, use

    git push --set-upstream origin NewReadme
```

So we enter the command it suggests and we can push the new branch to our fork on GitHub.

```
 * [new branch]      NewReadme -> NewReadme
Branch 'NewReadme' set up to track remote branch 'NewReadme' from '
origin'.
```

So now the content is pushed and saved. We can continue to make changes on this branch without fear of losing work, or interfering with other people work. Branches are often used to add features or fix bugs.

Once everything works, we can then merge the work into the master branch. The idea here is to save work in progress, and when the feature is done, we can contribute our work to the main timeline and not break the build.

To merge the new README.md into the master branch we first jump back into the master branch with the command:

```
git checkout master
```

```
$ git checkout master
Switched to branch 'master'
Your branch is up to date with 'origin/master'.
```

This is followed by the git merge command:

```
git merge NewReadme
```

```
git merge NewReadme
$ git merge NewReadme
Updating e34f565..4835c5e
Fast-forward
 Chapters/Chapter8/README.md | 3 +++
 1 file changed, 3 insertions(+)
 create mode 100644 Chapters/Chapter8/README.md
```

To see the work, we can read the log. In this case, we didn't do a whole lot of changes, so the log doesn't look very interesting. In a case where multiple check-ins occurred, the log would have more interesting details. Our goal shouldn't be to make interesting looking git graphs, perhaps not in this chapter anyway.

Branches can be managed as a `feature/NewMonster` or perhaps `bugfix/FixingScoreChart`. Adding a slash makes the branches easier to differentiate. To facilitate this, an add on to Git called Git flow was created. Release versions and development branches are used to separate work.

It's not always necessary to merge branches. This is an important feature of Git. Branches can be used as an experimental divergence from the main timeline. You could for instance test a concept which might not work. This means that you can very easily check in work, test, and fail. Should your experiment not bear fruit, that's okay. You can checkout master and your experiment will have never touched the master branch.

8.4.2 Merge Conflicts

Not everything goes as planned. Merging code can often result in a merge conflict. A conflict occurs when changes from one branch do not match changes in another branch.

```
/* original function */
void FirstFunction()
{
    // doing things here
}
/*              | original                                                    */
/*              ┴                                                             */
/*        ┌─────────────────────────────────────────────┐                    */
/*        ↓ changed in Branch A                  ↓ changed in Branch B        */
/*    void FirstFunction()                      void FirstFunction()          */
/*    {                                         {                             */
/*        // doing things here                     // doing things here       */
/*        // This line changed in Branch A         // Same line changed in Branch B  */
/*    }                                         }                             */
/*                                                                            */
```

In the above we see a line changed in both `Branch A` and `Branch B`. When we are working in Branch A and we merge changes in from `Branch B` we'd get the following conflict:

```
    void FirstFunction()
    {
        // doing things here
<<<<<<< HEAD
        // This line changed in Branch A
=======
        // Same line changed in Branch B
>>>>>>> origin/BranchB
    }
```

The changes you're working on are at the HEAD or the latest you have. When merging, the changes appear after yours. From here you'll need to determine which line to keep and which to discard. For this you'll want to try out which version works better or is more important, or maybe you'll keep both lines. The result is your decision.

```
void FirstFunction()
{
    // doing things here
    // This line changed in Branch A (I like mine more)
}
```

Before pushing your code, always check that everything works. After you finish your changes commit and push. To use Unity as an example we'll look at the following:

```
// Start is called before the first frame update
void Start()
{
    Debug.Log("Player 1 Start");
}
```

Simple and to the point. This gets added this to a check-in and you commit the code. Then you merge from Git and get this message.

```
$ git merge origin/FirstBranch
Auto-merging Chapters/Chapter8/Assets/GitRevisited.cs
CONFLICT (content): Merge conflict in Chapters/Chapter8/Assets/GitRevisited.cs
Automatic merge failed; fix conflicts and then commit the result.
```

Git has changed the branch title from (develop) to (develop|MERGING) just to remind you there are conflicts that need resolution before you can push your code. At least we know what file needs merge. The CONFLICT points to the file where the content needs attention.

```
        // Start is called before the first frame update
        void Start()
        {
<<<<<<< HEAD
            Debug.Log("Player 1 Start");
=======
            Debug.Log("Player Two Start");
>>>>>>> origin/FirstBranch
        }
```

To help you see the conflict, you get some characters which will not let your C# compile. There is also text indicating where and what changed. The HEAD indicates what you've changed, the text below indicates the branch from which the code conflict came from. In most cases it might be easy to talk to the author of the conflicting code. Discuss which change to keep, clean up the code, and check it all in.

This is a simple case, and there are sure to be larger, more severe conflicts in the real world. To help resolve these issues it's often useful to find a stand-alone diff-merge app. These won't be covered in this book since there are so many to choose from. However, the tools do the same thing, they look for the <<<<<<< and >>>>>>> to identify where the conflict came from. Then the ======= is used to find which block came from what source.

After the conflict is resolved, add, commit, and push as usual. There are times when you may have changed a file and forgot to add and commit before pulling. This results in the following:

```
$ git merge origin/SecondBranch
error: Your local changes to the following files would be overwritten by merge:
        Chapters/Chapter8/Assets/GitRevisited.cs
Please commit your changes or stash them before you merge.
Aborting
```

This tells you that you need to commit changes or stash them before merging. Git aborts the pull and you can choose to do either.

Stashing is a way to temporarily undo the changes to a file. To do this enter:

```
git stash
```

This creates a local check-in with a hash id. Now you're able to pull or merge as though none of the files you were working on had any changes. To un-stash the changes enter:

```
git stash pop
```

The pop command after stash infers a stack. And yes, stashes can be stacked. And as you pop stashed changes, the changes come out in order. However, if you pull and pop a stash you may still run into merge conflicts.

```
        // Start is called before the first frame update
        void Start()
        {
<<<<<<< HEAD
            Debug.Log("Change From Second Branch");
=======
            Debug.Log("Merge ahead of stash pop");
>>>>>>> bcc91fb3303769cee3d942d023b4af38f3437cb9
```

When you pop a stash after a pull you'll get a hash rather than a branch indicating where the conflict came from. After all this branching, merging, and stashing, the git graph is starting to look a bit more interesting:

```
*   43f6d41 (HEAD -> develop) Merge branch 'develop' of https://github.com/CSharpWithUnity/BookContents into develop
|\
| * bcc91fb (origin/develop) before unstashing
* |   cccc327 Merge remote-tracking branch 'origin/SecondBranch' into develop
|\ \
| * | bd9cbeb (origin/SecondBranch) Second Branch Change.
| |/
* | 2db04ae my code
* |   d4100bf Merge remote-tracking branch 'origin/FirstBranch' into develop
|\ \
| * | 7e10323 (origin/FirstBranch) changes 1 to Three
| | |   2398359 fixed
|\ \ \
| | |/ /
| * | 59202ba Update GitRevisited.cs
* | | f526b43 changed 1 to Two
| |/
|/|
* | b46d1d4 (SecondBranch) Second Change
|/
* 500fcd1 (FirstBranch) change to one
```

If something seems to have changed and you remember a line acting differently from a different check-in, you're able to checkout a file from a specific hash. Each node in the graph is preceded by a 7-digit hash. This helps identify specific check-ins in the git repos history.

```
git checkout <hash> <path to file>
```

alexokita@Buggy MINGW64 ~/Documents/BookContents (develop)
$ git checkout 2398359 Chapters/Chapter8/Assets/GitRevisited.cs

The command above takes the version of the file indicated from that point in time and checks it out to your directory. The file replaces the one currently in the directory. The checkout also ignores any changes that are currently in progress. To read the history related to a specific file use:

```
git log --oneline <file name>
```

alexokita@Buggy MINGW64 ~/Documents/BookContents (develop)
$ git log --oneline Chapters/Chapter8/Assets/GitRevisited.cs
bcc91fb (origin/develop) before unstashing
b46d1d4 (SecondBranch) Second Change
500fcd1 (FirstBranch) change to one
30d7302 added git stuff

This shows the hash IDs for the file at each change. This will help when you want to pick a specific version of a file knowing the specific hash to use to check out the file will help.

8.4.3 What We've Learned

Once all the merges have been made and you've tested your code to make sure that everything still works as intended, it's time to push your changes back up to the server. At this point, it's a good idea to remind your fellow programmers to get the latest version before they make too many more changes.

Communication remains the best form of code conflict resolution. Making sure that your code integrates well involves talking to everyone to make sure your changes don't stomp on something others have been working on. Everyone has his or her own coding style. C# is flexible enough to allow different philosophies to work together.

Knowing your way around git is important. Even when working independently, using Git helps a great deal every step of the way. All too often the phrase, "This was working a few minutes ago; what did I break?" will be saved by reverting a file to a previous version. Using checkout with a hash can save a lot of time.

Git diff can show you what changed between check-ins, so if you checkout a specific file at a specific hash:

```
alexokita@Buggy MINGW64 ~/Documents/BookContents/Chapters/Chapter8/Assets (develop)
$ git checkout 3b87392 GitRevisited.cs
```

You can see what's different between that version and another with the following git diff command:

```
alexokita@Buggy MINGW64 ~/Documents/BookContents/Chapters/Chapter8/Assets (develop)
$ git diff 500fcd1 GitRevisited.cs
diff --git a/Chapters/Chapter8/Assets/GitRevisited.cs b/Chapters/Chapter8/Assets/GitRevisited.cs
index 1946902..c3ec366 100644
--- a/Chapters/Chapter8/Assets/GitRevisited.cs
+++ b/Chapters/Chapter8/Assets/GitRevisited.cs
@@ -9,7 +9,8 @@ namespace Chapter8_4
        // Start is called before the first frame update
        void Start()
        {
-            Debug.Log("Player One Start");
+            Debug.Log("Player 1 Start");
+            Debug.Log("Stashed Line");
        }

        // Update is called once per frame
```

In your Console, the + indicates added lines and the – indicates removed lines. Lines above and below the change are visible to help identify the context where the changes were made. You can also use `git diff` at any time to see what your current changes are.

The scenarios here are basic, but the commands are the same. There are still plenty of git commands that have not been revealed, but to do so would require an entire new book. Git is popular enough, that most questions have several answers findable through a quick internet search.

8.5 Recursion

"To understand recursion, you must first understand recursion."

—James Teal

We've studied most of the basic iteration loops. The for, while, do while, foreach, and even goto can be used to iterate through a task. Of all these options, we're left to adding them to the body of a function.

The for loop:

```csharp
//for loop
for (int i = 0; i < 10; i++)
{
    Debug.Log("for:" + i);
}
```

The while loop:

```csharp
// while loop
int i = 0;
while (i < 10)
{
    Debug.Log("while:" + i);
    i++;
}
```

The do loop:

```csharp
// do loop
int i = 0;
do
{
    Debug.Log("do:" + i);
    i++;
} while (i < 10);
```

The foreach:

```csharp
// foreach loop
int[] ints = { 0, 1, 2, 3, 4, 5, 6, 7, 8, 9 };
foreach (int i in ints)
{
    Debug.Log("foreach:" + i);
}
```

Enumerators:

```csharp
// enumerator
int[] ints = { 0, 1, 2, 3, 4, 5, 6, 7, 8, 9 };
IEnumerator enumerator = ints.GetEnumerator();
while (enumerator.MoveNext())
{
    Debug.Log("enumerator:" + enumerator.Current);
}
```

And the unlikely goto:

```
{    // goto
    int i = 0;
BEGIN:
    if (i < 10)
    {
        Debug.Log("goto:" + i);
        i++;
        goto BEGIN;
    }
}
```

Each one of these loops will count from 0 to 9, and all of them operate within the UseLoops() function. However, if we wanted to create a self-contained function, we might want to consider a recursive function. A recursive function, or method, is any method that calls upon itself.

Recursion is often used to deal with complex sets of data. If we're not sure how many layers of data are buried within a set of parameters, we need to have a flexible system to deal with what we're given.

8.5.1 A Basic Example

In the Recursion_Scene the Recursion script attached to the game object of the same name has the following:

```
// begin function   /*                              */
recurse(0);         /* ↓ start recurse              */
void recurse(int i)/* ← ──────────┐                 */
{                   /*             |                 */
    if (i < 10)     /* ↓ check i   |                 */
    {               /*             |  ┌──────────┐   */
        Debug.Log("recurse:" + i);/* ┤start over |   */
        i++;        /* ↓ iterate i |  └──────────┘   */
        recurse(i);/* → ──────────┘                 */
    }               /*                              */
}                   /*                              */
```

8.5.2 Understanding Recursion

Using a recursive function can be a bit mind-bending at first. It's all too easy to set yourself up for a loop that never breaks. It's important that we understand why recursion works in order to use it more effectively. The first rule for a recursive function is to have a clear condition where the function returns without calling on itself. This is how the function breaks out of itself. If we look at the above example, the if statement has a clear escape condition where the recurse function will not call on itself.

```
int i = 11;

if (i > 10)
{
    Debug.Log(i);
    i++;
    // code isn't
    // reached.
}
```

This statement does not call on the `recurse()` function again, so the recursion stops here. The reason recursion repeats itself is that the function calls on itself at some point. Once the function stops calling itself, the recursion terminates. To observe this with another example consider the following:

```
CountDownRecursion(10);

void CountDownRecursion(int i)
{
    Debug.Log(i);
    if(i > 0)
    {
        i--;
        // Only called when
        // the if statement
        // is true.
        CountDownRecursion(i);
    }
}
```

Here we can see that int i is decremented just before recurring. Once i is no longer greater than 0, the function doesn't call on itself. Once the function stops calling on itself, the function ends, we've reached the end of the recursive loop.

8.5.3 In Practice

When dealing with a set of data with many child objects, we might have to use for loops within for loops to get through all the data. If there's another tier of data underneath that, then we might pass over it without even knowing. To get started, building a simple blob of game objects will be our first goal. This way we'll have something to sort through.

```
GameObject top = new GameObject("6_0");
CreateHierarchy(top, 5);
void CreateHierarchy(GameObject parent, int a)
{
    GameObject[] subObjs = new GameObject[a];
    int b = 0;
    while (b < a)
    {
        subObjs[b] = new GameObject(a + "_" + b);
        subObjs[b].transform.SetParent(parent.transform);
        b++;
    }

    // decrease the iterations
    a--;
    foreach (GameObject sub in subObjs)
    {
        CreateHierarchy(sub, a);
    }
}
```

The above code will produce a hierarchy of game objects in the scene. Some of the game objects were left collapsed. The above code is a recursive function to create a number of objects under a parent object. Each iteration is one less than the previous iteration. Once in the scene they're parented in such a way that they create the nested game object you see in the following hierarchy:

Now we'll want to make our recursive function that calls on itself to iterate through the whole lot of the game objects with a single call. After the recursive function is added, we just need to call it after the hierarchy of objects has been created.

```
LogObjects(top.transform);
void LogObjects(Transform a)
{
    Debug.Log(a.gameObject.name);
    foreach (Transform b in a)
    {
        LogObjects(b);
    }
}
```

With a complex hierarchy in the scene, we want to see each one of the game object's names printed to the Console panel with the recursive function LogObjects() by passing it a game object. It looks pretty simple, but there's a very interesting behavior that's going on with this simple function LogObjects(); in the Console panel.

```
! 1_0
  UnityEngine.Debug:Log(Object)

1_0
UnityEngine.Debug:Log(Object)
Recursion:<UseHierarchy>g__ListObjects|3_1(Transform) (at Assets/Recursion.cs:155)
Recursion:<UseHierarchy>g__ListObjects|3_1(Transform) (at Assets/Recursion.cs:158)
Recursion:<UseHierarchy>g__ListObjects|3_1(Transform) (at Assets/Recursion.cs:158)
Recursion:<UseHierarchy>g__ListObjects|3_1(Transform) (at Assets/Recursion.cs:158)
Recursion:<UseHierarchy>g__ListObjects|3_1(Transform) (at Assets/Recursion.cs:158)
Recursion:UseHierarchy() (at Assets/Recursion.cs:152)
Recursion:Start() (at Assets/Recursion.cs:195)
```

If you look at the log, you'll notice a single function is listed more than once! The first part of this log Recursion: indicates the class where the call is originating. It tells us what file is sending the Console output command.

After that we get the function name where a call is being made, UseHierarchy, which indicates what function has created the Debug:Log, highlighted in the Console panel.

The function has called several times! This is proof that the recursion is calling itself correctly. Also, it's quite interesting to see this behavior in action in the Console panel. Rather than just printing out the names of each game object in the hierarchy, we'd make something more useful with the information we're iterating through.

To build something more interesting to look at, we'll add in some GameObject primitives that spawned rather empty GameObjects with a name in the hierarchy. We'll add in some simple transforms and rotations to some primitives. To set a goal, we're going to build a set of objects parented to one another; like in the hierarchy, we're going to have them orbit around one another.

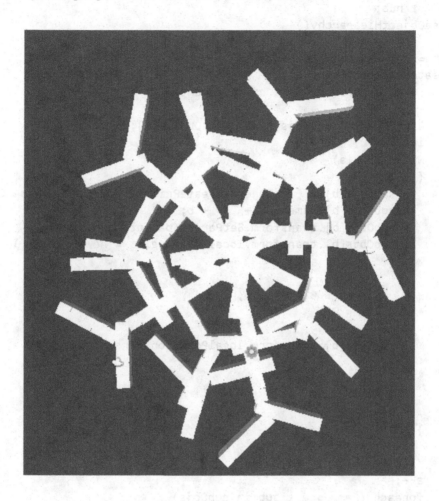

The above example will clearly show us a rotational relationship connected through the hierarchy. We'll start off with the following GameObject:

```csharp
GameObject hub;
void UseObjectHieararchy()
{
    hub = new GameObject("hub");
    CreateHierarchy(hub, 5);
    void CreateHierarchy(GameObject parent, int a)
    {
        GameObject[] subObjs = new GameObject[a];
        int b = 0;
        while (b < a)
        {
            subObjs[b] = GameObject.CreatePrimitive(PrimitiveType.Cube);
            subObjs[b].name = a + "_" + b;
            subObjs[b].transform.SetParent(parent.transform);
            subObjs[b].transform.localEulerAngles = new Vector3()
            {
                x = 0,
                y = (360 / a) * b,
                z = 0
            };
            subObjs[b].transform.localPosition = new Vector3()
            {
                x = 1 * a + b,
            };
            b++;
        }

        // decrease the iterations
        a--;
        foreach (GameObject sub in subObjs)
        {
            CreateHierarchy(sub, a);
        }
    }
}
```

The GameObject hub is used at the class scope to begin. From here we'll try to stick to the same operation as we did before. However, after this we'll want to set some local offsets and rotations.

```
subObjs[b] = GameObject.CreatePrimitive(PrimitiveType.Cube);
subObjs[b].name = a + "_" + b;
subObjs[b].transform.SetParent(parent.transform);
subObjs[b].transform.localEulerAngles = new Vector3()
{
    x = 0,
    y = (360 / a) * b,
    z = 0
};
subObjs[b].transform.localPosition = new Vector3()
{
    x = 1 * a + b,
};
b++;
```

The above code takes over the construction of the hierarchy that we created before. Notice here that the parent object from the previous for loop has its `localEulerAngles` set before the child is parented. This makes it critical to get the rotation to affect the child. Without this function the child object rotates in place rather than having an orbit set.

In addition, I've also created each set of objects to different `PrimitiveTypes`; this gives some variety to the final solution to make different levels of hierarchy more clear. Then we'll add in a simple recursive function that rotates objects in the hierarchy.

```
void RotateHierarchy(Transform a)
{
    a.transform.Rotate(new Vector3()
    {
        y = 0.5f
    });
    foreach (Transform b in a)
    {
        RotateHierarchy(b);
    }
}
```

Rather than `Debug.Log()`, we'll use `transform.Rotate` and slowly rotate each object's *y* axis. Using the first command `go.transform.Rotate(new Vector3(0, 0.5f, 0));`, we'll simply grab the object and add some rotation to it. Now it's only a matter of adding the `RotateHierarchy()` function to the `Update()` function.

As programmers have a knack for giving clever names for systems, we've experienced what is commonly called linear recursion or sometimes single recursion. This is a recursive function that calls itself only once as a condition is met.

Linear recursion is the simplest type of recursive function. Basically, if we need to recurse then we do; otherwise we end the recursion. Because the linear recursion we wrote has the call to itself at the end of the function, it's in a subcategory of linear recursion functions called tail recursion.

Another common type of recursion is called indirect recursion. This occurs when two or more functions call on one another before ending. Indirect recursion is often useful for one function to be called that returns a completed set of data from the recursive function.

```
ArrayList arrayList = GetList(hub);
ArrayList GetList(GameObject go)
{
    ArrayList list = new ArrayList();
    BuildList(go, list);
    return list;
}

void BuildList(GameObject go, ArrayList list)
{
    list.Add(go);
    foreach (Transform t in go.transform)
    {
        BuildList(t.gameObject, list);
    }
}

Debug.Log(arrayList.Count);
```

The first function called `GetList()` calls the recursive function and gives it a list to fill in. This function is commonly referred to as a wrapper function. The task in the recursive function adds the incoming game object to the list given by the wrapper function. Then if there are children, it repeats the process for every child. Once it's done, the recursion ends and the function which called it gets the completed list. For instance, can use these two functions with the following call:

```
ArrayList arrayList = GetList(hub);
Debug.Log(arrayList.Count);
foreach (GameObject g in arrayList)
{
    Debug.Log(g);
}
```

The above code fragment creates a list, then iterates through the list, and logs the names of each object in the `arrayList` that was returned from the `GetList()` function. There are similarities between simple iterative loops like the one that created the original hierarchy of primitives and the recursive systems that look through them.

However, there are more differences at play than the superficial appearance of the code. In many cases, recursion functions often operate faster in the computer's memory than iterative functions. With increased complexity, the iterative function will slowdown more. Without going too far into how a computer's memory is managed, it's good to know that by using a recursive function you might be speeding things up, even if just by a tiny bit.

8.5.4 What We've Learned

As you might have guessed, there's a lot of information on recursion out on the vast sea of the internet. It's one of those topics that people tend to write about to prove their competence. Aside from the somewhat confusing nature of a function calling on itself, the more important part of the recursion function is when the function *doesn't* call on itself.

The programmers writing Unity must know that recursion is a tricky topic. Many functions provided like `GetComponentsInChildren()` do some recursion to iterate through all of the components in the gameObject's hierarchy. These functions supplant the necessity of writing your own function to do the same thing. That being said, at least now you know how the inner workings of the `GetComponent()` functions work.

8.6 LINQ

LINQ (language-integrated query) sorts objects and data.

Let's think for a moment about a data driven game in Unity 3D. A game where statistics, like hit points, magic, abilities, skills and the like are tracked and updated. You'll likely store a mass of data in either a spreadsheet, XML, Json file or database. This generates a long list of items with respective stats.

How then will we need to find and organize the items? One simple method is using LINQ, pronounced "link." LINQ stands for *language-integrated query,* something Microsoft introduced to C# and the .NET Framework several years ago. LINQ draws techniques created for database query systems like SQL. A database is a collection of information grouped and organized for searching and retrieval.

8.6.1 Lambdas and Arrays

Wading through a vast database of information can be intimidating. Writing a loop to search through an array and acting on each bit of data could be a verbose long-winded task. LINQ to the rescue. Instead of what might have been a rather tedious manual task of sifting through a scene with a bunch of monsters looking for the ones with the most hit points, you can now use the Linq library to sift through that data for you.

8.6.1.1 A Basic Example

We'll start with a simple way to find even numbers in an array of ints. This is found in the Chapter 8 Unity Project in the Linq_Scene in the Linq script on the game object of the same name.

```
int[] numbers = { 0, 1, 2, 3, 4, 5, 6, 7, 8, 9, 10 };
var evenNums = from n in numbers
              where (n % 2) == 0
              select n;
// Linq adds the keywords, from
// where and select.
foreach (int n in evenNums)
{
    Debug.Log(n);
}
// 0
// 2
// 4
// 6
// 8
// 10
```

The above code will produce the even numbers output when the game is run. The syntax involves the from keyword. The following n becomes a reused variable. Much like a foreach statement. Syntax in a Linq statement appears different, but the more it's seen the more sense it makes.

```
int[] numbers = { 0, 1, 2, 3, 4, 5, 6, 7, 8, 9, 10 };
/*         └──────────────❶──────────┐ numbers is an array    */
/*                 ┌──❷──┐   ↓ n is each object in          */
/*                 ↓     ↑   ↓ the number array.             */
var evenNums = from n in numbers
/*     ↑ the result ↓                                         */
/*     ❺ is added to └❸┐ an operation is performed           */
/*     │ evenNums      ↓ on each object in the array         */
/*     │        */where (n % 2) == 0                         */
/*     │                ↓ if this operation is true          */
/*     │                ❹ the value is added to              */
/*     │                ↓ the result of the statement        */
/*     └──────←*/select n;                                   */
```

The value n represents each element in an array. Operations follow the extraction of each element. The where statement is a Boolean operation, if the statement is true, n is added to the result output array.

8.6.2 Var

The System.Linq library introduces many new keywords, the depth to which Linq can be used may actually surpass the scope of this book. We will cover the basics and a few cases in which Linq can be applied.

If we look at the variable we created called evenNums, we'll see that it's an IEnumerable<int> of values. Though the var can be different everywhere, it's used in your code as the type is assigned dynamically depending on how it's used.

```
int[] numbers = { 0, 1, 2, 3, 4, 5, 6, 7, 8, 9, 10 };
var evenNums = from n in numbers
```

    [❂] (local variable) IEnumerable<int> evenNums

Hovering over each variable in Visual Studio can reveal quite a lot, especially when working with Linq where the result output type might not always be obvious. For instance, if we create a few different things assigned to var, we can see how C# sees the types being assigned to var.

```
var aThingHere = 7;
var anotherThingThere = (object)19;
var aDifferetThing = (float)23;

System.Type firstType = aThingHere.GetType();
System.Type secondType = anotherThingThere.GetType();
System.Type thirdType = aDifferetThing.GetType();

Debug.Log(firstType);
// System.Int32
Debug.Log(secondType);
// System.Int32
Debug.Log(thirdType);
// System.Single
```

The first is seen as int, the second as an object, and the third as a float. The var type is fine with any type of assignment, even arrays. The GetType is assigned based on the value it is first assigned. Once var has a type, it cannot change.

```
var someThing = 1;
var anotherThing = new GameObject();
someThing = anotherThing;
```

In the above, someThing has become an int. The other value anotherThing is a GameObject type. Once assigned, the int type someThing cannot accept GameObject type anotherThing.

8.6.3 LINQ From

For a more informative use for Linq, we'll add more detail to the operation of the Linq expression in a manner which might actually come up in use.

```
class Zombie
{
    public int hitPoints;
    public Zombie()
    {
        hitPoints = UnityEngine.Random.Range(1, 100);
    }
}
```

A nested class called zombie has some hit points that will be randomly assigned between 1 and 100 when a new Zombie is instanced. Then in we create a hundred zombie objects with the following block of code:

```
// make a bunch of zombies
Zombie[] zombieArray = new Zombie[100];
for (int i = 0; i < 100; i++)
{
    zombieArray[i] = new Zombie();
}
```

After the array is populated with some Zombie objects, we can find zombies with less than 50 hit points, with the following Linq expression.

```
// select weak zombies;
var weakZombies = from z in zombieArray
                  where z.hitPoints < 50
                  select z;
```

Then to prove that we've got a list of zombies with less than 50 hit points, we'll print out the `hitPoints` of each zombie in the new `weakZombies` var.

```
foreach (Zombie z in weakZombies)
{
    Debug.Log(z.hitPoints);
}
// a bunch of numbers < 50!
```

From this little exercise, we'll get the following output to the Console panel.

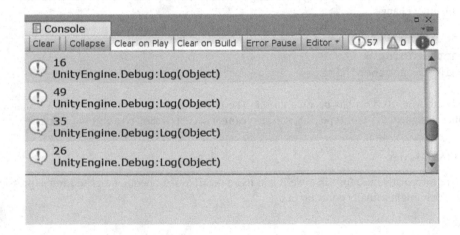

The multitude of tricks you can deploy using Linq can fill a book on its own. When dealing with a large number of objects to sort through, Linq is often the most flexible option. Another bonus is that it's surprisingly fast.

8.6.4 Strange Behaviors in LINQ

When a Linq query is created, it's not immediately executed. We can see the numbers array that we started with and observe some interesting behaviors by adding to the list after the Linq statement is used.

```
//declare an array
int[] numbers = { 0, 1, 2, 3, 4, 5, 6, 7, 8, 9, 10 };
var divisibleByThree = from n in numbers
            /*   ⌐     */where (n % 3) == 0
            /*    |    */select n;
numbers[0] = 1;/*   | */
numbers[3] = 1;/*   |   changes made to numbers not to         */
numbers[6] = 30;/*  |   divisibleByThree but divisibleByThree  */
numbers[9] = 300;/*↓   still knows it's function               */
foreach (int i in divisibleByThree)
{
    Debug.Log(i);
}
// 30
// 300
```

After the `divisibleByThree` Linq query is created, we can change the numbers in the array to new values after the Linq operation. After the `divisibleByThree` var is created, it's source data can be modified. It's only when the foreach statement uses the var from the Linq statement the actual query is made.

The above code prints out 30 and 300 values which were not in the numbers array when the Linq query was applied to the array. The operation applied to the variable assigned by the Linq operation remains alive.

```
numbers[0] = 3000;
numbers[1] = 30000;
Debug.Log("look again!");
foreach (int i in divisibleByThree)
{
    Debug.Log(i);
}
// 3000
// 30000
// 30
// 300
```

Even after the first foreach statement we can make changes to the numbers array again, log the items in the array, and get the new values in the output.

8.6.5 LINQ on Lists

The Linq statements offer additional functionality through the dot operator as well. Here we have an array of numbers where the `.Where()` function can be used with a lambda instead of the previous `where select` statement. After the statement an additional function can be applied to change the result to an array.

```
int[] setA = { 1, 2, 3, 4 };
int[] setB = setA.Where(x => x % 2 == 0).ToArray();
foreach (int i in setB)
{
    Debug.Log(i);
}
// 2
// 4
```

The last `ToArray()` function avoids the strange behaviors by converting the query into an array by using what is called a greedy operator. If we encapsulate the Linq statement in () and add.ToList() afterward, we can force the Linq statement to fulfill the var into an array.

This tells us that the `divisibleByThree` query is set before the numbers array is modified. This becomes a very important change to the operation of this query. The var type is important to the query, but not to how it's used. Because var is flexible, we don't have to figure out what we're getting back from the query.

```
int[] setA = { 1, 2, 3, 4 };

// Lambda
Func<int, bool> even = (x) => { return x % 2 == 0; };
int[] setB = setA.Where(even).ToArray();
foreach (int i in setB)
{
    Debug.Log(i);
}
// 2
// 4
```

In the case were we used different lambda statements, we can also use a Func type to assign to the `Where()` function on the array. The `Func<int, bool>` even can be used to satisfy the `Where()` function. In addition to Where we can also use a function called `Distinct()` on an array.

```
int[] setA = { 1, 1, 2, 2, 3, 3, 4, 4 };
// Distinct removes repeated values
List<int> setB = setA.Distinct().ToList();
foreach (int i in setB)
{
    Debug.Log(i);
}
// 1
// 2
// 3
// 4
```

The `Distinct()` function removes repeated values. Adding the `ToList()`, rather than `ToArray()` function at the end creates a `List<int>`. So what else can we use Linq to do?

```
int[] setA = { 1, 2, 3, 4 };
int[] setB = { 3, 4, 5, 6 };

// union merges the two lists together
// distinct removes duplicates
int[] setC = setA.Union(setB).Distinct().ToArray();
foreach (int i in setC)
{
    Debug.Log(i);
}
// 1
// 2
// 3
// 4
// 5
// 6
```

Here we take two arrays and use Union() to merge them together. The values 3 and 4 are repeated. To remove repeated values we chain Distinct() and then finally ToArray() at the end. The result is a single array with all of the unique values of both arrays.

```
int[] setA = { 1, 2, 3, 4 };
int[] setB = { 3, 4, 5, 6 };

// only shows things unique to setA
int[] setC = setA.Except(setB).Distinct().ToArray();
foreach (int i in setC)
{
    Debug.Log(i);
}
// 1
// 2

// only shows objects unique to setB
int[] setD = setB.Except(setA).Distinct().ToArray();
foreach (int i in setD)
{
    Debug.Log(i);
}
// 5
// 6
```

Functions like Except can take values seen in one array from the other. This can show you what was added or what values were taken away.

8.6.6 Monsters Linq

Starting with some definitions of a monster class we begin with an Alignment enum. We also give the monster class a few attributes for a name, Alignment, HP, and Position. Each monster is likely to be unique when it's created. Functions like `Distinct()` will take into consideration all attributes when filtering an array of these objects.

```csharp
public enum Alignments
{
    Good,
    Neutral,
    Evil
}

class Monster
{
    public string Name;
    public int HP;
    public Alignments Alignment;
    public Vector3 Position;
    public Monster()
    {
        string[] nameParts = { "Ba", "Ga", "Da", "Wa", "Pa", "Na", "La", "Ta", "Fa" };
        Name = "";
        for (int i = 0; i < 2; i++)
        {
            int p = UnityEngine.Random.Range(0, nameParts.Length);
            Name += nameParts[p];
        }
        Alignment = (Alignments)UnityEngine.Random.Range(0, 3);
        HP = UnityEngine.Random.Range(1, 11);
        Position = new Vector3()
        {
            x = UnityEngine.Random.Range(-1f, 1f),
            y = UnityEngine.Random.Range(-1f, 1f),
            z = UnityEngine.Random.Range(-1f, 1f)
        };
    }
}
```

To customize how Linq is used we have several options. Linq and C# are very flexible in that regard. Lambda functions interface classes and Linq all diverge the C# syntax for better or for worse. Not to get too confused, we can still pick a syntax that's comfortable, however it's also important to be able to read code if someone else writes in a different style than you are accustomed to.

```csharp
int numMonsters = 100;
Monster[] monsters = new Monster[numMonsters];
for (int i = 0; i < numMonsters; i++)
{
    monsters[i] = new Monster();
}
{
    var distinct = monsters.Distinct();
    string log = "Distinct default: \n";
    int count = 1;
    foreach (Monster m in distinct)
    {
        log += count++ + ") name: " + m.Name + " " + m.Alignment + "\n";
    }
    // odds are that all 100 are still in the list.
    Debug.Log(log);
}
```

In this array of monsters, we have 100 objects. Using the default `Distinct()` parameter, we find that there have been no monsters taken out of the array. We can use an `IEqualityComparer` interface for the `Monster` type object and write a custom parameter for the `Distinct()` function.

```
class MonsterNameEqualityComparer : IEqualityComparer<Monster>
{
    public bool Equals(Monster x, Monster y)
    {
        return x.Name.Equals(y.Name);
    }

    public int GetHashCode(Monster obj)
    {
        return obj.Name.GetHashCode();
    }
}
```

To take two monster objects and only use the name to qualify the two objects are equal we name the class a `MonsterNameEqualityComparer`. This allows us to use the `Distinct()` function using only names as a comparison rather than all properties of each monster.

```
/* this will use the Name Comparer to filter out
 * monsters with the same name
 */
MonsterNameEqualityComparer nameEqualer = new MonsterNameEqualityComparer();
var unique = monsters.Distinct(nameEqualer).ToArray();
//about a third of the names will be removed.
string log = "";
int count = 1;
foreach (Monster m in unique)
{
    log += count++ + ") name: " + m.Name + " " + m.Alignment + "\n";
}
Debug.Log(log);
```

The `nameEqualer` object is given to the `Distinct()` function and now about a third of the objects in the array have been removed. No two monsters have the same name in the array. We can also make a custom sort. We could rearrange the array in alphabetical order based on the name.

```
class MonsterNameComparer : IComparer<Monster>
{
    public int Compare(Monster x, Monster y)
    {
        return string.Compare(x.Name, y.Name);
    }
}
```

The name is isolated from each monster to make the comparison rather than equality check. A list that's both ordered alphabetically and only contains unique names can be generated.

```
MonsterNameComparer compareNames = new MonsterNameComparer();
MonsterNameEqualityComparer nameEqualer = new MonsterNameEqualityComparer();
var distinctOrdered = monsters.OrderBy(m => m, compareNames).Distinct(nameEqualer);

string log = "using classes to compare and filter: \n";
int count = 1;
foreach (Monster m in distinctOrdered)
{
    log += count++ + ") name: " + m.Name + " " + m.Alignment + "\n";
}
Debug.Log(log);
```

To get here we had to write two classes, one to compare name equality and another to compare name ordering. We can avoid extra code by using a lambda function instead.

```
/* this uses lambdas to sort the names
 * then we filter out repeated names but ignores
 * alignments.
 */
var distinctOrdered = monsters.OrderBy(m => m.Name)
                              .GroupBy(m => m.Name)
                              .Select(group => group.First());

string log = "using lambda to compare and filter: \n";
int count = 1;
foreach (Monster m in distinctOrdered)
{
    log += count++ + ") name: " + m.Name + " " + m.Alignment + "\n";
}
Debug.Log(log);
```

With the function `OrderBy` we can arrange an array of monsters alphabetically. Follow this with `GroupBy` unique names are selected. The last statement `.Select()` uses `group` which is a keyword for the values inside of the Linq statement. This might seem to appear out of nowhere, and to be honest, it kind of does. But this behavior is similar to how `value` appears in a get set property. The `.First()` function on the group selects the isolated group we just created using the `GroupBy()` function.

```
/* this does the same name sorting and
 * also filters out repeats, but ignores
 * alignment.
 */
var distinctOrdered =  from monster in monsters
                       orderby monster.Name ascending
                       group monster by monster.Name into uniqueNames
                       select uniqueNames.First();

string log = "using linq to compare and filter \n";
int count = 1;
foreach (Monster m in distinctOrdered)
{
    log += count++ + ") name: " + m.Name + " " + m.Alignment + "\n";
}
Debug.Log(log);
```

Another form of the same function is using only Linq commands. This last version uses a few more key-words unique to Linq. We have `orderby` as a keyword and not a function. We see `group monster by` and `into` appear as well.

The `into` keyword creates a new group of objects and again we see `.First()` appear on the `uniqueNames` object. This should raise the question, Is there a `.Second()` function as well?

So what else is hiding in the Linq statement?

```
var distinctOrdered = from monster in monsters
                      orderby monster.Name ascending
                      group monster by monster.Name into uniqueNames
                      select uniqueNames;

string log = "What is in uniqueNames \n";
int count = 1;
foreach (var group in distinctOrdered)
{
    var groupKey = group.Key;
    foreach (Monster m in group)
    {
        log += count++ + ")" + groupKey +" " + m.Alignment + "\n";
    }
}
Debug.Log(log);
```

The value `uniqueNames` without the `.First()` function returns a group of items with a Key, much like a Dictionary. Then each object in the new group can be accessed like a dictionary. What's going on here is that all 100 objects are still in the `uniqueNames` object, but the `.First()` gives you the unique names and not the whole array.

8.6.7 What We've Learned

The Linq library is a powerful tool made available through System.Linq. For sorting through and finding bits of information, we are able to use Linq to find and use data quickly and easily. Rather than using for loops and complex foreach loops for inspecting each object in an array, we're better able to use Linq to find what we're looking for.

Practically any data type can be sorted out with a Linq expression, even if it's a list of zombies, weapons, or colors. A Linq expression can use an external function to provide additional logic or a lambda or even some built in functions.

```
/* This produces a list of all 100 monsters
 * they are grouped together based on their
 * names and alignments.
 */
var sorted = monsters.OrderBy
(
    m =>
    m.Alignment.GetHashCode() + m.Name.GetHashCode()
);

string log = "Sorted Monsters using lambda \n";
int n = 1;
foreach (Monster m in sorted)
{
    log += n++ + ") name: " + m.Name + " " + m.Alignment + "\n";
}
Debug.Log(log);
```

The flexibility of C# really begins to show when we start to use lambdas mixed in with other function types with Linq.

```
/* This picks out monsters with HP above 9
 * then lists them out.
 */
var strongMonsters = monsters.Where
(
    monster =>
    monster.HP > 9
);
string log = "Strong Monsters: \n";
int n = 1;
foreach (Monster m in strongMonsters)
{
    log += n++ + ") " + m.Name + " " + m.HP + "\n";
}
Debug.Log(log);
```

We can continue to explore many different variations of the same thing with the Monsters Linq experiment.

```
/* This picks out monsters with HP above 9
 * then lists them out. This and the above
 * statements are equivalent. The only difference
 * is the syntax and use of keywords in place
 * of anonymous lambda like syntax.
 */
var strongMonsters = from monster in monsters
                     where monster.HP > 9
                     select monster;

string log = "Strong Monsters: \n";
int n = 1;
foreach (Monster m in strongMonsters)
{
    log += n++ + ") " + m.Name + " " + m.HP + "\n";
}
Debug.Log(log);
```

One of the most important lessons here is the use of a local lambda and LINQ allow for capturing local variables.

```
/* Objects in the linq statement can see
 * variables in its immediate scope
 */
Monster ComparedTo = new Monster();/* ──────┐      ComparedTo can  */
var weakerThan = from monster in monsters/* ↓       be used in the  */
                    where monster.HP < ComparedTo.HP/* where statement */
                    select monster;

string log = "Weaker than " + ComparedTo.Name + ":" + ComparedTo.HP + "\n";
int n = 1;
foreach (Monster m in weakerThan)
{
    log += n++ + ") " + m.Name + " " + m.HP + "\n";
}
Debug.Log(log);
```

When using the open natural version of Linq, you're more able to integrate local variables into the function statement easily. The above function shows a local variable `ComparedTo` being used to against `monster.HP` in the `where` statement. The topic of Linq allows for a fun variety of uses when it comes to sorting through data. We could spend more time on the subject, but it's time to move on!

8.7 Reflection

A type like `int` or `string` is a clearly defined type of data. To that point, when you create your own class, you're also define a new type. While you're busy writing new classes, it's often the case that you'll want to check for attributes of an object.

It's important to start with clearly defined sets of parameters. All classes of characters should have matching parameters. Constraining parameters with a base class can help. Making changes to different parameters depending on different combinations can mean writing a function for every possible combination. This could end up a cumbersome process. One way to avoid writing many special case functions, inspecting properties and making decisions based on what a class has can vastly improve the flexibility of the code you write.

```
class Stuff
{
    public float PubFloat;
    public int PubInt;
    public void AFunction()
    {
    }
    public int IntFunction()
    {
        return 1;
    }
}
```

Code can read code. You're able to make decisions based on the members of a class. Reflection enables you to see into a class and read the variables it contains. When you look at a class, you can normally get its name; from its name, you might be able to assume what it contains. Something like MyZombieMonster() might be fairly clear, but what does the zombie monster do?

```csharp
Stuff stuff = new Stuff();
Type type = stuff.GetType();
foreach (MemberInfo member in type.GetMembers())
{
    Debug.Log(member);
}
```

With System.Reflection MemberInfo allows you to read the public contents of a class. In this case, the Type Stuff has a float an int and two public functions.

> ! Void AFunction()
> UnityEngine.Debug:Log(Object)
>
> ! Int32 IntFunction()
> UnityEngine.Debug:Log(Object)
>
> ! Boolean Equals(System.Object)
> UnityEngine.Debug:Log(Object)
>
> ! Int32 GetHashCode()
> UnityEngine.Debug:Log(Object)
>
> ! System.Type GetType()
> UnityEngine.Debug:Log(Object)
>
> ! System.String ToString()
> UnityEngine.Debug:Log(Object)
>
> ! Void .ctor()
> UnityEngine.Debug:Log(Object)
>
> ! System.Single PubFloat
> UnityEngine.Debug:Log(Object)
>
> ! System.Int32 PubInt
> UnityEngine.Debug:Log(Object)

Along with Object's inherited functions like ToString() or GetType() the AFunction() IntFunction() and PubFloat and PubInt are printed out to the console. These members are all publicly visible. Private functions, if present, will not be presented as MemberInfo properties.

8.7.1 A Basic Example

In the Reflection_Scene the Reflection script attached to the game object of the same name has a very simple string comparison to find a function:

```
class HasAFunction
{
    public void TheFunction()
    {
        Debug.Log("You found me");
    }
}


void UseHasAFunction()
{
    Type hasAFunctionType = typeof(HasAFunction);
    HasAFunction hasAFunction = new HasAFunction();
    foreach(MemberInfo info in hasAFunctionType.GetMembers())
    {
        if (info.Name.Equals("TheFunction"))
        {
            hasAFunction.TheFunction();
        }
    }
}
```

This simply searches for a function with a name we're looking for. As a superficial example, this doesn't accomplish much if we already knew what the function was named. If we knew that much, we could just call it. However, this does illustrate the use of the type of object and not the object itself. Reflection uses the type definition of an object to discover the object's properties.

8.7.2 Reflection MethodInfo

Aside from the fields found in a class, it's also possible to inspect a function. The complexity of a class grows over time. With that growth comes added a growing number of functions to act on the class.

If your game has powerups which all act in a specific manner, it's often cumbersome to write into a character functions like "ActivateExtraDamage" or "EnableHealthRecovery", etc. In cases where you want the powerup.

In a MonoBehaviour we have an enumerator that processes a queue of delegate tasks.

```csharp
public void DoTheThings()
{
    IEnumerator DoesThings()
    {
        while (ThingsToDo.Count > 0)
        {
            Delegate thing = ThingsToDo.Dequeue();
            string thingName = thing.Method.Name;
            // figure out which function is in the Queue.
            MethodInfo methodInfo = thing.GetMethodInfo();

            // read the name of the incoming parameter
            ParameterInfo[] paramInfos = methodInfo.GetParameters();
            switch (paramInfos[0].Name)
            {
                case "life":
                    Func<int, int> life = (Func<int, int>)thing;
                    Life = life.Invoke(Life);
                    break;
                case "money":
                    Func<int, int> money = (Func<int, int>)thing;
                    Money = money.Invoke(Money);
                    break;
            }
            Debug.Log("Did " + thingName + " Life:" + Life + " Money:" + Money);

            yield return new WaitForSeconds(1f);
            if (Life <= 0)
                Destroy(this.gameObject);
        }
    }
    StartCoroutine(DoesThings());
}
```

The delegate pulls out a task from the queue and gets its name. Then we pull out the method's information with `GetMethodInfo()`. This returns everything we'd ever want to know about the method assigned in the queue. One of the values in the `MethodInfo` is a list of names in the parameters of the function.

For this exercise we can assume that every function assigned to the queue has at least one parameter and it's named either life or money. The `Person : MonoBheaviour` has three parameters,

```csharp
class Person : MonoBehaviour
{
    public Queue<Delegate> ThingsToDo;
    public int Life = 0;
    public int Money = 0;
    private void Awake()
    {
        ThingsToDo = new Queue<Delegate>();
    }
```

`Life`, `Money`, and `ThingsToDo`, reflecting on this Person reveals a very simple existence. When Person is created it initializes a Queue of things to do. This person is unaware of what will become of its life or money. One thing is for sure, with each loop through the switch statement we wait for a second, then we check if life is <= 0 and we destroy the gameObject.

When we look at the parameter of the incoming delegate function we check the name and assign the function either Life or Money. This could be expanded to any number of properties your class might have.

```
int BeBorn(int life)
{
    Debug.Log("You've got one life...");
    return life + 10;
}

int GoToWork(int money)
{
    Debug.Log("You're Welcome.");
    return money + 10;
}

int Accident(int life)
{
    Debug.Log("Oops.");
    return life - 5;
}

int PayTaxes(int money)
{
    Debug.Log("Thankyou come again.");
    return money / 2;
}

int Die(int life)
{
    return life - life;
}
```

Person has instore the above functions. Each one acts on the parameter as you might expect. The different functions are assigned to Persons ToDo list using enqueue.

```
GameObject capsule = GameObject.CreatePrimitive(PrimitiveType.Capsule);
Person bob = capsule.AddComponent<Person>();
Func<int, int> born = BeBorn;
Func<int, int> work = GoToWork;
Func<int, int> accident = Accident;
Func<int, int> taxes = PayTaxes;
Func<int, int> death = Die;
bob.ThingsToDo.Enqueue(born);
bob.ThingsToDo.Enqueue(work);
bob.ThingsToDo.Enqueue(accident);
bob.ThingsToDo.Enqueue(taxes);
bob.ThingsToDo.Enqueue(death);
bob.DoTheThings();
```

Once the person's queue is populated, the Function `DoTheThings()` is called and the queue begins its invocation process.

```
(!) You've got one life...
    UnityEngine.Debug:Log(Object)

(!) Did BeBorn Life:10 Money:0
    UnityEngine.Debug:Log(Object)

(!) You're Welcome.
    UnityEngine.Debug:Log(Object)

(!) Did GoToWork Life:10 Money:10
    UnityEngine.Debug:Log(Object)

(!) Oops.
    UnityEngine.Debug:Log(Object)

(!) Did Accident Life:5 Money:10
    UnityEngine.Debug:Log(Object)

(!) Thankyou come again.
    UnityEngine.Debug:Log(Object)

(!) Did PayTaxes Life:5 Money:5
    UnityEngine.Debug:Log(Object)

(!) Did Death Life:0 Money:5
    UnityEngine.Debug:Log(Object)
```

With each process of the queue we step through the short and dismal life of Person. As unassuming as what's happened here, we can take for granted we know what happens to life and money, aside from death and taxes. Person had no idea what the function was going to do. We only had the information of what the incoming parameter was asking for, and Person assigned its life and money to the incoming function not knowing what it would do.

The outcome is still clear, we saw the name of the incoming function and that's something we could have processed. But if we didn't know ahead of time what to expect then that wouldn't have mattered. The important take away is that we only knew the name of the parameter of the function.

```csharp
void LifeInMoneyOut(int life, out int outMoney)
{
    outMoney = life * 2;
}


delegate void InOutDelegate<T, U>(T input, out U output);
InOutDelegate<int, int> lifeInMoneyOut;
```

Additional parameters named in the function can be assigned to change how a function can be discovered and used from the assigned function.

8.7.3 What We've Learned

To explore the idea that a class might have a list of properties and a delegate coming in might want to modify those properties we could do so by reflection alone.

```csharp
class HasStuff
{
    public int number = 0;
    public Vector3 position = Vector3.one;
    public GameObject gameObject = new GameObject();
```

In the `HasStuff` class we have a few class members, a number position, and a gameObject. These are names of members which reflection can find. To match this, a delegate is setup that mirrors the property names.

```
delegate void ThreeInputs<T, U, V>(T A, U B, V C);
ThreeInputs<int, Vector3, GameObject> GiveThreeInputs;
void TheThreeThings(int number, Vector3 position, GameObject gameObject)
{
    Debug.Log("Got called!");
    Debug.Log(number + " " + position + " " + gameObject);
}
```

The input parameters number position and gameObject can also be seen through reflection. We can iterate through the properties of the class and compare them to the properties of the delegate.

```
public void CheckOnStuff()
{
    GiveThreeInputs = TheThreeThings;
    Delegate threeIns = GiveThreeInputs;

    var delegateMethodInfo = threeIns.GetMethodInfo().GetParameters();
    var myFields = this.GetType().GetFields();
    object[] pars = new object[delegateMethodInfo.Length];

    for (int i = 0; i < delegateMethodInfo.Length; i++)
    {
        for (int j = 0; j < myFields.Length; j++)
        {
            if (delegateMethodInfo[i].Name.Equals(myFields[j].Name))
            {
                pars[i] = myFields[i].GetValue(this);
            }
        }
    }

    threeIns.DynamicInvoke(pars);
}
```

A small touch of magic here seems to happen. The array `object[] pars` gets populated through getting the classes property by name. The class properties are turned into an object in an array. The `threeIns` delegate is assigned the array of parameters in the `DynamicInvoke` call. The fields in the class that match the names of the parameters in the delegate are assembled and called.

```
HasStuff hasStuff = new HasStuff();
hasStuff.number = 42;
hasStuff.position = new Vector3(3, 5, 7);
hasStuff.gameObject = new GameObject("magic");
hasStuff.CheckOnStuff();
```

The values of `hasStuff` get set to something unique. Then the delegate gets assigned. The delegate's values are name checked against the fields of the class. When matching string names are found the values are added to an array. The delegate is called with the object array populated with the classes properties.

> (!) Got called!
>   UnityEngine.Debug:Log(Object)
>
> (!) 42 (3.0, 5.0, 7.0) magic (UnityEngine.GameObject)
>   UnityEngine.Debug:Log(Object)

By using Reflection, the class was able to identify parameters and assign a function values from its own members. Add this functionality to incoming delegates and you'll be able to assign any variety of modifications to a game character or object.

8.8 Dynamic

C# is a strong typed language, usually. As we've seen with var, the type of data that can be stored in a variable isn't always clearly defined. The var type gets defined after it receives a value. This is useful when the value assigned is assumed to be changing, as with the case with Linq values. The dynamic type is a bit different.

Opening the Dynamic_Scene find the Dynamic script attached to the game object of the same name. The dynamic type, unlike var can be reassigned at any time to anything. This defies what it means to be a string typed language. Especially since the `GetType()` function returns no clue that the variable is being stored in a type that isn't set.

```
dynamic d = "im a string";
Debug.Log(d.GetType());
// System.String

d = 1;
Debug.Log(d.GetType());
// System.Int32

d = (Action)(() => { });
Debug.Log(d.GetType());
// System.Action
```

The dynamic isn't commonly used, and for clarity it shouldn't be used very often. The practice of defining a type is important. Type definition and use restricts a variable from changing accidentally. Even with generic types, the `<T>` becomes a type when it's assigned and after assignment the type can't change.

Variables in most cases remain static or unchanged once assigned or created. The dynamic type can change. The chaos this may introduce allows for errors Visual Studio might have been able to catch. Compile-time error checks are skipped on the dynamic variables; use with caution.

```
d = 1;
d++;
Debug.Log(d.GetType() + " " + d);
// System.Int32 2

d = d / Mathf.PI;
Debug.Log(d.GetType() + " " + d);
// System.Single 0.6366197
```

In some cases, the dynamic can change types even without a specific assignment. By dividing an int by a float, the type gets reassigned. The type mutation occurs without error or warning. This behavior mimics that of other languages like LUA or Python where a variable's type changes as the assignment changes.

```
/* in Visual Studio we don't get an error     */
/* only when you run the game, will an error   */
/* be produced!                                */
d = 1;
d = "im a string again!";
d++;
// RuntimeBinderException:
// Operator '++' cannot be applied to operand of type 'string'
```

Where the dynamic type causes problems is when the variable is used in an unexpected way. The data stored in the dynamic variable still functions as a specific type, so operations like ++ cannot function on a string. Though in most cases the error would have been caught in Visual Studio before the game is played.

8.8.1 ExpandoObject

The unique ability of dynamic to change type can be expanded upon. The System.Dynamic name space includes a strange object called the ExpandoObject.

```
dynamic expando = new System.Dynamic.ExpandoObject();
expando.thing = "im a thing";
expando.dodad = 1;
expando.widget = 1.0f;
expando.gizmo = (Action)(()=>{ Debug.Log(expando.thing);});

Debug.Log(expando.thing.GetType() + " " + expando.thing);
// System.String im a thing
Debug.Log(expando.dodad.GetType() + " " + expando.dodad);
// System.Int32 1
Debug.Log(expando.widget.GetType() + " " + expando.widget);
// System.Single 1
expando.gizmo();
// im a thing
```

The dot operator allows a new `ExpandoObject()` to create add name and define a type of a member dynamically. The near magic powers of the `ExpandoObject()` should be used with caution. Once assigned, the type and function of each member of an ExpandoObject cannot be debugged before it's used.

The expando object can reference itself, as we can see in the Action assigned to the `expando.gizmo` object. And a value in the ExpandoObject can be a delegate of some kind as well, not just a plain old data type. The ExpandoObject can also be used as different types.

8.8.2 Expando Reader

Data is quite often stored as text. Properties for game objects are parsed from string values into an expected data type for use elsewhere in the Scene of the game. A Zombie could have a name, some hit points, and a position in the world. These would be stored as a string, int, and a Vector3, but in text form there's no type other than string.

```
/* some data in string format */
string data = "" +
    "Name:Rob\n" +
    "HP:10\n" +
    "Position:1.23,4.56,7.89";
```

The data could originate from anywhere, but we begin with a few lines of data separated with the `\n` character and put together with a + character. We'll forgoe reading and writing a text file to disk since we've already done that before.

```
dynamic expando = new System.Dynamic.ExpandoObject();
// convert expando to a dictionary!
var expandoAsDictionary = (IDictionary<string, object>)expando;
```

To make the `ExpandoObject` into a type we can dynamically add new members to convert the `ExpandoObject()` into an `IDictionary<string, object>`. In this form we can use the Dictionary's interface member `Add()` to create new members.

```
var parts = data.Split('\n');
foreach(string part in parts)
{
    var pair = part.Split(':');
    // ExpandoObject doesn't have Add
    // but Dictionary does!
    expandoAsDictionary.Add(pair[0], pair[1]);
}
```

The data string gets turned into three strings when it's split with the `\n` char. The result is `Name:Rob`, `HP:10`, and `Position:1.23,4.56,7.89`. These three strings are then split at the : character into a string object key value pair. Each key value pair is added to the `expandoAsDictionary` var.

```
expando = expandoAsDictionary;
Debug.Log(expando.Name + ":" + expando.Name.GetType());
// Rob:System.String
```

The expando value is then assigned the expandoAsDictionary to convert the dictionary back into an ExpandoObject. The expando object now has a Name, HP, and Position property. For the first pair Name we didn't have to convert the value. So expando.Name is the string Rob.

```
expando.HP = int.Parse(expando.HP);
Debug.Log(expando.HP + ":" + expando.HP.GetType());
// Rob:System.Int32
```

The values of a ExpandoObject object are also dynamic, so the string "10" can be parsed and to itself and become an int. Now expando.HP is an int 10 after the Parse function has been applied to itself.

```
Vector3 toVector3(string s)
{
    var v = s.Split(',');
    return new Vector3()
    {
        x = System.Single.Parse(v[0]),
        y = System.Single.Parse(v[1]),
        z = System.Single.Parse(v[2])
    };
}
expando.Position = toVector3(expando.Position);
Debug.Log(expando.Position + ":" + expando.Position.GetType());
// (1.2, 4.6, 7.9):UnityEngine.Vector3
```

The expando.Position gets converted with a split and more parsing. This also shows that dynamic can be assigned types from Unity as well.

The example shown here has no error checking. There's no guarantee that a text file from disk won't have an unexpected character or an extra space. The interesting effect though is converting a string to an int without jumping through any tricky conversions or type assignments. The dynamic type is suited for situations like the one shown.

8.8.3 What We've Learned

The dynamic type was added to C# to add compatibility with languages like LUA or Python. In LUA variables were all just names. The only definition added to a LUA variable was it's scope, either Local or Global. Python did the same thing were you simply wrote "bob = 10" and now bob is a value of 10.

By using dynamic you can use variables in a similar fashion. This does open more opportunity for unexpected behavior with fewer safeguards in place. The dynamic is also useful for parsing more complex types like Json or XML. With C# on a web server, dynamic is often used to read and build complex HTML web pages. Each <ELEMENT> becomes a new expando.object with values.

```
expando.Transform.Position = expando.Position;
expando.Transform.Rotation = Quaternion.identity;
expando.Transform.Scale = Vector3.one;
```

It doesn't stop there. Each object in an ExpandoObject can have members with values with members and more values as well. ExpandoObject lives up to it's name and it's quite expansive.

8.9 Bitwise Operators

When you are taught to count, you're learning the decimal system. The decimal system is a base-10 numeral system, but there are many other systems as well. Your computer uses binary or a base-2 numeral system. The transistors in your computer have only two states; they are either on or off. To be more technically correct, they are in either a charged state or a ground state.

Manipulating individual bits seems a bit low level for the common game-building tasks, but once you get the hang of flipping individual bits, they can be used for many different tricks. Going back to the basics, we'll review about how numbers are stored in the computer's memory.

```
ShowBits(1);
// bits in 1:
// 10000000

ShowBits(128);
// bits in 128:
// 00000001

ShowBits(255);
// bits in 255:
// 11111111
```

A byte is a collection of eight 1s and 0s. Therefore, the binary 0000 0000 represents the decimal 0. The binary representation is what is stored in the computer's memory. A decimal 1 is stored as binary 1000 0000, and a computer represents decimal 2 as 0100 0000. The second place is a decimal 2. Therefore, decimal 128 is binary 0000 0001.

```
bool isLittleEndian = System.BitConverter.IsLittleEndian;
Debug.Log("Is Little Endian?: " + (isLittleEndian?"Yes":"No"));
// Is Little Endian?: Yes
```

8.9.1 Big Endian and Little Endian

The arrangement of the digits we're looking at is called *little endian*. The name comes from the position in the line of 1s and 0s where the biggest value is stored at the far end of the stream of ones and zeros. Since the lowest value is stored at the start of the number, it's called little endian. If we were to represent 128 in binary as 10000000, where the largest values are stored first, then we're looking at a big-endian number.

Each digit is a value of a power of 2. The first number is either 0 or 1; the first value is either 0 or 1 to the power of 0. The second digit is either 0 or 2 to the power of 1, which is 2. The third digit is 0 or 2 to the power of 2, which is 4. The pattern repeats for each digit in the binary number.

To explain how binary works and what the 1s and 0s represent, consider first that binary is made up of 1s and 0s. If each represents a power of 2, then 1, 2, 4, 8, and then 16, 32, 64, 128 are what each digit in a byte means. With these we're able to represent each number between 0 and 255.

As a simplified example, we'll look at a 2-bit number. To count to 3, we'd start with 00, 10, 01, and then 11. The first digit is 0 or 1 followed by 0 or 2. To count 0, we use 00. The combination 10 counts 1. To count to 2, we use 01. Last, the number 3 is indicated with a 10 and a 01, added together as 11. If you add 1 and 2, you get 3. This is how your computer counts.

This arrangement comes from backward compatibility with older processors that go back to the 8008 made by Intel in 1972. This was a tiny processor which used little endian byte storage to more easily communicate with a serial bus, a computer interface to send bytes between systems. This dictated that the lower values needed to be calculated first.

Today most modern CPUs are big endian since, as humans, we read the largest values first, not last. A million one hundred eleven thousand one hundred and eleven begins with the large value and works down to the smallest value. Modern assembly is organized in the same way.

8.9.2 Signed or Unsigned

The same system as above works for a byte that is eight 1s and 0s. An int stores 32 1s and 0s, but there's a catch. The words signed and unsigned indicate if a number is allowed to have negative values. If the number is signed, then you lose a bit to indicate a plus + or minus − sign; though you don't usually see a plus + symbol in front of a positive number, it is inferred.

To go back to our 2-bit number, we'd only be able to count to three values again. To begin we can start with 10 that would translate into −1. When the first bit represents a value, the second bit indicates a sign.

We can use 00 to indicate a 0 and 11 to indicate a +1. We still have three usable values: −1, 0, and +1. Whether or not a bit is used to indicate a plus + or minus − sign is called signed or unsigned. When we have only positive values, we consider that an unsigned number; if we can show both positive and negative numbers, programmers call this signed.

```
sbyte sbite = (sbyte)-127;
ShowBits(sbite);
// bits in -127:
// 10000001
```

A signed `byte` or `sbyte` is a number from -127 to +127. Using little endian bits, the last bit is 1 if the value is negative and 0 if the value is positive. In the case with -1 we get a lot of 1s. The reason for this is that with negative numbers we change how we use the value of the bits. The system is more like, what value do you subtract from 128 to reach the value in the signed byte?

```
ShowBits((sbyte)-1);
// bits in -1:
// 11111111

ShowBits((sbyte)1);
// bits in 1:
// 10000000

ShowBits((sbyte) 0);
// bits in 0:
// 00000000

ShowBits((sbyte)127);
// bits in -127:
// 10000000

ShowBits((sbyte)-127);
// bits in -127:
// 10000001
```

An int is a number between −2,147,483,648 and 2,147,483,647. Notice that the number reaches one more negative than positive; we will see why in a moment. A uint or an unsigned int is a number from 0 to 4,294,967,295. To get these numbers, the last bit is the only one that controls the sign of the number.

So the regular math operators work as we'd expect, but we get an interesting behavior when we reach the limit of these numbers.

```
int max = 2147483647;
Debug.Log(max);
// 2147483647

max += 1;
Debug.Log(max);
// -2147483648
```

Normally, you might expect c to print out 2147483648; however, we get -2147483648, a negative number. There's also an unsigned version of int called the uint where the u means unsigned.

```
uint umax = 4294967295;
Debug.Log(umax);
// 4294967295

umax += 1;
Debug.Log(umax);
// 0
```

The increment of 1 on the unsigned int starting at 4294967295 results with 0. When umax is assigned 4294967295, you can imagine 32 1s filling up the 32-bit number. When we add 1, they're rolled over and the result turns into 32 0s instead. Therefore, the numbers in the computer, because they are binary, act weird. This is a simple awkward fact of computing. In a small example, rather than looking at 32 numbers, we'll look at just a few digits.

A 4-bit number, 0000, sometimes called a nibble, starts off as a collection of four digits. If we add 1, we get the following result 0001, which is then pushed to the left; when we add another 1, we get 0010 to get 2. Remember that the second digit is 2^1.

Adding another 1, we get 0011 to get $1 + 2$ or $2^0 + 2^1$, so we have 3. By adding another 1, we get 0100; the first two numbers are reset and the 1 is pushed to the left again, so we have 4. Adding another 1, we get 0101 to get $1 + 4$. To continue we add another 1 and we get 0110; then we add another 1 and we get 0111 or $1 + 2 + 4$ to get 7.

Finally, by adding another 1, we get 1000, which is the last digit for 8. The process continues until we have 1111, and following the pattern of adding another 1 will push the 1 to the right, but there's no space left, so we get 0000. The 4-bit number has rolled over. With a 4-bit number, we get a range from 0 to 15. If we have a signed 4-bit number, we get a range from −7 to 7.

This whole business of counting with $2^0 + 2^1 + 2^2 +...$ was invented in 1679. A mathematician named Gottfried Wilhelm von Leibniz concocted the system. He also happened to invent calculus, so if you're having trouble in math class, you can blame Gottfried.

Though without him we wouldn't have computers. After he created the system, he said, "When numbers are reduced to 0 and 1, a beautiful order prevails everywhere." Indeed, computers have led to many beautiful things.

The system works for larger numbers. In the case of a 32-bit number, we'd be counting till we hit the 4294967296 number before we roll the number. When we use a signed number, we lose either the first or last digit to store the sign, either + or −. Technically, it's a 31-bit number with a sign whose range is either $+2^{31}(-1$ for holding a 0) or -2^{31}, which means 2147483647 to -2147483648. Even though computers are limited by the bits per number, we can work with this, so long as we keep these limitations in mind.

8.9.3 Bitwise Or |

The bitwise operators |, &, ^, and ~ are used to manipulate numbers on the bit level rather than on the math level. These are referred to as "Bar" where we assume $1 + 2 = 3$. We can also use $1 | 2 = 3$, though this is not working in the way you might think it is. The or operator | is used to merge bits together. Looking at the previous 4-bit number, we can use the following notation:

```
  1248
  1001 =   9
  1010 =   5
|
  _____
  1011 = 13
```

Or in C# we can use the following notation:

```
uint a = 5;      // 1 + 0 + 4 = 5
uint b = 6;      // 0 + 2 + 4 = 6
uint c = a | b;  // 1 + 2 + 4 = 7
Debug.Log(c);
```

The above example looks at the 1s, and if either bit is 1, then the resulting bit is set to 1. If both numbers are 1s, then the result is only another 1. Therefore, in the above example, we get the result 7, not 11 as you might imagine.

At first glance, we might not immediately see the advantage of using numbers by the bits that they are made of. However, programmers like to think in strange ways, and to learn how to write code is to think like a programmer, which is never an easy task.

8.9.4 Enums and Numbers

If we use an enum, we can set each value to a number.

```
enum CharacterClasses
{
    Farmer  = 0x00,
    Fighter = 0x01,
    Thief   = 0x02,
    Wizard  = 0x04,
    Archer  = 0x08
}
```

If we use the above enum, you can see some assignments to number values. You should also notice that they are being assigned the same values that are used when counting in binary. Therefore, if 0000 is a farmer, then 0001 is a fighter. This means 0010 is a thief, 0100 is a wizard, and 1000 is the archer. What should happen if we want to have a multiclass character who is a fighter wizard?

```
CharacterClasses fighter = CharacterClasses.Fighter;
ShowBits((byte)fighter);
// bits in 1:
// 10000000

CharacterClasses wizard = CharacterClasses.Wizard;
ShowBits((byte)wizard);
// bits in 4:
// 00100000

CharacterClasses multiClass = fighter | wizard;
ShowBits((byte)multiClass);
// bits in 4:
// 10100000
```

Therefore, we can use the statement multiClass = fighter | wizard; to merge both values
into the enum. Hidden on the inside of the multiclass value is a 01010000 from using 0001 | 0100
to combine the bits. This might seem strange, since the result is 5, and there is no numeric value in the
CharacterClasses enum assigned 5. However, that's assuming we're using the enums as numbers,
not bits, or in this case, we're using them as flags. We'll read more into what this means in the following
section.

8.9.5 Bitwise And &

To find out which bits are in use, we use the bitwise operator and, &. Therefore, to see if the bits match
up, we can use the & operator to compare two sets of bits.

```
   1248
   1001 =  9
   1010 =  5
&  _____
   1000 =  1
```

This shows the value for each bit, then using the & operator we can see how the bits are modified in the
result of the operation. With an enum we get the following result.

```
CharacterClasses fighter = CharacterClasses.Fighter;
ShowBits((byte)fighter);
// bits in 1:
// 10000000

CharacterClasses wizard = CharacterClasses.Wizard;
ShowBits((byte)wizard);
// bits in 4:
// 00100000

CharacterClasses fighterAndWizard = fighter & wizard;
ShowBits((byte)fighterAndWizard);
// bits in 0:
// 00000000
```

The above notation returns a 1 only when bits in both values match 1. To use this to check what classes our character is, we can use the following fragment:

```
CharacterClasses multiClass = fighter | wizard;
ShowBits((byte)multiClass);
// bits in 5:
// 10100000

byte andFighter = (byte)(multiClass & CharacterClasses.Fighter);
ShowBits(andFighter);
// bits in 1:
// 10000000

byte andWizard = (byte)(multiClass & CharacterClasses.Wizard);
ShowBits(andWizard);
// bits in 4:
// 00100000
```

The multiclass has a 1 in the first and third place of the byte. Using & CharacterClasses.Fighter we can see if multiClass has a value in the first place. The same works for checking if multiClass has a value in the third place.

```
byte andArcher = (byte)(multiClass & CharacterClasses.Archer);
ShowBits(andArcher);
// bits in 0:
// 00000000
```

The check of multiClass is an Archer that we check with & CharacterClasses.Archer and we see that there are no bits that match.

8.9.6 Bitwise Exclusive Or ^ (xor)

We can also see which bits are mismatching.

```
   1248
   1001 =   9
   1010 =   5
^
  ─────────
   0011 =  12
```

The ^ operator in the following fragment shows us where two sets of bits misaligned. The 0s are ignored, but if there are 1s, then we take action. In this case, we get the first and second bits mismatching. The following bits are the same, so they are left at 0.

```
// ^ "Xor" also known as caret
uint a = 5;    // 1 + 0 + 4 = 5
uint b = 6;    // 0 + 2 + 4 = 6
uint c = a ^ b; // 1 + 2 + 0 = 3
Debug.Log(c);
// 3
```

To go back to the enum we were just using, we have a multiclass fighter and wizard, but how do we take the fighter out from the enum? This is what the xor operator is for. MultiClass is a combination of the bits from the fighter and the bits from the wizard. The fighter was 10000000 and the wizard was 00100000, so multiClass is 10100000. To remove the wizard, we want to end up with 10000000 again.

```
/* using | we add in a wizard to the fighter
 * to take the wizard flag back out use ^
 */
CharacterClasses wizard = CharacterClasses.Wizard;
CharacterClasses fighter = CharacterClasses.Fighter;
CharacterClasses multiClass = wizard | fighter;
ShowBits((byte)multiClass);
// bits in 5:
// 10100000

CharacterClasses result = multiClass ^ CharacterClasses.Fighter;
ShowBits((byte)result);
// bits in 4:
// 00100000
```

Using the ^ on multiClass, we get remove the 10000000 from 10100000 and the result is 00100000.

To add bits we use the or operator |, to check for bits we use the and operator &, and to remove bits we use the exclusive or operator ^. In the above case, we'll be looking at the multiClass and we get fighter sent to the Console. This works with any number of classes.

```
multiClass = CharacterClasses.Fighter | CharacterClasses.Thief | CharacterClasses.Wizard;
ShowBits((byte)multiClass);
// bits in 7:
// 11100000
```

The | operator can compound as many values as there are bits to work with. In the above code, the multiClass is now a fighter, a wizard, and thief. To check which of these classes multiClass is, we use the same statement as we did earlier. To check if multiClass contains the bits required to be a thief, we use the same statement:

```
bool isThief = (multiClass & CharacterClasses.Thief) == CharacterClasses.Thief;
Debug.Log("multiClass is Thief:" + isThief);
// multiClass is Thief:True
```

Therefore, isThief in this case is true. However, now we're starting to repeat ourselves, and as any programmer should do, we should make our lives easier by writing a function to do all this stuff for us. So where do we start? Logically, we'll want to begin with the same processes. We started with adding bits to a value, so we should begin there.

8.9.7 Setting Bitwise Flags

After assigning a characterClass, it's time to add one. The enum isn't something we can extend, so we'll want to use something like addClass(my current class, class im adding) that would look like the following:

```
CharacterClasses addClass(CharacterClasses a, CharacterClasses b)
{
    return a | b;
}
CharacterClasses newbie = CharacterClasses.Farmer;
newbie = addClass(newbie, CharacterClasses.Wizard);
```

Now newbie is a wizard. To continue, we can use the following.

```
newbie = addClass(newbie, CharacterClasses.Archer);
```

By using newbie in the addClass() function, we're adding a second value to the newbie enum. To remove a class, we'll want to do something similar.

```
CharacterClasses removeClass(CharacterClasses a, CharacterClasses b)
{
    return a ^ b;
}
newbie = removeClass(newbie, CharacterClasses.Wizard);
```

This means that if we use removeClass(newbie, characterClass.archer);, we'll take the archer flags back out.

Of course, we could use a bool to check if a class contains a value with the following function:

```
bool hasClass(CharacterClasses a, CharacterClasses b)
{
    return (a & b) == b;
}
bool isFarmer = hasClass(newbie, CharacterClasses.Farmer);
Debug.Log("newbie is a farmer:" + isFarmer);
// newbie is a farmer:True
```

This simply checks if the flag is present, and if it is then our return is true; otherwise it's false. This can be used to check if a character, given its characterClass, can be allowed to fire a bow or pick a lock. This changes the nature of the enum that is usually intended to be fixed at a single value. Of course, it would be easy to store these as boolean values, but where's the fun in that?

8.9.8 Bitwise Shortcuts | = and ^ =

When assigning these enums, we can shorten some of the assignments by using the same operators. If we want to assign a = a | b;, we can use a |= b;. Similar looking syntax appears when adding a value to a where a = a + b; and a += b; from Section 5.6. The same goes for a = a ^ b;, which can be replaced with a ^= b;.

```
CharacterClasses character = CharacterClasses.Farmer;
character |= CharacterClasses.Fighter;
character |= CharacterClasses.Wizard;
character |= CharacterClasses.Archer;
character |= CharacterClasses.Thief;
ShowBits((byte)character);
// bits in 15:
// 11110000

character ^= CharacterClasses.Fighter;
ShowBits((byte)character);
// bits in 14:
// 01110000
```

8.9.9 Bits in Numbers

Remember that we're still dealing with numbers, not just bits. Being numbers, we can use this to check for odd or even numbers with a simple & operator. Odd numbers always have a 1 in them, but even numbers do not. What does that mean? We can use bool even = (number & 1) == 0; to check if a value is odd or even.

This system has the same result as checking number % 2 == 0.

```
int number = 758;
bool even = (number & 1) == 0;
Debug.Log("number:" + number + " is even:" + even);

bool evenMod = number % 2 == 0;
Debug.Log("number:" + number + " is even:" + evenMod);
```

This returns true, quick and easy. In addition, performing checks like this happens very quickly on most CPUs. We'll want to keep this in mind for some later math tricks in C#.

8.9.10 Bit Shifting >> and <<

Our enum was written in the form farmer = 0x00, fighter = 0x01, through archer = 0x08, and so on. However, if you had many different classes, we might easily miscalculate one of the numbers. It's not too easy to remember what 37^2 is; your higher numbers turn into—rather difficult to remember— power of two values. Therefore, again bitwise operators can help here as well. We can add the >> and the << between numbers to indicate a movement of bits.

```
enum Alignments
{
    Neutral         = 0,
    CrazyNeutral    = 1 << 0,
    NormalNeutral   = 1 << 1,
    CrazyGood       = 1 << 2,
    NormalGood      = 1 << 3,
    ReallyGood      = 1 << 4,
    CrazyEvil       = 1 << 5,
    NormalEvil      = 1 << 6,
    ReallyEvil      = 1 << 7,
    Unknown         = 1 << 8 //is this valid?
}
```

The above code is simply numbered 0–8, and if we need a ninth class, we simply add monk = 1<<9 at the end. What does the << do? It's taking the value of 1 and moving it over to the right the number of digits indicated by the number following the operator. Therefore, in the bits we start off as 1000, which is 1. Then if we look at fighter, we shift the bits 0 places, and we still get 1.

The opposite works in a similar way: 0011 or 3 turns into something else altogether when shifted one space. Looking at 3 or 0011 << 1 = 0110, which is 6. Then, 6 << 1 = 12 or 1100, so there is a pattern! This is the same as multiplying by 2—altogether another useful math operation that can be done by shifting bits!

Of course, we're just looking at the little end of the value range of a 32-bit int; it's just as simple as writing out 0011 0000 0000 0000 0000 0000 0000 0000 to show 12. Shifting the values << can happen many times before we run out of digits.

```
Alignments neutral = Alignments.Neutral;
ShowBits((byte)neutral);
// bits in 0:
// 00000000

/* 1 << 0
 * remember, 0 is the first index! or zeroth index
 */
Alignments crazyNeutral = Alignments.CrazyNeutral;
ShowBits((byte)crazyNeutral);
// bits in 1:
// 10000000

/* 1 << 1
 * shifted skipping the 0th index into the first
 * index, which is the second from the zeroth
 * position.
 */
Alignments normalNeutral = Alignments.NormalNeutral;
ShowBits((byte)normalNeutral);
// bits in 2:
// 01000000
```

When using the bit shifted enum we can see how the bits are shifting around in the bits themselves. Things are easy to understand, though conceptually the direction of the << and >> might seem a bit off. It's important that << is pushing into higher values and ignores the little or big endian direction. The bit we're pushing seems to be traveling to the right even though the arrows << point to the left to shift the bits. The enum for Alignments has not been set to a specific type. It's an enum. What happens when we push the bit past the range of a byte?

```
/* 1 << 7
 * in a byte there are only 0 to 7 positions
 * the last position for a 8 bit byte.
 */
Alignments reallyEvil = Alignments.ReallyEvil;
ShowBits((byte)reallyEvil);
// bits in 128:
// 00000001

/* 1 << 8
 * in a byte there are only 0 to 7 positions
 * past the last bit, we've rolled a byte!
 */
Alignments unknown = Alignments.Unknown;
ShowBits((byte)unknown);
// bits in 0:
// 00000000
```

The last unknown value in the enum has rolled the byte over and shows a 0 when printing out the bits as a byte. The same enum for alignments given to ShowBits produces an int with a value of 256, with one bit beyond the byte range.

```
/* 1 << 8
 * in a byte there are only 0 to 7 positions
 * past the last bit, we've rolled a byte!
 */
Alignments unknown = Alignments.Unknown;
ShowBits((byte)unknown);
// bits in 0:
// 00000000

Debug.Log("use an int?");
ShowBitInt((int)unknown);
// bits in int:256
// 00000000100000000000000000000000

void ShowBitInt(int number)
{
    int bitLen = 32;
    string log = "bits in int:" + number + "\n";
    for (int i = 0; i < bitLen; i++)
    {
        int mask = 1 << i;
        if ((number & mask) == mask)
        {
            log += "1";
        }
        else
        {
            log += "0";
        }
    }
    Debug.Log(log);
}
```

An int is 32 bits long and we can still count the values in each position by using a bit mask. Shifting over each value to check what bit is turned on in the number.

8.9.11 What We've Learned

Computers do math in a unique way, different from what we are accustomed to. Thinking in 1s and 0s requires a fundamental restart in learning how to do math. Multiplication, addition, subtraction, and even counting require a whole unique system.

Some of these systems have effects outside of math. Using the binary system as a collection of flags or using them as enums allows for a greater ability to control a breadth of information in a single value. A 64-bit integer allows for 64 unique boolean values to be stored.

So why study how bits work? In classic video games top scores are usually stored as some number form where 65,575 was the maximal limit. Score one more point and the score was reset to 0 or "The score was rolled." Knowing the limitations of numbers will help avoid bugs or, at the very least, you'll know what to expect when using some number types.

Even today many pieces of hardware that communicate over Bluetooth use number types with very limited ranges. Game controllers can often send analog joystick values using a single int with bits masked for each axis.

A wireless controller may send a single 16-bit value as an orientation. The first 5 bits are used as pitch, the following 6 as yaw, then the last 5 as roll. Color can also be compressed into a single 16-bit number using similar encoding for red blue and green.

Knowing how to mask values, shift bits, and decode a usable number can greatly extend your game development beyond the built-in controllers and types in Unity. Devices like Arduinos can send custom inputs to your game if you know what the bits are doing.

8.10 Attributes

When working with the editor, we can add new menu items, windows, and other useful tools for helping with the level design. Many of the new menu items are done through Unity 3D-specific attributes. Attributes is another layer added to the C# language that augment how the code is read by the computer.

Attributes in some ways look out of place; like preprocessor directives, they have their own set of rules and uses. They use the square brackets [] to indicate their use and function. Attributes allow your code to read additional information about your code. Reflection occurs when your code can look up additional information on a function or type. This includes any field in a class as well as any function or the class itself.

Often in Unity 3D we use [Serializable] to indicate a field or value which you want to have saved by the game. For instance, you've created custom data structures and other public settings that show up in the editor; normally any form of plain old data (POD) will be automatically serialized. However, in times where you've written your own data, you need to tell Unity 3D that your new data types must also be serialized to be saved.

In many cases, you might be getting used to using a struct or class to store a complex assortment of different types of data. This is fine; however, it's better to consider using a class to hold data rather than a struct.

This serves two purposes: first, you're better able to handle data coming in and going out of each variable, and second, you're able to use the class in Unity 3D as a clever container for your variables which you can edit in the Inspector panel.

8.10.1 A Basic Example

We'll need to add the using System; directive to start. This will give us the [Serializable] attribute for use in the editor. Our code will start off like the following:

```
[Serializable]
public class DataParameters
{
    public int Players;
    public int MinRange, MaxRange;
}


public DataParameters ParameterData;
```

This gives us a simple public class DataParameters to which we'll add a some data fields. The public int Players will serve as our basic example of serialization. After this is public DataParameters ParameterData; where we can hold data we just set up in DataParameters class. Without the [Serializable] attribute, the editor's Inspector panel doesn't show any new information.

To get the `ParameterData` to show up, we simply add a single attribute to the class, not the variable.

After the Serializable attribute was added to the `DataParameters` class, the public members of the class become visible under the `ParameterData` object in the Unity 3D Inspector panel. The result in the editor is our DataParameter information in the editor.

Adding the Serializable attribute makes the data stored inside of the class savable. Once we make changes to the values in the serialized class, the editor can save them with the scene. The attribute tells Unity 3D to look at the class as a chunk of information which it needs to both expose to the Inspector panel and save with the scene.

The other attributes that System gives us are also useful for different reasons.

Should we add an int to the class outside of the nested class, we'd get what you'd normally expect to see in the Inspector panel.

```
public int PlainOldInt;
```

This shows up as an int value in the editor as we have seen earlier.

However, we can add an attribute to keep this out of the editor, but also maintain the variable's public accessor selling.

```
[NonSerialized]
public int PlainOldInt;
```

Adding the attribute magically hides the value from the Inspector panel. This has two effects: first, any values assigned to the PlainOldInt variable will not be saved with the scene, and second, the value cannot be set from the editor. The variable still acts as any normal public int, only that we're not able to manipulate it from within the editor.

Adding serialized attributes for the Inspector is handy, however for a game to have some additional features it's useful to enable the serialization of that data for saving to file.

```
[Serializable]
class CharacterData
{
    public string Name;
    public int HitPoints;
    public int Defense;
    public int Offsense;
}

class GameData
{
    public CharacterData[] Characters;
    public string Town;
    public int players;
    private int GameID;
}
```

By adding the [Serializable] attribute to the CharacterData class you allow GameData to save the Characters array. Let's see how this works.

```
// make some data
GameData data = new GameData();
data.players = ParameterData.Players;
data.Characters = new CharacterData[data.players];
data.Town = "Someville";
for (int i = 0; i < data.players; i++)
{
    data.Characters[i] = new CharacterData();
    // give the character some random name.
    string[] nameParts = { "La", "Da", "Fa", "Ma" };
    for (int j = 0; j < 2; j++)
    {
        data.Characters[i].Name += nameParts[UnityEngine.Random.Range(0, 4)];
    }
    // populate the rest of the player's data with random values
    int min = ParameterData.MinRange;
    int max = ParameterData.MaxRange;
    data.Characters[i].HitPoints = UnityEngine.Random.Range(min, max);
    data.Characters[i].Defense   = UnityEngine.Random.Range(min, max);
    data.Characters[i].Offsense  = UnityEngine.Random.Range(min, max);
}

// store the data to file!
string path = Directory.GetCurrentDirectory() + "/Data.json";
string text = JsonUtility.ToJson(data);
Debug.Log(text);
File.WriteAllText(path, text);
```

In the fragment we create a new set of data to save. In here we create a number of characters. The `ParameterData` settings in the Inspector panel in the editor will make modifications to the data being saved.

▼ Parameter Data	
Players	5
Min Range	3
Max Range	10

The data here turns into settings to be saved in the data.

```
{
    "Characters": [
        {
            "Name": "FaFa",
            "HitPoints": 9,
            "Defense": 5,
            "Offsense": 9
        },
        {
            "Name": "MaFa",
            "HitPoints": 8,
            "Defense": 9,
            "Offsense": 8
        },
        {
            "Name": "LaLa",
            "HitPoints": 4,
            "Defense": 8,
            "Offsense": 3
        },
        {
            "Name": "MaMa",
            "HitPoints": 8,
            "Defense": 3,
            "Offsense": 3
        },
        {
            "Name": "LaDa",
            "HitPoints": 7,
            "Defense": 9,
            "Offsense": 7
        }
    ],
    "Town": "Someville",
    "players": 5
}
```

Characters are saved and written to a Data.json file in the Chapter 8 Unity Project directory. When the file is first opened it'll be a long unbroken stream of text. In Visual Studio you can reformat the Json file into what is seen above. If the [Serializable] tag is left out, then the array of characters gets omitted from being written to the data file being saved.

```
// to read the file back again
GameData ReadData(string dataPath)
{
    string dataText = File.ReadAllText(path);
    return JsonUtility.FromJson<GameData>(dataText);
}

data = ReadData(path);
```

To read the data that was written to the Data.json file we simply use the JsonUtility.FromJson() once the text from the data is read back. The combination of [Serializable] and writing data to Json is a useful combination. With this it's possible to save game data between sessions.

8.10.2 Custom Attributes

A custom attribute allows us to prepare information we'd like to apply to an object. The setup appears quite simple, but allows us to create a tag of our own creation.

```
[AttributeUsage(AttributeTargets.All)]
class CustomAttribute : Attribute
{
    public string customString = "A Custom Attribute";
}

[CustomAttribute]
class Something
{
}
```

Once created and assigned over an object we can look for the specific attribute with Reflection.

```
// using Reflection, get the custom attributes of the
// Something class.
var memberInfos = typeof(Something).GetCustomAttributes(true);
foreach (var i in memberInfos)
{
    CustomAttribute custom = i  as CustomAttribute;
    Debug.Log(custom.customString);
}
// A Custom Attribute
```

The GetCustomAttributes() function returns any tag given to the class type. We can create categories of objects we'd like to process for any number of classes. This gives us a system to highlight some objects as special. What makes the attribute usable on the class or any other specific type is that the attribute tag is applied to the custom attribute. In this case, the AttributeTargets.All is provided.

8.10.3 Custom Attributes for Default Values

Setting default values for fields in Unity is usually something set up in a Prefab or setting values in the Inspector. The values become difficult to retrieve in runtime.

```
[AttributeUsage(AttributeTargets.Field)]
class DefaultValue : Attribute
{
    public object Value;
    public string Name;
    public DefaultValue(string name, object value)
    {
        Name = name;
        Value = value;
    }
}
```

Another example for Attributes is to hold a value for a class value. Attributes can only hold onto values that inherit directly from object. This means that most of Unity's specific data types like Vector3 and GameObject cannot be stored in an attribute. Attribute constructors are limited to storing simple type literals or POD types.

```
class Character
{
    [DefaultValue("Health", 10)]
    public int HP;
    [DefaultValue("Magic", 10)]
    public int MP;
    // excluded from default settings
    public int XP;
    public float Time;

}
```

The field tagged by the attribute shows the constructor creating the attribute. The syntax reveals the values the attribute will store when it's created.

```
Character character = new Character();

var fields = typeof(Character).GetFields();
foreach (var f in fields)
{
    DefaultValue d = f.GetCustomAttribute(typeof(DefaultValue)) as DefaultValue;
    if (d != null)
    {
        f.SetValue(character, d.Value);
    }
}
Debug.Log("character.HP " + character.HP);
// character.HP 10
Debug.Log("character.MP " + character.MP);
// character.MP 10
Debug.Log("character.XP " + character.XP);
// character.XP 0
Debug.Log("character.Time " + character.Time);
// character.Time 0
```

The `GetFields()` function is provided by `System.Reflection`. The character type reveals a list of the available fields in the class. A simple search through each field allows us to check and set values if the tag exists.

As a human reading a function like `int AddInts(int a, int b);`, you're able to understand that it's a function with two arguments and an `int` return type. Reflection gives us the ability to read the function's arguments, return type, and its name. However, this might not be enough information to work with.

Reflection allows your code to make decisions based on attributes assigned to struct or class members. Once your code can read these attributes, you're able to apply logic and make decisions on which function to use. If we were able to assign additional information to a function or field, we would be able to better scheme up new ways to make our code smarter.

Attributes need to be prepared before they are used. A custom attribute is a class that inherits from the System.Attributes class. The class itself is also labeled as a special class that is used to define custom attributes.

8.10.4 Multiple Attributes

Each custom attribute should be specific. The special instructions or hint which you mark a field or function with should be for a specific use. If you need to add multiple attributes to a class member, then you can stack them.

[AttributeUsage(AttributeTargets. All, AllowMultiple = true, Inherited = true)]

The addition of `AllowMultiple = true` tells the attribute that you can stack different attributes over a class member. In addition, we can add the `Inherited = true` option to this attribute as well. This code tells anything inspecting this attribute that any child class inheriting the member will also have the accompanying attribute.

```
[AttributeUsage(AttributeTargets.All, AllowMultiple = true, Inherited = true)]
class SpecialAttribute : Attribute
{
}
[AttributeUsage(AttributeTargets.All, AllowMultiple = true, Inherited = false)]
class SuperficialAttribute : Attribute
{
}


[Special, Superficial]
class BaseThing
{                    ⊗ SuperficialAttribute.SuperficialAttribute()
}


class SuperThing : BaseThing
{
}
```

In use, the above `BaseThing` class has both Special and SuperficialAttributes tagged. The superficial attribute has Inherited = false. This means that `SuperThing`, which inherits from `BaseThing`, will not have the superficial attribute.

```
Debug.Log("BaseThing's Attributes:");
var attribs = typeof(BaseThing).GetCustomAttributes(true);
foreach (var attrib in attribs)
{
    Debug.Log(attrib);
}
// BaseThing's Attributes:
// Attributes+SpecialAttribute
// Attributes+SuperficialAttribute
```

Logging the custom attributes on the BaseThing reveals both the Special and SuperficialAttributes. The SuperThing only has the special attribute.

```
Debug.Log("SuperThing's Attributes:");
var attribs = typeof(SuperThing).GetCustomAttributes(true);
foreach (var attrib in attribs)
{
    Debug.Log(attrib);
}
// SuperThing's Attributes:
// Attributes+SpecialAttribute
```

The attributes are also applied to the BaseThing as [Special, Superficial] where the Attribute part of the name has been omitted. A simple feature of the Attribute class has allowed trimming the end of the name of the attribute. You're still allowed to use SpecialAttribute, but C# has allowed the obvious part of the name to be used alone.

To make things simple, we can check the types of attributes and cast them as they are found. Once they have been cast, we can extract the expected information and make use of it. In this example, we're just looking at simple casts to find the attributes. Once the attribute is found, we have both the information from the attribute and the member of the class the attribute is associated with.

8.10.5 Putting Attributes to Work

To make an attribute useful, we can make special classes that don't rely on an active Update() function. The MonoBehavior base class makes them considerably more controllable. To make these classes controllable we use a MonoBehaviour class to inspect and start co-routines for more simple classes.

```
[AttributeUsage(AttributeTargets.Method |
                AttributeTargets.Event |
                AttributeTargets.Delegate,
                AllowMultiple = true,
                Inherited = true)]
class UpdateAttribute : Attribute
{
    public float Delay;
    public UpdateAttribute(float delay)
    {
        Delay = delay;
    }
}
```

This attribute is named `UpdateAttribute` and it's got a `Delay` `float` value. In a simple class we can use this to tag functions for updating with a frequency.

```
class HasUpdates
{
    // updates every half a second
    [Update(0.5f)]
    public void RequiresUpdateOften()
    {
        Debug.Log("Got Updated");
    }
    // updates every three seconds
    [Update(3f)]
    public void AlsoRequiresUpdateSlowly()
    {
        Debug.Log("Also Got Updated");
    }

    // doesn't get updated.
    public void DontUpdate()
    {
        Debug.Log("Exclude me.");
    }
}
```

A simple class named `HasUpdates` contains two tagged functions and one that's not tagged. The first has a frequency of `0.5f` or an update every half a second. The second function has `Update(3f)`, which means to update every three seconds. To serve as a starting point we simply print out either `Got Updated` or `Also Got Updated` when the functions are actually called.

```
// this class has methods
// that need updating.
HasUpdates needsUpdates = new HasUpdates();

// now we know what method has the attribute
// in the class type
var updateMethods = from m in needsUpdates.GetType().GetMethods()
                where m.GetCustomAttribute<UpdateAttribute>() is UpdateAttribute
                select m;
```

To start we'll make an instance of the class. The instance could occur anywhere as long as we can find the variable referencing the object. After that, we need a list of methods based on the object type. This contains the method names and if the method has the `UpdateAttribute` then we'll add it to the updateMethods from the Linq statement.

```
/* hold onto the coroutines incase
 * we want to kill them later.
 */
List<IEnumerator> routineList = new List<IEnumerator>();

// has methods with update attribute
foreach (var method in updateMethods)
{
    /* inner function for each
     * method with custom attribute
     * inner function can pretty much
     * appear anywhere.
     */
    IEnumerator updater()
    {
        while (true)
        {
            UpdateAttribute upa = method.GetCustomAttribute<UpdateAttribute>() as UpdateAttribute;
            method.Invoke(needsUpdates, new object[] { });
            yield return new WaitForSeconds(upa.Delay);
        }
    }
    routineList.Add(updater());
}
```

Once the LINQ statement has filtered out and selected the tagged methods, a new co-routine is made for each one. The `updater()` inner function appears inside of the foreach loop. This means that for each instance of an `updateMethod` in the class we create a new `IEnumerator` function. A `List<IEnumerator>` stores each function after it's been populated with the method info data.

To find the `Delay` value we use the `method.GetCustomAttribute()` function to get to the `Delay` value in the attribute the function was tagged with. Then we add that value to the `yield return WaitForSeconds` function in the while loop in the `updater()` function. Once that's setup, the `Updater()` is added to `routineList`.

```
foreach (IEnumerator e in routineList)
{
    StartCoroutine(e);
}
```

Once we finish the `updateMethods` foreach loop we iterate through any items that were added to the `routineList` and start the co-routine. The result makes Got Updated and Also Got Updated appear in the Unity console window. Twice a second we get "Got Updated" and every three seconds we get "Also Got Update" as expected.

By storing the `routineList` we can also go through the list and stop the co-routines. This makes the system a bit more robust. By keeping the co-routine around we can start them up again if they're needed. This could be handy when switching scenes or pausing the game, etc.

8.10.6 Attribute Flags

Attributes can be applied to classes, functions, and variables. We should also consider keeping track of what an attribute should be applied to, limiting where an attribute can be used to prevent an attribute being applied to an object for which you don't want to have a specific attribute assigned.

When declaring the new attribute class, we've got several options we can apply.

```
[AttributeUsage(AttributeTargets.Method |
                AttributeTargets.Event   |
                AttributeTargets.Delegate,
                AllowMultiple = true,
                Inherited = true)]
```

Additional `AttributeTargets` can be added using the bitwise operator | to add multiple flags. Such flags were covered in Section 8.9.

```
[Flags]
public enum AttributeTargets
{
    Assembly = 1,
    Module = 2,
    Class = 4,
    Struct = 8,
    Enum = 16,
    Constructor = 32,
    Method = 64,
    Property = 128,
    Field = 256,
    Event = 512,
    Interface = 1024,
    Parameter = 2048,
    Delegate = 4096,
    ReturnValue = 8192,
    GenericParameter = 16384,
    All = 32767
}
```

This changes the option to include both functions and variables. As we've just seen the bitwise operator | in Section 8.9.3, we know that the `AttributeTargets` enum is set up for bitwise checks.

8.10.7 What We've Learned

With a custom attribute, we can simplify with many tasks. An Update attribute with a time delay `[UpdateAttribute (3.0f)]` helps functions update at their own pace. Not all functions need to be updated at the beginning of each frame.

Each monster could have a different parts of their behavior update at different time values. Smarter, faster monsters can update more often than slower, dumber monsters that have long delays between updates.

If you revive a character, various stats may need to be reset to their default values. If each different character had a different set of stats, the bookkeeping might get more difficult. A `[DefaultAttribute(int restoredAmount)]` attribute would make the bookkeeping automatic. Just get all the fields that need to be restored and restore them to the indicated restored amount.

Custom attributes provides an easy readable system to attach important information to a function or variable.

8.11 Bitwise Math

The strange thing about bits is that they are numbers that operate with a system different from what we've been taught in your usual math class. If you wanted to make 10 into -10, you might normally think to simply multiply 10 by -1. However, the usual tricks don't work in the context of the computer's binary world.

Remember what happens when we add 1 to a number at the limit of the binary range. For a nibble of a 4-bit number, that would be 1111 or 15. However, the nibble we're looking at is unsigned, or rather the four digits are all used for counting. If we use a signed nibble, or perhaps a snibble, our limit would be either -8 or 7, which is either 1000 or 0111. Maybe we're talking about a unibble, or unsigned nibble that can count to 15. In any case nibbles, snibbles, and unibbles don't exist in C# so let's move on.

The interesting fact going on binary numbers is that it's a range from 0 to a limit. Often we observe the values as hexadecimal. You come across this term often when making colors for a web page.

When we're in base 10, we start at 0 up to 9. To count to 10, we add another digit to fill in the 10s' place. When we count past 99, we add another digit for hundreds, and so on. When computers count, they use 16, or a nibble; we've come back to that again. To represent each hexadecimal, we use a few letters to fill in the extra digits.

To count like a computer, we use the sequence 0, 1, 2, 3, 4, 5, 6, 7, 8, 9, a, b, c, d, e, f, before getting to another digit. For the computer to count from 0 to 255, it uses eight binary digits, but if we use two nibbles we can represent that with two digits. This is two nibbles, not one nibble, or a byte. A byte is a specific number of bits in a computer's memory. This can tell the computer to store a 1 in decimal it actually thinks "0x01" in hexadecimal. Where the computer uses ff in hex we see 255 in decimal.

```
byte ff = 0xff;
Debug.Log("ff: " + ff);
// ff: 255
```

The above code prints "ff: 255" to the Console panel in Unity. Here the prefix 0x informs C# that we are representing a byte followed by two digits in hexadecimal. The syntax is used to avoid something like "byte b = 11111111;". If we want to use a signed byte or an sbyte, we can represent negative numbers with the following:

```
sbyte sff = -0x80;
Debug.Log("sff: " + sff);
// sff: -128
```

This shows us -0x80 in hex is -128 in decimal. If we try to assign a value outside of the range of the sbyte, we get an error reminding us that we can't assign 255 to an sbyte. However, after a valid assignment, anything can happen.

```
sff--;
Debug.Log("sff--: " + sff);
// sff--: 127
```

If we decrement sff by 1 from -0x80, we get 127 printed to the Unity's Console panel, not -129. Again, we roll numbers even though we're using a different notation. The difference in notation hasn't changed the nature of how the data is stored or calculated. Not surprisingly, the int type has a larger range.

```
int hexMax = 0x7fffffff;
Debug.Log("max in hex:" + hexMax);
// max in hex:2147483647
```

```
int intMax = int.MaxValue;
Debug.Log("max from int:" + intMax);
// max from int:2147483647
```

The int is 8 nibbles long. Or rather 8 hexadecimal digits long. The max value of which is 0x7fffffff. The max value is also stored in the int.MaxValue accessor. Smaller values, like 0xff will fit into an int, so assignments using fewer hex digits are perfectly valid.

8.11.1 Two's Complement Unary Operator ~

The unary operator ~ referred to as a tilde works on int values, and if you use byte b = 0 x 01;, then ~b; C# will automatically up-cast the byte to an int before performing the operation. In general, the int type is the more universal of the different integer numbers used in C#. It's just 8 nibbles long, or 4 bytes.

Aside from the casting implications of using the ~ operator, this operator does an interesting trick. If we have 0001, the ~ operator applied to this nibble gives us 1110. This two's complement is used for many different things, including addition.

To change an int from 10 to -10 using binary operations, we use a method known as two's complement. If we wanted to use multiplication, we could go that route; however, by using a bitwise operation, we can speed up the process. Starting with a value, say an int -1 that would look like binary 32 1s.

```
int negOne = -1;
ShowBits(negOne);
// bits in int:-1
// 11111111111111111111111111111111
```

With a slightly more interesting number like 10 which in hex is 0x0a have 0101 followed by a bunch of 0s.

```
int ten = 0x0a;
ShowBits(ten);
// bits in int:10
// 01010000000000000000000000000000
```

We can use the complement bitwise operator ~ to flip the bits. Therefore, if we look at the important value after ~ we see the following:

```
int nTen = ~ten;
ShowBits(nTen);
// bits in int:-11
// 10101111111111111111111111111111
```

Therefore, to get the correct value, add 1 to ~n and assign that to p.

```
int nTenOne = ~ten+1;
ShowBits(nTenOne);
// bits in int:-10
// 01101111111111111111111111111111
```

In a very simple form rather than `int a = 100; a = a*-1;` we can instead use the following:

```
int complement = 100;
complement = ~complement + 1;
ShowBits(complement);
// bits in int:-100
// 00111001111111111111111111111111
```

And we get the same as if we had used `int p = -n;` on the value. So why do things this way? In short, bitwise operations are fast. Because bitwise operations are fast, we often see them in optimized code seen in some C++ projects. The syntax looks unusual, and it is. By seeing this here, you'll have a better chance of reading code written by programmers in other fields.

8.11.2 Bitwise Addition and Subtraction

The computer's CPU has no + and – circuits built into it. It's a collection of these bitwise operators. Because of this reason, it's an interesting exercise to understand what is actually going on when you do something simple like $7 + 3$.

Looking at the nibble again, we have the decimal 7 represented as 1110 and 3 being 1100; adding these together makes the bits look like 1010 or 10. There isn't a direct process by which 0111 and 0011 can be added together in one operation. To add we need to move bits from one number into the other.

```
int a = 7;
int b = 3;
int c = a & b;
int r = a ^ b;
while (c != 0)
{
    int s = c << 1;
    c = r & s;
    r = r ^ s;
}
Debug.Log(r);
```

Where `while (c != 0)`, we are done taking all of the bits from the carry c and adding them to the result r. A breakdown of the code, one line at a time, shows what's happening to the bits and their decimal values. There are only three significant lines we need to observe. The first line `int s = c << 1;` is temporary storage for clarity.

The loop begins by finding all the digits that match. This loop will tell us which digits need to be carried over. The carried-over digits are the ones where 1s appear in both numbers. So, `a & b` shows us where 1s appear in both numbers, and we get `0111 & 0011 = 0011`. After this we need to find where the digits are mismatched with `0111 ^ 0011 = 0100`.

```
int c = a & b;
//a  1110 0000
//b &1100 0000
// =1100 0000

int r = a ^ b;
//a  1110 0000
//b ^1100 0000
// =0010 0000
```

In the first line where we begin adding the numbers, we start with a shifted digit.

```
int s = c << 1;
//[ s = 0110 0000 << 1]
```

We move the digits over by one space and find the next digit to carry over.

```
c = r & s;
//[ r    0010 0000        ]
//[ s & 0110 0000         ]
//[ c = 0010 0000         ]
```

After shifting the digit and finding the one that needs to be carried over, we need to reassign r to the next digit to carry.

```
r = r ^ s;
//[ r    0010 0000        ]
//[ s ^ 0110 0000         ]
//[ r = 0100 0000         ]
```

We've reduced the number of carry digits by 1. However, we still have one digit to merge in, so we go back to the beginning of the loop.

```
int s = c << 1;
[ s = 0001 0000 << 1] → actual direction
```

We have a digit carried over from the previous loop that needs to be merged back into the result. But we need to check whether there are any digits overlapping to check if we need to do the loop again.

```
c = r & s;
[ r    0100 0000        ]
[ s & 0001 0000         ]
[ c = 0000 0000         ](c == 0)
```

Here we see that 0010 & 1000 has no overlapping digits. Therefore, we can merge to our final result.

```
r = r ^ s;
[ r    0100 0000        ]
[ s ^ 0001 0000         ]
[ r = 0101 0000         ](final result)
```

Now our result is a correct merging of 0100 and 0001, which is 0101 or decimal 10. Inside the computer's CPU, there is a section of circuits called an adder that does the same thing. When you have a computer running several billion operations per second, this operation happens incredibly fast. However, if you need to do this operation a hundred million times, then you'll see a performance difference between this operation and perhaps a more complex operation.

To turn the above code into a function, we'll use the following:

```csharp
int BitwiseAdd(int a, int b)
{
    int c = a & b;
    int r = a ^ b;
    while (c != 0)
    {
        int s = c << 1; //shift digits to add
        c = r & s;      //find overlapping digits
        r = r ^ s;      //merge digits that don't overlap
    }
    return r;
}
```

Subtraction is an addition with a negative number. To get the negative number, we use the previous two's complement. So, in the case of the following

```csharp
int a = 7;
int b = 3;
int c = BitwiseSub(a, b);
```

subtraction involves flipping the b into a negative number using two's complement and then adding them together. To use this feature, we can simply reuse the BitwiseAdd() function a couple of times. The first one is basically two's complement without using a + 1 to get the negative version of b, and then we use BitwiseAdd() again to get a result.

```csharp
int BitwiseSub(int a, int b)
{
    b = BitwiseAdd(~b, 1);
    return BitwiseAdd(a, b);
}
```

8.11.3 Bitwise Multiplication

The bitshift operators can be used to multiply by 2: $4 << 1 = 8$ or $0100 << 1 = 1000$; this is rather handy when finding a specific half or double of a value. However, when multiplying, we need to do something like that of addition. We need to find out how many times we can multiply by 2, and then to an odd number we add the last number. So, in the case of $7 * 3$, we use $(7 * 2) + 7$; the code that can do this operation is shown below.

```
int BitwiseMultiplication(int a, int b)
{
    int r = 0;
    while (b != 0)
    {
        if ((b & 1) != 0)
        {
            r = BitwiseAdd(r, a);
        }
        a = a << 1;
        if (b == 0)
        {
            r = a;
            break;
        }
        b = b >> 1;
    }
    return r;
}
```

The above code shifts a `<< 1` for each multiple of 2 we find in b. Each time b is shifted `>> 1`, it's moved toward 0. When we check if b is odd using `(b & 1) != 0`, we add to int r whatever is at int a before it's shifted again. When we're done shifting and thus done multiplying by 2, our while loop exits, and we're done.

Division can be simplified to the number of times b can be subtracted from a.

```
int BitwiseDiv(int a, int b)
{
    int divideStart = a;
    int timesDivided = 1;
    while (true)
    {
        divideStart = BitwiseSub(divideStart, b);
        if (divideStart <= 0)
            break;
        timesDivided = BitwiseAdd(timesDivided, 1);
    }
    return timesDivided;
}
```

The above code is a very simple version of an integer division solution using our `BitwiseAdd()` and `BitwiseSub()` functions. Multiplication can also be a simple addition of a to a by b times. Though not as efficient as the system used in the multiplication function, the division system is a very rudimentary example of how the most basic bitwise operators can be used to do mundane math functions. The problem with an integer is that you're not allowed any fractions, so division will end up with an incorrect value unless a is evenly divided by b.

8.11.4 Bitwise Tricks

Now that we know how bits work on a more fundamental level, we can use them to our advantage to perform quick operations. Rather than checking if an int is odd or even by using `n % 2 == 0`, we can use the faster n & 1 == 1 to check for an odd number. We can tell if a number is negative using a bit; if (someNumber & (1<<31)) != 0, then we have a positive number. This checks for the last digit, which is at 1<<31 and looks to see if it's a 1 or a 0. If it's 1, then it's negative; otherwise it's positive.

Not all these tricks are necessarily faster than using more regular math functions. We can check the 1<<31 bit. But perhaps it's just easier to check if someNumber > 0 to see if it's positive or not. However, knowing how bits work is interesting.

If you need to know whether two values are both negative, both positive, or different, then you can check with the following:

```
int a = 20;
int b = 1;
bool same = ((a ^ b) > 0);
Debug.Log(same);
```

If a and b are positive, the same is true; otherwise if a and b are different signs, then the same is false. This condition works only when the bit at 1 holds a sign for positive or negative. Simple tricks like this can be used in various situations.

The following function will help with the above examples by printing out each digit.

```
string BitsToString(int number, int digits)
{
    char[] binary = new char[digits];
    int digit = digits - 1;
    int place = 0;
    while (place < digits)
    {
        int d = number & (1 << place);
        if (d != 0)
        {
            binary[digit] = '1';
        }
        else
        {
            binary[digit] = '0';
        }
        digit--;
        place++;
    }
    return new string(binary);
}
```

```
Debug.Log(BitsToString(42, 8));
// 00101010
```

The above code uses int d, which is a check for a 1 or a 0 at the place in the given number. Each iteration of the while loop increments the place and decrements which digit we're looking at. If d is 0, then we add a 0 to the char[] array; otherwise we add a 1. With the above code, we can check out the first 4 bits or all 32 bits of an int.

8.11.5 What We've Learned

These tutorials got into quite low-level concepts. Finding practical game play applications for these concepts may not be readily evident. However, the concepts do provide an important foundation for your understanding of C#.

The ability to create complex algorithms means being able to create more complex and more interesting game play scenarios. Adding in various logical parameters and making use of them in creative ways means providing more interesting puzzles.

Outside of games, many of these concepts are also useful for processing data. A modern game requires many different tasks, from collecting and analyzing data from users to sorting through databases for building leader boards.

8.12 Architectures and Organization

So far in this book we've focused on writing individual classes or inheriting one class to another. This is fine to learn the mechanics of the language, but it doesn't help toward building a larger project. Take a moment, step back, and think about how all your classes fit together to build an entire project. This takes another frame of mind altogether.

When you're building a structure for your game, it's important to keep C# files separated by task. Tasks can be added or merged as needed far easier when separated into different files. The more separation you keep, the less often files will have to be merged when working in a team of engineers.

If each class is limited in scope to just a few related tasks, you also decrease the number of places you need to look to fix bugs. This also helps when using the debugger; if the file isn't long and the scope is limited, you can find a problem and fix it in a smaller file.

When you're working by yourself, it's easy to claim ownership over your code base. You know where everything is, and you have a better idea of what it's doing. However, when it comes to working in a team, each person needs to focus on smaller, more specialized part of the code base. When you're able to focus on a specific task, you're better able to limit your scope and build a more thoughtfully crafted class.

Once each task lives in its own file, it's unlikely that too many people will have to touch the file while you're working on it. This reduces the number of merging you'll need to do when using version control systems like Git. If a single C# script file spans many different operations, then more and more people will need to make changes to the file. When you check in the file, having to merge your changes with many other changes can create problems if the merge isn't done correctly.

Approaching a project with the intent to build a complex game involves a great amount of thought; luckily, if you've written functions that have little or no side effects, then you're better able to rearrange and separate the classes and functions into different files much more easily.

The following work is seen in the GameCo directory in the Assets of the Chapter 8 unity Project.

8.12.1 Planning Structure: Namespaces and Directories

Even the smallest project can grow into a huge undertaking. There's almost no such thing as overly organized when it comes to programming. When programming is well organized, it also becomes much easier to both read and write. Your specific tasks become precise and sometimes easier.

In the root of Assets should be a directory for either your game company or the game title. This serves as a container for the most generic functions and classes for your project. We'll come back to what sort of classes should live in this namespace.

If you intend to make only one game ever, then a game-specific namespace may not be necessary, but I'm sure that you've got bigger visions than that. After a broad namespace, a slightly more specific namespace for your game should be considered. So we might be looking at `AwesomeGameCo.ZombieGame` that would contain classes that are particularly useful for a zombie game.

Directories and namespaces should match. The scripts running in the game should live in your game scripts `ZombieGame`. The `GameCo.ZombieGame` namespace should implement game behaviors. This could be further divided into `GameCo.ZombieGame.Player` or `GameCo.ZombieGame.Monster` to further isolate and encapsulate specific functions.

The purpose of a namespace and the following directory structure is to divide the different tasks in your game. A namespace for the player, the environment, effects, monsters, and weapons will ensure focus and specialization.

Tools that help debugging tasks can be fit into a GameCo.Utilities. Repeated functions and methods can be moved into lower level base class functions so implementations further up the inheritance hierarchy can implement them.

In the `ZombieGame` directory lives the `BasePlayer` for implementation in the `ZombieGame.ZombiePlayer` object. The specialization also divides how many files need to be checked into Git. By separating classes, the engineer can also find a bug and fix it in relative isolation from other bugs.

8.12.2 Divide and Conquer

The use of partial comes into play when needing to extend a specific class with different Interface classes. Consider something like a pick-up item. Various Interface classes like the `IComparer` and `IEnumerable` allow for LINQ to compare items in the scene or in the player inventory.

The using partial in a class allows you to break up a single file across multiple appropriately named files. This ensures that a bug in an Interface is contained to a specific file. Naming files also serves as a system to divide work.

You may have noticed that MonoBehaviour uses a particular spelling which isn't common in American English. If this bothers you, it can easily be fixed with a starting namespace for your own game company. Here we can create a simple renaming of MonoBehaviour to Behavior.

```
using UnityEngine;
namespace GameCo
{
    public class Behavior : MonoBehaviour
    {
    }
}
```

8.12.3 Refactoring

When you've decided that a class or type name needs to change, the work to change it has multiplied once the name has spread across many different files. Searching for every place that a specific name appears isn't always so easy.

```
namespace GameCo.ZombieGame
{
    public class Damage
    {
        public DamageInfo Info;
    }

    public class DamageInfo
    {
        public DamageTypes DamageType;
        public int DamageAmount;
    }

    public enum DamageTypes
    {
        Projectile  = 0,
        Poison      = 1,
        Fire        = 2,
        Explisove   = 4,
        Cutting     = 8,
        Dimensional = 16,
        Freezing    = 32,
        Crushing    = 64,
        Falling     = 128
    }
}
```

A Find and Replace may find something like Damage in DamageType and DamageInfo. This means inspecting each instance and deciding whether it should be changed. So long as the name only appears in a few places, this might not be too bad. If the word were more common, then you might be looking at many dozen instances that can easily lead to creating bugs.

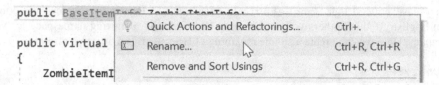

The Rename tool in Visual Studio as well as many other IDEs was created to help this process. The rename tool is aware of the name's use and where it appears. In addition, conflicts will also be pointed out as you change the name.

```
public class Damage
{
        public Damage Info;
}
```

```
public class Damage
{
        public DamageTypes DamageType;
        public int DamageAmount;
}
```

The Rename tool helps redefine identifiers throughout the project. It's important to avoid conflicting with names already in use. If the conflicts are ignored, Visual Studio will not remember how the classes were separated. The tool is also aware of namespace and will not change identifiers in another namespace that has the same identifier.

8.12.4 What We've Learned

Creating and using a structure for your game takes a lot of experience and practice. Coming to a final decision on structure before you've started writing the code for your game is unlikely. By creating namespaces and writing small classes in each one, you're also giving yourself a much easier way to reorganize the files into new namespaces and new directories.

Even after things get established, it's not so difficult to make widespread changes. One of the best ways for making these changes is by keeping categories and types clearly separated. Ensuring that the crossover between classes is limited to only specific functions is difficult, but no less important.

The less each class needs to depend on another class to operate, the less chance you have of one object causing a cascade of errors. If each function can act on its own, then you have a better chance of preventing bugs. If a class can be fragmented into many different parts, then assigning work to different team members is easier.

By splitting off functions to different people, you've also made decisions that make the design more clear. If the design is still undecided to make clear tasks for a given project, then it might be a good idea to spend more time thinking about what you're building before writing any code.

8.13 Design Patterns

We can't get the feeling that we've learned how to speak the same language as a programmer unless we've studied something called a design pattern. Computer programmers have been solving the same problems time and again, so it should come as no surprise that some common solutions for similar problems have been discovered and shared.

The solutions to these re-occurring problems became known as design patterns. With the long history of programming, many complex problems are solved with known patterns. The more common the problem, the more likely there's already a known pattern. These solutions are described by how the problem has been solved.

Design patterns are reusable solutions. The patterns become established when they are reusable, and they are proven to work. They are also general enough to be modified to suit the situation you need it for.

Often the patterns have been tested enough and optimized to the smallest fastest code required for a solution to the problem. When properly understood and applied, the pattern will often prevent edge cases from escaping the solution. If a pattern stands the test of time, it becomes established and relied upon.

Learning patterns means you get to build up your vocabulary and overall ability as a programmer. There are a great number of established design patterns. The list of design patterns is extensive and the topic concerns many matters beyond the scope of this book. However, we can still talk to some of the main points behind why the design patterns matter.

There are three categories of design patterns in computing: creational, structural, and behavioral. When writing software for the first time, you're going to be coming across tasks thinking that they're all new. In fact, they're the same problems which everyone has had to solve many times before you.

8.13.1 Creational Design Patterns

Creational design patterns are named so because they relate to how an object is created and later used. These systems are often used in games to instance new creatures and items. When you start a game, it's a good idea that you're starting one game and referencing the one game that was started. Other patterns are useful for creating a variety of similar objects.

Creational design patterns represent the idea of creating and setting up any object from a class using a consistent system. To list a few common creational design patterns, we can start with the Factory, Prototype, Singleton, and Builder.

8.13.1.1 Singleton Pattern

A singleton pattern is a creational pattern which limits the number of instanced objects to one instance. If a problem comes up like "I'd like to make ensure there's only one instance of an object," then you might look on the internet to how someone has solved this particular problem. After a few searches, you'll come across a "Singleton pattern" which ensures that only once instance of an object is ever created.

The first time the object is asked for like CommandCenter MyCommander = CommandCenter. Commander;, you can use an accessor to create and return the commander. If the commander has already been created, then you can pass him along, and not create a new one.

The Singleton pattern is useful to ensure that a game only has a single game state controller. If you want to keep track of the player's navigation through your menus and into your game, it's better to have a single class instructing the rest of your game to start, stop, and post results through one class.

The reason why we don't simply use a lot of static fields and functions is more an effect to memory. If everything was static, then they're never be cleared out of memory. If you're managing a lot of data, then the static field storing them will never be freed, and your game's memory will bloat and take up all the room left for the rest of your game.

Like the "Singleton pattern," many different patterns have a specific role and description. The "factory pattern" uses a class whose only purpose is to instance and create objects. Much like a candy factory produces various sweets. The "builder pattern" is similar to the "factory pattern," but requires another class called a director to control its activity. The "prototype pattern" is another variation on the factory pattern, but copies from a pre-existing copy of a class to create a new object.

8.13.2 Structural Design Patterns

Structural design patterns help consolidate how data and functions are organized and arranged in a class. In this category, we've got the Decorator, Facade, Flyweight, Adapter, and Proxy. Of these the Decorator pattern comes up often in games.

The Decorator pattern is used when instancing objects into a scene. We use this pattern extensively in Unity 3D. For each component you attach to a gameObject, you're decorating it with new behaviors. See that you've been using design patterns all this time and didn't even know it.

When you create a template for creating a zombie or a vampire, you're creating a system to decorate a gameObject with the appropriate components. By keeping movement, armor, attack patterns, and other behaviors separated into different components, you're allowing yourself more freedom to create new objects with different decorations.

Add a blood-sucking component to a Plymouth Fury and you've got a 1980s movie car. Add a talking component to a toaster and you've got a British situation comedy in space. Various components allow for unexpected and sometimes fun results.

8.13.3 Behavioral Design Patterns

Behavioral design patterns focus on communication between objects in a system. Some behavioral patterns include Iterator, Mediator, Observer, and Visitor. In this section, we'll take a close look at the Iterator and Observer patterns.

The Observer pattern is a common system of behavioral design. Combine this with the Singleton, and you've got a game state manager. Combine this with a character, and you've got a level boss. The Observer pattern means that a single class orchestrates the behavior of many child classes.

The children are actually the observers; they watch a central class for changes in the game. Based on the events in the game, a condition will change, and they'll all change their behavior, or rather they observe a state change and react accordingly.

When building your game, it's often a good idea to make sure that data isn't duplicated anywhere it's not necessary. If every child had a record of the player's health, then you're wasting space on redundant data. The player's health should only ever be located in the player object.

When new conditions are met, an event can be raised to tell the game state that the player's health is low. When this event is raised, anyone observing this change should be notified. Then the observing objects can rush in to finish off the player.

8.13.4 What We've Learned

It's unfortunate that we don't have another few hundred pages for this book to go into more depth on the different design patterns. Each one has not only benefits but also some interesting drawbacks. A Singleton pattern is great for centralizing all of your object management. The main problem here is the fact that the Singleton tends to get very big once it's managing a lot of different things.

There's no perfect answer for which pattern any situation should use. In the end, a blend of a few different patterns is usually how the final implementation ends up. Holding too close to any single pattern will only accomplish slowing down overall development time and limit what your game can do.

The final product should be something fun for your player. Even if the code is a little bit awkward in some places, your player isn't reading your code. So long as the code runs fast, reliable, and is easy to read, you're on the right track.

8.14 Continuing on Your Own

Where to go from here? You'll want to explore more of the different function calls that are found within .NET and the Unity 3D application programming interfaces. Google and Bing are both great to help search for answers. Also, now that you know a lot of different programmer jargons, you're less likely to be ignored when asking questions on forums.

One of the hardest lessons to learn is less about code and more about time management. The time management I speak of is not the amount of work any given task is going to take. The amount of time your work takes up of your life is more about what I'm speaking of.

After talking to many vets in the games and software industry is the amount of time left after work and dedicated to living *away* from your keyboard. When first getting into any new topic, it's natural to want to dedicate a large portion of your life to learning more and getting better. However, when this becomes the majority of your life to the degradation of your health, it's time to pull back.

Only after experience can one clearly see that overzealous dedication was a mistake. Of course, getting to that point leads to the experience necessary to see where things went wrong, a horrible catch-22 if there ever was one. Because of this, I'll just leave you with a final word of caution to not let your computer take over your life.

Personally, I've realized that I don't draw as often as I used to. I appreciate my weekends more, and I'm learning a wider variety of things, trying not to focus so heavily on a single topic any more. This comes after realizing that putting your life's work into a single project can all too easily lead to disaster. Though I haven't really had any giant plans crushed by being over-focused, I have seen friends and co-workers having family problems and personal issues grow due to lack of a life outside of work.

Anything can happen, and a project can get canceled before it sees the light of day. The end result can be months or, worse yet, years invested into a lost cause. Nothing is worse than walking away from a gigantic project with nothing to show for your work.

The games industry is volatile; it's filled with politics and instability. The more you know, the easier it is to remain relevant. The more skills you have, the wider your opportunities. Eventually, once you've accumulated enough skill, it's time to work on personal projects that mean more to you.

9

Stuff We Couldn't Cover

Writing in C# means being able to write software for many platforms. This includes embedded systems like the Arduino. Although the C# for Arduino is limited to older versions of .NET and thus older features of C#, a lot of the basic C# functionality is available. You can build software to drive little affordable processors for building robots or internet connected sensors.

You also can build stand alone software applications for the Windows Store, Linux, OSX. You can build for both Android and iOS using Xamarin and Visual Studio. You can write stand-alone apps that aren't necessarily games. The boundaries for where C# has reached span far past the bounds of this book.

Really interesting bits like writing assembly with C# is also possible.

9.1 The Extern Keyword

We could inspect a simple dynamically linked library (DLL) project in Visual Studio. The included project can also build an external library for osX and Linux as well. UnityEngine is a DLL. A DLL is a pre-built binary file that contains any one of the constructs that were covered in this book.

Open the MyUnityLibrary.sln in Visual Studio. Until now, most of the projects in the BookContents repository were created by Unity. This Visual Studio project was created in Visual Studio from a DLL template.

```csharp
using System;
public static class MyUnityLibrary
{
    public static string MyString()
    {
        return "Hello World.";
    }
}
```

The one C# file in the Solution Explorer has a static class and a static function. This is just a simple starting point, but the project isn't to serve as anything more than a simple example of how to import methods from a DLL.

```
🔒 Solution 'MyUnityLibrary' (1 project)
  ▲ 🔒 C# MyUnityLibrary
      ▷ 🔒 🔧 Properties
      ▷ ■-■ References
      ▷ ✓ C# MyUnityLibrary.cs
```

From looking at the content of the DLL you could imagine that you're able to get a "Hello World." string from the MyString() function. To build the DLL, you'll find the "Build" command in the Visual Studio menu as Build -> Build Solution.

A DLL is created and stored in the project directory MyUnityLibrary\MyUnityLibrary\bin\Debug\, where you'll find MyUnityLibrary.dll. To use the library, copy the dll file into a Plugins directory in Unity's Assets directory.

```csharp
using System.Runtime.InteropServices;
using UnityEngine;

public class TestLibrary : MonoBehaviour
{
    [DllImport("MyUnityLibrary")]
    public static extern string MyString();

    void Start()
    {
        Debug.Log(MyUnityLibrary.MyString());
    }
}
```

Once Unity is aware that there's a DLL in the Plugins directory, the project is updated with some additional files reflecting how the DLL is to be used. Cross platform compatibility is also allowed when writing a plugin with C#. A C# library built with .NET can conveniently run on any platform that runs Unity.

The classes in Unity need to know how to operate with an external library. The `System.Runtime.InteropServices` enables the external library connection. The `[DLLImport()]` attribute searches for a DLL with the `MyUnityLibrary` name. The `MyString()` function has an extern accessor assigned telling C# to look outside of the class and into external sources for the `MyString()` function. When the game is played, the "`Hello World.`" string is pulled from the DLL and printed to the Unity console.

This is a very simplified example of an external Library. A DLL can also be written in C++, C, or any other language, assuming that the target platform matches the target of your Unity game project. Special optimizations can be built into a DLL that cannot be built in C# with Unity. This allows for heavy calculations to be done with faster optimizations and packed into a DLL using C++ or assembly language.

If some code is special and you're not willing or able to share the code with a project, this can also be built into a DLL and only an interface to the code needs to be exposed in Unity.

10

Good Luck

If you've gotten this far, thank you. Even though you've read through miles of material, you've still got a long way to go to be a full-fledged game engineer. However, don't let this dull your motivation.

The most important advice I can give you is to remain focused on learning with your first few projects rather than finishing that massively multiplayer online role-playing, first-person World War II zombie shooter game. It's important that you understand what you're capable of, and to do this, you need to learn your own limitations.

Your strengths aren't just about what you're able to do, but how long it takes to do them. Eventually, you'll be able to write a fairly complex multiplayer game. It might take a few years, but it'll eventually get done. If you think you'll still be interested in working on one project for many thousands of hours, then I commend your focus and dedication.

For many people, a weekend or an evening project should remain fairly simple and small. A puzzle game, an endless runner, or a simple adventure game can still be done by one person. Once your game requires several hundred assets, sounds, effects, and the like, you're now looking at a product requiring a large-scale effort.

Such efforts require teams of people simply because of the hours involved to finish the product. Even a team of less than a dozen people means that there is several times more hours dedicated to a project than you can dedicate alone. Even if you dedicate 2000 hours a month to a project, it would not be enough, as many large-scale projects require tens of millions of hours to complete.

Finishing a project, even a small one, means you have something to show for your effort. You may well start down the path of a super cool game that no one has ever seen before, but is it something you can stay focused on for a few million hours? It's likely that even after a few hundred hours into the project, you'll realize that you need to start over anyway.

Learning how to write code is an ongoing process. Halfway through a large project, you'll learn that the beginning of your project had many mistakes because of bad programming habits. Usually, fixing all of the problems means throwing everything out and starting over. Don't let this discourage you. You've learned something, and you've become a better programmer!

Index

A

accessibility, 123
accessing structs, 336–337
access modifiers, 125–127
accessors/properties
    encapsulation, 453
    `MyNumberProperty` class, 453
    read-only, 457–458
    set event, 455–457
    simplification, 458–459
    value, 454–455
`Action` func/expression, 575–577
`AddComponent()` function, 307–309
algorithms, 70–73
ambiguous namespaces, 133–134
anonymous expressions, 574–577
application programming interface (API), 6, 10, 58, 196
architectures and organization, 653
    divide and conquer, 654–655
    namespaces and directories, 653–654
    refactoring, 655–656
arguments (args), 287–288
    `Input.GetKey()` function, 290
    `Movement()` function, 291
    multiple, 288–290
ArrayList
    `ArrayList.Contains()`, 265–266
    drawback, 262
    fixed-sized arrays, 262
    GameObjects, 263–265
    performance issue, 268
    `Remove()`, 266–267
    sort and reverse, 267–268
arrays
    `AddComponent()` function, 307–309
    breakpoint, class inheritance, 395–399
    discovery, 393–394
    dynamic initialization, 246–247
    fixed-sized, 241–245
    foreach loop, 246, 390–393
    `GameObject`, 302–304
    length and count, 389–390
    `Mathf`, 306–307
    multidimensional, 252–262
    `Time.fixedTime`, 306–307
    type casting, 309–311
    while loop, 247–248
    `zeroth`, 304–306
    zombies and humans, 394–395
artificial intelligence (AI), 6, 251
Assets directory, 31–32
assignment operators, 292–294

attributes, 635–639
    custom, 639–641
    flags, 644–645
    multiple, 641–642
    to work, 642–644

B

`BaseClass`, 461–463
    generalization, 459–460
    `partial`, 463–466
    `protected`, `private` and `public`, 466–467
    specialization, 461
    `virtual` and `override`, 459
behavioral design patterns, 658
big endian, 624
bitwise math, 646
    addition/subtraction, 648–650
    multiplication, 650–651
    tricks, 651–652
    unary operator ~ , 647–648
bitwise operators, 624
    and &, 628–629
    big/little endian, 624–625
    bit shifting >> and <<, 632–634
    bits in numbers, 632
    enums and numbers, 627–628
    exclusive or ^ (xor), 629–630
    flags, 630–631
    or |, 627
    shortcuts |= and ^ =, 631
    signed/unsigned, 625–627
blank scope, 151–152
Bombe, 3
BookContents, 22
Boolean logic, 3
booleans, 162–163
`BreakAndContinue()` function, 248–249
    foreach loop, 251–252
    ZombieData, 249–250
BumpyCase, 94
byte code, 3

C

cast operator, 102
central processing unit (CPU), 10
ChaseCamera, 294–295
`ChildAbility()` function, 209
class construction, 121–123
    access modifiers/dot operator, 125–127
    adding data fields, 125
    declaration, 123–125

class construction (*Continued*)
    members, 128
    scope, 127–128, 146–149
    value/reference types, 124–125
class constructors, 491–492
    TreadmillManager, 495–498
    TreadmillSegment, 493–495
    Zombie() function, 298–301
ClassData, 338–339
    character base class, 339–340
    const, 340
    readonly, 341–342
classes, 74–75
    complex code, 198
    C-style languages, 196–197
    definition, 81
    inheritance, 362–364
    modular code, 199–202
    MonoBehaviour, 198
    objects, 82–86
    partial, 81
    UnityEngine and System.Collections,
        197–198
class members
    data gathering, 283
    FirstFunction(), 283
    GetKey(), 284–285
    Start(), 282
    Update(), 285–286
    void FirstFunction(), 282
clock math, 143
code
    blocks, 70, 79–81
    folding, 78, 111–113
    fragment, 33–34
    style, white space, 78–79
code smell
    comments, 583
    duplicated code, 584
    naming, 584
    responsibility rule, 583
code structure
    class construction, 123–128
    directives, 129–134
    functions, 134–140
    game building, 118–121
    leveling up, 194
    logic and operators, 162–173
    loops, 173–186
    operation order, 140–145
    scope, 146–152
    this, 152–155
command line, 20
comments, 108–110
    code folding, 111–113
    line numbers, 111
    navigating code, 114
    organized code, 115
    summary, 113–114
compilation unit, 61

compile-time errors, 34–35, 192
compiling, 9–10
computer
    languages, 4
    layer abstraction, 10
    science, 3–4
ComputerCat, 206
concurrency/co-routines
    arrays of delegates, 561–562
    setting up timers, 558–561
    stopping, 562–565
    yield keyword, 555–558
console, 20
const keyword, 340
ContainsKey(), 567–568
controlling inheritance
    abstract classes, 430–433
    Ended() function, 435–436
    ExtensionFunction(), 429–430
    GameTimer, 434–435
    sealed, 128
creational design patterns, 657
C# paradigm, 5
cube-generating system, 277
custom attributes, 639–641

D

data, 88–89
debugger, 192–194, 443
debugging code, 186
Debug.Log(), 140, 200, 272, 322, 480, 574, 580
declaration/assignment statements, 69
delegates, 474–475
    arrays of, 561–562
    destructors, 549–550
    signatures, 476
    stacking, 476–477
    updating, 478–480
    UseDelegate, 477–478
design patterns, 656
    behavioral, 658
    creational, 657
    structural, 657–658
destructors, 546–547
    clearing events/delegates,
        549–550
    garbage collection, 552, 554
    OnDestroy(), 550–552
    SelfDestructor, 547–548
    UsesOnDestroy, 553
Dictionary data type, 565–568
Difference Engine, 3
directives
    ambiguous namespaces, 133–134
    libraries, 130–133
    using UnityEngine, 129–130
dot operator, 125–127
do-while loops, 177–178
DrawRay, 379–380

DrawWords, 450–452
Duck-typed languages, 102
dynamic, 620
     ExpandoObject, 621–622
     Expando Reader, 622–623
dynamically linked library (DLL), 130, 345,
          661–662
dynamicFloats, 246–247
dynamic typing, 102–103

E

8-bit unsigned integer, 100
encapsulation, 85, 146
enumeration (enums), 311–312, 515–517
     MonsterState, 315–316
     options, 317
     PrimitiveType, 312–315
equality operators, 163–164
escape sequences, 270–271
evaluation
     math, 141–143
     operator, 144–145
events, 533
     delegates, 534–535
     EventArgs, 537–538
     GenericEventArgs, 539–540
     HandleDelegate and HandleEvent variables,
          535–536
     Listener class, 535
     proper, 536–537
ExpandoObject, 621–622
explicit *vs.* implicit casting, 104–108
expressive statements, 70
extension functions, 540–541
     GameObject, 541
     Mirror, 544–546
     namespace Tricks, 541–542
     overloading, 543–544
     Reset(), 543
     static keyword, 542
extern keyword, 661–662

F

FindObjectsOfType() function, 212
finite state machine, 328–330
fixed-sized arrays, 241–245
floating point numbers, 414
floating point unit (FPU), 415
floor generator, 295–297
foreach() loop, 246, 581
fork, 19
for() loop, 175–177
function overloading, 444–445
     CreateObject(), 448–449
     DrawWords, 450–452
     HalfValue(), 445
     signature, 446–448
     UseCreateObject(), 448–449

functions
     arguments, 348
     call, 134
     defined, 135–136
     foreach *vs.* for loop, 350–351
     members, 60, 123
     overrides, 359–362
     parameter lists, 346–350
     scope, 149–151
     side effects, 347–348
     Unity 3D entry points, 136–137
     white space/tabs, 139–140
     writing, 137–139

G

game-building, 118–119
     components, 155–158
     mouse point, 119–120
     mover, 229–230
     move to point, 120–121
     physics settings, 232–233
     player, 228–229
     projectile, 158–159
     shooter, 230–231
     target, 160–161
game engines, 2, 5–6
     class declaration, 39
     creating/assigning, C# file, 40–42
     file naming, 42–43
     high-level programming, 37
     MyFunction(), 39
     opening scene, 50
     operating system, 38
     saving scene, 50
     Unity 3D tools, 48–50
     Update(), 39
     using new file, 43–48
     working, live scene, 50
GenerateRooms, 436–439
GenericEventArgs, 539–540
generics, 521
     anonymous objects, 530–533
     identifier T, 522–523
     types, 526–527
     use of, 523–526
     values, 529–530
     var keyword, 527–529
GetComponent(), 309–311
GetKey(), 284–285, 290
GetMethodInfo(), 616
GetType(), 416–417
Git, 584
     branch and merge, 585–588
     flow, 587
     merge conflicts, 588–591
     submitting changes, 54–56
Git SCM installation, 11
     basics, 20–22
     first repo, 22–25

Git SCM installation (*Continued*)
   GitHub, 18–20
   software download, 17–18
   Unity Hub, 25
Gizmos, 377–379
   DrawRay, 379–380
   Gizmos DrawLine(), 380
   sort optimization, 381
global access, structs, 337
global scope, 188–190
goto keyword, 327–328, 381–383
   HumanWithStates, 386
   skipping down, 383
   Zombies, 386–388
   ZombieWithStates, 383–386
graphics processing units (GPUs), 5, 415
greater/less than operators, 166–167
greedy operator, 606

H

handling structs, 335–336
hard-coded value, 67
hash codes, 55
high-level programming, 37

I

IComparer, 488–491
identifiers, 87
IEnumerator, 514
   enumeration, 515–517
   implementation, 517–520
   interfaces, 521
if statement, 169–173
implicit *vs.* explicit casting, 104–108, 372–373
indirect recursion, 600
inheritance, 86
   class, 362–364
   Component, 203
   function overrides, 359–362
   InheritingMembers, 205
   instancing, 206–208
   Is-A and Has-A, 206
   MonoBehaviour, 202–203
   != null, 213–214
   object, 209–212, 364–367
   parent child, 208–209
   using UnityEngine, 204
instance variables, 126
instancing, 84, 214–215
   class initialization, 215
   constructors, 216–219
   new keyword, 215–216
integrated development environment (IDE), 7, 12
interface
   abstract class, 480
   accessors, 483–485
   IComparer, 488–491
   IPickup, 491
   IThis, 481–483

   multiple, 486–488
   naming convention, 481
   object-oriented programming, 481
   property, 481
International Business Machines Corporation (IBM), 4
interpolation, 120
invocation expression, 70
iteration, 9

J

JumpStatements
   BreakAndContinue(), 248–252
   return, 233–240

K

keywords, 73–76

L

Lambda expressions, 573
   anonymous expressions, 574–577
   queue of, 577–578
language-integrated query (LINQ), 601
   Distinct(), 606–607
   lambdas and arrays, 601–602
   monsters, 608–611
   strange behaviors, 604–605
   ToArray(), 606
   var type, 602–603
   Where(), 605–606
   zombie objects, 603–604
lexical analyzer, 62
libraries, 130–133
License management panel, 14
linear recursion, 599
line feed character, 76
line numbers, 111
LINQ, *see* language-integrated query (LINQ)
literals, 66–67
little endian, 624–625
logic and operators
   and/or, 168–169
   booleans, 162–163
   equality operators, 163–164
   greater/less than, 166–167
   if/branching, 169–173
   logical not!, 165–166
looping condition, 69
loops
   breakpoints, 185–186
   do-while, 177–178
   for(), 175–177
   within loops, 182
   postfix/prefix notation, 178–179
   return and break, 183–185
   unary operators, 173–174
   using, 179–181
   while(), 174–175
low-level programming, 10

M

MagicComponent project, 278–279
mantissa, 103
math, 141–143
Mathf class, 306–307
mechanical computers, 3
megabyte, 100
mobile development, 502–504
modern computer language, 4
Mono history, 443–444
MonsterGenerator, 375–377
monsters LINQ, 608–611
mouse point, 119–120
movement
    experiments, 57–58
    stack, 569–571
multidimensional arrays, 252–253
    camera and screen setup, 257–259
    columns and rows, 253–255
    GameObjects, 262
    puzzle board, 255–257
    range checking, 259–261
multiple attributes, 641
MyColors, 314–315

N

named parameters, 471–473
namespaces, 75, 342–344
    alias directives, 345–346
    ambiguous references, 345
    directives, 344–345
native machine code, 10
nested class, 121
nested code blocks, 80
NewBehaviourScript, 40
NewUnityUser, 23
non-transitive operations, 67
nullable types, 101
numeric literals, 66

O

object oriented programming (OOP), 82–86
OnDestroy(), 550–552
operators, 422–423
    overloading*, 424–426
    overloading < and >, 65, 426–427
    Puzzle object, 423–424
    tokens, 65–66
optional parameters, 469–470
    arguments, 470–471
    CreateACube() function, 468
    function declaration, syntax, 467
    named parameters, 471–473
    out and ref, 473
OutParameter
    GetSevenEleven(), 400–401
    GetSevenOut(), 401–403

simple sort (bubble sort), 403–405
simple sort proof, 405–406
override keyword, 359–362

P

ParentAbility() function, 208
parsers, 35
partial classes, 81, 463–466
PeanutButter.cs, 42
PianoCat, 205–207
Plankalkül, 4
POD (plain old data), 88, 215
polymorphism, 85, 373
postfix/prefix notation, 178–179
preprocessor directives
    mobile development, 502–504
    organizing, 505
    TESTING, 499–500
    UNITY_EDITOR, 500–502
    warning, 504–505
primitive types, 101
programming, 7–8
    classes, 8
    computer science, 3–4
    C# files, 8–9
    documentation, 58–61
    expression form, 2
    iteration, 9
    learning, copy/paste, 9
    logic, 3
    mechanical computers, 3
    modern computer language, 4
    software origin, 4
    source code, 7
    style, 583
projectile, 158–159
prompt, 20
proper event, 536–537

Q

queues, 571–572
    of Lambdas expressions, 577–578

R

readability, 581
    code smell, 583–584
    if statement, 582–583
    ?: notation, 581–582
readonly keyword, 341–342, 457–458
recursion, 579
    do/foreach/while loops, 592
    enumerators, 592
    GameObject, 594–601
    goto loop, 593
    for loop, 592
    understanding, 593–594
refactoring process, 94, 583

ref keyword, 410–411
    code fragment, 407–408
    code portability side effects, 408–410
reflection, 613–614
    MethodInfo, 615–618
reserved keywords, 74
return keyword, 286–287
    GetZombie(), 236–238
    keyword void, 234
    MyNumber(), 235
    null is not void, 240
    objects, 235–236
    tuples, 238–240
Rule of Three, 349
run-time errors, 34–35

S

sample code, 33
    code fragments, 33–34
    comments, 36–37
    compile-time/run-time errors, 34–35
    Unity Hub, 35–36
SampleGame Unity Project, 56–57
    movement experiments, 57–58
    programming documentation, 58–61
scope
    blank, 151–152
    class, 127–128, 146–149
    encapsulation, 146
    function, 149–151
    global, 188–190
    visibility/accessibility, 187–188
separator tokens, 64–65
signed numbers, 414
single line comments, 64
Singleton pattern, 657
software origin, 4
source code, 7, 12
source files, 31, 61
stacking delegates, 476–477
stacks
    movement, 569–571
    Push(), Pop() and Peek(), 568–569
statements, 88
    algorithms, 70–73
    code execution, 70
    declaration and assignment, 69
    and expressions, 70
static, 220–221
    functions, 224–225, 228
    variables, 222–224
    zombie script, 225–227
strings, 64
    declaration, 268–270
    escape sequences, 270–271
    verbatim, 271–272
strong typing, 102–103
structs, 330–331
    accessing, 336–337
    vs. class, 332–334

global access, 337
    handling, 335–336
    PlayerData, 332
    without, 334–335
structural design patterns, 657–658
style guides, 194
switch() statement
    advantage, 319
    data types, 323
    default, 319–322
    fall-through, 326–327
    finite state machine, 328–330
    goto, 327–328
    if-else, 317
    integral types, 319
    nested, 324–325
    parameters, 318, 330

T

tail recursion, 600
this keyword, 152–155
tile floor generator, 295–297
timers, 273–278
tokenization, 62
tokens, 61, 67–69
    comments, 63–64
    literals, 66–67
    operator, 65–66
    separator, 64–65
    transitive/non-transitive operations, 67
    writing C#, 62–63
ToString(), 367
transitive operations, 67
TreadmillManager, 495–498
TreadmillSegment, 493–495
try-catch-finally process, 506–508
    custom exceptions, 510–512
    exception messages, 508–510
    file.txt, 514
    finally{} statement, 512
    UnauthorizedAccessExceptions, 513
turing completeness, 4
type casting, 103–104, 309–311, 411–413, 417–419
    explicit *vs.* implicit, 104–108, 372–373
    floating point numbers, 414
    integers, 413–414
    numbers, 413
    user-defined type conversion, 370–371
    (Type) *vs.* as cast, 368–370
types/operators, 415–416
    boxing and unboxing, 420–422
    GetType(), 416–417
    type aliasing, 420
    type casting, 417–419

U

unary operators ~, 173–174, 647–648
Unity 3D
    code execution, 70
    C#, 6–7

entry points, 136–137
game engines, 5–6
installation, 13–17
learning, 6
and Microsoft Visual Studio, 7
tools, 48–50
useful variables, 94–100
Unity 3D execution order
Awake() function, 354–356
component, 356–358
ExecutionOrderFirst.cs class, 353
Start() and Update() functions, 352
UNITY_EDITOR directive, 500–502
Unity Editor interface
Assets directory, 31–32
Git ignore, 32
Hierarchy panel, 28
Inspector panel, 29
Packages directory, 32
Project and Console panel, 29–31
Project Settings directory, 32
Scene and Game view, 28
toolbar, 27–28
Unity.gitignore, 32
Unity Hub, 13–14, 35–36
Unity version numbering, 16–17
Update() function, 285–286, 292, 406
user-defined type conversion, 370–371

V

value/reference types, 100–101
variables, 86–87
assignment, 96–98
collision, 147

data, 88–89
dynamic initialization, 90–91
identifiers, 87
manipulation, 89–90
names, 91–100
var keyword, 527–529
Vector3, 101, 141
vectors
Gizmos, 377–381
MonsterGenerator, 375–377
objects, 374–375
verbatim strings, 271–272
Version Control System, 11
Visual Studio, 442–443
debugger, 443
installation, 15–16
Mono, 443–444

W

warnings *vs.* errors, 190–194
wash/rinse/repeat, 73
while() loop, 174–175,
        247–248
white space, 76–79

Y

yield keyword, 555–558

Z

Z1 computer, 3

Printed in the United States
by Baker & Taylor Publisher Services

The Catholics of Ulster

MARIANNE ELLIOTT

The Catholics of Ulster

A HISTORY

ALLEN LANE
THE PENGUIN PRESS

ALLEN LANE
THE PENGUIN PRESS

Published by the Penguin Group
Penguin Books Ltd, 27 Wrights Lane, London w8 5tz, England
Penguin Putnam Inc., 375 Hudson Street, New York, New York 10014, USA
Penguin Books Australia Ltd, Ringwood, Victoria, Australia
Penguin Books Canada Ltd, 10 Alcorn Avenue, Toronto, Ontario, Canada m4v 3b2
Penguin Books India (P) Ltd, 11, Community Centre, Panchsheel Park, New Delhi – 110 017, India
Penguin Books (NZ) Ltd, Private Bag 102902, NSMC, Auckland, New Zealand
Penguin Books (South Africa) (Pty) Ltd, 5 Watkins Street, Denver Ext 4, Johannesburg 2094, South Africa

Penguin Books Ltd, Registered Offices: Harmondsworth, Middlesex, England

First published by Allen Lane The Penguin Press 2000
3 5 7 9 10 8 6 4 2

Typeset in 10.5/14 pt PostScript Linotype Sabon
Typeset by Rowland Phototypesetting Ltd, Bury St Edmunds, Suffolk

Printed and bound in Great Britain by The Bath Press, Bath

A CIP catalogue record for this book is available from the British Library

ISBN 0–713–99464–9

For Marc
a book in a life

Contents

List of Plates   ix
Maps   xiii
Acknowledgements   xxix
Prologue   xxxiii

1 FROM CÚ CHULAINN TO CHRISTIANITY: I
   RELIGION AND SOCIETY IN EARLY ULSTER

2 GAELIC ULSTER: LAND, LORDSHIP AND PEOPLE   23

3 RELIGION IN ULSTER BEFORE THE REFORMATION   57

4 THE LOSS OF THE LAND: PLANTATION AND   81
   CONFISCATION IN SEVENTEENTH-CENTURY
   ULSTER

5 THE MERGER OF 'IRISHNESS' AND CATHOLICISM   123
   IN EARLY MODERN ULSTER

6 LIFE UNDER THE PENAL LAWS   161

7 REFORM TO REBELLION: THE EMERGENCE OF   211
   REPUBLICAN POLITICS

8 THE REVIVAL OF 'POLITICAL' CATHOLICISM   267

9 THE FAMINE AND AFTER: CATHOLIC SOCIAL   303
   CLASSES IN NINETEENTH-CENTURY ULSTER

10 ACROSS THE DIVIDE: COMMUNITY RELATIONS   333
   AND SECTARIAN CONFLICT BEFORE PARTITION

11 CATHOLICS IN NORTHERN IRELAND 1920–2000   371

CONTENTS

12 A RESENTFUL BELONGING: CATHOLIC IDENTITY   429
     IN THE TWENTIETH CENTURY

     Notes   483
     Select Bibliography   562
     Index   601

Plates

1a) *Belfast from the River Lagan. Cave Hill in the Distance*. Engraving by Marcus Ward & Co., 1863, in the collection of the Ulster Museum, Belfast (Photograph reproduced with the kind permission of the Trustees of the National Museums and Galleries of Northern Ireland)

1b) *West Belfast Peace Wall separating the Loyalist Shankhill Road and Nationalist Falls Road*, 1994 (Photograph: © Pacemaker)

2a) Aerial photograph of Emain Macha (Navan Fort) (Photograph: Environment and Heritage Service, Belfast © British Crown Copyright 2000. Published by permission of the Controller of Her Britannic Majesty's Stationery Office)

2b) Statue of Cú Chulainn, republican plot, City Cemetery, Brandywell, Derry (Photograph: © Allan Leonard)

3a) *The Dartmouth College Map of the North East of Ireland*, Map 25, *c.* 1586. Detail showing Tullahoge, County Tyrone (Photograph: © National Maritime Museum, London)

3b) Aerial photograph of Tullahoge Fort (Photograph: Environment and Heritage Service, Belfast © British Crown Copyright 2000. Published by permission of the Controller of Her Britannic Majesty's Stationery Office)

4   *The Chief of the MacSweeneys seated at Dinner*, Plate III in *The Image of Irelande* by John Derrick, 1581, republished by Adam and Charles Black, Edinburgh, 1883

5a) Hedge Row School Mural, Ardoyne Avenue, Belfast (Photograph: © Allan Leonard)

5b) Orange banner, Loyal Orange Lodge 273, Portadown No. 1 District (Photograph: Carleton Orange Hall, Portadown)

6a) Mural of a Mass Rock, Ardoyne Avenue, Belfast (Photograph: © Allan Leonard)

6b) Mural of the Virgin Mary, Berwick Road, Ardoyne, Belfast (Photograph: © Allan Leonard)

7a) 'The Station' taken from *Traits & Stories of the Irish Peasantry, Vol. 1*, by William Carleton, William Curry, Jun., and Co., Dublin, 1844

7b) *Cabins, Mourne Mountains, Co. Down* by R. J. Welsh, *c.* 1900. In the collection of the Ulster Museum, Belfast (Photograph reproduced with the kind permission of the Trustees of the National Museums and Galleries of Northern Ireland)

8   *Battle of Ballynahinch, 13th June 1798*, (detail) by Thomas Robinson, *c.* 1798/99 (Photograph reproduced by permission of the Office of Public Works, Ireland)

9a) *Cardinal Paul Cullen*, artist unknown, nineteenth century (Photograph reproduced with permission from St Patrick's College, Drumcondra, Dublin)

9b) *At Doon Holy Well, Kilmacrenan* by R. J. Welsh, 1912. In the collection of the Ulster Museum, Belfast (Photograph reproduced with the kind permission of the Trustees of the National Museums and Galleries of Northern Ireland)

10a) *An Gorta Mór: 'Britain's Genocide by Starvation'*. Mural of the Great Famine, Whiterock Road, Ballymurphy, Belfast (Photograph: © Allan Leonard)

10b) *An Gorta Mór: 'They buried us without shroud nor coffin'*. Mural of the Great Famine, Ardoyne Avenue, Belfast (Photograph: © Allan Leonard)

11a) *Rioting in Sandy Row Belfast*, 1864, artist unknown. In the collection of the Ulster Museum, Belfast (Photograph reproduced with the kind permission of the Trustees of the National Museums and Galleries of Northern Ireland)

11b) *Riots in York Street, Belfast, 1922* (Photograph: © *Belfast Telegraph* Newspapers Ltd)

12a) *Walker's Pillar, Walls of Londonderry* drawing by W. H. Bartlett, engraved by R. Wallis, *The Scenery and Antiquities of Ireland – illustrated in One Hundred and Twenty Engravings, from the Drawings by W. H. Bartlett with historical and descriptive text by J. Sterling Coyne, N. P. Willis etc. – Vol. II*, James S. Virtue, London, *c.* 1825/1840 (Photograph: National Museums and Galleries of Northern Ireland, Ulster Folk & Transport Museum)

12b) Parliament Building, Stormont, Belfast (Photograph: © Pacemaker)

13a) Terence O'Neill with Councillor Robert Hart after opening O'Neill Road (Photograph: © *Belfast Telegraph* Newspapers Ltd)

13b) *"Biased!! How dare you, you long haired Fenian agitator."* – illustration by Martyn Turner from *Pack Up Your Troubles – 25 Years of Northern*

Ireland Cartoons, by Martyn Turner, The Blackstaff Press Ltd, Belfast, 1995 (Picture: © Martyn Turner/*Fortnight* Magazine)

14a) *Questionnaire* illustration by Martyn Turner from *Pack Up Your Troubles – 25 Years of Northern Ireland Cartoons*, by Martyn Turner, The Blackstaff Press Ltd, Belfast, 1995 (Picture: © Martyn Turner/*Irish Times*)

14b) August 1969 (Photograph: © *Belfast Telegraph* Newspapers Ltd)

15a) '*Free Ireland*' 1916 commemoration mural, Beechmount Avenue, Belfast (Photograph: © Allan Leonard)

15b) Bobby Sands Funeral, 1981 (Photograph: © *Belfast Telegraph* Newspapers Ltd)

16 Last rites by Father Alex Reid said over the body of one of the two British Army corporals killed at Andersonstown, March 1988 (Photograph: © *Mirror* Syndication International)

Maps

Map 1. Modern Ulster

N

30 mi

40 km

Inishowen

Ailech

R. Bann

Lough
Neagh

Navan Fort
(Emain Macha)

Clogher

Strangford
Lough

R. Bann

Downpatrick

Black
Pig's Dyke

Slieve Gullion

Black
Pig's Dyke

Dundalk

Linear earthworks

Map 2. Prehistoric Ulster

N

40 mi
50 km

L. Foyle

DÁL
RIATA

CENÉL   CENÉL   ULAID
            nEÓGAIN
Ailech   DÁL
NORTHERN   nARAIDE
UÍ NÉILL
            Uí   DÁL
CONAILL   Thuirtri   FIATACH

            Airthir   Uí ECHACH
                         COBO
            Armagh

AIRGIALLA
                         Newry

                                    Leth
                                    Cuinn

CONNACHTA   SOUTHERN
             UÍ NÉILL   Tara

             MIDE

                                    Leth
                                    Moga

EÓGANACHT

AIRGIALLA   Overkingdoms

DÁL   Subkingdoms
RIATA

Airthir   Other dynasties
             and subject peoples

.... Boundaries between
             overkingdoms

─────   Boundary between Leth
             Cuinn and Leth Moga

Map 3. Political divisions to *c.* 800

Map 4. Gaelic and Anglo-Irish lordships by the fifteenth century

Map labels:

N

30 mi
40 km

Rathlin Is.

INISHOWEN

Coleraine

Kilmacrenan

Derry

(LONDON)DERRY

ANTRIM

Island
Magee

DONEGAL

Templepatrick

TYRONE

Lough
Neagh

ONEILLAND

Augher

DOWN

FERMANAGH

ARMAGH

Enniskillen

Fews

MONAGHAN

Orior

Mourne
Mts

CAVAN

Legend:

■ Assigned to Scottish undertakers
▫ Assigned to English undertakers
■ Assigned to servitors and Irish
▤ Exceptional areas
✳ Granted to Sir Turlough McHenry O'Neill

0   30 mi

0   40 km

Ballymoney

43%

ANTRIM 19%

(London)Derry

DERRY 24%

DONEGAL

Maghera

Ballymena

Strabane

Randalstown   Antrim

Strangford Lough

TYRONE

Templepatrick

Barons Court (Abercorn Estate)

Stewartstown

Belfast

Lough Derg

52%

Lisburn

Killinchy

Dungannon

Lurgan

Saintfield

Ballynahinch

DOWN

Armagh

Downpatrick

FERMANAGH

Monaghan

ARMAGH

27%

Ards

42%

MONAGHAN

35%

Ballybay

Newry

64%

Carlingford

CAVAN

76%

*   Charter Schools

●   Main brown linen markets by size

%   Percentage of Catholics in 1732

◇   Places referred to in account of 1798 rebellion

Map 6. Eighteenth-century Ulster

The Catholic population increased rapidly in the latter half of the century, particulary in south Ulster, where it reached 50% in Armagh by 1766 and 60% in south Down. By 1834 Catholics outnumbered Protestants in the province

Map 7. Sectarian conflict in Armagh and Down, late eighteenth century

Map 8i. Ulster in the famine era: dependence on soup kitchens after 1847
(after Frank Wright, *Two Lands in One Soil*)

N

30 mi
40 km

Broughshane
Ballymena

Omagh

Portadown •Lurgan

Enniskillen
Dolly's Brae

Tanderagee

Mackan
Clones
Ballybay

Numbers of Orange lodges 1–28+

Map 8ii. Ulster in the famine era: number of Orange lodges
(after Frank Wright, *Two Lands in One Soil*)

N

40 mi

50 km

Glenveagh

Cloghaneely

Letterkenny

Burtonport

Drumoghill

Strabane

Dundalk

● Harvest migration

○ Illicit distillation

Map 9. Harvest migration and illicit distillation,
early nineteeth century

Map 10. Belfast in 1911
(from Sybil Baker, 'Orange and Green')

Map 11. Religious segregation in Belfast, 1990s

Labels on map:
Belfast Lough
Squires Hill
Cave Hill
Harbour
Black Mountain
Ardoyne
Shipyards
Shankhill Road
City Centre
Clonard
Ballymacarrett
River Lagan
Andersonstown

Legend:
More than 90% Catholic
Mixed areas
More than 90% Protestant

Acknowledgements

This book started out in conversations with Brian Friel and Anne Tannahill, after I had written a Field Day pamphlet about Ulster Protestantism. It has taken many turns and twists since then and ended up a much bigger project than first envisaged. It has been researched and written while I have been a full-time academic in the British University system, in the last three years as a Head of Department. In view of the current audit culture – a virus-like infection spreading through every aspect of British higher education, a culture which actively penalises long-term research projects such as this book – I am somewhat in despair about my ability to embark on such a major project again. It is unlikely that this one would have been brought to fruition without periodic research grants awarded by Birkbeck College, the University of Liverpool, the Leverhulme Foundation and most notably the Nuffield Foundation, which gave me time to write when it was becoming increasingly difficult to find. I acknowledge their generosity with deep gratitude. Like any writer, I have paid a price in neglected friends and family. I would like to pay particular tribute to my mother, Sheila Burns, my sisters Geraldine Walsh and Eleanor Dent, to friends like Susan Paton, Joanna Bourke, Anne Laurence, Moya Paul, Margaret and David Rankin, Angie and David Stovell, and Annie and Robin Gwyn, who have repaid such negligence with constant loyalty and support.

I have been blessed in my colleagues, notably Richard Evans, Hilary Sapire and Joanna Bourke at Birkbeck College, University of London; Linda Christianson, Elizabeth Malcolm, Dorothy Lynch, Ulli Kockel, Máiréad nic Craith, Conor mac Carthy and Harvey Cox at the Institute of Irish Studies, University of Liverpool, and Angela MacEwan in the School of History.

ACKNOWLEDGEMENTS

The staff at numerous libraries and archives have been consistently helpful, and I am deeply grateful to those at the libraries of Liverpool University, Birkbeck College, Boston College, the National Library of Ireland, the National Archives of Ireland, the Royal Irish Academy (notably Síobhain O'Rafferty), the Department of Irish Folklore (UCD), Queen's University Library, the Ulster Museum, the Ulster Folk and Transport Museum (especially Linda Ballard, Bill Crawford and Roger Dixon), Belfast Central Library (particularly Darren Topping and Suzanne Drake), the Public Record Office of Northern Ireland (notably Marian Gallagher and, formerly, Allan Blackstock), the Scottish Record Office, the Public Record Office, the British Library and the Institute of Historical Research. But I must single out the staff at the Linenhall Library in Belfast, most notably John Gray, John Killen, Mary Delargey, Yvonne Murphy, Bern Kane, Ciaran Crossey and Allan Leonard (particularly for his assistance with the illustrations), for making my innumerable visits there so rewarding and enjoyable.

I am humbled by the remarkable generosity of so many fellow scholars. Séamus Ó Catháin helped on many occasions with the riches and pitfalls of the folklore material; Aídan Mac Poílin, Bréandain Ó Buachalla and Art Hughes with the early stages of locating the Irish-language sources; Anthony Buckley shared his expertise on ethnicity, Trevor Parkhill his on local history and the riches of the Ulster Museum. Brian Walker was unstintingly generous with his time and expertise. Roy Foster was always there with helpful tips, support and friendship. Donnacha Ó Corraín, Katharine Simms, Cathy Swift, Bernadette Cunningham, Nicholas Canny, Roy Foster, Paul Arthur, Michael Parker and Maurice Hayes read and commented upon individual sections. Tracey Holsgrove and Phil Jimmieson of Liverpool University have helped defuse numerous crises. Tim Walsh helped with last-minute checking. Ian McBride, Don Akenson and Christopher Woods read the entire manuscript against a tight deadline, which, in retrospect, I had no right to ask. My debt to them is incalculable. Vincent Morley has provided research assistance (and critical commentary) throughout the research and writing of the book, most notably with the Irish-language sources. He brought a particular expertise to the translation of the poems. The book – and indeed my own experience in researching and writing it – would have been considerably impoverished without him.

My agent, Peter Robinson, and publisher, Simon Winder, have been patient beyond belief and the team at Penguin (particularly Jennifer Munka, Sophie Wright, Claire Pollak, Jennie Todd and Cormac Kinsella) have been a pleasure to work with. My thanks also to Oula Jones for the index.

But I owe more than I can ever repay to my immediate family: to my son Marc, for all those missed childhood experiences, and most of all to my husband Trevor, for all the times that he did the chores to let me write, or had to forgo holidays because I had no time, and most of all for his love and sense of humour and for making me laugh even on the dark days.

Prologue

'Whatever you say, say nothing'

(Ulster saying)

I still consider myself an Ulster Catholic, for that was the tradition into which I was born and in which I was raised and educated until the age of eighteen. I have always felt different from Catholics elsewhere in Ireland and this is a common feeling among Ulster Catholics. Yet I have found them consistently neglected in the histories of Ireland and of Irish Catholicism in particular, as if Irishness and Catholicism so dominated their sense of themselves that they could be safely included with all other Irish Catholics. The assumption is that Ulster is primarily Protestant. Had this been so, we would not have been left with that overwhelming insecurity which is such a feature of the Ulster personality, or such daily agonising over culture and identity. By the second half of the nineteenth century Catholics were in a small majority in Ulster. On the eve of partition they remained at 43.7 per cent and today (from the most recent 1991 census) account for 38 per cent. To a considerable degree their modern identity has been shaped by the Ulster Protestants and not always in a simple oppositional way. They needed a separate history which located them firmly in Ulster.

I have chosen to define them as 'Ulster' Catholics because it accurately describes that cultural and religious grouping for most of the period covered in this book. In addition, four-fifths of the book deals with the centuries before the state of Northern Ireland came into existence. However, I recognise that few Catholics today would admit to an 'Ulster' identity. Indeed, some go even farther in rejecting the very term 'Northern Ireland', dismissively calling the state the 'Six

Counties', with all its connotations of incompleteness and illegitimacy. In the recent past they disliked the way in which Unionists flaunted the term 'Ulster', when the new northern state contained only six of the so-called 'historic' nine counties (Cavan, Monaghan and Donegal having been included with the southern state). So they chose to reject it, except, pointedly, for all-Ireland occasions such as Gaelic Athletic Association sports fixtures. It is one of the many terms by which one can still identify the cultural and religious identity of the speaker in Northern Ireland. It is surely high time for Ulster Catholics to re-assert their regional identity and challenge the view that 'Ulster' necessarily means Protestant.

Conversely, I have opted on most occasions to use the name 'Derry' for both the city and county rather than the more politically correct 'Derry/Londonderry', except when the context dictates otherwise. I do so in the knowledge that County 'Londonderry' is technically more correct, since the county only came into existence after the seventeenth-century Ulster Plantation and was called after the London companies to whom it had been transferred. More than any place name, this one traditionally singles out Catholic from Protestant, for Catholics consider the ancient monastic site of Derry (Doire) as peculiarly theirs and seldom use the 'London' prefix. But since I am writing about the Catholics, it makes sense to adopt their terminology. Besides, I am beginning to tire of those mental contortions required before saying anything about Northern Ireland. We would like to believe that it is because we do not wish to offend. But there are equally valid and less complimentary explanations, including an effort to disguise our own background or to fathom that of others.

I have found this book very painful to write, not because the experience of Ulster's Catholics has been the doom-laden one of nationalist tradition, though there was enough of that to dispel any idea of this image as pure mythology, but because I have discovered in myself lingering prejudices and sensitivities which I either believed I had left far behind or never recognised in the first place, and I know that I am not alone. I do not subscribe to the belief voiced by many public figures associated with Northern Ireland that we must leave the past behind. The mistrust, prejudices and fears which lay behind the recent Troubles and many earlier periods of conflict have existed for a very long time and are unlikely to disappear overnight. I now know why I viewed the Bible College behind my school bus-stop as sinister, why I tagged certain areas and towns as Protestant or Catholic and felt uncomfortable in the former, why I, like my community, was instinctively anti-Scottish and anti-English, when I had no direct experience of either. I have since learnt that few people conform to stereotypes.

Although I was born in County Down, near Strangford, my family moved shortly afterwards to Belfast, my father's home city. We had moved to a new housing estate on the edge of North Belfast. Surrounded by fields rolling down from the Cave Hill and overlooking the sea, the White City never quite felt like urban living. The beauty of Belfast's setting has often figured in writings by its authors, a poignant contrast to the living conditions and sectarianism in the streets below, a form of escapism allowing that deep love of the place which I noted in my father and which I have retained, even through the Troubles. It is a love often heightened by a sense of embattlement, and I have noted similar feelings in the people of Liverpool, where I work.

The White City in the late 1940s was something of a new beginning in Northern Ireland, and so indeed it was remembered by my parents. The Northern Ireland government had a poor record in the provision of housing for its people and the Belfast blitz of 1941 highlighted the serious over-crowding and inadequate housing of the city. The White City was one of the model estates of the post-war Housing Trust, a body which has won general acclaim for its record in supplying affordable housing and allocating it on a non-sectarian basis. In our corner of the estate there were three Catholic families and five Protestant, just about reflecting the religious make-up of the population then. Large tracts of North Belfast and adjacent areas in those days were genuinely mixed religion. The jaggedness of sectarianism impinged rarely enough to be truly memorable. But in general one knew the codes of behaviour and said nothing to upset in mixed company. That perhaps was the problem. The undercurrents were always there, but suppressed in the interests of good neighbourliness. I recall, as a teenager, my first experience of what I now recognise as a particular characteristic of Ulster humour: using Ulster Catholics' and Protestants' stereotyped views of each other to induce laughter and a more relaxed atmosphere.

But it was a very long time indeed before I could do this myself and even now it does not come naturally. I am angered that I still have a habit of treading carefully in conversation with people in and from Northern Ireland, instinctively seeking out the tell-tale clues to their background before I can totally relax. And yet, when that point comes, it is so refreshing, so much we have in common. I am glad to say that younger generations – many who have grown up entirely in the Troubles – are much less reticent on such matters. On the downside, there are many other areas of Northern Ireland life which are very much worse. Today the White City is a loyalist stronghold, one of the many mixed neighbourhoods which fell victim to the polarisation of the Troubles, one of the latest (1999) to acquire a peace 'wall' (for which read 'barricade'), dividing it off from Catholics on the Whitewell Road. Those streets, where I used to play and walk safely, have become another sectarian frontier zone.

There was genuine friendship and total mixing of the children at play then. But we went to different churches (often several times a week), different schools (the uniforms publicly proclaiming our religion from an early age) and attended different social functions, more often than not associated with our church. By the time we had become teenagers, the childhood friendships had given way to ones with class-mates of our own religion. My family read the *Irish News* (the Catholic daily newspaper), bought southern papers outside Sunday mass, had a Catholic GP (even though there were others much closer), never voted in elections, and, like thousands of other Catholic families, took our summer holidays south of the border. For the mandatory 12 July shut-down, then as now, was the Orangemen's marching season, and as the estate became festooned with Union Jacks, it took on a new character. Admittedly we had more reason to go south than most, for my mother came from County Kerry. It meant that I was more familiar with every other province in Ireland than my own. Long summer days spent in Counties Antrim and Down (straddled by the city of Belfast) created a great affinity with the people and landscape of these areas, while the largely rural territory west of Lough Neagh and the River Bann seemed like a foreign country.

I was cured of much of my early prejudice by my first experience of working with Ulster Protestants and English and Scottish people. With many of my schoolfriends, I applied for holiday work to the newly opened British Home Stores in Belfast. The 'Religion?' portion of the application form and the very term 'British' interacted with my prejudices to convince me that no Catholic would be hired. In fact, we were all offered jobs. I learnt that the Protestant stereotype of the untrustworthy and lazy Catholic, about which our parents' generation had heard so much, was here turned on its head, for we found that our new 'British' employers thought quite the contrary.

After attending Catholic primary and grammar schools in north Belfast, I went up to Queen's University in Belfast in 1967 to study History and (in the first and second years of a four-year degree) I also took French and Scholastic Philosophy. Of course, the choice of the latter instantly marked me out as Catholic, for the Department had been created in response to a successful campaign to create separate Catholic teaching programmes in controversial subjects. But there was no obviously Catholic bias in the programme and, throughout my years at Queen's, I never experienced any sectarianism whatsoever. It is unlikely that I, the other members of my family or indeed very large numbers of Ulster Catholics would have gone through higher education without Queen's University and the grants provided by the Northern Ireland Ministry of Education. We were in a much more privileged position than the bulk of University students today. It was the time of Terence O'Neill's premiership and the civil rights marches and I remember a new optimism in the air. I think O'Neill was a courageous man, ahead of his time. I also remember one of his major critics, Bernadette Devlin, as an inspiring student leader and was saddened that her talents, alike with those of so many other Catholics, were lost in Ulster's sectarian undercurrents.

Although in this book I am critical of the Catholic Church when I believe it has deserved criticism, I do not remember an occasion when the clergy were not there for their flock at times of need. The authoritarianism of the Catholic Church in Ireland generally (and in Ulster in particular, because of the prevailing lower social status of Ulster Catholics after the seventeenth century) was a late development. It has not always worked in the interests of either the Church itself or its people and it played into the hands of those who never wanted to see Catholics in power in any event. The Church's dislike of internal criticism through the ages, its ethos of endurance, submissiveness and guilt has tended to crush initiative and individuality. There *is* something in the Ulster Protestant tendency to assume a herd-like mentality in Catholics. But the Church has never been able to take its people where they did not want to go and it gave much-needed leadership in the absence of a secular one in past centuries. For better or worse, it has played a major role in fashioning Catholic identity.

However, that other perception of Catholicism as some kind of dangerous conspiracy, with Rome at its head, is entirely misconceived. This most conformist of religions has sought rather to belong to the system and I have highlighted a number of occasions in past centuries where failure to so involve leading Catholics in the state structure (a resistance often insultingly expressed) not only transferred that leadership to the clergy and turned the Catholic community into a state within a state, but also created that sense of alienation and victimhood which deterred criticism of the Church and upon which militant nationalism was to feed. The post-1999 power-sharing executive is what most Catholics would have settled for in the past. But reasonable demands have a tendency to increase when resisted and only time will tell whether this is what they will settle for in the future.

But this is not a book about the Catholic Church. It is about the people who have called themselves Catholics, about their culture and sense of identity, about their relationship with people in the rest of the island and, above all, with their immediate neighbours: the Protestants and Presbyterians of Ulster. It is important to recognise that Ulster Catholics have been on the losing side for most of the past four centuries, and that the almost complete loss of the top tier of Catholic leadership, and progressive loss of land to Protestants from the time of the Ulster Plantation, placed them on a lower social and economic level than most of their co-religionists elsewhere on the island. From this it was perhaps predictable that the images of the downtrodden and dispossessed Gael or feckless 'taig' (depending on one's religion) established themselves several centuries ago. But the common assumption that Ulster Catholics are pure Gaels is wrong, as I have argued in the main body of the book, even though the association of Gaelic culture and Catholic religion from the time of the Reformation is accurate enough.

This is why I have felt it so necessary to go back to the very earliest of times when Catholics, strictly speaking, did not exist. I am very aware of how controversial this will be and of the centuries-old 'slanging match' (it can scarcely be dignified by the term 'debate') between Protestantism and Catholicism as to which was the true heir of Christ. However, it made no sense to commence this study at the end of the Gaelic order (1603–7), for Ulster was then the most Gaelic province in Ireland and Gaelic traditions were subsumed into Catholic culture. A return to the earliest history (even the pre-history) of Ulster people is, I believe, also essential because of the nationalists' claim to racial purity. The related issue of my treatment of the Irish language requires some clarification. I have taken advice from a number of early Irish historians and on the whole used Old Irish spellings in the early chapters. Thereafter I have adopted Irish or anglicised versions of names according to which had most currency at the time and have used English translations of Irish-language sources throughout. Although the counties of Ulster were only created between 1570 and 1613, I have chosen to use their names also in preceding centuries to facilitate understanding of the location of the events discussed. I have taken a largely chronological approach in structuring the book, chapters broadly outlining political developments prefacing those dealing with the social, religious, cultural and economic issues of a given period.

Ulster's physical environment has played a significant part in the development and reinforcement of cultural identities. Its proximity to Scotland – visible from the north-east coast on most clear days – is immediately apparent. Even before the Ulster Plantation and subsequent population movements made Scottish Presbyterianism such a dominant influence in the province, Scots had been arriving and settling for many centuries. Antrim and Down have remained the most Protestant in the province (with Presbyterianism the largest Protestant denomination).

The eastern counties, along with Armagh, also contain the main concentration of urban dwellers and industry in the province. Pivotal to this has been the spectacular growth of Belfast over the past two centuries, from a small market-town of some 8,000 inhabitants in the eighteenth century, to around 400,000 (a quarter of the province's entire population) in the twentieth. Ulster Catholics in the past have had an ambivalent relationship with the city. Incorporated in 1613, it was then a Protestant settler town, and has remained an essentially Protestant city both in reality and in the perception of Catholics elsewhere in Ireland. In the eighteenth century Catholics accounted for only 8 per cent of its population, largely clustered on its western fringes (from where the Catholic west-Belfast enclave would later develop). By mid-nineteenth century they were 33 per cent of its population, the rapid influx of often poor rural Catholics in preceding decades forming the backdrop to the ugly sectarian riots for which Belfast has become notorious. Because of the recent Troubles, there are more areas in Belfast today which Catholics (notably working-class males) would find inhospitable, even dangerous. On the other hand, members of the fast-growing Catholic middle class are moving in large numbers into those areas which I would have considered posh and Protestant as a child.

Even east Ulster, however, like the rest of the province, is largely rural. The volcanic plateau, which covers most of County Antrim, drops sharply to the coast and is dissected by deep gulleys. The result is one of Europe's most scenic coastlines. But much of it is bleak and inaccessible, today's coastal road – the product of a public works scheme of the Great Famine – only opening it to the outside world in the middle of the nineteenth century. Its remoteness locked in older traditions and, like other hillier and remote areas, the Glens of Antrim were and have remained a traditionally Catholic and nationalist area – though the county as a whole is largely Protestant.

In contrast County Down, south and east of Belfast, has a landscape of rolling, fertile countryside, home in past centuries to some of Ireland's most influential landed gentry. But the south and south-west of the county is more varied topographically, with the Mountains of Mourne rising to 852 metres and a belt of lower mountains stretching into south Armagh. This – alike with much of south Ulster – is largely Catholic territory and was in the seventeenth and eighteenth centuries the haunt of bandits and escapees from the defeated Jacobite forces. South Ulster also has a distinctive drumlin topography – a wide belt of hummocky hills, small lakes and boggy hollows – stretching from County Down to the Atlantic coast of Sligo and Donegal, causing particular distortion on the borders of Cavan, Monaghan and Fermanagh, where it opens into larger lakes and gives this county the appearance of a water wonderland. It makes for difficult access and has been a cultural and defensive barrier since prehistoric times. These drumlins defined such 'border' areas for many centuries before political units emerged.

Another such barrier between east and west was the River Bann, connecting with the outsized Lough Neagh (some 24km in width, 48km in length). It was one of the reasons why the Anglo-Norman settlement of the eleventh and twelfth centuries was largely confined to Antrim and Down, and all but collapsed a century later. Ulster was to remain much less culturally diverse than most of the rest of the island, the strongest Gaelic area in Ireland until the defeat of the Ulster chieftains in 1603 and subsequent Ulster Plantation. This resulted in large tracts of six counties (Armagh, Tyrone, Cavan, Fermanagh, Derry and Donegal) being confiscated and settled with imported English and Scottish Protestants. The religious demography has altered very little since then. The religious map of Armagh would remain particularly significant: the low-lying fertile north assigned to Protestants, the rising and higher ground from mid to south to Irish Catholics. Armagh was left with a number of internal religious frontiers and potential flashpoint areas. It was the only Ulster county with near-numerical parity of Protestants and Catholics, leaving neither feeling secure. In general, as in Armagh, low-lying areas were occupied by Protestants, with notable corridors along the Bann, Foyle and Lagan river valleys, while political and economic factors over the centuries tended to concentrate Catholics in poorer upland areas. It is important to add, however, that not all Catholics were poor and not all Protestants rich. Indeed, the poor Protestant has tended to be forgotten in all the propaganda about the downtrodden Catholic and superior Protestant.

Because of a very general absence of natural woodland and an inhospitable weather pattern – with two-thirds of the province experiencing 225–250 raindays per year, the north-west in particular, battered by Atlantic gales – much of Ulster is covered by blanket bog, most notably Donegal, but also much of Derry, Tyrone, Fermanagh and Antrim. The broad mountainous band of the Sperrins, spanning north Tyrone and south Derry, does not relieve this sense of barrenness, for even its highest point, Sawel Mount (683 metres), is flattish and bog-covered, and the Glenshane Pass, through which travellers from the east must access Derry City, is notoriously the first road to be closed in adverse weather. Although Tyrone has long been something of a religious patchwork quilt (with Protestant majorities in the south, east and west) the Sperrins area has remained largely Catholic, its inaccessibility, as with the Glens of Antrim, locking in old traditions. With Fermanagh, Tyrone has had a marginal Catholic majority, making for very close electoral contests between Nationalists and Unionists. County Derry has had a small Protestant majority. Derry City was, like Belfast, very much a Protestant town at the outset, incorporated in 1613 as part of the Ulster Plantation. Because it was a defensively walled town and because of its lengthy and successful resistance to Jacobite (Catholic) attack at the close of the seventeenth century, it has been considered as something of a siege city. As working-class Catholics began to arrive in large numbers from Donegal in the early nineteenth century (giving Derry a Catholic majority by 1851) that siege mentality intensified. Catholics clustered on the Donegal side of the city, in the Bogside and outside the city walls. The city has long had a dual personality, the Donegal side exercising a powerful emotional pull for many of its Catholic populace.

Donegal, like Monaghan and Cavan, has long had a Catholic major-ity, and on this crude numerical basis all three counties were joined with the south in 1920. But they all retained significant Protestant populations (as much as a quarter in Donegal) on the eve of partition. The magical mountainscape and Atlantic coastline of Donegal has made it a favourite holiday destination for many Ulster people. But its barren and boggy soil also made it the poorest county in Ulster, its people figuring prominently in the seasonal search for work in Scotland and travelling to the hiring fairs in Tyrone well into the twentieth century. The western parts of Donegal have remained Irish-speaking, even though the language had all but died out elsewhere in the province by the middle of the nineteenth century.

The boundary of Ulster has been something of a moveable feast in the two thousand years or so covered in this book. I have accordingly followed the political definition of the province current at a given period, so that Cavan, Monaghan and Donegal are included in my discussion until partition, alike with some areas of north Leinster and north Connacht which have had common experiences. After 1920, however, my analysis is largely confined to the six counties of Northern Ireland.

In 1992–3 I was invited to serve on the independent Opsahl Commission in Northern Ireland, headed by the international human rights lawyer, Torkel Opsahl. It was the brainchild of the then editor of the current affairs magazine *Fortnight,* Robin Wilson, and Queen's University law professor, Simon Lee, and was one of the early landmarks in the current peace process. There were particular years in the Troubles when raw sectarianism overflowed into random assassinations, and this was one of them. Inter-party talks had just broken down, and with every initiative seemingly exhausted there was a very widespread sense of helplessness. The Commission sought to give everyone involved in and with Ulster the chance to talk, even if it produced no infallible blueprint for peace, and talk they did: a huge range of people, pacifists and paramilitaries, unemployed and executives, schoolchildren and teachers, clergy and voluntary workers, and a lot of what is often termed 'ordinary' people. There was not much of the naked hatred that outsiders have come to associate with the province, but a lot of mutual fear, suspicion and misunderstanding. We concluded that Ulster's problems were very largely internal to the communities themselves, that the desire for peace was overwhelming, but that securing it required an examination of the roots of their mistrust and a more honest acceptance of responsibility. I hope that this book will be a small contribution to that process.

I

FROM CÚ CHULAINN TO CHRISTIANITY: RELIGION AND SOCIETY IN EARLY ULSTER

'In the days when this took place there was in those parts a great king, a fierce pagan . . . by name Loíguire son of Níall . . . He had around him sages and druids, fortune-tellers and sorcerers . . . [who] prophesied frequently that a foreign way of life was about to come to them, a kingdom, as it were, with an unheard of and burdensome teaching, brought from afar, over the seas, enjoined by few, received by many; it would . . . seduce the crowds, destroy all their gods, banish all the works of their craft, and reign for ever . . . And so it happened afterwards: when Patrick came the worship of idols was abolished and the catholic Christian faith spread over our whole country.'

Muirchú, *Life of St Patrick*, seventh century AD
(Deane, ed., *Field Day Anthology*, i, 78–9)

1. Pre-Christian Ulster

Prehistoric man arrived in Ulster around 7000 BC and settled along the sea and lake shores, in the valley of the Bann, around Lough Neagh and the Antrim coast, later extending to Strangford Lough and the Inishowen peninsula. Defended by a band of hummocky drumlins,[1] interspersed with boggy marshes and lakes, human settlements in prehistoric Ulster were lost amidst primeval Atlantic forests and a carpet of prickly vegetation. Man made no catastrophic alteration to the landscape, its very inhospitality becoming part of outsiders' perception of its people: romantic and mysterious to primitivists, barbaric and threatening to those seeking to subdue it. Its multitude of tiny kingdoms defied easy conquest and its final subjugation in the seventeenth century was ironically facilitated by the novel, if unstable, political unity achieved under Hugh O'Neill.

The Mesolithic hunter-gatherers who first inhabited the province have left their mark in archaeological finds around the coast, lakes and river valleys. But our knowledge of this uncharted period is poor and uncertain. It was thought until recently that these northern arrivals were the first inhabitants of Ireland and that they had travelled over land-bars from Scandinavia and Scotland. This is no longer accepted by archaeologists as certain, despite the land-bar theory being well represented in Irish mythology, and the heaviest distribution of Meso-lithic sites and megalithic tombs from the Neolithic period (c.4000 BC onwards) being in the northern part of Ireland.[2] To argue any cultural distinctiveness from these times before written records, however, would be impossible. Early Ulster man was well travelled and receptive to outside influences. As he entered history, he was already a mongrel.

By around 4000 BC Ulster had acquired its pastoral economy. But evidence of domestic and communal life is elusive. Survivals come rather in the form of sophisticated burial tombs and suggest well-developed religious cults long before Christianity. When Celtic-speaking peoples emerged as a distinctive entity in Europe or when they arrived in Ireland is a matter of some controversy.[3] However, despite some speculation that Ireland may have received large numbers of Celtic Gauls fleeing before the Roman invasions, the introduction of the more famous La Tène Celtic culture in the first century BC is thought to have come from Britain and Scotland.

In the 1940s, T. F. O'Rahilly put forward an elaborate schema for the arrival of successive waves of Celtic peoples in Ireland.[4] The first he identified as the Cruithin. Since they were also found in Scotland, they have been used by some Ulster Protestants to create an origin legend, separate and apparently older than the equally spurious claim that the Catholics are the pure descendants of the Gaels.[5] However, we simply do not know the origins of any people during Ireland's Iron Age.[6] Although the predominance of court tombs in Ulster suggests some element of cultural and regional distinctiveness, they are inter-mixed with other varieties which show substantial links with other parts of Ireland, notably the south-east. There is little agreement on whether the Ulster peoples of this age arrived from continental Europe via the Atlantic and western route, or through northern England and Scotland. But scholars now dismiss the idea of waves of invasion displacing one people by another, preferring to explain cultural change by contact with other countries. The names Cruithin, Ulaid and Érainn represented ruling dynasties, their territorial and military power based on confederations. Prehistoric Ireland was a considerable racial mix. Other parts of Ireland besides Ulster shared populations with Britain. In truth, little is certain about this period before written records. The fact remains, however, that, whatever the origins of the inhabitants of Ireland, Ulster, with the rest of the island, became thoroughly Celticised in language and social institutions half a millennium before Christ and remained so until early modern times.

But it is the Ulaid who dominate the sagas transmitted by the medieval writers to the future and who gave their name to the province. In the *Ulidian Tales* or *Ulster Cycle*, with their legendary hero Cú Chulainn, and their royal centre at Emain Macha (Navan Fort in County Armagh) the Ulaid have left one of the most striking records of

Celtic society. Though largely mythological and bearing the hyperbolic mark of generations of storytelling before it was committed to writing in the seventh century, the *Ulster Cycle* has come to epitomise Ireland's heroic age. It tells of the Ulaid king Conchobar (Conor) mac Nessa and his champions, the youthful hero, Cú Chulainn, Fergus mac Róich, his foster-father, and Conall Cernach, his foster-brother. Each is inexorably pulled along by his heroic destiny, doomed by irrational codes of honour to kill those whom they love most. It is also a tale of strong and passionate women: the vampish and ruthless Medb (Maeve) of the enemy Connachta, the faithful Émer, who was to die for love of Cú Chulainn, and the heroine who was to exercise most influence on modern Irish writing, the tragic Deirdriu (Deirdre).

She is a woman of startling beauty whose fate as destructress – 'a woman over whom there will be great slaughter' – was foretold at birth. Destined to wed Conchobar, she leaves him for love of Noíse, son of Uisliu, and goes into exile with him and his brothers. Enticed back by an offer of immunity from Conchobar, Deirdriu commits suicide after Conchobar has the sons of Uisliu murdered. Fergus takes 3,000 warriors into exile with the Connachta, in protest at such treachery. Thus is set the scene for the centrepiece of the *Ulster Cycle* and perhaps the most important tale in Irish literature, the *Táin Bó Cuailnge* (Cattle Raid of Cooley). The *Táin* recounts an episode in the long wars waged by the Connachta against the northern province. The conflict centres on the Boyne valley in County Meath.

It is an aristocratic warrior society, in which the traditional Irish preoccupation with lineage is already present – boastful, heroic, hospitable, much given to feasting and drunkenness, fine music and long stories. But it was only in raids and warfare that their aristocratic values could be measured and demonstrated. The theme of the *Táin* concerns a cattle raid, and the main festivals of the ritual year – Beltaine and Samain – mark the beginning and the end of the grazing season. There may have been some thirty-five *tuatha* or petty kingdoms in Ulster, each with its king – chosen from the kin-group of his predecessor – its nobles, its free commoners and its unfree population. Larger units were brought into being by more powerful kings exchanging military protection for hostages and tributes. But the kin-group (those sharing a common great-grandfather, the *derbfine*) was the important unit of social control. Usually no one had any legal rights outside one's own *tuath*. There were no urban centres, no state institutions as such. Assemblies were held by the king at festival times, and kings proclaimed law and regulations to meet emergencies. But the law was for the most part customary, accurately committed to memory in the law schools, and applied and transmitted by learned lawyers, whose status was equal to that of the nobles and who held positions of great respect in this pre-literate society. With the poets and other learned men, they alone in Celtic society had free right of movement between *tuatha,* and were fundamental to the extraordinary unity of language and tradition in early Ireland. They remained an important and revered element in that society into modern times and the customs and laws they transmitted were central to its stability.

The people of pre-Christian Ulster generally lived in circular structures known as raths. Like the identical ring-forts elsewhere in Ireland, they are distinctive to the island. Some fifty to sixty thousand have survived throughout Ireland, and County Armagh alone contains three to four hundred.[7] Excavations show that they – like the similar crannog lake-dwellings – tended to be built over existing settlements, sometimes of great antiquity. Such continuity belies the image of constant conflict portrayed by the sagas, and excavations of these domestic structures, for example, show no sign of warlike activity.[8] Certainly these predominantly single-family farms appear to have had no military purpose, their circular earthworks designed to keep animals in or out. They are generally located just below the tops of low-lying hills and their very wide distribution throughout the province suggests a close relationship between dwelling and pasture, short-range transhumance determined by the geography. Ancient field patterns suggest small, perhaps less wealthy, even unfree, communities involved in arable farming and pooling resources.[9]

It is the more spectacular ringed enclosures or hill-forts, however, which have left their mark on Irish mythology, even if archaeological excavations limp a long way behind. Four prominent hill-forts have been identified in Ulster. Grianán of Ailech in County Donegal, Clogher in County Tyrone, Downpatrick in County Down, and most important of all, Emain Macha (Navan Fort) in County Armagh. With the exception of the first, however, even these have no obvious defensive purpose. Rather, the presence of Megalithic burial mounds within the enclosures suggests a ritual importance and ceremonial function. Certainly excavations of Emain Macha suggest as much. The tradition of Armagh as the religious capital of Ireland does not start with St Patrick. There is a high density of pagan artefacts in the north, with the heaviest concentration around Armagh – lending credence to the Patrician legend that he chose the site because it had been a pagan cult centre.

It was the recognised centre of Ulaid power, said to have been named after the horse-goddess, Macha, a site which even today is staggering in its grandeur. A massive circular edifice, built in timber over the site of earlier structures, Emain figures prominently in the Ulidian tales. It was the scene of the Ulaid's great celebrations, and artefacts found nearby – including a splendid ceremonial bronze trumpet, some 186cm in length – amply bear this out. Indeed, Celtic feasting was a topic of much fascination with the classical authors. An entire pig was said to be the reward for the most fêted warrior (the so-called 'champion's portion'), voracious appetites incongruously linked with strict etiquette and codes of hospitality. It is not without reason that some of the greatest acts of treachery noted in Irish mythology and folklore should have been associated with betrayals of traditional hospitality. The highlight of such festivities was provided by the musicians and the bards and the tradition of courtly eulogies survived as long as the Gaelic order itself.[10]

The imaginary world of the *Táin* depicts a high-spirited, excitable and recklessly brave warrior society, one that was almost childishly fond of adornment. In the *Táin Bó Cuailnge*, the three companies of Ulster exiles gather with the Connachta armies to march against the Ulaid. One company was distinguished by speckled cloaks, clipped hair, knee-length tunics and full-length shields; the second, by dark-grey, wrap-around cloaks and calf-length, red-embroidered tunics, swept-back hair and bright shields; the third, purple cloaks, red-embroidered, full-length tunics, shoulder-length hair and curved, scallop-edged shields. The longer the cloak, the greater the wealth and status of the wearer. Physical beauty is central to their idea of perfection, and parading it part of the ritual of war.[11]

This warrior aristocracy also believed the afterlife to be very much like the present and was buried with enough earthly chattels to tide them over. The location of the otherworld is very often associated with water, which may explain why so many artefacts have been found in the Shannon and Bann valleys, and the longstanding fascination with the outsized Lough Neagh (the largest freshwater lake in the British Isles). In the twelfth century Giraldus Cambrensis found Lough Neagh fishermen claiming to have seen the submerged towers of the horse-god Eochu, from whom the lake derived its name (Loch nEchach).[12] Early Irish religion, however, was very much of this life. The gods were polymorphic and prominent actors in Irish mythology. The entire emphasis was on ensuring the well-being of the *tuath*. The gods were highly localised and the importance and strict observance of ritual was deemed to tame them and ensure prosperity. The king was ritually married to the earth-goddess and the well-being of the territory taken as a sign of her endorsement of his reign. All the great festivals were likewise designed to enlist the supernatural on the side of earthly prosperity and their importance was such that all were assumed into the Christian calendar. One of the effects of such close linkage between this and the otherworld was a sense of the beauty and enjoyment of this life.[13] These gods and goddesses, however, are rarely benign – the male gods, giant, club-wielding figures, presiding over magical cauldrons; the goddesses treacherously alternating from beautiful maiden to frightful hag, predicting catastrophe. Irish paganism appears to have been as localised as its politics. Every district had its *síd* (hill or mound) another possible location of the otherworld.[14] But the pervasiveness of the deities, both for good and evil, is a token of the intermingling of the real and the divine, the natural and the supernatural which has always characterised Irish folk religion. It is no accident that the Irish word for fairies is *síde* (from *aés síde*, or people of the hill) for they were believed to reside in such hills.[15]

The historic division of Ireland into four provinces was already in place. A fifth, Mide – defining an area roughly coterminous with modern Meath and Westmeath – was an artificial creation by the Kings of Tara. During the ascendancy of the Ulaid (450 BC to AD 324), according to the pseudo-historical dating of the medieval chronicles,[16] the boundary of Ulster seems to have fluctuated between a line from the modern counties of Donegal, Fermanagh, Monaghan, Armagh and

Down, to one taking in Leitrim, Cavan, Louth, Longford and parts of
Meath and Westmeath. The events of the *Táin* show 'the border
country' well defined by natural phenomena and in people's minds by
the time it came to be written down. The 'province boundary' –
traditionally extending from the River Drowes in the west, to the
Boyne in the east – was guarded from Slíabh Fuait (the Fews mountain,
between Dundalk and Armagh), protecting the route to Emain. 'Each
of Ulster's heroic warriors had his day on Slíab[h] Fuait, to take care
of every man who came that way with poetry, and to fight any others.'[17]
It may have been reinforced by earthworks, thought to have predated
Hadrian's Wall and popularly known as the Black Pig's Dyke. Surviving folk traditions tell of a monstrous black pig tearing up the earth
and disappearing into the sea. Sometimes the story is associated with
the defence of Ulster. But usually it has assumed portents of war to
come, and in modern times has even been linked to predicted sectarian
attacks.[18] Known to have been erected at the same time as Emain
Macha around 100 BC, it runs across south Ulster, from Armagh to
Donegal. Historically such earthworks appear to have been linked to
a series of attacks on Ulster, the similar Dorsey and Dane's Cast of
County Armagh acting as secondary lines of defence of the route to
Emain Macha.[19]

Although the jewel of the Ulster Cycle, the *Táin Bó Cuailnge* portrays the Ulaid already in decline. The *Táin* recounts an episode in the
long wars waged against the northern province by the Connachta,
centred on Meath and the Boyne valley, the location of the conflict of
the *Táin*, and the Black Pig earthworks. It is for the Uí Néill, sprung
from the Connachta, that the most elaborate and entirely fictitious
origin legend was created by the Christian compilers of the *Lebor
Gabála* or *Book of Invasions*. They were said to have been a Goidelic
(Gaelic) people. In fact, we have no real evidence of the ethnic origins
of these dynasties. The term Goidelic more accurately describes the
Irish form of the Celtic language, although it was in usage as an ethnic
term by the eighth century.[20] However, the ascendancy of the Ulaid,
and with it their capital at Emain, was destroyed around the time of
the introduction of Christianity in the fifth century AD. The Ulaid were
henceforth largely confined to the small kingdom of Dál Fiatach (most
of eastern County Down), their kinsmen to Dál Riata (north Antrim).

The Cruithin were organised into the two sub-kingdoms of Dál nAraide (around Belfast Lough), and Uí Echach Cobo (central and west Down). This area east of the Bann acquired the general denomination of Ulidia. According to later historical speculation, the three sons of Niall of the Nine Hostages, King of Tara – Eóghan, Conall and Enda – set up kingdoms approximately covering Donegal, Derry and Tyrone. Two, Cenél Conaill and Cenél nEógain, later rose to prominence. Thus came into being the northern Uí Néill. In central and south Ulster were a number of vassal states, collectively known as the Airgialla (Oriel) – the group of ruling families now governing much of Armagh, Tyrone, Monaghan and later Fermanagh and including many from the midlands who had fought with Niall. As written history commences with the arrival of Christianity in the fifth century AD, Ireland is almost completely Gaelic in speech. So commenced the golden age of Gaelic Ireland, which would endure until the Norse invasions.

2. The historiography of pre-Christian Ireland[21]

In the realm of prehistory nothing is certain. Oral traditions were probably not written down till the seventh century AD, and the earliest written version of the *Táin* to survive dates from the eleventh century. Taming the past to suit the present is a process not unique to Ireland. Even so, the humanising of pagan gods to create fictitious dynastic ancestors or the portrayal of a golden Celtic age has had a particularly long history in Ireland. In this process the *Ulster Cycle* holds a special place. It was the most highly developed of all the mythological tales – possibly, as Robin Flower suggests, because they were first written down in Ulidian territory at the great monastic house of Bangor – and enjoyed considerable prestige into the Middle Ages. Although some scholars now think that the tales of the *Ulster Cycle* may have contained some genuine oral traditions and may well have initially been compiled by Ulaid literati, they can no longer be accepted as the reliable 'window on the Iron Age' that they once were.[22] However, their idealised picture of early Irish society as wedded to its land and its traditions was to exercise a powerful influence over future generations.[23]

Although that other great epic of Finn and the Fianna has enjoyed more popular appeal because of its lyrical romanticism, the *Ulster Cycle* became the perfect symbol of Ireland's glorious past. Its portrait of a heroic and aristocratic society was particularly adapted to rebut accusations of savagery and barbarism, which characterised English accounts from Giraldus Cambrensis onwards. By the early sixteenth century the Ulidian tales had long been out of fashion. In seventeenth-century poetry – after the destruction of the Gaelic order – they reappear in the bardic lament for a golden age when the poets moved in royal circles. 'They [the English] will be in our places', writes the late seventeenth-century poet Ó Bruadair, 'thick-hipped, mocking, after beating us from the flower of our towns . . . English-speaking, cosy, tasteful . . . [They are now] where Deirdre . . . Emer and the Liath Macha (Cú Chulainn's grey steed) used to be'.[24]

On the whole, however, the *Ulster Cycle* was 'a rediscovery of the romantic period', as Patrick Rafroidi has put it, a period when Catholic emancipation was the main issue of the day and when liberals generally saw the Celtic past as a period capable of reconciling all sides. In presenting the past to an English audience, its sophistication and aristocratic nature had much to recommend it. The intensity and violence of the *Ulster Cycle* did not lend itself easily to romantic primitivism. Yeats and Lady Gregory hoped to harness its energy to a new heroic present and, with Standish O'Grady, were largely responsible for the revival and survival of the Cú Chulainn myth. But it was perhaps predictable that its intensity would make the perfect vehicle for Patrick Pearse's fusion of heroic action and Christ-like sacrifice and that Cú Chulainn should have become the back-stage actor in the 1916 rising. It was used by O'Grady to argue that the qualities which advanced the North far beyond that of the rest of the island lay in its Gaelic past rather than its importation of Scottish and English settlers in the seventeenth century.[25]

O'Grady and other writers of Ireland's late-nineteenth-century literary revival were particularly interested in promoting the image of an organic link between an ancient Irish civilisation and a haunted landscape, such that it is sometimes difficult to disentangle later nationalism's tendency to associate mysterious landscape with ancient culture from genuine folk survivals. Indeed, Sinn Féin early last century made south Armagh's Slieve Gullion – overlooking the route to Emain Macha – a special place of pilgrimage. Suffice it to say that there is a wealth of Ulster folk material linking key figures from the *Ulster Cycle* with features of the landscape, features to which modern Catholic traditions often lay particular claim in the widespread (though largely unproven) belief that theirs is a culture rooted in a more ancient tradition than that of Protestantism.[26]

3. The arrival of Christianity

As Ireland emerges into history in AD 431, much of the world reflected in the heroic tales had already passed. A new order of things was emerging which would survive until the Normans. Fundamental to this was the arrival of Christianity. It is the only example in western history of Christianity establishing itself in a culture untouched by Roman conquest. As elsewhere, it did so by adapting to that culture, thereby preserving many of its features. It introduced a notional unity just when the political concept of High Kingship was itself developing and the two became mutually supportive. As early as the seventh century AD, St Patrick had been accepted as the country's saint and Armagh was promoting its claim to be its religious capital.

Patrick was the son of a minor Roman noble living somewhere in north-west Britain. At sixteen he was captured by a raiding party from Ireland and spent the next six years in slavery. Why Patrick's name became associated with the religious centre at Armagh is as mysterious as almost everything else about his life. There are suggestions that it occurred before the destruction of Emain Macha and it was common for early Christian bishops to seek the patronage of local rulers. This would explain the need of early Christian hagiography to invoke Cú Chulainn, the Ulaid's legendary hero, and Patrick's associations with Downpatrick, new capital of the Ulaid after they were defeated and forced east of the Bann.[27] Despite the seventh-century hagiographic lives of Patrick, depicting him moving about the country, converting huge numbers, anointing bishops, performing miracles and everywhere conquering paganism, the earlier establishment of Christianity in the south of Ireland seems to have come mainly from non-Patrician sources. It was another two centuries before Christianity became firmly established in Ireland and Patrick himself tells of early resistance. Indeed, the traditions of the bullish saint who could do no wrong are less than the man. In the two authentic documents left by Patrick – his *Confession* and *Letter to Coroticus* – he reveals himself as more than willing to accommodate native ways, provided they did not openly conflict with Christ's teachings.[28] It was to be the key to Christianity's remarkable success in Ireland. There are no martyrs in the history of early Irish Christianity. Giraldus in the twelfth century considered this a weakness, symptomatic of his notion of the general laxity of the Irish church, though he appreciated the barbed witticism of one Irish bishop's response that his own people, the Anglo-Normans, would soon change that. The Irish 'have always paid great honour and reverence to churchmen, and they have never put out their hands against the saints of God. But now a people has come to the kingdom which knows how, and is accustomed, to make martyrs. From now on Ireland will have its martyrs, just as other countries.'[29]

In later centuries both Protestants and Catholics claimed the early Irish church as their own. The former argued that the early Irish church was free from Roman control until imposed by Henry II in the twelfth century, that it was therefore never really 'Roman' Catholic in any significant sense and that the Reformation church was simply attempting to return it to its primitive purity.[30] Certainly Patrick's mission seems to have been unofficial and entirely British in origin and support. Indeed, he was frowned upon by other ecclesiastics as some kind of vulgar itinerant. Charges of unworthiness he readily admitted and he was desperately anxious to explain his conduct in Ireland to his fellow clerics in Britain. Claims for loose ties with Rome are accurate enough for the very early church. However, the collapse of the Roman Empire elsewhere caused Irish Christianity to be isolated for several centuries. But if native peculiarities were the result, historians have identified a strong emotional attachment between the early Irish church and Rome and a sense of belonging to one church with Rome as its head.[31] In the seventh century, Armagh successfully used native and Roman law to establish its primacy, interlinking its claims with those of the Uí Néill to the High Kingship, on the one hand, and to Rome's claims to be the final appeal court in Christendom on the other. Central to its case was the active promotion of the cult of Patrick (despite the embarrassing tradition of his burial at Downpatrick). It was then that the popular image emerged of Patrick the all-conquering hero, outwitting the druids and securing submission from Lóegaire, king of Tara (though given his patronage by the Ulaid, this could never have been the case).

It is unlikely that a Roman-type episcopacy, based on Roman administrative centres, would have succeeded in Ireland and, although bishops played an important role in the early Irish church, it was to develop largely as a monastic and rural organisation until the reforms of the twelfth century.[32] There was little in the way of parochial development until the time of the Normans, and later in Ulster, where Norman settlement was weak. The monasteries became important social centres, fulfilling many of the social functions normally associated with towns and attracting major settlements, lay and clerical alike, within their precincts. Monasticism accommodated Irish society's familial structure, and as Christianity gained ground, it became fashionable for the Irish aristocracy to help found monasteries on their family's land. But under Irish law, land could not be alienated from the family grouping without its consent, and so the tradition developed of monastic leadership and property being passed on naturally to the heirs of the founder. Abbots became the equivalent of territorial overlords, they were succeeded by their kin and family succession to land was guaranteed. The abbot was often elected from the family of the founder and the family retained that right of presentment for centuries.[33] Christianity did not fundamentally alter the existing social system. The communities settled in raths, crannogs and cashels (e.g. Nendrum in modern County Down) and the Irish monastic tradition of living in small huts rather than monastic houses was such that the introduction of great monasteries with the Cistercians in the twelfth and thirteenth centuries was frowned upon as un-Irish.[34] They followed Irish rather than continental rules that mirrored the diverse local traditions in which they operated. Far from opposing pagan survivals, they often simply Christianised them. They Christianised the native practice of fasting to enforce unmet claims.[35] Pagan festivals became feastdays, pagan deities Christian saints. The saints took over the druidical weapon of malediction, assumed responsibility for bestowing hospitality and holding public assemblies. The early saints' lives written in the seventh and eighth centuries reflected many barely Christianised beliefs. Qualities hailed by heroic societies are uppermost; miracles replace magic, litanies druidical incantations. Christianity had gone native. The saints, bishop-abbots and monks were members of royal houses. It is they who were responsible for collating and writing the country's history, traditions and laws.[36]

For, most of all, the saints took over the mantle of the learned classes and in Irish law the clerics enjoyed the same respect as the *file* (poets) and equal social status with the kings of *tuaths*. They were not only tolerant of Irish secular learning, they took most of it over. They created a new Irish identity by constructing the genealogies, sagas and tales of early medieval Irish literature. By the seventh century the early Irish church had become a deeply integrated one. In the new writings the heroes of the past are summoned from the dead to bear witness. Christianity has become the heir to native traditions.[37] By the eighth century, poet, cleric and king are represented as co-operating in the compilation of that great body of Irish law, the *Senchas Már*. The sixth to ninth centuries are recognised as Ireland's 'Golden Age'. As early as the sixth century, the monastic schools acquired a reputation for learning and Bede tells of many students being attracted from Britain by their reputation. Over the next two centuries many had developed highly professional scriptoria and the golden age of monasticism arrived the following century with the epitome of the successful combination of native and Christian: the illuminated manuscripts.

It is no accident that the earliest written chronicles, annals and vernacular poetry should have originated in south-east Ulster, or that some of the earliest recorded sagas are dominated by the Ulaid, by now a declining dynasty. For it was on Ulidian territory that the great monasteries of St Comgall at Bangor and St Finnian at Movilla actively cultivated vernacular literature and educated or influenced many of the leading scholars and saints of the period. In the *Book of Invasions* or *Book of the Taking of Ireland* (the *Lebor Gabála*) – the most influential of the narrative pseudo-histories, compiled between the eighth and twelfth centuries – a holy man is said to have come to Finnian. He claimed to be of the royal house of Ulaid and to have lived through many lives and shapes, witnessing the entire history of Ireland, which he then related. Thus was born that tradition of genealogical and historical lore, which became standard teaching in the schools for centuries to come and which produced the mythology of the Milesian (Spanish) origin-myth of the Irish race, a myth of such durability that a special blood relationship with Spain was still being claimed as late as the eighteenth century.[38]

In Ulster Catholic tradition, however, it is Colum Cille (Columba, AD 521–97) rather than the national Patrick who emerges as symbolising their particular identity.[39] A member of the Uí Néill royal house and particularly associated with Donegal and Derry, Colum Cille represents the merger of the early church with Irish society. A bard in his own right, he is particularly remembered for having saved the bards from expulsion at the famous Convention of Druim Cett near Limavady in AD 575. He came to symbolise that attachment to nature and the land so characteristic of Gaelic poetry, and the sense of physical wrenching from that land through exile which was to form such a part of Irish nationalist tradition. For Colum Cille is said to have gone to war with Finnian in a dispute over possession of a copy of St Jerome's gospel and to have accepted permanent exile as penance. It is not surprising to find that it is Colum Cille, as a saint with human failings, rather than Patrick, who is invoked as the Catholics' vengeful ally in prophesying the destruction of the Protestant heretics during periods of sectarian conflict in Ulster.[40] Folk traditions of the native saint ready to avenge his people probably have good groundings in reality.[41]

Ulster's domination of early Irish learning had faded by the beginning of the eleventh century. Central to its passing was the eclipse of Bangor, almost certainly through the continued decline of its political patrons in Dál nAraide. But the process was hastened by the destructive Viking attacks from the eighth century onwards. Christianity was confidently established and monastic art and learning was at its height when the Vikings struck in AD 795. They raided the defenceless coastal monasteries, destroying the manuscripts and plundering the precious objects. Iona, Bangor, Downpatrick and Armagh were raided repeatedly. They sailed up the Bann, Foyle, and Boyne, raiding from Lough Neagh, Strangford and Carlingford Loughs. The northern kings fought back with considerable success. The Ulaid attacked victoriously in 811 and again in 825, and Viking encampments were finally destroyed in the north by the Uí Néill in 866.[42] Thereafter there were no Viking settlements north of Dublin, though the Dublin Norsemen continued to raid the northern coasts and lakelands well into the tenth century. But the monasteries never recovered their earlier character. Many more monks fled to the Continent. Scholars are still guessing at the many manuscripts destroyed and the art of illuminating manuscripts never revived. Although the campaign against the Vikings may have achieved a fragile political unity, ultimately it simply aggravated dynastic quarrels and prepared the way for the Normans.

4. Dynastic changes: eighth–twelfth centuries

From the time of St Patrick to the establishment of Brian Boru's claim to High Kingship in the early eleventh century, the political history of Ireland is dominated by the Uí Néill and their claims to dynastic overlordship were encouraged and legitimised by the church. From around the eighth century the terms *Leth Cuinn* and *Leth Moga* began to be used to describe Uí Néill and Eóganacht hegemony in the northern and southern halves of the country respectively. Later monastic writings gave prominence to dominant lines and the Irish practice of kingship and succession was already modified in a feudal direction before the Anglo-Norman invasion. The twelfth-century church reforms which introduced a diocesan organisation mirrored closely the territorial and political changes that had occurred. The monastic familia of the early Irish church reflected a society based on the small units of *tuatha* and family groupings. By the twelfth century provinces had replaced peoples as the essential political unit and the development of strong provincial kingships provides the backdrop to the diocesan reorganisation.[43]

The period witnesses constant pressure by ascending dynasties on older or declining ones. It was this pressure which was behind the expansion of Dál Riata into Scotland in the fifth century and they were overrun entirely by Dál nAraide in the eighth century. The Ulaid (now confined to east Down) had shared the kingship of Ulidia with the Cruithin of Dál nAraide (roughly occupying the southern two-thirds of Antrim, half of Down and north Louth) until 972 when they killed the last Cruithin king, Áed mac Loingsich. They had been helped by the attacks on Dál nAraide by Uí Thuirtri of the Airgialla, who by the twelfth century had replaced them as the dominant element in Antrim. By then, however, the Ulaid themselves no longer held any authority in Ulidia, much of which had been subsumed into the expanding overlordship of the Cenél nEógain.

In the eighth and ninth centuries, the Cenél nEógain branch of the northern Uí Néill emerged from a long struggle with their rival branch Cenél Conaill and expanded from their Donegal–Derry centre to take control of the mid-Ulster territories of the Airgialla and become High Kings of Ireland.[44] During the centuries of the Norse attacks, the annals also record a bewildering series of dynastic feuds in Ulster. As the tenth century opened, the climate deteriorated, food was scarce and comets appeared in the sky.

Great snow and cold and unprecedented frost, in this year, so that the chief lakes and rivers of Ireland were passable, which brought great havoc upon cattle, birds and fishes. Horrid signs besides. The heavens seemed to glow with comets.[45]

Internal feuding in the Uí Néill facilitated the rise of Brian Boru to the High Kingship and destroyed their centuries-old monopoly. Thereafter Ulster became increasingly isolated from the affairs of the rest of the country.

But the continued aggrandisement of the Cenél nEógain and their allies was bringing about significant changes in Gaelic society. There was a considerable narrowing of power at the top, and there are hints in the annals of a growing distance and hostility between upper and lower orders.[46] The idea of the *tuath* and its king as the essential unit was being eroded by the surge towards dynastic aggrandisement. Familial land is no longer sacrosanct; there is a growing territorialisation of the idea of kingship, power over property as well as peoples, and the Cenél nEógain's subjugation of the Ulaid included the alienation of large tracts of territory in a way which would have been unacceptable at an earlier period. The early Middle Ages thus witnessed the oft-repeated process in Irish history of subject-peoples being pushed down the social scale and on to less fertile land.[47] Notable too in this period was the tendency both of conquered and conquerer to simply assume the pedigrees of the more ancient peoples.[48] Falsification and confusion of genealogies became a matter for complaint by the poets, one complaining in 1150:

Bad brotherhood within the *túath*, iniquitous law and great arrogance in kings, the needy transitory king will subdue the miserable husbandman, . . . many judges without justice, sovranty destroyed by base kindreds.[49]

By the time of the Norman invasion in the twelfth century, it had become impossible to trace lineages with certainty to an ancient past.

One sign of this narrowing of power was the trend towards surnames from the eleventh century onwards, further separating dominant from inferior family groupings. Most notable is the emergence of the Ó Néill from Cenél nEógain and, over the next two centuries, their defeat and reduction of their once-dominant kinsmen, the Mac Lochlainns, to the status of minor lords in Inishowen. The Ó Catháin (O'Cahan) likewise emerged from the proliferation of Cenél nEógain families in this period and established themselves in north Derry. At the end of the twelfth century the Ó Dochartaigh (O'Doherty) rose to dominance from the internal feuding of Cenél Conaill, only to be replaced themselves as overlords by the Ó Domhnaill (O'Donnell) at the beginning of the following century. The pressure of the Uí Néill dynasties had greatly reduced Airgialla territory by the twelfth century to that roughly co-existent with Fermanagh, Monaghan, Armagh and part of Louth. The Ó Cerbaill (O'Carroll) dynasty were replaced as kings of Airgialla in the twelfth century by the Mac Mathgamna (MacMahon), who remained effective rulers of Monaghan to the end of the old order at the beginning of the seventeenth century. Their lineage could be traced back to AD 700. More dubious was the Airgialla descent claimed by the Fermanagh Mag Uidir (Maguires), who only emerged into history at the end of the thirteenth century. The Airthir of Armagh had been chief rivals to the O'Carrolls, but their power was eventually eclipsed by Uí Néill encroachments and the only branch to retain prominence into modern times were the O'Hanlons. Further east, only the Cruithin, Mag Aonghusa (Magennises), and their kinsmen the Mac Artáin (MacCartans) of Down survived the dynastic aggression of the pre-Norman age and the Anglo-Norman invasion of Ulster.

Such developments, however, were largely confined to the upper echelons of society and did not alter the lives of most people in these centuries. Apart from a general increase in tillage, Ulsterman lived much as he had done in the past. He was still largely engaged in raising livestock; his home was still a circular wooden structure, heated by central fires and as ill ventilated and smoke-filled as those still remarked on by the Williamite forces in the seventeenth century. In this, little differentiated the upper from the lower social levels, despite the enormous noble contempt for the lower orders. Slavery persisted into the twelfth century, and, as elsewhere, pagan survivals continued to be complained about by the church into modern times.

5. The Irish church on the eve of the Norman invasion

What was the nature of the Christianity bequeathed by Gaelic society? Giraldus complained of the absence of a pastoral mission in the Irish church of the twelfth century. It is one of the few areas in which his criticism is well founded. There is little evidence that the monasteries gave much priority to preaching or to the care of souls, whatever the genuine asceticism of some, particularly during the period of the Céili Dé (Culdee) movement of the eighth century (which practised strict self-sacrifice and also included reclusive anchorites).[50] But the twelfth-century reformers exaggerated the worldliness of the early Irish church. They underestimated the elements of genuine piety and, more importantly, the deep impact it had made on Irish society.[51] The simple fact is that the Irish church on the eve of the Norman conquest was a 'popular' one. It had accommodated pagan survivals and existing secular society and succeeded in turn in permeating the culture of that society on common ground.[52] The authors of the early saints' lives had consulted popular tradition, so that the images transmitted to future generations were very often those developed by Irish society in the eighth century. The saints are endowed with virtues esteemed by that society, not least of which is their role in providing hospitality and entertainment and in later times they were deemed to have blessed the merriment and festivities of the patrons' days (or patterns) celebrated at local holy wells. The veneration of local saints almost as familial figures was a particular facet of Irish rural society.[53] 'Saint Patrick . . . didn't discourage the sport or myth that used to be at these places', a Fermanagh storyteller claimed in the 1970s, 'but he made these places holy places' – places still known to be good for 'a day's outin'.'[54] The relics of the saints became important tools of power for the leading dynasties, their bells in particular being vested with supernatural powers, their hereditary custodians becoming venerated figures. The holy wells and other pagan sanctuaries are still places of pilgrimage to the present day, damned as 'mere remnants of heathen superstitions, practised by our forefathers before the Christian era, and afterwards appended to the rites and ceremonies enjoined by the Church of Rome in the darker ages of Christianity', as one of the many critics put it in the nineteenth century.[55] Whatever the controversy about which church was the natural successor to Patrick's, Irish Protestantism generally – alike with the Catholic hierarchy of later centuries – would remain dismissive of the pagan survivals which were as much part of that church as its biblical teachings, and the rural nature which had transformed it at the outset remained to conserve those elements into later times.

2

GAELIC ULSTER: LAND, LORDSHIP AND PEOPLE

'It may be easily perceaved by this slender and brief description of Ulster, what hath ben and ar the reasons why this Province hath ben . . . more chargeable to Her Maj^ie than any other Province, an namlie, the want of good townes and Fortified places . . . the sufferance of the Oneils to usurp the government of the Severall Captens and freeholders . . . [enabling them] to wage and mainteine the greater number of Scottes . . . and lastlie, the want of due exercises of religion and justice . . . the occasion of much impietie and barboresnes.'

Hore, ed., 'Marshal Bagenal's Description of Ulster, anno 1586', 157–8

The beginnings of English rule in Ireland, or what became English rule in later centuries, came when Henry II, with papal support (granted by the letter *Laudabiliter* in 1155), arrived in 1171. This twelfth-century Anglo-Norman[1] 'invasion' was to alter fundamentally the cultural landscape of Ireland, though not by replacing one people or one culture by another. That never happened. Indeed, the Anglo-Norman colony contracted, virtually collapsed entirely in Ulster, and had been reduced to the eastern seaboard of the Pale around Dublin by the fifteenth century. The changes which occurred came about rather through the process of acculturation. Gaelic chieftains, initially defeated by superior Anglo-Norman military talent, soon copied their methods. These centuries witnessed a remarkable escalation in the militarisation of Irish society, the establishment of mercenary armies and a growing exploitation of Gaelic society to support them. Gone were the checks and balances, the strong personal bonds inherent in the old Irish law codes. Gaelic polity had not remained static, but on the eve of its destruction at the end of the sixteenth century it had deteriorated so far that many welcomed the Tudor changes. That said, Gaelic mores and culture remained as vital as ever, defying attempts at church reform, continuing to shape the landscape and people's lives. Ulster was to remain the most Gaelic part of Ireland till the opening of the seventeenth century and the lives of the people were not fundamentally affected by the changes at the top. This is why the events of the seventeenth century were to come as such a shock.

1. Anglo-Norman Ulster

The population increases of the twelfth and thirteenth centuries produced new migratory movements throughout western Europe. The move of the Anglo-Norman lords from south Wales was part of this process.[2] They moved into the fertile valleys of Leinster and Munster and held Connacht as a tributary kingdom. That they never settled throughout Ulster was as much a result of its natural defences as the defiance of the Gaelic lords. In Ulster, only the coastal territory of Antrim and Down was partially brought into the new system by the daring of John de Courcy (1177). It was not an 'invasion' in the strict sense of the word, but the kind of individual and localised exploit already so common in Ireland, and de Courcy was quickly accepted as just another element in traditional dynastic feuding.[3] By sponsoring local traditions and saintly cults, he was even seen as a leader who might revive the fortunes of ancient Ulidia. He was responsible for the heavy concentration of religious establishments and promotion of the Patrick cult in what became modern County Down. In the thirteenth century, de Courcy's successors built a strong power-base, laying claim also to the old 'Ulster' title (the earldom of Ulster was created in 1205). The Anglo-Normans had entered a region where the River Bann was already a cultural divide and had established themselves with the support of many of the lesser chieftains as a buttress against Cenél nEógain aggression. Thus did the O'Flynns of Uí Thuirtri (mid-Antrim), the MacCartans and Magennises of the Ulaid (Iveagh and Kinelarty, mid and south Down), that branch of the O'Neills later to become the Clandeboye O'Neills of Antrim and Down, the borderland Maguires of Fermanagh, the O'Hanlons of Armagh, the O'Reillys of Breifne (Cavan) and the O'Cahans of Derry survive and strengthen as allies of the Anglo-Normans.[4] Such pragmatism – allying with whatever side offered the most – was to characterise the Gaelic chiefs until the seventeenth century.

Likewise, the Anglo-Normans survived by adapting. They fitted easily into the complex network of Gaelic alliances. There was considerable intermarriage, so that most of the great families at the end of the period would have been of mixed descent. By the fourteenth century the Anglo-Irish in Ireland were in retreat and the Ulster colony effectively collapsed. Always insecure, occupying little more than an eastern coastal strip some 25km wide from Fair Head to Carlingford Lough, and excluding much of mid-Antrim and west and central Down, the colony's survival had depended on exploiting the perennial Irish dynastic divisions and on adaptability. The Anglo-Normans had imported settlers at every level, English peasants, merchants and crafts-men being brought into Ulster, largely from the north-west of England. There was displacement of native lords, notably in the Ards peninsula and Lecale, where the descendants of Anglo-Norman families such as the Russells, Whites and Savages retained a precarious and diminishing foothold throughout the period.[5] They did not, however, displace Irish tenants. Indeed, the sharp demographic decline of the fourteenth century made tenants a scarce commodity.[6] They adopted the native land system and very often native ways and outside observers came to make little distinction between them and the native Irish chiefs. There was some hostility between settlers and natives, notably with the O'Neills, but on the whole the relationship seems to have been one of compromise.[7] Flashes of nationalistic fervour occurred at the top, notably at the time of the invasion of Ulster by Edward Bruce of Scotland (1315). But the only sustained record of nationalistic or, more accurately, ethnic conflict is to be found in the church.[8]

We have little information about settlement on the ground. Broadly speaking, in Ulster east of the River Bann the hills, woodland and bogs remained the preserve of the native Irish and the lowland coastal areas that of the Anglo-Irish. Certainly in Ireland as a whole the uplands came to be associated in the minds of the authorities with a peculiarly Irish way of life.[9] It was a tendency accentuated by the colony's retreat from the fourteenth century onwards. North Antrim was lost around 1400 through marriage to the MacDonnells of the Isles. The Clandeboy O'Neills, driven from Tyrone, occupied south Antrim and north Down and the Anglo-Irish Savages and Whites became confined to the Ards peninsula and south Down.[10] By the time of Marshal Bagenal's famous description of Ulster in 1586, the descendants of the original colonists had contracted to the area around Strangford Lough (Ards, Lecale and Dufferin), 'somewhat degenerate [i.e. Gaelicised] and in poore estate', yet still having freehold rights to their lands and never totally assimilated into native society.[11] This area around Strangford Lough was to continue a special, if at times purely nominal, allegiance to England throughout this period. The result was to be a particularly striking cultural diversity, to which was added 'New English' such as Bagenal in the late sixteenth century (i.e. a new cohort of Protestant English arriving during the Tudor conquest, in turn giving rise to the terms 'Old English' and 'Old Irish' to describe the Catholic descendants of the Anglo-Irish and Gaelic Irish respectively). It was considered culturally different from the rest of Ulster and by the late sixteenth century naughty children would be threatened with removal east of the Bann 'where you never hear a word of Irish'.[12]

Neither the MacLochlainns nor the O'Neills were successful in subjecting eastern Ulster to their overlordship, despite successive attempts. It is one of the best examples of topography shaping the history of the province. Cut off by the Bann, the woods of Glenconkeine and the Mountains of Mourne, the area was accessible in only four eminently defensible places: over the Bann at Coleraine, the ford at Toomebridge, Glenn Righe (Vale of the Newry River) and the Moiry Pass (parish and townland of Moira, north-east of Magherlin).[13] Inland topography, therefore, and coastal location prevented the remnants of the Anglo-Irish colony from being totally overrun.

2. The Scottish influence

The cultural landscape was also altered by the importation of large numbers of Scottish mercenaries after the thirteenth century – Gaelic Ireland's response to the more sophisticated warfare of the Anglo-Normans. Gaelic in speech and tradition, and, unlike the seventeenth-century Scottish planters, largely from the Gaelic/Scandinavian Western Isles, they intermarried, settled (mostly along the coast from the Foyle to the Glens of Antrim), and assumed Gaelic Irish genealogies.[14] Marriages were contracted by the Gaelic lords for the purpose of recruiting more mercenaries, thereby producing a succession of formidable wives to the O'Neills and O'Donnells in particular. By the sixteenth century the greatest of the overlords – O'Neill of Tyrone and O'Donnell of Tyrconnell – were of mixed blood, the former contracting

Anglo-Irish, the latter Scottish marriages. Although the Anglo-Irish in the north-east looked south to the Pale, Gaelic Ulster's cultural and economic frontier had long operated on an east–west, rather than a north–south, axis. It already formed part of a cultural and linguistic community with the Isles and western Scotland, the poets in particular enjoying an easy interchange. Scots were settled by King John around Coleraine and in the Glens of Antrim at the beginning of the thirteenth century. The MacDonnells of the Isles established an hereditary claim in Antrim through marriage with the Bissets c.1400. They and other mercenaries, like the MacQuillans of the Route (north Antrim, probably Welsh in origin), were amongst the major beneficiaries of the decline of the Anglo-Irish colony in the fourteenth and fifteenth centuries.[15] By the latter half of the sixteenth century the collapse of the Lordship of the Isles had added successive waves of MacDonnells to the Ulster settlement and destabilised neighbouring territories. They eventually pushed out the MacQuillans from the Route and the Whites from Dufferin. They were to remain a law unto themselves, supporting whichever side furthered their interests, miraculously emerging at the beginning of the seventeenth century (despite the hostility of successive English governments) as untainted by treason and with a commanding hold over most of Antrim.

The greatest of these hereditary mercenary or gallowglass families, the MacSweeneys, were territorial lords in Donegal by the fourteenth century, while another branch of the MacDonnells, serving O'Neill in Tyrone, came to own the area around Ballygawley. Others came in the wake of the Bruce wars (1315–18) and stayed. By the fifteenth century we find the gallowglass families of MacSheehy, MacDowall (MacDougal), MacCabe (who became the Maguires' and Mac-Mahons' hereditary gallowglass), MacGill, MacRory and MacConnell, most, alike with the east Ulster hereditary poets, the Ó Gnímhs (Agnews), coming from the same Hebridean stock as the MacDonnells. Although these families spread into the other parts of Ireland, they did not do so until the sixteenth century and on the whole remained peculiar to the northern part of the country. They were treated like the hereditary professional families and were settled on gifts of free land. They became thoroughly absorbed into Ulster Gaelic society, establishing territorial lordships in their own right and becoming major patrons of the poets.[16] The high costs of their maintenance gradually altered the character of Gaelic lordship, replacing the personal service and periodic hospitality of the old law tracts with increasing exactions and billeting (or 'coyne and livery'). The numbers of Scots mercenaries increased dramatically in the wars of the sixteenth century, reaching an estimated 25,000 between the 1560s and 1590s, and placing an intolerable burden on the host population.[17] They were quartered throughout the province, most notably in convenient locations like the Inishowen peninsula and O'Cahan's country around Coleraine, while Rathlin Island became the MacDonnells' military way station between the Isles and the Antrim coast. There were Irish mercenaries too (kerne), likewise quartered by 'coyne and livery'. But the Scots gallowglass and mercenaries became a particular feature of warfare in the north, causing heightened English anxiety at the prospect of the Scottish enemy using Ireland as a base and producing that novel preoccupation with Ulster which would characterise Elizabethan policy.[18]

3. Daily life and social relations in Gaelic Ulster

Such localism was to intensify after the Anglo-Normans halted the eleventh- and twelfth-century moves towards unity and high kingship, and a European-wide decline in population impacted on Ireland from the fourteenth century onwards. Ireland, even by contemporary standards, was grossly underpopulated. This fostered assimilation in colonised areas. Labour and tenants were scarce. But it also made labour-intensive arable farming difficult. In Gaelic areas pastoralism increased. Once-cultivated land reverted to forest, intensifying outsiders' perception of Ulster in particular as another world, primitive and threatening. They were struck by the comfortless and impermanent housing of even the lordly classes. A people who seemed to move and live with their cattle, their largely outdoor life reflected in their distinctive clothing.[19] Although towards the end of the period there are signs of Gaelic lords periodically adopting the externals of European nobility in more comfortable housing and formal attire, many aspects of Gaelic life had remained unchanged since the dawn of history and power was still reckoned in terms of people and livestock rather than property and land.

Certainly the Irish were contemptuous of Anglo-Irish attachment to stone buildings. Even in church life the showiness of the new continental-inspired monasteries was ridiculed. 'He was not engaged to keep stone walls', MacMahon at the end of the twelfth century is reputed to have replied to the accusation of having abandoned his alliance with John de Courcy and destroyed his forts, 'he scorned to confine himself within such cold and dreary enclosures while the native woods were open for his reception and security'.[20] His words neatly capture the difference between Anglo-Irish and native Irish perception of man's relationship with the land: to the former native Irish areas seemed wild and wooded, hilly and hostile, full of 'narrow corners and glennes under the mountaines foote, in which they lurked',[21] a landscape requiring taming, clearing and civilising through building and enclosure. House-building was made compulsory in later plantation leases. The extension of English law depended on the existence of administrative centres. In 1606 Sir John Davies found it impossible to conduct court because of the absence of buildings in which to site sessions and gaols, 'for the habitations of this people are so wild and transitory as there is not one fixed village in all this county', Fermanagh.[22] Even the apparel of the Irish was adapted to the boggy terrain – most going bare-legged, breechless and shoeless. 'The bogs are so great on this island', wrote a fourteenth-century Spanish pilgrim after passing through Ulster en route for Donegal, 'that scarcely upon the highest mountains can one pass through the waters, and even if one goes knee-deep, so that on foot there is great difficulty, and on horseback even greater.'[23] The wildness – still a feature of the immediate northern side of the border today – was a threatening cordon for the medieval Pale, deterring settlement well into the eighteenth century. And just as such wild terrain protected the east from absorption by O'Neill, so the mountain ranges of Tyrconnell (Donegal) made the latter virtually unconquerable. The province was thus effectively divided politically and geographically into three blocks.

In the absence of towns and modern communications, physical relief dominated everyday life and local identity. Even O'Neill's country – though the largest and most powerful territorial lordship in Ireland, extending from Inishowen(Donegal) to south of the river Blackwater (Tyrone/Monaghan/Armagh border) – did not have a natural locus of power. The annals record a very real mental division created by the Sperrins, one part looking north-west to Derry and its hinterland from Omagh to Lough Foyle, the other south-east towards Armagh and beyond. It was a physical and mental divide reflected in the semi-independent status of O'Cahan's country and eventually in the creation of the separate county of Londonderry in the seventeenth century.

The insubstantial housing of the Ulster Gaels may have contributed to the remarkable mobility noted by all commentators. But to government officials they betokened the rootless man, and such mobile abodes were outlawed in 1608. The beehive wattle-and-daub, windowless and chimneyless huts – such a feature of early seventeenth-century maps – are very much a survival of ancient vernacular housing, more common in early modern Ulster than in areas influenced by the Anglo-Irish. They are depicted as clustered round the few towns, abbeys and royal residences. By the sixteenth century they would have been the housing of the poorer elements in society, regardless of race, and in the plantation surveys they were reported from every part of Ulster. The great lords were already living in tower houses, and middling septs like the O'Hagans of Tyrone in two-storey houses. But for most of this period the living styles of the lords did not differ greatly from the people at large. Cattle were the only valuable property and the quickly erected, temporary wood-framed house was the norm and a standard of great antiquity. In its most basic form, it permitted considerable mobility to the Irish during the Nine Years War, 1593–1603 (or Tyrone's – after Hugh O'Neill, earl of Tyrone – Rebellion). It came to represent for Elizabethans all that was worst in the Irish character and was heavily legislated against. The change to stone as a building material was one of the more visible revolutions in the cultural landscape of seventeenth-century Ulster. But like almost everything else in the medieval rural lifestyle, the nature of its housing was dictated by circumstances. Local building stone was in short supply, whereas wood was plentiful. The destruction of the forests in the seventeenth century soon changed that.[24]

The general disregard for domestic comfort by all classes was another cause of complaint. In this respect even the lifestyle of the lords seems not to have changed much over the centuries, and was lived out in great halls adjoining their fortresses, surrounded by crowds of people, including the mandatory poets, harpists and storytellers. It was even claimed of the early fourteenth-century Aedh Reamhar O'Neill that he maintained sixty houses other than his chief residence, twenty for entertaining the poets, forty for performers of the lesser arts.[25] The carelessness and lack of privacy in sleeping arrangements was thought to encourage promiscuity, the constant presence of animals squalor, the lack of etiquette and social distinction at table (or lack of one, as Fynes Moryson proclaimed) irreverence and want of social deference. Meat was cooked in skins, meals taken out-of-doors, tables and beds notable by their absence. 'They care not for pot, pan, kettil, nor for mattrys, fether bed, nor such implements of household', remarked one Tudor visitor.[26] Judging by similar comments from later centuries, the reality was probably not far removed from such statements, even if the idea of depravity requiring rescue was. Pastoral habits do not inspire order and cleanliness, and the promotion of tillage was as much a part of the Tudors' and Stuarts' mission to 'civilise' the Irish, as enclosures, towns, villages and stone houses.[27]

In contrast the typical native warrior lord disdained the apparent tameness of settler farming and housing, and Conn O'Neill in Henry VIII's reign cursed those who sought to 'learn English, sow wheat, or make any building in Ulster'.[28] It was, after all, not through good husbandry that one became *The* O'Neill or *The* O'Donnell, but rather through the skilled horsemanship, for which Gaelic lords were noted, the daring cattle-raid and generous gifts of the spoils.[29]

> Conn vow'd his race
> For ever to the fight and chase,
> and curs'd him of his lineage born,
> Should sheathe the sword to reap the corn,
> Or leave the mountain and the wold
> To shroud himself in castled hold.[30]

'Every prince eligible for high Kingship is taught love of plunder and hatred of peace', ran one fourteenth-century praise poem of the O'Donnells. In contrast those who slept in feather beds, cropped their hair and wore ruffs, hose and jewelled spurs, were satirised by the poets as effeminate and unmanly.[31] They seemed to be forever on the move, their very dress denoting lives generally pursued out of doors. The famous Irish mantle – a huge shag, a brightly trimmed and russet-coloured rug or cloak, worn over saffron tunics – was in general use, by male and female alike, in the sixteenth century. Acting both as bedding and clothing, and enabling woodkerne, cattle-herders and, Spenser thought, rebels and outlaws, to sleep rough and move rapidly, it was 'their house, their bed, and their garment . . . a fit house for an out-law, a meet bed for a rebel, and an apt cloke for a thiefe'. Spenser also thought it encouraged promiscuousness, providing the 'bad hus-wife' and 'wandring woe men . . . a coverlet for her lewde exercise'.[32] In dress and lifestyle little would have differentiated the lowly from the lordly, although, with the general trend towards greater distancing between lord and subject by the sixteenth century, this too was chang-ing. In common with their peers elsewhere in Europe, there was a move towards what English officials applauded as 'civility' among sixteenth-century Irish lords, both in dress and housing. Indeed, Mac-Mahon levied protection rents on the Pale in fine cloth, and Magennis of Iveagh (deemed the 'most cyviliest of all the Irishrie'[33] in Ulster), Manus O'Donnell and Turlough Luineach O'Neill wore satin and velvet on ceremonial occasions. In fact, Irish dress, like Irish housing, had been adapted to suit the terrain and way of life, and the Anglo-Irish settlers in Ulster adopted both, the Savages becoming wholly 'degener-ate' in Tudor terminology. And while the poor like the poor everywhere can have had little but rags below their mantles (which might explain the aforementioned Spanish pilgrim's belief that they were naked beneath their shag cloaks), all the evidence, visual and otherwise, from the heavily bejewelled women, with their elaborate linen head-dresses, to the long-flowing sleeves of the standard tunic and the long, fringed, curled (almost dreadlocked) hair of the men, betrays as much stylis-ation as that of the ancient Celts – primitive certainly, in the sense of being locked in an earlier age, but scarcely the symbol of barbarity as perceived by Spenser and others.

4. *The land and its 'ownership'*

To the Irish, the hills and forests were places of refuge – as much from the predatory Gaelic lord as the English. It was complained of O'Neill during an invasion of his lands in 1541 that he 'never made show of no power, but kept him and his and their cattell in grete woodes and fastnes, where we could not attayn them, nor yet have perfect knowledge where they were'.[34] They were also essential elements in the agrarian economy. The hills provided summer pasturage for the large herds which dominated that economy and in many cases were considered communal land for neighbouring communities. The forest clearings permitted arable farming in the unenclosed lowland ground, which would otherwise have been difficult to protect against livestock. Most estates were arranged to include a hilly area.[35] Often whole septs would move with their cattle to adjacent hill areas for summer pasturage. This was that seasonal movement of livestock termed trans-humance, at the time called booleying (from the Irish word *buaile* for enclosure or byre) or creaghting (after the Irish word *caoraigheacht*, Hiberno-English 'creaght', signifying 'a herd of miscellaneous livestock with its attendants, grazing or passing through other people's lands').[36] It gave rise to the misconception that the native Irish were a nomadic people. Although there are early signs of a cash economy (particularly in areas bordering Anglo-Irish settlements), cattle still formed the basic unit of value till the end of the Gaelic period. Most people would have been involved in herding livestock – the cattle being moved to summer pastures on 1 May and returned at the end of October. The economic basis for booleying was little understood by English observers. Its association with those maligned hills and fastnesses damned it as a rebelly way of life; its temporary nature conjured up the image of the rootless man, even though it was very often conducted by milkmaids. Rather it was a long-established response to local terrain; it was a particular feature in boggy and hilly areas and as such it continued in these areas, in various forms, down to the twentieth century.[37] But it would be wrong to romanticise this image of the Gael living in poorer, upland regions. In medieval society considerable power attached to the command of mountain passes, and throughout this period the

Magennis castles controlled the accesses to the Anglo-Irish of Lecale, whilst in the largely pastoral economy of Gaelic Ireland extensive woodland was no deterrent to settlement and pasturage. Creaghting was first described in the annals in the fourteenth century as a particularly northern phenomenon practised by Irish and Anglo-Irish alike. At times it was used aggressively, particularly by the Fews branch of the O'Neills – the cattle being deployed as a weapon to devastate enemy lands and was a particular feature of Ulster conflict in the seventeenth century.[38]

This association in the minds of the authorities between landscape and Gaelic and rebelly ways is particularly noticeable in the case of inauguration ceremonies for Gaelic chiefs. Here the symbolism of nature was allied with that of an ancient pagan past. Such ceremonies always took place on hills, which were usually ancient burial mounds or in some other way associated with the ancient history of the people or place, and the poet played a key role in linking the candidate to that past. Frequently the inauguration stone was encircled by trees, like some ancient druidical grove. Such ancient survivals seem to have died out or were suppressed after the Anglo-Norman invasion. But, in a clear anti-English political gesture, they were revived with particular emphasis on the Gaelic past in the fourteenth century and were adopted even by hibernicised Anglo-Irish families. There was considerable local variation in the ceremony, Donegal in particular originally retaining many more ancient, even pagan, rituals, though later O'Donnell inaugurations took place in the church at Kilmacrenan. By the sixteenth century the most powerful chief in Ireland was O'Neill of Tyrone, and his inauguration site at Tullahoge, just east of Lough Neagh, attracted particular attention from Tudor cartographers. Before the twelfth century, the church had played a major role in such ceremonies. But although the role of native monks seems to have continued undiminished, and that of the poets as perceived heirs to ancient druids was magnified, there was a marked turning away from the institutional church which had associated itself with Henry II and English ways.

By the sixteenth century, the narrowing of power in Gaelic Ireland was also reflected in changes in the inauguration ceremonies. The main overlords, for example, were now claiming the right of naming and inaugurating the sub-chiefs. The MacSweeneys claimed to have been inaugurated by Colum Cille's successors at Iona before they came to Ireland. It may well have been this tradition which explains their inauguration in 'Colum Cille's precinct', Kilmacrenan, 'and if any were inaugurated elsewhere, he could not be long in power'. But this seems to have been on the suffrage of O'Donnell, who exacted a hereditary tribute for the honour and inflicted bitter retribution when such approval was not sought.[39] Most notable, however, was the significance being attached to the surnames of the leading families and the public declaiming of 'the name' – *The* O'Neill, *The* O'Donnell – at the inauguration. To be called 'The O'Neill' signified lordship of the whole of Ulster, a counter-sovereignty to that of the Crown. Thus was Conn O'Neill obliged to forsake 'the name of O'Neill' prior to becoming earl of Tyrone in 1542 and his son Shane's use of it was part of his attainder in 1569:

Forasmuch as the name of O'Neill, in the judgements of the uncivil people of this realm, doth carry in itself so great a sovereignty as they suppose that all the lords and people of Ulster should rather live in servitude to that name than in subjection to the crown of England: be it therefore enacted that the same name of O'Neill ... shall from henceforth cease ... and be utterly abolished and extinct forever.[40]

To English governors Gaelic inauguration ceremonies held such potential for rebelliousness that they had symbolic sites such as the O'Neill inauguration stone at Tullahoge destroyed in 1601. Indeed, the revival of lapsed inauguration rites became a symbol of rebellion by many chiefs during the Nine Years War. Assisted by the cultivated antiquarianism of the learned men, the retention of such ancient customs became part of a chief's armoury and the old idea of the marriage between chief and land continued to be voiced by the bards well into the seventeenth century. Although the sacral element had by then long been replaced by a more secular definition of the lord as head of a dominant family, the practice itself symbolised an alternative definition of power to that being assumed under English law (often readily so) towards the end of the period. In this respect it was also a reminder of the ancient status of declining families, the O' Cahans and O'Hagans for instance retaining the ceremonial role of conferring authority on

The O'Neill. For later nationalists, such sites were to retain their symbolic significance, as remnants of a Gaelic landscape which was considered peculiarly theirs.[41]

This traditional association of land with Gaelic tradition, however, owed little to secure ownership, and we must look to later centuries for the development of what Ulster folklorist Michael J. Murphy terms 'the peasant complex – which puts prestige, house, lands, cattle and everything else above people'.[42] But as the land surveyors set about assessing 'ownership' on the eve of the Ulster Plantation, they aroused an acute consciousness of who had rights to what. Gaelic landholding differed from region to region and even from kin-group to kin-group within the same area, and custom was often stronger than right. At the top of the landholding system the overlord controlled his 'country' (equivalent to the old *tuath*[43] or the modern barony). Each 'country' consisted of the lord's private family lands (technically the property of the sept rather than the individual); the mensal lands, which supplied him with food, probably farmed by freeholding septs; the demesne lands which went with his office, and which were farmed by rent-paying tenants; the freeholders' lands, owing him dues and services; and church lands, traditionally free from such exactions. But for most of this period, the lord's power was defined not in terms of landownership, but in a complex series of rights and clientship. Thus, although there might have been certain hereditary lands attached to his office (desmesne lands), more often than not such lands belonged rather to his particular sept. Indeed, he actually owned only about one-fifth of the land held. More important were the lands from which he could demand certain rights, and when these were not fulfilled he would simply take such land into his hands as forfeit, and time and custom established ownership. The process was mirrored on church lands, the bishop or abbot having assumed many of the lord's secular trappings and powers.[44]

Within each lordship actual ownership of land was confined largely to the lord and his relatives, officials, soldiers, poets, brehon (a lawyer or judge) and ecclesiastics. But there would also have been a number of formerly important landowning families reduced in status through the expansion of ruling lineages, and thereby several layers of presumed ownership, with groups theoretically reduced to tenants-at-will still claiming title. This downward social process was a particular feature of the period and was aggravated by the nature of Irish succession. Every male with a common great-grandfather in the chiefly line had a right to be considered for succession to the sept title. But very often force spoke louder than right, and the history of Gaelic Ulster is riven by bloody succession disputes, which, even when temporarily resolved, could leave behind aggrieved family factions ready to join forces with the new lord's traditional enemies. Even depressed septs and the lowliest farmer would have retained a keen sense of status – a point noted in 1607 by Sir John Davies (James I's attorney-general in Ireland). In Fermanagh he had interviewed the inhabitants of every barony, particularly the scholars, 'who know all the septs and families and all their branches, and the dignities of one sept above another, and what families or persons were chief of every sept, and who were next, and who were of a third rank, and so forth, till they descended to the most inferior man in all the baronies'.[45]

The patent rolls of 1615 list a multitude of small grants to persons described as 'gentlemen', revealing the existence of something approaching a peasant gentry.[46] 'All the Irish almost boast themselves to be gentlemen, no lesse than the Welsh', noted Spenser, 'for if he can derive himselfe from the head of any sept, (as most of them can, they are so expert by their Bardes), then hee holdeth himselfe a gentleman, and thereupon scorneth to worke, or use any hard labour, which hee saith, is the life of a peasant or churle.'[47] Lineage notions of status were to persist through and beyond the plantations. Stronger amongst those who had lost out than among those who had gained by the changes, it was to fuel a sense of grievance into modern times.

This downward social process was intensified by the much-criticised system of gavelkind or partible inheritance, whereby the sept's land was subject to periodic redistribution, as co-heirs died or families increased in size. Gavelkind also operated in Gaelicised areas of the Anglo-Irish colony. There was a wide regional variation in this practice; where it did occur regularly it was a disincentive to improvement. In some areas, however (e.g. Fermanagh), it happened so infrequently that by 1600 most farmers would have held their farms much as they do today. More powerful families could compensate for proliferation by extending control over other lands, further adding to the depression of status of those overrun. Given the right of illegitimate children to inherit, the sexual permissiveness of Gaelic society, and the enormous number of male heirs produced, by the end of this period the leading families had acquired possession of vast tracts of their respective counties, as much as three-quarters of Fermanagh, for example, being in the hands of the Maguires.[48] Consolidation by the dominant lord at the expense of freeholders, and their decline in status to that of tenants, was a prominent feature of late medieval Ireland, even the inauguration ceremonies changing in content to reflect the progressive transformation from king to landlord.[49] The tendency in the fifteenth and sixteenth centuries was for overlords such as O'Neill or O'Donnell to reduce free subjects to the status of tenants and transform their territories from lordships to estates. Such was their success that, in 1603, Hugh O'Neill was recognised as owning virtually the whole of Tyrone. The expansion of the junior branches of the O'Neills had caused the once-prominent Mac Cathmhaoil (McCawll, McCall) sept to disperse eastwards through Armagh and Down, and likewise encroached upon the territories of minor lords such as Magennis, O'Hanlon, MacMahon and O'Reilly (occupying the heavily wooded borderlands between Ulster and the Pale and Gaelicised midlands).[50] It was this class of minor lord which unsurprisingly responded most positively to the Tudor policy of 'surrender and regrant'.

Such depression in status would have been a recurrent feature of Gaelic Ireland, though we do not know enough about medieval landholding to assess how it was absorbed. In a society where linear succession did not operate, the sons of former chieftains also risked losing their father's lands to the sons of succeeding rulers. One way of avoiding this was to break away and form a new sub-chieftainship, as did the O'Neills of Clandeboy, those of the Fews in south Armagh and the Maguires of west Fermanagh, in the fourteenth and fifteenth centuries. Such an unsatisfactory system of landholding was one of the main factors in the violence of medieval Irish society. When power attached to overlordship rather than ownership, it required constant assertion through enforced tributes and services. Yet ancient customs die hard. Despite the proclamation of 1605 against Gaelic land tenure, older inheritance customs survived and were even recognised by the Dublin authorities until 1641.[51] Studies of land usage and settlement in County Derry show that such subdivision within a defined kin-group persisted, the same families occupying the lands of their ancestors and continuing to live in kin-groups into the twentieth century. At the most basic level, subdivision may not have been as destructive or anarchic as studies of the upper reaches of Gaelic society would suggest, and where rough land, bog or mountain adjoined restricted arable land, an element of communal farming was not incompatible with independent holdings within the family land.[52]

This picture of kin-groups possessing a long-standing stake in identifiable pieces of land would seem to conflict with the total absence of written proof. However, in a society without written land titles, no tradition of mapmaking or surveying, and where outright ownership was the exception rather than the rule, customary right and an acute awareness of who had what rights over what territory were vital. In the plantation scheme it could mean the difference between retention and dispossession to know whether one's land was demesne or freehold, as many in Fermanagh argued successfully, and in Cavan less so. It would appear that the humblest farmer knew every inch of the territory to which he was entitled.[53]

A particularly notable association of land and people was that of the O'Hagans of Tyrone, whose prominent role in the inauguration of the O'Neills seems to have come from their lengthy occupation of the Tullahoge site itself and the surrounding territory, an occupation which continued from at least the eleventh to the early seventeenth centuries.[54] The modern association of local people with certain townlands would appear to go back far beyond the keeping of records, and divisions became more precise where partition occurred, as under gavelkind. Indeed, Davies says as much of Fermanagh in 1607, where he found 'an exceeding great' number of freeholders, even occupiers of 'petty fractions and divisions' under gavelkind claiming such.[55] In Anglo-Irish areas, where occupation was more continuous, measurement was more rigorously defined. But in Gaelic areas units would have been seen as little more than 'a bundle of spade ridges',[56] boundaries loosely defined and periodically re-defined by the medieval practice of 'perambulation', symbolic location of burial grounds and crosses, and handed-down custom. When asked in 1543 to adjudicate in a territorial dispute between O'Donnell and O'Neill, Lord Deputy

St Leger complained that they produced no legal proof besides 'certain old parchments or bills, confirmed by no seal, signature or other testimony but such as are composed by vain poets ... blinded by affection for their lords'.[57] The extreme localism of Gaelic society and the apparent confusion of land title was to bewilder the Elizabethans. But it was a medieval concept of landholding defined by tradition which was to persist into modern times and to provide the emotional groundwork for the land campaign of the late nineteenth century. Moreover, although the trend by the early seventeenth century was towards individual ownership and primogeniture, the old identification of family groups with certain areas continued, and in the absence of other records was frequently accepted by seventeenth-century crown officials in the parcellation of land to new owners.[58] It would be wrong, therefore, to assume blanket instability of title. Historical geographers have identified an underlying stability in medieval Irish society which conflicts with the picture of mayhem in contemporary English accounts. Indeed, in areas of Ulster not torn by warfare at the end of the sixteenth century, crown officials were surprised to find a relatively well-ordered landscape.[59] In this mapless society, there was nevertheless a network of small territories whose boundaries were well-known to the resident population, and a well-established association between particular communities and certain parcels of land. Even the unfree gained a right of inheritance after thirty years' occupation.[60]

The lowest level of land unit was called different things in different areas – the 'poll' of Cavan, the 'tate' of Fermanagh and Monaghan, the 'ballybo' of Tyrone, Derry, Donegal and Down. But at the end of this period they were standardised as the modern townland, their local names and boundaries retained, thereby fossilising Gaelic settlement patterns. Averaging some sixty acres, these base units represented not so much a fixed geographic area as the measurement of agricultural potential, or land considered capable of grazing a certain number of cattle. It was a notional and fluctuating form of land assessment which survived the Ulster plantation and was still remarked upon in the eighteenth century.[61] The larger land units of ballybetaghs (averaging sixty ballyboes) were controlled by middle-level sept leaders, the inferior septs of the dominant lord. These were the free septs, the future freeholders of Tudor settlements, those most at risk from the system of periodic redistribution to the benefit of the senior lord, and those who increasingly resorted to English law for protection.

At the lower level of the 'churls' or under-tenants who actually worked the land (and we know that substantial areas of Ulster were under tillage, whatever the dominance of pastoral farming), their scarcity should have ensured some security. Certainly the appeals of Hugh O'Neill and the other Ulster lords for the return of those who had exercised the customary right to change lords and had fled to the Pale during the ravages of Shane O'Neill's rebellion and the Nine Years War, show them to have been a scarce and valued commodity. But this involved a further deterioration in their condition, removing traditional freedom of movement and reducing them to total subservience. There can be no doubt that this is exactly what the Ulster lords were attempting to do and it was specifically forbidden by royal proclamation in 1605.[62] The idea of a personal bond between lord and subject had long disappeared. The position of the Irish peasant generally was one of the worst in Europe, and, after the ravages of the Nine Years War, that of the Ulster peasants was the worst in Ireland. The poor and weak would have had little redress under what was left of the brehon laws, a fact noted by Spenser.[63] Little wonder that many saw England's common law as frequently providing more protection and the Anglo-Irish and English as the lesser taskmasters. Although we know very little about the people of Ulster during the Middle Ages, it is clear that ownership of land and memory of past ownership were more important in Gaelic Ulster than once thought and enmity between dominant and declining septs persisted through many generations.[64] Low densities of population would have cushioned the impact of dispossession. But by the end of the sixteenth century insecurity of tenure, erratic and increasing military exactions and absence of fixed payments were emerging as major grievances. The middling rank of chieftains might have welcomed the greater security offered by the introduction of English Common Law. But the confiscations and influx of settlers after the Ulster Plantation was quite another matter, exacerbating tensions which had been brewing for some time.[65]

An even more tortuous layering of landholding occurred in the case of church lands. These so-called termon lands dated from the very generous grants of land to the early monasteries, and to all intent and purposes had become the hereditary possessions of certain families. By the late medieval period the term encompassed coarb (technically heir or successor to the founding saint) and erenach (monk-steward) lands. The holders were not necessarily in orders, though many were. Even then hereditary transmission was still possible, given the continu-ance of clerical marriage, regardless of the statute of the Synod of Cashel (1101) forbidding it. Such families traditionally provided the members of the clergy.[66] They symbolised the economic basis of the medieval church, paying tithes, in addition to rents, fines, and tributes to the bishop or archbishop – as they would have done to the secular lord – providing supplies, upkeep of church buildings and hospitality. They were technically free from lay exactions, but suffered encroach-ment by Gaelic lords, notably the O'Neills.[67] Whatever their different status, however, these lands came to be treated by their erenach families in the normal Gaelic manner. There was as much precise local know-ledge of their extent and their attendant duties and rights, as there was of neighbouring secular lands. The Inquisition of Dungannon in 1609 found 'that these septs or erenachs have, tyme out of mind, inherited the said lands accordinge to the Irish custome of tanistrie' (whereby the successor was appointed by the existing holder within his own lifetime), and that neither abbot nor bishop had any right to remove them.[68]

Such lands were extensive in Ulster, particularly in those areas of early Patrician and Columban foundations. They may have accounted for as much as a third of the land in the Irish part of the diocese of Armagh (i.e. County Armagh, east Tyrone and south-east Derry). When the English archbishop of Armagh, John Colton, made a visita-tion to the see of Derry in 1397, hospitality and security was arranged through termon lands along the entire route from Termonagurk in east Tyrone. The contemporary account of Colton's visitation reveals the ubiquity of erenachs in Gaelic Ulster, suggests a large degree of co-operation between different areas and, most importantly, shows that the lands and positions had remained in the hereditary possession of the families of the founders. Even though they had fallen down the scale of power, they nevertheless still retained considerable local prestige through their erenachies. Notable examples were the O'Boyles in Donegal, the O'Loughrans of south Tyrone and the MacCawells of Clogher.[69]

Such lands were not considered part of native territory under the territorial arrangements of the late sixteenth and early seventeenth centuries, in which much land was regranted to native freeholders. In fact, they became the earliest effective plantations, most going to 'servitors' who were largely Palesmen.[70] Given the noted attachment of the people to holy places associated with the early saints, former church lands retained a special attraction for local Catholics even though no longer in their hands. 'The country around Downpatrick is now mostly Protestant', wrote Walter Harris in 1744, 'yet some remains of popery still continue, and will probably always do so as long as St Patrick's Wells . . . are held in such high veneration by the credulous vulgar.'[71] Special significance seems to have attached to the termon land of Colum Cille's successors, and MacSweeney family tradition claimed that the branch which despoiled it without restitution perished, while that branch which made restitution prospered.[72]

5. The poets and the preservation of tradition

Gaelic society on the eve of its extinction was a contradictory mix of remarkable survival, adaptation to the new circumstances and internal decline. The role of the learned men was unchanged for most of this period, bound by the continuing hereditary principle and centuries-old convention. If anything, their importance in proclaiming the lord's noble lineage and praising his prowess was greater than ever in the aggravated localism and instability of the fifteenth and sixteenth centuries. The brehon was still an important figure at the end of the sixteenth century, undergoing the same lengthy training, enjoying the same hereditary status as his forebears, presiding over the open-air arbitrations, and repeating passages from the law codes drawn up in the seventh and eighth centuries. But little remained of the ancient laws in practice. Their repetition by the brehons was little more than 'antiquarian window-dressing',[73] and the protection for the church and free landowning families, in-built in the early law codes, was long gone. The brehon was not seen as particularly dangerous by English officials, and Davies was clearly touched by the sight of Maguire's aged brehon, who had been summoned to give information on the lands and dues to which Maguire was entitled. No such sympathy, however, was reserved for the 'chroniclers, gallowglasses, and rhymers . . . persons that merit no respect . . . for they are enemies to the English government'.[74]

The poet and the musician were still mandatory figures in the Gaelic lords' retinue. Indeed, bardic poetry remains the most important surviving Gaelic source for the thirteenth to seventeenth centuries, even though its true significance continues to be hotly debated by historians.[75] There is little sign of immediate nationalistic response to the Anglo-Norman incursions. But it is a frequent element in bardic poetry – of its very nature a glorification of past traditions – which called up a pagan past and nature itself to produce a native messiah who would expel the 'foreigner'. In the conventional bardic format the 'foreigner' (*Gall*) always implied non-Gaelic, though it often referred to local enemies, and as time went on the distinction was made between 'fair foreigners' (*Fionnghallaith*) or Old English, and the *Saxain* or *Sax-Ghaill*, the New English. Traditional bardic calls to their hosts to rise against the intruder have sometimes been misinterpreted as reactions to English conquest, whereas many Ulster poets, whilst lamenting the passage of the old order, were, by the early seventeenth century adapting and accepting changed conditions.[76] Bardic poems mislead if interpreted as some early nationalistic expression, though no one has yet come up with a satisfactory concept to encapsulate the pride in culture and place clearly there in medieval Ulster. Moreover, although the content of the sixteenth- and seventeenth-century poems differs little from those of the thirteenth and fourteenth centuries, the poets excelled in their antiquarianism and sense of historical connectedness. The Gaelic revival of the fourteenth century in particular produced a new interest in Gaelic history and genealogy which continued to the seventeenth century.[77] But unless the context and identity of the patron are also taken into account, these praise poems can be unreliable source material and on that point Spenser made one of his more acute observations: 'Through desire of pleasing perhaps too much [the Bards] . . . have clouded the truth.'[78]

Bardic conventions were intensely conservative. Their training remained unchanged throughout the centuries, and they were critical of those few poets who broke free from the straitjacket of convention.

The turn of phrase, the cultivated irony and ambiguity of these poems are admirable. But one cannot expect to find much sense of vision or spirit or any fresh commentary on current events. We would learn more of popular opinion from songs – if any survived.[79] But these were disdained by the poets as the preserve of the unlettered, and Thomas Moore's nineteenth-century romantic image of the bard as minstrel has no basis in reality. The poets represented a highly elitist profession, which disdained the lowly-born of every race and whose lament for the demise of the Gaelic order often rose no higher than a criticism of the *arriviste*, the 'churl' and 'serf' who knew not their place in society. Indeed, there is in these poems a sense of respect for breeding, nobility and royalty regardless of nationality. The poets were typical of Gaelic society in their professed loyalty to the English monarch, whilst some-times making the unreal distinction between the person of the monarch and the monarch's representatives in Dublin. Their main role was to praise their host chieftain and for this they were – and expected to be – richly rewarded in land and the spoil of battle.

But historians are often too dismissive of bardic poetry. The poets did reflect the interests of the elite, otherwise they would have been – indeed, some were – rejected by their patrons. Their real importance – with that of the other professional families – was their linkage between past and future, their task, 'to spin the threads of lore' and to 'follow up the branches of kinship'.[80] They were valued by their employers as genealogists, historians and preservers (sometimes creators) of princely lineages, and their poems were preserved by generations of the recipient family as proof of status. Their authority was equivalent to that of the clerics and lawyers as guarantors of legal agreements, as attested by the 1543 dispute between O'Donnell and O'Neill, mentioned above. In their claims to overlordship of all Ulster, the Great O'Neill and his son Niall Óg chose the symbolic site of Emain Macha to entertain a great gathering of the learned men of Ireland, the O'Neill poets tracing a fictitious connection with the ancient Ulaid dynasty.[81] The poets liked to be considered as heirs to the druids, their verses endowed with magical powers, their satire and criticism so influential in destroying reputation, that the famous west Ulster poet Tadhg Dall Ó Huiginn was said to have been murdered in 1591 by those who had been the subjects of his satire. 'Vain and Childish', wrote English Jesuit scholar

Edmund Campion in 1571 of the Irish, 'greedy of prayse they bee, and fearful of dishonour. And to this end they esteeme their Poets who write Irish learnedly, and penne their sonnets heroicall, for the which they are bountifully rewarded. But if they send out libells in disprayse, thereof the Gentlemen . . . stand in great awe.'[82]

The exact role of the poets in Gaelic society is elusive, but it was such a part of the fabric of authority that even such New English as Sir John Perrot felt compelled to employ them.[83] They tended to admire power in any quarter and had no difficulty serving those English who patronised the poets, or in adapting to the new anglicised order after the initial shock at the collapse of the society which had supported them. Indeed Maguire's chief poet, Ó hEódhasa, was among the 'deserving Irish' allotted land in the Ulster Plantation.[84] Their real importance to the later development of Catholic identity lies in their role as antiquarians and pseudo-historians. Although as custodians of historical tradition they could and did accommodate change, the history they perpetuated was that of the *Lebor Gabála* or *Book of Invasions* – the pseudo-history of Ireland which had created the myth of the Gaelic race. The *Lebor Gabála* was one of the central texts of the bardic schools. It was particularly popular in the first part of the seventeenth century, and through the learned classes became central to the writings of the Counter-Reformation, a distiller of the elements on which later nationalism was to draw. Ironically, it was the progressive decay of the bardic order which projected such historical readings to a wider audience; for, deprived of lordly patronage after the destruction of the Gaelic order in the early seventeenth century, the poets were obliged to abandon their former exclusiveness and write for a more popular audience. It was only then that they became purveyors of nationalist sentiment.

6. Gaelic lordships in late medieval Ulster

If we turn from the poems to reality, the idea of national consciousness is even less credible. Gaelic polity remained that of dynastic aggrandisement right up to the sixteenth century and in the giddy swings of alliances the Anglo-Normans and Anglo-Irish were just another factor.

Thus we find the Dunleavys (Mac Duinn Sléibhe), the Clandeboye O'Neills, the Magennises and the O'Hanlons successively in alliance with the Anglo-Irish against MacLoughlin, then O'Neill aggression; or the O'Neills and Whites in alliance against the Savages and Magennises; or the Anglo-Irish themselves as often as not in revolt against the crown and capitalising on the collapse of royal authority in Ulster. But there is a sense of provincial pride, and a constant effort to link into the lineage of ancient Ulster. The Mac Duinn Sléibhe kings of Dál Fiatach were profoundly conscious of their illustrious Ulidian past and, after the disappearance of the family from politics at the end of the thirteenth century, that claim was taken up by the Magennises of Uí Echach Cobo (Iveagh), a powerful if minor sept in south-west Down, who successfully resisted Anglo-Norman and O'Neill aggression alike and who taunted the O'Neills on their groundless claims to dynastic succession from Conchobar mac Nessa and the Ulaid. Their patronage of the poets outstripped their importance in numbers and power and they were rewarded by poems tracing the antiquity of their lineage back through the ancestors of the Ultonian heroes. Likewise, the O'Hanlons, though frequently vassals of the O'Neills, were conscious of their descent from the ancient Airthir and their association with Emain Macha, and there are signs that they too considered the O'Neills upstarts. Expelled by the O'Neills from north Armagh, where they had been kings of Loughgall, they were able to use the Anglo-Normans and the Dublin government to halt the O'Neill advance. They remained deadly enemies to the O'Neills of the Fews and the related McCanns, who had displaced them. Such identity with Ulster's past was therefore no premise for provincial unity, but another dynastic tool in the power struggle. It is significant here because it shows how doggedly the minor septs clung on to traditional definitions of status and lineage, preserving the elements from which a future Catholic and Gaelic identity would be forged.[85]

At the beginning of the sixteenth century the political situation in Ulster was much as it had been for centuries. The Gaelic lords had never challenged the validity of the papal grant of Irish lordship to England. They simply ignored it.[86] Throughout the period Gaelic Ulster contained a host of semi-independent lordships, paying nominal fealty to the English crown, each following their own interests and lacking any sense of common purpose. Indeed, it has been suggested that Gaelic Ulster before the Tudor 'conquest' was moving towards a Polish situation, an enserfed peasantry controlled by a host of territorial magnates.[87] Crown officials found agreements made with dominant lines would founder on the vagaries of the Irish succession system, new leaders simply ignoring those made by their predecessors. There was a long history of the crown supporting strong chiefs who could bring stability to Ulster and Tudor support for Hugh O'Neill was very much in this tradition. In the new thinking that followed Henry VIII's act of 1541 transforming the medieval Irish lordship into a kingdom, the Gaelic system of succession and landholding was identified as the main cause of instability. Tudor policy did not envisage the destruction of Gaelic Ireland, rather its accommodation in an extension of English law throughout the country. Central to this policy was the system of 'surrender and regrant', whereby the lord surrendered his traditional rights and lands, and received them back from the crown in outright ownership, normally to be held according to English inheritance custom. The Irish title of the O'Neill or the O'Donnell would likewise be converted into English-style earldoms, O'Neill becoming earl of Tyrone. It was a voluntary policy, to be worked out by slow accommodation over a lengthy time-span, and it was applied with much sensitivity to local custom. The aim was to create freeholders, holding directly from the crown and this, followed up by 'composition' – whereby fixed dues would replace the arbitrariness of 'coyne and livery' – would inject a stability so noticeably lacking in Gaelic areas. The policy, started in the 1540s, was continued into the seventeenth century by James I, progressing from the principal lords to much smaller landholders.[88]

Given the constant downward pressure exerted in Gaelic society by expanding dominant lineages, the process held obvious advantages for the lesser lords. It was espoused with particular eagerness by those borderland septs caught between O'Neill and the Pale: the O'Reillys of Breifne (Cavan), the Magennises of Iveagh (south Down), the Mac-Mahons of Monaghan, and there are signs of support for the administrative structures – including the shiring of Ulster in 1585 and the introduction of sheriffs and courts – which accompanied the process. It is wrong to think of some kind of independent Ireland pitted against an expanding colonial power in this period. The refusal of the English crown to extend the protection of the law to the Irish, was, claimed Sir John Davies, one of the key reasons why English rule had never been made effective in the country.[89] Such inequality of treatment before the law had indeed been a frequent complaint by the Irish throughout the Middle Ages, and even the greater lords welcomed the certainty of hereditary title. The O'Neills had been trying to introduce lineal succession since at least the fourteenth century,[90] and Conn O'Neill was among the first to accept the new policy, taking the title earl of Tyrone in 1542. But under Irish law such title was not in the possession of an individual lord to surrender, and customary law continued to be practised by all but the immediate kin of the parties to the original agreement.[91] In a system where so many had legitimate claims to the lordship, 'surrender and regrant' consolidated individuals at the expense of the family group and the collateral septs, and a series of major succession disputes destabilised Ulster in the latter half of the century. The most notable led to the rebellion of Shane O'Neill (d.1567), and dynastic instability continued in Tyrone for the rest of the period. Dynastic disputes in all the lordships weakened and ultimately destroyed 'surrender and regrant'. They were most destructive in those very counties – Monaghan, Fermanagh and Cavan – where the new policy had found most support. But it was the coincidence of similar dynastic challenges in the two strongest lordships of Tyrconnell and Tyrone which created the climate for rebellion in the 1590s.

With so many threats no lord could afford to be seen as entirely abandoning the Gaelic system of succession. No one had walked the tightrope between the English and Gaelic systems as successfully as Hugh O'Neill, seen by contemporary crown officials and modern historians alike as the key mediator between the two traditions and the one native leader capable of modernising Ulster and adapting to the new circumstances. But even he found himself compelled to join the rebellion against government policies in 1595, recognising that if he failed to do so, he would provoke rebellion from his rivals within the lordship. His taking of the title of the 'O'Neill' at Tullahoge was an open act of rebellion against the crown, and may have been his way of placating those septs who adhered to Gaelic ways.[92]

The policy also collapsed through lack of adequate crown support for those who had entered into such agreements. All the Tudors had preferred accommodation to confrontation. Dispossession was not official policy. But the introduction of English adventurers and settlers on to confiscated church lands after the Reformation (particularly in view of the kind of occupation system outlined above), the inefficient and sometimes brutal attempts at colonisation, and the activities of freebooting officials who exploited the weaknesses of the Gaelic system to acquire land for themselves, alienated even friendly Gaelic lords and contributed to the unusual, if transient, sense of unity in the end-of-century revolt.[93] The appearance of sheriffs and officials and perhaps, most of all, of mapmakers and surveyors was all very unsettling, and the best cartographer of the period – Barthelet – was beheaded by the Irish in Donegal. Government officials seemed to be everywhere. 'The greatest advantage that the Irish had of us in all their rebellions', commented Davies, 'was our ignorance of their countries, their persons, and their actions; since the law and her ministers have had a passage among them, all their places of fastness have been discovered and laid open ... how they live and what they do ... insomuch as Tyrone [Hugh O'Neill] hath been heard to complain that he had so many eyes watching over him as he could not drink a full carouse of sack but the State was advertised thereof within few hours after.'[94]

There was little consciousness that the Gaelic order was under threat. The lords entered into 'surrender and regrant' agreements and abandoned them with similar unconcern, when they wished to continue the traditional occupation of attacking their weaker neighbours. But to a situation already unsettled by the aggrandisement of Hugh O'Neill, the application of new crown policies and the build-up of mercenary forces, was added a remarkable concurrence of succession disputes. That in Monaghan resulted in the summary execution of Hugh Roe MacMahon by the Lord Deputy Fitzwilliam and the subsequent partition of the county. The denunciation of Hugh Maguire as a traitor in neighbouring Fermanagh, for claiming succession under Gaelic practice in defiance of an existing 'surrender and regrant' agreement, set in motion the train of events which by 1595 had brought almost the whole province into rebellion, finally bringing to a close the Tudor experiment and the collapse of Gaelic Ulster.[95] It was a collapse which was as sudden as it was unforeseen.

Internally it was collapsing anyway.[96] The downward pressure which had been part of the Gaelic land system was accelerated by 'surrender and regrant'. At the end of the sixteenth century there was a growing recognition of land as a commodity and this, accompanied by the painful introduction of a money economy, started the process of indebtedness through which the land system was progressively eroded. This was a much more corrosive process than the more dramatic Ulster Plantation and it affected plantation and non-plantation counties alike.[97] Ironically where government policy of 'surrender and regrant' was made effective lower down the scale, native landholders were cushioned from the new economic realities for longer (as in Monaghan), for the result was a host of independent landowners technically protected from the dispossession which followed the flight of their previous overlords in 1607. It was because 'surrender and regrant' had not proceeded beyond the top in the major lordships of Tyrone and Tyrconnell that the entire territory lay open to confiscation when O'Neill, O'Donnell and the other lords went into exile in 1607. But even before this it was becoming clear that the favourable terms granted in 1603 would not be allowed to stand.

By the Treaty of Mellifont in 1603, which ended the Nine Years War, O'Neill had been effectively granted the freehold of his entire earldom (modern Tyrone, most of Armagh and Derry), with the clear implication that all living within its confines – including some like O'Cahan who had fought on the English side – were dependent on him.[98] He had also successfully resisted the establishment of an Ulster presidency along lines of those already existing in Connacht and Leinster and restricted the interference of crown officials to periodic visits by justices, thereby effectively establishing his claim to be considered chief lord west of the Bann. But all this conflicted both with official policy to break the power of the overlords by creating freeholders and with the latter's ambitions to so be liberated, and created dissatisfaction on all sides. As O'Neill continued lineage expansion at the expense of collateral septs, their complaints were taken up by dissatisfied officials. Measures such as the 1605 proclamation compelling all principal landowners to introduce English landholding practices, followed by the 1606 commission for defective titles, bode ill for the lords who had survived the war so successfully. Both, in fact, were aimed against the power of the chief lords and were yet another attempt to weaken it by granting secure title to the inferior septs. A test case was brought against O'Neill by O'Cahan, with government backing. The recognition of O'Neill's ownership of O'Cahan's country (Coleraine) was contrary to both Gaelic law and assurances received by the latter from government. O'Neill was preparing to travel to London to answer the challenge when an invitation by O'Donnell and Maguire to join them in flight to the Continent dramatically altered the situation, baffling contemporaries and historians alike as to his motives for accepting. Through a skilful use of diplomacy and knowledge of English ways on the one hand, and a ruthless exploitation of Gaelic custom on the other, O'Neill appeared to have survived the end-of-century crisis rather well and there seemed little reason for his sudden abandonment of a position still apparently powerful. The activities of his younger and more volatile allies Maguire and O'Donnell threatened to involve him in new charges of conspiracy and when they announced that they were about to take ship for Spain in September and invited him to accompany them, he agreed. This event, closely followed by renewed rebellion in Inishowen and Derry, produced an abrupt change in government policy: from accommodation and gradual anglicisation (in the belief that the people were reformable) to outright confiscation and plantation.

Traditionally the Flight of the Earls in 1607 is taken as the end of the Gaelic order in Ireland and there can be no doubt that the events of the seventeenth century marked a sharp break with the past. The poets were the first to register the shock at this sudden destruction of the world which had sustained them. But it was to be many generations before Ulster generally did so and Gaelic practices continued far into the seventeenth century. The Nine Years War was in no way a popular rebellion. It was fought largely by mercenaries, and the experience of Fermanagh, where only two freeholders could be found to have actually participated in the rebellion, may not have been unusual. The Ulster chiefs were independent of their people and when they were removed, government officials experienced extraordinarily little resistance. In 1606 when Lord Deputy Mountjoy visited Monaghan he needed only 120 to 140 soldiers. In previous years he would have required between 800 and 1,000.[99] At first it seemed that those free septs and minor lords who had been seeking independence from over-lords like O'Neill would benefit from the attainder of their former overlords – and indeed many were confirmed in their land titles. But the Gaelic system, whatever its flaws, had allowed them considerable local autonomy – that famous 'liberty' which English observers thought made them such bad subjects. The operation of the new system pushed some into revolt, others into penury. Even Donal O'Cahan ended his days in the Tower of London, his case against O'Neill never resolved.[100]

Few at the end of the Gaelic period wished to perpetuate the old system of landholding. What seems to have been unrecognised, how-ever, was that with the introduction of the English system went a change in the notion of status, definable in future by ownership of land. In the seventeenth century there was a steady decline of native freeholders to the status of tenants. There were now many Palesmen and New English settled in Ulster, conversant with the new legal system and exploiting the very obvious weakness of Gaelic title to acquire more land. The support for measures which promised to give freehold-ers and tenants more security gave way to confusion at the operation of the new system. Inability to cope with an economy which required payment of money rents soon led to indebtedness. English officials eventually excluded the Irish entirely from operating the new legal system, because ties of kin stopped jurors convicting locals to whom, by the very nature of Gaelic society, they were invariably related.[101] Although the annals record frequent atrocities among the elite, medi-eval Irish society was not generally a violent one. People were much too valuable a commodity – lordship, after all, was defined by control of people rather than possession of land – and warfare generally took the form of 'harrying' (systematic destruction of property) and cattle raids, rather than the killing of people.[102] There was, moreover, no criminal code in Irish law, only collective fines and distraint, and the rural Irish never did quite come to terms with English laws which put people to death for attacks on property.[103]

Ironically the Flight of the Earls had removed the chief modernising element from Gaelic society in Ulster, an element prepared to operate within the new anglicising process.[104] But that process, coming so suddenly into the one part of Gaelic Ireland which had been left relatively untouched by English ways, did not allow for gradualism or accommodation, and the myth of the golden Gaelic past was already in the making among the first casualties of the process – the poets, the clerics, and the continental exiles.

3

RELIGION IN ULSTER BEFORE THE REFORMATION

Twisted their consciences, perverse their minds,
they desire no bishop or cleric;
they say no pater or creed –
I refuse to be one of their sort.

Fasts or feasts of the saints –
bad is the whim – they keep them not;
Mary is no more to them than a wisp,
a rude breed unblessed by God.

They hate baptism, cross and church,
a treacherous stock; a pity, O God,
is the decline of Patrick's faith
and a faith without direction being promoted.

> 1640 poem *Truagh mo Thurus ó mo Thír* ('Regretted
> is my Journey from my Country') of uncertain
> authorship, though attributed to Patrick Dunkin
> (Ó Muirgheasa, *Dhá Chéad*, 13–14)

At the end of the Nine Years War a general fear of religious persecution was preventing remaining rebels from surrendering.[1] O'Neill had identified religion as a common unifying force which would attach the Old English and the Spanish to his cause and win the support of the papacy. Certainly the new breed of English-born official in Ireland in the latter part of the sixteenth century was making Protestantism rather than obedience to the crown the test of loyalty, and increasingly identifying 'civility' with the new religion.[2] But even the Pope doubted O'Neill's sincerity and Jesuit and Spanish travellers to Ulster considered its inhabitants more pagan than Christian. Such tension between the 'universal' and 'national' church was quite common and in Ireland generally a central standard was not successfully imposed until the nineteenth century. But in Ulster in particular the old religion was too embedded in traditional ways to be easily supplanted and by the mid seventeenth century its future was reasonably secure. More dramatic was the speed and success with which the clerics and literati moved to create the image of the Gaelic past and Catholicism as an organic entity, providing the documentation for that exclusive nationalism which was to emerge two centuries later.

1. Decay and revival in the medieval church

The long isolation of the Irish church ended in the twelfth and thirteenth centuries with a series of church councils which introduced a system of dioceses and sought to end the many 'abuses' into which the Irish church had fallen. Bishops now replaced abbots as leaders of the church. More important in the decline of Gaelic monasticism, however, was the introduction of new continental orders: the Augustinians, Franciscans and, most of all, the Cistercians. With their strict rules, community life, grandiose buildings and distinctive dress, they remained apart from the laity. Although patronised by a few Ulster kings in the twelfth century, they were concentrated in Anglo-Norman areas and remained weak in Irish areas. Certainly, apart from the coastal strip of the earldom of Ulster, the province was relatively unaffected by the changes. The Columban tradition remained extraordinarily dynamic. Irish monks continued to prefer separate huts outside churches to the communal dormitories of the new orders, and many of the other 'abuses' associated with the Gaelic church continued.[3]

That the reforms of the twelfth and thirteenth centuries had such limited impact in Ulster owed not a little to the divisions that developed in the church between Irish and Anglo-Irish areas after the Anglo-Norman invasion. By the fourteenth century the see of Armagh was in the control of English or Anglo-Irish clerics and was to remain so till the sixteenth century. Ulster remained split between *ecclesia inter Hibernos* and *ecclesia inter Anglicos*. Whilst the Archbishop of Armagh chose to reside permanently in County Louth rather than in the cathedral city, the dioceses of Raphoe, Derry, Clogher and Kilmore remained relatively free from Anglo-Irish interference in church affairs, and although Down, Connor and Meath were *inter Anglicos*, a separate diocese of Dromore was created to take account of the increasing power of the Magennises. Even then it proved difficult to fill the see because it was considered 'as beynge . . . amonges wilde Irysh men'.[4] The ethnic conflict within the formal structure of the medieval church is undeniable, creating numerous incidents. The church leaders had welcomed Henry II as an ally in their programme for ecclesiastical reform. In consequence the Gaelic chiefs came to see the church as something foreign, and there was a significant revival of pagan practices in the early thirteenth century.[5] Indeed, Alan Bruford's study of medieval Irish romance and folk-tales shows that, unlike continental romances, Christian themes scarcely figure in the Irish ones. The traditional heroes were pagan, as was the landscape: 'They still lived for the most part in the world of Cú Chulainn.' Clerics when they do appear seem rather sinister, enchanters or abductors of women, whereas the druids are the poets.[6] It is important, however, not to exaggerate the internal conflict; the Ulster clerics and erenachs were perfectly happy to welcome the English primate of Armagh on his 1397 visitation.[7]

Although successive popes urged the Irish clergy and people to be loyal to the king of England under the terms of the initial 'grant' of *Laudabiliter*, they also intervened frequently to moderate the persistent tendency of English clerics to treat their Irish counterparts as inferior. The Irish clergy became great 'Rome-runners' in this period, and, as in later centuries, the papacy was widely recognised as a supranational arbiter in perennial local disputes. As elsewhere in late medieval Europe, there appears to have been genuine popular devotion to the Pope. 'In this place I could not walk in the street', wrote Bishop Chiericati, papal nuncio to the court of Henry VIII, of Downpatrick in 1515, 'because everyone ran to kiss my dress, understanding that I was nuncio from the Pope, so that I was almost compelled by force to stay in the house, so strong was their importunity, which arose from strong religious feeling.'[8]

As administrator-bishops continued to be appointed, however, and many English appointees to abbacies became absentees, formal religion declined. Monasteries attracted fewer vocations and fell into disrepair and as the Anglo-Irish colony retreated in the fourteenth century, so too did the monastic foundations which had spread with it. Border areas between the crown colony and the independent lordships – once seen as buttresses against encroaching rebelliousness – were particularly affected. Such was the decline in the Downpatrick area, that only the Franciscans survived the absorption of all the other foundations (five in all) into the cathedral in 1513.[9] Certainly the formal structure of the medieval Irish church was in poor shape on the eve of the Reformation. The first stages of the dissolution of the monasteries in the sixteenth century did not affect predominantly Irish areas in the west and north, where there were few large monasteries to dissolve. But to look for a formal, church-based religion in Ulster in this period would be unproductive. A preference for older monastic forms not only thwarted the medieval reforms but gave rise to a remarkable revival on the eve of the Reformation.

The rural, familial structure of Gaelic society provided an alien environment for the great continental orders. More congenial were the mendicant (or Observant) orders of friars, notably the Franciscans, with their emphasis on poverty and preaching, and travellers in sixteenth-century Ulster were impressed at the flourishing state of their friaries.[10] The revival had developed in the fifteenth century from an existing trend within the Franciscans for laity to follow a version of the rule while continuing to live in the community. This was the Third Order Secular, and, even though adopting a regular rule, it continued in closer communion with the locality than the older and now declining orders. Medieval Irish Christianity had retained the strong ascetic urge so notable in early centuries. Communities of Culdees survived in Ulster into the seventeenth century and holy men and places continued to be venerated.[11] Even Campion, often so critical of native Irish ways, found the people 'such mirrours of holiness and austeritie, that other nations retaine but a shewe or shadow of devotion in comparison of them'.[12]

These existing tendencies help explain the phenomenal popularity of the mendicant orders. They were noted for strict observance of their vows and preference for simple dwellings, often sited in remote and barren areas. It was almost a reversal to early church organisation. Unlike the Cistercians, their buildings and dress were simple and their mission was to minister to the religious and social needs of the local people. They did not have extensive lands, and they lived, not by tithes or compulsory dues, but by charitable alms usually given in kind. As they were credited with leading exemplary lives and sponsoring a spiritual literature in simple Irish, their criticism of fellow clerics who became Protestant as having 'sold Mary for meat and a wench', carried a particular relevance.[13] Their development seems to have had no parallel outside Ireland, and their existence must surely explain the failure of anti-clericalism to take root there. In contrast to English and Scottish preference for colleges of secular priests, the popularity of the friars testifies to Ireland's continuing attachment to monasticism and to the general conservative nature of Irish society. At the time of the dissolution of the monasteries, it proved particularly difficult to suppress the orders of friars. When ejected, they simply continued in the neighbourhood, sustained, as before, by the goodwill of the locals. Those of Armagh, when expelled at the beginning of the seventeenth century, split into two communities, one to Brantry, County Tyrone, the other to Creggan, south Armagh, and remained in the area into the eighteenth century.[14]

Their friaries in Ulster were founded by leading local families – the O'Donnells, the MacSweeneys and the O'Neills being particularly notable patrons in Gaelic areas, where they were most widespread. But we also find foundations by the MacQuillans, the MacDonnells and the Savages in Antrim and Down. The spiritual rewards of burial in the cemeteries and habit of the friars helped cement the links between Gaelic lord and the mendicant order. Indeed, this centuries-old attachment to monastic burial had made the monastic burial grounds ancestral mausoleums. It was very often the neglect into which these had fallen which motivated a local chieftain (or his wife) to introduce the mendicant orders.[15] The holy dead retained their powers in late medieval religion: penances were typically performed in cemeteries, the unworthy dead were thought to be repulsed by their worthier neighbours and families took great care to ensure the continued protection of their ancestral dead. There was much discontent among the descendants of the Armagh O'Neills in 1715 when a tree over the family vault was felled. It had been planted in the sixteenth century on the south side of the church just opposite the altar, so that the branches would grow over the O'Neill vault.[16]

To the Elizabethan mind the friars were particularly associated with native Irish culture and rebelliousness. John Derricke's woodcuts and commentary of 1581, claiming to depict the lifestyle of the Donegal MacSweeneys, is perhaps the most famous expression of this. Here the friar is constantly involved in the chieftain's everyday life and exploits, and while Derricke is hostile, and hardly a reliable source, he captures the respect for the friars among the Irish lords.[17] Nearly all were native Irish; many were members of hereditary learned families, closely linked with ruling dynasties, and almost all the Third Order friaries in Ulster owed their origins to local chiefs. Kinship with the exiled Gaelic lords made them spearheads of the continental Counter-Reformation and introduced a highly politicised tone into its literature.

The Franciscan Observant friars were particularly popular in Ulster.[18] Their spread was often a reaction against the exclusivity of the older orders (which were declining at the same time), and given their largely pastoral role, their expansion reflects a surviving popular piety independent of the fluctuations in church history. The debate over the failure of the Reformation in Ireland has singularly neglected the nature of popular piety.[19] It is wrong to think of medieval Christianity as rotten and ripe for reform. The problems lay rather in the higher church structure and its inflated bureaucracy. At local level it was flexible and accommodating of popular beliefs and practices. Few actually wanted a Reformation.[20]

2. Official and unofficial religion

In his study of devotional literature in the centuries before the Reformation, a Franciscan priest, Canice Mooney, found a ready availability of literature in Irish, much of it perpetuating pagan leftovers or peculiarly Gaelic interpretations of scripture. Significant is the continuing devotion to local saints, the familiar association of saints (and Mary in particular) with kin, and a sense of the vengefulness of the saints reminiscent of the heroic tales.[21] 'St Patrick is of better credit than Jesus Christ', it was observed in the 1580s, and Colum Cille was considered 'a god of great veneration with . . . all Ulster.'[22] Relic and image-worship was common throughout pre-Reformation Europe. But in Ireland both were symbols of power, part of the hereditary element so common throughout the history of the Irish church, and as such they were jealously guarded by secular rulers and families. Medieval churches seem to have been very ornate, their ornaments and relics prized by the local people and protected during the perennial warfare. Despite the ruthlessness of one of the Maguire chiefs in the fifteenth century, he was hailed by the Annals as one who had 'frequently set up oratories and churches and monasteries and holy crosses and images of Mary'.[23] While the complaint in 1530 of Nelan O'Neill against 'certain ecclesiastics' (including a McGurk and an O'Mellan) for 'fasting' and 'ringin bells' against him (including the bells of St Colum Cille and St Patrick, of which these families were respective hereditary keepers) represents the remarkable unbroken link of certain families with the early saints and their relics.[24]

Because of the failure of the medieval reform movement in Gaelic areas, the religion which continued to flourish in Gaelic Ulster retained traits left over from earlier times. Clerical marriage continued into the seventeenth century, as did hereditary clerical succession, lay claims to patronage and presentation (the right to nominate clergy), and a stronger attachment to kin than to church – resulting in persistent participation by clerics in inter-clan warfare. There was little social stigma attached to illegitimacy, concubinage and marriage to near relatives, and little inducement among the native clergy to enforce church decrees in such matters when clergy were as culpable as laity. As late as 1613 one Counter-Reformation missionary to Ulster still found it necessary to compel priests 'to put away their wives'.[25] Indeed most of the Rome-running of the period was in pursuit of dispensations for clerical illegitimacy, which Rome was more than happy to grant.[26] 'The clergy have more dispensations here than anywhere', commented Campion, 'and like to return a wife after only a year, if even a small quarrel.'[27] Indeed, clerical marriage was an essential part of the hereditary succession of professional clerical families like the O'Loughrans of Armagh and Tyrone. Benefiting from frequent papal dispensation for illegitimacy and marriage, members of the family dominated nearly all the important positions in the fifteenth-century *ecclesia inter Hibernicos* in the Armagh diocese. They were hereditary erenachs of Donaghmore near Dungannon, held various offices also under the O'Neills, and remained prominent in both church and politics throughout the seventeenth century. By then they were leading figures in the Counter-Reformation.[28] Cases of local clerical dynasties can be replicated from all over Ulster: the O'Corrys of County Armagh, whose descendants were still prominent in the twentieth-century parish of Lissane; the O'Boyles of Clondehorky parish, Donegal;[29] the Mac-Cawells of Clogher in Tyrone. A number of the leading clerical families were also members of ruling local dynasties, the names of the Maguires, the O'Donnells, the O'Gallaghers, the O'Reillys recurring regularly in episcopal succession lists.[30] The Protestant church's legitimisation of clerical wives and children both improved the legal status of women and had much to offer the hereditary Irish churchman. For such a cleric to support the Counter-Reformation, required, as Katharine Simms has forcibly argued, 'a transformation of outlook and ideals hardly less revolutionary than that involved in embracing Protestantism'.[31]

By the end of the sixteenth century little formal religion remained in Ulster. 'The people without discipline [and] utterly devoid of religion', complained Lord Deputy Sussex in 1562, 'come to divine service as to a May game.'[32] Nor was there much sense of belonging to the Roman church. The bishop was a distant figure, requiring the local lord's protection to enter an area, and seemingly unable to administer the one sacrament designed to bring bishop and laity together – confirmation. We have no positive information that sermons supposed to be delivered from the basic doctrinal handbook, the *Ignorantia sacerdotum*, were so delivered, and a good deal of evidence to the contrary – Elizabethan observers finding the Ulster Irish totally ignorant of doctrine and commandments. 'They are very religious', wrote Bishop Chiericati in 1515, 'but do not regard theft as a crime, and do not punish it.'[33] Nor was the taking of life considered wrong. Campion recounts an old tale of an Ulsterman attending confession for the first time with a travelling monk, who, when asked if he had committed murder, replied that he never knew before that it was a sin and confessed to five.[34] The novelty of Tuathal Balbh O'Gallagher capturing rather than killing prisoners in the early sixteenth century was attributed to a sermon in which he had heard a friar condemning homicide.[35] There are many such examples of the popularity and efficacy of these sermons (though the absurdity of some of the moral stories should guard against excessive romanticisation of the friars' integrity).[36]

Popular religious culture was largely one of localised folk practices and, with most of rural Europe at the time, the Ulster people would have been ignorant of the most basic elements of formal religion. Religion was rather a functional spirituality directed towards the needs of the community, honouring local saints like local chieftains, as much for their powers of protection and vengeance as for their spiritual example. A sense of sin scarcely existed, and confession – that most potent channel through which the Counter-Reformation sought to refashion the moral perception of the people – was largely unknown. But there was an age-old reverence for local devotional rituals and for learned and holy men which had transferred itself to the friars. Clerical training in Gaelic areas – though still a largely uncharted field – appears to have operated on a system of fosterage to clerical teachers operating in their own homes. Everything testifies to the complete integration of religion into Gaelic society, even the churches, as often as not, serving local secular needs.[37] So integrated, then, was religion with Irish society, particularly traditional kinship structures, but so lacking in formal structure, that the Reformation would have had to reform from the bottom up.

This must not, however, be confused with irreligion and Campion's dismissal of the religion of the 'uplandish' Irish as composed of 'idle miracles and revelations vaine and childish' was typical of that ageless disdain of the urban intellectual for the rural mind.[38] As in Europe generally, popular religiosity in Ulster was a mixture of the sacred and the superstitious, a profound identification of the mystical with local places and objects, a kind of pantheism which was a direct continuation of pre-Christian traditions.[39] In this mix, the friars supplied a devotional need. Surviving evidence – notably in the devotional literature translated from Latin into simple Irish, religious poems, many reflecting strong social preoccupations, and rhymed sermons testifies to the strength of their pastoral mission and to a genuine popular spirituality creating the demand. There exists in manuscript a considerable collection of compendia of moral tales used by Franciscan preachers in the late middle ages. Commentators note a lightness of touch, an absence of high moral theology, and a naturalness which helps explain why many of the tales survived into modern folklore.[40] Most are meditations on the life of Christ from the *New Testament*. But there is nothing sterile or inaccessible about them and they make moving reading. A notable example – and perhaps the most popular of all – is *Smaointe beatha Chríost*, a fifteenth-century translation by a Franciscan friar at Killala of a fourteenth-century Latin text. At least thirty-eight manuscript copies have survived, when less than half a dozen would be the norm, and some twenty survive for the nearest rival in popularity, a thirteenth-century life of Mary. *Smaointe* is shot through with typical Franciscan ideals of poverty, but even more significant is its sheer humanity. Christ is a loving son, close to his Mother, solicitous for her suffering. Mary is not the plaster-cast image of serenity and virtue as promoted by the modern Catholic Church, but a real person, suffering normal maternal anguish at loss, separation and death. This is Mary as the representative of humanity rather than the icon of the church, a theme common also in secular literature of the period.[41]

There is, moreover, some evidence that amongst the literate and aristocratic elite, particularly among those actively involved in the sixteenth-century revival, religion may not have been quite so divorced from the church's ideal as imagined. Maire MacSweeney was one of several aristocratic Irish women who commissioned pious and religious works in the sixteenth and seventeenth centuries. In 1513–14 she commissioned a 'Book of Piety' from a local scribe, which includes stories about the 'Finding of the True Cross', 'Christ's Descent into Hell', the infancy and passion of Christ, Adam and Eve's banishment from Heaven, lives of saints Margaret, Catherine, Colum Cille and Patrick, the vision of St Paul, some passages of St Patrick's Purgatory, various papal indulgences, a treatise on the Eucharist, the benefits of hearing mass, advice on how to make confession, a description of venal and mortal sins, a passage on the twelve golden Fridays (a precursor of the first Fridays practice), various homilies on drunkenness, hypocrisy and true piety, and advice for holy living. There is also evidence of the celebration of Easter as special. Maire, we are told, heard daily mass (sometimes more than once), fasted three days a week and during the fasts of Lent and winter, and observed the golden Fridays. She founded many churches in Ulster and Connacht, and was buried in the friars' habit and in the monastery which she founded.[42] Support for the Counter-Reformation by the Gaelic aristocracy may not have been so entirely cynical as once imagined.

3. The impact of the Reformation and Counter-Reformation

Lacking a working parochial structure and regular religious practice, however, Gaelic Ulster presented a problem to Reformation and Counter-Reformation alike and both proceeded on the premise that the populace required 'civilising' before they could be formally instructed in religion. Both were equally unsuccessful in the short term. Although Counter-Reformation Catholicism had a working church structure in Ireland by the 1630s, it was concentrated in Anglo-Irish areas and it would be some time before it penetrated Gaelic Ireland. But equally, the Reformation failed entirely to make any impact on Gaelic areas. Until quite recently even leading Irish historians wrote of a Catholic people predestined to triumph, ignoring the fact that other European states had been just as renowned for their popular piety, yet still adopted Protestantism.[43] It was not a case of positive choice between one or the other. In the seventeenth century people just continued as they had done before. The long-term difference lay in Protestantism's cultural rejection of Gaelic ways and Catholicism's compromise with them.

Until the seventeenth century, the progress of the Reformation was minimal in Ireland and non-existent in Ulster, outside Carrickfergus.[44] At the time there was certainly no great popular outburst against it, no immediate association between rebelliousness and religion. After the dissolution of the monasteries, there was some spectacular destruction and iconoclasticism[45] – a wanton destructiveness which left the Protestant church impoverished and dependent on the hated tithe. But such attacks on church property had been a common feature of Gaelic society,[46] and it was the earlier foundations in the urban areas which suffered most. Recusancy fines could only be implemented in the few areas where local government was in the control of the Protestant gentry, and overall there was a lack of will and consistency in the implementation of the religious reforms. Personal greed rather than religious zeal was often the motivating force. 'The ministers for disability, and greediness', remarked Lord Deputy Sussex in 1562, 'he had in contempt, and the wise fear more the impiety of the licentious professors, than the superstition of the erroneous papists.'[47] The New English, who had most to benefit, would have preferred a more repressive policy and the few spectacular executions of clergy which occurred (that of Bishop O'Devany of Down and Connor in 1612 being the most notable) were gratuitous acts by those in power in Ireland rather than policy developed in London. James I's government preferred accommodation.[48]

There is still considerable debate on the reasons for the success or failure of the Reformation in different localities. But much seems to have depended on the accessibility of the reformers, their residence in the area, their assiduous application to preaching and involvement of the laity in the new religion.[49] They were preconditions for success which proved unattainable in Ireland. James I believed that the native Irish areas would be more amenable to instruction, and successive English monarchs and their advisers were against forced conversion.[50] It was a policy of persuasion, however, which foundered on the absence of sufficiently trained preachers to bring the gospel to the Irish, and most of all on the developing exclusivity of the Church of Ireland.

Staffed predominantly with English and Scottish clerics – the existence of some genuinely Protestant native clergy not surviving into a second generation – the Church of Ireland pursued a policy of winning the Irish from their 'stubborn traditionalism and ignorant superstition' through compulsion and Anglicisation and simply succeeded in setting itself apart as elitist and foreign. Failure fed its existing assumption that the Irish were perhaps irredeemable in any event. More Calvinist than its English parent, its belief in predestination and justification by faith alone and its early identification of the Pope with Antichrist caused it to see the Irish generally as already damned. It fixed in Protestant imagination the fiercely anti-Catholic, apocalyptic and embattled identity which would afflict its relationship with Catholicism into modern times. Above all it was hostile to Gaelic ways and the pull of kin ultimately eroded the loose conformity of native Irish clergy.[51] Calvinism's hostility to the temporals of Catholicism alienated it from a native culture in which local saints were so revered. They 'neither fast nor keep the feasts of the saints and they don't care a rush for Mary', complained one poet of the Puritan ministers brought to County Down by the Scots planters.[52]

At first Counter-Reformation Catholicism too seemed at war with Gaelic mores. In particular it condemned those very elements in popular religious practice which had developed from existing kin and community structures: contractual, private and clandestine marriages, polygamy, excessive feastings and communal gatherings at wakes and funerals, money fines and compensation as part of penance; burials in monastic rather than church grounds. Tridentine Catholicism (as set out by the Council of Trent, 1545–63, in response to the Protestant Reformation) sought a priestly, church-centred religion, directly communing with the individual rather than the family or community. Most of all it sought instruction through catechism and education. Until the continental seminaries produced enough priests to serve such needs, which they did not before 1641, such aims remained unfulfilled. Before then the need for an Irish-speaking clergy required the frequent vesting of episcopal authority in the friars, and they mediated the strictness of Tridentine decrees. There was also only limited circulation of the vernacular catechisms and religious tracts issuing from the sole existing Irish-language printing press, which was in Louvain.[53] The Catholicism which survived the Reformation in Ulster was more the medieval than the Tridentine kind, and owed more to simple survival on the one hand, and the exclusiveness of Protestantism on the other, than to the Counter-Reformation.

Calvinism represented a move from religion based on locality and a sacralised view of the world, to an inward-looking one based on the individual and one's co-religionists.[54] As such it was in sharp opposition to the intertwining of religion, place and kin prevalent in rural Ulster (and in rural Europe generally). Tridentine Catholicism, strictly interpreted, was also hostile to popular religion. The Old English tended to be more strictly Tridentine and elitist, and in this there was some continuation of the medieval divisions between *ecclesia inter Anglicos* and *ecclesia inter Hibernicos*. There was no meeting of minds between Old English and native Irish prior to 1641. The Jesuits – the advanced guard of the Counter-Reformation – were concentrated in and around the Pale and had little contact with the Ulster chieftains. They persistently objected to the influence of Hugh O'Neill (even in exile) over episcopal appointments to Ulster, and to the continuing dominance of the friars, when Tridentine reforms envisaged authority flowing from the bishops.[55]

And yet, in the circumstances, it made sense to utilise the only clergy left in place – which in most cases meant the Franciscan friars. In 1561 papal permission had been given to hold masses in places other than churches, and half a century later the friars were fulfilling many of the duties of the absent secular clergy. Some religious communities simply set up again near their destroyed buildings, and by 1615 many were returning to re-occupy their old houses. Two years later the Franciscan provincial and guardian of their college at Louvain, Donatus Mooney, reported 18 houses of Franciscan tertiaries in Ulster, against 9 in Connacht, 2 in Meath and one in Leinster.[56] Because these were more dependent on the support of the laity than previously, traditional lay influence continued. The result was that by the 1620s, though there was an episcopal structure in place (something which failed to materialise in England till 1685), the kind of change envisaged by Counter-Reformation reformers had not materialised. For most of the sixteenth century the friars were still trained in the traditional manner in the localities (one of the factors, it was thought, rendering them hostile to Counter-Reformation changes). There were still married clergy and friar-bishops still closely connected with local Gaelic dynasties. Peter Lombard, the absentee Old English Archbishop of Armagh, attributed the otherwise inexplicable execution of O'Devany (when government policy was one of general leniency towards the clergy) to his association with O'Neill.[57] As the leading Irish cleric at the papal court he contributed to papal reconciliation with the Stuart monarchs and to the acceptance of the idea that Irish Catholics could be loyal to a Protestant monarch.[58]

But in Ulster, where organised religion had been so closely identified with aristocratic society, old traditions died hard and aristocratic lineage remained a major recommendation to church preferment long after the dismantling of the Gaelic superstructure. The Franciscan Bonaventure Magennis, appointed Bishop of Down and Connor in 1630, was recommended to the Pope as of true noble blood, kindred to the O'Donnells, the MacDonnells of Antrim, the O'Neills of Tyrone and of course, the Magennises.[59] The Ulster clergy as a result remained the most pro-Spanish, the most suspected of political subversion. They did not receive a welcome at the new continental seminaries set up by the Old English – a major factor in the institution of one of their own at Louvain, in the Spanish Netherlands.

In turn the Ulster clergy resented the appointment of outsiders to benefices, much as they had done throughout the Middle Ages. They considered the clergy outside Ulster soft on the Protestants, and prone to resist Ulster appointees as 'those who could give offence to the English'. In a lengthy memorial on the subject in 1626, Bonaventure Magennis explained that 'ecclesiastics have frequently to hide in woods and mountains and there assemble the people for the reception of the sacraments and for instruction, and the people have to carry to those places food and requisites for their ecclesiastics'. How then, he asked, would an outsider survive, unknown to the area, even if he did reside, which recent experience had shown to be unlikely? This was a thinly veiled attack on Lombard, who never took up residence in his archdiocese of Armagh. Magennis continued by pointing to the Ulster princes as preservers of the faith there. It is their influence, wrote another Ulster cleric the same year, through whom 'the faith is preserved whole and inviolate in the province of Ulster, more than in all the other provinces of Ireland'.[60]

Such provincialism was entirely typical of Gaelic society.[61] All the colleges on the Continent were subject to such rivalry. Provincial pride aside, the continuing strength of the Gaelic lords had preserved much of Ulster from the full force of the Reformation until James I's reign. When steps were taken to establish a Protestant episcopate after 1603, the first bishop, George Montgomery, found the medieval church infrastructure still intact.[62] Signs are that those remaining after the Flight of the Earls – even so-called 'deserving natives' who received land under the plantation scheme – continued to provide the focus of Catholic religious practice and sustenance to the friars. In May 1613 Shane McPhelimy O'Donnelly attended a Sunday mass in a glen in Brian Maguire's country between Fermanagh and Tyrone. Several of the Maguires, an O'Quin and an O'Neill were there, O'Neill 'enthusiastically saying they'd rather go into rebellion than lose religion'. The friar, the thirty-year-old Turlough McCrudden, a native of Tyrone 'lately come from beyond the seas', preached for most of the day, stating 'that he was come from the Pope to persuade them not to change their religion, but rather to go into rebellion'.[63]

The scene may have been repeated many times, for another deposition some months later told of McCrudden having preached while staying with the O'Hagans and again in the woods of Lisselby Roodan in the barony of Loghenesolyn, Londonderry. The informant estimated attendance at 1,000, including 'all the priests of those parts . . . to the number of 14'. Again he preached against the English 'damnable doctrine', inferring that greed alone induced their countrymen to turn. 'He told the people that the Pope had sent him unto them to comfort them . . . and that every year the Pope would send unto them holy men, lest they should be seduced and reasoned by the English, and that they should not despair or be dismayed; though for a time God punished them by suffering their lands to be given to strangers and heretics, it was a punishment for their sins; and he bade them fast and pray ... for it should not be long before they were restored to their former prosperities.'

Information on this Franciscan mission reveals an already established system of local funding for the Louvain seminary through gifts to preachers such as McCrudden and more regular collections by the priests. 'There is nobody in the country of the Irishry, but has given somewhat according to their abilities', reported Teag McGlone, the informant, 'the poorer sort' giving twelve pence on the above occasion. His sermons also highlight the moral strictness of the Counter-Reformation, even if the Ulster clergy hardly measured up to its standards. 'He prayed long, exhorting them to reform their wicked lives, telling them of drunkenness, whoredom, and lack of devotion and zeal.' He deprived a number of priests of their livings 'some for keeping women, others for presuming to exercise the function of priest, who had not been properly called, and for having more benefices than one'. McCrudden is an example of the new continental-trained Franciscans, who were more politicised and pro-Spanish than their predecessors. It was these the authorities most wanted to exclude, and in a year when fears ran high of a Spanish-backed return by the exiled chiefs, McCrudden told his audience that Tyrconnell was returning with 18,000 men sent by the King of Spain 'and that, according to a prophecy in a book at Rome, England had only two years more to rule in Ireland'.[64]

In the long term continental-trained clergy were to play a vital role in bringing a certain uniformity to Irish Catholicism. But they remained a minority in Ulster. In the 1670s and 1680s Archbishop Oliver Plunkett was still complaining at the weakness of episcopal control and parish structure in Ulster, the poor quality (in his view) of the clergy, and, above all, the continuing dominance of the Franciscans over the spiritual life of the people. The influence of the local lords over Catholicism in their localities was still greater than that of the bishop. Various synods, such as that at Drogheda in 1614, may have promulgated the decrees of the Council of Trent, but half a century later there was little sign of change on the ground.[65] In this Ireland was not unique. The Tridentine reforms were rarely implemented in all their purity and the general picture throughout Europe was one of harnessing rather than repudiating popular practices.

4. The friars and the beginnings of 'patriotic antiquarianism'

Given this continuing position of the friars as part of the Gaelic elite, it is hardly surprising that it was the Franciscans who led the way in anchoring the Gaelic past to Catholicism. Such a development was not unusual to Ireland: the Counter-Reformation generally produced a kind of 'patriotic antiquarianism', prompted initially by humanist contempt for barbaric pasts.[66] The ancient traditions of monasteries as repositories of learning had continued with the friars, who recruited heavily from the families of hereditary poets and genealogists. And just as the crises of the Viking and Anglo-Norman invasions had sparked off major Gaelic revivals, so also did the Tudor conquest. From Ulster the leading figures were all Franciscans associated with the new Franciscan seminary in Louvain. It had been founded in 1606 by Florence Conry (Flaithrí Ó Maoil Chonaire), chaplain to Hugh O'Neill, confessor to Red Hugh O'Donnell, and member of a Connacht family of hereditary historians. He was the epitome of the politicised native Irish priest, conducting missions on behalf of Tyrone and Tyrconnell to Spain.[67] In similar mould was Hugh Mac Caghwell (Mac Aingil). Born in County Down, but descended from the hereditary erenachs, the Clogher Mac Cathmhaoils, he trained at one of the bardic schools still operating in Ulster in the late sixteenth century and became tutor to Hugh O'Neill's sons. On the Continent he became a noted theologian, and, like Conry, was appointed to an Irish see at O'Neill's request. He too had carried out political missions to Spain and, it seems, a papal mission to Ulster in 1613.[68] Over the next three decades Louvain produced a remarkable outpouring of Gaelic scholarship and devotional texts in Irish.

In 1626 Michael O'Clery was sent to Ireland by Aodh Mac an Bhaird (Hugh Ward), professor of theology at Louvain and member of the family of hereditary poets to the O'Donnells, to collect all the available manuscript material for an ecclesiastical history of Ireland. O'Clery had been a lay brother of the Franciscan Abbey in Donegal and, like Ward, a member of a family of ollamhs (poets/historians) to the O'Donnells. O'Clery was a trained historian, and he and his associates are credited with saving many of the Irish manuscripts now extant. Working mainly out of the remnants of the Donegal friary, they scoured the north and midlands of Ireland, and were given ready access to the manuscript collection of the Protestant Archbishop Ussher (himself a noted antiquarian, who shared the Franciscans' ambitions of defending Ireland's reputation as the island of saints and scholars from its detractors). Only in the western parts of Ulster and in Connacht did O'Clery find the chroniclers following the old ways. The outcome of the Louvain Franciscans' efforts was a number of saints' lives, in simple Irish, which set the standard of hagiographical religious writing thereafter, a new edition of the *Lebor Gabála*, a new martyrology, and, most famously, the *Annals of the Four Masters*.[69]

It has frequently been argued that the activities of O'Clery and his like represent the coming together of Catholicism, Gaelic heritage and anti-English nationalism, and that the works emanating from the continental seminaries played a major role in the process. If so the process was lengthy in its gestation for the Louvain works are not noticeably anti-English and were aimed at an Irish and continental elite rather than at the Irish people.[70] The portrayal of an unbroken link between the Irish people, Catholicism and learning, is however, unmistakable, as is the replacement of the multitude of local saints with the national trio of Patrick, Brigid and Colum Cille, and the denunciation of Protestantism as heretical – a word entering the Irish language for the first time. Certainly the purpose behind the 1625 Louvain life of Patrick, Brigid and Colum Cille, the compiler told his reader, was that 'you may learn the sympathy between us moderne Catholikes and St Patricke and the Primitive Christians, and on the contrary discover the discrepancy of the Protestants, not only with S. Patrike whome I am sure they will discarde for a very superstitious papist, but from all the current of the ancient Catholiks'.[71] Likewise the devotional work of someone like Florence Conry also incorporated contemporary religious issues, the repression of the clerics, the recusancy fines, an attack on Protestant bishops, interference of the state in religious matters, and an early claim that government derived its authority from the governed.[72]

Much of this continental-inspired revival falls into the established pattern of antiquarianism, the retrieval and copying of older Gaelic manuscripts, and scholars differ on the extent to which one can detect early glimmerings of nationalism in it. Certainly much of the Gaelic poetry of the early seventeenth century – like bardic poetry through the centuries – shows a pragmatism which attempts to accommodate the new political situation, hostility to Luther's and Calvin's 'breed' and praise for James I existing in equal measure. The coronation of James I was welcomed by many of the Ulster poets as ushering in a new age of tolerance. The king's Scottish and Catholic background, his past friendship with Hugh O'Neill, and most of all their belief that he was in fact descended from the third-century Irish king Feargal, all combined to reconcile clerics and poets to the new order. O'Neill's call for a religious crusade now found less favour with Rome and a pious formula on the theme of rendering unto Caesar what is Caesar's was put forward to allow Irish and English Catholics to reconcile their religion with loyalty to a Protestant monarch. As Breandán Ó Buachalla has detailed in a seminal article on the subject, the traditional occupation of the learned classes in supplying impeccable genealogies to victorious lords played a major role in the acceptance of the Stuarts as Ireland's rightful kings.[73]

This did not stop them, however, from lamenting their lost status and proclaiming a holy war against the new breed of upstarts, *Gael* and *Gall* alike; thus Eochaidh Ó hEódhasa (O'Hussey), Maguire's *ollamh*,

> Where have the Gaels gone?
> What is the fate of the mirthful throngs? . . .
> They have been given billeting far and wide,
> Away from bright, smooth Ireland; . . .
> They find no sweetness in devotion to poetry
> The sound of harps or the music of an organ
> Nor the tale of the Kings of Bregia of the turreted walls
> Nor the numbering of the ancient generations of their
> forefathers . . .[74]

And yet the same poet welcomed the accession of James as the end of mourning, a new dawn. Ó Gnímh (*ollamh* to the O'Neills) could write the haunting

> My heart is in woe,
> And my soul is in trouble,
> For the mighty are low,
> And the abased are the noble.[75]

> (A more literal translation would be:
> My woe at the condition of the Gaels!
> seldom a joyful mind
> has any of them at this time –
> all their nobles are annihilated!)

But he could also sing the praises of those who were profiting from the new system. Fearghal Óg Mac an Bhaird's 1608 lament on the death of O'Donnell spoke of the threat to Ireland from 'the sect of Luther, the legions of Calvin . . . the stewards of heretic bishops'. Yet he too accepted James as rightful king:

> Three crowns the right of James . . .
> For the King of the hosts of the Gael and the Gall . . .
> To you is the place of Ireland as well
> You are her husband and equal.[76]

Given such apparently mixed sentiments, scholars have questioned nationalistic readings of these poems.[77] Despite the remarkable outpouring of Gaelic literature which occurred at the beginning of the seventeenth century, it would be unrealistic to expect a major break by the poets and learned men with the strict, centuries-old conventions in which they were trained. Their preoccupations were still the elitist ones of the Irish bards, praising their traditional patrons by tracing kinship with the Irish saints. Moreover, in a continuing oral culture where few (even among the elite) could actually read, the direct influence of the printed works emanating from Louvain can have been minimal. The key link here would have been the clergy and particularly friars like McCrudden who would have used such works as manuals, and clearly had the power to draw large crowds. For over a century, even in times of practical tolerance, successive governments sought to curtail the influence of the continental-trained clergy: 'for they spare not to come out of Spaine, from Rome, and from Remes, by long toyle and dangerous traveyling hither, where . . . no reward or richesse is to be found, onely to draw the people into the Church of Rome . . . lurking secretly in their houses, and in corners of the country'.[78]

The Catholic Church, dominated as it was by members of the Gaelic elite, had moved quickly to define Catholicism as the 'ancestral religion', that 'received by their forefathers'.[79] In so doing it created the texts which fed into later nationalism. These texts were not generally printed until the nineteenth century. But to claim lack of impact because not in print till then would be to misunderstand the process of the transmission of ideas in the two preceding centuries. Gaelic manuscripts were highly prized by their owners. They were frequently copied, widely circulated, and often memorised for recitation in public. As the scribal tradition gradually disappeared with the cessation of the schools which had operated in the Gaelic system, clerics and schoolmasters increasingly became the main practitioners. Often older Gaelic manuscripts survive only in their seventeenth-century form, some corrupted by contemporary readings of the past. Ten surviving manuscripts would suggest that such a work had entered popular oral tradition. By this yardstick, the most celebrated work by Catholic priest, poet and historian of Anglo-Norman ancestry, Geoffrey Keating (*Foras Feasa ar Éirinn*, *c*.1634) must rank as the most influential Irish-language manuscript of all time. Though not printed in full until the twentieth century, hundreds of manuscript copies have been located from all over Ireland.[80] A popular history of Ireland written in Irish by a French-trained Munster cleric, it updated the pseudo-history of the *Lebor Gabála* to include the Old English and conveyed the notion of Catholicism and Ireland as an organic unit. The Louvain-produced devotional works in Irish would have been used as religious manuals, the sources of homilies and sermons by the clergy in Ireland. In time their message would have entered popular consciousness. Certainly the trend by the eighteenth century was for Irish scribes to write in a more popular idiom. The material from which 'the origin legend of the emergent Irish nation'[81] later developed was being created by these exiled clerics. The clergy were replacing the learned classes and frequently acting as patrons in this new order of things. The old elitism is still there and it is the Irish upstarts and churls who are objects of scorn in the poetry.[82] But the association between the Irish and Catholicism is unmistakable and the two would merge in the second half of the seventeenth century.

4

THE LOSS OF THE LAND: PLANTATION AND CONFISCATION IN SEVENTEENTH-CENTURY ULSTER

'Before the war the nobility of Ulster enjoyed their possessions . . . But now, only three Catholic gentlemen in all Ulster have recovered their estates and property . . . All the others have difficulty obtaining a lease of a part of their property . . . The peasantry – those who cultivate the land – are all right . . . But the gentlemen are completely ruined.'

Archbishop Plunkett, 1671 (Hanly, ed., *Plunkett Letters*, 247)

It would require over two centuries of erratic development for the kind of Catholic nationalism previewed in the continental writings of the early seventeenth century to emerge. However, the association between religion and dispossession – so central to modern nationalism – was well established by the close of the seventeenth century. The plantation of Ulster with British settlers was not initially intended as a religious campaign against Catholics. But it took on its own dynamic and effectively became such by the turn of the century. For Protestant settlers too the century established the perception of Catholics poised to take revenge and dispossess them at the first opportunity. The Ulster Irish had risen in 1641 and 'massacred' large numbers of the settler population. That the Ulster Plantation was never as total, nor the 1641 uprising as brutal, as tradition allows matters little. Both have continued to be axioms of respective communal identities for over three centuries, the one played up, the other played down according to one's religious affiliation. 'I was watching a programme on TV about the conquest of Northern Ireland and the setting up of the Plantation,' Paddy Doherty, prominent Catholic civic leader in Derry, told the 1993 Opsahl Commission.

'It featured the building of houses in order to protect the inhabitants. The seizing of the land and all of the activities and atrocities to maintain the ownership of that land is the root problem of the present troubles. They [the Unionists] are still building walls and it looks as if there has been no movement from those days when they saw everybody outside as being uncouth, violent and prepared to take their lives.'[1]

This 'seizing of the land' – the land confiscations of the seventeenth century – was to remain a symbol of communal injustice in the minds of Ulster Catholics long after it had ceased to be an issue in the rest of Ireland. It pervaded popular tradition and much otherwise scholarly local history. The post-1969 Troubles were to dispel much of that bitterness as a majority of Catholics became increasingly aware of the monster to which it had given rise. But it informed rural republicanism possibly more than is recognised. The sinister campaign against Protestant border farmers during the Troubles, the justification of hard-line attitudes by references to the sufferings of Catholics at the plantation, the implication that the settlers and their descendants are un-Irish, all fuelled the equally persistent Protestant fears of another 1641.[2]

The problem about the chaos which engulfed seventeenth-century Ireland (as indeed it did contemporary Britain and the rest of Europe) is that we know very little about the ordinary people, the 'churls' so valued by Hugh O'Neill and equally by the new settler landlords. The 'churls' may well have fared a good deal better under the new dispensation than under the Gaelic land system.[3] But the elite did not, and it is their voice we hear. Moreover, because of the nature of Gaelic society – with its extended kinship networks, multiple layers of declined and declining families, and regular division of lands – there were many more people claiming status as gentry than had land to support such claims, and this at a time when social status was increasingly measured in land-ownership rather than lineage. It was this, the sharp decline in status, the resentment at being lorded over by upstarts and *parvenus*, which most determined the reaction of that 'elite' to the plantation, rather than actual dispossession.

1. The Ulster Plantation

The Irish chiefs were scattered and King James was well content. He declared that all Ulster was forfeit to him . . . The bad land, bog and mountain and forest was divided among the Irish. The good land was given to the King's favourites or sold to Englishmen . . . This was called the Plantation of Ulster; for the king planted there men whom he could count on to be loyal to him, since they would always be at enmity with the Irish they had driven out; many of whom were living miserably on the bleak hillsides, in sight of their old homes.[4]

So ran a popular early twentieth-century school textbook. Like all popular history it contains both truths and distortions. From the government's point of view, the Ulster Plantation, like earlier plantations in Leix, Offaly and Munster, was driven largely by security and fiscal considerations. The Flight of the Earls, the subsequent rebellion of Sir Cahir O'Doherty and the vast tracts of church land (some 20 per cent of the province, technically confiscate, but relatively untouched till James I's reign) placed an unprecedented amount of territory at the disposal of the crown – virtually the whole of modern Armagh, Cavan, Tyrone, Fermanagh, Derry and Donegal. The sudden availability of so much territory presented the new monarch with the opportunity of creating a defensible colony and infusing Ulster Irish culture with habits of 'civility' and industry. Like all colonial ventures it was shot through with the cultural elitism of the colonising power. But it was not a blueprint for a general dispossession of the existing inhabitants. Sir John Davies, the attorney general, credited with master-minding the plantation, thought earlier plantations had failed because all the land was given to adventurers, forcing the local people into the hills and woods where they became outlaws.[5] He and the Lord Deputy, Chichester, considered the creation of a secure Ulster Irish population alongside the new planter element as vital to the scheme's success. Having cut off the 'heads of that hydra of the North', he predicted a rosy future.

'All the possessions shall descend and be conveyed according to the course of the Common Law. Every man shall have a certain home and know the extent of his estate, whereby the people will be encouraged to manure their land with better industry than heretofore hath been used, to bring up their children more civilly, to provide for their posterity more carefully. These will cause them to build better houses for their safety and to love neighbourhood. Thense will arise villages and towns, which will draw tradesmen and artificers. So as we conceive a hope that these countries in a short time will not only be quiet neighbours to the Pale, but be made as rich and civil as the Pale itself.'[6]

In other words, he thought the Irish could be made 'civil'. Time would reveal this cosy image of a settled peasantry to be inappropriate for a pastoral people, accustomed to transhumance and the mobile lifestyle dictated by it. But it held a certain attractiveness for those continuing to seek security of land title.

Such had been the insecurity (and resentment) created in Gaelic Ulster by the aggrandisement of overlords like Hugh O'Neill that a number of rival chieftains had not only fought in the war against him, but fully participated in and initially welcomed the Ulster Plantation as giving them greater security of title under English law. It was the Gaelic system of overlordship and all its trappings which England sought to destroy. Bringing the Irish into the benefits of the common law, granting rent relationships and leases in place of the customs tying man to lord in the Gaelic system was as important as planting British settlers in early schemes, and widespread dispossession of the Ulster Irish was not envisaged.

Ulster was to remain severely under-populated for most of the seventeenth century.[7] Loss of life in the Nine Years War, followed by famine and harvest failure, had taken a heavy toll. In contrast England and Scotland were over-populated and severe land-hunger was fuelled by a flood of pamphlets extolling the attractiveness of Irish land. At a time when voyages of discovery and colonisation were in vogue in Europe, a natural migration of peoples from Scotland and England to Ulster was already underway before the official plantation was conceived. We know of new settlements of Catholic Scots (almost certainly gallowglass families) at Strabane (in Tyrone), Inishowen (in Donegal), and there were almost certainly others.[8] But Counties Antrim and Down are the best documented and here we have a foretaste of how the indigenous population (or at least their lords) responded to settlement by newcomers. In these two counties that chronic instability of land rights, so noticeable in the closing decades of the sixteenth century, made many Gaelic lords eager participants in the new schemes. Partial surrender of family territory in return for secure title over the remainder seemed a good bargain. The hibernicised Catholic descendants of the old Anglo-Norman colony in County Down, around Downpatrick and Lower Ards (the Savages, Whites, Russells, Echlins, Audleys, Mandevilles, Smiths, Bensons, Jordans and

Fitzsimmonses) had participated in abortive attempts at new British settlements in the late sixteenth century, largely as part of their continued resistance to O'Neill's expansion.[9] The three leading Gaelic lordships in Down (those of Magennis, the MacCartans and the Clandeboye O'Neills) had all voluntarily accepted a reduction of their landed power in return for such title. However, there was more than a hint of shady dealing by Scottish speculators like Sir Hugh Montgomery and Sir James Hamilton in their agreement with Conn O'Neill in 1605, whereby they used their influence at the Stuart court, and O'Neill's parlous political situation (in prison for rebellion) to acquire one-half and then two-thirds of his land. Even still it granted O'Neill secure title to the remainder of his existing estate, recognised status as a figure of consequence in the new system, and guaranteed succession to his sons.[10] All of this reflected a recognition that the best chance of secure title now lay with the crown, and there was a rush to gain it from a new Scottish monarch who was expected to be more sympathetic. In fact, Conn's inheritance was whittled away in little over a decade by indebtedness and the need for ready cash, which he raised by selling off most of the remnants of his estate to Hamilton, Montgomery and Moses Hill. Few Gaelic lords would handle the new rent and money economy well and indebtedness was to cause more loss of land than confiscation.

But one east Ulster Catholic family was to profit spectacularly under the new regime of crown grants. When James became king of England in 1603, the MacDonnells of Antrim held a precarious, though legally unrecognised, hold over the whole of Antrim (including the Route, where they had displaced the MacQuillan lords). Good timing ensured that they had survived the Nine Years War, untainted by treason and favoured by James (whom they had helped against internal enemies in Scotland). The upshot was a royal grant of the entire territory of the Glens and the Route. The MacDonnells (soon to become earls of Antrim) were survivors. Despite a number of major setbacks, they succeeded in retaining both their estates and their Catholicism throughout the seventeenth century. The result was a Scottish-Irish hybrid population, speaking a 'Highland Irish'. Antrim became a haven for Catholicism, to which streams of Scottish Catholics resorted periodically, and one of the final remnants of Gaelic overlordship. It survived as such because of the earl's strong position within the Anglicised power structure. A leading courtier who married the widow of the duke of Buckingham and periodically raised troops for the Stuarts, he effectively straddled both worlds. His power and position at court also allowed him to retain all the trappings of a Gaelic chief which elsewhere the authorities were trying to stamp out. Like all Gaelic lords, his kinship network was wide, with the result that a call for help in 1639 to recover his family lands in the Western Isles elicited offers from nearly all the Gaelic families in Ulster – 'as many Oe's and Mac's as would startle a whole council board', according to Lord Deputy Wentworth.[11]

The unofficial settlement of the eastern counties set a pattern for the plantation. Even the earl of Antrim encouraged some three hundred families of Lowland Scots Protestants to settle on his land. There is no sign that they displaced sitting Catholic tenants, many of whom sub-let to incoming Protestants.[12] In contrast the Clandeboye estates were de-populated and waste, and the acquisitions by Montgomery and Hamilton produced the most concentrated settlement of Scots in Ulster in the first half of the seventeenth century, extending from the south shore of Belfast Lough to the Ards peninsula. Conn O'Neill had given away more territory than he was strictly entitled to, and, since the area was flooded with new settlers, it is likely that existing Irish were displaced.[13] By 1609 a vigorous building programme was already underway to accommodate the new settlers. The ruins of local monasteries disappeared in the search for building materials, much to the disgust of the Franciscan priest Edmund MacCana who toured the area in the 1640s. 'Of these monasteries not even the ruins remain, for a colony of Scots, who settled there, employed the stones of them for building houses for themselves – so great is the passion of heretics for demolishing sacred objects' – a statement seized upon two centuries later by Revd James O'Laverty, in his scholarly, though passionately partisan, history of the diocese of Down and Connor.[14]

However, Chichester (Lord Deputy, 1604–14), though he profited handsomely from the land deals of the period, disapproved of major clearances of the Irish. His was a continuation of the Tudor policy of breaking the powers of the overlords by making the lesser lords freeholders of the land they occupied. This is what happened in County

Monaghan in 1591, and the reason that Monaghan, like Antrim and Down, was excluded from the plantation settlement. But the new policy – first hinted at in Clandeboye – was directed from London and represents the missionary zeal which the new king was to bring to the policy of 'civilising' Ulster through plantation. In the nineteenth and twentieth centuries a series of legal contests of the Lough Foyle fisheries was to challenge what rights the crown possessed over such territory.[15] It has to be said that such rights were not challenged at the time. The Ulster Plantation was implemented with considerable co-operation from the Ulster Irish. The Irish elite responded as it had always done: as individuals, using England when it suited them against their enemies. The learned men too, after initial panic at the Flight of the Earls, accommodated themselves to the new situation.

A roll-call of the main Irish beneficiaries under the plantation settlement would read like a list of the rivals of the O'Neill, O'Donnell and Maguire lords who had fled in 1607. The O'Hanlons who had fought against O'Neill were rewarded with a total of 1,340 acres.[16] Maolmhuire MacSweeney, who had testified against Hugh O'Neill and attacked the crews of the ships taking the chieftains to the Continent, received 2,000 acres, as did Turlough O'Boyle and two other Mac-Sweeneys.[17] The various O'Neill branches in Tyrone and Armagh who had suffered in Hugh O'Neill's lineage expansion received grants. Notable among these were the O'Neills of the Fews in south Armagh, frequent allies of the Dublin administration in the sixteenth century. Turlough MacHenry O'Neill had been pardoned in 1603 and received a grant of 9,900 acres (the largest grant to any Gaelic lord), on which he was to settle considerable numbers of British tenants.[18]

In Fermanagh the senior Maguire, Conor Rua, had expected to be rewarded for his loyalty and surrendered his three baronies in Fermanagh. But it was not government policy to replace one overlord with another.[19] Usually the great were lowered and the middle-ranking consolidated. Conor Rua received less than a third of his territory back and lost the ancestral seat at Lisnaskea to a Scottish undertaker. The decline of the once great had been a running sore in Gaelic society. With the dismantling of that society in the seventeenth century such traditional restiveness found a new focus. Conor Rua's grandson was to be one of the initiators of the Ulster rebellion in

1641.[20] Paradoxically it was the junior Enniskillen branch, which had fought on O'Neill's side in the Nine Years War and participated in the Flight of the Earls, which became most reconciled to the new situation. Brian Maguire received 2,000 acres in the plantation scheme, and by pragmatically avoiding future involvement in rebellion, transmitted them to his descendants. For this he was posthumously damned by later nationalist tradition, a fate awaiting all the Irish landowners who survived the plantation. Other Maguires received smaller grants, a practice repeated in all the plantation counties to reconcile a handful of key 'deserving Irish' to the scheme.[21]

The descendants of Shane O'Neill, thwarted in their succession to the O'Neill title by successive earls of Tyrone, likewise received recognition in the new scheme, with land grants in Armagh and Fermanagh. But their position was a pale shadow of their former glory, and resentment at continuing decline (even if started long before the plantation) was undoubtedly a factor in Sir Phelim O'Neill's drift to rebellion in 1641.[22] Cavan was already settled by many Englishmen and the county's position had accustomed its chiefs to Pale ways. They were accordingly the first to use the English common law to argue their rights to the land, engaging a Pale lawyer and travelling to London to push their claims. Grants of land totalling 13,950 acres raised the O'Reillys to a position second in importance to the O'Neills in the new order.[23]

Despite Sir John Davies' dislike for Ireland's 'chroniclers . . . and rhymers', the government recognised that it was ignorance of the Gaelic land system which had prejudiced previous plantations and that it was the learned men who were the repositories of local knowledge. The multitude of surveys and commissions which accompanied the plantation – many conducted personally by Chichester and Davies – consciously sought out such 'clerks or scholars of the country who know all the septs and families and all their branches, and the dignity of one sept above another . . . till they descended to the most inferior men of all the baronies . . . [and] what quantity of land every man ought to have by the custom of their country'.[24]

No doubt there was an element of compulsion in this for Davies and Chichester in their 1609 inquisition were accompanied by a strong military force. But the very many cases of the learned men receiving grants under the plantation system, of the Gaelic gentry serving as sheriffs, jurors, justices, or electors, and using the new legal system to settle disputes, show that a substantial number were prepared to work within the new system. The Ulster Plantation was not imposed on a universally reluctant population. It was nonetheless a major revolution in land ownership. In all, two hundred and eighty Irish became land-owners of some 94,013 acres. But seen against an estimated 365,097 acres acquired by various English and Scottish grantees in the six plantation counties alone, the scale of the revolution in land ownership can be appreciated. These figures also disguise cases such as that of Hugh O'Neill's half-brother Art McBaron O'Neill. He had fought against O'Neill in the recent war. But his reward of 2,000 acres was to revert to the crown after the deaths of himself, his wife and their survivor. It also included an agreement to move from his O'Neilland (north Armagh) territory centred on Loughgall – then given to English undertakers – to the less fertile area of Orior in the south of the county. His son was Owen Roe O'Neill, military leader of the Irish Catholic Confederacy after the 1641 rising.[25] Always remembering the novelty and limited appeal of the modern concept of 'ownership' in Gaelic society, how did those not included among these two hundred and eighty fare in the new order?

The plantation scheme involved the division of six counties (Don-egal, Londonderry, Tyrone, Fermanagh, Armagh and Cavan) into three categories: first, land to be granted to English and Scottish undertakers; second, land to be granted to servitors (usually English government officials) and 'deserving' Irish; third, land belonging to or to be granted to the established church and Trinity College. The undertakers were required within three to five years to settle English or Scots on their lands at a rate of 24 per 1,000 acres, and to pro-vide defences and build stone houses and bawns, or risk hefty fines. No one who did not conform to Protestantism and no Irish could rent these lands. The other two categories were granted with no condition to plant or conform, and here the Irish inhabitants could remain. In fact, although some displacement did occur, the Irish re-mained even on undertaker land, for tenants were scarce. The Irish remained likewise on the lands given to the London companies: the new county of Londonderry, encompassing Derry and its immediate

Inishowen hinterland, part of north Tyrone, and O'Cahan's lands around Coleraine.

On the whole the Irish remained in occupation of the land. Only the remaining swordsmen of the Irish lords or 'kerne' were totally expelled, some transported to continental service, others taking refuge as outlaws in the woods. But 'occupation' and 'ownership' are quite different things. Those Gaelic lords who had participated in various 'surrender and regrant' schemes recognised as much, and so increasingly did the minor septs. The abundance of Irish families claiming freehold over the land they occupied, even though most such claims would have been untenable, testifies to this. Only a small number were to be satisfied. This and the loss of the top tier of Gaelic lordship (through the Flight of the Earls and death in battle) pushed the gentry of Catholic Ulster down a tier. A new tier of chief lords had been substituted for the old and generally the main undertaker in each barony ended up occupying the residence and demesne land of the former Irish chief.[26]

We simply do not know how the bulk of the Ulster Irish reacted to the plantation. The continuation of year-to-year leases on the estates of some Irish grantees (e.g. MacSweeney) suggests that they may have enjoyed greater security in new leases from the undertakers and servitors. Generally the Irish were supposed to receive shorter leases. But the 1619 and 1622 surveys suggest that many British settlers fared little better. In fact, such was the general insecurity of title under the plantation, with British grantees constantly under threat of confiscation for non-compliance with the original terms of their grant, and frequent prying commissions to check on them, that few were in any hurry to give tenants legal title.[27] The plantation had caused a frisson of anxiety about land title, and the investigations into defective titles during the lord deputyship of Thomas Wentworth, future earl of Strafford, continued such uncertainty into its third decade. Certainly the original concept of a strong, segregated British (and Protestant) colony had to be abandoned. The Irish remained in the majority on all estates. Many of the settlers showed a preference for Irish ways and did not always comply with the terms of the original grants. Indeed, the requirements for conformity to the established religion and the abandonment of Irish dress and agricultural methods were quietly set aside.

What then of popular tradition, of the dispossession of the Ulster Irish and their forced transfer to less fertile ground? In the 1940s a farmer in Killeavy parish, County Armagh, told the Irish Folklore Commission of a family tradition about their people having been driven from the good land in the north of the county to the boggy land of the south. Similar traditions were reported from Cavan, north Louth and Tyrone.[28] Such population movement certainly did occur in Armagh. As one of the most fertile areas of Ulster, it had already been more densely populated in Hugh O'Neill's time than elsewhere in his lordship, and was to prove particularly popular with British settlers.[29] In other areas the trend would have been more gradual, part of the progressive erosion of Catholic landholding over the century. It is not always clear why this movement took place. But judging from reports of Irish tenants, unable to pay rents or fines, and simply leaving with their stock in time-honoured fashion, compulsion may not have been the only factor. In the original plantation proposals there is no requirement to locate the Irish on less fertile land, even though the bulk of better land went to the English undertakers.[30] By the 1660s, however, although Irish and settler still occupied the most fertile land in about equal numbers, the tendency for marginal land to be occupied almost exclusively by Irish was already far advanced. These were to be the areas of Irish cultural survival and to a remarkable degree the figures show that the plantation and subsequent Cromwellian settlement had already set the pattern for the province's future political divisions: with the Ulster Irish heavily concentrated in Donegal, mid-Ulster, the Glens of Antrim, and the southern part of Armagh and Down.[31] 'The natives for the most part remained on their former lands, but degraded from the status of proprietors to that of tenants-at-will', commented T. W. Moody in a seminal article in 1938. 'The process by which they were driven out of the more fertile land and their places taken by British colonists was a gradual one, and was the product of economic forces rather than of any deliberate act on the part of the state.'[32]

However, it is difficult to find contemporary evidence of sustained Irish resentment against the settlers. Most complaints came from the other direction, as settlers told the various commissions of their inability to get secure leases because of landlord preference for Irish tenants, who were always willing to pay higher rents.[33] There were many stories of grumbling and restiveness in the early years of the plantation and, until his death in Rome in 1616, persistent expectations of a return of Hugh O'Neill with continental help. Another period of high tension occurred during the war between England and Spain (1625–30) and family connections with the continental exiles fanned lingering discontent. There was no open rebellion, yet a wide enough range of reported conspiracy among minor players to show rumbling discontents among the disappointed or declining. Anything like 'popular' support is impossible to gauge – though it was vaguely reported in a Fermanagh conspiracy to repossess the confiscated lands in 1625.[34] But however much the impositions of the overlords were disliked and burdensome in the closing days of the Gaelic political system, it is quite clear that the Ulster Irish continued to look for social leadership to the former Gaelic lords, however fallen in fortune, and would continue to do so well into the following century. What lay behind these rumblings was not so much loss of land (though that was a feature) as loss of status and failure to cope with the new landed and money economy.

Rents in the Gaelic system were largely nominal. Evidence suggests that many Ulster Irish grantees continued to exercise traditional lordships, when the various impositions of the new system required ready cash and good estate management. The remaining lands of Conn O'Neill, the O'Cahans, the O'Donnells, the Magennises, the Mac-Mahons and many more were progressively mortgaged or sold off for this very reason.[35] The reported poverty of the conspirators of 1615 and rebels of 1641 was clearly a major contributory factor in their actions. 'It may seem strange that those men who were accounted so great . . . should have no better revenues', wrote Chichester of O'Cahan's and O'Donnell's poverty on the eve of the plantation, 'but it may be answered that their maintenance is not from the money they receive but from their provisions of meat, butter, cuttings and coshierings which [since the two men were then in prison, and remained so till their deaths in the 1620s] none of the people will afford to them . . . whilst they are in prison or absent from their countries.'[36] Another aspect of Gaelic lordship which continued was the lavish hospitality. Maolmhuire MacSweeny was not the only beneficiary of the plantation to die in poverty, having, according to local tradition 'drank out his estate and mortgaged it'.[37]

Most of all, the plantation played havoc with this intensely status-conscious society. Suddenly people deemed their social inferiors (Irish and British alike) were rising in the social ladder while those who would normally have been in the elite were rapidly declining. This elitism and social snobbery of Gaelic society is frequently overlooked. But more than any loss of land it explains the sense of lost glory which later infused developing nationalist tradition. 'The people in general are great admirers of their pedigree,' commented an English traveller in 1674, 'and have got their genealogy so exactly by heart that though it be two hours work for them to repeat the names only from whence they are descended lineally, yet, will they not omit one word in half a dozen several repetitions; from whence I gather they say them instead of their Pater noster.'[38] This older lineage definition of status was to continue in Ulster Catholic society alongside the newer landed one, quite independently of wealth and property, and was undoubtedly responsible for the long memory of customary land rights.[39]

Randal MacDonnell (created earl of Antrim in 1620) and Brian Maguire were not alone in their attainment of a social position which would not have been theirs without the new dispensation. Even more obscure would have been the lot of the O'Haras of Crebilly in Antrim, who, through marriage alliances (in particular with the MacDonnells) and astute land deals, had pulled themselves from minor lords in the sixteenth century to become one of the most important lords in east Ulster in the seventeenth.[40] Brian Crossagh O'Neill, an illegitimate nephew of the earl of Tyrone, could have expected little under the old system. But he was granted 1,000 acres in the Ulster Plantation, as another of those potentially restless middle-ranking lords considered worth 'buying off' by government administrators. The plantation settlement gave rise to a new social category: the middleman, people like Patrick Groome O'Dufferne in north Tyrone, who managed to acquire a lease to Sir Claud Hamilton's entire estate at Gortin and then sub-let it to Irish and settler alike.[41] Certainly by the 1630s there was a sudden upsurge of Gaelic families applying to the Ulster Office (the Irish chief herald's office) signifying, if not a total acceptance of the new system, at least a recognition that new symbols of noble status were required.[42] Status, its retention or acquisition, appears to have been the crucial determinant of the Gaelic lord's response to plantation. The experiences of those creators of tradition, the learned men, may well be the key to much of the future bitterness and will be discussed more fully in a later chapter.

One class of learned men fared particularly badly: the septs holding the termon and erenach lands. These formed the lion's share of land deemed to belong to the established church (some 48,158 acres of a total 74,852 acres of church land). Parcelled throughout the counties involved in the Ulster Plantation, they amounted to 24 per cent of the confiscated territory in Tyrone, and from 21 per cent to 18 per cent in Londonderry, Donegal and Armagh. Technically the holders did not own the land. But their families had held them for many centuries and could be expected to be particularly sensitive to the changing interpretation of land title. Some may have done as well as the O'Loughrans of Donaghmore (County Tyrone), who survived as chief tenants to 1666. But the McCaseys of Tynan in County Armagh – granted a 21-year lease in 1615 of much diminished land and losing even this by mid-century – may have been more typical.[43] Such families seem to have remained on church lands where they were traditionally concentrated. But there are many cases of leases being questioned by former coarbs and erenachs and by 1641 most Irish on church lands had been depressed to the category of sub-tenants.[44]

Although the poets who remained quickly adapted, seeking patrons, as they had always done, among English and Irish alike, they were the traditional guardians of Gaelic ancestry and were the first to register their distaste for the pretensions of those not born to gentry status.

> Man after man, day after day,
> Her noblest princes pass away
> And leave to all the rabble rest
> A land dispeopled of her best.[45]

Already a highly politicised class, they were prepared to accommodate the new situation provided their own elite position continued to be recognised. The most accommodating were those who continued to be patronised by surviving Gaelic lords. Fear Flatha Ó Gnímh, the east

Ulster poet, at first fiercely critical of the new system, but latterly more accommodatory, is perhaps the best known of such pragmatists. Such accommodation by lord and poet, however, led to the traditional charge of 'selling out' by other poets who preferred a return to a heroic warlord past. And even Ó Gnímh had to admit that the craft of the poet was lost on 'men of low crafts' and 'serfs'.[46] The most comprehensive attack on this new breed of upstarts was the satirical *Pairlement Chloinne Tomáis*. Though Munster in origin, it epitomises the professional classes' reaction to the turmoil in the social hierarchy introduced by plantation policies. It recounts the history of Clan Tomáis, a low-born brutish breed, suddenly raised by the collapse of the old nobility. Then Clan Thomas began to accumulate land, create bogus genealogies, seek marriage alliances and educate their children to rhetoric and the priesthood – a 'race of churls', aping noble ways, but lacking the breeding to carry it off.[47]

2. The 1641 rebellion

By the 1630s evidence suggests that the plantation was settling down. Some 40,000 settlers had arrived. But this out of a likely population of between 200,000 and 300,000 left the Irish in the majority everywhere.[48] There was tacit religious tolerance, and in every county Old Irish were serving as royal officials and members of the Irish Parliament, inherent in which was the conferment of new status within the post-plantation settlement. Indeed, local government effectively collapsed in 1641 because so many such officials were among the rebels.[49] But all was not well with the Irish grantees. Most Gaelic lords were heavily in debt and the amount of land in their hands was being steadily eroded.[50] Declining branches of the Maguires or the O'Neills would have been a volatile element at any time in Gaelic society, but they would have been kept in check by their Gaelic overlord. With the overlords gone, their restlessness fed on every slight by English officials, many of whom would have been their social inferiors. The economic troubles of the 1630s had introduced a lesser breed of landowner than the original undertakers. The resentments of at least one future rebel (Hugh MacMahon) were aggravated by the lack of respect of one such newcomer. Old English cleric John Lynch would later describe the leaders of the Ulster rising of 1641 as 'a rabble of men of ruined fortunes and profligate character'.[51] There may too have been a restlessness for old ways and the earl of Antrim's call in 1638-9 for military recruits savoured of former 'hostings' by Gaelic chiefs.[52]

It would be wrong, however, to seek the causes of the 1641 rebellion in the restlessness of individuals among the old Gaelic elite or to see it as a delayed reaction to the Ulster Plantation. Many of the main surviving Gaelic families such as the Maguires of Tempo, the O'Neills of the Fews, the Antrim MacDonnells, the O'Neills of Killeleagh, the Magennises of Iveagh, did not take part – though their wider kin groups were heavily involved. There is every likelihood that the new system would have settled down had it not been for the heightened tensions and fears caused by the developing conflict between king and parliament in England, an economic crisis, the presence of thousands of unemployed soldiers and a general breakdown of order at every level. It was a classic revolutionary situation, and like all revolutionary situations, it did not start as such.

The lord deputyship of Viscount Wentworth, from 1633 to 1640, when he was made earl of Strafford, had succeeded in making a crisis out of existing insecurities over land title and religion. In principle his actions should have pushed settler and Ulster Irish closer together, for every sector of Irish society was affected by his 'thoroughness'. His renewal of a confiscation and plantation policy – this time in Connacht – sent a frisson through the remaining Catholic landowning class. But they were not alone. His failure to confirm earlier concessions on land titles – notably those modifying the articles of plantation in Ulster – was accompanied by new, unfavourable leases, higher rents and in some cases extortionate fines. The activities of his commission on defective titles meant that no landholder could rest easy. The high rents consequent on Wentworth's policies affected every level of Ulster society at a time when it was already deep in recession. By spring 1641, harvest failure, high food prices and a general deterioration of material well-being were already producing disorders in the east of the province, where an unusual concentration of military quartering was intensifying the religious and economic fears of the local population.[53]

The soldiers thus being quartered in Ulster were no ordinary soldiers. They constituted the largely Catholic 'New Irish Army', which had been raised for Charles I by Wentworth in 1639 for use against the Scottish Covenanters. It was to figure prominently in the anti-popery mania of the English parliament which was to provoke the Ulster Irish into the protective pre-emptive strike with which the 1641 rebellion began. Thereafter it was to supply the rebellion with its trained troops. More immediately it contributed to the unusually heightened religious tensions of 1640–41. Prior to Wentworth's deputyship there had been an easy-going tolerance in religion. The Catholic Church was able to re-establish some of its structures and to develop a *modus vivendi* over the increasing numbers of inter-faith marriages in Ulster.[54] All this was put in jeopardy by Wentworth's religious policies. The established Church of Ireland was to be brought into strict conformity with that in England, raising the spectre of revived recusancy fines for those who did not attend Anglican services and repossession of church lands. The covenanting war in Scotland brought Wentworth's religious policies to bear most heavily on the Ulster Presbyterians – till now accommodated within the Church of Ireland. In 1639–40 Wentworth sent agents into Ulster to force them to swear the so-called Black Oath against the Covenant, forcing some to flee back to Scotland, others to take to the hills and many more to riot. It is a token of the chaos and confused identities of the period that many English settlers thought the early stages of the 1641 rising was a Scots–Irish conspiracy against themselves.[55] The tensions of the period were causing people to look at their neighbours in a new light, for Ireland was about to be pulled into the vortex of impending civil war in England.

The calling of the Long Parliament in England at the end of 1640 unleashed a flood of puritan propaganda to implicate Charles I in a popish conspiracy, of which Wentworth's 'New Irish Army' was deemed the centrepiece. The net effect was to provoke in reality what was feared in theory, for the Ulster Irish rebelled in October 1641 in the firm conviction that they were themselves about to be attacked. It was a County Antrim English planter of puritan sympathies (Sir John Clotworthy, later Lord Massarene, and a member of the Long Parliament), who first alerted parliament to the threat posed by Wentworth's 'popish army' in Ulster. His accusations were seized upon and used first against Wentworth himself, then against the king. In language which thereafter became the stock-in-trade of anti-popery, John Pym denounced this international papist conspiracy to destroy Protestants' 'law and religion'. A host of pamphlets denied that papists could be loyal and Catholics in Ulster feared that Scottish puritans were poised to attack them. The propaganda further fuelled the developing crisis in Ulster and was claimed by the rebellion's leaders as one of the main reasons for their action.[56] The tragedy of the situation was that negotiations between London and the Catholic Old English that summer had started to remedy their grievances, notably over land title. But the Ulster Irish had not been included in the negotiations and they viewed the prorogation of the Irish parliament as another ploy by their enemies to silence their protests.[57]

On 22 October 1641 a number of Ulster Irish, headed by Sir Phelim O'Neill, attacked the principal fortified positions in Ulster. By the following day most of the province from Newry to Donegal was in their hands. It had been a comparatively bloodless rising which had taken most people completely by surprise. Thus opened eleven years of extraordinary confusion and complexity, which even now historians cannot completely unravel. It was to see the Ulster Irish successively in uneasy alliance with the Old English Catholics, the Protestant royalists and ultimately even Cromwell (against their former Catholic allies). Owen Roe O'Neill had returned from nearly four decades of service with the Irish regiment in Spanish Flanders to lead the Irish 'Confederate' army. But his Counter-Reformation zeal – and even more so that of the papal nuncio Rinuccini, who arrived in 1645 with the aim of fully restoring Catholicism – alienated the Old English and put paid to any chance of a negotiated settlement. It was very far from being the great Catholic nationalist uprising of later tradition. But its significance for the future of Ulster's Catholics, and for their relation-ship with their Protestant neighbours, cannot be overestimated.

Early proclamations from the leaders assured the English and Scots settlers that no harm would come to them and that the Irish were acting under a commission from the king. The latter was in fact a forgery, but most of the Ulster Irish were genuine enough in their belief that they were supporting the king. Certainly there was some disposition – particularly among the Scots – to believe them, and, at the very least, to remain neutral.[58] It was a disposition encouraged by many personal links between the Irish and the settlers, with whom many were now related by marriage. Certainly the early stages of the rising were marked more by plunder than bloodshed, suggesting envy among the lower Irish of new, more materialistic conditions among the settlers. 'He never saw such base covetousness as did show itself in these Irish robbers, such bitter envyings and emulations,' commented George Creichton, a Presbyterian minister who spent many months a prisoner among the rebels.[59] Lack of investment in chattels and material comforts had always been a feature of Gaelic society much commented upon by visitors. Aspiration to such comforts as symbols of civility had already been noted among the gentry and would have started to set apart the 'haves' and 'have-nots'.

The Catholic leaders, however, very quickly lost control in what fast became a total breakdown of order in Ulster. Miles O'Reilly was simply rejected by his men when he intervened to prevent the killing of Protestants at Kilmacrenan in Donegal.[60] Phelim O'Neill's notes of protection were ignored, and Philip O'Reilly, after numerous attempts to protect prisoners in Cavan, had to admit his loss of authority over his men and advised prisoners to flee to Dublin.[61] However moderate the aims of the initial rising, that breakdown of order generated vigilantism. Popular indiscipline gave rise to localised vendettas. Scotland's troubles finally spilled over into the province early in 1642 and the presence of thousands of unoccupied soldiers from Wentworth's now disbanded army added to the powder-keg.

Even today historians lavish thousands of words denying any general massacre of Protestants in 1641. Such denials are undoubtedly necessary, given the wild exaggerations of genocide and dreadful barbarities which were to exercise anti-Catholic opinion for centuries after the events and form the basis of dispossession and penalisation of religion until the nineteenth century. Pamphlet literature in England laid claim to anything up to 150,000 Protestants massacred, when the number of Protestants in Ulster may not have been much above 30,000. None the less, as many as 12,000 may have perished, the majority from cold and exposure after being stripped of clothes and possessions during an unusually cold winter. In this state thousands made their way to Dublin in a seventeenth-century preplay of famine-induced population movements in the Third World. Their sufferings were

extensively documented in the commissions of 1641–2 and 1652 and
in the trials of 1652–4. However unreliable they have been proved,
one cannot read the statements of people such as Elizabeth Price
of County Armagh, who had lost her husband and five children in
circumstances of considerable brutality, without coming to understand
the terror and suffering which occasioned the rumours and wild exaggerations of the period. Even Catholic folk memory is critical of the
extreme brutality of the Irish leaders in 1641.[62]

We know less about losses among the Ulster Catholics. But retaliatory massacres of Ulster Irish at Templepatrick and Island Magee in
County Antrim were not isolated incidents. Some 500, mostly women
and children, were reportedly killed in a revenge attack in the Mourne
Mountains in County Down, another 295 in Fermanagh. In the
Mourne incident Sir James Montgomery could not contain his men,
for they 'had seen . . . their houses burned, their wives and children
murdered. So they were like robbed bears and tygers, and could not
be sattisfied with all the revenge they took', and instead of open battle
as Montgomery wished, they attacked the Irish from the rear 'being
full of revenge . . . most partys killing many, and giving no quarter'.[63]
Certainly the period decimated many Ulster Catholic families: an
analysis of those of the Fews in Armagh shows a numerical decline of
between a third and four-fifths.[64] The failure of the Irish Catholics –
above all the Old English – to mount any effective defence until long
after the event is surprising, particularly since it was their political
enemies in Ireland who were effectively manipulating the evidence. It
can surely only be adequately explained by their own anger at the Ulster
Catholics' lack of moderation, which had given their parliamentary
enemies the excuse to associate them too in the Ulster's guilt.[65] The
fact remains, however, that even if the slaughter was spontaneous and
not planned, even if there were barbarities on all sides, even if every
Catholic was not involved, 1641 destroyed the Ulster Plantation as a
mixed settlement and made religion for the first time the main justification for dispossession.

The first indiscriminate killings appear to have been those of a small
force of Scots (some 300 to 400) at Augher, County Tyrone, in the
first days of November, after they had already surrendered. The exact
train of events has been impossible to trace. The main Irish leaders

were horrified and, still anxious to keep the Scots neutral, they issued
a number of statements, blaming the massacre on 'lewd people' or the
'common sort'. But bloodshed begot bloodshed. It was largely carried
out by inferior leaders over whom the key figures quickly lost control.
There was widespread plunder of property and livestock and cases
of Irish and settler alike either fleeing from their homes for fear of
neighbourly enmities escalating, or pre-empting such by killing the
neighbour concerned.[66] There was a concentration of atrocities in that
swathe of territory covering north Armagh and south Tyrone which
had been most densely settled by English. All were the result of freebooting by local captains as groups of prisoners were transferred.
There is no sign of a general assassination policy, and alcohol was
frequently a factor. But local captains tended to be residents of the
area, local sept leaders. The most notorious incident – which lives on
in the commemorative banner of the local Orange lodge – was that at
Portadown in County Armagh. Sometime in November 1641 a group
of prisoners being moved from Loughgall were drowned in the River
Bann in circumstances of extreme cruelty. No one, then or since, has
discovered the precise reason or who gave the order, but ultimate
responsibility would have fallen to the local captain, Toole McCann.
Some 80 to 100 men, women and children perished and rumours
quickly spread of portents and visions, ghosts of the victims rising
from the water to call for vengeance. Other killings, such as that at
Shewie in County Armagh, were carried out by Irish soldiers fleeing
from defeat, helped by locals pursuing personal vendettas. At Kinnard
(Caledon) in Tyrone, some Protestant tenants and servants of Sir
Phelim O'Neill himself were murdered, an event which so angered him
that he had a number of the attackers hanged.[67]

The first such killings in County Antrim were representative of this
lack of any overall pattern, for the attackers were led by a Catholic
Scot, recently arrived from Scotland. Alisdair MacDonald (Alexander
MacDonnell), a kinsman of the earl of Antrim, was part of a mixed
religion force of the earl's tenants, assembled to protect his estates
against the rebels. On 2 January 1642 they were crossing the Bann at
Portnaw to protect a Protestant settler, when MacDonnell turned his
men on the Protestants within his own force and killed sixty of them.
Thereafter all the earl of Antrim's Catholic tenants joined the rebels,

largely in self-protection as the Portnaw incident set off a train of reprisals. Some days later settlers, reacting to news of such killings of Protestants, massacred the Irish in Islandmagee and Templepatrick, which in turn triggered killings of Protestants at a number of besieged locations in the north-east of the province. By now local leaders were unable to contain their followers, and it had become something of a rebellion without a cause, as fear turned low-level resentments at English fashions and language into murderous attacks.[68] But it was never general and there are innumerable incidents of clemency on all sides – the terrible events at Portadown being criticised by local Irish for their 'inhumanity and unchristianlike murder'.[69]

The action of Alisdair MacDonnell was symptomatic of the lack of common aim in the Ulster rising. He had joined as part of his own ambitions to use the Irish against his family's traditional enemies in Scotland, the Campbells. It was, in part, the same reason which kept his uncle, the earl of Antrim, neutral. Notwithstanding his neutrality, his Scottish Campbell enemy, in the form of the earl of Argyll, was permitted by the English parliament to occupy the earl of Antrim's estates and base his army on Rathlin Island, the population of which was systematically massacred.[70] Argyll was part of a Scottish force under General Robert Monro which arrived in Ulster in April 1642 and swept through Antrim and Down by May, wasting much of the land and destroying the Irish strongholds.

By the summer the Ulster Irish had all but acknowledged defeat. That the war continued for another ten years owed more to the eruption of England's civil war into Ireland than any coherent sense of purpose. In effect, the future of Catholic Ulster had already been sealed in those first few months of the Ulster rising. The Old English had been sucked into it by the spreading disorder at the end of 1641. But the next ten years witnessed persistent friction between them and the Ulster Irish, the former dismissing the other as 'a rabble of men of ruined fortunes and profligate character'; the Old Irish responding with taunts of 'sons of heretics and remonstrators'.[71] This was not the great Catholic uprising of tradition.

Early reports of the rising filled the press in England with histrionic and often fictional accounts. Thus began England's lurid fascination with 1641 which was to outlast anything similar in Ireland. More popular literature was generated in England by 1641 than by any other single event in Irish history, all alike depicting the rising as a popish conspiracy to exterminate Protestants. A particularly influential tract was the *Remonstrance* of Henry Jones. In March 1642, Jones, Dean of Kilmore and future Bishop of Clogher, delivered his own account to the English House of Commons. He portrayed the rebellion as 'a long-laid conspiracie' by the Church of Rome to extirpate Prot-estantism and undermine allegiance to the king. Popery was thus a political as well as a religious threat. The events of 1641 firmly implanted this notion of Catholicism as a dangerous political system and as such underpinned state policy for almost two centuries and Ulster Protestant perceptions for even longer.

And out of that ancient hatred the Church of Rome beareth to the Reformed Religion . . . There hath been beyond all paralell of former ages, a most bloody and Antichristian combination and plot hatched, by well-nigh the whole Romish sect, by way of combination from parts foreign, with those at home, against this our Church and state; thereby intending the utter extir-pation of the reformed Religion, and the possessors of it: In the room thereof, setting up that idol of the Masse, with all the abominations of the whore of Babylon.[72]

In an effort to persuade parliament to send help, Jones then detailed the atrocities, dwelling on particularly horrifying details such as reports of babies having been ripped from the womb and fed to the dogs. Jones took much of his information from the much-maligned 'Depositions' (taken from Protestant refugees who had reached Dublin), which are now housed in Trinity College, Dublin. To those of 1641–2 were added a further set of 1652, the main purpose of which was to acquire evidence against the rebellion's leaders. The hand of Jones, prime interlocutor on each of these occasions, is clearly visible, and there are good grounds for the centuries-old doubts about the reliability of the depositions.[73] Yet their more extreme claims provided the basis for a new English policy towards Ireland and in Sir John Temple's *Irish Rebellion* – an Irish equivalent of Foxe's *Book of Martyrs* – a formative influence on Protestant psyche. Jones and Temple were virulently anti-Catholic New English, whose understanding of Ireland would have been influenced by the timeless stereotypes of Giraldus Cambrensis.

The message of Temple was of heroic endurance against a barbarous infidel. He was the first to paint what was to become an enduring picture of the Catholic Irish as untrustworthy dissemblers. Their aim had always been the dispossession and extirpation of Protestants and such it would remain if they were given a chance. It confirmed Calvinistic belief in the Catholics as irredeemable and the message was reinforced in annual sermons on the anniversary of the rebellion which only ceased in 1784.[74] However propagandistic Temple may have been, such blanket reports of massacre became part of genuine belief among Irish Protestants generally in later centuries, a kind of 'occult force', informing Protestant consciousness particularly in times of crisis.[75] The cry of 'remember 1641' proved a powerful counter to would-be reformers in the next century. Incidents such as the discovery of bones of the reputed victims in County Down in the 1720s kept local traditions alive, and a century and a half later the United Irishmen failed to make headway in areas which had been the scene of killings in 1641. It was always at key political moments that the horrors of 1641 were recalled and manipulated by interested parties.[76]

More immediately the lurid accounts of cruelties, on which most of the popular English versions seized, transposed the centuries-old English perception of the barbarous Irish exclusively to the Catholics. Certainly many of the Cromwellian soldiers were fired by the accounts of the massacres into considering their campaign one of revenge. But the image of a religious crusade should not be carried too far, and ultimately Cromwellian policies towards Ireland were governed by fiscal, not punitive, concerns. If English Protestants had had more sympathy for the sufferings of their Irish co-religionists, the propaganda campaign mounted by the like of Jones and Temple would have been unnecessary. As it was, the entire parliamentary war effort in Ireland was funded by loans from speculators or 'adventurers', who would be repaid in Irish land. But much of the money was diverted to the English campaign and the soldiers in Ireland were left unpaid. Only in 1652 was Ireland finally subdued and Cromwell's campaign there was waged as much against Protestant (and Presbyterian) royalist as against the Catholic Irish. It was Cromwell's intention to crush support for Charles II rather than destroy either the Irish or their religion and by 1652 London was more inclined to moderation.

At that point Henry Jones resurfaced with an abstract of the 'barbarous . . . cruel, murders and massacres' in 1641. The four parliamentary commissioners sent to Ireland to arrange the terms of settlement later explained how he had overcome their 'temptation' to lenity. 'So deeply were [we] all affected . . . that we are much afraid our behaviour towards this people may never sufficiently avenge the same; and fearing lest others, who are at greater distance, might be moved to the lenity we have found no small temptation in ourselves', they sent a lengthy extract from Jones's depositions to deter parliament from making concessions.[77] Thus had Jones 'saved the settlement from moderation'.[78] It is the terms of the subsequent land settlement on which much of Cromwell's evil reputation in Ireland rests.

3. The Cromwellian settlement

Under Cromwell's land settlement those who had participated in the first stages of the rebellion or in the killing of civilians or who failed to surrender arms within twenty-eight days, together with 105 named persons (including Sir Phelim O'Neill, but also a large number of Protestants and leading Presbyterians like Viscount Montgomery of Ards), were exempted from pardon. All other landowners would be subject to partial forfeiture, depending on the extent of their 'delinquency' and required to move across the Shannon to Connacht or Clare. Forfeited lands in ten counties of the other three provinces would then be assigned to soldiers and adventurers. But the implications of 'blood guilt' on a national level were never carried through. Wives and children of 'delinquents' were to be allowed to retain up to a fifth of the confiscated estate, and 'Irish not guilty of blood' were to receive protection.[79] Cromwell was more worried by the radical Protestant sectaries in his own camp (who controlled the Irish administration) and his son, Henry Cromwell, sent to Ireland in 1655, became a moderating influence. The court set up to try those exempted from pardon (which, it has been estimated, could have encompassed as many as 80,000 people), was clearly designed to intimidate rather than to punish. We do not know how many were executed, perhaps about fifty. But many – including even key leaders – were acquitted or permitted to go into exile. Even Sir Phelim might have been spared had he not continued to deny that he received his commission from Charles I.[80] Some 34,000 swordsmen were permitted to enlist in the continental armies, and several thousand followed English and Scots royalists already transplanted to the new English colonies in the West Indies.[81]

The policy of transplantation to Connacht got under way in 1654 amidst confusion and uncertainty, and doubts remain as to how far it was actually implemented. No reliable survey of the acreage involved was completed until 1659, by which date the policy, though only partially implemented, had been abandoned. The commissioners, installed at Loughrea (County Galway) to parcel out the land in Connacht, were quickly overwhelmed and generally open to bribery. Cromwellian policy made a clear distinction between the people and their social leaders, and, under further pressure from Protestant landlords who needed their Catholic tenants and labourers to work the land, only Catholic landlords and those tenants who chose to accompany them were subject to transplantation.[82] It took more than a generation for the Cromwellian land settlement to work itself out. Local government was not sufficiently restructured to ensure a smooth operation of such a potentially massive policy. Some officials in Connacht simply dispensed with paperwork and assigned land according to the number of cattle requiring grazing. Some Ulster Irish and Scots, due for transplantation, simply moved their cattle into the hilly areas of neighbouring County Leitrim.[83] Many Cromwellian soldiers had not wanted land and quickly sold their small portions, often to original tenants who were anxious to return. Of those soldiers who stayed (some 12,000) many inter-married with and became Catholics. Cromwellian ambitions to establish a resident Protestant yeomanry from the soldiery did not materialise. What it did achieve, however, was the virtual eradication of a Catholic landed elite, for despite original outlawry of certain Protestants, in the end only Catholic landowners were transplanted.[84] In their place the Cromwellian settlement established the backbone of a Protestant proprietary. The host of small grants to reluctant soldiers ensured a speculator's paradise. The vast estates of the Massarenes, Annesleys, Beresfords and Cootes, and many more who would dominate the country's political future, were accumulated in this manner.[85]

Historians seem strangely ignorant of the consequences of the Cromwellian settlement on the ground.[86] In fact, despite Jones's propaganda, Ulster suffered less than any other province, one of the reasons, possibly, why Cromwell is less a force of evil in popular tradition here than elsewhere.[87] The amount of land left in Old Irish hands had dramatically declined even from 1609 levels as a result of sales. This is why the map of Cromwellian confiscations for Ulster shows levels as low as 4 per cent for Tyrone, 11 per cent for Donegal, rising to a maximum of 41 per cent for Antrim and 43 per cent for Cavan (as against 77 per cent for Tipperary and 91 per cent for Galway). Moreover, although most Ulster landowners would have been royalist during the war, they were permitted to compound for their estates, so that fewer confiscations were necessary to pay the Cromwellian soldiers.[88] Of just under 2,000 landowners estimated to have been transplanted, around thirty were from Ulster. However, of the fifty-eight Gaelic Catholic landholders in 1641, only five retained their property in 1660, whilst Scottish and Old English Catholics generally fared better.[89] In fact, even some of the Ulster figures do not reflect the final outcome, for 'any lawful right, title or interest' to the forfeited lands were to be honoured before satisfaction of the adventurers' and soldiers' claims could be entertained. Efforts were made to prevent any precipitate land grabbing, while evidence of separate agreements made with individual leaders on their surrender suggests a large element of flexibility. Terms made with Philip O'Reilly, for instance, permitted his men 'enjoyment of their personal estates by such of them as desire to live in the nation', or freedom of sale if they go abroad, provided they had had no hand in murder or robbery.[90]

It was the confiscation of a third of the earl of Antrim's estates for distribution among some 800 soldiers which explains the disproportionally high figure for that county. This had been against the wishes both of Cromwell and his supporters in Ireland, since the earl had been instrumental in winning Ulster (and indeed the Papacy) over to the Cromwellian side in the last years of the war. In fact, only five adventurers and some 100 soldiers took up residence. Most of the soldiers quickly sold their small portions, often to Antrim's tenants, who were anxious to return or acting on behalf of the earl himself. The result was that some two-thirds of the earl's tenants remained either Irish or Scottish Catholics, and such indeed was the general picture all over the country.[91]

Sir Henry O'Neill of the Fews (son of Sir Turlough MacHenry) was not quite so fortunate. He had succeeded peacefully to his father's estates of 9,305 acres in 1639 and had studiously avoided involvement in the 1641 rising. He successfully contested the depositions against him, as witnesses confessed that their accusations were based on hearsay. However, all his children and kin were involved and he had supplied the Irish armies. He therefore lost his estates in Armagh and was partially compensated by two-thirds the equivalent in Mayo. In fact he only received a third, and this experience of receiving less land in compensation than initially promised was a common one throughout the country.[92] Maguire of Tempo alone of the Irish land-owners in Fermanagh remained. But it was the host of small Catholic proprietors created by the Ulster Plantation who lost most. Typical were the gallowglass families of MacDonnell in Armagh and Tyrone. They had received nine grants of land varying from 60 to 120 acres in the Ulster Plantation. By 1641 only two of the grants remained, and these were lost in the Cromwellian settlement.[93] Some were partially compensated in Connacht. Others went into exile, became outlaws or tenants.

But it was a decline that was accelerated rather than caused by the Cromwellian settlement. The vast majority of the Catholic population remained unaffected by the dramatic change in property at the top, and in many ways their position was a strong one because of the continuing acute shortage of tenants and the massive re-leasing of lands at low rents in the 1650s.[94] The Cromwellian settlement, unlike previous ones, did not involve any importation of large numbers of new tenants. The Ulster Catholics largely remained on their lands. In June 1652 the Magennises of Iveagh used a device which would become common under the penal laws of the eighteenth century, of conveyancing their lands to a friendly Protestant to be held until such times as they could be lawfully retrieved.[95] But, far more effectively than any of the plantations, the Cromwellian land settlement cemented the link between Protestantism and land ownership, prompting Lecky two centuries later to proclaim it as the originator of that 'lasting division between the proprietary and the tenants which is the chief cause of the political and social evils of Ireland'.[96] Lecky was writing at the height of the campaign to establish a peasant proprietorship. But he captured the essence of the Cromwellian settlement well enough. That it proved so complete and so enduring, however, owed as much to the thwarted efforts of the restored monarchy to reach a fairer settlement as to Cromwellian policies.

4. *The Restoration settlement*

One of the reasons for the foot-dragging over the implementation of the Cromwellian settlement was the heightened expectation of a change in the political situation. Hopes of a reversal of the Cromwellian land settlement ran high with the restoration of the Stuarts in 1660, though it is noteworthy that those petitioning for such did not question the original Ulster Plantation. At the outset the new king promised all things to all men. Protestants would be allowed to retain their lands and Catholics who had been loyal to the crown or deprived of their lands on the grounds of religion would be restored – prompting the duke of Ormond's cynical comment that the king would then have to discover a second Ireland to satisfy his promises.[97] Such promises nevertheless caused local skirmishing, some former owners simply seizing their old lands.[98]

But if Catholics thought a restoration of the Stuarts signalled a return to the *status quo ante*, they were to be rudely disabused. The Cromwellian settlement had established for the rest of the island what was already in place in Ulster: a new landed base of power which was firmly Protestant. Many Protestants had been royalist in the recent conflict. But the threat to land ownership posed by Charles II's court of claims united old and new Protestants as never before. It was this united Protestant front in the face of a still-divided Catholic elite which set the seal on the Cromwellian land settlement.[99] Even the Act of Settlement passed by the Irish parliament in May 1662, undertaking to look into the claims of 'innocent papists', was prefaced by a strongly anti-Catholic preamble which implied that an 'innocent papist' was a contradiction in terms. A court of claims commenced hearing cases in January 1663. But it was quite suddenly discontinued after only eight months, with less than a seventh of the claims heard. Some 540 Catholics over the whole island had been declared innocent, leaving over 7,000 claims unheard.[100] Although not all of these would have been major landowners, for widows and children were also allowed to petition, the entire 'scramble', as the Lord Lieutenant, the earl of Essex, described it, left no one satisfied. An additional act requiring adventurers and soldiers to surrender a third of their acquisitions was to have created land to compensate Protestants who had made way for innocent papists. But the uproar caused in the English parliament, and the unruly last session of the Irish parliament (December 1665) – where members confronted each other with half-drawn swords – revealed the depth of dissatisfaction also in this quarter.[101]

Again the situation provided many opportunities for sharp practice by speculators. So-called 'discoverers' were out searching for concealed lands. No one could feel secure. One public official writing in 1684 was very critical of the injustices created by the Restoration settlement. He was particularly critical of those with access to power who abused the system to the detriment of both the crown and the former pro-prietors:

For many years after the closing of the Court of Claims, those who had favour in Court got commissions of inquiry to look after concealed lands ... And therefore these favoured grantees bought up unsatisfied debentures (which they might buy for a song) ... It were to be wished that a considerable part of such money were distributed to those Irish families as have been notoriously disappointed of the good intended them by the acts, and by which their condition is most miserable, many of the English allowing some sort of gifts or poor subsistence to the old proprietors, who evermore haunt and live about those lands they were dispossessed of, and cannot forbear to hope and reckon upon a day of re-possession.[102]

The former proprietors in Ulster suffered particularly badly, not simply because of their support of the ultra-papal party in the recent war, though this was a factor, nor Charles II's bitterness at the eleventh-hour conversion of the Ulster Catholics to the Cromwellian side.[103] The main reason was the continuing disunity among the Catholic elite and the lack of influence by the Ulster Gaelic lords in the corridors of power. The outcome of the Restoration settlement was decided by influence and string-pulling. The position of the earl of Antrim in the pre-1641 power network, with all the contacts that brought, determined his restoration.[104] Likewise the influence of many Old English lords ensured that they would be the principal beneficiaries of any lands restored to Catholics and they made little effort to extend the operation of the court of claims once their own claims had been satisfied.[105] It was the claims of the small proprietors above all which were ignored and the bulk of the remaining Ulster Catholic proprietors in 1641 fell into this category. Another badly treated grouping were the so-called 'ensignmen' (perhaps as many as 30,000) who had joined the king in exile on the Continent. But since their claims were to have been considered only after the 'innocents' and Cromwellians, theirs remained largely unsatisfied.

Prominent among the losers was Viscount Magennis of Iveagh, County Down, one of the ensignmen, who ended up with only 2,000 acres out of an estimated 45,000. The Kilwarlin branch also suffered losses. In 1611 Brian Oge McRory Magennis alienated 5,204 acres of the Kilwarlin lands to Sir Moses Hill. Thus began a steady process of acquisition by the Hill family which was to see them become the most important landed family in Ulster by the next century. His son joined the Cromwellian forces and was rewarded with another 3,000 acres of the Kilwarlin lands in 1656. These he retained at the Restoration, contrary to the expectations of the Magennis family. Among those Magennises dispossessed was Father Patrick Maginn, chaplain to Charles II's queen (Catherine of Braganza, a devout Catholic), who was to remain a very influential figure on the Continent till his death in 1683. Nevertheless, despite a vigorous petitioning campaign by Maginn and his Magennis kin, the lands remained with the Hill family, the consequences of which would form an important element in the religious and political history of the area.[106] Phelimy Magennis and his son Ever were restored to their Castlewellan estates, Henry O'Neill of Killeleagh in County Antrim to his, as was Daniel O'Neill, son to Conn O'Neill of Clandeboye, who, though a Protestant, had used his strong familial ties among the Catholics to assist Charles II during Cromwell's time. But all were contested for many years, the latter two most effectively by the Presbyterian adventurer, Sir John Clotworthy, earl of Massarene.[107] The Scottish settlers Sir George Hamilton and his brother Claud, Lord Strabane, were restored in Tyrone, as was the Old English Patrick Russell to Killough in County Down. The chief line of the Savage family had become Protestant by this time and the main surviving Catholic proprietor in the family lost his lands as a Jacobite supporter in the Williamite settlement.[108] Colla MacBrian MacMahon of Tullyglass in Monaghan was restored, as was Miles MacSweeney in Donegal.[109] But such survivals were insignificant in the new power structure, for outside Antrim, less than 4 per cent of the land in Ulster remained in Catholic ownership.[110]

5. The Williamite land settlement

Dissatisfaction with the Restoration land settlement made its repeal the Catholics' main priority when Catholic James II became king in 1685. Under the Restoration Lord Deputy Ormond, with the benefit of direct experience through his many Catholic relatives, was irritated by Protestants' paranoia. After James II's accession, however, a wave of triumphalism swept through Catholic Ireland, particularly when his lord deputy, Richard Talbot, earl of Tyrconnell, was replacing Protestant officials with Catholics. Old prophecies were invoked to depict James as the saviour of the Gael, a 'sovereign sprung of their own most ancient royal race ... would forthwith restore ... to the natives their properties and estates of which they had been for so many years so unjustly despoiled'.[111] It was a triumphalism picked up in the most famous Protestant song of the period – 'Lillibullero' – a parody of Catholic hopes that their day had finally come.

> Now Tyrconnel is come ashore,
> Lillibulero bullen a la;
> And we shall have commissions gillore,
> Lillibulero bullen a la.

And he dat will not go to mass,
Lillibulero bullen a la;
Shall turn out and look like an ass,
Lillibulero bullen a la.

Now, now de heretics all go down,
Lillibulero bullen a la;
By Chreist and St Patrick de nation's our own,
Lillibulero bullen a la.[112]

Predictably, Talbot's activities raised fears of another 1641, and James himself infuriated his Irish supporters by suggesting them capable of such.[113] James's Irish parliament of 1689 had proclaimed Temple's book a seditious libel, which only increased its popularity among Protestants.[114] Catholic writers later accused Protestants of cynical manipulation of the religious issue to confiscate land.[115] But with James's ally Louis XIV ruthlessly suppressing Protestants in France and his Irish parliament attainting over 2,000 people on mere hearsay, there was good cause for concern.

It was, however, the land issue which was and would remain the main cause for that concern. Tyrconnell's actions had ensured an overwhelmingly Catholic return to the parliament of 1689 – only six of its 230 members were Protestants. It immediately repealed the Act of Settlement and sought to re-establish the court of claims, at a stroke providing the main justification for withholding political rights from Catholics over the next century.[116] Most land in Ulster was already in Protestant hands, and the actions of the 1689 parliament sent tremors through the province. This was 'the Irish summer', when former pro-prietors like Edmond Oge Magennis 'expelled, but without cruelty or effusion of blood, those whom Cromwell had introduced to his estates and replaced them by those who had been the ancient vassals of his house'.[117] These were the lands of William Waring – acquired by purchase in 1663 – and since he was not in arms against James, the Catholic MP for Newry, Rowland White, intervened on his behalf to secure continued ownership.[118] The ensuing war (1689–91) between James and William of Orange, more than any previous conflict, divided the province along religious lines. But the relatively generous terms granted to James's Irish army on its surrender at Limerick (leaving some 14 per cent of land in Catholic ownership, when Protestants called for total confiscation) determined the bitter mood in which William's first, totally Protestant, Irish parliament met in 1692. This was the parliament which passed the first of the penal laws. Several key clauses of the Treaty of Limerick, notably those extending its generous terms to everyone in areas under Jacobite control and granting religious freedom to Catholics, were omitted when it was finally ratified in 1697. But although the latter omission laid the ground for the penal laws, it made very little difference to the Williamite land settlement.

The vast majority of those outlawed by name in Ulster were Old Irish. Although a sizeable number of Old English were also outlawed (notably Savages, Whites and Russells), about one in three received pardons against one in seventeen Old Irish.[119] The last Catholic O'Neill proprietor (Sir Neill O'Neill of Killeleagh, County Antrim) had died after fighting on James's side at the Boyne (1 July 1690) and his Londonderry and Monaghan estates were confiscate. Cú Chonnacht Maguire (grandson of Brian Maguire of Tempo) died at the Battle of Aughrim (12 July 1691) on James's side. But the forfeiture of his estates was successfully contested by his widow and son. A string of County Down Magennises figure among King James's officers. One was killed at Aughrim, two more at Athlone; others, including Lord Iveagh, joined the Irish regiments on the Continent, though the bulk of Iveagh's Ulster regiment opted to transfer to William's forces. The exchange of letters between William Waring and the Magennises of Clanconnel during these fraught months suggests relatively friendly relations, and there is evidence that Waring gave some assistance to surviving members of the family who had fallen on hard times. This does not mean, however, that the loss of the land ceased to rankle with future generations, and the grandson of Bryan Magennis who was killed at Aughrim (John MacCartan) made another unsuccessful bid to recover some land early next century (interestingly claiming rights as a 'discoverer' of concealed crown property).[120] Ironically the largest forfeiture was the 9,861 acres of the Scottish Catholic, Claud Hamilton, earl of Abercorn, though it was later re-purchased by his Protestant nephew.[121] The earl of Antrim was restored, though initially outlawed. By the 1720s the Antrim MacDonnells had conformed to the established religion, as had other remaining Catholic landowners, sometimes under pressure from Protestant members of their own family.[122]

6. The Ulster Irish and the land at the end of the seventeenth century

Despite their loss of land, these formerly important Gaelic families retained 'gentle' status into the eighteenth century and did not marry beneath that. A history of the Magennises of Iveagh, written by a descendant at the height of the Catholic campaign of 1792, clearly illustrates this point. Successive generations had intermarried with other gentry families (of Irish and English descent) and were described as having retained the stature and manners of nobility even after their land had been lost.[123] Heads of families, though landless, still retained enough influence to raise large numbers of men from their traditional followers at the end of the seventeenth century.[124] The traditional Irish concept of status was to be a crucial determinant of identity through the next century, and the popular picture of an impoverished Catholic peasantry opposed to a Protestant elite does not survive close scrutiny.

It is equally true that the policy which had motivated the Ulster Plantation – that of curtailing the power of the overlords – continued into the eighteenth century, as Protestant landlords proved reluctant to let lands to leading Gaelic families.[125] And it is with these families that we must, first and foremost, seek the origins of the bitter traditions about the loss of the lands, never forgetting that the bulk of people adapted as they had always done.[126] It was such families that continued to supply successive generations of priests, now replacing the disappearing lords as social leaders. They were likewise the families who supplied most of the continental exiles and much of the bandit culture of south Ulster in particular. With the dismantling of the Gaelic warlord society early in the seventeenth century, vast numbers of masterless men remained in Ulster to haunt Stuart officials. Prior to 1641 some 32,660 were given British blessing to enlist in the forces of the continental powers (normally those of France and Spain). After each upheaval further contingents left and the turmoil of seventeenth-century Europe sustained the demand for troops. The geography of recruitment is telling. Gaelic lords tended to recruit from within their own kin, which explains the staggering number of O'Neills, O'Donnells and their relatives among the continental military class. It was difficult for such men to return to Ireland, but when they did, their influence was considerable. They were very largely based in Flanders, a key centre of the Counter-Reformation, and were militantly Catholic. They were fiercely resistant to recruiting for Protestant countries or fighting against Catholic ones and many defected from the levies raised for Sweden (1609–10) for this very reason.[127] In exile they preserved their former status, pride and territorial affinity with their birthplace, continental-born descendants citing their father's Ulster birthplace as their own and bequeathing their confiscated estates there.[128] They also retained their retinue of learned men (now usually clerics). In 1662 Captain Art O'Neill, upon applying for entry to one of Spain's highest military orders, called upon the family's hereditary genealogist, one of the Conrys, to prove his lineage back to the tenth century.[129]

Those military retainers who remained in Ulster in the early part of the century became the woodkerne who preyed on settler and Irish alike. Their more organised successors, the tories (from the Irish *toraidhe* or 'raider') and rapparees (*rapaire*, a form of pike), came to prominence in the Cromwellian period and continued intermittently until the middle of the eighteenth century. They operated in remote hilly and wooded districts in Cork, Kerry, south-west Connacht, but most notably in south-west Ulster and to a lesser extent in Donegal, the Sperrins in Tyrone, Londonderry and the Glens of Antrim. They have been seen by some writers as the dispossessed conducting an early nationalist struggle against the oppressor. Many were indeed survivors of such dispossessed families. The tories of Armagh and Tyrone, wrote Archbishop Oliver Plunkett to Rome in 1671, were 'certain gentlemen of the leading families of the houses of O'Neill, MacDonnell, O'Hagan etc . . . together with their followers';[130] while leaders in Leitrim were known to be men disappointed in their hopes of regaining their lands at the Restoration. Warrants issued in 1666 for their arrest in Counties Leitrim, Sligo, Londonderry, Down and Tyrone contain the names of almost all the leading Gaelic families in Ulster.[131] They also included those soldiers who managed to return from the Continent, and during the Williamite war they shaded into the Jacobite campaign as irregulars attacking Williamite forces. Old customs and traditions were not eroded overnight by the changes of the seventeenth century. Toryism in many respects was a continuation of the Gaelic order by other means. Successful cattle raids, feasting and accumulation of a personal following – all features of Gaelic lordship – remained the tory's route to leadership. There is too a territorial continuity in such activities, the Cavan O'Reillys for example continuing to raid into Louth, much as their ancestors had done in the past. In the sixteenth century areas like the baronies of Farney in Monaghan and the Fews in south Armagh and other wooded and boggy areas had been notorious sources of raiding parties into the adjacent Pale.[132] By the late seventeenth century they are identifiable frontier zones between surviving Gaelic and extending Scottish and English cultures.[133]

But nothing is ever quite so straightforward in Irish history and every attempt to look to the tories as an 'example of the passionate and indomitable resistance of the Celts to foreign despotism' is destined to be frustrated.[134] There is evidence of English and Scots amongst them, of 'settler' collusion in the black economy they operated, of men falling in and out of gangs according to their employment situation. Rather than protectors of Catholics, they robbed and murdered Catholic and Protestant alike and (usually) they were denounced by the priests.[135] What can be said with more certainty was that the folklore which developed around them helped generate the legend of 'Gentleman Robber[s]' and 'Protector[s]' of their people. The words are those of John Cosgrave's chapbook history of Redmond O'Hanlon (the most famous of all the tories), one of the most popular works of the eighteenth century. O'Hanlon had seen French service after his family had lost their lands in Armagh. Under the Restoration he became so famous for his exploits in Armagh and surrounding counties that he was a regular news item in the London press. He was eventually betrayed by another tory (a Franciscan friar) and murdered in 1681 by his foster-brother, under orders from the authorities. The story of O'Hanlon and his like would later inform nationalist traditions of the struggle of the dispossessed and betrayal by their own.[136] The traditions were particularly strong in the border zone of south Armagh, south

Down and north Louth – which were his major haunts – and the unfortunate descendants of those who had betrayed him were still being taunted by schoolchildren in the twentieth century.[137] The geography of tory and rapparee activity, whilst owing much to inaccessibility and deliberate concentration in those 'fastnesses' of old, also defines for the historian those areas where Gaelic ways survived longest. By the second half of the seventeenth century the upland areas had the heaviest concentration of people defined in official statistics as 'Irish' – places like the baronies of Omagh in Tyrone, Loughinsholin in Londonderry, Bannaugh and Boylaugh in Donegal, and the Fews in Armagh. It was in such areas that creaghting and lavish hospitality continued, practices which were part and parcel of bandit life. The Williamite officer George Story wrote in 1691, with barely concealed admiration, of the peripatetic lifestyle of these semi-militaristic bands in 'the wildness of the country between Newry and Dundalk'.[138]

It would have required superhuman qualities to have devised a just land settlement in the seventeenth century. It was not even clear cut who was the rebel, who the loyalist, and the Old English in particular claimed that the Catholics had been the only 'loyal subjects'.[139] The Restoration had recognised that much of the land had been legitimately acquired, or re-sold to new owners (many Catholic) who could not then be dispossessed. For most Catholics in Ulster the wrangles over the court of claims and the subsequent Jacobite attempt at reversing earlier land settlements would have been entirely academic. Both campaigns had been driven largely by Old English Catholics, and nothing points up the gulf between them and the Old Irish so much as the former's demands for a return to the situation as it existed in October 1641, by which time all but a few of Ulster's Gaelic Irish proprietors had disappeared. At the rate with which they were selling off their lands, little would have remained to them by the end of the century regardless of the political upheaval.[140] Even in the non-plantation county of Monaghan the Gaelic land-holding system had largely succumbed to more mercenary attitudes by the second decade of the seventeenth century.[141] In County Antrim, cushioned from the full impact of the century's land fluctuations because of the powerful position of its earl, only seven out of the hundred declared forfeit by the Williamite settlement had anything left to lose, and of these six were leaseholders, not outright owners.[142] Any of the sought-for changes in the second half of the century would have made very little difference to the existing proprietorship in Ulster. There was to be no return to the old Gaelic system.

The transformation of Ulster into a predominantly Protestant province in the eighteenth century would also contribute to Ulster Catholicism's distinctive qualities. In the seventeenth century Ireland became the receptacle of the largest movement of population in Europe. That it would have happened without official policies of confiscation and plantation is indisputable. Most land was lost unofficially to aggressive speculation, and the original British settlers of the Ulster Plantation also suffered because of progressive new immigration. The type and intensity of settlement also changed, jumping from 40,000 in 1630 to 270,000 by 1712. The influx of Scottish Presbyterians in the 1690s was to cause one of the most significant indents in what was still a substantially Catholic tenantry, with a massive re-leasing of lands to the new arrivals.[143] But the full impact of the land changes of the seventeenth century took generations to unfold and may not have registered fully with Ulster's Catholic tenantry till the sudden rise of population in the second half of the eighteenth century. The persistent shortage of good tenants would have placed existing ones in a strong position. Archbishop Oliver Plunkett noted this in 1671. 'The peasantry – those who cultivate the land – are all right and it is these who support the priests and friars; they even give some help to those who were once their masters.' But, he added, 'the gentlemen are completely ruined'. Only three had recovered their estates and all were in debt. 'All the others have difficulty in obtaining a lease of a part of their property, and it is regarded as a great favour when they succeed in this.'[144]

It would be difficult to exaggerate the social consequences of the seventeenth-century land settlements for the future of Ulster Catholicism. Only a handful of Catholic landowners survived into the eighteenth century and very soon these too disappeared, most conforming to the established church. The net result was to place the Ulster Catholics on a lower social level than their co-religionists elsewhere in the country. The Catholics of Ulster and adjacent north Connacht were generally the poorest in the country. This, and the absence of the kind of surviving Catholic gentry which sustained an institutionalised Catholic church elsewhere, dictated its different character in Ulster. Ulster never had a significant Old English class, an elite accustomed to the practice of power and politics. The absence of such a political tradition is still felt today. The Protestant gentry in Ulster never had to deal with equals, and the distance between them and the socially inferior Catholics bred unrealistic fears of subversion. The picture of an impoverished Catholic peasantry clinging to the hills is far-fetched. But they had lost their natural social leaders, they were to play little part in the eighteenth century's campaigns for Catholic rights until alerted to them by Catholics from the south and enlightened Presbyterians, and highly charged local resentments against those who got the land have festered to the present day.

5

THE MERGER OF 'IRISHNESS' AND CATHOLICISM IN EARLY MODERN ULSTER

That 'you may learn the sympathy between us modern Catholikes and St Patricke and the Primitive Christians; and on the contrary discover the discrepancy of the Protestants, not only with S. Patricke, whome I am sure they will discarde for a very superstitious papist, but from all the current of the ancient Catholiks, having no more alliance with them than truth with falsehood'.

Introduction to Fr. Rochford's 1625 *Life of Patrick, . . . Brigid . . . Columb* (Jennings, *Michael Ó Cléirigh*, 38)

Fionnuala O Connor's *In Search of a State* (1993) has a revealing interview with a woman from the working-class Catholic community of Ardoyne in north Belfast. She was speaking about the first stages of the Troubles in the early 1970s.

I was in Toby's Hall and a British foot patrol came in. Both sides exchanged insults. A glass was thrown. One soldier panicked and strafed the hall with bullets, leaving one of the crowd dead. Other soldiers outside – thinking themselves under attack – also started firing. When the shooting stopped somebody got up and started to sing an old hymn which was well-known in the Ardoyne. 'Faith of our Fathers'. I think it was to calm people down. Everybody stood and started singing it.

Recalling the incident over twenty years later, she could appreciate the incongruity of the situation.[1] And yet this nineteenth-century hymn was one of great political symbolism for northern nationalists on the eve of the Troubles. It linked fidelity to faith with the sufferings of ancestors. Though commemorating English saints and martyrs (a fact unknown to most Irish Catholics until recently), it had become something of a nationalist battle hymn: suffering, sacrifice and victimisation carrying with them the ultimate promise of victory.

> Our fathers chained in prisons dark,
> Were still in heart and conscience free
> How sweet would be their children's fate,
> If they like them could die for thee.
> Faith of our fathers living still,
> We will be true to thee till death.

The basic premises of later nationalism, of an ancient national faith, of unswerving fidelity and of ultimate triumph had already been laid by the end of the seventeenth century.[2]

Catholicism, like Presbyterianism, experienced intermittent persecution throughout the seventeenth century, the adherents of both projecting remarkably similar self-images as a persecuted people. Tacit if begrudging tolerance was, however, the norm – even under Cromwell. Indeed, it was arguments that Catholicism stood a fairer chance of toleration under Cromwell than under the exiled Stuarts which enlisted papal approval when the Ulster Catholics transferred their support to the Commonwealth.[3] But public displays of Catholic ritual were discouraged and the nascent church reorganisation crumbled. The result was the perpetuation of Ulster Catholicism's peculiarities – so persistently attacked by church authorities – into modern times. As in the eighteenth century so in the seventeenth, state penalisation of Catholicism most directly affected the elite and the social pressures to conform to the religion of one's class eventually eroded the few remaining Catholic gentry in Ulster. But lower down the social scale, traffic was often in the other direction. Although a relatively prosperous tier of Catholic tenants survived the land upheavals of the period, Ulster Catholicism was rapidly becoming the religion of the 'have-nots', mostly of Irish ancestry, but with a significant sprinkling of English and Scots.

Equally, Catholicism is unlikely to have survived at all without the connivance of some Protestant neighbours.[4] How such daily accommodations operated, how indeed the identity, religious or otherwise, of the Ulster Irish evolved in this period is now all but lost to history. The Irish language goes into rapid decline from the seventeenth century, not because of oppression but because the new legal system required the populace to come to terms with the English word and the written document.[5] Irish language culture's most accessible expression is still to be found in the poetry, although before the end of the seventeenth century it is an unsatisfactory source for the opinions of the people at large, and the interests of the patron who had commissioned the work would still have dictated the message. Katharine Simms warns: 'The bards are . . . professional wordsmiths paid to give the patron's desired public image a literary form. Thus a sharp change in tone from medieval warlike compositions of the late sixteenth century to pious preaching of Counter-Reformation morality and Catholic nationalism in the seventeenth does not necessarily reflect a sudden conversion of society at large, so much as the role of Counter-Reformation clerics as parsimonious substitute patrons, when the fall of the Ulster lords left many bards unemployed.'[6] The culture transmitted in these poems is that of a declining elite, for whom loss of land, status and the Gaelic order is a searing experience. Poetic language is often stark and exaggerated, concepts and images pared to their suggestive minimum. Yet the language of such poems had become stereotypical by the nineteenth century, and poets and priests were often one and the same.[7]

It is with these groups that an answer may be found to the question: why did Ulster Irish society not absorb the influx of new people in the seventeenth century as it had so often done in the past? State backing for the new Protestant culture is of course a major factor. But so also is the failure to accommodate the elite of the old culture as had been the original intention. For it was they who had created the pseudo-histories and genealogies to incorporate the *nouveaux arrivés* and had then transmitted such refashioned 'history' to future generations. In the seventeenth century these were the very groups against which most of the penalisation was directed. They were pushed down the social scale and their bitterness helped form the cultural identity of the future.

1. *Who were the Catholics of Ulster?*

Given the uncertainties of the seventeenth century, it should not surprise that the consequences of developments then were still only unfolding a century later. Nowhere is this more noticeable than in the area of religious identity. Little is known of the relationship between the various religious groupings before 1641. The extreme statements of sectarian identity produced by the events of that year played a formative role in emerging stereotypes. But they are not a reliable window on reality. Neither 'native' nor 'settler' would have had any clearly defined sense of religious identity before 1641.[8]

Nor should one assume that all the new arrivals were necessarily Protestant. Stories abound of Scots Catholics on the Inishowen peninsula of Donegal. They appear to have been on good terms with their Presbyterian neighbours, who by all accounts were just as superstitious – an accusation more normally made, then as now, about Catholics.[9] The religion of the tenancy on an estate was often dictated by that of the landowner. Thus, through the influence of the Catholic Sir George Hamilton of Greenlaw, the Hamilton and Abercorn estates in Tyrone continued to attract Scottish Catholic tenants well into Charles I's reign.[10] The MacDonnells in Antrim provided a haven for Scottish Catholics from the Highlands and the Isles. The Franciscan monastery at Bonamargy, near Ballycastle in north Antrim, was the focal point of a Catholic mission to convert the Scots and by 1640 was reputedly attracting five hundred Scots every year. By 1625 some 20 per cent of Scots settlers were Catholic.[11] Although the tendency was for greater distinctiveness by the end of the seventeenth century, by then there had been significant cultural and religious cross-fertilisation. The image of the Calvinist Scot introducing civilisation and the work ethic into Ulster was a nineteenth-century fabrication to explain the *status quo* then. In reality, the early Scots settlers were closer to their Irish counterparts, in dress, work practices and housing, than to the English.[12] We still do not know whether the new settlers included Gaelic speakers. But Scots – that regional dialect of English which has so affected the Ulster accent – had been present since the high Middle Ages, and was particularly strong in Donegal.[13]

The belief that Protestants were insincere in their religious beliefs, motivated by pure self-interest and reluctant to convert the Irish for fear of losing land and power, was first voiced in the seventeenth century.[14] *Ireland's Case Briefly Stated*, published in Louvain in 1695, by the Jacobite exile Hugh Reily, and popularised in numerous editions over the next century and a half as *The Impartial History of Ireland*, made the point particularly forcefully:

It was Saint Paul's sentiment that *Godliness is great Gain*, but the Reform'd saints of this Age invert the Maxim, and do rather conclude, that *Gain is great Godliness*. Upon this Godly motive it was, that our zealous Reformers went into Ireland to propagate their Gospel, where they took more pains to make

the land turn Protestant [than] the People; the confiscation of Men's estates
... being more beneficial, than the charity of saving their Lives, or reforming
their errors.[15]

In fact, the accusation was less appropriate for Ulster than for any
other province. The migration of people from Scotland in particular
would have occurred and did occur without either the official plantation or the Reformation, and the land transfer had already taken
place before the more overtly religious confiscations of the latter half
of the century. The accusation, however, was to become a central
element in Ulster folklore. Moreover, apart from the hiatus of the
1640s, there were regular attempts at conversion and criticisms of the
Church of Ireland for neglecting the spiritual welfare of 'the poor
Irish'.[16] Lamenting 'what small effect reformation hath taken in this
country', Henry Leslie preaching in Drogheda in 1622 attributed its
failure to 'custom and long continuance in error', 'fear of breaking
with their friends', 'busy trafficking of priests and Jesuits', 'want of
sufficient ministry' and 'miseducation of our youth'.[17]

The lack of Irish-speaking preachers and organisational infrastructure dogged the spread of Counter-Reformation Catholicism and all
but confined any successful Protestant evangelisation to the lowlands,
where native Irish were more influenced by the culture and language
of the settlers. The only Irish-language printing press in Ireland had
mysteriously disappeared – torn apart for heresy by the friars, so it
was rumoured.[18] A partial translation of the Bible was published in
1603, a full version in 1685, but little appears to have been done with
it and a general lack of knowledge of the Bible was one of the things
separating Catholic from Protestant, giving rise to the still-current
accusation that Catholicism is an unscriptural faith. Henry Jones's
antipathy may have been a contributory factor. During the Cromwellian period he was also provost of Trinity College, Dublin, where
Irish-speaking Protestant clergy were to have been trained. He
inherited the completed portions of an Irish translation of the Old
Testament, prepared by his predecessor, Bishop William Bedell –
a supporter of Irish language and culture – but did nothing with
them. Certainly the language problem is an important element in the
development of formal religion, as the respect of the Ulster Irish for

Irish-speaking Protestant divines like Bedell and Ussher illustrates. One might have expected Bedell's funeral in 1642, in the immediate aftermath of the 1641 rebellion, to have been a fraught event. Instead, the 'Irish of Cavan in considerable number' attended, including their main military leaders, respectfully observing the Protestant service and according the burial full military honours.[19]

'Conversion' presupposes some knowledge of the religion one is converting to. The vast majority of Ulster Irish had no knowledge of written language, Irish or English. This essential difference between Protestantism, a religion of text and the written word, and Catholicism, one of the spoken word and oral tradition, was fundamentally to affect the two religious cultures and goes a long way to explaining the failure of the Reformation in Ireland. Religious texts required oral explanation, usually by clergy. Although Ulster was better supplied with Protestant schools than elsewhere, most religious change came through cultural seepage and personal relations. 'Persecution, neglect and mixed marriages' were the causes adduced by the Revd James O'Laverty in his influential nineteenth-century history of Down and Connor to explain why Ulster Catholics turned away from 'the faith of their race'. And many did, large numbers reverting to Catholicism in 1641, and again after the Restoration, suggesting continued fluidity of religious affiliation.[20]

Intermarriage appears to have occurred at every social level and by 1639 Catholic clerics were discussing what provision to make for the children of mixed marriages.[21] Generally the tendency was for the remnants of the native landowning elite to intermarry with and conform to the dominant religion of their class, whilst lower down the social scale the drift was in the opposite direction. Thus the Clandeboye O'Neills, the Ardkeen Savages, the Tollymore Magennises intermarried with English or Scottish Protestants and the land descended through their Protestant heirs.[22] Such elite conversions did not mean an abandonment of Gaelic ways, however, and the Protestant descendants of a number of the Gaelic lords remained patrons of the poets into the eighteenth century. The new Cromwellian tenantry quickly succumbed to cultural pressures to conform to the practices of the society they had joined. The numerous references to Cromwellian soldiers marrying papist women and to widows of English extraction among the transportees to Connacht suggest as much.[23] It was those areas heavily settled by Scots and English that experienced the highest levels of bilingualism, conformity, intermarriage and participation in the new market-orientated culture by the Ulster Irish. In contrast the uplands, where the Irish progressively became concentrated, did not experience such levels of cultural seepage and remained strongholds of Irish culture. Although Gaelic culture would continue to suffuse Catholicism, there were enough English, Old English and Scottish Catholics and enough Ulster-Irish Protestants to make the claim of Catholicism as the religion of the Irish race untenable, even if that was the assumption (or more often the accusation) made by successive governments.

How and when did such fluidity change? The reorganisation of the churches played a part, but the real battle for the popular soul did not develop until the next century, and Presbyterianism, like Catholicism, experienced considerable organisational difficulties.[24] Of more immediate importance were the dramatic demographic changes in Ulster in the course of the seventeenth century. Although considerable numbers of settlers returned to Scotland in times of political tension – notably in the 1630s and 1640s – in the latter half of the century waves of immigration from Scotland (perhaps as many as 80,000 people in the 1660s and a further 50,000–80,000 in the 1690s) altered the religious makeup of the province.[25] This provided a youthful basis for population increase among Presbyterians, while there was a simultaneous decline in the equivalent Irish base with the exile of so many military men after James II's defeat in 1691. By 1732 Ulster had become the predominantly Protestant province of modern times, with an estimated 313,120 Protestants and 192,295 Catholics.[26] There was a corresponding shift of Irish into more marginal lands, concentrating the casualties of a rapidly changing economy. But the main effect of the demographic change was to place those Irish in areas of Scottish penetration in economic dependency on the settlers, for, as W. H. Crawford writes, 'a new layer of tenants had been slipped into the Ulster social pyramid so that most of the Irish paid their rents and duties not to the landlords but to substantial Protestant tenant farmers.'[27] The result was a transformation of Irish attitudes towards the Scots by the end of the seventeenth century. By 1679 Archbishop Plunkett was identifying the Presbyterians as the most anti-Catholic in his province:

The secular clergy have been granted a certain amount of toleration up to now, but in many places, and especially around Armagh, they are considerably harassed . . . so strict are the Presbyterians. The latter are very numerous in these parts . . . one could travel twenty-five miles in my area without finding half-a-dozen Catholic or Protestant families, but all Presbyterians, i.e. strict Calvinists.[28]

Thus in Ulster Irish did the word for Scot (*Albanach*) become that for Protestant, much as *Sasanach* (Englishman) did in Munster Irish. Likewise *Gael* and *Gall* (Irish and foreigner) had come to mean simply 'Catholic' and 'Protestant'.[29] The seventeenth century had thus set in place one of the essential ingredients of Ulster Catholic identity: its confusion between its local Protestant neighbour and some distant imperial state.

However, the image of the suppressed Gael stoking up thoughts of revenge is far-fetched. Participation in the new system, where permitted, was more likely. Poets sought patrons from all quarters. The presence of Ulster-Irish officials in the new legal and administrative system was such that it entirely collapsed in 1641 and that presence continued throughout the century, though in a steadily decreasing form. Even the father of the future Catholic archbishop of Armagh, Hugh MacMahon, acted as a tithe-collector for the Church of Ireland.[30] An awareness of religious difference was slow to emerge. It is most marked among the literate elite and it was they who provided its linguistic parameters.

2. *The poetic tradition*

The decline of the Gaelic elite brought in its train the disintegration of the bardic order, and it was within the Catholic Church that both dispossessed chiefs and learned men now sought social status. It is only when the main political families such as the O'Neills and the O'Donnells lost their lands that they entered the church in large numbers. They had not done so before. Priests and clerics were now hailed as saviours in a way once reserved for the Gaelic chiefs.[31] The coming together of these two classes of learned men explains the association of religion and dispossession which appears in many of these poems. The poets had long been part of the second league of landowners behind the main chieftains.[32] They were highly politicised as a class, but any new message in their poetry tended to be obscured by the standard themes and motifs of the bardic tradition. By the 1630s, however, the beginnings of non-professional poetry were already visible.[33] As the century wore on, the poets were of recognisably lower status. The metres of the poems changed. They became more comprehensible to the untrained ear and very often were set to music. The diplomatic veneer of the bards disappeared and often the language was stark and bitter. Much of this bitterness was economically driven, reflecting their own impoverishment. They tended to blame the new Protestant or English dispensation for the decline of their order, but were particularly resentful of those Irish who had prospered, thereby establishing a notable theme in future nationalism.

The five political poems from the mid-seventeenth century published by Cecile O'Rahilly in 1952 strike a new note. Only Munster and Ulster are represented – a reflection of the continuation of a literary Gaelic tradition in these regions alone. There is some suggestion that they were composed by continental-trained clerics, and, given their enormous popularity (with transcriptions being made far into the nineteenth century), they clearly had resonance far beyond their time – at least for the literary class. Only one, *An Síogaí Rómhánach*, is of Ulster origin; the other four are from Munster. All are highly propagandistic and politicised. The Munster poems reflect the bitterness of a dispossessed landowning class, the many English loan-words indicating dealings with the new legal system: King's Bench, Assizes, Exchequer, Court of Wards, all tending to the same end, 'the mangling of property'. Another, written on the morrow of the Cromwellian transplantation, reflects the searing impact it had on Munster in particular.[34]

Significantly, *An Síogaí Rómhánach* (c.1650) dwells less on the land than on religion, for little remained of Ulster's Gaelic landed elite. Members of the old noble families were joining the clergy in large numbers, particularly the Franciscans. Therefore when Ulster poets composed poems in praise of certain priests, they were often merely fulfilling their traditional obligation of praising a noble family.[35] *An Síogaí* is scathing of those who did not support Rinuccini's party during the Confederacy, and shows the consciousness of the Ulster clergy to have been far more Rome-centred than that of the rest of the country.

It is an early version of the emotional vision-poem, the aisling, which became the preferred format of the genre after the disappearance of the bardic schools. It tells of a vision of a beautiful maiden by the author as he lay on the tombs of O'Neill and O'Donnell in Rome. She bewails the fate of the Gaels. Why should they, alone of the race of Adam, they who had preserved the faith since Patrick's time, be punished by God, while the 'Saxon brood', the 'Lutherans', 'the heretics' who had 'scoffed at the Mother of the only son', were exalted? Most English monarchs were denounced, from the 'lecherous' Henry and 'whorish' Elizabeth, and the Stuarts fared little better. It is their attack on the mass and the Irish language which is singled out for particular scorn. Then Ulster arose to save them, first with Maguire and Mac-Mahon 'for love of the faith they would not forsake', then with Owen Roe (for whom *An Síogaí* is very much a praise poem). They failed because of the disunity of the Gael – the 'treacherous foreign Gaels [Old English]' – and those clerics who compromised with 'the heretic horde' and were cursed by the papal nuncio. The vision ends with a hope that the Gael will unite 'to drive out the strangers and set Ireland free'.

> Then none shall league with the Saxon,
> Nor with the bald Scot,[36]
> Then shall Erin be freed from settlers,
> Then shall perish the Saxon tongue.
> The Gaels in arms shall triumph
> Over the crafty, thieving, false sect of Calvin.
> . . .
> True faith shall be uncontrolled;
> The people shall be rightly taught
> By friars, bishops, priests and clerics.

Unlike the Munster poems, however, the poem ends on a passive note of despair – the poet is too weak, too alone to fulfil the maiden's dream. It is a theme which was to be a characteristic of Ulster poetry, a symbol perhaps of the passive nature of Ulster Catholicism which future commentators would note. Whereas the English are the over-arching threat, the poem speaks of the Scot with the petty jealousy of a neighbour. He is 'crafty', 'thieving', 'shitty', 'cowardly' – a significant shift from the early years of the century when some thought the plantation was a government ruse to sour relations between Irish and Scots 'who from ancient times were on most friendly terms . . . and to unite the Scotch and English against the Irish'.[37] The association of religion and culture, and the reduction of the generalised bardic theme of expelling the foreigner to the more specific English-speaking 'churl' and 'Luther's' and 'Calvin's brood', marks a significant break with the literary past. Hugh O'Neill does not figure prominently in popular oral tradition. It is quite the reverse with Owen Roe, who linked faith and fatherland and was represented as such in the poetry. It would take time to evolve into the embittered nationalism of Art Bennett's poetry in the nineteenth century, but the direct evolutionary link to the component themes is unmistakable.[38]

Although later versions of these poems are often criticised as unreliable, it is wrong to think their central themes twisted to suit later anti-English nationalism. There was no need to manufacture the bitterness of the elite at loss of land or religious persecution. Indeed, the early texts are far more insulting about the Protestant settlers. What the later versions have done is to remove most of the personal insults, the uncouth, scatological elements, thought to debase the noble message which the early nineteenth-century translators wished to convey. The intense regionalism (so prominent in seventeenth-century Ulster Irish), the dislike of the Scots as much as the English, have also been toned down and a more simplified message conveyed of the suppression of the Gael by the Saxon. The publication of *An Síogaí Rómhánach* in Hardiman's *Irish Minstrelsy* of 1831 was a landmark in this filtering process, since subsequent translations and transcripts tended to follow this version. Hardiman set out to portray Irish poetry as a dignified tradition destroyed by the English. The translations 'for the most part transmuted the originals into pallid imitations of Thomas Moore in an attempt to make them seem respectable by the standards of the day'.[39]

Transitional poets were the blind poet-harpist Séamus Dall Mac Cuarta (McCourt, *c.*1650–1733), born at Omeath in north Louth, and Patrick McAlindon (*c.*1665–1733), born in the Fews, south Armagh. Neither had yet fallen to the impoverished position of their immediate successors, and McAlindon appears to have been a prosperous farmer who gave hospitality and support to a host of lesser poets in the region.[40] Both were also accomplished harpists, ardent Jacobites and devout Catholics. McAlindon's home was regularly used for religious services and his most historically interesting works were often poems praising the clergy. Mac Cuarta's family had traditionally close links with the Franciscans and his devotion and sobriety were legendary. An analysis of the language used by poet and priest reveals the close identification which is occurring in these years (even if the priest who does not live up to the ideal continues to be the butt of satire). The use of the word 'heretic' as a blanket description for Protestants appears early in clerical material, matched by the equally prevalent use of 'papist' for Irish in Protestant sources. The beginnings of the '800 years of English tyranny' concept, traceable back to Henry II and the bull *Laudabiliter*, also appears in early seventeenth-century Ulster clerical and exile literature prior to its adoption by the poets.[41]

McAlindon's praise-poem for Hugh MacMahon, Catholic archbishop of Armagh, 1715–37, *A Rí lér fuasclaíodh*, contains the usual (by now) references to heretics and Luther and the association of Ireland's plight with that of the people of Israel.[42] He points to Mac-Mahon's noble lineage, suggesting that this head of the church in Ireland has inherited the mantle of the Gaelic princes of old. McAlindon's clear support for Armagh, in yet another episode in the long-running controversy with Dublin over which episcopal see merited metropolitan status, reflects the strong provincial pride of these transitional poems. The steadfastness of Ulster is compared to the weakness of the south, which sold out on so many occasions, from Dermot MacMurrough's 'evil deed' in inviting in the Anglo-Normans in the twelfth century, to its refusal to assist Owen Roe 'in sustaining the faith of Christ against Oliver Cromwell'. The metre of a number of McAlindon's poems suggests that they were consciously written for popular consumption. Politically they are firmly Jacobite, but pessimistic about Ireland's ability to help herself.[43]

But beside such fatalism a powerful reorientation of popular culture was taking place. Keating's reordering of the past was part of an increasing identification of race and religion. It is epitomised in Mac Cuarta, the most religious of these transitional poets and undoubtedly the most popular. Lineage and rightful belonging is pitted against foreign possession, 'deceiving English law', and a heretic religion.[44] Mac Cuarta's poems deal with the apparent finality of defeat under King William. The bones of the true nobility lie scattered at Aughrim or in ruined castles, the very land itself abandoning them in the bleakness of defeat. As in bardic poetry, land and people have lost their vigour and bountifulness 'under the domination of the heretics' and 'the puffed-up New English'.[45] Houses which once provided hospitality to poet and cleric have adopted the new culture, language and religion. '*I cannot understand your Gaelic*, so speak in the foreign manner', the returning poet is told, as he denounces the house's inhospitality and preference for '*prayers* . . . explained in English' and a 'foreign Bible' over a clergy, with powers delegated from Christ, 'reading the passion' in Irish and administering the sacraments. Such refusal to change consigns your people to serfdom, responds the house. No, retorts the poet:

> . . . the English-speaking stock,
> it was who left the Gaels as serfs,
> their rents, their riches, their wealth, their property,
> it is you who have their value.

But like the Israelites in Egypt, such bondage will end: 'The saints and *true* clerics [my italics] say/ that the Englishry will be destroyed.'[46]

The numerous priests celebrated in Mac Cuarta's poems (even those of Old English extraction) possess 'the noble blood of the Gaels', reaching back to the Milesians.[47] And that true Gaelic blood has the imprint of Rome, linking them to the early church and a wider Catholic community on the Continent. His praise-poem for James O'Sheil, bishop of Down and Connor, 1717–24, also guardian of the Franciscan houses at Downpatrick and Dromore, is particularly significant, since O'Sheil was also involved in a public controversy concerning Catholicism as 'the only religion that is truly conformable to the express word of God'.[48]

> Your trumpet is sweeter in Rome
> and in Louvain of the orders amongst the clergy,
> than in Ireland to Luther and John,[49]
> who would extinguish the right by means of lies.

> Dear, wise Colm Cille,
> the good son of the king of Inis Fáil;
> your ancestry is the same as his –
> with Niall of the gold your lines separated.[50]

Nearly all the leading Ulster Catholic families appear in Mac Cuarta's poems as the unjustly deposed and rightful heirs of the true Gael. His litany also includes Gaelicised Scots like the MacDonnells, the O'Boyles and the MacSweeneys, and Old English like the Flemings of County Meath. Mac Cuarta lived on Fleming's Slane estate until it was lost under King William, so the poet felt the impact of the new Williamite dispensation particularly keenly.[51] But it is the O'Neills of the Fews and the Magennises of Iveagh who take pride of place – suggesting continued patronage of the poets by the descendants of both families – their priests and above all those who had gone into exile after the defeat of James II. Hope now lies with them and Mac Cuarta sets the tone for subsequent Irish-language poetry in his call for them to return with the hosts of Spain and France to free them from the foreigners:

> May I not retreat to the grave until I see hosts
> coming in victorious strength to pleasant Ireland;
> the kindred of Owen Roe in their ships [full] of true worthies
> who will place hundreds of foreigners in a new subjection.
> I'd be happy to be gazing
> on long-eared Britain running in terror from us;
> and the triumphant champion as leader of the hosts
> proclaiming a new battle against swarthy heretics.[52]

Mac Cuarta's poetry reflects the scale and finality of the defeat inflicted by the new order on the Jacobite cause and its Irish supporters, and the battle of Aughrim fought on 12 July 1691 – possibly the bloodiest episode of Irish history when over 7,000 were killed by the Williamite forces – haunts his verse. 'Aughrim of the slaughter' introduces his most popular poem: 'A lament for Sorley MacDonnell' (1691). A powerful poem which lists the members of the noble families who fell at Aughrim, it interlinks MacDonnell's death with the passion of Christ, the sufferings of the Christian martyrs, 'the only faith of Patrick', with Cú Chulainn and the people of the *Táin*. The poem is as elitist in content as the bardic poetry of old, for the lament is for the nobles who patronised the poets and clergy, but of its popularity there can be no doubt, for it survives in a staggering forty-one known manuscripts.[53]

However, in an exchange with another poet, Hugh MacGerrity, on whether the tories were the true descendants of the Gaelic nobility (as Mac Cuarta claimed), he comes off much the worse. To a small band of tories under their leader McDaid, Mac Cuarta attributes the standard virtues of the nobility: generosity to the poets, valour, vigour, comeliness, defying 'the men of England ... and all the greatest attorneys', holding the fort 'until the Gaels arrive with the prayers of the clergy/ on the waves from afar to liberate us'. Nonsense, responds MacGerrity, there is nothing noble about them. Their 'proper status' is 'applying their talents to the shovel'. 'Ugly churlish crouchers', 'setting themselves up as nobility', where were they when the true nobility was fighting with James? They wouldn't know how to read a letter or poem; they confront no enemy, but pass their time 'plundering the cattle of every tenant', and are scorned by 'the old women of Cooley and Carlingford'.[54] The tories, in other words, were committing that mortal sin of Gaelic society: getting above their station.

Many poems had already become popular songs by the end of the seventeenth century: 'infamous ballads ... bawled about the streets' composed by 'hired wretched scribblers' and prophesying the destruction of Protestantism.[55] By the time we reach Art MacCooey (*c.* 1738–73) and Peadar Ó Doirnín (*c.*1700–69) the remnants of the old poetic order have entirely disappeared. Although there are signs that Mac-Cooey was educated in one of the classical hedge-schools (and a very definite familiarity with *An Síogaí Rómhánach*), there are few literary flights in MacCooey. Most of his poems were written for singing and they were still being sung in the twentieth century.[56] MacCooey's poetry is rich in detail about the preoccupations of the Catholic poor. Indeed, he is the nearest we can get to a peasant poet. His family were small farmers in Creggan (Fews barony), south Armagh. But Art would have appeared to both Protestants and well-off Catholics as the archetypal feckless papist, drinking himself to an early grave, living from hand-to-mouth on odd jobs as a gardener, herdsman, or *spailpín* (a migrant harvest labourer), and praising (and expecting to receive) the old 'hospitality' to which poets traditionally laid claim. Although the most common theme in his poetry is a lament for the final destruction of the Gael at Aughrim and the Boyne (above all the O'Neills of the Fews), like other Ulster poetry in Irish, it is not a call to arms, but a nostalgic lament. Even his editor, the late Cardinal Ó Fiaich, thought his poetry 'a form of escapism'.[57] In his *Castle of Glasdrummond* (a former O'Neill castle), the ruined walls tell the poet:

> I shall not be restored in future, I will be swept away
> With all the loyal noble sons who won renown in me,
> They are under the slabs in Creggan and I'll not see them
> till death there.

Nor is there that mystical bitterness for the loss of land deemed to be naturally theirs, but the immediate problem of Catholics renting *any* land under the penal laws, particularly in the densely populated area of south Armagh. MacCooey speaks of 'the land sighing in sorrow/ our leases and our happiness yielding to the contemptuous brood'. Notable too is the way in which social, linguistic, cultural and religious loss are intertwined. Thus in his *Aisling Airt Mhic Cumhaigh*:

> My heart is shattered in a hundred thousand pieces,
> and even balsam will not ease my pain
> when I hear Irish all being abandoned,
> and a torrent of English in everyone's mouth,
> Wully and Jane are taking leases,
> on the lands of Ireland of the lovely golden spots,

and when I make enquiries I receive the reply:
'You're a Papist, I know not thee.'

The last line is in English in the original. Most of the English loanwords in other poems of the post-bardic era reflect similar insults, and Mac-Cooey was not the only one to express Catholic resentment at the word 'papist'.

His most bitter satire on the new Protestant culture is his allegorical dispute between the ruined medieval Catholic church at Faughart, County Louth, and the Anglican church at Forkhill – *Tagra an dá Theampall* or 'The Argument of the Two Churches'. In this the 'Foreign Temple' addresses the 'Roman Churchyard' in curt, abusive English. It is both 'Popery's vain devotion' and 'ignorant papist notions' which are responsible for the decay of its people's fortune and culture:

> My flock has estates, with land and demesnes,
> all riding in state in their coaches,
> while taxes arrears, and cesses severe
> upon your Gaedhelian broaches.[58]

The contrast he draws is that between the antiquity, nobility and cultured Roman faith and the novelty, worldliness and boorishness of Protestantism. MacCooey's poems contain all the stock references to Calvin, Luther, Henry VIII and Anne Boleyn, heretics, churls and foreigners.

However, one would be hard put to find in MacCooey some proto-type nationalist rebel. His resentments are often social rather than religious and the Catholic made good was the butt of one of his most vicious satires: 'The Churls of the Barley' – directed at the O'Callaghans, successful distillers and entrepreneurs in south Armagh. Much of his spite may have been caused by the failure of the *nouveaux riches* – unlike the gentry of old – to entertain the poets ('the breed and the seed of the vipers/ who threaten each day and never would pay/ a penny to poets or pipers'). But Art Bennett was to take up the theme from MacCooey and the O'Callaghans entered nationalist tradition as unpatriotic (a tradition totally without foundation).[59]

Also MacCooey, like so many other Ulster Irish, was not so

consumed with bitterness that he could not develop a *modus vivendi* with his Protestant neighbours. He was even married by a Protestant clergyman (a not uncommon event among Catholics, who resented the high level of priests' fees). Indeed, in one poem he suggests that he was even on the point of converting to Presbyterianism. His praise of the clergy (particularly the Franciscans), if from old noble (even Old English) stock, is unstinted. But those he considers upstarts receive the same verbal lashing as their secular counterparts, and his celebrated satire on Mary Quinn, the sister and housekeeper of the parish priest of Creggan, flailed the two for aping the new rich whilst fleecing the Catholic poor. The fact that the Revd Lawrence Taaffe, vicar-general of Armagh, had to intervene to defuse the situation is testimony to the power the poet could still wield as late as the 1760s. However, for a poet to so openly attack a priest in this way was highly unusual and he risked victimisation of his family by his community if he did so.[60]

All these key poets had come from old Oriel – the south Ulster/ north Leinster borderlands of Monaghan, south Armagh and Louth. Literary scholars have noted a greater bitterness in the poems of such Gaelic areas juxtaposed with more Anglicised areas.[61] This was an area where enough Old English landowners survived to act as patrons and protectors of poet and priest alike, and where the poets still thought of themselves as an elite.[62] The importance of such poetry cannot be overestimated, particularly that of the seventeenth-century transitional poets. It was known and admired by succeeding poets and scribes and set the tone and many of the themes for the future.[63] Their importance gathered pace as the poems began to be printed and translated from the end of the eighteenth century (feeding and inspiring Irish Romanticism). But what we are dealing with here are the 'hits' of Irish poetry, selected by the scribes, who did not usually concern themselves with the writings of lesser individuals. The corpus of the work of Simon Macken, a scribe and schoolmaster in County Fermanagh (active 1770s – 1820s) would have been typical. Among his transcriptions of popular medieval romance tales, various catechisms and continental devotional works, some tales and poems on death and the otherworld, humorous skits and burlesques, and the usual love poems and drinking songs, we find two poems attacking those who changed their religion, poems by Mac Cuarta (including his 'A Lament for Sorley MacDonnell') and MacCooey's *Tagra an dá Theampall* ('The Argument of the Two Churches'). No local folk poem or song is included. Macken, a linguistic purist, clearly despised such verse and is known to have transcribed only one during his lifetime.[64]

3. Persecution and 'political' Catholicism

In the first half of the seventeenth century Catholicism in Ireland did not experience major persecution. The oath of supremacy in the terms of the Ulster Plantation was not generally administered, the London companies even building mass-houses and receiving 'Popish priests' at their tables, as one aggrieved planter complained in 1631.[65] Active persecution returned under Cromwell, particularly in the initial stages of the military campaign (1649–50), when a number of priests and regulars were executed. The main difference during the first years of Cromwellian rule (1649–58) – and it was a difference commented upon by contemporaries – was that for the first time the laws could not be evaded.[66] Thereafter clerics were more likely to be exiled, and though the country was not entirely cleared of priests, their numbers were greatly reduced and the reorganisation of previous decades collapsed. Cromwell recognised the contradiction this posed to his general policy of liberty of conscience, and though 'popery' was not permitted such liberty and various acts of abjuration and discovery were placed on the statute book, there was a relaxation of official policy after 1654, and evidence of priests returning from exile. The persecution was short-lived, and, in the view of Monsignor Patrick Corish in what is the best short account of Irish Catholicism in this period, scarcely lived up to 'the national legend of Cromwellian ruthlessness'.[67] None the less, it helped establish the emotive tradition of the mass-rock and the hunted priest which until recently deterred dispassionate enquiry.[68] The effect on church organisation, however, was catastrophic. The synods held on the return to toleration at the Restoration (1660) record a reversion to 'superstitious' practices and widespread ignorance of the fundamentals of the faith.[69] It took over a century for church structure to recover.

For the next three decades tolerance and 'connivance'[70] was the norm. Political rather than religious conformity was the test, and most government officials recognised that, given the numbers of Catholics, their clergy required practical tolerance, 'since they must have Romish clergie whylst they are papists'.[71] For most of the seventeenth century private practice of Catholicism was tolerated, but public demonstrations or anything too ostentatious might provoke new restrictions. Responding to a complaint by the Spanish ambassador to London concerning recent edicts against Catholic clergy in Ireland, the future Charles I 'said he did not really know what prompted his father to issue such an edict, but he thought the occasion for it was a procession held by a bishop in Ireland with cross and lights etc.'.[72] Plunkett was irritated by those priests who drew attention to themselves by annoying the Protestants. Not until William and Mary's reign after 1688 did penalisation become systematic. How then can we explain the execution of Primate Oliver Plunkett in 1681, which was so out of character with the policy of the period, particularly since Plunkett was undoubtedly the most amenable Catholic bishop of the century where government was concerned?

The Ulster clergy (particularly the Franciscans) resented the appointment of an Old English outsider like Plunkett to the archbishopric of Armagh and they made innumerable complaints to Rome in ensuing years.[73] His absence from surviving Gaelic poetry (when nearly every other archbishop of Armagh was celebrated) is noteworthy. His preference for Protestant gentry and government supporters over his native Irish co-religionists was a particular charge made against him, and he would undoubtedly have attracted the taunt of 'Castle Catholic' – one who had gone over to the enemy or joined the system – had such a term of abuse then existed. There can be no doubt that his care to placate the authorities moderated government policy towards the Catholics and was appreciated by the higher clergy in particular.[74] Yet his bitter disputes with the Franciscans have given rise to a belief that they were responsible for his downfall. Certainly such internal bickerings were not unwelcome to the authorities. The Lord Lieutenant, the Earl of Essex, did not consider these friars the dangerous popish conspirators of English parliamentary propaganda. They 'alwaise have their little wrangles with the secular clergy', he wrote in his protest against the proclamation of 1673 banishing bishops and regulars.[75] He also made a personal appeal on behalf of Plunkett, 'who seems to me to be one of the best men of his persuasion . . . of a more peaceable temper and more conformable to government than any of their titular bishops in this country'.[76] Despite such disputes, however, and the presence of one renegade friar among the witnesses against him, the charges against Plunkett of plotting a French invasion were entirely manufactured in England. They were the Irish angle of the 'popish plot' devised by opposition English politicians to exclude the future James II from the throne. Plunkett was acquitted by a Protestant jury in Dundalk and the witnesses against him were utterly discredited. But a re-trial in London found him guilty of treason and he was executed at Tyburn on 1 July 1681.[77] His arrest and execution can only be explained by the rabid anti-popery of the English House of Commons, which even Charles II found impossible to control.

The authorities in Ireland had acquiesced in the implementation of security measures demanded by the discovery of the so-called 'plot'. A new proclamation ordered bishops and regulars to leave the country and a large number were arrested. Catholics were forbidden to keep weapons and mass-houses in towns were closed. But the English witch-hunt was not replicated in Ireland and, sporadic scares apart, the tendency to ignore inoperable laws and respect 'due process of the law' marked the entire penal era. Local magistrates seemed confused about the laws and the constant reminders suggest patchy implementation. In 1682 Franciscan vicar-general of Armagh, Bernard McGurk, defied the laws for the expulsion of regulars by taking the precaution of informing the local magistrate of any meetings held with his clergy and inviting official observance. This, and his acquittal of 'foreign jurisdiction' at successive assizes, highlights such confusion, and despite the high sheriff's determination to have him convicted, Lord Mountjoy ordered his release. He cannot simply be tried at one assize after another for the same offence, he argued: 'I believe this Maguirke a great rogue, but if he were a devil he must have right.'[78] He was to die in prison in February 1713 at the age of ninety, but his re-arrest the previous September gave rise to similar reminders that he had been acquitted of all charges at the earlier assizes. Nor were Catholics above taking their own priests before 'the Protestant tribunals' or themselves benefiting from the rewards offered for the capture of priests. Terence

Kelly, vicar-general of Derry, had used this very threat against success-ive primates to prevent his removal for misconduct.[79]

But if the measures against religion were easy enough to evade, the political and material discrimination against Catholics had now become part of the fabric of society. The historiography of the hunted priest and the mass-rock tends to miss this point. Given the unformed nature of Catholicism for much of the seventeenth century, the incur-sion of militant continental Catholicism with Owen Roe O'Neill and Rinuccini gave a false impression of its political dimensions and cast a long shadow over ecclesiastical and political relations. Not all the Ulster clergy supported the extreme stance of Rinuccini; but most did, and the northern province acquired a reputation for political extremism thereafter. This was, and remained, the touchstone of anti-popery: could Catholics be loyal to a Protestant state, given their recognition of papal jurisdiction? Periodically acts were passed requir-ing Catholics to 'abjure' or renounce the Pope's temporal power, just as the Black Act of 1639 had required the Presbyterians to renounce certain beliefs before their political loyalty could be accepted. This 'foreign jurisdiction' or perceived political threat from international Catholicism had already become part of New English propaganda; but it was not fully developed as a popular war-cry until the Williamite campaign of the 1690s introduced the full force of Dutch fears about the progress of the Counter-Reformation.[80] The Jesuits certainly upheld the right to depose an unjust ruler. Similar Presbyterian teaching put them into the same category of potential traitors. But such conditional loyalty, even if it was generally believed, and there is evidence of confusion about papal authority even among the clergy themselves,[81] went against the dominant political ethos of the seventeenth century. This presumed the undivided sovereignty of the divine-right monarch, which required religious as well as political loyalty. Even against such a background of heightened religious tension, however, Catholic clergy resorted to the time-old subterfuge of asserting that they were seculars or had been ordained at home, and we find Ulster priests who had been attainted in 1691 still registered for the same parishes in 1704.[82] Protestant perceptions of Catholics as masters of subterfuge, dissemblers, wheeler-dealers may well have had their origins in the daily accommo-dations which permitted a fragile religious tolerance.

The Old English had a long tradition of compromise with the English crown. The few remaining Old Irish gentry followed the same course. The difference was that the latter's almost total loss of political leadership gave excessive power to the clergy. The Old English would have been happy with tacit toleration. The Rinuccini party sought to make Catholicism the established religion and rejected the peace offered in 1646 by the Lord Lieutenant, the marquis of Ormond, which did not grant it. Rinuccini then excommunicated those who had subscribed to it, convincing Ormond that this was 'papal jurisdiction in action'.[83] But Rinuccini was an extremist. The Old English Catholics who dominated James II's Irish parliament of 1689 did not seek to create an established Catholic Church, or to deprive the Church of Ireland of its property. Rather they sought liberty of conscience for all, and the more moderate Catholic demands for religious and civil liberty were to remain the hallmark of Catholic relief campaigns for the next one hundred and forty years. The memory of the Rinuccini split in the Confederation and Ulster's role in transferring support to the Commonwealth dictated Ormond's religious policies thereafter, and he dominated the political scene until his death in 1688. Thus began a policy towards the Catholics which was pursued by successive governments until the nineteenth century: wooing those prepared to accommodate Protestant rejection of papal authority and playing upon internal Catholic disagreements to isolate the ultras.

Generally speaking, those areas which retained a Catholic gentry tended to be politically moderate. That gentry was usually Old English and disagreements over allegiance invariably fell along the traditional Old English–Old Irish fault lines, with the former quite ready to abandon the latter as they had already done over the Restoration land settlement. Since the Reformation had thrown the clergy into economic dependence on the richer Catholic laity, they too were similarly divided, supporting such gentry in areas where they had survived, remaining more politically 'turbulent' in areas like Ulster where they had not.[84] Issue was joined in 1661 when the Catholic gentry and some clergy proposed a loyal 'Remonstrance' to the restored monarchy, to prove that Catholicism was not incompatible with loyalty to a Protestant king.[85] In fact, many Catholics had little difficulty with declarations of allegiance or loyalty. But the issue of finding a satisfactory formula always foundered on Protestant belief that they could not serve two masters. Simple declarations, even oaths, of loyalty were deemed insufficient by the authorities, and, as with the Remonstrance controversy, specific rejection of any external papal power was required. The issue was clouded by continuing rifts left over from the Confederate War (1641–53). At the centre of the controversy was the archbishop of Armagh, Edmund O'Reilly, an ardent supporter of Rinuccini and mediator with the Cromwellians against Ormond, rendering him *persona non grata* with the restored Stuarts.[86] Against him was the Franciscan Peter Walsh, an opponent of Rinuccini. Following O'Reilly's lead, most of the clergy rejected the Remonstrance. Yet they accepted part of a compromise set out by the Sorbonne, declaring the king's divine right in temporal matters and rejecting the deposing power of the Pope, only to have it rejected by Ormond and the Pope alike. This very public confrontation simply perpetuated the notion of Catholic disloyalty and provoked leading Catholic laity to accuse the more ultramontane Ulster clerics of supplying the justification for continued persecution. In fact, there was a great lack of clarity throughout Europe about the relationship between the papacy and secular rulers of whatever denomination and some fifteen to twenty priests in Ireland took the 1708 oath of abjuration before the Pope's condemnation of it arrived.[87]

Dithering by the papacy only contributed to the confusion. Thus the Pope could reject the Irish compromise accepted even by O'Reilly, yet discipline the Franciscan author of a thesis at Louvain which asserted the Pope's supremacy over secular power. On the whole successive popes were anxious to avoid giving cause for persecution of Catholics. At the height of the Remonstrance controversy the Pope authorised a circular letter to the Irish clergy and nobility denouncing as malicious those who argued the impossibility of Catholics combining loyalty to king and pope.[88] James III's continued claim to monarchical rights to nominate Catholic bishops to Ireland encountered papal resistance for this very reason.[89] In essence this conflict between Old English Gallicanism (or acceptance of some state involvement in church organisation) and the ultramontanism (or unfettered papal authority) favoured by the Ulster clergy continued in some form until resolved in favour of the latter in the nineteenth century. But this was high church, high state politics, of little relevance to ordinary laymen, save those with any property left to lose. The way in which it dominates the printed literature is a further indication of the ecclesiastical dominance of Irish Catholic historiography over the past century. In this both Ormond and Walsh are arch-villains and even the late Cardinal Ó Fiaich succumbs to this overriding tendency by clerical scholars to back the anti-Remonstrants.[90]

4. The sacred and the secular in emerging Catholic identity

Free of the kind of control which made the Anglican Church in England and the Catholic Church in France extensions of state departments, free of the Inquisition to pull deviants into line with the Counter-Reformation, the Irish Catholic Church developed apart. Intermittent persecution – aimed most consistently at the hierarchy and papal jurisdiction – postponed Tridentine reforms indefinitely. The limited restructuring which had taken place under the first two Stuarts collapsed after 1641, and Plunkett had barely started to rebuild episcopal authority under the Restoration when it fell apart again under renewed persecution. Ulster was considered the most backward part of Ireland by ecclesiastical criteria. By 1704 only one bishop remained.[91] All the 'abuses' for which the Ulster church had been noted in the Middle Ages persisted, and the difficulties of the times reinforced existing tendencies for excessive interference by the laity. The tendency for the laity to regard the church as a localised family fiefdom had persisted since the arrival of Christianity, and 'lay' claims to the right to nominate priests continued to be made into the nineteenth century. In this the 'inferior clergy' were as much disputees with their superiors as the people, those of Inishowen developing an ingenious justification. 'The inferior clergy pretend to constitute their superior by their own election', wrote the parson of Inishowen to the Protestant Bishop of Derry in November 1682, 'and by this artifice and evasion think to secure themselves from the penalty of the law for extolling of and exercising foreign jurisdiction.'[92]

Poverty and persecution forced the clergy into even closer dependence on the laity, and both became common justifications for living among their relatives.[93] This was a laity, moreover, now devoid of its gentry class (amongst whom the Counter-Reformation had made most progress). Catholicism had become a religion of cabins, as Rinuccini dismissively referred to it.[94] It scarcely did much for a bishop's dignity, to be left wondering in his granary hide-out (as Plunkett did in 1674) whether he would be fed by his peasant protector or left to fast if his host drank away his earnings at the local market.[95] Poverty also adversely affected the quality of the clergy. By the beginning of the eighteenth century Ulster had the lowest number of continental-trained clergy in the country. The former gentry were too poor to fund their sons' education abroad, and bursaries at such seminaries were usually confined to families of the benefactors, which effectively restricted Counter-Reformation training to the elite and put the poorer Ulster students at a decided disadvantage. Archbishop O'Reilly even suggested the sale of hidden chalices in 1660 to fund such continental training.[96]

It clearly did not deter vocations, for if anything the Ulster church was oversupplied with clergy, and successive bishops complained about the inability of the Catholic laity to support them.[97] It was rather the quality of candidates which produced most criticism. The Ulster clergy's lack of education was legendary. Plunkett waxes lyrical about it. The Franciscans, still the most powerful element on his arrival, remained the butt of his criticisms, as they had done of all Old English clerics. It was also the topic of an extremely popular contemporary satire, *Mac Clave of Aughnamullen*, reputedly composed by the reforming Armagh cleric and poet, Owen O'Donnelly. He was typical of a number of priest-poets of the seventeenth century, his family having been Gaelic lords, closely attached to the Tyrone O'Neills, now producing dynasties of clerics. As evident from his verse, he had all the contempt of his class for the lowly born.

The satire concerns the advice given to 'Red Arsey Litis . . . Sean son of Brian son of Fiachra son of Gloomy Donal son of Sean son of Turlagh etc.' on how he can change his miserable existence for the comfortable one of a priest, despite his lowly birth and lack of education. Simply 'pick up a little Latin from me . . . [and] you can be a fully-fledged priest like the rest of them', he is advised. And as further inducement he is told the story of a low-born peasant, whose innumerable relatives push him forward to fill a vacant parish. His only qualifications are 'seven years a clerk of water and wafers' to the recently deceased incumbent, 'as well as that he is very plentiful with *amen* during Mass and likewise at a baptism or marriage'. The bishop cudgels him for his ignorance, which the ill-educated relatives mistake for ordination with his crozier and fall down on their knees to receive the blessing of the new priest. 'And he raised his hand cleverly and cleric-wise, smartly and pious over their heads and gave them general absolution.' The moral: you do not need a continental education to minister to the common people.[98] Certainly it would appear that the kind of religious instruction reaching the people was highly irregular. The low-born or worldly priest remained a common theme in poetic satire over the next century. But *Mac Clave* also captures that unquestioning reverence for the cleric which was such a feature of Ulster Catholicism.

Rigidly Tridentine in his separation of private and public religion, Plunkett seriously misconceived the nature of Ulster's Catholicism, in particular the strength of its societal and familial network. His comments bore many similarities to traditional English and Protestant criticism, a feckless church for a feckless people. He mistook the easy relations of the Franciscans with the local community for indiscipline. The ancient traditions of hospitality had always frayed into excess at the edges. But they were still strong in Ulster and there were clear expectations that the clergy should fulfil the role once held by the now dispersed gentry. Conviviality, drinking, meetings in taverns by the clergy all figure prominently in Plunkett's complaints. But there is a sense here of the 'outsider' of which the Ulster clergy complained, of the hierarchy standing apart from the people as they were to do in so many incidences over ensuing centuries, and it is hard at times to escape the conclusion that Plunkett was a social snob. He was most comfortable amongst the nobility – Protestant and Catholic alike – and, as was traditional for Catholic archbishops of Armagh, he resided in County Louth (where a Catholic gentry survived). There can be no doubt that his good relations with government officials moderated the application of penal legislation, and his mediation ensured that Ulster suffered less in this respect than Munster. It is equally true that the accusations of toadying to the Protestant authorities had much foundation in fact. Plunkett was highly sensitive to Protestant criticisms of popular Catholic religious practices. The Protestant and Catholic reformations had, after all, come from the same stable. The tight, centralised and controlled church which finally emerged in the nineteenth century was not a natural development from a society more accustomed to a highly localised and personal religion.

For most Ulster Irish, religious belief and practice had changed little from medieval times. The poems, like the ecclesiastical correspondence, reflect the concerns of the elite. There is little information on the interaction of people and clergy, and often no documentary evidence for priests who have nevertheless left their mark on folklore.[99] And yet it is with these clerics that the emerging identification of popular Catholicism with Gaeldom may lie. What knowledge we have of the lower clergy in Ulster reveals whole dynasties of former erenach and termon families or cadet branches of other leading Gaelic families continuing to supply most of the clergy.[100] It is clear that some of them adapted church teachings to local situations, as hinted at in the various ecclesiastical decrees condemning clergy who preached that the activities of the tories or thefts from Protestants were not sins.[101]

Plunkett was a very active primate and his many letters to Rome and to successive internuncios in Brussels are a mine of information on the state of religion in Ulster. But they only allow us to skim the surface, because they are largely regulatory, determined by an ideal of institutionalised religion that did not exist in reality. His early letters speak volumes for the collapse of ecclesiastical discipline: some 60,000 people unconfirmed in the archdiocese, tales of very old men in remote parishes who had never seen a bishop, and everywhere often untrained Franciscans administering the sacraments. The 'ancient custom' of questing for alms he found particularly offensive at a time when those Catholics with leases were supporting the now impoverished former nobles as well as their own and the established church's clergy (through tithes). And surely the practices of saying masses in private houses to increase fees or interrupting mass to inveigle alms from the congregation and cursing the ungenerous went against everything ordained at Trent?

There is hardly a Sunday in the Year that the Franciscans, Dominicans or Augustinians, etc., do not quest at the altar for barley, corn, lambs, geese, hens, onions, etc., and even the Franciscans of the Reform quest for money and put it in their pockets. They have an Our Father and Hail Mary said at the Mass for whoever speaks up first, and gives grain or a giulio, they hurl threats whenever the people are slow to give – they say 'may the devil close your mouths, your hearts and your purses!' In fine, it is a most indecent business.[102]

Drunkenness and worldliness were common failings in the clergy, and again the Franciscans came top of Plunkett's list of transgressors. 'Novices are taken in at random without any selection, and they are not trained as they should be . . . Certain friars do nothing else all day in those convents except scratch their tummies.'[103] What has become of 'the holy rule of Saint Francis', he lamented, when 'in your convents here hardly a priest is found who does not himself use a horse and have a servant on horseback', and many 'buy themselves, at considerable expense, rich clothing of French material . . . adorned with woven goffered fringes, and such like.'[104]

This was the Tridentine version of the Europe-wide diatribe against the worldly and dissolute friar, who became the synonym for Catholicism in the critical literature of the Enlightenment. It appears too in *Mac Clave* (unsurprisingly, since O'Donnelly was one of Plunkett's ordinands), as Arsey is intoned in the virtues of the ideal priest. 'As for the learned folk in your congregation, they will overlook your ignorance of Latin, your scarcity of learning . . . because they find you good, cheerful, and a fat mast-fed pig of Manannan in public taverns . . . stretching the neck of every bottle.'[105] Protestants, Plunkett writes, regularly pointed out such abuses to him in order to discredit the mass, and if they did so to him we can be sure they did so to others lower down the social scale. But his letters also highlight great variety in relationships between Ulster Catholics and Protestants: intermittent persecution and taunts on the one hand, but greater tolerance in Ulster than elsewhere in Ireland because of the liberality of the provincial president, Lord Charlemont, and, perhaps surprisingly, Protestants also paying alms to the friars and carousing at patterns.[106]

The practices condemned by Plunkett – burial in a monk's habit, excesses at wakes and holy places, primacy of burial places over any other physical representation of religion – reflect a continuation of medieval religion. But the problems were accentuated by the clergy's growing need for money. The destruction of the monasteries and churches (never in great supply in Ulster in any event) accentuated the tendency for a 'domestication' of religion. Cut off from continental developments to a greater extent than the rest of the island, Ulster remained immune to the growing emphasis on scripture in the Catholic Church.[107] Judgement Day, the torments of hell, the seven deadly sins, the passion of Christ and above all devotion to Mary remained the touchstones of both priestly and popular religion, aided by the popular-isation of medals and above all of rosary beads – the pope's 'apish toys', as one Anglican divine described them, 'drugs of Rome, dregs of superstition . . . relics, hallowed beads . . . [which] Rome send[s] . . . to delude the people of this land'.[108] Religious verse is dominated by images of 'the pains of hell', and even in the eighteenth century there is little sense of Enlightenment-induced softening of such images of religious demonry. This is why Mary's protection, particularly at the hour of death, was such a part of popular devotion, why 'the habit of the saints'[109] was still considered a talisman of salvation, and why devotion to Rome as a semi-supernatural channel to the other world still figured so strongly in the religion of the people.[110] Nearly all the travel accounts of the period are very critical of the religion of the people, particularly in Ulster. But the criticism is based on textbook religion, by which standards most people of early modern Europe would have been found wanting. Even so, they pick up an un-questioning and instinctive religiosity focused on 'the Church of Rome'. 'The native Irish are very good Catholics, though knowing little of their religion', commented the French traveller Boullaye le Gouz in 1644, '. . . but their faith is great in the Church of Rome.'[111] It is a description echoed by another English traveller at the end of the century:

Ask many of them, what was the name of the blessed Virgin Mary, and 'tis ten to one, but they'll answer, it was Jane or Susan, and that St Patrick was her Godfather . . . so that if Ignorance be the true Mother of Devotion, the

City of Rome itself cannot produce such devout Catholicks, as those Teagues; and therefore it's a pitty but they should be transplanted into the Territories of the Holy Church, as being the most submissive Members thereof.[112]

Whatever the opinion some friars had of their archbishop, huge crowds came to hear Plunkett preach and to receive the sacraments during his visitations. The French traveller Jouvin de Rochefort reported in the 1660s 'astonishing' numbers 'travelling across the woods and mountains' to attend mass.[113] But the religious enthusiasm of the people was not church-based and it remained largely untutored until late in the eighteenth century, when the Catholic Church finally embarked on a programme of popular catechesis.[114] In the seventeenth century Ulster Catholicism would not have differed radically from that in continental Europe. Everywhere reforming bishops complained of ill-educated and wordly clergy, of lay interference and popular superstition; while Plunkett's complaints of a number of the Ulster clergy keeping mistresses and families could have been replicated throughout Catholic Europe. In France it was the female religious orders who first experienced Tridentine reforms. There were no female religious in Ulster until the eighteenth century, and Plunkett dismissed the handful he found in County Down as 'four Franciscan zealots'.[115]

Even so, judging from the content of some of the poetry, although regular sacraments are not yet the norm, there is a growing consciousness of what church-based religion expects. 'The general confession of Fiachra Mac Brádaigh', a Cavan poet, c.1700–55, is typical in this. It also reflects the social envy among what by now was a generally poor stratum of Ulster society.

> I commit pride, I break the Sunday holiday, . . .
> I am avaricious, too quarrelsome with the clergy
> and with gentle pleasant women who are married.
> I commit envy towards those with boots and coaches
> and anyone who is covered with coats, . . .
> I commit gluttony with no fast on Friday from meat,
> I do not enjoy the restriction of Lent, a soul-fast;
> I am often drunk from what I drink,
> and I swear against law and clergy . . .

> I love poems and songs,
> I am cosy in my bed when I should be
> Going to mass . . .[116]

Knowledge of canon law was largely irrelevant to this popular simplification of what differentiated Catholic from Protestant: mass and Mary versus the Bible; poverty and the people versus wealth, materialism and empty churches. The evolution of Ulster Catholicism in this period is a classic example of identity formation in opposition to traits disliked in 'the Other'. Because 'that idol of the Mass', as Henry Jones termed it, was so persistently attacked by Protestants, it was treated with the same reverence as the priests, though its religious significance was only dimly understood.[117] Although we know of regular social dealings with Protestants, they were considered a damned breed, and the Presbyterians were doubly damned.

> Twisted is their consciences, perverse their minds,
> they desire no bishop or cleric;
> they say no pater or creed . . .
> Fasts or feasts of the saints –
> bad is the whim – they keep them not;
> Mary is no more to them than a wisp,
> a rude breed unblessed by God.
> They hate baptism, cross and church,
> a treacherous stock; a pity, O God,
> is the decline of Patrick's faith . . .[118]

The 1641 rising was treated as a religious war by Protestant commentators and some accounts are suspect. But the account of the County Monaghan priest Hugh O'Dugan Maguire converting forty to fifty Protestants, then ordering them killed in case they lapsed, may not be entirely apocryphal.[119] Such hostility was also triggered by the political stance of Protestantism. The Bible was used as an anti-popish symbol and political weapon. The 'Parliament of England', protested the General Remonstrance of the Catholics of Ireland in October 1641, had planned 'to send over the Scottish army with the sword and Bible in hand against us . . . to supplant us and raze the name of Catholike and Irish out of the whole kingdom.'[120] By then the Ulster Irish were displaying a marked antipathy to the Bible, and the depositions tell of attacks on it in 1641.[121] Mac Cuarta's Protestant house testing every Catholic belief against scripture was most likely a common experience, and it is in this period that the concept of the 'foreign Bible' enters popular tradition.[122]

Mary too has been politicised. She is now the protectrice exclusively of the Irish; the Saxons won't defeat her.[123] It is taken as read that one only converted to Protestantism for worldly pleasures, the convert priest rejecting Mary for sexual satisfaction in this world. Stories of priests becoming Protestant ministers abound in Ulster-Irish poetry and folklore, the most frequently related being that of two County Donegal brothers at the end of the seventeenth century, one a priest, the other a minister. The treatment of the Gael who converted to Protestantism is uniform: it is of Judas-like betrayal of people and religion, deserting them both when times got bad – 'a lopped off branch ... far from your people' – his motives invariably the flesh or profit, his church opulent and empty, his earthly and heavenly mothers alike in sorrow.[124] In the standard histories written by clerics they are 'renegades' and 'apostates', an outlook which was to remain remarkably consistent among the clergy from the seventeenth century onwards.[125]

> O Manus dear, is the news true,
> which I heard yesterday in the neighbourhood,
> that you recently abandoned God's church,
> and the mighty Pope of Rome,
> and that you were reading your *recantation*
> in the Protestant church on Sunday?
> [to which Manus replies]
> Even if they go to God's paradise
> it's certain I'll be with them,
> my shining sword hanging by my side,
> and my lease in my pocket.[126]

The 'turncoat' Gael is even more heinous than the foreigner, or the Gael who anglicises his name (a practice which increases in the eighteenth century), in this case Phelim O'Neill of County Tyrone assuming the name Felix Neel:

> Scorning to spend his days where he was reared,
> To drag out life among the vulgar herd,
> Or trudge his way through bogs in bracks and brogues,
> He changed his creed, and joined the Saxon rogues
> By whom his sires were robbed. He laid aside
> The arms they bore for centuries with pride –
> The ship, the salmon, and the famed Red Hand,
> And blushed when called O'Neill in his own land!
> Poor paltry skulker from thy noble race,
> Infelix Felix, weep for thy disgrace![127]

Whatever the efforts made by Protestantism to proselytise through Irish speakers, it appears that these may have been even less acceptable than English-speakers:

> . . . false prophet of Conn's Half, . . .
> The stammerer of the senseless mishmash . . .
> you'll receive no respect from anyone descended from the gaels;
> coming to us with your babbling like the wheezing of a goose.[128]

The seventeenth century marked the beginnings of a composite tradition. It is not the loss of the land alone which is so resented in folk tradition; it is the loss of the land to Protestants – and those who 'turned' to keep it in the family are considered the worst villains of all. Such themes thread through many local histories, the minute listing of Old Irish family names against the new Protestant landowners in Father Éamon Ó Doibhlin's *Domhnach Mór* (1969) being a notable example. Forgetfulness would become a luxury not permitted to Ulster's Catholics. The Maguires of Fermanagh are considered 'traitors' in nationalist folklore. In 1978 in Blacklion, a village on the Fermanagh-Cavan border, between Northern Ireland and the Republic, Myles Dolan told Irish Folklore Commission collector, Michael J. Murphy: 'The people, our forefathers, was banished for their faith; they gave up their land and everything, and kept on to their faith . . .

And all the Maguires down about the banks of the Erne is all Protestants, because they turned their coats and stayed.'[129] In 1945 Murphy
was told in Hilltown, County Down, of O'Neill land going to Protestants when John O'Neill's sister married a Protestant lord. Her
offspring were then buried in 'Luther's Hole', the Protestant cemetery
of Rostrevor.[130] 'Thems not Irish at all', those that 'turned' to keep
their land, one of the most respected storytellers in Tyrone, and a firm
republican, commented in 1950.[131] And so indeed had Catholicism
become the prerequisite for Irishness.

These are the sentiments which have been part of Catholic sub-culture
over the past two centuries. They would not have been universally
shared in the seventeenth century. Moving in and out of different
religious denominations as practicalities demanded was not unusual
and no evidence has been found of contemporary ostracisation of 'land
Protestants' by their peers.[132] At first a middling group of Ulster-Irish
society benefited from the acquisition of long leases, but increasingly
as the century wore on the tendency was to re-let to Protestant tenants.
Religious persecution coincided with the beginnings of a modern
definition of property and wealth, by which political and social
status and power would be defined thereafter. By this new definition
even the great warlords of the sixteenth century would have been
found wanting. The demotion of this top tier of Ulster-Irish society
before this new definition entered into popular currency meant that
the remnants of that elite retained their status in the popular mind. It
was from this group, traditionally the producer of the clergy and the
learned men alike, and among whom there was already a much more
acute recognition of religious difference, that the sentiments which
were to become so instinctive to Ulster Catholicism first emerged.
Anti-Englishness and anti-Protestantism is largely absent from literature in Irish before the early seventeenth century.[133] By its close it is a
prominent theme and the two are usually intertwined. The fundamental point of departure was the religious persecution. It was never as
brutal or sustained as popular tradition would have us believe, and it
affected the elite more than the foot soldiers. But lay Catholics no
longer held positions of prominence. Power was Protestant. In such
circumstances the clergy emerged as the new social leaders and a

culture developed of separateness from a power structure which did not include them.

Historians of religion are divided over the issue of what constituted 'popular' or 'elite' religion and whether indeed the two can be legitimately separated.[134] The problem is even more acute when identifying at what point essentially secular notions were sacralised as part of a religious community's tradition. It was perhaps inevitable that a clerical elite would articulate them first. It is equally true that the centrality of the mass, with its message of sacrifice, and deliverance through suffering and victimhood, would already have provided the basis for the ready absorption of such ideas. The sense of occupying the moral heights against the victimiser, as expressed by the Ardoyne Catholics in the early 1970s, was a tradition which entered Catholic consciousness in the seventeenth century. Today's nationalists in Northern Ireland do not define their identity in anything other than cultural and political terms and are irritated by outsiders who more accurately portray it as religious. This is because that religion was so successfully subsumed into political culture over three hundred years ago.

6

LIFE UNDER THE PENAL LAWS

... the Scottish Calvinists, with whom the Province is swarming, put very serious difficulties in my way ... Although all Ireland is suffering, this province is worse off than the rest of the country, because of the fact that from the neighbouring country of Scotland Calvinists are coming over here daily in large groups of families, occupying the towns and villages, seizing the farms in the richer parts of the country and expelling the natives ... Prelates and regular clergy have, for some years, been proscribed by Act of Parliament, but the ordinary secular clergy are allowed to exercise their ministry ... a difficult situation but not unbearable ...

Bishop Hugh MacMahon, 1714
(Flanagan, 'Diocese of Clogher', 40–41)

The eighteenth century is the period when information about the Ulster Catholics is most scarce. They barely figure in the press; the records of the lower courts, which would have told us how they fared under the law, were destroyed in 1922; there are no *causes célèbres* to throw up information, no surviving landed class and even the continental archives contain little information, for the bulk of Ulster Catholics were too poor to send their sons to continental seminaries, and like the rural poor elsewhere in Europe, they do not make their mark on historical record until the end of the century. For some three hundred years after 1500 a process had been developing in Europe which historians call the emergence of polite society. This saw the gradual moving apart of the social classes from the shared rough lifestyle of the Middle Ages to the pursuit of refinement, good taste and social codes of restraint which would set the upper classes apart after the seventeenth century. The development coincided with the emergence of separate cultural and religious communities in Ulster. With no significant gentry class, few of the Ulster Catholics qualified for entry to this newly defined polite society and the modern stereotypes of social and mental inferiority were already well formed by the close of the eighteenth century.

Traditionally, it is the penal laws which have been held responsible for the disadvantaged situation of the Irish Catholics in the eighteenth century. 'This is the period of the Penal Code', reads a typical entry in a school textbook of the early twentieth century, 'when for more than sixty years, Ireland lay in helpless misery, ground down by an inhuman tyranny – the blackest known to history.'[1] It was a system, continues the traditional reading, designed by the 'Planter population' of Ireland with the backing of England to deprive the Catholics of their land, their civil rights and their religion. 'Priests were hunted, hanged, or banished', secretive penal day altars sprang up 'among the lonely mountains and in the quiet glens', and stories of priests gunned down at mass-rocks proliferate. Protestant 'discoverers' could deprive Catholics of their horses, arms and property; sons were encouraged to turn Protestant and disinherit their fathers; children were educated in hedge-schools because Catholics were banned from running schools. The penal laws lie at the heart of a composite reading of history in which the handful of clerical executions, the land confiscations of the seventeenth century and sectarian atrocities in the 1790s, have been subsumed into an image of biased authority, religious discrimination against an entire people and behind it all English domination. It is a popular image of such power that it has remained to the present day, undermining nascent Ulster Catholic trust when British governments, Unionist politicians and Orangemen seem to revert to type.

Little wonder that recent historians have been at pains to question this view. They argue that there was no systematic penal 'code'; that legislation was piecemeal and erratic, produced by genuine political crises and rarely fully implemented; that in terms of social relationships Ireland differed little from contemporary Europe; that far from being decimated, the Catholic Church actually flourished in the period. Nor was the political threat of 'popery in the gross' as groundless as the traditional reading makes out, for Jacobitisim dominated Catholic political thinking and Rome's ambivalence about Catholic loyalty to the state was real enough. Although historians accept that Ulster comes nearer than any other province to fitting the stereotypical image of the 'penal era', even here good neighbourliness was the norm.

All of this is indisputable and has gone a long way to defusing the explosiveness of the penal myth. However, it deals largely with the penal laws as cause and effect rather than symptom. The effects traditionally ascribed to the penal laws did not always materialise. But the penal laws were products of and enshrined a frame of mind about Catholics which continued long after their effectiveness had passed. It pervaded all aspects of civil society, affecting lower as much as higher social classes, and whilst it was honoured as much in the breach as anything else, it created an undercurrent of sullen Catholic resentment and swaggering, if insecure, Protestant imperiousness which would surface at times of crisis. Arthur Young, even though he was writing in 1776, at a time when religious penalisation was out of fashion, captures the situation perfectly. He had been staying with Anthony Foster, Lord Chief Baron of the Exchequer, who was famous for his improvements on his estate in County Louth. 'In conversation upon the popery laws', writes Young, 'I expressed my surprise at their severity: he said they were severe in the letter, but were never executed', which prompted Young to recall Edmund Burke's comment in the English House of Commons that '"Connivance is the relaxation of slavery, not the definition of liberty".'[2]

1. The Penal Laws

The penal laws were passed in a brief period of heightened political tension between 1695 and 1707, after the reign of James II had shown how vulnerable was the seventeenth-century land settlement and when the Protestant succession to the English throne was by no means secured. The Irish parliament was angry at William III's generous terms in the Treaty of Limerick, and even before it was ratified it passed the first penal law. The 1695 acts prohibited Catholics from carrying arms, keeping horses valued at more than £5, sending their children abroad for education and teaching school. The aim was to prevent Catholics from assisting or communicating with the foreign enemy. In 1697 another act banished ecclesiastics and regular clergy. But there was considerable opposition in the House of Lords to measures against the Catholic religion itself – not least from a handful of senior Anglican ecclesiastics. Secular priests were given legal recognition in 1703, provided they registered and gave security for good behaviour; 1,089 over the whole country did so, though only 189 of these were from Ulster.[3] Another invasion scare, however, prompted the imposition of an oath of abjuration in 1709 on the registered clergy. This required the denial of James III's right to the throne. It was denounced by the Pope and only thirty-three priests took it, in effect rendering the whole Catholic Church illegal. But this was certainly not the original intention, and after a brief period of priest-hunting the authorities turned a blind eye.[4] Ironically the validity of priestly orders was accepted and Catholic marriages celebrated by a priest were recognised by the state. Presbyterians suffered greater inconvenience on these accounts, their ministers securing official recognition only in 1737.[5]

It was not that Catholics were being denied freedom of conscience. Indeed many Anglican divines made this very distinction and protested at measures that affected the ability of Catholics to practise their religion. *Raison d'état* might justify laws against the property and 'some moderate restraints' on the civil rights of those adhering to a religion so at odds with the ethos of the state, argued Edward Synge (future Bishop of Elphin) in an influential sermon preached on the 1725 anniversary of the 1641 rebellion. But this should not involve 'forcing men's consciences'. He pointed to France where Catholics had rejected papal claims to depose heretical princes and argued that such Gallicanism should be supported. 'All persons . . . whose principles in religion have no tendency to hurt the public have a right to a toleration.' Declaring their religious assemblies unlawful simply forced them underground, out of sight of the magistrates.[6]

After an initial period of persecution of the clergy, the actual practice of Catholicism was not interfered with. Mass-houses went up without protest. Cemeteries continued to be shared by Catholic and Protestant. Catholic patterns and pilgrimages were rarely disturbed, though prohibited under the 1704 Popery Act, and since the Catholic Church did not oblige clerics to wear distinctive dress until 1850, they did not always attract attention. It was a gap between public rhetoric and private practice which amused Arthur Young.

I must be free to own that when I have heard gentlemen who have favoured the laws as they now stand urge the dangerous tenets of the Church of Rome, quote the cruelties which have disgraced that religion in Ireland and led them into the common routine of declamation . . . I could not but smile to see subscriptions handed about for building a masshouse . . .[7]

Even so, the 1697 Banishment Act remained on the statute book throughout the century, notwithstanding various Catholic relief acts in the later decades. The legal position of the regulars remained perilous, old clauses against their very existence still being invoked as late as 1865, while each Catholic relief act – even the unsatisfactory one of 1829 – tended to reinforce petty and often insulting clauses retained from earlier laws. Not until Gladstone's act of 1869, disestablishing the Church of Ireland, were Catholic bishops finally permitted legal use of their titles.[8]

But the main target of the penal laws was property and its associated political power. Catholics were prevented from purchasing land or acquiring leases longer than thirty-one years; Protestant heiresses lost their claim on marrying a Catholic; Catholic estates had to be divided amongst the male heirs, unless the eldest turned Protestant, in which case he became sole owner, even during the lifetime of the father; Catholics could not act as guardians to minors; a Protestant 'discoverer' could acquire the Catholic's share in any transaction if he could prove any infringement of the 'Popery laws'. Faced with the loss of their land, most remaining Catholic landowners conformed. Honoria McManus, wife of Oliver O'Hara of Ballymena, County Antrim, raised her sons as Protestants, explaining that if she did not do so 'she might as well make tailors or shoemakers of them as their prospects in life would be destroyed'.[9] Such 'land-conformism' was generally accepted by eighteenth-century Catholics – whatever its notoriety in later folklore.[10] Some remained crypto-Catholics, a liberalising force against the passage of new penal measures and the application of existing ones. Indeed, the O'Haras retained their estates through occasional conformity, while continuing to marry Catholics.[11] Less acceptable was the Catholic who conformed to dispossess members of his own family and Paul MacLorinan of Ahoghill, County Antrim – killed in 1772, four years after conforming to acquire family land – cannot have been the only case of rough justice being meted out for doing so.[12] After 1693 Catholics were effectively debarred from sitting in parliament by the requirement of oaths against the Pope's deposing power and transubstantiation. But they could continue to vote if they took oaths of allegiance and abjuration, until that right too was removed in 1728.[13] Other measures debarred them from local government, the higher levels of the legal profession and from Ireland's only university.

The fears of the Protestant gentry for their land never entirely disappeared. It was these which made the Irish parliament, dominated by the country's major landowners, more anti-papist than the country at large. 'In a country where every man holds his estate and political consequence by dispossession of Catholics', one Lord Lieutenant, Lord Westmorland, in 1793 cautioned an English government inclined by then to dismiss Protestant fears, 'allowance must be made for even unreasonable apprehension.'[14] Affinity with the American colonies – to which as many as 150,000 Ulster Presbyterians had emigrated by 1775[15] – made Ulster particularly sensitive to the treatment of Catholic Canada. Correspondence to the *Belfast News Letter* linked the North American Indian threat to that of popery, 'as they are all Roman Catholicks', and the Quebec Act of 1774, granting toleration to Catholicism, prompted rumours that Catholic regiments would be used to crush the American colonists.[16]

The individual acts of the penal laws were not so-styled. Rather they were acts to prevent the growth of 'popery'. Protestants then as now had little difficulty separating the individual from the perceived concept and the less offensive term 'Roman Catholic' became more common in the second half of the century when fears receded. But fears of 'popery' as a political 'system' were never far below the surface. So embedded in Protestant consciousness was this spectre of popery that the ethos underlying laws passed to protect a ruling elite came to pervade all sections of Protestant society. Even reformers as sympathetic towards the Catholics as Henry Grattan and Theobald Wolfe Tone came to espouse Catholic emancipation only because they believed that 'popery' was withering.[17] What was this spectre of 'popery' and were Protestant fears justified?

'Popery' was political. It united a faith which was deemed corrupt, superstitious and persecutory to the foreign political threats of Jacobitism and absolute monarchy, and the image was sustained by frequent wars with the Catholic powers on the Continent. The Protestant archbishop of Armagh instructed his clergy in October 1745:

You are to raise in your people a religious abhorrence of the Popish government and polity, for I can never be brought to call Popery in the gross a religion . . . Their absurd doctrines . . . their political government . . . makes it impossible for them to give any security of their being good governors, or good subjects in a Protestant kingdom . . .[18]

The very concept of liberty as Protestant and embedded in constitution and state was part of popular Protestant psyche throughout Britain and Ireland. Morever, every state in *ancien régime* Europe considered uniformity of religion as part of state security and penalised those who did not conform. Certainly the Jacobite threat in Ireland was no illusion, even after the military defeat of Charles Edward, the Young Pretender, in 1746. Continued Stuart intrigues on the Continent, residual popular Jacobitism in Ireland, and the presence of huge numbers of Catholics training in continental seminaries or serving in continental armies – some 120,000 in the first three decades alone – sustained such perceptions long after the threat had evaporated. Moreover James III, the Old Pretender, resided in Rome, recognised by the Pope as legitimate monarch and continuing to exercise his right to nominate Catholic bishops until his death in 1766.

But the ultimate 'foreign jurisdiction' was the papacy itself. It was believed that the papacy exercised a temporal as well as a spiritual jurisdiction over Catholics, that it taught them not to keep faith with heretics and that 'princes excommunicated by the pope may be deposed or murdered by their subjects'. Fears were sustained by papal refusal to reject this medieval doctrine (even as late as the 1770s), to the dismay of Catholic reformers, lay and clerical alike.[19] Catholics were willing to swear a simple oath of allegiance and such an oath was agreed in the Treaty of Limerick. But oaths of abjuration, renouncing the Stuart succession and the deposing power of the pope, were another matter, and successive attempts to impose one foundered on papal disapproval. The Vatican temporised on these matters and scuppered various attempts at accommodation, because any concession to win toleration for Catholics in Ireland would open up the whole issue of church persecution of Protestants elsewhere in the world. Frederick Hervey, Protestant bishop of Cloyne, soon to become Bishop of Derry, was a prominent supporter of Catholic rights. Yet even he was baffled at the resistance to such an oath, as he explained to a Catholic friend in 1768.

Surely the *oaths and declarations* which I have myself drawn are such as any loyal subject would not scruple and any conscientious Catholic may safely swear. My object is to leave you your faith entire, but to secure your allegiance to the present government and to make you independent of all foreign jurisdiction whatever. For, depend on it that there is not an iota in the scriptures to warrant the least temporal jurisdiction in the Bishop of Rome . . . *penal laws* . . . can never take place against loyal subjects.[20]

The frequent re-issue of Hugh Reily's *Impartial History*, which asserted that Catholics were loyal subjects, was mirrored by the equally frequent re-issue of Temple's *Irish Rebellion*, testifying to continuing Protestant belief that they never could be.[21] Catholics were referred to as 'enemies' in the first decades of the century. Their clergy were 'dangerous', 'insolent', 'subtle', 'presumptuous'. Catholics could not be trusted. Their claims to loyalty showed their hypocrisy, for 'perjury' was 'a principle of the Popish religion'.[22] The range of insults reveals the mixture of fear and contempt for Catholics. Even though the impact of the penal laws was short-lived and the worst was over by 1730, Protestants preferred to keep them on the books as a form of security. Indeed, in 1762, on the very eve of their repeal, new acts were being passed to calm Protestants' fears for their property.[23] Wars and political crises invariably reactivated the law against the carrying of arms; and a century before they occurred in England, Ireland was obsessed with religious censuses, documenting any increase in the already overwhelming numbers of Catholics.[24] Nor did such attitudes retreat as the penal laws were repealed. The London Hibernian Society, with 326 proselytising schools in Ulster in the early nineteenth century, explained its crusade as follows:

The great body of the Irish wander like sheep, that have no faithful shepherd to lead them. Legendary tales, pilgrimages, penances, superstitions, offerings, priestly domination . . . abandoned practices, and all that shocks and disgusts in the mummery of the mass house, cannot fail to fix a mournful sentiment in the heart of every enlightened and pious observer . . . The hope, therefore, that the Irish will ever be a tranquil and loyal people, and still more that piety and virtue will flourish among them, must be built on the anticipated reduction of popery.[25]

Catholicism was believed to induce sloth and slavishness of mind in its adherents, making them incapable of liberty, virtue and entry to polite society. Catholic children reared in the Charter schools, where Protestant doctrine and practice were imposed, were paraded as examples of the association of Protestantism and cleanliness. If the effects of popery were so pernicious, why then was there such little effort made to convert its adherents to Protestantism?

Certainly the process of conversion was a deterrent in itself, and was meant to be so, particularly for those who nominally converted to preserve estates. The convert had to recant 'the errors of Rome' publicly, before an Anglican clergyman and his congregation at Sunday service. Great crowds would turn out to observe the occasion and very often the names appeared in the press.[26] In fact, the Protestant elite was as divided on the desirability of converting large numbers of Catholics as on many other issues. Many – including notable figures like the Anglican archbishop of Dublin, William King – would have liked an Irish-speaking ministry to explain Protestantism to the people, and in a much-quoted phrase from the Bible, he accused his co-religionists of preferring to maintain the Catholics as 'hewers of wood and drawers of water' rather than attempting to convert them through their own language.[27] The most notable campaigner for such was Dr John Richardson, rector of Belturbet, County Cavan, for he had experienced particular success in south Tyrone, Fermanagh, Donegal, and the Glens of Antrim – where Gaelic-speaking Scottish highlanders were rescued from their slippage to popery by Irish-speaking preachers. The Presbyterian Synod also sought to evangelise through the Irish language in the early years of the century, with seventeen preachers in the field by 1720. Such campaigns were not sustained, but persistent internal criticisms of the established church for failing to take its message to the Catholic people, and the success of Irish-speaking Methodist preachers in south Ulster at the end of the century, casts doubt on the view that the penal laws were entirely motivated by cynical materialism.[28]

The most sustained attempt at converting the natives was the establishment of the Charter schools. They were conceived by an enlightened group of gentry in the 1730s as a way of luring the poor from the perceived backwardness and indolence of popery by a mixture of proselytism, anglicisation and education into useful pursuits. The idea was to encourage poor Catholic families to send their children to these boarding schools, away from their home districts, where they might risk continued papist influence from their families and clergy. They would then receive some elementary education, particularly in practical skills (notably linen weaving in the Ulster schools), and above all religious instruction. Thereafter they would be apprenticed to Protestant families. The belief that the perfect recipe had been found for converting Ireland to Protestantism informs the initial crusading enthusiasm. By the 1750s ten such schools were functioning in Ulster (out of forty-seven for the entire country). At Killough in County Down, one of three schools in the county, Walter Harris (a Dublin man of letters) found '20 poor popish children trained up to useful labour and carefully educated in the principles of the Protestant religion'. He disapproved of the penal laws and thought the Charter schools a far more 'effectual and rational scheme' of winning the people from 'the superstitious and idolatrous worship of the church of Rome' and creating 'a race of honest and industrious Protestants'.[29] Harris's language deserves comment. It would have been instantly recognisable to Enlightenment thinking generally in eighteenth-century Europe, for it too saw Catholicism as backward, superstitious and oppressive, a dead weight on rational pursuits, improvement and prosperity.

However, sufficient Catholic poor were unforthcoming and from an early stage the original function of the schools was being diluted by the admission of poor Protestant children. A good deal of stigma also seems to have attached to those children reared in the schools.[30] The Charter schools acquired a villainous reputation in popular Catholic tradition, in which they became intertwined with the better-known proselytising activities of militant evangelicalism in the nineteenth century. By then attitudes had changed sufficiently for both the established church itself and the government to pronounce the aims of the schools offensive and self-defeating. The parliamentary report of 1825 into education in Ireland found considerable evidence of malpractice and cruelty in the schools, towards Protestant and Catholic children alike. 'But however great and numerous the instances of mismanagement and abuse which prevail in these establishments, it appears to us, that the main objection arises from the mistaken principles on which they are founded.'[31]

The Charter schools were not a success, even in Ulster. All but two of the ten had been closed by the 1770s, and in response to the damning report of 1825 the remainder were progressively closed. But other public charitable institutions such as almshouses also brought the children up as Protestants. This, and a number of well-documented cases of heirs being sent out of the country to Protestant guardians,[32] had already laid the basis for a long-standing belief among Catholics that Protestants targeted the innocent child to brainwash with their beliefs. The Catholic bishop of Clogher, Hugh MacMahon, refers to it as early as 1714. The context was the implementation of Church impediments against marriage to close relatives. If married before a priest, as required by the Church, this could be guarded against. But this clearly was not happening. He feared that if he were to enforce church law couples would simply 'pervert', or, if children were involved, they would 'fall into the hands of heretics who are always anxious to pick up children of this kind and have them reared as heretics'. Thus did marriage become one of the areas where the penal laws caused the church to compromise on its own teachings, for dispensations were regularly on offer.[33]

The friars caused as much concern to governments in the eighteenth as in the seventeenth century. But increasingly the reason was their rootlessness and their ability to wander freely. The Catholic Church shared such fears – coming to the aid of the state by suppressing the regulars' novitiates in 1751. As elsewhere, so in Ireland – this is the period of the 'Catholic Enlightenment', a time when sections in the Catholic Church were not only sensitive to Protestant criticisms but shared them. The efforts by the Catholic episcopacy and gentry to be accepted as part of the social hierarchy from mid-century onwards were not insincere. The British – if not the Irish – political establishment finally conceded such when a more potent threat to existing society than 'popery' emerged with Jacobinism at the end of the century.

Historians have struggled to find some clear intention behind the penal laws. But their researches into the labyrinthine processes of Anglo-Irish legislation reveal as much division as agreement among the law-makers.[34] Earlier tendencies to simply reproduce the acts them-selves, or the descriptive heads of bills, have clouded understanding for almost two centuries. Some of the most influential accounts (Butler's

Digest of Popery Laws, 1792, Lecky's *History of Ireland*, 1892, Burke's *Priests in Penal Times*, 1914) did just that, and have been raided by scholars ever since. However, as in contemporary England, so in Ireland a huge gulf separated the practice from the letter of the law. In a society without a regular police force, the enforcement of the law depended on a level of popular acceptance. Attempts to arrest priests had to be abandoned, as they were regularly rescued by threatening crowds.[35] The folklore of innumerable priests killed at mass-rocks, usually at midnight mass, is largely unproven. In his detailed investigation of the clergy of Clogher, the Revd P. Ó Gallachair found such stories substantiated in only two cases, both in the seventeenth century, and one in the aftermath of 1641.[36]

There was also widespread Protestant collusion and connivance at Catholic evasion of the laws. The penal laws cut horizontally across the early modern concept of vertical social relations. Society throughout Europe operated along recognised lines of social division and responsibility, whereby elite paternalism and protection was repaid by deference and co-operation by the common people. The many relief and charitable schemes sponsored by the Protestant gentry carried no religious label. Irish Catholics had some power to make laws unworkable, which they did so effectively with the agrarian protest of the Whiteboys (1760s–1770s), mainly in Munster.[37] It would have been more difficult for Ulster Catholics to have engaged in such social protest, and in general they did not do so until towards the end of the century. Whatever their insecurities, many of the Protestant elite winced at laws which permitted inferior Protestants to challenge Catholics who were their social superiors. There are a number of cases of Protestant neighbours taking out leases or holding property in trust for Catholics, and stories of Protestants hiding Catholic clergy at times of persecution are legion. The Dickey family of Ballydonellan, County Antrim (who came from Ayrshire in the seventeenth century), was known to have sheltered priests and held land in trust for Catholic neighbours, and I have encountered a number of similar cases from Fermanagh, Donegal, Antrim and Down.[38] Ulster Catholics benefited less from the survival of a strong Catholic landed element which elsewhere mitigated the impact of the laws. Even so, many landlords tended to grant the longest leases permissible under the penal laws to their Catholic tenants. Although Protestant tenants were usually preferred, where Catholics of social standing remained they retained their leases and as often as not landlords who had converted from Catholicism to Protestantism remained favourably disposed towards their former co-religionists.[39] There are, of course, marked regional differences. The extreme Protestantism of the gentry in parts of south Down for example was to become legendary. Lord Hillsborough offered a reward in 1771 to every papist on his estates who would conform and declared that no papist in future would be given a lease.[40] However, until the 1780s Ulster society was very stable and landlords tended to use their rights of eviction sparingly.[41]

Priest-catchers, discoverers and sons conforming to disinherit fathers were as unpopular with the eighteenth-century legal system as they were to become in later Catholic folklore. Complaints by the chief law officers in England about the law being placed at the whim of 'an unfaithful wife, a disobedient child, an impatient heir and a common informer', were made in the more liberal climate of 1778.[42] But they could also have applied to the legal world earlier in the century. It was extremely difficult to disinherit Catholics under the penal laws. Judges and magistrates regularly stretched the law, and the legal establishment in Dublin, where property cases were dealt with by the higher courts, was frequently accused of being staffed by converts and crypto-Catholics. A case in point was brought by a Protestant 'discoverer' to the Court of Exchequer in 1749. Since the penal laws confined Catholics to leases of a maximum of thirty-one years, he challenged the leases for lives held in Monaghan by Nugent McKenna, who had inherited them from his father. A host of people (including the landowner and the sheriff) appeared for McKenna to prove that his father had been covered by the articles of Limerick (permitting certain categories to retain their land).[43] Nor, given the reservations of many Anglican divines, should it surprise to find the wills of Catholic bishops being registered unopposed in the ecclesiastical courts of the established church. Registered Catholic clergy were given legal status, and whilst bishops were not supposed to exercise ecclesiastical jurisdiction, a blind eye was regularly turned and magistrates, forced by the complaints of ultra-Protestants to arrest bishops in Ulster in 1739 and again in 1756, ensured that no further action was taken against them.[44]

Such incidents highlighted the unsatisfactory halfway house of the penal laws. They created a society attuned to evading the law. The 1704 Registration Act – by banning bishops from exercising ecclesiastical authority – failed to provide for a future priesthood and threatened to deprive Catholics of any religious direction whatsoever (not at all what the authorities, civil or ecclesiastical, had wished). In 1756 Lord Clanbrassil, a landowner in County Down, who had been sympathetic towards the Catholics since sitting as MP for Dundalk 1715–18, sought a new act to regularise their covert existence. The act was rejected by the English Privy Council and Clanbrassil's good intentions were denounced by the extremes of both religions.[45] But it highlighted the unsatisfactory nature of the legislation and was the immediate cause of the establishment of the Catholic Committee to campaign for its repeal.

Catholics were most likely to experience the penal laws in the workings of the law. The destruction of eighteenth-century assize records – apart from those for Antrim – makes generalisations difficult. The Antrim records till 1731 reveal surviving toryism in south-east Ulster, the Glens of Antrim and along the Derry/Tyrone borders. If caught, execution would be automatic, and, as in England, the heads of those executed were displayed as a deterrent to others. Even so, eighteenth-century Ulster was not a particularly violent society. Although there may well be other cases, now lost, in these surviving papers I have found only one case of a Catholic being accused of carrying arms against the law. This was Fergus McVeagh of Drumadoon in the Glens of Antrim, who terrorised the shopkeepers of nearby Ballycastle in 1725, threatening to burn their houses and hough their cattle if they appeared against him.[46]

As noted earlier, the higher courts tended towards relative impartiality – a cause for resentment among Armagh Protestants during the sectarian clashes of the 1780s and 1790s.[47] In the lower courts, however, although Catholics could serve on juries they could be challenged by a plaintiff or counsel in cases between Protestants and Catholics or those involving any aspect of the penal laws. The opportunities for prejudice were extensive. The United Irishman and magistrate in Tyrone, Thomas Russell, resigned from the bench for this very reason in October 1792, criticising his fellow JPs for asking plaintiffs their religion before trying the case.[48]

Certainly the opportunities afforded 'petty bigots' and the unscrupulous were legion. Under both English and Irish law, localities where crimes were committed could be made to pay the damages. In Ulster there are tales of the so-called 'Robbery Cut', whereby Protestants disposed of sickly farm animals, claimed they were stolen and had the costs levied from local Catholics by the Grand Juries.[49] In the last decades of the century, when Catholics were becoming more assertive, they put a stop to the rights apparently exercised by Protestant tenants of entering Catholics' lands to shoot fowl.[50] There were also times when the penal laws *were* enforced. Till mid-century every foreign war or political scare witnessed the arrest of priests and the seizure of arms from Catholics, and at such times sectarian tensions ran high.[51] Catholics were debarred from serving in the British army in Ireland until 1793 (and there were similar restrictions on Protestants until 1745), though in effect numbers of both were secretly enlisted. Nevertheless, the defence forces contained a disproportionate number of Ulster Protestants. Recruiting parties, troop movements and a knowledge of the use of arms were greater in the province than elsewhere. In 1756 106,295 Ulster Protestants joined the militia against just over 42,000 for all the other provinces together.[52]

A very full account of the position of the clergy in the more difficult times at the beginning of the century exists for the diocese of Clogher (covering much of south Ulster, including nearly all of parts of Fermanagh and Monaghan, and parts of Tyrone and Donegal). In this 1714 account Bishop Hugh MacMahon describes the great difficulty of functioning as a bishop in a province 'swarming' with Scottish Calvinists, of travelling in disguise, of his fear of being exposed by the 'incautious talk' of Catholic servants in Protestant houses, of priests hiding their faces from mass-goers to protect them if interrogated, of magistrates compelled to apply the oath of abjuration when previously they could be bribed. It was a year of particularly heightened tension after the death of Queen Anne and things were generally easier for the clergy after the succession of George I in 1714. By 1720 the worst of the penal laws were over. Even so, MacMahon's verdict that they made life 'difficult . . . but not unbearable' accurately summarises their general impact.[53]

2. *Community relations*

There is sometimes a tendency to read social relationships in Ulster back from the sectarian troubles of the 1780s and 1790s and to assume that it was ever thus. It would appear, however, that the eighteenth century was not a period of open religious conflict in Ulster. Territorial and linguistic segregation are part of the explanation. In 1744 Walter Harris reported only one Catholic living in Holywood, north Down. He was a coachman employed by a Mr Isaac, and when he first drove through the village people ran to their doors to see him, for most had never before seen a Catholic.[54] Where conflict occurred it was often because Protestants and Catholics invaded each other's recognised districts. Regular faction fights occurred between the inhabitants of Irish, Scottish and English streets in Armagh, Lurgan and Newry.[55] However, the famous incident in 1743 when Catholics burnt down a Presbyterian meeting house at Freeduff, south Armagh, was unusual. It came on the heel of the importation of Presbyterian tenants and the establishment of a Charter school in 1737 in this largely Catholic area. The meeting house was replaced by an enlarged one in 1760 (to cope with the expanding Presbyterian population) on the proceeds of fines levied on all the Catholic inhabitants for its destruction.[56]

Are we to assume then that Catholics settled down to co-existence with their Protestant and Dissenting neighbours? For the most part yes – awareness of difference should not be confused with bigotry – or they conformed. And Protestant, Catholic and Dissenter alike tended to conform to the majority religion in their area.[57] Social pressures to conform to the established church also eroded the small Presbyterian landed interest. Large numbers of Gaelic-speaking highland Scots turned Catholic in Inishowen and north Antrim, though in the north and east of the province, the religious traffic was in the opposite direction.[58] There is no record of any serious sectarian disturbance in Ulster before the 1780s. Though the Catholic clergy lamented the drunken tumult which generally accompanied funerals, there is no mention of inter-religious feuds at shared cemeteries. Lord Macartney's family of Lissanoure in north Antrim had been noted for their religious tolerance, and both he and other Protestant landlords in the area had contributed to the construction of 'a large handsome mass-house' nearing completion in 1789. But since the Catholics were refusing to pay tithe for the upkeep of the Protestant church, it had no minister and had fallen into ruin. As a result many 'Church people' now worshipped in the Catholic mass-house or Presbyterian meeting-house and were baptised by the priest 'for there is no other minister to do it'.[59] Indeed Macartney's informant thought this reflected the general situation throughout the country.

Mixed marriages were common, and wandering friars – so-called 'couple-beggars' – who earned a living from conducting them, drew scorn from the civil authorities and the Catholic Church alike, though only occasionally was action taken against them. In law a priest who conducted mixed marriages could incur the death penalty. This act remained in force till 1833, and was only repealed in 1870. But they were only illegal if they involved property, and all sides trod carefully. The Catholic bishops, anxious not to provoke the state, resisted promulgation of the papal decree *Tametsi* which required such marriages to be solemnised by a priest. Indeed, the 1766 case of the Catholic widow on the Abercorn estate in Tyrone – whose Protestant suitor tried to deny the validity of her marriage to an equally grasping Catholic by claiming that she had recanted and could not marry a Catholic – suggests that the lower orders entered mixed marriages without much hesitation, though it also shows the potential for mischief makers.[60] In the early 1800s, long after most of the penal laws had been repealed, the popular Catholic Tyrone writer (later turned Protestant) William Carleton was to meet a rather sorry degraded priest in Mullingar jail. 'His crime was the marriage of a Protestant and Catholic, and as it was a case in which there was property concerned, he had been prosecuted upon a statute dug up from the penal laws; while . . . the poor fellow knew no more about the property involved than I did.'[61]

In the English language at least, there was also a shared popular culture, particularly in the hedge-schools. Increasingly the hedge-schools were vehicles for the poor to learn English, and most of those children (Catholic and Protestant alike) who received any education in the eighteenth century received it in such schools – often together. The hedge-schools were irregular affairs, usually conducted in barns or disused farm buildings. Their staffing was equally irregular, many poets and scribes finding intermittent employment in such schools. They were not exclusively Catholic, whatever the folklore which has built up around them. Run on a shoestring, these hedge-schools had always used as readers whatever was available in cheap print. Chap-books and tales of romance and adventure doubled as school texts. Both Carleton and the Presbyterian controversialist Henry Cooke told of almost identical experiences as pupils at hedge-schools.[62] Carleton also recalled how the most popular play of the century, *The Battle of Aughrim*, was both used as a hedge-school 'reader' and attracted mixed religion audiences when staged in local barns. Although it celebrates 'the entire subversion of popery and arbitrary power' and contains most of the Protestant stereotypes of 'Romish tyranny' (Jacobitism, 'Romish worship', 'incense', monks, Jesuits, and the Spanish Inquisition), it distinguishes 'popery' from the defeated Irish, who are treated as a noble race. The central theme is the coming together of *Gael* and *Gall* in a Romeo-and-Juliet-style tragic romance.[63] Inevitably the flood of cheap literature put out by the United Irishmen in the 1790s also reached the hedge-schools – though never as universally as the authorities claimed.

Under the penal laws Catholics could not keep schools. But in practice they commonly did so. There is a reference in the 1731 *Report on the State of Popery* to 'straggling schoolmaster[s]' being threatened by churchwardens, but generally hedge-schools escaped penalisation. The same report details the numbers of 'popish' schools in each diocese and county: only six in Raphoe (Donegal), Armagh diocese with thirty-seven being at the other end of the scale. There is no sign of any clerical involvement in the schools – except in the case of Owen O'Gallagher 'an old fryer, [who] instructs a great many popish students' on the Fermanagh–Donegal border. The Catholic Church did not take an interest in schooling until the 1750s, and then only when prompted by anxiety at the activities of the Charter schools. The 1731 report cites only one case of Protestant children being 'taught to read together with natives'.[64] But unless there was a change in the course of the century, there must have been many more cases of this, for by the end of the century most hedge-schools would have been interdenominational, as were their teachers. An interesting case was reported from County Cavan in 1787, where the parish priest of Cress-stoney, Revd

Michael O'Reilly, had established a Sunday school where some four hundred children were taught reading and writing together, but given religious instruction by teachers of their own denomination.[65] In the more prosperous classical schools in the towns, catering for the sons of the middle class, it was the same story, but with clerical involvement more apparent. William Crolly, future Catholic archbishop of Armagh, attended such a school in Downpatrick in the 1790s, run by Dr James Neilson, a local Presbyterian minister.[66]

But although many hedge-school teachers may have taught through Irish, they were employed for their ability to teach classics, arithmetic and above all English. The surging demand for literacy lies behind these hedge-schools and that literacy was in English. It was a drive by the common people to advance themselves, for English was the language of everyday practicalities. Carleton was surprised at the 'number of books, pamphlets and odd volumes' that he found in the homes of Catholics in his parish in County Tyrone. Even if they could not read themselves – and half could not – such works were carefully preserved for the young relative who some day might do so. The ability to speak English had become a badge of status and in Carleton's *The Three Tasks*, when Jack Magennis moved up in the world through a pact with the devil, people marvelled at 'how high-flown and Englified he could talk'.[67] The poets might decry the English language, but they were usually bilingual and proud of it. In areas where Irish was declining, such bilingual speakers spoke English with a Scottish accent. Very few Irish speakers could either write or read their language and were becoming literate only through English.[68]

However, despite the general picture of good neighbourliness, mutual suspicions were easily aroused. There was a perception of Catholics as potential traitors, even on the most liberal of estates. In times of political tension, landlords would look to the religious makeup of their tenants and ensure that their Protestant tenants were well armed. In 1739 when war broke out between England and Spain some two hundred 'Protestant gentlemen' rode through Dundalk, beating drums and playing 'The Protestant Boys Will Carry the Day', and similar ceremonies occurred in Carrickfergus, Monaghan, Newry, Strabane, Belfast, Dromore and Enniskillen.[69] Election times also had the potential to underscore divisions, for although Catholics could still influence returns (much as the unenfranchised could in England) and landlords regularly ensured temporary conformity of tenants to increase the number of voters, opponents just as regularly campaigned to have such 'Catholic' votes discounted and at times Catholic tenants were turned out to create Protestant freeholders. Catholics could be trusty servants, but if even advanced thinkers like Mary Anne McCracken of Belfast hesitated on being asked if she completely trusted the family's Catholic servant, Betty, we can be sure that the sentiment was widespread.[70]

Statements in Irish were often more strident than those in English, much the same as in Northern Ireland of today Catholics and Protestants reserve different language for in- and out-groups. Awareness of difference expressed itself sometimes in mutual irritants, sometimes in mutual fascination. The firing of guns offended all sides and intentionally so. The Presbyterian wedding is a case in point, involving the ostentatious display of firearms in the pre-nuptial ritual. Describing the continuation of the ritual by Ulster emigrants in America, Edward Parker, writing in 1851, commented:

This practice it seems originated in Ireland, in consequence of the Catholics having been, after the Revolution, deprived of the use of firearms. The Protestants, proud of their superior privilege which they then enjoyed, made a display of their warlike instruments, on all public occasions.[71]

On the ground, jibes and insults about the inferiority of Catholics under the law would appear to have been commonplace and Catholics found the term 'papist' offensive. In *Adeir Clann Liútair* ['Luther's Children Say'] MacCooey contemplates the rewards of conforming:

> 'The children of Luther who are in court and in coaches say
> that I would have a vote in their own religion,
> cheap land and accurate guns,
> and my hat adorned with a cross-cockade;
> [i.e. able to join the army]
>
> . . .
>
> and wouldn't it be better for me to sign up with them
> than to be a waster in the Gaelic style?'[72]

However in such oral traditions Protestantism was deemed material-istic and acquisitive and woe betide any Catholic who rose in the world. The younger generation of the Gael, in their new prosperity, were becoming 'full of English pride', complained MacCooey.[73] One Donegal priest, Dominick O'Donnell (1700–93), who converted to Protestantism, was warned:

> It were better for you to be herding cattle,
> a stick in your hand and a blanket covering you,
> than to be seated under great windows,
> listening to the sounds of a minister.[74]

Catholics' belief in the antiquity, superiority and greater spirituality of their religion and traditions, however down on their fortunes, pervades the poetry – as it would do popular folklore in ensuing centuries – and we can be sure that it would have been given voice frequently, the jest veiling serious belief. However neighbourly, Cath-olics believed Protestants ultimately doomed. 'You must come over to our church,' Father Ned advised Andy Morrow in Carleton's *Ned McKeown*; 'you're a good neighbour, and a worthy fellow, and it's a thousand pities you should be sent down' – to which McKeown responded in agreement: 'It's a great thing entirely to be born in the true church – one's always sure, then.' There may too have been a peculiarly Irish version of the one-upmanship which poorer, older continental nobles indulged in against the newer, richer ones. The earl of Roden wrote to his sister in 1811:

There is a curious old woman here, a Mrs. Nugent one of the most decided Brogueniers you ever heard. She is of a very good Irish family, Mother to Count Nugent who is in the Austrian service, but she says she is not a Nugent at all but a McDonough who are a thousand years older than the Nugents. I told her to take care the Hutchinsons [whom Roden thinks 'decided Methodists'] did not convert her – she replied that there was no danger, if they talked to her she would tell them she was an *ould Papish* as their grandfather was, and would have nothing to do with their *fagairier*.[75]

As in every other rural society at the time, there is also a culture of outwitting the law and of celebrating those who did so. But one had to understand it first. Irish-language interpreters were available to the courts, but there is little evidence on their performance and a lot of evidence to suggest that monoglot Irish speakers were at a distinct disadvantage. In a Donegal folk song, the *Gall* taunts the *Gael*:

> What is your business at the sessions
> when you have no word of English?
> You'd not be given permission to speak there
> to plead any case.[76]

It is the priests, the educated men, who are celebrated for their understanding of the 'foreign' law and for protecting their people. A recurrent story in Ulster folklore is one where an eighteenth-century friar bottled the spirits of the local law officers, the site remaining an object of fear far into the nineteenth century.[77]

Although Protestant clerics who were not anti-Catholic were generally accepted by Catholics, Catholic youths were known to disrupt Protestant services of particularly anti-papist preachers. But they might also stay to listen, just as Protestants of all hues looked on with bemused fascination at popular Catholic practices – our people being as likely to join as condemn them, as one Protestant divine complained.[78] In the 1790s William Putnam McCabe, a United Irish leader noted for his impersonation skills, was able to turn this mutual fascination to good account in recruiting for the United Irishmen. He would spread word that 'a converted Papist would preach the Word in a certain barn ... and explain how he became convinced of the true doctrines of Presbyterianism', then recruit among the assembled mixed-religion crowd.[79]

Lough Derg in County Donegal had been a place of pilgrimage since medieval times. Although destroyed under Cromwell, it had been re-established and was undisturbed during the entire period of the penal laws, even though prohibited by the 1704 Act 'to prevent the further growth of popery'. With upwards of five thousand pilgrims converging on the south Donegal site every August, any interference risked popular tumult, and, like other penal legislation carrying such risks if implemented, this ruling was generally ignored. It was, after all, a tidy little earner for the local Protestant gentry who leased the island and a source of some fascination for the many more Protestant 'tourists' who came to witness Catholics act out their 'superstitious' beliefs.[80] Certainly the ritual demanded endurance of heroic proportions: the pilgrims fasting for up to nine days, traversing some fifty miles in bare feet over jagged stones, constantly reciting the rosary and finishing up being incarcerated in a cave or vault (the 'purgatory' proper). Here they neither ate nor slept for twenty-four hours, kept awake by clerical warnings that their soul would be seized by the devil should they succumb to weariness. Predictably the combined effects of sleep deprivation, fasting and religious ecstasy produced the many visions and hallucinations associated with the pilgrimage. Little wonder that Catholic people came to regard such pilgrims as having acquired saintly powers and the pebbles brought back from the lake as miraculous talismans. Lough Derg epitomised for Protestants the credulousness and superstition which they associated with the Catholic mind. For centuries it had been run by the Franciscans. But it too experienced the reforming sweep of a new breed of Catholic bishop later in the eighteenth century, when it was taken over by secular clergy and its primitive rigour considerably reduced. Even so, Carleton's courage failed him at the sight of the island early in the next century.[81]

3. Social status of Ulster Catholics

People of all denominations were poor in Ulster until the rapid expansion of the linen industry in the second half of the eighteenth century. The descendants of the Cromwellian soldiers in Monaghan, for example, subsisted on tiny, poor farms.[82] Catholic tenants were not always the poorest and if they were good tenants they were as secure as Protestants (though again it depended on the landlord). In the early decades of the century general insecurity made even Protestant tenants unwilling to take on long leases because of the contractual obligations. There is even a recurrent complaint of Catholics outbidding Protestants for leases.[83] The province was particularly badly affected by the series of natural disasters in the first decades – the terrible famine of 1741 alone thought to have brought the deaths of 300,000 people. The situation in Armagh inspired Swift's *Modest Proposal* of 1729 (in which he proposed the eating of the country's children to alleviate its poverty). The provision of churches, meeting-houses and schools was just as inadequate for Protestants and Dissenters as for Catholics, the discontent at tithes and ecclesiastical courts just as strong. The rewards of conformity were ideals which most Protestants could not aspire to. In the first half of the century firearms were generally in short supply because Protestants could not afford them and there are enough reports of firing at specifically Catholic celebrations to suggest easy defiance of the 1695 act.[84] Catholics were just as anxious to turn in malefactors to the law; landlords just as likely to use Catholic chapels as churches and meeting-houses to disseminate information among their tenants.

Under the Gaelic system the native Irish had not put much store on comfort, and later commentators noted a greater willingness by Catholics to endure hardship.[85] By the close of the century, however, most Catholics were prospering, linen-induced prosperity giving even the poorer a higher standard of living than their counterparts elsewhere in Ireland. Even if most Catholics were involved at its lower levels – spinning yarn, rather than weaving – the pace of change was such that marginal areas (traditionally dominated by Catholics) were being reclaimed and brought into production to feed a rapidly expanding population.[86] Landlords, still living in the castles and bawns of plantation times in the first part of the century, with all their overtones of division and insecurity, were building fashionable country mansions by the second half, planting new woods, laying out demesnes and deer parks, all alike providing new employment opportunities. In areas of linen prosperity landlords sought to increase their revenue by letting directly to the sub-tenants, granting secure leases to those who could pay and placing many Catholics, for the first time, in direct economic competition with Protestants. By the time MacCooey came to write his poetry in the second half of the century, leases for lives were the most coveted and the obstacles placed in the way of Catholics obtaining them had become live issues.

Despite the penal laws, the eighteenth century was a period of opportunity for Irish Catholics. There were no restrictions on the accumulation and transfer of non-landed wealth and a wealthy Catholic middle class emerged despite the laws. A sub-gentry also developed, largely consisting of original landowners who had survived as chief tenants and middlemen. However, Ulster diverges from this national pattern. The large Catholic merchant, strong farmer and middleman classes that came into existence elsewhere in Ireland, driving the rise of Catholic political power from mid-century onwards, are absent, as is a class of 'comfortable' Catholics at lower levels.[87] The top tier of Irish Catholic society, which survived to provide the base for upward mobility elsewhere in Ireland, had disappeared in Ulster. In the old O'Neill territories and in south Down there are even signs of reluctance to grant leases to old gentry.[88] The absence of Ulster from the early campaigns of the Catholic Committee is unmistakable. Financial contributions to its campaign were also lower from Ulster than from the other provinces. That campaign was urban-driven and Ulster's urban development was retarded until the second half of the century. Even then its urban culture remained largely Protestant. Few if any Catholics participated in the commercial end of the linen industry before the 1740s and when they settled in towns they tended rather to be publicans, grocers, small traders and shopkeepers.[89] By the 1790s, however, successful Catholic families – notably from County Down, where they had reached the top of the linen industry – were represented in the Catholic Committee's campaign, even though there were few from the other Ulster counties. Magennises, Savages, O'Neills and Teelings were among the Down representatives, Patrick Russell, Esq., represented Louth, Andrew MacShane, Esq., Donegal, Daniel Reilly Esq., Monaghan.[90] The Loinsigh (Lynch) family had been able to sustain a classical and Irish-language school at Loughinisland, County Down for generations.[91] A Catholic middle class was beginning to emerge by the end of the century, but it was tiny in comparison with the rest of the country.

However, the complexity of the Ulster situation has not yet been properly researched. It is not one of unrelieved social decline, and if we move away from the main families (who have fallen on bad times), we find enough examples of secondary lines remaining on the land and prospering. Where Catholics had a strong presence, they remained important figures, either as tenant farmers or small proprietors. This is particularly so in south Ulster: the Maguires of Fermanagh; McKennas, MacMahons, Plunketts and Murphys of Monaghan; O'Callaghans and O'Neills of Armagh; O'Reillys of Cavan; O'Neills, Magennises, Savages and Whytes (formerly White) of south Down. The O'Neills of the Fews in Armagh had retained some of their former status, Daniel being listed in 1766 as a 'yarn merchant' and manufacturer, with a number of weavers in his employment. In 1767 he was appointed petty constable for Creggan. His children intermarried with old Irish families of similar status.[92] The Coigley (Quigley) family of Armagh, with O'Neill and O'Donnelly ancestry, were also leading linen entrepreneurs by the last decades of the century.[93]

Likewise in south Down a number of old Catholic families retained positions of social importance. The Whyte family of Loughbrickland weathered the penal laws by a series of collusive trusteeships in the hands of Protestant relatives.[94] The O'Neills of Banvale, Hilltown (linear descendants of the Clandeboye O'Neills) prospered in the linen industry. John was owner of a bleach green and member of the 1792–3 Catholic Convention – 'old gentry' as Tone was to call him.[95] The MacCartans of Loughinisland are noted in the 1766 return of papists as employing seven servants. They also supplied large numbers of the local clergy, including a bishop of Down and Connor, Theophilus MacCartan (bishop, 1760–78) – who continued to reside in Loughinisland during his episcopacy. His will of 1777 goes some way to telling us why this small but powerful Catholic network survived. Not only did his family intermarry with the Magennises, O'Neills and Kellys, but they remained close to those Magennises and Savages who had conformed to the established church, and his grandnieces were warned that they would be cut out of his will if they married any 'base or inferior person'.[96] Another case of horizontal social relations between descendants of the old Gaelic elite and the new Protestant establishment is related in the account of a tour of Ireland made in 1752 by Richard Pococke (Protestant bishop of Ossory, 1756–65). At Castle Caldwell, on the Donegal/Fermanagh border, home of Sir James Caldwell, aide-de-camp to General O'Donnell in the Austrian service, Pococke, another Anglican minister, Sir James and the father of General O'Donnell dined together. O'Donnell 'they say is the head of that family descended from the Earl of Tyrconel and tho' he has only leases, yet he is the head of the Roman Catholicks in this country'.[97]

The most intriguing case of a once-important landed Catholic family retaining their status and prospering in the new linen industry is that of the Teelings. An Anglo-Norman family, in Ireland since the twelfth century, they had forfeited their estates in County Meath in 1657 and moved to County Louth, where they intermarried with another leading Catholic family, the Taaffes of Smarmore Castle. In the eighteenth century they had become linen merchants in Lisburn, County Antrim, also acquiring property in Dublin and amassing a fortune said to have been worth £30,000 by 1798. The then head of the family, Luke Teeling, figured prominently in Catholic politics. But his career and his business were ruined by the conflict of the 1790s and he was bitter at the continuing penal restrictions which barred Catholics like himself from a full participation in public life. As positions progressively opened up to Catholics in the nineteenth century, however, his descendants were found behaving like any members of the Irish upper class, some becoming officers in the British army and dying for it in World War I.[98]

The first real insight into this emerging tier of prosperous Ulster Catholics is in the Catholic Qualification Rolls.[99] To avail of the provisions of the Catholic relief acts after 1778 Catholics had first to take an oath of allegiance at the assizes in their county town. Apart from a small handful of Catholics appearing as gentry (the O'Rorkes, O'Haras and O'Neills of Antrim, the O'Neills and Savages of Down, the O'Callaghans of Armagh), there are some 111 undifferentiated merchants, a handful of linen drapers (7), distillers (11), and at the top of the linen industry 5 bleachers (Terence Hughes, Antrim, Michael McFall, Londonderry, Daniel McNeill, Antrim, Charles O'Hara, Randalstown, John Toole, Armagh). Although the vast majority describe themselves as 'farmer', there are also numbers of quite lowly Catholics (labourers, weavers, servants, shoemakers, carpenters) – a trend increased in the 1793–96 returns (1,899), and this when they actually had to pay to take the oath.[100] It testifies to the heightened expectations of change at the end of the eighteenth century among every class of Catholic.

Older wealth tended to enter the Church and there is usually a direct connection between those who became bishops and families who retained a landed base. Indeed the very existence of the Catholic Church in Ulster depended on the ability of such families to shoulder the expense of training their sons abroad. Ulster Catholicism is not an undifferentiated impoverished mass, as the supporters of Catholic emancipation at the end of the century tried to argue. 'If we drive the rich Catholic from the Legislature and from our own society,' argued pro-emancipist MP for County Tyrone, George Knox, 'we force him to attach himself to the needy and disaffected.' We shall admit him eventually, he predicted with more accuracy than he could have realised. 'But we shall withhold that admission so long, that at length we shall give without generosity what will be received without gratitude.'[101] There was a continuing undercurrent of disaffection among the poorer Catholics, which had all but disappeared from the Catholic elite. That elite argued that the very nature of Catholicism was conservative and far more likely to sustain the existing hierarchy in state and society than the Protestant sects.[102] There was little Catholic support in Ulster for any of the disturbances of the 1760s and 1770s, and some evidence that the uncharacteristic involvement of some Catholics was due to the temporary weakening of clerical control after the demise of the regulars. Likewise, at the end of the century even the by then radicalised Catholic Committee held back from association with the United Irishmen until pushed into it by the very rejection of which Knox had warned.

The case of Edmund McGildowney, younger son of a Catholic gentry family in the Glens of Antrim, was typical. A landlord in his own right, he also acted as agent to a number of prominent Protestant families (not least the Earl of Antrim) – which may have protected him from legal interference. He in turn seems to have protected his Catholic tenants from the worst effects of the penal laws. But he was also highly politicised. His papers reveal a knowledge of the arguments being put forward by the Catholic Committee for a relaxation of the penal laws. He took the Catholic qualification oath in 1782, became the representative for Antrim on the Catholic Committee in 1791, and a JP in 1797. At local level he had been active in promoting the welfare of the Catholic Church, and as an old man he was one of the organisers of O'Connell's campaign in Ulster.[103] Another highly successful Ulster Catholic was Armagh-reared Bernard Coile (1766?-1829), who was related to the Catholic bishop of Raphoe and who rose through the linen industry to become a cambric and muslin manufacturer. As with his friends the Coigleys, his success and prominence in Catholic politics attracted the wrath of the Orangemen, and his webs and yarns were destroyed in 1795. He went on to participate in the campaign for Catholic emancipation in the early decades of the next century. Again he is an example of good inter-communal relations at the higher social levels. Both his mother and aunt (who reared him) had converted to Catholicism on their marriage.[104]

At first there was little Catholic participation in the commercial side of the linen industry; and although this changed in the second half of the century, the most profitable side of the industry remained in Protestant hands. There are even signs of some resistance in Catholic areas to an activity being promoted by landlord importation of Prot- estant craftsmen.[105] By the 1780s, however, the market economy and the process of modernisation had reached even remote districts, and linen had opened up new opportunities unavailable through agricul- ture. As prosperity spread, so did 'polite' culture, the *Gael* (particularly the women) aping the fashions of the *Gall* and progressively aban- doning the Irish language.[106] Surviving Irish-language scholars mis- trusted print and Irish-language culture was becoming increasingly enclosed. There was a conscious shunning of Irish by the upwardly mobile, a trend reflected in the disappearance of large numbers of Irish-language manuscripts – stories surviving of them being found in rivers and fields and being used as wrapping paper in general grocers stores.[107] Surveys of Irish-speaking reveal continuing strength (50–70 per cent) in south Ulster, particularly in the main area of poetic activity (south Armagh, north Louth, east Monaghan and an isolated area around Newry), significant pockets in Tyrone and north Antrim (40 per cent) and the bulk of the populace in Donegal. But the trend was downwards, and within a century Irish-speaking had disappeared almost everywhere in Ulster apart from the extreme west and north of Donegal.[108] Irish-speaking becomes increasingly associated with the poorer labourer and the migrant *spailpín*.[109]

It would be difficult to exaggerate the impact of linen on the lifestyle of eighteenth-century Ulster. Although linen production was native to Ireland, it was the British colonists who began weaving the broad linen required for export. The Ulster Irish were slow at first to produce for the market, but were later won over by the higher prices it could command (particularly after 1743 when Britain placed a bounty on exports to the colonies). Between 1730 and 1790 exports of linen increased from 4 to 37 million yards. Since weaving and spinning techniques had changed little, the phenomenal expansion was the result of increasing numbers of spinners and weavers joining the industry. It was linen which paid the rent even on uneconomic farms, encouraging larger families, increased demand for food and a drive to bring even barren land into production. The result was 'a landscape of intensively cultivated small holdings reaching out into the bogs and up into the mountains, thronged by an industrious peasantry enjoying a higher standard of living than elsewhere in rural Ireland'.[110] Even before the repeal of the penal laws, such was the demand for linen that landlords were offering leases to weavers of any denomination. As competition for land intensified, Catholics outbidding Protestants for leases was one of the ingredients in the end-of-century sectarian troubles. The so-called 'Oultachs', who fled from Ulster to other parts of Ireland as a result of these troubles, were comfortably off, for it was mainly Catholic property-owners that the Orange gangs targeted. In the linen triangle (Belfast, Armagh, Dungannon) and the Newry–Drogheda axis, a recognisable Catholic middle class was emerging and belatedly joining the campaign of the Catholic Committee.[111]

Prior to the economic take-off of mid century, all denominations sought career outlets abroad. Dissenters left in large numbers for North America. According to Arthur Young, Catholics were less willing to leave: 'The Catholicks never went; they seem not only tied to the country but almost to the parish in which their ancestors lived.'[112] Emigration, he continued, was not an option for the very poor. But with the upswing of the economy Catholics too began to participate in the transatlantic flow. At one stage the apparent religious imbalance in emigration gave rise to fears that the country would be denuded of its Protestant population – 'the papists being already five or six to one, and being a breeding people', as archbishop King commented in 1718.[113] Traditionally Catholics had looked to the Catholic countries on the Continent, thousands joining the continental armies and seminaries in the period. Once considered a harsh consequence of the penal laws, this is now recognised as an important career outlet for the sons of Catholic gentry. The impact of those returning and the social and political consequences of such extensive family networks is only beginning to be investigated. Again Ulster's lower participation is commented upon. Yet, for a province whose upwardly mobile Catholics were starting from a lower base, it is significant enough.[114] Austrian and Spanish service hosted several generations of Ulster families, notably O'Donnells, Maguires, Plunketts and O'Neills, their absence lamented by the poets, but their status abroad sustaining the image of a surviving Gaelic nobility.

A survey of eighteenth-century tombstones in the ancient Fermanagh cemetery of Devenish is revealing. Every denomination still used it. Catholic tombstones reveal a number of old Gaelic family names (Reillys, Magraths, Gallaghers, Kellys, Cassidys, Maguires, Seerys (Ó Saoraigh), many displaying coats of arms. Indeed, the later eighteenth century witnessed an upturn in members of Gaelic-Irish families seeking to register their pedigrees prior to leaving for the Continent, and the Ulster (Heraldry) Office in Dublin Castle showed itself more than willing to collaborate with priests and Gaelic scholars to assist them.[115] The occupational history of a number of the families is recorded on these tombstones: the Cassidys, ancient physicians to the Maguires, still functioned as doctors and begat dynasties of priests. Edward Kelly is recorded as an Enniskillen merchant at the time of the death of his two daughters in 1793. The Maguire tombstones include those of Denis Maguire, bishop of Dromore, and Bryan Maguire, erected by his son, a captain in the Imperial (Austrian) service.[116] The Monaghan MacEnaneys, who left Ulster after the defeat of James II, had also found fame and fortune in Austrian service (Patrick MacEnaney becoming secretary of state, his son counsellor of state).[117] When the latter died in 1800, he left his fortune to his Monaghan relatives, suggesting the maintenance of ties in such dispersed families and no little contribution to the Catholic economy from those abroad.

The Cassidys are typical of other ancient professional families who continued their traditional calling. The Kernans became apothecaries and attorneys; the Hoods of Maghera – descendants of *ollamhs* to the O'Neills of Clandeboye – poets and schoolteachers;[118] the Quins – quartermasters to the O'Neills – owners of corn mills in Armagh.

Contrary to the accepted image, therefore, there is a nascent middle class in Catholic Ulster, its size underestimated because of the failure to take into account the large numbers entering and prospering in the church. But it is geographically confined (largely south and south-east Ulster) and does not dent the general image of the bulk of Catholics as an underclass. Even so, they form a potentially stronger support group than their Protestant equivalent, largely because of their group solidarity and close family ties with the clergy. Dr William Drennan (1754–1820), leading Presbyterian reformer and United Irishman, and, after early doubts, a lifetime campaigner for Catholic emancipation, was nevertheless to complain about the tendency of Catholics only to employ professionals of their own denomination – their group identity as Catholics overriding all others.[119]

4. The religious geography of eighteenth-century Ulster

However, such developments did not radically alter the religious geography of the province except in the few areas at the heart of the linen industry. Areas deemed native after the Ulster plantation remained so. The preoccupation with the religious make-up of the populace, mentioned earlier, took the form of a certain amount of social engineering in the first half of the century. At first many landlords went to great lengths to attract Protestant tenants in preference to Catholics, and the recent influx of Scots was reducing many Irish to the level of under tenants. Bishop MacMahon complained in 1714:

Although all Ireland is suffering, this province is worse off than the rest of the country . . . from the neighbouring country of Scotland Calvinists are coming over here daily in large groups of families, occupying the towns and villages, seizing the farms in the richest parts of the country and expelling the natives.[120]

There was too an economic motive as Protestant tenants were generally thought more likely to improve their lands and pay their rents. This attitude was to change as the economic standing of Catholics improved later in the century.

But the religious map remained much the same. Territorial segregation often kept the different religious communities apart. The 1766 religious census shows mixed communities to have been in the minority and a large number of predominantly Catholic juxtaposing predominantly Protestant areas. Areas where recognisably 'Catholic' territory bordered on recognisably 'Protestant' territory were to become traditional flashpoint areas. This was certainly the case in parts of south Ulster, on the Tyrone/Fermanagh border and the western shores of Lough Neagh and north Armagh (ancient O'Neill territory), where there was virtual parity in numbers of Catholics and Protestants and where the common eighteenth-century pastime of faction fighting first assumed a sectarian hue. 'In these parts, and in the adjacent parts of Cavan', wrote one commentator in the early 1790s, 'there reside numerous tribes of Presbyterians, called by the common people Scotch. Between these and the lower order of Catholics there has prevailed for many years an hereditary Animosity, and it is hard to say on which side preponderate ignorance and religious prejudices.'[121] The tories and rapparees of the early century successfully beat off Protestant incursion in the south of the province. The poorer terrain of Donegal, the Glens of Antrim, south Ulster and the Sperrin mountains of Tyrone and Derry proved unattractive to Protestant tenants until reclamation and population increase brought even these into the competition for space in this increasingly crowded territory.

By the second half of the century Catholics were in a minority in Antrim, Down and Derry, equal in numbers in Armagh and Tyrone, but in the majority in the other counties. Until then poverty, traditional immobility, lack of communications and surviving Gaelic culture – which, like its poetry, tended to be backward rather than forward looking – shut in traditional practices. With areas like the Glens of Antrim, almost totally inaccessible to wheeled vehicles and incapable of growing their own flax, these uplands came late to the linen industry, and in the case of the Glens not at all. In such areas, where the Protestant population was small, Catholics did have more chance of acquiring leases. But they could often only do so by joining with others in partnership groups, which would continue communal farming practices – giving a distinctive 'open' appearance to landscape which already contained large tracts of barren bog. This was subsistence farming; and whilst it protected vulnerable members of the community, it also curbed initiative and did not lend itself to improvement.[122]

In stark contrast to 'Protestant' landscape which was enclosed and neat – the model having been set by the late seventeenth-century English immigrants who reproduced their English landscape in the Lagan valley and north Armagh – this was seen as primitive terrain, avoided by the typical eighteenth-century traveller or traversed in trepidation. The Fews area of south Armagh – through which travellers from Dublin had to pass to reach Armagh city – was particularly dreaded. A landscape of 'very wild mountains', wrote Dr Thomas Molyneux of his journey in 1708, 'of a boggy, heathy soil, the road through them of a rocky gravel', scarce a house to be seen and no meadows or enclosures. After sixteen or seventeen miles of this, his relief was tangible as he left the mountains and entered 'pleasant, enclosed country' and 'new made roads to Armagh'.[123] It was still noted for bandits in mid-century, another traveller observing in 1750 that no one would risk a journey through 'the dreaded defiles' of south Armagh without an escort. It was an area which seemed to have stood still, its sparse population still ploughing by the tail.[124] In 1759 Chief Baron Willes likened the difficulty of journeying between Downpatrick and Newry through the Mourne Mountains of south Down to that through the Alps or Apennines:

Within these twenty years it was an absolute uncivilised country, and anyone who ventured to go among them did it at his peril, it being almost the inaccessible retreat of Tories and Rapparees and outlaws. But a good road being made . . . it is much civilised to what it was . . . it is the wildest and most mountainous country I have seen . . . The cabins one sees on the sides of the hills are the most miserable huts I ever saw, built with sods and turf, no chimney, the door made of an hurdle, the smoke goes all out of the door, the cocks and hens, pigs, goats and if perchance they have a cow, inhabit the same dwelling. They seem much upon a rank with the American savages, except that they have some notion about making the sign of the cross and stand much in awe of their priests. And yet there must be times when the master and mistress of the family are merry and jolly, for one sees the cabin doors crowded with little naked boys and girls.[125]

Until romanticism and the novels of Lady Morgan altered perceptions, this was unfashionable landscape. Towns, roads and canals were Protestant. The economy of whiskey, barley, black cattle and smuggling of the uplands was contrasted with that of linen in the lowlands. James McParlan commented in 1802:

In the mountain region, where the culture of barley, and use of whiskey . . . are suffered to predominate, industry and the habits of it are shamefully degraded. In the champain parts, where agriculture and manufactures employ the time of the peasant . . . industry and all its habits prevail; . . . in those parts of the mountain . . . where the linen manufacture is gaining ground, drunkenness and idleness are decreasing considerably.

He also noted Irish speaking generally in the mountains, but English with a 'Scotch twang' in the lowlands.[126] Although some of the mountainous districts, such as those on the Fermanagh/Donegal border, were still haunted by outlaws as late as the 1770s, there is a sense of the primitive rather than of actual danger in the many travel accounts. In the tenser atmosphere of the 1790s, however, awareness of Catholic concentration in 'the wild parts' once again caused alarm in adjacent Protestant areas.[127]

Nor was this religious tagging of the very land an exaggeration by outsiders. There was a heightened awareness of the location of ancient families' lands. In Carleton's *Poor Scholar*, the McEvoys, evicted from their farm by a Protestant land agent, look down from the barren hills where they now live to the fertile farms below. 'Look at thim . . . only look at the black thieves! how warm an' wealthy they sit there in our own ould possessions, an' here we must toil till our fingers are worn to stumps.'[128] The different habitats of the religious communities is thought accountable for their contrasting characteristics: 'The Catholic being, like his soil, hardy, thin, and capable of bearing all weathers; and the Protestants, larger, softer, and more inactive.'[129] This religious division of the economy can be pushed too far. The Scots were just as traditional in their farming methods as the Irish. Poorer Protestants also joined together in partnership leases.[130] But there can be no denying that different territorial allegiances and religious segregation had developed in the course of the eighteenth century and there was an acute awareness of who lived where. The process was accentuated by the very high mobility amongst Presbyterians and the reluctance of Catholics to move outside their immediate locality. The 1766 religious returns also show Protestants more resistant to living among Catholics than the reverse.[131] Little wonder that observers spoke of Catholics and Protestants inhabiting different districts and behaving and speaking like different peoples.[132]

John Gamble's invaluable tour of 1810 shows that the practice of seeking the stereotypical cues to identify one's religion – a practice ingrained in contemporary Northern Ireland consciousness – was already well established by the turn of the eighteenth century. Travelling through south Tyrone, he sought shelter from a rainstorm in a roadside cabin.

I stepped into a cabin, which by good luck was on the roadside. It was really good luck, for there was a large dunghill in front, which nearly hid it from view ... 'ten thousand welcomes...', said the man of the house, starting up: 'Susy, draw his honour a creepy'. I knew now I was the guest of a Catholic. The dunghill was suspicious; 'your honour' was decisive. A Protestant never gives this appellation lightly, a Presbyterian never gives it at all.[133]

The incident (and there are many such in Gamble) shows that the old traditions of hospitality and deference had not been eroded by the bitter experiences of the 1790s – even if, as with Gamble, awareness of difference was probably rarely far below the surface.

5. Recovery of the Catholic Church

Despite the penal laws, the eighteenth century was a period of major recovery for the Catholic Church throughout Ireland. The penal laws had not destroyed church organisation, for there had been little recovery since the beginning of the previous century. Several Ulster sees had been vacant for much of the seventeenth century and by the new century there was widespread slippage among the faithful and a lack of clerical discipline.[134] However, from 1730 onwards episcopal succession was maintained. Despite the penal laws, the authorities had recognised the practical need for bishops to maintain discipline, and generally left them alone. By the second half of the century a succession of reforming ecclesiastics had laid the basis for the take-off of the nineteenth century. They were able to operate with a remarkable degree of independence, more indeed than their colleagues in countries where Catholicism was the established religion, and where state interference, the Enlightenment's attack on religion and growing religious indifference saw the church in retreat all over Europe. It is unlikely that the Catholic Church in Ireland would have become such a powerful institution had the Stuarts survived as Catholic monarchs. Under James II there had been tensions as he tried to assert the kind of state control which already existed in the other European monarchies. The long-term result was a more Tridentine, more severe, more conservative religion than elsewhere, a religion which, according to a leading Church historian, 'stood alone as a kind of affront to contemporary living in the West, even within the Church' until the second half of the twentieth century.[135] The drive for internal reform came mainly from Munster and south Leinster, Ulster and north Connacht clinging to old practices much longer than anywhere else. It took three forms: the restructuring of the visible church (notably the construction of mass-houses and chapels); the instruction of the faithful; and the imposition of ecclesiastical authority.

The preponderance of mass-rocks and other open-air places of worship in Ulster reflects the poverty of the people and the absence of a supporting gentry, much more than legal penalisation. Clogher was by no means the poorest of the Ulster dioceses. Yet even here Bishop MacMahon in 1714 reported the people 'in dire poverty' and unable to support their clergy. 'Indeed the sight of them would move one to compassion, as they go around unkempt, ill-clad, without companions, with no fixed abode, spending the night here and there in huts by the wayside . . . [celebrating] Mass in soiled or tattered vestments', using 'tin' chalices and cracked altar stones.[136] Pococke reports similar poverty from his tour of 1752. He was able to travel all over Ireland and was welcomed in the cabins of the poor. By now he was using the terms Roman Catholic and Papist interchangeably, with no sense of threat, and he comments on Catholic religious practice without any reference at all to the existence of the penal laws. Near Dunfanaghy, Donegal, he witnessed an open-air mass:

In the Side of one of them [the mountains] a Sort of Amphitheatre is formed in the rock; here I saw several hundred people spread all over that plain spot, the Priest celebrating Mass under the rock, on an altar made of loose Stones . . . I observed his Pontifical Vestment with a black Cross on it; for in all this Country for Sixty miles west & south as far as Connaught, they celebrate in the open air, in the fields or on the mountain; the Papists being so few & poor, that they will not be at the expense [sic] of a public building.[137]

In predominantly Protestant areas the provision of Catholic places of worship was worse. In 1764 the hearth-money collector for Carrick-fergus reported neither seceding Presbyterian nor Catholic places of worship in the area, but a priest, Phelix Scullion, saying mass in the fields in the summer, and in his parishioners' homes in the winter. In the nearby parishes of Templecorran and Kilroot mass had not been said 'in the memory of the oldest man living'.[138]

Ulster Catholicism had never been church-based and, in this drive of the episcopacy to restore the church's visible structures, it had to start from a much more undeveloped base than in much of the rest of Ireland. From at least the beginning of George I's reign (1721–27) mass-houses began to replace mass-rocks and other temporary structures. In some cases the sites were donated by Protestant landlords and they tended to appear in areas where relations with local Protestants were good. They were humble structures, resembling one-storey thatched cottages. Catholicism was not alone in this. Early Presbyterian meeting houses were remarkably similar and Protestant churches remained in a lamentable condition until the end of the century.[139] But the 1731 report into the state of popery shows Ulster and parts of north Connacht lagging far behind the rest of the country in the provision of mass-houses (though with neighbouring Louth the wealthiest in the country), and still dependent on itinerant friars.[140] The situation improved rapidly from mid-century, one commentator reporting as early as 1764: 'Till within these few years there was scarce a mass-house to be seen in the northern counties of Ulster; now mass-houses are spreading over most parts of that country.'[141]

Although Derry was registered as the poorest diocese in the country in 1731, and Philip McDevitt still found no churches there when he became bishop in 1766, by the time of his death in 1797 there were many churches and a seminary at Claudy near Strabane. His will reveals a man of comfortable means and social standing – a far cry from the fugitive priest at the beginning of the century.[142] But elsewhere the restructuring was slower and Carleton recalled of his south Ulster childhood that 'there was nothing in existence for the Catholics for the worship of God except the mere altar, covered with a little open roof to protect the priest from rain', and such mass-rocks figure prominently in his stories. But with no protection for the congregation he concludes 'that during the winter months the worship of God was . . . a very trying ceremony'.[143]

The church's teaching called for 'outward profession' of the faith, and after the early years of persecution, there were regular episcopal exhortations to construct mass-houses.[144] The kind of pragmatism which encouraged occasional conformity to retain family land was condemned by a new breed of bishop intent on tightening discipline and might explain why hostile folk traditions differ from contemporary acceptance of land conformism.[145] Mass-attendance was to become the cornerstone of such 'outward profession' and there has been considerable historical debate on this as a yardstick for Catholic practice.[146] In the absence of statistics, any analysis for the eighteenth century must remain impressionistic. In Europe generally, however, regular attendance was not expected, and there is no sign in these new religious texts that it was causing concern one way or another. Issues which *were* causing concern were the huge number of holy days (criticised by the state authorities for taking people away from their work and by the bishops themselves for the attendant drunkenness and bawdy behaviour); and above all the need to make the sacraments of penance and confirmation readily available. In all cases the aim was to impose church control, and on the issue of holy days – where the number was reduced but observance of the remainder made obligatory – they appear to have been successful, at least in the towns. 'This being Assumption-day, the shops were shut in every town,' remarked an English traveller, *en route* from Drogheda to Derry in 1804, 'and in the streets it looked like Sunday, as observed in the more remote and decent parts of England or Scotland.'[147] However, such was the continued shortage of churches in rural areas that in the south Ulster diocese of Kilmore the Bishop was conducting confirmation at the fairs and markets in the 1750s and 1760s – a period when an acute shortage of priests was depriving large tracts of the poorer districts of any ministry whatsoever.[148] It also gave rise to a practice known as 'stations', whereby once a month mass and confession was held in a private house in the parish.

Given Catholic Church teachings on the necessity of interpreting scripture for the laity – indeed, reading the Bible in the vernacular had been prohibited since 1559[149] – the absence of public places of worship in Ulster and the inability of most Catholics to read (in either English or Irish), were clearly major barriers to the Tridentine goal of instruction. Priests were obliged to provide instruction at mass. However, the considerable independence of priests in the eighteenth century made it difficult to enforce uniformity, and the extravagant praise heaped by the poets on those few clergy who provided instruction suggests that it was uncommon. An early eighteenth-century sermon in Irish, reputedly written by a Franciscan friar in Armagh, says as much:

The clergy don't consider it worthwhile to spend their time on catechism, but on great, highly-learned, ingenious sermons of which people don't understand the tenth part, and it is because of that, alas, that many have been listening to Mass and to sermons throughout their lives without much benefit and who are still ignorant of the faith of Christ.[150]

It was a complaint echoed by the Dominican Provincial in Ireland in 1730, who criticised clerical training at Louvain as too 'speculative' and called instead for instruction in matters 'of more use to this mission', particularly 'the subjects controverted between the Catholics and Protestants of this country'.[151]

It was in the eighteenth century that the Catholic Church began finally to address the issue of survival in a Protestant kingdom. In this, Ireland was not behind the times, for it was only in the eighteenth century that the Church throughout Europe accepted responsibility for giving sustained spiritual instruction to the laity. A new kind of bishop finally produced popular teaching texts and catechisms – texts which would define popular Catholicism into modern times and provide the basis for the Catholic publishing industry in the second half of the century. Two in particular, O'Reilly's catechism (c.1720s) and Gallagher's 1736 sermons, remained popular favourites into the twentieth century, notably in Ulster and Connacht. They undoubtedly played a key role in instilling that particularly authoritarian strain in Tridentine teaching into Irish Catholicism and in replacing the genuine affection for the friars with that fearful respect for the clergy which was cultivated by the Church in the next century. Both are extremely stern in tone, but their content would be recognisable to any Ulster Catholic who was a child before Vatican II. They also finally succeeded, where all their predecessors had failed, in destroying the power of the friars, and with it a more earthy, easygoing faith.

Michael O'Reilly (c.1690–1758) was born in County Cavan, trained in Paris, and served successively as parish priest of Cavan, vicar-general of Kilmore, bishop of Derry and primate of Armagh (1749–58). Kilmore and Derry had been without a bishop for fifty and one hundred years respectively before O'Reilly's arrival, and the resulting laxity of discipline would have had a major impact on his outlook. A 'rigid disciplinarian', he would arrive unannounced at Sunday mass and rebuke any priest who failed to provide instruction. His catechism was produced in phonetic Irish and English versions, the latter 'for the newly converted colonists'. It contains some two hundred simple questions and answers setting out the basic tenets of Catholicism. There are specific condemnations of drunkenness, 'carnal knowledge' outside marriage, and 'impure thoughts'. Those failing to confess and communicate at least once a year are to be debarred from divine service and denied a Christian burial. Readers are warned that there is 'but one true Church . . . the holy Catholic Church' and they should be prepared 'to suffer all hardships and extremities' rather than renounce it. This would be typical of the Irish hierarchy in the future, a tendency to reject any improvement in the lot of its adherents if it involved any weakening of church authority.

But if the English text is stern, the Irish is more so, with 'its tendency to multiply the heads in hell'.[152] O'Reilly was to stir up a hornets' nest in Ulster as he spearheaded its reform. But, Ó Doirnín apart, anti-clerical poetry is notably absent in Ulster; deference to the clergy and unquestioning acceptance of Catholic teachings remained a characteristic of Ulster Catholicism. Gallagher's sermons (1736) and Pulleine's catechism (1748) are likewise in phonetic Irish. The sermons of James Gallagher, bishop of Raphoe, were designed as clerical preaching aids, but by the nineteenth century they had become treasured possessions throughout Ulster, Connacht and Munster. Early this century Rose O'Doherty of Falcarragh, County Donegal, though illiterate and knowing little English, could recite entire sermons in Irish from Gallagher.[153] 'My father always had a few Irish books of his own, mostly on religion, the Irish catechism and Dr Gallagher's sermons,' recalled Patrick McGlinchey, Inishowen weaver (1861–1954). 'He could read the sermons well. There was a great sermon on the Day of Judgement ... Dr Gallagher's sermons were great reading. No one going now will be saved according to these sermons, for there's nobody living up to them.'[154]

The sermon which made such an impact on young McGlinchey was sermon II, 'On the Last Judgement', based on a reading of St Luke's Gospel. It presents a terrifying vision of the last day, the end of the world, and the 'Judge' taking 'vengeance on sinners': the lustful, the glutton, the drunkard, those who sold Christ 'for a bottle of whiskey', or the housewives selling their hanks of yarn in short measure. Women fare badly in these sermons, constantly measured up to the impossible ideal of Mary. These are the petty crimes of the common people. Other classes scarcely figure, giving some support to MacCooey's criticisms of the clergy. They are medieval in their vision and sternness: God is a terrible judge, Mary and the saints necessary intermediaries. There is considerable emphasis on sin, confession and communion (particularly at Easter), a suggestion that absolution was more often withheld than not and a consequent resort to 'a strolling priest [i.e. a friar]', or to a priest 'no longer in active service' or 'exiled from his diocese', and there is some evidence that O'Reilly himself often suspended priests.[155] As for any political message, there is none. Gallagher's message is typical of that coming from the hierarchy generally: the sufferings of the people of Ireland were brought upon themselves by their own sins and loss of piety.

Another, even simpler and very popular catechism in Irish (1748) is that by the Catholic dean of Dromore, James Pulleine. It is the earliest Irish-language catechism for children and is firmly addressed to the laity rather than the clergy.

The Council of Trent, sess. 24 c. 7 binds not only the Church, but also fathers and mothers, sponsors and teachers and all heads of hearths and homes to teach Christian doctrine to their families and charges so that the light of untarnished faith may shine in the hearts of the people in spite of all the storms of evil, in spite of every persecution or unjust power which is or may be ranged against them.

It also indicates an ability to read English far in advance of areas in the west, for the instructions on Irish pronunciation suggest that the reader was expected to have been able to read English, but not Irish. Irish speaking died out earlier in County Down than anywhere else in Ulster.[156]

In a county where Catholics were outnumbered by Protestants and where bitter memories of seventeenth-century events were vivid, it reveals a sectarian consciousness absent from Gallagher's and O'Reilly's works and a political message unusual to these new popular religious works. Like the chosen people in captivity in Babylon, the Irish are now 'under the yoke of slavery, under oppression and persecution at the hands of the foreigner', Down, Saul and Faughart, 'home of the saints . . . of Patrick, Brigid and Columcille', are now in spiritual ruin and the need for proper instruction was urgent.[157] The reason for this unusually strident tone is that something of a battle was being waged in south Down for the hearts and minds of the Catholic people. Three Charter schools had recently been established in the county at Killough, Ballinahinch and Moira, and another was planned at Donaghmore. Walter Harris, who described these developments in detail, hailed the progress of the linen industry, the spread of the English language and the decline of 'popery' in the area.[158]

The kind of proselytising literature used by the Charter schools was clearly having some impact in the area, for Pulleine only four years later was warning his readers 'not to place any erroneous or heretical book in the hands of your children, for the bad instruction and bad knowledge which they obtain from those books . . . ruins and pollutes them, and . . . will not easily leave them.' [p.vi] The catechism is a conscious effort to counteract such Protestant proselytising through the medium of Irish, and there is a suggestion that it was enjoying a fair degree of success, for the catechism contains specific detail about what distinguishes a Catholic from others. For Catholics the sign of the cross is 'a distinguishing sign between us and the Turks, Pagans, Gentiles, and every other accursed group that is without God and the church'.[p.7] 'What is the holy Catholic church? It is the general assembly of the faithful who . . . profess the law of God, under the rule and direction of the Pope . . . And just as none were saved at the time of the flood, except for those who were with Noah in the Ark; so nobody will be saved who is not in the Catholic church'.[p.13]

Part of Harris's crusade involved detailing every local atrocity carried out against Protestants, largely in 1641, and the local memory seems to have been extraordinarily vivid. Here we have two separate and antagonistic traditions of victimhood building up. Pulleine was also a minor poet, and in his *Óráid* or praise-poem for Owen O'Neill of Clandeboye, who died at Hilltown in September 1744, he detailed past atrocities against the Irish in remarkably similar terms to those of Harris. It is thought that Pulleine resided with O'Neill at Hilltown and acted as private chaplain, while serving as parish priest to the surrounding Clonduff parish. His *Óráid*, like the poetry of south Ulster generally, shows a detailed knowledge of the ancestry of O'Neill and ascribes to him all the noble virtues formerly associated with his forebears. It is bitter about the downfall of Conn O'Neill in the seventeenth century, who lost 'his country and his lordship' to 'the deceitful quarrel-raising Galls . . . by treachery, murder, and beheading of men', the remainder left 'wandering to strange foreign countries, leaving their land and their tribal inheritance . . . to strangers and to Scotchmen'. But Owen had been a constant 'surety' to his people, 'a protecting defensive branch between them and those who wronged them' and nothing could tempt him 'to forsake the Holy Catholic Church'.[159]

Pulleine is unusual, and although little is known about him he was almost certainly a friar. His catechism seems to have had a largely localised circulation, for O'Reilly dominated the rest of the province. Although 'the holy Catholic Church' is claimed as the 'one true church' in all these new catechisms, they tended to be less anti-Protestant than preceding ones. Most of the new breed of crusading clergy were acutely aware of Protestant criticisms and the need for clergy to be better prepared to answer them.[160] There is a drive to eradicate superstitious practices and excessive devotion to the saints. And it is the friars whom they hold most responsible for perpetuating such 'abuses'. Most of the secular diocesan bishops in Ireland were educated in France and brought back with them the Enlightenment's dislike of the regular orders, whose scandalous behaviour they blamed for the intermittent persecution in Ireland. They were more anxious to conciliate Protestants and the Irish government than the regulars, and O'Reilly's depoliticised catechism was typical. He also had personal reasons, having been replaced in Clogher by a younger Dominican on the recommendation of James III. Stuart nomination to bishoprics was another object of their attack, for it promoted too many regulars. O'Reilly was personally to debar the bishop-elect to Derry, John Brullaghan, notwithstanding Stuart nomination (1750), and he joined forces with other reforming bishops in their campaign against the friars. The outcome was the papal closure of the regulars' novitiates in Ireland in 1751. Henceforth numbers were to be strictly limited by the requirement to study abroad, few of whom could have afforded to do so.[161]

The crisis would point up the different nature of church organisation in Ulster and parts of Connacht from the rest of the country. 'The priests had no settled way upon them', McGlinchey recalled from stories circulating in his youth, 'wandering friars went about and said mass here and there among the hills . . . They were a droll lot of men, and I heard old rhymes about them arguing and bantering and joking with the people.' But that had all changed, he continued, sometime around the 1780s.[162] All the old accusations about questing at the altars, inadequate training and education and general scandalous behaviour resurfaced in the eighteenth-century campaign and there is an acute awareness that, with Protestantism's efforts to win the people from their popery, Catholicism needed to be better equipped to respond.[163]

In Carleton's rural Ulster the priest is the central figure of authority, and respect for the 'clargy' has become an eleventh commandment. In this the eighteenth-century reformers had been entirely successful.

Although problems of lay interference resurfaced into the nineteenth century – the Maguires of Tempo, though now Protestant, still claiming ancient rights of presentment – and further measures would be necessary to restrict excessive fraternisation between priest and flock, the trend, which would peak in the so-called 'devotional revolution' of the nineteenth century, had already begun. The dominance of the friars had disappeared. Those that remained were firmly under the authority of the parish priest. The mendicant friar who turns up at Carleton's *Shane Fadh's wedding* had been questing for alms – but only with the parish priest's permission, and there is clearly no love lost between them. Like Darby More in *The Midnight Mass,* he is fat and jolly, and closer to the people (in his vices as much as his virtues) – 'an admixture of fun and devotion, external rigour and private licentiousness, love of superstition and of good whiskey, as might naturally be supposed . . . [of] men thrown among a people in whom so many extremes of character and morals meet'.[164] The irony is that the superstition and foreign power which Protestants associated with popery were increasingly antagonistic, as the papacy and the episcopacy alike tried to rid Catholicism of such pagan leftovers.

O'Reilly's actions were very much in line with those of the hierarchy generally and accompanied the first stages of the campaign to prove to government that Catholics were loyal citizens. In Ulster, however, he had not had the support of all the bishops, the majority of whom supported the friars' claims that they had been grossly misrepresented. Ulster Catholicism had been dependent on the friars, and by the late 1760s there was a serious shortage of priests in rural areas – particularly in the province of Armagh, where the population growth was the highest in the country. Moreover, it was argued, the Protestant press had seized on the dispute to fabricate details of orgies in the convents, much as the continental press thrived on stories of lascivious friars. In 1769 eight Irish bishops appealed to Rome on behalf of the friars. Five of these were from Ulster, all (Denis Maguire of Dromore, Philip McDevitt of Derry, Philip O'Reilly of Raphoe, Daniel O'Reilly of Clogher and Theophilus MacCartan of Down and Connor) were from those Old Irish families which had traditionally supported the friars.[165]

Even after O'Reilly's death in 1758, turmoil continued under his successor, Anthony Blake, who raised a storm for his appointments, his overturning of old practices, his exactions and, above all, for his non-residence. A member of an Old English landed family in County Mayo, he resided for the whole of his primacy in Galway. But although he gave good cause for complaint, it was the old accusation of being an outsider (and of ignoring local opinion when making appointments) which surfaced most regularly in such complaints.[166] Blake's appointment in 1758 looked like a veiled censure of the Irish hierarchy, for he had stood aside from the attempt to devise a loyalty oath the previous year and his stance was known to have been regarded favourably in Rome. Rome made a succession of such appointments in later decades of the century – including that of the redoubtable Dr Thomas Troy to the Dublin archdiocese in 1786 and Richard O'Reilly as Blake's successor in Armagh in 1787. It was not that the papacy endorsed any political or civil discord. But it steadfastly opposed anything savouring of Gallicanism or diminution of its authority, and all of the oaths devised to prove Catholic loyalty (including that eventually adopted and signed by many clergy after 1774) involved rejection of the pope's temporal power. There is a sense that the quietude during the office of Richard O'Reilly (primate 1787–1832) was self-imposed after decades of turmoil. It goes part of the way to explaining the unusual turnaround in clerical political attitudes in Ulster and the overwhelming support for government during the crisis of the 1790s.[167]

More important, however, was the destruction of the power of the friars, traditionally far more politicised than the secular clergy. Although the papacy surrendered to pressure and restored the novitiates in 1774, they were now firmly under ecclesiastical control and they never recovered their former strength. Under the 1829 Catholic Emancipation Act, regulars were required to register. Only one appears to have done so in Ulster, a Dominican in County Tyrone, who had had no regular contact with the order for twenty-nine years.[168] The tendency for most priests to be secular was firmly anchored by the opening of the new seminary at Maynooth in 1795. Despite protests from Connacht and Munster, O'Reilly's stance was more representative of the Irish Church's desire for better relations with the government, and the papacy's 1769 conditions for reopening of some novitiates included a requirement to site them where they would give 'the least cause of suspicion' to government.[169] But the centuries-old attachment to the friars died hard, and they continued in the hillier, more Irish areas like south Armagh, Monaghan and Donegal.[170]

The penal laws had reversed the long-standing government policy of punishing the chiefs but helping the people. In the long term they performed the highly unusual process of cutting through class divisions to produce a common identity. Often it was those at the lowest levels who were affected most. And whilst those who did not draw attention to themselves got by well enough, the potential for 'annoyance' by 'some little local persecutor' was always there.[171] That potential was much greater in Ulster than anywhere else in Ireland. It helps explain why the province accommodated itself to the replacement of the friars by a more rigorous, distant and authoritarian clergy; why Ulster Catholicism lacks that earthy religious scepticism so common to rural Catholicism elsewhere in early modern Europe and why the central tenets of Catholic teaching were rarely questioned. Everywhere else people were straining at confessional controls and embracing new religious movements like pietism, evangelicalism and Methodism. Resentful, the Ulster Catholics certainly were. But the Protestants were simply another factor in life to be endured. Endurance and submission was part of Catholic teaching. Religion itself had come to the assistance of that medieval mindset which accepted evil as part of life. Protestantism tended to personalise evil and consider it capable of defeat. Protestants might be hopelessly lost to salvation in Catholic perceptions, but they were left to it and their places of worship were scarcely ever attacked. Protestant tendencies to see the Ulster Catholics as some kind of coiled rebellious spring were misconceived and such misconceptions were to produce some incongruous results in the last years of the century.

7

REFORM TO REBELLION: THE EMERGENCE OF REPUBLICAN POLITICS

A lamentable story dear people I'll tell you,
That happened in Armagh this very last year;
The landlord combined, with others they joined,
To plunder and rob us of all we held dear:
For as we were Catholics they vow'd to oppress us,
Because at elections we had not a vote;
But by St Patrick, as we can't get justice;
Before a year passes we'll alter their note!

United Irish song, 'Granu's Lamentation', 1797

The 1790s marked a watershed in Irish history and set the pattern which has not yet been broken. But there was nothing inevitable about its legacy of militant Catholic nationalism, despite the intensity of the religious suspicion. The decade opened optimistically. The French Revolution, with its message of religious and political equality, temporarily eroded old antagonisms. The main outcome was the Society of United Irishmen, founded in 1791 in the belief that old religious fears were things of the past. In their enthusiasm for the French Revolution, elements of Protestant patriotism and Presbyterian radicalism formed what many considered an 'unnatural' alliance with the new middle-class leadership of the Catholic Committee, and together they embarked on the political education of the Catholic masses. In the space of a decade the Catholic populace was exposed to the full gamut of contemporary political thinking. But French-inspired republicanism and counter-revolution, superimposed on the attitudes analysed in previous chapters, and the outbreak of war between Britain and France in 1793, caused underlying tensions to explode. The United Irish ideal of creating 'the common name of Irishman in the place of the denominations of Protestant, Catholic and Dissenter' was still-born.[1]

1. Catholic political awareness prior to the 1790s

For much of the eighteenth century, Ulster Catholicism seemed quiescent and de-politicised. In the first decades its poets and clergy, particularly the bishops, were as Jacobite as elsewhere in Ireland. There were periodic reports of recruiting for the Pretender until 1745[2] and the Jacobitism of poets like MacCooey and Ó Doirnín is real enough. But

Jacobitism was weaker in Ulster, and in the Jacobite scare of 1726 fewer troops were posted to Ulster than anywhere else in the country.[3] The Ulster poetry reflects a sense that the battle has been lost and the Stuarts themselves were responsible for the destruction of the Gael. Forgetfulness has already set in by the 1730s and, by the 1750s, the Ulster bishops were in the forefront of the campaign to prove the Catholics loyal. The Gael must shift as well as he can in the new system.[4]

> We lost the Boyne through superior strength that day,
> . . . King James – a cowardly king who took to flight, . . .
> leaving nine-fold affliction on the poor Gaels.
>
> . . .
>
> and it's easy for the churls who didn't see that time
> to speak most severely about James' boys.[5]

Yet behind such apparent fatalism lay sullen resentment and a conspiratorial ethos which excluded the stranger. The subversive message of deliverance and victory over the foreigner remained long after the Jacobite cause had been defeated. The metaphor of the Gael as the chosen people in captivity ran through much of the poetry and even today Jacobite songs form part of the repertoire of traditional musicians.[6] Mac Cuarta's 'Lament for Sorley MacDonnell' seemed as relevant to the new age as it had been at the time. The new Moses might have changed through time – from the Stuarts to the French revolutionaries, from Bonaparte to Daniel O'Connell – but the old message remained the same.

The penalisation of Irish language and culture was a thing of the distant past and for much of the eighteenth century the Protestant gentry not only participated in traditional Irish pastimes but promoted a major revival. But its conspiratorial nature for the in-group is already a feature of the poetry.[7] The prophetic twentieth-century threat 'our day will come' has a long antecedent. In conversation with the Hill of Tara – ancient seat of the High Kings of Ireland – Ó Doirnín (d.1769) laments the fate of Ireland. Worry not, replies the Hill, 'if the prophesy of the saints who have gone is fulfilled' the foreigners will be 'vanquished forever by Gaels . . . the Pope's faith will be held by every high prince ... and Martin's children will be put up without a saddle or reins'.[8] The theme was stereotypical of many poems and was not a call to action. The most traditionally Irish parts of Ulster were not prominent in the 1798 rebellion. But the Ulster Catholic was anti-Protestant before he was nationalist. Where the two merged – as they did in the Defenders (though only in certain areas) – it was not always clear whether the *Gall* to be got rid of was English rule or their Protestant neighbours. There was a linear connection between *An Síogaí Rómhánach* and the Defender who told the trial judge in 1794 that he and his like expected to knock the Protestants on the head and replace them in positions of power.[9]

But the train of events which brought the Ulster Catholic to such active resistance was not at all straightforward. Even at the height of penalisation early in the century, the Catholic Church urged 'endurance' on its flock.[10] The history of the Ulster Catholics in the eighteenth century was neither one of resistance nor even of open defiance, but rather a withdrawal into themselves and a tendency to cling onto old practices and values.

Even so, there is not the rush to placate government and display their political loyalty which characterises the Catholic gentry and clergy in other parts of Ireland.[11] Ulster displays little of the Gallicanism which dominated the Catholic campaign for recognition as loyal subjects. Is it because Ulster Catholicism had retained its traditional ultramontanism when the general trend throughout Europe and the rest of Ireland ran against it? Certainly there is an element of this and, as in other poorer areas, traditions were slow to change in Catholic Ulster. Earlier in the century Archbishop MacMahon had successfully resisted publication of the papal bull *Unigenitus* (1713) – which, though technically against the Jansenist movement within French Catholicism, sought to establish unquestioning obedience to papal authority. In France the monarch's insistence on implementing *Unigenitus* was a disastrous misjudgement, setting in train an attack on church and monarchy which would culminate in the French Revolution. MacMahon's judgement was sound in resisting it. He argued against drawing unwelcome attention and giving the excuse to their enemies 'to give the impression, as they usually do, that an attempt is being made to overthrow the government'. Besides he thought it unnecessary since the Irish catholics are very submissive in matters of religion, and believe on good faith anything which they are told, has been decided upon . . . at Rome; so there is no need to make a formal publication of such things . . . a homely instruction . . . is sufficient; the catholics in Ireland believe that the faithful of the whole catholic world are united by the same beliefs and by submission to the Holy See and that there is no contradiction among them; the bishops let them live this way in their simplicity, and do not bring disputed points to their notice . . . in case they might scandalize them in their weakness and because any other approach might do harm to their faith.[12]

Such statements would seem to justify Protestant perceptions about Catholicism's tendency to mentally enslave. Even Presbyterian radical Dr William Drennan, though a good friend to the Catholics, thought it a religion of 'faith' and 'trust' rather than reason: 'For the restless power of reason, once introduced, brings in doubt' – so he mockingly told his sister. 'Trust like a Papist, for if you doubt as a Dissenter, the same restless faculty that rejects the Athanasian Creed . . . will begin to nibble at the Incarnation, the Miraculous Conception etc.' He was impatient at what he perceived as Catholics' 'milk and water spirit', their 'slovenliness of mind', their clannishness. But he also thought their group identity as Catholics gave them a unity lacking in other religions; and he admired their clergy's total independence from the state and found his own clergy wanting in comparison.[13]

Ulster Catholicism also displays that distrust of government and its agents found in all poor societies. Even as the penal laws were being repealed, large swathes of Ulster did not take the oath which would have allowed Catholics to benefit. The Catholic Qualification Oath of 1774 permitted Catholics to swear their allegiance to the existing monarch. It also contained clauses renouncing the Stuarts, denying the temporal power of the pope and the whole notion that he could absolve Catholics from their loyalty to heretic princes. The oath split both the church and the Catholic Committee. But when the first major relief act was passed in 1778 and it was clear that only those who had taken the oath could benefit, large numbers, clergy and laity alike, came forward to do so. The pattern of acceptance was greater in the more anglicised and prosperous counties, with particularly powerful group-ings in Dundalk and Drogheda (both in County Louth), respectable showings in Fermanagh and Antrim, but tapering to only seventy-six in Donegal. Indeed although Lord Abercorn wished to place his Catholic and Protestant tenants on the same footing after the relief measures, his agent reported reluctance to register on his Donegal lands. The numbers of clergy are also well below those elsewhere in the country: six priests and one bishop in Fermanagh,[14] nine in Monaghan, one in Donegal.[15] The depth of suspicion amongst the poorer Ulster Catholics finds expression in the McCrackens' trusty Catholic servant who mourned when her son went into the army (after the Catholic Relief Act of 1793 permitted Catholics to enlist), not because she was losing him 'but his taking the oath that's so much against him'.[16] In contrast, the next phase of oath-taking after the 1793 act – which returned the franchise to Catholics – witnessed a steep increase, with some 667 coming forward in Down alone (a token of the rapid politicisation of Ulster Catholics in the interim).[17]

The lower social status of Ulster Catholics may have accounted for the slow uptake in the 1770s. Certainly, few people in Ireland would have had any direct experience of politics before the 1760s. Until 1768, elections occurred only on the death of the monarch and contests were largely urban events. The higher percentage of Protestants gave Ulster the largest electorate in the country, with County Down the largest single constituency. How far the hotly contested elections impacted on Catholics – though ineligible to vote – is difficult to say. But the opposing electoral interests of the major landlords in Armagh, and their mobilisation of election mobs in the 1753 election was certainly a factor in the deteriorating situation in that county over the next few decades.[18] Here intense dislike of the many payments required by the established church had brought cross-denominational protests earlier in the century.[19] Then they were landlord inspired. By July 1763, however, the unusual independence of the Ulster tenantry was a matter for comment, and in the Oakboys they organised their own protest. Starting in the linen-producing districts of north Armagh, the protest rapidly spread to most of south and mid-Ulster and within a few weeks gentry and law officers were intimidated into concession. The beating of drums and blowing of horns 'their martial music' – such a feature of the 1753 election contest – had by now become something of a permanent feature of protest in Armagh.[20] MacCooey's hero, Art Óg

O'Neill, was an Oakboy captain, and the Oakboys became folk heroes in Gaelic poetry – even though they were predominantly Presbyterian.

In areas which would see some of the worst of the sectarian outbreaks after the 1790s, it is tempting to see the absence of sectarianism in the Oakboy disturbances as unusual. Certainly Catholic involvement in riot was not common, and may well have owed something to the shortage of priests following the suppression of the friaries and resultant weakening of social control. It may also reflect the early stages of politicisation. There was enough common ground, for tenants of all denominations had shared grievances.[21] From at least mid-century there was a greater invasiveness by authority in the social and economic life of the people. Rents were rising as leases fell in and landlords tried to capitalise on an expanding Ulster economy. Tithes were increased as clergy too tried to cope with rising costs and more efficient collection was creating widespread discontent. The government was becoming more active in collecting taxes and as early as 1752 Pococke reported poor people around Lough Swilley simply abandoning their makeshift houses on news of the approach of the hearth-money collector.[22] But acts in 1774 and 1779 forbidding distilling except in towns and refusing licences to smaller stills soon brought poorer Catholics into direct conflict with the authorities. The net effect was to make illegal one of the most pervasive elements in the economy of Catholic districts. Illicit whiskey was everywhere, widely believed by the common people to be something wholesome – and the increasing raids on illicit stills from this time on became part of popular folklore. As taxes increased into the 1790s, so government agents became more aggressive in their collection. Hearth-money collectors and excise officials were regularly accompanied by military and bloody clashes became a feature in the increasingly tense atmosphere of the 1780s and 1790s, particularly in south Ulster and the north midlands.[23]

But timing and local situation is everything and in some districts sectarianism never disappeared. Thus in 1762 when Lord Hillsborough was mobbed and the Lisburn market suspended, the linen weavers and manufacturers in neighbouring Lurgan protested at such activities having disgraced 'this Protestant civilised country'. And ten years later the exclusively Protestant Hearts of Steel in Magherally, County Down, rejected accusations that theirs was a popish plot. We are loyal subjects, they wrote to the editor of the *Belfast News Letter* and 'will, with our lives and properties, defend his majesty's person and government against the unjust attempts of all popish pretenders to the crown of these realms ... Not one Roman Catholic is ever suffered to appear amongst us.'[24] After nearly two decades of intermittent disturbance in Ireland, France sent the American Edward Bancroft in 1779 to investigate news of discontented Presbyterians and Catholics coming together. He reported that they appeared to be 'too divided by the difference of their religions to be too jealous one of the other and of the designs which they imagine that foreign powers could have upon them to be able to unite in friendship, or to risk taking up arms even to obtain satisfaction for their grievances'.[25]

2. *The Armagh Troubles*

For most of the eighteenth century, a *modus vivendi*, based on recognisably different spheres, maintained the peace between Protestant and Catholic in Ulster. Paradoxically it was the breaking down of demographic, cultural and most of all political divisions which sparked the conflict of the 1780s and 1790s. The dramatic rise of population, more than doubling in Ulster between 1750 and 1790, involved significant encroachment on the kind of poorer, upland territory so often occupied by Catholics. This was particularly noticeable in Armagh – the most densely populated county in Ireland – where the success of linen and vastly improved communications were opening up more remote areas to outsiders. Catholics were belatedly entering the commercial end of the linen market, and the sight of successful Catholics outbidding Protestants for land, was a particular affront to the plebeian ascendancy of the lower-class Protestant. Another leftover from the Ulster Plantation was the unusually large number of lower-class Anglicans in Armagh and neighbouring parts of Tyrone.[26] A rash of chapel-building around this time would have further contributed to the image of Catholics as more visible, confident and organised. Worse still was the sight of Protestant gentry espousing the cause of the Catholics.

So-called Protestant or 'colonial' nationalism – whereby Protestant politicians saw themselves as the Irish 'nation' defending its rights against the colonial power, with no recognition of the apparent contra-diction when Catholics, and to some extent Dissenters, were excluded from politics altogether – had been a feature of Irish politics since the beginning of the century. From the 1750s it had flowered as the 'patriot' movement, with Ulster politicians in particular perfecting an anti-Englishness which would have been inconceivable to future generations. When war broke out in 1775 between England and her American colonies (with whom Protestant Ulster had a particular affinity), the patriots armed themselves as the Volunteers, ostensibly to defend Ireland when most of the troops had been withdrawn for the American campaign. At first the landed gentry were apprehensive. Then, as so often in the future, they assumed leadership to assert control, and the lower-class Protestants who later joined were satisfied that the Volunteers were a further embodiment of the Protestant nation. The Volunteers had originated in Ulster, and as they increas-ingly became the patriots' major prop, Ulster became the fountainhead for the most extreme anti-government propaganda. For the first time large numbers of Ulster people were exposed to a campaign denounc-ing British rule in Ireland. The timing of this campaign ensured a larger audience for such ideas than ever before, for the war with America had closed the safety valve of emigration, and increased prosperity kept more at home thereafter.[27] The outcome was that thousands of younger, more turbulent men – who would normally have emigrated – remained in Ulster, and they included Catholics, for they too were now emigrating in large numbers.

The significance for Catholics of this upsurge in political activity, this Volunteer rhetoric about the rights of Irishmen, was not immedi-ately apparent, for the Volunteers were as ardently anti-papist as the early patriots. The process of repealing the penal laws had already begun – with two acts in the 1770s permitting Catholics to hold land on the same terms as Protestants. But they had been imposed by the London government and the opposition in the Irish parliament from MPs who were also Volunteers spoke volumes for the limits of their reformism. Although reforming Protestants outside parliament came to support the campaign for Catholic emancipation, the anti-popery of those inside increased apace over the next two decades. In this they represented the feelings of many Ulster Protestants, who viewed with mounting concern Catholics now competing with them on equal terms for increasingly scarce land. Catholics were theoretically excluded from the Volunteers, because the law banning them from carrying arms remained in force until 1793. The Ulster Volunteers had been the most reluctant to accept Catholics into their ranks. Even in Antrim – one of the more enlightened counties – no company had more than seven Catholics serving. Louth – with its significant Catholic propertied class – admitted Catholics as early as 1780. Derry, Donegal and Tyrone admitted small numbers as privates. But although the Loughgall Volunteers in Armagh publicly rejoiced at the relaxation of the penal laws and welcomed Catholics joining, none had been admitted by the end of 1784.[28]

In areas of traditional tension such as Armagh, the very suggestion that Catholics be admitted was enough to increase tensions. Some Armagh gentry had been taking a relaxed attitude to arming their Catholic tenants for general agricultural purposes. Protestants were offended at the sight of numbers taking the oath of allegiance during the assizes. How could these people whom they had long been told were disloyal be welcomed into the system? Prominent among those who first showed their displeasure by raiding Catholic homes was a disgruntled group of Protestant tenants from the Cope estates at Portnorris, attracted to Mayo to start the linen industry only to run into controversy because of their displacement of existing Catholic tenants. Irritants multiplied. Protestants began to disarm Catholics, claiming to be enforcing the penal laws. Petty juries acquitted those Protestants brought to trial in consequence, much to the horror of many gentry who rightly thought such biased justice would further inflame the situation. A heated exchange between the parish priest of Armagh and the Protestant minister of Benburb unleashed old bigotry, which in the more tolerant climate of the 1780s few would have publicly owned. Attacks began on Catholic chapels and services, although, as our main source for all these events, John Byrne, commented, attendance at high mass in Armagh had become a great treat for all denominations in recent years.

This indeed is what strikes most about the troubles in County Armagh: how quickly very localised feuds and insults escalated out of control, how quickly neighbour turned on neighbour. 'It was lamentable to see poor, quiet peasants, coming to Armagh, every day,' comments Byrne, 'with grief painted in the emaciated figure of a poor old man, making a complaint against his neighbour, with whom he lived in peace and quietness since the days of his nativity.' It was a sentiment echoed by the prominent Whig magnate and Volunteer commander-in-chief Lord Charlemont : 'How strange is the inconstancy of the people! A few years ago I was compelled . . . to prevent the Protestants from ruining themselves and their country by giving up all to the Papists; and now I am forced . . . to prevent them from cutting each others throats.'[29]

The religious and occupational geography of late eighteenth-century Armagh was quite distinctive. A flat northern part was the centre of the most lucrative end of the linen industry. Here the dominant group was Anglican, with only a sprinkling of Catholics. In the middle, south of Armagh City, and where the gentle rise of the land created that pleasant vista so admired by many travel writers, Protestants were still in the majority, but here Presbyterians and Catholics were more numerous – even though the combined total put Protestants marginally in the ascendancy. Moving towards the south of the county, the landscape changed dramatically, with a band of mountains, stretching south-west from Keady's 600 feet (200 metres) to Slieve Gullion's imposing 1,894 feet (630 metres). This was in every respect a cultural barrier, with Catholics increasing dramatically, until, as the mountains dropped, the parishes of Creggan, Forkhill and Jonesborough, at the other side of the barrier, were almost exclusively Catholic and largely Irish-speaking. However, the erection of the Freeduff meeting house in 1734 marked the early stages of sustained Presbyterian immigration into this traditional Catholic area. The tensions created formed the backdrop to the Armagh troubles of the 1780s and 1790s.[30]

The troubles, which by 1785 had produced the Catholic Defenders and Protestant Peep O'Day Boys, had built on localised faction fights and party parades over the past two decades. Parading to Anglican or Presbyterian church services, in full military regalia, had been a particular feature of Volunteering, as had its public celebration of William of Orange. The map of the spread of the troubles reveals incidents radiating out from areas of mixed settlement (the Portnorris malcontents prominent in the second wave of 1786–7).[31] Outsiders were then attracted to the scene. By all accounts lower-class Protestants were the original aggressors. But very soon the Catholics returned like for like. Boycotts of traders of the opposing religion (by both Defenders and Peep O' Day Boys) extended the circle of malcontents. Parades and social events became factionalised. Fights at fairs increased. New regiments of Volunteers were raised on a purely Protestant basis. Neighbours began to withdraw goodwill from those of the opposite religion. Converts and those in mixed marriages became particular targets of Protestant rancour, and swaggering youths were to the fore in deliberately provocative actions. On Sunday 21 November 1788, one of the new, more lower-class Volunteer companies from Benburb marched to church at Armagh along the Eglish road. They planned to return by another road. However, their anti-papist comments and provocative drum-beating drew insults from Catholic countrywomen along the outward route. To avenge the insults of the morning, the Volunteers stocked up on arms and additional drums in Armagh and returned by the same route, 'playing tunes ['The Protestant Boys' and 'The Boyne Water'] which were an insult to Catholics'. Moderate negotiators failed to calm the young hotheads. At Drumbee stones were thrown, the Volunteers fired and two Catholics, one a Defender, were killed. Their funerals then became occasions for major shows of Defender strength and the following Sunday the Volunteers (reinforced by ex-soldiers from the American war) marched along the same road and cheered at the spot where the Catholics were killed. And so the situation rippled out of control, gathering pace as it spread farther afield.

By 1789 the troubles had reached more traditional Catholic territory in south Armagh and south Down. That year the traditional Drumban-agher pattern on St John's Eve was attacked by Peep O' Day Boys and Volunteers, and there were attacks on priests and chapels around Tanderagee and Portadown. The Defenders were already well-organised around Creggan, while at Forkhill an attack on the Prot-estant rector, Edward Hudson, was followed some days later by the destruction of the vestments and chalice in the Catholic chapel. This was Ó Doirnín and MacCooey territory and the language used by the Defenders suggests that old scores and historical grievances were fundamental to the escalating conflict.[32]

The landlord of Carrive and Forkhill had been attracting Protestant tenants on to wasteland which the Catholics had long thought their own. The same landlord left a hornets' nest in his will endowing Protestant missionaries in the area. It was rumoured that the will stated that 'whenever a Papist's lease was expired, that they should be banished their rocky habitations, and Protestants reinstated into the land of their fathers'.[33] The people were still largely Irish-speaking in these mountainous districts, and the situation was further enflamed by the replacement of an Irish-speaking schoolteacher in Forkhill – who had undertaken to teach forty children 'popish prayers' in Irish – by Alexander Barkely, the brother-in-law of an unpopular magistrate who was held responsible for the execution of a local Defender. On the night of 28 January 1791, Barkely and his family became the victims of the mounting tension in south Armagh. A group of Catholics, including the brother of the executed Defender, broke into his house and mutilated and cut out the tongues of himself and his family – wounds from which his wife later died. It was an act reminiscent of 1641, and in the years which followed the old belief that Catholics were out to massacre Protestants fuelled an upsurge in militant loyalism.

Virulent sectarian warfare was now sweeping south Ulster and north Leinster. Most contemporary accounts of the Armagh Troubles blamed the magistrates and local gentry for failing to nip them in the bud. Certainly contagion was prevented from spreading to neighbouring areas of Tyrone because of the impartiality of its gentry and clergy. The Armagh gentry were not at first partisan, though their Protestant tenants clearly expected them to be so, and those showing favour to the Defenders became particular objects of attack. But the petty juries consistently acquitted Peep O' Day Boys and convicted Defenders. And with landlord control challenged by both sides, it was all too easy to accept the invitation of the ultra-Protestants as a way of restoring control, at least over this section of the tenantry. Such a tendency was further prompted by the post-1793 war crisis and escalating domestic subversion. Ultimately many leading gentry added their weight to the unplanned, but ultimately welcome, graduation of armed loyalism from Peep O' Day Boyism to Orangeism.[34]

By now Armagh's sectarian troubles had spilled into Down, Louth,

Monaghan and parts of Tyrone, and a pitched battle between Defenders from all these areas and Peep O' Day Boys took place at the Diamond, near Loughgall, on 21 September 1795. The Defenders were routed and 'on the field of action' the victors drew up plans for 'a defensive association of Protestants', their resolution 'in no small degree excited by men . . . of very advanced age who had in the early period of their lives lived with those who . . . had been partakers in the War of the Revolution of 1688 and who had heard from the lips of those patriarchs of the Boyne and Aughrim of the sufferings which had driven them to the field in arms'.[35] The following 12 July Orangemen paraded through Lord Gosford's demesne at Markethill, where a decade earlier armed Catholic tenants had guarded his orchards. Gosford was the area's leading magistrate, and had been a friend to the Catholics. But increasingly Catholics felt they could expect little from the law. At least that is what the United Irish propaganda machine now told them, and Catholic refugees from these sectarian disturbances were singled out for their particular attention.

> A lamentable story dear people I'll tell you,
> That happened in Armagh this very last year;
> The landlord combined, with others they joined,
> To plunder and rob us of all we held dear:
> For as we were Catholics they vow'd to oppress us,
> Because at elections we had not a vote;
> But by St Patrick, as we can't get justice;
> Before a year passes we'll alter their note!
>
> The jails they are filled with your nearest relations,
> Your wives and your children are sorely oppressed;
> Your houses are burned, your lands desolated,
> By a band of ruffians with Orange cockades.
>
> The clergy and landlords they have oppressed you,
> Because that poor Ireland they wished to keep slaves;
> They bribed your own neighbours to ruin your labours,
> says they 'you are Papists, and so must be knaves'.[36]

When threatening notices signed 'Oliver Cromwell' were affixed to Catholics' homes, ordering them to quit or be burnt out, most chose to leave without question. Thousands of Catholics were thus intimidated out of Armagh and Down during 1795 and 1796, usually moving to known Catholic districts elsewhere. In 1945 Thomas Mulholland told of how his great-grandfather had thus fled from their ancestral home in Rich Hill, County Armagh, to Rostrevor in County Down. Later Donegal nationalist and writer, Seamas MacManus, told a similar story of his family fleeing to Donegal from Armagh. Others went as far as Tipperary, where they were still referred to as 'Oultachs' and still spoke 'Ulster Irish' in the twentieth century.[37] These so-called 'Armagh Outrages' sent hordes of Catholics into the United Irishmen. The government was fully aware of the possible consequences of thus alienating loyal Catholics and sought at first to curb such attacks by preventing provocative Orange marches.[38] But increasingly its emergency counter-insurgency measures seemed to give countenance to United Irish claims that such attacks on Catholics had government sanction. Certainly the United Irishmen later attributed the upturn in its membership to the Armagh Outrages. There can be no doubt that their alliance with the Defenders was made good that year as the United Irishmen mounted a major recruiting drive among the Catholics.[39]

The sectarian disturbances in Armagh were to set the tone for future politics in Ulster. But at the outset they were highly unusual and spread only to similar cultural frontier zones such as south-west Down. Here recognisably Protestant and Catholic territories abutted, and clashes between Defenders and Peep O' Day Boys prompted a joint Catholic Committee-United Irish peacekeeping mission in 1792. They were told, by the Whig peer, Lord Moira, among others, of how the notorious anti-popery of some of the local gentry was creating the image of biased authority. The main landlord (Lord Annesley) in the worst-affected area around Rathfriland and Castlewellan, was widely held to be 'a mere brute' with a 'trick of knocking down the Catholics on the roads or wherever he meets them for his amusement'. The Defenders could expect little mercy from him at the assizes, for he would always find another charge even against those acquitted. His naked sectarianism was a worry to the authorities – still at this stage convinced that the Catholics were infinitely more loyal than the Presbyterians. But Annesley was not alone. Lord Downshire – governor of County Down, head of the Hill family and one of the most powerful magnates in Ulster – shared his anti-popery and was noted too for his intense dislike of the Presbyterians. He had been barely civil to the Catholic Committee delegates and made no secret of his belief that they and the illegal Defenders were one and the same. They had more support from Catholic leaders, like the O'Neills of Banvale and the O'Hanlons of Newry, and the priests undertook to read out statements urging calm on the Defenders. But opposition from the Protestant gentry ensured a hostile reception when they returned in the autumn.[40]

Downshire was not representative of the gentry even in Ulster – many of whom supported the Catholic case for total repeal of the penal laws – and the hostility between such Anglican magnates and the Presbyterians was an additional factor in the latter's espousal of the Catholics' cause. But Downshire did speak for a large number of the most influential people in the country, who now increasingly defined themselves as a 'Protestant Ascendancy'. Although the London government was in favour of Catholic relief, each new measure had to be wrenched from the Dublin parliament which made its opposition known in increasingly strident terms.

3. The United Irishmen and the education of public opinion

Given traditional Catholic teaching on subordination and deference to authority, the hierarchy's gradualist approach had dominated Catholic Committee dealings with government since its formation in the 1760s. But to a new breed of middle-class Catholic leader educated into the politics of 'natural rights', such traditional deference increasingly looked like grovelling. In 1791 these had finally replaced the conservative gentry at the head of the Catholic Committee in a widely publicised coup, and thereafter conducted an aggressively radical campaign for Catholic emancipation. The new mood among these middle-class Catholics was the backdrop to the formation of the United Irish Society, for it had been the belief that Catholics were not yet ready for admission to political life which had split the reformers in the 1780s.

Certainly this was a key theme of Tone's *Argument on Behalf of the Catholics of Ireland* of 1791. It was largely directed at the northern Presbyterians, since their reservations about the Catholics had prevented the inauguration of the Society of United Irishmen the preceding summer. It argued that Protestants were themselves victims of unscrupulous governments because their fear of Catholics was the ultimate deterrent to reform. The government knew it and played upon it. Protestants had denied Catholics education, then complained of their ignorance; persecuted their religion, then wondered why they drew together with their priests; and having shut off every avenue of improvement, they then claimed that they were incapable of liberty. 'We plead our crime in justification of itself.' Proclaiming the *Rights of Man* and the downfall of tyranny sat uneasily with the degradation of three million Catholics. The choice was clear : they must admit the Catholics into their demands for reform, or abandon it altogether.[41]

Such fears Tone saw as based on stereotypes, and he dismissed each in turn. He might have found them more difficult to dismiss had he examined lower-class Catholic culture, with its pervasive resentment. But this as yet had found no political outlet and he was right in his assessment of the propertied and middle-class Catholics, who would have repaid their re-admission to political rights by bringing their brethren with them, rather than giving a head to that resentment. Their 'weapons', commented Tone, were still those of 'constitutional loyalty', even if 'sulky' and 'complaining'. Such was the topicality of the issue that Tone's pamphlet became an instant bestseller. However, since the stereotyped Catholic was as alive in Ulster Protestant imagination at the end of the twentieth century as it was in the eighteenth, it should be no surprise that Tone continued to encounter it. His journals recount 'a furious battle' at a private dinner in Belfast, where the Whig reformers (mostly Presbyterians alike with those setting up the United Irish Society) stated their objections to Catholic emancipation :

1st. Danger to true religion, inasmuch as the R[oman] C[atholics] would, if emancipated, establish an inquisition. 2nd. Danger to property by reviving the Court of Claims . . . to substantiate Catholic titles. 3rd. Danger, generally, of throwing the power into their hands, which would make this a Catholic government, incapable of enjoying or extending liberty ... Sad nonsense about scavengers becoming members of Par[liamen]t &c.[42]

But the newly radicalised Catholic leaders were just as suspicious of the Presbyterians. Tone's gentle mocking of their mutual suspicions, during a historic visit of the former to Belfast in 1792, makes for amusing reading. But the suspicions were never entirely removed. The bulk of the rural Catholic populace did not join the United Irish Society until after 1796, when fears of Orangeism drove them to the only other body likely to provide protection. Although the northern United Irish Society would remain largely Presbyterian, and had a significant presence among Presbyterians in the Laggan area of east Donegal, outside Antrim and Down lower-class Presbyterians commonly became Orangemen, reinforcing traditional Catholic suspicion of Presbyterians generally.[43]

Once again, the religious geography of Ulster is crucial to understanding what happened in the 1790s. In areas of ancient animosities the alliance between Dissenter and Catholic was weaker, though even here it rather depended on which form of Presbyterianism prevailed. South Ulster in particular witnessed a dramatic spread of revivalist evangelicalism in the 1790s, the anti-Catholicism of the Methodists noticeably to the fore.[44] The different varieties of Presbyterianism also had different perceptions of the Catholics. The 'New Light' Presbyterians were concentrated in the wealthiest areas and in the towns, particularly Belfast. These were the more radical and libertarian, who believed in freedom of conscience and dominated the early United Irishmen. But the Seceders and Covenanters – who were more rigidly Calvinist and anti-papist – were more likely to be lower class and resident in those areas like south Armagh and west Down, where Catholics were perceived as a threat. They more than doubled their congregations towards the end of the century.[45] That some, nevertheless, found their way into the 1798 rebellion has been explained in terms of a peculiarly Presbyterian form of millenarianism which would have been just as exclusive as the anti-Protestant variety which propelled many rural Catholics into it.[46]

The message of the Catholic clergy throughout the 1790s remained the traditional one of non-involvement in politics and the number of

Ulster priests caught up in the 1798 rebellion was the lowest in the country.[47] In a telling statement Archbishop Troy denounced the idea of state payment of priests as holding out a 'danger that the people would become Presbyterians, Methodists or politicians'.[48] The Catholic Church had good reason to fear the United Irishmen, for they actively spread Presbyterian belief in the primacy of individual conscience and an end to priestcraft. 'The Catholics of Ireland', proclaimed the United Irish newspaper the *Northern Star,* 'are now beginning to look to the position of free men and cast away that indolent disposition which tied up their senses and made them insensible as it were of their debasement.'[49] That newspaper's satirical column, 'Billy Bluff and the Squire', has the Catholic priest proposing the toast: '*Every man his own road to Heaven.*'[50] The Catholic hierarchy had always argued a natural affinity between Catholicism, a naturally hierarchical and conservative religion, and the *status quo* – an argument which the London government had largely conceded by 1793. Eighteenth-century Catholic culture may have aspired to a Catholic victory, but it was not particularly anti-government and was entirely antithetical to the notions of democracy and individual rights unleashed by the French Revolution. Indeed, early overtures from the United Irishmen to the Defenders seem to have foundered for this reason. The Defenders 'looked to France, in the earlier period of her Republic, with a two-fold feeling of alarm, alike regarding the invasion of the altar and the throne . . .' wrote Charles Teeling, one of the architects of the union between the two movements. 'Indeed, they rather prided themselves, as being the descendants of men, whose devotion to monarchy had long been proverbial; though their fidelity was badly requited!'[51] How then can we explain the rapid radicalisation of the Catholic populace and its almost total alienation from government as a result?

The Volunteer movement had become split on the issue of further Catholic reforms. But a sizeable element in Ulster (including Armagh) continued to espouse the principle. There was a long tradition of suspicion of government in Ulster Presbyterianism and its attempt to kill reform by playing upon religious divisions was all too obvious. The belief that the mass of Catholics were still in thrall to a tyrannical religion, unthinking and as yet 'unfit for liberty', held many advanced reformers back. It was the more benign wing of a very general Protestant fear of 'popery'. But the dismantling of Catholic absolutism in France and the religious tolerance of the early French revolutionaries caused many to rethink such traditional stereotypes. If the government would not change, then, as in France, the reformers would bring the weight of the people into the fray. The United Irish Society was formed in 1791 'for the promotion of constitutional knowledge, the abolition of bigotry in religion and politics, and the equal distribution of the rights of man through all sects and denominations of Irishmen'. It saw its role first and foremost as creator and educator of public opinion, and to do so it brought together one of the most formidable gatherings of talent in Irish history.[52] Although the tactic of mobilising traditionally unpoliticised sectors of the populace had already begun with the Volunteers and the Anglo-Irish 'patriots' of the previous decade, the scale and character of the United Irish propaganda machine was quite unprecedented and it impacted on a Catholic populace just emerging into political awareness and experiencing the greatest surge of Catholic literacy that century.

The United Irishmen fostered an explosion of print, subsidising key texts like Paine's *Rights of Man*, Tone's *Argument*, Butler's *Digest of Popery laws*, which were run off in tens of thousands, many United Irishmen exhausting private fortunes in the process. 'Such writers were extensively put into the hands of the people', Henry Cooke later testified; 'it was very common to drop them on the road, and leave them at the door of the poor man, or push them under the door.'[53] The Catholic Committee's nationwide elections – based on the organisational unit of the parish – set a precedent. United Irish broadsheets were affixed to chapel doors or nailed to nearby trees. Handbills were distributed to mass-goers and United Irish newspapers read to huddled groups after the service. The United Irishmen capitalised on that traditional reverence for the printed word and the learned man so notable among the rural Irish. Most of the society's declarations were printed as handbills, in simple language which made the most sophisticated political ideas accessible to the common man.[54]

Their main propaganda weapon was song and satire, both threading through the reports from Europe, the letters, the polemical editorials, the serialised radical works which were the standard fare of the enormously popular *Northern Star* newspaper. Established in Belfast at the end of 1791 by that same group of middle-class Presbyterians which had set up the Society of United Irishmen some weeks earlier, the newspaper became the society's main mouthpiece till its suppression in 1797. It was frequently distributed *gratis*, and its popularity so worried the government that it hounded its printers and proprietors and gave free licence to a number of military attacks on its offices. 'At every cabin around us you will see them reading the *Northern Star* (a paper which has sharpened them all for rebellion)', commented an English visitor to Ulster in 1797, 'and I often meet Sir John's labourers walking to work, and reading this paper as they move along.'[55] It utilised every aspect of popular culture which could be turned to propaganda purposes. Its songs were set to popular tunes, so that the most common-place came to have the kind of double, subversive meaning so beloved of the poorer people; and their popularity is attested by the frequent re-issue of the United Irishmen's most notable song collection, *Paddy's Resource*. 'They dispersed liberty-songs composed for an Irish climate', complained one Protestant minister from the Armagh–Tyrone border.[56] And so they did: songs in the Scots dialect for the Presbyterians, songs that used the themes and style of Gaelic verse for the Catholics. The United Irish leaders shared the enthusiasm for the patriotic antiquarianism of the 1780s which produced Charlotte Brooke's influential *Reliques of Irish Poetry* (1789). But they ignored (if indeed they recognised) the strident sectarianism of the Ulster poetry and instead they told of Ireland's ancient glories, when freedom prevailed, until treachery and disunity let the 'foreigner' in.[57]

At first the pro-French songs spoke of abstract rights, of equality versus tyranny, of the cause of the French being the cause of mankind. But increasingly – particularly as the war crisis after February 1793 brought repression and economic hardship – the songs identified with the plight of the poor. By 1797 – as the military clampdown intensified – the theme of Ireland as 'Granu' or the 'Shan Van Vocht', a suffering old woman, prophesying help from overseas, became more common. Thus did the United Irishmen erode the Catholics' traditional deference and direct their vague sense of grievance to the entire structure of government.

Typical of such tactics was the skit 'Billy Bluff and Squire Firebrand', which first appeared as pseudo-letters in the *Northern Star* (May to

December 1796). It was published as a pamphlet that same year and freely distributed among the peasantry. The liberal Presbyterian divine, the Revd Henry Montgomery (1788–1865) recalled the peasantry of south Antrim committing it to memory and such was its popularity that it was still being reprinted in 1840. It was this kind of propaganda which helped reduce traditional Catholic suspicion of the Presbyterians. The writer 'A Presbyterian' or 'R' – in reality the Revd James Porter, Presbyterian minister of Grey Abbey (County Down) – is worried that he will be prosecuted for shaking hands with a priest, because his neighbour Squire Firebrand has ordered his tenant Billy Bluff to spy on him. Firebrand and his immediate superior Lord Mountmumble were satires on the Earl of Londonderry and the magistrate and agent the Revd John Cleland. The two were prime movers in the campaign against the United Irishmen in north Down and through them Porter represented the entire Ascendancy, on which the government relied, as stupid and intolerant. Firebrand is scandalised by the idea that Presbyterians and Catholics might sink their old animosities. The new rights granted to the Catholics were upsetting his notions of the proper ordering of society, for R was encouraging them to register their freeholds [i.e. to vote, after the 1793 Catholic Relief Act restored the franchise to Catholics] 'filling their head full of notions and setting them all a thinking'.

D — m thinking, Billy, 'tis putting the world mad. O, what a happy world we had before men turned their thoughts to thinking! Catholics thought nothing but just getting leave to live, and working for their meat; Presbyterians thought of nothing but wrangling about religion and grumbling about tithes; and Protestants thought of nothing but doing and saying what their betters bid them; and the gentlemen thought of nothing but drinking and the game laws. O! how times are changed, and all for the worse. Your Catholic college – your Catholic schools – your Catholic emancipation . . . your book societies, your pamphlets . . . all turning the people's head and setting them a thinking about this, that, and t'other.

And as for those songs – and the whistling of them was even worse – his own tenants were singing them and ballad-singers were carrying baskets full of handbills and seditious tunes. A poor Catholic, Bryan

O'Carolin, whose home had been burnt and son murdered by Orangemen, came to seek justice from the Squire, but was subjected instead to a torrent of perverted reasoning such as could have come from Voltaire's mock-philosopher Dr Pangloss. 'Did you resist?' asks the Squire. 'We did, please your Worship,' answers Bryan. 'You resisted, that is, you defended. Are you a Defender? I would like to defend myself. I thought so. I am sorry you come under the act against Defenderism. Let me see again; you had firearms and you are a Catholic? Worse and worse. I am sorry Bryan, I must commit you; my duty demands it as a Magistrate.'

The series ends – like the many heroic tales so beloved of the eighteenth-century public – with a moral. R is damned by the Squire for his 'reading, and thinking, and talking, and planning'. 'I make use of plain understanding, Sir, and compare the promises of the GREAT with their performances . . . when their own wickedness has brought them into danger . . . they throw the blame on the innocent and unoffending, should they dare to complain.' F: 'You drink with the priest . . . And yet you are a Presbyterian . . . And your fathers persecuted the Catholics . . . And now you are friends . . . D-n-n to such friendship, so new, so unexpected, so *unnatural*!' R: 'They persecuted each other . . . we are wiser than our ancestors . . . our absurd dissensions were the cause of our national poverty, ignorance, degradation, and slavery.'[58]

The early success of United Irish tactics was remarkable. The outbreak of war with France in 1793 met with almost immediate grumbling from ordinary people, and soon they were refusing to pay their debts in expectation of some major upheaval. Thomas Russell was told that the

great majority of the people [were] in favor of the French in the mountains [of Cavan, Fermanagh and Leitrim] where you could not conceive that any news could reach . . . Know of the abolition of tythes in France and infer therefrom. Few republican. Fond of the King. Hate the gover[n]ment. Angry at the King's ent[e]ring into war agains[t] France. Strong for reform.[59]

It is an extraordinary mixture of sentiments which Russell's informant attributes to these mountain people, who would almost certainly have been Catholic, and his information almost perfectly mirrors the conflicting messages of Defender oaths. It is the hatred of government which is so new and it was not simply the outcome of United Irish propaganda. Such hatred started with the public exposure of the depth of anti-popery in the top echelons of government. It had always been there. But the general body of Catholics would have been unaware of it. As the penal laws were gradually repealed, it became more strident, particularly since repeal was evidently being forced on Irish politicians by the British government. And both the reconstituted Catholic Committee and the United Irish Societies – there was common leadership – had a vested interest in disseminating information about their resistance. Thus were the bitter parliamentary debates on the Catholic Relief Bills of 1792 and 1793 publicised as never before.

4. The Catholic Convention, 1792–3

Ireland was unfortunate to have been governed by a succession of weak Lord Lieutenants in one of the most crucial decades in its history. As a result, the opinions of her ultra-Protestant officials at Dublin Castle came to prevail, and British rule in Ireland was tarred with their prejudices, even though they were unrepresentative of Protestant political opinion as a whole. It was the Catholic Committee's interference and perceived threat to Protestant social control which had so incensed men like Downshire and Annesley in the summer of 1792. But in demanding the traditional submissiveness from the Catholic Committee the Irish government miscalculated the public mood. Initially the credibility of the Catholic gentry and prelates with their people was severely damaged and there is a noticeable turning away from the leadership of the priests in these years. Tone feared 'that the Catholic clergymen are bad friends to liberty'. But he noted that when the parish priest of Saintfield preached against the United Irishmen and warned his parishioners not to join, he was publicly rebuked in his chapel by one of the congregation.[60] The Catholic Committee and United Irishmen were providing defence lawyers (and very often material help) to the families of arrested Defenders, and in a masterly publicity campaign in the summer of 1792, the Catholic Committee effectively became the real director of Catholic opinion in the country.[61]

In the 1792 Irish parliamentary session – in which London sought to have a bill passed to extend to Irish Catholics concessions recently made to their English co-religionists – petitions in favour of the Catholics were treated with an unprecedented contempt, and insults were showered upon the Catholic Committee. In response the Committee launched a country-wide election (based on the principle of universal manhood suffrage – a revolutionary departure), which would copper-fasten its truly representative character. Members were to be elected for each town and county to sit on the existing Dublin Committee. The whole body of 233 would then meet in a Convention in Dublin to draw up a petition to the King. The Catholic parish was the base unit of organisation for the election. Committee members had stumped the country that summer, drumming up support and flooding it with propaganda. There had been a split in the Committee the previous year, with a number of clergy and gentry (particularly from Munster) seceding. This was now mended. However, the Catholic bishops and gentry largely shared government distaste for the radicals and were to spend most of the rest of the decade recalling Catholics to their old habits of deference.

The elections and Convention (meeting but a short walk away from the Irish Parliament building) were perceived as a threat to the whole structure of government as it had existed since the 1690s. But the strident anti-popery which had informed it sounded out of place in the new mood of the 1790s and only served to further discredit government in the eyes of Catholics. Commencing with the Grand Jury of London-derry, grand juries throughout the country proclaimed the Convention a threat to 'Protestant Ascendancy'. The attacks (and the continued insistence of the Castle on traditional submissiveness) incensed the Catholic delegates and gave the radicals an unusual (though short-lived) victory. The Convention decided to go over the heads of the Dublin administration and make a direct plea to the King for complete emancipation. The delegates chosen to take the petition travelled via Belfast, pushing home the message that the 'Ascendancy' could no longer rule by dividing. Here the leading Convention member from Ulster (Luke Teeling) had forged a close working alliance with the

United Irishmen and it was he who had argued the case for demanding total emancipation. En route through the town, the Catholic delegates were greeted by supporters, who insisted on removing the horses from their carriages and drawing them over the bridge across the River Lagan. 'To those who looked beyond the surface, it was an interesting spectacle', commented Tone, '... to see the Dissenter of the North drawing, with his own hands, the Catholic of the South in triumph through what may be denominated the capital of Presbyterianism.'[62]

That the Convention members endorsed such radical action was a symptom of how far they had been goaded by government. But it was out of character. Fewer than thirty of its members can be identified as United Irishmen and Tone would later fume at their docile acceptance of the partial concessions of the 1793 act. Two of the Ulster representatives, Edmund McGildowney of Ballycastle, County Antrim, and Owen O'Callaghan of Cullaville, County Armagh, would have been typical – successful entrepreneurs, anxious to participate in the establishment rather than overturn it. Both were to hold public office soon after the 1793 act permitted them to do so. The Ulster county representatives reveal a high level of participation by old families: Philip, Constantine and Terence Maguire for County Fermanagh, John O'Neill, Hugh and Thomas Savage and John Magennis for County Down, Terence O'Neill of Ballybawley, Tyrone and a number of McLaughlins and McShanes for Donegal and Derry. Only in Antrim and Down did Convention members later emerge as republican leaders. One of the three representatives of County Antrim was Luke Teeling, linen bleacher and wine merchant in Lisburn, whose influence also extended into Down, Armagh and Louth. He was the richest and most prominent Catholic in Ulster and his son, Charles, was treated with considerable deference by Lord Castlereagh, even as he was in the process of arresting him. Luke Teeling was already in close contact with the Belfast United Irish leaders in 1792 (though he never became a member) and his family (particularly his two sons Bartholomew and Charles) were to play a central role in republican organisation in Ulster. John Magennis, also a successful linen dealer, and a representative for County Down in the Convention, was Teeling's son-in-law, and with the youthful Charles Teeling was instrumental in bringing the Defenders into alliance with the United Irishmen.[63]

In north Down and most of Antrim (including Belfast) relations between Catholic and Dissenter were good, and Down would become the strongest United Irish county in the country. The county had produced the most advanced Presbyterian supporters of Catholic political rights during the 1780s, even after their co-religionists elsewhere were beginning to pull back, and the many chapels erected during these years – Belfast, Lisburn, Dromore, Saintfield, Ballynahinch, Saul, Ballee, Portaferry – were all built with substantial Protestant, and particularly Presbyterian, assistance.[64] Sectarian tensions would weaken the movement almost everywhere else in Ulster and provide government with its most important informers. But it was the perceived spinelessness and 'popery' of some of the Dublin-based Catholics in the United leadership which turned a Newry Presbyterian and United Irishman, Samuel Turner, into an informer. The Teeling brothers he appears to have respected, sharing their militancy and mistrust of the Dublin moderates, whom he accused of betraying the Ulstermen.

The Catholic delegates were favourably received in London and many believed that full emancipation would be forthcoming. War was declared between England and revolutionary France in February 1793 and, in a sharp exchange with the Dublin government, ministers in London insisted on concession to the Catholics. A Catholic Relief bill was forced through the Irish Parliament on Britain's instructions, but traditional government supporters made no secret of their distaste – and this at a time when anti-popery was very much on the decline, and when a Catholic reading public now took note. All the old stereotypes of Catholics being incapable of loyalty to a Protestant power were raked up, prominent government supporters taking a lead in the accusations. The most vociferous attack came from Dr Patrick Duigenan, Judge in the Prerogative Court, who, although (or perhaps because) he had been twice married to Catholics and had a Catholic mother, plundered history to show the Catholics as incorrigible traitors, whose real objects were 'power and the recovery of the forfeited estates'.[65] A riposte from the Catholic hierarchy denying such accusations only worsened matters. The upshot was the imposition of yet another Catholic loyalty oath requiring any Catholic wishing to benefit from the new concessions to deny papal infallibility and recognise the Protestant establishment in property and politics.

Certainly the concessions were substantial: the franchise was restored, civil and military offices opened up (with some exceptions); Catholics could now take degrees at Dublin University and, most controversial of all, could carry arms, subject to a property qualification and the taking of the new oath of allegiance. But the concessions were permissive rather than obligatory and a newly awakened Protestant Ascendancy chose as often as not to withhold them. As late as 1836 a government report on municipal corporations found that no Catholic had ever been a member of Bangor corporation, its provost, seemingly unaware of the 1793 change in the law, still thinking that only Protestants qualified.[66] Moreover the withholding of the right to sit in parliament, having granted everything else, seemed petty and was interpreted by the newly politicised Catholic populace as final proof that the existing government was their natural enemy. That year – one torn by an escalating crisis and riots against the embodiment of a new militia – demonstrated more than ever before that even lower-class Catholics had renounced the time-old Catholic principle of patience and endurance. Indeed, reports from Donegal told of a turning away from the priests – one was even accused of being a Protestant for advising subordination.[67] The local elections to the Catholic Convention had particularly unnerved Protestants in areas of ongoing sectarian tension and a new 'insolence' among lower-class Catholics was being reported.[68] 'The clergy, who formerly misled the minds of the Catholic body', wrote Leonard McNally, United Irishman and Dublin Castle's most talented spy, in December 1794, 'have within a few years lost all influence over the better sort and retain very little authority over the lower classes.' He held the distribution of Thomas Paine's works by the northern United Irishmen responsible. 'One consequence of these publications is a strong union between the better classes of Papists and Dissenters. They have been brought to think alike.'[69]

5. Defenderism

Defenderism was the prototype for the pervasive secret societies which were to become so common in Ireland in the next century. It reflected the communal values of its locality, its bitter anti-Protestantism in its south Ulster/north Leinster heartland, shading into more agrarian concerns in Munster and Connacht (where it was generally weaker) and more political ones in United Irish strongholds. Its mix of oaths and sign language gave its members a sense of importance and belonging at a time of major dislocation. In this it had much in common with freemasonry, which was everywhere in late eighteenth-century Ireland, as it was elsewhere in Europe. But its stated aims seemed so contradictory and nonsensical that they baffled the government of the day, as they have done so many later commentators. They are entirely comprehensible, however, if we remember that Defenderism flourished in a deeply conservative, semi-literate (sometimes illiterate) society, where the values expressed in the oral poetry were widely shared, and where the intensification of sectarian attacks by Peep O' Day Boys and Orangemen would have unleashed existing undercurrents of anti-Protestantism. Just like the poetry, so in Defender oaths, Biblical imagery is mixed with the idea of deliverance, of the restoration of 'the true religion ['the true Catholic church'] . . . lost at the reformation', of obtaining the conditions of Limerick, of help from France. But there is confusion in the nature of that assistance and the end to be achieved. The very many references to French revolutionary symbols and institutions, to fraternity and equality, to pulling down 'the British laws', show that the significance of post-1789 events and ideas have made an impact. Against this, however, is the apparently contradictory belief that the Stuarts were somehow involved, for it is the Stuart 'duke of York [who] will save us', and an apparent allegiance to the British monarchy. The Monaghan-born Gaelic League scholar Énri Ó Muirgheasa (Henry Morris) collected the following song in the Rosses of Donegal, where it was and has remained popular:

> Oh rise up you finest of men
> and put a pike on top of every shaft,
> strike them down, the evil-hearted ones,
> and establish French law.
>
> And O woman of the house, what's your trouble? . . .
> we'll have land without rent from this year forth;
> . . .

the Duke of York has army enough,
the Frenchman and the Spaniard are on the seashore[70]

However, Charles Teeling later denied that the Defenders were highly politicised or revolutionary at this stage – and he should have known as he was to play a lead role in their political education – arguing that they had retained the largely defensive role of their origins.[71] Certainly the often incongruous language of Defender oaths and statements bears the hallmark of Carleton's part-educated rustic, impressing his compatriots with high-sounding phrases and snippets of Latin. His own account of being sworn in 1814 into the Ribbonmen (the new name for Defenderism) could have applied equally in the 1790s. Ribbonism, like Defenderism, like the United Irishmen, were societies of young men. Peer pressure made it difficult (and at times positively dangerous) not to belong. The nineteen-year-old Carleton noticed a certain coolness among his acquaintances as he failed to respond to their signs and passwords. Eventually, at an open-air dance, and in between several glasses of poteen, he found himself and many more young men sworn in by Hugh Roe McCahy. 'He was one of those important individuals who make themselves active and prominent among their fellows, attend dances and wakes, are seldom absent in fair or market from a fight.' He insinuated that Carleton should be ashamed at his ignorance of 'what is going on ... over the whole country', and almost before he knew what was happening, Carleton was sworn in, with 'dexterous rapidity' of language, on a Catholic prayer-book. Although McCahy was illiterate, he kept some works of Catholic theology in his home and had committed to memory lengthy Ribbon oaths and catechisms.[72] He was typical of the petty godfather which enclosed cultures, alienated from authority, tend to throw up. Among the Defenders there was much talk of getting rid of the heretics, massacring the Protestants, and taking their places, similar to the wishful thinking of the poetry. However, the widespread attacks on Protestant homes in south Ulster and north Leinster in the winter of 1793 were for arms, almost certainly for defensive purposes, and nearly all the casualties were the Defenders themselves. Even so, such talk fed the old Protestant fear of popish massacre and dispossession. Protestants fled to the towns for safety and – as the Catholic Committee had feared – gave substance to the ultra-Protestant attack in the Irish Parliament.[73]

The year 1793 was the most violent that century and set the tone for the remainder of the decade. With the outbreak of war, the government began a series of measures against the radicals. Belfast was ransacked by troops and warrants issued for the arrest of the proprietors of the *Northern Star*. A House of Lords secret committee report lumped the Defenders, United Irishmen and Catholic Committee together in an alleged Catholic conspiracy, and over the next year key Committee members were targeted for prosecution. A Convention Act made it impossible for a body like the Catholic Convention to convene again. A stringent Arms Act suggested that the right of Catholics to carry arms given with one hand in 1793 (and very reluctantly so) would be whipped away with the other. A new Militia Act was deeply unpopular, for it involved compulsory balloting to replace regular troops withdrawn for the war against France. A new wave of Defenderism sweeping through south Ulster and north Leinster in the winter of 1792–3 was met with an unprecedented show of force by the authorities. In Meath the Defenders were routed in a botched bid to rescue a captured colleague. Forty-seven were killed and nearly all the remainder captured in this one incident alone, and at the ensuing trials the authorities sought to make a dreadful example by handing down the death verdict on twenty-one Defenders and transporting a further thirty-seven. The *Northern Star* made much of the 'summary justice' meted out to the 'deluded Defenders', intertwining its reports of the hostile debates on the Catholic bill with accounts of the new security measures to show that the country was being rushed to 'arbitrary government'.[74]

In fact, at this stage, the Defenders were still a mirror image of those in Armagh and south Down, a deeply sectarian defence force. But their systematic arming was now unmistakable. The anti-militia riots which swept through the country in the summer of 1793 were initially unconnected, and they were worse in more rural counties where neither the United Irishmen nor the Defenders had penetrated. But a general alienation from government was evident and a recognition that the Catholic Relief Act had been granted with ill grace. There is evidence too that ordinary Catholics were looking to their secular leaders rather than to their clergy – a decline in respect intensified by the role of the priests in drawing up lists of their parishioners for the militia ballot.[75] Predictably, trouble in Ulster was mainly in areas where the Protestant gentry were already considered enemies. After eight weeks of riots, five times as many casualties had been sustained as in the previous thirty years, even though such years had witnessed persistent agrarian trouble.[76] The old *modus vivendi* between rulers and ruled, which had underpinned stability throughout *ancien régime* Europe had entirely broken down in Ireland. The rupture was the background to the development of militant republicanism in succeeding years.

6. The alliance between the United Irishmen and the Defenders

In the spring of 1793 when a United Irishman, Joseph Cuthbert, was sentenced to an hour in the pillory and twelve months' imprisonment for attempting to seduce the soldiers from their loyalty, some 25,000 people converged on Belfast for the event, and a rescue attempt was only prevented by military saturation. Belfast was considered the fount of all sedition in the country, and General Whyte, the military commander in Ulster, thought his lot comparable to that of General Gage in Boston on the eve of the American Revolution.[77] But Belfast and its hinterland in Antrim and Down was unusual. In these non-plantation counties, where Catholics were very much in the minority, a libertarian spirit had long existed and Charles Teeling was later to reflect with affection on the enlightened spirit in which he had been nurtured in the 1780s and 1790s.[78] The handful of upwardly mobile Catholics in these two counties were ready to identify their own cause with that of the advanced political reformers. Thus in 1795 when they were thwarted once again with the sudden removal of the emancipationist Whig Lord Lieutenant, Earl Fitzwilliam, and revelations that the King himself opposed Catholic emancipation, they publicly threw in their lot with the United Irishmen. In a meeting of the Belfast Catholics on 29 March 1795 at St Mary's Chapel, they proclaimed their cause the same as that of their Protestant brethren in the United Irishmen.[79] Further meetings took place in Antrim, Down and

Drogheda, with a final angry one in Dublin pronouncing the end of the Catholic Committee.

Shortly afterwards the decision was taken by the United Irishmen to seek an alliance with the Defenders, the secretary of the Belfast Catholics, the attorney's clerk Daniel Shanaghan, acting as intermediary. But the two most important Defender–United Irish axes were those centred on the linen triangle (involving the mediation of the Teelings and the priest, James Coigley) and the south Down–north Louth area, notably around Rathfriland, Newry and Carlingford. In this latter area Louis Cullen has traced a particularly high number of Catholics among the most radical United Irishmen, and those in Newry seem also to have spearheaded the reorganisation in Leinster.[80] These Catholics involved in the enlistment of Defenders appear to have already been United Irishmen, a 'junto of d–d United Papists [which included the Magennises] . . . instilling into the minds of a numerous banditti of cottiers under them, that you are only entitled to a chiefry upon the lands, and cannot dispossess them', as Downshire's agent claimed.[81] They were, however, concentrated in the east, and generally in the wealthy linen areas. Ulster has always been a patchwork of highly localised regions. Presbyterians only tended to join the United Irishmen in areas where Catholics were in a minority. In poorer rural areas, areas where old sores from confiscation persisted, or those where Catholics predominated or where they equalled Protestants in numbers, Presbyterians tended not to join the United Irishmen. Yet even in mid- and west Ulster, where Catholics had been relatively quiescent, a very sudden change had occurred by spring 1797, and Abercorn's agent began also to suspect the Catholics, though until then he had considered them ten times more loyal than either the Presbyterians or the Methodists.[82] The main reason was the upsurge in Orange attacks.

In July 1796 – in response to a government request for advice on how to extinguish animosities – John Ogle, high sheriff of County Armagh, warned Dublin Castle to avoid the mistakes of the past in failing to control Orange aggression. Catholics claimed as their excuse for turning equally aggressive that the Peep O' Day Boys had always been acquitted by Protestant juries. 'As this have been so or not, their minds were strongly impressed by it, & with the alledged oppression of their sect & having no cordiality toward a Protestant Government when they broke out under the style of the Defenders they became a ready prey to any sort of miscreants, whether United or Disunited Irishmen.' He had not known the Catholics to show any discontent at their exclusion from political power until enflamed by this Peep O' Day Boy turned Orange 'Protestant banditti', with their 'absurd bravados', not satisfied 'with the security & advantages they possess unless they may be allowed to bawl out Protestant ascendancy, as in the 12th Instant [July, when the Orangemen paraded through Lord Gosford's estate]'.[83] As late as 1797 even the Armagh gentry had been anxious about appearing to countenance the Orange Order. But as disaffection spread in 1796–7 and their inability to control their own areas became all too evident – to say nothing of the persistent French threat of invasion – they came increasingly to depend on the ultra-loyalists. The march through Gosford's estate was highly symbolic. This was the Orangemen reasserting the concept of the Protestant state, which the recent Catholic legislation had so obviously weakened. With the embodiment of a yeomanry force in September 1796, which would become a predominantly Orange institution, despite the recruitment of some Catholics, the reassertion of Protestant supremacy seemed complete.

The yeomanry was a part-time policing force, organised by the gentry for local service. But it could – and increasingly was – used like a regular army at times of crisis. Fitzwilliam had hoped to embody such a force as part of a Catholic emancipation package, uniting the propertied of all denominations, who would then be expected to enrol their own tenantry. But he was concerned at the prospect of a yeomanry recruited on a purely Protestant basis. At first his successor, Lord Camden, Lord Lieutenant 1795–8, shared such fears. But, in the absence of Catholic emancipation and given the escalating security threat, Fitzwilliam's fears were realised. Outside Ulster, Catholics did enrol in the yeomanry. In Ulster, however, there was fierce resistance to admitting Catholics. Entire Orange lodges were recruited, and, as time progressed, and rebellion and invasion seemed ever more likely, increasingly with the Castle's tacit blessing. The bulk of the yeomanry were located in Ulster, their local knowledge and Orange sympathies adding to the perception that they were arrayed against 'papists' rather than rebels. A 1798 version of the popular loyalist tune 'Croppies lie down' had the chorus changed to 'Papists lie down'.[84] The predominantly Catholic militia was particularly targeted. On 12 July 1797 in Stewartstown, County Tyrone, an affray occurred between the Kerry militia and a crowd sporting Orange ribbands, leaving a number killed on both sides. The following day the yeomen and fencibles took their revenge, attacking another group of Kerry militia and killing three.[85] The militia remained a politically suspect force and increasingly the authorities came to depend on a mixed force of yeomanry and fencibles to contain the rising tide of Ulster's disaffection.[86] Both forces were heavily infiltrated by Orangemen, ostentatiously displaying Orange emblems as they disarmed people in disturbed areas. The fear of Orange attack became the main reason for a sudden Catholic influx into the United Irishmen after 1796.

This growing ascendancy of Orangeism in the mechanics of counter-subversion was frowned upon by many who were not necessarily anti-government, and the action of General Lake (the British military commander in Ulster) in reviewing huge gatherings of Orangemen and yeomen in Belfast and Lurgan on 12 July 1797, was thought singularly inappropriate.[87] Nor was the spirit of radical reform entirely dead – many leading Protestants and Dissenters still calling for Catholic emancipation and parliamentary reform.[88] Ultimately however, even critics had to admit that Orangeism was a necessary evil to combat disaffection, which had got entirely out of hand. Even so, a French traveller, the chevalier de Latocnaye, moving through Ulster towards the end of 1796, found reports of sedition there greatly exaggerated. When he returned the following year, however, the situation had entirely changed.[89] A failed French invasion attempt on Ireland in December–January had exposed the country's vulnerability. The military forces at government disposal were inadequate and London refused to send reinforcements. The French attempt had boosted disaffection in the north and at the spring assizes no juries could be found to convict those arrested. A terrible change had come over Ulster. In Tyrone and Donegal whole baronies which had been quiet in January were in a rebellious state only weeks later, the United Irishmen having successfully spread among 'all religions'. Elsewhere new mansions, recently built in the heyday of Protestant confidence, were bricked up for defence. In County Down Lord Londonderry had to be guarded in his home by soldiers, though his father had rarely bolted his windows.[90] United Irish agents in France assured the French government of widespread support among the country's defence forces and there is no denying that they were having things very much their own way in the early months of 1797.[91]

In March 1797 government decided on a crackdown in Ulster. Martial law was proclaimed and the populace required to surrender arms and take an oath of allegiance. Infected militia units were purged and exemplary punishments meted out to militiamen who had taken the United Irish oath. Four Catholics from the Monaghan militia stationed near Belfast were executed beside their coffins in a macabre showpiece *pour encourager les autres*. Their fate was immediately immortalised in a popular ballad.[92] For the first time in a century Ulster was exposed to the full rigours of martial law. House burnings and floggings became routine and prison ships were anchored off the coast to accommodate the large numbers of those arrested. De Latocnaye found Ulster given over to military licence, the 'poor peasant' suffering the brunt of the military campaign, the real rogues 'very careful themselves to stay behind the curtain'. He found the people in the mountainous areas near Newry had suffered far more than their neighbours, their houses routinely burned to extort information about arms. Here the most notorious fencibles' regiment, the Ancient Britons, was quartered. Certainly south-east Ulster seems to have experienced particularly harsh treatment – even the noted government supporter John Giffard observing that the Ancient Britons' route could be traced by 'the smoke and flames of burning houses and by the dead bodies of boys and old men'. Since such atrocities were aired in the English parliament by Lord Moira they have become the stock of every historical account of the period. But even Lecky – a noted critic of government – warns that the authorities were obliged to take strong measures, such was the seriousness of the situation in the north. The existence of a formal United Irish assassination committee was roundly denied by its leaders. Certainly when told about it by one of its most useful informers – Edward Newell – government effectively incorporated it into its propaganda campaign. But a number of informers and active magistrates met violent deaths in these months and, as Nancy Curtin has shown, Ulster was in the grip of both republican-inspired terror and government counter-terror in the year before the 1798 rebellion.[93]

Not every county experienced the lash of the Ancient Britons. In those areas which underwent the worst military licence, however – notably Down, Antrim and adjacent areas of Derry – there was major Catholic involvement in the rebellion. Although even peaceable Protestants were abused, it was the poorer Catholic populace which suffered most in the disarming of Ulster. For the first time they joined the United Irishmen in great numbers, intensified efforts having been made to woo them via specifically Defender oaths.[94] The suddenness of this transformation among the Catholics from passive loyalty to active subversion was a matter of comment. The final date to surrender arms was 25 June 1797 and a great flurry of activity was noticeable among the United Irishmen as they attempted to bring about a rising before their undoubted strength was eroded. The attempt highlighted the traditional animosities between Ulster and Leinster, for the leaders in Dublin (many Catholic or pro-Catholic) opposed a rising before French help arrived. However, nothing separated the Catholic United Irish leaders in east Ulster from their Presbyterian counterparts, and people like the Teelings, the Revd James Coigley, and John Magennis were among the leading militants attempting to bring about a rebellion and a French invasion.

Catholics, however, also came forward in large numbers to take the oath of allegiance and to subscribe to the flood of declarations of loyalty orchestrated by their parish priests, while the Revd Patrick MacCartan, the parish priest of Saul, was prominent among those trying to woo their flocks away from subversive activities. The Catholic hierarchy had finally won its long campaign to convince the government that it was a force for conservatism, and that government's establishment of a Catholic seminary at Maynooth in 1795 saw them firmly on the side of the authorities throughout the crisis of 1798. Only one Irish bishop (Thomas Hussey, bishop of Waterford and Lismore) was to speak out against Orange and military atrocities, and the Ulster bishops – under Archbishop O'Reilly's firm anti-political lead – were the most silent of all. It is no accident that fewer Catholic clergy were involved in the 1798 rebellion in Ulster than anywhere else in the country. O'Reilly's excommunication of the Defenders, however, made little difference and the declarations of loyalty still accounted for a tiny proportion of Ulster Catholics (though it looks as if most of the Catholic middle class were among them). The United Irishmen had urged their adherents to take the oath and surrender some arms to prevent worse damage and we have the evidence of Abercorn's agent that, quite out of character, Catholics by 1797 had no reservations about perjuring themselves.[95] There was nothing unusual in Catholic tradition of the faithful ignoring the priest who stepped outside his community and there was no denying the widespread disaffection of the Catholic populace by 1798.

7. The 1798 rebellion in Ulster

In such a conservative society, whose world had been literally turned upside down, millenarianism was rife. Defenderism made public the kind of visionary expectations so common in the poetry. Old prophecies spread rapidly; those of the thirteenth-century Thomas the Rhymer, the seventeenth-century Scottish Covenanter, Alexander Peden, and the sixth-century Colum Cille, converged in foretelling deliverance at the hands of the French. A widespread belief in cataclysmic change was the backdrop to the dramatic, almost trance-like atmosphere of the years 1796–8.[96]

But the power of prophecy, particularly in times of distress and dislocation, and particularly in poorer rural communities, lies in its ability to foretell whatever the community wants it to. And whilst it served to unite at the height of United Irish confidence, ultimately it fed the increasing sectarian polarisation. The Defenders operated at many different levels, their chameleon character and transmutation over time confounding historical efforts at explanation. In their south Ulster heartland, however, they acted as the bridge linking the prophetic vision of the poetry with the political ideas of the 1790s. The idea of a French saviour picked up the old Jacobite message and translated it for a new age. In a contemporary poem in Irish, the Messiah was the French rather than the Stuarts, but the message of a radical overthrow of the existing order was the same.

The French at this time are relegating rank,
and there'll be no prince over them but a pure new régime;
Germany and Flanders will be subject to them in that state,
and I suspect that Scotland and Ireland will be in the bloc.

There'll be no Louis or any other king from now on
in the countries forever oppressing each fine son;
people will be full of wisdom, unfettered, unthreatened,
and the children of Milesius will have free will
            and prosperity until Judgement Day.

Remember the conditions the Gaill gave you at Limerick, my woe!
you were betrayed, and no mistake, since the time of King William
which left your poor children in distress, without property but in pain
like a blind beast running for a prize while the one guiding it has no reins.

Not by inheritance did Luther or anyone of the descendants obtain
all the bright new courts from Limerick to the Boyne
a scourge will come on these boors from the Gaels in battle
and they'll have no estate or fortress in Ireland any more.

The province of Munster is controlling its multitudes sensibly
and every famed man among the victorious Leinstermen is happy
the mighty, active Ulstermen will be defending the hosts
as they rout the race of Luther, and may they not escape them.[97]

French help would 'get [them] the conditions of Limerick', their followers were told; 'that the Protestants had the power of the country
long enough, and that they would have it as long more'.[98]

The main United Irish leaders and the Catholic middle class (however radical) distanced themselves from the increasingly sectarian readings of the prophecies. But many others were not averse to playing on
fears of Orangeism and hopes for a reversal of the land settlement as
a means of recruiting Catholics. The United Irish press became much
more shrill after the destruction of the *Northern Star* in May 1797.
The prophecies of Colum Cille foretelling a dreadful massacre of the
Catholics, which had circulated in 1641 and would again in the next

century, gained particular currency. Catholics in Antrim, Derry and Donegal were reported to have fled to the hills because of the prophecy.[99] In Armagh de Latocnaye thought such prophecies had been spread by Orangemen to force the Catholics to flee to the west.

The poor folk, who are after all the most timid and credulous of the universe, with their families and small remains of furniture, started in crowds to put themselves in safety on the other side of the Shannon. I myself have met often these wandering families moving to the line of safety . . . It was in talking to some of these on the road that I learned of the prophecy of St. Columba.[100]

At first widespread intimidation swelled the ranks of the United Irishmen – 'designing men who buzzed in our ears Catholic emancipation, and the danger of being massacred by Orangemen', as the parishioners of Arboe, County Tyrone, told their priest in June 1797.[101] Certainly the ease with which Ulster was disarmed suggests that many had enlisted through fear rather than commitment. Neighbours were now perceived as potential murderers where once they had lived in peace. Even converts to Protestantism were suspect. Thomas Macan, who converted in 1751, was a Volunteer captain and sovereign of Armagh until 1794. But he retained a liberal attitude towards the Catholics. His son Arthur succeeded him as sovereign and was a yeomanry commander. He was nevertheless nicknamed 'Papist Macan' and it looks very much as if his departure for India in December 1797 was for his own safety.[102]

By 1798 the prophecies were intensifying the sectarian polarisation of Ulster. After spring 1797 Ulster was effectively a military camp, and many of the troops were billeted on the people. The other provinces did not experience martial law till the spring of 1798 and the terror induced was a major factor in the outbreak of the rebellion. As a result of military repression and sectarian polarisation, little of the United Irish movement survived outside Antrim and Down by 1798. The United Irishmen still expected support from parts of Donegal and Derry, but in the event only Antrim and Down rose in June 1798, an attempted turn-out at Maghera, County Derry, collapsing on news of the approaching troops.

By the last week in May 1798, nearly all the main United Irish leaders were in prison, and confusion reigned in Ulster, when the planned rebellion finally erupted in Dublin on 23 May and spread to the other counties in Leinster. The entire country had been proclaimed at the end of March and as the floggings, torture and houseburning made infamous by the disarming of Ulster now spread south, affected counties witnessed a similar upsurge in sectarian tensions. Reports of anti-Protestant activities by the rebels in the southern counties – coming through in late May and early June and peaking with the brutal massacre by defeated rebels on 5 June of some 184 prisoners at Scullabogue in Wexford (all but 10 to 15 of them Protestants) – further dampened support for the United Irishmen.

I am happy to be enabled to assure your Lordship', wrote Abercorn's agent in Strabane on June 3, 'that the zeal and loyalty of almost all ranks in this part of the North have of late been increasing in proportion to the disaffection of the South. The Presbyterians (however late) now plainly see that the disaffection to government which originated with their party, must, without a speedy check, end in the total annihilation of them, in common with the church establishment . . . they will now fight in earnest to keep down the Catholics.

He now looked upon the Catholic populace as the most disaffected – only months after he had reported the exact opposite – and apprehended 'a rising of the Catholics in the wild parts of Donegal . . . [where they were] as numerous as sand', to say nothing of the 20,000 or so then gathering at Lough Derg only sixteen miles from Barons Court (Abercorn's seat). News of the rising in Antrim and Down on 7 June came as a shock: 'So long as it appeared a Catholic business I was quite easy about the North, but Antrim is quite a Protestant county.'[103]

On 5 June the Down commander, the non-subscribing Presbyterian minister of Portaferry, the Revd William Steel Dickson, was arrested. Down's succession of United Irish leaders friendly towards the Catholics (Russell, Dickson and finally Henry Munro) maintained an unusual unity right through the tensions of 1797–8. In Antrim, the last-minute assumption of command by Henry Joy McCracken would have had the same effect and assured a high Catholic turnout. Along with Russell, McCracken was one of the few highly placed United

Irishmen who was popular with the common people. A telling instance of this occurred days before the rebellion, as he was leaving Belfast. In Hercules Street (today's Royal Avenue), then a Catholic enclave, he was rescued from a group of yeomen by a woman wielding a huge knife – almost certainly one of the Catholic butchers operating in the area. McCracken had been central in the United Irish–Defender alliance, reputedly chosen by the Defenders shortly before the rising as their deputy for communication with the United Irish Society.[104]

But the omens were bad. Many of the Antrim colonels refused to act, and it was younger men, occupying positions of less social prominence, who were pushed to the fore. Martial law had been intensified and spies at the very heart of the United Irish command were supplying the military commander, General Nugent, with accurate information about their plans. A vital letter to co-ordinate the movements of the Antrim and Down rebels was secreted by the key informer, Nicholas Magin, a Catholic farmer from north Down and member of the United Irish provincial committee. The Antrim rising began on 7 June, with perhaps as many as 22,000 turning out in battles at Randalstown, Antrim and Ballymena, and countless skirmishes in almost every other town and village.[105] But the rebels were ill armed and poorly led, and after early victories they succumbed to Nugent's forces. When one of the military commanders offered an amnesty, McCracken's rebel army melted away.

Much has been made of religious dissensions among the rebels. Indeed, given the atmosphere of the time, their absence would have been unusual and there was much greater dissension among the rebels generally. But most of the incidents reported come from the pens of two hostile writers, the loyalist politician Sir Richard Musgrave and the former yeoman Samuel McSkimin, and should be treated accordingly. The early stages of the Antrim rising had a carnival atmosphere. Old banners, flags and ensigns were resurrected (many from former volunteering days); columns sang the *Marseillaise* en route to the battlefield, and in his excitement, Larry Dempsey, an army deserter from Munster, exclaimed: 'By J—s, boys, we'll pay the rascals this day for the Battle of the Boyne.' The story is McSkimin's and is plausible given the bad relations between the Orangemen and southern soldiers noted earlier. 'The great Orange fear' of 1798 tended to assume greater proportions the further removed from Ulster itself. But threading through McSkimin's account is a suggestion of separate Defender forces, often involved in dissensions with the rest.

As the largely Presbyterian leadership began to fall apart, there is some evidence of escalated recruiting among Catholics – United Irishmen capitalising on the Orange scare by using specifically Defender oaths to entice them to join. James Hope, the Presbyterian weaver from Templepatrick (and still something of a folk-hero in those parts), was McCracken's closest aide in the recruitment of Defenders. 'Charles Teeling was labouring . . . to unite the Defenders and Catholics of the smaller towns of Ulster', he later told the historian of the United Irishmen R. R. Madden, 'and joining in sworn brotherhood, they became United Irishmen. At a later period, Henry Joy McCracken advised and assisted in the special organisation of a body of seven thousand men, *originally* of the Defenders, to act as a forlorn hope, in case of necessity, out of the twenty-one thousand that were returned fighting men in the county of Antrim.'[106] This is an intriguing passage suggesting a later strategy in tune with reports of separate recruiting of Defenders. It receives further endorsement from the account of events in these crucial early days of June from one of the commanders in north Down, David Bailie Warden – a young Presbyterian schoolmaster and trainee minister. On 3 June he was present when an express arrived from Antrim announcing: 'That the Colonels of United Irishmen in the County of Antrim were averse to action but that the Defenders were 5,000 all ready for action.' On 1 June, the Ulster commander-in-chief, Robert Simms – one of the few original leaders still at liberty and, along with most leaders of that vintage, adamant against rising without the French – resigned. On 2 June, as the remaining commanders still vacillated, when faced with demands from the inferior officers for immediate action, McCracken was raised to the command, his elite force of Defenders apparently becoming part of the argument for action.

However, the image of Catholics and Presbyterians fighting under different banners can only be taken so far. When the so-called 'regenerated Defenders' emerged after the collapse of the United Irish rebellion, it is clear that their leaders had been United Irishmen in the rebellion year.[107] Catholics only seem to have coalesced in separate Catholic divisions when the demography of their particular area was exclusively Catholic and such would have been the case in parts of County Down. Predictably it is from here that the main case of religious division is reported, for more than any other county in Ulster, huge numbers of County Down Catholics joined the standard of rebellion.

In the split of 1797 over the timing of the planned rising, a meeting was reported to have taken place near Newry at which over 1,000 were said to have attended. Prominent among those calling for an immediate rising were leading Catholics John Magennis and Alexander Lowry, and they appear to have won their case, for it was a minority (some 300) who withdrew in protest.[108] Thereafter the same group took the initiative in Ulster in support of a militant faction within the Dublin leadership. Their immediate strategy, short of avoiding arrest – a distinct possibility for warrants were out against them – was to organise supporters in Britain and France. They were joined by Coigley, Bartholomew Teeling, Anthony McCann from Carlingford, and Patrick and John Byrne from Dundalk. By now Down was the United Irishmen's most organised county and the most vocal in pushing for rebellion.[109] With most of the main leaders either out of the country or in prison, it is difficult to keep track of the vicissitudes among the leadership. Yet even after the great Orange scare which immediately preceded the rising, Catholics were well represented among the United Irish leadership – a list of six colonels of April 1798 included three Catholics: Patrick McDonnell, the priest Bernard Magennis and Hugh O'Hanlon of Newry.

Down and Antrim were to have risen on the same day, but McCracken's message had not arrived and most of the Down commanders had been arrested. The rising in Down started belatedly with an attack on Saintfield on Saturday 9 June. Warden, 'having gone through several stages of promotion' in one day, was made commander of the Ards brigade. By the following day the Ards peninsula was in rebel hands. But Warden could barely contain the disposition among his ill-trained men to flee, arms and all, at the slightest rumour of attack. The insubordination escalated en route to the main rebel camp. This had been established at Creevy Rocks – just south of Saintfield on the road to Ballynahinch – but as yet it had no overall commander. On Sunday Henry Munro appeared and was 'appointed by acclamation, to the chief command'. Munro was a young linen draper from Lisburn with an established reputation as a reformer. Ironically he was a direct descendant of the same Major-General Munro who had been sent to quell the 1641 Ulster rising, and who introduced Presbyterianism to Ireland.[110]

The rebellion in County Down had been a largely Presbyterian one until now. But the Ards men hoped to cross Strangford Lough to link with the Defenders in an attack on Downpatrick. The main battle occurred at Ballynahinch on 11 June. On its eve, 'the mutinous disposition . . . [and] spirit of insubordination', which Warden found among the footsoldiers from the outset, had reached such a height, that entire units, officers and all, threatened to decamp and return home. The rebels were poorly armed and ill equipped and Munro hesitated. Troops converging from Belfast and Downpatrick could be tracked by the plumes of smoke on the horizon, for towns taken by the rebels were torched and a statement put out by General Nugent offered a choice of clemency on surrender or utter destruction. Whether it was this or clear indecision among the rebel command which caused it, there can be no doubt about the hundreds defecting on the eve of battle. The twelve-year-old James Thompson watched the battle from a neighbouring hill, where his family had sought refuge, and in later life left a vivid account of the day's proceedings. 'The chief injury sustained by the rebels . . . consisted in the gradual desertion of a great part of their army . . . we distinctly heard their more determined fellows shouting to stop the runaways . . . during every hour of the night fugitives were seen passing our station.'[111] Musgrave claimed these were Catholics.[112] But this cannot be proved. Nor can the continuing speculation that John Magennis had returned on the eve of the rebellion and that it was he who had argued with Munro and withdrawn with the Catholics from Ballynahinch.[113] Such were the stories still circulating in 1834 about the defection of the Catholics, that Hope felt compelled to confront them. He told Madden:

A party, which was assembling near Rathfriland, was advised to disperse by John O'Niel, of Eight-mile Bridge; they did so and traitors represented them as Catholics who had deserted the people. There was another false report that was industriously spread, and which is current to this day, that Maginnis had gone to Ballinahinch, with a body of Catholics, but in consequence of a dispute with Munro, had abandoned the people, and taken away his party with him. Maginnis was not there at all, nor any body of men, exclusively Catholics; the Catholics that were there were mixed with the Dissenters, and fought side by side with them, in a common cause ... the Killinchy people were the men who deserted, and they were Dissenters.[114]

The story first surfaced in information given to the Revd James Mac-Cary – a Dominican priest who had been compromised by the information of another priest into informing. He had it from a Felix Conroy or Converoy from Armagh, who had it from a Lisburn innkeeper and cotton manufacturer named Clarke, said to be one of the rebel commanders at Ballynahinch. Clark blamed the defeat on 'an ambitious and religious contest' between Munro and a Magennis. The dispute over who should lead the forces was decided in Magennis's favour by the toss of a coin. But Munro drew his sword, crying out that 'his intentions was[sic] to establish a presbiterian independant Government' – unlikely, since he was a Protestant of the established church – and called to his side all who supported him. Magennis did likewise and that night they left the rebel camp. Several hundred Catholics who were to have joined the camp the next day heard of Magennis's departure and failed to turn up.[115]

In the south of the county a military council was held to decide whether to march north to join Munro at Ballynahinch, or to capture Newry, extend along the Armagh–Louth border and cut Ulster off from Dublin. After much time was wasted, the latter strategy was adopted. But before it could be implemented, news arrived of the defeat at Ballynahinch. It may well have been from this group of United Irishmen that young Charles Teeling escaped into the mountains of south Ulster, his journey charting the widespread military licence and destruction which had occurred since the previous year. But about sectarian quarrels among the Down rebels, Teeling is silent. Catholic rebels also set out from Monaghan to join the Down men,[116] and, as with the Derry United Irishmen who tried to reach Antrim, others too may have been stopped in their tracks by news of the swift suppression of the rising in the two counties. It is difficult to know what to make of the Magennis story, for Clark was clearly no bigot and seems to have used his business dealings to spread the United Irish system among the Defenders of Connacht. It does not at all square with what we know of Munro. Yet there is a possibility that it was rather Bernard Magennis or another relative, Roger, who took part in the Down rebellion, for they were arrested after the battle of Ballynahinch.[117] A far more reliable witness – David Bailie Warden – blamed their defeat on a failure of command, 'the arrestment of most of our principal officers – the neglect or ignorance of the next superiors [all accounts agree on Munro's courage and honour, but absence of military acumen], the disordered embodyment of the people and the too great eagerness in General Munro for engaging – together with some improprieties committed at Ballynahinch'. In his long account of the Down rising, he does not single out religious dissension as a major factor in its failure.[118]

Hope may be guilty of special pleading in what he told Madden. But in the aftermath of 1798, there was no shortage of those trying to shift the blame on to the other side and the tendency was actively promoted by government supporters. Indeed, the Ballynahinch incident, like so many from the events of 1798, was exaggerated to suit party purposes. Frank Wright was told of it by some Protestants in Newtownards in the late 1980s. The point of such stories, he reflected, 'is that they create a picture of a United rising that really had very little to do with the Catholics, and which was anyway seen as a mistake later . . . They dispose of the romantic rubbish about how the 1798 Republicans were 1916 rebels little over a hundred years before their time.' To paint the 1798 Ulster rebels as somehow deluding themselves until Wexford had alerted them to the real threat of Catholic power, concluded Wright, is 'to accept uncritically the claims of later political actors who wanted to destroy the very idea that there might be any unity of purpose between Protestant and Catholic'.[119] The reality was that in those areas where the rebellion did erupt, Catholics were too few and too insignificant to appear in any other guise than the victims of military and Orange atrocities, and on the whole those Catholics were beholden to the Presbyterians who had given such support to the campaign for Catholic rights in recent years.

Government had long sought to drive a wedge between Catholic and Dissenter. The withdrawal of the propertied Presbyterians on the eve of the Ulster rising caused intense bitterness among lower-class Catholics throughout Ireland. Their action, Hope reflected, 'gave our enemies an opportunity of shaking the confidence of our countrymen in the other provinces, by constantly reminding them how the Dissenters of the north began the business, and in the time of need were the first to abandon it'.[120] The truth, as ever, probably lies somewhere in between. The Catholic Church in Ulster was almost totally united in its condemnation of disaffection and barely half a dozen Ulster clergy out of seventy for the entire country were involved. The *Belfast News Letter* took comfort from the inaction of the bulk of Ulster Catholics during the rebellion:

The different character maintained by the Catholic of the north and the Catholic of the south is well understood by everyone acquainted with Ireland. God be praised the former has better information than the latter and has we believe a degree of liberality with which the other is unacquainted.[121]

Given the religious demography of the rest of Ireland, it was inevitable that the foot soldiers of the rebellion there should have been largely Catholic. The possible consequences of this clearly worried some United Irishmen. The Antrim leader James Dickey's oft-quoted declaration, immediately prior to his execution, 'that if the *north* had been successful, they would have had to fight the battle over again with the Catholics of the *south*',[122] echoes Turner's suspicions the previous year.

The propertied of all denominations had steadily withdrawn from the United Irishmen after Lake's disarmament, and lack of leadership and continued military licence, more than any dissension, was responsible for the steady stream of defections. Disillusionment was widespread. James Orr, the Ulster-Scots folk poet of Ballycarry, whose entire village was 'out' in '98, graphically described the feelings in the main rebel camp at Donegore Hill in Antrim. Many were half-hearted:

> Repentant Painites at their pray'rs,
> An' dastards crousely craikin',
> Move on, heroic, to the wars
> They meant na to partake in,
>   By night, or day.

And when the soldiers appeared, they took flight:

> For Nugent's red-coats, bright in arms,
> An' rush! the pale-fac'd randies
>   Took leg, that day.

> The camp's brak up. Owre braces, an' bogs,
> The patriots seek their sections;
> Arms, ammunition, bread-bags, brogues,
> Lye skail'd in a' directions;

> Come back, ye dastards! – Can ye ought
> Expect at your returnin',
> But wives an' weans stript, cattle hought,
> An' cots, an' claughin's burnin?
> Na, haste ye hame: ye ken ye'll 'scape,
> 'Cause martial worth ye're clear o';
> The nine-tail'd cat, or choakin' rape,
> Is maistly for some hero,
>   On sic a day.
> Better he swing than I, on
>   Some hangin' day.

What might have been, asked Orr, 'Had they no been deserted'; but flesh is weak and:

> In tryin' times, maist folk, you'll fin',
> Will act like Donegore men.[123]

We may never know the exact number who lost their lives during the rebellion. But when Lord Cornwallis arrived as the new Lord Lieutenant in late June he was shocked by the military licence, the Catholic militia to the fore in an effort to counter previous charges of disaffection. The military had given no quarter in the aftermath of battle, bodies were left hanging from trees at Antrim, others stripped and buried in shallow graves on the shores of Lough Neagh, while rebels fleeing from Ballynahinch were cut down in the surrounding woods. The leaders were executed shortly afterwards, their heads displayed on market-house spikes throughout the affected counties. The Revd Robert Magill was a child in 1798, 'I particularly remember . . . the awful spectacle of human heads fastened on spikes and placed on the Market-house of Ballymena,' he later recalled, '. . . the hair of the heads waving to and fro in the wind.'[124] The physical scars also would have remained, the towns burnt by Nugent's forces, the Catholic chapels burnt to the ground, their sites continuing to be used for services until passions calmed and they could be rebuilt. It was a reversion to an uglier past, wiping from memory the many gains that had been made in the interim.[125]

Another casualty was the Irish parliament itself. An unusual combination of loss of faith by the British government in its capacity to cope with the security situation and its willingness to buy off vested interests, radical and republican contempt for a reactionary, aristocratic institution, and confidence by the Catholic establishment that London would reward its support by granting emancipation, produced the abolition of the Irish parliament by the Act of Union of 1800. But the King's implacable opposition to Catholic emancipation thwarted Catholic expectations (largely encouraged by Pitt) that further reforms would reward their support and nearly three decades were to pass before emancipation finally came.

8. The Fall-out

The sufferings and horrors of the 1798 period seemed a world apart from the euphoria of 1792, and all sides had cause to pause and reflect. The fact that most Ulster Catholics remained uninvolved and their clergy conspicuously loyal was soon lost in the return of the belief that, given the chance, Catholics would always behave as they had done at Scullabogue. Religious stereotypes were already well formed by the 1790s, and the decade provides an awful example of how the underlying fears of Protestants and resentments of Catholics were allowed to become a self-fulfilling prophecy. Even without the anti-Catholic propaganda circulating in the aftermath of the rebellion, former Presbyterian rebels needed little persuading that they had been snatched from the jaws of a popish conspiracy. Presbyterian radicalism did not die in 1798. James Orr's continued support for Catholic emancipation well into the nineteenth century was not untypical, though, as his editors suggest, it might not have survived its link with O'Connellism, which for Ulster Presbyterians came to symbolise the kind of Catholic tyranny forecast by Turner and Dickey.[126] As long as the possibility of French aid survived – which it did, at least theoretically, until 1815 – government feared the 'few Protestant traitors' still active around Belfast.[127]

Within months of the collapse of the Ulster rising the main flow of disaffection was into revived Defenderism. 'The word "Protestant", which was becoming obsolete in the north,' commented the Revd Edward Hudson in a graphic description of the new polarisation, 'has regained its influence, and all of that description seem drawing closer together.' He considered the spread of 'the Orange mania' the main culprit. It had been introduced to his area by a corps of yeomanry in the aftermath of the rebellion, and those, like himself, who tried to stop it were denounced as 'Catholic lovers'. It was said to be countenanced by the government and notices began to appear carrying 'the old inscription: "To hell or Connaught" '. United Irishmen were joining the Orangemen to hide themselves, and these he considered the most violent against their former Catholic associates. These in turn began to inform, and suspicions that the Catholics had betrayed the popular rebel commander at Antrim, George Dickson – captured and executed in May 1799 – contributed to the growing religious gulf.[128]

For Presbyterians 1798 has left a much more confused legacy than for Catholic nationalists, for whom it holds out the simplified vision of Ulster Protestantism once again accepting 'the common name of Irishman'. Even after the religious and political transformations of the late nineteenth and twentieth centuries, which saw Presbyterianism fully integrated into a common Protestant unionism, there was a residual pride that their ancestors had been 'out' in '98. But this could only be sustained through the Catholic nationalist 'hi-jack' of the United Irish story by adopting the myth that the Ulster rising had been a Presbyterian one, quite different in character from that in the rest of the country. The story of *Betsy Gray and the Hearts of Down* was once a favourite with the people of Down, Catholic and Protestant alike. It was immortalised in the 1896 novel of W. G. Lyttle, a liberal newspaper editor in Bangor, north Down. The short novel became a minor classic and I remember my father retelling the story as late as the 1960s and 1970s. It is the story of Elizabeth Gray, who had joined her brother and lover at the battle of Ballynahinch – all three being killed by yeomen in the aftermath of the defeat. Far into the nineteenth century the descendants of these yeomen were shunned at the Anahilt Protestant church and their children stoned at school. But when Catholics and Home Rulers tried to use Betsy's grave for the 1898 centenary celebrations, local loyalists smashed it to pieces to prevent its takeover by nationalists. Ballynahinch loyalists turned out on 13 June to parade in honour of the victory by royal troops in 1798, placing union jacks on the courthouse and the hills overlooking the battle site. Nationalists, thwarted in their desire to lay a wreath at Betsy Gray's grave by the destruction of the headstone, moved to the grave of another rebel only to find that the owner of the land had called in the police to block them. The following month a 'monster' Orange demonstration on Edenavady hill was addressed by the Revd L. A. Pooler. Why Catholics should want to celebrate '98 anyway, he could not understand. 'They had little or nothing to do with it. The night before the Battle of Ballynahinch the Roman Catholics deserted . . . They decorated the grave of Betsy Gray, but they had not the courage to fight beside her', and were she alive today, she would be a Unionist.[129]

The events of 1797–8 had indeed transformed relationships in Ulster. For the first time that century the bulk of lower-class Catholics were disaffected, the bulk of lower-class Protestants and Presbyterians were loyalist. Lord Castlereagh, always an astute observer of long-term trends, described the transformation which had occurred in popular politics:

The Protestant dissenters in Ulster have in a great degree withdrawn themselves from the Union, and become Orangemen. The Northern Catholics always committed in feeling against the Presbyterians, were during the early period of the conspiracy loyal – the religious complexion of the Rebellion in the South gradually separated the Protestants from the Treason, and precisely in the same degree, appear'd to embark the Catholics in it – defenderism was introduced, and it is principally under that organization . . . that whatever there is of Treason in the North, is at present associated. They are destitute of Leaders, and the people of substance, manufacturers as well as farmers have withdrawn from them.[130]

Normally suspicious Catholics had been taught by the likes of Henry Joy McCracken to accept leadership from sympathetic Presbyterians and Protestants, and a turning away from the priests has already been noted. But as the Presbyterians in particular drew back, Catholics felt they had been misled and then made the scapegoats. An anonymous correspondent writing to the military under-secretary at Dublin Castle, warned that although not all Catholics had been rebels, nevertheless they now believed 'that they had been first misled, then forsaken, and lastly betrayed by the leaders of the Rebellion'. Even so the actions of the Orangemen kept them disaffected. 'Being made to believe that these outrages are committed on them under the authority, and sanction of government, their antipathy against it and against the Orange party is exactly the same: for they conceive on this account Government to be the real source of all their real or ideal sufferings.'[131] When Thomas Russell came north to organise the Ulster part of 'Emmet's Rebellion' in 1803, he found little support, except from 'the lowest order of the Catholics', even if their clergy again organised loyal addresses against the latest attempt.[132]

Catholics were now profoundly alienated from the state, where once they had looked to England as a better friend than their Protestant fellow Irishmen. Such alienation was deepened by the continuing influence of Orangeism over the forces of law and order. In the new century, the suspect Catholic militia was progressively whittled down, the numbers of British troops and yeomanry simultaneously increased (reaching 21,000 and 31,000 respectively by 1823).[133] The countenance given by government to the Orange takeover of counter-insurgency in 1797–8 proved difficult to shake off – even though almost every government thereafter sought to do so. Orangeism did not always attract support from higher social orders, and most of its history has been a continuation of Armagh's lower-class sectarianism, just as Ribbonism (the direct descendant of Defenderism) perpetuated lower-class Catholic sectarianism into the nineteenth century. The enemy for Catholic Ulster remained the Protestant and above all the Orangeman. Ribbonism, like the early Defenders, was a largely reactive force and when the Orange Order was temporarily dissolved and parades ceased (1836–45) Ribbonism likewise declined.

But for the future character of Ulster Catholicism, perhaps the most important casualty of these years was the sudden curtailment of that secular Catholic leadership which had started to emerge. Many like to think of the 1790s as one of the great might-have-beens of Irish history, when Catholic, Protestant and Dissenter came together. But the union was only really successful at the leadership level – a coming together of the excluded middle class. The great might-have-been was not that they could have realistically carried out a revolution without exacerbating existing sectarian divisions but that a secular Catholic leadership might have been peacefully incorporated into the state, pre-empting the emergence in the nineteenth century of the kind of clerical nationalism which so fed Protestant terrors of political Catholicism. The claims of repentant United Irishmen that they would have been satisfied with such a move (accompanied by a measure of parliamentary reform) have been dismissed as an attempt to distance themselves from the catastrophe of 1798. However, it was such rejected middle-class Catholic leaders who effected the alliance between the Defenders and the United Irishmen, and whilst it is likely that sectarian animosity would have persisted in some form, both the 1790s and the subsequent history of Ribbonism showed that lower-class Catholics were as status-conscious as ever and as willing to follow the leadership of their own kind or, (as in Antrim and Down) even of sympathetic Protestants and Presbyterians. Dr Haliday writing to Lord Charlemont from Belfast at the close of 1791 caught the mood of a Catholic middle class no longer willing to grovel for recognition:

I understand that the Catholic members of the Belfast United society . . . have . . . insisted on their Protestant associates pledging themselves to go all lengths with them in that business of franchise . . ., and he warned that the Whigs could not afford to alienate 'a body who are likely to rise into prominence'.[134]

The awful experiences of 1798 had done nothing to weaken this new mood. An attempt to secure an oath of allegiance from Luke Teeling in return for his liberation in December 1798 produced the stinging retort that it was 'contrary to honour and religion, and, therefore ought not to be required. It is unreasonable to expect, and dishonourable, in any person who is not of the established religion, to swear that "he will, to the best of his power, support the laws", when one law (without going further) degrades and taxes his mode of worship, and is contrary to the free will which God has given to man.' He believed that his only crime lay 'in being considered the head of the Catholics in this county and active in their cause at the time of our convention', and in no uncertain terms he denounced the 'faction' in the Irish government for its 'mysterious policy . . . of arming and inflaming the minority against the majority, who were distinguished for loyalty and peaceable behaviour'.[135] For the Ulster Catholics a sense of rejection by the state, the apparent takeover of state apparatus by Orangeism, and a reassertion of Catholic church authority (so shaken in these years) were ultimately more important legacies from the 1790s than republican nationalism.

8

THE REVIVAL OF 'POLITICAL' CATHOLICISM

'To be a Catholic is still a political thing . . . [Catholics] have an affinity with the Church which has to do with its history in Ireland . . . the Church was part of the people's struggle.'

Gerry Adams, speaking in 1992
(O Connor, *In Search of a State*, 291)

There is a belief held by some Ulster Protestants that Catholics are under the domination of their priests and that those priests teach them biased politics and history.[1] Such beliefs represent a continuation of the fears of 'political popery', present in Protestant psyche since the Reformation and acquiring a new stridency in the nineteenth century. However, like all stereotypes, this one is only partly true and is largely based on developments elsewhere in Ireland. The Ulster Catholic clergy have traditionally been averse to political involvement. Attuned to operating in a climate of sectarian sensitivities, they have been much less aggressive than their southern colleagues. However, Catholicism and Protestantism in Ulster – particularly the militant varieties – have always fed off each other. The two communities' identities owe far more to sectarian awareness than to any Irish or British nationalism. It should not be surprising therefore that in the period when those identities were acquiring their modern form, it was the extreme representations which dictated the pace.

1. The 'Second Reformation' and the re-organisation of the Catholic Church

By the close of the nineteenth century the Catholic Church had acquired almost all its modern characteristics: a highly visible organisational structure, a disciplined clergy, a high level of religious instruction and practice, church control of Catholic education and social activities, and visible allegiance to Rome. The revival and restructuring was already in progress by the end of the eighteenth century. None the less the term 'devotional revolution' to describe developments within

Catholicism in the nineteenth century – however much it has been criticised and modified since it was coined by Emmet Larkin a quarter of a century ago – still seems an appropriate description for such a remarkable transformation, in particular the activities of the redoubtable bishop and cardinal, Paul Cullen.[2] In Ulster the pace was dictated by equally dramatic developments within Ulster Protestantism and Presbyterianism. There were similar religious developments throughout the western world in the nineteenth century, as papal authority revived after the shock of revolution in the late eighteenth century. 'The essence of their creed', writes Hugh McLeod in the best short overview of such developments in the western world, 'was the combination of a highly dogmatic and anti-rationalist theology with a warmly emotional piety, and a preference for life within a Catholic ghetto, where the faith of the masses could be preserved from Protestant or rationalist contamination.'[3]

Until mid-century (and beyond that in Belfast), the Ulster Catholic hierarchy continued in the O'Reilly mode, preferring a *modus vivendi* with Protestant society and keeping as low a political profile as possible. Church building – such a feature of the Catholic revival – lagged behind in Ulster, because of the continuing poverty of most of the Catholic people. In the western rural areas – where mass-attendance was significantly lower than elsewhere in the province – there was a distinct reluctance to subscribe.[4] Belfast, in Corish's analysis, was 'a disaster area' in this period, in its shortage of places for public worship – a judgement which the Halls even in the 1840s would have fully endorsed, for they found Catholics had but two chapels, ' one large and commodious . . . in Donegal St [sic – i.e. St Patrick's]; and the other, a dingy brick building, in Chapel-lane' [St. Mary's].[5] Even so, the appearance of such visible signs of 'popery' still caused tensions in traditional areas of conflict like Armagh. But since the land was predominantly in Protestant hands, the Catholic Church in Ulster remained heavily dependent on Protestant goodwill and generosity for sites and financial assistance. Provided Catholicism appeared as unthreatening as it did in Ulster in the early 1800s, liberal Presbyterians, particularly in the towns, remained supportive. But the prognosis was not good. Developments in Catholic politics elsewhere in Ireland and within Ulster Protestantism suggested that neither had changed their spots, and the middle ground was steadily eroded.

Daniel O'Connell's campaigns for Catholic emancipation (notably 1824–9) and the repeal of the Union (1832–47) raised the old spectre of political popery, and eroded much of what was left of Presbyterian liberalism. Many former United Irishmen continued to support Catholic emancipation, as did the Presbyterian Synod. But even they came to accept the Union as immutable. To leading Catholics, their betrayal by the government after the Union, the insistence by successive British governments that Catholic emancipation should be accompanied by some form of 'securities' – notably a veto over episcopal appointments – and the known hostility of successive monarchs did not inspire confidence. As successive bills were defeated, so statements from the Dublin-based Catholic Association became more aggressive, so the temperature rose in Ulster. Even though he accepted limited emancipation, the fiery Presbyterian minister Henry Cooke caused a furore in 1825 by revisiting stories of atrocities in 1641 and other past examples of popery's attack on liberty and religion. Although he was denounced by leading Presbyterians, all the signs were that Cooke was speaking for a growing tide of lower-class opinion, Presbyterian and Anglican alike.[6]

Faced with the same begrudgery as the campaigners of the 1790s, O'Connell too resorted to mass mobilisation and again utilised the best network available: the priests. But there the comparison with the Catholic campaign of the 1790s ceases. The priests were mobilised not for one election, but as organisers of the Catholic rent – the scheme under which individual Catholics paid a penny per month in support of the campaign's activities. This, it has been argued, with perhaps pardonable exaggeration, did more than anything which had gone before to create a nationwide Catholic community.[7] The sums raised were then mobilised to fund Catholic legal expenses, education and political activities. It prefigured the future by facilitating alternative Catholic social and political structures. But it was undoubtedly O'Connell's mobilisation of the Catholic vote which made demands for 'Catholic emancipation' irresistible. It was finally granted in 1829, when the right to sit in parliament, belong to corporations and hold high civil and military office, was restored to Catholics.

Support for O'Connell's campaign had been muted in Ulster. The low returns for the Catholic rent may have reflected relative poverty (as it did in Connacht).[8] But there was also considerable clerical ambivalence about its wisdom. The bishops were anxious about its effect on the always delicate community relations in Ulster, and cautioned those priests who became too publicly involved. One of those cautioned was Edward Maginn, parish priest of Inishowen, later bishop of Derry (d.1849) – a highly politicised priest and ardent supporter of O'Connell. He was no revolutionary, and was as critical of agrarian outrage as his predecessors. But he argued that if England expected loyalty, then Catholics expected justice.[9] A more moderate figure was bishop Crolly of Down and Connor, who had carefully nurtured relationships with Belfast's liberal Presbyterians and was particularly worried about O'Connell's antagonistic statements. Knowing little about Ulster, O'Connell spoke of it almost as a foreign country, and that is how his deputy, John Lawless, behaved in the one effort made to mobilise the province. In September 1828 Lawless announced the 'invasion of Ulster'. Great crowds joined him as he advanced through Meath and Louth, and in a mood of incautious triumphalism he pre-announced his plans to enter Ballybay, a Presbyterian enclave in Monaghan. It was a time of heightened sectarian tension. Both sides were spoiling for a fight and Orangemen called in their brethren from neighbouring counties. The local military commander persuaded Lawless to retreat, as did the Catholics of Armagh – his next venue. Lawless's conduct was condemned by the Catholic clergy and liberal Protestants as 'foolish and improper'. But the Orangemen of south Ulster viewed his retreat as a major victory and marched in triumph through Armagh, prompting the liberal *Northern Whig* to comment sadly on the apparent bias of the law in preventing one side's triumphalism, but not the other's.[10]

The O'Connellite campaign was only one element in the atmosphere of heightened religious tension in the 1820s, 1830s and 1840s. The so-called 'Second Reformation' not only added a new tier to persistent anti-popery, but forced the Catholic Church to rethink its pastoral role. In these early decades of the nineteenth century a number of evangelical societies set out to convert Irish Catholics to Protestantism. In doing so they activated an alarmed Catholic clergy, whose successful fight back in many other parts of Ireland effectively concentrated the proselytising campaign in the north – notably in the densely populated south Ulster counties. The activities of the evangelicals were based on the fundamentalist Protestant perception of Catholicism as a backward, superstitious, even unchristian religion, and of its adherents as in thrall to a crafty priesthood. Catholics were bombarded with leaflets outlining the errors of their church. At its worst, the campaign assumed apocalyptic proportions, a final effort to rescue Catholics from the abyss of resurgent political Catholicism. Catholic clergy were challenged to theological disputations, children taken aside secretly by itinerant preachers, and a kind of missionary paternalism operated whereby Protestant landlords offered Catholics material rewards for conversion. To the fore was Lord Farnham of Cavan, who in 1828 claimed a total of 428 converts, mostly from his own estates.[11] There was, moreover, a distinct correlation between such evangelical landlords and Orange sympathisers, and there can be no doubt that the movement heightened religious tensions.

Such abuse of landlord power over their tenants was not widespread. But it left a lingering sore in Catholic tradition, for it became the 'souperism' of the Great Famine, 1845–9, when as many as a million people may have died of starvation and disease, and when a few districts experienced the trade of food for conversion to Protestantism. Even in Donegal – where responses to the 1945 Irish Folklore Commission's famine questionnaire did not throw up strong memories of 'souperism' – the word evoked stories of the proselytising schools, the *Cait Bhreaca* (literally 'speckled cat', the bi-lingual primer used in such schools) and the *Bíobla Gallda* (literally foreign but doubling too for Protestant) Bible. The Donegal writer, Seamas MacManus (1870–1960), recalled a brother and sister who gave themselves airs and despised the common people. These 'were the children – the cursed children, everyone agreed – of a turn-coat father, one of the very few who traded their religion for the land with which a proselytising Protestant landlord would bribe them'. A country ballad mocked the father for his action and the son was taunted as 'Orange' by local boys.[12]

Art Bennett was inspired by the activities of the Revd Henry Young around Forkhill, County Armagh (1846–58), to compose a bitter attack on proselytisers' use of the Irish language. 'I went to the Post

Office of Forkhill on Good Friday last', he explained to Father Patrick Lamb in April 1852, 'and there I seen *(sic)* a large multitude of the most wretched fugitives trudging after Mr Young to church. Each of them had an Irish Bible. I was told that they attended that synagogue every day during that week, and received their communion. Those shameful doings set the feathers on end upon me, and prompted me to give vent to my feelings [in the attached poem].' The poem traced the history of the use of the Irish-language Bible to 'seduce' and 'bait' 'our people'. But it is the 'dregs' of the people who are enticed by offers of food and drink.

> It was shame enough, on Holy week, the vile lunatics
> who were gathered from all directions around the foreign church, each
>   with his Bible,
> there's not one of the party who didn't receive a piece of cake and a little
>   drop of wine
> for insulting the Pope and the Virgin of graces and the Church of Christ

As far as Carlingford and Dunleer in County Louth, Bennett accused Young of seeking out every donkey-man, bag-man, street-sweeper and woman carder. But they are 'weeds' whom the church can do without. In death no priest will come near them and their 'bribes and prizes and their false Bible' will not save them from damnation on Judgement Day.[13]

Although both Irish-language poetic and scribal traditions were in rapid decline in the nineteenth century, surviving poems register the bitterness of some Catholics at the activities of the proselytisers in Irish-speaking areas. 'Do you hear me, O children of the Gaels?' went a poem still recited in Ulster in the twentieth century. It warned the Gael not to exchange his religion for worldly wealth. It is not natural for the Gael to take on the language and religion of the foreigner, for the foreigners will go to hell and the Gael to eternal happiness.[14] Many Irish-speaking poets found employment with the Bible societies. But the poems of Hugh McDonnell (Aodh Mac Domhnaill), like those of Bennett, suggest a good deal of cynicism on their part. McDonnell was employed as a Bible teacher in Meath, Cavan, the Glens of Antrim and later in Glenties, County Donegal. He tells of how he was recruited to the Presbyterian Home Mission by Henry Cooke, who showed him 'the Bible written in Irish' and of how he, like the other teachers, made inflated claims about the numbers of pupils to obtain more money. These inflated figures were published in good faith by the Home Mission, till exposed as a fraud by the Catholic Church in 1844. His poems tell of the activities of the societies in Cavan, particularly Lord Farnham's teacher, Francis Brennan, 'arranging schools on bogs and on mountains' and seducing the ignorant with miraculous claims:

> 'And O beloved Mary, isn't he the spouter of lies!
> I don't believe any more in the lies of the traitors
> since my eyes have seen every deceit and wrong.'[15]

McDonnell was dismissed from the Antrim mission when his daughter was discovered to have called in a Catholic priest during an illness. Indeed Antrim – after Cavan – witnessed much of the sectarian skirmishing in Ulster during the second quarter of the nineteenth century. One magistrate addressing the 1835 parliamentary enquiry into Orange Lodges in Ireland attributed much of the trouble in the Ballymena-Broughshane area to the evangelical fervour created by local preachers.

> I saw at one time, 2,000 or 3,000 children brought for many miles to march in procession, each child holding a bible in its hand, and there ... were trumpets to go before each party ... I saw this Revd Mr McClelland ... trying to break into a [Catholic] chapel at the head of all these children ... and when he was not admitted, I saw him ride out of town ... followed by 10,000 well-dressed respectable persons.[16]

MacClelland was later condemned by the Presbyterian Synod and such activities were denounced by very many Protestants. But the 'Second Reformation' ultimately had more impact on Ulster Protestantism than on Ulster Catholicism, infusing it with a new fundamentalism which would steadily erode Presbyterian liberalism and, in time, paper over the cracks which divided the various Protestant denominations. It also heralded a tradition of fiery populist preachers, stretching from Henry Cooke to Ian Paisley, tarring the whole of Protestantism in Catholic eyes with their anti-popery. In a highly symbolic gesture, the statue of perhaps the most prominent exponent – the Revd Hugh Hanna (1821–92) – was blown up in Belfast in 1970, at the beginning of the Troubles.

The intensity of this sectarian strife in the years before the Famine saw a revival of the old prophecies which had also been circulating before the 1798 rebellion, particularly those attributed to Colum Cille. In Ulster they were claimed to have foretold the massacre of the Catholics by the Protestant clergy, but that the Catholic nations would intervene to destroy Protestantism and restore the Gael. Such prophecies were widely believed among the Catholic lower classes, though they were embarrassing to those of the Catholic middle class trying to make their way in politics. One of McDonnell's best poems – 'On the prophecy of Colum Cille son of Phelim' (*Ar Thargair Cholmcille mhic Féilim*) – probably accurately reflects popular belief. It tells of how Colum Cille had predicted the English 'swarm', the massacre of Islandmagee in 1641, the loss of the Irish parliament in 1800 and the Famine; of how 'the descendants of the Gael' would take their parliament back from England, which would 'incite the dogs to murder through the north'. But then the Spaniards would come, Britain would be split, Wully (England) and Sandy (Scotland) gnawing over the bone, and Ireland would be freed. McDonnell had been a fervent O'Connellite and a large number of his poems are devoted to O'Connell. But 'On the prophecy of Colum Cille' reflects the disillusionment at the defeat of repeal in 1843: 'It isn't the Repealers who'll relieve the distress/ or who'll give their land to the Gaels', but the 'mighty champion' from Spain.[17] It is a reminder that the same gulf existed between the Catholic poor and the Catholic political leadership as in the time of the Defenders, even though the power of that leadership to harness the poor's more militant tendencies remained strong, provided it continued to play to their traditional prejudices.

The 'Second Reformation' also intensified denominational divisions in another way. The good relations between Protestant and Catholic clergy early in the century distintegrated from the 1820s because of the proselytising campaigns. The Catholic hierarchy – thoroughly alarmed by such proselytism – took up the challenge, and for the first time mobilised the kind of religious instruction which the Council of Trent had called for three hundred years earlier.[18] Denominational education now became the key dividing issue. Despite their initial anxiety about the Charter schools the previous century, the Catholic hierarchy had not given much priority to Catholic education below that required for educating the priesthood. But the activities of the Protestant missionary societies in the early nineteenth century coincided with an increasing desire for education among the populace. Increasingly unable to afford even the traditional hedge-schools, poorer Catholics (and Protestants) were being attracted to the free schools offered by the proselytising organisations. By 1818 the London Hibernian Society alone was operating 194 schools in rural Ulster (almost as many as for the rest of the country put together) and the Irish Society – with its emphasis on Bible study in the Irish language – was targeting predominantly Catholic areas.

The Ulster hierarchy – more accustomed to mixed denominational teaching – did not respond to the perceived threat as early as those elsewhere in the country. In Belfast Catholics still attended mixed Sunday schools until the early 1820s. But as signs of proselytism grew, even Crolly became worried, opening a Catholic Sunday school in 1822 and the first Catholic day school in Belfast in 1830. But his problems in financing even such small beginnings were symptomatic of Catholic education generally, and this venture only got off the ground through generous Protestant subscriptions. The establishment in 1831 of state-funded National schools was a godsend, and they were very generally welcomed by the Ulster clergy. Crolly's Belfast school was among the first in the country to join the national system. Protestants continued to attend National schools in the first years of their existence, and those in Antrim and Down were generally of mixed religion. In effect, however, the religious demography of Ulster meant that large numbers of such schools were one religion from the outset. At this stage the hierarchy was prepared to tolerate common religious teaching. But Presbyterians and especially Anglicans were not. Cooke conducted a heated campaign against the schools, claiming that they were channels of popery. The Anglicans founded the Church Education Society to rival the commissioners of national education. Groups of angry Protestants in Counties Antrim, Down and Tyrone forced the closure of a number of National schools after daubing them with anti-papist graffiti.[19]

Catholic opposition came not from within Ulster, but from the anglophobe archbishop of Tuam in Connacht, John MacHale. Having effectively split the hierarchy on the issue, banned the schools from his own archdiocese (much to the mental impoverishment of his own people, as was later admitted), and all but destroyed the scheme entirely in the eyes of the papacy, it was the reasoned arguments of Crolly and his like which won the day. The Catholic people simply could not afford the education for which they clamoured. Without such state support, they would take it where they could and many would fall victim to proselytisers. The papacy accepted such arguments, and by 1840 was prepared to delegate judgement to the local bishops. Control of education was one of the earliest campaign issues in the Catholic Church's revival and its resistance to interdenominational education would be long-lasting.[20] However, in the first half of the nineteenth century it was the withdrawal of Presbyterians and Anglicans, and their refusal to permit priests in their schools, which brought about the development of exclusively Catholic schools. The religious teaching orders, like the Christian Brothers, were to play a vital role. But until the 1860s, the vast majority of Catholic children, who were receiving education in Ulster, did so in the National school system.

However, the move towards separate denominational education was proceeding apace in all the religious groupings and archbishop Crolly's final years were darkened by the row over the Queen's Colleges. After his elevation to Armagh in 1835, he and his successor at Down and Connor, Cornelius Denvir (bishop, 1835–65), and the equally accommodating archbishop of Dublin, Daniel Murray (bishop 1809–52), were already being bypassed within the hierarchy because of their support for the Charitable Bequests Act of 1844. Although genuinely intended by government as a conciliatory measure (opening up to Catholics public offices hitherto monopolised by Protestants), the act contained some anti-Catholic restrictions and in a heated attack the three bishops were accused of gullibility in their relations with government.[21] The dispute over the same government's establishment of non-denominational colleges in 1845 caused Crolly and Murray to become even more isolated. It was perhaps not unreasonable for the government to think that the colleges would mirror the success of the National schools. But opinion had hardened since the 1830s.

O'Connell's repeal campaign had failed, leaving nationalists embittered. His denunciation of the colleges was an important factor in the mustering of Catholic opinion against them. Pointing also to the increase of religious indifferentism produced by such 'secular' higher education in Prussia and elsewhere in Germany, the *zelanti* among the Irish bishops, following MacHale's lead, and now including Cullen, persuaded the Pope to issue condemnations in 1847–8. Their case was that without a Catholic professor of theology and Catholic appointments in sensitive subjects like history, logic, metaphysics, moral philosophy and geology, the religion and morals of Catholic students would be undermined. Many Anglicans and Presbyterians had made the same point for their students. Given the influence of Cooke's brand of Presbyterianism in Belfast, Crolly always knew that the establishment of the College there would draw episcopal opposition, and he had campaigned for its establishment at Armagh. Unlike the Colleges at Cork and Galway, that in Ulster would always have been predominantly Presbyterian in any event, since these were colleges designed to educate the middle classes, and Ulster's Catholic middle class was still insignificant. Crolly had had no problem with Catholic students attending what passed for a university till then – the Royal Belfast Academical Institution, a Presbyterian foundation. But his was a minority voice among the Irish bishops, and after his sudden death from cholera in 1849, the Synod of Thurles in 1850 formally condemned the colleges as dangerous to faith and morals. It was the first national synod to have been held since 1642, and it marked the arrival of Paul Cullen as Crolly's successor at Armagh, and with him an entirely new era in Catholic church development.[22]

Cullen had spent most of his life, since the age of seventeen, in Rome. These were the years of a resurgent papacy and Cullen was to stamp the Irish Catholic church with its ultramontanism. For nearly a century the Ulster bishops were generally known for their political quietism. Cullen claimed that this had made Crolly and his like too uncritical of government, and during his long reign as effective head of the Catholic Church in Ireland (1849–78), he appointed bishops in his own image. By the 1860s Cullen's own anti-Englishness and anti-Protestantism had made such quietism a thing of the past. His arrival had coincided with an unseemly and unnecessary furore –

sparked off by the British Prime Minister's anti-papist scare-mongering – over the restoration of a Catholic hierarchy in England. But the fall-out was largely felt in Ireland, where it brought nationalist feeling in behind the church and undermined the spirit of accommodation which had marked its relationship with the state for over a century. Shortly after Cullen's arrival at Armagh, an incident occurred which symbolised the changing climate. The Protestant archbishop called to pay his respects. He was told that Cullen was not at home and such niceties were never repeated.[23] It is, however, important to put this in the context of the heightened religious suspicion of the day, and even Cullen could distinguish a liberal or apathetic Protestant from a bigot. He was also quite prepared to work with reforming English politicians in pursuit of Catholic policies and did so very effectively with the emerging Liberals.[24]

Cullen was very critical of the state of religious practice in Ulster. His own appointment was a token of things to come. The Ulster clergy were just as resistant to the appointment of outsiders to the see of Armagh as they had been in Oliver Plunkett's time. But Cullen was appointed over the heads of the local candidates, and in his drive to impose internal church discipline, he would steadily erode Ulster's long-standing claim to lay control of clerical appointments. Like those continental clerics who visited Ulster at the time, Cullen remarked on the extreme neglect of the externals of religious devotion. 'The exterior ceremonies of religion', he reported in 1851, 'are very neglected, and matters proceed as in the time of persecutions.' By the following year he had already introduced some of the Italianate devotions which would become such a feature of the Irish church generally, adding further credence to the attack by Ulster's newly evangelised Prot-estantism on popish idolatry. 'The people are beside themselves with joy at seeing processions, functions etc. [during Holy Week]', wrote Cullen, 'which formerly were not to be seen.'[25] Over the next few decades 'missions', where thousands would come for spiritual renewal, benediction, new devotions to the Sacred Heart, exposition of the Blessed Sacrament, novenas, and other services little known to the easy-going ways of the past, became permanent features of Ulster Catholicism. Superstitious practices, rowdy festivals, patterns and wakes, were already under attack at the time of the ordinance survey of 1834.[26] By the close of Cullen's life, most were a thing of the past as the Catholic Church was transformed by the new puritanism of Victorian middle-class morality. New religious orders were introduced to Ulster: the Redemptorists, the Passionists (opening in 1877 the first monastery in Belfast since the Reformation), the Sisters of Mercy (establishing convents in Belfast 1854, Downpatrick 1855, and six more the following decade), and the Christian Brothers (1856). By 1920 some sixty convents had been established in Ulster, all but two or three of them since 1840.[27] Progressively education and a number of other social and medical facilities were transferred from lay to clerical hands, as the church came to dominate Catholic community life. By the turn of the century Catholics and Protestants were operating in separate social spheres.

The new bishop of Down and Connor, Patrick Dorrian (bishop, 1865–85), though critical of the quietism of his predecessors, admitted that had he been bishop in the 1830s he too would have welcomed the National schools. Indeed he continued to support them for the benefits they brought to Catholics. But as the communities became increasingly polarised, the concern of the Catholic clergy at covert proselytism and inbred hostility to Catholic practices grew apace. There were too many signs of Catholic pupils still attending scriptural education in school hours, their parents too illiterate, too poor or too intimidated to exercise their right to withdraw them, as permitted under the National school system. Even the books in use for general education had a Protestant ethos. By the 1860s a more confident episcopate was more prepared to challenge the government's claims of fair play. A special commission established in 1868 investigated their complaints and many reforms followed. The introduction of fully denominational education in Ulster did not occur until 1923, but even before then the trend was unstoppable. By the time of the Powis Commission of 1868–70 the bishops had already formulated a philosophy of Catholic education which went far beyond protection against proselytism, a philosophy which is still in place today. Dorrian explained this to the Commission in 1868. He did not think that secular and religious education could be separated and since information was received as much through the senses as the intellect, the surroundings, religious symbols and general tone of the place were as important as its teaching.[28]

Above all Trent had finally arrived in Ireland. The 1834 data collected by the parliamentary commissioners into public instruction in Ireland revealed very low levels of formal religious practice in Ulster (alike with parts of Munster and Connacht). Churches were still in short supply, the ratio of priests to population was unfavourable, and poverty, particularly in the western counties, all played their part. The church was not yet at the centre of religious life. Cullen made this one of his central missions: the transfer of religious practice from the home to the church, by increasing the number of church-based devotions and masses on offer. From mid-century new churches were to have baptismal fonts and confessionals with grilles. Administration of the sacraments in private houses, particularly in the form of the so-called 'stations' – so open to abuse by the clergy, and the topic of one of Carleton's most revealing satires on the avaricious priest[29] – were progressively discontinued. Priests themselves were better educated and set apart from their parishioners as holy men (black clerical dress being widely adopted for the first time after the 1850 Synod of Thurles). There would be far less criticism of the negligent or scandalous priest in the nineteenth than in any previous century. Regular religious education of the laity also appears to have been achieved. Admittedly it was the regular religious education through the National and new religious schools which brought this about.

But even Carleton's peasants had the basics of modern Catholicism. Gallagher and his like had already secured this. The 'Second Reformation' also spurred the Catholic clergy into a frenzy of print. Alarmed at the dissemination of Protestant bibles, the Antrim and Down bishops alone had 308,600 Douay Bibles printed between 1817 and 1852 and the Catholic Book Society produced five million books in its first ten years of existence (1827–37).[30] Certainly commentators noted a new sobriety and sharp upturn in religious practice among Catholics at the end of the century. The new public rituals, the display, the new array of religious aids and decoration of churches, picked up the emotionalism of nineteenth-century romanticism and seemed to supply the need previously met by folk ritual. Moreover, under Pius IX (pope, 1846–78) indulgences came back into vogue, proving as popular as they had done in the Middle Ages. There is an Ulster folk tradition that the 'Big Wind' of 1839 banished the fairies. Another version has the angelus bell doing away with them at the time of the Boer War (1899–1902). Thus did memorable events come to be associated with the changes wrought on Catholic society by the 'devotional revolution'.[31]

An associated factor was a wave of Catholic triumphalism – for which Cullen has been much criticised. Its main physical legacy was the great nineteenth-century Gothic churches, with their towering spires and heavy ornamentation. There was already more than a hint of sectional rivalry in the surge of new church-building in the first half of the century.[32] But they were often great empty structures, unadorned through either lack of money or lack of will. In many cases, however, they were knocked down and replaced with far more elaborate buildings, costing six or seven times as much as the original.[33]

Developments in Belfast (even though its Catholic population was far less wealthy than urban Catholics elsewhere) were typical. Bishop Dorrian was a Cullenite expansionist. His predecessor, Denvir, had been a bishop in the old mould, keeping a low profile and pursuing a policy of quietism. Dorrian, in contrast, oversaw a massive expansion of Catholic church organisation in Belfast. As co-adjutor in Down and Connor since 1861, Dorrian's frustration at the lack of amenities for Catholics had been sharpened by his knowledge that some 1,000 Catholics a year were converting to other religions. During his term as bishop the ratio of priest to people jumped from 1:5,000 to 1:1,600. He invited the Christian Brothers and a number of other teaching and charitable orders to Belfast, their schools, orphanages and convents springing up in all the Catholic districts. He purchased land for a new Catholic cemetery at Milltown in west Belfast (after a row with the corporation over separate provision), he orchestrated the building of a host of new churches (including the replacement of the old St Mary's and St Patrick's along the Gothic lines outlined above), and in 1883 a hospital, the Mater Infirmorum. Almost the entire physical structure of modern Catholicism in Belfast was in place by the time of his death. By then Belfast's 70,000 Catholics were served by twenty-eight priests, twelve Christian Brothers, seventy nuns and seven churches.[34] The Catholic Church had become the main provider of needs for the Catholic populace and with that Catholicism had become a community, not just a church.

Although it is traditional to trace the authoritarianism of twentieth-century Catholicism to this period, the Catholic Church could never force a reluctant Catholic people in a direction of which they did not approve. The new devotions were popular. It was the first injection of confidence for several centuries, and by all accounts ordinary Catholics were thrilled at the new profile and public display of their Church. The magnificent pomp attending the opening of St Peter's pro-cathedral on the Falls Road in Belfast in 1866, just after Dorrian took over, had Cullen and twelve other bishops celebrating high mass, to the music of a full orchestra. Dorrian had none of his predecessor's inhibitions about offending Protestants with such displays.[35] Such developments already had a basis in widespread respect for the priest as the learned man of the community. The absence of visible church structure before this period by no means should be assimilated to irreligion. Quite the contrary; although Carleton was to become a Protestant in his adulthood and worked for the proselytising societies, this is not apparent in his fiction, because, as he states himself, respect for the priest and the rudiments of Catholicism were part and parcel of the simple people's lives which he was celebrating. There is not even a hint of a lapsed Catholic in his stories.[36] A particular feature of peasant devotion in his fiction is the saying of the rosary, and he remembered his father constantly with his beads in his hands.[37] Significantly this was one of the items in established popular devotion which the church did not jettison.

Nor should one carry too far the image of the newly authoritarian church at war with the more superstitious beliefs of its people. Rather it was part of the process of civilising and taming which was such a part of middle-class culture everywhere in Europe. Although the Ordnance Survey Memoirs of the 1830s reveal considerable progress by the Ulster priests in curbing popular excesses, the main success came later in the century and owed as much to changing social conditions and outlook as to priestly intervention. Most important were the decimation of the cottier class in the Famine, growing urbanisation, changing work-patterns and modes of behaviour, and the prevalence of Maynooth-trained priests among the clergy, thereby providing a lower middle-class leadership to nineteenth-century Catholicism. The pursuit of respectability which was implicit in the 'devotional revolution' also involved priestly damnation of the rowdier and irreverent side of Catholic culture. The novels of the Donegal writer Patrick MacGill expose the snobbery of the Father Devany character, the scourge of country dances and popular pastimes, whilst admiring the 'polite' gatherings of the 'quality'. It was a trend which was not confined to Catholic society, for the removal of country dances from the cross-roads was also a product of the new fashion for ballroom dancing.[38] The seriousness and prudishness which infused extreme nationalism and which saw the sentimental songs of Thomas Moore replace traditional singing and storytelling, owed not a little to this triumph of lower middle-class morality within the Catholic Church.[39]

The new puritanism of the Catholic Church was also a response to developments within Protestantism. In many ways the 'devotional revolution' was Catholicism's equivalent of the Second Reformation. It was partly initiated by fears of proselytising and tended to focus on those aspects of Catholicism most criticised by the Protestant reformers. The churching of folk religious practices was the main response to attacks on superstition, rowdiness and excessive drinking. But the Church went even further: it founded the Pioneer Total Abstinence Association in 1898 and effectively destroyed the illicit distillation of poteen – something of an industry in Donegal in particular – by declaring it a reserved sin which only the bishop could absolve.[40] Predictably it would be a sanitised version of the Irish Catholic peasant which became the ideal of the Gaelic revival. Don't by your drunkenness give Ireland's 'enemies' the excuse to sneer, Matthew Russell, a Jesuit priest from County Down and editor of the popular Catholic periodical, the *Irish Monthly*, appealed to the Irish peasant in June 1894:

> Dear Irish peasant, brave and pure and true,
> Ah! let this scandal rest no more on you
> Honest, contented with your scanty score,
> And Catholic, aye to the very core;
> Yet why let Pharisees their eyebrows lift
> At your intemperance and lack of thrift?
> If by no nation are ye left behind
> In generous qualities and gifts of mind,
> Why not do justice to your creed and race
> By stamping out this vulgar, vile disgrace?[41]

The 'devotional revolution' was, moreover, a continuation of the clergy's long-standing campaign against practices which might reinforce hostile Protestant stereotypes of the Catholics.

The wakes and even some patterns at holy wells remained, but shorn of their former excesses. The priest himself became the master of ceremonies, leading the faithful in prayer. In the early decades of the twentieth century Ó Muirgheasa plotted the location and history of holy wells in Donegal. He found over a hundred, many having gone out of usage or declined in importance – notably at the end of the previous century – but others having been adopted officially by the church. St Patrick's well, at Inishowen, was actually re-opened and re-dedicated by clergy from Derry City, while the 'most frequented' well in Donegal – Doon Well, near Kilmacrenan – was relatively modern, having been founded by one priest and blessed by another. Although some older inhabitants remembered patterns on St John's eve and May eve, and many of the older wells listed by Ó Muirgheasa celebrated aspects of the Colum Cille legend, by the early twentieth century most ceremonies had been transferred to 15 August (the Feast of the Assumption of the Blessed Virgin Mary).[42] The 'missions' – Catholic versions of the renewal and emotionalism of Protestant evangelical revival meetings – came to supply a demand once met by the patterns, but again now firmly under clerical control. Just as in the early centuries of Christianity, so in the nineteenth and twentieth centuries, localised saints' cults and relic veneration were replaced by cults formally approved by the Church itself. Cults to the Sacred Heart and Mary, and to the relics of the 'True Cross' would dominate Catholic popular devotionalism into modern times – as well as a small number of 'legitimised' cults (St Anne, St Jude, St Joseph and later the Little Flower and St Martin de Porres). Anthropologist Lawrence Taylor, whose *Occasions of faith* provides one of the best local studies of the changing nature of popular Catholic devotional practices, comments on this process in relation to holy places formerly associated with local saints. 'It is difficult to find poor Brigid among the Marian images and Sacred Hearts . . . Then again, that is probably no more than what Brigid herself did to whatever goddesses preceded her . . . one is tempted to conclude that the once wild pilgrimage so often condemned by the clergy is now but an extension of the church.'[43]

Religion is woven into the fabric of Michael MacGowan's Donegal childhood in the 1870s. En route to the hiring fair in Letterkenny, his mother insisted on doing the 'station' at Doon Well. Nearby they stayed with friends, for whom extensive prayers were part of the evening cycle. Fifteen decades of the rosary were succeeded by 'the little prayers'. 'The old woman prayed for seven generations that preceded her, for the neighbours and for those who were away in foreign parts, for protection against sickness, against devils of the earth and air, against any other harm that might be hanging over us.' Young Michael regarded this as excessive piety. But nightly rosary and Sunday mass were part of Donegal Catholic life in the 1870s and were carried to the Klondike by the Irish Catholic miners.[44]

Mrs MacGowan's list of 'intentions' is a reminder that the 'magical' – such a feature of poorer rural societies everywhere – was not eradicated in the 'devotional revolution'. Indeed, there appears to have been quite a mix of clerical attitudes towards such non-Christian customs. There are signs of adaptation by the clergy of those supernatural elements in popular belief which could be 'churched', and leaving well alone those which could not. The belief that Catholic priests possessed magical powers remained strong, even in the twentieth century. Although a survival from pagan times, it continues in the popular belief that priestly exorcism is the only effective remedy against satanic possession. The idea that the Catholic sacrament of extreme unction or 'last rites' held the passport to heaven not only made it the most important rite of the Church for Catholics, but has informed a rich folklore tradition of converts to Protestantism reconverting at the time of death. A visit to the priest for the 'cure' was commonplace – a special power more traditionally attributed to the unfrocked priest.[45]

But again, just as the holy wells had acquired rituals legitimised by the church, so the 'cures' now sought were often in the context of Catholic devotionalism. There is, writes the folklorist Linda May Ballard, a tendency for Ulster Protestants to think of folklore as something peculiarly Catholic, thereby leaving them a convenient excuse to reject aspects deemed undesirable.[46] The belief that Catholics may well have a better link to both folk customs and the supernatural has remained extraordinarily durable throughout Europe. Gamble comments on it in his travels in Ulster in 1812; whilst in 1992 Dr Bob

Curran recalled similar experiences from his childhood at the edge of the Mourne Mountains in County Down. His grandmother, 'a staunch Ballymena Presbyterian', losing faith in conventional medicine's remedies for her grandson's ringworm – which had all failed – took him (much against her will, he suspected) 'to an old Catholic woman who lived in the Dromara Foothills and who was supposed to have had "a cure" given to her by the fairies for sickness and irritations'. The old woman passed some 'sally-rods' over the skin, muttering something which his grandmother thought 'very Catholic' and Dr Curran remembered as the Apostles Creed. The 'cure' worked, but in the 1950s when his grandmother was reminded of the visit, she was clearly embarrassed, trying at first to accommodate it within the non-denominational concept of faith-healing. 'Catholics, on the other hand, believed that such things came from fairies. Their priests both encouraged and reinforced this view to keep them servile. As long as they believed in the supernatural – fairies, cures, visions and miracles – the priests had them in their grip.'[47]

Despite such disclaimers, all the evidence shows that Ulster Protestants were just as superstitious as Catholics. Indeed, some practices appear to have been entirely Presbyterian in origin. Father James O'Laverty was at pains to detail these Scottish-imported 'superstitions' in his 1884 *History of Down and Connor*, particularly when such 'charms' did not work or needed the addition of Catholic prayers to do so.[48] The difference was that Protestant culture located religion and the supernatural in different spheres, whereas Catholic culture intertwined them. And while some Protestants could be supercilious about yet another sign of Catholic inferiority and some Catholics could be overly defensive about it, it also informed Catholics' self-perception that theirs was an older, more organic culture. Protestants were uninterested in the souterrains, one north Antrim Catholic told Ballard in 1976, because they knew they were earlier than their time. Hence they had less respect for the fairies: 'A fairy thorn had no time in a Protestant field.'[49] This idea of sacred landscape and Catholicism as organically linked with it is commonplace, a tradition of sacred landscape at least traceable to the early Christian compilers of the heroic tales.[50] This was also the view promoted by the Gaelic revival, in which the priests played a major part.

However, the fairy-lore associated with specific features of the landscape and belief in the fairies as the sources of everyday misfortunes proved less adaptable to official Catholic devotionalism. Why Irish Catholic folk-beliefs do not subscribe to the witchcraft mania which affected Protestant and Catholic countries alike in the early modern period has never been adequately explained. Aside from a famous Kilkenny trial in the fourteenth century, accusations of witchcraft since the seventeenth century have been largely confined to the east Ulster Presbyterian community, suggesting some foundation for the apparently prejudiced Catholic view that it was brought from Scotland.[51] It may be that the fairies – believed to be the angels who had fallen with Lucifer – provided quite adequate explanation for evil. The most prevalent and long-lasting of such traditions were those of the fairy thorn and the changeling. Fairies could express their displeasure in all manner of ways and could even replace humans, particularly children and young women, with changelings. Unsurprisingly, less orthodox beliefs remained strong in rural Ulster, where the friars held sway for so long, where Irish speaking locked in tradition and where the Catholic populace remained largely peasant and rural. 'Official' Catholicism had always been more successful in richer areas and in the towns.

Certainly clerical denunciations of fairy beliefs did not deter a County Tyrone man in the twentieth century from having his wife's body exhumed because he believed her death in childbirth to be a case of fairy abduction.[52] 'My native place was a spot rife with old legends, tales, traditions, customs and superstitions', recalled Carleton of his early youth in south Tyrone; 'even beyond the walls of my own humble roof, they met me in every direction.' His father's 'unrivalled' stock of tales and legends consisted of 'all kinds of charms, old ranns, or poems, old prophecies, religious superstitions, tales of pilgrims, miracles and pilgrimages, anecdotes of blessed priests and friars, revelations from ghosts and fairies'.[53] And lest we think the 'devotional revolution' made any significant dent in this aspect of rural belief, listen to Seamas MacManus's account of the 'fairy faith' in his late nineteenth-century upbringing in Donegal:

My Mother's faith in the Good People wasn't just static but missionary. She brought up her children to reverence all fairy haunts, the Mount, the raths, their playgrounds on many a Glen Ainey hilltop, their *sciog* [from *sceach* – whitethorn or hawthorn] bushes from which one mustn't break a twig, any more than they'd break a Commandment. She taught the youngsters always to pray, 'God bless you!' when anyone sneezed – the fairies having, for that instant, power over the victim. Her children from her learned, no matter how hungry they'd be at quitting the table, never to finish their portions – to leave ... the fairy bit – a modest offering which reassured the watching Good People that they were not forgotten by anyone in *her* house.

She had twice heard the banshee cry and claimed to have seen the white-clad figure 'raising her blood-curdling lament for one of the family about to leave the world'. She told salutary tales of the fate of those who had doubted the fairies' power. The half-Scottish Bab McClay, 'scorning "fairy superstitions", built his house on a fairy rath which everyone else respected, and suffered the consequences in the deaths of his livestock and failure of his crops.[54]

The prevalence of lone thorn trees and undisturbed mounds in the middle of so many Irish fields indicates that Mrs MacManus's belief in the power of the fairies was widely shared. Thus were ancient raths preserved from plough or spade, as Gamble noted early in the century, because people thought them fairy forts.[55] Although most people will claim not to believe such old superstitions, yet there are still those who will not pick the whitethorn, just in case. The tradition of the sacred or magical tree goes back to pre-Christian times, their association with royal sites a feature of the *Ulster Cycle* and other ancient legends. They were particularly associated with inauguration sites, leaving their traces in placenames like Lisnaskea (or 'whitethorn fort', the Maguire place of inauguration in Fermanagh). Like much else, the tradition was christianised in early medieval times, when they also became associated with local saints and ecclesiastical sites. It was, however, the association with the supernatural which was to be most enduring, and tales of misfortune befalling those who interfered with the thorn-trees were still told in the twentieth century.[56]

2. The Catholic Church and the development of nationalist politics

Did the Cullenite 'revolution' amount to the political Catholicism which Protestants so feared? Certainly until the 1890s there seemed little leadership of the Catholic community in Ulster other than clerical. But this is not the same as clerics promoting nationalist politics – which the fear presupposes – and the relationships between rising nationalism and even the newly aggressive Cullenite Catholicism is by no means clear cut. Crolly's nervousness about political campaigns was generally true of the Ulster hierarchy throughout the nineteenth century, and militant nationalism in particular continued to be denounced from the altar.

The religious polarisation of the late nineteenth century occurred also in politics. Catholics and Presbyterians traditionally voted Liberal before the rise of Parnell in the 1880s. But whereas Catholics regularly voted for Protestant Liberal candidates, Protestants did not reciprocate if the candidate was Catholic, a trait which the clerical-backed *Ulster Examiner* noted with some resentment.[57] Protestant politicians making interdenominational gestures were given a rough ride by their constituents. The basis was already there for Ulster politics to divide into separate religious blocs, but there was no specifically Catholic political leadership until the end of the century and when it first arrived it was largely imported from the south. The development of Ulster Catholic political consciousness in the nineteenth century is still one of curious apartness from the rest of the island. Few had the vote until the major electoral changes of the 1880s. Although the stereotype of the Ulster Catholic as a natural rebel continued unabated into the modern era, the Catholic population was not highly politicised. The frequent use of the terms 'invade', 'invasion' of Ulster by successive nationalist movements is telling. Organised nationalism took a very long time to gain a foothold in Ulster, and when it did it was solidly constitutional. Militant republicanism held little attraction. The amnesty campaign for Fenian prisoners secured emotional support throughout Ireland, some 30,000–40,000 turning out in Belfast in September 1867 for the funeral of a Fenian who had died in jail there. While in the summer of

1872, a mass demonstration for the release of prisoners gathered some 30,000 at Hannahstown on the western edge of Belfast, and set off another round of sectarian riots.[58] Even so, Fenianism itself was weaker in Ulster than in any other province. As Parnell's movement was beginning to make an impact on Ulster in the 1880s, Catholics remained more concerned about local Orange parades than about national politics.

The key to all this, ironically, was the Catholic clergy. Protestant perceptions of the sinister role of the priests, brainwashing their people and bent on a popish political tyranny, have never entirely disappeared. But the true picture of clerical involvement in nationalist politics is very far from the stereotype. Throughout the century the Catholic Church performed a delicate balancing act of damning violence, without losing the support of the mass of the Catholic people. By the second half of the century its politics were decidedly nationalist, but above all it sought to protect Catholic church interests. The pursuit of non-denominationalism in any body affecting those interests was frowned upon and increasingly crushed. In this the Church undoubtedly played a major role in squeezing out the Protestant voice in Irish nationalism. Such was the identification of Catholicism and nationalism by the end of the century, that both the state and successive national movements had to recognise the Church's special position and to consult it. No nationalist movement could hope to survive without clerical support. Acceptance of this spelt the end to the concept of an Irish nationalism which espoused all creeds, 'except for rhetorical purposes'.[59] However, the clergy were rarely initiators or leaders of political movements.

O'Connell's campaign for Catholic emancipation – involving as it did the mobilisation of the Catholic clergy as agents and collectors of the Catholic rent – created the illusion of the political priest. O'Connell became a particularly heinous figure for Protestants, to the extent that the sectarian riots of 1864 in Belfast were sparked off by the unveiling in Dublin of a statue to his memory. And yet O'Connell was entirely constitutional in his politics, a Whig for most of his political life, utterly loyal in terms of seeking justice for Catholics within the British connection. In as much as the Catholic clergy had a consistent political approach in the nineteenth century, it was O'Connellite. Even the highly politicised and nationalist Dorrian was loyal to the British crown and utterly opposed to republicanism – which returned the compliment by retaining the anti-clericalism of its founders (a trait largely absent from constitutional nationalism). Indeed, the papacy was against *any* political activities by clergy and issued frequent declarations to that effect throughout the century. Nevertheless the Ulster clergy did eventually become heavily involved in nationalist politics (more so than those in the rest of Ireland, largely because of the absence of any significant lay leadership in Ulster) and their involvement both alienated the handful of Protestant nationalists and established the dominant Catholic ethos of modern Irish nationalism. But they were also a moderating force, and they ensured that on the eve of the 1916 rising Ulster nationalism remained overwhelmingly constitutional.

Despite their inherent distrust of secular politics, the Catholic clergy had no problem involving themselves in campaigns seeking justice for Catholics. In this they usually followed rather than led and Dorrian responded to the Pope's attacks on the Land League by warning that priests would lose all influence with their people if they did not stand by them in their sufferings:

The exasperation of our people at the neglect of the government and want of sympathy of those who ought to be their friends, alienates many and drives our people to Fenianism . . . priests and people must keep united and I hope nothing shall induce the Holy Father to interfere against the friends of the distressed and famishing poor.[60]

Between the death of O'Connell and the rise of Parnell, although the clergy still intervened to defend Catholic interests (on poor law boards, for example), there was no strong national lead and clerical politics too became 'fragmented'.[61] In 1864 the establishment of the National Association of Ireland to press various Catholic demands, drew a very mixed response from the hierarchy. Five Ulster bishops refused to endorse it. Even Archbishop Cullen hung back. But Dorrian believed that if nothing was done for the Catholic people by constitutional means they would turn to Fenianism, and he persuaded Cullen to sign up. Dorrian was also among the earliest supporters of Parnell. But the Home Rule campaign initially caused great confusion among the Ulster clergy. In its early stages suspicion of initial Orange support and the predominance of Protestants among electoral candidates caused the Ulster bishops to trust more in Gladstonian reforms. The Home Rule movement's first foray into Ulster politics at the 1874 general election was a failure – returning only two of the twenty-nine Ulster seats, though holding most of the seats outside Ulster.[62] It was perhaps inevitable, therefore, that it had to become more 'Catholic' to succeed, for, given the growing strength of conservatism among the Protestant populace, only the Catholic Church had the organisational structure to increase the nationalist vote on the ground. By 1885 Parnell's parliamentary party had won the full support of the Catholic hierarchy in its promotion of specifically Catholic aims (notably denominational education). That year it nominated candidates only in constituencies with Catholic majorities, held its meetings in Catholic church halls and schools, and publicly involved the clergy on its political plat- forms. Predictably early Protestant support faded and the Liberal party (which for decades had secured Catholic and Presbyterian backing) was eliminated.

After 1885 Ulster electoral politics were almost entirely denomi- national, Catholics voting Nationalist, Protestants voting Conserva- tive or Liberal Unionist. Till then Catholics had little political clout. But the 1884 Franchise Act (establishing household suffrage) brought many thousands of lower-class Catholics and Protestants into politics for the first time. This – combined with clerical mobilisation and effective Nationalist central organisation from Dublin – transformed the political map. Nationalists won over half the Ulster seats (17) on a massive turn-out of 93 per cent. There had been no Catholic MPs in Ulster in 1868. In 1885 there were sixteen. In the rest of the island Nationalists swept the board, taking 68 seats against only two con- servatives. With the bulk of non-nationalists representing Ulster con- stituencies, the differences between the province and the rest of the island had never seemed greater, even if the Ulster Catholics were now visibly part of an island majority.[63] But Ulster Catholicism was anti-Protestant before it was anti-English. Such leanings would have to be reversed before Ulster Catholicism's traditional apartness could be overcome and there was little evidence of the newly powerful clerical lead doing so. Rather they were much less worried about Protestant sensitivities than they were at the beginning of the century.

It seemed as if clerical domination of Ulster Catholic politics was complete. Even then, however, the clergy did not set the pace, and it was not until the Nationalist Party itself had decisively rejected Parnell after the O'Shea divorce that they too became anti-Parnellite. The weakness of an alternative Catholic leadership and that tendency to close ranks against possible Protestant criticism, caused the bulk of the Catholic vote to swing in behind them. In the 1892 elections Ulster was much more anti-Parnellite than any other province. In the four constituencies contested by both factions of the Irish Nationalist Party, the anti-Parnellites obtained 97.8 per cent of the combined vote, and in thirteen other constituencies anti-Parnellites stood without opposition. The Catholic clergy played a highly visible role against the Parnellites, even to the extent of swallowing up the Parnellite Catholic newspaper, the *Belfast Morning News*, into the new anti-Parnellite *Irish News*.[64] However, Ulster clerical support for the Irish Parliamentary Party returned after 1900, when it was reunited under John Redmond. Militant republicanism continued to find few supporters among the Ulster clergy and they were unprepared both for the 1916 rising and for partition.

Protestants, however, might be forgiven for not seeing in the prospect of Home Rule or independence anything other than submergence in Catholic culture – given the espousal by Irish-Irelanders of everything in Irish culture which they had traditionally considered popish and backward-looking – though Catholics too could be forgiven for now seeking to enhance everything in their own culture which had been so maligned for the past three centuries. And yet, however 'popish' the undoubted authoritarianism of the Ulster hierarchy in these years, theirs was actually a much more 'Ulsterish' approach than their critics recognised. Their chief concern remained – even in the dramatic climate of 1916 and afterwards – the defence of Catholic interests in the predominantly Protestant society of Ulster.

But there emerged at the turn of the century a new kind of Catholic, whose political base was the Catholic ghetto and who was less welcoming of clerical politicking than the old elites. In the 1860s an attempt to establish a Catholic Institute outside clerical control had been effectively crushed by Dorrian. 'Some of our Catholics in the North have been imbued with too much Presbyterianism', he claimed in this failed effort at what he considered 'lay dictation'.[65] However, in 1899 to 1905 when a similar contest occurred under another bishop of Down and Connor, Henry Henry, this time the leader of lay Belfast nationalism was the legendary Joe Devlin. In a foretaste of those tensions between a predominantly middle-class constitutional nationalism and a working-class republicanism – still apparent in Ulster nationalism in the late twentieth century – Devlin challenged Henry's efforts to control nationalist politics. Henry had set up a local political association in Belfast in opposition to the Parliamentary Party and totally devoted to local Catholic interests. Although an exaggerated version of the Ulster hierarchy's tendency still to view national trends through their localised view of the Protestant peril, such overt and aggressive political involvement was not the norm and disquiet at Henry's political activities within the Church itself helped in Devlin's successful challenge. Yet even Devlin's brand of Ulster nationalism – shorn of clerical domination – could not divorce itself from Catholicism.[66] Secular nationalism in Ulster still had to be seen to defend Catholic interests, for by now there was no other constituency to court and although Ulster nationalism did identify with that in the rest of the island, it retained distinctive features. The old Irish Nationalist Party remained the main political voice of Catholics in Ulster, even as Sinn Féin was sweeping nationalist support elsewhere, and most notably it expressed itself in the Ancient Order of Hibernians, whose core strength, under its president, Joe Devlin, was in Ulster.

The AOH was a mirror image (if never as strong) of the Orange Order in its sectarian identity and its mesmerisation with parades. Also, like the Orange Order, it was largely working class. Even though it functioned as a friendly society throughout Ireland, it was considered too sectarian and it never quite gained the hold which it did in Ulster – where, by 1909, it was the main nationalist organisation. Although it traced its lineage back to the Defenders and Ribbonmen, it was firmly constitutionalist in its activities.[67] The AOH looked after its own kind within existing sectarian politics and the headlong rush of Catholics and Protestants in apparently opposite directions in these years disguises one very important fact: it brought about a measure of stability. With their separate social, educational, religious and political institutions, both communities could feel a certain kind of security.

Until the outbreak of the First World War the Irish Parliamentary Party under Redmond seemed to be regaining some of its former strength. The next decade, however, witnessed a crisis in Ireland which ended in partition, and the form it took was about the worst of all options for Ulster Catholics. It was the Catholic bishops, fearing for the future of Catholic education in a Unionist state, who foresaw this far more clearly than the politicians and desperately tried to urge unity on them. The Third Home Rule Bill, giving limited autonomy to Ireland, was passed shortly after the outbreak of the First World War, and was due to be put into effect when the war ended. But the Ulster Protestants were already preparing to resist, some 471,414 having signed up to the principles of the Solemn League and Covenant, and 90,000 having joined the paramilitary Ulster Volunteer Force. Partition had already been discussed before the war, the Ulster Unionists demanding that the nine counties of Ulster be excluded from the scope of the bill. Eventually it was accepted that Cavan, Monaghan and Donegal, with their overwhelming Catholic majorities, must be included. The fate of Tyrone, Fermanagh and Derry City, with small Catholic majorities, was less easily resolved. By 1916, however, the six-county option – Antrim, Down, Armagh, Tyrone, Fermanagh and Derry (both city and county) to be excluded from any home-rule scheme – had emerged as the Unionists' minimum demand.

Redmond and Devlin believed such exclusion would be temporary and tried to recommend the scheme to their followers on that basis. They also believed that the excluded counties would continue to be governed from London and rejected as 'absurd' claims that the excluded area would have its own government. In June 1916 they addressed a stormy meeting of Nationalists in Belfast, when 776 delegates from all over Ulster packed into St Mary's Hall. Although a majority of 475 to 265 voted in favour of the scheme, the result was reached only through Devlin's deft management and Redmond's threat to resign. Only Belfast, Antrim and Down – reflecting Devlin's standing in the north-east – fell in behind them. Nationalists west of the Bann remained anti-partitionist and this east–west split in Ulster nationalism was to endure after partition. Delegates included a priest from every parish in Ulster. Significantly most of the clergy supported the anti-partitionists. Foremost among them were the bishops. Both the bishops and the constitutional nationalists were far more worried about the treatment Catholics would receive in such a state than about partition itself. All the Derry clerics had voted against the resolution and the city's bishop, Charles McHugh, had been a powerful spokesman for those fearful of the consequences of partition. Asked by Redmond two years previously to intervene against a march by the Irish Volunteers, which might have added fuel to Unionist criticism, the bishop – normally no friend to the militants – nevertheless made clear his mistrust of extreme Protestantism in power:

The Orange Order is never done crying out intolerance and publishing what they would suffer under home rule, but there is not a word about what the Catholics and nationalists would suffer if the Orangemen got control and what they have already suffered at their hands. The great object of the [Volunteers] meeting was to give the liberals to understand that the nationalists have their rights and that while agreeable to making concessions, they were not prepared to accept a state of things that would be worse than if they never stood up for home rule.[68]

The Irish Parliamentary Party had sent delegates to all the Ulster bishops to try to win them over, but found them totally opposed to any solution which would give extra administrative power to a devolved Belfast administration. 'What a prospect for Ulster Nationalists to be put under Belfast Orange Rule', McHugh wrote in a letter to the press. 'Unionist bigotry will then have full control over the lives and liberties of Catholics.'[69]

The Nationalist leader in County Tyrone, John McGlone, had warned the Belfast meeting: 'Catholics would again, after years of heroic struggle for equality of rights, be subjected to an odious oppression, and become the hewers of wood and drawers of water which the Unionists thought good enough for the papists.' Experience of sitting with Unionists on the new county councils for the past sixteen years, he continued, showed how intolerant they were and unwilling to co-operate when in a majority, and nationalists would be betraying their forefathers if they yielded to such an 'ascendancy' party.[70] After a century of reform, often extracted with difficulty, but of late accelerated to the point where a reversal of roles was a distinct possibility, here were Catholics like McGlone faced with the possibility of a return to the bad times of the past. Historic resentment prevented them from recognising their own double standards, for they were unwilling to concede the kind of separate identity to Protestants which they were claiming for themselves.

A bewildering array of political bodies claimed to represent nationalists by now, and militant nationalism was on the upturn. The 1916 rising received as little support in Ulster as it did elsewhere in the country and the Catholic hierarchy was caught off-guard. But the ensuing arrests and executions – as Pearse had foreseen – popularised militant republicanism and in the elections of 1918 Sinn Féin swept the board. Only six members of the old Parliamentary Party were returned – four of them from Ulster. But although Sinn Féin had begun to make headway in Ulster, particularly among the young, its success should not be taken as proof that the Ulster Catholics had abandoned their long tradition of constitutional nationalism. For the Ulster bishops – in time-honoured tradition of avoiding division in the face of Protestantism – had stepped in to force some pragmatism on the warring nationalist factions, who were in danger of splitting the Catholic vote and ensuring an Ulster Unionist landslide. The outcome was a shareout of winnable seats. A remarkable personal victory for Devlin in Belfast Falls – where he defeated the Sinn Féin leader Eamon de Valera by 8,488 to 3,245 votes – prefigured the future split in nationalist politics between east and west Ulster, and there were significant tensions too in south Down and south Armagh.[71]

But Sinn Féin's abstention from Westminster all but handed the Unionists a victory in any event. As the fine details of partition were being debated, the once-filled benches of the Irish Nationalists were empty, apart from the dispirited rump of Parnell's party, six in all, including the four Ulstermen – Devlin, Patrick Donnelly (south Armagh), Jeremiah MacVeagh (south Down) and Thomas Harbison (north-east Tyrone). And yet they still represented the bulk of Catholic opinion in Ulster – both lay and clerical – and with much justification they chided Sinn Féin for allowing partition through by their abstention. Sinn Féin used its landslide victory in the 1918 election to set up their own parliament in Dublin the following year, the first Dáil. Thereafter the party's attention was fully absorbed in its pursuit of an independent republic.[72] For the moment – the critical moment – it had little time for the partition issue, and northern nationalists felt increasingly abandoned.

The preferred option of the constitutionalists, including the archbishop of Armagh, Cardinal Logue, was that of dominion status for the whole of Ireland within the British empire. If the outcome was permanent partition, under a home government in Ulster, they would prefer to return to the *status quo ante* of rule from London. But with a weakened Nationalist presence at Westminster and an increased Ulster Unionist one in Lloyd George's Conservative government, and against a backdrop of the worst sectarian troubles for over a century, partition and home rule for Ulster became a reality in December 1920. The Boundary Commission – thought by Ulster nationalists to hold out some prospect of renegotiation – came to nothing. Ironically, despite Catholic bitterness, the 1918 election result had turned out to be a false dawn for Sinn Féin. The bulk of the hierarchy had been wary of republicanism, and, as on previous occasions when republicanism revived, clerical influence waned. Militant republicanism continued to be weaker in Ulster than elsewhere in Ireland and after 1922 nationalist politics settled back into its stable constitutional nationalist mould, in alliance with the Catholic clergy.

The partition of Ireland and the emergence of a Northern Ireland state with a sizeable Catholic minority had come about almost accidentally, and owed as much to the southern politicians' disinterest as to Unionist intransigence. At crucial moments southern nationalists were too preoccupied with attaining 'independence' for their part of Ireland to resist partition, and the balance of power at Westminster slipped from the pro-nationalist Liberals in 1914 to a pro-Unionist Conservative government which decided the details of the fourth Home Rule Bill in 1919–20. The resulting Government of Ireland Act (December 1920) provided for two Irish parliaments and administrations for the north and south, and a Council of Ireland to consult on common interests. As the rest of Ireland then became embroiled in civil war over the form of government to be established there, the northern state was able to settle into early permanency. By the time the civil war ended and the Boundary Commission finally came into existence (November 1924) most Irish people – even in the south – had become accustomed

1a. *Belfast from the River Lagan. Cave Hill in the Distance*, 1863.

1b. *West Belfast Peace Wall separating the Loyalist Shankhill Road and Nationalist Falls Road*, 1994. One of seventeen such barricades still separating Belfast Catholics and Protestants – usually at their own request – often physically dividing streets in apparently 'mixed' areas.

2a. Aerial photograph of Emain Macha (Navan Fort). Emain Macha in Armagh is believed to have been the capital of ancient Ulster, the centre of the Ulaid dynasty until its demise in the fourth to fifth century AD, and location of many of the legendary exploits of Cú Chulainn.

2b. Statue of Cú Chulainn, republican plot, City Cemetery, Brandywell, Derry. Legendary youth warrior of Ulster as depicted in the medieval Ulster Cycle tales, Cú Chulainn was reinvented by late nineteenth-century nationalism, his death (depicted here) becoming the key inspiration in the 'blood sacrifice' tradition of Patrick Pearse and twentieth-century Irish republicanism. Ironically he has also become a symbol for Ulster loyalism, because of his mythical role as defender of Ulster against the south.

Tullahoge was the inauguration site of the O'Neills, the most powerful Gaelic lords in Ulster. It was destroyed by the Elizabethans in 1602, symbolically ending O'Neill power.

3a. *The Dartmouth College Map of the North East of Ireland*, Map 25, c.1586. Detail showing Tullahoge, County Tyrone.

3b. Aerial photograph of Tullahoge Fort.

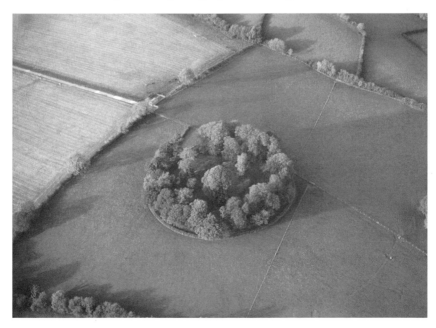

A *Now when into their fenced holdes the knaues are entred in,*
  To smite and knocke ths cattell downe, the hangmen doe beginne.
  One plucketh off the Oxes cote, which he euen now did weare,
  Another lacking pannes, to boyle the flesh his hide prepare.
C *These theeues attend vpon the fire for seruing vp the feast,*
B *And fryer smelfeast sneaking in, doth preace amongst the best.*
  Who play'th in Romish toyes the Ape, by counterfetting Paull;
  For which they doe award him then, the highest room of all.
  Who being set, because the cheere is deemed little worth,
  Except the same be intermixt and lac'de with Irish myrth.
D *Both Barde and Harper is preparde, which by their cunning art,*
  Doe strike and cheare vp all the gestes with comfort at the hart.

4. *The Chief of the MacSweeneys seated at Dinner* by John Derrick, 1581.
Derrick's engravings, though typical of the anti-Irishness of the Elizabethans,
nevertheless provide a contemporary image of the importance of the bards,
musicians and friars in the retinue of the Gaelic lord (in this case the
MacSweeneys of Donegal).

5a. Hedge Row School Mural, Ardoyne Avenue, Belfast. A romantic portrayal of a hedge-school in this late 1990s mural in a nationalist estate of north Belfast (note the depiction of the Cave Hill in the background, identifying it with the locality). The caption in Irish translates 'speak the Irish language to me'.

5b. Orange banner, Loyal Orange Lodge 273, Portadown No. 1 District – representing the drowning of Protestants by Catholics in the River Bann during the Ulster rising of 1641. The events of 1641 are regularly retold by some Ulster Protestants as an example of Catholics' inherent treachery.

6a. Mural of a Mass Rock, Ardoyne Avenue, Belfast. Late 1990s mural in nationalist North Belfast, near that of the Hedge School, this represents the most common nationalist image of the eighteenth-century penal era: the Catholic priest, saying mass in secret and hunted by the 'red-coats' (British military), in the distance.

6b. Mural of the Virgin Mary, Berwick Road, Ardoyne, Belfast. This 1990s mural in a North Belfast nationalist estate (Holy Cross Catholic church depicted in the background) is also something of a shrine, with an altar and monthly rosary meetings announced in an attached plaque.

THE STATION.

7a. 'The Station'. Before the so-called 'devotional revolution' of the nineteenth century, the 'station', whereby the priest would periodically visit the house of a selected parishioner to hear the confessions and give communion to Catholics in the parish, was a significant part of Catholic devotion in rural areas.

7b. *Cabins, Mourne Mountains, Co. Down* by R. J. Welsh, *c.* 1900. Though a later photograph, these cabins would have been inhabited since the eighteenth century.

8. *Battle of Ballynahinch, 13th June 1798*, (detail) by Thomas Robinson, *c.* 1798/99.

9a. *Cardinal Paul Cullen*, artist unknown, nineteenth century – redoubtable leader of the Catholic Church in Ireland between 1849 and 1878, he is largely credited with fashioning modern Irish Catholicism.

9b. *At Doon Holy Well, Kilmacrenan* by R. J. Welsh, 1912. Devotions and 'cures' sought at holy wells have been a feature of 'popular' religion in rural Ireland since early Christian days. Denounced by successive generations of clergy for the excesses which often accompanied the gatherings, some, like Doon Well in southwest Donegal, have nevertheless survived and been incorporated into the Catholic Church's devotional calendar.

The Great Famine of 1845–9, when over a million people died from starvation and disease, came to feature prominently in Irish nationalism's attack on British rule. The more polemical and unfounded accusation of genocide by Britain has been a feature of republican propaganda. But the bitterness at such suffering (well represented here) is real enough, even among nationalists who denounce violence.

10a. *An Gorta Mór: 'Britain's Genocide by Starvation'.* Mural of the Great Famine, Whiterock Road, Ballymurphy, Belfast.

10b. *An Gorta Mór: 'They buried us without shroud nor coffin'.* Mural of the Great Famine, Ardoyne Avenue, Belfast.

11a. *Rioting in Sandy Row, Belfast*, 1864, artist unknown. Belfast was torn by regular sectarian riots in the nineteenth century, often centred on the Protestant Sandy Row/Catholic Pound districts, the Boyne Bridge (pictured here) marking the interface.

11b. *Riots in York Street, Belfast*, 1922. Severe inter-communal violence marked the birth of the Northern Ireland state, 1920–22, claiming the lives of 453 people in Belfast. York Street, just north of the city centre – a district of internal segregation between Protestant and Catholic streets – was one of the flashpoint areas.

12a. *Walker's Pillar, Walls of Londonderry*, drawing by W. H. Bartlett, engraved by R. Wallis, *c*. 1825/1840. The walls of Derry/Londonderry hold a special place in Protestant tradition because of the walled city's resistance to the forces of James II in 1690. The Walker Pillar (commemorating the joint-governor of the city in 1690) was erected in 1826. It was intended as a symbol of Protestant dominance and considered so by the Catholic Bogside area over which it towered. It was blown up in 1973.

12b. Parliament Building, Stormont, Belfast – the massively imposing seat of the Northern Ireland Parliament, built in 1932. Situated in Protestant East Belfast, and transferring its name to the entire period of Unionist rule (1920–72), it was considered another symbol of Protestant dominance by most Catholics.

13a. Terence O'Neill with Councillor Robert Hart after opening O'Neill Road. This photograph was reproduced by Terence O'Neill in his *Auto-biography* as an example of his constant taunting by Paisleyites (in the background) during his premiership (1963–9).

13b. "*Biased!! How dare you, you long haired Fenian agita-tor.*" Martyn Turner – best-known caricaturist of the Troubles in Northern Ireland – capturing (in *Fortnight*, May 1971) Catholic perceptions of discrimination.

14a. *Questionnaire* is Turner's satire on the verbal ambivalence associated with Northern Ireland – usage of certain terms identifying the religious and political leanings of the speaker – and first appeared in the *Irish Times* where he has worked since 1976.

14b. Residents leaving Divis Street, in West Belfast in August 1969, after their homes were destroyed in sectarian riots.

15a. *'Free Ireland'* 1916 commemoration mural, Beechmount Avenue, Belfast – reproducing Patrick Pearse's 1915 oration at the grave of the Fenian, O'Donovan Rossa.

15b. *Bobby Sands' Funeral, 1981.* The funeral of Bobby Sands – first and the most famous of the republican hunger strikers to die in May 1981 – was attended by some 100,000 people.

16. Last rites by Father Alex Reid said over the body of one of the two British Army corporals killed at Andersonstown, March 1988.

to the border. The final report involved tinkering rather than major changes – and most of the Catholic areas of Tyrone, Fermanagh, Derry City and south Down would have remained within Northern Ireland. Even so, 31,000 people would have been shifted into the Irish Free State and 7,500 in the other direction. By now even the Dublin government thought it better to concentrate on consolidating what they already had and to leave the border unchanged. The Boundary Commission report was shelved, much to the distress of its chairman, and one Irish cabinet member felt that the Ulster Catholics might with some justification think that they had been sold down the river.[73] However, such were the levels of mistrust on both sides by the time of partition that neither Nationalists nor Unionists showed any understanding that their fears of being ruled by parliaments dominated by the other religion (whether in Dublin or Belfast) were mirror images of each other.

9

THE FAMINE AND AFTER:
CATHOLIC SOCIAL CLASSES IN
NINETEENTH-CENTURY ULSTER

But if there survived in high station in this place champions of old,
 Mac Cumhaill and the son of Dáire not to mention King Conchobhar,
Cú Chulainn, Conall Cearnach and all who were vanquished in battle,
 it wouldn't be long before Wully [Protestants] were dumped in the
 slime.

But since they've gone without trace, the bands who trained in our country,
 and we have nothing in their place but want, hunger and thirst,
 warbling and singing on the branches isn't heard in the valleys,
and there are no trout in the stream as is normal in the Island of Saints.

There's no man in the land of Fál, or woman and suckling baby,
 there's no strapping youth or elegant stately woman,
there's no beggar in the street whose lament isn't tortured and deep
 since the plague came upon the potatoes . . .

Hugh McDonnell, *Milleadh na bPrátaí*
(The destruction of the Potatoes), 1846
(Beckett, *Aodh Mac Domhnaill: Dánta*, 46)

In time the growth of Catholic organisations outlined in the preceding chapter opened up new career opportunities for a small Catholic middle class. But the trend for Catholics to be disproportionately represented in the lower social levels reinforced the kind of stereotype which became the standard fare of the evangelical preachers. The Ulster Catholics, the Revd Henry Cooke claimed in 1825, 'are generally inferior in point of education; they are greatly inferior, generally, in point of farming ... they are not generally so industrious as the Protestants; they put up with far less comfort'.[1] Even as late as 1861, Catholics, though 51 per cent of the Ulster population, supplied only 15 per cent of the professions and 22 per cent of the merchant class. Catholics had no monopoly on suffering and disadvantage.[2] Even so, the rural crisis which hit Ulster in the nineteenth century disproportionately affected Catholics, who predominated in the areas worst affected – south and west Ulster, with Cavan and Monaghan suffering most, followed by Tyrone and Armagh.

1. *The Famine*

As early as 1776, Arthur Young had foreseen the rural crisis which hit Ulster in the early nineteenth century.[3] The expansion of domestic linen had produced excessive sub-division, exhaustion of tiny plots of land and a dangerous reliance on the potato. Archaeological excavations in the Sperrins on the Tyrone/Derry border have shown potato cultivation spreading far into hitherto uncultivated, mountainous land during the eighteenth and early nineteenth centuries.[4] In predominantly Catholic areas social observers noted a particular tendency to sub-divide among children – a side-effect of that reluctance to leave the land noted earlier. Successive slumps, partial harvest failures and most of all the collapse of the domestic linen industry after 1815 had already weakened the once flourishing Ulster rural economy when natural disaster struck with the Great Famine (1845–9).[5] Much has been made of British government laissez-faire economic policy which allowed grain ships to sail from Ireland at the height of the Famine. But increasingly it is recognised that the underemployment of the huge agricultural labourer and cottier class when the Famine struck meant that few had the resources to buy other foodstuffs when the potato failed.[6]

Henry Glassie in his study of Ballymenone in Fermanagh discovered that the two issues which recurred most often in folk memory were the Famine and 'the days of the landlords'. Although cases can always be found to match the stereotype, the image of the tyrannical Irish landlord has been largely discredited along with that of the feckless absentee. Indeed nationalist literature often ignored the petty tyranny of the large Catholic tenant farmer or shopkeeper, because it was largely written by them or their offspring.[7] But it is notable that stories of bad landlords and evictions in the folklore records come mainly from south Ulster, where the disappearance of rural weaving was almost complete by 1841. Social commentators noted a listlessness and sense of hopelessness among the rural poor.[8] The terrible suffering of Ireland's Great Famine would become the centrepiece of Catholic nationalist tradition, driving a further wedge between the rest of Ireland and Ulster (for not suffering enough), and permitting extreme Protestants to claim the heavy losses in the south as yet another token of Catholic fecklessness. Beneath all the propaganda, it was easy to forget that Protestants also died in the Famine.[9]

The Great Famine, which started with the first potato blight of 1845, was drawn out over a number of years, successive potato blights, bad weather and the failure of other crops leaving the most vulnerable sectors without seed and without the income to purchase other food-stuffs at soaring prices. Fever and disease followed. Emigration soared. Ireland lost an estimated 1 million people through starvation or disease, another 1.2 million through emigration, and the trend of demographic decline continued until the end of the century. Ulster's population declined less than that of the rest of Ireland in the Famine decade of 1841–51 – 16 per cent against 20 per cent for Ireland as a whole. Even so, that 16 per cent accounted for 374,000 people and it disguises considerable regional variation. Thus while Antrim lost 10 per cent of its population, Cavan and Monaghan lost 30 per cent, with Tyrone and Armagh falling into the next worst-affected areas.[10] The Famine, in other words, had hit most in those areas least able to cope. On the very eve of the first potato blight, the Devon Commission reported the cottiers in Monaghan as largely unemployed. And yet no Ulster county escaped, even in prosperous Newtownards the soup kitchen was distributing 100 gallons of soup per day by 1847.[11]

Although the misery of the Famine was very widely shared in Ulster, and there are many oral traditions of decent Protestant landlords and clergy, there can be no doubt that in the long term the experience further soured communal relations. Prominent in these oral traditions of the Famine was that of the heartless landlord, the image of Protestants doling out soup to Catholics, proselytism, people dying in the open and the demeaning experiences associated with relief. Unsurprisingly the bulk of such stories come from areas where communal relations were already poor and overcrowding and poverty already extreme.

In general, Ulster landlords appear to have been rather better than their southern counterparts at remitting rates and rents for distressed tenants, though each county threw up examples of the best and the worst.[12] Both Derry and Donegal benefited from improving landlords such as Sir George Hill in Dunfanaghy – who actively flouted stringent government guidelines, by selling Indian meal early and cheaply. Indeed, the hate figures in Ulster folklore were not the grandees, but the middling farmers.[13] There were also counties in which criticism of the absentees like Lords Londonderry and Waterford were most heated. In fact the likes of Londonderry – who had estates in Antrim, Down and Derry – were more guilty of insensitivity than tyranny, and other landlords dreaded his tendency to air his 'mischievous' private opinions publicly.[14] His agent on the County Down estates, John Andrews, was representative of a particularly narrow-minded approach, which although untypical, came to be associated with Tory Ulster's reponse to the national disaster. As the crisis deepened, successive relief schemes – imports of Indian meal, public works, inside relief in the workhouses – all proved insufficient to cope, and by 1847 the government belatedly instructed the Poor Law Guardians to offer outdoor relief. Antrim, Belfast and Down were the only Poor Law unions in the country to refuse it. Andrews had viewed the Famine as a way of 'civilising' the country, of weaning the people of the south and west in particular from that lethargy and indolence which he thought resulted from the culture of the potato. It was the 'discipline' and the 'cleanliness' of the workhouses which they disliked, he claimed, and outdoor relief would simply give them 'the means of enjoying petty luxuries in their own filthy cabins'.

Andrews and his like were lambasted even by the Protestant press.[15] However, the outcry with which the so-called rate-in-aid scheme was met in Ulster was a token of things to come. In 1849 London decided to levy a rate on the more prosperous poor law unions to subsidise the impoverished ones in other parts of Ireland. The outcry from the north was not specifically anti-Catholic. Indeed, most protests were based on the belief that the rest of the British Empire should be sharing the cost of Famine relief, not foisting it all on Irish property. But many complaints were tinged with the kind of stereotyping of Irish poverty which often served as shorthand for Catholicism. Thus the Lisnaskea board of guardians in County Fermanagh told the Poor Law Commissioners:

it is with indignation we learn it is recommended . . . to impose a rate-in-aid on the peaceable and industrious inhabitants of the North of Ireland for the support of the lazy, vicious and indolent population of the south and west of the kingdom who neither fear God, honour the queen nor respect the laws of the land.[16]

It was this kind of mentality which eventually produced what Frank Wright called Ulster's collective amnesia of the Famine, denying memory even to the many Protestants who died or emigrated in it (a third of the population of Lisnaskea workhouse itself throughout the Famine being Protestant).[17] Many landowners were ruined by the Famine, as tenants could not pay rents and some 50 per cent of the total costs for relief was levied on Irish property. Catholics too protested at escalating rates. In truth everyone could have done better during the Famine; and if Lord Londonderry attracted criticism for lavish expenditure on Mount Stewart at the height of the Famine, the Catholic Church too was still trying to raise money for its ambitious building programme during it – one priest was even accused of levying contributions on the meagre earnings of his parishioners from public works.[18] However, the Famine would have been a good deal worse without the clergy's efforts, and many died in the process.

Given the heightened religious tensions of the previous decade, it is the co-operation of all the churches in relief schemes which is most impressive. When the workhouses were collapsing under the strain, increasing numbers being evicted for non-payment of rent and destitute people having to walk miles for any kind of relief, clergy of all denominations, like those in Cavan, joined to appeal to the poor law commissioners.[19] In Antrim, particularly in the Glenarm area, the churches had been co-operating on relief since the shortages of 1817 – and were early in establishing soup kitchens – the most effective of all the relief measures adopted during the Famine.[20] Before the end of 1846, soup kitchens were already in operation in Belfast – and clergy of all denominations were involved in the Belfast Relief Fund (which raised money not only for Ulster, but for Cork and Mayo). The rate-in-aid controversy should not be overplayed.

With such widespread co-operation by the clergy, why is 'souperism' – proselytising activities attending food relief – such a vibrant memory? Oral traditions throw up a number of memories of Protestant evangelicals using the weakened state of Catholics to trade food for conversion. But, in contrast to the south and west of the country – which saw a concentration of such missionary efforts – the few modern histories which pay any attention to Ulster do not give much prominence to this during the Famine period. What seems to be happening – as so often in folk memory – is a compression of stories over a longer period of time. These then become associated with the Famine period because of sensitivities about the general image that Catholics more often than not were those coming to the soup kitchens and Protestants more often than not were those administering them. Traditions of such occurring are very strong in north Antrim, where earlier proselytising activities had already aroused such hostility. 'Taking the soup' meant turning, taking soup for proselytism, and the families who did so were still remembered when folklorist Michael J. Murphy visited in the 1950s.[21] The Donegan family of Ballintoy spoke in 1956 of traditions of 'a soup kitchen run by people named McKinnan in the townland of Cloughcur. They called them the "Brockan-men" [from *brachán*, porridge or stirabout, associated with the Indian meal used during the Famine]. It was porridge they would give if you would change your religion ... The children would bless themselves before they would ate; and these ones would have their hands tied behind their backs so's they couldn't bless themselves. . . . And another thing I hear them tell, they would offer to give you brogues and a top coat if you would ate bacon on a Friday.'[22]

Other stories of intentional usage of meat in the soup kitchens on Friday come from Cavan, and were particularly associated with Lord Farnham's continuing activities. It was said that a number of Catholics 'turned' for the food, only to return to Catholicism when the Famine was over. But they were not allowed to forget that 'they ate Lord Farnham's bacon', and there is a tradition that Catholics so enticed through sheer necessity were denounced by their priests.[23] Certainly a series of embittered letters from both Farnham and local priests to the *Freeman's Journal* in 1848–9 suggests very bad relations and a perception of religious discrimination operating in the evictions which followed the Irish Poor Law of 1847. 'There never was perhaps a more terrible persecution carried on against the poor than at the present moment', wrote Matt McQuaid, parish priest of Killsherdany, County Cavan.

There seems to be a hellish rivalry among some agents as to who will banish the most. . . . It is not enough to drive out the mother and flock to tumble their cabin, wound their feelings and see their tears, but it is said some of these monsters grinned at their victims' devotions and mocked them ... Everyone knows that the mere Irish are being banished from some estates and Protestants substituted for them on long leases.[24]

Similar traditions survive from the Armagh–Monaghan borders. 'Of course it was all Planter Protestants about,' Robert McAlester of Crossmaglen, speaking in 1945, recalled of his grandfather's stories of the Famine, 'an' they had the soup kitchens of course, trying to convert ... the Catholics.' They had to go to Castleblayney, where 'big Hamilton, a Protestant of course ... could afford to boil a big pot'. People were dismissive about the ingredients and composed a rhyme about it.

> Oh, Mister Hamilton, you're big an' your [sic] fat;
> With plenty of grease on top of your pot.[25]

Such traditions were particularly associated with bad landlords – the soup being stigmatised with black humorous names such as 'Benson's gravy' or 'Downshire's porridge', and those who took it chided as 'turncoats' long afterwards. Several of these landlords and their agents, including the Catholic O'Callaghans of Armagh, Monaghan and Louth, who had evicted tenants during the Famine, became objects of retaliatory attack by Ribbonmen.[26] Although there is considerable folklore material on the good Protestant landlord, I have found no recognition of the genuine philanthropy which often co-existed with such missionising, particularly in the women's branches of the evangelical movement. Indeed, the dropping of tracts by these women on routes to the soup kitchens are a feature of the bitter memories.[27] There is not much criticism of government in these accounts. Again the cause of the suffering is much closer to home and invariably the shame of it all involves resentment of the Protestants who (as the more prosperous) figured prominently in the relief schemes.[28]

Most of the workhouses in Ulster had only recently been built when the Famine struck. Given that the Irish Poor Law of 1838 forbade public-financed relief outside the workhouse, many thought the new buildings ill-attuned to Irish needs. The Ulster-born Young Irelander John Mitchel – despite his typically melodramatic language – captured some of this in his dismissal of the Glenties (County Donegal) workhouse as 'rearing its accursed gables and pinnacles of Tudor barbarism, and staring boldly with its detestable mullioned windows as if to mock those wretches who still cling to liberty and mud cabins ... like the fortress of Giant Despair, whereinto he draws them one by one, and devours them there.'[29]

There was certainly a great reluctance among the Ulster poor to enter the workhouse and the preponderance of females and children amongst the inmates undoubtedly reflected male emigration or migration for work, but may also reflect the shame attached to males (of all religions) entering. Likewise with the soup kitchens. The *Newtownards Independent* recalled:

Oh to see those emaciated and half-famished souls surround the dog kennel where the soups was distributed. How to get a shawl, or cape or an old petticoat to envelop the head and fit to be seen, even at a dog kennel, was a question difficult to answer. And for the men to go with a can or jug was out of the question.[30]

The 'wee tin cans' carried along the roads for the daily ration while the soup kitchens operated made it hard to disguise one's plight.[31] 'If the parliament has gone without returning to this nation', the proselytising Irish Society's teacher Patrick Brady taunts the poet in Hugh McDonnell's *Agallamh idir Brádaigh an spiadhóir agus Bard Gaeilge* (A conversation between Brady the spy and an Irish poet):

> don't you have there in its place English schools
> and a prison building [the workhouse],
> where your women will receive more than a quart
> of mutton broth,
> drugget and an apron to cover their shame . . .[32]

Many soup kitchens and other direct relief schemes were financed directly by private charity, landed families like the Leslies of Monaghan, the Adairs of County Antrim, the Gwynns of south Down, along with the Quakers and innumerable clergy, emerging as heroes of the hour.[33] Even so, it was generally in the houses of Protestant landlords or in Protestant churches that the soup kitchens were set up.

It would be some time, however, before the sufferings of the Famine era came to reinforce pre-existing grievances and resentments. There is little evidence of attachment of blame at the time. Mitchel's attack on England for having 'slain' the Irish in the Famine finds little echo in oral memory, and where it does it is directly attributable to later printed sources – notably the immensely popular A. M. Sullivan's *The Story of Ireland* (1867).[34] In Monaghan – by far the worst-hit county of Ulster – its most recent historian, Patrick Duffy, has found that it 'left no trace in the collective memory'.[35] Something similar to the suppression of memories too awful after 1798 may be happening in the case of the Famine and there was a very general shame at death from starvation.[36] South Armagh and north Antrim (neither so badly hit) and south Down (which, like south Ulster generally, suffered most) may well be throwing up such bitter memories because a tradition of such was already well established before the Famine. South Down too became the area where many evicted from neighbouring counties settled. There is, however, some evidence in McDonnell's poetry of talk about the Famine being part of England's plot against the Gael – a precursor of a trend in later nationalism. But this is rare and may reflect the concentrated bitterness of the many migrants to Belfast, where McDonnell was living at the time of the Famine.[37]

2. *Seasonal Migration*

Predominantly Catholic counties continued to register the greatest decline in population in the latter half of the century, Ulster's Catholic population declining from 50.5 per cent in 1861 to 43.7 per cent in 1911, while all other denominations increased.[38] The rural decline meant that the hiring fair and seasonal migration, often to Scotland and England, became increasingly important to poor rural communities. By all accounts those experiences were often demeaning, and hiring fairs continued in Ulster into the twentieth century – long after they had disappeared elsewhere in Ireland.[39] Michael MacGowan's autobiography vividly recalls the typical experience of the rural poor in the nineteenth century. One of twelve children brought up in County Donegal, he was first taken by his mother to the hiring fair at Letterkenny at the age of nine. He was hired as a herd for six months to a kindly Catholic family at Glenveagh. By the time he was fifteen he had gone through five or six seasons of the hiring fair, having good and bad experiences. At ten he was taken on by a Presbyterian brother and sister at Drumoghill, five miles from Letterkenny. 'In my day, it was all "Scotsmen" who were there, but I heard that it is much changed and that some of our own people were now [1941, when his story was written down] getting the places that their forefathers had been driven from.'

MacGowan's account of his stay with the Presbyterians tells us more of inter-communal relations than any statistics. It should also raise a question mark over many of the stereotypes about the manner in which the different communities lived, for Michael, though coming from an overcrowded three-roomed cottage, was shocked by the personal and domestic slatternliness of the couple. The floor of the house was thick with dirt, food for the pigs and human food cooked side-by-side, and chickens scratching about on the floor. Their stinginess about food and money he saw as a characteristic of their people. But despite the acute awareness of difference, there is absolutely no prejudice on either side. Young Michael came to respect and like them, and although he clearly expected ill will towards Catholics – and there is a suggestion that there was enough of it around – he found none in Sam and Jane. On Sunday they made sure he went to mass and when their own minister came around for a 'lesson' he was never compelled to stay. He also found them just as superstitious and fond of storytelling about the fairies as 'our own people'. Michael was an Irish speaker, with just a smattering of English picked up the previous season. At first there were communication difficulties as he could scarcely understand their Ulster-Scots dialect. Another Irish-speaking Donegal migrant – Aodh Ó Domhnaill – had similar difficulties after he was hired at the Letterkenny fair in 1867. But he too experienced kindness, when the farmer and his wife brought in another Irish speaker to help him communicate.[40] However the initial difficulty in communication would have underscored the gulf between the Protestant and English-speaking culture of the richer areas, and the Catholic Irish-speaking one of those supplying the labour. Early last century Ó Muirgheasa collected in Donegal a poem still recited and thought to have been written a century earlier. 'The Gael amongst the Gaill' tells of the loneliness of the young Irish-speaking worker going to the English-speaking Protestant district (almost certainly the Laggan district in east Donegal):

The day that I went north through Barnesmore Gap
there was a coldness and a great tiredness on my shoulders,
my cheeks were wet with loneliness and I was crying,
such a pitiable man I've not yet met with in the province of Ulster.

When I was at home with my father and mother,
I did nothing for them, and they were no better off for my work;
but now I'm overcome and I'd prefer to be with them,
and if the day was a month long I'd be glad to be working.

It's I who am tormented and I'm not ashamed to recount it,
for since I left home many is the day that I spent,
listening to voices, Oh! such as I was not used to,
bleating on Sundays like a cow to its calf.[41]

The hiring fairs remained the fate of many rural poor in west Ulster until the Second World War – by which time they were confined to Omagh and Strabane in Tyrone. This was 'the slave market' in Patrick MacGill's *Children of the Dead End*, where boys and girls 'stood huddled together like sheep for sale in the market-place'.[42] In Tyrone Colm Tóibín was shocked to discover how powerful were the memories and resentments about the fairs as late as 1986. Few wanted to talk of their experiences because of the stigma attached, and Irish speakers from Donegal felt conscious that their very language singled them out in Tyrone as having come in to be hired. Rose McCullough told of her experiences in the 1920s when she first went to the hiring fair at Strabane aged thirteen, and of how she and her sister cried with homesickness as they stood in the snow. She remembered harsh treatment and inadequate food for the six years that she was hired out. 'They were all Protestants, the farmers', but the hiring included permission to attend mass every fortnight.[43]

When at the age of fifteen MacGowan first joined the very large numbers of seasonal migrants from Donegal to Scotland, the communication problems were even greater. There was no difficulty getting work and he regularly encountered 'great hordes' of people from Donegal 'on the "tramp"' like himself. By all accounts it was not a pleasant experience. 'Nothing was thought of the Irish in Scotland those days and as well as every other ill-usage they received, they certainly weren't paid in any way commensurate with the work they did.' He does not recount in detail any incident apart from general hardship. But the old people spoke of a village on their route through Scotland where they were regularly attacked. Carrying their own sickles and wearing the distinctive Irish homespun greatcoat, they were easily recognisable as Irish migrant workers.[44]

Migrant experiences differed greatly. In general conditions were worse for those migrants travelling to other parts of Ireland, and better in England than in Scotland, where resentments against the Irish were greater than anywhere else – and where more Ulster migrants went than from any other province. Within Ireland there was a keen awareness of the religion of the employer. There is some folklore evidence of bad employers creating difficulties about workers observing Sundays and holy days, and serving up meat on Fridays. However, Protestants – even in areas of traditional sectarian tensions – were generally considered better employers than Catholics and were more concerned with 'fair play'. Indeed, workers from Dromintee in County Armagh did not attend the hiring fair in Dundalk, County Louth, since the southern Catholic farmers did not have so good a reputation for attention to the comforts of their workers as the northerners.[45]

After some fifteen years in America, Michael MacGowan returned to his Donegal home of Cloghaneely in 1901. On arrival at Derry he was told of the great changes which had come over the area. In the first place he would no longer have to walk to his home, for a railway now ran from Letterkenny to Burtonport.

A Board was set up called the Congested Districts Board and some years ago a man named Balfour visited your parts. He enquired about the condition of the people and when he had done that, he conferred with people in authority about schemes to help the poor districts that stretch from here westwards to the sea. As a result of that, the railway . . . was started. . . . Changes there are . . . and the people down by the sea where you live can be thankful to this new Board for many of them. They've done well for the fishing all around the coast; roads and bridges were built; grants were given to poor people to help them to build new houses; they're helping home industries and the weavers are very busy now making bawneen. There are twenty ways in which they're trying to help the people, late and all as it is. But better late than never.[46]

MacGowan is the human face of economic and social trends in post-Famine rural Ulster. The continued decline in rural population after the Famine was largely due to increasing emigration, delayed marriage and urban expansion. The net outcome by the early twentieth century was the kind of improvement in rural conditions noted by MacGowan on his return home. By then peasant proprietorship was almost complete, the old rundale system had largely disappeared as farms were consolidated and 'the days of the landlords' were a thing of the past. Indeed, MacGowan himself became one of a growing class of strong Catholic farmers, having bought his house and 150 acres from the landlord who had been in financial difficulties for some time.

3. Tenant Right

Return emigration with 'Yankee' money, however, was unusual and, until the government-inspired improvements of the late nineteenth century, rural poverty remained a factor of life. The letters of small tenant farmers (Catholic and Protestant alike), written in the 1860s, 1870s and 1880s and analysed by David Fitzpatrick, show the same insecurities, the same long hours, the same meagre diet, the same watchful eye on the potato 'Since the year of the Failure', the same fear of expropriation in lean years, the same extended emigrant network.[47] These subsistence farmers could not have survived without the traditional help of neighbours often across the religious divide, however important the cultural and religious differences. Indeed, it would be difficult to explain the very high levels of religious co-operation in Ulster in the various land campaigns of the nineteenth century, and the lower levels of agrarian violence, except in the context of such shared grievances or perceived grievances.

By the early twentieth century the land acts of successive governments had created peasant proprietorship and effectively removed the land problem from Irish politics, except as an emotive memory. The passing of landlordism was not achieved in the rest of Ireland without

considerable violence – notably during the Land War of 1879–82 –
and in the more traditionally Catholic areas of south and west Ulster
there were sufficient similarities in the campaign to create a community
of interest. But in Ulster generally the land campaign was waged with
remarkably little violence. This was partly the result of rather better
landlord–tenant relations than elsewhere (with some glaring exceptions), but also of the interest of a powerful Presbyterian tenant interest, which politically the landlords could not ignore. The main social
development in Ulster Catholicism in the second half of the nineteenth
century was the massive influx into the towns. But the bulk of Catholics
continued to live in the predominantly rural parts, and although they
still tended to occupy smaller holdings than Protestants, there was
enough antagonism between Presbyterian tenants and Anglican landlords to create a community of interest between Catholics and Presbyterians – even after the recognised Nationalist–Catholic/Unionist–
Protestant polarisation that occurred after 1886. Brian Walker, in his
study of the religious make-up of the different social groupings in Ulster
between 1868 and 1886, highlights considerable diversity within the
overall picture of Protestants at the top end of rural life (owning some
72.5 per cent of the land), Catholics at the bottom (some 57.3 per cent
of agricultural labourers, 63.1 per cent farm servants). Protestants of
all denominations also accounted for a considerable portion of the
poorest. The landowner class was dominated by Anglicans, wealthier
tenants by Presbyterians, with Catholics making up a significant portion of medium-sized farmers.[48]

The campaign for Tenant Right came to the fore in the 1850s.
Essentially it sought to legalise the so-called Ulster Custom (which was
just that, a 'custom', not always generally practised, even in Ulster
where it was traditionally thought to be the reason for the rather better
landlord–tenant relations than elsewhere in Ireland). Although there
was considerable confusion over its interpretation, essentially it gave
outgoing tenants the right to compensation for improvements or for
the remaining 'interest' in their property, which they could sell to the
incoming tenant. During the Famine, its operation was particularly
important in helping to finance emigration. What it did not do was
give any guarantee against eviction.[49]

The problem then and since was the belief that Catholics should have been the natural inheritors of the land which had once belonged to their ancestors. It had sufficient weight even among Protestant tenants for them to vote with the landlords.[50] The task of getting them to identify with the largely Catholic tenant-right campaign elsewhere in Ireland seemed an almost insurmountable challenge. The editor of the Presbyterian *Banner of Ulster*, Dr James McKnight, assumed the challenge and presented an intriguing interpretation of the Ulster Plantation. By this the original undertakers were simply trustees rather than outright owners. Their tenants had carved out their estates from uncultivated wastes. The landlords only had the right to the rent of the 'raw' earth and not the inflated rates of the land improved by the tenants themselves. The argument found a ready audience among Catholics. There are intriguing echoes of it in the Revd James O'Laverty's history of the *Diocese of Down and Connor* (1878–95), where the Gaelic chieftains are also included among those who had no right to the land separate from the people who farmed it.[51] The tenant-right campaign soon ran foul of the anti-popery generated by the restoration of the Catholic hierarchy to England and the ensuing Ecclesiastical Titles Act (1851), which prohibited Catholic bishops from including a British or Irish placename in their titles. The landlord interest fanned the flames of sectarianism to defeat the popular challenge. But for a short while the campaign had the backing of both Catholic and Presbyterian churches. Even in areas of acute religious tensions, like Ballybay in County Monaghan and the Downpatrick area in County Down, priests and ministers shared platforms. There were also some signs of Catholic–Orange co-operation on the ground, which became even more prominent at the time of the Land League.[52]

McKnight was also editor of the *Londonderry Standard*, and his stand was undoubtedly influenced by the Donegal experience – the one part of Ulster where the stereotype of the tyrannical landlord found supportive examples. When MacGowan went to herd cows for the old Presbyterian couple of the Laggan, he found a police barracks oddly situated in the middle of nowhere. It had been built in 1861 to protect the landlord John Adair at the time of the notorious Glenveagh evictions. After the murder of his agent and the loss of many of his sheep, he took revenge by evicting hundreds of his tenants and pulling down many of their houses. McKnight, through the *Standard*, made the harrowing scenes an international scandal.[53] Simultaneously McKnight was conducting a campaign against the landlord from hell: the Third Earl of Leitrim, whose activities on his large north Donegal estate, from the 1850s till his murder in 1878, would rival any fictional account of aristocratic antics in *ancien régime* France. No one mourned his demise, not even the authorities. 'He was what we call a bad land Lord', wrote the Fermanagh small farmer and Methodist William Fife, whose letters to his emigrant daughter in Australia reveal the continued community of interest on the land issue across the religious divide.[54]

The tenant-right issue went into abeyance during the post-1850 economic recovery. But it was fanned into renewed activity in the late 1860s by Gladstone's disappointing Land Act of 1870 and by the agricultural depression of the late 1870s, which spelt disaster for the poorer farmers, particularly in the hilly areas. Again it produced some highly unusual alliances: Catholics voting for Conservatives who promised land reform (Tyrone by-election, 1873), where traditionally they would have been Liberal,[55] and again Orange–Catholic co-operation, even as Fenianism was contributing to the tensions which would see political polarisation reach new dimensions in the following decade. In the 1880 election the Orange Order in County Armagh refused to endorse any candidate who did not support tenant right, but repudiated the ultra-nationalist Land League which made its first appearance in Armagh that same year.[56]

The most surprising and notable example of this was Catholic support for the ultra-Protestant William Johnston of Ballykilbeg near Downpatrick, most remembered for coining the phrase 'Home Rule is Rome Rule'. Johnston's writings and speeches bristle with all the traditional anti-papist stereotypes of the fundamentalist Protestant. But, whilst never abandoning his Orangeism, he seems to have been sufficiently affected by the sufferings of the Famine to have decided that he had a destiny to take on the landlords and the government, and he was returned as an independent Conservative MP for Belfast in 1868 with significant Catholic support. There were similar stories from County Antrim, where the strongly pro-tenant-right Ballymoney was the first of any Ulster town to elect a Catholic to the town commission. Ulster Liberalism was paying the price of complacency about the Catholic vote, just when more and more Catholics were becoming enfranchised and resentful of continuing Protestant dominance of the party. Over the next decade organised nationalism under Parnell was able to sweep their vote, sending even radical Protestants back to Conservatism. Although tenant right continued to occupy rural voters of all denominations in Ulster – and initially the Land League recruited considerable Protestant support there – by 1885 renewed sectarianism had confined the tenant-right campaign to mainly Catholic areas.[57] The passage of a number of other Land Acts in the 1880s (particularly beneficial to the hill farmers) followed by the Wyndham Act of 1903 effectively removed tenant right as a common grievance.

4. Belfast

Although Catholics still tended to live predominantly in rural areas – they were 53 per cent of the farming population in 1871, though only 48.9 per cent of the Ulster population as a whole[58] – the nineteenth century witnessed a dramatic increase of Catholics in the towns, notably from internal migration by rural Catholics. The experiences of Catholics in Victorian Belfast in particular played a major role in shaping Catholic identity on the eve of partition. By 1911 40 per cent of Ulster's population was town-based. Most dramatic of all was the growth of Belfast. By the end of the nineteenth century, Belfast, in its size, economic activities and social problems, had more in common with Glasgow and Liverpool than with any town elsewhere in Ireland, Dublin included. It had grown from 19,000 in 1801 to 349,180 by 1901. Increasingly Ulster people were urban-dwellers, while the population on the rest of the island remained largely rural. In the 1780s Catholics formed only 8 per cent of Belfast's population. By 1808 their numbers had jumped to 16 per cent, by 1834 to 34 per cent. This represented a five-fold increase over twenty-six years.[59] The arrival of increasing numbers from rural areas was already causing tensions in this predominantly Presbyterian town, and in 1813 it experienced its first sectarian rioting.

It was the mechanisation of the textile industry which both ruined the rural industry and attracted increasing numbers to the town.

Already by the 1840s, the huge mills – still a feature in the 1950s – were defining the skyline. Mr and Mrs S. C. Hall in 1842 commented approvingly of the sense of bustle and full employment which they gave to the city: 'Such an "aspect" of business; a total absence of all suspicion of idleness in contrast to the south, that we thought we were in clean Manchester.'[60] The numbers employed in the Irish linen mills and factories increased ten-fold between 1839 and 1917 and the industry was almost exclusive to Ulster. But within Ulster the regional focus shifted dramatically eastwards. As early as the 1830s Belfast had ten steam-powered spinning-mills, four of them in the already recognisably Catholic Falls Road. By 1861 there were thirty-two mills and the port had begun its legendary expansion to accommodate the textile trade.

Belfast's sectarian geography was already being defined by these mills. Rural Catholics, seeking employment, tended to move in family groups and settled near each other. Despite the upsurge in the number of Catholics, in 1861 they still only accounted for a third of Belfast's population and only a quarter by 1911. Belfast remained very much a Protestant town. Thackeray, visiting in 1842, found theatre-goers damned from the pulpits of meeting-houses and churches, and the bookshops stuffed with evangelical literature. 'I was not very sorry to leave the town behind me, and its mills and its meeting-houses, and its commerce, and its theologians, and its politicians.'[61] The tiny Catholic middle class felt uncomfortable with their social peers and increasingly channelled their activities into Catholic social organisations. The changing nature of organised Catholicism in Belfast in the second half of the nineteenth century was also a response to this upsurge in the Catholic population. The building of chapels, convents and other social institutions further defined the Catholic areas and increasingly provided a social outlet for the often dreary lives of the Victorian working class.[62]

Thackeray was as impressed as the Halls by the huge mills and bustle of Belfast. But his main observation concerned the large numbers of young females in the city. He noted 500 in Mulholland's mill alone working twelve hours a day 'in huge long chambers, lighted by numbers of windows, hot with steam, buzzing and humming with hundreds of thousands of whirling wheels'.[63] What Thackeray did not note was that 60 per cent of the employees in Mulholland's mill were children, many as young as eight; that the average age of death in Belfast was said to be nine; that the employers resisted many of the reforms of workers' conditions imposed from Westminster; that Belfast Town Council (on which only three Catholics had sat that century) was notoriously resistant to providing any social amenities for its working class, even to the point of rejecting a bequest to provide Sunday music for the workers in the parks.[64]

Ten years after Thackeray's visit the Revd W. O'Hanlon – a Congregationalist minister, originally from Lancashire – conducted his famous walks among the poor of Belfast. Among Catholic and Protestant working class – inhabiting the rookeries and airless 'courts' in its centre – he found wretched poverty, strangers sleeping seven to a room, few practising any religion (though they knew what religion they were born into, and occasionally priests were invited in for specific needs). Drunkenness was rife and public houses proliferated. It is a reminder that a Protestant underclass also existed – though heavily disguised by Protestant and Catholic myth-making deeming such a thing inconceivable.[65]

Even so, the structural disadvantage of Catholics – there since the seventeenth century – assumed new and more visible proportions in Belfast. In 1853 they constituted 48 per cent of workhouse inmates. Fifty years later they still accounted for 46 per cent, though only 24 per cent of the population. Moreover economic developments and discrimination ensured that they remained clustered in the lower levels of the labour market. There is a perception among Ulster Protestants that Catholics are culturally pre-conditioned towards arts-type disciplines and averse to the 'useful' sciences and technology. But this – if proven – may be because they had little choice. All the commissions and surveys of the nineteenth century show low percentages of Catholics in the skilled trades and among the middle classes. In the second half of the century, the activities of the Harland & Wolff shipyard began to define the employment profile of more and more male workers, just as the mills had done that of females. But few Catholic workers were employed (only 225 out of 3,000 in 1886), and when they were, they were unlikely to figure among the skilled workers. At the end of the century Catholics accounted for 41 per cent of the dockers but only 7 per cent of the shipwrights. Battles between the two groupings became a feature of Belfast's sectarian rioting, and intimidation seems to have played a part in the decline in the proportion of Catholic shipyard workers from perhaps as much as 20 per cent in 1861 to 7 per cent in 1901. In 1886 only one of the town's large employers, the Combe, Barbour and Combe foundry in North Howard Street (today's interface between the Falls and Shankill Roads) had a religious balance, with 40 per cent of the workforce Catholic. This may have been because of the mixed religious makeup of the area, and Catholic employers in Catholic areas seem to have been equally discriminatory in employment practices. Sectarian rioting (at its height in the period 1857–86) accelerated segregation in both the workplace and housing. And – just as in rural areas landlords preferred to let to co-religionists of an outgoing tenant – so managers and foremen were simply taking the 'line of least resistance' to maintain the peace: 'Where one community dominated a workplace, its position was allowed to drift towards exclusivity.'[66] Belfast's Catholic population did not occupy an inferior position in relation to the overall workforce in the United Kingdom. The key point is that the Protestant population had secured a particularly privileged position.

Worst of all in employment practices were the public bodies, particularly local government, where Orange political influence was in the ascendant. The Belfast Riots Inquiry of 1886 found that only five of the ninety-five officers of Belfast Corporation were Catholics, on a salary only half that of Presbyterian officers. By 1911 only 9 per cent of those employed in local government and poor law administration were Catholic. In municipal elections the £10 household franchise had discriminated against Catholics who tended to be amongst the poorest. But increasingly they had allies in Dublin Castle and at Westminster. Central government employment of Catholics in Belfast was nearly proportionate to their numbers. In 1887 a special extension of the British household franchise to Belfast, and in 1896 Westminster's creation of two new wards (Falls and Smithfield) for these predominantly Catholic areas, resulted in the automatic election of eight Catholic councillors.[67]

By the end of the nineteenth century some 91 per cent of west Belfast was Catholic, and the trend throughout the century was one of increased religious segregation. The Falls area of west Belfast had developed from the Catholic districts of Smithfield, Hercules Street (now Royal Avenue), Millfield, and the Pound. It was in west Belfast that competition for employment and territorial rivalry was most intense from early in the century. For the expanding Catholic population was pushing up against the Orange weaving districts of Brown Square and Sandy Row. Until the Famine, Protestant Orangemen and Catholic Ribbonmen or Repealers were equally aggressive. The upsurge in Catholic numbers, the ascendancy of O'Connell, the banning of party processions, 1832–45, the distancing of the gentry from the plebeian Orangemen – all seemed to give the Catholics the edge on triumphalism, and in the 12 July riots of 1843, thousands of Catholics marched along the edge of the Protestant enclaves, just as the Orangemen had always done to Catholic areas. After the Famine, however, the tide had turned decisively, with the decline of Catholic numbers from pre-Famine heights, the re-entry of the 'respectable' classes to Orangeism, the accession of Protestant working-class strength from the expansion of the shipyards and the addition of anti-popish street preaching and newspaper coverage to election campaigns.

The 1852 riots – sparked off by shots fired from the Sandy Row area into the neighbouring Catholic one – witnessed the first extensive use of firearms and the intimidation of families out of mixed areas. Thereafter, each successive riot marked an intensification of previous ones – 1857, 1864, 1872, 1880, 1884, 1886, 1898, 1901, 1907, 1909 – the four months of rioting on the defeat of the first Home Rule Bill (1886) resulting in 32 deaths and 371 injuries. Most of the riots were still confined to the Sandy Row/Pound, Falls/Shankill interface, with conflict between Protestant shipwrights and Catholic dockers becoming a regular feature. The Royal Commission investigating the 1857 riots could not understand why Orangemen felt such a need to incite Catholics in a town that was predominantly Protestant. But the rise of organised Catholicism and nationalism in the second half of the century, and Gladstone's Home Rule Bills fed traditional Protestant belief that political popery was in the ascendant. All the more so since Catholics were emulating them and insisting on their right to march. Sybil Baker describes the trend at the end of the century: 'Marches to

Hannahstown by the Ancient Order of the Hibernians; torchlight processions by the '98 Centenary Clubs; [fundamentalist Protestant preacher] Trew's anti-ritualist demonstrations; Twelfth parades; Lady Day [15 August] excursions . . . bands with their followers playing nightly through the town – Belfast's mobs had never exerted with such tireless vigour their right to parade the streets.'[68]

The persistent riots and intimidation had made safety among one's own a priority for the working class of Belfast. By 1901 over two-thirds of Catholic householders lived in Catholic areas, the 'tribal map' of the late twentieth century already recognisable: the Falls Road/ Smithfield area, New Lodge Road, Markets, Ardoyne, with smaller groups in Dock and Greencastle. But the percentages of Catholics living in one-religion areas jumped to 75 per cent among manual workers and Belfast-born Catholics. The rural influx had stopped. A specifically Belfast working-class culture was developing and the trend towards separate cultures grew apace. By the beginning of the twentieth century most Catholics could attend exclusively Catholic educational establishments, exclusively Catholic public houses, shops and parks and often even exclusively Catholic workplaces. It suited most Protestants and Catholics alike and was an important factor in the increasing role of the Catholic Church in Catholic social life.[69]

Here was a world very different from the rural one of MacGowan, where the agricultural cycle and relative isolation did not permit the development of such antagonistic identities. However, Tony Hepburn has identified segregation also between towns, all the main industrial centres becoming more Protestant in the 1861–1911 period, establishing the enduring perception of towns and localities as predominantly of one ethos or the other. Thus in Portadown – though registering a percentage population increase as great as that of Belfast – the proportion of Catholics fell by 12 per cent and there were similar falls in Larne, Ballymena and Lisburn. Even in Derry City – whose Catholic population, drawn mainly from neighbouring Donegal, outnumbered Protestants by 1850 – there was a 2 per cent decrease during the period. Whilst net increases of 7–12 per cent occurred in perceptively Catholic towns like Downpatrick, Newry and Strabane, Lurgan experienced a 67 per cent Catholic increase, with a 149 per cent Protestant increase in neighbouring Portadown. Of course the religious segregation and polarisation were already intense in this historic flashpoint area, and there was a pre-existing Catholic linen-weaving population in Lurgan to act as a magnet.[70] But the development of different religious cultures in the neighbouring Armagh towns of Portadown and Lurgan was setting fast the area's historic divisions.

5. Catholic social classes

The structural disadvantage of Catholics in Ulster even impeded genuine attempts at reform. Protestant domination of the magistracy continued because traditionally its members were taken from among the major landowners.[71] Magistrates had to be of sufficiently independent means and standing so that influence could not be brought to bear on them. The problem was that, although there were many Catholics among medium-sized farmers by the late nineteenth century, the landowners were still largely Church of Ireland and the numbers of magistrates in 1884 – 72.6 per cent Church of Ireland, 14 per cent Presbyterian, 8.5 per cent Catholic – was a fair reflection of the social situation. Among the middle class, Catholics continued to make slow progress, though more among its lower than its upper levels. Thus, although their share of the legal profession increased from 14.1 per cent to 22.3 per cent between 1871 and 1891, it was in traditional areas of Catholic employment like the retail and drinks trades that they came to dominate – some 55.5 per cent of hoteliers or publicans being Catholic in 1871. Lest one think that this rising social class would emerge as lay champions of their fellow Catholics, however, it is important to remember that they were part of that reviled breed of gombeenmen, small retailers who sold on credit, then exacted a high price, often the forced sale of smallholdings, for unpaid bills.[72]

Significantly, other areas of employment in which Catholic numbers soared were closely connected with the expansion of Catholic social organisation. Thus the growth in Catholic schooling is reflected in a Catholic percentage of 39.5 per cent of teachers by 1871, while the number of Catholic clergy by 1891 accounted for 31.7 per cent of clergy in the province. Thereafter they continued to increase, reaching a ratio of 1:1,276 in Belfast by 1926, up from 1:4,601 forty years earlier.[73] This picture of social advancement within their own community marks an important change of outlook among Ulster Catholics. Even in O'Connell's time the ambition of those who prospered was to join the existing social and political system. And whereas the old, small elite tended to live outside the exclusively Catholic areas, this new middle class did not. These would become the leaders of nationalist politics in Ulster. They also produced the clergy, since they alone could afford the costs of clerical training. Given the greatly expanding power of the Catholic Church by the end of the nineteenth century, it was very much the values of this lower middle class which came to infuse the modern Church.[74]

This is not to say that religious identity had totally overtaken that of social class. Indeed, in Belfast the rivalries between the Christian Brothers (imported to cater for the education of the working class) and the more elitist St Malachy's College, run by the diocesan clergy, was a factor in organised Catholic life until the second half of the twentieth century. But inter-denominational class identity was severely impeded and indeed discouraged. The Catholic Church did not approve of socialism. Trade union organisation among teachers was specifically banned in the Armagh archdiocese. The activities of the Society of Saint Vincent de Paul, and the organisation of sodalities, evening classes and early morning religious services to accommodate the mill-workers were more typical of the kind of self-help culture fostered by the church.[75]

Such ghettoisation greatly assisted the expanding power of the Catholic Church. But Ulster Catholics showed little resistance. They had always been less anti-clerical than their co-religionists elsewhere and, by the end of the nineteenth century, there was none of the resistance to church payments, which had been such a feature of earlier times. There were some wealthy Catholics. Bishop Dorrian, assessing the prospects on the eve of the remarkable expansion of church building during his episcopate, thought there were between seventy and ninety in Belfast who could spare £100 each for church purposes. Prominent among these were John Hamill, the landowner, whose home (Trench House on the Falls Road), was later donated to become the Catholic teacher-training college; William Watson, the property developer in west Belfast; George Murney, the shopkeeper and tobacco importer; William Ross, owner of the Clonard flax mill; and the Armagh-born Bernard Hughes, who began his apprenticeship as a baker in 1827, later starting a bakery empire which was still a significant Catholic institution in the 1960s.[76]

Despite their generosity, however, it was the Catholic people as a whole who funded the second wave of major church building in Ulster (in the 1870s and 1880s) and the acquisition of buildings for Catholic social institutions. The door-to-door collections, the charity sermons, special appeals and bazaars became a significant feature of Catholic life. Accounts published by the parish priest of Ballymoney in 1881 show that the funds for a new church, reading room, schools, parochial house and offices had been raised very largely from parishioners' subscriptions, collections, charity sermons and a bazaar.[77] On the whole Catholics were proud of such external displays of new wealth and status by their church and were anxious to donate to it.[78]

But in predominantly Catholic areas – lacking the potential for priests to pull critics into a common Catholic line against local Protestants – there may well have been tensions. The most publicised case of such was that of Canon James MacFadden of Glenties, County Donegal, an arrogant and authoritarian figure, whose political militancy became an embarrassment to his superiors. His extensive building programme on behalf of the church in the 1890s was typical. But his lavish expenditure on his own parochial house, often extracted from the poorest of his parishioners, while he 'hobnobbed' with Catholic gombeenmen, earned for him the savage 'image' as Father Devany in the autobiographical novels of Patrick MacGill – for which the young author was denounced by MacFadden from the altar.[79] Seamas MacManus remembered a similar priest in Kinawley (County Fermanagh), though he lived at Swanlinbar, County Cavan. Father Tom O'Reilly chased drinkers from the public houses and loiterers from the street with his stick, and would publicly shame any parishioner who did not put the weekly halfpence into the Sunday collection box.[80]

However, wealthy Catholics seeking to run their own denominational bodies outside the control of this newly powerful church were quickly pulled into line. The most notable example of this was Dorrian's dispute with the businessmen founders of the Catholic Institute in Belfast. In 1859 they bought property on the edge of Hercules Lane to serve as a kind of residential club for the Catholic middle class. Dorrian distrusted such 'Catholic' institutions outside episcopal control – citing the 1864 *Syllabus of Errors* to underscore his claim that no one should be running Catholic societies whose religion and character did not have his approval – and feared its possible use for political purposes. It is a significant commentary on the changed times that such wealthy Catholics (Hughes among them) did not attempt to put him in his place as their social peers on the Catholic Committee would have done at the beginning of the century. The Protestant press, picking up on the dispute and portraying it as proof of Romish priestly tyranny, simply rallied Catholic opinion behind Dorrian – an early example of how Ulster Catholics would suppress internal differences in the face of hostile Protestant attention. Joe Devlin was later to win his contest against the autocratic Bishop Henry, in part because Henry had broken this widely accepted rule of Catholic politics.

This confessional basis of northern nationalist politics caused predictable problems to trade union and labour organisations. Although the leader of the 1907 Belfast dock strike, James Larkin, was a Catholic – a factor which the employers used to great effect to play on sectarian tensions among the strikers – he was a Liverpool Catholic. Joe Devlin, despite his impeccable working-class credentials, did not appear on strike platforms till very late in the day and then largely to take up traditional nationalist complaints about the activities of the police and the army. The difference was that Catholic workers were far less likely to turn on employers of their own denomination than Protestant workers. 'Catholic workers viewed the Protestant ruling elite as their chief agent of oppression', writes John Gray, historian of the 1907 strike, 'and were thus far less likely to develop specifically working-class opposition to their own middle class which, whatever its faults, was in no sense a ruling class in the north.'[81] Nor did the early stages of Labour politics in Belfast inspire confidence among Catholics. Working-class Protestants had invariably demanded traditional anti-popery from their candidates, and even William Walker, champion of the unskilled in the shipyard, and Labour candidate for North Belfast in the elections of 1905–7, seemed more than happy to defer to their expectations by agreeing to oppose any Catholic succeeding to the monarchy, resist Home Rule and always place the interests of Protestantism above those of party. Needless to say, the Catholic electorate deserted him and Ramsay MacDonald despaired at the failure of socialism to surmount Belfast's traditional sectarianism.[82]

10

ACROSS THE DIVIDE:
COMMUNITY RELATIONS AND
SECTARIAN CONFLICT BEFORE
PARTITION

[The Catholics'] fires are kept up in a kind of party spirit, in contradistinction to the British and Caledonian settlers, who, principally on that account, annually commemorate by bonfires on the 1st and 12th of July their delivrance from Popish domination, by the victories gained by their ancestors at the battle of the Boyne and Aughrim in 1690 ... The descendants of these primitive [the old Irish] and more modern British and Caledonian settlers ... have not yet assimilated, so as to form one general character; this in a great measure may be attributed to the difference of their religious tenets ... [they] are extremely jealous with the British and Caledonian settlers, whom they are taught to believe are intruders and foreigners.

[John Donaldson, *Historical and Statistical Account
of the Barony of the Upper Fews* (1838)]

By the time of partition Ulster Protestants and Catholics had acquired separate political identities. But they were simply superimposed on long-established communal and religious differences. They were identities which fed off one another. This is why sectarian and highly localised Ribbonism was never replaced in Ulster by the avowedly non-sectarian Fenianism, and why it ebbed and flowed in response to levels of Orange activity. Outsiders were (indeed, still are) surprised at how apart Protestants and Catholics were in Ulster, when racially, culturally and linguistically they seemed so similar. The resurgent Catholic Church and increased papal authoritarianism, the greater Catholic visibility as they poured into the towns, outnumbering Protestants in their original city (Derry) by the end of the century, the growing confidence and political assertiveness of Catholicism – all had the effect that every sign of Catholic assertiveness had in the past: Protestants of all denominations closed ranks and liberalism faded. Catholics saw this as conforming to type, Protestants thought them inferior and would always try to dominate, given the chance – and so the simplified stereotypes were reinforced.

1. Across the divide

What all this produced was a mutual wariness merging into hostility at the extreme, and always a sensitivity about name calling or mockery from the other side. But local situations ensured wide variations. In the second decade of the nineteenth century Dr John Gamble, a native of Strabane in County Tyrone, made a number of tours on foot through the north of Ireland. The impression is of roads full of human traffic, of walkers invariably seeking companionship, of hospitality to excess. He was particularly interested in how Catholics and Protestants viewed each other. He too commented on how alike they were. But Protestants were very anxious to assure him that they were not papist – particularly if they had Catholic-sounding names. Near Larne he spoke with an innkeeper named O'Sullivan: 'He was very anxious to assure me that he wasn't Catholic, despite the name, but descended from a Huguenot' – 'a zealous Protestant would as soon call his son Judas as Pat.'[1] The lesser gentry he found particularly anti-papist. His host in Omagh regaled him with a typically lurid commentary on the 'scarlet whore' of Rome because he thought Gamble had 'a good Protestant face'. 'You don't know *thim* as I do', he confided, having drawn his chair near; 'you *hivn't* lived amon them, and can't tell what sort of *varmin* they are: why, man, my own *sarvants* would murder me in my bed, if they durst.' Certainly a young male Catholic servant whom he met on the road a day or so later showed scant respect for the gentry and expressed a hope that the 'croppies' would have their day. 'Emancipate the Catholics to make friends of them', his host continued [for Gamble supported Catholic emancipation]; 'J–s, what fools our great people be! if they were to give them the crown of England today, they would be quarrelling for the diamond (that I'm *tould* once dropped out of it) to-morrow' – a traditional Protestant complaint still made today – that Catholics would never be satisfied.[2]

Further along the road to Omagh, Gamble found a parish priest lodging with a Presbyterian landlady. He thought it unusual enough to query. Catholics were good customers, she told him, and the priest in particular. Their pounds were the same as Protestant ones, and who's to know they might not be right in the end! Gamble thought such comments unrepresentative and he was right. Friendships between individuals there were – particularly in rural areas – but the idea of 'popery in the gross' was as strong as ever and one is struck by anti-papist perceptions unchanged since the Reformation, now riveted in popular Protestant consciousness. As in all societies, the school-children reduced such perceptions to their simplest expression. The future Young Irelander, Charles Gavan Duffy, attended a classical school in Monaghan in the late 1820s and early 1830s, where he was the only Catholic. At first the boys were resentful about a 'papist' joining them. The resentment did not last and Duffy made close friends. But he found books like Foxe's *Book of Martyrs* circulating among them. One lad was particularly steeped in the lore of popish atrocities, which he regaled to his school-mates during recreation, his favourites being the old tale of popish priests absolving murderers of Protestants.[3]

At the other end of the century nationalist playwright Seamas Mac-Manus told a similar tale of the largely Protestant model school in Fermanagh, where he went as a teenager. But the intermingling brought tolerance and he too built strong friendships, particularly with John Irvine. Though 'a loud Orangeman', and drummer in an Orange band, he was nevertheless warm-natured and developed such a liking for 'the Fenian' that he taught him Orange tunes which he drummed on the school's revolving globe, while MacManus tried to beat out the pink patches that marked the British empire.[4] A Protestant perspective from Downpatrick-born writer Lynn Doyle (1873–1961) shows that no side had a monopoly on sectarian awareness. At his overwhelmingly Catholic National school there were frequent after-school fights provoked by religious taunts and, even during class, protagonists would flash scrawled slogans on their slates: 'To H– with the Pope', 'To H– with King William'. One day the Catholic master caught the Catholic culprit and he was caned for his 'unchristian' action. The master was respected as a fair man, but even he could not help adding, besides, 'It's . . . *unnecessary*.' 'One dogma, maintained equally firmly by Catholic and Protestant when I was a boy [was] – the eternal damnation of all adherents of the opposite faith.'[5]

The ease with which all creeds resorted to stereotypes was noted too by Gamble – though the Catholics' imagery was impoverished by contrast. King Billy came too late to attract the purple prose of the Reformation era. On the road to Ballymena, Gamble was rescued from some disorderly farm animals by a kindly Catholic. He surmised as much, for the good Samaritan did not recognise his biblical allusions. 'Of course then you are not a Presbyterian,' commented Gamble. 'No; I thank God,' replied he, 'I don't belong to the black-hearted breed.' However, when asked why he called them such, he was at some loss to explain. 'Why, – why,' said he, somewhat puzzled, 'because I always heard them called so.' And when urged further for some rational explanation, none was forthcoming, save that they had sold their king for silver (i.e. Charles I) and abandoned the Catholics in 1798. Gamble found this opinion pretty general amongst Catholics.[6]

The nineteenth century was a defining time for such prejudices, because of the developments in politics and organised religion discussed earlier, and sectarian conflict was on the increase. But it was still locally confined and the experiences of Duffy and Doyle would have been the norm: heightened mutual awareness, suspicion and, at times, fear, tempered by genuine friendship and neighbourliness and an ability to laugh at their prejudices. Doyle reflected:

Yet none but an Ulster man can fairly criticise Ulstermen. The foreigner, looking at the surface of things, judges both sides too hardly. There was a good deal of convention in our attitude towards each other in those days . . . In theory we hated one another bitterly, but practise did not follow at theory's heels, in country districts at least. Our childish freaks apart, in all my boyhood I never knew of anyone being insulted on account of his religion. . . . We possess in the North one great corrective of bitterness, that dry sense of humour that is so often infused with self-criticism. We are conscious of our bitterness, and see the ridiculous side of it now and then.[7]

Nor was he the first to comment on the tendency for people from Ulster, when thrown together outside the province, to make sport of their mutual feud. It is also crucial to recognise that even in the worst of times Ulster communities were never totally polarised. The Catholic grandfather of William McComiskey (b.1875) emigrated to America from County Down, boarding a Liverpool-bound ship at Warrenpoint. Nearly all aboard were from the south of Ireland and 'he didn't have much to do with them'. But there was an Orangeman from Derry called Walker on board; they recognised each other's Ulster accents and stayed together the whole voyage. Mass was said on board every morning. But when the captain tried to stop it the Irish all rose and captured him and the Orangemen took their side.[8] At its edges, sectarianism shades into that particular brand of Ulster black humour, so appreciated by natives, so appalling to outsiders. Hugh McEnhill told of the local landlord in late nineteenth-century Tyrone taunting the Catholics with a chamber-pot carrying a picture of the pope at the bottom. 'But he wasn't a bad man,' he continued. And unlike his wife, he never gave himself any airs and graces. He walked everywhere and would always treat them to breakfast at Omagh fair.[9]

A degree of local accommodation was normal when political issues did not intervene and an awareness of what might offend (or give others the excuse to do so) often smoothed over potentially divisive situations. The difficulty of finding neutral venues – such a feature of late twentieth-century Ulster – was already a problem a century earlier. It was particularly noticeable during the cross-community tenant-right campaign of the early 1850s in south Ulster, where the large number of evictions after the Famine and resultant agrarian incidents exacerbated persistent sectarian tensions.[10] Lynn Doyle's tales of *Ballygullion* – his fictional Ulster village, with its equal numbers of Catholics and Protestants – charts the perennial efforts of the more moderate to surmount communal tensions, and they make for hilarious reading. Even the setting up of a creamery society in the town seemed doomed to be thwarted by petty sectarianism. Disputes over the location of the initial planning meeting nearly scuppered the project at the outset, for how to choose between Orange or Nationalist halls. Even if both were used in rotation, one would necessarily be first, and there were far too many who would not concede even that to the other community. Very well, responded the priest – one of the community leaders called upon to mediate – let there be two creameries, a Catholic one and a Protestant one. 'The only thing that bothers me . . . is the difficulty av doin' it. It's aisy enough to sort out the Catholic farmers from the Protestant; but what about the cattle?' – a variant on the standard theme in humorous Ulster writing: nobody and nothing could be anything other than Protestant or Catholic.[11] Stories of good neighbourliness and genuine friendship are legion, from the MacManuses in Donegal leaving payment for the apples they had picked from their Methodist neighbours' orchard – because they could not trade on Sundays – to the Brennans of Drumcullen in Fermanagh sponsoring the passages to Australia of their Methodist friends, the Fifes, between 1859 and 1865.[12]

Even so, it was friendship *across* the divide. Generations of friendship between the Presbyterian Hamiltons and the Catholic Floods in Tyrone did not lead to any greater religious understanding. May Brunt, née Hamilton, speaking of her childhood friendship with one of the

Floods in the early twentieth century, recalled that they could never agree on religion and she still thought theirs 'a peculiar blend of religion, politics, and superstition under the domineering influence of their church and its lust for power'.[13] The greater visibility and assertiveness of the Catholic clergy in the nineteenth century were finally giving substance to such ancient perceptions. It can be found even in the works of a sympathetic Protestant novelist from Fermanagh, Shan Bullock (1865–1935). Sarah and Felix are poor Protestant farmers in his *Dan the Dollar* (1906). They had taken in the orphaned children of distant relatives and they became like their own. But young Mary was a Catholic, and a particularly devout one at that. Sarah could not quite reconcile Mary's undoubted goodness with her fervent Catholicism. She 'fasted and did penance, prayed to the Virgin and the Saints, confessed to a priest, knelt to idols. Such practices in Sarah's eyes were abominable.' Mary too had all the stereotypical traits of a Catholic. She was utterly guided by and uncritical of the priests, whatever evidence was put to her of their worldliness. Despite her goodness, she still felt herself unworthy. Her excessive humility and sense of guilt is commented upon by the other characters, as if being miserable was a Catholic duty. Mary, for her part, was always aware of Sarah's dislike for her Catholicism – however much they loved each other – and she was convinced her religion was at peril if she married a Protestant (even a lapsed one like Dan, Sarah's son). Another theme is the perceived Catholic disdain for comfort and their tendency to live in run-down and ill-kept houses. The stereotypical Catholic lack of domestic comfort and cleanliness may have made a virtue of necessity, for, as noted earlier, the majority of Ulster Catholics were generally to be found in the lower social categories. For their part Catholics viewed materialism as a vice associated with Protestants.[14]

Whilst rural life imposed necessary mixing and co-operation, denominational cultural spheres were becoming increasingly separate. The practice of sharing at least some cemeteries seems to have continued for much of the nineteenth century.[15] National schools were still mixed in rural areas till the end of the century, but at the secondary level Catholics left in droves from mid-century on, given the choice of denominational education.[16] However, it is in the thorny area of 'mixed marriages' that the intimate social tensions caused by religious difference are most apparent. The very term raises eyebrows outside Ireland, where it is understood as mixed race. And yet in Ireland, and more especially in Ulster, the cultural taboos and impediments have been just as strong. Neither Catholic nor Protestant clergy or laity liked them. The Catholic Church progressively tightened up its controls until its notorious *Ne Temere* decree of 1908 insisted that all children of mixed marriages be brought up Catholic – where the tradition had been for sons to be raised in the faith of the father, daughters in that of the mother – and banned the couple from remarrying before another clergyman. But although it made many couples' lives unnecessarily difficult and delivered a major propaganda weapon to anti-popery, pressures from the Protestant churches were equally effective. Such marriages were treated as popish in any event, and in sectarian rioting mixed-religion couples were hounded out of Protestant areas, just as Protestants who married Catholics were dismissed from the Orange Order. Nor should the churches be held entirely responsible. As D. H. Akenson observes in his investigation of inter-communal relationships, *Small Differences*, no church could impose restrictions which its adherents did not endorse.[17] It looks as if the mixed marriage between Mary Brennan and Joseph McKee of north Down compelled the couple to emigrate. Certainly their letters from Australia (1865–76) reveal little evidence of friendly relations between the families at home.[18] Once out of the country, they were not so inhibited by communal pressures.

Relations were undoubtedly becoming more strained from quite early in the century. The rapid growth of population – particularly in the poorer sectors and traditionally Catholic districts – was creating tensions beyond the purely economic. If Gamble noticed it, then others less tolerant would also have done. Catholics were tolerated if an unthreatening minority. To this was added the economic stereotyping underpinned by the Ulster Catholics' concentration in the unskilled and labouring end of the employment market. David Fitzpatrick's analysis of the 1901 census figures for one parish in north Down reveals only Protestants employing domestic servants, and all those servants were Catholic.[19] Such was the limited experience of the rural poor that, when they moved for work to more prosperous areas, they could appear backward. H. A. Lafferty recalled the Donegal servant girls on his father's farm at Ardstraw, County Tyrone, coming down stairs backwards because their only experience of a second storey was climbing by ladder into the loft of their single-storey houses.[20] Many of the lower-class Protestants who still dominated Orangeism in the nineteenth century were just as underprivileged, but eagerly accepted the rhetoric of superiority *vis-à-vis* the Catholics. After the Union the anti-Catholicism of English politicians was less disguised by the presence of an Irish parliament, and the thirst for political news created by the United Irishmen did not evaporate. The Catholic emancipation issue dominated debate for much of the first three decades. In the end, emancipation had to be extracted from a reluctant parliament and, as before, the concession did not meet the high expectations. But in the process O'Connell had mobilised a Catholic movement of staggering power. Tory politicians were not slow to play on the anti-papist paranoia which it gave rise to, particularly among Ulster's lower-class Protestants.

Irish-language poems are awash with references to 'Luther's breed' and Protestant 'heretics' – with particularly scathing references to Elizabeth I – and such poems were still being recited in Armagh in the twentieth century.[21] Indeed, the last bardic contention to have taken place in Ireland, at Dundalk in 1822, had as one of its themes: 'The faith which Christ left a while ago . . . now under a cloud since the greed of the *Gaill* began; but . . . near is the hour when Clan Luther will be exhausted and weak.'[22] But it is resentment at Protestant slights which most comes through. Ó Muirgheasa collected an Irish-language prayer in Monaghan dated 1824:

> O loving Mary, O gentle virgin . . .
> send down your heavy blow and rudely fell the heretics of Ireland;
> expel the English language from our country, and leave the dear Irish in
>   its place,
> the children of Luther it was who left us without life, like an old faggot
>   you'd find in a hedge.
> Give a heavy damaging blow to the deceitful children of blind Calvin,
> it's the Scots I mean, lay your hand down on them fiercely.[23]

A poem composed by Hugh McDonnell in the 1840s picks up the dismissive language being employed by the teachers of the proselytising societies.

> O heedless lackey who never puts aside
> nonsensical chatter,
> stuff up the throat which won't stop your mouth
> from talking about oppression
> . . . layabouts of your nation,
> poets and druids,
> who'd normally go without shelter or shade,
> or a place to spend the night.[24]

An early nineteenth-century sectarian doggerel also collected by Ó Muirgheasa in Donegal – 'The Orangeman' ('*An tOrangeman*') – dreams of the Orangeman 'ploughing the land for us'.[25] At the Belfast meeting of June 1916, McGlone's choice of phrase in the heat of the moment to express Catholic resentment at being presumed inferior by Protestants is entirely representative of Catholic opinion: give Protestants the chance and they'll reassert their old ascendancy over us and treat us like 'hewers of wood and drawers of water'.[26] The Revd John Tohill, a professor at St Malachy's College, Belfast, said much the same during the 1887 Belfast Riots' Inquiry. He complained of 'an aggressive Protestant ascendancy' being exercised by all classes of Protestants, and of Catholics being 'treated as if they were an inferior and conquered race'.[27] Catholics were generally very aware that Protestants thought them inferior and that for much of the century they still held most of the state power. 'The Protestants are generally of higher rank and pride themselves on being Protestants and freemen,' Gamble concluded. 'The Catholic is depressed and dispirited; he hates the Protestant, but fears him for the party to which he belongs . . . which he thinks is supported by the magistrate and the state.'[28]

In fact, as the century wore on, the state was making considerable efforts to ensure impartiality in policing and the administration of justice. Although Belfast and Derry retained borough police forces until 1865 and 1870 respectively (both of which were regularly accused of anti-Catholic bias), a new centralised police force was established for the entire country, which became the Royal Irish Constabulary in 1867. Many Catholics were recruited into this, and a system of stipendiary magistrates was introduced from 1836 onwards. Evidence to the numerous riots commissions in the second half of the century show the beginnings of a greater trust among Catholics in the central government's desire to ensure equal justice. A Protestant doctor who ministered to the working-class Catholics of Derry told the 1870 commission: 'I know that party [the Catholics] are very much inclined to accept the protection of the law, if they have any expectation of it.' Indeed, the Catholic clergy had dissuaded their people from clashing with the loyalist Apprentice Boys of Derry the previous year, on the understanding that the government commission would indeed introduce reforms.[29] However, although government enquiries regularly rebuked Orange magistrates, the belief among Catholics and often the reality was that the forces of law and order were inherently anti-Catholic, even Orange. The tendency for such magistrates to see Orange parades as legitimate loyal displays and nationalist meetings – however constitutional – as rebellious, becomes particularly marked during the Home Rule campaign. The problem, as always, about such imperiousness and lack of generosity was that it created the very evil which it claimed to prevent. It also disguised the legitimate concerns of many Protestants.

2. Parades and sectarian riots

Lower-class Protestants were unnerved by Daniel O'Connell's often inflammatory rhetoric and heeded warnings that Catholic emancipation would adversely affect their community.[30] Orangeism witnessed a phenomenal growth in the early decades of the nineteenth century. Gamble found it everywhere. 'Beyond all other things, Orange processions are become offensive to the Catholics; they remind them forcibly of their ancient misfortunes, and what they think their present degradation. They regard them not only as injuries but insults, and writhe at the sight of them.'[31] 'We did not know much of history', Gavan Duffy recalled, 'but we got . . . "object-lessons", to keep it alive in our memory. The Orange drum was heard on every hill from June till August to celebrate the Boyne and Aughrim . . . To be a Protestant of any sort was a diploma of merit and a title to social rank . . .'[32] In time the Orange parades became part of popular Protestant tradition and Lynn Doyle remembers the little boy's ambition to participate in the flute bands. But for much of the nineteenth century Orange parades were aggressively and provocatively anti-Catholic and were central to Catholic complaints throughout the century.

It was at this time too that such parades became Protestantism's most cherished symbol of a fading Protestant ascendancy. Until the end of the Napoleonic war in 1815, the security policy of successive governments was still dependent on the yeomanry (20,000 of its total force of 30,000 being Ulstermen), which had always been highly susceptible to Orange infiltration, and Orangeism still had many friends in high places. After 1815, however, the yeomanry increasingly fell into disfavour. The reorganisation of the police and the introduction of stipendiary magistrates began to challenge respectively the yeomanry's role and that of the local Orange gentry who occupied the bench. One of these new magistrates – John Hancock – waged such a campaign against the Orangemen of County Armagh that his home came under armed attack.[33] By the 1820s the movement seemed under siege. O'Connell's campaign, however – particularly Lawless's ill-advised 'invasion' of Ulster – brought about a major revival. The yeomanry was needed to cope with a serious 'tithe war' in the Irish midlands (1830–33) and it was re-armed. Its 'new' arms now began to feature prominently in an upturn in sectarian clashes. This did not mean a renewal of government approval. On the contrary, Orange processions continued to be frowned upon and were banned under the first Party Processions Act in 1832; while a major parliamentary enquiry in 1835 was so critical that the Grand Lodge of Ireland voluntarily dissolved itself the following year, even though the local lodges continued their activities.[34]

But in areas of traditional confrontation, notably County Armagh, they clearly had, and expected to have, the side of the law. A map of Orange lodges in 1836 reveals a very heavy concentration in the old linen triangle, centred on north Armagh and south Tyrone. Since the 1790s both the yeomanry – and to all intents, the justice system – seemed to be entirely under Orange control. Colonel William Blacker was a yeomanry commander with impressive Orange credentials: he had been present at the Battle of the Diamond, was the Grand Master of County Armagh and had been Deputy Grand Master of all Ireland. He was also chairman of the petty sessions. Orangemen were confident he would take no action against them. The parliamentary report of 1835 into Orange Lodges concluded likewise, and he and several other Orange magistrates were stood down. The Portadown, Tanderagee, Lurgan area is the prime example of the kind of league between Anglican gentry, clergy and labourers which gave the latter such a sense of 'owning' the system. Lord Mandeville (owner of the Tanderagee estate) and the Revd Dean Carter were known to have kept up Protestant fears by prophecies of popish plans to massacre Protestants and dark references to a 'Sicilian vespers'.[35]

A number of liberal landlords and legal men were encouraging Catholics to complain to the government and from the late 1820s it took action to curb such activities. But by then a pattern of behaviour had been established. 'For most of the year', one Protestant witness told the 1835 enquiry, people are usually good neighbours, 'but prior to the 12 of July in every year, say for a month, the people become estranged from each other as if they were foreigners.'[36] Although Carleton had become a Protestant by the time he came to write his autobiography towards the end of his life (he died in 1869), he recalls with some bitterness the early nineteenth-century Orange ascendancy in County Tyrone and how Protestant neighbours could so easily turn on respectable Catholics to show they were in control:

This [early nineteenth century] was the period of Protestant, or rather of Orange, ascendancy ... Every yeoman with his red coat on was an Orangeman. Every cavalryman mounted upon his own horse and dressed in blue was an Orangeman. ... Merciful God! In what a frightful condition was the country at that time. I speak now of the North of Ireland. It was then, indeed, the seat of Orange ascendancy and irresponsible power. To find a justice of the peace not an Orangeman would have been an impossibility. The grand jury room was little less than an Orange lodge. There was then no law *against* an Orangeman, and no law *for* a Papist.

These yeoman were in the habit – especially when primed with whiskey, or on their way from an Orange lodge – of putting on their uniform, getting their guns and bayonets, and going out at night to pay domiciliary visits to Catholic families under the pretence of searching for firearms; and it is painful to reflect upon, or even to recollect, the violence and outrage with which these illegal excursions were conducted.

He went on to relate a night-time raid on their house by a group of Orangemen, all of whom were their neighbours.[37] Protestant friends and neighbours turning aggressive during the marching season would have been a common experience for Catholics – particularly at the lower end of the social scale. Lynn Doyle's Catholic narrator of Bally-gullion claims:

I'm no party man, myself; but whin I see William Robinson, that has been me neighbour this twenty years, goin' down the road on the twelfth av July wi' a couple av Orange sashes on, me heart doesn't warm to him as it does av another day. The plain truth is, we were bate at the Boyne right enough; but some av us has more than a notion we didn't get fair play at the fightin'; and between that and hearin' about the batin' iver since, the look of ould Billy on his white horse isn't very soothin.[38]

Groups of young men would roam the countryside playing party tunes, attacking their opponents, organising 'drumming parties' outside the homes of liberal magistrates or clergy – who would be damned as 'papists', 'a term they deem very offensive'. Huge parades would take place on 12 July – 10,000 parading at Tanderagee in 1831 – fed by long marches from other areas.[39] Drink would be taken and Catholic areas attacked on the homeward march. Catholics would retaliate and very often end up convicted by Orange juries. The following year during the marching season, anniversaries of 'incidents' would draw even greater numbers. 'Orangemen' or 'Ribbonmen' became generic terms of abuse – even though neither represented the majority of either community. However, it is clear that the Orangemen still believed that they were defending the interests of a Protestant state against rebellious Catholics, and in 1831 attacks were reported on Catholic houses in the Portadown area by young labouring Protestants who believed that Catholics were still not entitled to keep arms.[40]

In fact the 'Protestant state' *was* being slowly dismantled – too

slowly to attract Catholic gratitude, but too quickly for Ulster Protestants. Again O'Connell's campaign, however constitutional,
enflamed a raw nerve, and it coincided with the kind of Protestant
revival which depicted popery as a disease in need of cure. One incident
in County Monaghan gives some idea of the communal bitterness of
these years in areas of long-standing conflict. On the night of 13
February 1828 in Drumswords churchyard, four miles from Clones,
the body of David Burke was disinterred and hung from a nearby tree.
It seems to have been an area of long-standing religious conflict and
was the scene of a massacre of Protestants in 1641.[41] Burke was
master of Drumanan Orange lodge; a yeoman and a leading figure in
suppressing rebellious activities in 1798, he was considered also as a
scourge of the local Catholic population. Of late the area had witnessed
a number of clashes between Orangemen and Ribbonmen, including
one over whether a Protestant convert to Catholicism should be buried
in a Catholic graveyard. One press report described it as the action of
'Dan's [O'Connell's] worse than savage pupils'.[42]

Catholic emancipation brought little immediate benefit to the average Catholic. But it did wonders for him psychologically and from
1829 onwards Orange parades were challenged at every level. At its
crudest it involved Catholic youths challenging the marchers. A notable
example of this occurred at Mackan in Fermanagh in July 1829. The
marchers seem to have attacked a group of youths who had jeered
them on the outward march that morning. That evening the Catholics
gathered with their pitchforks and billhooks and took revenge, killing
three of the Orangemen. Four Catholics were later capitally convicted
for the killings. They claimed to have acted in self-defence, that none
of the original perpetrators had been called to account, and that they
could not expect a fair trial because of the notoriety of the Orange
juries in the area – a claim the Lord Lieutenant seemed to accept, for
he later commuted the sentences to transportation, though too late for
one of the men, who was hanged at Enniskillen.[43]

Like so many more local affrays, that at Mackan gave rise to strong
local traditions, which were embellished over time. By the last decades
of the century, the hanged man had died 'for God and Ireland', for
'faith and fatherland'. By the next century it had entered a composite
picture of a time when the Catholics were enslaved and the Protestants

in control – though none of those who related the tale to Henry Glassie were particularly militant. One of the commemorative songs incorporates the kind of insults which the Orangemen would have used:

On the 13th of July,
Of the year of twenty-nine,
Being the time of these bloody No Surrender,
They were cheering loud and shrill,
To they came to Mackan Hill,
For the face of a papish pretender.

Where they drew up their lines,
In square and rank and file,
The cry was for No Pope or No Surrender.
But with steadfast hope,
They who consmate [sic] the Pope,
All his nuns and crucifix pretenders.[44]

As the affrays grew worse, the respectable people began to abandon the Orangemen, and Catholics made their feelings clear to government that 'they will not suffer themselves to be insulted, or their feelings outraged by these senseless parades, of what they have hitherto considered a domineering faction'.[45] Certainly once government clamped down on the marches (Party Processions Act of 1832), there was a visible relaxation in tension for almost three decades and the propertied Protestants remained aloof from Orangeism until the 1880s.

When the Party Processions Act lapsed in 1845, there was an immediate resurgence of Orange parades. Catholic clergy called for re-routing and urged Catholics not to react – but to no avail. Ribbonism was reactivated. Invariably the Orangemen were better armed. A famous incident occurred at Dolly's Brae near Castlewellan in County Down. Communal relations in the Rathfriland–Castlewellan area had long been fraught and an incident earlier in the century had convinced residents in the largely Catholic Dolly's Brae area that no more Orange marches would be permitted to pass. A new road skirting below the pass of Dolly's Brae allowed Catholic clergy and local magistrates to ensure a peaceful resumption of marches in July 1848. But local Ribbonmen treated the failure to go through the pass itself as a great victory and celebrated it as such in printed songs. Predictably Orangemen rose to the challenge the following year and succeeded in marching through the pass itself. But tensions were high. They had been taunted by Catholic women along the way with threats that they were walking into a trap. In fact, although the Ribbonmen had been potting shots all day to show that they were armed, their threat was to prove something of an illusion. The Orange parade had marched through the pass to their grand master's (Lord Roden's) estate at Tollymore. There they were told of how recent measures by the government had placed the Protestant constitution in jeopardy and of how their loyalty was needed to defend it. On the route back some shots were heard – whether from the Orangemen or Ribbonmen on the hill no one could later ascertain. A general affray ensued. But the Orangemen emerged unscathed, while at least thirty Catholics were killed and Catholic homes in the area fired. The descriptions of attackers and assailants in the government report into the incident shows the deadly nastiness of these sectarian feuds among the under-privileged. The armed Orangemen had fired on children fleeing across the fields, shot domestic animals and strangled chickens.

But the report singled out those in higher places for particular censure. The two local priests were praised for their efforts to keep the peace, but criticised for then formally blessing the Ribbonmen as they knelt on the hill – a gesture the commissioner felt gave unintended legitimacy to the Ribbonmen's actions. But his major criticism was reserved for those magistrates (including Lord Roden), who, though aware of 'a population consisting of two contending bodies, whose prejudices and feelings are inflamed against each other from old recol-lections and religious differences', nevertheless – because they were leading Orangemen, had failed to stop what he regarded as an unlawful march.[46] Once again propertied Protestants took flight from Orangeism. The government reimposed the Party Processions Act (1850) and added a Party Emblems Act in 1860. But lower-class Catholics might have been forgiven for not appreciating that the authorities were no longer the Orange supporters of the past, for the local magistrates had again shown themselves partial (and three, including Roden, were stood down after a government enquiry). Moreover, the event entered Orange mythology as another great victory over popery.

> Twas on the 12th day of July, in the year of '49,
> ten hundreds of our Orangemen together did combine,
> In the memory of King William, on that bright and glorious day,
> To walk all round Lord Roden's park, and right over Dolly's Brae.
> . . .
> And as we walked along the road not fearing any harm,
> Our guns all over our shoulders, and our broadswords in our hands,
> Until two priests came up to us, and to Mr. Speers[Beers, a magistrate]
>   did say,
> 'Come, turn your men the other road, and don't cross Dolly's Brae.'
>
> Then out speaks our Orangemen, 'Indeed we won't delay,
> You have your men all gathered and in a manger lay;
> Begone, begone, you Papist dogs, we'll conquer or we'll die,
> And we'll let you see we're not afraid to cross over Dolly's Brae.'
>
> And when we came to Dolly's Brae they were lined on every side,
> Praying for the Virgin Mary to be their holy guide;
> We loosened our guns upon them and we gave them no time to pray,
> And the tune we played was 'The Protestant Boys' right over Dolly's
>   Brae.
> . . .
> Come all ye blind-led Papists, wherever that ye be,
> Never bow down to priest or Pope, for them they will disown;
> Never bow down to images, for God [you must] adore,
> Come join our Orange heroes, and cry 'Dolly's Brae no more'.[47]

Orangeism to Catholics represented hatred of their religion and insulting dominance, and they were increasingly unwilling to stand for it. But their own assertiveness, the growing visibility and power of the Catholic Church, and the renewed dogmatism of the papacy exacerbated the fears which translated into a murderous sectarianism at the lowest levels of Orangeism. Many Protestants frowned on Orangeism – notably the Presbyterians, who disliked its overwhelming

Anglicanism. But evangelicalism and revivalism were bringing the different Protestant denominations closer together and the development of nationalism reacted upon centuries of tradition about political popery to make the Home Rule campaign of the 1880s the deciding moment in consolidating a common Ulster Protestant identity. That identity was firmly rooted in anti-popery and in a belief that their very religion made Catholics inferior, disloyal and persecutory.[48] This is why Ulster Protestants never made a distinction between so-called moral-force and physical-force nationalists. It was their 'popery', not their methods, which threatened the Protestant way of life. Orangeism witnessed a remarkable revival in the 1880s – in response to the growth of organised nationalism – and provided much of the organisational basis for developing Unionism. Both communities, accordingly, approached the Home Rule crisis in the belief that the other would persecute and tyrannise if successful. 'Home Rulers to my childish mind were a dark, subtle, and dangerous race,' Lynn Doyle recalled of his childhood in County Down; 'they were ready to rise, murder my uncle, possess themselves of his farm, and drive out my aunt and myself to perish on the mountains ... in my aunt's stories it was on the mountains we always died.' Later he reflected on how such fears could co-exist with the friendship and trust which his family felt for a number of Catholics. He also learnt that the young Catholic maid in his house was as fearful about going near Orange Lodges as he had been of the nationalists' meeting places.[49] By the 1870s the Government's ban on marching had become unenforceable because of widespread civil disobedience and was replaced with a policy of equal marching rights within confined areas.[50]

Lynn Doyle characteristically put a humorous slant on the way the marching season impacted on the smaller villages. In Ballygullion, where 'although we're just about half-an'-half, nationalist an' Orange ... we can live side by side friendly enough until both of us begin to make ready for the party processions in the summer time. But from the first blatter on an Orange drum comin' up to the Twelfth of July, ill-will an' bitterness sets in like the flowin' tide, an' only ebbs with the last wallop of a Nationalist drumstick on the night of the fifteenth of August.' By the early twentieth century, party quarrels had become so bad during Ballygullion's marching season that the police had confined

the parades of each side to that half where their own religion predominated. But no occasion for annoyance was let pass. On the Catholic
side a priest's ordination was made the excuse to bedeck their area
with 'such a flyin' of flags as never had been in Ballygullion before',
arousing predictable ire from the other side and leaving the sorry
Protestant grocer serving the Catholics in a quandary about what to
do. His efforts – helped by a Catholic friend – to find some flag which
would offend no one, and the impossibility of such, forms the core
narrative.[51]

But in the towns, where social intercourse between working-class
Protestants and Catholics was increasingly disappearing, such sectarian stereotyping left a dreadful legacy. Belfast in particular became a
by-word for sectarian riots, in which more people died in the nineteenth
century than in rioting in any other European city. 'I had not the least
idea that religion could cause such rancour between people until I
came here', John O'Donovan wrote during his ordnance survey visit
to Belfast in 1834. 'It is principally fomented by clever men, who are
well acquainted with the nature of the human mind, and whose interest
it is to paint the failings of other sects in the strongest lights possible.'[52]
In Belfast Orangeism, Ribbonism and the Ancient Order of Hibernians
found their main strengths, and new waves of rural migrants came
prepared. In 1864, Sandy Row Protestants attacked the Catholic
Pound area in protest at the great rally in Dublin to unveil a statue to
O'Connell. Mrs Mullins prepared to defend the Catholic enclave. Her
husband had taught her to use a gun when they first came to Belfast.
'When she heard the Protestant shipwrights were coming, she put her
three children in the piggery at the back of the house, loaded her gun
and went off to defend the church.'[53] The riots had started out with
the crowd from Sandy Row conducting a mock requiem mass and
funeral for O'Connell within sight of the Pound, and continued with
groups of Protestant shipwrights and Catholic navvies terrorising the
city. It was a particularly nasty attack by the navvies on a Protestant
school in Brown Square, Millfield, which mobilised the Shankill Road
crowd to attack Mrs Mullins's church on the Falls Road. Repeated
armed attacks by Protestant gangs on Catholic churches and convents
had Catholics arming and rallying to their defence.

The emergence of a common Ulster Protestant identity firmly

anchored in anti-popery was also accelerated by a series of demagogic open-air preachers – particularly in Belfast. They played to the lowest form of anti-popery and were tremendously popular with lower-class Protestants. Indeed, the Revd Thomas Drew's inflammatory sermons were said to have sparked off the 1857 riots. On the evening of 12 July he regaled the Sandy Row boys – who had marched to church with their Orange regalia secreted under their hats, the ban on such parades being still in force – with terrifying images of papal prisons paved with human blood and hair and of wicked Catholic prelates in bygone times dabbling in the gore of Protestant women being tortured on the rack. Popery's wiles were traced from James II's reign through to the contemporary outrage of 'Romanists' actually occupying state office and 'Jesuit intrigues' polluting 'our Protestant Universities'. Britain's mission ought to be one of 'Protestantizing the world' and Protestants were urged to vigilance against 'the arrogant pretences of Popes and the outrageous dogmata of their blood-stained religion', with its 'detestable machinations of the Confessional, of Jesuitism, and of the Inquisition'.[54] Drew's church was situated at the corner of Durham Street and College Street North, at the end of Sandy Row, and therefore on the interface between working-class Protestant and Catholic areas, a traditional location of confrontation around the 12 July. As opposing mobs gathered outside Drew's church, it only took the prank of a tipsy Catholic youth waving an Orange lily to set off a week of rioting. The subsequent parliamentary enquiry criticised both sides, for they had been preparing for conflict, and the mobs included entire communities, men, women and children – even little girls singing sectarian street-rhymes. However, it laid particular blame on the Orange Order and on preachers like Drew. 'The feeling which leads to the separation of these districts in July . . . is a feeling of dominancy and insult on the one side, and of opposition to its display on the other.' It attributed the origins of the riots to the celebration of 12 July, 'a festival which is used to remind one party of the triumph of their ancestors over those of the other, and to inculcate the feeling of Protestant superiority over their Roman Catholic neighbours'.[55]

The parliamentary enquiry also found a near monopoly of 'insulting language' on the Protestant side. Betty Donohue lived on waste ground between the Pound and Sandy Row, a widow with four children, who sold eggs and milk from her cows and poultry. Early one morning she was confronted behind her home by a gang of youths who tried to get her 'to curse the Pope'. Catholic mill-girls walking to Grimshaw's mill near Sandy Row were stoned, told the water being poured on them was 'holy water', that they were 'Papish whores', that their attackers 'had burned Dan O'Connell [a straw man having been burnt as such], and that they would burn the Pope, and ... the Blessed Virgin'.[56] Some of the language reveals the continuing belief that Catholics were disloyal. A militiaman went through the Protestant streets calling on the people to arm against 'the rebels coming down the Blackstaff' [the river running between the districts], whilst Catholics being intimidated out of their homes during the night were called upon to 'rise up and surrender'.[57] The commissioners were dismissive of the Orange Order's justification that it was arming in self-defence against the Ribbonmen. They thought the latter organisation nearly gone from Belfast, and anyway such measures were hardly needed in a town where Protestants were in the majority.[58]

The 1857 riots were localised to the Sandy Row/Pound areas, with ripples in neighbouring frontier zones, Shankill Road/Peter's Hill/ Millfield areas, and, as with the late twentieth-century Troubles, people in other districts could live almost unaffected by them, except through heightened press coverage. Those intimidated out of their homes told of good neighbourliness before 1857 and of friendly acts even at the height of the riots. One Protestant woman in Quadrant Street was seen to point out the houses of her Catholic neighbours. But very many more covered up for them. Anne Cummins – one of the mill-workers at Grimshaw's – heard her landlady deny that she had a 'Papist' lodger when they came to turn her out. Betty Donohue told of how a Protestant woman from Sandy Row had brought her to the police for protection in 1854, when her house was wrecked, while another Protestant neighbour had carried out the repairs without charge. In 1857 she was finally forced out, but the Presbyterian neighbour who had alerted her had been a family friend and the warning was 'friendly intended'.[59] However, a pattern had been set and the intimidation of Catholics and Protestants (and those in mixed marriages) from working-class areas would be a prominent feature of all future riots.

Drew's sermons were an embarrassment to his religious leaders. He was banned from open-air preaching and shortly afterwards moved away from Belfast. But his brand of fundamentalism was popular and the *Belfast News Letter* saw his silencing as putting Belfast on the same level as 'Romish cities' like Cork or Limerick, where Protestant ministers risked stoning or murder from priestly mobs.[60] The arrival of Catholic convents also added to the reactivation of popular Protestant stereotypes of popery. Just like the confessional, here again was priestly power destroying the family and using the helpless female as its instrument, and calls were regularly made for inspections to ensure the nuns were not being held against their will.[61] Another Orange preacher, the Revd Hugh Hanna, called on Protestants to unite against this same threat from political popery which had confronted their forefathers three centuries earlier and even less messianic commentators on the threats of Home Rule were to take the same line.

The right to 'walk' was vigorously exercised by Belfast Orangeism throughout the recent bans, which had heightened their sensitivities on the issue of marches. The repeal of the Party Processions Act was followed in 1872 by huge Orange displays all over Ulster. It was unusual for Catholics to insist on marching. But this year on the Feast of the Assumption (15 August) they planned to march from Carlisle Circus, just north of the city centre and the site of Hanna's church, to Hannahstown, west of the town. It was the first occasion on which a Catholic procession sparked off major rioting, for Hanna had assembled a huge crowd of 5,000–10,000 to stop it.[62] No one could remember a Catholic parade in Belfast that century. But increasingly Catholics emulated the Orangemen, and 15 August vied with 12 July as riot seasons – particularly when AOH lodges organised seriously. The growth of Orangeism and the Hibernians in the city was truly phenomenal in these years – the Orange Order up from 1,335 in 1851 to 18,800 in 1913, the bulk of the AOH's 60,000 membership being based in Belfast and County Tyrone by 1909. Both had a grip on their respective religious ghettos and it would have been difficult for the working class to find employment outside these sectarian organisations. Orangeism came to have a particular stranglehold on the Belfast shipyard, to the extent that the seventh Belfast district of the Orange Order was concentrated there.[63] In Belfast, writes Sybil Baker,

A century of Orange and Green rivalry had conditioned its communities to violent confrontation. The influence of the lodges upon Belfast's working classes had always exceeded their numerical strength, for they reflected much wider circles of family, neighbourhood, and trade, and crystallised much sectarian competition and ethnic enmity. Their indoctrination fed prejudice. Their disciplinary codes enforced chauvinistic intolerance. Their celebrations taunted the opposition to retaliation. Their ballads perpetuated an impassioned urban folklore where victories on seventeenth-century battle-grounds and nineteenth-century brickfields [open ground on the Falls/Shankill interface] were entwined. Separate education began ethnic isolation: the culture of the lodges turned it into ethnic alienation.[64]

After further riots in Belfast in 1864, the Government criticised the anti-Catholicism of the Town Council and abolished the largely Orange police force which had been under its control. Replacing it with the largely Catholic (and militarised) RIC, however, set the scene for the 1886 riots – the worst of the century. The 1885 parliamentary election had delivered virtually the whole of Ireland to Parnell's Nationalists, decimating the Liberals and leaving Ulster (with sixteen Conservative-Unionists and seventeen Nationalists) as the only province registering any significant opposition to Home Rule. Ulster had voted along almost exclusively denominational lines, Belfast in particular returning Conservatives for all four of its constituencies.[65] There had been a closely fought contest in west Belfast – which also included the Protestant Sandy Row and Shankill Road. After Gladstone introduced his Home Rule Bill in April 1886, tensions ran high, particularly in the shipyard, which drew most of its skilled workers from Protestant districts.

On 3 June word went out that a Catholic navvy in dispute with a Protestant one had claimed that under Home Rule none of his sort would get leave to work.[66] The story was clearly embellished in the telling, but the next day the Protestant shipwrights descended on the Catholic labourers and forced them to swim for their lives. One was drowned, and his funeral cortège from his home in Ballymacarrett in east Belfast to Milltown cemetery turned into a huge nationalist demonstration. But the defeat of the Home Rule Bill on 8 June caused the ensuing riots to merge into Protestant victory celebrations, and Catholic-owned public houses and grocery stores in Protestant areas were wrecked. So many Catholics were put out of work that the Catholic Church organised a diocesan collection for their relief.[67] Disturbances continued through the marching season and Catholic and Protestant mill-girls turned on each other – the former now giving as good as they got, cries of 'Fenian whore' and 'Orange whore' echoing through the streets, and the segregated map of working-class Belfast growing apace. The term 'Fenian' (from the republican movement of the 1860s), and its association with political disloyalty, had now become the preferred term of abuse for Catholics. The old battle-fields surfaced again: the interface between the Shankill and Falls Roads, the Falls Road and Sandy Row, the Catholic enclave of Carrick Hill and the Old Lodge/Clifton Street area, York Street, and Ballyma-carrett, near the shipyard. Thirty-two were killed, 371 injured and over £90,000 of damage was sustained in the riots.

Another commission was severely critical of the borough corporation – not one Catholic officer serving on it, nor on its police committee. But once again it was the parades, processions, and party music which was deemed to keep religious tensions alive – prompting the president of the Commission, Mr Justice Day, to comment that perhaps music in Belfast should be restricted to the more neutral barrel-organs. Certainly the parading of Orange bands had got out of hand. Even the Sunday-school parades to the Revd Hanna's church and school at Carlisle Circus were accompanied by them, attracting crowds of 'roughs' who would then attack Catholic property. Michael Kernan was a publican on the corner of Carrick Hill and Clifton Street. His property was attacked by such crowds on almost every significant political occasion (the Prince of Wales's visit in 1885, Lord Randolph Churchill's in 1886) and on numerous occasions every year during the school parades. Certainly the commissioners concluded that 'the principal actors in the rioting were what is known as the Protestant mob'.[68]

Derry escaped the repeated sectarian riots of Belfast until later in the century. Residential segregation there was. But the predominance of Catholics in the Bogside was the result of geography, not sectarian confrontation – it was situated on the Donegal side of the city, from which county most of the Catholic families had originated. In predominantly Catholic Donegal there was not the history of sectarian conflict of the counties further east. Possibly because of the largely lower-class nature of Derry's Catholic population, the Catholic Church exercised considerable moderating control, encouraging its members to seek political remedies from the Liberals rather than from Fenian revolutionaries. Apart from the years of Edward Maginn's term as bishop of Derry (1845–54), the hierarchy tended to divert activities into internal Catholic organisation. Certainly Derry Catholics were still voting for Protestant Liberals as late as 1913 and a significant number of Presbyterians – irritated at the Tory–Orange dominance of local politics – joined them. One of these, Dr James McKnight, addressing the 1870 Commission of Inquiry into the riots and disturbances in Derry the previous year, thought the people would live peaceably together were it not for parades stirring up animosities.

Whenever these periodical displays are intended as a commemoration of the victories of one political party in the State over another they tend inevitably to perpetuate the original feud . . . in the city of Derry and throughout the north of Ireland, every celebration of that kind, both historically and otherwise, is regarded by [the] conquered party as a triumph of the representatives of the opposite party over them; and in some of our platform oratory . . . I am sorry to see a wish repeatedly expressed to fight the battles of Aughrim and the Boyne over again.

He cited the annual commemorations by the Apprentice Boys of Derry of the shutting of the gates in 1688 (18 December) and the lifting of the siege by James II's forces in 1689 (12 August). He queried their claim to long tradition and condemned in particular their ritual of choosing that part of the city walls which overlooked the Catholic populace below, 'and firing in practical triumph over the heads and houses of these people'.[69] He might have added the presence on the same spot of the 90-foot-tall monument to the Revd George Walker – joint governor of Derry at the time of the siege – built at the height of the Catholic emancipation campaign in the 1820s. Thereafter it became the focal point of Orange celebrations, a reinforcement of the seventeenth-century fortified walls to keep out popish pretenders. It was fiercely resented by local Catholics and was blown up in 1973.[70]

Although poor Protestants also lived outside the city walls by this stage (largely in the Fountains area), the Apprentice Boys – with the support of significant numbers of the city authorities and police – viewed the walled city area as peculiarly their own and one to be defended at all costs against Catholic incursions. From the 1860s Catholics began to challenge this by organising their own parades and the young hangers-on were just as provocative as those who followed the Orange parades.[71] The various riots suggest that a definite territorial battle was in train. As the Home Rule campaign became more aggressive and a monster nationalist rally was planned for St Patrick's day in 1883, the Apprentice Boys of Derry called on Orangemen to come from all over Ulster (the extension of the railways bringing in thousands of Orangemen to controversial venues) 'to oppose this renewed attempt to erect the standard of rebellion on sacred historic ground ... and from her [Derry's] walls declare your firm determination to oppose treason and the dismemberment of the empire.'[72] Some months later, the Apprentice Boys seized Corporation Hall in the Diamond and raised their flag over it to prevent another nationalist meeting. Nationalists were diverted by police into the Bogside. That night there were armed clashes between the two factions. Catholic leaders complained of 'an insolent minority' who controlled civic office and thereby the instruments of the law, a complaint which was largely upheld by the various Royal Commissions.[73] However, the growth in Catholic numbers (which had already made Catholics a majority by 1861), and the rise of Catholic political organisation and aggressive nationalism after the 1880s was bringing about the same kind of Protestant realignment in Derry as elsewhere in Ulster.[74]

It is worth noting that the many reports of sectarian riots in the nineteenth century may give a false picture of communal relations. They are also geographically confined, largely concentrating on Belfast and to a lesser extent on Derry. However, they highlight already well-established patterns of conflict and the tendency for each side to turn on those within their own community who tried to remain neutral or worse, who actually helped victims of the other religion.[75]

A notable feature of the 1886 riots was the sustained attacks by Protestants on the police. RIC reinforcements had been brought in from other counties in Ireland and there was a belief among the

Protestant working classes – actively fanned by some of their political and religious leaders, notably Hanna – that they were brought in to subdue the Protestant populace. There was also considerable irritation among the Protestant magistracy at any hint that 'loyal' Belfast might be subjected to the Coercion Act, just like disturbed counties in the south and west.[76] A pamphlet, sponsored, if not actually written, by Wesley De Cobain (former Orange Grand Master and independent Conservative MP for East Belfast) depicted the riots, whatever the evidence to the contrary, as having been produced by priestly tyranny. Had priests not been seen talking to those who later joined the riots and to the police (those 'Royal Irish' [RIC] – with obvious stress on the assumed incongruity of the two terms), who then fired on Protestants, and weren't those same police those big, stupid 'southern' Catholics, from the 'poteen making and poteen drinking districts' who talked funny, with their 'foinest' southern accent? And since all papists were 'poor credulous fools ... brought up and trained in a church founded on lies', they would believe anything their priest told them. The pamphlet is a meandering, gossipy and often prurient piece of propaganda, a suggestion that convents were in reality prisons for young girls to satisfy priestly wiles continuing Drew's imagery. It reproduced the boast reputedly made by the Catholic navvy that when Home Rule came, no Protestant 'would get leave to earn a loaf of bread'. 'In fact', observes the writer, 'I believe that the Papists – poor mortals that they are – under priestly rule, and thereby not enjoying anything like true liberty themselves, neither would know or could know how to give liberty to others.'[77] It was the old Protestant belief, prevalent since the seventeenth century, that given half a chance Catholics would prove just as persecutory and triumphalist as themselves.

3. The refining of Catholic nationalist identity

Protestant culture had subsumed Elizabethan stereotypes of the Irish and transposed them to the Catholics. Popular folklore even in contemporary Northern Ireland holds that Catholics and Protestants can distinguish each other by appearance and speech. The Belfast Police Committee Chairman, Samuel Black, claimed as much before the 1865 Commission.[78] At its most extreme, ultra-Protestantism thought the assumed mental oppression of popery was reflected in the demeanour of its adherents. 'Contrast the Protestant and Romish physiognomy,' Thomas Drew told his audience, 'and say where you will find such depressed, saddened, drooping-looking men, as the poor, oppressed, mentally aggrieved Romanist.'[79] History books written by Catholic clerics, which appear in great abundance in the later nineteenth century, are steeped in resentment at these attitudes and it has left its legacy in the Ulster Catholic's heightened sensitivity about the potential 'put-down'. Catholics still dislike the 'Roman' prefix, for the emphasis had always been put on that in the past. The historian of Monaghan, D. C. Rushe, thought the prefix only became common among Protestants in the nineteenth century: 'And the bigots rumbled the word Roman round their mouths with a spice of contempt, which is still noticeable.'[80] The Revd Ambrose Coleman who in 1900 produced a Catholic version of James Stuart's 1819 *Historical Memoirs of the City of Armagh*, was pleasantly surprised at the absence of bigotry in this future editor of the *Belfast News Letter*. But communal relations had deteriorated since then and Coleman systematically replaced Stuart's 'Roman Catholic' with 'Catholic'.[81] The Revd James Connolly, who delivered a highly emotional centenary sermon at St Mary's church in Belfast in November 1883, spoke at length of 'the taunt and insults', 'the scorpion sting of calumny', 'the withering sneer of scorn' endured by the Ulster Catholic.[82]

Out of that resentment developed a specifically Catholic reading of history, in which the Catholic is always the underdog, the victim. To a remarkable degree Ulster Catholic culture became one of grievance, each new grievance copper-fastening all those which had gone before. 'It is impossible, without a sinking of the heart', Gamble mused, 'to think of the fate of these generous and warm-hearted, though often misguided and misled people, of their sufferings, their proscriptions, their expulsions, and when actual violence had ceased, of the contempt which unceasingly pursued them – the brutal scorn, the idiot laugh, the pointed finger, ... which has made past recollection almost pre-dominate over future hope.' The past, he noted, held an unusual sway over their imagination, with present grievances sustained by the memory of past ones.[83]

Modern commentators note similar victim psychologies in contemporary northern Protestants and Catholics alike. These outlooks have lengthy roots, Jacqueline Hill identifying 'beleaguered Protestant' and 'long-suffering' Catholic readings of history from as early as the seventeenth century.[84] Ulster's Catholics and Protestants had long been equally sectarian, with one very fundamental difference. The latter had been in the seat of power for several centuries. Liberal Protestants only tended to support Catholic causes when Catholics were unmistakably the underdogs or when they had a common purpose. However, with the steady rise of Catholic nationalism in the nineteenth century, the Catholic clergy were markedly less concerned about Protestant sensitivities than their predecessors.

The Gaelic revival of the late nineteenth century and associated political developments did not create the notion of the Catholics as the Irish nation proper. That was already a widely held Catholic belief. But it made it fashionable and politicised it in an unprecedented way. It coincided with an explosion of Catholic print-culture and a dramatic increase in literacy as a result of the expanded education system, and it ensured that future Catholic readings of the past would be based as much on the heroes and villains in the popular histories, novels and plays of this period, as on accurate memory.[85] In William Johnston's evocative image of 'Home Rule' being 'Rome Rule', Protestant Ulster expected triumphalistic Catholicism to be in the driving seat of Gladstone's Home Rule Ireland.

The perception of Protestants as foreign usurpers is a long-standing feature of Ulster Catholic mentality. John Donaldson writing in the *Newry Register* for 1818 of the Upper Fews barony in south Armagh, could still speak of the different religious groupings as separate peoples: they 'each . . . retain a portion of their national customs, manners etc . . . [and] have not yet assimilated, so as to form one general character . . . [the Catholics] are extremely jealous with the British and Caledonian settlers, whom they are taught to believe are intruders and foreigners'.[86] The theme was a common one in Watty Cox's racy *Irish Magazine* (1807–15), as was that of the Catholics as the nation proper.[87] Protestants felt sensitive and insecure on the topic, however much they tried to attribute loss of land to Catholic fecklessness.[88] As the Home Rule campaign belatedly got under way in Ulster, its posters calling for 'the land' to be 'restored to the people' – though in reality calling for agrarian reform – were deemed particularly inflammatory by the Orange leaders. Lord Rossmore, county Grand Master of Monaghan, depicted such publicity as 'separatist' and 'communistic' and was only narrowly prevented from orchestrating a bloody counter-demonstration at Rosslea in County Fermanagh (1883).[89]

The common belief that Protestants are somehow un-Irish, not just Protestants, but 'British' Protestants and symbols for all England's wrongs against Ireland, becomes standard in the writings of Catholic priests in the late nineteenth century. But it was simply proclaiming publicly, in a time of more confident Catholicism, a view which had long been held in private. The Young Irelander and editor of the *Nation*, Charles Gavan Duffy, tells of how the senior curate in Monaghan taught him Irish history as a child. He told of religious persecution, of the dispossession of the native princes 'who were Catholics' by Scots and Englishmen; of how the natives were almost 'exterminated' when they tried to reclaim their lands; of how after the Boyne there were passed 'laws designed to exterminate the Irish race', after which they became 'serfs' on the land; of how they were denied education, their priests liable to be hanged for performing religious functions; of how their churches were taken away from them, and of how their humiliation was celebrated in annual processions and 'insulting celebrations'.[90] One of Art Bennett's most bitter poems 'O Gentle Cleric' ('*A Chléirigh Cheansa*'), tells 'of the unrelenting cruelty exercised over conscience by English rulers in order to annihilate Catholicity'. It paints a picture of frightful slaughter, listing the names of clergy who actually did lose their lives and suggesting that no member of any religious order was left alive. It was addressed to Bennett's friend Fr Patrick Lamb of Lower Creggan, and it would be unlikely for him to have presented such a picture, had he not believed that the priest shared his sentiments.[91]

When Ulster Protestants accuse the priests of teaching their people biased history and hatred of Protestants, they have a point, even though their own clergy had been doing likewise for much longer.[92] The post-Cullenite priest was in a powerful position to dictate the shape of emerging cultural nationalism. Anthropologist Lawrence Taylor tells of just such a priest in the 1870s, who, quite against the facts, was able to define himself and the Church as the defender of the oppressed against the *Gall*. John Magroarty, parish priest of Glencolumbkille, County Donegal, was a particularly litigious priest, who engineered his own eviction by his Protestant landlord, and then created his own legend of 'An Sagart – the heroic priest', fighting the cause of the Irish Catholic against the foreign Protestant. 'The discourse', Taylor concludes, 'managed (and still manages) to link a comfortable clergy to the outlaw prophets of Penal times, and keeps class-conscious anti-clericalism at bay.' In other words, the existence of Protestant power allowed the clergy to set up a competing power structure and defeat anything like internal criticism. Taylor encountered a similar situation a hundred years later with another parish priest of Glen-columbkille, who denounced critics from the altar, squeezed them out of employment in Catholic schools and then also portrayed himself as the father of his people in his memoirs.[93] It is important to recognise, however – and he does – that the theme of oppression of the *Gael* by the *Gall* was one widely held by all Catholics. It did not need to be created, even if it could be manipulated.

The world-wide campaign of the Catholic Church against secularism and modernism at the end of the century also added yet another vice to England's villainies, whilst the Catholic Irish had clung heroically to their faith. Father Connolly's centennial sermon at St Mary's made much of this.

Look across the sea at that country which for centuries trod under foot our most sacred liberty – liberty of conscience – and put forth its giant strength to impose upon the people of this land an alien faith at the point of the bayonet, and what a sorry spectacle, religiously speaking, it presents before the nations of the world to-day! England is now a battle-ground for sects, her people, robbed of their priceless inheritance of Catholic Faith, are running after every form of human error ... But you – you, children of Catholic Ireland, you, Catholics of Ulster, you still hold in your midst the sacred and untarnished deposit of Catholic faith.[94]

Likewise O'Laverty's *History of Down and Connor* is replete with comments about the heroism of the people clinging to 'the ancient faith of their race' and assumptions that all Orangemen would come to a sticky end.

In a sophisticated attack on the Catholic ethos of modern nationalism and republicanism, Conor Cruise O'Brien argues that the lip-service paid to Tone's ideal of a 'common name of Irishman' has allowed both to appear non-sectarian and all-inclusive, whereas they are anything but. He points in particular to cultural nationalism's most talented propagandist, D. P. Moran (1872–1936), and draws a direct link to the belief of modern-day Sinn Féin that once you 'de-anglicise' Ireland, Unionists will fall into line and become good Irishmen. He finds too in Moran's newspaper *The Leader* – 'the journalistic flagship of Irish Ireland' – that belief common to all shades of Ulster Catholic opinion, that only Protestants are bigots. 'Just as black racists in modern America think that only whites can be racists, so *The Leader* thought that only Protestants could be bigots: "Why should Irish Catholics try to prove their tolerance when they have never been intolerant? Let those who have been intolerant prove that they have given it up." '[95] By the turn of the century Protestants were no longer welcome as members of the 'Irish-Irelander' wing of the Gaelic revival.[96]

Admittedly Conor Cruise O'Brien's agenda is informed by his conversion to Unionism from a nationalist background, and the main Northern Ireland nationalist leader of contemporary times, John Hume, accuses him of 'paranoia' in this book. In a similar mould is the critique of contemporary republicanism by Ulster journalist Malachi O'Doherty. But both are courageous efforts to draw to the attention of non-militant nationalists the kind of brainwashing behind their own culture which made them unwitting accomplices to republican atrocities. Both single out Catholic education for criticism, particularly as it has been delivered by the Christian Brothers. In the nineteenth century I do not find popular Catholic emphasis on Ireland as an organic whole, divinely ordained to nationhood. Rather there is considerable local pride in Ulster. In the works of both Art Bennett and Hugh McDonnell (Aodh Mac Domhnaill) there is still a sense of competition with the other provinces and a feeling that the Ulster men have always been let down by them. Gavan Duffy also feels himself an 'Ulster man' first and foremost, and rejects the common perception of Ulster in the south as 'the enemy's country; a territory where Nationality could only appear under some decent disguise'.[97] O'Doherty recalls how the largely southern Christian Brothers who taught him 'sneered' at such local and regional identification.[98] It is this regional identity which is sublimated to the national one in nationalist literature and so successful was that change of emphasis that after partition few Ulster Catholics could conceive of a specifically 'Ulster' identity outside the whole island context.

It is the popular school histories of the Christian Brothers which are usually credited with finely tuning the Catholic nationalist reading of Irish history. The early National school readers were very sanitised histories. Indeed, the teachers were supposed to avoid political controversy. This did not stop teachers such as Seamas MacManus imparting their nationalist readings of the past in the 1880s and 1890s. It was from him and his successor as teachers at Kinawley National school in Fermanagh that the local storyteller who provided Henry Glassie with much of his material learnt of the Mackan fight and the time when the Catholics *were slaves* and the Protestants *in control*.[99] The Christian Brothers' texts were assertively Catholic, Irish and anti-English. Their works were central to the Irish-Ireland movement, glorifying Ireland's Gaelic past and culture. Their literature was by no means confined to use in their schools. Their *Our Boys* magazine (launched in 1914) sold outside the churches and was still regularly taken by Ulster Catholic homes for much of the twentieth century. Their motto of 'faith and fatherland' tripped easily from the tongue of those educated in their schools, as did their dismissal of the more middle-class Catholic schools for not being nationalist enough.[100] Although they sent a number of ex-pupils into the 1916 rising, the Christian Brothers, like the Church generally, were neither militant nationalists nor particularly anti-Protestant. Besides the anti-English rhetoric, there was much of that romantic nationalism which remained the dominant strain in that of Ulster, even after partition, and there is much in Conor Cruise O'Brien's contention that the Catholic Church endorsed and developed the intensely Catholic nationalism of the cultural revival as an antidote to the more inclusive but anti-clerical varieties of both Parnellism and the Fenians.[101] There is an equally compelling explanation voiced earlier by Cardinal Cullen that if you did not give the people constitutional outlets for voicing their discontent, they would drift to unconstitutional ones.[102]

However, the clergy had a somewhat ambiguous relationship with the Gaelic revival. The majority of the bishops, for example, opposed the Gaelic League's campaign for compulsory Irish in the schools.[103] The history of the Irish language in the nineteenth century was one of dramatic decline. By 1851 only 6.8 per cent of Ulster people could speak it; by 1911 only 2.3 per cent (very largely in Donegal and Antrim) – though there were small pockets of Irish speakers in Counties Armagh, Londonderry, Cavan, Monaghan and Tyrone. The clergy themselves played a significant role in its decline and children were punished at the National schools for speaking it.[104] It came to be seen by the people as a badge of inferiority. It was, one elderly lady in Tyrone told the folklorist Michael J. Murphy, equated with 'low intelligence, social backwardness and ignorance, a verbal emblem which an inferiority complex compelled them to treat with derision and contempt'.[105] The Gaelic League was to have more success in the towns than in the rural areas where such attitudes were rife. Francis McPeake, of the famous Belfast family of traditional Irish musicians, remembered Ulster Protestant Gaelic Leaguers – Bulmer Hobson, F.G. Bigger, Roger Casement, Alice Stopford Green – initiating the Gaelic revival in the city. They were in a long tradition of Presbyterian and Protestant Irish-language speakers, which included James McKnight, editor of the *Belfast News Letter*.[106] However, when news of Roger Casement's execution reached the Falls Road in 1916, Paddy the local tram-driver said to McPeake's father: 'Ach we're better without them people anyway' – by which he appears to have meant upper-class Protestants – '. . . you never can trust them.' McPeake's grandfather was not an Irish speaker. But the likes of Bigger and Casement travelled around 'to tell the people that they were Irish in the North', and at Bigger's home in north Belfast there were lantern slides on the O'Neills and the O'Donnells 'because the ordinary people didn't know anything about it'. The Gaelic League succeeded in rescuing the Irish language from its terminal decline. It taught people how to write their names in Irish. But its later republicanism and involvement of some of its prominent members in the 1916 rising began that association of the language with rebelliousness in the minds of Unionists. One Falls Road coal-man painted his name in Irish on his cart, and was arrested.[107]

It had been several centuries since Irish culture was perceived as subversive. For a while after 1798 there was a similar reaction – the blind harpist, Art O'Neill, who had always been patronised by Catholic and Protestant alike, was chided on his journey to Tyrone in 1803 by 'illiterate loyalists' who saw his harp.[108] But on the whole Irish culture was not used for political purposes in the nineteenth century. Nor was the turn-of-century Gaelic revival intended to be. But its aim of de-anglicising Ireland was a perfect fit for militant republicanism. The attempt to de-couple the Irish language from this association with extreme nationalism continues to the present day.

The celebration of Irish peasant culture at the heart of the Gaelic revival firmly associated Catholicism with Irishness. Local priests both transmitted the central ideas of the new nationalism, but also virtually made loyalty to that ideal 'a moral obligation'.[109] The linkage infused the penny pamphlets of the newly formed (1899) Catholic Truth Society of Ireland and made the increasing Protestant rejection all but inevitable. The Gaelic revival sanitised the Gaelic past, discarding anything deemed vulgar or crude. And this pursuit of 'respectability' continued into the collections of the Irish Folklore Commission (established 1935).[110] The Gaelic League and associated Gaelic Athletic Association (which banned English sports) increasingly fell under the control of the Catholic clergy and the association of Protestantism with foreignness becomes a standard in clerical writing.[111] 'Irish' culture had become 'Catholic' culture. 'There is an assumption among locals', the folk-collector Michael J. Murphy was told in Tyrone in the 1950s, 'that only Catholics [were] able to speak it [Irish] and it's subconsciously seen as their own particular code.'[112] Catholics had finally, it seemed, found their own form of 'ascendancy' with which to belabour Protestants and members of their own community who did not sign up to the 'Irish-Irelander' philosophy in its entirety. It was perhaps, as Roy Foster suggests, 'the logical response to generations of English and Anglo-Irish condescension towards "priest-ridden", "backward" Ireland'.[113]

11

CATHOLICS IN NORTHERN IRELAND 1920–2000

Not since the foundation of Ulster [*sic*] have they been prepared to contemplate assimilation. They rejected the concept of the state from the beginning and refused to participate in its institutions ... The inevitable consequence has been that they have drawn to themselves the very antagonism and suspicion of which they complain.

Harold Jackson, *The Two Irelands*
(Minority Rights Group, 1971)

It all turns on the question of 'loyalty' ... The Six Counties is a 'loyal' area and it is natural sometimes that 'disloyalists' should get hurt ... [and] fail to get jobs. And so on. 'Well, they must expect it if they are "disloyal",' says the outsider. But then the outsider does not know that the words 'loyalist' and 'disloyalist' have a meaning all their own in Northern Ireland.

'Ultach', 'Orange Terror', 1943

1. Birth of the new state

The state of Northern Ireland came into being in 1921 amid confusion and violence. The continuing IRA campaign provoked similar paramilitarism on the 'loyalist' side, largely in the form of the hastily recruited Ulster Special Constabulary (USC or 'Specials'). But most of the confusion was on the nationalists' side. They remained as split after 1920 as before, and had no contingency plans to deal with the new situation, short of recurrent appeals for help to Dublin. 'Surely this cannot be happening' just about sums up their reaction to partition, and all hopes were centred on the Boundary Commission to rescue them. In the meantime they embarked on a policy of passive non-recognition of the Northern Ireland state. Because of the continuing hostilities in much of Ireland (first with the brutal Anglo-Irish war 1919–21, then with the civil war in the Irish Free State, 1922–3) and the delay in the report of the Boundary Commission, a sense of insecurity and impermanence prevailed. Although the boundary imposed by the Government of Ireland Act of 1920 put some 90,000 Protestants in the largely Catholic southern state, the size of the Catholic minority left in Northern Ireland was far more problematic (430,000 against a Protestant majority of 820,000). In June 1920 local government elections were held under new proportional representation (PR) regulations. As a result Fermanagh, Tyrone, south Down, south Armagh and Derry City returned local councils with Catholic majorities, and they promptly voted their allegiance to the Dáil and the republican government in Dublin.[1]

Protestants in these areas felt vulnerable. Their fears were confirmed by the triumphalist speech of Derry's first Catholic mayor in 230 years, in which he asserted Ireland's right to decide its own destiny whether the Ulster Protestants liked it or not.[2] At the same time the other three provinces were engulfed in the Anglo-Irish war – largely consisting of guerilla IRA activities against the RIC – and while the northern IRA was not as organised as it was elsewhere, its intermittent attacks on RIC barracks (particularly along the border) and other public buildings added to a sense that the embryo northern state was under siege. It also further contributed to the image of Catholics as generically 'disloyal'. In fact, although Joseph MacRory, Catholic bishop of Down and Connor, made a number of highly provocative statements at this time, the clergy and Catholic middle class were opposed to violence and were instrumental in bringing Nationalist abstention from the Northern Ireland parliament to an end in 1925. Even so, reprisals now assumed a familiar pattern. Militant Protestantism, having long seen the institution of Catholicism itself as the enemy, took revenge for IRA attacks on Catholic civilians and church premises. This was 'the doctrine of vicarious punishment,' MacRory declared in his 1922 Lenten pastoral, 'according to which the Catholics of Belfast are made to suffer for the sins of their brethren elsewhere.'[3]

There had already been severe sectarian rioting in Derry City in April and June 1920, and the July funeral in Banbridge of an RIC commissioner shot in Cork sparked off a series of expulsions of Catholics from their homes and workplaces. In Lisburn the shooting of another RIC inspector was followed by the mass burnings of Catholic business premises and the expulsion of almost the entire Catholic community from the town. But predictably it was in Belfast – its traditional lines of conflict already so well mapped – that sectarian violence was worst. Over the next two years sectarian conflict resulted in 453 deaths (37 members of the security forces, 416 civilians – 257 of them Catholic), the expulsion of between 8,700 and 11,000 Catholics from their places of work and 23,000 from their homes – a quarter of the entire Catholic population of Belfast. In addition, some 500 Catholic-owned businesses were destroyed. Very many innocent Protestants also lost their lives, but since Catholics formed only 25 per cent of the city's population, they figured disproportionately among the casualties. In Catholic consciousness it became known as the Belfast 'pogrom' and it left a terrible legacy of bitterness to the new state.

In the charged atmosphere of the time, the inflammatory speeches of the Unionist politicians on 12 July 1920 may well have lit the fuse. On the first full day back at work after the holiday, the 'disloyal' Catholic workers were expelled from the shipyard. Once again many had to swim for their lives, and those who returned to collect valuable tools, or wages owing to them, were brutally beaten. Similar expulsions took place from other traditionally Protestant firms, where Catholics had acquired jobs during the war. Catholic enclaves in predominantly Protestant districts were then attacked and looted. St Matthew's Catholic church and convent in Ballymacarrett experienced semi-permanent siege over the next two years. It was bombed six times and worshippers attacked and murdered.[4] But the incident which has survived longest in Catholic folklore was the killing of the McMahon family in north Belfast. During the night of 24 March 1922, the house of Owen McMahon, a wealthy Catholic publican, was broken into by a group of men reportedly in 'police uniform'. The male members of the family, and a barman who lived with them, were lined up in the sitting-room and shot. The murders were thought to have been in retaliation for the killing of two 'Specials' the previous day. No one was ever brought to justice, but District Inspector J.W. Nixon was rumoured to have been involved with the murder squad. Certainly he was thought too extreme by James Craig's Unionist government, and was dismissed from the police two years later – only to remain a thorn in Craig's side as Independent Unionist MP for Woodvale in the Northern Ireland parliament (1929–49).[5] There were claims that police and military often protected the anti-Catholic rioters and even perpetrated some of the worst outrages. Certainly the image of a police force dominated by extreme Protestants, particularly after the RIC was replaced by the RUC (Royal Ulster Constabulary) in June 1922, was copper-fastened in these years. Police raids on Catholic homes singled out prayer-books and religious objects for particular scorn and Catholic members of the security forces often found themselves objects of attack.

The terrible events of 1920–22 form the backdrop to Michael McLaverty's 1939 novel, *Call My Brother Back*. The MacNeill family has moved from Rathlin Island to Catholic west Belfast after the death of their father. Colm, the young narrator, makes his perilous school journey from west to north Belfast through snipers' bullets and police searches. It is a nightmarish picture: people pinned in their houses by gunfire and curfew, the night-time sounds of armoured cars rushing through the narrow cobbled streets, shuddering the small houses, the screams of victims, the neighbourhood cries of 'Murder, murder', the sight of IRA men shooting from their streets into the neighbouring Protestant ones, the police raids. The MacNeill household is 'done' one night. The British soldiers are courteous. But the policeman is convinced they are hiding guns and when he cannot find any, he smashes the republican pictures. The eldest brother, Alec, is a soccer supporter. But he gives up the football after persistent sectarian riots at the matches and joins the IRA. His mother disapproves. He is a zealot and contemptuous of the 'spineless Hibernians' (the constitutional nationalists in the AOH) who won't talk to the republicans.

The surrounding hills and beautiful views afforded over the city provide a stark contrast to the murderous hatred unfolding in the streets below. At first Colm is startled at the sectarian conflict, which was entirely absent from Rathlin. But as he reads the papers, with their lists of those killed the previous nights, he falls into the Belfast habit of identifying them as Protestant or Catholic. It is instinct rather than prejudice. But his mother is appalled at the change which has come over him since their move to Belfast.[6]

The provisional government in Dublin, alarmed at the attacks on Catholics in the north, did not help matters by partially re-arming the IRA and supporting a boycott of Belfast goods and businesses. Thus was the image reinforced of the new northern state under siege, and the already deteriorating economic plight of Catholics as well as Protestants exacerbated. In the early months of 1922, Michael Collins (chairman of the provisional government in Dublin) seemed to be coming round to recognising the Northern Ireland state in return for measures to involve and protect the Catholic minority. This was increasingly the thinking of moderate nationalists, particularly in Belfast, and their influence helped fashion the second Craig–Collins pact between the London, Dublin and Belfast governments in March 1922. The most significant clauses implicitly recognised the particular plight of the Catholic minority in Belfast. The police there would be reorganised, with Catholics joining the Specials, mixed Catholic–Protestant patrols operating in mixed areas and Catholic ones in Catholic areas.

A Catholic police advisory committee would recommend recruits, a joint Catholic–Protestant Conciliation Committee would investigate outrages and try to prevent melodramatic reports in the press. Even the Belfast IRA seemed disposed to give the pact a trial.

But the opportunities offered by the pact were lost, for the extremes on both sides soon made it unworkable. The final split in the IRA in the south (between supporters and opponents of the Anglo-Irish Treaty and the provisional government), and the onset of civil war saw a re-imposition of the Belfast boycott by the anti-Treatyites. Collins was anxious at Craig's slowness in implementing the pact and his refusal to investigate a particularly brutal set of murders of Catholic civilians in Belfast in April 1922 when, in retaliation for the shooting of a colleague in the vicinity, uniformed police raided Catholic homes in Stanhope and Arnon Streets, killing five people, including a child, and wounding several more. He therefore sought to keep pressure up by sanctioning a renewal of IRA attacks in Northern Ireland in May. Predictably this provoked further reprisals against the Belfast Catholics, making May and June 1922 the bloodiest months of the two years of inter-communal violence and prompting the moderate nationalist *Irish News* to lash out at extremists on their own side for giving the excuse to others to terrorise innocent Catholics.[7] The northern IRA campaign collapsed the following month. Vastly outnumbered by security forces, it had always been ill-equipped and poorly armed, and was nicknamed 'the Rag man's army' in border areas.[8] The bulk of the northern IRA remained firmly pro-Treatyite in its support of Collins. His death in the civil war on 22 August 1922 removed the Ulster Catholics' most powerful protector. Thereafter, the attention of the Irish Free State turned inwards. A peace of sorts descended on the north. But it was one of exhaustion and disillusionment on the minority's part. The Craig–Collins pacts had held out the prospect of peaceful collaboration by the minority with the northern state. Not until the Sunningdale agreement of 1973 was another such effort made.[9]

It would be difficult to exaggerate the damaging impact of the sectarian attacks of 1920–22. Father Hassan, curate of St Mary's in Chapel Lane, and author of the fullest contemporary account of the Belfast 'pogrom' of those years, absolved the city's Protestant population generally from any part in them.[10] For they too now felt the need to move out of areas dominated by people of the other faith and there were large numbers of agreed exchanges of houses between Protestants and Catholics caught in such areas. But the movement had been overwhelmingly that of Catholics into the already bulging Catholic ghettos and when things calmed down after 1922 the mood was one of sullen resentment and introversion. The moderate Patrick Shea, arriving in Belfast for the first time in 1926 to take up a post as one of the very few Catholics in the Northern Ireland civil service, found the city still bearing the scars of the recent troubles:

The Catholics, large numbers of them crowded into streets along the Falls Road, were cowed and dispirited; they had seen riots and death, the burning of homes and business premises, the violent expulsion of their men from the shipyards and factories and building sites. They had stories of murder and cruelty, of the wild exploits of the Special Constabulary, the bigoted outbursts of political leaders. The Protestants had something to say about the involvement of the IRA in the city's troubles but the Catholics discounted any allegations that blame lay on their side. They feared their Protestant neighbours with the anger of people who had been subdued by force and left without any means of retaliating against their persecutors.[11]

The civil war south of the border took much of the pressure off the Northern Ireland government. It moved quickly to abolish proportional representation in local elections, a move so against the terms of the Anglo-Irish Treaty and so blatantly directed against nationalists, that Lloyd George's government withheld approval until obliged to do so by Craig's threats of resignation. This, the imposition of a declaration of allegiance upon local authorities and the redrawing of the local electoral boundaries, halved the number of councils left in nationalist hands. Londonderry County Borough, where Catholics were in the majority and where boundaries were repeatedly redrawn to create a Unionist majority on the council, acquired particular notoriety. Powers of allocating houses and jobs now became heavily biased in favour of Unionists and whilst Nationalist-controlled councils acted in a similarly biased fashion, as David Harkness concludes, 'there were not only more Unionist authorities, but more than there ought to have been'.[12]

Collins told Churchill that such measures to alter the outcome of local elections were designed to convince the Boundary Commission that nationalist areas were unionist. There can be no doubt that the delay of the Boundary Commission simply copper-fastened the uncertainties and divisions in the new state. Catholics fully expected a redrawing of the border which would bring those areas with Catholic majorities, Tyrone, Fermanagh and the border areas of Armagh and Down, into the the Irish Free State, and thereby render the rump state unviable. Patrick Shea recalled such certainty in nationalist-dominated Newry that a Newry unionist had exchanged his house with that of a republican businessman in Warrenpoint.[13] Unionists felt besieged and the pattern of calling and fighting elections on the one issue of 'the state in danger', which would characterise Northern Ireland's elections for the rest of the century, was first established by Craig in 1925. It was only in that year that the delayed Boundary Commission reported, by which stage even the Dublin government, battling with its own post-civil-war difficulties, had lost interest. The leaked report of October 1925 left most of the existing territory of Northern Ireland intact (including Newry, Derry City, Tyrone and Fermanagh). But it also proposed the transfer of small portions of territory from the Irish Free State, chiefly from east Donegal, and since the leak itself caused such a furore, Cosgrave's government in Dublin acquiesced in the ultimate suppression of the report. The border would remain as it was in 1920. The Catholics in Northern Ireland had been abandoned.[14]

2. Securing the state

But with such a large Catholic minority, and such entrenched sectarian fears, Craig's government felt little incentive towards generosity. The police proposals in the second Craig–Collins pact had been put together by a group of Catholic businessmen, led by two supporters of Joe Devlin, shipbroker Raymond Burke and Hugh Dougall, owner of a substantial carrying business.[15] At this stage the terms on which the Catholic minority might work with the new state were still negotiable. Since the pact was never implemented, however, it was in the area of security more than any other that Catholics were made to feel they did not belong.

A third of the RUC was to have been Catholic. In the event only 400 Catholic RIC men transferred to the new 3,000-strong force. At first Catholics were quite well represented among the senior officers (17.1 per cent by 1936), because of the transfer from the RIC. But such transferees encountered a prejudice in the new force which had not existed in the old one. As they gradually retired, fewer Catholics came forward to join and the proportion of Catholics had dropped to 11 per cent by 1963. The force became visibly more 'Protestant' as Specials were given favourable entry conditions, accounting for between a quarter and a third of recruits to the RUC, until the Specials' disbandment in 1970. Increasingly it came to be seen by Catholics as a partisan force, soft on the Orangemen, hard on the Catholics when they clashed.[16]

But it was the Ulster Special Constabulary, established in 1920 and numbering some 48,000 by the end of 1922, which effectively policed the new state. And here lies the problem, for not only were they exclusively Protestant, but they were built from a base of loyalist paramilitaries, the UVF (Ulster Volunteer Force), various Protestant vigilante groups and the Ulster Protestant Association (a loyalist group responsible for many sectarian murders in Belfast).[17] In part it was the authorities recognising the inevitable and gaining some control over the persistent tendency for unauthorised loyalist paramilitaries to take matters into their own hands. Although the IRA was weaker in Ulster than in the other three provinces, it still had 4,500 members in 1921, and, when set against a backdrop of IRA violence in the rest of the country and the withdrawal of British forces to deal with it, the growing sense of Protestant vulnerability is easier to understand. Protestants in border areas, in Tyrone, Fermanagh, Derry City and parts of Armagh, were particularly active in the demand for increased protection. Although the full-time A Specials were disbanded in 1926, the larger part-time force, the B Specials, continued until 1970. They restored to popular Protestantism that supremacy over Catholic neighbours (notably in the rural areas) so threatened in recent years. By mid-1922, over half the adult male Protestant population of Fermanagh had joined the Specials and similar figures were reported from other areas bordering the Irish Free State and where Protestants were outnumbered by Catholics. In addition to a number of revenge murders of Catholics which they were thought to have carried out, petty intimidation and harassment of Catholics were part and parcel of the history of the B Specials and their activities tainted the entire police force in Catholic minds. Moreover, because the force was financed from London, the impartiality of British justice was seriously affected. In fact, the very existence of the USC and its blatant lack of discipline gave such cause for concern in England that an attempt was made in 1922 to bring it under British military supervision. By then, however, the kind of militant popular Protestantism which it represented was essential for Ulster Unionist survival, and the notoriously bigoted Unionist Home Affairs Minister, Richard Dawson Bates, ensured that the critical reports of the British Military Adviser sent to investigate the USC were suppressed.[18]

Sir Arthur Hezlet's favourable history of the B Specials, whilst conceding that the USC was exclusively Protestant, points to Catholic political and religious bodies actively discouraging Catholic recruitment into the force. This indeed has always been a factor deterring Catholic recruitment into the police, and in the ghetto areas the IRA made it positively dangerous to join. The requirement of the oath of allegiance was another deterrent. Certainly such resistance gave an excuse to those who never wanted Catholics to join anyway. Selection committees discouraged Catholics and Protestant Specials refused to train with them. Thus did the loyalist ethos become established at a very early stage in the police force. Even the Catholic businessmen, who had once encouraged their co-religionists to join, now dismissed it as sectarian. Although the B Specials never again reached the numerical strength of the 1920s, they did tend to be called out at times of sectarian disturbances, IRA campaigns and general border scares, thereby reinforcing the image that they were mobilised against the Catholics. Their role was often that of mounting road-blocks, checkpoints, patrols and searches, giving ample opportunity for that petty harassment for which they became notorious in Catholic circles. Certainly as early as the summer of 1922, a senior English civil servant, sent to Belfast to report on the breakdown of the Craig–Collins pact, was profoundly disturbed by the reputation which the Specials were acquiring. 'Catholics', he stated, 'regard them with a bitterness exceeding that which the Black and Tans' – British ex-soldiers recruited temporarily into the RIC in 1920–21, who gained a reputation for brutality – 'inspired in the south', and even some leading Unionists warned him that 'this purely partisan and insufficiently disciplined force was sowing feuds in the countryside which would not be eradicated for generations'.[19]

Patrick Shea's autobiography shows that not all Unionist ministers were the villains of Catholic imagination. Craig had every intention of ensuring the impartiality of the law.[20] But he let himself be constantly overruled by his Ministry of Home Affairs, where the tendency to defer to Orangeism was all prevalent. Moreover, the emergency situation which had necessitated the Specials also produced the Special Powers Act and this too became a permanent feature of Northern Ireland until its repeal in 1973. This gave the Minister of Home Affairs, and through him the police, extensive powers to detain without warrant, and suspend civil liberties altogether when he thought it necessary. Similar emergency powers had been assumed by the provisional government in Dublin, and it proved far more brutal in suppressing the IRA than did the Northern Ireland government. The difference was that the Special Powers Act and the accompanying internment tended to be used routinely and more severely against Catholics, more 'circumspectly' against Protestants. Between May 1922 and December 1924, the overwhelming majority of the 728 men interned were Catholic, whilst of the twenty-one flogged in prison in 1922 – to the outrage of nationalists and the embarrassment of the London government which tried to persuade Craig to remit the sentences – only three were Protestants.[21]

As John Whyte warned, in his impressive 1983 overview of Unionists' treatment of Catholics, Northern Ireland was not a police state. But he, along with nearly every other scholar who has attempted a dispassionate analysis of security under the Northern Ireland state, found this area the most difficult of all to arrive at the truth. This is because of the maddening pettiness which has always infused everyday attitudes and behaviour in Northern Ireland and pettiness is not well documented. But, as the bitter popular traditions of the penal era show all too well, it is the petty oppressions rather than outright tyranny which impact most on a community. 'Baiting business', was how Daniel Mageean, Catholic bishop of Down and Connor, referred to police activities in 1942, 'multiplied instances of petty persecution, the perpetual pin-pricks of the "where's-your identity-card-from-the-same-policeman-four-times-a-day" variety'.[22] Recalling the beginning of the 1969 Troubles in his home town, Downpatrick, Maurice Hayes, one of the few Catholics to reach the top echelons of the Northern Ireland civil service, observed 'the build-up of aggro' between local youths and the B Specials. 'What you had really was two groups of louts, defined by religion, one lot of whom had uniforms and guns and the power to stop and harass the others on their way home from dances late at night.'[23] The experience of very many Catholics of policing in Northern Ireland consisted of this kind of petty, one-sided harassment by the B Specials. Both the Cameron Commission (1969) and the Scarman Tribunal (1972), reporting on events at the beginning of the Troubles, rejected the more hostile assessments of police activities. But they did find evidence of 'long-standing' sectarianism and lack of impartiality in the force. There had been a progressive improvement of police attitudes after the Second World War. Even so, Whyte concluded that for most of the century the police force in Northern Ireland was 'teetering uncertainly between impartiality and partisanship'.[24]

3. Discrimination

Nationalists boycotted the new Northern Ireland parliament when it opened at Belfast City Hall on 22 June 1921, as they did every other state body including the crucial Leech and Lynn Committees (set up to decide on the future structure of local government and education). This policy of abstention was disastrous, particularly in these early days when things were still open to change. It also absolved the Unionists from blame for the developing bias, since they could legitimately claim that Nationalists had been given the opportunity to influence developments, but refused, and by so refusing simply proved their disloyalty.[25]

The assumption that all Catholics were rebels was to permeate Unionist thinking for the next fifty years. In the violence and uncertainty of the 1920-22 period, emergency measures to protect the embryo state were understandable, as was the ambivalence of very many Catholics towards a state which might not have lasted. However, most Catholics did not actively work against the Northern Ireland state, even though they disliked its political leaders, and there were times like the late 1930s or the 1950s when increasing numbers would have accepted integration into the state had they been given any encouragement. But such a gesture of goodwill had to await the premiership of Terence O'Neill and, just as with many other liberal Unionists in the past, it proved his undoing. With monotonous regularity it was the Unionists with impeccable anti-Catholic credentials who rose to leading positions. It was the one issue on which they were sure of retaining popular Protestant support, and throughout the period 1921–73 urban working-class Protestants continued to vote into power big landowners with whom they had little else in common. Nor is the dismissive epithet 'Orange State' such an inaccurate description. Not all Protestants were Orangemen; indeed many, notably the professional classes, considered the Orange Order an embarrassment. But for Unionist politicians membership was almost mandatory and, as a result, Orangeism exerted a quite disproportionate influence on government.[26] Orange complaints about 'disloyalists' in public employment were made regularly to ministers and were just as regularly taken seriously.

Charges of state discrimination against the minority Catholic community have been the central theme of northern nationalism. Certainly the belief in blanket discrimination produced a highly sensitised victim psychology among Catholics, which has not yet disappeared. Fear of rebuff eventually stopped them applying for certain jobs and those who did risked the old accusation of 'selling out' or of becoming 'Castle Catholics'. Invariably, it was that ever-impeded Catholic middle class that was caught in between. That Catholics were more likely than Protestants to suffer discrimination in Northern Ireland is no longer in doubt. Even pro-Unionist historians accept this. Working-class Protestants, feeling the pinch of unemployment since the 1970s, as their traditional industrial base has collapsed, have been resentful at the implication that all the suffering and all the victimisation has been one-sided. 'We know that things were not right under Stormont and we can never return to that,' one highly respected community worker in the Protestant Shankill Road told the Opsahl Commission in 1993, 'but if we say so, all the wrongs of the past are heaped on our shoulders.'[27] Since the belief in systematic discrimination gave rise to the civil-rights campaign of the 1960s, the immediate background to the Troubles, and still survives in a streak of resentfulness, prickly defensiveness and reluctance to forgive among many Catholics, particularly in the republican community, it is vital to establish how far the accusations are sustained.

John Whyte, one of the most dispassionate writers on Northern Ireland before his untimely death in 1989, examined all the available literature on the issue. His conclusions largely, though not universally, sustain the charges made against the Unionist government that it discriminated against Catholics. Claims that gerrymandering and the abolition of proportional representation disadvantaged Catholics in parliamentary elections are upheld only in the case of Fermanagh and possibly Armagh. In local government elections, however, the Unionist record was bleaker. Here the number of councils in Nationalist hands declined from twenty-three – and two shared equally – to eleven, and these were less important than those held previously. Foremost among the losses was Londonderry County Borough, which had a substantial Catholic majority, and where boundaries were repeatedly redrawn to ensure Unionist control. The usual Unionist defence was that boundaries reflected rateable value of property as much as population. Owners of business premises also had a double vote, and since these were more often Protestants, and since Catholics were traditionally poorer, the outcome was predictable. This Whyte dismissed as a 'dubious defence', for democratic politics does not accept the rule of the rich over the poor and in general he found gerrymandering in local politics 'one of the clearest areas of discrimination' in the history of the state.[28] The Cameron report of 1969 also looked at the traditional Unionist explanation and dismissed it. 'Such validity as this argument ever possessed is one which is rapidly losing any force ... universal adult local government suffrage has for long been the rule in the remainder of the United Kingdom.'[29] A bad-tempered and highly unsatisfactory debate over reputed discrimination against Catholics took place between two American-based academics in the 1980s. Perhaps the only valid point to emerge was the reminder that Catholic families were larger, the stark statistics ignoring the fact that as children many of the Catholics would not have had the vote in any event. Whilst accepting some of these arguments, however, Whyte still reaches the conclusion outlined above.[30]

In 1938 the British government was sufficiently concerned at de Valera's accusations of discrimination against the Catholic minority in Northern Ireland to order an internal investigation. It found the accusations of gerrymandering in the Tyrone and Fermanagh local councils and discrimination in public employment generally substantiated, thought the Northern Ireland government had 'emerged with little credit' in recent cases involving the Special Powers Act, doubted the fairness of educational legislation, and expressed concern at the nature of Unionist party domination of the state.

It is everywhere inimical to good and impartial administration where Government and Party are as closely united as in Northern Ireland. In the South, Mr. de Valera was at one time largely dependent on the I.R.A. for support, but he has been able to throw off his dependence on that body – in a way in which the Government of Northern Ireland have not been able to throw off their dependence on the Orange Lodges. If the Government of Northern Ireland wish partition to continue, they must make greater efforts than they have made at present to win over the Catholic minority, just as on his side Mr. de Valera, if he wishes to end partition, can only do so by winning over the Northern Protestants. At present both sides are showing a lamentable lack of statesmanship and foresight.[31]

It was common knowledge that the gerrymandering also underpinned poor housing and employment opportunities in certain areas. Northern Ireland's housing record was generally poor. Unionist authorities – dominated by deeply conservative rural landlords – were not favourably disposed towards public housing schemes. The government preferred to leave the initiative to private enterprise and this proved woefully inadequate. Until the setting up of the Housing Trust in 1945, public housing schemes accounted for under 8,000 new houses since the foundation of the state. The first housing survey to be conducted in Northern Ireland in 1943 revealed an urgent need for some 200,000 new houses, existing shortages having been exacerbated by the German bombing of Belfast in 1941. The target still had not been met when the Troubles erupted in 1969. It was not so much the appalling shortage of housing which lay at the heart of nationalist complaints, however, as their politically motivated allocation. Indeed, it was the persistence of bad practices into a new era when more public housing was becoming available which fuelled much of the discontent in the 1960s.[32] 'Council housing policy has also been distorted for political ends in the Unionist-controlled areas to which we specially refer [i.e. Londonderry County Borough, and Omagh and Dungannon Urban Districts]', concluded the Cameron Commission. 'In each, houses have been built and allocated in such a way that they will not disturb the political balance . . . There have been many cases where councils have withheld planning permission, or caused needless delays, where they believed a housing project would be to their electoral advantage.'[33] The Cameron Commission's case-histories were taken from areas which had generated most complaints, and not all councils were at fault. But those were areas west of the Bann where Unionist-dominated councils often controlled Catholic majorities, and Whyte, like Cameron, found the case against them largely proven.

Whyte's analysis of discrimination in public employment is equally damning. Since the establishment of the Fair Employment Agency in 1976, a series of reports have shown that Catholics were twice as likely to be unemployed as Protestants. These figures are disputed by many working-class Protestants. They sometimes see Catholics as inveterate whingers and scroungers on the state, perfectly happy to live on the dole. In fact, research has shown that Catholic attitudes to work differ little from those of Protestants.[34] In the past other variants have come into play: lower educational achievements by Catholics, demographic concentration in areas far removed from urban industry, reluctance to apply for jobs in Protestant-dominated sectors such as the shipyard. Even so, Whyte found that discrimination did play an important part in Catholic disadvantage, even though, by the time he was writing, 1983, it was in decline.[35]

Discrimination against Catholics was particularly acute in public employment. A quick glance at the religious breakdown of public service employees reveals a Catholic percentage broadly in line with overall population breakdown. A close look, however, reveals the traditional bunching of Catholics in the lower levels – with 40 per cent of labourers employed by local councils being Catholics in 1951, but only 11.8 per cent in senior posts. Another survey in 1969 found little change. Catholics were also under-represented on other statutory bodies, the more educated finding it particularly difficult to break into the system. 'We are satisfied', the Cameron Commission concluded, 'that all these Unionist-controlled councils have used and use their power to make appointments in a way which benefited Protestants.' Even at the level of school bus-drivers, over 90 per cent were Protestant in counties like Fermanagh where Catholics were a majority. Cameron did find that Nationalist-controlled Newry Urban District employed very few Protestants.

But two wrongs do not make a right; Protestants who are in the minority in the Newry area, by contrast to the other areas we have specified, do not have a serious unemployment problem, and in Newry there are relatively few Protestants, whereas in the other towns Catholics make up a substantial part of the population.[36]

Many reasons besides discrimination have been put forward for the under-representation of Catholics in public employment, and there can be no doubting a definite antagonism within the Catholic community against those who entered public service. 'It was my experience', recalled Patrick Shea, 'that some Catholics, and especially those in Belfast where, I had been told, the Bishop had advised them against seeking Government employment, looked with suspicion on Catholic civil servants. We had joined the enemy.'[37] Unionists told Cameron that there were fewer Catholics in public employment because they did not apply – a claim that was still being made in the 1990s. 'No doubt that is factually true', concluded Cameron, 'but the answering comment, which is made with force and supported in evidence, is that from experience it is realised that an application made by a Catholic would stand no real prospect of success.'[38] Whyte, after examining all the evidence on both sides and accepting some of the Unionist explanations as partly valid, still found the case for discrimination overwhelmingly proven. Patrick Buckland, though he had started out broadly sympathetic to the Unionists in researching his *Factory of Grievances* (1979), reached the same conclusion and argued against ever restoring devolved government to the region.[39]

Even had there not been active discrimination against Catholics, the many sectarian public pronouncements by government ministers and officials would have been enough to deter applications. Much of the surviving evidence on discrimination was not the product of dispassionate government inquiries, but of investigations of numerous complaints from loyalist organisations about 'disloyal' elements in public employment. Protestant pressure groups, particularly the Orange Order, wielded a dominant influence on the structures and policies of the state. It was virtually impossible to be a Unionist politician without being an Orangeman. Every prime minister of Northern Ireland has been an Orangeman and between 1921 and 1963 only three cabinet members were not Orangemen upon election.[40] Orange complaints and delegations were readily received and acted upon, when nationalist ones were dismissed. In 1933 an allegation that the majority of the porters at Stormont were Catholic prompted John Andrews, minister of labour and a future prime minister, to investigate. He was then able to proclaim that of the thirty-one porters he had found, only one was a Catholic and he was only temporary. The following year a Catholic gardener at Stormont was dismissed because of Orange claims that he was a Sinn Féiner, despite his British army record and personal service with the Prince of Wales. Most famously, Home Affairs Minister Dawson Bates refused to have Catholics in his ministry and in 1934, upon learning 'with a great deal of surprise' that a Catholic telephonist had been appointed in Stormont, he refused to use the phone for important business and the telephonist was transferred. James Kelly, remembering his early days as a reporter with the Catholic newspaper the *Irish News*, recalled that one editorial writer's particular task was to scour the Ministry of Home Affairs' Gazette for details of the application of the Special Powers Act: 'A nationalist meeting banned, or another local anti-unionist served with an "exclusion order" . . . an obscure publication or patriotic gramophone record banned.' Bates was said 'to sleep with the Special Powers act and a revolver under his pillow'.[41]

The belief that Catholics stood little chance of entering public employment is well chronicled. The headteacher of the Christian Brothers' school in Newry, attended by Patrick Shea, had stopped entering his bright boys for the Northern Ireland civil service examination for this reason. But Shea applied in any event and no one was more pleased when he succeeded than the same headmaster. The story epitomised Catholic attitudes towards the Northern Ireland state – shunning state employment for fear of being shunned. Shea's lifetime experience in the civil service would confirm some, but by no means all, of the stereotypes. He did indeed, as a Catholic, find himself in a tiny minority within the Northern Ireland civil service.

To many of my colleagues Catholics were strange animals of which they had astonishingly little knowledge . . . I learned of their beliefs about the power of the Pope and his clergy and no words could persuade them that I was not subject to malevolent direction by black-robed priests to whom Rome had entrusted its master plan for world domination. I was astonished to meet youths of my own age who had never met a Catholic until I appeared in the office, who believed, as one of them told me, that in the event of their coming under a Nationalist government the Pope would require his obedient Irish flock to banish the Protestants from the land.[42]

Certainly Shea experienced discrimination and his promotion was impeded because of his religion, only coming under the more relaxed regime of Terence O'Neill in the 1960s. But he also learnt that the discrimination came from the politicians and angered and embarrassed the career civil servants. He singles out Sir Wilfred Spender in particular for his integrity. An Englishman and head of the Northern Ireland civil service until 1944, he is on record as protesting at the anti-Catholicism of the politicians and he particularly disliked Bates. He personally recommended Shea for promotion, but it was rejected by the 'political advisers' because of Shea's religion. Spender (and the other senior civil servants who had supported the recommendation) was angry. 'I thought it only right I should tell you about this,' he said. 'I can only say that I am surprised and disappointed and very sorry.' Shea was happy in the civil service. He found much 'native kindness' there and many in senior positions who would have liked more Catholics appointed. But he felt 'a cuckoo in the nest', Protestants wondering how he had 'got in', and Catholics, particularly those in Belfast, suspicious that he had. 'I was probably a "bad Catholic", perhaps secretly a Freemason . . . [I] had gone over to the "other side".' But although critical of Catholics for being fatalistic and for not always using opportunities that existed, he nevertheless believed that 'very serious discriminatory practices' operated against Catholics in public employment and that both Unionism and the Northern Ireland government were in thrall to the often 'malevolent' influence of the Orange Order. Only then could one explain 'how men for whom one could feel genuine respect could have acquiesced, even participated in, illiberal practices which, in the end, brought discredit on fifty years of government'.[43] Certainly the percentage of Catholics in the civil service had declined since partition and remained at 6 per cent between 1927 and 1959, while only one Catholic achieved the status of permanent secretary before Terence O'Neill's premiership. This was A.N. Bonaparte Wyse, permanent secretary at the Ministry of Education 1921–39, who had transferred from Dublin Castle after partition and travelled back to his Dublin home at weekends.[44]

Cameron was told by one local council that it only employed 'loyal' citizens. This belief that no Catholic could be loyal was the bedrock of Unionist thinking till the 1960s and was deeply resented by Catholics. It was at the heart of Ultach's damning indictment of Stormont in a series of pamphlets in the 1940s and of numerous *Irish News* reports. Ultach's challenge consisted of case after case in which leading Unionist figures, up to and including successive prime ministers, declared Catholicism as incompatible with allegiance to the state.[45] The fact that many of the public statements were made to massed Orangemen on 12 July further endorsed Catholics' sense that Northern Ireland was an 'Orange State'. The most famous of such claims was made by Sir Basil Brooke (Lord Brookeborough, Prime Minister of Northern Ireland, 1943–63). On 12 July 1933, Brooke, then Minister of Agriculture, spoke at Newtownbutler, County Fermanagh:

There were a great number of Protestants and Orangemen who employed Roman Catholics. He felt he could speak freely on this subject as he had not a Roman Catholic about his own place . . . Roman Catholics were endeavouring to get in everywhere. He would appeal to Loyalists, therefore, wherever possible to employ good Protestant lads and lassies.[46]

The speech became notorious and was retold by countless Catholic parents to their offspring. But Brooke refused to retract a syllable when publicly criticised. 'I recommended those people who are loyalists not to employ Roman Catholics', he told the Londonderry Unionist Association the following March, 'ninety-nine per cent of whom are disloyal.' When called upon to dissociate himself from the speech, the Prime Minister (created Lord Craigavon in 1927) simply dug deeper by stating that 'there is not one of my colleagues who does not entirely agree with him'.[47]

'Ultach' cites many instances of such attitudes at every level of the political and justice system and he blamed such 'inflammatory speeches from responsible public men' for the anti-Catholic riots of 1935, a criticism also made by the Belfast City Coroner. The public face of Ulster Unionism did a great disservice to the Protestant community generally, creating the illusion that all Protestants were victimisers and all Catholics were victims. Such 'injudicious public utterances [by Unionist leaders]', commented a 1938 brief to the British Home Secretary, 'seem to have been stored up by the Nationalist propagandists year after year and are constantly being brought forward again.'[48] The internal inquiry into the treatment of Catholics, of which the brief was part, concluded – after consulting the marquess of Dufferin – that 'there was nothing approaching persecution', but Dufferin 'did consider that gerrymandering . . . had taken place and that the attitude of the Northern Ireland Government towards the minority had been illiberal . . . He thought that many Ulstermen shared his view and were uneasy about the attitudes of their Government which had the effect of perpetuating a division which a more enlightened policy might close.'[49]

Though descended from the O'Neills of Antrim and spending long periods at the ancestral home, Shane's Castle, Terence O'Neill was brought up and educated in England. When he came to Stormont as MP for Bannside in 1946, he had a wider British view of Northern Ireland's constitutional position and was shocked at the parochialism of its politics. Predictably that parochialism often took the form of Unionist resistance to British-inspired legislation which might also benefit Catholics. In 1956, efforts were being made by some in the Unionist party to have him unseated as minister of finance, because it was rumoured that he was admitting more Catholics into the civil service. By that stage, however, relations between the two major traditions were improving. There were enough Unionists to support him and his threat to reveal the reasons for a smear campaign against him caused the conspirators to back down. He was particularly critical of Lord Brookeborough, 'a man of limited intelligence', who would never have been a minister in London. O'Neill thought that Brookeborough treated the whole business of government and politics as of secondary importance to hunting and fishing in Fermanagh; 'the tragedy of his premiership was that he did not use his tremendous charm, and his deep Orange roots to try and persuade his devoted followers to accept some reforms . . . [He] played safe. In twenty years as Prime Minister he never crossed the border, never visited a Catholic school and was never received or sought a civic reception from a Catholic town.'[50] This is why, perhaps, he assumed that all Catholics were out to overthrow Northern Ireland by force and why he felt the need to reiterate his views in opposition to O'Neill in 1969.[51]

The provocative statements of the Unionist politicians in the 1930s fed the rising tensions caused by the revival of militant Protestant evangelicalism in the Ulster Protestant League (founded 1931). In 1934 Brooke's call to boycott Catholic businesses was denounced by Nationalist MPs as inviting reprisals. 'Are we to take it', asked Alex Donnelly, Nationalist MP for Tyrone West, 'that it is but a prelude to another pogrom?'[52] Certainly there were ominous hints of renewed sectarian trouble in Belfast. Poverty and unemployment had briefly drawn the Protestant and Catholic poor together in the outdoor relief strike of 1932, when the huge numbers of unemployed in Belfast demanded adequate poor relief outside the workhouse. But this was highly unusual and a build-up of sectarian incidents in north Belfast's Dock ward saw both sides preparing for trouble when the factories closed for the 12 July holiday. As 40,000 Orangemen paraded back to Belfast on the evening of the 12th, there was mutual taunting and riots erupted. Many of the Orangemen had come from outside the area for the annual celebrations and it was a group of Glaswegian loyalists who led one of the most sustained attacks on Catholic houses in the area. For nine days the riots continued, leaving 10 dead, 83 injured and 2,500 intimidated out of their homes.

In the event it was the Catholic populace in mixed areas who suffered most, accounting for some 85 per cent of those displaced. Once again Belfast's sectarian map was redrawn, once again those in mixed-religion relationships were the object of loyalist attack. Catholic families intimidated or burnt out of York Street, the Old Lodge and Donegall Road areas, crowded into refugee huts on the Falls Road and a half-built housing estate (Glenard) adjoining Ardoyne. On the return to work on 22 July, thousands of Catholics were expelled from the mills and the shipyard. This time the employers, who tried to protect their workers, were absolved from any charges of sectarianism, and it was mobs at the gates to the shipyards, rather than fellow-workers, which were responsible for the expulsions. There were also attacks on Catholic enclaves near Portadown. But a number of retaliatory attacks on Protestants in the Irish Free State weakened the Nationalist argument that Protestants encountered no discrimination there. Not all Catholics were forced out of Dockside, for Fred Heatley remembered a return to neighbourly relations during his childhood in the 1940s.[53] But few political lessons were learnt. Indeed, it is hard not to sympathise with the Catholic bishop of Down and Connor, Daniel Mageean, in his dismissal of Ultach's 1943 recommendation that Britain be asked to intercede, for the Bishop had sought political action from London, Dublin and Stormont alike in 1935, but to no avail. Craigavon had taken himself off on holiday to Scotland and virtually ignored the Bishop's protest. De Valera was anxious to improve relations with Britain and made no more than consolatory noises, which Mageean was at much greater pains to excuse than what he considered the predictable lack of action from the Northern Irish and British authorities. The British Government continued its conventional reluctance to interfere in Northern Ireland, despite considerable English pressure to do so and the deployment of British troops during the riots – for the first time since 1922.[54] There had been no significant paramilitary involvement, though the IRA experienced a surge in membership in the aftermath. The combustible potential of Belfast's ethnic frontier zones had once again been demonstrated and once again reinforced, as had the 'ostrich'[55] mentality of the statesmen.

4. *Nationalist politics during the Stormont years*

One of the most fundamental and baffling aspects has been the apparently ineradicable tendency of the minority to attract discrimination. Not since the foundation of Ulster [sic] have they been prepared to contemplate assimilation. They rejected the concept of the state from the beginning and refused to participate in its institutions ... The inevitable consequence has been that they have drawn to themselves the very antagonism and suspicion of which they complain.[56]

So concluded a Minority Rights Group report in 1971, in an atmosphere where old-style nationalism was generally under attack. It is a token of how people can live in open harmony, yet never talk about what really concerns them, that Richard Rose could find 74 per cent of Protestants in 1969 believing that no discrimination against Catholics existed in Northern Ireland and exactly the same percentage of Catholics declaring that it did.[57] Only such a gulf of understanding can explain why the early civil-rights movement was perceived by Unionists as an IRA plot, long before it became just that. There was a terrible circularity of argument in Northern Ireland's political rhetoric, entrapping both communities, Nationalists saying 'we cannot give allegiance to the state because it is anti-Catholic', Unionists 'we cannot give them a stake in the state because they are disloyal'. Here were two absolutes, to which variations were inadmissible. How can the 'ascendancy party' defend its policies to England, asked 'Ultach' in 1943, for by then many Catholics considered England something of an honest broker and were baffled that it did not interfere more forcibly to ensure fair play.

Examine almost any 'defence' ... It all turns on the question of 'loyalty' ... loyalty to the King of England, to the flag, and to the Empire. The Six Counties is a 'loyal' area and it is natural sometimes that 'disloyalists' should get hurt. Riots break out in 'disloyal' areas. 'Disloyalists' fail to get jobs. And so on. 'Well, they must expect it if they are "disloyal",' says the outsider. But then the outsider does not know that the words 'loyalist' and 'disloyalist' have a meaning all their own in Northern Ireland.

He then reproduced endless quotations from Unionist politicians and Orangemen showing that for them ' "Disloyalist" and "Catholic" are synonymous'.[58]

So how 'disloyal' were Catholics after partition? It is certainly true that not until the 1960s were Catholics prepared to accept the legitimacy of the Northern Ireland state. But neither did they actively try to subvert it. An IRA campaign of sorts continued intermittently throughout the first forty-five years of the state's existence, though on nothing like the scale of the post-1969 Troubles. However, the bulk of northern Catholics remained, as they had always been, conservative, clerically-dominated, but utterly constitutional nationalists. Until the Boundary Commission reported in 1925 uncertainty reigned in nationalist politics, particularly in those areas thought likely to be transferred to the Irish Free State. Some Nationalist-controlled councils swore allegiance to the Dáil and were dissolved. Others were happy to vote temporary allegiance to the Northern Ireland government. For a while large numbers of Catholic teachers (as many as 50 per cent in Tyrone) were supported in their non-recognition stance by continued payment of their salaries from Dublin. But this was discontinued after Collins's death in 1922 and the Irish government then urged Catholics in Northern Ireland to recognise the Belfast regime.[59] Nearly half a century was to pass before the bulk of Catholics recognised that the border was not simply a temporary and unnatural imposition and demanded their rights as 'UK citizens'. Until then their ambivalence towards the state simply played into the hands of the ultra-loyalists.

For a while in the 1920s there was a co-operative mood among some Nationalist MPs. Backed by the leading nationalist press, most of the Catholic clergy and the Dublin government, the members for Belfast and Antrim decided that abstentionism was no policy at all and took their seats in the Belfast Parliament after 1925. Joe Devlin had been the first to take his seat, and his pragmatism, charisma and experience made the years before his death in 1934 the most favourable for any constructive relationship between Nationalists and Unionists. Most republicans continued to favour abstention and remained antagonistic towards Devlin. But his old Sinn Féin opponent, Cahir Healy, MP for Fermanagh-Tyrone, joined him in restructuring the Nationalist Party. By 1927 it had ten MPs in the Northern Ireland Parliament, leaving two republicans still abstaining. The revamped party promised conciliation and co-operation whilst pursuing nationalist aims. Devlin got on well with Craig. There were even some minor government gestures towards the Nationalists, most famously Craigavon's visit and concessions to the Catholic Mater hospital in Belfast in 1930. But the abolition of PR for parliamentary elections in 1929 was more symptomatic of the new political reality. Sick and disillusioned, Devlin saw himself going in directions which his whole career had fought against. Discrimination and the constant need to pursue purely Catholic issues made him realise that he was leading a Catholic party (and this when he had always been cold-shouldered by the local bishop and cardinal). Finally he led his followers out of the Northern Ireland parliament in May 1932, after delivering a bitter verdict on the Unionist government's treatment of the Catholic minority:

You had opponents willing to co-operate. We did not seek office. We sought service. We were willing to help. But you rejected all friendly offers. You refused to accept co-operation ... you went on on the old political lines, fostering hatreds, keeping one third of the population as if they were pariahs ... and relying on those religious differences and difficulties so that you would remain in office for ever.[60]

Thereafter the Nationalists became part-time MPs, abstaining more often than not, and remaining almost totally absent during the period of the Second World War. They sank into an already well-worn rut of sulkiness and whinging. For this they were to be criticised by northern nationalists in the 1960s and 1970s.[61] With constitutional nationalist politics so directionless, it cannot surprise that the party failed to develop any new vision. After Devlin's death it was deeply conservative, middle class and clerically driven. T. J. Campbell (Nationalist leader 1934–45), was a barrister and former editor of the *Irish News*. His successor, the MP for Mourne, James McSparran (1945–58), was another barrister with *Irish News* (and therefore clerical) connections, and as he handed over the leadership to his successor, East Tyrone MP and publican Joe Stewart (leader 1958–64), he was thanked for upholding 'Catholic and Nationalist interests'.[62] None have left their mark on the history books – although this is also a product of the historical neglect of northern nationalism, with the notable exception of the works of Michael Farrell, Eamon Phoenix and Brendan Lynn.

Within this political world of largely rural and conservative Catholic nationalism, Devlin's former Belfast constituency sat uneasily and after his death working-class areas with sizeable Catholic populations voted for a range of socialist and labour candidates. But these candidates also had to be anti-partitionist, and when the Northern Ireland Labour Party officially accepted partition in 1949, it lost its Catholic support to the newly formed Irish Labour Party. Then, as later, it proved impossible to build a labour movement drawing support from Catholics and Protestants alike.[63]

Catholics in the mid-twentieth century, however, were as conservative and predisposed to authority as they had ever been. Why then should they have so vehemently opposed the very existence of the Northern Ireland state? Why did it take so long for the disappointment and frustration at the time of partition to abate? Part of the answer lies in the continuing territorial link between those predominantly Catholic areas in the western and southern parts of Northern Ireland with the three Ulster counties that had become part of the Irish Free State. Few here would ever have travelled to Belfast. Belfast was the seat of the enemy. Belfast Catholics reconciled their residence in Unionism's capital by a kind of spatial alternative thinking. Protestant Stormont, east Belfast, the shipyards were worlds apart from the other world over the ring of hills – Colin Mountain, Black Mountain, the Cave Hill, which edged the Catholic areas.[64] Elsewhere, the mental world moved slowly from the local parish, to Dublin, to Rome. The regional nationalist press reflects all three. Northern nationalism was extraordinarily confused. Just as their religious leaders would have preferred continued rule from Britain to partition, so territorial unity was more important to northern nationalists than Irish national self-determination. The declaration of a republic by the Irish Government in 1948 was a shock, a token of southern rejection. It was the first time, recalled a retired Catholic academic in conversation with Fionnuala O Connor in 1992, that he and his like recognised that they would have to reconcile themselves to life in the northern state. Until then, they were totally convinced it would not last.[65]

Intermittently Nationalist MPs, when pushed to the limit, would seek permission to sit in Dáil Éireann in Dublin (always unsuccess-fully); would accept political funds from the south (usually counter-productively, as with the disastrous 'chapel-gate election' of 1949, when southern politicians organised collections after Sunday mass to assist anti-partition candidates in the north, thereby providing a propaganda gift to their Unionist opponents); and would further iden-tify themselves with the southern state by sporting the Irish tricolour. Because so many nationalists believed (or, rather, wanted to believe) the political rhetoric in the south claiming an overwhelming desire to unite the six Ulster counties with the republic, they began culturally to think of it as home. Of course it was not and never had been. But above all they wanted to belong to a state and their rejection of and by the northern one caused the identification with the southern state to become a necessary crutch. This was the essence of romantic nation-alism – a psychological need. However, their experience was often one of rejection. Northern Catholics were treated as troublesome and embarrassing by the south, at best lumped together with all the other 'black northerners', at worst treated as far more problematic than the Unionists (the latter tendency predominant after the onset of the Troubles). Certainly Fionnuala O Connor found that those Catholics who still nourished the idea of a united Ireland in the early 1990s 'had inherited a powerful sense of betrayal and rejection by the southern state', often from parents who had grown up in the 1930s and 1940s. 'We are the bastard children of the Republic', the Nationalist leader Eddie McAteer told civil-rights campaigner Dr Conn McCluskey in the 1960s; 'sometimes they must needs acknowledge us, but generally speaking they try to keep their distance'.[66]

But the Unionists were the old enemy, and they held exclusive power for over fifty years after the foundation of the state. Just after Devlin's departure from the Northern Ireland parliament, it was re-housed at Stormont in Protestant east Belfast. Even today it seems entirely over the top, a magnificent, over-sized Portland-stone mansion, completed in 1932 at a cost of some £1,150,000 at the height of the Depression. Craigavon now had his Protestant parliament for his Protestant people, commented the *Irish News*.[67] It was a reference to a speech delivered by Craigavon to Orangemen at Poyntz Pass in County Armagh on 12 July 1932, when he declared, 'Ours is a Protestant government and I am an Orangeman.' He was to reiterate the claim in the Northern Ireland parliament on 22 April 1934.[68] In Catholic mythology the parliament buildings became another symbol of Unionist domination. Nationalists duly boycotted the opening ceremony by the Prince of Wales. And yet the sequel had all the hallmarks of good old one-upmanship. After the opening of Stormont, the Prince of Wales paid a visit to the Mater Hospital in north Belfast. The crowd which gathered was, the *Irish News* boasted, the largest attending any of the events during his stay in Northern Ireland and the hospital's chapel the only place of worship visited by him.[69] For most nationalists, denials of the legitimacy of the state sat incongruously with a desire for participation and recognition. Although the nationalist press reveals an intense dislike of the Union flag as a symbol (largely because of its usage by some Protestants to denote exclusivist loyalism), attitudes to the British monarchy were respectful. In the 1980s and 1990s resistance to the playing of the British national anthem became common among younger, often republican-minded nationalists. But their more con-servative forebears were far more restrained. Catholic councillors were angry at being excluded from the City Hall lunch to welcome Queen Elizabeth to Belfast in 1953. One complained:

The Nationalist people of the city . . . paid more than lip sympathy to this young woman. Their wishes towards her were sincere and good . . . it is a damnable thing and most insidious thing to say we would attempt to insult or injure the Queen. We don't recognise her. But the British people are entitled to have monarchy if they want it.[70]

Civil rights campaigner in the 1960s, Dr Conn McCluskey, recalls being hurt that many Protestants assumed Catholics would not rise for the national anthem: 'My kind of Catholic would never dream of offering a discourtesy to the Queen.'[71]

MPs, local councillors and all other public employees (including teachers) were required to take the oath of allegiance. Nationalist MPs duly took the oath on George VI's accession to the throne in 1936. But it was one of the many areas where nationalists were not pressed too hard. As Maurice Hayes recalls his experience of taking it in the 1940s and 1950s, most Catholics did so, but squared their consciences by taking it before a Catholic JP. His own experience suggests that Protestant JPs were anxious not to offend. With all 'the pomposity' of the young graduate he wanted nothing to do with such double standards. He sought out a Protestant JP, took the oath and declared that were he ever to withdraw his allegiance he would return to inform him.

He looked at me with mounting horror and said he did not think that would be necessary, that it was no part of his function and that, in such a case, he would be better not knowing. We had a pleasant discussion about the novels he remembered from his Edwardian schooldays, and the proprieties had been attended to.[72]

Thus did daily life in Northern Ireland function between the apparent absolutes.

In the end the old Nationalist Party had no role except to 'maintain a protest'. It had no proper party organisation, no policy beyond that of ending partition and defending Catholic interests. In the mid-1950s it was thought to be on its last legs. In the elections for the Westminster parliament in 1955, when the party did not field candidates, there was a major transfer of the Catholic vote to Sinn Féin, not because Catholics necessarily supported the IRA, but because they appeared to be the only candidates able to sustain 'the traditional protest'.[73] The essential parliamentarianism of the Nationalist Party ensured a welcome for Terence O'Neill's conciliatory gestures, and for the first time since partition it agreed to act as the official opposition. It also caused it to misread the signs in refusing to respond to calls for civil disobedience just months before Northern Ireland was swept by civil-rights demonstrations. Eddie McAteer, leader of the Nationalists, was defeated by the civil-rights candidate, John Hume, at the next election for the Northern Ireland parliament in 1969.[74] By then, increasing numbers of Catholics were disillusioned with the politics of old-fashioned nationalism. But it had reflected their interests accurately enough for much of the century.

These then were the 'disloyalists' of Unionist rhetoric. Pure rhetoric it sometimes was and Unionist leaders respected some of the Nationalist MPs. But the Nationalists had put themselves in an impossible situation. They made no secret of their dislike of the state and ultimate ambition to see its demise. This allowed Unionists to dismiss charges that they were penalising the Catholic religion as such, and to assert that their quarrel was with nationalism in its 'political sense'.[75] To some commentators in the 1960s and 1970s it seemed incomprehensible that it had taken nationalists till then to accept the constitutional position of Northern Ireland.[76] However, they were hardly encouraged to do so. What would have happened had that encouragement been forthcoming must remain speculation. Moreover, Unionists were given every reason to think nationalists a threat. Even though most nationalists did not seek to overthrow the Northern Ireland state by violent means, they shared the religion and traditions of those who did: the IRA. Indeed, an IRA campaign of sorts had continued since partition. After 1942 it was largely directed at Northern Ireland and entirely so by the 1950s.

5. The IRA

The post-partition IRA was the direct descendant of the anti-Treatyites, completely dedicated to overthrowing partition by force. It was anti-political and those who chose a political path, from de Valera to the so-called Official IRA of the 1970s, tended to withdraw and change their name. Once independence had been established, the new Irish state took a far more vigorous line against the IRA than either the British or Northern Irish governments: some seventy-seven members were executed between November and May 1922–3; internment was introduced by successive Irish governments; IRA hunger-strikers were more likely to be left to die in Irish than in British or Northern Irish prisons; and after 1957 the tough measures of de Valera, once one of their own, effectively decimated the IRA in the south of Ireland. He was particularly incensed at their bombing campaign in England in 1939, since he was then involved in delicate anti-partition negotiations. Their meetings were banned and the leaders rounded up under a new Offences Against the State Act, June 1939. The IRA was denounced by the Catholic Church throughout the twentieth century, much as it had denounced previous violent movements. The success of the suppression south of the border shows how limited was the support for the IRA there.[77] But with bombs and volunteers being transported over the border and IRA funerals turning out thousands of followers, the Northern Ireland authorities might be forgiven for not entirely recognising the change of mood in the south.

The northern IRA was marginalised from the national leadership by the 1930s. But so long as sectarian tensions persisted, it played a traditional role of defending the Catholic community against attack, notably during the parading season around 12 July. This was particularly the case in Belfast and it was the attacks on Catholic homes in 1968–9 which effectively recalled it into existence. The riots of 1935 played a similar role and by 1938–9 it had a Belfast membership of 800.[78] The terrible economic conditions of the 1930s produced common suffering and considerable co-operation among working-class Catholics and Protestants. Peadar O'Donnell, the prime mover in taking some members of the IRA in the Irish Free State to the political left, thought only their sectarianism prevented the Ulster republicans from winning working-class Protestants to their cause. He recalled attending a 1916 commemoration in Belfast – traditionally held by republicans at Easter. He had persuaded some Protestants to come along. But when stopped by the B Specials: 'The whole republican procession flopped down on its knees and began the rosary. My Orangemen could have afforded to risk getting their heads cracked with a baton, but they couldn't kneel on the Belfast streets to say the rosary.' The Belfast IRA, he concluded, was no more than 'a battalion of armed Catholics'.[79]

The Belfast IRA developed a new, younger command structure, far more aggressive than that in Dublin. During World War II they ran a republican radio station out of west Belfast, organised symbolic burnings of gas-masks and were partly blamed for assisting the Belfast blitz by refusing to obey black-out orders. The IRA was in negotiation with Germany at this stage and collecting information on British military bases. There were a number of isolated attacks on the RUC and one IRA man was hanged in September 1942 for killing a policeman in Belfast. Internment was re-introduced for the duration of the war, with 243 interned by 1942.[80] In that mental framework which has ever been a part of Irish republican tradition, the IRA blamed the erosion of their campaign on traitors and informers. But the war was a time of shared suffering, particularly in Belfast: bomb attacks by the German air force on Protestant and Catholic working-class districts indiscriminately killed over 1,000 and wounded hundreds more, destroying workplaces and 53.5 per cent of the city's housing. Clonard Monastery gave refuge alike to people from the Shankill and the Falls. Once-crowded areas seemed eerily silent as an estimated 100,000 fled to the countryside.[81] The arrival of 120,000 American servicemen in 1942 brought jobs on their bases and excitement as international stars like Glen Miller and Bob Hope came in their wake. It was more difficult to depict the war as England's difficulty when such a friendly nation was involved. By the late 1940s the northern IRA had almost totally disintegrated. The support in the Catholic community, on which it relied, no longer existed.

Paddy Devlin, one of the founders of the SDLP and a future minister in the 1974 power-sharing executive, was an IRA man in this earlier period. His was not a particularly republican family. Indeed, his mother was an ardent supporter of Joe Devlin and he remembered fisticuffs between nationalists and republicans. But they lived on that ethnic frontier zone between Protestant and Catholic enclaves of west Belfast. There were family traditions of attacks from Protestants dating from the nineteenth century and more recent ones from the 1920s and 1935. Paddy Devlin joined the Fianna, a republican youth movement. These were a form of ideological boy scouts, which aspired to transform basic ghetto-defensiveness into a kind of spiritual martialism along the lines of the mythical ancient hero, Cú Chúlainn. Membership (which Paddy had from the age of eleven) raised even the most puny boy's prestige. Classes indoctrinating the boys in a particular brand of Irish history were punctuated by real drilling after Sunday mass. When war broke out in 1939 their teenage commanding officer, with all the pomposity of youth, told them that their time had arrived, for England's difficulty was Ireland's opportunity. They were ordered to daub the gables with suitable slogans. Paddy lied about his age and gained admittance to the IRA at fifteen. Contrary to Unionist belief in Catholic 'disloyalty', he found the IRA very generally disliked in west Belfast and people all too ready to give information to the police, who still walked the beat there.[82]

By early 1942 the Belfast IRA had all but faded away. In the post-war period the benefits of the British welfare state were progressively implemented in Northern Ireland, adding a new propaganda weapon to the Unionist case for partition – and one which Catholics found increasingly difficult to answer. These were the 'Quiet Years' and the historian Jonathan Bardon criticises the Unionist government for not taking the opportunity to offer some concessions to the nationalist population.[83] But it was matched by equal intransigence in the south, for with de Valera out of power after 1948, all political hues vied with each other to show their patriotism on the issue of partition. In the north the early 1950s witnessed a number of skirmishes over parades and flags. The result was a new series of Public Order Acts and the 1954 Flags and Emblems Act. This was to prove a long-running sore with nationalists, since it gave special protection to the Union flag, heightening the sense that its sometimes provocative use had state approval. A restive IRA group had broken away, and its leader, Liam Kelly of Pomeroy, County Tyrone, had built up a sizeable personal following. The climate was perfect for an IRA comeback. However, the fate of their renewed campaign (1957–62) showed yet again that the majority of northern Catholics eschewed violence.

But this would not have been immediately apparent to the authorities. There had been a number of small IRA raids and explosions and a noticeable increase of tensions along the border. It was partly to control such actions by splinter groups that the IRA launched its 'Operation Harvest' on 11 December 1956, with attacks on public buildings all over Northern Ireland. Over the next five years the newspapers regularly carried reports of IRA attacks. This time Belfast figured hardly at all, most IRA activity being confined to Tyrone, Fermanagh and Armagh. The campaign was a total failure, though characterisitically republicans tried to pull some kind of moral victory from defeat. Notable was the attempt on New Year's Eve (1956/7) to bomb Brookeborough police barracks and the consequent deaths in an exchange of fire of IRA men from the Irish Republic, Sean South from Limerick and Fergal O'Hanlon from Monaghan. Their deaths became immortalised in a popular song and massive crowds turned out for their funerals in the south. Taoiseach John Costello publicly denounced the IRA attacks and lost the support of some members of his unstable coalition government as a consequence. But outrage greeted the murder of an RUC constable at Forkhill, County Armagh, the following July. De Valera, Costello's successor as Taoiseach, re-introduced internment and swooped on IRA men in the south. In 1957 internment was re-introduced in Northern Ireland. By 1961 there was only a hard core of some thirty to forty IRA men still active. The northern campaign had continued intermittently, but was sufficiently low-key for the last of the internees to be released in the south by 1959, and in the north two years later. Even so, there had been some 600 'incidents', considerable destruction of property and a significant number of deaths. It had sustained the image of the Catholics as murderously disloyal and provided the backdrop to the rise of Paisleyism.

In fact, this IRA campaign of 1956–62 had failed largely through lack of Catholic support. The IRA admitted as much in its statement calling off the campaign on 26 February 1962:

TO THE IRISH PEOPLE

The leadership of the Resistance Movement has ordered the termination of the Campaign of Resistance to British Occupation launched on December 1956 . . . Foremost among the factors motivating this course of action has been *the attitude of the general public whose minds have been deliberately distracted* from the supreme issue facing the Irish people – the unity and freedom of Ireland.[84]

The IRA campaign had been condemned all along by the nationalist press and by the Catholic bishops, the bishop of Clogher perceptively catching the essence of the dilemma when the campaign opened in 1957:

That there is obstinate and subtle discrimination against Catholicism and Nationalists in the separated counties we are painfully aware. Nevertheless the opposing elements in our nation . . . constitute the people of one indivisible country, and nothing short of extreme provocation would justify a resort to violence . . . The border is not merely a geographical division. It is a spiritual division of minds and hearts which physical force cannot heal, but only aggravate.[85]

6. The O'Neill Era

There is a tendency to think of the premiership of Terence O'Neill (1963-9) as one of the great might-have-beens of recent Irish history – like Grattan's Parliament two centuries before, a regime apparently moving to heal its religious divisions, being derailed by the extremes on both sides. There are indeed many parallels, and no regime is so vulnerable as when it is reforming itself, for it raises expectations unlikely to be met in their entirety and the subsequent falling out sends the regime back into its shell. Despite Terence O'Neill's plummy accent and nervous, haughty ways, his arrival as Ulster's Prime Minister (after Brookeborough's resignation in 1963) seemed to match the mood of the sixties. Not only did he embark on an apparent whirlwind of regional development, but for the first time a Unionist Prime Minister made religious reconciliation part of government policy. Catholics had never forgiven Brookeborough his anti-Catholic statements of the 1930s and many came to see O'Neill as some kind of saving hero. That was his problem. It was hardly traditional Unionism and it left too many Unionists uneasy and ultimately hostile.

The legislation that established the welfare state in post-war Britain came to Northern Ireland in the various health and insurance acts of 1946-8. There was still some Unionist reluctance to share all its benefits with Catholics. The Health Services (Northern Ireland) Act of 1948 did not contain that clause of the 1946 British National Health Service Act, whereby hospitals with religious links could maintain their character within the health service. The Catholic Mater Hospital in Belfast was accordingly excluded from state funding. Such reluctance was also evident in the abortive attempt to reduce family allowance to larger (more typically Catholic) families in 1956. In education there was some Unionist grumbling at the apparent generosity of the 1947 Education Act towards Catholic voluntary schools. The following year the liberal Unionist Education Minister, Colonel Hall-Thompson, was forced out of office in favour of the former socialist, but now virulently anti-Catholic populist Unionist, Harry Midgley, to the dismay of civil servants in his department.[86] Even so, things were getting markedly better for the average Catholic. Northern Ireland's chronic housing shortage was beginning to be addressed, and the scrupulous fairness of the Housing Trust (established 1945) in allocating housing has been recognised in every social survey. Sadly, the new mood was not also reflected in the housing record of all local councils, one of the main reasons for the emergence of the Northern Ireland civil-rights movement in the late 1960s. Some 125,000 new jobs had been created in Northern Ireland between 1950 and 1969, many in the service industries, a traditional area for Catholic employment. Ominously, this made little difference to unemployment which was always higher than in Britain, for the industries on which Ulster had built its reputation – engineering, shipbuilding and textile manufacture – were in decline.[87] These were traditionally Protestant areas of employment and, unfortunately for O'Neill, there was no Protestant working-class 'feel-good factor' to match that of the Catholics during his premiership.

When he came to power, however, the omens were good. The IRA had just called off its campaign and admitted its failure to win Catholic support. The reforming papacy of John XXIII, the presidency of John F. Kennedy (the first Catholic, and one with Irish ancestry, to reach the White House), placatory gestures by the new Wilson government in London and a change of political opinion in Dublin were all adding to growing Catholic self-confidence. The media also played an important role in changing public perceptions. In retrospect critics like to see BBC Northern Ireland's early productions as anodyne. But this was simply making a policy of Northern Ireland's unwritten rules of social engagement: never raise controversial topics in mixed religious company. Its coverage in these years was scrupulously balanced. Northern Ireland's main daily newspaper, the *Belfast Telegraph*, had been moving steadily from its traditional Unionism to a centrist position. The young Cal McCrystal, later to become a top political reporter with the broadsheet press in England, recalled his appointment in the 1950s to its staff straight from Belfast's prime Catholic school, St Malachy's. He could tell that the interviewers genuinely wanted to appoint him. But his very Gaelic-sounding name (Cathal) appearing on its political columns would raise traditional Protestant hackles. So he was gently nudged to spell the name as it was pronounced and was duly appointed.[88]

O'Neill saw reconciliation as a fundamental part of his modernisation policies. He already had something of a reputation as one of the few Unionist ministers who would not block the promotion of Catholics. Patrick Shea finally won promotion under O'Neill, after waiting fifteen years for it.[89] O'Neill sent condolences to Cardinal Conway on the death of Pope John, visited a Catholic school, opened a civic reception in a nationalist town, invited two Irish premiers to Stormont, starting with Seán Lemass in January 1965. Nothing like this had ever been done by a Unionist leader. Nationalists took note. For the first time since the foundation of Northern Ireland the Nationalist Party agreed to assume the role of official opposition. The *Irish News*, after generations of anti-Unionism, swung behind O'Neill's efforts. In the general election of November 1965, some Catholics voted Unionist for the first time.[90] Surveys of voter behaviour in Belfast the following year showed Catholics more prepared to accept existing political arrangements than ever before. But although most Unionists seemed to favour the new conciliation, their words did not translate into actions. Nothing was being done to involve nationalists' representatives in existing institutions. Indeed, for four successive years one of the most moderate of Nationalist aldermen on Belfast City Council, Charles Daley, had been refused a chairmanship on its least important committee.[91] Richard Rose's 1967 pilot survey for his exhaustive 'Loyalty Survey' of the following year found respondents confused about O'Neill's policies.[92] Moreover, O'Neill's 'modernisation' programme contained some remarkable blunders. Most of the new economic development was going to predominantly Protestant areas in the east. Three issues in particular showed considerable insensitivity towards nationalists: the 1965 siting of a new university in the small Protestant town of Coleraine, rather than the predominantly Catholic, economically-depressed second city, Derry, which already had in Magee College the nucleus of a university; the naming of a model new town in County Armagh after Craigavon the same year; and the equally insensitive suggestion of 'Carson' – Unionist leader at the beginning of the century, closely associated with the threat of militant opposition to Home Rule – as the name for the new bridge over the Lagan.[93]

But the main challenge to O'Neill's concilation policies came from within his own camp. He had not been the Unionist party's first choice as leader and his most bitter recriminations after his downfall were reserved for Unionist rivals, notably Brian Faulkner.[94] His aloof, English manner alienated many, as did his reluctance to jeopardise his conciliatory policies by discussing them in advance with his party. Outside Stormont Ian Paisley was playing on traditional Protestant fears. Today the Revd Ian Paisley is a senior politician, commanding a huge popular vote at every election. But many hold him personally responsible for wrecking almost every attempt at fair government in Northern Ireland since the 1960s. His fundamentalist Protestantism sees Catholicism as the supreme evil, every drift towards conciliation part of popery's evil plot. His is an apocalyptic vision whereby Protestantism is fighting its last stand in Ulster. His Old Testament biblical imagery, and lurid images of popish persecution, appeals to that part of the Protestant psyche which genuinely fears the Catholic Church and the Irish Republic, with its claims over the whole of Ulster (only abandoned in 1999) and its dominant Catholic ethos. The decline of the Protestant population south of the border from 11 per cent before partition to 4 per cent by 1961 was used as irrefutable evidence of the end product of political popery.[95] The normally ultra-compassionate Dervla Murphy was shocked by the messianic violence of Paisley's sermons when she visited his church in 1976. She felt she had encountered pure evil. The only other occasion on which she experienced similar feelings was in the presence of an older, relatively prosperous guru of the Provisional IRA (the militant breakaway group in 1969, which went on to dominate the movement and was largely responsible for IRA activities throughout the Troubles).[96] Paisley came to symbolise for Catholics all that was wrong with the Northern Ireland state; whilst the Provisionals or Provos became the living symbol of Paisley's claims about the murderous threat of political popery.

Paisley first came to public notice in the 1950s, founding his own Free Presbyterian Church in 1951, 'rescuing' a young Catholic girl (Maura Lyons) from the popery of her parents in 1956, participating in the activities of the ultra-Protestant organisation 'Ulster Protestant Action'. The combination of the new ecumenism of the 1960s and O'Neill's invitation to southern leaders brought the Unionist prime minister into Paisley's gallery of enemies. His followers stalked O'Neill, waving placards: 'O'Neill must go', 'O'Neill the Real Enemy of Ulster', provoking riots and demonstrations not only against O'Neill but any other public figure or organisation guilty of ecumenism or dealings with 'popery'. The authorities clearly did not quite know what to do with him. Convicted in July 1966 of unlawful assembly and breach of the peace, he welcomed imprisonment and relished the martyr status which it gave him. As ever, the extremes fed off each other. Widespread republican rallies for the fiftieth anniversary of the 1916 rising produced Paisleyite counter-demonstrations and excessive deployment of armed police. That summer a young Catholic barman was murdered by the revived UVF, in an attack that was seen by Paisley's critics (and admitted by one of those convicted) as the direct outcome of his sectarian rhetoric. O'Neill was forced to invoke the Special Powers Act against Protestants, an action which further contributed to growing Protestant nervousness.[97]

One wonders if O'Neill would have survived had the traditional Catholic endurance continued through this period. As it was, Catholic restiveness at the slowness of reform took far longer to materialise than the Protestant backlash and in many ways was provoked by it. As Charles Carter wrote in 1972, when revising his and Denis Barritt's path-breaking study of ten years earlier, Catholics at first held their breaths on O'Neillism. This was not the Unionism they were used to and as the Paisleyite backlash gained momentum 'evidence suggested that there was little change at the grassroots of Unionism: that, whatever Captain O'Neill might say or do, the reality of what would happen would in the long run be nearer to what were then considered to be the wishes of the Revd Paisley'.[98]

In the western parts of Northern Ireland, where Catholics were more numerous, there was little to show for O'Neill's modernisation. In February 1967 unemployment in Derry City was 20.1 per cent, against a British average of 2.6 per cent and a Northern Ireland one of 8.1 per cent.[99] Some Unionist-controlled local councils had a record of neither building nor allocating houses in Catholic areas. O'Neill had begun an overhaul of local government which would eventually undermine such local Unionist autonomy. But a new breed of professional Catholics, frustrated by the negative whinging of traditional nationalism, had already started to demand equal rights within the state. Dr Conn McCluskey, a Catholic GP in Tyrone, who with his wife, Patricia, founded the Campaign for Social Justice (CSJ) in 1964, tells of older nationalist leaders dismissing their new approach, finding it incomprehensible that they could actually trust Unionists to deliver. Indeed, as they set about gathering statistics, wooing journalists, and most of all ensuring that English MPs were kept informed, they found the same traditional nationalists critical that they had so far accepted the system as to actually use the name 'Londonderry', instead of 'Derry', as preferred by nationalists![100] The instruction of the British political establishment had vastly improved with the election of the charismatic Gerry Fitt as Republican Labour MP for west Belfast in 1966. Lord Cameron criticised the authorities in his 1969 enquiry for misreading the CSJ and later civil-rights movement as somehow dangerously political:

These organisations concern themselves with immediate social reforms, such as opposition to housing and job discrimination by Unionists, support for universal adult franchise in local government elections and fairer electoral boundaries in local government. They are not concerned, as organisations, with altering the constitutional structure of Northern Ireland, and in this sense represent a quite new development among Catholic activists.[101]

In 1967 the McCluskeys' low-key efforts developed into the Northern Ireland Civil Rights Association (NICRA). As Lord Cameron was later to conclude, it arose largely because of the failure of normal politics in Northern Ireland. It had started out in the early 1960s with Patricia McCluskey's campaign to secure even low-standard prefabricated publicly-funded housing for needy Catholic families in the Dungannon area, where the two Unionist-controlled councils had a reputation for discrimination against Catholics and where efforts to secure redress through normal legal channels had proved fruitless. It was on the housing issue that the civil-rights campaign first broke through to attract widespread media attention. In June 1968 Austin Currie – Nationalist MP for East Tyrone – squatted in a council house in Caledon village to highlight the injustice of its allocation to the young secretary of a local Unionist candidate, when large Catholic families, living in squalor, had been repeatedly refused council housing. The media attention focused on these events at Caledon provided the impetus for the public marches which came to mark the civil-rights campaign and which started symbolically in Dungannon that August. This after all was 1968. The demand for 'civil rights' was mobilising vast crowds from Czechoslovakia to Mississippi.

But marching was never a neutral activity in Northern Ireland. Home Affairs Minister William Craig was already making the usual Unionist assumption that NICRA was a front for the enemies of the state (a claim which Cameron utterly dismissed). When the Apprentice Boys of Derry called a counter-march to that planned by the civil-rights campaigners on 5 October, Craig banned the latter. Why the authorities so consistently opposed these early peaceful demonstrations baffled many, even the Presbyterian Church in Ireland asking as much.[102] The 2,000 making their way to Dungannon in August dispersed when stopped by a police cordon. Now in Derry some of the original civil-rights leaders, including the McCluskeys, wanted their march called off.But this was the most economically depressed, most gerrymandered city in Ulster. The civil-rights campaign had unwittingly stirred up the resentment of centuries; 'we're not going to take this any more' just about summed up the mood, and the march went ahead. Even Eddie McAteer, leader of the Nationalist Party, joined the march, as did Gerry Fitt and three Westminster MPs, John Ryan, Russell Kerr and Anne Kerr.[103] Inexperienced at handling such situations, their manpower low after successive cuts, the police over-reacted, batoning and beating the unarmed demonstrators and spraying powerful water-cannon even over innocent bystanders. But the image flashed not only around the province that evening, but around the world (the first time international media attention had been focused on Northern Ireland) was of blood pouring from Gerry Fitt's head and vivid examples of police brutality.

Huge numbers became politicised overnight. The new term was just starting in Queen's University in Belfast, a relatively placid, even politically apathetic institution till then. But within a few days some 3,000 – including a number of academic staff – had mobilised for a peaceful protest march from the university to Belfast city centre. A short distance from the university the lawful student march was re-routed by police to avoid a counter-demonstration by Paisleyites, and then brought to a standstill within sight of its destination by the same

Paisleyites. For three hours the students sat in the rain as police and Paisleyites continued to block their route. It was one of the many occasions when police were noticed to stand with their backs to the loyalist protesters, while facing the peaceful and legal marchers. That evening those who had made it back to the university formed People's Democracy, from which emerged sociology student Bernadette Devlin as its most charismatic leader. Initially, People's Democracy was a radical extension of the civil-rights movement, but its tactics eventually played into the hands of those most anxious to destroy the movement altogether.

By now Northern Ireland was becoming badly destabilised. Civil-rights protests were continuing despite Craig's ban on 'non-traditional' (i.e. non-Orange) parades, and Paisley was mobilising increasing numbers against them. O'Neill was summoned to Downing Street and told to speed up his reform programme. On 22 November 1968 he announced a programme of reforms which granted most of what the civil-rights campaigners had been demanding: Londonderry's gerrymandered local authority was to be replaced, local authorities were to adopt a fair points system in allocating housing, an Ombudsman was to be appointed. On 9 December in a widely-viewed television broadcast, O'Neill appealed for the space to carry out further reforms without the increasingly provocative demonstrations. The response was overwhelming, some 150,000 messages of support and the media across the border in the republic voting him man of the year. NICRA called off its campaign and even his critics in the Unionist party seemed supportive. But a small portion of People's Democracy decided to keep up the pressure, against the wishes of most of its student supporters. During the Christmas vacation PD activists decided on a march from Belfast to Derry, in the belief that the Unionists could not be trusted to continue the reforms without such pressure. Certainly it would be another three years before O'Neill's promised reforms were forthcoming. But in the event this small, bedraggled group of student protesters helped destroy emerging Catholic confidence in O'Neill, because the excessive loyalist reaction did indeed seem to prove that Paisley and not O'Neill was still the authentic voice of Unionism.[104]

About eighty students set off from the City Hall in Belfast to march to Derry on the morning of 1 January 1969. Craig did not think the march sufficiently dangerous to ban. But all along the way it was harassed by loyalists, and at Burntollet Bridge outside Derry it was subjected to an orchestrated and bloody attack, in which, as subsequent inquiries proved, off-duty B Specials took a prominent part and the RUC seemed more in sympathy with the attackers than the victims. Attacks continued when they arrived in Derry and the RUC rampaged through Catholic areas in the city. As violence increased, moderates retreated into their traditional corners. O'Neill tried desperately to rally the middle ground in a snap election in February 1969. He was returned, but his mandate was not large and Paisley had fought a damaging campaign against him in his own constituency. A contemporary analysis of the election found traditional party structure very fragmented, but 'the sectarian divisions' unshaken. Anti-O'Neillism among Unionists was strongest in those areas where the Catholic presence was greater and in Protestant working-class constituencies, which would have lost most from civil-rights reforms. Although votes cast for pro-O'Neill candidates were more than double those for his opponents (pro-O'Neill twenty-four Unionists, anti-O'Neill twelve Unionists and three independent Unionists), Catholics had not been won over.[105] It was too small a mandate to go on forcing unwelcome reforms on his party and, when a number of explosions took place, many were convinced that Paisley and Craig had been right after all and that the civil-rights campaign was simply a Trojan Horse for the IRA. Later revelations showed the explosions to have been the work of loyalists determined to bring O'Neill down. They succeeded all too well and O'Neill resigned on 28 April 1969.

By then almost all the demands of the civil-rights movement had been granted and O'Neill himself admitted that its campaign had produced the kind of reforms which normally it would have taken government a decade to produce. He had also established the Cameron Commission to report on the reasons for the 1968 disturbances. There were queues outside Her Majesty's Stationery Office on the morning of 12 September 1969 when it reported.[106] The report was well disposed towards the civil-rights movement, generally absolving it from accusations that it was a cover for republicanism. Whilst it recognised that the RUC was in no way as sectarian as the USC, it nevertheless found it guilty of 'grave misconduct' and 'malicious damage' in Catholic areas in Derry. But most of all Cameron, in the words of O'Neill himself, 'blew sky high' 'the faithful [Unionist] Party line' that it did not discriminate against Catholics.[107] The Cameron Report found all the claims of discrimination made by the civil-rights movement to have been substantiated and, significantly, it found very many 'responsible' Protestants recognised this 'and called urgently for remedy'.[108]

The genuineness of O'Neill's reformism has been doubted by some commentators.[109] Others think Brian Faulkner, a more talented politician, should have succeeded Brookeborough. But all of this is to overlook the contribution of O'Neill to a real climate of hope in the 1960s which allowed many Catholics to identify with Northern Ireland, often for the first time. Here was a decent man who did not play the Orange card for political gain. It would have taken more time than was available to O'Neill to entirely remove Catholic mistrust of Unionists. But some Catholics did join the Unionist party in his day and there are few moderate nationalists who do not remember the O'Neill era without nostalgia. His problem was that despite his genuine Ulster roots – he really could claim descent from the ancient O'Neills – he never quite seemed to belong, never quite recognised the niceties and pitfalls of intercommunal living in Ulster. Even some republicans, however, credited him with trying. One Belfast IRA man told Dervla Murphy in 1976:

'We couldn't wait forever while O'Neill was pussy-footin' about trying to keep Paisley calm. He was a fool of a Prime Minister. Brave enough though, I'll say that for him. There was a time back in the sixties when a whole crowd of his own lot were itchin' to bump him. But he stuck with his principles, for all the good they were to anyone. Too much namby-pamby Eton carry-on. That kinda crap's no good in Belfast. He always went on like he was in London. Paisley could knock him flat with a look – and often did.'[110]

7. The Troubles

Whatever people at the time thought of the 'Burntollet' march – it had been opposed by the main civil-rights movement and many student supporters withdrew in its aftermath – it had achieved what some of its more radical leaders had sought. It had shown the bankruptcy of the Northern Ireland state and was a preliminary to its swift disintegration. In 1969 all the undercurrents which had gone to create that fearful and suspicious part of Ulster mentality suddenly exploded.

In Derry the battle between the police and the Catholic Bogside had continued intermittently since the beginning of 1969 – each case of over-reaction by a desperately overstretched police force (and there were a number of them) adding to the emotional time-bomb. By the time the traditional 12 August Apprentice Boys march passed along the walls overlooking the Bogside, the riots which ensued could have been predicted. Nothing had been done to take the heat out of the 'marching season' and there had already been ugly incidents elsewhere. There were hooligan elements spoiling for a fight. But the trigger seems to have been the tossing of pennies by Apprentice Boys, though a longstanding tradition, from the walls on to the Bogsiders below. It symbolised hundreds of years of Protestant contempt, and the area exploded. For three days a running battle was fought with police and there were supportive riots right across the province. In Belfast they assumed the all-too-familiar pattern. The *Sunday Times* Insight team reported:

In Derry a Catholic victory was always possible, for the Catholics have a local majority. In Belfast, on the other hand, the Catholics are outnumbered and hemmed into their ghettos: traditionally, the Belfast Catholics have seen themselves as hostages for the good behaviour of their co-religionists elsewhere.[111]

And so indeed did subsequent events enter Catholic folk-memory: another 'pogrom' on the Catholic ghettos, just as in the past, and again one in which the forces of the state seemed to have sided with their attackers. But this underestimates the real sense of fear and uncertainty which often lies behind the undoubted bully-boy tactics of elements of loyalist paramilitarism. That they really do fear and hate Catholics is beyond question. But they had been told by their political leaders that Catholics were out to destroy all that they stood for and the civil-rights movement was just another cover for the IRA. For years they had been experiencing their own economic recession, as the industries which had traditionally employed large numbers of Protestants, notably ship-building, went into terminal decline, while Catholics seemed to be getting better off. The demoralisation of the police in these months reflected that of their community. The misfortune is that both acted as if all Catholics were rebels.

In good civil-rights fashion, several hundred marchers had set off up the Falls Road to the Springfield Road RUC station on the evening of 13 August to present a petition against police action in Derry. But the inspector on duty refused to accept it, sending them instead to a station near Divis Street, at the lower end of the Falls, from where they had come in the first place. As they arrived at Divis Street, hooligans on the Catholic side stoned and petrol-bombed the police station, although the protest had been largely peaceful until then. But by all accounts the police panicked and unleashed armoured cars, armed with machine guns, on the area. The following day the B Specials were deployed. Not only did this action incense nationalists, but it created an impression on the neighbouring Protestant Shankill Road that the Divis Street riots were the prelude to a republican invasion of their area. That evening Catholic hooligans taunted the massed Protestants, waving tricolours and chanting the Irish national anthem the 'Soldier's Song'. Protestant mobs then invaded, torching Catholic houses in the streets connecting the Falls and Shankill. In the mêlée the RUC machine-gunned the Catholic Divis Flats and killed two innocent bystanders. There was similar police muddle in the north Belfast enclave of the Ardoyne, where Catholics were also being burnt out of their homes. The following night another Catholic street on the traditional frontier zone between the Falls and the Shankill – Bombay Street, near Clonard Monastery – was burnt out, the Protestant mob believing, with some justification, that they were being attacked by gunmen from within the monastery's precincts. It was the start of several years of intimidation which forced between 30,000 and 60,000 out of their homes in Belfast, further increasing the sectarian division of the city. An estimated 80 per cent of these were Catholic. Not all such intimidation during the Troubles was by 'the other side' and a distinctive feature of later years was increasing intimidation by paramilitaries within their own community. But there can be no doubt-ing the importance of such early intimidation to republicans' self-image as protectors of the Catholic community.[112] In the first days of the Troubles Catholics expelled from mixed areas elsewhere in the city poured into the already over-crowded Falls district – most with no possessions but the clothes they wore. Not all became IRA supporters, but such suffering explains the ambivalence of large numbers of ghetto Catholics towards the IRA (particularly in the first decade of the Troubles), for they might be needed again as defenders – at least that is what they were told by the emerging Provos.

There was no IRA organisation in Belfast at this time. The old – soon to be called the 'Official' – IRA had abandoned 'the armed struggle' and become socialist. They had recognised the legitimacy of the Belfast and Dublin parliaments, sought reform rather than revolution, and were largely content with the way the civil-rights movement was operating. Against accusations that NICRA was a front for the IRA, Cameron generally absolved the recognisable IRA members from any role in the riots.[113] In 1969 the IRA was called back into existence as the traditional defender of the Catholic ghettos. As slogans 'IRA – I ran away' appeared on gable walls, those leaders who had been discontented at the way in which the organisation had been moving took over. The people in these Catholic ghettos, some of the poorest areas in Northern Ireland, had little time for Marxist theorising by the Officials. The 'Provisionals', as they were now called, offered the traditional right-wing, pious national-ism and quite simply good old-fashioned defence. The feud between them and the Officials continued for several years. Amazingly, security intelligence was so poor in these early years of the Troubles that the military targeted the Officials rather than the emerging Provisionals, effectively undermining the former and recruiting for the latter. The Provisionals also found covert support from within the Irish Republic's Fianna Fáil government. Agriculture Minister Neil Blaney and Finance Minister Charles Haughey were sacked (May 1970) and later tried (September 1970) for alleged involvement in an illegal attempt to send arms to Northern Ireland.

The British army, when first deployed in Derry and Belfast in August 1969, was welcomed by the Catholics, in whose eyes the police had been totally discredited. Indeed, after further investigations the B Specials were disbanded in 1970, and the RUC disarmed and placed under the control of the military commander. This had provoked riots in the Protestant Shankill, which seemed to justify Catholics' complaints about the partiality of the police. But sending young, heavily armed soldiers, with little local knowledge and no experience of civil disturbance, into ghetto areas, with existing social tensions and high male unemployment, was a recipe for disaster. Being roughed up at the point of a soldier's rifle was more often than not an initiation rite into the IRA. Paddy Devlin, since February 1969 Northern Ireland Labour Party MP for Falls, watched with dismay as such tactics recruited for the Provisionals. Interestingly he spoke highly of the local RUC officers at this time, who were increasingly becoming the scapegoats for the army's mistakes.[114]

Several disastrous security decisions were taken after a Conservative election victory in England in June 1970 ushered in a more hard-line approach. That no effort was being made to curb provocative Orange parades for a second year running further enflamed the situation. During the last weekend of June, Orange parades from all over Belfast converged on the troubled Shankill Road–Crumlin Road area, some passing the recently burnt-out Catholic streets. There were gun battles between the two sides and riots all over the city. The army retaliated some days later by placing the Lower Falls under curfew. For an entire weekend the area was cordoned off by the army; homes systematically raided, often with gratuitous violence, and large amounts of CS gas utilised. An arms' haul was indeed made. But otherwise the exercise was a disaster. There were five civilian deaths, seventy-five injuries, 'outright communal hostility' against the army in the whole Falls area and an eight-fold increase in Provisional recruitment by the end of the year. The Lower Falls had been one of the few remaining strongholds of the less threatening Official IRA. When the curfew was over two Unionist ministers – one the son of Lord Brookeborough – were toured round the devastated Falls by the army. If anything else was needed to convince people that this was a replay of Unionist and security force collusion to crush the Catholic ghettos, this was it. Future Northern Ireland Ombudsman Dr Maurice Hayes, who held the post of Chair of the Community Relations Commission at the time of the curfew, writes with unconcealed anger at this event – a stupid decision, conducted by stupid leaders, political and military – which he sees as one of the disastrous turning points in the Troubles.[115]

It now became a vicious circle – misguided security decisions feeding the IRA machine. The most disastrous of these was the introduction of internment in August 1970. Both police and army commanders were against it. But the IRA had now resorted to what was to become their preferred weapon – the bomb – and the security chiefs could offer no alternative. Internment had been used before, most successfully by the Dublin government, but so recent was the upswing in recruitment into the Provisionals that sound intelligence was lacking. Accordingly it was largely old IRA members and their relatives who were initially taken. Between 9 August 1970 and 5 December 1975, 2,158 were interned. Very many internees emerged hardened republicans and as word leaked of torture of internees (for which Britain was later condemned by the European Court of Human Rights) another wave of riots and violence was unleashed. Thousands more were put out of their homes, this time many Catholics fleeing over the border to be housed in camps made available by the Irish army.

It was one of the many anti-internment marches which produced 'Bloody Sunday' in Derry (30 January 1972). Although, as I write, there is yet another public inquiry under way to establish exactly what happened on that day, it looks as if the soldiers may have over-reacted to the taunts and missiles of a youthful Catholic crowd and shot dead fourteen unarmed civilians. It was incidents such as this which recruited for the IRA and deterred Catholics from standing up to its hoodlum activities in their own community. 'Bloody Sunday' became one of the defining movements for a younger generation of republicans. That the IRA went on to become the most ruthless, callous and efficient terrorist movement in modern times should not detract from the early mistakes made by the authorities which helped it on its way. Notwithstanding bombing campaigns in England, the main theatre of the Troubles remained those same crowded streets of Belfast that had witnessed the main sectarian disturbances in the past. Over the next thirty years two frightened, defensive and resentful working-class communities systematically terrorised each other. In the first twenty years of the Troubles, there were 924 fatalities in north and west Belfast (586 Catholic, 338 Protestant) almost four times as many as in Derry or Armagh/Newry – the next in scale – and over a hundred times as many as in neighbouring north Down. By 1993 working-class north

Belfast, with some 600 fatalities, had become the blackest spot in Northern Ireland for sectarian murder.[116]

After 'Bloody Sunday' the British government suspended Stormont and imposed direct rule (March 1972). Working-class Protestants believed they had been on the losing side since the beginning of civil-rights movement. They saw nationalist areas – many for the first time – flashed on their television screens. They had long been told they were better-off than the Catholics. Now they saw housing which was no worse than their own, their traditional industries declining, low levels of educational achievement, the population of working-class Protestant areas declining whilst neighbouring Catholic ones were bursting at the seams.[117] In addition they saw their traditional protectors, the B Specials and the Stormont regime, vilified and then abolished. The vacuum created after 1972 (and there were similar occasions in the 1980s and 90s) produced some of the bleakest moments of the Troubles. Random and brutal sectarian murders made ghost towns of city centres after dark. Places of amusement closed down, and mass fear trapped people (particularly those young men most likely to be both the recruits and the victims of the paramilitaries) in their own areas. And yet, even in the very first years of the Troubles, the fundamental lesson had already been learnt: no stability could exist in Northern Ireland till the nationalist community was brought into the political system. The state of permanent opposition had bred a sense of alienation and frustration among the old nationalists. It was this sense of powerlessness (even when times seemed to be getting better) which lay behind the violence.

8. Nationalist politics 1970–99

The civil-rights movement was the first experience very many Catholics had of participatory politics. In 1970 it spawned a coming together of constitutional nationalists and other non-Unionist groups in the Social Democratic and Labour Party. The old Nationalist Party slowly withered. The initial leadership of the SDLP brought together a formidable array of talent. The two most experienced politicians were Paddy Devlin and Gerry Fitt. Both were working-class Belfast men, with strong socialist leanings and republican roots. Indeed, Devlin had been interned as a member of the IRA in the 1940s, but had long since renounced violence. They were both popular with British politicians for their gutsy, down-to-earth approach, and Gerry Fitt, as Westminster MP for West Belfast since 1966, had played a major role in breaking down the convention that Britain should not interfere in the internal affairs of Northern Ireland. Austin Currie was Nationalist MP for East Tyrone, credited with kick-starting NICRA's campaign of direct action. Paddy Wilson was a Republican Labour Senator. The other three had emerged through the civil-rights movement: Paddy O'Hanlon, Ivan Cooper (the only non-Catholic among the founders) and John Hume.

The SDLP was an unprecedented alliance of rural and urban constitutional nationalism. The product of the new mood of the 1960s, its policy was to work within the existing structures and its MPs were to be full-time politicians, unlike the old Nationalist Party. But in the disintegration of political structures and rapid communal polarisation caused by the Troubles, the kind of political participation by Catholics sought both by the SDLP and by successive British governments proved more and more elusive. The problem was further compounded by a dilemma at the heart of the new party's stand on the constitutional issue. Despite some flirtation by the SDLP with the idea of a negotiated independence for Northern Ireland, its aim of Irish unity by consent has remained one of its most consistent policies. However, this necessarily involved participation in and recognition of the legitimacy of the Northern Ireland state, a dilemma only resolved with the acceptance of power-sharing in 1973.[118]

Britain's policy after partition had been to steer clear of embroilment in Northern Ireland. Terence O'Neill recalled the British Prime Minister's surprise that he should have expected to talk about anything other than the weather. At the outset of direct rule from London there was appalling ignorance of the niceties of the situation, and throughout the Troubles too great a tendency to see it merely as a security problem. But as time went on, information improved as did the calibre of the teams of politicians and senior civil servants sent over. Sadly – in retrospect – the most exciting initiatives came in the very early days of direct rule. In October 1973 Maurice Hayes (the first Chairman of the

Community Relations Commission) was called in for advice by Ken Bloomfield – then under-secretary at the Northern Ireland Office. He was told that the NIO was opening negotiations with the SDLP, but knew nothing about them. He wanted to learn. Hayes reflected:

Here were people, elected members of parliament, some of whom . . . had been around for years, yet they had rarely, in the days of government at Stormont, met government ministers or senior civil servants . . . This might be said to reflect their failure as an opposition. More seriously it reflected the failure of successive governments to accommodate, much less encourage a responsible opposition.

For the next two hours they spoke about the different strands of opinion in the Catholic community and the 'politics of accommodation'. The SDLP were being looked upon as 'the spokesmen of an oppressed people, as the best bet to avoid a descent into anarchy . . . and as men whose time had come'.[119] And so indeed it appeared. In elections for a new Northern Ireland Assembly in June 1973, and with proportional representation restored, the SDLP, with 22 per cent of the vote and eleven seats, had emerged as the dominant voice of nationalism in Northern Ireland.[120]

The Hayes–Bloomfield conversation was one of the opening moves in what became the Sunningdale Agreement and the power-sharing executive of 1974. The Heath government in London recognised that no solution was possible without recognition of the so-called 'Irish dimension' – nationalists' desire to involve the Irish government in some way – whilst the Dublin government in turn recognised, for the first time that century, that there could be no re-unification of Ireland without the consent of the majority of people in Northern Ireland. Both were major shifts in policy and the concept of power-sharing with an Irish dimension has remained the bedrock of British policy ever since. It was on this basis that, in January 1974, nationalists entered government in Northern Ireland for the first time. The six SDLP ministers made a point of choosing portfolios in those areas which had exercised the civil-rights movement, and reforms were on the way which might, in time, have transformed some of the more contentious elements of northern life. Potential investors were clearly impressed at being greeted by both a Unionist chief executive (Brian Faulkner) and an SDLP deputy (Gerry Fitt), whilst John Hume as minister of commerce had made a successful start on what was to become his own particular mission: transforming Irish-America's misguided support for the IRA into investment in the Northern Ireland economy. Indeed, the teamship and professionalism of the power-sharing executive surprised even themselves. Brian Faulkner, its leader, had been something of a hate figure among Catholics, as the hardline Unionist who had forced Orange marches through Catholic areas in the late 1950s and later engineered the demise of O'Neill. Yet he now won the respect of the SDLP, and many in retrospect recognised him as the most talented politician Northern Ireland had ever had. Paddy Devlin, by his own admission a rough diamond, developed a particular fondness for Faulkner. He recognised that Faulkner was being asked to swallow too many nationalist demands at once and might not be able to bring his party with him.[121]

In fact, a unified Unionist party was no more, with the largest number of unionist people now supporting an array of anti-Sunningdale splinter parties. Like Ian Paisley, now leading his own Democratic Unionist Party, most wanted a simple return to majoritarian rule and disliked sharing power with nationalists. But the Council of Ireland, which was to give the Dublin government a share of executive power in Northern Ireland (without any corresponding concession on those clauses in the Irish constitution which laid claim to its territory) was simply unacceptable to the general body of Unionists. Faulkner's supporters were heavily defeated in a general election, called unexpectedly by Prime Minister Edward Heath on 28 February 1974. The timing was disastrous – before the executive had time to prove its worth. The final coup came in a most extraordinary display of loyalist strength – the so-called Ulster Workers' Strike of May 1974. It was orchestrated by loyalist paramilitaries, but with the support of large numbers of Protestant workers. The directing committee also contained a number of Unionist politicians: Ian Paisley, Harry West and Bill Craig. The strike succeeded in bringing Northern Ireland to a standstill, much to the satisfaction of the IRA, which, according to Brian Faulkner's memoirs, was actually assisting the Ulster Workers' Strike by intimidating the largely Catholic workforce at the Derry power-station and preventing them going to work. Progressively all the essential utilities were closed down, roads blocked, businesses forced to close. When its organisers threatened to swamp the cities with raw sewage, Faulkner resigned. The leaders of the strike later admitted that it would never have gathered momentum had the security forces been moved against it. Ironically, security was one of the areas reserved to London under direct rule and the recently arrived Labour Secretary of State for Northern Ireland, Merlyn Rees, chose not to confront the leaders of the strike – even though Brian Faulkner had asked him to do so.[122] Certainly the whole episode marked an appalling abdication of responsibility by Wilson's Labour government. But lessons were learnt, and when another strike was tried in 1977, swift military action brought it to a premature end.

Politically – although many efforts have been made since – no one has come up with a better answer to Northern Ireland's difficulties than that found in 1974.[123] The Good Friday [Belfast] Agreement of April 1998 involves the same principle of power-sharing with an Irish dimension. Because it is operating in a climate of relative peace, it just might succeed. If Sunningdale could have delivered peace, it too might have lasted. But its failure added yet another element which would have to be accommodated – paramilitary politics. The SDLP and Unionists can now work constructively together. But the failure of the first power-sharing experiment created a political vacuum from which Sinn Féin in particular emerged to threaten the constitutional nationalists.

In time direct rule from London came to be accepted as the least unpleasant of all the options, if rarely anyone's first choice. But it gave Northern Ireland politicians no direct responsibility for the running of the state and no opportunity whatsoever of participating in any change of administration in London and inevitably spread the irresponsibility of permanent opposition to all Ulster politicians, nationalist and Unionist alike. The demoralising effect of this on the foot-soldiers – those who did the constituency spadework, but with little chance of rising to any position themselves – was becoming particularly notice-able in the SDLP, as a revived Sinn Féin (the political wing of the IRA) began to eat into its natural constituency. The success of Sinn Féin can be traced to the political outcome of the 1981 hunger strikes by republican prisoners in Northern Ireland, in which ten died. Even supporters of the IRA had shown that they did not like mindless killing or civilian casualties and the new strategy – proclaimed at the Sinn Féin *ard fheis* of November 1981 – of the 'Armalite' and 'the ballot box' was popular. But they were never again able to mobilise the emotional Catholic support which they had done during the hunger strikes. Indeed, very many Catholics were angered by the clear 'moral blackmail' which they had exercised at that time and far more bitterness existed between Sinn Féin and SDLP supporters than between any of the groupings on the Unionist side.[124] But after the hunger strikes, the thought of Sinn Féin becoming the voice of northern nationalism was enough to frighten London and Dublin alike into rescuing the SDLP from the doldrums. The outcome was the New Ireland Forum of 1983–4 (which involved a wide-ranging rethink of Irish nationalism's response to the problems of Northern Ireland) and the Anglo-Irish Agreement of 1985, involving the Irish government in the search for a solution. Needless to say, both provoked Unionist anger. But they had achieved one of their key purposes in restoring credibility to constitutional nationalism.

The SDLP had started out with southern financial backing; this and its tendency to see its natural partners as successive Dublin governments had always provided a hostage to Paisleyite rhetoric about the 'pan-nationalist' threat to the very existence of Northern Ireland. But although the Forum still endorsed re-unification as nationalism's ultimate goal, and the Anglo-Irish Agreement recognised the Irish government's role by actually giving it an executive presence in Northern Ireland, both marked a major alteration in nationalist thinking about the majority Protestant population in the north. No longer was the central problem seen to be partition or the British presence, but rather the conflict of two identities, which would have to be resolved before any change in Northern Ireland's constitutional status could take place. It also restated the 1974 position on power-sharing. It was a great victory for John Hume and over the next few years it helped restore the SDLP to its position as the main voice of northern Catholics. Peter O'Hagan, an SDLP councillor in Lisburn, remembered its impact on the moderate Catholics whom he represented. He had been involved in civil-rights activities since the early 1960s, one of 'the "poor bloody infantry" . . . who has slogged through the Troubles at the SDLP's grassroots, and occasionally come close to despair . . . "Give-up time was the '79 to '85 period". But then came the Anglo-Irish Agreement. It was "unbelievable".'[125]

The Troubles divided Catholics in Ulster as never before. Hume has often baffled and infuriated some of his followers. Indeed, Fitt and Devlin were lost to the SDLP at an early stage because of its apparent retreat backwards to old-fashioned nationalism, for which Hume was often blamed. Brian Faulkner found the Belfast SDLP less 'Dublin-orientated' than its rural (and Derry) supporters. Derryman John Hume he described as 'a formidable political thinker with great personal integrity but a sometimes exasperating dogmatism'.[126] Republicans disliked the SDLP as too middle class and too church-orientated. John Hume denounced them as 'whingers', wallowing in their victimhood. As the Troubles polarised people according to religion, and the old Labour vote (notably in Belfast) collapsed, Sinn Féin became the voice of the Catholic working-class ghettos. But the SDLP – and particularly John Hume – has given most Catholics what they so desired: respectability, recognition and political clout. The fall of the power-sharing executive in 1974 had shown that the involvement which they had so craved would never be conceded unless there was peace. Time will tell whether John Hume's high-risk strategy (embarked upon in 1993, but with a precedent in 1988) of bringing Sinn Féin out of the political wilderness, will pay off. Power-sharing is now on the books again, only this time with the potential for finally neutralising the physical force tradition in nationalism, for it also encompasses the 'men of violence'. But it was already neutralised in the 1960s and it is hard not to reach the conclusion that the awful trauma of the last thirty years – which has so fortified that tradition – need never have happened.[127]

12

A RESENTFUL BELONGING: CATHOLIC IDENTITY IN THE TWENTIETH CENTURY

[A] man of about fifty, poorly dressed . . . began to air all the old obsessions . . . 'I could tell you where the land that was ours is, away below in the Co. Down – and rich planters gettin' fatter on it every day and talking all the time about the lazy Taigs who wouldn't work for a livin' but go drinkin' on the dole!' . . . It was impossible to unhook Gerry from the past; he seemed to need his grievance, to have built his whole personality around it . . . so much resentment – generations of resentment, forming the very marrow of his soul.   Dervla Murphy, *A Place Apart* (1978)

Since the outbreak of the Troubles, society in Northern Ireland has been analysed as never before. These studies make bleak reading. They confirm how attitudes developed several centuries ago have become fixed. Religion is a very public weapon. In the 1961 census only 384 in a population of 1.5 million did not accept a religious identity. There has been a decline in weekly church attendance among Catholics, from the 95 per cent in 1968, to 86 per cent in 1989, and overall an increasing number of people willing to admit 'no religion'. Even so, in 1994 scarcely anyone from a Catholic background professed to having no religion.[1] Converts are not easily integrated into their new community, for they carry the cultural baggage of their upbringing. Yet the studies also show great variety within the underpinning religious and cultural categories, and above all a widespread recognition of shared prejudice. This explains the black humour which is such a feature of Northern Ireland and the following of comedy acts like the Hole in the Wall Gang, a group of four Queen's University graduates, whose humour is based on Northern Ireland's stereotypes and obsessions. At some of the bleakest moments of the Troubles it has allowed us to laugh at ourselves. Dervla Murphy caught this aspect of Ulster life perfectly in the mid-1970s, a time of particularly acute fear.

It is impossible to be gloomy for long in Belfast. I was feeling rather depressed one afternoon when I turned a corner and saw on the gable-end the familiar NO POPE HERE. And underneath, in different coloured paint, LUCKY OLD POPE![2]

Likewise within hours of the issue of the Patten Report on policing (September 1999), North Belfast's gable-wall artists were at work.

Overnight 'Disband the RUC' murals became 'Disband NIPS' – the setting up of a Northern Ireland Police Service being Patten's key recommendation – confounding those not in the know, amusing those who were.[3] Comedy indeed has been one of the few areas which uses sectarianism to rise above it, one of those 'modes of reassurance' that emphasises 'shared or interchangeable experience'.[4]

1. Northern Ireland stereotypes

In March 1993, David McKittrick, one of Northern Ireland's most respected journalists, produced a startling report on the levels of segregation in Northern Ireland. He found that half its residents lived in areas which were over 90 per cent one religion (often reflecting a three-fold increase during the Troubles), that less than 110,000 of its 1.5 million populace lived in truly mixed areas and that even these might be divided by the so-called peace-lines (twenty-foot-high reinforced walls to keep Catholic and Protestant – at their own desire – apart).[5] The Opsahl Commission, which reported that same year, found ample evidence of such self-imposed segregation in working-class areas, with young males in particular fearful of travelling outside their own community, even to take up much-needed employment.[6] There are also considerable communal pressures deterring people from selling property to members of the opposite religion, thereby inten-sifying spatial segregation.[7] Direct intimidation there undoubtedly has been. There are particularly high levels of intolerance in predominantly Protestant areas to Catholics living there. The attempt, at the beginning of the Troubles, to intimidate Mary Beckett's fictional 'Belfast Woman' out of her home in the Falls/Shankill frontier zone, simply followed a pattern already set in 1921 and 1935. Her fictional account finds ready evidence in reality, though this particular feature of Belfast is not always replicated across the province.[8] But direct intimidation is only part of the story. More often it is the anticipation of such that sends families to the perceived safety of their own communities. They are influenced by the stereotypical view of how the other side will behave.

Catholics are very quick to sense a slight. It is a touchiness developed through centuries of being considered and treated as inferior. Mrs McFadden, recalling her youth in early twentieth-century west Belfast, told of how she was sent by the 'Boru' (the labour exchange or job centre) to a job in a mill in Protestant north Belfast. It was little over two miles from her home, but it was foreign territory. When asked by her new employer 'what are you', she defensively replied 'an RC', when the man had simply wanted to know whether she was a fine or coarse spinner.[9] At the other end of the century, Martha's emotional support for the IRA in Mary Beckett's *Give Them Stones* (1987) had come from her hope that in a united Ireland 'the Catholics wouldn't be despised any more and we could have a bit of confidence in ourselves'.[10] Since there was a long history of Catholics being deemed inferior in Ulster, it is not surprising that such attitudes should have become part of the fabric of the post-partition state. The anything-but-extreme Patrick Shea – after a lifetime in the Northern Ireland civil service – recalled the patronising of Catholics by Unionists:

The Catholics of Northern Ireland did, of course, benefit in many ways from the Government's progressive legislation; any fair-minded person would be bound to admit that in material things they would not have fared so well in a united Irish Republic. But when Unionists point to these benefits and ask why Catholics did not more actively support the Government, they talk as though the Protestant community has been sharing its wealth with the less well-deserving. (This attitude was outrageously typified by the comment of a schoolmaster in my presence; "We should never have given them Maynooth'.) [Catholic seminary, founded 1795 by the exclusively Protestant government.][11]

It was a sentiment echoed as recently as 1996 by a member of the Northern Ireland Conservative Party, who complained about 'this lawless and ungrateful minority', who had been in receipt of 'the largesse of our country'.[12] Little wonder then that the advent of the welfare state and attendant educational reforms should have increased this tendency. Protestants, particularly poor Protestants, tended to view these as gifts from *their* state, the British state, to which Catholics were most reluctant to give allegiance. The sight of all those Catholic university students on civil-rights marches touched a raw nerve among working-class Protestants with no tradition of sending their children into higher education: 'They'd taken the State's money for grants to get themselves educated at university, and repaid it by fomenting trouble', an unemployed loyalist from Londonderry complained in 1993.[13] This sector of Northern Ireland's Protestant population is embittered. They feel they have lost out through the anti-discrimination measures, fair-employment legislation and a host of other reforms arising from the civil-rights campaign. All this talk of discrimination working-class Protestants consider as typical Catholic whinging. They do not believe the statistics which show that one is still twice as likely to be unemployed if Catholic. Whilst Catholics and Protestants are more alike on a range of social issues, Catholics are more likely to attribute social evils to 'injustice', Protestants to 'laziness', 'drinking' and 'too many children'.[14]

The historic Protestant stereotype of Catholics was reinforced by developments in the twentieth century. This is what Ken Heskin, in an intriguing early study of the Troubles, has called the concept of the 'negative reference group', against which Protestants and Catholics alike define themselves in Northern Ireland. But it is the Catholic Church and religion itself which is the most common 'reference' point in an otherwise diverse Protestant community. Anti-Catholicism is an important defining element in Protestant identity, as it was throughout Britain. The fears of 'political popery' are still very much alive, the fragmentation of northern Protestantism exaggerating the view of Catholics as an undifferentiated and threatening mass, in thrall to their priests and pope. At its extreme it has produced the 'religious pornography' of the Paisleyite *Protestant Telegraph*.[15] Even the more highly developed community activity among Catholics, though envied by some community workers in working-class Protestant areas, is perceived as part of this herd instinct.

A series of focus groups were organised in 1992 as part of the Opsahl Commission. In Belfast and Counties Derry, Tyrone and Armagh, every group, whether Catholic or Protestant, expressed an over-riding desire for peace. Even so, every Protestant group had the same perception of the power of the Catholic Church. It was the Church, they believed, which dictated the size of Catholic families and taught 'perverted history' and 'hatred of Protestants', and whilst these

Protestants supported integrated education, they feared Catholic teachers might inculcate their views 'in subtle ways'.[16] Catholics were disloyal. Through their church they were linked with a Catholic state south of the border, whose territorial claims over Northern Ireland were enshrined in its constitution.[17] Predictably it was border Protestants (including those in Derry City) who subscribed most to such views of Catholics during the Troubles. And with an undoubted IRA campaign to murder and intimidate Protestant farming families out of their properties, they had good reason to think that this was 'political popery' in action.[18]

Like majorities living beside sizeable minorities elsewhere in the world, Ulster's Protestant population has always been very sensitive to demographic change. The widespread publicity accorded the 1991 census in particular had horrific consequences. To a Protestant working-class community visibly in decline in Belfast, whilst Catholic areas were bursting at the seams, media reports conveyed the news that such had been the percentage increase in Catholics over the preceding twenty years that it was only a matter of time before Catholics became the new majority. Although such conclusions were later discredited, they fuelled a terrifying escalation of murders, particularly of Catholics, in the years preceding the first ceasefires of 1994.[19]

The fear of being outbred by Catholics feeds continuing Protestant horror of the mixed marriage, for such are the pressures from the Catholic Church, that the offspring are as likely as not to be reared as Catholics. The Catholic Church's *Ne Temere* decree of 1908 – which required that children of mixed marriages be raised as Catholics – has been largely enforced until very recently. The result has been a steady erosion of the Protestant population in the south (from 11 per cent to 4 per cent between 1911 and 1961) and a reinforcement of Ulster Protestant stereotypes that 'popery' is out to destroy Protestantism. There are signs, however, that this decline is about to be reversed, a 1993 report showing 40 per cent of mixed-religion couples in the Republic opting to raise their children as Protestants.[20] Currently it is only the Catholic partner who has to make such an undertaking. But in a society as divided as Northern Ireland still is, such an undertaking could only be fulfilled with considerable strain on the other partner. In fact, *all* churches in Northern Ireland discourage mixed marriages and, because of the quite separate socio-religious networks operating, such partnerships frequently encounter difficulties. Couples often feel compelled to move away from their communities; either they cease formal religious practice entirely, or the children go one way and the other partner cuts links with his or her kin. There is a heady folklore – based on reality – of the outrage caused when the widow (for usually it was) had her dead husband buried in her cemetery, away from his community.[21] 'I've got a Protestant girlfriend', a 16-year-old Catholic from the Falls Road told Tony Parker in 1993, 'but I wouldn't like my parents to know that, and she hasn't told hers.' Little wonder that his ambition was to get away to England or America, or that doomed love across the divide should be such a feature of contemporary Northern Ireland fiction. A loyalist song of 1970 takes up the theme:

> Come gather round kind Protestants.
> A tale I'll tell you all
> Of deeds and recent happenings
> In the town of Donegal
> When my sister to a rebel wed
> And broke our happy home
> To live in fear and darkness
> With a popish son of Rome.[22]

A survey of 1986 showed that 98 per cent of Protestants and 95 per cent of Catholics married within their own religious grouping. By 1993 the equivalent figures were 91 per cent and 83 per cent.[23] 'Fear and hatred of Rome are instilled into the [Protestant] children from their earliest days', wrote 'Ultach' in 1943. 'They are taught that the [Catholic] Church has a specially-trained troop of sirens to bewitch young non-Catholics with their insidious charms and lure them into the dreaded mixed marriage, so that the children may be reared Catholic and the non-Catholics gradually swamped. (This, notwithstanding repeated condemnations of mixed marriages from Catholic pulpits.)'[24]

The reverse of Protestant self-perception as an honest, hard-working, straight-talking and law-abiding people is theirs of Catholics as devious, untrustworthy, lazy, slovenly, happier to 'diddle' the state and whinge, than turn an honest penny. 'Rebels beware', proclaims a loyalist mural featured in the 1943 pamphlet by 'Ultach', painted on a wall near a Catholic Church. 'To Hell with Popery. Where Popery Reigns Poverty Remains. God Save Our King.'[25] Catholics are alternatively hurt and amused by all of this. They tell self-mocking jokes about beating the system and of nationalist areas devoid of television licences.[26] This Ulster version of the 'Protestant ethic' explanation of economic development is of considerable vintage, and, as earlier chapters have demonstrated, it was frequently reinforced by real situations. In 1989 a sociologist, Leo Howe, examined two working-class housing estates, one in Protestant east Belfast, the other in Catholic west Belfast. In the latter he found over 56 per cent unemployment, no tradition of skilled industry and a reluctance to travel into Protestant areas, where almost all the major industries have been traditionally located. It was not only fear which was the deterrent, but a belief that Catholics do not get the jobs anyway – hence the greater readiness (and indeed necessity) to 'do the double' (drawing unemployment benefit whilst involved in casual work). It then becomes a way of life, accepted by a community traditionally averse to 'informing' and hostile to DHSS inspectors operating in the area. All of this only reinforces Protestant stereotypes of Catholic laziness and lawlessness and Catholic stereotypes of a system which discriminates against them and thereby deserves to be 'diddled'.[27] In many ways it had all been culturally and demographically determined even before partition. Most of the traditional engineering industries were located in Protestant areas and Protestants came to see such jobs as 'theirs' by right. So although in 1989 there were also high levels of unemployment in Protestant east Belfast (26 per cent) and many cases of real hardship, there was nevertheless an expectation that they would eventually get back to work. The weakness of a black economy, the greater ability of inspectors to operate and willingness of people to 'inform', endorsed Protestants' image of themselves as honest, hardworking and law abiding, and of Catholics as totally the reverse. This was notoriously epitomised in 1991 when, in response to a complaint by nationalists that their voice was not heard on Belfast City Council, DUP councillor Sammy Wilson retorted: 'Taigs don't pay rates.'[28]

This is why it is so important to ascertain the religious affiliation of the other person before serious conversation is engaged. There are topics which are best left alone, lest they reveal the stereotypes which inform most people's attitudes in Northern Ireland. Since there really are two mind-sets behind the apparent similarity of Ulster people, there are so very many areas where offence can be inadvertently caused unless the 'off-switch' is triggered by the stereotypical cues. One's school, name, place of residence, pronunciation and use of certain words are the most obvious clues. Some claim an ability to identify Catholics or Protestants from their very appearance and most have developed a sixth sense for such niceties. The random sectarian killings, which were such a feature of the Troubles in Belfast in particular, were very often preceded by this sectarian identifier process. Bernard MacLaverty uses it as the theme of his 1994 story 'Walking the Dog'. The hero (apparently Protestant) is picked up on a lonely road by two loyalist terrorists posing as IRA men in order to entrap and murder a Catholic. The grilling included all the set questions: name, school, how he pronounced the alphabet, where he worked, whether he could say the Hail Mary. Fortunately for him he passes the test and is let go. It is a chilling – and all-too-true – version of how the everyday social codes of Ulster so easily adapt themselves to terror. Frank Burton's 1978 study tells of a Quaker social worker, with an address in a Catholic block of flats, wrongly identified by a loyalist assassination gang as Catholic and murdered as such.[29] In one of the better analyses of the Troubles by a foreign journalist, Rian Malan, a South African, commented in 1993 on how finely tuned such indicators had become. He found Belfast a place 'full of people with nervous tics and trembling hands and eyes that gleam paranoically at the most innocent of questions. They can't tell the enemy by looking at him, so they've invented all these obscure codes and arcane riddles to distinguish friend from foe.'[30]

In fact it is an unthinking feature of everyday life, triggered as much by a desire to avoid offence as anything more sinister – at least that is what we like to think. It is why there has been such a tendency to patronise shops, businesses, professional practices, social gatherings and sporting fixtures sponsored by members of one's own religion – for only then can the guard come down. In Catholic-owned shops, one is likely to find newspapers from south of the border, Catholic news-sheets, Catholic charity boxes, mass-cards and produce advertised on the southern radio stations – preferred listening in many Catholic households. This is why mixed marriages can cause such discomfiture in a society which has only been prevented from falling apart by mutually agreed distance between the communities and where most social visiting occurs within the kin-group, which by the same unwritten rules tends to be of the same religion.[31]

The stereotypes are frequently reinforced and there are limited opportunities for re-assessment through direct experience. Although there is a small and growing number of children in integrated education (and in Belfast at least a trend for some middle-class Catholic parents to send their children to state – in effect Protestant – schools, because of the better facilities offered), the vast majority of children in Northern Ireland attend either Protestant or Catholic schools, soaking up quite different cultures in the process. Since very many social activities tend to revolve around the churches and schools, even here there are few neutral venues. Sociologists warn against attaching too much blame to the schools and churches, for the stereotypes and heightened awareness of difference are inherited. Sectarian street-rhymes have always come naturally to children, as generations of Ulster's children 'skipped to songs of cheerful hatred'.[32]

Catholics like to think that only Protestants are bigoted and in a purely religious sense they have a point. They certainly have no equivalent of the anti-popery so readily resorted to by every rank of Protestant, and their lexicon of insults is impoverished by comparison.

> I am Ulster, my people are an abrupt people
> Who like the spiky consonants in speech
> And think the soft ones cissy
> . . .
> Anything that gives or takes attack,
> Like Micks, Tagues, tinker gets, Vatican.
> An angular people, brusque and Protestant,
> For whom the word is still a fighting word,
> Who bristle into reticence at the sound
> Of the round gift of the gab in Southern mouths . . .'

(W. R. Rodgers, Ulster poet of Presbyterian background 1909–1969)[33]

439

Catholics are not obsessively hostile to Protestant clerics in a way that Protestants are to Catholic clergy. Because most of the pressure is on the Protestant partner to conform, Catholics have fewer problems living among and inter-marrying with Protestants than the reverse, and no problems with ecumenism. But Catholics *are* obsessed about the political ramifications of Protestantism in the Northern Ireland state, the Orange Order and the excessive displays of loyalism to Britain, its flag and its monarchy, and they are far more resistant to being educated with Protestants than the reverse. Ironically the situation in the Irish Republic today is quite the reverse, a high proportion of pupils in Protestant schools being Catholic, except in Ulster Counties Cavan, Monaghan and Donegal where the situation resembles that in Northern Ireland.[34] The reason for such apparently contradictory positions is the same. Catholic culture and identity is far more secure and all-embracing than that of Protestants. It has suffused – some might say 'hi-jacked' – 'Irishness' and, with the essentials of Catholic church teachings, Catholic schools also deliver what amounts to a nationalist 'ideological package deal'.[35]

2. A grievance culture

The anti-Catholicism (or more accurately the anti-popery) which underpins Ulster Protestant identity is rarely admitted. It is indeed difficult to articulate (even if recognised) in a largely secular age, which sees Ian Paisley as antediluvian. In a 1997 survey of the press in Northern Ireland, John Brewer found this Protestant fear of 'political popery' to be alive and well – anti-Catholicism underpinning Protestant identity generally, even though at different levels of intensity. As Heskin had concluded in his earlier study, 'Protestants object primarily to Catholics as Catholics, but not as people.' And whilst Catholic attitudes to Protestants changed in reaction to political events (in general mellowing during the Troubles), Protestant attitudes have proved more deeply-rooted psychologically and more unchanging.[36]

Complaints by groups of 'concerned residents' in the late 1990s that Orange insistence on marching through Catholic areas is simply to 'maintain an ascendancy over us', echoes down through the ages, sustained by a host of popular songs and literature of oppression and suffering. This culture of grievance and self-perception as the victim, the underdog, has united Catholics in the past (and to some extent still does). 'Discrimination' was the ready explanation for all manner of wrongs – and certainly the main reason evoked for unemployment and poor housing conditions, even if not always the real reason. During the Troubles petty verbal abuse by young soldiers and policemen of residents in Catholic ghettos fed this long-standing tradition of victimhood. Such suffering became something of an entrance require-ment for full membership of the ghetto community. Those who pros-pered no longer conformed to the identikit and became an easy target for republican sarcasm.

At the outset of the Troubles, Richard Rose found Catholics less willing to use violence in pursuit of their political aims than Protestants. This surprised him. And yet, as I have argued throughout this book, Ulster Catholics were not natural rebels. Certainly the IRA campaign – particularly when it became more ruthless and, ironically, more successful – caused a major dilemma for Ulster's Catholics, for it lost to them the moral high ground. 'The perception of Catholics as rebels is the trap into which the Provos have fallen,' Monsignor Denis Faul told the Opsahl Commission in 1993.[37] How could Catholics continue to proclaim themselves victims, when the IRA were carrying out dreadful atrocities in their name? Even one Sinn Féin councillor admit-ted to nearly giving up republican politics after the IRA bomb in Enniskillen in 1987, which killed eleven and injured sixty-three of those attending the Remembrance Day ceremony, for it had taken away the 'moral dignity' of being the oppressed.[38] Just as the bullied become the bullies, so the victims of the Northern Ireland situation had become the victimisers and in the process they destroyed the legitimacy of their cause. Psychiatrist John Mack writes:

The egoism of victimisation is the incapacity of an ethno-national group, as a direct result of its own historical traumas, to empathise with the suffering of another group. [They] have little capacity to grieve for the hurts of other peoples, or to take responsibility for the new victims created by their own warlike actions. Victims kill victims through unendingly repeated cycles that are transmitted from one generation to another, bolstered by stories and myths

of atrocities committed by the other people, and by heroic acts committed . . .
by one's own.[39]

As the reforms called for by the civil-rights movement started to come
through, middle-class Catholics in particular began to turn the old
Unionist complaint about Catholics as scroungers and whingers on to
the republicans. The Troubles shattered that Ulster Catholic identity,
based on a common sense of grievance and a tailored version of history.
Many found themselves in the same moral dilemma as the woman
from County Tyrone who told her tale to Fionnuala O Connor in
1993. She had gone to England in 1972, but as IRA killings mounted,
she found herself in tears of frustration as she tried to explain to
English friends her Catholic view of the underlying historical reasons
for the conflict. To them it sounded like justification for IRA actions.
'For years I had a very idealistic thing about nationalism and the
rebellion against British domination. Emotionally, I don't want them
[the IRA] to be bad guys.'[40]

Like her, the only way that constitutional nationalists could salvage
their traditions was by treating the Provisional IRA as distinct from
the 'noble' republicans who had gone before. 'We were fightin' a
decent clean war and killin' on'y the Queen's men,' an IRA man from
a previous generation told some Provos in a west Belfast republican
shebeen in 1977, 'not blowin' up women and babies an' anythin' else
that happens to be around.' But it was only a criticism of their methods,
for he went on to talk about 800 years of 'torment' by 'the Brits', land
which belonged to his forebears taken by 'rich planters' who then
berated the 'lazy Taigs' for 'drinkin' on the dole'. It was impossible to
divert the speaker from his rendering of the past, as Dervla Murphy
(who witnessed the episode) recalled: 'he seemed to need his grievance,
to have built his whole personality around it . . . so much resentment
– generations of resentment, forming the very marrow of the soul.'[41]

It was a persona which the majority of Catholics in Northern Ireland
would have identified with before the Troubles. The bitterness at
centuries of patronising and contempt by those considered 'blow-ins'
and usurpers became a peculiarly northern thing in the twentieth
century, shared even by successful Catholics with little sympathy for
republican separatism. Few recognised how much they themselves

subscribed to republican readings of history until the Troubles. Bernadette Devlin came from a strongly republican household – at least on
her father's side. Her early introduction to Irish history was in bedtime
stories, rebel songs and the actor Micheál Mac Liammóir's rendering
of the speeches of Patrick Pearse and Robert Emmet. Her father was
typical of the working-class Catholic unable to find work except in
England, yet blaming the English that he should have to do so. At her
convent grammar school the Reverend Mother was so pathologically
anti-English that she tore posters representing events in English history
from the walls and stamped upon them. Even Bernadette thought
this extreme and accused the nun of bigotry.[42] My own childhood
memories of the 1950s and 1960s, of Catholic families and friends in
north and west Belfast, are of stirring tales about nationalist heroes,
fortified by films about the fight for Irish independence such as *Mise
Éire, Saoirse* and the Hollywood rendering, *Shake Hands with the
Devil*. All of which would be interspersed with stories of sectarian
attacks in the 1920s and 1930s, the McMahon murders, the attacks
on pilgrims to the 1932 Eucharistic Congress and the ever-present
villain: the B Special. None of these families had republican backgrounds. Most were and remained romantic nationalists. Yet even
amongst these, it was Pearse's messianic republican message which
was favourite.

Whatever one thinks of Patrick Pearse, his power as a propagandist
beggared that of any of his predecessors – even his heroes, the United
Irishmen. A devout Catholic and consummate Gaelic scholar, whose
children's books were often the stock of Irish-language classes in the
Catholic schools, Pearse combined the visionary elements of Gaelic
poetry with Catholic themes of endurance and sacrifice to produce a
new republican theology which remains the dominant inspiration in
militant Irish republicanism. The theme is of a pure Gaelic Catholic
race finally being restored to what is rightfully theirs, not by overnight
victory, but by endurance and sacrifice, notably the ultimate blood-
sacrifice of 'dying for Ireland'. From the examples of the mythological
Cú Chulainn, to Robert Emmet and the Fenian O'Donovan Rossa, he
preached 'redemption' through 'death', the perfection and 'Christ-like'
nobility of the ultimate blood-sacrifice. The hopeless rising of 1916
(as Pearse himself had envisaged) drew triumph from failure, when he

and fourteen other leaders were executed by a British firing squad. Thus was he added to the pantheon of glorious dead, who – in the words of one of his most famous speeches, his 'Oration' at the grave of O'Donovan Rossa – could never be taken away and whose inspiration would eventually triumph. The idea of 'dying for Ireland' – much as it appears in the refrain of Frank McCourt's Ulster Catholic wastrel father – now seems pathetic and ludicrous.[43] And yet, just as with Malachy McCourt, that principle had been enunciated by generations of constitutional nationalists and militant republicans alike as somehow giving meaning to otherwise insignificant or intolerable existences. Many constitutional nationalists admit to paying lip-service to it at some time or another. It is why bungled actions such as that in 1956 which brought about the deaths of Fergal O'Hanlon and Sean South could be turned into hugely popular rebel songs and draw massive crowds to their funerals. It is why the sense of betraying the patriot dead can still prove such a major obstacle to the inching of republicans towards consensual politics. It allows republicans – with more success than nationalists care to admit – to pull at their guilt strings with taunts of 'selling-out', 'collaborating', 'shoneen' [seoinín, toadying to, aping English ways], 'West Briton', 'Brit-lover'. It is why the IRA hunger strikes of 1981 presented nationalists with such a dilemma.

Until very recently Catholics generally would have been reluctant to accept the forces of law and order as impartial. In return soldiers and police were more likely to consider Protestants as friends and Catholics as suspect.[44] Many Protestants considered these attitudes tantamount to supporting the Provos, and said as much. In February 1993 I watched a generally good-humoured sixth-form debate in Belfast fall apart and polarise along the traditional religious divisions on this very issue. The Catholic teenagers – male and female alike – commented on how often they were stopped by the security forces and how they feared the police, even though they had done nothing wrong. This triggered in some of the Protestant pupils the traditional assumption that all Catholics supported the IRA in their hearts, which in turn incensed the Catholics, prompting even those who had been critical of Catholic culture to draw together with their co-religionists. On core issues they were voicing inherited values and the girl from west Belfast who had sparked it all off was exasperated: 'I am thoroughly disgusted the way we are behaving . . . just like . . . the older generation.'[45] And so indeed had been the experience of the 'older generation' – they knew why the Provos had arisen, they worshipped at the same altar of romantic nationalism, they distrusted the security forces controlled by a Unionist state. But if they said so they risked being taken as apologists for the Provos. And so it joined those many 'no-go areas' of mixed-company conversation which is such a feature of Northern Ireland society.

This troubled silence, where once there would have been righteous indignation aimed exclusively at Unionists and Protestants, is part of the confusion into which the Troubles have thrown the once secure Catholic identity. In many ways it is only the extreme republicans who have retained that old identity, and they blame everyone but themselves for the widespread questioning of the myths which once gave meaning to real sufferings. The Dublin intelligentsia and present-day historians have been favourite targets. They 'tell people they can't be satisfied with what they came from', Gerry Adams commented in a 1993 interview. 'That's putting things you thought of as constants under attack: the effect's like a family trauma, like discovering you've been adopted.'[46] Those readings of their past were a necessary crutch for the bulk of Ulster Catholics after partition. Like all crutches they provided relief from suffering, but scarcely an inducement to move on. Even so, Adams was right in identifying them as such an integral part of Catholic culture that to deny the relationship between this past and the IRA campaign is self-delusion. There is no need to seek banned publications or republican declarations for such readings of history. They were the constant drip-feed of the Catholic press and other Catholic writings for much of the twentieth century.

The most widely read Catholic newspaper, the *Irish News*, and its Unionist counterpart, the *Belfast News Letter,* have moved a long way in recent years from their past sectarianism, and both have been instrumental in producing the current peace process. In this change the *Irish News* has reflected readership opinion. But for much of the twentieth century that opinion would have been virulently anti-Unionist. The *Irish News* accordingly (and its weekly spin-off, the *Irish Weekly*) thought partition unnatural and the term 'Ulster' – because truncated – incorrect usage for the political entity of Northern

Ireland. The editorials and commentary sections were highly polemical, and the tendency to blame Britain for everything was a regular theme. Partition was the old policy of 'divide and conquer'(1932), the ills that stem from it the product of 'alien rule' (1953). 'British hypocrisy' was a favourite theme, and the 'causes' opposed by Britain (India, Franco) received automatic endorsement. There were still too many Catholic ex-British-army soldiers around in the 1930s for the *Irish News* not to have commemorated Armistice Day, and the relevant issue in 1932 carries a reverential editorial and a half-page advertisement for the poppy appeal.[47] But increasingly Catholic ex-soldiers were marginalised. At an early stage Unionists had subsumed the ceremonies into their own blood-sacrifice mythology; whilst the imperialist overtones of the Remembrance Day ceremonies and downright opposition from republicans sidelined them within their own communities.[48]

However, just as with today's republicans, the belief that Unionists would recognise their Irish identity if Britain pulled out, and a nostalgia for the 1790s when their ancestors did so, was never reconciled with the persistent tendency to see Protestants as blow-ins, planters, with no history and an inferior religion.[49] Assertions that they would have nothing to fear in a united Ireland were contradicted by the most abiding theme of the nationalist press: that Irishness and Catholicism were one and the same. Distasteful as this may now seem, however, it is important to recognise such attitudes as fundamental to the self-protective mechanism developed by generations of Catholics in response to traditional 'put-downs'. In post-partition Ulster the protective myths of Catholicism as the one true faith, indelibly bound up with the 'Irish struggle', seemed all the more necessary. In recent years the once highly politicised Catholic clergy of the late nineteenth and early twentieth centuries have, with a few exceptions, become very nervous of politics. Republicans are bitter and confused about the critical attitude of the Catholic Church, since they usually come from working-class areas where traditionally conservative Catholicism has been strongest. Moreover, they still see Catholicism as an integral part of their political identity. 'To be a Catholic is still a political thing,' Gerry Adams told Fionnuala O Connor in 1992; 'it identifies you as a Fenian, a Taig. People are killed for being Catholic . . . And they have an affinity with the Church which has to do with its history in Ireland, echoes of the penal days, punishment by death for being a priest or a bishop – the Church was part of the people's struggle.'[50] And who can deny that this is exactly the picture promoted by the Catholic Church since at least the seventeenth century?

It is no accident that among the 'cultural' rapidly replacing the 'armed struggle' murals in post-ceasefire republican Belfast will be found that most stereotypical image of the penal laws: the priest at the mass-rock, the crown forces closing in.[51] The message is hardly a conciliatory one. It is also false, since it was never unlawful under the penal laws for a priest to say mass. However, this image was a central part of Ulster Catholic culture in the twentieth century. Editorial attacks by the Catholic press on Unionist politicians sometimes alluded to their ancestors' persecution of priests in the eighteenth century. Clerical sermons published by the press regularly referred to religious persecution in the past.[52] The hedge-schools, which had not been exclusively Catholic, were also appropriated as part of the story of persecution, endurance and superior culture, linking penal-day persecution to the fight to retain separate Catholic education under Stormont. 'Can't you see a ring of eager little faces, with eyes that looked up at him [the hedge-schoolmaster] with all the clear bright courage of a great race?' the Revd Francis Connolly S.J. wrote in a full-page article in the *Irish Weekly* for 15 March 1958.

Can't you hear him as he starts one of the old-time songs about Granuaile . . . or the Dark Rosaleen calling for her Sarsfield to come back from over the sea to ransom her? . . . Besides, what can great souls do when they are chained and crushed to the earth by force – what can they do but sing . . . here was a whole people ground down and destitute for centuries, who never lost their urbanity, their spirit of gaiety, their consciousness of obvious superiority . . . in the darkest days of penal times. If it was the martyred and fugitive priests who kept the soul of Ireland alive, it was the Hedgemaster who kept its eyes open.[53]

The 1932 Eucharistic Congress – attracting a million pilgrims to the mass in the Phoenix Park in Dublin and a number of other events – was proclaimed the 'Triumph of Catholic Ireland' by the *Irish News* in a prominent feature article on the Revd B. McLaverty's sermon at

St MacNissi's Church in Larne. The Congress, he said, represented 'the triumph of Catholic Ireland over 750 years of persecution such as even the early Romans or the Jews had not endured'.[54] Thirty years later (1962, the year in which the second Vatican Council began its transformation of worldwide Catholicism) the theme remained unchanged in the nationalist press. 'The Irish people are rightly proud of their country's stand for the Faith throughout fifteen hundred years,' ran the *Ulster Herald* editorial for 10 March 1962 – praising the Catholic bishops' Easter pastorals – 'a stand that endured the longest of the persecutions known in European history, proud that, with Spain, our land was the one territory in which the "Reformation" failed to gain even a foothold ... the valiant souls of the Penal Days who rejoiced to suffer and endure that our land might hold its religious heritage.'[55]

Throughout Northern Ireland every county and sizeable town had separate Catholic and Protestant newspapers. Such was the difference in tone and news items that readers might as well have lived in different countries. Even the successful middle-class father in Brian Moore's (1965) novel *The Emperor of Ice-Cream* looked to the *Irish News* in the 1930s and 1940s to reinforce his prejudices:

[He] read the newspaper as other men play cards, shuffling through a page of stories until he found one which would confirm him in his prejudice. A Jewish name discovered in an account of a financial transaction, a Franco victory over the godless Reds, a hint of British perfidy in international affairs, an Irish triumph on the sports field, an evidence of Protestant bigotry, a discovery of Ulster governmental corruption: these were his reading goals.[56]

Given such acculturation over many generations, it is little wonder that the IRA hunger strikes of 1981 posed such a dilemma for Ulster Catholics. The IRA's claim that they were fighting a war rather than mounting a terror campaign found partial recognition in the special-category status of their prisoners until 1976. This was removed under the Thatcher government's 'criminalisation' programme. They immediately mounted a campaign to secure the return of their 'political status', of which the hunger strikes were the culmination. Bobby Sands was the first to refuse food on 1 March 1981. His family, burnt out of the Rathcoole housing estate on the northern edge of Belfast in 1972, had moved to the Twinbrook estate in Catholic west Belfast. There Sands joined the Provisional IRA at the age of eighteen, eventually becoming commander of its 'active service' unit on the estate. At the time of the hunger strikes, he was five years into a fourteen-year prison term for possession of firearms. In prison he had become a republican intellectual, learning Irish and orchestrating a brilliant public-relations campaign. The IRA prison protest had been making little progress. Now Margaret Thatcher's famous intransigence provided the perfect foil to the image being built of the noble rebel, battling against insurmountable odds. It was Pearse's vision all over again and Sands recognised it. A failing movement would emerge re-fortified when Britain fulfilled its traditional role in republican mythology. Granting leave to wear civilian clothes would have pre-empted the hunger strikes. But by October 1981 ten men had died, beginning with Sands on 5 May. By then he was a Westminster MP, having stood as a protest candidate in the Fermanagh–South Tyrone by-election on 9 April. The IRA had been given new life.

The election of Sands in Fermanagh–South Tyrone capitalised on previous divisions among the nationalists and republicans which had let Unionists win this predominantly nationalist constituency. In a highly emotional atmosphere, in which the republican campaign centred on the need to save Sands's life (rather than on the IRA prisoners' campaign for political status), intense pressure and 'moral blackmail'[57] secured the withdrawal of the constitutional nationalists, and victory (though by a small margin) for Sands. A hundred thousand people attended his funeral in west Belfast some weeks later. Members of the SDLP, Fianna Fáil ministers and TDs from the Irish Republic, Catholic bishops and even a special papal legate tried to mediate between government and hunger strikers, but to no avail. They were being pulled by their own past into being the apparent spokesmen for a tradition of violence which they abhorred. Moreover, the officiation by Catholic priests at the often elaborate republican funerals of the dead hunger-strikers seemed to confirm the most extreme loyalist vision of 'popery'. Ambivalence about the use of violence, and a tendency to view its use by the 'others' as worse than by 'one's own', has been common to all sides in the recent Northern Ireland conflict.

Even so, there has been what Dervla Murphy termed 'a massive muddle' in the Catholic mind about this – particularly before the rules for the use of firearms by the security forces were tightened up.[58] Even non-violent Catholics tended to have less sympathy for members of the security forces killed during the Troubles – particularly since Protestants have traditionally considered the security forces as part of *their* community – than for Catholics killed in sectarian attacks.[59]

The discomfiture and helplessness of constitutional nationalism during the hunger strikes was palpable. How could it denounce what the hunger-strikers were doing without also damning the traditions of Tone, Emmet and Pearse – the 'good' republicans of the past who had laid the basis for the Irish state? Moreover, the results of a series of elections over the next eighteen months saw Sinn Féin capturing 30–45 per cent of the Catholic vote in Northern Ireland. The constitutional nationalists in the SDLP seemed to have nothing to show for their years of condemning IRA violence, and the hunger strikes had touched all the right nerves in Catholic consciousness. The SDLP needed a lifeline. It came in the form of the New Ireland Forum report of 1984 and the Anglo-Irish Agreement of 1985. The 'poor bloody infantry' of constitutional nationalism, who had come close to giving up at the time of the hunger strikes, seemed at last to have been rewarded.[60]

3. Catholicism as cultural and political identity

However critical republicans were of the Catholic Church, their criticism had to be muted, so intertwined had Catholicism and Irish nationalism become. For Catholics their religion *was* their political identity, and the Church provided all the necessary institutional infrastructure. This is why secular nationalist institutions, including the Nationalist Party itself, remained so weak in Northern Ireland. There was no need for them.[61] This is why, in contrast to the unionist press, the nationalist press was so dominated by Church matters, and why the presumption that nationalism depended on Catholicism for its survival is such a common theme in Catholic statements (both lay and clerical) throughout the twentieth century.[62] A friend recently told me of his memories of reading the *Irish News* in the 1960s. 'It was the most appallingly bad daily paper for news I ever read. It was noted for reports of greyhound races and priests' funerals.' As I look through its past issues in the Belfast Newspaper Library the prevalence of Catholic Church news and pictures of priests in the *Irish News* stands out, as does the association of Catholic religious practice with often quite extreme nationalist sentiments. The highlight of the republican year – the commemoration of the 1916 Easter rising – was intertwined with the Church's liturgical calendar. Indeed, public religious practice by Catholics became something of a defiant political act after partition. Whatever the hierarchy's traditional denunciation of violence, priests regularly led the recitation of the rosary in Irish at commemorations of the 1916 rising. Crowds of Catholics, falling on their knees and reciting the rosary when blocked by police from attending republican demonstrations, were a common occurrence, and recital of the rosary was still a feature of republican demonstrations in the 1970s and 1980s.[63] In 1957 public recitation of the rosary was the chosen form of defiance by the crowd outside the Enniskillen morgue where the bodies of South and O'Hanlon were laid.[64] Why it should have been the rosary which became the traditional form of protest is not entirely clear, but it may have developed from the recognition of how much it was disliked by Protestants. The Catholic Truth Society of Ireland had been founded in 1899 and became part of the Church's armoury against modern evils such as socialism and communism. Sales of the CTS booklets in Down and Connor alone amounted to 174,937 in 1957, with Ardoyne, Clonard, St Peter's and St Mary's – at the heart of working-class Catholic Belfast – accounting for over a third of these.[65] Ash Wednesday provided many a Catholic child the opportunity for his or her first gesture of political defiance, as the black ash on the forehead was flaunted and preserved long after the day itself. Ulster Catholicism had now become a defiant religion, which emphasised difference.

It was much the same with symbols of Irishness: Irish games, Irish dancing, Irish language. As in the rest of Ireland, Irish-speaking had gone into terminal decline by the early twentieth century. Even before partition, only 2.3 per cent of Ulster people were Irish speakers.[66] In the nineteenth century the Catholic clergy had been willing assistants in the decline of the Irish language.[67] But after partition, they were prominent in Gaelic League activities, which were in decline everywhere else in Ireland. As the Free State drained revivalist enthusiasm by making the language a compulsory part of Irish identity, Unionist condemnation of it had the opposite effect in Northern Ireland. In the years immediately preceding partition, the British government had been according the Irish language an increasing place in the schools' curriculum.[68] But loyalist claims that Irish language and Irish history were subversive secured a progressive attack on their funding and timetabling. In their efforts to produce highly qualified Catholics to disprove the Protestant stereotype, the Catholic schools progressively abandoned the subjects. State exams did not require the formal teaching of Irish history, so it was often picked up from amateurs and enthusiasts outside the school system.[69]

Protestant interest in Irish language and culture did not entirely disappear after partition. Jack O'Rourke – a traditional piper who came to live in Belfast in 1940 – recalled people from the Protestant Shankill Road and Sandy Row at *céilís* (Irish dancing events), and cross-religious enthusiasm for Irish music, particularly from people he termed 'old Presbyterians', by which he seems to have meant the old United Irish type. It was, he claimed, the Troubles which finally destroyed such interest.[70] In 1992 Dr Bob Curran, a teacher in Portrush, County Antrim, remembered his Protestant grandfather from south Armagh as a fluent Irish speaker and traditional musician. But his Ballymena grandmother's reaction would have been more typical.

My grandfather was frequently told to 'stop filling the child's head with nonsense' and I was told . . . he had come from 'a Catholic part of the country' and that the traditions which he held were 'very Catholic'. There were many good Catholics, she insisted . . . but 'they had a very different culture to us' and it was best not to have too much to do with that.[71]

Successive ministries of education after 1921 had to combat the dominant Unionist prejudice and paranoia towards Irish language and culture. Even Craigavon was persuaded that outright suppression would be ill advised. But most of his party considered the language subversive, and cited the prominent role of Gaelic League members in the 1916 rising as proof. *Any* official sanction was tantamount to supporting 'an anti-British and disloyal faction', protested the Loyalty League in 1928. 'As loyal subjects . . . we strongly resent this pandering to a cunning foe.' It would 'enable rebellious spirits to propagate sedition . . . The language is of no practical utility, but may be of much value to incipient traitors.'[72]

Like so much in Northern Ireland, Unionist association of rebelliousness and Irish culture became a self-fulfilling prophecy. The Irish language became something of a Catholic code, since only Catholics were presumed to speak it. Inability to do so often meant a double marginalisation, particularly for Catholics outside traditional Catholic areas, where classes and *feiseanna* tended to be located. Ever since the foundation of the Gaelic League in 1893 there have been tensions between those supporting the revival of Irish for scholarly or preservationist reasons, and those who use it for political ends.[73] In Northern Ireland the language came to be used as a weapon by the more republican-minded – brief statements in Irish, usually rejecting the 'sassanachs' [sic *Sasanaigh*], marking the appearance of IRA men in courts, which they otherwise refused to recognise.[74] 'Every word of Irish spoken', claimed a prominent Sinn Féin member in the early 1980s, 'is like another bullet being fired in the struggle for Irish freedom.'[75] In prison republicans often studied the language for the first time and the current revival owes much to the increased numbers of prison 'graduates' in the Catholic community. It has also provoked internal tensions in that revival. The various community ventures which have produced a number of Irish-language schools in west Belfast and other educational projects, have invariably involved such republicans and just as invariably attracted 'political vetting' in the allocation of funds.[76] Although the 1991 census recorded a large increase in interest in the language, and new bodies such as the Cultural Traditions Group (1988) and the Ultach Trust (1989) are promoting an apolitical approach, its public face has tended to be that of militant nationalism. 'In the North the IRA has all but appropriated the Irish language,' wrote the writer Sam McAughtry in 1993,

and the other Catholic Irish speakers are silent on the issue; Fianna Fáil politicians at their conferences have made the language elitist; the Gaelic

Athletic Association's ban on the army and the RUC is seen as sectarian; the task of persuading Protestants to encourage the growth of Irish culture, never mind embracing it to themselves, is a huge one. But Catholics can help. Already there is support within the GAA for the removal of the Ban . . . Irish-speaking Catholics should ease the concerns of Protestants by condemning politicians who use the language for political ends.[77]

Many Irish-language speakers and most Catholics would like to depoliticise the language issue, but given recent tensions about bi-lingualism in the new Northern Ireland Assembly – when Sinn Féin and some SDLP members conducted proceedings in Irish, some Unionists mocking and most insisting on equal rights for Ullans or Ulster-Scots – a resolution still seems a long way off.[78]

An awful piety infected northern nationalism and the Irish-language movement for much of the twentieth century, both alike infused with the puritanism of post-Cullenite Catholicism. 'Canoodling' in the Donegal Gaeltacht was the most heinous of crimes and treated as such in the Catholic schools. Cal McCrystal recalls priests patrolling the roads and hills in the 1940s Gaeltacht in search of courting couples. He also recalls the time in 1955 when his Irish-speaking father was denounced from the pulpits, forced out of his twenty-year chairmanship of the Gaelic League in Belfast, and dropped as a regular columnist in the *Irish News* for flouting that other taboo of Catholic cultural nationalism then, consorting with dangerous leftist movements. As a life-time socialist, he had led a cultural delegation to Moscow that year.[79]

The *fáinne*, a gold or silver tie or lapel pin, signifying levels of proficiency in the Irish language, was one of the most respected symbols of such nationalism. It often accompanied an array of other pins and motifs in a defiant gesture to the majority Protestant culture: the Pioneer Total Abstinence Association, the Legion of Mary, the Sodality of the Holy Name and sometimes an Irish tricolour pin too. The use of the tricolour, however, had a chequered history and symbolises the largely reactive nature of such displays. Its usage, though often in a relatively unobtrusive way, sparked a considerable overreaction by the authorities, culminating in the Flags and Emblems Act of 1954 and the Paisleyite attack on the flag in Sinn Féin's Belfast office in 1964. Predictably such action produced the opposite result to that intended, and for a while the tricolour became the main emblem of nationalist defiance. Bernadette Devlin recalled being prompted to flaunt a tricolour pin as a teenager by the knowledge that it was banned by the 1954 act. But when a policeman simply laughed good-humouredly at her impudence, she lost interest and ceased wearing it.[80] The act was repealed in 1986. The adoption of Gaelic forms of names was another way of expressing separate identity and defiance of Unionist pettiness. They marked the bearer as Catholic just as much as the name Patrick had done a century earlier. As such they acted as an effective bar to Catholic employment in certain areas. As late as 1984 the Ulster Unionists' annual conference could treat the numbers of Róisíns and Séamuses in the local media with a mixture of contempt and fear that they somehow posed a threat to Ulster's Protestant heritage.[81]

The kind of ascetic pious nationalism encapsulated in the array of symbols noted above is typical of the defensiveness of embattled minorities. It was the underlying theme of Irish-language school textbooks, printed south of the border, and of the Gaelic revival generally. The promotion of rural values as the ideal of Irishness struck a particular chord with northern nationalists, who had long dignified their inglorious lot with the conviction that they were Ulster's native sons. Little wonder that after partition the Gaelic League's most missionary elements should now be in Ulster. The Irish cultural revival was also espoused by the Catholic Church as a channel for promoting a more wholesome culture against the perceived atheism and immorality coming in from England. *Céilís* were often the only dances permitted in parish halls and the only ones permitted by the Gaelic Athletic Association until 1973.[82] The GAA epitomises the best and the worst of such Catholic cultural nationalism. The increase in the number of clubs in Ulster after 1920 was politically inspired. However, sporting success gave large numbers of Catholics the opportunity to participate in team games and the GAA's cultivation of local pride sometimes brought Protestant support for team victories. But the organisation was dominated by priests and country school teachers, who conducted organisational meetings in Irish, played 'Faith of Our Fathers' and 'The Soldier's Song' at fixtures and generally acted as 'cultural policeman and gauleiter'[83] of the Catholic community, particularly in rural areas. It policed its ban on 'foreign [for which read English] games' by sending vigilantes to patrol the gates at soccer matches and came to symbolise the new political correctness of Catholic nationalism, lampooned in a satirical song of the 1960s.

> Come all you boys that vote for me, come gather all around,
> A Catholic I was born an' reared an' so I'm duty bound
> To proclaim my country's misery and express our Papish hope,
> To embarrass all the Orangemen an' glorify the Pope.

> Our allegiance is to Ireland, to her language and her games,
> So we can't accept the border boys, as long as it remains,
> Our reason is the Gaelic blood that's flowin' in our veins,
> An' that is why our policy is never known to change.[84]

This parade of stereotyped 'Irishness' was both unwelcome to and unwelcoming of Protestants, and its political overtones, notably the GAA's exclusion of members of the security forces, tarred all those involved with the stigma of 'disloyalty'. *Céilí*-goers, Irish-speakers and GAA members often attracted hostile attention from the police (and latterly from loyalist terrorists), thus reinforcing Catholics' self-image as a persecuted people, with right on their side. Catholics claim that their Irish culture rather than their religion is the key to their identity.[85] But the time has not yet arrived (at least not in Northern Ireland) when Catholicism, Irish culture and political nationalism can be disentangled, for they have been consciously intertwined for centuries. This was the 'package deal' from which Catholics deviated at their peril. It had played an important social function before the recent Troubles, often dignifying the lives of those who genuinely were victims. But it also set up an internal elitism, unaccepting of Catholics who did not subscribe to or fit the composite image of Gaeldom. It was a total identification of religion and culture which, whilst it could just about accommodate Catholics from other European countries as part of the auld alliance against England, found 'British' Catholics discomfiting and something of a contradiction in terms. There was a story told in Tyrone about a Scottish Catholic family who had moved there towards the end of the Second World War and whose celebration of things British, including the flying of the Union Jack, met with such thorough disapproval from local Catholics, that they eventually had to move.[86]

4. Catholicism as religion

In 1993 I listened to some Catholic teenagers in Belfast argue for an ideal future in which their faith could be separated from the traditions associated with it. By this they inferred its traditional association with political nationalism, and, at its extreme, militant republicanism. Certainly the Ulster hierarchy has attempted to do just this in its consistent condemnation of the IRA. As a result it has incurred the wrath of republicans, particularly since it has been more reticent in its condemnation of state violence. In this it has reflected the opinions of the vast majority of its adherents. Even so, it has embittered and confused a significant number of Catholics who vote for Sinn Féin, particularly in working-class areas, where there has been a noticeable drop in religious practice. This is because Catholicism and nationalism have traditionally been one and the same thing. For much of the twentieth century the clergy have been the real political leaders of the Catholic populace. Republican leaders recognise the connection and are careful not to offend the religious sensibilities of their followers. When Gerry Adams accuses the Church of going back on its own traditions in its criticism of republicans, he has a point, even though he conveniently ignores that other longstanding Church tradition – opposition to violence.[87]

In the absence of effective nationalist politics under Stormont, the clergy were expected to be the main voice of the Catholic people. Nationalist politicians could not survive without their endorsement. So much coverage was given by the Catholic press to their statements, sermons and pastorals that critics could be forgiven for thinking them penned by the same people. In these writings the debt nationalism owed the church was a regular theme as was the idea of St Patrick as 'ours'. Indeed, Cardinal MacRory – a dominant influence in the Catholic Church in Ulster, first as bishop of Down and Connor, 1915–28, then as archbishop of Armagh, 1928–45 – declared the Protestant churches to be no part of the church of Christ, took great exception to

Protestantism using the name 'Church of Ireland', and sought to have a clause inserted in the new Irish constitution of 1937 declaring Catholicism the true faith established by Christ. De Valera was too astute a statesman to accept this and cultivated the papacy in successfully resisting it.[88] MacRory was supported by his successor in Down and Connor, Daniel Mageean (bishop, 1929–62). Their formative years were the traumatic ones of post-partition Ulster and like the rest of the older clergy they carried their scars and prejudices into the early 1960s. They rarely made representations to government on behalf of their community other than on educational matters, and it is perhaps unsurprising that they lacked any civic culture. Even in towns like Downpatrick, with a Catholic majority on the council, there was no easy relationship, and Protestant clergy turned up to civic occasions more readily than their Catholic counterparts.[89] Since the Catholic clergy had not been made welcome at state functions in any event, and had alternative administrative and welfare systems, their parishes remained their essential administrative units. There was little internal challenge to the authority of the Catholic Church as long as Catholics generally felt themselves excluded from the state.

The main impact of church authority on Catholic lives has been in the field of education. The prevalence of devotional symbols distinguishes Catholic from state schools, and preparation for the sacraments takes place in school hours. The Catholic Church is passionate in its defence of separate Catholic education, believing that 'the faith is caught as much as taught'.[90] 'We stress that Religious Education', wrote the Ulster bishops in 1988, in a strongly-worded protest at new government education proposals, '. . . is *the* foundation on which all aspects of the curriculum in the Catholic school are based. For that reason we must demand that Religious Education be given its rightful place *before* the other "foundation subjects" '.[91] Bishop Farren of Derry had put it more forcefully in the 1950s – the Church 'required' Catholic parents to send their children to Catholic schools to preserve the faith of the next generation, otherwise the children of those attending non-Catholic schools would be 'perverts'.[92]

However, what once was a justifiable reaction to Protestant proselytism has solidified into dogmatism. Catholic parents going outside the Catholic school system encounter considerable hostility from their clergy when they seek help to prepare their children for the sacra-ments.[93] The Catholic Church's opposition to integrated education takes the same line, and were it not for the more charitable approach of the religious sisters and brothers, Catholic children in integrated schools would be deprived of such instruction. In this stance the Church is out of step with a majority of lay Catholics, who approve of integrated education in principle.[94] This does not necessarily mean that they are correspondingly critical of the Catholic educational system. Catholic parents are generally content for their children to receive their religious instruction during school hours. But since those who were closest to the Church's official hostility to integrated edu-cation were Sinn Féin and the IRA (organisations which the hierarchy disliked intensely) – largely because of the nationalist which accom-panies the religious ethos in Catholic schools – it should at least have caused the Church some unease. However, since Sinn Féin's Martin McGuinness took over the Education ministry in the new (1999) devolved administration in Northern Ireland the party's public pro-nouncements on integrated education have been more positive.

Educational surveys from the 1960s to the 1990s reveal percentages in the high nineties of children in totally segregated schools. Although there is a steadily-growing integrated school movement in Northern Ireland, it accounts for only 4.5 per cent of the school population. One of the best accounts of the early debate on integrated education is that by the Revd Eric Gallagher (former President of the Methodist Church in Ireland) and Stanley Worral (former headmaster of Methodist Col-lege in Belfast). It shows educational segregation to have been such an everyday 'fact of life' that few gave much thought to it and the high numbers registering support for integration did not translate into pressure to achieve it. The fact is that Northern Ireland society gener-ally supports denominational schooling. Gallagher and Worrall's study also suggests that the Catholic Church's declared opposition has allowed the other churches to avoid taking a stand on the issue. 'As long as Catholicism insists on its special role in education, the others are absolved from any requirement to develop their apparent or alleged call for radical change.'[95]

The court is still out on the role that separate education may have played in the problems of Northern Ireland. Yet the very ethos in maintained (religious, mostly Catholic) and state (Protestant) schools must surely have been a factor. John Whyte concluded in his study published in 1990 that segregated education *was* divisive 'not so much because of what was taught, but because of the "hidden agenda", the values – political more than religious – which are informally put across to the pupils'.[96] In Catholic schools children were more likely to pick up negative attitudes to the state and civic society. Until quite recently, it was believed that Catholics had little chance of employment in a range of public services, and so everything in this area might be the subject of unfavourable comments by teachers.[97] Similar perceptions of the Union flag as a symbol of dominance were also transmitted, while in some schools there was a tendency to shun British and Imperial history in favour of Irish history and sometimes a particularly national-istic version of it.[98] In addition, most Catholic religious brothers and sisters – a significant element in Catholic education, particularly in boys' schools – were trained south of the border. Indeed, in 1962 Barritt and Carter found only two of the forty-three teachers at St Mary's Christian Brothers' School in Belfast had been trained in Northern Ireland.[99] The differences in school curricula, however, had narrowed by the 1980s. As elsewhere, the Troubles have caused a questioning of what was being taught and today one is as likely to learn Irish history in state as in Catholic schools.

The story of how Northern Ireland's educational system became almost totally segregated is not a pleasant one. Indeed, D. H. Akenson chose to call his pioneering study of the issue *Education and Enmity* (1973). The proselytising activities of fundamentalist Protestants in the nineteenth century had made the Catholic clergy wary of education over which they did not have control, and even before partition they were already blocking government reforms. The MacPherson Bill of 1919 would have introduced education authorities and rate support for schools. But it was denounced by the Catholic Church, often in shrill anti-English and anti-Protestant language, and had to be withdrawn. By the time of partition, the entire educational system was overdue for reform.[100] The establishment of a central Ministry of Education (such as happened in 1922) had already been advocated by educational reformers. But the required transfer of schools to its authority was resisted not only by the Catholic Church but by some

Protestant clergy also. Indeed, it was the extremism of many Protestant clerics rather than the difficulties created by the Catholic bishops – though there were enough also of these – which turned the state system into a Protestant one and brought down the enlightened regimes of education ministers Lord Londonderry in 1926 and Hall Thompson in 1949.[101] The religious sensitivity of the educational issue was recognised, and, with the possible exception of the deeply anti-Catholic Harry Midgley (1950–59), successive ministers of education were to prove remarkably ecumenical in their approach.[102]

Even so, the Catholic Church's early opposition to educational reform threw away its main chance of negotiating equitable treatment for Catholic pupils, and Catholic children have remained relatively deprived to this day. The refusal of the church to co-operate with the Lynn Committee (established in September 1921) and of about a third of Catholic elementary schools to recognise the new ministry's responsibility – until October 1922 their teachers were being paid from Dublin – were political gestures that made it more difficult to argue a religious case. Indeed, the political nationalism of Catholic clergy in the twentieth century often confused religious and political issues, both in their own minds and in those of their opponents. It was unfortunate that Sir Robert Lynn's Orangeism and distinct hostility towards Catholic cultural values should have provided an additional excuse for non-co-operation, for it was not until the mid-1920s that the Unionist party abandoned its efforts at non-sectarian government. But with political leaders in the Irish Free State beginning to use the schools as the channel for their vision of a de-anglicised and Gaelic new order, and the Lynn Committee equally bent on a school curriculum that would inculcate British civic values, the future of Irish education was being decided in a highly intolerant atmosphere.[103]

The 1923 Education Bill sought to make primary education free, compulsory and largely secular. The secular aspect of such provision was incompatible with Catholic practice of providing religious instruction as part of the curriculum. The Bill therefore accepted a category of schools totally independent of local control. Teachers' salaries and half the running expenses of the schools would be paid from public funds, but no capital costs. Education Minister Lord Londonderry had tried to be impartial, and rewrote the Lynn Committee's proposals on religious education to ensure that the fully-funded state sector did not provide denominational religious education in school hours. But a heated campaign by Protestant clerics won concessions on Bible instruction which made state schools Protestant in all but name. Continuing agitation by the Protestant clerics finally roused the Catholic bishops. A concession of 50 per cent capital funding to Catholic schools was granted under the 1930 Education Act. This was increased to 65 per cent in 1947, and 100 per cent by 1992 – a level of public funding for denominational schools much more generous than that provided in the Irish Republic.

But this point could have been reached much earlier had the bishops accepted the middling route offered under the 1923 Act. By this, schools with committees composed of four members of the original owners (i.e. the clergy) and two lay representatives of the new authorities (who would certainly have been Catholics) would have received substantial capital grants. Understandably Catholic authorities were most reluctant to grant any influence to the gerrymandered local authorities. But Akenson argues forcefully that this obstacle could have been surmounted and that it was rather the Catholic clergy's insistence on maintaining control (even against their own laity) which condemned generations of Catholic children to antiquated and inferior school facilities. A number of retired Catholic teachers concluded as much in their interviews with Fionnuala O Connor in 1992.[104] Bishop Farren of Derry had argued in 1945 that the government's requirement of lay members was spurious, since the clergy were always accepted by the Catholic people as their natural representatives. When in 1968 capital grants of 80 per cent were offered if voluntary schools accepted government representatives on to their committees (essentially the middling route offered in 1923) almost all the Catholic primary schools came over.[105]

Such relative deprivation was also reflected in the secondary sector. There was no free secondary education at the time of partition. Indeed, only 6,237 pupils of all denominations were receiving secondary education in 1921. Real progress in this area only came in 1947, when the government – following the 1944 Butler Act in England – extended compulsory education to the age of fifteen. It was only in 1951 that a means test was abolished for grammar school pupils (selected through the eleven-plus examination) and it took over another decade for the real benefits to filter through. Even then Catholic schools struggled to provide enough places for those qualified, and they levied a small fee to help make up the deficit in the capital grant – a real hardship for the larger number of poor parents among the Catholic population.[106]

As with other matters in Northern Ireland no side could claim the moral high ground. Immediately prior to partition a largely denominational system of state-funded education was already in place and the Catholic bishops were nearing victory in their long battle over education. Now they were faced with a state whose ethos and school system exuded anti-Catholicism. Any gesture of more generous funding of Catholic schools by government invariably raised Protestant ire. Protestant clerics were regularly invited on to the boards of management of 'state' schools. Catholic clergy never were. Advertisements sought Protestant staff for state schools, even in school kitchens.[107]

Much the same battle was engaged over teacher training. On the eve of partition there were seven teacher-training establishments in Ireland. The Marlborough Street College in Dublin was intended to be non-denominational, but effectively operated as a largely Presbyterian establishment. The other colleges were entirely denominational. Only one was based in Northern Ireland, St Mary's in Belfast, for Catholic women. The new northern Ministry of Education accordingly had an immediate problem to resolve: how to ensure continued facilities for male students generally and Protestant students in particular. It tried to reach an arrangement to continue training in the southern colleges, but its overtures were rejected. Indeed one of the Irish Free State's first actions was to close the Marlborough Street College, thereby depriving Presbyterian students of any training facility whatsoever. The northern government accordingly established Stranmillis [Training] College in Belfast, and initially Catholic men also attended. But when, in 1925, the government rejected the hierarchy's demands for the establishment of a separate Catholic establishment for male students, the bishops reached an arrangement with a Catholic training college in England (St Mary's Strawberry Hill) and informed Catholic students at Stranmillis that if they did not transfer, it would seriously jeopardise their chances of obtaining employment in Catholic schools in Northern

Ireland. Thereafter Stranmillis effectively became a Protestant college, although that had not been the government's intention.[108] It is at the very least some tribute to the Northern Ireland Ministry of Education, whatever about the known discriminatory policies of other ministries, that it continued to subsidise Catholic students who attended Strawberry Hill in England. The Catholic bishops were opposed to *any* state control over areas traditionally considered the church's domain, and since three had dioceses which straddled the border, they would have been acutely aware of the Irish Free State's acceptance of undisputed ecclesiastical supervision in matters educational.[109]

The Ulster bishops were also ambivalent about the extension to Northern Ireland of the British welfare state after 1946, which involved unprecedented interference with their role as a voluntary provider of social services. As in southern Ireland, they tended to see the increasing role of the state as smacking of socialism and communism and, from recent experience with state agencies, they had good reason to think the new system would interfere with Catholic social teaching.[110] In 1951 the Catholic bishops' objection to limited state welfare in the south helped bury Noel Browne's 'Mother and Child' scheme (to provide free medical care to mothers and children under sixteen), and they had already resisted nursery schemes which would have assisted the many Catholic women employed in the mills of Derry and Belfast.[111] It was an extra stigma on poor communities that their women went out to work while their men were idle, and the Catholic clergy and Unionists were unlikely allies in treating it as such.[112] Although the activities of Catholic welfare societies such as St Vincent de Paul had been praised by social reformers, there is evidence that poorer Catholics preferred the anonymous state to the shame of relief from the better-off in their own community.[113] The very real benefits which the welfare state brought to the traditionally poorer Catholic population in Northern Ireland soon made the quality of life very different from that in the Irish Republic, where church influence had positively conspired against the less well-off.

But one running sore remained: the position of the Mater Hospital in north Belfast. At the outset run largely by Sisters of Mercy, this small hospital has always catered also for the needs of the largely working-class Protestant population in the area. It had good relations with the Queen's University and was a recognised teaching hospital. But, although provisions had been made in British legislation for protecting the ethos of such voluntary hospitals within the welfare state, the Northern Ireland Act of 1949 left the Mater out of the system. The Catholic Church had objected to the proposed transfer of the Hospital to state control as a form of 'theft', and it continued to function on voluntary assistance until 1972. In many ways Catholics have been disproportionately the beneficiaries of the welfare state, having started from a lower economic base. Indeed, the benefits of the welfare state played a major role in the softening of many Catholics' attitudes towards continued inclusion in the United Kingdom. But there can be no doubt that the limbo status of the Mater left a running sore. Again there was fault on both sides and the normally balanced study by Barritt and Carter had considerable difficulty reaching a conclusion on where the main fault lay. Their suggestion that the Minister should have made more effort at accommodation had also been made by more traditional supporters of the state, including the *Belfast Telegraph*.[114] Denied consultancies in the National Health Service, Mater Hospital doctors were to the fore among the rising Catholic middle class which spawned the civil-rights movement.

This absence of full state funding for Catholic educational and medical institutions became part of the Catholic folklore of unfair discrimination. The northern state's 'penalisation' and 'persecution' of Catholic education was a recurrent theme in the nationalist press and in clerical sermons and homilies, particularly during school renovation ceremonies or fund-raising events. Such fund-raising was woven into the pattern of everyday life for generations of Catholics, binding their identity ever more closely to that of an apparently embattled church. The YP pools, which helped fund the Mater Hospital, were collected on Friday evenings, giving pin-money to many a Catholic teenager and demarcating Catholic households which subscribed in mixed areas. The 'white babies' and 'black babies' collections in aid of the Catholic orphanages and missions, the imaginative 'buy-a-brick' school-building-fund schemes involved even those on the lowest income in that culture of 'supporting your own', which Catholics were nurtured on. Necessity shaded into defiance, school-building campaigns built up fighting funds to deter government interference. 'All our days were spent organising concerts or raffles or draws or competitions to raise more money to get equipment for the lab,' recalled Bernadette Devlin of her convent grammar school's 'struggle to do without government help and interference'.[115] Eamonn McCann, journalist, writer and former civil rights activist, recalled the high profile of such fund-raising activities in his working-class Derry community and their role in bonding church and community. 'The collection of money and articles for sale and the selling of tickets for weekly functions kept every household in almost daily contact with the church, provided the occasion for constant, repeated renewal of commitment to it.'[116]

A long tradition of necessity and self-help made Catholics adept at community organisation – a feature increasingly recognised in recent years by community workers in deprived Protestant areas. The drawback was that it created the image (and frequently the reality) of a grasping church. Stories abound of favouritism towards the children of publicans, bookmakers and the like in Catholic schools. Because of their estrangement from the dominant culture in Northern Ireland, Catholics have generally been reluctant to criticise their church in public. It is highly significant, therefore, that in the otherwise highly sectional-minded rural community of south Tyrone, analysed by Rosemary Harris in the 1950s, she should have found Catholics preferring to seek financial advice from a Protestant minister, rather than reveal their financial circumstances to their parish priest.[117]

Such communal self-help also intensified authoritarian tendencies within the Catholic Church and its resentment at Mother Teresa's interference in 1973 and most of all at Sinn Féin activities during the recent Troubles had much to do with its perceived role as sole arbiter of Catholic community projects. Maurice Hayes is a prominent lay Catholic. His lifelong experience of working closely with the Catholic Church involved some time training for the priesthood. He found that the most talented and spirited clergy tended not to be promoted and the limited experience and training of the others simply reinforced old stereotypes by returning priests to their communities in positions of leadership but without any new thinking.

The Down and Connor priests tended not to serve abroad. They were drawn from closed communities, educated within them in a segregated system, propagated in a sort of enclosed clerical hothouse, and returned straight to the community again in a position of status and leadership, where their views were not questioned or challenged. This was a recipe for the continuous reinforcement of values – the bad as well as the good. In a good sense, it meant that the clergy might be closer to the people, but the system also induced a lack of vision, an unwillingness to take risks, and an inordinate dwelling on old sores.

As chairman of the newly established Community Relations Commission in 1969, he found that the Catholic clergy had a highly developed sense of working within their own community, but none whatsoever of cross-community contacts.[118]

Until recent years there has been a sense of a repressive culture in the Catholic press, where clerical views were faithfully reproduced and never criticised, where communism, materialism and 'impurity' were regularly and hysterically denounced. The Catholic Church syllabus for religious instruction in second-level schools (in place until 1966) was particularly concerned about 'the subversive influences of the age'.[119] Little wonder that the faddish addition of a CND pin to a lapel in the 1960s was grounds for severe disciplining in the Catholic schools, or that Vatican II came as such a shock to most of the Irish hierarchy. Indeed, there are many well-educated Catholics in Northern Ireland today who still carry the same psychological scars of their education as those articulated to Fionnuala O Connor in 1992. Besides the wanton violence in some Catholic boys' schools, one university lecturer recalled his schooling in the late 1950s and early 1960s as one of 'ferocious humiliation and destruction of the personality'. Others remembered the victimisation of those from working-class backgrounds and favouritism towards the rich.[120]

It is an ethos most famously depicted in the fiction of Brian Moore, in his life-long critique of his native Belfast, the Catholic Church and (but thinly disguised), St Malachy's College, the Catholic boys' grammar school attended by Moore himself. It is a school where even the teachers are victims of its repressive violence and sexual puritanism [*The Feast of Lupercal*]. Judith Hearne had found meaning to her loneliness and suffering in the teachings and devotions of the Church. But as she loses her faith, the unsympathetic priest, to whom she turned for solace, was incapable of dealing with those who did not conform unquestioningly [*The Lonely Passion of Judith Hearne*]. And just as with Gavin in *The Emperor of Ice-Cream*, her questioning involves stark reappraisal of the ever-present holy statues and pictures, when stripped of their devotional significance – the Infant of Prague becoming a nagging little martinet, the picture of the Sacred Heart retained simply because it was familiar, part of the furniture.[121]

But Moore wrote at a distance. For most Catholics in the 1950s, when Moore's writing career started, the idea of criticising your own was unthinkable. It still is. Many of those talking with Fionnuala O Connor in 1992–3 asked for the tape-recorder to be switched off when they criticised the Church. Catholics, even lapsed ones, recognise Catholic culture as part and parcel of their identity. To attack it is to play the Protestant card. Catholic culture south of the border is altogether more confident and unthreatened. But in Northern Ireland the Church is still protected from internal criticism by that Catholic sixth sense of saying nothing which would feed anti-Catholicism. When Protestants claim that Catholicism is an authoritarian religion, which crushes debate and individualism, they have a point. But when they carry that criticism through to an assumption that Catholics are an unthinking herd, they entirely miss the real reason for such apparent lack of critical instincts within northern Catholicism. The same person who keeps mum in mixed company is as likely as not to let rip in the company of fellow Catholics.

Nor should one confuse internal criticism of the clergy with a rejection of the faith, still less of the community defined by it. Many commentators have noted a qualitative difference between Protestant and Catholic bigotry in Ulster. As noted earlier, Protestant bigotry seems to be more against the Catholic religion itself, whereas Catholics do not see Protestantism as threatening. This is because of a belief in the superiority of their religion and the time-old Church traditions of triumph through suffering and endurance: 'the Church suffering', 'the Church militant', 'the Church triumphant' were regular refrains. Maurice Hayes recalls the in-talk of his friends at the Catholic school in Downpatrick, of ghostly monks and bells below the river Roughal awaiting the reversal of the Reformation and return of property stolen by the Protestants.[122] Eamonn McCann tells of childhood pilgrimages to a rock near Buncrana, where the 'redcoats' were said to have murdered a penal-day priest, of other stories about the penal laws and the English offering food during the Famine if the people would 'turn' – 'but through it all the people stayed faithful'. 'An essential part of the Irish Freedom for which patriots had fought through the centuries was, we understood, the freedom to be Catholic.' There were daily reminders of the threat from red communism: the church attacked in Spain (prior to the 'Catholic victory' of Franco), in Mexico, in Yugoslavia, in Hungary, in China. The plight of Cardinal Mindszenty (Hungarian prelate, imprisoned by the Communists) was known to every Catholic schoolchild in the 1950s. 'That, one gathered, was what communism was about. The church was persecuted everywhere. The fact that it had survived was proof positive of its divine mission.'[123]

This sense of being part of a world-wide community was reinforced by references to the internationalism of the Latin mass, and many felt that something had gone out of their lives when the vernacular replaced it after Vatican II. The 'devotional revolution' reached its apogee in the twentieth century as daily lives revolved around the church's liturgical calendar. Aside from family rosary, daily mass and weekly confession, there was an extraordinary array of Catholic devotions on hand, recalled Maurice Hayes of his childhood in the 1930s and 1940s.

There were novenas for this and that which meant nine evenings on the trot, and nine Fridays, which involved mass and communion every Friday for nine weeks in succession . . . November Devotions and May Devotions and Lenten Devotions and Advent and Saint Patrick's Day and Corpus Christi and Sundays and Holy Days of Obligation and almost anything else anybody could think of, and the Men's Confraternity once a month and the Women's sodality and Perpetual Novena every Friday night so that there seemed to be few days in the year on which we did not go to church.[124]

Added to this were the large number of Catholic societies and committees to which one might belong. In 1939 tributes to the new bishop of Derry, Neil Farren, came from bodies ranging from the Knights of St Columbanus, the Irish National Foresters, the Ancient Order of Hibernians and St Vincent de Paul to St Columb's Past Pupils Union, the Derry Catholic Club and the Catholic Ex-Combatants

Association.[125] There would have been little time for social activity outside such a densely packed Catholic timetable. Catholicism provided a great big comfort blanket for its adherents, and far from repressiveness at this level, most remember a communal togetherness, crowded services, a place to meet friends and a sense of well-being in the dimly lit warmth of the perpetually open chapel.

There was too the pomp and pageant. In addition to the great processions for the feast of Corpus Christi and the thousands who would turn out for the various confraternities, investitures or funerals of bishops were like alternative state occasions. The Congress of the Catholic Truth Society of Ireland held in Belfast in 1934 attracted 120,000 to its pontifical mass. Tens of thousands lined the streets of Derry for Dr O'Kane's funeral in January 1939 and those of west Belfast for Dr Mageean's funeral in January 1962. Figures of 10,000 and 6,000 were estimated to have processed with the male and female confraternities to Clonard monastery in west Belfast in June and July 1958, whilst the golden jubilee of the Holy Family Confraternity had attracted 40,000 to the services at Clonard and accompanying street festivities in 1947.[126] But it was the activities surrounding the 1932 Eucharistic Congress which provided the most stunning example of triumphal pageantry and Catholic devotionalism as a leisure activity. An estimated 100,000 Catholics travelled south for the Phoenix Park ceremony, and a special high mass was said in Corrigan Park in Belfast for another 80,000. Numbers were further swollen by pilgrims disembarking at Belfast from other parts of the world. Open-air shrines and arches appeared all over Catholic Belfast and the press was full of pictures of the crowds who participated in the street devotions. It was, proclaimed the *Irish News* in bold headlines, the 'Triumph of Catholic Ireland', and so indeed it was treated by gangs of loyalists who stoned the trains as they departed.[127]

5. The Catholic Church and the Troubles

The post-war years saw a more conciliatory approach by the Catholic Church to the state. But in 1962 when William Philbin, bishop of Down and Connor, sought to pay a courtesy call on the Lord Mayor of Belfast – the first bishop of Down and Connor to do so since partition – he was snubbed, and a meeting between a Unionist Prime Minister and the head of the Catholic Church did not occur until 1970. An invitation to appoint a chaplain to the Northern Ireland parliament first came in 1968. It took the bishops three years to concede. By then the Troubles were already under way and there was some pressure from radical priests for the appointment to be suspended until the Stormont regime had reformed itself. Such internal criticism was highly unusual. Cardinal Conway could afford to ignore it. But the Troubles shook the Catholic Church – as they did the entire Catholic community – in a way not experienced since the 1790s.

When the civil-rights movement got under way, the Archbishop of Armagh was Cardinal William Conway, a Queen's University-educated Belfast man. He and Bishop Philbin had arrived within a year of each other in the early 1960s and in outlook were quite different from their recent predecessors. Both were intellectuals who had participated in Vatican II. Though religiously orthodox, they brought to the hierarchy a political reticence unthinkable since the time of the 'devotional revolution'. The civil-rights movement, with its call for reforms within the state, matched this new mood precisely, and there was considerable involvement by the clergy in its early stages. When violence erupted the bishops followed tradition by condemning it, Philbin personally intervening in 1972 to have the barricades removed in Catholic 'no-go' areas. As such they increasingly ran foul of the emerging republican movement.

Although many accuse the Catholic Church of having partly assisted the rise of the Provisional IRA – as an antidote to the socialist Official IRA – a survey made in 1986 could identify only three priests as having had any sympathy for the Provos, and *they* were ostracised. Likewise barely nine showed any inclination to vote Sinn Féin.[128] The northern church, whilst it has remained as thoroughly nationalist as before (or, more correctly, as anti-Unionist), has been solid in its condemnation of IRA violence. This has often placed it in an ambiguous situation, which critics have been all too ready to exploit. It sought to explain the apparent contradiction of supporting past rebels, whilst condemning present ones, by depicting the Provos as something entirely different. But its lack of moral certainty on a range of associated issues laid it open to attack in a majority culture so attuned to seeing priests as the real enemy. Whatever its public condemnations, it has not actually deprived the IRA of any of its theological services or sacraments, continuing to bury IRA men and refusing to bend to pressures to excommunicate them. In fact, history was on its side, for such actions in the past were counter-productive. Even so, its explanations sounded unconvincing to outsiders. Its refusal to denounce the hunger-strike deaths as suicide revealed its theology to be compromised by its nationalism and occasioned something of a rebuke from Cardinal Hume, then head of the Catholic Church in England.[129]

There can be no doubt that the clergy has walked a tightrope in its attitudes to republican activities, sensing they would be damned if they did and damned if they didn't. At times it has been near impossible to argue church teaching on Catholic funerals, when they have been made such occasions for republican propaganda. The clergy also recognised that any criticism of the state, when before the Troubles they would have had no such inhibitions, would be twisted to insinuate that they were Provo sympathisers. In 1969 one priest, Father Denis Faul, was publicly criticised by Cardinal Conway for his attacks on the judiciary. His subsequent campaign with another priest, Father Raymond Murray, to highlight injustice and misbehaviour by the security forces, also caused embarrassment to his superiors.[130] Promotion was a long time in coming. But even among many lower clergy there was concern in these early years that their church was not speaking out against state violence. It has to be said that as IRA violence (and even more so the political threat from Sinn Féin) increased, most clergy fell in behind their bishops. Although many, in protest at internment, had refused co-operation with the 1971 census, none supported the republicans' campaign against the next census in 1981.

The position of the Catholic Church has been an unenviable one during the Troubles. Its tendency to discourage internal debate at a time when it was never more necessary has weakened it. But the awful position of many clergy, at the centre of a bloody vortex, partly produced by their own predecessors and largely centred on their own community, must surely be epitomised by that terrifying picture of Father Alex Reid, despair in his face, as he prayed over the semi-naked body of the dead British soldier, battered to death in west Belfast in the spring of 1988. He subsequently became a key player in bringing about the IRA ceasefires of 1994 and 1997.

The Catholic Church had already become more accommodating towards the state even before the Troubles and was broadly supporting an internal power-sharing rather than an anti-partitionist constitutional solution. But just like the constitutional nationalist politicians, particularly after the downfall of the power-sharing executive in 1974, it had little to show for its denunciation of republican violence. In a moving interview with Fionnuala O Connor, Bishop Edward Daly of Derry spoke of the almost impossible position of the clergy during the Troubles, every incautious word pounced upon by one side or the other. Born in south Fermanagh, with impeccable nationalist credentials, Daly had been a popular priest in Derry and was the priest most associated with his community at the time of Bloody Sunday (1972). One senses that his promotion to the bishopric of Derry in 1974, at the young age of thirty-nine, was an effort by the Church to stem the flow of recruits to militant republicanism, as was the elevation of Tomás Ó Fiaich to Armagh in 1977.

Ó Fiaich was a charismatic, generous and plain-spoken man, whose historical studies of his native Armagh were masterly. His ten-year 'reign' as head of the Irish Church was nevertheless a mixed blessing for the northern Catholics. Popular with republicans, because he called for Irish unity and British withdrawal, he aroused mixed feelings in other Catholics. They sometimes admired his outspokenness on issues where they were traditionally reticent. But this native of Cullyhana in south Armagh, near Crossmaglen, who had spent most of his adult life outside Northern Ireland, did not always observe those unspoken conventions by which northern Catholics and Protestants regulate social interaction. When, with the best of intentions and genuine emotion, he apologised on behalf of the entire Catholic community for the 1987 bombing of Enniskillen by the IRA, many Catholics were outraged that he should have so identified them with republican atrocities.[131] His misfortune was to have been leader of the Catholic Church in Ireland at the time of the hunger strikes. His own ultra-nationalism and open support of the prisoners' cause both hardened theirs and the British government's resolve, where a more neutral figure might have had more success in securing concessions.

The successor to Cardinal Ó Fiaich could hardly have been more different. It was as if the Church had gone on the offensive against the growing strength of republicanism after the hunger strikes. Dr Cahal Daly was from County Antrim and had been bishop of Down and Connor since 1982. His was the most anti-republican of all the clerical voices. Politically a nationalist, like all the clergy, he nevertheless adopted the line that the future lay in respect for both traditions in Northern Ireland, and unification, if it ever came, could do so only with the consent of all. On the ground he began seriously to combat the growing challenge to church authority posed by the rise of Sinn Féin.

Catholic voluntary social activity – aside from that of the St Vincent de Paul Society and the Legion of Mary – was underdeveloped, as was the Church's communication with the providers of state social funding.[132] Philbin and Conway had a rather better record than their predecessors in this area. Even so, the fact that the Church itself sought and became the main channel for government funding to job-creation schemes in Catholic west Belfast by the 1980s was quite a reversal of previous practice and owed much to the new bishop's crusade to combat the growing community activity of Sinn Féin. Mass attendance had dropped alarmingly in some west Belfast communities, falling as low as 33 per cent in one parish by 1983. The increased communal involvement by the Church, notably by the nuns, brought the figures up again, though there has been no return to Richard Rose's findings in 1968 of 95 per cent Sunday observance in such areas. The bitterness of republican response was some measure of the Church's success, one outraged republican declaring of a competing church-run community centre that it had even called in the police to deal with trouble![133] The sum total of such accusations was that the Church had joined the enemy, and indeed this is one of the most fascinating, though rarely-noted,[134] aspects of the church-republican battle. Since the clergy have rarely been out of touch with the pulse of popular acceptability, such a very public stance against the IRA speaks volumes for general Catholic opinion. The decline in Church influence in working-class areas is undisputed. But for the first time it now has considerable influence both within the state and a range of other opinion and policy-forming bodies. The ghetto church has gone.

Has the Catholic clergy been as profoundly changed by the Troubles as the laity? On religious issues, and above all on education, it still seems profoundly authoritarian. The 'pick-and-mix' or 'café' Catholicism of so many of its flock today evokes little sympathy and it is significant that the most innovative thinking is coming from the religious orders or from clergy who have come to Northern Ireland from the south. Traditional Catholic reluctance to criticise one's own was reinforced by the Troubles and the northern Church has been spared the rethinking which criticism by a more confident Catholic populace in the Republic has produced. Edna Longley, professor of English at Queen's University, is critical. 'The Northern Catholic Church, still locked into a nineteenth-century relationship with nationalism, is also pursuing its own interests, in that Northern Catholics can be kept thirty years less liberal than their Southern counterparts.'[135]

However, there would need to be a significant decline in the anti-Catholicism of the majority community in Northern Ireland for such Catholic revisionism to take hold. In the most comprehensive survey of northern clerical attitudes this century (Gerald McElroy's questionnaire of 1986), there was a significantly higher rate of response from religious orders than from diocesan clergy (58.5 per cent – rising to 100 per cent in Derry – against 31.7 per cent). Even so, McElroy's findings do reflect internal debate within the Church, even if it has not yet erupted on to the public arena. From 232 responses, he concluded that, whilst respondents were uniformly nationalist in political orientation, they were almost exclusively constitutional nationalists. Younger, urban-based priests tended to more flexibility on the issue than older or rural-based ones. They also were more aware of the need to accommodate Protestants than their southern counterparts, as many as 50.4 per cent of the respondents favouring the liberalising of church attitudes either on divorce or mixed marriages (and in this they reflected Ulster Catholic lay opinion at the time). Again it was the younger clerics and the religious who were more willing to criticise their church on a range of issues associated with the Troubles: failure to condemn state violence, to help the poorer communities, to encourage intercommunal reconciliation. All were broadly happy on the Church's denunciation of republican violence. The only area on which the clergy were discovered to be out of step with lay Catholic opinion was that of education. The bulk of northern-born clergy (as against the southern-born) were opposed to integrated education, 67.2 per cent and 39.7 per cent respectively, the figures for those accepting that it would reduce Northern Ireland's problems: 14.5 per cent parish priests, 31.2 per cent curates, but 66.1 per cent religious. These findings largely correspond with the conclusions of the Opsahl Commission in 1993. Significantly it was the religious sisters, who do not appear to have been included in McElroy's questionnaire, who were then more prepared to comment on the shortcomings of their church. The dramatic post-Vatican-II transformation of the role played by nuns in Northern Ireland still awaits research.[136] During the Troubles they were certainly instrumental in reversing the mounting criticism of the clergy in deprived communities.

As I complete this final chapter, Ulster Catholic identity is in transition. The Troubles have shattered many of the old certainties and for a number of years the resulting confusion eroded much of that nascent Catholic confidence so noticeable in the civil-rights movement. 'This is the reason for the withdrawal into private life and apparent apathy of so many Northern Ireland people', I concluded in 1993, 'the fragmentation of the old identities, the abuses to which they have given rise, but the inability to arrive at anything new which carries the same clarity.'[137] The Troubles have completed the clergy's withdrawal from vocal nationalist politics, a process also hastened by the emergence of a strong nationalist party in the SDLP and latterly in Sinn Féin. Although the Troubles witnessed periods when political Catholicism retreated into traditional moulds – notably at the time of Bloody Sunday (1972) and the Hunger Strikes of 1981, the aspirations of the civil-rights movement for justice and equality within Northern Ireland have remained the dominant political aim of a majority of Ulster Catholics. This, and the recognition that an aspiration to eventual unity is a legitimate aim, if pursued by peaceful means, is enshrined in the Belfast-Good Friday Agreement of April 1998. Anti-discrimination laws, job-creation schemes, the Parades Commission, reforms within the RUC and more to come following the report of the Patten Commission, have gone some way to bringing Catholics into a sense of legitimate belonging in Northern Ireland.[138] Seamus Mallon, in that black humour so characteristic of Northern Ireland, has called the 1998 Agreement 'Sunningdale for slow learners'. The humour only barely disguises the tragedy that similar arrangements were on offer a quarter of a century ago.

Certainly the literature coming out of Northern Ireland in the past twenty-five years, particularly its fiction, makes bleak reading. The sectarianism is so prevalent that it is almost a caricature. Authors are still recognisably from one community or the other. Inevitably, as the largest concentration of population, Belfast has been the setting for the majority of such fiction. Often presented in monotones, fated to its grimness and violence as much as to its climatic wetness. It was in itself such an accepted stereotype that, as Edna Longley amusingly observes, camera crews, arriving to make the equally stereotypical Troubles thriller, were reluctant to film a sunny Belfast.[139] Seamus Deane's semi-autobiographical *Reading in the Dark,* shows an equally bleak Derry, where the countryside across the border in County Donegal serves the same function of escape to another world as that of the Cave-Hill for Belfast writers. Here is a parable of a community carrying the scars of the 1920s and nurturing its grievances into the 1960s. The result blights their own families and community as much as the society around them.

This is a feature of late Troubles novels by Catholic writers: a recognition of the imperfect past which helped produce the Troubles, but a bafflement at the outcome. In Deane, as in others, England is the conqueror who should get out of Ireland, but also a place of refuge and freedom for escapees from the claustrophobia of charity-less Catholic vendettas. And when the enemy appears as the mourning Yorkshire miner father of the soldier son shot by an IRA sniper, even Deane's staunchly republican family is moved to pity.[140] Mary Beckett's Belfast working-class Catholic heroine in *Give Them Stones* (1987) also carries the experiences and rhetoric of the past into the present, but again it provides an awkward fit. 'The IRA [of which her father had been a member in the 1940s] would never hurt ordinary people', comments Martha, 'only the system they were going to pull down. And the border would disappear and we'd all be one united country with our government giving fair play to everyone' – at least this is what they were supposed to do, 'not fighting Protestants'.[141]

'Catholic' writing, like Catholic identity, is in transition.[142] There is little romanticisation of the past, little left of the belief in the old panaceas of 'freeing Ireland', and a recognition that the problem like the solution lies with the two communities themselves. A plague on all your houses, is the most extreme version of this in Robert McLiam Wilson's *Ripley Bogle*. Catholic west Belfast in upbringing, and thrown on the streets as an adolescent by his mother – for dating a Protestant – the young male anti-hero blames his fate on the traditions of his blighted upbringing and the 'senseless sentimentality' of stock Irishness. The reality inspires some of the most unromantic descriptions of IRA activity to appear in any Troubles-inspired fiction. Here they are petty, jumped-up young hoods – their leaders aping leadership by sporting cheap suits and gangsterish hairstyles – their fight for Ireland consisting of stripping and tarring a young girl for consorting with the army.

The Troubles have been a dehumanising trauma, with the very communities which produced the paramilitaries at the sharpest receiving end of their violence. The New Ireland Forum of 1983–4 published a demography of the violence in Northern Ireland showing a heavy concentration in nationalist areas. 'In other words the IRA was causing greater damage to those it was supposed to be defending.'[143] People in Catholic west Belfast felt treated as outcasts, assumed to be Provo supporters simply because of their religion and location. One Catholic man at the Falls Road session of the Opsahl Commission hearings in February 1993 was dismayed at the 'set' pieces and resort to the time-worn themes of old nationalism. 'All the new thinking is among the Prods . . . All the old thinking is among the Taigs. We're stuck,' he lamented. It was hard not to sympathise with his sense of frustration, after listening to the presentation and discussion that had provoked his outburst and which had argued that the Northern Ireland situation was a 'colonial' problem.[144]

There are still some in Northern Ireland who will reiterate the old orthodoxy of 800 years of British misrule as the root cause of the Troubles and its removal as the ultimate solution. But even Sinn Féin is inching away from this – however belatedly. Too often it transferred the blame elsewhere, and disguised the ethnic nature of Ulster Catholic nationalism. In this the successful transformation of a religion into an all-encompassing culture may yet prove quite an obstacle to harmonious communal relations. Catholics are startled by the continuing anti-popery of political Protestantism, at the insults to their clergy, at the attacks on their churches. Even the newly successful members of the Catholic middle class carry scars of prejudice encountered. Many Ulster Catholics are indeed still 'stuck', still the prisoners of their past, or what they have been told is their past. They are deterred from constructive criticism both of their Church, because their culture is so entwined with it, and of their culture, because it is still under attack. The workings of the eighteenth-century penal laws and seventeenth-century Ulster Plantation have been partly misunderstood and consciously used for partisan purposes. But they did happen. They represented defeat for a way of life and later injustices gave them added value. It is largely among an older generation and committed republicans that such historic bitterness remains strong. But that such respected community leaders as Paddy Doherty in Derry can still view them as dictating the fate of a people, can still speak of 'settlers' and 'natives', that nationalists can still polarise at election time, that even the growing Catholic middle class is still reluctant to give full allegiance to the state testifies to the continuing burden of the past.[145] There is a view that Ulster Protestants are not really interested in Irish history because they will always be depicted as the victimiser, the 'blow-in', the 'planter', and blamed accordingly. Indeed, it is baffling the extent to which they have thus subscribed to nationalist historiography and accepted both the 'settler' category and the predominance of the land issue. The ethnographer Henry Glassie spent the late 1970s studying the rural community of Ballymenone, not far from the Fermanagh/Cavan border. Basic neighbourliness within this mixed (though largely Catholic) small farming community was predominant. Even so he found knowledge of local history confined entirely to Catholics. 'Protestants say they are not interested in history, and Catholics say that is because they cannot be; Irish history is filled with the mistreatment of Catholics'.[146]

Intellectuals in the Republic of Ireland have spent several decades questioning the anti-English underpinnings of their nationalist past – often in a language which shocked the greener nationalists. But the debate, even the shock-therapy, was a necessary prerequisite to the emergence of the now confident Irish state as a player in world politics. The Troubles embarked nationalists on a more painful process of self-examination. It was easier for the republic to exorcise the ghost of the long-absent British. In the north, however, the people held responsible for the land confiscations and persecutions are one's neighbours. Orange marches through Catholic areas still have the potential to open half-healed sores about territoral conquest.

The acceptance of Northern Ireland as home, warts and all, has been a feature of recognisably Protestant writing. It has not been prominent in Catholic writing, though in reality intense local pride (or defensiveness) has been common to both communities. Mary Beckett's short story, *A Belfast Woman,* is a more mature writer's reflections on how working people negotiated their lives in those bleak streets of Belfast. The central character, Mary Harrison, had been intimidated out of her home twice before (1921 and 1935). But when the threatening notice came in 1972, she decided this time to stay. She had been the only Catholic in a Protestant street. Her husband's people had been Protestant; but he had been raised a Catholic in accordance with his dead mother's wishes. It took Mary some time to get used to the Protestant street, where neighbours kept themselves to themselves. They had been good neighbours none the less, and when they in turn were intimidated out and Catholic families moved in, she found the Catholic expectations of constant sociability and open doors hard to take. Her daughter had moved to Canada and wrote of how ashamed she was of those at home. Mary was stung. 'It's not right to put the blame on poor powerless people. The most of us never did anything but stay quiet and put up with things the way they were', and they warned the young ones that went on marches that it would all end in 'shooting and burning and murder'. One day a salesman came trying to sell Venetian blinds. But she told him she liked to see the sunset behind the Divis Mountain. He agreed that if through the smoke and dirt and pollution of Belfast you could still have sunsets like that, 'then there's hope for all of us'.

This pride of place is (and always has been) widespread in Ulster. But it is rarely heard above the political rhetoric, and the mutual mistrust of Protestant and Catholic is too ingrained to be easily overcome. However, it is high time that we 'poor powerless people' stopped blaming everyone else for what has happened and took control of our future by accepting responsibility for our past. For several centuries Catholics have felt no sense of ownership of Ulster and their rejection even of the name 'Ulster' since partition was part and parcel of an extraordinary nihilism and communal fatalism which thankfully appears to be coming to an end. There was little forgiveness in the past for the Unionist takeover and redefinition of the ancient Gaelic territory. The future of the peace process in Northern Ireland may yet be determined by the ability of all to agree on what 'Ulster' means. Until then 'Irishness' and 'Britishness' will remain the fig-leaves disguising the underlying local quarrel. The structures set up under the Good Friday Agreement involve something of a forced marriage of normally antagonistic parties. But it is the first time in history that Catholics and Protestants have been placed on an equal footing, with political structures to match, and the more the militant wings of the two traditions can be tied into constitutional procedures which work, the more they will decline.

I have argued throughout this book that it is a myth to see Ulster Catholics as natural rebels. Even today, their dislike of the Union flag derives not from any particular wish to overthrow the state, but rather from its aggressive (and very widespread) intimidatory usage by loyalists. There is no corresponding attachment to the Irish tricolour, except by republicans. Nor is there any immediate desire for Irish unification, except as an aspiration. A significant number of Catholics (ranging from 16 to 31 per cent in the 1990s) are content with the British connection, and the overwhelming majority support the current constitutional arrangement based on majority consent.[147] This is not to say that dissident republicanism does not have some power to destabilise this fragile consensus. But militant republicanism requires some communal support to flourish, and today the bulk of Catholics want decommissioning of weapons just as much as Protestants do. Moreover, republican violence during the Troubles badly shook nationalist self-confidence. There has been a noticeable return of such confidence since the Good Friday Agreement. There has, unfortunately, been a corresponding decline in confidence among Protestants – conditioned to think that Catholics can only prosper at their expense. A certain amount of republican and nationalist triumphalism is contributing to such Protestant insecurity. But I would suggest that such confidence may be no bad thing, for their new-found 'place in the sun' is firmly located in Northern Ireland. A sense of 'belonging', without the resentment, may yet prove to be the most important legacy of the Good Friday Agreement.

Notes

Short titles for books and abbreviations for journals are used in the notes. Please refer to the Bibliography for full references to the books and the following list of abbreviations for the journals.

Anal. Hib.	*Analecta Hibernica*
Archiv. Hib.	*Archivium Hibernicum*
BL	British Library
BNL	*Belfast News Letter*
Cal. S.P. Ire.	*Calendar of the State Papers relating to Ireland*
Coll. Hib.	*Collectanea Hibernica*
E.H.R.	*English Historical Review*
FDJ	*Faulkner's Dublin Journal*
FJ	*Freeman's Journal*
Hist. Jn.	*Historical Journal*
Ir. Eccles. Rec.	*Irish Ecclesiastical Record*
IFC	Irish Folklore Commission, University College, Dublin
I.H.S.	*Irish Historical Studies*
Jn. Med. Hist.	*Journal of Medieval History*
CKS	Centre for Kentish Studies, Maidstone
NAI	National Archives of Ireland, Dublin
NICH	*Northern Ireland House of Commons Debates*
NLI	National Library of Ireland
NS	*Northern Star*
NUI	National University of Ireland
Proc. R.I.A.	*Proceedings of the Royal Irish Academy*
PRO	Public Record Office, London
PRONI	Public Record Office of Northern Ireland
QUB	Queen's University, Belfast
R.S.A.I. Jn.	*Journal of the Royal Society of Antiquaries of Ireland*
UFTM	Ulster Folk and Transport Museum, Cultra
U.J.A.	*Ulster Journal of Archaeology*

1 FROM CÚ CHULAINN TO CHRISTIANITY

1 Duffy, 'Geographical Perspectives on the Borderlands', in Gillespie and O'Sullivan, eds., *The Borderlands*, 11, shows this to be 'the most extensive drumlin belt in western Europe'. See also Mallory and Hartwell, 'Down in Prehistory', in Proudfoot, ed., *Down. History and Society*, 1–31.

2 De Paor, *The Peoples of Ireland*, 20–21, and O'Kelly, *Early Ireland*, 85–7; Aalen, *Man and Landscape in Ireland*, 52; Mallory and McNeill, *The Archaeology of Ulster from Colonization to Plantation*, 8–10, 20–21.

3 Piggott, *The Druids*, 55; but see Waddell, 'The Question of the Celticization of Ireland', *Emania*, ix, 5–16.

4 O'Rahilly, *Early Irish History and Mythology*, though pioneering and exerting much influence on later writings, many of his findings are now dismissed as speculation.

5 Notably Adamson, *The Identity of Ulster*; Buckley, '"We're Trying to Find Our Identity"', in Tonkin, McDonald and Chapman, eds., *History and Ethnicity*, 183–97.

6 Mallory and McNeill, *Archaeology of Ulster*, 176–9.

7 Mitchell and Ryan, *Reading the Irish Landscape*, 255; McCormick, 'Farming and Food in Medieval Lecale', in Proudfoot, ed., *Down. History and Society*, 34–38.

8 O'Kelly, *Early Ireland*, 305; Aalen, *Man and Landscape*, 86–7.

9 Norman and St Joseph, *The Early Development of Irish Society*, 60, 68–72.

10 Kelly, *A Guide to Early Irish Law*, 36.

11 Kinsella, trans., *The Tain*, 58–60, 157–8; what O'Riordain, *The Gaelic Mind and the Collapse of the Gaelic World*, 117–18, calls 'the Cuchulainn factor': generosity, valour, immortality.

12 O'Rahilly, *Early Irish History and Mythology*, 291–2 (also taken up in one of Moore's melodies).

13 See Gantz, *Early Irish Myths and Sagas*, 15.

14 O'Rahilly, *Early Irish History and Mythology*, 289–90.

15 Livingstone, *Monaghan Story*, 14–16.

16 Moody, Martin and Byrne, eds., *A New History of Ireland*, viii, 13, 15.

17 Kinsella, trans., *The Tain*, 86.

18 Rogers, 'The Folklore of the Black Pig's Dyke', *Ulster Folklife*, iii, 29–36, and see response in *ibid.*, iv, 75.

19 O'Kelly, *Early Ireland*, 322; Livingstone, *Fermanagh Story*, 4; Mallory and McNeill, *Archaeology of Ulster*, 150–153.

20 On the debate over the origins of the 'Irish' language and the whole problem of 'Celticization', see a number of contributions to *Emania*, ix, notably by Waddell (5–16), Raftery (28–32) and Mallory (53–8).

21 For later interpretations of the Celtic past see: Bjersby, *The Interpretation of the Cuchulainn Legend in the Works of W. B. Yeats*; Flower, *The Irish Tradition*; Hill, 'Popery and Protestantism, Civil and Religious Liberty: The

Disputed Lessons of Irish History 1690–1812', *Past and Present*, 118, 96–129; O'Halloran, 'Irish Re-creations of the Gaelic Past: The Challenge of MacPherson's Ossian', *Past and Present*, 124, 69–95; MacCartney, 'The Writing of History in Ireland, 1800–30', *I.H.S.*, x, 347–362; Jeffares, 'Place, Space and Personality and the Irish Writer', O'Driscoll, 'Return to the Hearthstone', both in Carpenter, ed., *Place, Personality and the Irish Writer*, 11–40 and 41–68 respectively; Vance, 'Celts, Carthaginians and Constitutions: Anglo-Irish Literary Relations, 1780–1820', *I.H.S.*, xxii, 219–22; Dunne, 'Haunted by History: Irish Romantic Writing, 1800–50', in Porter and Teich, eds., *Romanticism in National Context*, 68–91; Rafroidi, 'Imagination and Revolution: the Cuchulain Myth', in MacDonagh, Mandle and Travers, eds., *Irish Culture and Nationalism, 1750–1950*, 137–48; Green, *History of the Irish State to 1014*; MacNeill, *Celtic Ireland*; Comyn and Dineen, eds., *The History of Ireland by Geoffrey Keating*, 4 vols.

22 Mallory, ed., *Aspects of the Táin*, 33, 58–62, 111–13; Jackson, *The Oldest Irish Tradition: A Window on the Iron Age*; but see critique of Jackson in Aitchison, 'The Ulster Cycle: Heroic Image and Historical Reality', *Jn. Med. Hist.*, 13, 87–116; also McCone, *Pagan Past and Christian Present in Early Irish Literature*, 4, on the proper context for understanding early Irish literature being the early Christian period, despite assumed oral origins; and Ó Cathasaigh, 'Early Irish Narrative Literature', in McCone and Simms, eds., *Progress in Medieval Irish Studies*, 58. However, Murphy, *Saga and Myth in Ancient Ireland*, 43, accepts 'the general historicity of their background', a similar conclusion to that of Mallory and McNeill, *Archaeology of Ulster*, 167–71.

23 Mallory, ed., *Aspects of the Táin*, 29–30; Green, *History of the Irish State to 1014*, 93–4; O'Grady, *History of Ireland*, 22.

24 Cited Hyde, *A Literary History of Ireland*, 592.

25 O'Grady, *The Heroic Period*, 25.

26 Flanagan in Vaughan, ed., *A New History of Ireland*. v, 515–20. On Cú Chulainn in modern folklore see Murphy, *Tyrone Folk Quest*, 69; Murphy, *At Slieve Gullion's Foot*, 17; Murphy, *Ulster Folk of Field and Fireside*, 83–4, 151–2; Murphy, *Rathlin: Island of Blood and Enchantment*, 6, 174–5; Livingstone, *Monaghan Story*, 10–11; Livingstone, *Fermanagh Story*, 1–3.

27 See, however, Sharpe, 'St Patrick and the See of Armagh', *Cambridge Medieval Celtic Studies*, 4, 33–59 on the debate surrounding Patrick's association with Armagh; also Binchy's seminal study, 'Patrick and his Biographers, Ancient and Modern', *Stud. Hib.*, ii (1962), 7–173.

28 Kelly, *Early Irish Law*, 60; Etchingham, 'Early Medieval Irish History', in McCone and Simms, eds., *Progress in Medieval Irish Studies*, 127; Hanson, *Saint Patrick*.

29 Gerald of Wales, *The History and Topography of Ireland*, translated by O'Meara, 115–16.

30 Linenhall Lib., NI Pol. Coll., P. 1740, *The Rise of Papal Power in Ireland* (London and Cork, 1983), P. 3479; Griffin, *Anglican and Irish*; Linenhall Lib., Joy MSS, 8, 113–35; Ussher, *An Epistle Written by the Rev. James*

Ussher, Bishop of Meath, Concerning the Religion Anciently Professed by the Irish and Scottish (Dublin, 1631); Mason, *The Testimony of St Patrick against the False Pretensions of Rome to Primitive Antiquity in Ireland*; Hamilton, *Letters Concerning the Northern Coast of the County of Antrim*, 50–70. For an excellent survey of the eighteenth-century debate on the nature of the early Irish church see Hill, 'Popery and Protestantism', 96–129.

31 See good discussion in Corish, *The Irish Catholic Experience, A Historical Survey*, 8–10, also his 'The Early Irish Church and the Western Patriarchate', in Ní Chatháin and Richter, eds., *Ireland und Europa, die Kirche in Frühmittelalter*, 9–15; Richter, *Medieval Ireland*, 62; Hanson, *Saint Patrick*, 203.

32 For the ongoing debate on the nature of early Irish ecclesiastical settlements see Etchingham, 'Early Medieval Irish History', 137–8; Etchingham, 'The Implications of Paruchia', *Ériu*, xliv, 139–62.

33 For the survival of such claims by the leading Gaelic families, see Ó Doibhlin, 'The Deanery of Tulach Óg', *Seanchas Ard Mhacha*, vi, no. 1, 141–82; Martin, 'Derry in 1590: a Catholic demonstration', *Clogher Record*, vi, no. 3, 597–602; Faulkner, 'The Right of Patronage of the Maguires of Tempo', *Clogher Record*, ix, no. 2, 167–86. This proprietorial outlook by the coarbs and erenachs (as the successors were called) extended to the relics and religious artefacts; see, for e.g., IFC, MS 1215/44–76, the bell of Drumragh in Tyrone, said to have been in the keeping of the McEnhill (MacConchoille) family for eleven hundred years.

34 Ryan, *The Monastic Institute*, 49–50.

35 See Binchy, 'A Pre-Christian Survival in Medieval Irish Hagiography', in Whitelock, McKitterick and Dumville, eds., *Ireland in Early Medieval Europe*, 165–178.

36 Ó Corráin, 'Nationality and Kingship in Pre-Norman Ireland', in Moody, ed., *Nationality and the Pursuit of National Independence*, 13–19.

37 Binchy, 'Opening Address', Mac Niocaill, 'Christian Influences in Early Irish law', and Ó Corráin, 'Irish Law and Canon Law', all in Ní Chatháin and Richter, eds., *Irland und Europa*, 4, 151–6 and 157–66; all three see native traditions and laws as transforming Irish Christianity rather than the reverse. In the same collection, Ó Cathasaigh, 'Pagan Survivals: The Evidence of Early Irish Narrative', 291–307, examines the heated controversy over the contribution of oral native traditions to the early church. See also McCone and Simms, eds., *Progress in Medieval Irish Studies*, 62, 124–6.

38 Flower, *The Irish Tradition*, 1–23 and 74–5; the *Annals of Ulster* are traditionally seen to have originated with Colum Cille's community in Iona, then continued probably at Armagh and Clonard, see Richter, *Medieval Ireland*, 82–4. See also Hamlin, 'The Early Church in County Down to the Twelfth Century', in Proudfoot, ed., *Down. History and Society*, 47–70.

39 Glassie, *Irish Folk History*, 32; for the strength of local tradition on Colum Cille, see also Murphy, *Rathlin*, 3; O'Laverty, *An Historical Account of the Diocese of Down and Connor, Ancient and Modern*, 5 vols., ii, 11–20; IFC, MS 102/25–30, 42–6; UFTM, Field Recording, R80.55, and Transcript 7/

28–9, Tyrone traditions of Colum Cille; also Lacy's accessible *Colum Cille and the Columban Tradition.*

40 IFC, MS 1364/36, 120/55–6, and UFTM, R85.10, traditions of Colum Cille's association with curses; O'Laverty, *Down and Connor*, i, 126; Gillespie, *Devoted People*, 138.

41 See Corish, *The Christian Mission*, 4–5. Colum Cille is frequently seen as Ireland's first exile; see Ó Laoghaire, 'Irish Spirituality', in Ní Chatháin and Richter, eds., *Irland und Europa*, 73–5, on how this notion of wrenching from country appeared in very early writings. Also de Paor, *Peoples*, 62. See Livingstone, *Fermanagh*, 8–19, on the royal lineages of the early saints and the rich folklore attaching to them.

42 Hennessy, ed., *Annals of Ulster*, 4 vols., i, 377.

43 Byrne, 'Tribes and Tribalism in Early Ireland', *Ériu*, xxii, 128–66, 160–66; though see McCone's attack on the idea of 'cosy' tiny kingdoms before the Viking raids in *Pagan Past and Christian Present*, 8ff.

44 *Annals of Ulster*, i, 323. Livingstone, *Monaghan Story*, 38–9, gives good account of local consequences of these developments.

45 *Annals of Ulster*, i, 433, see also entries for 899 and 917.

46 de Paor, *Peoples*, 75; Simms, *From Kings to Warlords*, 10–11; though see Etchingham in McCone and Simms, eds., in *Progress in Medieval Studies*, 141.

47 Gillespie and O'Sullivan, eds., *The Borderlands*, 33; Byrne, 'Tribes and Tribalism', 156.

48 See for e.g. Livingstone, *Fermanagh Story*, 23–4; Ó Corráin, *Ireland before the Normans*, 15.

49 Cited Byrne, in Cosgrave, ed., *New History of Ireland*, ii, 39; also Ó Corráin, *Ireland before the Normans*, 172.

50 Corish, *Christian Mission*, 86–7; Etchingham, 'The Early Irish Church', 99–118.

51 Hughes, 'Sanctity and Secularism in the Early Irish Church', in Dumville, ed., *Kathleen Hughes*, 21–37.

52 Hughes, *The Church in Early Irish Society*, ch. 20.

53 Doherty, 'The Use of Relics in Early Ireland', in Ní Chatháin and Richter, eds., *Irland und Europa*, 95: Livingstone, *Monaghan Story*, 24–8; O'Laverty, *Down and Connor*, i, 248–53; *Fermanagh Herald*, 9 September 1981 (Holy Wells).

54 Glassie, *Irish Folk History*, 21.

55 Philip Dixon Hardy, *The Holy Wells of Ireland*, iv; Ó Muirgheasa, 'The Holy Wells of Donegal', *Béaloideas*, vi, 141–62; Doherty, 'The Use of Relics in Early Ireland', 89–101. O'Laverty finds holy wells in almost every townland, *Down and Connor*, iii, 419–20, 443; also IFC, MS 102/62–31, for holy bells and their traditional custodians.

2 GAELIC ULSTER: LAND, LORDSHIP AND PEOPLE

1 There is some confusion over respective usage of the terms Anglo-Norman or Anglo-Irish during the two centuries following the 'invasion'. The practice here is that suggested by F. X. Martin: Anglo-Norman for the period up to 1216, Anglo-Irish thereafter (Cosgrove, ed., *New History of Ireland*, ii, li–liii). Medieval historians now tend to play down the 'invasion' as some kind of turning point, see Cosgrove, 'The Writing of Irish Medieval History', *I.H.S*, xxvii, 97–111. For a comprehensive survey see McNeill, *Anglo-Norman Ulster*, also his chapter in Brady, O'Dowd and Walker, eds., *Ulster: An Illustrated History*, 44–76.

2 Though see Seán Duffy's argument for a Cumbrian origin of John de Courcy, 'The First Ulster Plantation: John de Courcy and the Men of Cumbria', in Barry, Frame and Simms, eds., *Colony and Frontier in Medieval Ireland*, 1–27.

3 See e.g. in the case of Monaghan – Livingstone, *Monaghan Story*, 42–4 – how the MacMahons established their ascendancy under the mantle of the Anglo-Normans; also Simms, 'The O'Hanlons, the O'Neills and the Anglo-Normans in Thirteenth-century Armagh', *Seanchas Ard Mhacha*, ix, 70–94; idem, 'The O'Reillys and the Kingdom of East Breifne', *Breifne*, vi, 305–19; idem, 'The Medieval Kingdom of Loch Erne', *Clogher Record*, ix, 126–41.

4 Frame, *Colonial Ireland, 1169–1369*, 26–32.

5 *The Ancient and Noble Family of the Savages of the Ards*, compiled by G.F.A., 121–3, 154–5, 161; Davies, 'A Discovery of the True Causes Why Ireland was Never Entirely Subdued', in Morley, ed., *Ireland under Elizabeth and James I*, i, 304.

6 Frame, *English Lordship in Ireland 1318–1361*, 137; Simms, 'Nomadry in Medieval Ireland: the Origins of the Creaght or *Caoraigheacht*', *Peritia*, v, 383.

7 Aalen, *Man and Landscape*, 113; Simms, '"The King's Friend": O'Neill, the Crown and the Earldom of Ulster', in Lydon, ed., *England and Ireland in the Later Middle Ages*, 214–36.

8 See the discussion of Domnail O'Neill's famous 'Remonstrance' to the Pope in *c.*1317 by Phillips, 'The Irish Remonstrance of 1317: An International Perspective' *I.H.S*, xxvii, 112–29. Among other things, this complained that the English had abused the grant of Ireland in the papal bull *Laudabiliter*. But the complaint was against the English colonists, not the king. Simms, 'Gaelic Lordships in Ulster in the Later Middle Ages', 545, shows that Aedh O'Donnell had little sympathy with O'Neill's call for Irish unity to expel the English and indeed that such unity was illusory. See also Duffy, *Ireland in the Middle Ages*, 138.

9 Andrews, 'Geography and Government in Elizabethan Ireland', in Stephens and Glasscock, eds., *Irish Geographical Studies*, 186; Davies, 'A Discovery', in Morley, ed., *Ireland Under Elizabeth and James I*, i, 268, 288; Frame, *English Lordship in Ireland*, 74–84.

10 Brady *et al.*, eds., *Ulster*, 63–4.

11 Hore, ed., 'Marshal Bagenal's Description of Ulster, Anno 1596', *U.J.A.*, 1st ser., ii, 153–4; Davies, 'A Discovery', in Morley, ed., *Ireland under Elizabeth and James I*, i, 304. Anglo-Irish interest in the area was sustained through landed acquisitions of the descendants of Janice Dartas, which passed through Alice Fitzeustace to the Great Earl of Kildare. See Curtis, 'Janice Dartas', *R.S.A.I. Jn.*, lxiii, 182–205.

12 Gillespie, *Colonial Ulster*, 17.

13 Simms, 'Gaelic Lordships in Ulster', 277–8.

14 McCall, 'The Gaelic Background to the Settlement of Antrim and Down, 1580–1641', 14, on the importance of their Gaelic culture; Walsh, *Leabhar Chlainne Suibhne*, xvii–x.

15 See Simms, 'Gaelic Warfare', in Bartlett and Jeffery, eds., *A Military History of Ireland*, 108–10.

16 Moody, Martin and Byrne, eds., *A New History of Ireland*, iii, *Early Modern Ireland, 1534–1691* (Oxford, 1978), 522; Hayes-McCoy, *Scots Mercenary Forces in Ireland*, 27–35; Cunningham and Gillespie, 'The East Ulster Bardic Family of Ó Gnímh', *Éigse*, xx, 106–14; Walsh, *Leabhar Chlainne Suibhne*, especially i–xliv.

17 Brady, 'The Failure of Tudor Reform', in Brady, O'Dowd and Walker, eds., *Ulster*, 90.

18 Hayes-McCoy, *Scots Mercenary Forces in Ireland*, 146; Simms, *From Kings to Warlords*, 124; Morgan, 'The End of Gaelic Ulster', *I.H.S.*, xxvi, 16–17.

19 Cosgrove, ed., *New History of Ireland*: ii, 332; Simms, 'Nomadry in Medieval Ireland', 379–91.

20 Livingstone, *Monaghan Story*, 44.

21 Spenser, *A View of the State of Ireland* [1596], in Ware, ed., *Ancient Irish Histories*, i, 23.

22 Davies, 'A Discovery', in Morley, ed., *Ireland Under Elizabeth and James I*, i, 374.

23 Mahaffy, 'Two Early Tours in Ireland', *Hermathena*, xl (1914), 9. There is another translation in *The Medieval Pilgrimage to St Patrick's Purgatory: Lough Derg and the European Tradition*, ed. by M. Haren and Y. de Pontfarcy (Enniskillen, 1988).

24 Patterson, 'Housing and House Types in County Armagh', *Ulster Folklife*, vi, 9–10; Robinson, 'Vernacular Housing in Ulster in the Seventeenth Century', *Ulster Folklife*, xxv, 1–28. See also O'Danachair, 'Representations of Houses in Some Irish Maps of 1600', in Jenkins, ed., *Studies in Folk Life. Essays in honour of Iorwerth C. Peate*, 101–2; Evans, 'The Ulster Farmhouse: A Comparative Study', *Ulster Folklife*, iii, 14–18; Simms, ' "Warfare" in the Medieval Gaelic Lordships', *Irish Sword*, xii, 102–8.

25 Simms, 'Guesting and Feasting in Gaelic Ireland', *R.S.A.I. Jn.*, 108, 91; idem, 'Gaelic Lordships in Ulster', 699–700; Bergin, *Irish Bardic Poetry*, 129–32, 271–3, good poem on this from Maguire's poet; Livingstone, *Fermanagh*, 33–4.

26 Cited Cullen, *Life in Ireland*, 46.

27 See Quinn's summary of the elements of sixteenth-century English cultural nationalism in *The Elizabethans and the Irish*, 7–11, 62–3.

28 *Cal. S. P. Ire.*, 1598, 440; also Patterson, 'Housing and Housing Types in County Armagh', 9.

29 Cosgrove, ed., *New History of Ireland*, ii, 329–30; Knott, ed., *The Bardic Poems of Tadhg Dall Ó Huiginn*, I, li.

30 Hore, 'Bagenal's Description of Ulster', 139; also Bergin, *Irish Bardic Poetry*, 129–32, 271–3 for poem by Maguire's poet, Ó hEódhasa, 1595, in celebration of the gathering of Maguire's hosts.

31 Bergin, *Irish Bardic Poetry*, 9–10, 231–2; Morgan, 'End of Gaelic Ulster', 23; Simms, 'Gaelic Lordships in Ulster', 568.

32 Spenser, *A View of the State of Ireland*, i, 86–8.

33 Hore, 'Bagenal's Description of Ulster', 152; Morgan, 'The End of Gaelic Ulster', 23–4.

34 Quoted Hore, 'Bagenal's Description of Ulster', 139; Livingstone, *Monaghan*, 59.

35 McErlean, 'The Irish Townland System of Landscape Organisation', in Reeves-Smyth and Hammond, eds., *Landscape and Archaeology in Ireland*, 315–39; Graham, 'Rural Society in Connacht', 195–9.

36 Simms, 'Nomadry in Medieval Ireland', 379.

37 See e.g. McCourt, 'Surviving Openfield in County Londonderry', *Ulster Folklife*, iv, 17–28.

38 Simms, 'Nomadry in Medieval Ireland', 379–91; Story, *A True and Impartial History*, 15; Graham, 'Rural Society in Connacht', 199. See also Quinn, *Elizabethans and the Irish*, 125–6; Spenser, *A View of the State of Ireland*, i, 247, 258–9; and *A Historie of Ireland Written in the Yeare 1571 by Edmund Campion*, in Ware, ed., *Ancient Irish Histories*, i, 19, for Tudor criticism of such practices.

39 Walsh, *Leabhar Chlainne Suibhne*, 51, 73.

40 Hayes-McCoy, 'The Making of an O'Neill', *U.J.A.*, xxxiii, 89; see modern-day photographs of the site in Mallory and McNeill, *Archaeology of Ulster*, 239–40, and Donnelly, *Living Places*, 74.

41 Information on the inauguration ceremonies is taken largely from Simms, *Kings to Warlords*, 21–40 (the fullest account); idem, 'Gaelic Lordships in Ulster', 4–35; Livingstone, *Monaghan Story*, 46–7; idem, *Fermanagh Story*, 479; also Nicholls, *Gaelic and Gaelicised Society*, 28–30; Watt, in Cosgrove, ed., *New History of Ireland*, ii, 320–22; Morgan, *Tyrone's Rebellion*, 85–6.

42 Murphy, *Ulster Folk*, 7.

43 Nicholls, *Gaelic and Gaelicised Ireland*, 23, thinks the term obsolete by the twelfth century in its original sense as a political unit, though clearly still being used as a notional measurement in north-east Ulster in the early seventeenth century (see Gillespie, *Colonial Ulster*, 18–19).

44 Glancy, 'The Primates and the Church Lands of Armagh', *Seanchas Ard Mhacha*, v, no. 2, 375; for Gaelic landholding generally see O'Dowd, 'Gaelic

Economy and Society', in Brady and Gillespie, eds., *Natives and Newcomers*, 125–7; Nicholls, 'Gaelic Society and Economy in the High Middle Ages', in Cosgrove, ed., *New History of Ireland*, ii, 425–6, 430–32.

45 Davies, 'A Discovery', in Morley, ed., *Ireland under Elizabeth and James I*, i, 372 (also 291).

46 Butler, 'Irish Land Tenures: Celtic and Foreign', *Studies*, xiii (1924), 530.

47 Spenser, *A View of the State of Ireland*, i, 227–8; Livingstone, *Fermanagh Story*, 59; Graham, 'Rural Society', 200, on local definitions of 'gentleman'; Watt in Cosgrove, ed., *New History of Ireland*, ii, 329; Gillespie, *Colonial Ulster*, 113–20.

48 Nicholls, *Gaelic and Gaelicised Ireland*, 11; Simms, 'Gaelic Lordships in Ulster': Toirdhelbhach O'Donnell had eighteen sons by ten women, late fourteenth to early fifteenth centuries (p. 563), and land hunger may have contributed to the disputes in families with a large number of sons (p. 492).

49 Simms, *From Kings to Warlords*, 31.

50 Duffy, 'Geographical Perspectives on the Borderlands', 7; Hore, 'Bagenal's Description of Ulster', 149–50; Ó Dufaigh, 'The Mac Cathmhaoils of Clogher', *Clogher Rec.*, ii, 44–45.

51 O'Dowd, 'Gaelic Economy and Society', 141; Simms, *From Kings to Warlords*, 55, 58–9.

52 McCourt, 'Surviving Openfield in County Londonderry', *Ulster Folklife*, iv, 19–28; Graham, 'Rural Society', 198–9; see also Currie, 'Field Patterns in County Derry', *Ulster Folklife*, xxix, 70–80.

53 Andrews, *Plantation Acres*, 11; Simms, *From Kings to Warlords*, 39–40; Hore, 'Bagenal's Description of Ulster', 362, also 370. Hugh Maguire was found to have used mainly mercenaries in the recent rebellion, leaving most of the freeholders in Fermanagh unscathed.

54 Simms, *From Kings to Warlords*, 32; the O'Friels of Kilmacrenan fulfilled the same role for the MacSweeneys (Walsh, *Leabhar Chlainne Suibhne*, 51).

55 Hore, 'Bagenal's Description of Ulster', 363.

56 Andrews, *Plantation Acres*, 13.

57 Quoted in Simms, *From Kings to Warlords*, 2.

58 Gillespie, *Colonial Ulster*, 17–20; Duffy, 'Patterns of Landownership in Gaelic Monaghan in the Late Sixteenth Century', *Clogher Rec.*, x, 314–17, when the modern county of Monaghan was created in 1585, the five baronies into which it was divided were the traditional territories of the various branches of the MacMahons. Andrews, 'Geography and Government in Elizabethan Ireland', 178–91, shows how they were unwilling to invest in proper surveys and simply accepted old territorial units. O'Laverty, *Down and Connor*, ii, 450–61: certain ancient standing stones (this at Mallusk) still marked territorial boundaries till the early nineteenth century, while certain modern names derive from old family territorial units.

59 Aalen, *Man and Landscape*, 138; also McCoy, *Scots Mercenary Forces in Ireland*, 257.

60 Glancy, 'The Primates and the Church Lands of Armagh', 375.

61 Duffy, 'Geographical Perspective', 146, n. 16.

62 Canny, 'Hugh O'Neill, Earl of Tyrone, and the Changing Face of Gaelic Ulster', *Stud. Hib.*, x, 27–32.

63 Spenser, *A View of the State of Ireland*, i, 16.

64 O'Dowd, 'Gaelic Economy and Society', 125–6.

65 Simms, 'Late Medieval Donegal', in Nolan, Ronayne and Donlevy, eds., *Donegal*, 191–3; Hamilton, *Elizabethan Ulster*, 152–3; Canny, 'Hugh O'Neill', 13–14; Davies, 'A Discovery', in Morley, ed., *Ireland Under Elizabeth and James I*, i, 294–5; McAfee, 'The Population of Ulster, 1630–1841: Evidence from mid-Ulster', 73–4.

66 See Alexander, ed., 'The O'Kane Papers', *Anal. Hib.*, xii, 94–6: in the deanery of Derry Donald O'Cahan was rector of four different churches, Dermot O'Cahan erenach of five and p. 101 shows extraordinary complexity of who had what rights on church lands; Ó Doibhlin, 'The Deanery of Tulach Óg', *Seanchas Ard Mhacha*, vi, 141–182, notably 157–9, identifying the erenach families, the O'Loughrans, O'Conlons, McGirrs, O'Cullens, Mac Kathmaylls (Mac Cawell, McCall or Campbell) in this future Barony of Dungannon; Simms, 'Frontiers in the Irish Church – Regional and Cultural', in Frame *et al.*, eds., *Colony and Frontier in Medieval Ireland*, 177–200 *passim*.

67 Mooney, *The Church in Gaelic Ireland*, 10–15; a detailed case history in Glancy, 'The Primates and the Church Lands of Armagh', 370–96; Simms, 'The Archbishops of Armagh and the O'Neills, 1347–1471', *I.H.S*, xix, 38–55.

68 Reeves, ed., *Acts of Archbishop Colton in his Metropolitan Visitation of the Diocese of Derry*, 5n. Ó Doibhlin, 'Deanery of Tulach Óg', 167–75, reproducing findings of the 1609 and 1620 Inquisitions.

69 Reeves, ed., *Acts of Archbishop Colton*, particularly 5–7, 10, 12, 16, 19–21; Hamilton, *Elizabethan Ulster*, 152–3; Canny, 'Hugh O'Neill', 13–14; Robinson, 'Settlement in Tyrone', 61. See excellent map in Simms, 'Frontiers in the Irish Church', 179.

70 See e.g. McCall, 'The Gaelic Background to the Settlement of Antrim and Down', 69 and 81; Gwynn and Hadcock, eds., *Medieval Religious Houses. Ireland*, 268–74; Ó Doibhlin, 'Deanery of Tulach Óg', 179–82. See Morley, ed., *Ireland Under Elizabeth and James I*, i, 364–8, for Davies' survey of Church lands, 1607.

71 Harris, *The Ancient and Present State of the County of Down*, 35.

72 Walsh, ed., *Leabhar Chlainne Suibhne*, 39 – the MacSweeneys had been inaugurated by Colum Cille's successors.

73 Binchy, cited in Nicholls, *Gaelic and Gaelicised Society*, 44; but see Simms' critique of this view in 'The Contents of Later Commentaries on the Brehon Law Tracts', in *Ériu*, xlix, 23–40.

74 Morley, ed., *Ireland Under Elizabeth and James I*, i, 368–71.

75 For recent overviews of the debate see McCone and Simms, eds., *Progress in Medieval Irish Studies*, 211–15; also Caball, *Poets and Politics; Reaction and Continuity in Irish Poetry, 1558–1625*, 7–12.

76 Cunningham and Gillespie, 'The East Ulster Bardic Family of Ó Gnímh', *Éigse*, xx, 106–14; also Cunningham, 'Native Culture and Political Change

in Ireland, 1580–1640', in Brady and Gillespie, eds., *Natives and Newcomers*, 148–70.

77 Simms, *From Kings to Warlords*, 16–17; idem, 'Bards and Barons: the Anglo-Irish Aristocracy and Native Culture', in Bartlett and Mackay, eds., *Medieval Frontier Societies*, 188–94; Stalley, 'From the Twelfth Century to the Reformation', in de Breffny, ed., *The Irish World*, 97; O'Riordain, *Gaelic Mind*, particularly pp. 3–8, 22–3, 37, 131–3 (though see Ó Buachalla's critique of O'Riordain in 'Poetry and Politics in Early Modern Ireland', *Eighteenth-Century Ireland*, vii, 149–75.

78 Spenser, *View of the State of Ireland*, i, 62–63; but see Simms, 'Bardic Poetry as a Historical Source', in Dunne, ed., *The Writer as Witness*, 58–75. I am deeply grateful to Dr Simms for her advice on these issues.

79 Though see Ó Cuív, in Moody *et al.*, eds., *New History of Ireland*, iii, 537. Popular folk tales seem to have consisted of the ageless romantic tale and cast doubt on the average person's interest in high politics.

80 Ó Gnímh, hereditary poet to the Magennisses, quoted by Bergin, *Bardic Poetry*, 120.

81 Simms, 'Propaganda Use of the Táin in the Later Middle Ages', *Celtica*, xv, 142–9; idem, 'Gaelic Lordships in Ulster in the Later Middle Ages', 711–20.

82 Campion, *Historie of Ireland*, i, 19. On the poets' claims to druidic antecedents see Simms, 'Literacy and the Irish Bards', in Pryce, ed., *Literacy in Medieval Celtic Societies*, 250.

83 Quinn, *The Elizabethans and the Irish*, 44; Brian Ó Cuív, 'The Irish Language in the Early Modern Period', in Moody *et al.*, eds., *New History of Ireland*, iii, 514.

84 Cunningham, 'Native Culture and Political Change', 152; O'Riordan, *Gaelic Mind*, 120–22, 141; Breatnach, 'Metamorphosis 1603: Dán le hEochaidh Ó hEódhasa', *Éigse*, xvii, 171.

85 Simms, 'The O'Hanlons, the O'Neills and the Anglo-Normans', op. cit.; Bergin, *Bardic Poetry*, 120–23, Ó Gnímh's poetry; Simms, 'Propaganda Use of the Táin', 144–6.

86 Martin, in Cosgrove, ed., *New History of Ireland*, ii, l.

87 Morgan, 'The End of Gaelic Ulster', 30; Simms, 'Gaelic Lordships in Ulster', 711, also shows how successive generations of O'Neills could make a distinction between the crown and the Anglo-Irish.

88 Brady, 'Sixteenth-century Ulster and the Failure of Tudor Reform', in Brady *et al.*, *Ulster*, 77–103; O'Dowd, 'Gaelic Economy and Society', 132–4; idem, *Power, Politics and Land*, 32–5, 50–53.

89 Davies, 'A Discovery', in Morley, ed., *Ireland Under Elizabeth and James I*, i, 259–75; Hamilton, *Elizabethan Ulster*, 151; and see O'Dowd, 'Gaelic Economy and Society', 144–5, on the lower sectors of Gaelic society who prospered from the process. Also Canny, *Reformation to Restoration*, 118–19. However, there was only a limited extension of the machinery of English law, and it was not introduced into the main lordships of Tyrone and Tyrconnell until after their defeat in 1603.

90 McCarthy, 'Ulster Office, 1552–1800', 21–3.

91 See O'Sullivan, 'The March of South-East Ulster in the Fifteenth and Sixteenth centuries', in Gillespie and O'Sullivan, eds., *The Borderlands*, 64.

92 As suggested by Canny, 'Hugh O'Neill, Earl of Tyrone, and the Changing Face of Gaelic Ulster', *Stud. Hib.*, lx, 33.

93 See e.g. Morgan, 'The Colonial Venture of Sir Thomas Smith in Ulster, 1571–1575', *Hist. Jn.*, xxviii, 261–78.

94 Davies, 'A Discovery', in Morley, ed., *Ireland under Elizabeth and James I*, i, 335.

95 For an excellent account of the lead-in, see Morgan, *Tyrone's Rebellion*, particularly 139–66.

96 Nicholls, in Cosgrove, ed., *New History of Ireland*, ii, 426–7, sees this happening by the sixteenth century.

97 See e.g. Chart, 'The Break-up of the Estate of Con O'Neill, Castlereagh, County Down', *Proc. R.I.A.*, xlviii, sect. C, 119–45.

98 See Canny, 'The Treaty of Mellifont and the Re-organisation of Ulster, 1603', *Irish Sword*, ix, 249–62.

99 Davies, 'Letter to Robert, Earl of Salisbury', in Morley, ed., *Ireland Under Elizabeth and James I*, i, 352.

100 Falls, *The Birth of Ulster*, 111–14, 148.

101 Davies, 'Letter to . . . Salisbury', in Morley, ed., *Ireland under Elizabeth and James I*, i, 359–60; Falls, *The Birth of Ulster*, 145.

102 Simms, ' "Warfare" in Medieval Gaelic Lordships', *Irish Sword*, xii, 98ff.

103 See G. Mac Niocaill, 'The Contact of Irish and Common Law', *N. Ireland Legal Quarterly*, 23 (1972), 16–23. Campion writing in 1571 recounts the tale of a northern 'gentleman' attending confession with a travelling monk, asked if he committed homicide, said he never knew it was such before – Campion, *Historie*, 21–2; and when, under Lord Deputy Fitzwilliam's term of office (1571–5), a sheriff was to be sent to the new county of Fermanagh, Maguire asked to know beforehand his 'eric' or price of his head, 'that if my people cut it off I may cut the ericke upon the country', Davies, 'A Discovery', in Morley, ed., *Ireland Under Elizabeth and James I*, i, 290.

104 Simms, 'Gaelic Lordships in Ulster in the Later Middle Ages', 801, points out that even in the Middle Ages it was not the chieftains (who adapted to new conditions after the Anglo-Norman invasion) who were backward-looking, but the poets and preservers of tradition. See also O'Riordan, *Gaelic Mind*, 117–18, on the way Gaelic society could accommodate even those who had been militarily victorious, but not the increasing presence of such an expansionist and culturally different social grouping.

3 RELIGION IN ULSTER BEFORE THE REFORMATION

1 Moryson, *Itinerary*, ii, 274–5.

2 Canny, in Foster, ed., *Illustrated History of Ireland*, 128.

3 The point is that the church in Irish areas remained integrated into the

traditional kinship structure (see Watt, in Cosgrove, ed., *New History of Ireland*, ii, 335).

4 Costello, *De Annatis Hiberniae*, xix, Primate Octavian writing in 1508.

5 Simms, *Kings to Warlords*, 27–8.

6 Bruford, *Gaelic Folktales and Medieval Romances*, 24–6.

7 Reeves, ed., *Acts of Archbishop Colton*; also Corish, 'Two Reports on the Catholic Church in Ireland in the Early Seventeenth Century', *Stud. Hib.*, xxii, 141.

8 Mahaffy, ed., 'Two Early Tours in Ireland', *Hermathena*, xl, 13; Monter, *Ritual, Myth and Magic in Early Modern Europe*, 6; Watt, 'The Papacy and Ireland in the Fifteenth Century', in Dobson, ed., *The Church, Politics and Patronage*, 133–43. And yet under Henry VIII senior ecclesiastics in Gaelic areas accepted the early states of the Reformation, see Canny, *Reformation to Restoration*, 53–4.

9 Bradshaw, *The Dissolution of the Religious Orders in Ireland under Henry VIII*, 37; Costello, *De Annatis*, xviii–xix.

10 Mahaffy, ed., 'Two Early Tours', 10, 13; Watt, *Church in Medieval Ireland*, 193.

11 See e.g. account of Culdees in Armagh, Cathaldus Giblin, 'The Processus Datariae and the Appointment of Irish Bishops in the Seventeenth Century', in Franciscan Fathers, eds., *Father Luke Wadding*, 540–41. Murray, 'The History of the Parish of Creggan in the 17th and 18th Centuries', *Louth Arch. Soc. Jn.*, viii, no. 2, 134. In Creggan parish, South Armagh, the name Killyloughran (O'Loughran's church) recalls the fifteenth-century prior of the Armagh Culdees, John O'Loughran.

12 Campion, *Historie of Ireland*, i, 19.

13 Mhág Craith, *Dán na mBráthar Mionúr*, ii, poem no. 27, pp. 58–67, verse 66; O'Dwyer, *Mary*, 187; O'Duffy, *The Apostasy of Myler Magrath, Archbishop of Cashel*, 5 – this translation from Irish has him bartering his faith for flesh on Fridays.

14 Murray, 'The History of the Parish of Creggan', 131–2. Local folklore in Donegal, for example, is rich in stories and folk memory of their haunts and refuges, see Mooney, *Franciscan Donegal*, 13, 17–18, 33; also Millett, *The Irish Franciscans 1651–1665*, 74.

15 Costello, *De Annatis Hiberniae*, 49–50; Gwynn and Hadcock, eds., *Medieval Religious Houses*, 254; Walsh, *Leabhar Chlainne Suibhne*, 69: in 1516 Maolmhuire and Maire MacSweeney built a Carmelite monastery at Rathmullan because one of his sons was buried in the church there.

16 Murray, 'The History of the Parish of Creggan', 130–31; Murray and Gwynn, eds., 'Archbishop Cromer's Register', *Louth Arch. Soc. Jn.*, viii, 44, 179, in the early sixteenth century a typical penance is for the offender to be obliged to perambulate the cemetery in white linens on successive Sundays; Walsh, *Leabhar Chlainne Suibhne*, lvii.

17 John Derricke, *The Image of Irelande*, 54, plates III, IV.

18 Gwynn and Hadcock, eds., *Medieval Religious Houses*, 10, 240–47, 263–6.

19 Canny, 'Why the Reformation Failed in Ireland: *une question mal posée*', *Jn. Eccles. Hist.*, xxx, 423–50; Bottigheimer, 'The Failure of the Reformation in Ireland: *une question bien posée*', ibid., xxxvi, 196–207; the fullest account of the Reformation in Ireland is Ford, *The Protestant Reformation in Ireland, 1590–1641*.

20 Cameron, *The European Reformation*, 12–19.

21 Bergin, *Irish Bardic Poetry*, 93–100, 254–7, a good thirteenth-century example of this; O'Dwyer, *Mary*, 91, 100, 106, 289; Simms, 'Frontiers in the Irish Church', 200. In the Middle Ages the saints were seen in same light as the king or overlord, honour-bound to avenge his vassals; Giraldus Cambrensis also had noted the peculiar vengefulness of the Irish saints.

22 Quoted in Mooney, 'The Irish Church in the Sixteenth Century', *Ir. Eccles. Rec.*, xcix, 111; the foregoing from 'A Discourse for the Reformation of Ireland [1583]', in Brewer and Bullen, eds., *Calendar of the Carew Manuscripts Preserved in the Archiepiscopal Library at Lambeth*, ii, 1575–1588, 367.

23 Cited Simms, 'Gaelic Lordships in Ulster', 477; O'Reilly, 'Remarks on Certain Passages in Capt. Cuellar's Narrative of His Adventures in Ireland . . . 1588–89', *Proc. R.I.A.*, iii, 211 and 201; Costello, *De Annatis*, xiv, xviii.

24 'Archbishop Cromer's Register', *Louth Arch. Soc. Jn.*, ix, 41; Simms, 'Frontiers in the Irish Church', 197; Canny, ed., 'Rowland White's "The Dysorders of the Irishery, 1571"', *Stud. Hib.*, xix, 155.

25 *Cal. S.P.I.*, 1611–14, 430.

26 Costello, *De Annatis*, xxi, 46–7; 'Archbishop Cromer's Register', *Louth Arch. Soc. Jn.*, viii, 44, 322.

27 Campion, *Historie of Ireland*, i, 23.

28 Watt, 'The Papacy and Ireland in the Fifteenth Century', 142–3; Corish, *Irish Catholic Experience*, 97–8.

29 Reeves, *Acts of Archbishop Colton*, 12n, 16n.

30 Watt, 'The Papacy and Ireland in the Fifteenth Century', 136–7; Simms, 'Gaelic Lordships', 485–90.

31 Simms, 'Frontiers in the Irish Church', 200; idem, 'Women in Gaelic Society', in MacCurtain and O'Dowd, eds., *Women in Early Modern Ireland*, 32–42.

32 Shirley, ed., *Original Letters and Papers in Illustration of the History of the Church in Ireland*, 117.

33 Mahaffy, 'Two Tours', 14.

34 Campion, *A Historie of Ireland*, i, 21 – he also admitted to never having received communion. K. Simms tells me this tale may have originated in the preface to the Vision of Knight Owen.

35 Mooney, 'The Friars and Friary of Donegal, 1474–1840', in O'Donnell, ed., *Franciscan Donegal*, 9.

36 See for e.g. the Franciscan manual for preachers, Little, ed., *Liber Exemplorum*, British Society for Franciscan Pubs., i.

37 Burrows, 'Fifteenth-century Irish Provincial Legislation and Pastoral Care', in Sheils and Wood, eds., *The Churches, Ireland and the Irish*, Studies in

Church History, no. 25, 55–67; Watt, *The Church in Medieval Ireland*, 210–11; Jones, *The Counter-Reformation*, 37. See also Mooney, 'The Friars and Friary of Donegal', 7, 13, the O'Donnells holding important meetings in the Franciscan Abbey which they had endowed.

38 Campion, *A Historie of Ireland*, i, 19.

39 See Scribner, 'Interpreting Religion in Early Modern Europe', *European Studies Review*, xiii, 89–105, and particularly 94, for a survey of findings on popular religion in Europe.

40 Flower, *The Irish Tradition*, 119–29; Cosgrove, ed., *New History of Ireland*, ii, 704, 722–6.

41 Ó Maonaigh, ed., *Smaointe Beatha Chríost*; O'Dwyer, *Mary: A History of Devotion in Ireland*, 140–54.

42 Walsh, *Leabhar Chlainne Suibhne*, xliv–lviii, 37, 67–9; Walsh, *Irish Men of Learning*, 179–80.

43 Lennon, 'The Counter-Reformation in Ireland, 1542–1641', in Brady and Gillespie, eds., *Natives and Newcomers*, 76; see also Monter, *Ritual, Myth and Magic*, ch. 2.

44 Where a vigilant mayor and deputy-governor secured funds to rebuild the church and compel attendance, so that by 1605 most of the priests were said to have taken the oath of supremacy, see O'Laverty, *Down and Connor*, iii, 101–2; Bradshaw, *The Dissolution of the Religious Orders in Ireland*, 97, 121, 142; White, ed., *Extents of Irish Monastic Possessions, 1540–1541*.

45 Mooney, 'The Friars and Friary of Donegal', 11: in 1588 the soldiers attacked Donegal friary, destroying statues and pictures; Murray, 'Franciscan Monasteries after the Dissolution', *Louth Arch. Soc. Jn.*, viii, 275–82: in 1589 the large monastery in Monaghan was reduced to rubble, the Guardian and five friars put to death.

46 *The Ancient and Noble Family of the Savages of the Ards*, 176: in the 1570s the O'Neills burned the abbeys of Moville, Bangor and Holywood in a campaign against Sir Thomas Smith; Simms, 'Gaelic Lordships', 794, 1455, conflict between Arch. Mey of Armagh and the O'Neills for making territorial claims on church lands; O'Laverty, *Down and Connor*, iii, 60; the unnamed author of *Les martyrs de la Province dominicaine d'Irlande*, 71, tries to argue that the deaths of friars at the hands of Sorley Boy MacDonnell (sixteenth century) must have been instigated by the English.

47 Shirley, ed., *Church in Ireland*, 117–18. Moryson, *Itinerary*, in Falkiner, *Illustrations of Irish History and Topography*, 319: 'In christenings and like rites of religion they use generally the rites of the Roman Church, the which they persist with obstinacy, little care having been taken to instruct them in the reformed doctrine.'

48 Ford, *Protestant Reformation in Ireland*, 53–7; Clarke in Moody *et al.*, eds., *New History of Ireland*, iii, 210.

49 Cameron, *The European Reformation*, 311–13; see Steven G. Ellis, *Ireland in the Age of the Tudors*, 205–42, for the most recent analysis of the Reformation in Ireland.

50 See e.g. Shirley, ed., *Church in Ireland*, 90–91: extract from Queen Elizabeth's 'Instructions', 1559; Sir John Davies' similar belief that they could plant true religion 'among these rude people, who are apt to take any impression', in Morley, ed., *Ireland under Elizabeth and James I*, i, 378.

51 There is a useful survey of the literature on the Reformation in Ireland in, 'The Church of Ireland: A Critical Bibliography', Part I: 1536–1603, by James Murray, and Part II: 1603–41, by Alan Ford, *I.H.S.*, xxviii, 345–8.

52 O'Dwyer, *Mary*, 221.

53 Bossy, 'The Counter-Reformation and the People of Catholic Ireland, 1596–1641', in Williams, ed., *Historical Studies*, viii, 155–69, and idem, 'The Counter-Reformation and the People of Catholic Europe', *Past and Present*, no. 47 (May, 1970), 51–70.

54 Scribner, 'Interpreting Religion in Early Modern Europe', *European Studies Review*, xiii, 89–105.

55 Hagan, ed., 'Miscellanea Vaticano-Hibernica, 1580–1631', *Archiv. Hib.*, iii, 284; Jones, *The Counter-Reformation*, 37–8.

56 Murray, 'Franciscan Monasteries after the Dissolution', 275–82; Giblin, ed., 'Catalogue of Material of Irish Interest in the Collection *Nunziatura di Fiandra*', Vatican Archives: Part I, vols. 1–50, *Coll. Hib.*, i, 57. Franciscans administering the sacraments in Ireland; Gwynn and Hadcock, eds., *Medieval Religious Houses*, 11, for papal permission to hold mass in places other than churches.

57 Hagan, ed., 'Miscellanea Vaticano-Hibernica', 285; Clarke in Moody *et al.*, eds., *New History of Ireland*, iii, 210; O'Laverty, *Down and Connor. The Bishops*, 369–71 – he resided in Tyrone after his appointment, protected by the O'Neill family.

58 Silke, in Moody *et al.*, eds., *New History of Ireland*, iii, 629.

59 O'Laverty, *Down and Connor. The Bishops*, 404–11.

60 *Ibid.*, 411–14.

61 Cunningham, 'Native Culture and Political Change in Ireland, 1534–1641', 162–3; also Silke, op. cit., 628–9.

62 'The O'Kane Papers', *Anal. Hib.*, xii, 79–111; Morgan, 'The End of Gaelic Ulster', 28. Miler Magrath names twenty monasteries still operating in Ulster in 1594.

63 *Cal.S.P. Ire., 1611–14*, 431; Maxwell, *Irish History from Contemporary Sources, 1509–1610*, 150–51; Lodge, ed., *Desiderata Curiosa Hibernica*, i, 394–6.

64 *Cal.S.P. Ire., 1611–14*, 429–31.

65 Gillespie, 'The Transformation of the Borderlands, 1600–1700', in Gillespie and O'Sullivan, eds., *The Borderlands*, 86–8.

66 Bossy, 'Catholicity and Nationality in the Northern Counter-Reformation', in Mews, ed., *Religion and National Identity*, Studies in Church History, xviii, 285–96; also Cunningham, 'The Culture and Ideology of Irish Franciscan Historians at Louvain 1607–1650', in Brady, ed., *Ideology and the Historians*, Hist. Studs., xviii, 11–30.

67 Giblin, ed., 'Catalogue of Material of Irish Interest ... Part I', 61,

63; Lucian Ceyssens, 'Florence Conry, Hugh de Burgo, Luke Wadding and Jansenism', in Franciscan Fathers, eds., *Father Luke Wadding*, 295–331; O'Rahilly, ed., *Desiderius, Otherwise Called Sgáthán an Chrábaidh*, by Flaithrí Ó Maolchonaire, ix–x.

68 On MacCaghwell see Ó Cuív in Moody *et al.*, eds., *New History of Ireland*, iii, 526–7, 562–3; O'Laverty, *Down and Connor. The Bishops*, 398–401; Tomás Ó Cléirigh, *Aodh Mac Aingil Agus an Scoil Nua-Ghaeilge i Lobháin* (Dublin, 1935).

69 Jennings, *Michael Ó Cléirigh: Chief of the Four Masters and His Associates*; Ó Briain, 'Three Friars of Donegal', in O'Donnell, ed., *Franciscan Donegal*, 82–92; Ó Cuív, op. cit., 531–2; Walsh, *Four Masters*, 34.

70 These points are also made in Cunningham, 'The Culture and Ideology of Irish Franciscan Historians at Louvain', especially 20–21.

71 Quoted in Jennings, *Michael Ó Cléirigh*, 38.

72 Ó Cuív, op. cit., 533.

73 Ó Buachalla, 'Poetry and Politics in Early Modern Ireland', *Eighteenth-Century Ireland*, vii, 149–75; idem, 'Na Stíobhartaigh agus an tAos Léinn: Cing Séamas', *Proc. R.I.A.*, 83, sect C, 4–129.

74 Gillies, 'A Poem on the Downfall of the Gaodhil', *Éigse*, 13, 203–10; Ó Buachalla, 'Cing Séamas', 90–91.

75 Hardiman, *Irish Minstrelsy*, i, 102; Hyde, *Literary History*, 522.

76 Ó Buachalla, 'Cing Séamas', 85.

77 Leerssen, *Mere Irish and Fíor Ghael: Studies in the Idea of Irish Nationality, Its Development and Literary Expression prior to the Nineteenth Century*, 220; Cunningham, 'Native Culture and Political Change', particularly 165–70; Millett, in Moody *et al.*, eds., *New History of Ireland*, iii, 568–9. Hyde, *Literary History*, 517.

78 Spenser, *View of the State of Ireland*, i, 254–5.

79 Hagan, ed., 'Miscellanea Vaticano-Hibernica', 260–64: 'Brief of Paul V to the Irish People', c.1607; Corish, *The Irish Catholic Experience*, 95.

80 Bruford, *Gaelic Folktales and Medieval Romances*, 58–63; Breatnach, 'Early Modern Irish Prose', in McCone and Simms, eds., *Progress in Medieval Studies*, 195–6; Hyde, *Literary History*, 558–9; Cunningham, 'Native Culture and Political change', 165–7.

81 Ó Buachalla, 'Foreword' to Geoffrey Keating, *Foras Feasa ar Éirinn, The History of Ireland*, ed. by Comyn and Dineen (London, 1987), 5.

82 There is considerable disagreement over what messages can be taken from the poetry in this period. See Cunningham, 'Native Culture and Political Change', 164; Knott, *Bardic Poems*, xxxiv, arguing against reading too much into bardic conventions regarding the foreigner etc.; Ó Buachalla, 'Poetry and Politics in Early Modern Ireland', *Eighteenth-century Ireland*, 7, 149–75; idem, 'Jacobitism and Nationalism: the Irish Literary Evidence', in Michael O'Dea and Kevin Whelan, eds., *Nations and Nationalism: France, Britain, Ireland and the Eighteenth-century Context* (Oxford, 1995), 103–16. But see Simms's sensible overview of the controversy in McCone and Simms, eds., *Progress in Medieval Irish Studies*, 210–15.

4 THE LOSS OF THE LAND:
PLANTATION AND CONFISCATION IN
SEVENTEENTH-CENTURY ULSTER

1 Lin. Lib., Opsahl Comm., no. 184.

2 See Bernadette McAliskey, in O Connor, *In Search of a State*, 364, also her article explaining why republicans rejected the Downing Street Agreement, *Guardian*, 28 December 1993; Donegal writer Seamus MacManus, *Rocky Road to Dublin*, 131–2, the descendants of 'the hard-headed Scottish planters whom James I loosed upon Ulster, to grab everything in sight', being shunned in modern Donegal; see also Brewer with Higgins, *Anti-Catholicism in Northern Ireland, 1600–1998*, 86, showing how, by the twentieth century, 1641 is being raked up for purely political reasons. However, Clayton, *Enemies and Passing Friends*, particularly ch. 2, portrays present-day Ulster Protestants as retaining their 'settler' mentality.

3 Mac Suibhne, 'Canon James McFadden (1842–1917)', in Moran, ed., *Ten Radical Priests*, 173, shows that the *seanchas* of Donegal depicted the O'Donnells as 'harsh overlords who coerced labour to build roads and a castle', quite unlike the image created by later cultural nationalism.

4 UFTM, School Textbook Coll., E2/61/13: Mrs Stephen Gwynn, *Stories from Irish History*, 108.

5 Davies, in Morley, ed., *Ireland under Elizabeth and James I*, 276–81.

6 *Ibid.*, 379.

7 See e.g. map of population density in 1660 in Smyth, 'Society and Settlement in Seventeenth-century Ireland', in Smyth and Whelan, eds., *Common Ground: Essays on the Historical Geography of Ireland*, 66.

8 Harkin [Maghtochair], *Inishowen*, 74–6.

9 Robinson, *The Plantation of Ulster*, 45–52.

10 Chart, 'The Break-up of the Estate of Con O'Neill', *Proc. R.I.A.* xlviii, sect. C, 119–51; Perceval-Maxwell, *The Scottish Migration to Ulster in the Reign of James I*, 49–52.

11 Quoted in Ohlmeyer, *Civil War and Restoration in Three Stuart Kingdoms*, 83–4.

12 *Ibid.*, 25–40.

13 Perceval-Maxwell, *Scottish Migration*, 58–67.

14 O'Laverty, *Down and Connor*, ii, 137; Reeves, ed., 'The Irish Itinerary of Father Edmund MacCana', *U.J.A.*, ser. 1., vol. ii, 55.

15 *Report of the Lough Foyle Fishery Case ... tried ... at Omagh, 1856* (London, 1857).

16 Hunter, 'The Ulster Plantation in the Counties of Armagh and Cavan, 1608–41', 33–4; Robinson, *Plantation*, 201.

17 Walsh, *Leabhar Chlainne Suibhne*, xxx–xxxi; Hugh O'Neill scarcely figures in popular Irish poetry, see Ó Muirgheasa, *Céad de Cheoltaibh Uladh*, 192.

18 Gillespie and O'Sullivan, eds., *The Borderlands*, 61, also 84–5; Ó Fiaich, 'The O'Neills of the Fews', *Seanchas Ard Mhacha*, vii, 55–6; Robinson,

Plantation, 199. See also Moody, ed., 'Ulster Plantation Papers, 1608–13', *Anal. Hib.*, no. 8, 214–15, a host of lesser grants in Tyrone to the smaller allied septs, the O'Quinns, O'Devlins, O'Hagans, O'Mellans, O'Corrs, etc.

19 *Cal. S.P. Ire.*, 1608–1610, 68.

20 Hamilton, *The Irish Rebellion of 1641*, 99–101; Livingstone, *Fermanagh Story*, 61–2; George Hill, *An Historical Account of the Plantation of Ulster*, 109–10, 411; Gilbert, ed., *A Contemporary History of Affairs in Ireland*, vol. i, pt. 1, xx–xxi.

21 Moody, ed., 'Ulster Plantation Papers', 206–7.

22 Hamilton, *Rebellion of 1641*, 98–9; Robinson, *Plantation*, 200.

23 Hunter, 'Ulster Plantation', 52–78; Davies, in Morley, ed., *Ireland under Elizabeth and James I*, i, 384; Ó Gallachair, '1622 Survey of Cavan', *Breifne*, i, 60–75; Robinson, *Plantation*, 201.

24 Davies in Morley, ed., *Ireland under Elizabeth and James I*, 371–2; see also Ó Doibhlin, *Domhnach Mór*, 97ff, for the jurors at Dungannon; Hill, *Plantation*, 153–90, lists all the jurors involved in the 1609 commission's enquiries – also very good outline of the difficulties over termon and erenach lands.

25 Robinson, *Plantation*, 86; Hill, *Plantation*, 218, 311, 410–11, 569; Moody, Martin and Byrne, eds., *A New History of Ireland*, ix: *Maps, Genealogies, Lists*, 142.

26 Robinson, *Plantation*, 89–90.

27 Perceval-Maxwell, *Scottish Migration*, 210–14; see Hill, *Plantation*, extensive notes to pp. 454, 456, 480, 487, 490, 518 for yearly leases, but also examples of life leases, 533, and substantial tenancies, 503 and 535.

28 IFC, MS 976/167 and 1215/212; Gillespie and Sullivan, eds., *Borderlands*, 80.

29 Hunter, 'Ulster Plantation', 41, also 240; 1622 survey sees Armagh with almost twice the number of British settlers as Cavan (1,200 against 765).

30 Robinson, *Plantation* (his tables), 87.

31 *Ibid.*, 97–100; Macafee, 'The Population of Ulster, 1630–1841', 56.

32 Moody, 'The Treatment of the Native Population', 63.

33 Hunter, 'English Undertakers in the Plantation of Ulster', *Breifne*, x, 483; Moody, *Londonderry Plantation*, 327–31.

34 Hunter, 'Ulster Plantation', 149–53, 248.

35 Gillespie, *Colonial Ulster*, 140–41; also in *Natives and Newcomers*, 195.

36 Quoted in Gillespie, *Conspiracy*, 29.

37 Walsh, *Leabhar Chlainne Suibhne*, xxxv–xxxvi.

38 Buckley, ed., 'A Tour in Ireland in 1672–4', *Cork. Hist. and Arch. Soc. Jn.*, 2nd ser., x (1904), 89.

39 Gillespie, *Colonial Ulster*, 114.

40 *Ibid.*, 118–19; Hill, *An Historical Account of the MacDonnells of Antrim*, 61–2, 236.

41 Gillespie, *Conspiracy*, 31–3.

42 McCarthy, 'Ulster Office', 172.

43 Marshall, *History of the Parish of Tynan in the County of Armagh*, 42–3; Hill, *Plantation*, 207–10, 217.

44 Hunter, 'Ulster Plantation', 545–8, 574; Glancy, 'The Primate Lands . . . Armagh', 387, the 1714 list of the sub-tenants on these former erenach lands registers that decline.

45 Cited Flower, *Irish Tradition*, 167.

46 Cunningham, 'Native Culture and Political Change in Ireland', 161; Gillespie, *Colonial Ulster*, 150–51.

47 Williams, ed., *Pairlement Chloinne Tomáis*.

48 Macafee, 'The Population of Ulster', 52–4.

49 See Gillespie in Mac Cuarta, ed., *Ulster 1641*, 109.

50 Hunter, 'Ulster Plantation', 324–5 – 25% to 19% in Armagh, 22.5% to 16.5% in Cavan in the period between the plantation and 1641.

51 Kennedy, 'Eagla an Ghallsmacht. The Religion and Politics of Irish Catholics 1620s–1670s', 178.

52 Ohlmeyer, *Civil War and Restoration*, 83; Gillespie, in *Natives and Newcomers*, 198–9.

53 *Cal. S.P. Ire., 1633–1647*, 274; Gilbert, *Contemporary History*, vol. i, pt. i, 'Aphorismical Discovery', 12.

54 O'Riordain and Gillespie, in Mac Cuarta, ed., *Ulster 1641*, 83 and 110; Dunlop, ed., *Ireland under the Commonwealth: Being a Selection of Documents Relating to the Government of Ireland, 1651–9*, ii, 363, 423.

55 Gillespie, 'Destabilising Ulster, 1641–42', in Mac Cuarta, ed., *Ulster 1641*, 112.

56 [John Lodge] ed., *Desiderata Curiosa Hibernica, or, a Select Collection of State Papers*, ii, 78, 86–8; Perceval-Maxwell, 'Ulster 1641 in the Context of Political Developments in the Three Kingdoms', in Mac Cuarta, ed., *Ulster 1641*, 100–103; Lecky, *Ireland in the Eighteenth Century*, i, 94; Canny, 'What Really Happened in 1641?', in Ohlmeyer, *Ireland from Independence to Occupation 1641–1660*, 29–30.

57 *Desiderata Curiosa*, ii: 'The Humble Remonstrance of the Northern Catholicks of Ireland, Now in Arms', 99. But see Moody, *et al.*, eds., *New History of Ireland*, ix, 605, which does not support their accusation about the prorogation of parliament.

58 But see Stevenson, *Scottish Covenanters and Irish Confederates*, 83–102, for the confusion of attitudes towards the Scots.

59 Hamilton, *The Irish Rebellion of 1641*, 106.

60 Hickson, *Ireland in the Seventeenth Century or the Irish Massacres of 1641–2*, ii, 216–17.

61 Hamilton, *Irish Rebellion*, 150.

62 IFC, MS vol. 1215/214; Hickson, *Irish Massacres*, i, 176–82.

63 Hill, ed., *The Montgomery Manuscripts (1603–1706)*, 131–2; Hamilton, *Irish rebellion*, 256.

64 Murray, 'The History of the Parish of Creggan in the 17th and 18th Centuries', *Louth Arch. Soc. Jn.*, viii, no. 2, 124.

65 John Lynch, *Cambrensis Eversus*, 1, 12. Clarke, *The Old English in Ireland, 1625–42*, 224–6.

66 Gillespie, 'Destabilising Ulster', 112–13.

67 Simms, 'Violence in County Armagh, 1641', in Mac Cuarta, ed., *Ulster 1641*, 130–31.

68 McCall, 'The Gaelic Background to the Settlement of Antrim and Down 1580–1641', 130; McSkimin, *Carrickfergus*, 41–57, detailed account of the controversy over the numbers of Catholics killed.

69 Simms, 'Violence in County Armagh', 127; Hamilton, *Irish Rebellion*, 217–18, 149–52; Russell and Prendergast, eds., *The Carte Manuscripts*, 147–51.

70 Ohlmeyer, *Civil War and Restoration*, 110–13; Stevenson, 'The Desertion of the Irish by Coll Keitach's Sons, 1642', *I.H.S.*, xxi, 75–84.

71 Kennedy, 'Eagla an Ghallsmacht.', 178–83.

72 Jones, *A Remonstrance of Divers Remarkable Passages Concerning the Church and Kingdome of Ireland*, 1.

73 Most historians would not now go so far as Lecky in totally denying the stories of massacre (*Ireland in the Eighteenth Century*, i, 45–100), but would accept the Depositions as a valuable source, if used with utmost caution; see e.g. Canny, 'What Really Happened in Ireland in 1641', in Ohlmeyer, ed., *Ireland . . . 1641–1660*, 24–42.

74 Barnard, 'The Uses of 23 October 1641 and Irish Protestant celebrations', *E.H.R.*, cvi, 892.

75 Stewart, *The Narrow Ground. Aspects of Ulster*, 49.

76 Elliott, *Partners in Revolution*, 8–9; Stewart, *Narrow Ground*, 108; *Northern Star*, 22 August 1792; Harris, *The Ancient and Present State of the County of Down*, 106, also 35, 81, 84–6, 92–3, 97; David Hayton, 'The Propaganda War', in Maguire, ed., *Kings in Conflict*, 118–19.

77 Dunlop, ed., *Ireland under the Commonwealth*, i, 179. In August 1652 Jones was instructed by the commissioners to discover the perpetrators of such outrages with a view to their punishment (*ibid.*, 242).

78 The words are Walter Love's, quoted in Bottigheimer, *English Money and Irish Land*, 127–8.

79 Young, *Historical Notices of Old Belfast and Its Vicinity*, 75; Dunlop, ed., *Ireland under the Commonwealth*, ii, 370.

80 Corish, in Moody *et al.*, eds., *New History of Ireland*, iii, 359–60; Dunlop, ed., *Ireland under the Commonwealth*, ii, 322.

81 Dunlop, ed., *Ireland under the Commonwealth*, ii, 323–4.

82 *Ibid.*, ii, 486, 499, 515, 516, 542, and i, 299; 29 November 1652, Sir Charles Coote being reprimanded for moving Donegal creaghts, their families and stocks to his lands in Connacht. Simington, *The Transplantation to Connacht, 1654–58*, xii–xiii.

83 Dunlop, ed., *Ireland under the Commonwealth*, ii, 614, also i, 78–96, and ii, 339, 346–50, 351–4, 360–61 for the Scots to be transplanted, 254 from Antrim and Down alone, including a John Tennent from Lecale.

84 See *Montgomery Manuscripts*, Viscount Montgomery, like most other outlawed Protestants, 'composing' for their property, 218–19; Dunlop, ed., *Ireland under the Commonwealth*, ii, 363, 580, 711, and Burke, *The Irish Priests in Penal Times*, 42–3, on Cromwellian soldiers marrying Catholic

Irishwomen; Ohlmeyer, *Civil War and Restoration*, 245, on Cromwellian soldiers selling up; IFC, MS vol. 815/361–2: traditions in Cavan about purchase of the soldiers' portions.

85 Duffy, 'The Evolution of Estate Properties in South Ulster, 1600–1900', in Smyth and Whelan, eds., *Common Ground*, 100–104; Bottigheimer, 'The Restoration Land Settlement in Ireland', *I.H.S.*, xviii, 17; Barnard, 'Planters and Policies in Cromwellian Ireland', *Past and Present*, no. 61, 31–69.

86 The most recent general survey ignores it entirely: Fitzpatrick, *Seventeenth-century Ireland*. The most comprehensive (Bottigheimer) concentrates largely on the Adventurers, Barnard, 'Planters and policies', on the 'Old Protestants'. Given its place in popular demonology, it is at least odd that the best overall account of the consequences for the Catholic populace remains Butler, *Confiscation in Irish History*, whilst Ohlmeyer's *Civil War and Restoration* provides some valuable material on Antrim. A welcome exception for west Ulster (Tyrone, Londonderry, Donegal) is McKenney, 'The Seventeenth-century Land Settlement in Ireland', in Ohlmeyer, ed., *Ireland ... 1641–1660*, 181–200.

87 Kerry and Tipperary saw most transplantation, which probably explains the strength of anti-Cromwellian sentiment there, reflected in the bitterness of the Munster poetry and in living popular tradition. It was a tradition very much alive in my Kerry mother's family and Tipperary grandmother's.

88 Gillespie, 'Continuity and Change', in Brady *et al.*, *Illustrated History of Ulster*, 117.

89 McKenny, 'The Seventeenth-century Land Settlement in Ireland: Towards a Statistical Interpretation', 196–8; Butler, *Confiscation*, 150–53; also map in Bottigheimer, *English Money and Irish Land*, 214–15; see also Dunlop, ed., *Ireland under the Commonwealth*, ii, 702–3.

90 These were the Articles of Cloughoughter signed with O'Reilly, Lord Enniskillen, Miles O'Reilly, Col. MacMahon, Hugh Maguire, Con O'Neill, Dan O'Cahan, and various others of 'the Ulster party', Dunlop, ed., *Ireland under the Commonwealth*, ii, 336–7n, 362, 429.

91 Ohlmeyer, *Civil War and Restoration*, 234–48; Dunlop, ed., *Ireland under the Commonwealth*, ii, 369.

92 Ó Fiaich, 'The O'Neills of the Fews,' ii, *Seanchas Ard Mhacha*, 2, 287–92; Murray, 'The History of the Parish of Creggan', 121–3; Russell and Prendergast, eds., *The Carte Manuscripts*, 147–51. But Bottigheimer, 'The Restoration Land Settlement', 17, suggests he was eventually declared innocent. Archbishop Plunkett refers to him in 1671 as one of only three Catholic landowners left in Ulster (Hanly, ed., *The Letters of Saint Oliver Plunkett*, 247).

93 Schlegel, 'The MacDonnells of Tyrone and Armagh: A Genealogical Study', *Seanchas Ard Mhacha*, x, 193–219; Ó Doibhlin, *Domhnach Mór*, 140–54.

94 Cullen, *Emergence of Modern Ireland*, 42; Livingstone, *Monaghan*, 124; Maguire, 'The Estate of Cú Chonnacht Maguire of Tempo', *I.H.S*, xxvii, 141, shows throughout the century hardly any British settlement on his estate.

95 Lin. Lib., Joy MSS, Commonplace Book, fos. 33–7, 'An Account of the

Ancient Family of Magennis of Iveagh'. The outcome of this case, however, was to show that the original trust was not necessarily guaranteed if the offspring of the Protestant friend were ill-disposed. Edmond Oge Magennis was still trying to recover the lands from the son of the family friend when he joined James II's cause in 1688 and was later killed at the battle of Aughrim (1691). By the second half of the eighteenth century some of the Magennises of Waringstown had converted to the established church, see Atkinson, *An Ulster Parish*, 62, 86, also Coote, *Statistical Survey of County Armagh*, 126. Ó Doibhlin, *Domhnach Mór*, 159–63, the 1666 hearth-money rolls show the O'Loughrans still on former erenach land.

96 Lecky, *Ireland in the Eighteenth Century*, i, 106.

97 Bagwell, *Ireland under the Stuarts*, iii, 22–3.

98 Connolly, *Religion, Law and Power*, 13; also Ohlmeyer, *Civil War and Restoration*, 263–4.

99 Bottigheimer, 'Restoration Land Settlement', 19.

100 Russell and Prendergast, eds., *The Carte Manuscripts*, 87; Butler, *Confiscation*, 188.

101 Bagwell, *Ireland under the Stuarts*, iii, 49; Connolly, *Religion, Law and Power*, 13–17; *Cal. S.P. Ire., 1663–1665*, 687–9, 699.

102 Russell and Prendergast, eds., *The Carte Manuscripts*, 91–2.

103 Giblin, ed., 'Catalogue of Material of Irish Interest in the . . . Vatican Archives', Part I, 102–5.

104 Bagwell, *Ireland under the Stuarts*, iii, 39–43; *Cal. S.P. Ire., 1663–1665*, 29, 44, 90, 115, 208–21, 338, 687; Hill, *MacDonnells of Antrim*, 290–344.

105 Butler, *Confiscation*, 172, 191; and see Moody *et al.*, eds., *New History of Ireland*, iii, 572–3.

106 Butler, *Confiscation*, 192, 196, 203; Laverty, *Down and Connor*, ii, 243, lx–lxxii.

107 *Cal. S.P. Ire., 1663–5*, 361–2, 714, and *1669–70*, 433, 460, 523–4, 534–5; Butler, *Confiscation*, 203.

108 *Savages of the Ards*, 195, 250; O'Laverty, *Down and Connor*, ii, 145–6.

109 Livingstone, *Monaghan Story*, 123.

110 Moody *et al.*, eds., *New History of Ireland*, iii, 428; *Cal. S.P. Ire., 1666–1669*, 543–9, long, forceful memorandum showing utter amazement and a sense of deep injustice at the way the interest of former Cromwellians had been placed above those who had been loyal royalists.

111 Cited Ó Buachalla, 'Jacobitism and Nationalism: the Irish Literary Evidence', in O'Dea and Whelan, eds., *Nations and Nationalism*, 104.

112 Ó Buachalla, 'Lillibulero agus eile', *Comhar* (April, 1987), 29.

113 Bagwell, *Ireland under the Stuarts*, iii, 231; Connolly, *Religion, Law and Power*, 35.

114 Barnard, 'The Uses of 23 October 1641', 894.

115 Hugh Reily, *The Impartial History of Ireland*, iv.

116 Elliott, *Wolfe Tone*, 137; Simms, *The Jacobite Parliament of 1689*, 21–6.

117 Lin. Lib., Joy MSS, Commonplace Book, fo. 35.

118 Atkinson, *An Ulster Parish*, 37–8.

119 Simms, ed., 'Irish Jacobites', *Anal. Hib.*, xxii, 22–187, lists of outlawries and pardons; idem, 'Land Owned by Catholics in Ireland in 1688', *I.H.S.*, vii, 180–90, in which he also explains why more land survived in Catholic hands in the west of Ireland.

120 Atkinson, *An Ulster Parish*, 34–48.

121 Maguire, 'The Estate of Cú Chonnacht Maguire', 133–5; Simms, 'Land Owned by Catholics', 185. He died at sea en route to France after being outlawed. His brother Charles, who had become a Protestant, was granted the estate by William on payment of a fine. But this was voided by the Act of Resumption (Russell and Prendergast, eds., *The Carte Manuscripts*, 101).

122 See case of Antrim O'Haras in Connolly, *Religion, Law and Power*, 309; also Quinn, 'Religion and Landownership in County Louth 1641–*c*.1750', chap. 2.

123 Lin. Lib., Joy MSS, Commonplace Book, op. cit.; Ó Fiaich, 'O'Neills of the Fews', ii, 294–5, 300, 302, also shows O'Neills of the Fews intermarrying with Magennises, Clandeboye O'Neills and O'Donnells into the eighteenth century.

124 Maguire, ed., *Kings in Conflict*, 64.

125 Ó Fiaich, 'O'Neills of the Fews', iii, 386.

126 See Roebuck, in Mitchison and Roebuck, eds., *Economy and Society*, 85–6, showing considerable bargaining power of tenants in Ulster, even under the penal laws.

127 Silke, 'The Irish Abroad, 1533–1691', in Moody *et al.*, eds., *New History of Ireland*, iii, 593; Hill, *Plantation*, 205.

128 Henry, 'Ulster Exiles in Europe, 1605–1641', in Mac Cuarta, ed., *Ulster 1641*, 37–60. This is the best short survey of this topic. See Dunlop, ed., *Ireland under the Commonwealth*, i, cxxxvi, for a reported 27,000 leaving in 1656.

129 Ó Fiaich, 'O'Neills of the Fews', ii, 283; Silke, 'The Irish Abroad', in Moody *et al.*, eds., *New History of Ireland*, iii, 606.

130 Hanly, ed., *Letters of Saint Oliver Plunkett*, 160; Connolly, *Religion, Law and Power*, 206, which sheds new light on the tory phenomenon.

131 Russell and Prendergast, eds., *The Carte Manuscripts*, 98; Ó Fiaich, 'The Registration of the Clergy in 1704', *Seanchas Ard Mhacha*, 6, 52. Brian McHugh, priest in Longford, imprisoned 1708 for marrying a Catholic and Protestant, escaped and became a tory.

132 Gillespie, 'Transformation of the Borderlands', 84–6; Dunlop, ed., *Ireland under the Commonwealth*, i, 49–50.

133 Smyth, 'Society and Settlement . . . "1659 Census"', 75.

134 See for e.g. Ó Doibhlin, *Domhnach Mór*, 167ff. Glassie, *Ballymenone*, 110: in this region of Fermanagh popular tradition has the rapparees robbing the rich to give to the poor, rather than submit to 'English law and religion'.

135 For examples of English and Scots tories see McSkimin, *History of Carrickfergus*, 459–61; *Cal. S.P. Ire., 1666–1669*, 608; and 'Protestant Rapparees', Story, *Impartial History*, 161.

136 Casey, 'Carleton and the Count', *Seanchas Ard Mhacha*, viii, 7–22;

Adams, *The Printed Word and the Common Man*, 15, 90; Bardon, *History of Ulster*, 143–5; Moody, 'Redmond O'Hanlon, c.1640–1681', *Proceedings and Reports of the Belfast Natural History and Philosophical Society*, 2nd ser., i, pt 1, 17–33.

137 IFC, MS 1113/50 and 975/31; Story, *Impartial History*, 15; Murphy, *Ulster Folk of Field and Fireside*, 10. See also Murray, 'A Previously Unnoticed Letter of Oliver Plunkett's', *Seanchas Ard Mhacha*, viii, 23–33; Dunlop, ed., *Ireland under the Commonwealth*, i, 17.

138 Story, *Impartial History*, 15, 59; Macafee, 'Population of Ulster', 56; *Cal. S.P. Ire., 1666–1669*, 256–7.

139 Reily, *Impartial History of Ireland*, 39.

140 Livingstone, *Monaghan Story*, 123, makes this point; Simms, *The Williamite Confiscation in Ireland*, 16, shows that the successive land upheavals of the seventeenth century affected the Gaelic proprietors far more adversely than the Old English.

141 Duffy, 'The Territorial Organisation of Gaelic Landownership and Its Transformation in County Monaghan, 1591–1640', *Irish Geography*, xiv, 19.

142 Hill, *MacDonnells of Antrim*, 362.

143 See e.g. on Brownlow estate in Armagh, Cunningham and Gillespie, 'An Ulster Settler and his Irish Manuscripts', *Éigse*, xxi, 30; Macafee, 'Population of Ulster', 75, 92.

144 Hanly, ed., *Letters of Saint Oliver Plunkett*, 247, also 74–5, 410, 455; MacCurtain, 'Rural Society in post-Cromwellian Ireland', in Cosgrove and McCartney, eds., *Studies in Irish History*, 133.

5 THE MERGER OF 'IRISHNESS' AND CATHOLICISM IN EARLY MODERN ULSTER

1 O Connor, *In Search of a State*, 11.

2 The hymnn was used by the GAA until the 1960s as a kind of anthem for major fixtures, see Hayes, *Minority Verdict*, 56.

3 Ohlmeyer, *Civil War and Restoration*, 35–6, 287. 'Travels of Sir William Brereton in Ireland, 1635', in Falkiner, *Illustrations of Irish History and Topography*, 372–3; see e.g. Russell and Prendergast, eds., *The Carte Manuscripts*, 124; *Cal. S.P. Ire., 1663–5*, 138, 566, for sense of persecution.

4 Hanly, ed., *Letters of Saint Oliver Plunkett*, 144, 452; O'Laverty, *Down and Connor*, i, 313; Harkin, *Inishowen*, 142–3.

5 Cullen, *The Emergence of Modern Ireland, 1600–1900*, 131–2.

6 McCone and Simms, eds., *Progress in Medieval Irish Studies*, 212.

7 See e.g. Ó Muirgheasa, *Céad de Cheoltaibh Uladh*, 9–12, by Patrick Plunkett, early nineteenth century, contains all the standard themes first used in the seventeenth century, Catholicism the true religion of the Gael, the Protestants insincere, the Catholic who converts doomed, the Irish language exclusively theirs; idem, *Dánta Diadha Uladh*, 257, an 1824 poem of Thomas O'Connor.

8 Hanly, ed., *Plunkett Letters*, 546, shows Phelim O'Neill and his son Gordon adopting Catholicism and Protestantism at different points in their life.

9 Harkin, *Inishowen*, 74–5; Gillespie, *Devoted People*, 121–2, 140–41.

10 Perceval-Maxwell, *Scottish Migration to Ulster*, 272–3; *Cal. S.P. Ire.*, *1625–32*, 512–13; Hanly, ed., *Plunkett Letters*, 226, Captain John Hamilton 'a Scottish gentlemen', a Catholic 'and a great support of our religion in those parts', 1671.

11 Hill, 'The Origins of the Scottish Plantations in Ulster to 1625', *Jn. Brit. Studs.*, 32, 40; O'Laverty, *Down and Connor*, 430; Ohlmeyer, *Civil War and Restoration*, 75.

12 Gillespie, 'Continuity and Change', 124–9; Robinson, *Plantation of Ulster*, 187–8.

13 Even before the plantation a number of the Ulster Irish had studied in Scotland and were credited with speaking 'Scots' (as well as Irish, English and Latin), this 'The O'Kane Papers', *Anal. Hib.*, xii, 100–104. See also Adams, 'The Emergence of Ulster as a Distinct Dialect Area', *Ulster Folklife*, iv, 68–9. Montgomery and Robinson, 'The Linguistic Landscape of Seventeenth-century Ulster', unpublished paper delivered to the annual ACIS conference, Belfast, June 1995.

14 See e.g. Morgan, 'The End of Gaelic Ulster', 30; Ó Fiaich and Ó Caithnia, *Art Mac Bionaid*, 66–8, Art Bennett's 1852 poem 'A ghleann na suailce' ('O valley of virtue'), the belief that you only became Protestant if bribed or deceived; also IFC, MS 815/289, Cavan story of a woman in Cromwell's time 'turning to keep her land', struck down by supernatural forces as a result.

15 Reily, *Impartial History of Ireland*, iv–v.

16 Dunlop, *Commonwealth*, ii, 515, 517, also 355–7, 370, 413; Hill, *Plantation*, 414–15.

17 Phil Kilroy, 'Sermon and Pamphlet Literature in the Irish Reformed Church, 1613–34', *Archiv. Hib.*, xxxiii, 113–14.

18 Barnard, *Cromwellian Ireland*, 179n, and 90–91, 171–82 for this section; the press seems to have been taken to London in the 1650s and then lost – see McGuinne, *Irish Type Design*, 22.

19 Gilbert, *Contemporary History*, vol. I, pt. i, xviii; Burnett, *The Life of Bishop Bedell*, 140–41; Moody *et al.*, eds., *New History of Ireland*, iii, 574.

20 Burke, *Irish Priests in Penal Times (1660–1750)*, 43; Canny, 'Why the Reformation Failed', 443.

21 'Miscellanea Vaticano-Hibernica', *Archiv. Hib.*, v, 105; Gillespie, 'The End of an Era', in *Natives and Newcomers*, 197; Gillespie, 'Destabilizing Ulster, 1641–2', 110.

22 Ohlmeyer, *Civil War and Restoration*, 55, 249–50; O'Laverty, *Down and Connor*, i, 399–401, 423–4, ii, 316–27; Maguire, 'Estate of Cú Chonnacht Maguire', 140; Hill, ed., *Montgomery Manuscripts*, i, 89–91.

23 Dunlop, *Ireland under the Commonwealth*, ii, 363, 423; PRONI, T3022/4/2A–C, shows Gaelic names among the Cromwellian commissioners in Antrim, 1657; IFC, MS 976/92, folk traditions of Cromwellians turning

Catholic; MacCurtain, 'Rural Society in Post-Cromwellian Ireland', 131; Burke, *Irish Priests in Penal Times*, 43; Tynan, *Catholic Instruction in Ireland, 1720–1950*, 19–20: c.1720s, O'Reilly, Bishop of Derry, published an English language catechism for 'the newly converted colonists'.

24 Gillespie, 'The Presbyterian Revolution in Ulster, 1660–1690', in Sheils and Wood, eds., *The Churches, Ireland and the Irish*, 159–70.

25 Macafee and Morgan, 'Population in Ulster, 1660–1760', 47–59.

26 See Elliott, 'Origins and Transformation of Early Irish Republicanism', *Internat. Rev. Soc. Hist.*, xxiii, 415.

27 Crawford, 'The Ulster Irish in the Eighteenth Century', *Ulster Folklife*, vol. 28, 26; Gillespie, 'The Transformation of the Borderlands', 80–81.

28 Hanly, ed., *Plunkett Letters*, 530.

29 I am grateful to Dr Art Hughes, Institute of Irish Studies, Queen's University, Belfast, for advice here. Ó Baoill, *An Teanga Bheo: Gaeilge Uladh*, 123; see also Day and McWilliams, eds., *Ordnance Survey Memoirs of Ireland*, vol. 15, 15.

30 Flynne, 'Hugh MacMahon, Bishop of Clogher 1707–15 and Archbishop of Armagh 1715–37', *Seanchas Ard Mhacha*, 7 (1973), 110; Gilbert, *Contemporary History*, vol. I, pt i, xx; PRONI, T.3022/4, op. cit.; Gillespie, 'Destabilizing Ulster, 1641–2', 109.

31 See e.g. Ó Muirgheasa, *Dánta Diadha Uladh*, 227–32, Lament for Daniel Mackey, Bishop of Down, 1673, clearly a patron of the poets; translator Eugene O'Curry, in *Louth Arch. Soc. Jn.*, 267–72. Ó Fiaich, 'The Political and Social Background of the Ulster Poets', *Léachtaí Cholm Cille*, i, 30–32. Carrigan, 'Catholic Episcopal Wills in the PRO, Dublin, 1683–1812', *Archiv. Hib.*, i, 173–4, dynasty of MacCartan priests at Loughinisland. Heusaff, *Filí agus Cléir san Ochtú hAois Déag*, 5–6: Fr Phelim O'Neill, so beloved of the poets, direct descendant of Turlogh MacHenry.

32 Hughes, 'Landholdings of Gaelic poets', unpublished paper, kindly made available to me by the author.

33 Kennedy, *'Eagla an Ghallsmacht'*, 49–59.

34 O'Rahilly, ed., *Five Seventeenth-century Political Poems*, 140–41; Leerssen, *Mere Irish and Fíor Ghael*, 239–41.

35 Ó Fiaich, 'Filíocht Uladh', 92–3.

36 *Maol* – bald, bare, naked – possibly a reference to clean-shaven, shorn, cropped hair, singling them out from the bearded and long-haired Irish.

37 Walsh, ed., 'The Memorial Presented to the King of Spain on Behalf of the Irish Catholics, A.D. 1619', *Archiv. Hib.*, vi, 54.

38 Bennett acknowledges as much in his praise of Ó Doirnín, Mac Cuarta, Mac Cooey, in 'Don Sagart Pádraig Ó Luain' ('For the priest Patrick Lamb', parish priest of Cullyhanna), in Ó Muirgheasa, *Céad de Cheoltaibh Uladh*, 165; Heusaff, *Filí agus Cléir*, 56, Fr Phelim O'Neill (much respected by the poets), transcribing Keating, 'An Síogaí' and 'Tuireamh na hEireann', in the eighteenth century.

39 Welch, *The Oxford Companion to Irish Literature*, 237. Hardiman, *Irish Minstrelsy*, ii, 306–39. O'Rahilly, *Five . . . Political Poems*, 12–16.

40 Mag Uidhir, *Pádraig Mac a Liondain: Dánta*: the works of these poets were never published.

41 See e.g. Hagan, ed., 'Miscellanea Vaticano-Hibernica', *Archiv. Hib.*, iii, 302–5, the Irish Earls (O'Neill, O'Donnell etc.) to Pope Paul V. *c.*1613; Corish, ed., 'Two Reports on the Catholic Church in Ireland in the Early Seventeenth Century', *Archiv. Hib.*, xxii, 141–2.

42 Mag Uidhir, *Pádraig Mac a Liondain*, 6–8.

43 *Ibid.*, 19–22. There is a similar fatalism in church documents (Moran, *Spicil. Ossor.*, i, ccxv, 1654); also Maguire, 'Pádraig Mhac a Lionnduinn of the Fews', 20, 106–7.

44 "*Sé mo Ghéardheachair Chlíse mar d'Éag Treibh no dTíortha* (Painfully troubled is my heart for the way the tribe of the countries died), in Ó Gallachóir, 'Filíocht Shéamais Dhaill Mhic Cuarta', 263; Mag Uidhir, *Pádraig Mac a Liondain*, 7, Keating's influence.

45 Ó Gallachóir, 'Filíocht', 259, and '*Ní maith is léir damh*' ('It's not well that I see), 239.

46 '*Ceist agam ort a Chúirt na Féile*' (I've a question for you, O Court of Hospitality), O'Gallachóir, 'Filíocht', 121–7.

47 '*A Phlanda*' (O Scion), *ibid.*, 58.

48 His treatise had gone through six editions by 1733, see O'Laverty, *Down and Connor: The Bishops*, 514–15.

49 Either Calvin or Seán Buí ('swarthy John'), the Irish reference for the English.

50 Niall of the Nine Hostages, a favourite figure in Ulster nationalist rhetoric and iconography; this poem taken from Ó Gallachóir, ed., *Séamas Dall Mac Cuarta: Dánta*, 52.

51 QUB, Belfast, Gaelic Manuscripts 17: Mic A/428 (xviii), 'An essay on Séamus Mac Cuarta'.

52 '*Ní maith is léir damh*', in praise of Brian, son of Art O'Neill of the Fews, Ó Gallachóir, 'Filíocht Shéamais Dhaill Mhic Cuarta', 239.

53 Ó Gallachóir, *Séamus Dall Mac Cuarta: Dánta*, 63–9, 90. However, Ó Fiaich, 'Filíocht Uladh mar Fhoinse don Stair Shóisialta san 18ú hAois', *Stud. Hib.*, no. 11, 82, sees the poem as a lament rather than a call to action, a proclamation that Jacobitism is no more. See also Ó Buachalla, ed., *Nua Dhuanaire*, ii, 2–3, 'Eachroim,' *c.*1730, another Ulster poem of stark imagery at the scale of the defeat at Aughrim.

54 '*Sé is léir liom uaim*' ('What's evident to me'), Ó Gallachóir, 'Filíocht . . . Mhic Cuarta', 191–4.

55 Ó Buachalla, 'Lillibulero agus Eile', *Comhar*, 27.

56 Murray, *History of the Parish of Creggan*, 61–7.

57 Ó Fiaich, 'Art Mac Cooey and His Times', *Seanchas Ard Mhacha*, vi, 235; idem, '*Filíocht Uladh*', 82–4, says Jacobitism was much weaker in Ulster.

58 Ó Muirgheasa, *Dánta Diadha Uladh*, 376.

59 Ó Fiaich, 'Art Mac Cooey and His Times', *Seanchas Ard Mhacha*, vi, 242–3; the poems are in Ó Fiaich, *Art Mac Cumhaigh: Dánta*, 102–4.

60 Heussaff, *Filí agus Cléir san Ochtú hAois Déag*, 74–5, 161–2; Murray,

'Three Documents Concerning the Deanery of Dundalk during the Eighteenth Century', *Archiv. Hib.*, v, 68–73.

61 Ó Buachalla, *Cathal Buí: Amhráin*, 21ff.

62 The key scribes are also from this area, Maguire, 'Pádraig Mhac a Lionnduinn of the Fews', 18–19. Even after Cromwellian persecution this area, next to Meath, had the largest numbers of priests in the country. See Ó Fiaich, 'Edmund O'Reilly', 192–3; also Dunlop, *Commonwealth*, ii, 491, for the numbers of schoolmasters operating there; Hanly, ed., *Plunkett Letters*, 73–5, on the Old English families.

63 Maguire, 'Pádraig Mhac a Lionnduinn of the Fews', 9–10; Pádraig Ó Pronntaigh (Patrick O'Pronty), a minor County Down poet, but considered one of the finest scribes of the eighteenth century, was an assistant to Mac-Alindon; on the scribes see also Cullen, 'Patrons, Teachers and Literacy in Irish: 1700–1850', in Daly and Dickson, eds., *The Origins of Popular Literacy in Ireland*, 15–44.

64 Ó Mórdha, 'Simon Macken; Fermanagh Scribe and Schoolmaster', *Clogher Rec.*, ii, 432–44. For other examples of the most dramatic of the Irish-language material being passed on see Duffy, *Nicholas O'Kearney: The Last of the Bards of Louth*, 11–12; Art Murphy, the poet-teacher of Nicholas as a youth (he was born 1807), used Mac Cuarta's works (notably his *Tuireamh*), also Keating; Ó Muirgheasa, *Céad de Cheoltaibh Uladh*, 191, shows frequent later copies of this elegy for Owen Roe, written 1649 by a County Down priest.

65 Burke, ed., 'The Diocese of Derry in 1631', *Archiv. Hib.*, v, 2–3; Hunter, 'English Undertakers in the Plantation of Ulster', 486; Rogan, *Synods and Catechesis in Ireland, c.445–1962*, i, 4–5; Hill, *Plantation*, 494–5, 130 n.

66 Moran, *Spicil. Ossor.*, i, 407–12, 'An Account of the Irish Church in 1654', also pp. 415–16, 'The State of Ireland in 1656'; MacCaffrey, ed., 'Commonwealth Records', *Archiv. Hib.*, vi, 175–202, details Cromwellian policies, directed exclusively against clergy, though those willing to abjure papal supremacy allowed to stay.

67 Corish, *The Catholic Community*, 49; see also Barnard, *Cromwellian Ireland*, 172–5, and Edwards, 'Irish Catholics and the Puritan Revolution', in Franciscan Fathers, eds., *Father Luke Wadding*, 93–118. Barnard, 'Irish Images of Cromwell', in Richardson, ed., *Images of Cromwell*, 180–206.

68 See e.g. the influential little volume Millett OFM, 'Survival and Reorganis-ation 1650–1695', in Corish, ed., *A History of Irish Catholicism*, iii, ch. 7, 1–12. In his more recent bibliographical survey, 'The Seventeenth Century', in Ó Muirí, ed., *Irish Church History Today*, 42, he likens Cromwellian policy to that of the Nazis towards the Jews.

69 Rogan, *Synods and Catechesis*, i, 38–9.

70 According to Archbishop Plunkett, see Hanly, ed., *Plunkett Letters*, 145.

71 Russell and Prendergast, eds., *The Carte Manuscripts*, 124.

72 Giblin, ed., 'Catalogue of material of Irish interest . . . Part 1', *Coll. Hib.*, i, 60 (1624).

73 The word 'Palesman' appears frequently in Ó Doibhlin, *Domhnach Mór*, for Plunkett's activities contradict the association in this book between Catholicism and a Gaelic race, and his foreign roots can be the only explanation (see e.g. pp. 171–3). The appointment of Patrick Tyrrell to Clogher a few years later was similarly resisted. See Ó Fiaich, 'The Appointment of Bishop Tyrrell and Its Consequences', *Clogher Rec.*, i, no. 3, 1–14.

74 O'Connell, *The Diocese of Kilmore: Its History and Antiquities*, 448.

75 Russell and Prendergast, eds., *The Carte Manuscripts*, 125.

76 Quoted Burke, *Irish Priests in Penal Times*, 47.

77 Stuart, *Historical Memoirs of the City of Armagh*, by Revd Ambrose Coleman, OP, 237–9, deals at length with the Franciscan accusers. They are denounced as 'nefarious wretches' for betraying their own. Plunkett was canonised October 1975.

78 Burke, *Irish Priests in Penal Times*, 77, also, 61–5, 74–7, 282–3; Hanly, ed., *Plunkett Letters*, 442, 463; Lecky, *Ireland in the Eighteenth Century*, i, 255.

79 Hanly, ed., *Plunkett Letters*, 78, 86–7, 166, 306, 481; Moran, *Spicil. Ossor.*, i, 193 and 212–13; Burke, *Irish Priests in Penal Times*, 61.

80 Hayton, 'The Propaganda War', in Maguire, ed., *Kings in Conflict*, 113–18.

81 Flynne, 'Hugh MacMahon', 125; James MacCaffrey, ed., 'Commonwealth Records', *Archiv. Hib.*, vi, 191.

82 O'Laverty, *Down and Connor: Bishops*, 496; Burke, *Irish Priests in Penal Times*, 74–6.

83 Ryan, 'Religion and State in Seventeenth-century Ireland', *Archiv. Hib.*, xxxiii, 110–21.

84 Kennedy, '*Eagla an Ghallsmacht*', 177–86; Henry, 'Ulster Exiles in Europe', in Mac Cuarta, ed., *Ulster 1641*, 56, thinks fears of the Ulster clergy inciting rebellion were justified; *Cal. S.P. Ire.*, *1663–5*, 359–61.

85 See *Cal. S.P. Ire.*, *1669–70*, 560–63, for the full text and list of subscribers.

86 Giblin, ed., 'Catalogue of Material . . . in the Vatican Archives', Part I, 102–5; Stuart, *Historical Memoirs of the City of Armagh*, 242.

87 Flynne, 'Hugh MacMahon Bishop of Clogher', 125 – only three of these were from Ulster.

88 Giblin, ed., 'Catalogue of Material . . . in the Vatican Archives', Part II, 24ff, also Part I, 123.

89 Flynne, 'Hugh MacMahon', 136–40.

90 Ó Fiaich, 'Edmund O'Reilly, Archbishop of Armagh, 1657–1669', in Franciscan Fathers, eds., *Father Luke Wadding*, 214; Burke, *Irish Priests in Penal Times*, 11–14; O'Connell, *Diocese of Kilmore*, 433–4.

91 Ó Fiaich, 'The Registration of the Clergy in 1704', *Seanchas Ard Mhacha*, vi, 59.

92 Burke, *Irish Priests in Penal Times*, 65.

93 Moran, *Spicil. Ossor.*, i, 192; Giblin, ed., 'Catalogue of Material . . . in the Vatican Archives', Part I, 115–16.

94 Cited Corish, *Catholic Community*, 42.

95 Hanly, ed., *Plunkett Letters*, 407; Smyth, 'Blessed Oliver Plunkett in Down and Connor', *Down and Connor Hist. Soc. Jn.*, viii, 76–80.

96 Ó Fiaich, 'Edmund O'Reilly', 197; R. Gillespie, *The Sacred in the Secular*, 13–14; Gillespie, *Devoted People*, 152.

97 Flynne, 'Hugh MacMahon', 115; Crawford, 'Ulster Irish', 27; Ó Gallachair, 'Clogherhici. A Dictionary of the Catholic Clergy of the Diocese of Clogher (1535–1835)', *Clogher Rec.*, i, no. 3, 169; Hanly, ed., *Plunkett Letters*, 361–2, 380–81.

98 *Comhairle Mhic Clámha ó Achadh na Muilleann: The Advice of MacClave from Aughnamullen*, translated by Ó Dufaigh and Rainey.

99 See e.g. of Father McQuaid of Knockaraven, in Ó Gallachair, 'Clogherici', *Clogher Rec.*, xii, no. 2, 237.

100 See e.g. Ó Fiaich, 'The appointment of Bishop Tyrrell', 7; Ó Gallachair, 'Clogherhici', *Clogher Rec.*, i, no. 3, 68–9; Gallagher, 'Sources for the History of a Diocese', *Procs. Ir. Cath. Hist. Committee*, 29–30.

101 Hanly, ed., *Plunkett Letters*, 517–19, 522; also O'Laverty, *Down and Connor: Bishops*, 483; Bartlett, *Fall and Rise*, 5.

102 Hanly, ed., *Plunkett Letters*, 277.

103 *Ibid.*, 238; and Burke, *Irish Priests in Penal Times*, 75, for meetings of clergy in ale-houses.

104 Hanly, ed., *Plunkett Letters*, 340–41.

105 *MacClave from Aughnamullen*, 68–71.

106 Hanly, ed., *Plunkett Letters*, 75, 152–3, 277–8.

107 Gillespie, *The Sacred in the Secular*, 40.

108 The words are those of George Andrews, dean of Limerick, in 1625, cited in Kilroy, 'Sermon and Pamphlet Literature', 115.

109 Ó Muirgheasa, ed., *Dánta Diadha Uladh*, 139, also 97, 123, 125; Murray, 'A Previously Unnoticed Letter', 24, one of the papers found on the tory, Patrick Fleming, had prayers to the devotion of 'the print of Our Lady's Foot, with instructions for saying the Pater Noster and Ave Maria'.

110 Ó Muirgheasa, ed., *Dánta Diadha Uladh*, particularly useful here as it records poetry which survived in the popular oral tradition down to this century, e.g. poems by Ó Prontaigh, pp. 163–4, Cathal Buí, p. 139, Owen O'Donnelly, pp. 214–16.

111 Croker, ed., *The Tour of the French Traveller M. de la Boullaye le Gouz in Ireland in A.D. 1644*, 39 and 45.

112 Troyer, ed., *Five Travel Scripts Commonly Attributed to Edward Ward [1698]*, 10.

113 Litton-Falkiner, *Illustrations of Irish History*, 418 – the date is 1667–8, the location two miles from Drogheda.

114 Tynan, *Catholic Instruction in Ireland, 1720–1950*, 14; also Rogan, *Synods and Catechesis*, xiv–xv, showing very intermittent reference to such instruction in the synods of the seventeenth century.

115 Hanly, ed., *Plunkett Letters*, 141, 145; Briggs, *Early Modern France 1560–1715*, 172.

116 Ó Muirgheasa, ed., *Dánta Diadha Uladh*, 147–8.

117 Gillespie, *The Sacred in the Secular*, 2.

118 This is an Ulster poem of the 1640s. Its authorship is in contention,

sometimes attributed to a Protestant clergyman from Co. Down; if so, he is clearly of native Irish stock and/or the text must have been doctored by a scribe, given its content. Ó Muirgheasa, *Dhá Chéad*, poem 1, also in Ó Buachalla, *Nua-Dhuanaire*, i, 38.

119 Hickson, *Ireland in the Seventeenth Century*, i, 189–40; *An Account of the Bloody Massacre in Ireland*, 3.

120 *Cal. S.P. Ire.*, *1633–1647*, 355; Gilbert, *Contemporary History*, i (1), 360.

121 Hickson, *Ireland in the Seventeenth Century*, i, 173.

122 Ó Fiaich, 'Filíocht Uladh', 124; Ó Muirgheasa, *Céad de Cheoltaibh Uladh*, 13; Hanly, ed., *Plunkett Letters*, 220; *Montgomery Manuscripts*, 139, also says reading the scriptures has become the dividing line.

123 O'Dwyer, *Mary*, 232; the same image is reproduced in the nineteenth century, Ó Muirgheasa, ed., *Dánta Diadha Uladh*, 257.

124 Ó Muirgheasa, ed., *Dánta Diadha Uladh*, poems 50–51, 53, 54, 56.

125 Millett, 'Survival and Reorganization', 36; Moran, *Spicil. Ossor*, i, 120–21.

126 Ó Muirgheasa, ed., *Dánta Diadha Uladh*, 276–7; Robinson, *Plantation of Ulster*, 189: report of the woodkerne hanging an Irishman because he had conformed, 1615.

127 O'Donovan, *The Topographical Poems of John Ó Dubhagain*, 29–30; also Ó Muirgheasa, *Céad de Cheoltaibh Uladh*, 186–90, songs attacking priests who conformed still being sung in the twentieth century, particularly in Donegal and Tyrone.

128 Ó Muirgheasa, ed., *Dánta Diadha Uladh*, 348 (this about the two MacLochlain brothers of Inishowen; idem, *Céad de Cheoltaibh Uladh*, 186–90).

129 IFC, MS 1922/58.

130 IFC, MS 975/106.

131 IFC, MS 1275/212 and 214; see Murphy, *Tyrone Folk Quest*, 23. The original Catholicism of the Hamiltons is lost to local Tyrone traditions; see also Ó Fiaich, 'O'Neills of the Fews', 55, on local Armagh traditions of Turlough MacHenry changing his religion to keep his land.

132 IFC, MS 976/168, this from south Armagh; also MS 1923/97.

133 Cunningham, in *Natives and Newcomers*, 169–70.

134 See Edwards, 'The Priest, the Layman and the Historian', *European History Quarterly*, xvii, 87–93.

6 LIFE UNDER THE PENAL LAWS

1 UFTM, School Textbook Collection, E2/61/10: *The Programme of History Irish and English*, Book II, 34e; Ó Danachair, 'The Penal Laws and Irish Folk tradition', *Procs. Ir. Cath. Hist. Comm.*, 10–16.

2 Young, *Tour in Ireland* (1776–1779), i, 114; Cullen, 'Catholics under the Penal Laws', *Eighteenth-Century Ireland*, i, 71.

3 Ó Fiaich, 'The Registration of the Clergy in 1704', *Seanchas Ard Mhacha*, vi, 49.

4 Bishop MacMahon claimed this the situation as early as 1714: Flanagan, 'The Diocese of Clogher in 1714', *Clogher Rec.*, i, no. 3, 126. Many clergy would not have been averse to taking the oath, but disapproval from their flocks deterred them, see Fagan, *Divided Loyalties*, 45–6.

5 Corish, 'Catholic Marriage under the Penal Code', in Cosgrove, ed., *Marriage in Ireland*, 70–71.

6 Synge, *The Case of Toleration Considered with Respect Both to Religion and Civil Government*; Richardson, *A Short History of Attempts That Have Been Made … to Convert the Popish Inhabitants of Ireland*, 44; see also Connolly, *Religion, Law and Power*, 285–88; Fagan, *An Irish Bishopric in Penal Times*, 48–9, 74–5; and Lecky, *Ireland in the Eighteenth Century*, i, 271, 304, 306–7. These works by Synge and Richardson became bestsellers in their day, showing the level of debate on the issue.

7 Young, *Tour*, ii, 66.

8 Fagan, *Divided Loyalties*, 166–7, 189–92.

9 Shaw, *Cullybackey*, 132; Quinn, 'Religion and Landownership in Louth', 7.

10 Though not, it seems, by the Catholic clergy. The draft of a satirical pamphlet by Michael MacDonagh, Bishop of Kilmore, arrested near Lough Neagh in 1739, speaks scathingly of such converts: see Fenning, ed., *The Fottrell Papers, 1721–39*, 133–6; also Bishop MacMahon's criticism in Flanagan, ed., 'The Diocese of Clogher in 1714', *Clogher Rec.*, i, 128.

11 O'Laverty, *Down and Connor*, iii, 425, and i, 382, also iii, 407, for the continued pro-Catholic leanings of the McManuses. See Fagan, *An Irish Bishop in Penal Times*, 67–8, 94 and O'Brien, *The Great Melody*, 56–7, for similar examples from elsewhere in Ireland.

12 Bigger, *The Ulster Land War of 1770*, 51–2; see case also of Rowland Kane, a Protestant discoverer, PRONI, D.627/13; Lecky, *Ireland in the Eighteenth Century*, i, 47 on the sense of insecurity caused by this among propertied Catholics; Macaulay, *William Crolly: Archbishop of Armagh, 1835–49*, ix. Crolly's family lost land when one of the family conformed in 1774 and claimed all under the penal laws.

13 Simms, 'Irish Catholics and the Parliamentary Franchise, 1692–1728', in Hayton and O'Brien, eds., *War and Politics in Ireland, 1649–1730*, 224–34.

14 Cited in Elliott, *Partners in Revolution*, 37–8; Fagan, *Divided Loyalties*, 112, on the extreme prejudices of the Irish parliament.

15 Doyle, *Ireland, Irishmen and Revolutionary America, 1760–1820*, 70.

16 *BNL*, 23 January 1756; Ian McBride, 'Presbyterians in the Penal Era', *Bullán: An Irish Studies Journal*, i–ii, 82–3. Gebbie, ed., *An Introduction to the Abercorn Letters*, 144; Crawford and Trainor, eds., *Aspects of Irish Social History, 1750–1800*, 164.

17 *The Parliamentary Register Or, History of the Proceedings and Debates of the House of Commons of Ireland, 1781–97*, i, 258–9, xiii, 165, 169, xiii, 296; Moody, McDowell and Woods, eds., *The Writings of Theobald Wolfe Tone*, i, 121–2.

18 Brady, *Catholics and Catholicism in the Eighteenth-century Press*, 69. *A Test of Roman Catholic Liberality, Submitted to the Consideration of Both*

Roman Catholicks and Protestants. By a Citizen of London-Derry. Even this liberal Protestant feared that were Catholics to be given power they might close Protestants' churches and schools and persecute their religion.

19 Wall, 'Catholic Loyalty to King and Pope in Eighteenth-century Ireland', in O'Brien, ed., *Catholic Ireland in the Eighteenth Century*, 107–14. Fagan, *An Irish Bishop in Penal Times*, 97–8, 112.

20 PRONI, D.1514/9/71, Frederick Hervey to unnamed Catholic, 31 October 1767.

21 De Valera, 'Antiquarianism and Historical Investigations in Ireland in the Eighteenth Century', 39–43; Gamble, *View of Society and Manners in the North of Ireland in the Summer and Autumn of 1812*, 264–5.

22 Brady, *Catholics and Catholicism*, 111–25; Ó Gallachair, 'Clogherici. A Dictionary of the Catholic Clergy of the Diocese of Clogher (1535–1835)', *Clogher Rec.*, vol. 8, no. 2, 211; Leerssen, *Mere Irish and Fíor Ghael*, 361.

23 'Act for the Security of Protestant Purchasers' (I Geo. III, *c*.12) and 'Act for Quieting the Possessions of Protestants Deriving under Converts from the Popish Religion' (I Geo III, *c*.13).

24 Elliott, 'The Origins and Transformation of Early Irish Republicanism', *Internat. Rev. of Soc. Hist.*, xxiii, 415; Connolly, *Religion, Law and Power*, 144–9; Brady, *Catholics and Catholicism*, 96–7, 226; Crawford, 'The Political Economy of Linen: Ulster in the Eighteenth Century', in Brady *et al.*, eds., *Ulster: An Illustrated History*, 152–5.

25 Adams, *Printed Word*, 96–7.

26 O'Byrne, ed., *The Convert Rolls*, viii–ix; Brady, *Catholics and Catholicism*, 13–14, 58–9, 129–37, 146–50, 197; Bigger, *The Ulster Land War of 1770*, 51–2.

27 Quoted P. McNally, *Parties, Patriots and Undertakers*, 28.

28 Richardson, *A Proposal for the Conversion of the Popish Natives of Ireland to the Established Religion*; Hill, 'Popular Protestantism in Ulster in the Post-Rebellion Period, *c*.1790–1810', in Shields and Wood, eds., *The Churches, Ireland and the Irish*, 25, 191–202; Blaney, *Presbyterians and the Irish Language*, 20–27; Corkery, 'Gaelic Catechisms in Ireland', 56–63.

29 Harris, *The Ancient and Present State of the County of Down*, 17–18, 77, 109. Connolly, *Religion, Law and Power*, 304–7; Laverty, *Down and Connor*, i, 156–7.

30 Milne, *The Irish Charter Schools, 1730–1830*, 328.

31 Cited Milne, *Charter Schools*, 300; Stevenson, trans., *A Frenchman's Walk through Ireland, 1796–7*, 75, popular fear of such institutions in 1790s Munster.

32 Quinn, 'Religion and Landownership', 25.

33 Flanagan, ed., 'Clogher in 1714', 125–6; Fenning, ed., *Fottrell Papers*, 123.

34 The fullest accounts are in Connolly, *Religion, Law and Power*, 263–94, and his 'The Penal Laws', in Maguire, ed., *Kings in Conflict*, 157–72; also the articles by Simms, in Hayton and O'Brien, eds., *War and Politics in Ireland 1649–1730*, particularly 225–76.

35 Larkin, ' "Popish Riot" in south County Derry', *Seanchas Ard Mhacha*, 8, no. 1, 94–111.

36 Ó Gallachair, 'Clogher's Altars of the Penal Days', *Clogher Rec.*, 2, 103; idem, 'Clogherici', *Clogher Rec.*, i, no. 3, 68; IFC, MS 1359/153; Farry, 'Penal Day Traditions in Mourne', *Down and Connor Hist. Soc. Jn.*, ix, 42–9; Creighton, 'The Penal Laws in Ireland and the Documents in the Archives of Propaganda (1690–1731)', *Procs. Irish Cath. Hist. Committee*, 9, shows the penal laws against the clergy rarely fully enforced; McKeown, 'Friars Bush', *Down and Connor Hist. Soc. Jn.*, vi, 72–5; [Harkin], *Inishowen*, 68; Wall, 'Penal Laws', in O'Brien, ed., *Catholic Ireland*, 23.

37 Brady, *Catholics and Catholicism*, 16, 19; Lecky, *Ireland in the Eighteenth Century*, i, 258, 312; Flannagan, 'MacMahon', 127.

38 Shaw, *Cullybackey*, 127–9, Ó Danachair, 'The Penal Laws and Irish Folk Tradition', 15; Duffy, *Landscapes*, 36 (Caldwells of Fermanagh); [Harkin] *Inishowen*, 98–9, (Campbell family); Laverty, *Down and Connor*, i, 246–7, 313n., 317–8, 325, and ii, 353; Renehan, *Collections on Irish Church History*, 2 vols., ii, 93; UFTM, R.85.249, taped interview with Jim O'Neill of Warrenpoint, concerning the Presbyterian Glenny family holding land in trust for the Marmions and handing it back 'honourably'; Cogan, *Meath*, ii, 243, 266–7, 282.

39 Examples are the Hamiltons of mid-Ulster (Abercorn) and Louth (Clanbrassill); the O'Neills, McManuses and MacDonnells of Antrim; the Savages and Magennises of Down; the McCanns of Armagh.

40 Brady, *Catholics and Catholicism*, 146; also *BNL*, 9 July 1756, 12 July and 11 November 1757, advertisements for Protestant tenants exclusively; Laverty, *Down and Connor*, i, 317. In 1750 the recently rebuilt chapel at Struell, outside Downpatrick, was torn down by a mob headed by the Protestant curate and with the sanction of the landlord, the Southwell family.

41 W. H. Crawford, 'Economy and Society in Eighteenth-Century Ulster', 33–5; also his 'The Ulster Irish in the Eighteenth Century', *Ulster Folklife*, 28, 26; Roebuck, 'The Economic Situation and Functions of Substantial Landowners, 1660–1815', in Mitchison and Roebuck, eds., *Economy and Society in Scotland and Ireland, 1500–1939*, 84–9.

42 PRONI, D.207/5/46, report of the English Attorney and Solicitor-General to the English Privy Council, 16 July 1778.

43 Rushe, *Monaghan in the Eighteenth Century*, 131–7; Lecky, *Ireland in the Eighteenth Century*, i, 282, also 312; Brady, *Catholics and Catholicism*, 89, 272; Flynn, 'Hugh MacMahon', 129–30; Crawford, 'Economy and Society', 34; Osborough, 'Catholics, Land and the Popery Acts of Anne', in Power and Whelan, eds., *Endurance and Emergence*, 21–56.

44 Fenning, *Fottrell Papers*, xiii; Brady, *Catholics and Catholicism*, 90.

45 PRONI Mic.147/9/93–5, Clanbrassill to 'My Lord' [Roden?], November 1757; Lord Chesterfield (Lord Lieutenant 1745–6) had also tried to introduce such a bill.

46 PRONI, T.808/14895/7–10; also T.808/14895–6, Abstracts of County Antrim Assizes and quarter sessions, 1711–31 and ANT 4/1/1, Antrim Grand Jury Presentment Books for 1711–21.

47 The complaint 1788 'we had popish G[rand] Juries and Protestant Petit Juries', cited Miller, *Peep O'Day Boys and Defenders*, 65–7.

48 Mac Giolla Easpaig, *Tomás Ruiséil*, 56; *The Parliamentary Register: or, History of the Proceedings and Debates of the House of Commons of Ireland, 1781–97*, 7 vols., xiii, iii–2, speech by Dr Duigenan, 4 February 1793, in opposition to the Catholic relief bill, where he lists the incidences when Catholics can be debarred from juries.

49 O'Laverty, *Down and Connor*, iv, 129, 247.

50 Miller, *Peep O'Day Boys*, 73.

51 O'Laverty, *Down and Connor*, iii, 382, also ii, 49–50.

52 Gebbie, *Abercorn Letters*, 65–7; Brady, *Catholics and Catholicism*, 202.

53 Flanagan, ed., 'Diocese of Clogher', 40–41.

54 O'Laverty, *Down and Connor*, ii, 206.

55 James Stuart, *Historical Memoirs of the City of Armagh*, 349–50.

56 PRONI, T.1392: Memorial of the Proprietors of the Fews, 2 December 1743; Donaldson, *A Historical and Statistical Account of the Barony of the Upper Fews in the County of Armagh* (Dundalk, 1923), 10–16, 86–7.

57 Macafee, 'Colonisation of the Maghera Region', 88–9; McBride, 'Presbyterians in the Penal Era', 77.

58 Crawford, 'Ulster Irish', 26.

59 Crawford and Trainor, eds., *Aspects of Irish Social History*, 112–13; also Roebuck, ed., *Macartney of Lissanoure*, 146; and see Laverty, *Down and Connor*, iii, 294, 323, for other examples of liberal Protestant gentry in Antrim.

60 Gebbie, *Abercorn Letters*, 36; Corish, 'Catholic Marriage under the Penal Code', 72–5; Brady, *Catholics and Catholicism*, 50; Cogan, *Meath*, ii, 282, iii, 59.

61 Carleton, *Autobiography*, 235–6.

62 Adams, *Printed Word*, 12–14, 144–5; see also Ó Mórdha, 'Simon Macken; Fermanagh Scribe and Schoolmaster'; and Corish, *Catholic Community*, 109–10, on their dislike of the printing press and how they even transcribed things printed in English; Szövérffy, '*Rí Naomh Seoirse*: Chapbooks and Hedge-Schools', *Éigse*, 9, 114–17.

63 Ashton, *The Battle of Aughrim, or the Fall of Monsieur St. Ruth. A Tragedy*; Adams, *Printed Word*, 70–72; Ó Cíosáin, *Print and Popular Culture*, 107–11.

64 'Report on the State of Popery in Ireland, 1731', *Archiv. Hib.*, i, 10–27; Fenning, *Undoing of the Friars*, 196–7.

65 Brady, 'Catholics and Catholicism', 253.

66 Macaulay, *William Crolly. Archbishop of Armagh, 1835–49*, 2; see also O'Connell, *The Diocese of Kilmore: Its History and Antiquities*, xxxv.

67 Carleton, *Autobiography*, 72–3; idem, *Traits and Stories*, i, 41; Cullen, 'Patrons, Teachers and Literacy in Irish', in Daly and Dickson, eds., *Origins of Popular Literacy*, 30–31.

68 McPolin, 'An Old Irish Catechism from Oriel', *Ir. Eccles. Rec.*, 509–15;

Ó Cíosáin, 'Printed Popular Literature in Irish', in Daly and Dickson, eds., *Origins of Popular Literacy*, 50, discussed also in his *Print and Popular Culture*, ch. 9; Ó Casaide, *Irish Language in Belfast and County Down*, 45–6; Wall, *The Sign of Dr Hay's head*, 109–11.

69 Buttimer, 'An Irish Text on the "War of Jenkins' Ear"', *Celtica*, xxi, 80–82.

70 Young, *Historical Notices of Old Belfast*, 182–3; Brady, *Catholics and Catholicism*, 131.

71 Parker, *The History of Londonderry, Comprising the Towns of Derry and Londonderry, New Hampshire*, 74 – my thanks to Dr Ian McBride for drawing this to my attention. See also Sampson, *Statistical Survey of the County of Londonderry*, 457, for a description of such a wedding. Ó Danachair, in Cosgove, ed., *Marriage in Ireland*, 113, also notes this custom as being peculiar to the north, though he thinks it came from Scotland.

72 Ó Fiaich, *Art Mac Cumhaigh: Dánta*, 88, 186–7.

73 Ó Muirgheasa, *Abhráin . . . Mhic Chubhthaigh*, 56, 64; Ó Fiaich, *Art Mac Cumhaigh: Dánta*, 85.

74 Ó Muirgheasa, *Abhráin . . . Mhic Chubhthaigh*, 281.

75 PRONI, Mic.147/9/111–14, the earl of Roden to his sister Charlotte, 3 April 1811; for Count Nugent's family, see O'Callaghan, *Irish Brigades in France*, 154–5.

76 Ó Muirgheasa, *Dhá Chéad de Cheoltaibh Uladh*, 18; Rushe, *Monaghan*, 66–7, and McEvoy, 'The United Irishmen in Co. Tyrone', *Seanchas Ard Mhacha*, iii, no. 2, 288, for Irish interpreters at the courts.

77 McGarvey, 'The Heather Edge', *Seanchas Ard Mhacha*, ii, no. 1, 184; Ó Mórdha, 'Maurice O'Gorman in Monaghan', *Clogher Rec.*, ii, 20–24; Ó Gallachair, 'Clogherici', *Clogher Rec.*, ii, no. 1, 51; Carleton, *Traits and Stories*, i, 44n; see McMahon and Ó Fiaich, 'Inscriptions in Creggan Grave-yard', *Seanchas Ard Mhacha*, vi, no. 2, 330.

78 Francis Hutchinson, *A Defence of the Ancient Historians*, 128–9; Hutchinson, *The Reformed Presbyterian Church in Scotland*, 221.

79 Madden, *The United Irishmen, Their Lives and Times*, 3rd ser., i, 312–13.

80 See PRONI, D.668/3, lengthy description by Revd Philip Skelton, rector of Templecarn, Co. Donegal, 10 February 1776, to the Protestant bishop of Clogher. For continued gatherings at other holy wells see Harris, *The Ancient and Present State of the County of Down*, 25, 35; PRONI, D.605/1/12, detailed 1720 description of a pattern at Saint Ternan's well in Fermanagh.

81 Flanagan, 'Diocese of Clogher', 129–30; Donnelly Jr., 'Lough Derg' in Ronan *et al.*, eds., *Donegal: History and Society*, 491–507; Carleton, *Autobiography*, pp. 88–95.

82 Sir Charles Coote, *Statistical Survey of the County of Monaghan*, 39; Gebbie, *Ardstraw*, 52–61.

83 *The Distress'd State of Ireland Considered* ([Dublin], 1740); Macafee, 'Population of Ulster', 111–21.

84 Gebbie, ed., *Abercorn Letters*, 12–13; Day, *Letters from Georgian Ireland*, 215; Ó Gallachóir, *Séamas Dall Mac Cuarta. Dánta*, 70. 'Irish Catholics

Licensed to Keep Arms (1704)', *Archiv. Hib.*, iv, 59–65. Of 115 granted, only three went to Ulster, two Magennises, one Major Stafford, Co. Donegal.

85 Kirkham, 'Economic Diversification in a Marginal Economy', 80.

86 Young, *Tour*, i, 161, 166, 174–5, 184, 196–8, 205.

87 Cullen, 'Catholics under the Penal Laws', 23–36; Whelan, 'Regional Impact', 258–60; Dickson, 'Derry's Backyard: The Barony of Inishowen, 1650–1800', in Dunlevy, Nolan and Ronayne, eds., *Donegal. History and Society*, 417–18.

88 Ó Fiaich, 'O'Neills of the Fews', *Seanchas Ard Mhacha*, viii, 386; see Bigger, *Ulster Land War*, 125–6, MacCartans and their undertenants being turned out from lands of Clanvarraghan; Lin. Lib., Joy MSS, Commonplace Book, f. 32: similarly with the Magennises in Annachlone; Ó Fiaich, '*Filíocht Uladh mar Fhoinse don Stair Shóisialta san 18ú hAois*', *Stud. Hib.*, no. 11, 95–6; Ó Muirgheasa, *Dánta Diadha Uladh*, 276–7, Farney (Monaghan). Ó Mearáin, 'The Bath Estate, 1700–1777', *Clogher Rec.*, vol. 6, no. 2, 333–60, shows a great variety of leases, improving later in the century with Catholics letting directly from the landlord after 1777. The Irish generally maintained their presence on the old O'Neill lands around Dungannon (Crawford, 'Political Economy', 155), also Armagh (Glancy, *Primate Lands*, 387).

89 Crawford, 'Economy and Society in South Ulster', 246; Gebbie, *Abercorn Letters*, 49.

90 Plowden, *An Historical Review of the State of Ireland*, iv, 53; Tone, *Writings*, i, 365–71.

91 Ó Casaide, *Irish Language in Down*, 27.

92 Ó Fiaich, 'O'Neills of the Fews', *Seanchas Ard Mhacha*, viii, 389–90; idem, *Mac Cumhaigh. Dánta*, 148–9; idem, 'MacCooey and His Times', 242, the O'Callaghans; Crawford, 'Economy and Society in Eighteenth-Century Ulster', 25; Rushe, *Monaghan*, 38–9, for the MacMahons of Ballybay; Duffy, *Landscapes of South Ulster*, 66, 70, 74, for the McKennas and Murphys; Gebbie, *Abercorn Letters*, 76.

93 Simms, ed., *Rev James O'Coigley, United Irishman*, 11–12.

94 PRONI, Whyte Papers, D.298/1/11–26, D.2918/5/3/1–12, D.2918/8/63, various leases and legal papers. I am grateful to Dr Alan Blackstock for alerting me to the contents of these papers. *Burke's Irish Family Records* (1976), 1214–16.

95 Tone, *Writings*, i, 243; Ó Casaide, *The Irish Language in Belfast and County Down*, 12.

96 Carrigan, 'Catholic Episcopal Wills in the Public Record Office, Dublin, 1683–1812', *Archiv. Hib.*, i, 151–90; [Harkin], *Inishowen*, 186–7: this the account of a journey to the Collège des Lombards by Charles O'Donnell, future Bishop of Derry (1798–1823), his baggage every bit that of a gentleman; Crawford, 'Economy and Society in Eighteenth-century Ulster', 23; Duffy, *Landscapes of South Ulster*, 66.

97 McVeigh, ed., *Richard Pococke's Irish Tours*, 71.

98 *Burke's . . . Landed Gentry of Ireland*, 4th edn, 683–4.

99 However, since they were destroyed in the Four Courts fire of 1922, we

are dependent on highly deficient secondary lists. See excellent discussion of this in Fagan, *Divided Loyalties*, 176–88.

100 NLI, T.1,898 (Catholic Qualification Rolls, 1778–90); only twelve out of a national total of 1,526 took the 1774 oath, and those, it seems, in areas where the bishops endorsed the oath, or where there was a significant landed interest (Fagan, *Divided Loyalties*, 176–9).

101 Quoted Lecky, *Ireland in the Eighteenth Century*, iii, 339–40. A similar argument was made in *A Candid and Impartial Account of the Disturbances in the County of Meath, in the Years 1792, 1793, and 1794. By a County Meath Freeholder*.

102 Leighton, *Catholicism in a Protestant Kingdom: a Study of the Irish Ancien Régime*, 153–4.

103 PRONI, D.1325/3/35 and 37, for documents referred to above – also very useful 'Introduction' to the collection by Dr. A. P. W. Malcomson. I am grateful to Dr Alan Blackstock for drawing my attention to this collection.

104 I am grateful to Dr C. J. Woods for showing me this article on Coile for the *Dictionary of Irish Biography*.

105 Livingstone, *Monaghan Story*, 139–40.

106 This is the theme of MacCooey's 'Churls of the Barley', see Ó Fiaich, 'Art MacCooey and his times', *Seanchas Ard Mhacha*, vol. 6, no. 2, 242–3; idem, *Art Mac Cumhaigh. Dánta*, 102–4; Watson, '*Coimhlint an Dá Chultúr – Gaeil agus Gaill i bhFilíocht Chúige Uladh san Ochtú hAois Déag*', Eighteenth-Century Ireland, 3, 97; Crawford, 'The Ulster Irish in the Eighteenth Century', 29.

107 Ó Fiaich, 'MacCooey and his Times', 223.

108 Garret Fitzgerald, 'The Decline of the Irish Language', in Daly and Dickson, eds., *Origins of Popular Literacy*, 59–72.

109 Ó Fiaich, 'The Political and Social Background of the Ulster Poets', *Léachtaí Cholm Cille*, i, 29; de Brún, 'Some Irish MSS with Breifne Associations', *Breifne*, iii, no. 12, 560–61.

110 Crawford, 'Economy and Society in Eighteenth-century Ulster', 32, also 11, 28–32, 54–6.

111 In elections of 1773 only Enniskillen nominated representatives; in 1791 Carrickfergus, Monaghan, Armagh, Donegal, Derry, Newry, Belfast and Coleraine had joined, see Edwards, ed., 'The Minute Book of the Catholic Committee, 1773–92', *Archiv. Hib.*, 9, 12, 56–7, 92–3, 118–20; Whelan, 'Regional Impact', 262. For Orangemen attacking propertied Catholics see Brady, 'Catholics and Catholicism', 301–3; Hogan, 'The Migration of Ulster Catholics to Connaught, 1795–6', *Seanchas Ard Mhacha*, 9, no. 2, 286–301.

112 Young, *Tour*, ii, 57.

113 Cited Dickson, *Ulster Emigration*, 35.

114 Brockliss and Ferté, 'Irish Clerics in France in the Seventeenth and Eighteenth Centuries', 540.

115 De Valera, 'Antiquarianism and Historical Investigations', 195–8; McCarthy, 'Ulster Office', 208–12. Proof of noble rank would have been necessary to attain officer rank in the armies of the Continental powers.

116 [McKenna], *Devenish (Lough Erne) Its History, Antiquities and Traditions*, 125–34; also Simms in Moody and Vaughan, eds., *New History of Ireland*, iv, 642–3; Ó Gallachair, 'Clogherici', *Clogher Rec.*, i, no. 4, 137–56; Murray, *History of the Parish of Creggan*, 54; Ó Coinne and Ó Fiaich, 'Tombstone Inscriptions in Drumglass Cemetery', *Seanchas Ard Mhacha*, vii, no. 2, 316–19.

117 Livingstone, *Monaghan Story*, 591–2.

118 Ó Ceallaigh, *Gleanings from Ulster History*, 94–5.

119 Chart, ed., *The Drennan Letters*, 79.

120 Flanagan, 'The Diocese of Clogher in 1714', *Clogher Rec.*, i, no. 2, 40; Crawford, 'Economy and Society in South Ulster in the Eighteenth Century', 18.

121 *A Candid and Impartial Account of the Disturbances in the County of Meath, in the Years 1792, 1793, and 1794* (Dublin, 1794), 2; Crawford, 'Political economy', 153–6; Duffy, *Landscapes of South Ulster*, 42–4, 52, 64; Ó Fiaich, 'The 1766 Religious Census', *Seanchas Ard Mhacha*, iv, 147–70; Macafee, 'The Colonisation of the Maghera Region of South Derry during the Seventeenth and Eighteenth Centuries', 76–86, analyses this process of segregation; idem, 'Population of Ulster', Harris, *The Ancient and Present State of the County of Down*, 78, 97.

122 Crawford, 'Economy and Society in Eighteenth-century Ulster', 27, 61–80. Duffy, *Landscape of South Ulster*, 21; Houston, 'Literacy and Society in the West, 1500–1850', *Social History*, viii, no. 3, 285–7, shows how areas which do not speak the 'official' language are more traditional and economically less developed; in Scotland Highland Gaelic-speakers were viewed by the Presbyterian Lowlanders as popish and barbarous. But see Young, *Tour*, i, 161–2, showing Rundale in largely Presbyterian areas also; Anderson, 'Rundale, Rural Economy and Agrarian Revolution: Tirhugh, 1715–1855', in Nolan, Ronayne and Dunlevy, eds., *Donegal. History and Society*, 447–69. Macafee, 'The Population of Ulster', 56: in 1712 Catholics were still 60 per cent of the Ulster population and were largely concentrated in the remoter parts of the country.

123 Molyneux's Tour, 1708, in Young, *Historical Notices of Old Belfast*, 153. Crawford, 'Economy and Society in Eighteenth-century Ulster', 21; Duffy, *Landscapes of South Ulster*, 23; Sir Charles Coote, *Statistical Survey of County Armagh*, particularly 22–3, 35, 300; Gebbie, ed., *Abercorn Letters*, 205.

124 Patterson, 'The Territory of Ballymacone and Its Associations with the McCones', *Seanchas Ard Mhacha*, i, no. 1, 139; Donaldson, *A Historical and Statistical Account of the Upper Fews*, 139; Harris, *The Ancient and Present State of the County of Down*, 125, 'Booleying in the Mournes'.

125 Crawford and Trainor, eds., *Aspects of Irish Social History*, 90.

126 McParlan, *Statistical Survey of the County of Donegal*, 91–2, 100–101; Duffy, *Landscapes of South Ulster*, 79: in the hills of west Monaghan a 1760 commentator noted whiskey for sale in almost every house, though no inns in the area. Also Kirkham, 'Economic Diversification in a Marginal Economy:

a case study', in Roebuck, ed., *Plantation to Partition*, 65–81; Ó Muirgheasa, *Dhá Chéad de Cheoltaibh Uladh*, iii, 394–5: *c*.1780, poem about smuggling from Gortahork, Co. Donegal; *Sources for the Study of Local History in Northern Ireland. Northern Ireland Public Record Office*, 70; Gebbie, ed., *Abercorn Letters*, 126, 140, attempts to discourage whiskey production. Ó Fiaich, 'Filíocht Uladh', 117–19, on attitudes to new modes of travel in the poetry, limited popular use of new roads. Ó Muirgheasa, *Dhá Chéad de Cheoltaibh Uladh*, iii, poem 195.

127 Gebbie, *Abercorn Letters*, 205; Duffy, *Landscapes of South Ulster*, 26–7; Miller, *Peep O'Day Boys and Defenders*, 105, for Protestant fears of Catholics in the mountains in the 1790s, their distinctive great coats distinguishing them at the Battle of the Diamond, 1795.

128 Carleton, *Traits and Stories of the Irish Peasantry*, ii, 258; Madden, *United Irishmen*, 2nd ser., ii, 507, 125–6 n.

129 Carleton, *Traits and Stories*, i, 'The Party Fight and Funeral', 216.

130 Crawford, 'Economy and Society in Eighteenth-century Ulster', 26, 28.

131 O'Laverty, *Down and Connor*, iv, xxv–xxx.

132 John Dubourdieu, *Statistical Survey of the County of Antrim*, 429–48; Latocnaye, *A Frenchman's Walk through Ireland*, 217; Conolly, 'Spoken English in Ulster in the Eighteenth and Nineteenth Centuries', *Ulster Folklife*, xxviii, 33–9; Donaldson, *Upper Fews*, 165.

133 Gamble, *Sketches of History, Politics, and Manners in Dublin and the North of Ireland in 1810*, 246; Day, *Letters from Georgian Ireland*, 221.

134 O'Connell, *Diocese of Kilmore*, 461.

135 Tynan, *Catholic Instruction in Ireland*, 14.

136 Flanagan, 'Clogher in 1714', 127; Corish, *Catholic Community*, 129; Kelly, 'The Formation of the Modern Catholic Church in the Diocese of Kilmore, 1580–1880', in Gillespie, ed., *Cavan. Essays on the History of an Irish County*, 125.

137 McVeigh, ed., *Richard Pococke's Irish Tours*, 63.

138 O'Laverty, *Down and Connor*, iii, 107–9.

139 There is even a tradition of Catholics and Protestants sharing church accommodation at Loughinisland, County Down, till a dispute in 1720, see O'Laverty, *Down and Connor. Bishops*, 549.

140 'Report on the State of Popery, Ireland, 1731', *Archiv. Hib.*, i (1912), 10–27 (for Ulster), and for the rest of the country, ii (1913), 108–56, iii (1914), 124–59, and iv (1915), 131–77; Duffy, *Landscapes of South Ulster*, 29, 36, 40–44, 54, 58, 62–6, 92, PRONI, T.808/15261, 1744 religious return for Fermanagh; Donaldson, *Upper Fews*, 86, description of Presbyterian meeting house.

141 Crawford, 'Society and Economy in Eighteenth-century Ulster', 39.

142 [Harkin], *Inishowen*, 55–8; Carrigan, 'Wills', 262–4; Maguire, *Diocese of Raphoe*, i, 163; PRONI, T.808/15261, '1744 Committee on religion'.

143 Carleton, *Autobiography*, 43–4.

144 Tynan, *Catholic Instruction in Ireland*, 34; McPolin, 'An Old Irish Catechism from Oriel', *Irish Eccles. Rec.*, lxix, 510; Cogan, *Meath*, ii, 210, iii, 136, 139, 222–5: expansion in number of schools, churches, etc., reflecting a determined return to public worship.

145 Flanagan, 'Clogher in 1714', 128; Madgett, 'Constitutio Ecclesiastica', 81–2.

146 McGrath, 'The Tridentine Evolution of Modern Irish Catholicism, 1563–1962', in Ó Muirí, *Irish Church History Today*, 84–99.

147 [Richard Phillips] *Journal of a Tour in Ireland . . . 1804*, 16–17.

148 O'Connell, *Kilmore*, 505; Corish, *Catholic Community*, 108.

149 Delumeau, *Catholicism between Luther and Voltaire*, 9; Hennig, 'The First Liturgical Catechism in Ireland', *Ir. Eccles, Rec.*, 310.

150 Ó Maonaigh O.F.M., ed., *Seanmónta Chúige Uladh*, 42; Ó Muirgheasa, *Dhá Chéad*, ii, 159–63, 192–3; Heussaff, *Filí agus Cléir san Ochtú hAois Déag*, 61–2.

151 Fenning, *Fottrell Papers*, 10.

152 Tynan, *Catholic Instruction in Ireland*, 34, 49.

153 IFC, MS 102/231; also Taylor, *Occasions of Faith*, 99, 115, on their enduring popularity.

154 McGlinchey, *The Last of the Name*, 12.

155 Bourke, ed., *Sermons in Irish-Gaelic by the Most Rev. James O'Gallagher*.

156 Though see Ó Buachalla, *I mBéal Feirste Cois Cuain*, 58n, Irish still spoken between Ballynahinch and Newry until 1820.

157 Pulleine D.D., *An Teagasg Críosaidhe Angoidhleig (c.1782)*; McPolin, 'An Old Irish Catechism', 509–17.

158 Harris, *The Ancient and Present State of the County of Down*, 17–18, 76–7, 105–6, 109.

159 Hyde, trans., 'An Irish Funeral Oration over Owen O'Neill, of the House of Clanaboy', *U.J.A.*, vol. 3, 258–70 and vol. 4, 50–55.

160 Fenning, ed., *Fottrell Papers*, 13.

161 Fenning, *Undoing of the Friars*, vi–ix, 156, 178–9, 195.

162 McGlinchy, *Last of the Name*, 69–70.

163 Brady, 'Catholics and Catholicism', 85–9, 97–103; Millett, *Survival and Reorganization*, 47; Fenning, ed., *Fottrell Papers*, 37.

164 Carleton, *Traits and Stories*, i, 336; Ó Dufaigh, 'James Murphy, Bishop of Clogher, 1801–24', *Clogher Rec.*, vi, no. 3, 491–93.

165 Fenning, *Undoing of the Friars*, 282–3: my own account is heavily dependent on this excellent book.

166 Whelan, 'Anthony Blake, Archbishop of Armagh 1758–1787', *Seanchas Ard Mhacha*, v, no. 2, 289–323; Murray, 'Three Documents Concerning the Deanery of Dundalk during the Eighteenth Century', *Archiv. Hib.*, v, 70–71.

167 Brady, ed., 'A Pastoral of Arch. O'Reilly, 1788', *Seanchas Ard Mhacha*, 4, no. 1, 176.

168 'A List of Regulars Registered in Ireland Pursuant to the Catholic Relief Act of 1829', *Archiv. Hib.*, iii, 34–86.

169 Fenning, *Undoing of the Friars*, 294; see O'Laverty, *Down and Connor*, i, 40–41: the Dominicans had a small community at Kilcoo, near Castlewellan. In 1817 its last friar died.

170 Duffy, *Landscapes of South Ulster*, 74, 92; Murray, *History of Creggan*, 16; Ó Muirgheasa, *Céad de Cheoltaibh Uladh*, 187.

171 Lecky, *History of Ireland*, i, 147; Tynan, *Catholic Instruction in Ireland*, 24; IFC, MS 1215/215.

7   REFORM TO REBELLION: THE EMERGENCE OF REPUBLICAN POLITICS

1 The words of Theobald Wolfe Tone, cited Elliott, *Tone*, 411.

2 Rushe, *Monaghan in the Eighteenth Century*, 35; Adams, 'Ulster Folklife, 1738–40 from the pages of the Belfast Newsletter', *Ulster Folklife*, 31, 43, 46; Larkin, ' "Popish Riot" in Co. Derry 1725', *Seanchas Ard Mhacha*, viii, no. 1, 97–110; *BNL*, 1 and 26 June 1739.

3 Fagan, *An Irish Bishop in Penal Times*, 84.

4 Ó Fiaich, 'Filíocht Uladh', 82; Heusaff, *Filí agus Cléir*, 51, 170; Maureen Wall, 'Catholic Loyalty to King and Pope in Eighteenth-century Ireland', in O'Brien, ed., *Catholic Ireland*, 109.

5 Ó Buachalla, *Nua-Dhuanaire*, II, 2–3; Ó Muirgheasa, *Céad de Cheoltaibh Uladh*, ii, 151: 'Oró 'sé do bheatha abhaile' – Jacobite song collected in both Tyrone and Donegal, in support of victory by 'Young Charles', but a feeling that the author will never see it.

6 Woods, *Journals and Memoirs of Thomas Russell*, 66–7 – Russell describing how one of the Tyrone Grand Jury had thrown a glass at the head of a blind fiddler in Omagh for playing 'The White Cockade'.

7 Leerssen, *Mere Irish and Fíor-Ghael*, 275–6.

8 De Rís, ed., *Peadar Ó Doirnín: a Bheatha Agus a Shaothar* (Dublin, 1969), 7–8.

9 Howell, *State Trials*, xxv, 754.

10 Good example of this in Fagan, *Irish Bishop in Penal Times*, 58–9.

11 Brady, *Catholics and Catholicism*, 209: case of clergy Diocese of Derry subscribing to Volunteers when Catholic leaders generally stand aside from them, seeing London and Dublin governments as better allies than the Protestants.

12 Giblin, ed., 'Catalogue of Material of Irish Interest in the . . . Vatican Archives', *Coll. Hib.*, v, 80–82; Flynn, 'Hugh MacMahon', 144–5.

13 Chart, ed., *The Drennan Letters*, 72, 79, 115, 219, 232, 323.

14 This was the Bishop of Clogher, the Franciscan Denis Maguire, clearly residing in Fermanagh among his relatives.

15 The records are so deficient (only the index surviving the 1922 fire) that it is impossible to arrive at a totally accurate analysis. See Fagan, *Divided Loyalties*, 142–88 on this. Even so I have tried to reach some conclusions based on NLI, Pos. 1898, Index to the Catholic Qualification Rolls; Ó Gallachair, 'Catholic Qualification Rolls Index: Fermanagh and Monaghan', *Clogher Rec.*, ii, no. 3, 544–51; Ó Domhnaill, 'County Donegal in the Catholic Qualification Rolls, 1778–1790', *Co. Donegal Hist. Soc. Jn.*, i, no. 3, 204–5;

Wall in O'Brien, ed., *Catholic Ireland*, 110–14; Gebbie, ed., *Abercorn Letters*, 180.

16 Young, *Historical Notices of Old Belfast*, 183.

17 NLI, Pos. 1899: Index to Catholic Qualification Rolls, Ulster, 1793–6.

18 Miller, ed., *Peep O'Day Boys and Defenders*, 131.

19 Marshall, *History of the Parish of Tynan*, 50–51.

20 Crawford and Trainor, eds., *Aspects of Irish Social History*, 38–9; Rushe, *Monaghan in the Eighteenth Century*, 42–3.

21 Bigger, *Ulster Land War*, 12, 25–6, 50, 133–50.

22 McVeigh, ed., *Pococke's Irish Tour*, 60.

23 Dickson, 'Taxation and Disaffection in Late Eighteenth-century Ireland', in Clarke and Donnelly, Jr., eds., *Irish Peasants. Violence and Political Unrest*, 37–63; Crawford, 'Economy and Society in Eighteenth-century Ulster', 56–8; Miller, *Peep O'Day Boys and Defenders*, 14.

24 Bigger, *Ulster Land War*, 36, 101–3.

25 Beresford, 'Ireland in French Strategy, 1691–1789', 334.

26 Macafee, 'Population of Ulster', ch. 5.

27 *FDJ*, 10 June 1790; Young, *Tour*, i, 115, 164.

28 D. W. Miller, 'Politicisation in Revolutionary Ireland: the Case of the Armagh Troubles', *Ir. Econ. & Soc. Hist.*, 23, n. 46; Dickson, *A Narrative of the Confinement and Exile of William Steel Dickson, D.D.*, 10–11, says that Catholic offers were rejected and the Volunteers were anti-papist; Burns agrees: 'The Belfast Letters, the Irish Volunteers 1778–9 and the Catholics', *Review of Politics*, xxi, 678–91; Ó Snodaigh, 'Class and the Volunteers', 165–84. O'Laverty, *Down and Connor*, i, 472, thinks the Volunteers 'a very overpraised body', they generally excluded Catholics and, with a few exceptions, the Catholics 'remained unfriendly towards them'. PRONI, T.2541/IB1/4/12: G. Knox to Abercorn, 14 February 1793, shows even new corps of Volunteers divided; Gebbie, ed., *Abercorn Letters*, 15.

29 *Charlemont Mss*, ii, 76.

30 The religious topography of Armagh is an important topic in every work on the Armagh troubles. But there is a good overview in Wright, *Two Lands in One Soil*, 31–2; Cullen, *Modern Ireland*, 206–8.

31 Miller, 'Armagh Troubles', 158.

32 Ibid., 123; see also Stuart, *Historical Memoirs of the City of Armagh*, 417n. In 1784 people who had actually fought at the Boyne were still alive.

33 Miller, ed., *Peep O'Day Boys and Defenders*, 105. See Duffy, *Landscapes*, 42, 44, 52, 64, for other examples of population increase leading to movement by Protestants into hilly, Catholic areas, with inevitable sectarian clashes in the 1790s.

34 The most comprehensive account of the Armagh situation is Miller, ed., *Peep O'Day Boys*. See also his 'The Armagh Troubles, 1784–95', in Clark and Donnelly, eds., *Irish Peasants*, 155–91. Latocnaye, *Walk Through Ireland*, 258–60. *BNL*, 28 Aug. 1989: Armagh Assizes. *A View of the Present State of Ireland . . . by an Observer*, (n.p., 1797), 5–11.

35 Miller, *Peep O'Day Boys*, 123.

36 Cited Hogan, 'The Migration of Ulster Catholics to Connaught, 1795–96', *Seanchas Ard Mhacha*, ix, 286.

37 'Ulster Folk in Tipperary', *Béaloideas*, x, 300–301; Seamas Mac Manus, *Rocky Road to Dublin*, 90; IFC, MS 976/193: May 1945, recollections of Thomas Mulholland, aged sixty-five, of Newtown, Rostrevor; also account of attacks on the O'Coigleys in 1796, in Simms, ed., *Rev James O'Coigley, United Irishman*, 11–12.

38 Camden's correspondence with London: PRO, London, HO 100/62–64; NAI, SOC 1015/6–11, 21, also in Down, Tyrone, Cavan, Monaghan.

39 Elliott, 'Origins and Transformation', 414, 424–5; Lecky, *Ireland in the Eighteenth Century*, iii, 421–50 (also shows fugitive Catholics being sheltered by Presbyterians in Antrim and Down); MacNeven, *Pieces of Irish History*, 186–7; Kent, CKS, U840/0151/4, returns of Catholics who had fled to Mayo, December 1796.

40 Elliott, *Tone*, 180–81; Tone, *Life*, i, 172–5; Hillsborough had succeeded to the Downshire title in 1793; *FJ*, 8 September 1792 on Annesley.

41 *An Argument on Behalf of the Catholics of Ireland* (Dublin, 1791).

42 Tone, *Life*, i, 149–50.

43 McEvoy, 'The United Irishmen in Co. Tyrone', *Seanchas Ard Mhacha*, iii, 303–4, and v, 37; Mac Suibhne, 'Up Not Out: Why did North-west Ulster not Rise in 1798?', in Portéir, ed., *The Great Irish Rebellion*, 83–100.

44 David Hempton, paper delivered to Conference of Irish Historians in Britain, Oxford 1992.

45 Crawford and Trainor, eds., *Aspects of Irish Social History*, 42; Hill, 'Popular Protestantism in Ulster in the Post-Rebellion period, *c.*1790–1810', in Sheils and Wood, eds., *The Churches, Ireland and the Irish*, 196.

46 See Miller's Intriguing 'Presbyterianism and "Modernization" in Ulster', *Past and Present*, 80, 66–90.

47 McEvoy, 'United Irishmen in Co. Tyrone', v, 60–61.

48 Keogh, '*The French Disease*', 70.

49 *NS*, 11 July 1792.

50 *NS*, 30 May 1796; Keogh, '*The French Disease*', 50–51, for the hierarchy's fears of a Catholic-Presbyterian alliance.

51 Teeling, *Observations on the '. . . Battle of the Diamond*', 13.

52 Tone, *Life*, i, 367–8.

53 Adams, *Printed Word*, 86. The best analyses of the content of United Irish songs are Thuente, *The Harp Re-strung: The United Irishmen and the Rise of Irish Literary Nationalism*, and Zimmermann, *Songs of Irish Rebellion*. The best overview of United Irish propaganda is Curtin, *The United Irishmen*, chs. 8 and 9. PRO, HO 100/38/373: the gatherings at the churches to elect delegates to the Convention, also to sign a declaration against 'certain unpopular doctrines'.

54 Crawford and Trainor, eds., *Aspects of Irish Social History*, 76–7; Latocnaye, *A Frenchman's Walk through Ireland*, 204–5; McEvoy, 'United Irishmen in Tyrone', 307; Keogh, '*The French Disease*', ch. 6; *NS*, 5 December 1792.

55 BL, Add. Mss. 38, 759/37v, unsigned narrative, June 1797.

56 Miller, *Peep O'Day Boys*, 137.

57 NAI, 620/18/88a, A new song addressed to Irishmen, written by Wolfe Tone for the 1792 Belfast Harpers' Festival; also *NS*, 26 August 1796, 'Ireland: an Ode'.

58 *NS*, 30 May 1796; Curtin, *United Irishmen*, 185.

59 Woods, ed., *Journals and Memoirs of Thomas Russell*, 69.

60 Tone, *Life*, i, 377–8.

61 Madden, *United Irishmen*, 2nd ser., ii, 402–3, McCracken and Cuthbert employing counsel for those in Armagh; *FJ*, 20 April 1793; Elliott, *Tone*, chs. 12–14.

62 Tone, *Life*, i, 87–8.

63 Teeling, *History of the Irish Rebellion of 1798*, 12–14; Madden, *United Irishmen*, 3rd ser., i, 186–8; Tone, *Life*, i, 221–2; Elliott, 'The Defenders in Ulster', in Dickson, Keogh and Whelan, eds., *The United Irishmen*, 222–31.

64 Rogers, *The Irish Volunteers and Catholic Emancipation*, 144–66.

65 PRO, HO 100/42/248–51, Hobart to Nepean, 5 February 1792, summarising his speech; *Parl. Reg.*, xiii, 94, seq; Elliott, *Tone*, 202–5.

66 O'Laverty, *Down and Connor*, ii, 150.

67 PRO, HO 100/44/115–8: 'A Roman Catholic to Mr Braughall of the Catholic Committee', 29 May 1793.

68 Bartlett, *Fall and Rise*, 181–2.

69 PRONI, D.607/C/56: McNally to Downshire, 8 December 1794.

70 Ó Muirgheasa, *Céad de Cheoltaibh Uladh*, ii, 152.

71 Teeling, *Observations on the '. . . Battle of the Diamond'*, 7–13.

72 Carleton, *Autobiography*, 76–80.

73 Details of the very general arming of the Defenders in south Ulster are in PRO, HO 100/42/195–8, 270–72, 100/43/47–50, 145–51, 100/44/115–V8. More detailed accounts of the Defenders can be found in my articles, 'Origins and transformation', 'The Defenders in Ulster', and *Partners in Revolution*, 39–44. A sample of their oaths is conveniently located in Bartlett, 'Defenders and Defenderism in 1795', *I.H.S.*, xxiv (1985), 373–94. For Defenders' trials see Howell, *State Trials*, xxv, 750–84 and xxvi, 226–462.

74 *NS*, 23 March 1793; see PRO, HO 100/42/13–14, 27–8, 194–8 and 100/43/71–3, for the disturbances and trials; also Elliott, *Partners in Revolution*, 43–4.

75 PRO, HO 100/44/115–18, 'Extracts of various letters of information relative to the late insurrections', 8 June 1793; HO 100/38/243, [John Keogh] to the Revd. Hussey, 29 March 1792.

76 Bartlett, 'An End to the Moral Economy', *Past and Present*, xcix, 57–8.

77 PRO, HO 100/46/59, Gen. Whyte to Nepean, 8 April 1793; *NS*, 6 April 1793.

78 Teeling, *Observations on the '. . . Battle of the Diamond'*, 16–17; Coigley too praised the support the Catholics received from the Presbyterians and the Quakers (Madden, *United Irishmen*, 3rd ser., ii, 10).

79 *NS*, 30 March 1795.

80 Cullen, 'The Political Structures of the Defenders', in Dickson and Gough,

eds., *The French Revolution and Ireland*, 129–30; *Report from the Committee of Secrecy of the House of Commons of Ireland, 1798*, 58; PRONI, D.272/149, Cooke to Nugent [January 1796].

81 PRONI, D.607/G/200: T. Lane to Downshire, 12 October 1799; Elliott, 'The Defenders in Ulster', 225.

82 Gebbie, ed., *Abercorn Letters*, 175–6, 180.

83 Miller, *Peep O'Day Boys*, 138–9.

84 Zimmerman, *Songs of Irish Rebellion*, 297; Blackstock, *Ascendancy Army*, 92–7.

85 Madden, *Antrim and Down*, 25–6. The United Irishmen seem to have made particular headway among the Kerry Militia, *Report from the Committee of Secrecy, 1797* (Append. II of 1798 report), 82.

86 Blackstock, 'The raising of the Yeomanry in Ulster', in Dickson, Keogh and Whelan, eds., *The United Irishmen*, 234–43.

87 Chart, ed., *Drennan Letters*, 259; Dr Haliday too protests, *Charlemont MSS*, ii, 294, 303.

88 Lecky, *Ireland in the Eighteenth Century*, iv, 62–4; Ó Muirí, 'The Killing of Thomas Birch', *Seanchas Ard Mhacha*, x, no. 2, 298–300.

89 Latocnaye, *A Frenchman's walk through Ireland*, 221–2, 252–3.

90 Chart, ed., *Drennan Letters*, 252; Gebbie, ed., *Abercorn Letters*, 196–9.

91 NAI, 620/34/54: the notebooks of John Maxwell (member of the United Irish Ulster provincial committee, appointed colonel of Co. Down); PRONI, D.272/1: 1798 'Black Book'; also Ó Muirí, 'The Killing of Thomas Birch', 279, 284. McEvoy, 'United Irishmen in Co. Tyrone', v, 8–15.

92 Elliott, *Partners in Revolution*, 127. Later the regiment was part of the force which quelled the Ulster rebellion in 1798 (see PRONI, D.607/F/236 and 255).

93 Curtin, *United Irishmen*, 82–3; Newell, *The Apostasy of Newell*, partly reprinted in Madden, *United Irishmen*, 2nd ser., i, 345–425; Latocnaye, *A Frenchman's Walk through Ireland*, 255, 268–9. For folk memory of the military suppression, see IFC, MS 976/137, the Ancient Britons, MS 976/522, 'terrible time of the Light Horsemen' in Kilkeel, MS 1113/515, and Richill (Armagh); also the yeomanry, MS 976/522 and 555.

94 *Charlemont MSS*, ii, 321; *Report from the Committee of Secrecy, 1798*, Append. vi, information of Charles McFillin, a Derry Catholic United Irishman, on how they were specifically targeting Catholics at this time.

95 See also *Castlereagh Corr.*, i, 206; Dickson, *Revolt in North*, 240. However, Keogh, *'The French Disease'*, 169, thinks that most priests – under tremendous pressure from all sides – simply 'laid low'.

96 Adams, *Printed Word*, 88–9, the huge numbers of these prophecies were rolling off the presses in Ulster in these years; Curtin, *United Irishmen*, 188–9; Connolly, *Priests and People*, 109–10; Lecky, *Ireland in the Eighteenth Century*, iv, 125–6. See *Report from the Committee of Secrecy of the House of Commons of Ireland, 1798*, append. no. xxvi, and *Beauties of the Press*, 152–3 for reports of Orange oath to massacre all Catholics; Donnelly Jr., 'Propagating the Cause of the United Irishmen', *Studies*, lxix, 15–21, northern

United Irishmen adept at exploiting popular millenarianism. Dix, *Books and Pamphlets Printed in Strabane in the Eighteenth Century*, 14, lists a 1795 pamphlet, *Prophetical extracts . . . the Revolution in France and the Decline of Papal Power in the World*. Young, *Ulster in '98*, 28–35, suggests that Catholic United Irishmen in the south and northern Presbyterians may have been swearing different oaths.

97 NLI, MS G.200 (b), 'Ollamh Éigin. An Revolution. The French Revolution. By an Uncertain Author'. It seems to be from the Dundalk area, for the scribe was Ó Gallóglaigh of Dundalk. See also Ó Mórdha, 'Dán Faoi Mhuirthéacht na Frainnce', *Éigse*, 7, 202–4, on this poem.

98 Howell, *State Trials*, xxv, 754 – also McEvoy, 'United Irishmen in Co. Tyrone', *Seanchas Ard Mhacha*, iv, 11.

99 McSkimin, *Annals of Ulster*, 65.

100 Latocnaye, *A Frenchman's Walk through Ireland*, 263–4.

101 Keogh, '*The French Disease*', 163; NAI, SOC 1016/30: similar case from the Polls area of Meath/Cavan/Monaghan borders.

102 Miller, *Peep O'Day Boys*, 62; Ó Muirí, 'The Killing of Thomas Birch, United Irishman, March 1797 and the Meeting of the Armagh Freeholders, 19 April 1797', *Seanchas Ard Mhacha*, x, 289–90. See Dickson, *Revolt in the North*, 103, for more examples of sympathetic Protestants being harassed, and Steel Dickson, *Narrative*, 30–31, for new fears about neighbours.

103 Gebbie, ed., *Abercorn Letters*, 204–5. There is some dispute whether news from Wexford would have arrived in time to materially affect attitudes in Ulster on the eve of its rebellion. The following sources show that it did, likewise with reports from other counties: McBride, *Scripture Politics*, 202; PRONI Downshire Papers D607/F/185, 190, 192, 195, 196, 199, 218 (25 May–9 June); Lecky, *Ireland in the Eighteenth Century*, iv, 394–5; Stewart, *The Summer Soldiers*, 257; Gahan, *The People's Rising*, 132–3; Curtin, *United Irishmen*, 260–62; Hill, ed., *Rebellion in County Down*, 55.

104 Madden, *Antrim and Down*, 42–3.

105 Curtin, *United Irishmen*, 267.

106 Madden, *Antrim and Down*, 98, also 113 and 116, where, initially at least, the 'old' Defenders are being sworn as United Irishmen; *Charlemont MSS*, ii, 321.

107 Elliott, *Partners in Revolution*, 246; idem, 'The Defenders in Ulster', in Dickson, Keogh and Whelan, *The United Irishmen*, 222–33.

108 NAI, 620/31/128: [J. Lee] to George Anderson. 20 June 1797.

109 *Report from the Committee of Secrecy of the House of Commons of Ireland, 1798*, 162–4.

110 Stewart, *Summer Soldiers*, 206; Dickson, *Revolt in the North*, 227–31; Madden, *Antrim and Down*, 129 seq.

111 Cited Dickson, *Revolt in the North*, 227–31; also Teeling, *History of the Irish Rebellion*, 136.

112 Musgrave, *Memoirs of the Different Rebellions in Ireland* – the second edition published within two months of the first – 557: Musgrave claimed

that as many as 2,000 Catholics defected and watched from the Seaforde road with satisfaction as the Protestants were destroying each other.

113 On this see Cullen, 'The Internal Politics of the United Irishmen', in Dickson, Keogh and Whelan, *United Irishmen*, 194, 344. Cullen – in a revision of his earlier conclusions in 'The Political Structures of the Defenders', in Gough and Dickson, eds., *Ireland and the French Revolution* – argues that Magennis and Lowry returned prior to June 1798. If this were proved, it would significantly alter our understanding. There was a rumour reported by Leonard McNally on 2 June (NAI, 620/10/121/108) that Lowry was in the North. However since he signed a petition in Paris on 16 June (Elliott, *Tone*, 379 and 469) it seems unlikely that he was in Down at the time stated.

114 Madden, *Antrim and Down in '98*, 240.

115 NAI, 620/40/140: information contained in MacCary to Edward Cooke, under-secretary at Dublin Castle, 8 October 1798.

116 Rushe, *Monaghan in the Eighteenth Century*, 37; Teeling, *History of the Irish Rebellion . . . Sequel*, 202–3.

117 Keogh, 'The French Disease', 197–8; Hill, ed., *Rebellion in County Down*, 131.

118 NAI, 620/4/41: 'Narrative of the Rebel Army within C. Down'; Stewart, *Summer Soldiers*, 271.

119 Wright, *Two Lands in One Soil*, 42–3.

120 Madden, *Antrim and Down*, 131; see Elliott, *Partners in Revolution*, 237–8, for the many examples of this feeling throughout the country.

121 *BNL*, 24 July 1798. Priests involved in Ulster were: Magennis, and Coigley; two involved in the purely sectarian politics in Killevy, south Armagh; MacCary; Patrick Gribben – newly appointed parish priest of Glenravel – also imprisoned in Carrickfergus till 1803. The people of Rathlin seem to have been very generally involved and Father McMullen was arrested and brought to Ballyclare. However, to seek evidence of priests actually turning out may be inappropriate. Wexford was quite unusual in this. There is some circumstantial evidence that in the south Down, south Armagh, and the north Louth axis of successful United Irish-Defender co-operation, a number of priests at least subscribed to the political views of the United Irishmen. Keogh, 'The French Disease', 186–99; *Charlemont MSS*, ii, 340–41; O'Laverty, *Down and Connor*, iii, 111–13.

122 *BNL*, 24 July 1798; Musgrave, *Memoirs of the Different Rebellions*, 558.

123 D. H. Akenson and W. H. Crawford, *James Orr*, 10–11, 39–40.

124 Young, *Ulster in '98*, 14–17; Elliott, *Partners*, 205–6; Stewart, *Summer Soldiers*, 247, 264.

125 O'Laverty, *Down and Connor*, ii, 292, 329, 332, 352–3; NAI, SOC 1019/6: March 1800: anon to Col Littlehales, on how the yeomanry in 1798 did not distinguish between guilty and innocent, nor respect protections issued by the officers; that there were ten times more killed who had remained peaceably at home than took up arms or fled to the mountains.

126 Akenson and Crawford, *James Orr*, 16.

127 NAI, SOC 1567/10, Sir George Hill to Chief Secretary Peel, 9 March 1814.

128 *Charlemont MSS*, II, 327–55; for the spread of Defenderism see NAI, 620/46/38; Elliott, *Partners in Revolution*, 245–7; SOC 1091/4–7, 1020/ 3–7, 1383. *A Concise Account of the Material Events and Atrocities, Which Occurred in the Present Rebellion*, by 'Verdicus' (Dublin, 1799), claims that all the Defenders who migrated to Mayo from Ulster 'were virulent republicans, and drenched with superstitious credulity, being all of the scapular order'. He also cites Dickey's declaration to show it was a popish rebellion after 23 May.

129 McCoy, *Ulster's Joan of Arc* (Bangor, 1987), 30–33; Lyttle, *Betsy Gray or the Hearts of Down*, Append., 162–3; Stewart, *Summer Soldiers*, 227–9. IFC, MS 976/388, how Betsy Gray has been incorporated into the nationalist canon.

130 PRO, HO 100/87/5–7: Castlereagh to the Duke of Portland, 3 June 1799.

131 NAI, SOC 1019/6, anon to Col. Littlehales, March 1800; Elliott, *Partners*, 237–9.

132 O'Laverty, *Down and Connor*, i, 99–101, also iii, 356, for another loyalty address by Revd Hugh Devlin and 600 parishioners of Duncane, Grange, Cranfield and Ballyscullenbeg (Co. Antrim); Elliott, *Partners*, 311–12.

133 Donnelly Jr., 'Pastorini and Captain Rock', in Clark and Donnelly, eds., *Irish Peasants*, 127.

134 *Charlemont MSS*, ii, 180.

135 Teeling, *History of the Irish Rebellion ... Sequel*, 325, 328, 331–2; Madden, *United Irishmen*, 3rd ser., i, 192–4. Unlike his sons Luke Teeling had not become a United Irishman, even shunning his friend Thomas Russell in 1803.

8 THE REVIVAL OF 'POLITICAL' CATHOLICISM

1 See my 'Religion and Identity in Northern Ireland', in W. Van Horne, ed., *Global Convulsions: Race, Ethnicity and Nationalism at the End of the Twentieth Century* (New York, 1997), 152.

2 Emmet Larkin, 'The Devotional Revolution in Ireland, 1850–1875', *Amer. Hist. Rev.*, lxxvii, no. 3 (1972), 625–52; Rogan, *Synods and Catechesis in Ireland*, 73–9, uses evidence in the Vatican Archives to argue that the 'devotional revolution' was already in progress before Cullen. This my own research largely bears out.

3 Hugh McLeod, *Religion and the People of Western Europe 1789–1989* (Oxford, 1997), 47ff.

4 [Harkin], *Inishowen*, 172.

5 Mr and Mrs S. C. Hall, *Ireland: Its Scenery, Character etc.*, 3 vols. (London, 1841–3), iii, 57; Corish, *Irish Catholic Experience*, 169; David Miller, 'Irish

Catholicism and the Great Famine', *Jn. of Soc. Hist.*, ix, no. 1 (1975), 87; Ambrose Macaulay, *Patrick Dorrian, Bishop of Down and Connor 1865–85* (Dublin, 1987), 22, in 1834 there were only three priests for all Belfast; Revd Donal Kerr, 'James Browne Bishop of Kilmore, 1829–65', *Breifne*, vol. 6, no. 22 (1983–4), 128–9, poor state of church in Cavan 1820s–30s, though also shows reform already under way before Cullen.

6 MacAulay, *Crolly*, 63–5.

7 Bartlett, *Fall and Rise*, particularly 329–31.

8 See K. Whelan, 'Regional Impact', 265, shows the O'Connell 'rent' in Ulster the lowest in the country, except for Belfast and Newry, and a band stretching through south Ulster.

9 Desmond Murphy, *Derry, Donegal and Modern Ulster 1790–1921* (Londonderry, 1981), 41–6; Thomas D'Arcy M'Gee, *A Life of the Rt. Rev. Edward Maginn* (New York, 1857), 54.

10 Bardon, *History of Ulster*, 245–7; Macaulay, *Crolly*, 81; Livingstone, *Monaghan*, 190–91; HC 1835 (476) XVI: *Third Report from the Select Committee on Orange Lodges . . . in Ireland*, 36, 145.

11 Kerr, 'James Browne Bishop of Kilmore', 122–3; also S. Ó Dufaigh, 'James Murphy, Bishop of Clogher, 1801–24', *Clogher Rec.*, vi, no. 3 (1968), 422, 447–8, and Philip O'Connell, 'A Dublin Convert Roll: The Diary of the Rev. P. E. O'Farrelly', *Irish Eccles. Rec.*, lxxi (January–June 1949), 533–44 and lxxii (July–December 1949), 27–35, for the bitter contest going on between the proselytising societies and the Catholic Church for the souls of the young in particular.

12 MacManus, *Rocky Road to Dublin*, 159; IFC, MS 1,074/55 and 1,069/98.

13 Tomás Ó Fiaich and Liam Ó Caithnia, *Art Mac Bionaid: Dánta*, 66–8; Ó Muirgheasa, *Dánta Diadha Uladh*, 361.

14 See e.g. Ó Muirgheasa, *Dánta Diadha Uladh*, poem 58, pp. 363–4.

15 Colm Beckett, *Aodh MacDomhnaill: Dánta* (Dublin, 1987), poems no. 9 and 34, also the excellent introduction; Fr Luke Walsh, *The Home Mission Unmasked* (Belfast, 1844).

16 HC 1835 (476) XVI: *Third Report from the Select Committee on Orange Lodges . . . in Ireland*, 163.

17 Beckett, *Aodh Mac Domhnaill: Dánta*, 29–31, poem 2, and on O'Connell, poems 3, 4, 6, 7, 8, 12, 13 (on John O'Connell). There is also considerable admiration for Young Irelanders William Smith O'Brien, Thomas Davis and Charles Gavan Duffy. See also Seosamh Ó Duibhginn, *Séamas Mac Giolla Choille* (Dublin, 1972), 61–2, and Séan Ó Dufaigh and Diarmaid Ó Doibhlin, *Nioclás Ó Cearnaigh: Beatha Agus Saothar* (Dublin, 1989), 100–101, for other O'Connellite poetry from south Ulster, north Leinster. For the prevalence of the prophecies see Connolly, *Priest and People*, 109–10, and Donnelly, 'Pastorini and Captain Rock', 102–37.

18 The French priest, Adolphe Perraud, *Ireland under English Rule* (Dublin, 1864), describes Catholic 'fury' at such proselytising, 394–401; Ó Dufaigh, 'James Murphy, Bishop of Clogher', 422, 447–8.

19 Macaulay, *Crolly*, 155–7. Miller, *Church, State, and Nation*, 29–30, shows the Catholic clergy broadly happy with the National school system, despite a number of irritants.

20 Emmet Larkin, *The Consolidation of the Roman Catholic Church in Ireland, 1860–1870* (Dublin, 1987), 179; Rogan, *Synods in Catechesis in Ireland*, 107–8, 180–97.

21 Macaulay, *Dorrian*, 45–50.

22 Larkin, *Making of the Roman Catholic Church 1850–60*, 35–6.

23 Rafferty, *Catholicism in Ulster*, 139. See also Desmond Bowen, *The Protestant Crusade in Ireland 1800–70* (Dublin, 1978), 262–72 on Cullen's intense anti-Protestantism. Crolly he considered a 'Castle bishop' and he (Crolly) was severely criticised by the ultramontanes for his tolerance of Protestantism.

24 Patrick J. Corish, 'Cardinal Cullen and the National Association of Ireland', in Alan O'Day, ed., *Reactions to Irish Nationalism, 1865–1914* (London, 1987), 117–65; Larkin, *Making of the Roman Catholic Church 1850–60*, 387.

25 Connolly, 'Catholicism in Ulster', 165.

26 Mr and Mrs S. C. Hall, *Ireland: Its Scenery, Character etc.*, 3 vols. (London, 1841–3), iii, 271, found even Lough Derg much 'fallen' and 'superstition' generally in decline.

27 Marie O'Connell, 'The Genesis of Convent Foundations and Their Institutions in Ulster, 1840–1920', in Janice Holmes and Diane Urquhart, eds., *Coming into the Light: The Work, Politics and Religion of Women in Ulster 1840–1940* (Belfast, 1994), 179–206.

28 Macaulay, *Dorrian*, 263–5.

29 Carleton, 'The Station', in *Traits and Stories*, i, 145–80.

30 Corish, *Irish Catholic Experience*, 172; Macaulay, *Crolly*, 102; Rev. Patrick Rogers, 'The Minute Book of the Belfast Rosarian Society', *Down and Connor Historical Soc. Jn.*, viii (1937), 17–23 – this would explain why there was such a surfeit of New Testaments in its circulating library (estbld. 1819).

31 UFTM, field-recording transcripts vols. 17/101 and 23/1.

32 W. M. Thackeray, *Irish Sketchbook*, 35–6, 80, 100, 180, 241.

33 Keenan, *The Catholic Church in Nineteenth-century Ireland*, 114–25; Kerr, 'Browne, Bishop of Kilmore', 133.

34 Macaulay, *Dorrian*, particularly 106, 130, 140–57; A. C. Hepburn, *A Past Apart*, 131, 146–7.

35 Macaulay, *Dorrian*, 118–19; Fitzpatrick, *Oceans of Consolation*, 305; Vaughan, ed., *New History of Ireland*, v, 737–8, on their pleasure at Cullen's official welcome at the Castle; Taylor, *Occasions of Faith*, 169–70; Mary Louise Peckham, 'Catholic Female Congregations and Religious Change in Ireland, 1770–1870' (Univ. Wisconsin, Madison, Phd. thesis, 1993), 271–2. In the more prosperous counties in the east, there seems to have been no problem financing religious institutions – see Marie O'Connell, 'The Genesis of Convent Foundations and Their Institutions in Ulster', in Holmes and Urquhart, eds., *Coming into the Light*, 124–5.

36 Margaret Purdy, 'Some aspects of the Religious and Cultural Identity of Pre-Famine Rural Ulster as Portrayed in William Carleton's Traits and Stories of the Irish Peasantry' (Univ. of London, MA dissertation, 1992), 23; Connolly, *Priests and People*, 265–6, on the absence of popular irreligion among the Irish peasantry; McGlinchy, *Last of the Name*, 74–5.

37 Carleton, *Autobiography*, 61–2.

38 UFTM, V-19/22: recollections of Mrs Francilla Stevenson of her teenage days in Portrush at the close of the 19th century. For an excellent overview of priest-people relations see Connolly, *Priest and People*, 135–74.

39 Breandán Mac Suibhne, 'Canon James McFadden (1842–1917)', in Gerard Moran, ed., *Ten Radical Priests*, 149–84; Corish, *Irish Catholic Experience*, 235–6.

40 Murphy, *Ulster Folk of Field and Fireside*, 149–50. However Frank McKenna (b. Tyrone, near Omagh 1916) remembered the bishops' pastorals condemning poteen in his own time, so their success was not total – see UFTM, Tape R85.33.

41 Cited Brozyna, *Labour, Love and Power*, 176.

42 Enrí Ó Muirgheasa, 'The Holy Wells of Donegal', *Béaloideas*, 6 (1936), 141–62.

43 Taylor, *Occasions of Faith*, 66–7, also 18, 35, 43–4; Ronald H. Buchanan, 'Calendar Customs', *Ulster Folklife*, viii (1962), 15–34.

44 MacGowan, *Hard Road to Klondike*, 29; MacManus, *Rocky Road*, 291, also found in Donegal extraordinary 'praying powers' in the excessively long rosaries and other 'pedantic prayers'.

45 See IFC, MS 974/72–3, 146–8, MS 1057/7–8, 154–61, MS 2081/35–6; Murphy, *Tyrone Folk Quest*, 17, 77; Taylor, *Occasions of Faith*, 3, 26, 93; Linda-May Ballard, 'Three Local Storytellers: A Perspective on the Question of Cultural Heritage', in Gillian Bennett and Paul Smith (eds.), *Monsters with Iron Teeth*, 166–70; Gamble, *View of Society and Manners in the North of Ireland*, 324.

46 Ballard, 'Three Local Storytellers', 162; also UFTM Collectors' Books, V12/16/8: interview with Miss Campbell of Newcastle, 1956.

47 Opsahl Commission, 1993, submission no. 325.

48 O'Laverty, *Down and Connor*, iii, 395–7; Fionnuala Williams, 'A Fire of Stones Curse', *Folk Life*, xxxv (1996–7), 63–73; also UFTM, Collectors' Books V12/19/27 and V12/3/21–25; Glassie, *Ballymenone*, 66.

49 UFTM, Field Recording Transcripts, vol. 23/1–8; McLeod, *Religion and the People of Western Europe*, 54–74, for an excellent overview of popular attitudes to magic and the supernatural.

50 See e.g. Curley, 'Northern Irish Poets and the Land since 1800', 43, 56, 88–91, 113–20; Taylor, *Occasions of Faith*, 80, 98–100.

51 Seymour, *Irish Witchcraft and Demonology* (New York, 1992), notably 1–24 and 194seq.; O'Laverty, *Down and Connor*, iii, 395–7; [Harkin], *Inishowen*, 177; Connolly, *Priest and People*, 100–108.

52 Murphy, *Tyrone Folk Quest*, 27; Bourke, *The Burning of Bridget Cleary*, a study of an infamous case of fairy possession in Tipperary, 1895, in particular

pp. 24–38; Thuente, *W. B. Yeats and Irish Folklore*, 99; Andrews, *Ulster Folklore*, vi, 10–11.

53 Carleton, *Autobiography*, 18–19; Harris, 'The Schools' Collection', *Ulster Folklife*, iii, 12–13.

54 MacManus, *Rocky Road to Dublin*, 98–9.

55 Gamble, *View of Society and Manners in the North of Ireland*, 344–5; Glassie, *Ballymenone*, 64–8; Murphy, *Ulster Folk of Field and Fireside*, 82–4; Andrews, *Ulster Folklore*, 37–9.

56 Lucas, 'The Sacred Trees of Ireland', *Cork Hist. Soc. Jn.*, lxviii, 16–54, particularly 24–9, 46–8; Low, *Celtic Christianity and Nature*, 79–104; also Murphy, *Ulster Folk of Field and Fireside*, 82, 121–9; idem, *Tyrone Folk Quest*, 51.

57 Macaulay, *Dorrian*, 213.

58 Bardon, *History of Ulster*, 356; Comerford, *The Fenians in Context*, 147; Walker, *Ulster Politics*, 49.

59 Miller, *Church, State and Nation*, 31–6, 61; this is the central theme of this seminal study.

60 Macaulay, *Dorrian*, 240–41.

61 Hoppen, *Elections, Politics and Society*, 243.

62 Walker, *Ulster Politics*, 113–15; Corish, 'Cardinal Cullen and the National Association of Ireland'.

63 Walker, *Ulster Politics*, 219–21.

64 Bardon, *History of Ulster*, 408; Gray, *City in Revolt*, 52–5; Phoenix, ed., *A Century of Northern Life*, 15–17; Woods, 'The General Election of 1892', in Lyons and Hawkins, eds., *Ireland under the Union*, 310, 318–19; Walker, *Party Election Results, 1801–1922*, 144–9.

65 Macaulay, *Dorrian*, 149.

66 Hepburn, *A Past Apart*, 148–56; Miller, *Church, State and Nation*, 96–7; Harris, 'Catholicism, Nationalism and the Labour Question', 20.

67 Hepburn, *A Past Apart*, 157ff; Fitzpatrick, 'The Geography of Irish Nationalism', 420–27.

68 Murphy, *Derry, Donegal and Modern Ulster*, 180–81.

69 John B. Dooher, 'Tyrone Nationalism and the Question of Partition, 1910–25' (Univ. of Ulster M. Phil. thesis, 1986), 184 – Bishop McHugh's letter in the nationalist *Ulster Herald*, 24 June 1916. The bishops' utter insistence on denominational education further alienated moderate Unionists, see Miller, *Church and State*, ch. xviii.

70 Phoenix, *Northern Nationalism*, 32.

71 *Ibid.*, 49–53; Miller, *Church, State and Nation*, 422; idem, 'The Roman Catholic Church in Ireland: 1898–1918', in O'Day, ed., *Reactions to Irish Nationalism*, 197–203, charting the uncharacteristic confusion in church leadership about which horse to back in the 1916–22 period.

72 Hopkinson, *Green against Green: The Irish Civil War* (Dublin, 1988), 21–2.

73 Laffan, *The Partition of Ireland, 1911–1925*, 104; Darby, *Northern Ireland: Background*, 20.

9 THE FAMINE AND AFTER: CATHOLIC SOCIAL CLASSES IN NINETEENTH-CENTURY ULSTER

1 Connolly, 'Catholicism in Ulster', 158.

2 See e.g. Fitzpatrick, *Oceans of Consolation*, 366–9, for the terrible insecurity of a semi-literate Protestant peasant family in south Armagh, 1843–64.

3 Young, *Tour*, i, 150–51, 166.

4 O'Kelly, *Early Ireland*, 232–3.

5 Mokyr, *Why Ireland Starved*, 177, 244, 281; Atkinson, *Ireland in the Nineteenth Century* (London, 1833), 349, reports able-bodied poor 'with long trains of children' soliciting relief in the towns of Tyrone and Donegal.

6 Daly, 'Revisionism and the Great Famine', in Boyce and O'Day, eds., *The Making of Modern Irish History*, 71–89; Kennedy, 'The Rural Economy, 1820–1914', in Kennedy and Ollerenshaw, eds., *An Economic History of Ulster, 1820–1939*, 25–30; Wright, *Two Lands in One Soil*, ch. 4; Fitzpatrick, 'The Disappearance of the Agricultural Labourer, 1841–1912', *Ir. Econ. Soc. Hist.*, vii, 66–92; O'Neill, *Family and Farm in Pre-Famine Ireland*, 120–21; Mokyr, *Why Ireland Starved*, 268–75; Vaughan, ed., *New History of Ireland*, v. 351–4; Cormac Ó Gráda, *Black '47 and Beyond*, 77–83, 122–5.

7 Ó Gráda, *Economic History*, 122–4 – e.g. the London Companies, major absentees, considered caring landlords, also his *Black '47*, 126 seq.; Mokyr, *Why Ireland Starved*, 197–212; MacLaughlin, 'The Politics of Nation-Building in Post-Famine Donegal', in Dunlevy, Nolan and Ronayne, eds., *Donegal. History and Society*, 608.

8 Gamble, *Sketches of History, Politics, and Manners in Dublin and the North of Ireland in 1810*, 246–7; Grant, 'Some Aspects of the Great Famine in County Armagh', *Seanchas Ard Mhacha*, 8, no. 2, 353–4; Wright, *Two Lands in One Soil*, 76.

9 Akenson, *Small Differences*, 144–5, on how the Famine became the centre-piece of Catholic nationalist tradition.

10 Clarkson, 'Population Change and Urbanisation, 1821–1912', in Kennedy and Ollerenshaw, eds., *Economic History of Ulster*, 137–43; Fitzpatrick, *Oceans of Consolation*, 15–16, sees Fermanagh, Tyrone and Armagh as among those counties sending most emigrants to Australia in the decades after the Famine; Grant, 'The Great Famine and the Poor Law in Ulster: the Rate-in-Aid Issue of 1849', *I.H.S.*, xxvii, 30–47; Crawford, 'Poverty and Famine in County Cavan', in Gillespie, ed., *Cavan*, 140–41, 156; Mokyr, *Why Ireland Starved*, 267, shows excess deaths during the Famine at 43–57%, higher than any county in Munster, though not Connacht – the worst affected province.

11 McCavery, 'The Famine in County Down', in Kinealy and Parkhill, eds., *The Famine in Ulster*, 107.

12 Bardon, *History of Ulster*, 286.

13 See IFC, MSS 975/81–2, 976/163 and 168, and 1112/373; Quinlan, 'A Punishment from God: the Famine in the Centenary Folklore Questionnaire', *The Irish Review*, xix, 78–9. Begley and Lally, 'The Famine in County

Donegal', in Kinealy and Parkhill, eds., *Famine in Ulster*, 80; Kinealy, *The Great Calamity. The Irish Famine, 1845–52*, 349.

14 Parkhill, 'The Famine in County Londonderry', in Kinealy and Parkhill, eds., *Famine in Ulster*, 164.

15 McCavery, 'Famine in County Down', 120–21, 126–7.

16 Cunningham, 'The Famine in County Fermanagh', in Kinealy and Parkhill, eds., *Famine in Ulster*, 141; MacAtasney, '*This Dreadful Visitation*', 84–6; Grant, 'The Great Famine and the Poor Law in Ulster', 30–47.

17 Cunningham, 'The Famine in County Fermanagh', in Kinealy and Parkhill, eds., *Famine in Ulster*, 141; Wright, *Two Lands in One Soil*, ch. 5.

18 Wright, *Two Lands in One Soil*, 118, 124, see Ó Gráda, *Black '47 and Beyond*, 56–8; Gallogly, 'The Famine in County Cavan', in Kinealy and Parkhill, eds., *Famine in Ulster*, 69.

19 Bardon, *History of Ulster*, 296; MacAtasney, '*This Dreadful Visitation*', 32. 102.

20 Dallat, 'The Famine in County Antrim', in Kinealy and Parkhill, eds., *Famine in Ulster*, 21–3. McEvoy, 'The Parish of Errigal Kieran in the Nineteenth Century', *Seanchas Ard Mhacha*, i, 128, tells of the soup-kitchens in Armagh, but no tradition of souperism in this part.

21 IFC, MS 1361/103, unnamed interviewee, April 1953, also an excellent example of the elision of different periods and experiences into one historical narrative of oppression – in this case the penal laws, notably the £5 clause, spoken of as if they still operated at the time of the Famine.

22 Cited Póirtéir, ed., *Famine Echoes*, 167; also IFC MS 1359/129, 143.

23 IFC, MS 1360/143; Póirtéir, *Famine Echoes*, 169.

24 Gallogly, 'Famine in County Cavan', 72–3, citing *Freemans Journal*, 27 January 1849.

25 IFC, MS 1113/1G; also Póirtéir, *Famine Echoes*, 139, 140–41, 178–9.

26 IFC, MS 1072/315, 335 and 338, for the taunting of descendants of families who turned; MS 1072/359, it was always given out in the 'big Protestants' houses'; MS 1072/315, 335, 338 ('Benson's Gravy', Benson doling out the soup at Chambree's place); IFC, MS 976/163, and Póirtéir, *Famine Echoes*. 173, 178–9, on Ribbon retaliation; Ó Muirgheasa, *Dhá Chéad*, 31–2, Bennett's scathing poem on the O'Callaghans.

27 David Hempton and Myrtle Hill, *Evangelical Protestantism in Ulster Society 1740–1890* (London, 1992), 138–40 on the philanthropy.

28 See also Donnelly, in Vaughan, ed., *New History of Ireland*, v, 311–12, and Ó Gráda, *Ireland. A New Economic History*, 174, on widespread popular sense of the soup-kitchens as demeaning.

29 Cited Begley and Lally, 'Famine in County Donegal', 79; Ó Gráda, *Black '47*, 50–51.

30 McCavery, 'Famine in County Down', 107; Patrick Duffy, 'The Famine in County Monaghan', in Kinealy and Parkhill, eds., *Famine in Ulster*, 191.

31 Póirtéir, *Famine Echoes*, 139.

32 Beckett, *Aodh Mac Domhnaill: Dánta*, 41 – Brady is taunted as a spy because of his pro-English outlook.

33 UFTM, R85.249, taped interview with Owen O'Rourke, b.1889, Catholic farmer of Omeath, also favourable local tradition of the Protestant McGarrys running the soup-kitchen at Drumla 'there was no souperism, just charity'; Kinealy, *Great Calamity*, 164.

34 See Foster, *The Story of Ireland*, 8–13 on Sullivan's *Story*.

35 Duffy, 'The Famine in Monaghan', 195; Fitzpatrick, *Oceans of Consolation*, 536, also finds little mention of it.

36 Quinlan, 'A punishment from God', 72–3, 82; Ó Gráda, *Ireland: A New Economic History*, 174.

37 Beckett, *Aodh Mac Domhnaill: Dánta*, poems 15 and 16, '*Agallamh idir Aindrias Ó hÉigeartaigh agus an Bard um Mheath na bPrátaí*' ('A dialogue ... about the rotting of the potatoes'); *Report of Royal Commission on the Belfast Riots*, HC 1857–8 (2309), xxvi, 241.

38 Clarkson, 'Population Change and Urbanisation', 155.

39 Anne O'Dowd, *Spalpeens and Tattie Hokers. History and Folklore of the Irish Migratory Agricultural Worker in Ireland and Britain* (Dublin, 1991), 30–31, 42–3, 103–17, 233, 287–8. See Fitzpatrick, *Oceans' of Consolation*, 337 seq.; also his 'A Peculiar Tramping People', in Vaughan, ed., *New History of Ireland*, v, 623–4, 646–50; Foster, *Modern Ireland*, 345–9.

40 O'Dowd, *Spalpeens and Tattie Hokers*, 287–8.

41 Ó Muirgheasa, *Dhá Chéad de Cheoltaibh Uladh*, iii, 345–6.

42 Patrick MacGill, *Children of the Dead End* (London, 1985, reprint of 1914 original), 30.

43 Colm Tóibín, *Bad Blood*, 13–21; UFTM, Collectors' Books, V-19 (Tyrone), 46–7, hiring fairs in Tyrone after 1920; also Murphy, *Tyrone Folk Quest*, 13 and *Ulster Folk of Field and Fireside*, 151, on the sense of degradation of the hiring fair.

44 Michael MacGowan, *The Hard Road to Klondike* (London, 1962), 40.

45 O'Dowd, *Spalpeens and Tattie Hokers*, 130–31. 217–19.

46 MacGowan, *Hard Road to Klondike*, 142–3; Paddy [the Cope] Gallagher, *My Story*, 204 (*c*.1914) also highlights the real improvement in the life of the rural poor. His aged parents had feared eviction because he had spoken harshly to the Protestant minister. He assured them that eviction was no longer possible except for non-payment of rent.

47 Fitzpatrick, *Oceans of Consolation*, 446–7; UFTM, Collectors' Books V.19/7/18–20 also shows landlords having a bad name in Protestant traditions.

48 Walker, *Ulster Politics*, 18–21.

49 R. W. Kirkpatrick, 'Origins and Development of the Land War in Mid-Ulster, 1879–85', in Lyons and Hawkins, eds., *Ireland Under the Union*, 208, shows sudden increase in evictions in 1880, Ulster experiencing the highest of any province.

50 See e.g. Walker, *Ulster Politics*, 22, on Protestant fears that the aim of the Land League was to dispossess Protestants.

51 O'Laverty, *Down and Connor*, i, 389.

52 Paul Bew and Frank Wright, 'The Agrarian Opposition in Ulster Politics,

1848–87', in Clarke and Donnelly, *Irish Peasants*, 192–229; Wright, *Two Lands in One Soil*, ch. 7; Walker, *Ulster Politics*, 19–21; Samuel Clarke, *Social Origins of the Irish Land War* (New Jersey, 1979), 211–12.

53 *Report on the Derryveagh Evictions*, HC 1861 (316) lii, 539–79; Mac-Gowan, *Hard Road to Klondike*, 18–19; also Bardon, *History of Ulster*, 321–2; W. E. Vaughan, *Sin, Sheep and Scotsmen: John George Adair and the Derryveagh Evictions, 1861* (Belfast, 1983).

54 Fitzpatrick, *Oceans of Consolation*, 421; MacPhilib, 'Profile of a Landlord in Folk Tradition and in Contemporary Accounts – the Third Earl of Leitrim', *Ulster Folklife*, xxxiv, 26–40.

55 Walker, 'The Land Question and Elections in Ulster, 1868–86', in Clarke and Donnelly, eds., *Irish Peasants*, 238–9.

56 Kirkpatrick, 'Origins and Development of the Land War in mid-Ulster, 1879–85', 227–9.

57 Bew and Wright, 'Agrarian Opposition', 215, particularly in south Ulster where it sparks a major Orange revival; also Kirkpatrick, 'Origins . . . of the Land War', 228–35. Walker, *Ulster Politics*, 24–5: in the growing towns Catholics tend to be over-represented among the poorest and in consequence under-represented among the new town councils. The local government enquiry of 1877 shows only two Catholics out of forty on Belfast town council (though a third of its populace) and in Derry only two out of twenty-four. There were more elsewhere, but still less than their proportions warranted – and it was a source of grievance.

58 Kennedy, 'The Rural Economy', 60 n.127; Clarkson, 'Population Change and Urbanisation', 153–5.

59 Budge and O'Leary, *Belfast: Approach to Crisis*, 28–33.

60 Hall, *Ireland: Its Scenery, Character*, iii, 52–3; Ó Gráda, *New Economic History*, 285–6.

61 Thackeray, *Irish Sketchbook*, 310.

62 Macaulay, *Dorrian*, 122–8 – by 1884 over 20,000 Catholics were located on the Falls Road (almost a third of the city's Catholic populace), with a building programme of churches, schools and parochial facilities to match.

63 Thackeray, *Irish Sketchbook*, 308.

64 Baker, 'Orange and Green: Belfast 1832–1912', in Dyos and Wolff, eds., *The Victorian City*, ii, 806.

65 O'Hanlon, *Walks among the Poor of Belfast*, notably 4–19, 27, 38; also Hepburn, *A Past Apart*, 75, and Walker, *Ulster Politics*, 23–6, for the significant numbers of Church of Ireland (though not Presbyterian) members among the under-privileged.

66 Hepburn, *A Past Apart*, 38–40, 63; Baker, 'Orange and Green', 801. Morris, 'Inequality, Social Structure and the Market', 200–203, argues that one of the reasons for this is that skilled wages were tied to the Scottish urban model (from which many of the skilled tradesmen were imported), while unskilled labour wages were decided by the rural rates from which most of the unskilled came, producing a 'dual economy'.

67 Baker, 'Orange and Green', 802.

68 *Ibid.*, 799; Hepburn, *The Conflict of Nationality in Modern Ireland* (London, 1980), 24–31, reproduces a number of documents to illustrate the rising sectarian temperature in Belfast.

69 Hepburn, *A Past Apart*, 118–19, Budge and O'Leary, *Approach to Crisis*, ch. 3; John Gray, *City in Revolt: James Larkin and the Belfast Dock Strike of 1907* (Belfast, 1985), 15–17.

70 Hepburn, *A Past Apart*, 34–5, 39–44; Clarkson, 'Population Change', 138–41.

71 James H. Murnane, 'Dr James Donnelly, Bishop of Clogher (1865–1893) and the Ascendancy in Monaghan', *Clogher Rec.*, xiii, no. 1 (1988), 1–25.

72 Mac Suibhne, 'Canon James McFadden', 153–4; Ó Gráda, *New Economic History*, 268–70; Paddy [the Cope] Gallagher, *My Story*, 189, 267–8: how the gombeenmen try to stop the co-op by denouncing them as Orange and Unionist stooges; they were much worse than the landlords, indeed they reaped most benefit from the dismantling of landlordism. See Walker, *Ulster Politics*, 17–26, for the occupational statistics.

73 Hepburn, *A Past Apart*, 129; Jim MacLaughlin, 'The Politics of Nation-building in Post-Famine Donegal', 609–10; see also Hoppen, *Elections*, 171–2 for national ratios.

74 Jim MacLaughlin, 'The Politics of Nation-Building in Post-Famine Donegal', 615; James O'Shea, *Priest, Politics and Society in Post-Famine Ireland* (Dublin, 1983), 241–6.

75 Murphy, *Derry*, 173, church providing networks of support for incoming rural Catholics, permits employers to resist unionisation.

76 Macaulay, *Dorrian*, 36–7, 51, 105, 121–2, 128. Hughes was the first ever Catholic to be elected to municipal office in Belfast (1855): see Budge and O'Leary, *Approach to Crisis*, 61, and *Reports of the Commissioners of Inquiry into the Origin and Character of the Riots in Belfast, July and September, 1857*, HC 1857–8 [2309] xxvi, 1, 147, 242–4; Hughes thought some 100 to 150 Catholics in Belfast capable of being made Peace Commissioners, three – William Ross, McCue of Rosemary Street and Joseph Magill – being worth £100,000. The report into the 1886 riots found three-quarters of all the public houses in Belfast (even in Protestant areas) owned by Catholics, *Belfast Riots Commission*, HC 1887 [C.4925], xviii, 525, 533.

77 Macaulay, *Dorrian*, 124–5.

78 Fitzpatrick, *Oceans of Consolation*, 393, 408, 555, 560.

79 Mac Suibhne, 'Canon James McFadden', 150–51; MacGill, *Children of the Dead End*, 3–5, 11, 21–2.

80 MacManus, *Rocky Road to Dublin*, 228.

81 Gray, *City in Revolt*, 44, 152.

82 *Ibid.*, 33–8.

10 ACROSS THE DIVIDE:
COMMUNITY RELATIONS AND SECTARIAN
CONFLICT BEFORE PARTITION

1 Gamble, *View of Society and Manners in the North of Ireland in the Summer and Autumn of 1812*, 63, 83–4, 104.

2 Gamble, *Sketches of History, Politics, and Manners in Dublin and the North of Ireland in 1810*, 217–20, 233. In 1870 the Governor of the Apprentice Boys made a similar objection to granting equal marching rights to nationalists, *Royal Commission of Inquiry into Riots and Disturbances in the City of Londonderry*, HC 1870 [C.5*] xxxii, 575.

3 Duffy, *My Life in Two Hemispheres*, i, 6–8.

4 MacManus, *Rocky Road to Dublin*, 204, 214.

5 Doyle, *An Ulster Childhood*, 36–9.

6 Gamble, *View of Society . . . in the North of Ireland*, 116–7.

7 Doyle, *Ulster Childhood*, 39–40.

8 IFC, MS 975/87–88.

9 IFC, MS 1215/127.

10 Wright, *Two Lands*, 186–7; *Return of the Number of Murders and Waylayings in the Baronies of Upper and Lower Fews, in County Armagh, 1844–50*, HC 1850 [566] li, 577; *Return of . . . Murders, Waylayings . . . of Agrarian Character . . . Louth, Armagh and Monaghan, 1849–52*, HC 1852 (448) xlvii, 465–75.

11 Doyle, *Ballygullion*, 135; also his *Rosabelle and other Stories*, 200 (from *The Leprechaun*).

12 MacManus, *Rocky Road to Dublin*, 112; Fitzpatrick, *Oceans of Consolation*, 412–15.

13 UFTM, Collectors' Books V-19/7/64–5.

14 Bullock, *Dan the Dollar*. In Irish-language sources, this shunning of materialism is usually associated also with reminders that this world is not for long: see Ó Muirgheasa, *Dánta*, 164, 172–3, 271–4, 363, 365–6; idem, *Céad*, poem 4.

15 Ó Coinne and Ó Fiaich, 'Tombstone Inscriptions in Drumglass Cemetery'; however Corish, *Irish Catholic Experience*, 157, notes the beginning of its decline elsewhere in Ireland from 1820. This partly reflects the new ability of the Catholic Church to purchase land for its own cemeteries, whereas previously all cemeteries were in the hands of the established Church.

16 Wright, *Two Lands*, 392–3.

17 Akenson, *Small Differences*, 109–15.

18 Fitzpatrick, *Oceans of Consolation*, 391–5; Donaldson, *Historical Account of the Upper Fews*, 71, very few inter-faith marriages.

19 Fitzpatrick, *Oceans of Consolation*, 391n.

20 O'Dowd, *Spalpeens*, 281, 283.

21 Ó Muirgheasa, *Dánta Diadha Uladh*, no. 60; idem, *Dhá Chéad*, poem 14; frequent recitations of England's cruelty against Catholicism (very notable in

Bennett, see Ó Fiaich and Ó Caithnia, eds., *Art Mac Bionaid, Dánta*, notably poem 29.

22 RIA, MS 23B.19, p. 100.

23 Ó Muirgheasa, *Dánta Diadha Uladh*, no. 44.

24 Beckett, *Aodh Mac Domhnaill*, 40–43, 'A Conversation between Brady the Spy and an Irish Poet'.

25 Ó Muirgheasa, *Dhá Chéad*, 42–3, poem 14.

26 Indeed it looks as if the phrase may have been regularly used by Orangemen, Wright, *Two Lands*, 56.

27 *Belfast Riots Commission*, HC 1887 [C.4925] xviii, 535.

28 Gamble, *Sketches*, 287.

29 *Royal Commission of Inquiry into Riots and Disturbances in the City of Londonderry*, HC 1870 [C.5*] xxxiii, 428, 478, 497, 586.

30 Macaulay, *Crolly*, 92.

31 Gamble, *Sketches*, 269.

32 Duffy, *My Life in Two Hemispheres*, i, 13.

33 *Third Report from the Select Committee . . . [on] Orange Lodges*, HC 1835 [476], xvi, 110–21, 171–212; Hereward Senior, *Orangeism in Britain and Ireland, 1795–1836* (London, 1966), 247–8.

34 Senior, *Orangeism*, 267–8.

35 *Third Report from the Select Committee . . . [on] Orange Lodges*, 12–21, 32, 41, 69–70, 216–45. Milne, *Charter Schools*, 295, in 1822 it was revealed that the Blacker family had sent thirty-five boys and girls from the Portadown area to Charter schools at Strangford and Dundalk.

36 *Third Report from the Select Committee . . . [on] Orange Lodges*, 23.

37 Carleton, *Autobiography*, 34–40.

38 Doyle, *Ballygullion*, 131.

39 *Third Report from the Select Committee . . . [on] Orange Lodges*, 16.

40 Carleton, *Autobiography*, 188–9, 122–3.

41 Duffy, *Landscapes of South Ulster*, 62.

42 Ó Mórdha, 'The Rising of Burke', *Clogher Rec.*, iv, nos. 1–2. 50–53.

43 Livingstone, *Fermanagh Story*, 161–6; *Third Report from the Select Committee . . . [on] Orange Lodges*, 83 seq.; IFC, MS 1923/17–20; Ó Mórdha, 'Notes and Comments. Party Quarrels in Nineteenth-century Monaghan', *Clogher Rec.*, II, 2, 355–7, extracts from contemporary papers on sectarian clashes and killings in the Clones area, 1823–28; Murphy, *Derry*, 48–9.

44 Glassie, *Ballymenone*, 237, also 223–40; *Memorial of Prisoners Charged with Murder at Macken*, HC 1830 (150) xxvi, 301; also *Third Report from the Select Committee . . . [on] Orange Lodges*, 83 seq.; IFC, MS 1923/17–20, for folk memory of Mackan incident.

45 *Third Report from the Select Committee . . . [on] Orange Lodges*, Append. 129.

46 *Papers Relating to the Investigation held at Castlewellan into the Occurrences at Dolly's Brae, on the 12th July, 1849*, HC 1850 [1143] li, 331ff. IFC MS 975/267, 294–8, 584–5, 589: for memories of sectarian clashes in this area in the nineteenth century. Apparently five Catholics were executed and

two transported for killing an Orangeman in the 1840s; there was a commemoration of them a century later.

47 Zimmermann, *Songs of Irish Rebellion*, 311–13.

48 Hempton and Hill, *Evangelical Protestantism in Ulster Society*, ch. 9, 161–87.

49 Doyle, *An Ulster Childhood*, 54–5.

50 Hepburn, 'The Catholic Community in Belfast, 1850–1940', [though reproduced in his *Past Apart*, not the opening pages], in Engman *et al.*, eds., *Ethnic Identity in Urban Europe*, 41.

51 Doyle, 'A Flag and a Flapper', in his *Rosabelle and Other Stories*, 82–100.

52 'Letters written by John O'Donovan, relating to the History and Antiquities of the County of Down . . . in 1834' (unpubd. typescript in the RIA). The same outsider shock at the levels of sectarian bitterness is reflected in successive parliamentary reports into Belfast's riots, e.g. *Belfast Riots Commission*, HC 1887 [C.4925] xviii, 417. Boyd, *Holy War in Belfast*, 9, cites the occurrence of serious riots in 1835, 1843, 1857, 1864, 1872, 1880, 1884, 1886, 1898.

53 Boyd, *Holy War in Belfast*, 70–71; Baker, 'Orange and Green', 807. Duffy, *Life in Two Hemispheres*, i, 42, Catholics coming from predominantly Catholic counties regard Belfast as hostile territory.

54 *Report of the Commission of Inquiry into the Origin and Character of the Riots in Belfast in July and September 1857* HC 1857–8 [2309] xxvi, 248–51, also 3, 27. The September 1857 riots were likewise sparked by Revd Hugh Hanna's open-air preaching in the docks area (ibid., 11–14, 111); Hempton and Hill, *Evangelical Protestantism in Ulster Society*, 124–5; Boyd, *Holy War in Belfast*. 22–3, 26–7.

55 *Report of the Commission of Inquiry into . . . the Riots in Belfast in July and September 1857*, 8, 2, 124.

56 Ibid., 142, also 87, 123, 130.

57 Ibid., 138–9.

58 Ibid., 11.

59 Ibid., 87, 101, 124, 138–9.

60 Ibid., 125.

61 Brozyna, *Labour, Love and Power*, 22, 47–8.

62 Boyd, *Holy War*, 89–91.

63 Hepburn, *Past Apart*, 161; Budge and O'Leary, *Belfast. Approach to Crisis*, 92–4.

64 Baker, 'Orange and Green', 808.

65 Walker, *Ulster Politics*, 77–221.

66 *Belfast Riots Commission*, 1887, 638; Budge and O'Leary, *Belfast: Approach to Crisis*, 87–90.

67 *Belfast Riots Commission*, 1887, 538.

68 Ibid., 11, 533.

69 *Royal Commission of Inquiry into Riots and Disturbances in the City of Londonderry*, HC 1870 [C.5*] xxxiii, 581–5; The Apprentice Boys' annual celebrations were banned on the recommendation of the Commission.

70 Lacy, *Siege City*, 93, 173; McBride, *The Siege of Derry in Ulster Protestant Mythology*, 50–51.

71 Doak, 'Rioting and Civil Strife in the City of Londonderry during the Nineteenth and Early Twentieth Centuries', 147–58.

72 *Correspondence between Ld. Chancellor of Ireland and R. McClintock, in Reference to His Conduct as a Magistrate ... March 1884*, HC 1884 [C.5057] lxiii, 513.

73 *Report of the Royal Commission to Inquire into Disturbances in the City of Londonderry, 1 November 1883*, HC 1884 [C.3954] xxxviii, 611. For similar Orange counter-demonstrations elsewhere, and official rebuke of magistrates involved, see the various reports in HC 1884 [C.4065] lxiii, 517 (Newry), HC 1884 (95) lxiii, 461 (Dromore, Tyrone); HC 1884 [C.3891] lxiii, 547 (Rosslea, Fermanagh – also on magistrates in Monaghan and Cavan).

74 McBride, *Siege of Derry*, 54–57; Murphy, *Derry*, 133; Doak, 'Rioting and Civil Strife in ... Londonderry', 145–6, 249.

75 See Darby, *Intimidation and the Control of Conflict in Northern Ireland* (Dublin, 1986), 14–18.

76 *Belfast Riots Commission*, HC 1887 [C.4925] xviii, 448.

77 [W. Shankill], *The Belfast Riots, 1886. The Islandmen and Shankill Road Defended* (Belfast, 1886).

78 Budge and O'Leary, *Belfast: Approach to Crisis*, 83.

79 Cited, Macaulay, *Dorrian*, 79, 47n, see also Cogan, *Diocese of Meath*, iii, 86: 'We are told, a Catholic might be known by his stooped carriage and subdued manner.'

80 Rushe, *Monaghan in the Eighteenth Century*, 93.

81 Stuart, *Historical Memoirs of the City of Armagh*, new edn. by Revd Ambrose Coleman, OP (Dublin, 1900), vii, xxi–xxiii.

82 Connolly, *A Sermon Preached in the Church of St Mary Belfast, on the Occasion of the Centenary on Sunday, November 11th (1883)*, 16–17.

83 Gamble, *View of Society*, 267.

84 Hill, 'The Disputed Lessons of Irish History', *Past and Present*, 118, 96–129. For similarity of Catholic 'in the time of persecution' approach in O'Laverty, *Down and Connor* (e.g. iii, 468), also *Derry Journal*, 14 July 1957, and Presbyterian in 'time of tyranny' in Latimer, *A History of the Irish Presbyterians*, ch. xxix.

85 Quinlan, 'A Punishment from God', 73–4; Foster, *The Story of Ireland*; Adams, 'The Validity of Language Census Figures in Ulster, 1851–1911', *Ulster Folklife*, 25, 113–122, shows the impact being made on Ulster – particularly Belfast and particularly in the under-30s generation – of the Gaelic League's Irish language revival.

86 Donaldson, *A Historical and Statistical Account of the Barony of the Upper Fews*, 71.

87 See e.g. *The Irish Magazine*, i (1807–8), 36–37, ii (1809), 2, 162–5; Clifford, ed., *The Origin of Irish Catholic Nationalism*.

88 Duffy, *Life in Two Hemispheres*, i, 17–18.

89 *Correspondence and Reports Relating to the Removal of Lord Rossmore*, HC 1884 [C.3891] lxiii, 547.

90 Duffy, *My Life in Two Hemispheres*, i, 17–18.

91 Ó Fiaich and Ó Caithnia, eds., *Art Mac Bionaid: Dánta*, 71–5, poem 29.

92 Elliott, 'Religion and Identity in Northern Ireland', 150–53.

93 Taylor, *Occasions of Faith*. 118–44.

94 Connolly, *Sermon Preached in the Church of St Mary*, 26–7.

95 Conor Cruise O'Brien, *Ancestral Voices*, 43.

96 Miller, *Church, State, and Nation*, 61–2; Foster, *Modern Ireland*, 446–56.

97 Duffy, *My Life in Two Hemispheres*, i, 44; Ó Muirgheasa, *Dánta*, 270; Ó Muirí, ed., *Lámhscríbhinn Staire an Bhionadaigh*, 193.

98 Malachi O'Doherty, *The Trouble with Guns*, 18.

99 Glassie, *Ballymenone*, 223, also 199 and 234; MacManus, *Rocky Road to Dublin*, 304–5; Paddy [the Cope] Gallagher, *My Story*, 41.

100 *Irish History Reader* by The Christian Brothers [Br J. M. O'Brien from Co. Clare]. Coldrey, *Faith and Fatherland: The Christian Brothers and the Development of Irish Nationalism 1838–1921*, particularly ch. 6, also 68–76.

101 O'Brien, *Ancestral Voices*, 22–9.

102 Miller, 'The Roman Catholic Church in Ireland', 124–7.

103 Ó Cuív, 'Irish language and literature, 1845–1921', in Vaughan, ed., *New History of Ireland*, vi, 408.

104 IFC, MS 1360/279, 285–6, traditions from Antrim, MS 1215/262–3, from Tyrone; UFTM, R85.242, taped interview with Mrs Bridget Gilhooley, Mullaghbawn, Co. Armagh.

105 Murphy, *Tyrone Folk Quest*, 67.

106 Ó Snodaigh, *Hidden Ulster*, 80–81; also Blaney, *Presbyterians and the Irish Language*, particularly 143–51 and 175–82.

107 UFTM, M3 12: McPeake Transcripts, 109, 114–5; Blaney, *Presbyterians and the Irish Language*, 175–6.

108 C. Milligan Fox, *Annals of the Irish Harpers*, 198–9.

109 MacLaughlin, 'The Politics of Nation-Building in Post-Famine Donegal', 583–604.

110 Ó Danachair, 'The Progress of Irish Ethnology, 1783–1982', *Ulster Folklife*, 29, 7–10.

111 MacLaughlin, 'The Politics of Nation-Building in Post-Famine Donegal', 583–604, on the historical writings of the priests; also Miller, *Church, State, and Nation*, 308 on the anti-Englishness of the hierarchy. Fitzpatrick, 'The Geography of Irish Nationalism', 420–22.

112 Murphy, *Tyrone Folk Quest*, 64.

113 Foster, *Modern Ireland*, 453.

11 CATHOLICS IN NORTHERN IRELAND
1920–2000

1 Laffan, *Partition of Ireland*, 93; O'Halloran, *Partition and the Limits of Irish Nationalism*, 18; Farrell, *Northern Ireland. The Orange State*, 24–5.

2 Bardon, *History of Ulster*, 468.

3 Phoenix, 'Political Violence, Diplomacy and the Catholic Minority in Northern Ireland, 1922', in Darby, Dodge and Hepburn, eds., *Political Violence: Ireland in a Comparative Perspective*, 34.

4 The fullest contemporary account of the Belfast troubles is McKenna [Fr John Hassan, curate of St Mary's], *Facts and Figures of the Belfast Pogrom 1920–1922* – a private printing, only eighteen copies run off; Boyd, 'Father Hassan and the Pogrom', *The Irish Press*, 9 September 1970; *Irish News*, 5 January 1939, article on the death of Father Hassan.

5 'McKenna', *Belfast Pogrom*, 81; Phoenix, *Northern Nationalism*, 195–7; Farrell, *Orange State*, 51, 58, 96, 346; Hezlet, *The 'B' Specials: A History of the Ulster Special Constabulary*, 69, whilst condemning this, absolves the Specials of any involvement.

6 There are similar scenes in Frank Burton's account of another Catholic ghetto in Belfast in the Troubles of the 1970s, *The Politics of Legitimacy: Struggles in a Belfast Community*, 18–19. They could have been transposed to the 1920s and not seemed out of time.

7 *Irish News*, 22 May 1922.

8 UFTM, Collectors' Books, Tyrone, V-19-7, recollections of May Brunt, 1960; Bowman, *De Valera and the Ulster Question 1917–1973*, 72; Dooher, 'Tyrone Nationalism and the Question of Partition, 1910–25', 431; Hopkinson, *Green against Green: the Irish Civil War*, 83–6.

9 Phoenix, 'Political Violence', 29–47; Hopkinson, *Green against Green*, 248–52.

10 'McKenna', *Belfast Pogrom*, op. cit.

11 Shea, *Voices and the Sound of Drums*, 112.

12 Harkness, *Northern Ireland since 1920*, 89. Whyte, 'How Much Discrimination Was There under the Unionist Regime, 1921–68?', in Gallagher and O'Connell, eds., *Contemporary Irish Studies*, 3–7.

13 Shea, *Voices and the Sound of Drums*, 96.

14 Laffan, *Partition of Ireland*, 103–5.

15 Phoenix, *Northern Nationalism*, 197, 226, 237–9.

16 Farrell, *Arming the Protestants: The Formation of the Ulster Special Constabulary*, 1920–27, 267–9; Brewer with Higgins, *Anti-Catholicism in Northern Ireland*, 1600–1998, 93; Arthur, *Government and Politics of Northern Ireland*, 26–7.

17 It is extremely difficult to find a dispassionate account of the USC. The fullest accounts are the favourably disposed Hezlet, *The 'B' Specials: A History of the Ulster Special Constabulary*, and the hostile Farrell, *Arming the Protestants* – although both try to be fair and the latter is particularly well

researched. More recently Follis, *A State under Siege: The Establishment of Northern Ireland, 1920–1925*, 82, 88–9, vividly conveys Unionists' sense of siege in this period. But his case, largely absolving the USC from sectarianism, is marred by excessive pleading, particularly in his efforts to explain away the McMahon murders, 94–5, 111–12.

18 Bew, Gibbon and Patterson, *Northern Ireland 1921–1994*, 35–41.

19 Farrell, *Arming the Protestants*, 153.

20 Buckland, *James Craig*, 86–7.

21 Idem, *A History of Northern Ireland*, 46–7; idem, *Craig*, 87; Phoenix, *Northern Nationalism*, 223ff. There were only a handful of occasions when the Special Powers Act was used against Protestants and usually this was belatedly and reluctantly. It was not until 1966 that the power to ban an organisation under the Act was used against a non-republican body (in this case the UVF). See Whyte, 'Discrimination', 27–8; Farrell, *Orange State*, 63–4; and the traditional nationalist account of Gallagher, *The Indivisible Island*, 194–5.

22 Ultach, 'Orange Terror: the Partition of Ireland', reprinted from *The Capuchin Annual*, 25. Ultach speaks of young men being constantly stopped and harassed in Catholic areas (pp. 4–5). In my recollection actual incidents of this happening were central to nationalist consciousness in Northern Ireland.

23 Maurice Hayes, *Minority Verdict*, 74.

24 Whyte, 'How Much Discrimination Was There under the Unionist Regime?', 29; *Disturbances in Northern Ireland: Report of the Commission Appointed by the Governor of Northern Ireland [The Cameron Report]* (Belfast, 1969), para. 181, also 168.

25 See for e.g. PRO, DO 35/893/123/4, 40–43, 'Treatment of the Catholic minority in Northern Ireland', informal British enquiries, 1924 and 1938; Craigavon's dismissal of Nationalist complaints in 1934, *Northern Ireland House of Commons Debates (NIHC)*, vol. 16, 1933–34, cols. 1092–1094.

26 Barritt and Carter, *The Northern Ireland Problem*, 62; NIHC, 16, col. 1091, on a Nationalist motion about discrimination Craigavon declared himself 'an Orangeman first' ahead of his political status.

27 Opsahl Commission, private hearing, 18 February 1993.

28 Whyte, 'Discrimination under the Unionist Regime', 7; Barritt and Carter, *The Northern Ireland Problem*, 98; Gallagher, *The Indivisible Island* (London, 1957), 225–65; as a publicist employed by the Dublin government, Gallagher was able to use the gerrymandering issue to demonise Ulster Unionists in Irish nationalist thinking generally.

29 *Cameron Report*, para. 141.

30 See Hewitt, 'Catholic Grievances, Catholic Nationalism and Violence in Northern Ireland during the Civil Rights Period: a Reconsideration', *British Jn. of Sociology*, 32, 362–80; the subsequent debate between himself and O'Hearn, ibid., 34 (1983), 438–45, 446–51, 36 (1985), 94–101, 102–5; 38 (1987), 88–100; and the critique of both by Kovalcheck, 'Catholic Grievances in Northern Ireland: Appraisal and Judgement', ibid., 38 (1987), 77–87.

31 PRO, DO 35/893/251/6–9, 'Allegations made by Éire Govt. as to the

Maltreatment of the Minority in Northern Ireland, Arising out of the Partition Question', November 1938.

32 Bardon, *History of Ulster*, 591–3; Harkness, *Northern Ireland*, 71.

33 *Cameron Report*, paras. 139–40.

34 Heskin, *Northern Ireland*, 50.

35 Whyte, 'Discrimination under the Unionist Regime', 18; idem, *Interpreting Northern Ireland*, 54–64; Simpson, 'Economic Development: Cause or Effect in the Northern Irish Conflict', in Darby, ed., *Northern Ireland*, 100–107.

36 *Cameron Report*, para. 138; also Gallagher, *Indivisible Island*, 208–9; Barritt and Carter, *Northern Ireland Problem*, 97–8; Whyte, 'Discrimination under the Unionist Regime', 8–9.

37 Shea, *Voices and the Sound of Drums*, 112–13.

38 *Cameron Report*, para. 141.

39 Buckland, *The Factory of Grievances*, 278–9, 280.

40 Arthur, *Government and Politics*, 62–3.

41 Phoenix, ed., *A Century of Northern Life*, 41; Buckland, *Factory of Grievances*, 22.

42 Shea, *Voices and the Sound of Drums*, 113.

43 Ibid., 98, 142 and 197.

44 Ibid., 159; Barritt and Carter, *Northern Ireland Problem*, 96; Buckland, *Factory of Grievances*, 20; Whyte, 'Discrimination under the Unionist Regime', 13; Bew *et al.*, *Northern Ireland*, 57–94.

45 Ultach, 'Orange Terror', 10–15; this pamphlet went through four reprints, August–September 1943. The author was thought to be J. J. Campbell, then a teacher in St Malachy's, Belfast, later head of the Education Department at Queen's University and a BBC Governor.

46 *Fermanagh Times*, 13 July 1933.

47 *NIHC*, 16, cols. 612–19, 20 March 1934.

48 PRO, DO 35/893/123/44: note prepared by Mr Markbreiter for Sir Samuel Hoare, 3 March 1938.

49 PRO, DO 35/893/123/6, 'Treatment of the Catholic Minority in N. Ireland'; also Bowman, *De Valera and Ulster*, 182.

50 *The Autobiography of Terence O'Neill*, 27–9, 40, 47.

51 *Belfast Telegraph*, 17–18 February 1969.

52 *NIHC*, 16, cols. 1086–7.

53 UFTM, Tape R83.25, interview 9 November 1983.

54 Ultach, 'Orange Terror', 24–6; Hepburn, *A Past Apart*, 174–202; Munck and Rolston, *Belfast in the Thirties*, 46–56; Farrell, *Orange State*, 137–42; Jones, 'The Distribution and Segregation of Roman Catholics in Belfast', *Sociological Review*, 4, 174–5, on the increased residential segregation in this period.

55 Mageean's word (Ultach, 'Orange Terror', 24).

56 Harold Jackson, *The Two Irelands*, 10.

57 Richard Rose, *Governing without Consensus: An Irish Perspective*, 272–3.

58 Ultach, 'Orange Terror', 14. Despite the shock-horror title, Ultach is a

moderate nationalist, whose preferred solution is to publicise the plight of Catholics.

59 Dooher, 'Tyrone Nationalism and the Question of Partition, 1910–25', 321–3, 391–2, 420–25, 539.

60 *NICH*, 14, cols. 44–5; Phoenix, *Northern Nationalism*, 369; Kennedy, 'Catholics in Northern Ireland, 1926–1939', in MacManus, ed., *The Years of the Great Test, 1926–39*, 142.

61 See e.g. Dervla Murphy, *A Place Apart*, 76, 125, 126, interviewees' criticism of the Nationalist party for not accepting the state and getting what was rightfully 'theirs' in the early days of partition.

62 *The Irish Weekly*, 5 April 1958.

63 Farrell, *Orange State*, 194–6.

64 Robert Harbinson, *No Surrender*, 16.

65 O Connor, *In Search of a State*, 231.

66 McCluskey, *Up off Their Knees*, 16; O Connor, *In Search of a State*, 149–50; O'Halloran, *Partition and the Limits of Irish Nationalism*, particularly chs. 3 and 5.

67 *Irish News*, 17 November 1932.

68 *NIHC*, 16, col. 1095: 'We are a Protestant Parliament and a Protestant State'. See *BNL*, 13 July 1932 for the earlier speech, also Farrell, *Orange State*, 136.

69 *Irish News*, 19 and 23 November (editorial) 1932.

70 *Ibid.*, 2 July 1953, Alderman McKearney.

71 McCluskey, *Up off Their Knees*, 7.

72 Hayes, *Minority Verdict*, 15.

73 Barritt and Carter, *The Northern Ireland Problem*, 51.

74 Rose, *Governing without Consensus*, 229; McAllister, *The Northern Ireland Social Democratic and Labour Party*, 21.

75 *NIHC*, 16, cols. 1115–1117, Sir Basil Brooke, saying as much in a debate on the 'Rights of the Minority', 24 April 1934.

76 McCracken, 'The Political Scene in Northern Ireland, 1926–1937', in MacManus, ed., *The Years of the Great Test*, 154; Jackson, *The Two Irelands – a Dual Study of Inter-Group Tensions*, Minority Rights Group, Report no. 2, 10.

77 Bell, *The Secret Army: A Story of the IRA 1916–1970*, 156–69; Barritt and Carter, *The Northern Ireland Problem*, 129.

78 Hepburn, *A Past Apart*, 194.

79 Interview in the 1980s with O'Donnell, in Munck and Rolston, *Belfast in the Thirties*, 183–4. See *Irish News*, 28 March 1932: the march was to Milltown cemetery and had been banned by the Minister of Home Affairs. A priest led the marchers as they recited the rosary in Irish. The protest passed off peacefully.

80 Barritt and Carter, *The Northern Ireland Problem*, 133.

81 Bardon's moving description of the blitz, *History of Ulster*, 564–74.

82 Paddy Devlin, *Straight Left: An Autobiography*, 22–9; this dislike for the IRA in the 1940s finds confirmation in Ultach, 'Orange Terror', 45, 53.

83 Bardon, *History of Ulster*, 587–8.

84 My italics – Bell, *Secret Army*, 334; *Irish News*, 27–28 February 1962; *Ulster Herald*, 3 March 1962.

85 *Fermanagh Herald*, 9 March 1957 – Lenten Pastoral.

86 Shea, *Voices and the Sound of Drums*, 160–64.

87 Harkness, *Northern Ireland*, 126–7; Rose, *Governing without Consensus*, 98–9; Arthur, *Government and Politics of Northern Ireland*, 76–7.

88 Interview with McCrystal on BBC Radio Ulster, 4 June 1998.

89 Shea, *Voices and the Sound of Drums*, 183.

90 Arthur, *Government and Politics of Northern Ireland*, 93; Whyte, *Interpreting Northern Ireland*, 75–9; Brian Faulkner, *Memoirs of a Statesman*, 52.

91 Budge and O'Leary, *Approach to Crisis*, 220, 356 and 369.

92 Rose, *Governing Without Consensus*, 522, notes 55 and 61.

93 The final choice of name – Queen Elizabeth Bridge – was better, but only marginally so.

94 O'Neill, *Autobiography*, 114–17.

95 Arthur, *Government and Politics*, 69; Whyte, *Interpreting Northern Ireland*, 151–4, reaches the conclusion that Protestants in the south of Ireland did not suffer active discrimination. However, the rulings of the Catholic Church on the children of 'mixed marriages' did cause long-term decline in numbers; see also Livingstone, *Monaghan Story*, 447, shows discrimination against Protestants in the border areas and very high outward migration.

96 Murphy, *A Place Apart*, 157, 259–62.

97 O'Neill, *Autobiography*, 78–82. There is a sad little picture in the *Autobiography* of O'Neill opening a minor road in the Belfast suburb of Glengormley. Yet even here he had been sought out by placard-waving Paisleyites – the caption 'The Paisleyites in the background are an example of what I had to contend with'.

98 Barritt and Carter, *The Northern Ireland Problem*, 158–9.

99 Arthur, *Government and Politics of Northern Ireland*, 100.

100 McCluskey, *Up off Their Knees*, 19.

101 *Cameron Report*, para. 12.

102 McCluskey, *Up off Their Knees*, 122.

103 Devlin, *Straight Left*, 90–91.

104 The fullest account of the PD is Arthur, *The People's Democracy 1968–1973*; also Purdie, *Politics in the Streets*, 198–243; personal accounts in Bernadette Devlin, *The Price of My Soul*, 99ff. Devlin, *Straight Left*, 93–5; Farrell, *Orange State*, 247ff.

105 Boal and Buchanan, 'The 1969 Northern Ireland Election', *Irish Geography*, vi, 80–83.

106 Bardon, *History of Ulster*, 674.

107 O'Neill, *Autobiography*, 113.

108 *Cameron Report*, para. 127, also 128–47.

109 Gordon, *The O'Neill Years, Unionist Politics 1963–1969*; Bew et al., *Northern Ireland*, 114, 138–9; Devlin, *Straight Left*, 96–101, says much the same; he also found that O'Neill was being bullied by his own party.

110 Murphy, *A Place Apart*, 126 (but also generous tributes from moderate Catholics, pp. 126–67). Bernadette Devlin, *Price of My Soul*, 114, says much the same of O'Neill. Heskin, *Northern Ireland*, 114, substantiates the kind of perverse pride which Paisley evoked even among his opponents, signs of this also in IFC MS 1923/92–3. The above account of the O'Neill era is based on: his *Autobiography*, Faulkner, *Memoirs of a Statesman*, 38–56, Rose, *Governing Without Consensus*, 97–109, Harkness, *Northern Ireland*, 139–57, *Sunday Times* Insight Team, *Ulster*, chs. 3–5; Arthur, *The People's Democracy*, 1968–73, idem, *Government and Politics*, the most balanced analysis of the O'Neill years; personal memories and those of friends and colleagues.

111 The *Sunday Times* Insight Team, *Ulster*, 126ff.

112 Precise figures for such enforced relocation have remained elusive and controversial. Figures for 1969 were prepared for the Scarman Report: *Violence and Civil Disturbances in Northern Ireland in 1969: Report of the Tribunal of Enquiry (Scarman Report)*, 2 vols. (Belfast, 1972), i, 248–9. The Community Relations Commission updated the figures to 1972: Darby and Morris, *Intimidation in Housing*. See Darby, *Intimidation and the Control of Conflict*, 58–98, for an overview; and O Connor, *In Search of a State*, 108, 116, also Morrison, *West Belfast*, 107–14, and Adams, *The Politics of Irish Freedom*, 54, for their place in republican traditions.

113 *Cameron Report*, paras. 213–15.

114 Devlin, *Straight Left*, 127.

115 Maurice Hayes, *Minority Verdict*, 104.

116 'Where Death Stalks the Streets', *Irish News*, 25–29 January 1993; McKeown, *Two Seven Six Three*, 49–54; Burton, *Politics of Legitimacy*, 18–19.

117 Opsahl Commission, 18 February 1993 oral hearings, Argyle Business Centre, Shankill Road, Belfast.

118 McAllister, *Social Democratic and Labour Party*, 56–9, 130–31.

119 Hayes, *Minority Verdict*, 158.

120 Flackes, *Northern Ireland*, 167–8.

121 Devlin, *Straight Left*, 210.

122 Faulkner, *Memoirs of a Statesman*, 262, 271.

123 An opinion poll of March 1974 – just before the collapse of the power-sharing executive – revealed 65 per cent Protestant and 94 per cent Catholic support for the concept of power-sharing (McAllister, *Social Democratic and Labour Party*, 137).

124 Whyte, *Interpreting Northern Ireland*, 74; Arthur, *Government and Politics of Northern Ireland*, 138; Bardon, *History of Ulster*, 746. See Moloney, 'Where are the Provos Going?', in Bell, Johnstone and Wilson, eds., *Troubled Times*, 1983 commentary on the Provos' political threat to the SDLP; also O'Malley, *The Uncivil Wars*, 122–32.

125 Interview with O Connor, *In Search of a State*, 90–91.

126 Faulkner, *Memoirs*, 205, also 104, 110–11, 166–7, 187, 253. He found the Belfast SDLP less 'Dublin-orientated' than its rural (and Derry) supporters

– it was the latter who pushed the Council of Ireland. John Hume he described as 'a formidable political thinker with great personal integrity but a sometimes exasperating dogmatism'.

127 Though see Darby, *Northern Ireland*, 24–5, who suggests that this might be part of moderate mythology about 'the tolerant sixties' and that basic attitudes had not altered.

12 A RESENTFUL BELONGING: CATHOLIC IDENTITY IN THE TWENTIETH CENTURY

1 Breen, Devine, Dowds, eds., *Social Attitudes in Northern Ireland*, 149, also 90–91, 144; Rose, *Governing without Consensus*, 248, 496; *Belfast Telegraph*, 11 December 1992, Barry White's analysis of the 1991 census: 'Experience shows that when someone refuses to declare their religious denomination in a survey, a follow-up question such as "Do you consider yourself Protestant or Catholic?" usually gets a positive response, revealing true allegiance.'

2 Murphy, *A Place Apart*, 163.

3 My thanks to Vivienne Anderson, Director of the North Belfast Community Centre, for this information.

4 Longley, *The Living Stream*, 95.

5 McKittrick, *Independent on Sunday*, 21 March 1993, and follow-up in the *Independent*, 22 March 1993.

6 Opsahl Commission, oral hearings, Belfast 19–20 January and 16–17 February 1993 (particularly communications of Sally McErlean, Kathleen Feenan, Mary Leonard, May Blood, Kathleen Kelly and Geraldine Reagan on conditions in west Belfast); *Social Attitudes in Northern Ireland*, 184; also reports on the changing religious demography of north Belfast in 'Where Death Stalks the Streets', *Irish News*, 25–29 January 1993.

7 The extent to which this is practised was revealed in BBC Radio Ulster's 'Talkback' programme throughout the week beginning 11 January 1999. New regulations against the practice were brought in by government on 1 March 1999, but the views of many interviewed on 'Talkback' that day were that they would be unworkable.

8 Beckett, *A Belfast Woman*, 84–5; Devlin, *Straight Left*, 4, 16; Darby, *Intimidation and the Control of Conflict in Northern Ireland*, ch. 5. Breen *et al.*, eds., *Social Attitudes in Northern Ireland*, 190–91, found such stereotyping of the 'other' also determining job applications, where there was an expectation of discrimination, even though it was never directly experienced. McLaverty, *Call My Brother Back*, 122, reflects on how different Belfast is to Rathlin, where Protestants and Catholics mixed amicably. Boal, 'Territoriality on the Shankill–Falls Divide, Belfast', *Irish Geography*, vi, 30–50. An earlier study, Jones, 'The Distribution and Segregation of Roman Catholics in Belfast', *Sociological Review*, 4, 167–89, traced the segregation through the nineteenth and twentieth centuries.

9 UFTM, R.83/151: interview with Linda Ballard, 30 November 1983.

10 Beckett, *Give Them Stones*, 131. See discussion of this work in Smyth, *The Novel and the Nation*, 135–8.

11 O'Shea, *Voices and the Sound of Drums*, 196.

12 Brewer with Higgins, *Anti-Catholicism in Northern Ireland, 1600–1998*, 156; Clayton, *Enemies and Passing Friends*, 50–83.

13 Parker, *May the Lord in His Mercy be Kind to Belfast*, 331.

14 Linenhall Lib., NI Poll. Coll., P.637, Continuous Household Survey, June 1985.

15 Heskin, *Northern Ireland: A Psychological Analysis*, 28; for other examples of such stereotyping see my 'Religion and Identity in Northern Ireland', in *Global Convulsions*, edited by Van Horne, 149–67, Brewer, *Anti-Catholicism*, 100, and Parker, *May the Lord in His Mercy*, 129–30, 139–40.

16 Initiative '92-Opsahl Commission focus groups in Derry City, Castle-dawson, Keady, Auchnacloy and Belfast (Shankill Road). These are now in the Linenhall Library, Belfast.

17 Articles 2 and 3 of the Irish constitution were removed in December 1999 under the terms of the 1998 Good Friday Agreement.

18 'In these rural areas, a disproportionate number of the IRA's victims were the only sons of Protestant farmers', Fintan O'Toole, 'The End of the Troubles', *New York Review of Books*, 19 February 1998, 10.

19 White, 'Predicting the Balance', *Belfast Telegraph*, 11 December 1992. See Brewer, *Anti-Catholicism*, 92, for scares and prejudices concerning this issue since the foundation of the state.

20 Brewer, *Anti-Catholicism*, 87–8, 162–3, 234 n.1; Arthur, *Government and Politics of Northern Ireland*, 69.

21 Harris, *Prejudice and Tolerance*, 143–4; Boal, 'Shankill–Falls Divide', 43–7. This seems to have been a very long-running source of dispute, Ó Mórdha, 'The Rising of Burke', 52, details such an incident early in the nineteenth century.

22 Linenhall Lib., NI Pol. Coll. P.666, cheaply printed song-sheet 'Orange Loyalist Songs' (Belfast, 1970). Harris, *Prejudice and Tolerance*, 8, 88–9, 143–4, 171, provides an excellent account of how this ultimate taboo operates, even in communities with otherwise good communal relations.

23 Breen *et al.*, eds., *Social Attitudes in Northern Ireland*, 18–19; Whyte, *Interpreting Northern Ireland*, 40–42.

24 Ultach, 'Orange Terror', 10.

25 *Ibid.*, 23.

26 UFTM, R85.44, taped 1985 interview with Bridget and Brian Murphy of Forkhill, County Armagh, but this was also commonplace in everyday humour prior to the ceasefires.

27 Leo Howe, 'Doing the Double', in Curtin and Wilson, eds., *Ireland from Below*, 144–64; Heskin, *Northern Ireland*, 50, as in so many other areas, Heskin found attitudes to work remarkably similar in both communities.

28 BBC Radio Ulster, 'Talkback', Tuesday 8 January 1991.

29 Frank Burton, *The Politics of Legitimacy*, 187–8 n.43.

30 *The Guardian Weekend*, 3 April 1993; see also Burton's analysis of the importance of reading the sectarian signs correctly, *The Politics of Legitimacy*, 37–67.

31 Harris, *Prejudice and Tolerance*, 143–4; Stringer and Robinson, eds., *Social Attitudes in Northern Ireland: The Second Report*, 146.

32 McCann, *War and an Irish Town*, 81; also McCrystal, *Reflections on a Quiet Rebel*, 80–81; Harris noted such polarisation even in mixed rural schools, *Prejudice and Tolerance*, 137–8.

33 Cited Dunlop, *A Precarious Belonging*, 98–9.

34 I have learnt much of the situation in these Ulster counties which are part of the Irish Republic from conversations with Dr C. J. Woods.

35 McCann, *War in an Irish Town*, 73; Dervla Murphy, *A Place Apart*, 103–11; the best recent account of Protestant sensitivities about Catholic culture is by former Presbyterian moderator John Dunlop, *A Precarious Belonging*, particularly ch. 3.

36 Heskin, *Northern Ireland*, 44–7; Brewer, *Anti-Catholicism*, 124, 130–31.

37 Opsahl Commission, public hearing, Council Offices, Dungannon, 5 February 1993.

38 Tony Parker, *May the Lord in His Mercy*, 136.

39 The words of the psychiatrist John E. Mack, cited in Arthur, ' "Reading" Violence: Ireland', in Apter, ed., *The Legitimization of Violence*, 284.

40 O Connor, *In Search of a State*, 123–4; Cardinal Cahal Daly has always been vociferous in his condemnation of the IRA, yet even he saw earlier rebels as more noble, Daly, *The Price of Peace*, 69, though generally denouncing violence, 51–71, 191–3.

41 Murphy, *A Place Apart*, 203–4.

42 Devlin, *Price of My Soul*, 30, 39, 59–69.

43 McCourt, *Angela's Ashes*, e.g. 122, 162; *Irish News*, 2 January 1939 on the enthusiasm with which a rendering of Pearse's Oration over the grave of O'Donovan Rossa was received at the Christian Brothers past pupil association's annual *céilí* in Belfast; personal recollection of its recitation by Belfast nationalists.

44 See e.g. Breen *et al.*, eds., *Social Attitudes in Northern Ireland: the fifth report* (1996), 17.

45 Personal recollections and notes of the Schools Assembly, QUB, 25 February 1993; for a summary see *Citizens' Inquiry: the Opsahl Report on Northern Ireland*, 384–6.

46 O Connor, *In Search of a State*, 246.

47 *Irish News*, 11 November 1932.

48 Jeffrey, 'The Great War in Modern Irish Memory', in Fraser and Jeffery, eds., *Men, Women and War*, 148–51; Clayton, *Enemies and Passing Friends*, 117, 126–7. UFTM, Field Recording Transcripts, vol. 10, p. 71: Mary Sheehy's family were staunch republicans in Derry during World War I, yet she remembered the great sadness at the losses of the Somme.

49 *Irish News*, 9, 19, 20, 27 January, 19 March and 12 April 1932.

50 O Connor, *In Search of a State*, 293; Burton, *Politics of Legitimacy*, 73–4.

51 Dr Paddy McNally, paper read at Conference of Irish Historians in Britain, April 1998.

52 *Irish News*, 14 September 1953, Revd J. Maguire of St Malachy's College, at an open-air mass at Drumnaquoile, Co. Down; also *Irish News*, 20 and 23 February 1932 and *Fermanagh Herald*, 9 March 1957.

53 *Irish Weekly*, 15 March 1958, similar speech opening Strabane parochial carnival, by Revd Hugh Gallagher, *Derry Journal*, 14 July 1959.

54 *Irish News*, 21 June 1932.

55 *Ulster Herald*, 10 March 1962.

56 Moore, *The Emperor of Ice-Cream*, 29. Boal, 'Shankill–Falls Divide', 36, shows a massive 83 per cent readership of the *Irish News* in the Catholic Clonard area of west Belfast, although in Northern Ireland generally by then, British papers and the more neutral *Belfast Telegraph* were overtaking the *Irish News* and *Belfast Newsletter* in popularity, see Darby, *Conflict in Northern Ireland*, 142–3.

57 The words are those of the then Sinn Féin's publicity Director – Danny Morrison – reported in Padraig O'Malley's brilliant and disturbing account of the hunger strikes and their aftermath (on which much of the above account is based), *Biting at the Grave*, 60; see also Paul Arthur's revealing analysis of how the hunger strikes adapted the key concepts of Catholicism to their cause: ' "Reading" Violence', 234–91; Beresford, *Ten Men Dead*, notably 338–44, the Church's role.

58 Murphy, *A Place Apart*, 132.

59 McAllister, in Darby, ed., *Northern Ireland*, 77; Murphy, *A Place Apart*, 93–4, 132; Darby, *Intimidation and the Control of Conflict*, 136–7; Moxon-Browne, *Nation, Class and Creed in Northern Ireland*, 58, attitude survey of 1978 shows Catholics softer on IRA than on loyalist paramilitaries, but see 21–2, for an example of confused thinking; also O Connor, *In Search of a State*, 304, and McElroy, *The Catholic Church and the Northern Ireland Crisis*, 138–40 on the inadequacies of Church thinking on the 'just war' theory. An excellent analysis of violence in nationalist and republican traditions is Arthur, 'Republican Violence in Northern Ireland: the Rationale', in Darby *et. al.*, eds., *Political Violence*, 48–63; Clayton, *Enemies and Passing Friends*, 152–3, on similar ambivalence in Protestant thinking.

60 O Connor, *In Search of a State*, 88–9, interview with Peter O'Hagan, SDLP councillor.

61 Both Arthur, *Government and Politics of Northern Ireland*, 42, and Donnelly, 'Political Identity in Northern Ireland: An Issue for Catholic Theology', *Studies*, vol. 86, no. 343, 242–3, discuss this issue.

62 *Irish News*, 17 and 30 March 1932; Harvey, 'At the Edge of the Union': Derry Newspapers and the Rhetoric of Nationalism, 1937–39', 26.

63 Arthur, 'Republican Violence', 49 and 59; *Irish News*, 28 March 1932, 10 April 1939.

64 *Fermanagh Herald*, 12 January 1957.

65 *Irish News*, 19 April 1958; Harris, 'Catholicism, Nationalism and the Labour Question in Belfast, 1925–38', *Bullán: an Irish Studies Journal*, iii, no. 1, 25.

66 Ó Snodaigh, *Hidden Ulster*, 81.

67 Murphy, *Tyrone Folk Quest*, 67; idem, *Rathlin*, 96; UFTM, R85.249, interview with Mrs Bridget Gilhooley, Mullaghbawn, Co. Armagh, b. 1917, stories from her mother's time about the local priest discouraging Irish; IFC, MS 1360/285 and MS 1215/262–3, similar accounts from North Antrim and Tyrone.

68 UFTM, Collectors Books V-12-3/51, a Ballycarry Protestant's recollections of being taught Irish culture and history in her National school before partition.

69 Hayes, *Black Puddings with Slim*, 244; O Connor, *In Search of a State*, 318–19; also personal experiences in the 1950s and 1960s. Liam Andrews, ' "The very dogs in Belfast will bark in Irish." The Unionist Government and the Irish language 1921–43', in Mac Póilin, ed., *The Irish Language in Northern Ireland*, 69.

70 UFTM, Field Recording Transcripts, vol. 16, pp. 4–20: interview 12 May 1976; this claim about the polarising effect of the Troubles also finds endorsement in ibid., vol. 15, p. 171; see also Harvey, 'At the Edge of the Union', 31, for this notion of the '98-type Presbyterians.

71 Opsahl Commission, submission no. 325, summarised in *Citizens' Inquiry*, 341–2.

72 PRONI, CAB 9D/44/1, 1928 correspondence between 'The Loyalty League' and Government – this shows a decline in the numbers of children studying Irish from 5,531 in 1923 to 1,290 in 1927; Andrews, 'Unionist Government and the Irish language 1921–43', 74–6; Harvey, 'At the Edge of the Union', 76, citing Education Minister John Robb's 1943 rebuttal of the Orange Order's attempt to have the Irish language outlawed in the schools, on the grounds that it was 'part of that freedom of the individual for which we profess to be fighting this war'.

73 Mac Póilin, 'Aspects of the Irish Language Movement in Northern Ireland', in Nic Craith, *Watching One's Tongue: Aspects of Romance and Celtic Languages*, 156–9; also O'Reilly, 'Nationalists and the Irish Language in Northern Ireland: Competing Perspectives', in Mac Póilin, ed., *Irish Language in Northern Ireland*, 98–113.

74 *Newry Reporter*, 7 February 1957; UFTM, M3/12, McPeake Transcripts, the renowned traditional musician, Francis McPeake, recalls (1983) family traditions of early Gaelic League activities in Belfast. The language side seems to have been politicised at an early stage, even though he suggests that ordinary people on the Falls Rd (126) would have preferred it otherwise. The music side seems to have attracted much Presbyterian support (this finds endorsement in UFTM, Field Recording Transcripts, vol. 16, pp. 1–20, 1976 interview with the piper Jack O'Rourke).

75 O'Reilly, 'Nationalists and the Irish language in Northern Ireland', 100.

76 The poet Michael Longley recalls as an Arts Council officer being instructed to discontinue the funding to the Conway Education Project in west Belfast. This, together with the more notorious case of the removal of funding from the *Glór na nGael* language group in 1990, he thought short-sighted and

counter-productive (*A Citizen's Inquiry: The Opsahl Report*, 331–2); O'Reilly, 'Nationalists and the Irish Language', 118–27, examines the controversy in some detail, and comes to much the same conclusion.

77 Submission to the Opsahl Commission – *Citizen's Inquiry: The Opsahl Report*, 335. Although there is indeed a strong move elsewhere in the country to remove the GAA ban mentioned here.

78 See *The Agreement*, 19–20, for clauses on the language issue.

79 McCrystal, *Reflections on a Quiet Rebel*, 109–16, 142–6.

80 Devlin, *Price of My Soul*, 60; Loftus, *Mirrors, Orange and Green*, 88.

81 O Connor, *In Search of a State*, 178–9; McCrystal, *Reflections*, also his interview, BBC Radio Ulster, 4 June 1998.

82 May McCann, 'Belfast Ceilidhes', *Ulster Folklife*, 29, 55–105; Bardon, *History of Ulster*, 422–3; UFTM, Field Recording Transcripts, vol. 17, pp. 65–6; IFC, MS 976/203, Mrs Anne Mulholland of Rostrevor, recalling (in 1945) 'house *ceilidhes*': 'They'd only be wee dances of course, for the priest wouldn't allow a big dance. And you wouldn't stay late, for in them times you had to be home to say the Rosary.'

83 Hayes, *Minority Verdict*, 50.

84 Linenhall Lib., NI Political Coll., 'A New Song for Nationalist Heroes', in 'Micí bocht', *Dance to Democracy: A Collection of Broadsides with Insights into Our Present Troubles* (Belfast, n.d.); McCann, 'Belfast Ceilidhes', 64, for the GAA vigilantes.

85 As an articulate team of Tyrone sixth-formers did in their public presentation to the Opsahl Commission, Dungannon, 5 February 1993.

86 Harris, *Prejudice and Tolerance*, 176 (though it should be pointed out that her informant was a hostile source).

87 O Connor, *In Search of a State*, 293.

88 Keogh, *The Vatican, the Bishops and Irish Politics, 1919–39*, 212–15; *Irish News*, 9–20, 27–28 January, 8 February, 17 March 1932. Needless to say, MacRory's comments became part of the Unionists' association of Catholicism and 'disloyalty', see e.g. NIHC, 16, cols. 618 and 1115.

89 Hayes, *Minority Verdict*, 29–30.

90 The words are those of Monsignor Denis Faul (one of the very few senior clergy courageous enough to speak on the issue) to the public hearing of the Opsahl Commission at Dungannon, 5 February 1993; Rogan, *Irish Catechesis*, i, 22–3, shows that by the twentieth century the Irish hierarchy had established a control over education unique in the world, though somewhat similar situations obtained in Scotland, the Netherlands and Quebec.

91 'Submission from the Northern Catholic Bishops on the Consultative Document "Education in Northern Ireland – Proposals for Reform"', news release by the Catholic Press and Information Office, 23 June 1988, p. 3.

92 *Irish News*, 2 May 1953.

93 Murray, *Worlds Apart*, 23; Cardinal Daly's *Irish Times* interview (7 November 1990), in which he did not deny such when asked by the reporter; also McAllister, *Social Democratic and Labour Party*, 136, on reactions to integration proposals of 1974.

94 Breen *et al.*, eds., *Social Attitudes in Northern Ireland: The Fifth Report*, 19–20.

95 Gallagher and Worrall, *Christians in Ulster 1968–1980*, 169, 153–72.

96 Whyte, *Interpreting Northern Ireland*, 47, also 42–8; see also Education section of *A Citizen's Inquiry: the Opsahl Report*, 105–10.

97 Murray, 'Schools and Conflict', in Darby, ed., *Northern Ireland: The Background to the Conflict* (Belfast, 1983), 136–50.

98 Devlin, *Price of My Soul*, 62–70.

99 Barritt and Carter, *Northern Ireland Problem*, 89.

100 See Farren, *The Politics of Irish Education 1920–65*, 24–34.

101 Akenson, *Education and Enmity*, 95, 188 – much of this education section is based on Akenson's findings.

102 Shea, *Voices and the Sound of Drums*, 159–72. Indeed, in 1988 the Northern Ireland bishops paid tribute to 'the harmonious relationship' which had existed between them and the Northern Ireland Ministry of Education (see 'Submission from the Northern Catholic Bishops', op. cit., p. 9).

103 Farren, *Politics of Irish Education*, 49–58.

104 O Connor, *In Search of a State*, 311–14.

105 Murray, *Worlds Apart*, 21; Akenson, *Education and Enmity*, 117, 168.

106 Barritt and Carter, *The Northern Ireland Problem*, 87–8.

107 Murray, *Worlds Apart*, 26–30.

108 Akenson, *Education and Enmity*, 119–24.

109 Titley, *Church, State and the Control of Schooling in Ireland 1900–1944*, 106, 119, 132.

110 Harris, 'Catholicism, Nationalism and the Labour Question in Belfast, 1925–38', *Bullán: An Irish Studies journal*, iii, 17; Rafferty, *Catholicism in Ulster*, 248.

111 Akenson, *Education and Enmity*, 169; Farren, *Politics of Irish Education*, 167. Not all higher clergy were utterly opposed to state social welfare, notably Monsignor Arthur Ryan of Belfast (a professor at Queen's University) and the future bishop of Down and Connor, William Philbin (Whyte, *Church and State*, 272, also Hayes, *Minority Verdict*, 315 on Ryan); see Lee, *Ireland 1912–1985*, 318–19 for a reassessment of the hierarchy's role in the 'Mother and Child' episode.

112 UFTM, R83.135, Fred Heatley's memories of working-class Belfast in the 1940s: areas where the women did not work seemed to mark them out as 'decent working-class' areas; Harvey, 'At the Edge of the Union', 19–20.

113 Munck and Rolston, *Belfast in the Thirties*, 82–3.

114 Barritt and Carter, *Northern Ireland Problem*, 109–19; *Irish News*, 24 April 1953; Whyte, *Church and State in Modern Ireland 1923–1970*, 149–50.

115 Devlin, *Price of My Soul*, 63; also Farren, *Politics of Irish Education*, 89.

116 McCann, *War and an Irish Town*, 74.

117 Harris, *Prejudice and Tolerance*; 130, Hayes, *Sweet Killough*, 197; idem, *Black Puddings*, 154; idem, *Minority Verdict*, 117, 93–4.

118 Hayes, *Minority Verdict*, 117.

119 Rogan, *Synods and Catechesis in Ireland*, 436, 442, also 326–32, 431.

120 O Connor, *In Search of a State*, 314–17.

121 See also very good discussions of Moore's work in Norman Vance, 'Catholic and Protestant Literary Visions of "Ulster": Now You See It, Now You Don't', in *Religion and Literature*, 28, 134–6 and Sullivan, *A Matter of Faith: The Fiction of Brian Moore*.

122 Hayes, *Black Puddings*, 49, 102–4.

123 McCann, *War and an Irish Town*, 69–70.

124 Hayes, *Black Puddings with Slim*, 153–4; idem, *Sweet Killough*, 14–15, 186; Devlin, *Straight Left*, 3–4; O Connor, *In Search of a State*, 278.

125 Harvey, 'At the Edge of the Union', 35.

126 *Irish News*, 9 January 1939 and 23 January 1962, Bishop O'Kane's funeral in January 1939, and Dr Mageean's in 1962; also *Irish News*, 28 June and 5 July 1958, and Rafferty, *Catholicism in Ulster*, 236, 245–6, for the 1958, 1947 and 1934 references.

127 *Irish News*, 21 June 1932; every issue in June carries reports and there had been a build-up of preparation since the beginning of the year.

128 McElroy, *The Catholic Church and the Northern Ireland Crisis*, 144–5. The subsequent account relies heavily on this very interesting book.

129 O'Malley, *Biting at the Grave*, 173–8.

130 See e.g. Faul and Murray, *The Alienation of Northern Catholics*.

131 O Connor, *In Search of a State*, 172–4; Rafferty, *Catholicism in Ulster*, 275–81; David Beresford, *Ten Men Dead*, 178–91, 218–19, for Ó Fiaich's role in the hunger strikes and the dilemma of the Church.

132 Barritt and Carter, *Northern Ireland Problem*, 117–19.

133 Darby, *Intimidation and the Control of Conflict in Northern Ireland*, 111, also pp. 109–11, 121–2, 155–6; Burton, *Politics of Legitimacy*, 93–104, for a similar heart and minds battle in Ardoyne. However, for concern also within the Church that it was assuming a role better left to lay people see Lennon, *After the Ceasefires*, 97.

134 Except by the ever-impressive O Connor, *In Search of a State*, 282; also Dara O'Hagan, 'Sinn Féin and the Catholic Church', 17, 134–8, 142–59, also 194–5, on a general softening of relationships between republicans and the church since the 1994 ceasefire.

135 *A Citizen's Inquiry. The Opsahl Report*, 340.

136 There is an excellent overview of recent research into Catholic religious sisters in Ireland in Margaret MacCurtain, 'Late in the Field: Catholic Sisters in Twentieth-Century Ireland and the new Religious History', *Journal of Women's History*, 6–7, 49–63. This also highlights the struggle of female religious within the Catholic Church.

137 *A Citizen's Inquiry. The Opsahl Report*, 96.

138 See Moxon-Browne, *Nation, Class and Creed*, 49–51, useful survey of reforms since 1970; BBC Radio Ulster, 'Talkback', 12 January 1999, reporting the large increase in Catholic applications to the RUC since the Good Friday Agreement.

139 Longley, *The Living Stream*, 88–9.

140 Deane, *Reading in the Dark*, 231–2.

141 Beckett, *Give Them Stones*, 119, 130–31.

142 There is a good survey of Troubles writing in Michael Parker, *The Hurt World*, 1–8.

143 Arthur, ' "Reading" Violence', 282; for this concentration of violence in Catholic areas, both rural and urban. Michael Poole, 'The Geographical Location of Political Violence in Northern Ireland', in Darby *et al.*, *Political Violence*, 64–82, also shows Armagh top of the league.

144 *Citizen's Inquiry: The Opsahl Report*, 421.

145 See the interesting collection of papers to the 1995 conference: 'Beyond 2000 for Northern Ireland', published by the Jigsa Group in 1998 – notably those by Paddy Doherty and Michael Smyth. The extraordinary bitterness of much of Catholic historiography is exemplified in the otherwise excellent local history of Tyrone, *Domhnach Mór*, written in 1963, in which there are only two overarching themes, 'dispossession' and 'the Church'. It also characterises the work of the otherwise respected folklorist Michael J. Murphy, the most important collector and compiler for the Ulster section of the Irish Folklore Commission in Dublin.

146 Glassie, *Ballymenone*, 639.

147 There is an excellent overview of recent opinion in Joseph Ruane and Jennifer Todd, eds., *After the Good Friday Agreement: Analysing Political Change in Northern Ireland* (Dublin, 1999), notably the essay by Bernadette C. Hayes and Ian McAllister, 'Ethnonationalism, Public Opinion and the Good Friday Agreement', 30–48.

Select Bibliography

PRIMARY

Northern Ireland

Linenhall Library

Joy MSS
Broadside Collection
N.I. Political Collection
Opsahl Commission papers (originals in possession of the author)

Queen's University, Belfast

Gaelic Manuscripts 17: Mic A/428 (xviii), 'An essay on Séamus Mac Cuarta'

Public Record Office of Northern Ireland

Ant 4/1/1: Antrim Grand Jury presentment books, 1711–21
CAB 9D: N.I. Ministry of Education
D.272: McCance Collection
D.605: Survey of Col. Mervyne Archdal's estate, Co. Fermanagh, 1720
D.607: Downshire MSS
D.627: Family and estate papers of the Montgomery family, Blessingbourne,
    Co. Tyrone, 1880–94
D.1375: McGildowny Papers
D.1514: Hervey-Bruce Papers
D.2714/5H1: General notes on Viscount Magennis of Iveagh
D.2918: Whyte Papers
DIO (RC)/1: Clogher Diocesan Papers.
Mic.147/9: Papers and correspondence of the Roden family, Newcastle, Co.
    Down
T.808/14895–6:Tennison Groves Abstracts of the County Antrim assizes and
    quarter sessions
T.808/15261: 1744 Committee on Religion

T.1392: Memorial of the proprietors of the Fews, 2 Dec. 1743
T.2541: Abercorn MSS
T.3022/4/2A-C: Cromwellian Inquisition taken in the town and county of
  Antrim, 1657.

Ulster Folk and Transport Museum

Collectors' Books
Field Recordings, transcripts
Schools Text-Book Collection
Sound recordings (taped interviews), R83–90
M3 12: McPeake Transcripts

Republic of Ireland

Irish Folklore Commission, University College, Dublin

Collectors' books, vols. 57, 89, 102, 105, 270, 975–6, 1033, 1057, 1112–13,
  1215–17, 1359–60, 1364–5, 1386–7, 1483, 1844, 1922–6, 2034–5,
  2037–8, 2080–82, 2094, 2099, 2104, 2176

National Archives of Ireland

State of the Country Papers
Rebellion Papers, 620/1–67

National Library of Ireland

T.1898: Catholic Qualification Rolls, 1778–90
Pos. 1899: Index to the Catholic Qualification Rolls, Ulster, 1793–6
MS G.200(b): *Ollamh éigin. An Revolution. The French Revolution. By an
  uncertain author*

Royal Irish Academy

Ordinance Survey Letters

England

Public Record Office

HO 100/38, 42–4, 87, 62–4: Home Office Papers
DO 35/893/123: 'Treatment of the Catholic minority in Northern Ireland',
  1924, 1938

Centre for Kentish Studies

U840 Pratt Mss

PRINTED PRIMARY

Newspapers and periodicals

An Phoblacht. Republican News
Belfast News Letter
Belfast Telegraph
Derry Journal
Fermanagh Herald
Fermanagh Times
Fortnight Magazine
Guardian
Irish News
Irish Weekly
Newry Reporter
Northern Star
Ulster Herald

Official reports and papers (by date)

Cal.S.P.Ireland, 1598–1670
[David Bindon], *An Abstract of the Number of Protestant and Popish Families in the Several Counties and Provinces of Ireland taken from the Returns Made by the Hearth-money Collectors . . . in the Years 1732 and 1733* (Dublin, 1736)
The Parliamentary Register, or, History of the Proceedings and Debates of the House of Commons of Ireland, 1781–97, 17 vols. (Dublin, 1782–1801)
Report from the Committee of Secrecy of the House of Commons of Ireland (Dublin, 1798) – also reproducing 1793 and 1797 secret committee reports
Memorial of Prisoners Charged with Murder at Macken, H.C.1830 (150) xxvi, 301
Third Report from the Select Committee . . . [on] Orange Lodges, H.C.1835 (476) xvi,1
Papers Relating to the Investigation Held at Castlewellan into the Occurrences at Dolly's Brae, on the 12th July, 1849, H.C.1850 [1143] li, 331
Return of Number of Murders and Waylayings in the Baronies of Upper and Lower Fews, in County Armagh, 1844–50, H.C.1850 [566] li, 517

Report from the Lord Lieutenant . . . Proclaiming of a District in the County of Down, H.C.1851 (250) l, 435

Return of Numbers of Murders, Waylayings . . . or Other Crimes of Agrarian Character . . . Louth, Armagh and Monaghan, 1849–52, H.C.1852 (448) xlvii, 465–75

Report . . . into Conduct of Constabulary during Disturbances at Belfast, July and Sept. 1857, H.C.1857–8 (333) xlvii, 781

Royal Commission of Inquiry into . . . Riots in Belfast, July and Sept. 1857, H.C.1857–8[2309], xxvi, 1

Report on the Derryveagh Evictions, H.C.1861 (316), lii, 539–79

Notes of Trials at Armagh, Arising out of Riots at Derrymacash, H.C.1861 (315), lii,1

Papers relating to Donaghmore Riot, with Report of Commission . . . into Conduct of Justices of the Peace . . . at Dungannon, Oct. 1866, H.C.1867 [3906], lix,191

Royal Commission of Inquiry into Riots and Disturbances in the City of Londonderry, H.C. 1870 [C.5*] xxxii, 411

Royal Commission of Inquiry into Disturbances in the City of Londonderry, Nov. 1883, H.C.1884 [C.3954] xxxviii, 515

Correspondence Relating to the Action of Certain Magistrates . . . at Londonderry, Nov.1883, H.C.1884[C.4010] lxiii, 491

Correspondence between the Lord Chancellor of Ireland and R. McClintock, in Reference to His Conduct as a Magistrate . . . Mar. 1884, H.C. 1884 [C.5057] lxiii

Reports into other Orange meetings: H.C. 1884 [C.4065] lxiii, 517 and 527 (Newry); H.C. 1884 (95) lxiii, 461 (Dromore, Tyrone); H.C. 1884 [C.3891] lxiii, 547 (Rosslea, Fermanagh – also on magistrates in Monaghan and Cavan)

Correspondence and Reports Relating to the Removal of Lord Rossmore, H.C. 1884 [C.3891] lxiii, 547

Belfast Riots Commission, H.C.1887 [C.4925] [C.4925-I], xviii, 1, 25; [C.5029], xviii, 631

Northern Ireland House of Commons Debates, 1932–4

Disturbances in Northern Ireland: Report of the Commission Appointed by the Governor of Northern Ireland (Cameron Report), (Belfast, 1969)

Violence and Civil Disturbances in Northern Ireland in 1969: Report of the Tribunal of Enquiry (Scarman Report), 2 vols. (Belfast, 1972)

The Agreement: Agreement Reached in the Multi-party Negotiations [so-called Good Friday Agreement] (1998)

We Will Remember Them. Report of the Northern Ireland Victims Commissioner Sir Kenneth Bloomfield, KCB (April 1998)

Contemporary printed works

A. F. O'D. Alexander, ed., 'The O'Kane Papers. Bishop Montgomery's Survey of the Bishoprics of Derry, Raphoe and Clogher', *Anal. Hib.*, xii (1943), 67–127

'A List of Regulars Registered in Ireland Pursuant to the Catholic Relief Act of 1829', *Archiv. Hib.*, iii (1914), 34–86

An Account of the Bloody Massacre in Ireland . . . (London, 1678)

Annála Uladh: Annals of Ulster, edited by W.M. Hennessy, 4 vols. (Dublin, 1887–1901)

Annals of the Kingdom of Ireland by the Four Masters, from the Earliest Period to the Year 1616, edited and translated by John O'Donovan, 7 vols. (Dublin, 1851)

Robert Ashton, *The Battle of Aughrim, or the Fall of Monsieur St. Ruth. A Tragedy* (Dublin, 1756)

Thomas Bartlett, 'Select Documents: Defenders and Defenderism in 1795', *I.H.S.*, xxiv (1985), 373–94

Beauties of the Press (Dublin, 1800)

'Bodley's Visit to Lecale, County of Down, A.D. 1602–3', *U.J.A.*, ii (1854), 73–99

Revd Canon Ulick J. Bourke, ed., *Sermons in Irish-Gaelic by the Most Rev. James O'Gallagher* (Dublin, 1877)

John Brady, *Catholics and Catholicism in the Eighteenth-Century Press* (Maynooth, 1965)

J. S. Brewer and W. Bullen, eds., *Calendar of the Carew Manuscripts Preserved in the Archiepiscopal Library at Lambeth,* 6 vols. (London, 1867–73)

Cornelius G. Buttimer, 'An Irish Text on the "War of Jenkins' Ear"', *Celtica,* xxi (1990), 75–98

Michael J. Byrne, ed., *The Irish War of Defence, 1598–1600: Extracts from De Hibernia Insula Commentarius of Peter Lombard, Archbishop of Armagh* (Cork, 1930)

— *Ireland under Elizabeth . . . Being a Portion of the History of Catholic Ireland by Don Philip O'Sullivan Bear* (Dublin, 1903)

Edward Campion, *A Historie of Ireland Written in the Yeare 1571,* in James Ware, ed., *Ancient Irish Histories: The Works of Spencer, Campion, Hanmer, and Marleburrough,* 2 vols. (Dublin, 1809)

A Candid and Impartial Account of the Disturbances in the County of Meath, in the Years 1792, 1793, and 1794. By a County Meath Freeholder (Dublin, 1794)

Nicholas Canny, ed., 'Rowland White's "The Dysorders of the Irishery, 1571"', *Stud. Hib.*, xix (1979), 147–60

Charlemont MSS. The Manuscripts and Correspondence of James, First Earl of Charlemont, HMC, 12th report, append pt. 10 and 13th report, append pt. 8, 2 vols., (London, 1891–4)

D. A. Chart, ed., *The Drennan Letters* (Belfast, 1931)

The Christian Brothers, *Irish History Reader* (Dublin, 1905)

A Collection of Certain Horrid Murthers in Several Counties of Ireland Committed since 23 October 1641 (London, 1641)

A Concise Account of the Material Events and Atrocities, Which Occurred in the Present Rebellion, by 'Verdicus' (Dublin, 1799)

Revd James Connolly, *What Mean These Stones: A Sermon Preached in the Church of St Mary Belfast, on the Occasion of the Centenary on Sunday, November 11th (1883)* (London, 1883)

Charles Coote, *Statistical Survey of County Armagh* (Dublin, 1804)

— *Statistical Survey of the County of Monaghan* (Dublin, 1801)

Patrick J. Corish, ed., 'Two Reports on the Catholic Church in Ireland in the Early Seventeenth Century', *Archiv. Hib.*, xxii (1959), 140–62

M. A. Costello, *De Annatis Hiberniae: A Calendar of the First Fruits Fees Levied on Papal Appointments to Benefices in Ireland, 1400–1535* (Dublin, 1912)

W. H. Crawford and B. Trainor, eds., *Aspects of Irish Social History, 1750–1800* (Belfast, 1969)

Revd Séamus Creighton, 'The Penal Laws in Ireland and the Documents in the Archives of Propaganda (1690–1731)', *Procs. Irish Cath. Hist. Committee* (1961), 5–9

Sir John Davies, 'A Discovery of the True Causes Why Ireland was Never Entirely Subdued', in H. Morley, ed., *Ireland under Elizabeth and James I* (London, 1890)

Angélique Day, ed, *Letters from Georgian Ireland: the Correspondence of Mary Delaney 1731–68* (Belfast, 1991)

Angélique Day and Patrick McWilliams, eds.,*Ordnance Survey Memoirs of Ireland*, 40 vols. (Belfast 1990–98)

Seamus Deane, ed., *The Field Day Anthology of Irish Writing*, 3 vols. (Derry, 1991)

John Derricke, *The Image of Irelande* (Edinburgh, 1883)

William Steel Dickson, *A Narrative of the Confinement and Exile of William Steel Dickson, D.D.* (Dublin, 1812)

The Distress'd State of Ireland Considered; More Particularly with Respect to the North. In a Letter to a Friend ([Dublin], 1740)

John Dubourdieu, *Statistical Survey of the County of Antrim* (Dublin,1812)

Robert Dunlop, ed., *Ireland under the Commonwealth: Being a Selecion of Documents Relating to the Government of Ireland, 1651–9*, 2 vols. (Manchester, 1913)

R. D. Edwards, ed., 'The Minute Book of the Catholic Committee, 1773–92', *Archiv. Hib.*, ix (1942), 1–172

Patrick Fagan, ed., *Ireland in the Stuart Papers: Correspondence and Documents of Irish Interest from the Stuart Papers in the Royal Archives, Windsor Castle*, 2 vols., (Dublin,1995)

C. Litton Falkiner, *Illustrations of Irish History and Topography* (London, 1904)

Hugh Fenning, ed., *The Fottrell Papers, 1721–39* (Belfast, 1980)

Revd P. J. Flanagan, 'The Diocese of Clogher in 1714', *Clogher Record*, i (1954), 39–42, 125–30

John H. Gebbie, ed., *An Introduction to the Abercorn Letters* (Omagh, 1972)

Gerald of Wales (Giraldus Cambrensis), *The History and Topography of Ireland*, translated by John O'Meara (Harmondsworth, 1988)

Cathaldus Giblin, ed., 'Catalogue of Material of Irish Interest in the Collection *Nunziatura di Fiandra*', Vatican Archives: Part I, vols. 1–50, *Coll. Hib.*, i (1958), 7–136; Part 4, vols. 102–122, *Coll. Hib.*, v (1962), 7–125

J. T. Gilbert, ed., *A Contemporary History of Affairs in Ireland from A.D. 1641 to 1652 Containing the . . . Narrative Entitled an 'Aphorismical Discovery of Treasonable Faction'*, 3 vols. (Dublin 1879–80)

William Gillies, 'A Poem on the Downfall of the Gaodhil', *Éigse*, 13 (1969–70), 203–10

Mrs Stephen Gwynn, *Stories from Irish History* (Dublin and Belfast, 1920)

John Hagan, ed., 'Miscellanea Vaticano-Hibernica', *Archiv. Hib.*, iii (1914), 227–365; iv (1915), 215–318; v (1916), 74–185; vi (1917), 94–155; vii (1918–21), 67–356

Revd W. Hamilton, *Letters Concerning the Northern Coast of the County of Antrim* (Belfast, 1822)

John Hanly, ed.,*The Letters of Saint Oliver Plunkett* (Dublin, 1979)

William Harris, *The Ancient and Present State of the County of Down* (Dublin, 1744)

— *Translation of the Works of Sir James Ware* (Dublin, 1739)

George Hill, ed., *The Montgomery Manuscripts (1603–1706): Compiled from the Family Papers by William Montgomery of Rosemount Esquire* (Belfast,1869)

Herbert F. Hore, ed., 'Marshal Bagenal's Description of Ulster, Anno 1596', *U. J. A.*, 1st ser., ii (1854), 153–4

T. B. and T. J. Howell, eds., *A Complete Collection of State Trials*, 33 vols. (London, 1809–28)

Francis Hutchinson, *A Defence of the Antient Historians: with a Particular Application of It to the History of Ireland* (Dublin, 1734)

Irish Catholic Directory, 1932–79

'Irish Catholics Licensed to Keep Arms (1704)', *Archiv. Hib.*, iv (1915), 59–65

H. Jones, *A Remonstrance of Divers Remarkable Passages Concerning the Church and Kingdome of Ireland* (London, 1641)

Geoffrey Keating, *Foras Feasa ar Éirinn, the History of Ireland*, edited by D. Comyn and P.S. Dineen (Dublin, 1987)

John Lawless, *The Belfast Politics, Enlarged; Being a Compendium of the Political History of Ireland for the Last Forty Years* (Belfast, 1818)

Les Martyrs de la Province Dominicaine d'Irlande (Paris, 1890)

A. G. Little, ed., *Liber Exemplorum* (n.p., 1908)

[John Lodge], ed., *Desiderata Curiosa Hibernica, or, a Select Collection of State Papers*, 2 vols. (Dublin, 1772)

Marquess of Londonderry, ed., *Memoirs and Correspondence of Viscount Castlereagh*, 12 vols. (London, 1848–54)

John Lynch, *Cambrensis Eversus*, edited by Matthew Kelly, 3 vols. (Dublin,1848–52)

James MacCaffrey, ed., 'Commonwealth Records', *Archiv. Hib.*, vi (1917), 175–202; vii (1918–21), 20–66

G. B. McKenna [Fr John Hassan – curate of St. Mary's], *Facts and Figures of the Belfast Pogrom 1920–1922* (Dublin, 1922)

W. J. MacNeven, *Pieces of Irish History* (New York, 1807)

James McParlan, *Statistical Survey of the County of Donegal* (Dublin, 1802)

Francis McPolin, 'An Old Irish Catechism from Oriel', *Ir. Eccles. Rec.* (1947), 509–17

Samuel McSkimin, *Annals of Ulster from 1790–1798*, new edn. by E. J. McCrum (Belfast, 1906)

Dr Nicholas Madgett, 'Constitutio ecclesiastica', edited by Michael Manning, *Kerry Arch. Soc. Jn.*, ix (1976), 68–91

Cuthbert Mhág Craith, *Dán na mBráthar Mionúr* (Dublin, 1980)

Henry Joseph Monck Mason, *The Testimony of St Patrick against the False Pretensions of Rome to Primitive Antiquity in Ireland* (Dublin, 1846)

W. Shaw Mason, *A Statistical Account, or Parochial Survey of Ireland*, 3 vols. (Dublin, 1814)

C. Maxwell, *Irish History from Contemporary Sources, 1509–1610* (London, 1923)

Benignus Millet, O.F.M., 'Archbishop Edmund O'Reilly's Report on the State of the Church in Ireland, 1662', *Coll. Hib.*, ii (1959), 105–14

T. W. Moody, ed., 'Ulster Plantation Papers, 1608–13', *Anal. Hib.*, no. 8 (1938), 179–298

P. F. Moran, *Spicilegium Ossoriense, Being a Collection of Original Letters and Papers Illustrative of the History of the Irish Church from the Reformation to the Year 1800*, 3 vols. (Dublin, 1874)

— ed., *The Analecta of David Rothe, Bishop of Ossory* (Dublin, 1884)

Henry Morley, ed., *Ireland under Elizabeth and James I* (London, 1809)

Fynes Moryson, *An Itinerary*, new edition, 4 vols. (Glasgow, 1907–8)

Revd L.P. Murray, 'Three Documents Concerning the Deanery of Dundalk during the Eighteenth Century', *Archiv. Hib.*, v (1916), 39–73

— 'Archbishop Cromer's Register', *Louth Arch. Soc. Jn.*, vii (1929–32), 516–24; viii (1933–6), 38–49, 169–88, 322–51; ix (1937–40), 36–41, 124–30

— 'The History of the Parish of Creggan, *Louth Arch. Soc. Jn.*, viii (1933–6), 117–63; ix (1937–40), 135–61

— 'The Last Abbot of Mellifont', *Louth Arch. Soc. Jn.*, viii (1933–6), 223–33

Richard Musgrave, *Memoirs of the Different Rebellions in Ireland*, second edition (Dublin, 1801)

John Edward Newell, *The Apostasy of Newell* (London, 1798)

Eileen O'Byrne, ed., *The Convert Rolls* (Dublin, 1981)

Sean Ó Domhnaill, 'County Donegal in the Catholic Qualification Rolls, 1778–1790', *Co. Donegal Hist. Soc. Jn.*, i (1949), 204–5

Comhairle Mhic Clamha ó Achadh na Muilleann: The Advice of MacClave from Aughnamullen, translated by S. Ó Dufaigh and Brian Rainey (Lille, 1981)

Tomás Ó Fiaich, 'The 1766 Religious Census', *Seanchas Ard Mhacha*, iv (1960–62), 147–70

P. Ó Gallachair, '1622 Survey of Cavan', *Breifne*, i (1958), 60–75

— 'Catholic Qualification Rolls Index: Fermanagh and Monaghan', *Clogher Record*, ii (1959), 544–51

W. M. O'Hanlon, *Walks among the Poor of Belfast* (Belfast, 1853)

'The O'Kane Papers' presented by A.F. O'D. Alexander, *Anal. Hib.*, xii (1943), 79–111

Cainneach Ó Maonaigh O.F.M., ed., *Seanmónta Chúige Uladh* (Dublin, 1965)

— ed., *Smaointe Beatha Chríost* (Dublin, 1944)

Réamonn Ó Muirí, ed., *Lámhscríbhinn Staire an Bhionadaigh: Comhrac nGael agus na nGall le Chéile* [Bennett's historical manuscript: the conflict of the Gaeil and Gaill with each other], (Monaghan, 1994)

Thomas F. O'Rahilly, ed., *Desiderius, Otherwise Called Sgáthán an Chrábaidh,* by Flaithrí Ó Maolchonaire, 1616 (Dublin, 1941)

J. P. O'Reilly, 'Remarks on Certain Passages in Capt. Cuellar's Narrative of His Adventures in Ireland ... 1588–89', *Proc. R.I.A.*, iii (1893–6), 175–217

Adolphe Perraud, *Ireland under English Rule* (Dublin, 1864)

F. Plowden, *An Historical Review of the State of Ireland*, 5 vols. (Philadelphia, 1806)

Revd James Pulleine D.D., *An Teagasg Críosaidhe Angoidhleig* (1748 and 1782)

L. F. Renehan, *Collections on Irish Church History*, 2 vols. (Dublin,1861–74)

Revd William Reeves, ed., *Acts of Archbishop Colton in his Metropolitan Visitation of the Diocese of Derry* (Dublin, 1850)

— ed., 'The Irish Itinerary of Father Edmund MacCana',*U.J.A.*, ser.1., vol. ii (1854), 44–59

Hugh Reily, *The Impartial History of Ireland* (London, 1754; first printed Louvain, 1695)

Report of the Lough Foyle Fishery Case of Allen v. *Donnelly and Others Tried at the Tyrone Spring Assizes at Omagh, 1856 . . . Reported by W. McLaughlin, Londonderry Standard Office* (London, 1857)

'Report on the State of Popery in Ireland, 1731', *Archiv. Hib.*, i (1912), 10–27 (for Ulster); for the rest of the country: ii (1913), 108–56, iii (1914), 124–59, and iv (1915), 131–77

John Richardson, *A Proposal for the Conversion of the Popish Natives of Ireland to the Established Religion* (London, 1711)

— *A Short History of Attempts That Have Been Made ... To Convert the Popish Inhabitants of Ireland* (London, 1712)

E. Rogan, *Synods and Catechesis in Ireland, c. 445–1962*, 2 vols. (Rome, 1987)

C. W. Russell and J.P. Prendergast, eds., *The Carte Manuscripts in the Bodleian Library, Oxford* (London, 1871)

Revd G. Vaughan Sampson, *Statistical Survey of the County of Londonderry* (1802)

[W. Shankill], *The Belfast Riots, 1886: The Islandmen and Shankill Road Defended* (Belfast, 1886)

E. P. Shirley, ed., *Original Letters and Papers in Illustration of the History of the Church in Ireland* (London, 1851)

Sources for the Study of Local History in Northern Ireland. Northern Ireland Public Record Office: a catalogue for an exhibition (January–July 1968)

Edmund Spenser, *A View of the State of Ireland* [1596], in James Ware, ed., *Ancient Irish Histories: The Works of Spencer, Campion, Hanmer, and Marleburrough*, 2 vols. (Dublin, 1809)

[George Story], *A True and Impartial History of the Most Material Occurrences in the Kingdom of Ireland during the Two Last Years* (London, 1691)

'Submission from the Northern Catholic Bishops on the Consultative Document "Education in Northern Ireland – Proposals for Reform" ', news release by the Catholic Press and Information Office, 23 June 1988

Edward Synge, *The Case of Toleration Considered with Respect Both to Religion and Civil Government* (Dublin, 1726)

Charles Hamilton Teeling, *Observations on the 'History and Consequences' of the 'Battle of the Diamond'* (Belfast, 1838)

— *History of the Irish Rebellion of 1798* and *Sequel to the History of the Irish Rebellion of 1798* (Shannon, 1972, reprint of 1876 edition)

A Test of Roman Catholic Liberality, Submitted to the Consideration of Both Roman Catholicks and Protestants. By a Citizen of London-Derry (Londonderry, 1792)

Ultach, 'Orange Terror: The Partition of Ireland', reprinted from *The Capuchin Annual* (1943)

James Ussher, *An Epistle Written by the Rev. James Ussher, Bishop of Meath, Concerning the Religion Anciently Professed by the Irish and Scottish* (Dublin, 1631)

A View of the Present State of Ireland . . . by an Observer (n.p., 1797)

Reginald Walsh, O.P., 'The Memorial Presented to the King of Spain on Behalf of the Irish Catholics, A.D. 1619', *Archiv. Hib.*, vi (1917), 27–54

Fr Luke Walsh, *The Home Mission Unmasked* (Belfast, 1844)

N. J. A. Williams, ed., *Pairlement Chloinne Tomáis* (Dublin, 1981)

C. J. Woods, *Journals and Memoirs of Thomas Russell* (Dublin, 1991)

Georges-Denis Zimmermann, *Songs of Irish Rebellion: Political Street Ballads and Rebel Songs, 1780–1900* (Dublin, 1967)

Memoirs and Autobiography

Gerry Adams, *The Politics of Irish Freedom* (Dingle, 1986)

William Carleton, *Autobiography* (London, 1968)

Bernadette Devlin, *The Price of My Soul* (London, 1969)

Paddy Devlin, *Straight Left: An Autobiography* (Belfast, 1993)

Lynn Doyle, *An Ulster Childhood*, (Belfast, 1985, facsimile of 1926 edition)

Charles Gavan Duffy, *My Life in Two Hemispheres*, 2 vols. (London, 1898)

Brian Faulkner, *Memoirs of a Statesman* (London, 1978)

Paddy [the Cope] Gallagher, *My Story* (London, 1939)

Robert Harbinson, *No Surrender: An Ulster Childhood* (Belfast, 1987, reprint of 1960 first edition)

Maurice Hayes, *Sweet Killough: Let Go Your Anchor* (Belfast, 1994)

— *Minority Verdict: Experiences of a Catholic Public Servant* (Belfast, 1995)

— *Black Puddings with Slim: A Downpatrick Boyhood* (Belfast, 1996)

Eamonn McCann, *War and an Irish Town* (London, 1993)

Conn McCluskey, *Up off Their Knees: A Commentary on the Civil Rights Movement in Northern Ireland* (Galway, 1989)

Cal McCrystal, *Reflections on a Quiet Rebel* (Harmondsworth, 1998)

Patrick MacGill, *Children of the Dead End: The Autobiography of a Navvy* (London, 1985, reprint of 1914 original)

Charles McGlinchy, *The Last of the Name* (Belfast, 1989, reprint of 1986 edition)

Michael MacGowan, *The Hard Road to Klondike* (London, 1962)

Seamas MacManus, *The Rocky Road to Dublin* (New York, 1947)

Terence O'Neill, *The Autobiography of Terence O'Neill* (London, 1972)

Patrick Shea, *Voices and the Sound of Drums: An Irish Autobiography* (Belfast, 1981)

Samuel Simms, ed., *Rev. James O'Coigley, United Irishman* (Belfast, 1937)

William T. W. Tone, ed., *The Life of Theobald Wolfe Tone*, 2 vols. (Washington, 1826). (However, the most authoritative edition of Tone's writings is now T.W. Moody, R.B. McDowell and C.J. Woods, eds., *The Writings of Theobald Wolfe Tone, 1763–98*, 3 vols. (Oxford, 1998–) – only vol. i published to date.)

Fiction and poetry

Colm Beckett, ed., *Aodh Mac Domhnaill: Dánta* (Dublin, 1987)

Mary Beckett, *A Belfast Woman* (Dublin, 1987)

— *Give Them Stones* (London, 1991, reprint of 1987 edition)

Osbert Bergin, *Irish Bardic Poetry* (Dublin, 1970)

Shan Bullock, *Dan the Dollar* (Dublin, 1906)

William Carleton, *Traits and Stories of the Irish Peasantry*, 2 vols. (Gerrards Cross, 1990, reprint of 1844–5 edition)

— *Valentine McClutchy: The Irish Agent* (London, 1845)
— *The Black Prophet: A Tale of Irish Famine* (London, 1847)
(Both novels were used in the edition: *The Works of William Carleton*, 2 vols.
  (New York, 1970))
Seamus Deane, *Reading in the Dark* (London, 1996)
Seán de Rís, *Peadar Ó Doirnín: a Bheatha agus a Shaothar* (Dublin, 1969)
Lynn Doyle, *Ballygullion* (London, 1924)
— *Rosabelle and Other Stories* (London, 1933)
James Hardiman, *Irish Minstrelsy, or, Bardic Remains of Ireland*, 2 vols.
  (Dublin, 1831)
Douglas Hyde, translator, 'An Irish Funeral Oration over Owen O'Neill, of
  the House of Clanaboy', *U.J.A.*, ser. 2, vol. 3 (1897), 258–70 and vol.
  4 (1898), 50–55
E. Knott, ed.,*The Bardic Poems of Tadhg Dall Ó Huiginn*, Irish Texts Soc.,
  2 vols. (London, 1920–21)
Frank McCourt, *Angela's Ashes* (London, 1996)
Michael McLaverty, *Call My Brother Back* (Swords, 1976)
Seosamh Mag Uidhir, *Pádraig Mac a Liondain: Dánta* (Dublin, 1977)
Brian Moore, *The Emperor of Ice-Cream* (London, 1970)
— *The Lonely Passion of Judith Hearne* (London, 1956)
— *The Feast of Lupercal* (London, 1957)
Danny Morrison, *West Belfast* (Cork, 1989)
Breandán Ó Buachalla, *Cathal Buí: Amhráin* (Dublin, 1975)
— ed., *Nua-Dhuanaire II* (Dublin, 1976)
John O'Donovan, *The Topographical Poems of John Ó Dubhagain* (Dublin,
  1862)
Séan Ó Dufaigh and Diarmaid Ó Doibhlin, *Nioclás Ó Cearnaigh: Beatha
  agus Saothar* (Dublin, 1989)
Seosamh Ó Duibhginn, *Séamas Mac Giolla Choille* (Dublin, 1972)
Tomás Ó Fiaich, *Art Mac Cumhaigh: Dánta* (Dublin, 1973 and 1981)
Tomás Ó Fiaich and Liam Ó Caithnia, *Art Mac Bionaid: Dánta* (Dublin,
  1979)
Seán S. Ó Gallachóir, ed., *Séamas Dall Mac Cuarta: Dánta* (Dublin, 1971)
Séamus P. Ó Mórdha, 'Maurice O'Gorman in Monaghan: A Second Poem on
  Fr. Francis MacMahon', *Clogher Record*, ii (1957), 20–24
Énri Ó Muirgheasa, 'Domhnall Mac Craigh; easpag Dúin', *Louth Arch. Soc.
  Jn.* (1914), 267–72
— *Céad de Cheoltaibh Uladh* (Dublin, 1915)
— *Dhá Chéad de Cheoltaibh Uladh* (Dublin, 1934)
— *Dánta Diadha Uladh* (Dublin, 1936)
— ed., *Abhráin Airt Mhic Chubhthaigh* (Dublin, 1916)
Cecille O'Rahilly, ed., *Five Seventeenth-century Political Poems* (Dublin,
  1952)
Michael Parker, ed., *The Hurt World. Short Stories of the Troubles* (Belfast,
  1995)
Robert McLiam Wilson, *Ripley Bogle* (London, 1997 edn.)

Tours

A. Atkinson, *Ireland in the Nineteenth Century* (London, 1833)

Charles Topham Bowden, *Tour through Ireland* (Dublin, 1791)

William Brereton, *Travels in Holland the United Provinces England Scotland and Ireland, 1634–1635,* edited by Edward Hawkins (Manchester, 1844)

James Buckley, ed., 'A Tour in Ireland in 1672–4', *Cork Hist. and Arch. Soc. Jn.,* x (1904), 85–100.

T. Crofton Croker, ed., *The Tour of the French Traveller M. de la Boullaye le Gouz in Ireland in A.D. 1644* (London, 1837)

John Gamble, *View of Society and Manners in the North of Ireland in the Summer and Autumn of 1812* (London, 1813)

— *Sketches of History, Politics, and Manners in Dublin and the North of Ireland in 1810* (London, 1826)

Mr and Mrs S. C. Hall, *Ireland: Its Scenery, Character etc.,* 3 vols. (London, 1841–3)

Revd W. Hamilton, *Letters Concerning the Northern Coast of the County of Antrim* (Belfast, 1822 edition)

Chevalier de Latocnaye, *A Frenchman's Walk through Ireland,* translated by John Stevenson (Belfast, 1917 – 1984 facsimile)

Phillip Luckombe, *A Tour through Ireland* (London, 1780)

John McVeigh, ed., *Richard Pococke's Irish Tours* (Dublin, 1995)

J. P. Mahaffy, ed., 'Two Early Tours in Ireland', *Hermathena,* xl (1914), 13

Howard William Troyer, ed., *Five Travel Scripts Commonly Attributed to Edward Ward* [1698] (New York, 1933)

Molyneux's Tour, 1708, in Robert M. Young, *Historical Notices of Old Belfast and Its Vicinity* (Belfast, 1896)

Dervla Murphy, *A Place Apart* (London, 1978)

[Richard Phillips] *Journal of a Tour in Ireland . . . August, 1804 . . .* (1804) (London, 1806)

W. M. Thackeray, *The Irish Sketchbook* (Glos. 1990, 1st edition 1843)

Colm Tóibín, *Bad Blood: A Walk along the Irish Border* (London, 1994)

A Trip to Ireland, Being a Description of the Country . . . As Also Some . . . Observations on Dublin ([London] 1699)

Arthur Young, *Tour in Ireland* (1776–1779), 2 vols. (London, 1892 edition)

SECONDARY

The Ancient and Noble Family of the Savages of the Ards, compiled by G.F.A. (London, 1888)

F. H. A. Aalen, *Man and Landscape in Ireland* (London, 1978)

G. B. Adams, 'The Emergence of Ulster as a Distinct Dialect Area', *Ulster Folklife,* iv (1958), 61–73

— 'The Validity of Language Census Figures in Ulster, 1851–1911', *Ulster Folklife*, xxv (1979), 113–22

J. R. R. Adams, *The Printed Word and the Common Man: Popular Culture in Ulster 1700–1900* (Belfast, 1987)

— 'Ulster Folklife, 1738–40 from the Pages of the Belfast Newsletter', *Ulster Folklife*, xxxi (1985), 41–52

Ian Adamson, *The Identity of Ulster*, 2nd edition (Belfast, 1987)

N. B. Aitchison, 'The Ulster Cycle: Heroic Image and Historical Reality', *Jn. Med. Hist.*, 13 (1987) 87–116

D. H. Akenson, *Small differences: Irish Catholics and Irish Protestants, 1815–1922, An International Perspective* (Dublin, 1991)

— *Education and Enmity: The Control of Schooling in Northern Ireland, 1920–50* (Newton Abbot, 1973)

— and W.H. Crawford, *James Orr: Bard of Ballycarry* (Belfast, 1977)

Elizabeth Andrews, *Ulster Folklore* (London, 1913)

J. H. Andrews, 'Geography and Government in Elizabethan Ireland', in Nicholas Stephens and Robin E. Glasscock, eds., *Irish Geographical Studies* (Belfast, 1970), 178–91

Liam Andrews, ' "The Very Dogs in Belfast Will Bark in Irish." The Unionist Government and the Irish language 1921–43', in Aodán Mac Póilin, ed., *The Irish Language in Northern Ireland* (Belfast, 1997)

Paul Arthur, *The People's Democracy 1968–1973* (Belfast, 1974)

— *Government and Politics of Northern Ireland,* 2nd edition (London, 1987)

— 'Republican Violence in Northern Ireland: the Rationale', in John Darby et al., eds., *Political Violence: Ireland in a Comparative Perspective* (Belfast, 1990) 48–63

— ' "Reading" Violence: Ireland', in David E. Apter, ed., *The Legitimization of Violence* (New York, 1997), 284

E. D. Atkinson, *An Ulster Parish: Being a History of Donaghcloney* (Dublin, 1818)

Richard Bagwell, *Ireland under the Stuarts*, 3 vols. (London, 1909–16)

S. E. Baker, 'Orange and Green: Belfast 1832–1912', in H.J. Dyos and M. Wolff, eds., *The Victorian City: Image and Reality*, 2 vols.(London, 1973), ii, 789–814

Linda-May Ballard, 'Three Local Storytellers: A Perspective on the Question of Cultural Heritage', in Gillian Bennett and Paul Smith, eds., *Monsters with Iron Teeth: Perspectives in Contemporary Legend*, iii (Sheffield, 1988), 161–82

Jonathán Bardon, *A History of Ulster* (Belfast, 1992)

T. C. Barnard, 'Planters and Policies in Cromwellian Ireland', *Past and Present*, no. 61 (1973), 31–69

— *Cromwellian Ireland: English Government and Reform in Ireland, 1649–1660* (Oxford, 1975)

— 'The Uses of 23 October 1641 and Irish Protestant Celebrations', *Eng. Hist. Rev.*, cvi (1991), 889–920

— 'Irish Images of Cromwell', in R.C. Richardson, ed., *Images of Cromwell* (1993), 180–206

Denis P. Barritt and Charles F. Carter, *The Northern Ireland Problem: A Study in Group Relations* (Oxford, 1972)

Thomas Bartlett, 'An End to the Moral Economy: The Irish Militia Disturbances of 1793', *Past and Present*, xcix (1983), 41–64

— 'Defenders and Defenderism in 1785', *I.H.S.*, xiv (1985), 373–94

— *The Fall and Rise of the Irish Nation: The Catholic Question 1690–1830* (Dublin, 1992)

— and Keith Jeffrey, eds, *A Military History of Ireland* (Cambridge, 1996)

Brian Barton, *Brookeborough. The Making of a Prime Minister* (Belfast, 1988)

J. Bowyer Bell, *The Secret Army: The Story of the IRA 1916–1970* (London, 1970)

Robert Bell, *The Book of Ulster Surnames* (Belfast, 1988)

David Beresford, *Ten Men Dead* (London, 1987)

Paul Bew, Peter Gibbon and Henry Patterson, *Northern Ireland 1921–1994: Political Forces and Social Classes* (London, 1995)

F. J. Bigger, *The Ulster Land War of 1770* (Dublin, 1910)

D. A. Binchy, 'A pre-Christian Survival in Medieval Irish Hagiography', in Dorothy Whitelock, Rosamund McKitterick and David Dumville, eds., *Ireland in Early Medieval Europe: Studies in Memory of Kathleen Hughes* (Cambridge, 1982), 165–78

— 'Patrick and his Biographers, Ancient and Modern', *Stud. Hib.*, ii (1962), 7–173

B. Bjersby, *The Interpretation of the Cuchulainn Legend in the Works of W. B. Yeats* (Uppsala, 1950)

Allan Blackstock, *An Ascendancy Army: The Irish Yeomanry 1796–1834* (Dublin, 1998)

Roger Blaney, *Presbyterians and the Irish Language* (Belfast, 1996)

F. W. Boal, 'Territoriality on the Shankill–Falls Divide, Belfast', *Irish Geography*, vi (1969), 30–50

— and R.H. Buchanan, 'The 1969 Northern Ireland Election', *Irish Geography*, vi (1969), 80–83

John Bossy, 'The Counter-Reformation and the People of Catholic Europe', *Past and Present*, no. 47 (May, 1970), 51–70

— 'The Counter-Reformation and the People of Catholic Ireland, 1596–1641', in T.D. Williams, ed., *Historical Studies*, viii (Dublin, 1971), 155–69

— *The English Catholic Community, 1570–1850* (London, 1975)

— 'Catholicity and Nationality in the Northern Counter-Reformation', in Stewart Mews, ed., *Religion and National Identity: Studies in Church History*, xviii (Oxford, 1982), 285–96

Karl S. Bottigheimer, *English Money and Irish Land* (Oxford, 1971)

— 'The Restoration Land Settlement in Ireland: A Structural View', *I.H.S.*, xviii (1972), 1–21

— 'The Failure of the Reformation in Ireland: *une question bien posée*', *Jn. Eccles. Hist.* xxxvi (1985), 196–207

Angela Bourke, *The Burning of Bridget Cleary: A True Story* (London, 1999)

Andrew Boyd, *Holy War in Belfast* (Tralee, 1969)

Desmond Bowen, *The Protestant Crusade in Ireland 1800–70* (Dublin, 1978)

John Bowman, *De Valera and the Ulster Question 1917–1973* (Oxford, 1982)

Brendan Bradshaw, *The Dissolution of the Religious Orders in Ireland under Henry VIII* (Cambridge, 1974)

Ciaran Brady, Mary O'Dowd and Brian Walker, eds., *Ulster: An Illustrated History* (London, 1989)

Ciaran Brady and Raymond Gillespie, eds., *Natives and Newcomers: Essays on the Making of Irish Colonial Society 1534–1641* (Dublin, 1986)

John Brady, *Catholics and Catholicism in the Eighteenth-Century Press* (Maynooth, 1965)

W. J.Brady, 'The Story of Donaghmore', *Down and Connor Hist. Soc. Jn.*, x (1939), 36–43

P. A. Breatnach, 'Metamorphosis 1603: Dán le hEochaidh Ó hEódhasa', *Éigse*, xvii (1977–9), 169–80

Caoimhín Breatnach, *Patronage, Politics and Prose* (Maynooth, 1996)

Richard Breen, Paula Devine, Lizanne Dowds, eds., *Social Attitudes in Northern Ireland: The Fifth Report* (Belfast, 1996)

John D. Brewer with Gareth I. Higgins, *Anti-Catholicism in Northern Ireland, 1600–1998: The Mote and the Beam* (Basingstoke, 1998)

L. W. B. Brockliss and P. Ferté, 'Irish Clerics in France in the Seventeenth and Eighteenth Centuries', *Proc. R.I.A.*, C.87/9 (1987), 527–72

Andrea Ebel Brozyna, *Labour, Love and Prayer: Female Piety in Ulster Religious Literature, 1850–1914* (Ithaca and Belfast, 1999)

Alan Bruford, *Gaelic Folktales and Medieval Romances* (Dublin, 1969)

Ronald H. Buchanan, 'Calendar Customs', *Ulster Folklife*, viii (1962), 15–34

Patrick Buckland, *James Craig* (Dublin, 1980)

— *A History of Northern Ireland* (Dublin, 1981)

— *The Factory of Grievances: Devolved Government in Northern Ireland 1921–39* (Dublin, 1979)

Anthony Buckley, 'Neighbourliness – Myth and History', *Oral History Jn.*, xi (1983), 44–51

— 'Collecting Ulster's Culture: Are There Really Two Traditions?', in *The Use of Tradition*, edited by Alan Gailey (UFTM, Cultra, 1988), 49–60

— '"We're Trying to Find Our Identity": Uses of History among Ulster Protestants', in Elizabeth Tonkin, Maryon McDonald and Malcolm Chapman, eds., *History and Ethnicity* (London and New York, 1988), 183–97

— 'Collecting Ulster's Culture: Are There Really Two Traditions?', in Alan Gailey, ed., *The Use of Tradition: Essays Presented to G.B.Thompson* (UFTM, Cultra, 1988), 49–60

Anthony D. Buckley and Kenneth Anderson, *Brotherhoods in Ireland* (UFTM, Cultra, 1988)

Ian Budge and Cornelius O'Leary, *Belfast: Approach to Crisis: A Study of Belfast Politics 1613–1970* (London, 1973)

Burke's Genealogical and Heraldic History of the Landed Gentry of Ireland, 4th edition, edited by L.G. Pine (London, 1958)

Burke's Irish Family Records (London, 1976)

William P. Burke, *Irish Priests in Penal Tmes 1660–1750* (Shannon 1969, reprint of 1914 edition)

— ed., 'The Diocese of Derry in 1631', *Archiv. Hib.*, v (1916)

G. Burnett, *The Life of Bishop Bedell* (Dublin, 1736)

R. E. Burns, 'The Belfast Letters, the Irish Volunteers 1778–9 and the Catholics', *Review of Politics*, xxi (1959), 678–91

Frank Burton, *The Politics of Legitimacy: Struggles in a Belfast Community* (London, 1978)

W.F. Butler, 'Irish Land Tenures: Celtic and Foreign', *Studies*, xiii (1924), 530

William T. Butler, *Confiscation in Irish History* (London,1917), 291–305, 524–40

Francis John Byrne, 'Tribes and Tribalism in Early Ireland', *Ériu*, xxii (1971), 128–66, 160–66

— 'Seventh-Century Documents', *Irish Eccles. Rec.*, cviii (1967), 164–82

Marc Caball, *Poets and Politics: Reaction and Continuity in Irish Poetry, 1558–1625* (Cork, 1998)

Euan Cameron, *The European Reformation* (Oxford, 1991)

Nicholas Canny, 'The Treaty of Mellifont and the Re-organisation of Ulster, 1603', *Irish Sword*, ix (1969–70), 249–62

— 'Hugh O'Neill, Earl of Tyrone, and the Changing Face of Gaelic Ulster', *Stud. Hib.*, x (1970), 7–35

— 'Why the Reformation Failed in Ireland: *une question mal posée*', *Jn. Eccles. Hist.*, xxx (1979), 423–50

— *From Reformation to Restoration: Ireland, 1534–1660* (Dublin, 1987)

Andrew Carpenter, ed., *Place, Personality and the Irish Writer* (Gerrards Cross, 1977)

Revd W. Carrigan, 'Catholic Episcopal Wills in the PRO, Dublin, 1683–1812', *Archiv. Hib.*, i (1912), 151–90

Daniel J. Casey, 'Carleton and the Count', *Seanchas Ard Mhaca*, viii (1975–6), 7–22

Lucian Ceyssens, 'Florence Conry, Hugh de Burgo, Luke Wadding and Jansenism', in the Franciscan Fathers, eds., *Father Luke Wadding*, 295–331

D. A. Chart, 'The Break-up of the Estate of Con O'Neill', *Proc. R.I.A.*, xlviii (1942–3), sect. C, 119–51

Aidan Clarke, *The Old English in Ireland, 1625–42* (London, 1966)

Samuel Clarke, *Social Origins of the Irish Land War* (New Jersey, 1979)

— and J. R. Donnelly, Jr., eds., *Irish Peasants: Violence and Political Unrest, 1780–1914* (Dublin, 1983)

Pamela Clayton, *Enemies and Passing Friends: Settler Ideologies in Twentieth-Century Ulster* (London, 1996)

Brendan Clifford, ed., *The Origin of Irish Catholic Nationalism: Selections from Walter Cox's 'Irish Magazine'* (Belfast, 1992)

A. Cogan, *The Ecclesiastical History of the Diocese of Meath*, 3 vols. (Dublin, 1867–74)

Barry M. Coldrey, *Faith and Fatherland: The Christian Brothers and the Development of Irish Nationalism 1838–1921* (Dublin, 1988)

D. Comyn and P.S. Dineen, eds., *The History of Ireland by Geoffrey Keating,* Irish Texts Soc., 4 vols (London, 1902–14)

S. J. Connolly, 'Catholicism in Ulster, 1800–1850', in Roebuck, ed., *Plantation to Partition,* 157–71

— *Priests and People in pre-Famine Ireland 1780–1845* (Dublin, 1982)

— *Religion and Society in Nineteenth-Century Ireland* (Dundalk, 1985)

— *Religion, Law and Power: The Making of Protestant Ireland 1660–1760* (Oxford, 1992)

—ed., *The Oxford Companion to Irish History* (Oxford, 1998)

Linde Conolly, 'Spoken English in Ulster in the Eighteenth and Nineteenth Centuries', *Ulster Folklife*, xxviii (1982), 33–9

Patrick J. Corish, 'The Re-Organisation of the Irish Church, 1603–41', *Ir. Cath. Hist. Comm. Proc.* (1957), 9–14

— *The Origins of Irish Catholic Nationalism* (Dublin, 1968)

— *The Christian Mission* (Dublin, 1981)

— *The Catholic Community in the Seventeenth and Eighteenth Centuries* (Dublin, 1981)

— 'Catholic Marriage under the Penal Code', in Art Cosgrove, ed., *Marriage in Ireland* (Dublin, 1985), 67–77

— *The Irish Catholic Experience: A Historical Survey* (Dublin, 1986)

— 'Cardinal Cullen and the National Association of Ireland', in Alan O'Day, ed., *Reactions to Irish Nationalism, 1865–1914* (London, 1987), 117–65

Art Cosgrove, 'The Writing of Irish Medieval History', *I.H.S.*, xxvii (1990), 97–111

— 'The Early Irish Church and the Western Patriarchate', in Proinséas Ní Chatháin and Michael Richter, eds., *Irland und Europa, die Kirche in Frühmittelalter. Ireland and Europe, the Early Church* (Stuttgart, 1984), 9–15

— ed., *Marriage in Ireland* (Dublin, 1985)

— ed., *A New History of Ireland,* ii: *Medieval Ireland, 1169–1534* (Oxford, 1987)

W. H. Crawford, 'Economy and Society in South Ulster in the Eighteenth Century', *Clogher Record*, viii (1975), 241–58

— 'The Ulster Irish in the Eighteenth Century', *Ulster Folklife*, xxviii (1982), 24–32

— 'The Political Economy of Linen: Ulster in the Eighteenth Century', in Ciaran Brady *et al.*, eds., *Ulster: An Illustrated History* (London, 1989), 134–57

Donal F. Cregan, 'The Social and Cultural Background of a Counter-Reformation Episcopate, 1618–60', in Art Cosgrove and Donal McCartney, eds., *Studies in Irish History Presented to R. Dudley Edwards* (Dublin,1979), 85–117

L. M. Cullen, *Life in Ireland* (London, 1979)

— *The Emergence of Modern Ireland, 1600–1900* (Dublin, 1981)

— 'Catholics under the Penal Laws', *Eighteenth-Century Ireland*, i (1986), 23–36

— 'Patrons, Teachers and Literacy in Irish: 1700–1850', in Mary Daly and David Dickson, eds., *The Origins of Popular Literacy in Ireland: Language Change and Educational Development 1700–1920* (Dublin, 1990), 15–44

Bernadette Cunningham, 'The Culture and Ideology of Irish Franciscan Historians at Louvain 1607–1650', in Ciaran Brady, ed., *Ideology and the Historians* (Dublin, 1991), 11–30

— and Raymond Gillespie, 'The East Ulster Bardic Family of Ó Gnímh', *Éigse*, xx (1984), 106–14

— and Raymond Gillespie, 'An Ulster Settler and His Irish Manuscripts', *Éigse*, xxi (1986), 25–36

E. A. Currie, 'Field Patterns in County Derry', *Ulster Folklife*, xxix (1983), 70–80

E. Curtis, 'Janice Dartas', *Roy. Soc. Antiq. Jn.* lxiii (1933), 182–205

Cahal B. Daly, *The Price of Peace* (Belfast, 1991)

Mary Daly, 'Revisionism and the Great Famine', in George Boyce and Alan O'Day, eds., *The Making of Modern Irish History. Revisionism and the Revisionist Controversy* (London, 1996), 71–89

— and David Dickson, eds., *Origins of Popular Literacy in Ireland: Language Change and Educational Development 1700–1920* (Dublin, 1990)

P. de Brún, 'Some Irish Manuscripts with Breifne Associations', *Breifne*, iii (1969), 552–61

John Darby, ed., *Northern Ireland: The Background to the Conflict* (Belfast, 1983)

— *Intimidation and the Control of Conflict in Northern Ireland* (Dublin, 1986)

— and Nicholas Dodge and A.C. Hepburn, eds., *Political Violence: Ireland in a Comparative Perspective* (Belfast, 1990)

— and Geoffrey Morris, *Intimidation in Housing* (Belfast, 1974)

— and Geoffrey Morris, *Conflict in Northern Ireland: The Development of a Polarised Community* (Dublin, 1976)

Jean Delumeau, *Catholicism between Luther and Voltaire* (London, 1977)

Liam de Paor, *The Peoples of Ireland. From Pre-History to Modern Times* (London, 1986)

Liam and Máire de Paor, *Early Christian Ireland* (London, 1958)

Hugh Deery, 'Ancient Christian Burial places of Drumholm', *Donegal Annual*, iii (1956), 110–13

Charles Dickson, *Revolt in the North: Antrim and Down in 1798* (Dublin, 1960)

David Dickson and Hugh Gough, eds., *The French Revolution and Ireland* (Dublin, 1990).

— and Daire Keogh and Kevin Whelan, eds., *The United Irishmen* (Dublin, 1993)

E. R. M. C. Dix, *Books and Pamphlets Printed in Strabane in the Eighteenth Century* (Dublin, 1901)

John Donaldson, *A Historical and Statistical Account of the Barony of the Upper Fews in the County of Armagh, 1838* (Dundalk, 1923)

Colm J. Donnelly, *Living Places. Archaeology, Continuity and Change at Historic Monuments in Northern Ireland* (Belfast, 1997)

J. S. Donnelly, Jr., 'Propagating the Cause of the United Irishmen', *Studies*, lxix (1980), 5–23

— and Kerby A. Miller, eds., *Irish Popular Culture* (Dublin, 1999)

Peter Donnelly, 'Political Identity in Northern Ireland: An Issue for Catholic Theology', *Studies*, vol. 86, no. 343 (1997), 238–47

Martin W. Dowling, *Tenant Right and Agrarian Society in Ulster, 1600–1870* (Dublin, 1999)

David Noel Doyle, *Ireland, Irishmen and Revolutionary America, 1760–1820* (Dublin, 1981)

Patrick J. Duffy, 'The Territorial Organisation of Gaelic Landownership and Its Transformation in County Monaghan, 1591–1640', *Irish Geography*, xiv (1981), 1–26

— 'Patterns of Landownership in Gaelic Monaghan in the Late Sixteenth Century', *Clogher Record*, x (1979–81), 304–22

— 'The Evolution of Estate Properties in South Ulster, 1600–1900', in Smyth and Whelan, eds., *Common Ground*, 84–109

— *Landscapes of South Ulster: A Parish Atlas of the Diocese of Clogher* (Belfast, 1993)

Seán Duffy, *Nicholas O'Kearney: The Last of the Bards of Louth* (Tyrone, 1989)

— 'The First Ulster Plantation: John de Courcy and the Men of Cumbria', in T.B. Barry, Robin Frame and Katharine Simms, eds., *Colony and Frontier in Medieval Ireland. Essays presented to J.F. Lydon* (London, 1995), 1–27

— *Ireland in the Middle Ages* (Dublin, 1997)

David Dumville, ed., *Kathleen Hughes: Church and Society in Ireland A.D. 400–1200* (London, 1987)

John Dunlop, *A Precarious Belonging. Presbyterians and the Conflict in Northern Ireland* (Belfast, 1995)

Tom Dunne, 'Haunted by History: Irish Romantic Writing, 1800–50', in Roy Porter and Mikulás Teich, eds., *Romanticism in National Context* (Cambridge, 1988), 68–91

John Edwards, 'The Priest, the Layman and the Historian: Religion in Early Modern Europe', *European History Quarterly*, xvii (1987), 87–93

Marianne Elliott, 'Origins and Transformation of Early Irish Republicanism', *Internat. Rev. Soc. Hist.*, xxiii (1978), 405–28

— *Partners in Revolution: The United Irishmen and France* (London and New Haven, 1982)

— *Wolfe Tone: Prophet of Irish Independence* (London and New Haven, 1989)

— 'The Defenders in Ulster', in Dickson, *et al.*, eds.,*The United Irishmen*, 222–33

— 'Religion and Identity in Northern Ireland', in Winston A. Van Horne, ed., *Global Convulsions: Race, Ethnicity and Nationalism at the End of the Twentieth Century* (New York, 1997), 149–68

Steven G. Ellis, *Ireland in the Age of the Tudors 1447–1603. English Expansion and the End of Gaelic Rule* (London and New York, 1998)

Colmán Etchingham, 'The Implications of Paruchia', *Ériu*, xliv (1993), 139–62

E. Estyn Evans, 'The Ulster Farmhouse: A Comparative Study', *Ulster Folklife*, iii (1957), 14–18

Patrick Fagan, *Divided Loyalties: The Question of an Oath for Irish Catholics in the Eighteenth Century* (Dublin, 1997)

— *An Irish Bishop in Penal Times: The Chequered Career of Sylvester Lloyd OFM, 1680–1747* (Dublin, 1993)

Cyril Falls, *The Birth of Ulster* (London, 1936)

Michael Farrell, *Northern Ireland: The Orange State*, 2nd edition (London, 1980)

— *Arming the Protestants: The Formation of the Ulster Special Constabulary 1920–27* (London, 1983)

Sean Farren, *The Politics of Irish Education 1920–65* (Belfast, 1995)

Revd P.P. Farry, 'Penal Day Traditions in Mourne', *Down and Connor Hist. Soc. Jn.*, ix (1938), 42–9

D. Faul and R. Murray, *The Alienation of Northern Catholics* (Dungannon, 1984)

Anselm Faulkner, 'The Right of Patronage of the Maguires of Tempo', *Clogher Record*, ix (1977), 167–86

Brendan Fitzpatrick, *Seventeenth-Century Ireland: the War of Religions* (Dublin, 1988)

David Fitzpatrick, 'The Disappearance of the Agricultural Labourer, 1841–1912', *Ir. Econ. Soc. Hist.*, vii (1980), 66–92

— *Oceans of Consolation: Personal Accounts of Irish Migration to Australia* (Ithaca, 1994)

W. D. Flackes, *Northern Ireland: A Political Directory 1968–79* (Dublin, 1980)

Robin Flower, *The Irish Tradition* (Oxford, 1979 imprint of 1947 work)

Laurence J. Flynn, 'Hugh MacMahon, Bishop of Clogher 1707–15 and Archbishop of Armagh 1715–37', *Seanchas Ard Macha*, vii (1973–4), 108–75

Bryan A. Follis, *A State under Siege: The Establishment of Northern Ireland, 1920–1925* (Oxford, 1995)

Alan Ford, *The Protestant Reformation in Ireland, 1590–1641* (Frankfurt am Main, 1987).

R. F. Foster, *Modern Ireland, 1600–1972* (London, 1988)

— *The Story of Ireland: An Inaugural Lecture Delivered before the University of Oxford on 1 December 1994* (Oxford, 1995)

— ed., *The Oxford Illustrated History of Ireland* (Oxford, 1989)

Robin Frame, *Colonial Ireland, 1169–1369* (Dublin, 1981)

— *English Lordship in Ireland 1318–1361* (Oxford, 1982)

Franciscan Fathers, eds., *Father Luke Wadding: Commemorative Volume* (Dublin, 1957)

Eric Gallagher and Stanley Worrall, *Christians in Ulster 1968–1980* (Oxford, 1982)

Frank Gallagher, *The Indivisible Island: The History of Partition in Ireland* (London, 1957)

Revd Patrick Gallagher, 'Sources for the History of a Diocese: Seventeenth-Century Clogher', *Procs. Ir. Cath. Hist. Committee* (1957), 25–37

Jeffrey Gantz, *Early Irish Myths and Sagas* (Harmondsworth, 1988)

Cathaldus Giblin, 'The Processus Datariae and the Appointment of Irish Bishops in the Seventeenth Century', in Franciscan Fathers, eds., *Father Luke Wadding*, 508–616

Raymond Gillespie, *Colonial Ulster: The Settlement of East Ulster 1600–1641* (Cork, 1985)

— 'The Presbyterian Revolution in Ulster, 1660–1690', in W.J. Sheils and Diana Wood, eds., *The Churches, Ireland and the Irish* (Oxford, 1989), 159–70

— *The Sacred in the Secular: Religious Change in Catholic Ireland, 1500–1700* (Colchester, Vermont, 1993)

— ed., *Cavan: Essays on the History of an Irish County* (Blackrock, 1995)

— ed., *Devoted People: Belief and Religion in Early Modern Ireland* (Manchester, 1997)

— and Harold O'Sullivan, eds., *The Borderlands: Essays on the History of the Ulster–Leinster Border* (Belfast, 1989)

Michael Glancy, 'The Primates and the Church Lands of Armagh', *Seanchas Ard Mhacha*, v (1969–70), 370–96

Henry Glassie, *Irish Folk History: Folktales from the North* (Dublin, 1982)

— *Passing the Time in Ballymenone* (Bloomington, 1995, reprint of 1982 edition)

David Gordon, *The O'Neill Years: Unionist Politics 1963–1969* (Belfast, 1989)

B. J. Graham and L. J. Proudfoot, eds., *An Historical Geography of Ireland* (London, 1993)

Jean M. Graham, 'Rural Society in Connacht 1600–1640', in Glasscock and Stephens, eds., *Irish Geographical Studies*, 192–208

James Grant, 'Some Aspects of the Great Famine in County Armagh', *Seanchas Ard Mhacha*, viii (1977), 344–59

— 'The Great Famine and the Poor Law in Ulster: the Rate-in-Aid Issue of 1849', *I.H.S.*, xxvii (1990), 30–47

John Gray, *City in Revolt: James Larkin and the Belfast Dock Strike of 1907* (Belfast, 1985)

Alice Stopford Green, *History of the Irish State to 1014* (London, 1925)

Aubry Gwynn and R. Neville Hadcock, eds., *Medieval Religious Houses. Ireland* (London, 1970)

Lord Ernest Hamilton, *The Irish Rebellion of 1641* (London, 1920)

— *Elizabethan Ulster* (London, 1919)

R.P.C. Hanson, *Saint Patrick: His Origins and Career* (Oxford, 1968)

Philip Dixon Hardy, *The Holy Wells of Ireland* (Dublin, 1836)

Michael Harkin [Maghtochair], *Inishowen: Its History, Traditions and Antiquities* (Londonderry, 1867)

David Harkness, *Northern Ireland since 1920* (Dublin, 1983)

K. M. Harris, 'The Schools' Collection', *Ulster Folklife*, iii (1957), 8–13

Mary Harris, 'Catholicism, Nationalism and the Labour Question in Belfast, 1925–38', *Bullán: an Irish Studies Journal*, iii (1997), 15–32

Rosemary Harris, *Prejudice and Tolerance in Ulster: A Study of Neighbours and 'Strangers' in a Border Community* (Manchester, 1972)

G. A. Hayes-McCoy, *Scots Mercenary Forces in Ireland* (Dublin, 1937)

— 'The Making of an O'Neill: A View of the Ceremony at Tullahoge, Co. Tyrone', *U.J.A.*, xxxiii (1970), 89–94

David Hempton and Myrtle Hill, *Evangelical Protestantism in Ulster Society 1740–1890* (London, 1992)

A. C. Hepburn, *A Past Apart: Studies in the History of Catholic Belfast 1850–1950* (Belfast, 1996)

Ken Heskin, *Northern Ireland: A Psychological Analysis* (Dublin, 1980)

Anna Heussaff, *Filí agus Cléir san Ochtú hAois Déag* (Dublin, 1992)

Christopher Hewitt, 'Catholic Grievances, Catholic Nationalism and Violence in Northern Ireland during the Civil Rights Period: A Reconsideration', *British Jn. of Sociology*, 32 (1981), 362–80; the subsequent debate between himself and Denis O'Hearn, ibid., 34(1983), 438–45, 446–51, 36 (1985), 94–101, 102–5; 38 (1987), 88–100

Sir Arthur Hezlet, *The 'B' Specials: A History of the Ulster Special Constabulary* (London, 1972)

Mary Hickson, *Ireland in the Seventeenth Century or the Irish Massacres of 1641–2,* 2 vols. (London, 1884)

George Hill, *An Historical Account of the Plantation of Ulster* (Belfast, 1877)

— *An Historical Account of the MacDonnells of Antrim* (Belfast, 1978, reprint of 1873 edition)

Jacqueline R. Hill, 'Popery and Protestantism, Civil and Religious Liberty: The Disputed Lessons of Irish History 1690–1812', *Past and Present*, 118 (1988), 96–129

J. Michael Hill, 'The Origins of the Scottish Plantations in Ulster to 1625: A Reinterpretation', *Jn. Brit. Studs.*, xxxii (January 1993), 24–43

Myrtle Hill *et al.*, eds., *1798 Rebellion in County Down* (Newtownards, 1998)

Patrick Hogan, 'The Migration of Ulster Catholics to Connaught, 1795–6', *Seanchas Ard Mhacha*, ix (1978–9), 286–301

Michael Hopkinson, *Green Against Green: The Irish Civil War* (Dublin, 1988)

K. Theodore Hoppen, *Elections, Politics and Society in Ireland 1832–1885* (Oxford, 1984)

Rab Houston, 'Literacy and Society in the West, 1500–1850', *Social History*, viii (1983), 269–93

Leo Howe, 'Doing the Double', in Chris Curtin and Thomas M. Wilson, eds., *Ireland from Below: Social Change and Local Communities* (Galway, 1989), 144–64

Kathleen Hughes, *The Church in Early Irish Society* (London, 1966)

R. J. Hunter, 'The Settler Population of an Ulster Plantation County', *Donegal Annual*, x (1971–3), 124–54

— 'English Undertakers in the Plantation of Ulster, 1610–41', *Breifne*, iv (1973–75), 471–99

Revd Matthew Hutchinson, *The Reformed Presbyterian Church in Scotland: Its Origin and History 1680–1876* (Paisley, 1893)

Douglas Hyde, *A Literary History of Ireland* (new edition, London and New York, 1967)

Alvin Jackson, *Ireland: 1798–1998* (Oxford, 1999)

Harold Jackson, *The Two Irelands: A Dual Study of Inter-Group Tensions* (Minority Rights Group, London, 1971)

K. H. Jackson, *The Oldest Irish Tradition: A Window on the Iron Age* (Cambridge, 1964)

Neil Jarman, *Displaying Faith: Orange, Green and Trade Union Banners in Northern Ireland* (Belfast, 1999)

Henry A. Jefferies and Ciarán Devlin, eds., *History of the Diocese of Derry from the Earliest Times* (Dublin, 1999)

Keith Jeffrey, 'The Great War in Modern Irish Memory', in T.G. Fraser and Keith Jeffrey, eds., *Men, Women and War* (Dublin, 1993), 148–51

Revd Brendan Jennings, *Michael Ó Cléirigh: Chief of the Four Masters and His Associates* (Dublin, 1936)

Emrys Jones, 'The Distribution and Segregation of Roman Catholics in Belfast', *Sociological Review*, 4 (1956), 167–89

F. M. Jones, *The Counter-Reformation* (Dublin, 1967)

Desmond Keenan, *The Catholic Church in Ireland in the Nineteenth Century* (Dublin, 1983)

Fergus Kelly, *A Guide to Early Irish Law* (Dublin, 1988)

James Kelly, 'The Formation of the Modern Catholic Church in the Diocese of Kilmore, 1580–1880', in Gillespie, ed., *Cavan.*, 115–38

David Kennedy, 'Catholics in Northern Ireland, 1926–1939', in Francis Mac-Manus, ed., *The Years of the Great Test, 1926–39* (Cork, 1967), 138–60

Liam Kennedy, *Colonialism, Religion and Nationalism in Ireland* (Belfast, 1996)

— and Philip Ollerenshaw, eds., *An Economic History of Ulster, 1820–1939* (Manchester, 1985)

Daire Keogh, *'The French Disease': The Catholic Church and Radicalism in Ireland 1790–1800* (Dublin, 1993)

Dermot Keogh, *The Vatican, the Bishops and Irish Politics 1919–39* (Cambridge, 1986)

Revd Donal Kerr, 'James Browne Bishop of Kilmore, 1829–65', *Breifne*, vi (1983–4), 109–54

Phil Kilroy, 'Sermon and Pamphlet Literature in the Irish Reformed Church, 1613–34', *Archiv. Hib.*, xxxiii (1975), 110–21

Christine Kinealy, *The Great Calamity: The Irish Famine, 1845–52* (Dublin, 1994)

— and Trevor Parkhill, eds., *The Famine in Ulster* (Belfast, 1997)

Thomas Kinsella, trans., *The Tain* (Oxford, 1989)

G. Kirkham, 'Economic Diversification in a Marginal Economy: A Case Study', in Roebuck, ed., *Plantation to Partition*, 65–81

R. W. Kirkpatrick, 'Origins and Development of the Land War in mid-Ulster, 1879–85', in F.S.L. Lyons and R.A.J. Hawkins, *Ireland Under the Union: Essays in Honour of T.W. Moody* (Oxford, 1980), 201–35

Kassian A. Kovalcheck, 'Catholic Grievances in Northern Ireland: Appraisal and Judgement', *British Jn. of Sociology*, xxxviii (1987), 77–87

Brian Lacy, *Siege City: The Story of Derry and Londonderry* (Belfast, 1990)

— *Colum Cille and the Columban Tradition* (Dublin, 1997)

Michael Laffan, *The Partition of Ireland, 1911–1925* (Dublin, 1983)

Emmet Larkin, 'The Devotional Revolution in Ireland, 1850–75', *Amer. Hist. Rev.*, lxxii (1967), 852–4

— *The Making of the Roman Catholic Church in Ireland, 1850–60* (Chapel Hill, 1980)

— *The Consolidation of the Roman Catholic Church in Ireland, 1860–1870* (Dublin, 1987)

J. Larkin, '"Popish Riot" in South County Derry', *Seanchas Ard Mhacha*, viii (1975–6), 94–111

W. T. Latimer, *A History of the Irish Presbyterians* (Belfast, 1893)

W. E. H. Lecky, *A History of Ireland in the Eighteenth Century*, 5 vols. (London, 1892)

J. J. Lee, *Ireland 1912–1985* (Cambridge, 1989)

J. Leerssen, *Mere Irish and Fíor-Ghael: Studies in the Idea of Irish Nationality, Its Development and Literary Expression prior to the Nineteenth Century* (Amsterdam and Philadelphia, 1986)

Brian Lennon, *After the Ceasefires* (Dublin, 1995)

Peadar Livingstone, *Fermanagh Story* (Enniskillen, 1969)

— *Monaghan Story* (Enniskillen, 1980)

Belinda Loftus, *Mirrors, Orange and Green* (Dundrum, 1994)

Edna Longley, *The Living Stream. Literature and Revisionism in Ireland* (Newcastle Upon Tyne, 1994)

Mary Low, *Celtic Christianity and Nature: Early Irish and Hebridean Traditions* (Edinburgh, 1996)

A. T. Lucas, 'The Sacred Trees of Ireland', *Cork Hist. and Arch. Soc. Jn.*, lxviii (1963), 16–54

A. Lynch, 'Religion in Late Medieval Ireland', *Archiv. Hib.*, xxxvi (1981), 3–15

Revd John Lynch, *The Life of St. Patrick from Walter Harris's Translation of Sir James Ware's Works* (London and Dublin, 1870)

Brendan Lynn, *Holding the Ground: The Nationalist Party in Northern Ireland, 1945–72* (Aldershot, 1997)

Ian McAllister, *The Northern Ireland Social Democratic and Labour Party: Political Opposition in a Divided Society* (London, 1977)

Gerard MacAtasney, *'This Dreadful Visitation': The Famine in Lurgan/Portadown* (Belfast, 1997)

Ambrose Macaulay, *Patrick Dorrian, Bishop of Down and Connor 1865–85* (Dublin, 1987)

— *William Crolly: Archbishop of Armagh, 1835–49* (Dublin, 1994)

I. R. McBride, 'Presbyterians in the Penal Era', *Bullán: an Irish Studies Journal*, i–ii (1994), 73–86

— *Scripture Politics: Ulster Presbyterians and Irish Radicalism in the Late Eighteenth Century* (Oxford, 1998)

— *The Siege of Derry in Ulster Protestant Mythology* (Dublin, 1997)

May McCann, 'Belfast Ceilidhes', *Ulster Folklife*, 29 (1983), 55–105

Donal MacCartney, 'The Writing of History in Ireland, 1800–30', *I.H.S.*, x (1957), 347–62

Kim McCone, *Pagan Past and Christian Present in Early Irish Literature* (Maynooth, 1990)

— and Katharine Simms, eds., *Progress in Medieval Irish Studies* (Maynooth, 1996)

Desmond McCourt, 'The Rundale System in Donegal. Its Distribution and Decline', *Donegal Annual*, iii (1954–5), 47–60

— 'Surviving Openfield in County Londonderry', *Ulster Folklife*, iv (1958), 17–28

Jack McCoy, *Ulster's Joan of Arc. An Examination of the Betsy Gray Story* (Bangor, 1987)

J. L. McCracken, 'The Political Scene in Northern Ireland, 1926–1937', in Francis MacManus, ed., *The Years of the Great Test, 1926–39* (Cork, 1967), 26–39

Brian Mac Cuarta, ed., *Ulster 1641: Aspects of the Rising* (Belfast, 1993)

Margaret MacCurtain, 'Rural Society in post-Cromwellian Ireland', in Art Cosgrove and Donal McCartney, eds., *Studies in Irish History Presented to R.Dudley Edwards* (Dublin, 1979), 118–36

— 'Late in the Field: Catholic Sisters in Twentieth-Century Ireland and the New Religious History', *Journal of Women's History*, vi–vii (1995), 49–63

— and Mary O'Dowd, eds., *Women in Early Modern Ireland* (Edinburgh, 1991)

R. B. McDowell, *Ireland in the Age of Imperialism and Revolution* (Oxford, 1979)

G. McElroy, *The Catholic Church and the Northern Ireland Crisis* (Dublin, 1991)

Thomas McErlean, 'The Irish Townland System of Landscape Organisation', in Terence Reeves-Smyth and Fred Hammond, eds., *Landscape and Archaeology in Ireland* (Oxford, 1983), 315–39

Revd Brendan McEvoy, 'The Parish of Errigal Kieran in the Nineteenth Century', *Seanchas Ard Mhacha*, i (1954–5), 118–31

— 'The United Irishmen in Co.Tyrone', *Seanchas Ard Mhacha*, iii (1958–9), 283–314, and v (1969), 37–65

John McGarry and Brendan O'Leary, *Explaining Northern Ireland: Broken Images* (Oxford, 1995)

Revd Charles McGarvey, 'The Heather Edge', *Seanchas Ard Mhacha*, ii (1956–7), 178–88

Séamus N. Mac Giolla Easpaig, *Tomás Ruiséil* (Dublin, 1957)

Charles McGlinchy, *The Last of the Name* (Belfast, 1986)

Dermot McGuinne, *Irish Type Design* (Dublin, 1992)

[Revd G.E. McKenna], *Devenish (Lough Erne): Its History, Antiquities and Traditions* (Enniskillen, 1897)

Revd L. McKeown, 'Friars Bush', *Down and Connor Hist. Soc. Jn.*, vi (1934), 72–5

Michael McKeown, *Two Seven Six Three: An Analysis of Fatalities Attributable to Civil Disturbances in Northern Ireland in the Twenty Years between July 13 1969 and July 12 1989* (Lucan, 1989)

Jim MacLaughlin, 'The Politics of Nation-Building in Post-Famine Donegal', in Dunlevy, Nolan and Ronayne, eds., *Donegal History and Society*, 583–624

Hugh McLeod, *Religion and the People of Western Europe 1789–1989* (Oxford, 1997)

K. McMahon and T. Ó Fiaich, 'Inscriptions in Creggan Graveyard', *Seanchas Ard Mhacha*, vi (1971–2), 309–32

Paddy McNally, *Parties, Patriots and Undertakers* (Dublin, 1997)

Eoin MacNeill, *Celtic Ireland* (Dublin, 1921)

T. E. McNeill, *Anglo-Norman Ulster: The History and Archaeology of an Irish Barony 1177–1400* (Edinburgh, 1980)

Gearóid Mac Niocaill, *Ireland before the Vikings* (Dublin, 1972)

— 'The Contact of Irish and Common Law', *N. Ireland Legal Quarterly*, 23 (1972), 16–23

Séamas MacPhilib, 'Profile of a Landlord in Folk Tradition and in Contemporary Accounts – the Third Earl of Leitrim', *Ulster Folklife*, xxxiv (1988), 26–40

Aodán Mac Póilin, 'Aspects of the Irish Language Movement in Northern Ireland', in Máiréad Nic Craith, ed., *Watching One's Tongue: Aspects of Romance and Celtic Languages* (Liverpool, 1996), 156–9

Samuel McSkimin, *The History and Antiquities of the County of the Town of Carrickfergus, from the Earliest Records till 1839*, edited by E.J. McCrum (Belfast, 1909)

Breandán Mac Suibhne, 'Canon James McFadden (1842–1917)', in Gerard Moran, ed., *Ten Radical Priests* (Dublin, 1997), 149–84

R. R. Madden, *The United Irishmen, Their Lives and Times,* 3 ser., 7 vols. (London,1842–5), and revised edition, 4 vols. (London, 1857–60)
— *Antrim and Down in '98* (Glasgow, n.d)
W. A. Maguire, ed., *Kings in Conflict: The Revolutionary War in Ireland and Its Aftermath, 1689–1750* (Belfast, 1990)
— 'The Estate of Cú Chonnacht Maguire of Tempo: A Case History from the Williamite Land Settlement', *I.H.S.,* xxvii (1990), 130–44
J. P. Mahaffy, 'Two Early Tours in Ireland', *Hermathena,* xl (1914), 1–16
J. P. Mallory, ed., *Aspects of the Táin* (Belfast, 1992)
— and T.E. McNeill, *The Archaeology of Ulster from Colonization to Plantation* (Belfast, 1991)
John J. Marshall, *History of the Parish of Tynan in the County of Armagh* (Dungannon, 1932)
F. X. Martin, 'Derry in 1590: A Catholic Demonstration', *Clogher Record,* vi (1968), 597–602
Thomas D'Arcy M'Gee, *A Life of the Rt. Rev. Edward Maginn* (New York, 1857)
David Miller, *Church, State and Nation in Ireland 1898–1921* (Dublin, 1973)
— 'Irish Catholicism and the Great Famine', *Jn. Soc. Hist.,* ix (1975), 81–8
— 'Presbyterianism and "Modernization" in Ulster', *Past and Present,* 80 (1978) 66–90
— *Peep O'Day Boys and Defenders: Selected Documents on the County Armagh Disturbances 1784–96* (Belfast, 1990)
— 'Politicisation in Revolutionary Ireland: The Case of the Armagh Troubles', *Ir. Econ. Soc. Hist.,* 23 (1996), 1–17
Benignus Millett, *The Irish Franciscans 1651–1665* (Rome, 1964)
— *Survival and Reorganization 1650–1695* (Dublin, 1968)
Kenneth Milne, *The Irish Charter Schools, 1730–1830* (Dublin, 1997)
Frank Mitchell and Michael Ryan, *Reading the Irish Landscape* (Dublin, 1997)
Joel Mokyr, *Why Ireland Starved: A Quantitative and Analytical History of the Irish Economy, 1800–1850* (London, 1985)
William Monter, *Ritual, Myth and Magic in Early Modern Europe* (Sussex, 1983)
T. W. Moody, 'The Treatment of the Native Population under the Scheme for the Plantation of Ulster', *I.H.S.,* i (1938), 59–63
— *The Londonderry Plantation, 1609–4: The City of London and the Plantation in Ulster* (Belfast, 1939)
— 'Redmond O'Hanlon, *c.*1640–1681', *Proceedings and Reports of the Belfast Natural History and Philosophical Society,* 2nd ser., i, pt 1 (1937), 17–33
— and F. X. Martin and F. J. Byrne, eds., *A New History of Ireland,* iii: *Early Modern Ireland, 1534–1691* (Oxford, 1978)
— *A New History of Ireland,* viii: *A Chronology of Irish History to 1976* (Oxford, 1982)
— *A New History of Ireland,* ix: *Maps, Genealogies, Lists* (Oxford, 1984)

— and W. E. Vaughan, eds., *A New History of Ireland,* iv: *Eighteenth-century Ireland 1690–1800* (Oxford, 1986)

Canice Mooney, 'The Irish Church in the Sixteenth Century', *Ir.Eccles. Rec.,* xcix (1963), 102–13

— *The First Impact of the Reformation* (Dublin, 1967)

— *The Church in Gaelic Ireland, Thirteenth to Fifteenth Centuries* (Dublin, 1969)

— 'The Friars and Friary of Donegal, 1474–1840', in Terence O'Donnell, ed., *Franciscan Donegal* (Donegal, 1952), 3–49

Hiram Morgan, 'The End of Gaelic Ulster: A Thematic Interpretation of Events between 1534 and 1610', *I.H.S.,* xxvi (1988), 8–32

— *Tyrone's Rebellion: The Outbreak of the Nine Years War in Tudor Ireland* (Suffolk, 1993)

— 'The Colonial Venture of Sir Thomas Smith in Ulster, 1571–1575', *Hist. Jn.,* xxviii (1985), 261–78

R. J. Morris, 'Inequality, Social Structure and the Market in Belfast and Glasgow, 1830–1914', in S.J. Connolly, Rab Houston and R.J. Morris, eds., *Conflict, Identity and Economic Development* (Preston, 1995), 189–203

E. Moxon-Browne, *Nation, Class and Creed in Northern Ireland* (Aldershot, 1983)

Ronnie Munck and Bill Rolston, *Belfast in the Thirties. An Oral History* (Belfast, 1987)

James H. Murnane, 'Dr James Donnelly, Bishop of Clogher (1865–1893) and the Ascendancy in Monaghan', *Clogher Rec.,* xiii, no 1 (1988), 1–25

Desmond Murphy, *Derry, Donegal and Modern Ulster 1790–1921* (Londonderry, 1981)

Gerard Murphy, *Saga and Myth in Ancient Ireland* (Dublin, 1955)

Michael J. Murphy, *Tyrone Folk Quest* (Belfast, 1973)

— *At Slieve Gullion's Foot* (Dundalk, 1975)

— *Ulster Folk of Field and Fireside* (Dundalk, 1983)

— *Rathlin: Island of Blood and Enchantment. The Folklore of Rathlin* (Dundalk, 1987)

Dominic Murray, 'Schools and Conflict', in John Darby, ed., *Northern Ireland: The Background to the Conflict* (Belfast, 1983), 136–50

— *Worlds Apart: Segregated Schools in Northern Ireland* (Belfast, 1985)

James Murray, 'The Church of Ireland: A Critical Bibliography', Part I: 1536–1603, and Part II: 1603–41, by Alan Ford, *I.H.S.,* xxviii (Nov. 1993), 345–8

Revd L. P. Murray, 'The History of the Parish of Creggan in the 17th and 18th Centuries', *Louth Arch. Soc. Jn.,* viii (1934), 117–63, later reissued as *History of the Parish of Creggan* (Dundalk, 1940)

— 'Franciscan Monasteries after the Dissolution', *Louth Arch. Soc. Jn.,* viii (1934), 275–82

P. G. Murray, 'A Previously Unnoticed Letter of Oliver Plunkett's', *Seanchas Ard Mhacha,* viii (1975–6), 23–33

Kenneth Nicholls, *Gaelic and Gaelicised Ireland in the Middle Ages* (Dublin 1972)

Próinséas Ní Chatháin and Michael Richter, eds., *Irland und Europa, die Kirche in Frühmittelalter: Ireland and Europe, the Early Church* (Stuttgart, 1984)

William Nolan, Liam Ronayne and Mairead Donlevy, eds., *Donegal. History and Society* (Dublin, 1995)

E. R. Norman and J.K.S. St. Joseph, *The Early Development of Irish Society. The Evidence of Aerial Photography* (Cambridge, 1969)

Dónall P. Ó Baoill, *An Teanga Bheo: Gaeilge Uladh* (Dublin, 1996)

Conor Cruise O'Brien, *The Great Melody: A Thematic Biography of Edmund Burke* (London, 1992)

— *Ancestral Voices: Religion and Nationalism in Ireland* (Dublin, 1994)

Breandán Ó Buachalla, *I mBéal Feirste Cois Cuain* (Dublin, 1968)

— 'Na Stíobhartaigh agus an tAos Léinn: Cing Séamas', *Proc. R.I.A.*, 83, sect. C (1983), 81–134

— 'Lillibulero agus Eile', *Comhar* (April 1987), 27–9

— 'Poetry and Politics in Early Modern Ireland', *Eighteenth-Century Ireland*, vii (1992), 149–75

— 'Foreword' to Geoffrey Keating, *Foras Feasa ar Éirinn*, edited by D. Comyn and P.S. Dineen (1987 reprint of London, 1902)

— 'Poetry and Politics in Early Modern Ireland', *Eighteenth-Century Ireland*, vii (1992), 149–75

— 'Jacobitism and Nationalism: The Irish Literary Evidence', in Michael O'Dea and Kevin Whelan, eds., *Nations and Nationalism: France, Britain, Ireland and the Eighteenth-Century Context* (Oxford, 1995), 103–16

Cathal O'Byrne, *As I Roved Out* (Belfast, 1982, reprint of 1946 edition)

John Cornellius O'Callaghan, *Irish Brigades in the Service of France* (Shannon, 1968, reprint of 1870 edition)

Séamus Ó Casaide, *Irish Language in Belfast and County Down, 1601–1850* (Dublin,1930)

S. Ó Ceallaigh, *Gleanings from Ulster History* (Cork, 1951)

N. Ó Cíosáin, *Print and Popular Culture in Ireland 1750–1850* (Basingstoke, 1997)

Séan Ó Coinne and T. Ó Fiaich, 'Tombstone Inscriptions in Drumglass Cemetery', *Seanchas Ard Mhacha*, vii (1974), 316–19

Marie O'Connell, 'The Genesis of Convent Foundations and Their Institutions in Ulster, 1840–1920', in Janice Holmes and Diane Urquhart, eds. *Coming into the Light: The Work, Politics and Religion of Women in Ulster 1840–1940* (Belfast, 1994), 179–206

Philip O'Connell, *The Diocese of Kilmore: Its History and Antiquities* (Dublin, 1937)

— 'A Dublin Convert Roll: The Diary of the Rev. P.E. O'Farrelly', *Ir. Eccles. Rec.*, lxxi, (January–June,1949), 533–44 and lxxii (July–December, 1949), 27–35

Fionnuala O Connor, *In Search of a State* (Belfast, 1993)

Donnchadh Ó Corráin, *Ireland before the Normans* (Dublin, 1972)

— 'Nationality and Kingship in pre-Norman Ireland', in T.W. Moody, ed., *Nationality and the Pursuit of National Independence* (Belfast, 1978), 1–35

P. S. Ó Dalaigh, 'Sketches of Farney', *Clogher Record*, I, no. 2 (1954), 56–62

Caoimhín Ó Danachair, 'The Penal Laws and Irish Folk tradition', *Proc. Ir. Cath. Hist. Comm.* (1961), 10–16

— 'The Progress of Irish Ethnology, 1783–1982', *Ulster Folklife*, 29 (1983), 7–10

— 'Representations of Houses in Some Irish Maps of 1600', in Geraint Jenkins, ed., *Studies in Folk Life. Essays in Honour of Iorwerth C. Peate* (London, 1969), 91–104

Alan O'Day, ed., *Reactions to Irish Nationalism, 1865–1914* (London, 1987)

Éamon Ó Doibhlin, 'Conn O'Neill of Kilskeery', *Clogher Record*, vi (1967), 388–93

— 'The Deanery of Tulach Óg', *Seanchas Ard Mhacha*, vi, no 1 (1971), 141–82

— *Domhnach Mór (Donaghmore): An Outline of Parish History* (2nd edition, Dungannon, 1988)

Terence O'Donnell, ed., *Franciscan Donegal* (Donegal, 1952)

Anne O'Dowd, *Spalpeens and Tattie Hokers: History and Folklore of the Irish Migratory Agricultural Worker in Ireland and Britain* (Dublin, 1991)

Mary O'Dowd, *Power, Politics and Land: Early Modern Sligo 1568–1688* (Belfast, 1991)

Revd Seosamh Ó Dufaigh, 'The Mac Cathmhaoils of Clogher', *Clogher Record*, ii (1957), 25–48

— 'James Murphy, Bishop of Clogher, 1801–24', *Clogher Record*, vi (1968), 419–93

Revd Eoghan O'Duffy, *The Apostasy of Myler Magrath, Archbishop of Cashel* (No place of pub., 1864)

B. W. O'Dwyer, 'Gaelic Monasticism and the Irish Cistercians, *c.*1228', *Ir. Eccles, Rec.*, 108 (1967), 19–28

Peter O'Dwyer, *Mary: A History of Devotion in Ireland* (Dublin,1988)

Tomás Ó Fiaich, 'The Appointment of Bishop Tyrrell and Its Consequences', *Clogher Record*, i (1953–6), 1–14

— 'Diocese of Armagh: Sources and Problems', *Proc. Ir. Cath. Hist. Committee* (1955), 6–9

– ed., 'The 1766 Religious Census for Some County Tyrone Parishes', *Seanchas Ard Mhacha*, iv, no 1 (1960–61), 147–70

— 'The Political and Social Background of the Ulster Poets', *Léachtaí Cholm Cille,* i (1970), 23–56

— 'Filíocht Uladh mar Fhoinse don Stair Shóisialta san 18ú hAois', *Stud. Hib.*, xi (1971), 80–129

— 'The Registration of the Clergy in 1704', *Seanchas Ard Mhacha*, vi, no 1(1971), 46–69

— 'Art Mac Cooey and his Times', *Seanchas Ard Mhacha*, vi (1971), 217–46

— 'The O'Neills of the Fews', *Seanchas Ard Mhacha*, vii (1973–4), 1–63, 263–315, and viii (1977), 386–413

Revd P. Ó Gallachair, 'Clogher's Altars of the Penal Days', *Clogher Record*, ii (1957–9), 97–130

— 'Clogherhici. A Dictionary of the Catholic Clergy of the Diocese of Clogher (1535–1835)', *Clogher Record*, i, no. 3 (1955), 66–87, no. 4 (1956), 137–60; ii (1957–9), 170–91, 272–9, 504–11; iv (1960–62), 54–94; vi (1966–8), 126–36, 379–87, 578–96; vii (1969–72), 89–104, 514–28; viii (1973–4), 93–103, 207–20; ix (1976), 67–75; xi (1982–4), 374–86; xii (1986), 233–46

Cormac Ó Gráda, *The Great Irish Famine* (London, 1989)

— *Ireland: A New Economic History 1780–1939* (Oxford, 1994)

— *Black '47 and Beyond. The Great Irish Famine in History, Economy, and Memory* (Princeton, 1999)

— *An Drochshaol: Béaloideas agus Amhráin* (Dublin, 1994)

Standish O'Grady, *History of Ireland: The Heroic Period* (London, 1878)

Clare O'Halloran, *Partition and the Limits of Irish Nationalism* (Dublin, 1987)

— 'Irish Re-creations of the Gaelic Past: The Challenge of MacPherson's Ossian', *Past and Present*, 124 (1989), 69–95

Jane H. Ohlmeyer, *Civil War and Restoration in Three Stuart Kingdoms: The Career of Randal MacDonnell, Marquis of Antrim 1609–1683* (Cambridge, 1993)

— ed., *Ireland from Independence to Occupation 1641–1660* (Cambridge, 1995)

Michael J. O'Kelly, *Early Ireland. An Introduction to Irish Pre-History* (Cambridge, 1989)

Revd J. O'Laverty, *An Historical Account of the Diocese of Down and Connor, Ancient and Modern*, 5 vols. (Dublin, 1878–95)

Padraig O'Malley, *The Uncivil Wars* (Belfast, 1983)

— *Biting at the Grave: The Irish Hunger Strikes and the Politics of Despair* (Belfast, 1990)

Revd Lorcán Ó Mearáin, 'The Bath Estate, 1700–1777', *Clogher Record*, vol. 6, no. 2 (1967), 333–60

Séamas P. Ó Mórdha, 'Dán Faoi Mhuirthéacht na Frainnce', *Éigse*, vii (1953–4), 202–4

— 'Simon Macken: Fermanagh Scribe and Schoolmaster', *Clogher Record*, ii (1986), 432–44

— 'Maurice O'Gorman in Monaghan', *Clogher Record*, ii (1957), 20–24

— 'Notes and Comments. Party Quarrels in Nineteenth-Century Monaghan', *Clogher Record*, ii (1958), 355–7

— 'The Rising of Burke', *Clogher Record*, iv (1960–61), 50–53

Énrí Ó Muirgheasa, 'The Holy Wells of Donegal', *Béaloideas*, vi (1936), 141–62

Réamonn Ó Muirí, 'The Killing of Thomas Birch', *Seanchas Ard Mhacha*, x, (1980–82), 267–319
— ed., *Irish Church History Today* (Armagh, n.d.)
Kevin O'Neill, *Family and Farm in Pre-Famine Ireland* (Wisconsin, 1984)
T. F. O'Rahilly, *Early Irish History and Mythology* (Dublin, 1946)
Michelle O'Riordan, *The Gaelic Mind and the Collapse of the Gaelic World* (Cork, 1990)
Camille O'Reilly, 'Nationalists and the Irish Language in Northern Ireland: Competing Perspectives', in Mac Póilin, ed, *Irish Language in Northern Ireland*, 98–113
W.N. Osborough, 'Catholics, Land and the Popery Acts of Anne', in T.P. Power and Kevin Whelan, eds., *Endurance and Emergence: Catholics in Ireland in the Eighteenth Century* (Dublin, 1990), 21–56
James O'Shea, *Priest, Politics and Society in Post-Famine Ireland* (Dublin, 1983)
P. Ó Snodaigh, 'Class and the Volunteers', *Irish Sword*, xvi (1984–6), 165–84
— *Hidden Ulster* (Belfast, 1995)
Edward L. Parker, *The History of Londonderry, Comprising the Towns of Derry and Londonderry, New Hampshire* (Boston, 1851)
Tony Parker, *May the Lord in His Mercy be Kind to Belfast* (London, 1993)
T. G. F. Patterson, 'The Territory of Ballymacone and Its Associations with the McCones', *Seanchas Ard Mhacha*, i (1954–5), 132–50
— 'Housing and House Types in County Armagh', *Ulster Folklife*, vi (1960), 8–17
M. Perceval-Maxwell, *The Scottish Migration to Ulster in the Reign of James I* (1990 reprint of London, 1973 edition)
J. R. S. Phillips, 'The Irish Remonstrance of 1317: An International Perspective', *I.H.S.*, xxvii (1990), 112–29
E. Phoenix, ed., 'Political Violence, Diplomacy and the Catholic Minority in Northern Ireland, 1922', in John Darby, Nicholas Dodge and A.C. Hepburn, eds., *Political Violence: Ireland in a Comparative Perspective* (Belfast, 1990), 29–47
— *Northern Nationalism: Nationalist Politics, Partition and the Catholic Minority in Northern Ireland 1890–1940* (Belfast, 1994)
— ed., *A Century of Northern Life: The Irish News and 100 Years of Ulster History 1890s–1990s* (Belfast, 1995)
Stuart Piggott, *The Druids* (London, 1968)
Cathal Póirtéir, *Famine Echoes* (Dublin, 1995)
Andy Pollak *et al.*, *A Citizens' Inquiry: The Opsahl Report on Northern Ireland* (Dublin, 1993)
Michael Poole, 'The Geographical Location of Political Violence in Northern Ireland', in Darby *et al.*, *Political Violence*, 64–82
T. P. Power and Kevin Whelan, eds., *Endurance and Emergence. Catholics in Ireland in the Eighteenth Century* (Dublin, 1990)
Lindsay Proudfoot, ed., *Down. History and Society. Interdisciplinary Essays on the History of an Irish County* (Dublin, 1997)

H. Pryce, ed., *Literacy in Medieval Celtic Societies* (Cambridge, 1998)

Bob Purdie, *Politics in the Streets. The Origins of the Civil Rights Movement in Northern Ireland* (Belfast, 1990)

C. Quinlan, 'A Punishment from God: The Famine in the Centenary Folklore Questionnaire', *Irish Review*, xix (1996), 68–86

David Quinn, *The Elizabethans and the Irish* (Ithaca, 1966)

Oliver P. Rafferty, *Catholicism in Ulster 1603–1983: An Interpretive History* (Dublin, 1994)

Patrick Rafroidi, 'Imagination and Revolution: The Cuchulain Myth', in Oliver MacDonagh, W.F. Mandle and Pauric Travers, eds., *Irish Culture and Nationalism, 1750–1950* (Canberra, reprint 1985), 137–48

Michael Richter, *Medieval Ireland. The Enduring Tradition* (London, 1988)

Philip Robinson, 'Vernacular Housing in Ulster in the Seventeenth Century', *Ulster Folklife*, xxv (1979), 1–28

— *The Plantation of Ulster* (Dublin, 1984)

Peter Roebuck, 'The Economic Situation and Functions of Substantial Landowners, 1660–1815: Ulster and Lowland Scotland Compared', in Rosalind Mitchison and Peter Roebuck, eds., *Economy and Society in Scotland and Ireland, 1500–1939* (Edinburgh, 1988), 84–9

— ed., *Plantation to Partition: Essays in Ulster History in Honour of J.L. McCracken* (Belfast, 1981)

— ed., *Macartney of Lissanoure* (Belfast, 1983)

R. S. Rogers, 'The Folklore of the Black Pig's Dyke', *Ulster Folklife*, iii (1957), 29–36, and the response by T.G. Barron, ibid., iv (1958), 75–6

Revd Patrick Rogers, *The Irish Volunteers and Catholic Emancipation* (Belfast, 1934)

— 'The Minute Book of the Belfast Rosarian Society', *Down and Connor Hist. Soc. Jn.*, viii (1937), 17–23

Richard Rose, *Governing without Consensus: An Irish Perspective* (London, 1971)

Joseph Ruane and Jennifer Todd, eds., *After the Good Friday Agreement: Analysing Political Change in Northern Ireland* (Dublin, 1999)

D. C. Rushe, *Monaghan in the Eighteenth Century* (Dundalk, 1916)

Conor Ryan, 'Religion and State in Seventeenth-Century Ireland', *Archiv. Hib.*, xxxiii (1975), 110–21

John Ryan, *The Monastic Institute* (Dublin, 1971), 49–50

Donald M. Schlegel, 'The MacDonnells of Tyrone and Armagh: A Genealogical Study', *Seanchas Ard Mhacha*, x (1980–82), 193–219

R. W. Scribner, 'Interpreting Religion in Early Modern Europe', *European Studies Review*, xiii (1983), 89–105

Hereward Senior, *Orangeism in Britain and Ireland, 1795–1836* (London, 1966)

St John D. Seymour, *Irish Witchcraft and Demonology* (New York, 1992)

Richard Sharpe, 'St Patrick and the See of Armagh', *Cambridge Medieval Celtic Studies*, 4 (Winter, 1982), 33–59

William Shaw, *Cullybackey: The Story of an Ulster Village* (Edinburgh, 1913)

W. J. Sheils and Diana Wood, eds., *The Churches, Ireland and the Irish*, Studies in Church History, no. 25 (Oxford, 1989)

Robert C. Simington, *The Transplantation to Connacht, 1654–58* (Dublin, 1970)

J. G. Simms, *The Williamite Confiscation in Ireland* (London, 1956)

— ed., 'Irish Jacobites', *Anal. Hib.*, xxii (1960), 22–187

— 'Land Owned by Catholics in Ireland in 1688', *I.H.S.* vii (1950), 180–90

— *The Jacobite Parliament of 1689* (Dundalk,1966)

— 'Irish Catholics and the Parliamentary Franchise, 1692–1728', in D.W. Hayton and Gerard O'Brien, eds., *War and Politics in Ireland, 1649–1730* (London, 1986), 224–34.

Katherine Simms, 'The Archbishops of Armagh and the O'Neills, 1347–1471', *I.H.S.*, xix (1974), 38–55

— 'Warfare in the Medieval Gaelic Lordships', *Irish Sword*, xii (1975–6), 102–8

— 'The Medieval Kingdom of Loch Erne', *Clogher Record*, ix (1977), 126–41

— 'Guesting and Feasting in Gaelic Ireland', *Roy. Soc. Archives Jn.*, 108 (1978)

— 'The O'Hanlons, the O'Neills and the Anglo-Normans in Thirteenth-Century Armagh', in *Seanchas Ard Mhacha*, ix (1978), 70–94

— 'The O'Reillys and the Kingdom of East Breifne', *Breifne*, vi (1979), 305–19

— ' "The King's Friend": O'Neill, the Crown and the Earldom of Ulster', in J. Lydon, ed., *England and Ireland in the Later Middle Ages* (Dublin, 1981), 214–36

— 'Propaganda Use of the Táin in the Later Middle Ages', *Celtica*, xv (1983), 142–9

— 'Nomadry in Medieval Ireland: the Origins of the Creaght or *Caoraigheacht*', *Peritia*, v (1986), 379–91

— 'Bardic Poetry as a Historical Source', in Tom Dunne, ed., *The Writer as Witness: Literature as Historical Evidence* (Cork, 1987), 58–75

— *From Kings to Warlords: The Changing Political Structure of Gaelic Ireland in the Later Middle Ages* (Suffolk, 1987)

— 'Bards and Barons: The Anglo-Irish Aristocracy and Native Culture', in R. Bartlett and A. Mackay, eds., *Medieval Frontier Societies* (Oxford, 1989), 188–94

— 'Gaelic Warfare', in T. Bartlett and K. Jeffery, eds., *A Military History of Ireland* (Cambridge, 1996), 99–115

— 'The Contents of Later Commentaries on the Brehon Law Tracts', in *Ériu*, xlix (1998), 23–40

Peter Smith, *Oidhreacht Oirghiall. A Bibliography of Irish Literature and Philology Relating to the South-East Ulster–North Leinster Region: Printed Sources* (Belfast, 1995)

Gerry Smyth, *The Novel and the Nation: Studies in the New Irish Fiction* (London, 1997)

Revd J. Smyth, 'Blessed Oliver Plunkett in Down and Connor', *Down and Connor Hist. Soc. Jn.*, viii (1937), 76–80

William J. Smyth, 'Society and Settlement in Seventeenth-Century Ireland: The Evidence of the "1659 Census"', in Smyth and Whelan, eds., *Common Ground*, 55–83

— and Kevin Whelan, eds., *Common Ground: Essays on the Historical Geography of Ireland* (Cork, 1988)

Roger Stalley, 'The Long Middle Ages. From the Twelfth Century to the Reformation', in Brian de Breffny, ed., *The Irish World. The History and Cultural Achievements of the Irish People* (London, 1977), 72–98

David Stevenson, *Scottish Covenanters and Irish Confederates* (Belfast, 1981)

— 'The Desertion of the Irish by Coll Keitach's Sons, 1642', *I.H.S.*, xxi (1978), 75–84

A. T. Q. Stewart, *The Narrow Ground. Aspects of Ulster* (London, 1977)

— *The Summer Soldiers: The 1798 Rebellion in Antrim and Down* (Belfast, 1995)

Peter Stringer and Gillian Robinson, eds., *Social Attitudes in Northern Ireland: The Second Report* (Belfast, 1992)

James Stuart, *Historical Memoirs of the City of Armagh* (Newry, 1819), also new edition (Catholic version) by Revd Ambrose Coleman, OP, (Dublin, 1900)

Robert Sullivan, *A Matter of Faith: The Fiction of Brian Moore* (Westport, CT, 1996)

Sunday Times Insight Team, *Ulster* (London, 1972)

Joseph Szövérffy, '*Rí Naomh Seoirse*: Chapbooks and Hedge-Schools', *Éigse*, ix (1958–61), 114–28

Lawrence Taylor, *Occasions of Faith. An Anthropology of Irish Catholics* (Dublin, 1995)

Mary Helen Thuente, *The Harp Re-strung: The United Irishmen and the Rise of Literary Nationalism* (New York, 1994)

— *W.B. Yeats and Irish Folklore* (Dublin, 1980)

E. Brian Titley, *Church, State and the Control of Schooling in Ireland 1900–1944* (Canada and Dublin, 1983)

Michael Tynan, *Catholic Instruction in Ireland, 1720–1950* (Dublin, 1985)

Norman Vance, 'Celts, Carthaginians and Constitutions: Anglo-Irish Literary Relations, 1780–1820', *I.H.S.*, xxii (1980–81), 216–38

— 'Catholic and Protestant Literary Visions of "Ulster": Now You See It, Now You Don't', in *Religion and Literature*, 28 (1996), 127–40

W. E. Vaughan, *Sin, Sheep and Scotsmen: John George Adair and the Derryveagh Evictions, 1861* (Belfast, 1983)

— ed., *A New History of Ireland. v: Ireland Under the Union. i. 1801–70* (Oxford, 1989), 515–20

— ed., *A New History of Ireland. vi: Ireland Under the Union. ii. 1870–1921* (Oxford, 1996)

John Waddell, 'The Question of the Celticization of Ireland', *Emania*, ix (1991), 5–16

Thomas Wall, *The Sign of Dr Hay's Head* (Dublin, 1958)

B. M. Walker, *Party Election Results, 1801–1922* (Dublin, 1978)
— 'The Land Question and Elections in Ulster, 1868–86', in Clarke and Donnelly, eds., *Irish Peasants*, 230–68
— *Ulster Politics: The Formative Years, 1868–86* (Belfast, 1989)
Paul Walsh, *Leabhar Chlainne Suibhne. An account of the MacSweeney families in Ireland* (Dublin, 1920)
— *The Four Masters and Their Work* (London, 1944)
— *Irish Men of Learning* (Dublin, 1947)
— *Irish Chiefs and Leaders* (Dublin, 1960)
Seosamh Watson, 'Coimhlint an Dá Chultúr – Gaeil agus Gaill i bhFilíocht Chúige Uladh san Ochtú hAois Déag', *Eighteenth-Century Ireland*, iii (1988), 85–104
John Watt, *The Church in Medieval Ireland* (Dublin, 1972)
J. A. Watt, 'The Papacy and Ireland in the Fifteenth Century', in Barrie Dobson, ed., *The Church, Politics and Patronage* (Glos., 1984), 133–43
Robert Welch, *The Oxford Companion to Irish Literature* (Oxford, 1996)
Kevin Whelan, 'The Regional Impact of Irish Catholicism, 1700–1850', in Smyth and Whelan, eds., *Common Ground*, 253–77
— 'The Catholic Parish, the Catholic Chapel and Village Development in Ireland', *Irish Geography*, xvi (1983), 1–15
Patrick Whelan, 'Anthony Blake, Archbishop of Armagh 1758–1787', *Seanchas Ard Mhacha*, v (1970), 289–323
Newport B. White, ed., *Extents of Irish Monastic Possessions, 1540–1541* (Dublin, 1943)
John Whyte, *Church and State in Modern Ireland 1923–1970* (Dublin, 1971)
— 'How Much Discrimination was There under the Unionist Regime, 1921–68', in Tom Gallagher and James O'Connell, eds., *Contemporary Irish Studies* (Manchester, 1983), 3–7
— 'How is the Boundary Maintained between the Two Communities in Northern Ireland?', *Ethnic and Racial Studies*, ix (1986), 219–34
— *Interpreting Northern Ireland* (Oxford, 1990)
Fionnuala Williams, 'A Fire of Stones Curse', *Folk Life*, xxxv (1996–7), 63–73
C. J. Woods, 'The General Election of 1892: The Catholic Clergy and the Defeat of the Parnellites', in F. S. L. Lyons and R. A. J. Hawkins, eds., *Ireland under the Union: Essays in Honour of T. W. Moody* (Oxford, 1980), 289–319
Frank Wright, *Two Lands in One Soil: Ulster Politics before Home Rule* (Dublin, 1996)
R. M. Young, *The Town Book of the Corporation of Belfast 1613–1816* (Belfast, 1892)
— *Ulster in '98: Episodes and Anecdotes* (Belfast, 1893)
— *Historical Notices of Old Belfast and Its Vicinity* (Belfast, 1896)

UNPUBLISHED THESES

Marcus de la Poer Beresford, 'Ireland in French strategy, 1691–1789' (Univ. of Dublin M.Litt. thesis, 1975)

John Corkery, 'Gaelic Catechisms in Ireland' (NUI, MA thesis, St Patrick's College, Maynooth, 1944)

W. H. Crawford, 'Economy and Society in Eighteenth-Century Ulster' (QUB, PhD. thesis, 1982)

James Connor Doak, 'Rioting and Civil Strife in the City of Londonderry during the Nineteenth and Early Twentieth Centuries' (QUB, MA thesis, 1978),

John B. Dooher, 'Tyrone Nationalism and the Question of Partition, 1910–25' (Univ. of Ulster, M.Phil. thesis, 1986)

Patrick Harvey, 'At the Edge of the Union': Derry Newspapers and the Rhetoric of Nationalism, 1937–39' (Univ. Ulster, M.A. thesis, 1988)

R. J. Hunter, 'The Ulster Plantation in the counties of Armagh and Cavan, 1608–41' (Univ. Dublin, M.Litt. thesis, 1969)

Mary Catherine Kennedy, '*Eagla an Ghallsmacht*. The Religion and Politics of Irish Catholics 1620s-1870s' (NUI, Galway, MA thesis, 1987)

William McAfee, 'The Population of Ulster, 1630–1841: Evidence from mid-Ulster' (Univ. of Ulster, D.Phil. thesis, 1987)

T. P. J. McCall, 'The Gaelic Background to the Settlement of Antrim and Down, 1580–1641' (QUB, M.A. thesis, 1983)

Terence Francis McCarthy, 'Ulster Office, 1552–1800' (QUB, M.A. thesis, 1983)

Patrick J. Curley, 'Northern Irish Poets and the Land since 1800' (QUB, MA thesis, 1977)

Anne De Valera, 'Antiquarianism and Historical Investigations in Ireland in the Eighteenth Century' (NUI, UCD, MA thesis, 1978)

Hugh Joseph Maguire, 'Pádraig Mhac a Lionnduinn of the Fews' (QUB, PhD thesis, 1965)

V. Morley, 'The American Revolution and Opinion in Ireland, 1760–83' (Univ. of Liverpool, PhD. thesis, 1999)

Seán Seosamh Ó Gallachóir, 'Filíocht Shéamais Dhaill Mhic Cuarta' (MA thesis, St Patrick's College, Maynooth, 1967)

Mary Louise Peckham, 'Catholic Female Congregations and Religious Change in Ireland, 1770–1870' (Univ. Wisconsin, Madison, PhD. thesis, 1993)

Margaret Purdy, 'Some Aspects of the Religious and Cultural Identity of Pre-Famine Rural Ulster as Portrayed in William Carleton's Traits and Stories of the Irish Peasantry' (Univ. of London, Birkbeck Coll., MA dissertation, 1992)

Michael G. Quinn, 'Religion and Landownership in County Louth 1641 – c.1750' (Univ. Ulster, MA thesis, 1984)

Katharine Simms, 'Gaelic Lordships in Ulster in the Later Middle Ages' (Univ. of Dublin, PhD. thesis, 1976)

Index

abbots 14
Abercorn, Claud Hamilton, 4th Earl
116
Abercorn, Lord (John James
Hamilton, 1st marquis) 217
Abercorn estate, Tyrone 179
abjuration, oath (1708) 148
abstention, Nationalist 383, 396,
397
Act(s)
Arms (1793) 242
Banishment (1697) 166
Black (1639) 146
Catholic Emancipation (1829)
209
Catholic Relief (1793) 217, 233,
235, 242
Charitable Bequests (1844)
278
Coercion (1885) 361
Convention (1793) 242
Disestablishment (1869) 167
Ecclesiastical Titles (1851) 319
Education (1930) 462; (1944)
462; (1947) 407
Flags and Emblems (1954) 406,
454
Franchise (1884) 294
Government of Ireland (1920)
300, 373
Health Services (Northern
Ireland) (1948) 407
Home Rule Bills 297, 300, 325,
357

Irish Poor Law (1838) 311,
(1847) 310
Land 320, 321
MacPherson Bill (1919) 460
Militia (1793) 242
Offences Against the State (1939)
402
Party Emblems (1860) 350
Party Processions (1832) 345,
349, 356
Party Processions (1850) 350
Popery (1704) 166
Public Order 406
Quebec (1774) 168
Registration (1704) 176
Settlement (1662) 111–12, 115
Special Powers (1922) 382, 386,
411
of Union (1800) 261, 271, 342
Wyndham (1903) 321
Adair, John 319
Adair family 312
Adams, Gerry 445, 446
Adeir Clann Liútair (MacCooey)
182
Áed mac Loingsich 17
*Agallamh idir Brádaigh an spiadhóir
agus Bard Gaeilge* (McDonnell)
312
Agnew family 29
agriculture 305–6, 320
Ahoghill, Co. Antrim 167
Airgialla 10, 18, 19
Airthir 19, 49

Aisling Airt Mhic Cumhaigh
140–41
aisling poems 134
Akenson, D. H. 341, 460, 462
Albanach, use of word 132
alliances, medieval 48–9
America, emigration to 168, 192,
338
Ancient Britons regiment 247, 248
Ancient Order of Hibernians (AOH)
296, 326, 353, 356, 469
Andrews, John 307, 308, 389
Anglo-Irish 34, 48–9
Anglo-Irish Agreement (1985)
427–8, 450
Anglo-Irish Treaty (1921) 377, 378
Anglo-Irish war (1919–21) 373,
374
Anglo-Normans 13, 25, 26–8, 29,
30, 34, 48–9, 75
Annals of the Four Masters 64, 76
Annesley, Lord (Francis Charles, 1st
earl) 226, 227, 235
Annesley family 109
antiquarianism, patriotic 75, 232
Antrim, earls of 190
    land confiscation 109–10
    recruiting 98
    status 95, 113, 120
Antrim, Randal MacDonnell, earl of
95
Antrim county xxxix–xli
    Anglo-Norman 26, 27
    bog xli–xlii
    Catholics in 87, 195, 243, 252
    coast 3
    Coast Road xl
    community relations (1790s) 238
    Convention (Catholic) members
    237
    Cromwellian confiscations 109
    excluded from Plantation 89, 91
    Famine 307, 308, 309, 313
    Gaelic-speaking Scots 178
    National schools 277
    and oath of allegiance 217

1641 Rebellion 103–4
1798 Rebellion 252–4, 255
    religious demography xlii
    settlers 86–8
    'souperism' 309–10
    toryism 176
    United Irishmen 251, 252
    Volunteers 221–3
    Williamite settlement 120
Antrim plateau xl
Antrim town 253, 260
AOH
    see Ancient Order of Hibernians
Apprentice Boys of Derry 359, 360,
413, 417
Arboe, Co. Tyrone 251
Ardoyne, Belfast 125, 160, 326,
394, 418
Ards peninsula 27, 86–7, 255–6
Ardstraw, Co. Tyrone 341
*Argument on Behalf of the Catholics
of Ireland* (Tone) 228, 231
A Rí lér fuasclaíodh (McAlindon)
136
Armagh, *see* of 60, 61, 65, 136, 151,
180, 208, 209, 280, 328
Armagh city 7, 12, 13–14, 62–3,
221
Armagh county
    Boundary Commission and 379
    Cromwellian confiscations 110
    Famine 186, 305, 307, 313
    IRA activity 406
    local councils 373
    Oakboys 217
    Orangeism 345–6
    parliamentary elections 385
    Plantation 91
    poor land 93
    population 219
    population movement 93
    raths 6
    religious demography xli,
    222
    sectarian clashes (1780s and
    1790s) 176, 221–7

tories 118
Ulster Irish in 93
arms, Catholics and 182, 186, 242, 347
Arnon St, Belfast 377
Ar Thargair Cholmcille mhic Féilim (MacDonnell) 276
Ascendancy, Protestant 227, 233, 236, 239, 343, 440
asceticism, medieval 62, 101
Ash Wednesday 451
Athlone, battle (1691) 116
atrocities
   1641 101–7
   1790s 224, 247
Audley family 86–7
Augher, Co. Tyrone 102–3
Aughrim, battle (1691) 116, 137, 138, 139, 140, 344
Augustinian friars 60
Austria, military service 193

Bagenal, Sir Henry 27, 28
Baker, Sybil 325, 356–7
Ballard, Linda May 287
Ballintoy, Co. Antrim 310
Ballybay, Co. Monaghan 272, 319
ballybetaghs 42
ballybo 42
Ballycastle, Co. Antrim 176, 237
Ballydonellan, Co. Antrim 174
Ballygullion (Doyle) 339, 347, 352–3
Ballymacarrett, Belfast 357–8, 375
Ballymena, Co. Antrim 253, 261, 275, 326
Ballymenone, Co. Fermanagh 306, 479
Ballymoney, Co. Antrim 320, 329
Ballynahinch, Co. Down 256–7, 258, 260, 263
Banbridge, Co. Down 374
Bancroft, Edward 219
Bangor, Co. Down 239
Bannaugh, Co. Donegal 120

Banner of Ulster (McKnight) 319
Bann River xli, 26, 28, 103
Bann valley 3, 8
Bardon, Jonathan 405, 407
bards 45–8, 126–7
Barkeley, Alexander 224
barricades, Catholic 471
Barritt, Denis 411, 460, 465
Barthelet, cartographer 52
Bates, Richard Dawson 381, 389, 390
Battle of Aughrim (play) 180
BBC Northern Ireland 408
Beckett, Mary 432, 433, 477, 480
Bede, Venerable 15
Bedell, Bishop William 129, 130
Belfast 321–7
   attacked (1793) 242
   borough police 343
   Catholics in 283, 321, 322, 323–5, 374–8, 388, 398, 409, 417
   Catholic convention (1792) delegates and 236–7
   Catholic view of 398
   churches, shortage 270
   City Council 323, 324, 437
   death, average age 323
   dock strike (1907) 330
   east 437
   expansion xxvi, 321
   Famine 308
   in fiction 477
   first Catholic school 277
   as fount of sedition (1790s) 243
   household franchise 324
   intimidation 324, 325, 326
   Labour politics 330–31
   middle-class Catholics 322, 323
   murals 431, 447
   murder, sectarian 422
   IRA 403–4, 419
   'pogrom' (1920s) 374–6, 377–8
   population 321
   poverty 323

Belfast – *cont.*
  as Protestant 321, 322, 324
  Protestant demonstrations 181
  religious segregation 325, 326,
    432
  rural influx 321, 326
  sectarian geography 322
  sectarian riots 324, 325, 343,
    353–6, 357–8, 392, 393–4
  shipyard 323–4, 330, 356, 375,
    394
  soup kitchens 309
  state schools 439
  textile mills 321–3
  Town Council 357, 358
  Troubles (1969-) 418–21
  west 437, 478
  World War II xxii, 386, 403–4
Belfast Agreement (1998)
  see Good Friday Agreement
Belfast Morning News 295
Belfast News Letter 168, 259, 356,
  362, 368, 445
Belfast Relief Fund 309
Belfast Telegraph 408, 465
Belfast Woman, A (Beckett) 432,
  480
bells, saints' 21, 64
Benburb, Co. Tyrone 223
benefices, outsiders appointed to
  72–3, 280
Bennett, Art 135, 141, 273–4, 364,
  366–7
Benson family 86–7
Beresford family 109
Betsy Gray and the Hearts of Down
  (Lyttle) 262–3
Bible
  as anti-popish symbol 156, 157
  Catholics' ignorance of 129
  Douay version 282
  foreign 137
  Irish-language 129, 273, 274,
    275, 277
  Protestant 282
  in vernacular 202

Bigger, F. G. 368
bigotry
  Catholic 468
  Catholics and 366, 439
  Protestant 468
  qualitative difference 468
'Big Wind' (1839) 282
'Billy Bluff and Squire Firebrand'
  (satire) 232–3
Bíobla Gallda 273
bishops 71, 72
  authority 66, 71
  and Catholic loyalty 214
  church-building 199, 200, 201
  and landed families 190
  and mixed marriage 179
  penal laws and 167, 175, 176,
    177, 198–9
  political quietism 279
  status 59
  Stuart nomination 207
  support for friars 208, 209
  titles 319
  titles, use 167
  and welfare state 464
  see also hierarchy
Black, Samuel 361–2
black economy 437
Blacker, Col. William 345–6
Black Pig's Dyke 9
Blake, Anthony, archbishop of
  Armagh 208–9
Blaney, Neil 419
Bloody Sunday (Derry 1972) 421,
  422, 473, 476
Bloomfield, Ken 424
Boer War (1899–1902) 283
bog xxx, 27, 31, 195
Bogside, Derry 358, 417
Bonamargy friary, Ballycastle 128
Book of Invasions
  see Lebor Gabála
Book of Martyrs (Foxe) 336
Book of the Taking of Ireland
  see Lebor Gabála
booleying 35, 36

Boullaye le Gouz 154
boundaries, provincial 8–9, 378
Boundary Commission (1925) 300,
    301, 373, 378, 379, 396
boycotts 223, 383, 393
Boylaugh, Co. Donegal 120
Boyne, battle (1690) 116, 344
Boyne valley, Co. Meath 5
Brantry, Co. Tyrone 62
Brehon Laws 43, 45
brehons 45–6
Breifne (Cavan) 26, 50
Brennan, Francis 275
Brennan, Mary 341
Brennan family, Drumcullen 339
Brewer, John 440
Brian Boru, High King 17, 18
Brigid, St 76, 286
British Army
    Bloody Sunday (1972) 421, 422
    Catholics in 446
    mistakes leading to IRA
        recruitment 419, 420–21
    post-1798 264
    Troubles (1969–   ) 419–20
    welcomed by Catholics 419
British Government
    and discrimination 394, 395
    post-partition 423
    and prisoners 448, 449
    Troubles, view of 423
'Brockan-men' 310
Brooke, Sir Basil, Lord
    Brookeborough 391–2, 393,
    407
Brooke, Charlotte 232
Broughshane, Co. Antrim 275
Browne, Noel 464
Brown Square, Belfast 325, 353
Bruce Wars (1315–18) 27, 29
Bruford, Alan 60
Brunt, May 339–40
'B' Specials
    Catholics to join 376
    deployment (1969) 418
    disbanded (1970) 419, 422
    petty harassment 381, 382–3
    sectarianism 380–82
    see also Ulster Special
        Constabulary
Buckland, Patrick 388
Bullock, Shan 340
burial customs 63, 154, 178
Burke, David 348
Burke, Raymond 379
Burntollet ambush (1969) 415,
    416–17
Burton, Frank 438
business vote 385
Byrne, John 221, 222, 255
Byrne, Patrick 255

Cait Bhreaca 273
Caldwell, Sir James 188
Caledon, Co. Tyrone 103, 412–13
Call My Brother Back (McLaverty)
    375–6
Calvinism 70, 71
Camden, Lord (John Jeffreys Pratt,
    2nd earl) 245
Cameron Commission (1969) 385,
    387, 388, 412, 419
    and police 383, 415–16
Campaign for Social Justice (CSJ)
    412
Campbell, T. J. 397
Campbells, MacDonnells' enmity
    for 104
Campion, Edmund 48, 62, 65, 66,
    67
Carleton, William 179, 180, 181,
    185, 201, 207–8, 241, 284,
    289, 346
Carlingford, Co. Down 244
Carlisle Circus, Belfast 358
Carrickfergus, Co. Antrim 69, 181
Carrick Hill, Belfast 358
Carrive, Co. Armagh 224
Carson, Sir Edward 409
Carter, Charles 411, 460, 465
Carter, Revd Dean 346
Casement, Roger 368

Cashel, Synod of (1101) 44
cashels 14
Castleblaney, Co. Monaghan 311
Castle of Glasdrummond
(MacCooey) 140
Castlereagh, Lord (Robert Stewart,
Viscount) 237, 263
Castlewellan, Co. Down 349–51
Catherine of Braganza, Queen
Consort 113
Catholic Book Society 282
Catholic Church
authoritarianism xxxvii, 466,
468, 475
catechesis, popular 155, 202–5,
206, 207
as community 283–4, 469, 474
conservatism 230
criticism, internal 466, 468, 475,
476, 479
denounces IRA 402
'devotional revolution' 280–86
and education 180, 277
18th-century recovery 198–210
episcopal structure 71–2
and Gaelic Revival 455–6
and integrated education 459
internal debate 472, 475
Irish, separate development 149,
154
liberalisation 475
and MacPherson Bill (1919) 460,
461
and mixed marriage 341
modern characteristics 269
modernism, campaign against 365
in nationalist press 450–51
national *vs* universal 59
19th-century revival 269–70,
278, 280–86, 291
penal laws and 163–4, 165–77,
180, 198–9
power, growing 351
Protestant perception of xxiv, 273
and 1798 rebellion 259
secularism, campaign against 365

secular leadership 265, 293
and separate education 277–8,
458–9
and Sinn Féin 472, 474
social status within 132–3
and Troubles (1969–) 470–81
and United Irishmen 230
voluntary work 474
see also Catholicism; clergy
Catholic Committee 190, 227, 244,
330
Convention (1792–3) 236–9
and Defenders 235
elections 231, 236, 239
middle class and 192, 213
and oath of allegiance 216
perceived threat 235
Ulster and 187
and ultra-Protestantism 241–2
and United Irishmen 190
Catholic Convention (1792–3)
236–9
Catholic Emancipation 168,
220–21, 228–9, 236–7,
238–9, 271–2, 292, 342, 347,
348
Catholic Enlightenment 173
Catholic Institute, Belfast 295,
329–30
Catholicism
anti-English nationalism 76,
294
anti-Protestantism 294
Calvinist hostility towards 70
church-based devotions 282
as cultural and political identity
450–57
as dangerous political system
105–6
Gaelic heritage 75–80
middle-class morality in 284–5
militant continental 146
nationalism and 457
and oath of supremacy 143
oral tradition 130
persecution 126, 149

'pick-and-mix' 475
political 143–9, 168, 291
politics, clerical domination of
    294–6
private practice 144
public practice as defiance 451
as religion 457–70
and sacred landscape 288
southern 475
superiority, perceived 183
survival 126–7
see also Catholics, popery
Catholic Qualification Oath (1774)
    216
Catholic Qualification Rolls 189
Catholics, Ulster 127–32
    alienation from state xxiv–xxv,
        264, 266, 271, 422, 458
    arms, keeping 182, 186, 221, 242,
        347
    and arts 323
    assertiveness 335, 336, 351
    attendance at mass 431
    and Belfast xxvi
    bitterness 442–3
    British 456–7
    and British connection 481
    community organisation 323,
        466, 470
    conservatism 396, 398
    discrimination against 384–94
    disinheriting 175
    disloyalty, perceived 100, 106,
        146, 147–8, 170, 181, 221,
        226, 238, 248, 391–2, 393,
        395–6, 401, 406, 435
    distinctive qualities 121
    divided by Troubles 428
    and early church 13
    Elizabethan stereotypes 361
    emigration 192–3
    employment 194, 323–4, 327,
        330, 341, 384, 387, 460
    family size 192, 407
    and fundraising 328–9
    as Gaels xxv, 128, 363, 369

inferiority, perceived 182, 335,
    343, 432–3
and integrated education 459
jury service 176
land ownership 116
and the law 225, 343–4
as minority 131
mobility, resistance to 192, 198
moral dignity 441, 442
nationalism 215, 396
occupations 327–8
oppression, theme 365
as people 440
and polite society 163
political awareness, 18th-century
    213–19
political identity 335
and political Protestantism 479
population, percentage of xx,
    325, 435
powerlessness, perceived 422
Presbyterians, perceptions of 233
prosperity 186–91
in Protestant areas 432
Protestant perceptions of 146,
    170–71, 181–2, 210, 216, 221,
    230–31, 343, 417–18, 434–5,
    436–7, 440
Protestants, perceptions of 156,
    215, 337, 446
as 'real' Irish xxv, 4, 363, 369
rebelliousness, perceived 383–4,
    441, 481
'Roman' prefix 168, 362
romantic nationalism 367–8
rural 318
self-image 456
self-protective mechanism 446
sensitivity to scorn 362
social class 327–31
social life 326
and southerners 338
status 121–2, 185–94, 217,
    305
stereotypes 163, 228, 231, 238,
    432–40

Catholics, Ulster – *cont.*
structural disadvantage 323–5, 327
touchiness 432–3
as underclass 194
unemployment 358
victimhood xxxviii, 362–3
voting pattern 291, 294, 299
wealth 328–9
winners, perceived as 422
Catholic Truth Society of Ireland 369, 451, 470
cattle 32, 35, 36
Cattle Raid of Cooley
see Táin Bó Cuailnge
Cavan county xli–xlii
Cromwellian confiscations 109
English in 90
Famine 305, 307, 309
Home Rule 297
land grants 90
land tenure 41
and Partition xlii
Plantation 91
proselytism in 273, 275
succession disputes 51
ceasefires, IRA 473
Céili Dé movement 20
céilís 452, 455
Celtic Ulster 4–6, 7–10
cemeteries, sharing 166, 340
Cenél Conaill 10
Cenél nEógain 10, 18, 19, 26
censuses, religious 170, 195, 198
'chapel-gate' election (1949) 399
Charlemont, Lord (James Caulfield, 1st earl) 153, 222, 265
Charles I, King 108, 144, 337
Charles II, King 107, 111–14
Charter schools 171–3, 178, 180, 205, 277
Chichester, Arthur, Lord Deputy 85, 88–9, 90, 94
chiefs, Gaelic
inauguration ceremonies 36–8, 40
loss of 84, 85, 92

and Plantation 96
and settlers 86
see also lordships
Chiericati, Bishop 61, 66
children, in textile industry 323
Children of the Dead End (MacGill) 315
Chonaire, Flaithrí Ó Maoil 75, 76
Christian Brothers 278, 281, 283, 328, 389
history teaching 366, 367
Christianity 9, 10, 12–17, 20–21
Church Education Society 277
churches
building 270, 282, 283, 309, 328, 329
early Protestant 200
medieval 64
shortage 199–201, 202, 282
Churchill, Lord Randolph 358
Churchill, W. S. 379
church lands 38
attacked 69
confiscated 52
landholding 43–5
Plantation and 45, 96
repossession 99
Church of Ireland
Calvinism 70
conformity with England 99
disestablishment (1869) 167
exclusivity 70
land 91, 327
and National schools 277
and poor Irish 129
churls 43, 84
Cistercian friars 60, 62
civil liberties, suspension 382
civil rights campaign 385, 422
aims 476
bishops and 471
and Catholic confidence 476
emergence (1960s) 408
Protestant perceptions of 395, 415, 417
protests 411–15, 433–4

reforms, achieving 442
see also Northern Ireland Civil
Rights Association
civil service, Catholics and 378, 383,
388, 389–91, 393, 409
Clanbrassil, Lord (James Hamilton,
1st earl) 176
Clandeboye estates 88, 89
Clare county 107
Clark (Lisburn innkeeper) 257–8
Claudy seminary, 201
Cleland, Revd John 233
clergy
absentee 61, 72, 73
alms, questing for 152, 153
assertiveness 340
authority 207–8
civic culture, lack 458
and civil-rights movement 471
constitutional nationalism 299,
300
continental training 70–71, 74,
150, 169
dress 282
economic dependence 147,
149–50
education 150–51, 282
and education 459, 462, 476
18th-century 202
executions 69, 72
failings of 151, 152–3, 155
and Famine relief 309
hereditary succession 65
history, teaching 364–5, 366
increase 327–8
independence 202
and IRA 457, 471–2
and Irish language 67, 71,
451–2
and the law 184
lay nomination 149
lower 149, 152
loyalty 264
marriage 44, 65, 72
in medieval tales 60–61
and modern politics 446

and nationalism 292, 293, 295–6,
474, 476
oath of abjuration (1709) 165
and oath of allegiance 217
and O'Connell campaign 271
penal laws and 164, 165–6
persecution 149–50
and Plunkett 144
as political leaders 457
politics, non-involvement 229–30
poverty 149–50
pro-Spanish 72, 73
Protestant 461, 462
Protestant perceptions of 292
and republicans 446
respect for 151, 203, 239, 242–3,
264
role xxiv
'Rome-running' 61, 65
and 'Second Reformation' 272–3
secular 209
sheltering 174
shortage 208, 209
as social leaders 117
and state schools 461, 462
status 132–3, 151, 159
training 66, 202, 466–7
Troubles and 475–6
and United Irish Society 230
violence, opposition to 457
Clifton St, Belfast 358
Cloghaneely, Co. Donegal 316
Clogher, Co. Tyrone 6, 65
Clogher diocese 60, 177, 199, 406
Clonard Monastery, Belfast 404,
470
Clondehorky parish, Co. Donegal
65
Cloughcur, Co. Antrim 310
coarb land 44
Coigley, Revd James 244, 248, 255
Coigley family 188
Coile, Bernard 190–91
Coleman, Revd Ambrose 362
Coleraine, Co. Derry 29, 30, 92,
409

Collins, Michael 376, 377, 379, 396
Colton, John, archbishop of Armagh 44
Columba
  see Colum Cille
Colum Cille 16, 37, 64, 76, 249, 250–51, 276
Combe, Barbour and Combe foundry, Belfast 324
comfort, Gaelic disregard 32–3, 101, 186, 340
Common Law, English 85, 86
Commonwealth, Ulster Catholic support 126, 147
communism, Catholic Church and 469
community relations
  landlords and 307
  marching season 346–7, 349–51, 352–3
  O'Connell campaign and 272
  post-1798 263–4
  rural 317, 318, 319, 320
  1920s 374–9
  17th century 153
  18th century 178–85, 219
  19th century 272, 276, 338–42
Community Relations Commission 420, 424, 467
Conall Cernach 5
Conchobar mac Nessa, king of Ulaid 5, 49
concubinage 65
Confederate War (1641–53) 147, 148
confession, sacrament 66
Confessions (St Patrick) 13
confirmation, sacrament 66, 201, 202
Congested Districts Board 316
Connacht 98, 107, 108, 110, 118
Connachta 5, 9
Connolly, Revd Francis 447
Connolly, Revd James 362, 365
Conroy, Felix 257

Conry, Florence 75, 76
Conry family 118
conscience, freedom of 147, 166
Conservative party 320, 321, 357, 420, 422
Constitution, Irish (1937) 458
conversational topics, avoidance 437–8, 445
conversion, religious 251
  Charter schools and 171–3
  death-bed 287
  food-relief and 310, 311
  material reward for 273
  as treason 157–8
Conway, Cardinal William 409, 471, 472, 474
Cooke, Revd Henry 180, 231, 271, 275, 279, 305
Cooper, Ivan 423
Coote family 109
Corish, Monsignor Patrick 143, 270
Cork county 118
Cornwallis, Lord (Charles, 1st marquis) 260
Corrigan Park, Belfast 470
Cosgrave, John 119
Cosgrave, Liam, Taoiseach 379
Costello, John, Taoiseach 406
cottiers 284
council housing, discrimination in 378, 386–7, 408, 411
Council of Ireland (1920) 300, 425
Council of Trent (1545–63) 70, 75, 276, 282
Counter-Reformation 65, 66, 68, 70–72, 73–4, 75, 78, 129, 146, 150
'country', overlordship 38
'couple-beggars' 179
Court of Claims, Restoration 112, 115
Covenanters, Scottish 99, 229
Cox, Watty 363
'coyne and livery' 30, 50
Craig, James (Lord Craigavon) 375,

376, 377, 379, 382, 392, 394,
397, 399–400, 452
Craig, William 413, 414–15, 425
Craigavon, Co. Armagh 409
crannogs 6, 14
Crawford, W. H. 131
creaghting 35, 36
Crebilly, Co. Antrim 95
Creevy Rocks rebel camp 255
Creggan, Co. Armagh 63, 222, 223
Creichton, George 101
Cress-stoney, Co. Cavan 180–81
criminal law 55
Crolly, William, archbishop of
Armagh 181, 272, 277, 278,
279, 291
Cromwell, Henry 107
Cromwell, Oliver 100, 106–7,
107–11, 143
Crossmaglen, Co. Armagh 310–11
Cruithin 4, 10, 17, 19
CS gas 420
Cú Chulainn 4–5, 7, 139, 404, 443
Culdees 20, 62
Cullen, Cardinal Paul 270, 279–81,
284, 291, 293, 368
Cullen, Louis 244
Cullyhana, Co. Armagh 473
Cultural Traditions Group 453
culture, Irish 195, 369
Education Ministry and 452
medieval pride in 46
rebelliousness and 452–3
religion as 478–9
18th-century revival 214
written works in 78
Cummins, Anne 355
'cures' 287–8
curfew (1970) 420
Curran, Bob 287–8, 452
Currie, Austin 412, 423
Curtin, Nancy 247
Cuthbert, Joseph 243

Dáil Éireann 373, 396, 399
Daley, Charles 409

Dál Fiatach 9, 49
Dál nAraide 10, 16, 17, 18
Dál Riata 9, 17
Daly, Cardinal Cahal 474
Daly, Edward, bishop of Derry 473
Dane's Cast, Co. Armagh 9
Dan the Dollar (Bullock) 340
Davies, Sir John 31, 39, 41, 45, 51,
52, 85–6, 90
Day, Judge 358
Deane, Seamus 477
De Cobain, Wesley 361
decommissioning, arms 481
de Courcy, John 26, 31
Defenderism 239–43, 249
Defenders 215, 225, 235, 249, 296
excommunication 248
revived 254, 262
and United Irishmen 230, 237,
244–9, 253, 254, 265
deference, traditional 198, 227
Deirdriu (Deirdre) of the Sorrows 5
demesne lands 38, 41
Democratic Unionist Party 425, 437
demography
change, Protestants and 435
religious xxxix–xlii, 194–8, 229
17th-century changes 131
Dempsey, Larry 253
Denvir, Cornelius, bishop of Down
and Connor 278, 283
derbfine 5
Derricke, John 63
Derry city
Bloody Sunday (1972) 421, 422,
473
borough police 343
Catholic Church in 359
Catholics in 335
community relations 358–60
Council 373, 415
in fiction 477
first Catholic mayor 373
PD march (1968) 414–15
Plantation 91
religious demography xlii, 326

Derry city – *cont.*
  RUC behaviour 416
  sectarian riots (1920s) 374
  Troubles (1969-) 417
  unemployment (1960s) 411
  as university site 409
  use of name xx–xxi
Derry county 10
  bog xli
  Catholics in minority 195
  improving landlords 307
  land tenure 41
  United Irish Society 257
  Volunteers 221
Derry diocese 60, 201
detention
  powers (1920s) 382
  see also internment
De Valera, Eamon 299, 386, 394,
  402, 405, 406, 458
Devenish cemetery, Fermanagh 193
Devlin, Bernadette xxiv, 414, 443,
  455, 466
Devlin, Joe 296, 297, 299, 330, 379,
  396–7, 398, 399, 404
Devlin, Paddy 404, 420, 422–3,
  425, 428
devolved government, and
  discrimination 388
Devon Commission 307
devotional literature 64, 66
devotions, Catholic 469
Dickey, James 259, 262
Dickey family 174
Dickson, George 262
Dickson, Revd William Steel 252
difference, badges of 335
Digest of Popery Laws (Butler) 231
diocesan organisation 17
direct rule 422, 426
discrimination 384–94
  Catholic institutions and 465
  Protestant perceptions of 395
  use in explanation 441
dispensations 65
dispossession 52, 54, 83

Dissenters, emigration 192
distilling, forbidden 218
Divis Flats, Belfast 418
Divis St, Belfast 418
divorce, attitudes to 475
Dockside, Belfast 326, 393, 394
Doherty, Paddy 83, 479
Dolan, Myles 158–9
Dolly's Brae, Co. Down 349–51
domestic service 341
dominion status 300
Domhnach Mór (Ó Doibhlin) 158
Donaghmore, Co. Tyrone 65, 96
Donaldson, John 363
Donegal county 10
  Catholic life (1870s) 287
  Cromwellian confiscations 109
  as escape 477
  fairies, belief in 289–90
  hiring fairs 313, 314
  holy wells 286
  Home Rule 297
  inauguration ceremonies 36
  landlords 307, 319–20
  mountain ranges 31
  19th-century life 313–14, 316–17
  and oath of allegiance 217
  and Partition xlii
  Plantation 91
  and Protestant tenants 195
  1798 Rebellion 252
  tories 118
  Ulster Irish in 93
  United Irishmen 246
  Volunteers 221
Donegall Rd, Belfast 394
Donegan family 310
Donegore Hill, Co. Antrim 259–60
Donnelly, Alex 393
Donnelly, Patrick 299
Donoghue, Betty 354–5
Doon Well, near Kilmacrenan 286,
  287
Dorrian, Patrick, bishop of Down
  and Connor 281, 283, 284,
  292–3, 295–6, 328, 329–30

Dorsey, Co. Armagh 9
Douay Bibles 282
Dougall, Hugh 379
Down and Connor diocese 60, 451,
    466–7
Down county xl
    Anglo-Norman 26, 27
    Boundary Commission and 379
    Catholic Convention members
    237
    Catholics in minority 195, 243
    community relations (1790s) 238
    constituency size 217
    excluded from Plantation 89, 91
    Famine 308, 313
    Irish language in 205
    local councils 373
    National schools 277
    Patrick cult 26
    Protestant fears 352
    1641 rebellion 106
    1798 rebellion 255–8
    settlers 86–8
    Troubles (1780s/1790s) 223, 224,
    226–7
    Ulster Irish in 93
    United Irishmen 233, 238, 251,
    252
Downpatrick, Co. Down 6, 12, 14,
    45, 61, 86–7, 181, 319, 326,
    383, 458, 468
Downshire, Lord (Arthur Hill, 2nd
    marquis) 227, 235, 244
Doyle, Lynn 337, 338, 339, 344,
    347, 352–3
Drennan, William 194, 216
dress, Irish 34, 92
Drew, Revd Thomas 354, 355–6,
    362
Drogheda, synod (1614) 74
Dromintee, Co. Armagh 316
Dromore, Co. Down 181
Dromore diocese 60
druids 36, 61
Druim Cett, Convention of (AD
    575) 16

Drumbanagher pattern 223
Drumbee 223
drumlins xxix, 3
Drumswords churchyard,
    Monaghan 348
drunkenness, Catholic Church and
    285
Dublin, 1798 rebellion 252
Dublin University 239
Duffy, Charles Gavan 336, 338,
    344, 364, 367
Duigenan, Patrick 238
Dundalk, Co. Louth 181, 316
Dunfanaghy, Co. Donegal 200
Dungannon, Co. Tyrone 387, 412,
    413
Dunleavy family 49

earldoms 50
Easter Rising (1916) 299, 443–4,
    451, 453
Echlin family 86–7
ecumenism (1960s) 410
education xxxvii
    capital grants 462
    Catholic 277, 278, 407, 440, 447,
    452, 461, 462, 467–8
    history teaching 364–5, 366
    integrated 179–80, 336–7, 439,
    459, 476
    legislation, fairness 386
    means test 462–3
    monastic 15
    proselytising 273, 277
    segregated 276–8, 281, 294, 340,
    439, 458–64, 459, 462
    state 439, 463
Education and Enmity (Akenson)
    460
Education Bill (1923) 461, 462
Education Ministry xxxvii, 452,
    460, 463
elections
    Catholic Committee 231, 236,
    239
    Catholics and 181, 217

elections – *cont*
  'chapel-gate' election (1949) 399
  local government 373, 378, 385
  nationalists and 449
  parliamentary 299, 385, 397
  Westminster 401
elementary schools 461
  see also primary schools
eleven-plus examination 463
elite, Gaelic 126, 127
  decline 127
  disunity 111, 113
  and England 89
  and land settlements 84
  status 159
elite, Protestant 117
Elizabeth I, Queen 134
Elizabeth II, Queen 400
Emain Macha (Navan Fort), Armagh
  4, 6–7, 9, 11–12, 47, 49
Émer 5
emigration 192, 306–7, 317, 338
Emmet, Robert 443, 450
Emperor of Ice-Cream, The
  (Moore) 448, 468
employment
  Catholics 194, 323–4, 327, 330,
    384, 387, 460
  discrimination in 386, 387–92
  growth (1950s) 408
  religion and 378
endurance, Catholic tradition 239,
  468–9
engineering industry 408, 417–18,
  437
England
  Catholics and 481
  and Gaelic lords 49–52
  IRA campaign (1939) 402
  land-hunger 86
  Revolutionary wars (1793) 238
  rule over Ireland 25, 61
  war with Spain (1625–30) 94
  war with Spain (1739) 181
  see also British...
English language, status and 181

Enlightenment 172, 207
Enniskillen Co Fermanagh 451
  IRA bomb (1987) 441, 473
  Protestant demonstrations 181
Eóganacht 17
equality in government 481
Érainn 4
erenach land 96
erenachs 44–5, 152
Essex, Arthur Capel, earl of 112,
  144–5
Eucharistic Congress (1932) 443,
  447–8, 470
European Court of Human Rights
  421
evangelism, Protestant 129, 307,
  309–11
eviction, Famine and 309, 310–11
exorcism, priestly 287
extreme unction, sacrament 287

Factory of Grievances (Buckland)
  388
fáinne 454
Fair Employment Agency 387
fairies 8, 282–3, 288
'Faith of Our Fathers' (hymn) 125,
  455
Falls Rd, Belfast 358
  as Catholic area 325, 326
  mills 322
  Troubles (1969–) 394, 404, 420
family allowance 407
famine
  1741 186
  see also Great Famine
Farney, Monaghan 119
Farnham, Lord (John Maxwell, 5th
  baron) 273, 275, 310
Farrell, Michael 398
Farren, Neil, bishop of Derry 458,
  462, 469
Faughart, Co. Louth 141
Faul, Monsignor Denis 441, 472
Faulkner, Brian 410, 416, 425, 426,
  428

Feargal, king 77
feasting, Celtic 7
Feast of Lupercal (Moore) 467
Fenian, use of term 358
Fenians 291–2, 335, 368
Fergus mac Róich 5
Fermanagh county xli
  bog xli
  Boundary Commission and 379
  'B' Specials 380
  confiscated lands conspiracy
    (1625) 94
  Cromwellian confiscations 110
  elections 385, 386
  gavelkind 39
  genealogies 39
  IRA activity 406
  land tenure 41
  local councils 373
  Maguire lands 40
  Nine Years War 54
  and oath of allegiance 217
  Plantation xlii, 91
  succession disputes 51
Fews barony, Co. Armagh 119, 120,
  136, 140, 196, 363
Fews mountain 9
Fianna Fáil government 419
Fianna (Finn MacCumhail) 10–11
Fianna (republican youth) 404
fiction, Northern Irish 477–8, 480
Fife, William 320
Fife family 339
Finnian, St 15, 16
Finn MacCumhail 10–11
Fitt, Gerry 412, 413, 422–3, 425,
  428
Fitzpatrick, David 317, 341
Fitzsimmons family 87
Fitzwilliam, Sir William, Lord
  Deputy 52
Fitzwilliam, William Wentworth,
  2nd earl 243, 245
Flanders 118
flashpoints, traditional 195, 243,
  327

Flight of the Earls (1607) 53, 54, 55,
  85, 89, 92
floggings (1922) 382
Flood family 339–40
Flower, Robin 10
folklore, Protestant view 287–8
Foras Feasa ar Éirinn 79
forenames, as labels 455
forests 27, 30, 35–6
Forkhill, Co. Armagh 141, 222,
  223, 224, 273–4, 406
Fortnight magazine xliii
Foster, Anthony 165
Foster, Roy 369
France, and United Irishmen 246,
  249–50, 262
franchise
  business vote 385
  Catholics 291, 294, 324
Franciscan friars 60, 61, 62
  and Gaelic heritage 75–80
  missions 73–4
  and Plunkett 144
  Plunkett and 150, 151, 152, 153
  Third Order Secular 62
Franciscan Observant friars 63–4
Franco, General Francisco 469
Freeduff, Co. Armagh 178, 222
freeholders 40, 41, 42, 50–52, 53,
  88–9, 92
Freeman's Journal 310
Free State, Irish
  civil war (1922–3) 373, 377, 378
  and compulsory Irish 452
  and discrimination in NI 394
  emergency powers (1920s) 382
  and northern Catholics 376–7,
    379
  and northern sectarianism 376–7
  pact with Craig 376–7, 379, 381
  Protestants in 363, 373
  provisional government 376
  retaliatory sectarianism 394
  schools 461
  Ulster counties in 379
French Revolution 213, 215

friaries, foundation 63
friars 62–4
    abuses 207
    affection for 203, 207, 209–10
    Counter-Reformation 73–4, 78
    decline 207, 208, 209, 210
    devotional literature 67
    education abroad 207
    episcopal authority 71, 72
    as Gaelic elite 75
    itinerant 200, 207
    power 203
    pro-Spanish 73
    recruitment 75
    suppressing 173
    traditional training 72
    and weddings 179
friendship, across divide 126, 174,
    339
fundamentalist preachers 353–4,
    355–6, 410
fund-raising, Catholic 465–6

Gael, use of word 132
Gaelic Athletic Association (GAA)
    xxxiv, 369, 454, 455
Gaelic culture 195, 369
Gaelic League 368–9, 452–3, 454
Gaelic Revival 46, 285–8, 367–8,
    369, 455
Gaelic Ulster xxxviii, xxxix, 4, 25
    Counter-Reformation and 70–72
    disunity 111, 113
    familial structure 61–2
    frontier 29
    gallowglass families 29–30
    life in 30–34
    lords 30, 87, 94, 97
    power in 113
    pragmatism 26
    Protestantism and 69
    provincialism 73
    Reformation in 61, 68–70
    religious practice 60, 64–5, 66–8
    society in 84, 95
    status in 117

Gaeltacht, Donegal 454
Gall, use of word 46, 132
Gallagher, Revd Eric 459
Gallagher, James, bishop of Raphoe
    204, 205, 282
gallowglasses 29–30, 86, 110
Galway county 109
Gamble, John 198, 287, 290,
    335–7, 341, 362
gavelkind 39–40, 41
genealogy
    falsification 19, 77
    importance 5, 95, 118, 193
    religion and 72
    and status 39–40
    tracing 19
'general confession of Fiachra Mac
    Brádaigh, The' 155–6
General Remonstrance of the
    Catholics of Ireland (1641)
    156–7
gentry, Catholic 189, 190
geography, religious
    see demography, religious
George I, King 200
George III, King 243, 261
George VI, King 400
Germany, IRA negotiations with
    403
gerrymandering 378, 385, 388, 392
ghettos, religious 295, 326, 328,
    356, 378, 381
Giffard, John 247
Giraldus Cambrensis 8, 11, 13, 20,
    106
Give Them Stones (Beckett) 433,
    477
Gladstone, W. E. 167, 294, 320,
    357
Glassie, Henry 306, 348, 479
Glenard estate, Belfast 394
Glenarm, Co. Antrim 309
Glencolumbkille, Co. Donegal 365
Glens of Antrim 190
    Catholicism xl
    Gaelic-speaking 171

landscape xl, xlii
linen industry and 195
Protestant tenants 195
Scots settlers 29
toryism 118, 176
Ulster Irish in 93
Glenties, Co. Donegal 311, 329
Glenveagh evictions (1861) 319
gods, Celtic 8
Golden Age, Irish 15
gombeenmen 327, 329
Good Friday Agreement (1998) 426,
476-7, 481
Gortin, Co. Tyrone 95
Gosford Castle, Co. Armagh 225,
245
grammar schools, means test 462-3
grand juries 236
Grattan, Henry 168
Gray, Elizabeth (Betsy) 263
Gray, John 330
Great Famine (1845-9) xl, 305-13
Catholics affected by 305
collective amnesia and 308
cottiers decimated 284
in folk memory 306, 469
Protestants in 306, 308
relief schemes 307-8, 309-11,
312
souperism 273
Green, Alice Stopford 368
Greencastle, Belfast 326
Gregory, Augusta, Lady 11
Grianán of Ailech, Co. Donegal 6
grievance, culture of 362-3, 440-50
Grimshaw's Mill 354, 355
guns
see arms
Gwynn family 312

Haliday, Dr Alexander 265
Hall, S. C., Mr and Mrs 322
Hall-Thompson, Colonel 407,
461
Hamill, John 328
Hamilton, Sir Claud 95

Hamilton, Sir George 114, 128
Hamilton, Sir James 87, 88
Hamilton family 339-40
Hancock, John 345
Hanna, Revd Hugh 276, 356, 361
Harbison, Thomas 299
Harkness, David 378
Harland & Wolff shipyard, Belfast
323-4, 325, 330
Catholics in 323-4, 375, 394
intimidation in 324
Orangeism 356
Harris, Rosemary 466
Harris, Walter 45, 172, 178, 205,
206
Hassan, Revd John 377-8
Haughey, Charles 419
Hayes, Maurice 383, 420, 423-4,
466-7, 468, 469
healing 287-8
Healy, Cahir 396
hearth-money 218
Hearts of Steel 218-19
Heath, Sir Edward (later Lord) 424,
425
Heatley, Fred 394
hedge-schools 164, 179-81, 277,
447
Henry, Henry, bishop of Down and
Connor 296, 330
Henry II, King 13, 25, 36, 60, 61,
136
Henry VIII, King 50, 134
Hepburn, Tony 326
Hercules St (later Royal Ave),
Belfast 253, 325
hereditary land title 50, 51
heretic, use of word 136
Hervey, Frederick, Bishop of Derry
169-70
Heskin, Ken 434, 440
Hezlet, Sir Arthur 381
hierarchy, Catholic
authoritarianism 295
gradualist approach 227, 270
as outsiders 151

hierarchy, Catholic – *cont.*
  and partition 297–8, 300–301
  see also Catholic Church; bishops
higher education xxxvii, 433–4
High Kingship 12, 17
Hill, Sir George 307
Hill, Jacqueline 363
Hill, Sir Moses 87, 113
Hill family 113, 227
hill-forts 6–7
hills 27, 35–6, 131
Hillsborough, Wills Hill, 2nd
  viscount (later Downshire) 175,
  218
hiring fairs 313–15
Historical Memoirs of Armagh
  (Stuart) 362
history, Irish
  Protestants and 452, 479
  teaching 364–5, 366, 452, 460
Hobson, Bulmer 368
Hole in the Wall Gang 431
holy days 201–2
holy places, importance 45
holy wells 286
Holywood, Co. Down 178
Home Affairs Ministry 382, 389,
  390, 413
Home Rule
  campaign 293–4, 344, 360, 364
  opposition to 357
  Protestants and 295, 297
  and Protestant unemployment
  357, 361
  as 'Rome Rule' 320, 363
  Ulster excluded 297–9
Hood family 193
Hope, Bob 404
Hope, James 254, 256, 258, 259
horsemanship 33
hospitality, Gaelic 94–5, 198
housing
  allocation xxii, 378, 386–7, 408,
  411
  exchanges 378, 379
  Gaelic 30–31, 32–3

plantation 91
points system 411
provision xxxv
shortage 386–7, 408
two-storey 32
Housing Trust xxii, 386, 408
Howe, Leo 437
Hudson, Revd Edward 223, 262
Hughes, Bernard 329, 330
Hughes, Terence 189
Hume, Cardinal 472
Hume, John 366, 401, 423, 425,
  427, 428
humour, Ulster xxxv–xxxvi, 431,
  477
hunger strikes (1981) 426–7,
  448–50, 472, 473, 476
Hussey, Thomas, Bishop of
  Waterford and Lismore 248
huts, monastic 14, 60, 62

identity
  anti-popery in 440
  axioms of 83
  Catholicism as 450–57
  dual, conflict between 427, 437–8
  formation in opposition 156–7
  and past 445
  political 335
  republican 446–7
  sectarian awareness and 269
  secular 160
  social class and 328
  stereotypical cues 198
  in transition 476, 478
  Ulster Catholic xxxiii–xxxiv, 152,
  156, 361–9, 440, 442, 445,
  476–8
  Ulster Protestant 70, 352, 353, 440
Ignorantia sacerdotum 66
illegitimacy 65
illuminated manuscripts 15
image-worship 64
Impartial History of Ireland, The
  (Reily) 128–9, 170
inauguration ceremonies 36–8, 40

independence
  Northern Irish 423
  Protestants and 295, 297
indulgences 282
industry
  decline 408, 417–18
  location 437
informers
  IRA and 404
  and penal laws 175
Inishowen, Co. Donegal 3, 86,
    91–2, 128, 149, 178
Inquisition of Dungannon (1609) 44
In Search of a State (O Connor) 125
insecurity, Ulster xxxiii
insult, use 354–5
internment
  clergy and 472
  powers (1920s) 382
  torture in 421
  use (1957) 406
  use (1970) 421
  wartime 403, 423
intimidation 355
  anticipation of 432
  IRA campaign 435
  1790s 226
  Troubles (1969–) 418–19, 432
Iona abbey 37
Irish Catholic Confederacy 91, 134
Irish Church
  and England 61
  English influence 36
  Gaelic chiefs and 60, 70, 73, 74,
    79, 80
  in Gaelic Ulster 36
  indiscipline, monasteries 66–7
  as localised family fiefdom 149–50
  medieval reform 59–60, 61,
    64–5, 68–70
  popular culture 66–7
Irish Folklore Commission 93, 369
Irish Labour Party 398
Irish language
  as Catholic code 369, 453
  communication and 314–15

compulsory 452
decline 126, 181, 191, 205, 451
18th-century revival 214
evangelisation and 171
Gaelic League and 368
IRA and 453–4
mountain areas 197
19th-century decline 368
post-partition revival 451–4
Protestant interest in 452
and rebellion 369
religion and 67, 71, 129–30
sectarian vocabulary 132
Unionist condemnation 452–3
use in politics 182
Irish Magazine 363–4
Irish Minstrelsy (Hardiman) 135
Irish Monthly 285
Irish News xxxvi, 295, 377, 389,
    391, 399, 400, 409, 445–6,
    447, 448, 451, 454, 470
Irish Parliament
  abolition 261
  anti-Papist 167–8
  Catholic Relief Bill (1793) 238
  Catholics barred 167, 239
  Catholics in 294
  Old Irish in 97
  prorogation 100
  and Settlement Act 112
  and Temple 115
  and Treaty of Limerick 165
  Williamite 116
Irish Parliamentary Party 294, 295,
    296, 297, 298, 299
Irish Rebellion (Temple) 105–6, 170
Irish Republican Army (IRA) 396,
    442
  Catholics and 419
  and Catholics in police 381
  defence role 403, 419
  growth (1930s) 394
  internment (1970) 421
  1920s 373, 374, 377, 380
  Operation Harvest 406
  post-partition 402–6, 408

Irish Republican Army – *cont.*
  and Troubles (1969-) 419
  see also Official IRA; Provisional
    IRA
Irish Society 277
Irish Volunteers 298
Irish Weekly 445, 447
Irvine, John 337
Islandmagee, Co. Antrim 102, 104
Iveagh, Co Down 26, 49

Jacobitism 164, 168, 169, 213–14
James I, King 50, 69–70, 77, 78, 85,
  86, 89
James II, King 114–16, 131, 199,
  359
James III (Old Pretender) 148, 165,
  169, 207
Jesuits 71, 146
Jesus Christ 64, 67, 139, 154
John, King 29
Johnston, William 320, 363
John XXIII, Pope 408, 409
Jones, Henry, bishop of Clogher
  105, 107, 109, 129, 156
Jonesborough, Co. Armagh 222
Jordan family 86–7
juries
  kin ties 55
  Orange 347, 348

Keating, Geoffrey 79, 137
Kelly, Edward 193
Kelly, James 389
Kelly, Liam 406
Kelly, Revd Terence 145–6
Kennedy, John F. 408
Kernan, Michael 358
Kernan family 193
kerne 30, 92
Kerr, Anne 413
Kerr, Russell 413
Kerry county 118
Kerry militia 246
Killala friary 67
Killeavy, Co. Armagh 93

Killough, Co. Down 114, 172
Killsherdany, Co. Cavan 310
Kilmacrenan, Co. Donegal 36, 37,
  101
Kilmore diocese 60, 202
Kinawley, Co. Fermanagh 329, 367
Kinelarty, Co. Down 26
King, William, archbishop of Dublin
  171, 192
kin-group
  importance 65, 439–40
  as unit of social control 5–6
kingship, concept of 18
Kinnaird, Co. Tyrone 103
Klondike 287
Knox, George 190

Labour party
  and Ulster Workers Strike 426
labour politics 330–31
Lafferty, H. A. 341
laity, religious instruction 282
Lake, General Gerard 246, 259
Lamb, Revd Patrick 274, 364
'Lament for Sorley MacDonnell'
  (Mac Cuarta) 139, 142–3, 214
land
  as commodity 53
  competition for 221
  confiscation 84, 107–11
  Cromwellian settlement 93,
    107–11
  at Crown disposal 85
  discoverers 112
  dispossession 52, 54
  familial 14, 18, 37, 38–9, 41–2,
    318–19
  fertile, natives leave 93
  and Gaelic tradition 35–8, 40
  loss to Protestants 158
  marriage with chief 37
  mortgaged 94
  peasant proprietorship 317
  poor, assignation xl–xlii, 18, 93,
    195–7
  Protestant fears for 167–8, 170

redistribution by lord 40, 42–3
rents 55
Restoration settlement 111–14,
    120, 147
17th-century settlement 120–22
shortage 219, 221
subdivision 40, 41, 42, 305–6
tenure 38–45
tenure, Gaelic 86, 91
title 42, 86–7, 92, 96
units of measurement 42
Williamite settlement 115–17
see also freeholders; land-
    ownership
land-conformism 167
land law, early 14
Land League 293, 319, 320, 321
landlords
    Anglican 318
    Catholic 311
    18th-century 186
    electoral interests 217
    evangelical 273
    in Famine 307–8
    in folk memory 306, 307, 310–11
    improving 307
    Protestant 117
    removal 317–18
    as trustees 319
land-owners
    Catholic, transplantation 108
    Church of Ireland 327
    Protestant 108–9, 110–11, 115
    as tenants 187
land-ownership
    Catholic 114, 121–2
    Gaelic 38, 40–42
    increase 91
    as Protestant 270
    status and 55, 84
'land Protestants' 158–9, 167
landscape
    Catholic 195–7
    Protestant 196, 197
    sacred 288
    see also topography

Land War (1879–82) 318
Larkin, Emmet 270
Larkin, James 330
Larne, Co. Antrim 326
last rites 287
La Tène Celtic culture 4
Latocnaye, Chevalier de 246, 247,
    251
Laudabiliter papal bull 25, 61, 136
law
    Catholics and 225
    Catholics in 327
    Common Law 43, 85, 86
    criminal code 55
    and English language 126, 343–4
    evasion, and penal laws 176
    extension 31
    Irish language and 184
    and landholding 43
    outwitting, culture of 184
Lawless, John 272, 345
Leader, The 366
learning, respect for 231
leases 86
    annual 92
    long 159, 185
Lebor Gabála 9, 15, 48, 76
Lecale, Co. Down 27, 36
Lecky, W. E. H. 111, 247
Lee, Simon xliii
Leech Committee 383
Leinster 248, 252
Leitrim, William Sydney Clements,
    3rd earl 320
Leitrim county 108, 118
Leix county 85
Lemass, Seán 409, 410
Leslie, Henry 129
Leslie family of Monaghan 312
Leth Cuinn 17
Leth Moga 17
Letterkenny, Co. Donegal 313, 314
Letter to Coroticus (Patrick) 13
Liberal party 291, 294, 300,
    320–21, 357
liberty, as Protestant 169

'Lillibullero' 114–15
Limerick, Treaty of (1697) 116
linen industry
  agriculture and 305–6
  Catholics in 186, 187, 188, 189,
    191, 192
  collapse 306
  exports 192
  importance 191–2
  mechanisation 321–3
  Orangeism 345–6
  prosperity and 186
  Protestant 191
  United Irishmen and 244
Lisburn, Co. Antrim 218, 326, 374
Lisnaskea, Co. Fermanagh 290, 308
Lissane parish 65
Lissanoure, Co. Antrim 178–9
Lisselby Roodan, Co. Londonderry
  73
literacy
  English 181
  Ulster Irish 130
Lloyd George, David 300, 378
local government
  elections 373, 378, 385
  employment practices 324, 386,
    387–92
  gerrymandered 462
  Orange influence 324
  and 1641 Rebellion 97
localism, Gaelic 42
Lóegaire, King of Tara 14
Loghenesolyn, Londonderry 73
Logue, Cardinal 300
Loinsigh (Lynch) family 187
Lombard, Peter, archbishop of
  Armagh 72, 73
London companies 143
Londonderry
  County Borough 91–2
  boundaries redrawn 385
  creation 32
  housing, discrimination 387
  Grand Jury 236
  Plantation 91

tories 118
  see also Derry
Londonderry, Charles Stewart
  Henry, 7th marquis 461–2
Londonderry, Charles William
  Stewart, 3rd marquis 307, 309
Londonderry, Robert Stewart, 1st
  marquis 233, 246–7
Londonderry Standard 319–20
London Hibernian Society 170, 277
Lonely Passion of Judith Hearne
  (Moore) 468
Longley, Edna 475, 477
Long Parliament (1640) 99
Lord Lieutenants, weakness 235
lordship, Gaelic 48–56
  and English lordship 49–52
  hospitality 94–5
  and landholding 38
  leadership 94
  and power 38
  succession 51–2
  and toryism 119
  transformed to estates 40
Lough Derg, Co. Donegal 184–5
Lough Foyle fisheries 89
Loughgall, Co. Armagh 49, 91, 103,
  225
Loughgall Volunteers 221
Loughinisland, Co. Down 187
Loughlinstown, Co. Derry 120
Lough Neagh xli, 3, 8, 260
Loughrea, Co. Galway 107
Lough Swilly 218
Louis XIV, King of France 115
Louth county 151, 165, 216–17,
  221, 224–5
Louvain seminary 72, 73, 75–6,
  78–9, 148, 202
Lowry, Alexander 255
loyalty, use of term 395–6
Loyalty League 453
Lurgan, Co. Armagh 326, 327,
  346
Lynch, John 98
Lynch family 187

Lynn, Brendan 398
Lynn Committee (1921) 383, 461–2
Lyons, Maura 410
Lyttle, W. G. 263

MacAingil, Hugh 75
McAlester, Robert 310
McAlindon, Patrick 136–7
Macan, Arthur 251
Macan, Thomas 251
Mac an Bhaird, Aodh 75, 76
Mac an Bhaird, Fearghal Óg 78
Mac Artáin 19
Macartney, Lord 178–9
McAteer, Eddie 399, 401, 413
McAughtry, Sam 453
MacBrádaigh, Fiachra 155–6
McCabe, William Putnam 184
MacCabe family 29
Mac Caghwell, Hugh 75
McCahy, Hugh Roe 241
McCall sept 40
MacCana, Edmund 88
McCann, Anthony 255
McCann, Eamonn 466, 468–9
McCann, Toole 103
McCann family 49
MacCartan, John 116
MacCartan, Revd Patrick 248
MacCartan, Theophilus, bishop of
    Down and Connor 188, 208
MacCartan family 19, 26, 87, 188
MacCary, Revd James 257
McCasey family 96
Mac Cathmhaoil family 75
Mac Cathmhaoil sept 40
MacCawell family 44, 65
McCawll sept 40
MacClave of Aughnamullen
    (O'Donnelly) 150–51, 153
McClay, Bab 290
McClelland, Revd 275
McCluskey, Conn 399, 400,
    411–12, 413
McCluskey, Patricia 411–12, 413
McComiskey, William 338

MacConnell family 29
MacCooey, Art 139–42, 143, 182,
    183, 186, 204, 213, 217, 223
McCourt, Frank 444
McCourt, Malachy 444
McCracken, Henry Joy 217, 252–3,
    254, 255, 264
McCracken, Mary Anne 182, 217
McCrudden, Turlough 73, 74, 78
McCrystal, Cal 408, 454
Mac Cuarta, Séamus Dall 136,
    137–9, 142–3, 157, 214
McCullough, Rose 315
McDaid (tory leader) 139
McDevitt, Philip 201, 208
Mac Domhnaill, Aodh 274–5, 276,
    366
MacDonald, Alistair 103–4
MacDonald, Ramsay 331
MacDonnell, Alexander 103–4
McDonnell, Hugh 274–5, 276, 312,
    313, 342–3, 366
McDonnell, Patrick 255
MacDonnell, Sorley Boy 139, 142–3
MacDonnells of Antrim 72, 138
    friaries 63
    and James I 87
    lands 87–8
    and 1641 Rebellion 98
    religion 117
    restored 113, 116–17
    Scots Catholic tenants 128
    and settlers 88
    status 87–8, 95
McDonnells of Antrim
    see also Antrim, earls
MacDonnells of Ballygawley 29
MacDonnells of the Isles 27, 29,
    30
MacDowall family 29
Mac Duinn Slébhe 49
McElroy, Gerald 475, 476
MacEnaney, Patrick 193
MacEnaney family 193
McEnhill, Hugh 338
MacFadden, Canon James 329

McFadden, Mrs 433
McFall, Michael 189
MacGerrity, Hugh 139
McGildowney, Edmund 237
McGildowney, Eugene 190
MacGill, Patrick 285, 315, 329
MacGill family 29
McGlinchey, Patrick 204, 207
McGlone, John 298, 299, 343
McGlone, Teag 73
MacGowan, Michael 287, 313–14, 315–17, 319, 326
McGuinness, Martin 459
McGurk, Revd Bernard 145
Macha, horse-goddess 7
MacHale, John, archbishop of Tuam 278, 279
McHugh, Charles, bishop of Derry 298
Mack, John 441
Mackan, Co. Fermanagh 348–9
McKee, Joseph 341
Macken, Simon 142–3
McKenna, Nugent 175
McKenna family 188
McKittrick, David 432
McKnight, James 319–20, 359, 368
McLaughlin family 237
MacLaverty, Bernard 438
McLaverty, Michael 375–6
McLaverty, Revd B. 448
McLeod, Hugh 270
Mac Liammóir, Mícheál 443
Mac Lochlainn family 19, 28
McLorinan, Paul 167
MacLoughlin family 49
MacMahon, Colla MacBrian 114
MacMahon, Hugh, archbishop of Armagh 97, 132, 136, 177, 194, 199, 215–16
MacMahon, Hugh, bishop of Clogher 173
MacMahon, Hugh Roe 52
McMahon, Owen 375
McMahon murders 375, 443

MacMahons of Monaghan 19, 29, 31, 34, 40, 188
    mortgaged lands 94
    and surrender and regrant 50
McManus, Honoria 167
MacManus, Seamas 226, 273, 289–90, 329, 337, 339, 367
Mac Mathgamna 19
McNally, Leonard 239
McNeill, Daniel 189
McParlan, James 197
McPeake, Francis 368
McQuaid, Revd Matt 310
MacQuillans of the Route 29, 63, 87
MacRory, Cardinal Joseph 374, 457–8
MacRory family 29
MacShane, Andrew 187
McShanes 237
MacSheehy family 29
McSkimin, Samuel 253–4
McSparran, J. D. 397
MacSweeney, Maire 68
MacSweeney, Maolmhuire 89, 94–5
MacSweeney, Miles 114
MacSweeney family 29, 36–7, 45, 63, 89, 92, 138
McVeagh, Fergus 176
MacVeagh, Jeremiah 299
Madden, R. R. 254, 256
Mag Aonghusa 19
Mageean, Daniel, bishop of Down and Connor 382–3, 394, 458, 470
Magee College, Derry 409
Magennis, Revd Bernard 255, 258
Magennis, Bonaventure, bishop of Down and Connor 72–3
Magennis, Brian Oge McRory 113
Magennis, Edmund Oge 115, 116
Magennis, Ever 113
Magennis, John 237, 238, 248, 255, 256–7, 257–8
Magennis, Phelimy 113

Magennis family 19, 26, 36, 40, 49, 60, 87, 94, 116, 187, 188
Magennis family of Clanconnel 116
Magennis family of Iveagh 34, 50, 98, 110, 113, 117, 138
Magennis family of Kilwarlin 113
Magennis family of Tollymore 130–31
Maghera, Co. Derry 251
Magherally, Co. Down 218–19
magic, Catholicism and 286–90
Magill, Revd Robert 261
Magin, Nicholas 253
Maginn, Edward, bishop of Derry 272, 359
Maginn, Revd Patrick 113
magistrates
    Orangeism 345–6, 350
    Protestant 327
    stipendiary 343, 345
Magroarty, Revd John 365
Mag Uidir 19
Maguire, Brian 90, 95, 116
Maguire, Bryan 193
Maguire, Conor Rua 89
Maguire, Constantine 237
Maguire, Cú Chonnacht 116
Maguire, Denis, bishop of Dromore 193, 208
Maguire, Hugh 52
Maguire, Hugh O'Dugan 156
Maguire, Philip 237
Maguire, Terence 237
Maguire family 19, 29, 40, 64, 65, 110, 188, 193, 208
    and Anglo-Normans 26
    decline 97
    Flight (1607) 54
    genealogy 45–6
    land 40, 90
    and 1641 Rebellion 98
    as turncoats 158–9
Malan, Rian 438
Mallon, Seamus 477
Mandeville family 86–7, 346
manuscripts, Gaelic 76, 79

maps, making 52
marches, anti-internment 421
    see also parades
marching season
    community relations and 346–7, 349–51
    see also parades
Markethill, Co. Armagh 225
Markets, Belfast 326
Marlborough Street College, Dublin 463
marriage
    to close relatives 65, 173
    delayed 317
    religion and 436
    see also mixed marriage
martial law (1797–8) 247, 251, 253
martyrs 13
Mary, Virgin 154
    devotion to 70, 286
    as ideal 204
    politicisation 157
    portrayal 64, 67
mass
    attendance at 201, 474
    in vernacular 469
Massarene, Sir John Clotworthy, Lord 99, 114
Massarene family 109
mass-houses 166, 199, 200
mass-rocks 164, 174, 199, 200, 201, 447, 469
Mater Infirmorum hospital, Belfast 283
    Craigavon and 397
    funding 464–5
    Prince of Wales visits 400
    state funding 407
Maynooth, St Patrick's seminary 209, 248, 284, 433
meat, eaten on Fridays 310, 316
Meath diocese 60
Medb, Queen of Connachta 5
media 41, 440
    Catholic, repressive culture 467
    nationalist 445–6, 447

and peace process 445
meeting-houses, early 200
Mellifont, Treaty of (1603) 53
mendicant friars 62–4
mensal lands 38
mercenaries 25, 28, 30
    Scottish 28–30
    see also gallowglasses
Mesolithic Ulster 3
Methodists 171, 229, 339
Middle Ages 18
middle class
    culture of 284
    Presbyterian 232
middle class, Catholic 192–4, 243
    in Belfast xxvi, 322, 323
    in civil-rights movement 465
    18th-century 187, 228
    leadership 265
    19th-century 327
    prejudice encountered 479
    and prophecies 250
    and republicans 442
middlemen 95, 187
Mide, province 8
Midgley, Harry 407, 461
Midnight Mass, The (Carleton) 208
migration, seasonal 315–17
Milesian origin-myth 16, 137
militarisation, medieval 25, 29
militia 242, 246, 247, 260–61, 264
millenarianism 249
Miller, Glenn 404
Millfield, Belfast 353, 355
Milltown cemetery, Belfast 283
Mindzenty, Cardinal 469
Minority Rights Group 395
Mise Éire (film) 443
missions, Catholic 280, 286
Mitchel, John 311, 312
mixed marriage 340–41, 435–6,
    439, 475
    Catholic Church and 341, 435,
    475
    Catholics and 440
    18th-century 179

intimidation and 355
Protestants and 341, 435
sectarian violence and 394
    17th-century 130–31
mobility, Gaelic 30–31, 32, 33, 34,
    35, 86
Modest Proposal (Swift) 186
Moira, Francis Rawdon, 2nd earl
    226, 247
Molyneux, Thomas 196
Monaghan county xli, 19
    Cromwellian descendants 185
    excluded from Plantation 89, 91
    Famine 305, 307
    freeholders 88–9
    Gaelic land-holding system 120
    Home Rule 297
    militia 247
    and Partition xlii–xliii
    1798 rebellion 257
    sectarian incidents 347–8
    succession disputes 51, 52
    troubles (1790s) 225
Monaghan town 181, 336, 364
monarchy, Catholic support 400
monasteries
    buildings 31, 60, 62
    decline 59–60, 61
    dissolution 61, 62, 69
    land gifted 43–4
    and learning 75
    new orders 59–60, 61
    priorities 20
    as social centres 14
    succession within 14
    Viking raids 16–17
money economy 53
Montgomery, George, bishop 73
Montgomery, Revd Henry 233
Montgomery, Sir Hugh 87, 88
Montgomery, Sir James 102
Montgomery of Ards, Viscount 107
Mooney, Canice 64
Mooney, Donatus 71–2
Moore, Brian 448, 467–8
Moore, Thomas 46, 47, 285

Moran, D. P. 366
Morgan, Lady 197
Morris, Henry 240
Moryson, Fynes 33
'Mother and Child Scheme' 464
mountain people, and government
    234–5
Mountjoy, Charles Blount, 8th
    baron 54, 145
Mount Stewart, Co. Down 309
Mourne Mountains, Co. Down 102
Movilla, Co. Donegal 15, 16
Mulholland, Thomas 226
Mulholland's mill, Belfast 322–3
Mullins, Mrs 353
Munro, Henry 252, 255–6, 257,
    258
Munster 85, 133, 135
murders, sectarian 422, 435, 438
Murney, George 329
Murphy, Dervla 416, 431
Murphy, Michael J. 38, 158, 159,
    310, 368, 369
Murphys of Monaghan 188
Murray, Daniel, archbishop of
    Dublin 278
Murray, Revd Raymond 472
Musgrave, Sir Richard 253
music, sectarian 223, 358

names
    anglicisation 157–8
    Gaelic forms 455
Naoise 5
Nation, The 364
national anthem, Catholics and 400
National Association of Ireland 293
National Health Service 464–5
nationalism
    ascetic, pious 454, 455
    battle hymn 125–6
    Catholicism and 83, 450–51, 457,
        478
    clergy and 292, 293, 295–6
    constitutional 292–3, 299, 300,
        444

development 83, 351–2, 363
early 291, 294
politics (1970–99) 422–8
post-1921 373, 377, 383
as rebellious 344
romantic 367–8, 399, 443–4,
    445, 449
secular 295–6
and Stormont 396–402
nationalists
    abstentionism 396, 397
    Catholic disillusionment with 401
    division in elections 449
    in government 424–5
    and Irish Republic 399
    meeting (1916) 297–8
    middle-class takeover 397–8
    need to belong 399
    and oath of allegiance 400–401
    secular identity 160
    self-confidence 481
    self-examination 480
    southern 299, 300
    in Stormont 396–7
    and unity 481
    Westminster election (1955) 401
National schools 277–8, 281, 337,
    340, 368
Navan Fort
    see Emain Macha
Ned McKeown (Carleton) 183
neighbourliness 126, 339
Neilson, James 181
Nendrum, Co. Down 14
Neolithic Ulster 3
Ne Temere papal decree (1907) 341,
    435
Newell, Edward 247
New English 28, 46, 69
New Ireland Forum (1983–4) 427,
    450, 478
New Irish Army 99, 101
'New Light' Presbyterians 229
New Lodge, Belfast 326
Newry, Co. Down 181, 244, 326,
    379, 388

Newry Register 363
newspapers
  separate 448
  see also media
New Testament 67
Newtownards, Co. Down 307
Newtownards Independent 312
Newtownbutler, Co. Fermanagh
  391
Niall of the Nine Hostages 10
NICRA
  see Northern Ireland Civil Rights
  Association
Nine Years War (1593–1603) 32,
  37, 43, 53, 54, 59, 86, 87
Nixon, D.-I. J. W. 375
no-go areas, Catholic 471
nomadism, Gaelic
  see mobility
Normans 14
Northern Ireland, use of term xxxiii
Northern Ireland Assembly (1973)
  424–6
Northern Ireland Assembly (1999)
  454
Northern Ireland Civil Rights
  Association (NICRA) 412–14,
  419, 423
Northern Ireland Conservative Party
  433
Northern Ireland Labour Party 398,
  420
Northern Ireland Office 424
Northern Ireland state
  boundaries 373, 379
  Catholic Church and 470–71,
    472, 473
  Catholic minority 300, 373, 379
  Catholic ownership 384, 476,
    481
  Catholics and 384, 395, 396, 398,
    399, 402, 409, 458
  discrimination in 384–94
  foundation (1921) 300, 373,
    374
  'in danger' 379

nationalist recognition 373, 376,
  383, 423
sectarian pronouncements 389
Unionist domination 386
Northern Irish parliament
  see Stormont
Northern Star newspaper 230,
  231–2, 242, 250
novitiates, reopening 209
Nugent, Major-General George 253,
  256, 261
nuns 155
  and Church 476
  introduction 281, 283, 356
  modern role 474, 476
nursery schemes, Catholic Church
  and 464

Oakboys 217–18
oath of allegiance
  Catholics and 169, 189, 216–17,
    248
  Nationalist Party and 400–401
oaths of abjuration 169
O'Boyle, Turlough 89
O'Boyle family 44, 65, 138
O'Brien, Conor Cruise 366, 367
Ó Bruadair (poet) 11
Ó Buachalla, Breandán 77
O'Cahan, Donal
  case against O'Neill 54, 55
  in Nine Years War 53
O'Cahan family 19, 26, 30, 32,
  37–8, 92, 94
O'Callaghan, Owen 237
O'Callaghan family 141, 188, 189,
  311
O'Carroll family 19
Ó Catháin family 19
Occasions of Faith (Taylor) 286
Ó Cerbaill family 19
O'Clery, Michael 75–6
O'Connell, Daniel 325, 328
  campaign 271–2, 279, 347
  clergy as agents 271, 292
  Protestants and 353

support 271–2, 276, 342, 344
O'Connellism 262
O Connor, Fionnuala 125, 399, 442, 446, 462, 467, 473
O'Corry family 65
O'Devany, Bishop of Down and Connor 69, 72
Ó Dochartaigh 19
O'Doherty, Sir Cahir 85
O'Doherty, Malachi 366, 367
O'Doherty, Rose 204
O'Doherty family 19
Ó Doibhlin, Revd Éamon 158
Ó Doirnín, Peadar 139, 203, 213, 214–15, 223
Ó Domhnaill, Aodh 314
Ó Domhnaill family 19
O'Donnell, Dominick 183
O'Donnell, General 188–9
O'Donnell, Manus 34
O'Donnell, Peadar 403
O'Donnell family 19, 33, 72, 193
   and friaries 63
   hereditary poets 75–6
   inauguration ceremonies 36, 37
   lands 94, 132–3
   marriages 28–9
   as priests 65, 132–3
   territorial dispute with O'Neill 41–2, 47
   see also Tyrconnell
O'Donnelly, Owen 150–51, 153
O'Donnelly, Shane McPhelimy 73
O'Donovan, John 353
O'Donovan Rossa, Jeremiah 443, 444
O'Dufferne, Patrick Groome 95
Offaly, plantation 85
Official IRA 402, 419, 421
   targeted by military 419
Ó Fiaich, Cardinal Tomás 140, 149, 473–4
O'Flynn family 26
Ó Gallachair, Revd P. 174
O'Gallagher, Owen 180
O'Gallagher, Tuathal Balbh 66

O'Gallagher family 65
'O Gentle Cleric' (Bennett) 364
Ogle, John 244–5
Ó Gnímh, Fear Flatha 96–7
Ó Gnímhs 29, 78
O'Grady, Standish 11
O'Hagan, Peter 427–8
O'Hagan family 32, 37–8, 41
O'Hanlon, Fergal 406, 444, 451
O'Hanlon, Hugh 255
O'Hanlon, Paddy 423
O'Hanlon, Redmond 119–20
O'Hanlon, Revd W. 323
O'Hanlon family 19, 26, 40, 49, 89, 227
O'Hara, Charles 189
O'Hara, Oliver 167
O'Hara family 95, 189
Ó hEódhasa, Eochaidh 48, 77–8
Ó Huiginn, Tadhg Dall 47
O'Kane, bishop of Derry 470
O'Laverty, Revd James 88, 130, 288, 319, 366
Old English 28, 46
   and compromise 147
   and freedom of conscience 147
   and land 100, 109, 120
   and loyalty 120
   O'Neill and 59
   outlawed 116
   and 1641 Rebellion 100, 102, 104
   status 113
   Tridentine Catholicism 71
   and Ulster Irish 100, 104
Old Irish 28
   and compromise 147
   and land 109, 120
   outlawed 116
   in Parliament 97
   as royal officials 97
Old Lodge, Belfast 358, 394
ollamhs 76, 77, 193
O'Loughran family 44, 65, 96
Omagh, Co. Tyrone 120, 315, 387
Ombudsman 411

Ó Muirgheasa, Énri 240, 286, 314, 342, 343
O'Neill, Aedh Reamhar 33
O'Neill, Art 369
O'Neill, Captain Art 118
O'Neill, Art McBaron 91
O'Neill, Brian Crossagh 95
O'Neill, Daniel of Clandeboye 113–14
O'Neill, Daniel of the Fews 188
O'Neill, Henry of Killeleagh 113
O'Neill, Sir Henry of the Fews 110
O'Neill, John 188, 237
O'Neill, Sir Neill of Killeleagh 116
O'Neill, Nelan 64
O'Neill, Niall Óg 47
O'Neill, Owen of Clandeboye 206
O'Neill, Owen Roe 91, 100, 134, 135, 136, 146
O'Neill, Sir Phelim 90, 100, 101, 103, 107, 108
O'Neill, Phelim (Felix Neel) 158
O'Neill, Shane 37, 43, 90
O'Neill, Sir Terence xxxvi, 392–3, 423
    Catholics and 384, 390, 411, 414, 416
    modernisation programme 409
    Paisley and 410–11, 415, 416
    reconciliation policy 407, 409, 410, 414
    resignation (1969) 401, 407–12, 414–16, 415, 425
    Unionist party and 409–11, 414, 415
O'Neill, Terence (Convention representative) 237
O'Neill, Turlough Luineach 34
O'Neill, Turlough MacHenry 89
O'Neill family 187, 193
    alliances against 49
    and Anglo-Normans 26, 27, 28
    and church lands 44
    declining branches 97
    earldom 50, 51
    and friaries 63
    inauguration 41
    land grants 89
    land loss 132–3
    and lineal succession 51
    lordship 31–2
    marriages 28–9
    as priests 132–3
    territorial dispute with O'Donnell 41–2, 47
    'the', use of 37
    and Ulaid dynasty 47, 49
    see also Tyrone, earls
O'Neill family of Antrim 189, 392
O'Neill family of Armagh 63, 188
O'Neill family of Banvale 188, 227
O'Neill family of Clandeboye 26, 27, 40, 49, 87, 130–31, 188
O'Neill family of Killeleagh 98
O'Neill family of the Fews 36, 40, 49, 89, 98, 138, 140, 188
O'Neill family of Tyrone 36, 37, 72
Ó Néills, emergence 19
On the prophecy of Colum Cille son of Phelim (MacDonnell) 276
Opsahl, Torkel xliii
Opsahl Commission xliii, 83, 384, 432, 434–5, 476, 478
O'Rahilly, Cecile 133
O'Rahilly, T. F. 4
Óráid (Pulleine) 206
Orangeism
    aggression 240, 244–5, 262, 325, 346–7
    Catholics and 264, 351
    gentry and 224
    growth 344
    as necessary evil 246
    Presbyterians and 351
    and 1798 rebellion 253–4
    revival (1880s) 352
    and state apparatus 264, 266
    United Irishmen and 251
    working class and 264
'Orangeman, The' (verse) 343
Orange Order
    and Catholic employment 391–2

Glaswegians in 393
Grand Lodge of Ireland 345
influence of 389
lower-class Presbyterians in 229
and mixed marriage 341
parliamentary enquiry (1835) 275
temporary dissolution (1836–40)
    265
and tenant right 320
United Irishmen join 262
Ordnance Survey Memoirs 281, 284
O'Reilly, archbishop of Armagh 248
O'Reilly, Daniel 208
O'Reilly, Edmund, archbishop of
    Armagh 148, 150
O'Reilly, Revd Michael 181
O'Reilly, Michael, archbishop of
    Armagh 203–4, 206, 208, 209
O'Reilly, Miles 101
O'Reilly, Philip 101, 109, 208
O'Reilly, Revd Tom 329
O'Reilly family 26, 50, 65, 90, 119,
    188
Oriel
    see Airgialla
Orior, Co. Armagh 91
Ormond, James Butler, 1st duke
    111, 114, 147, 148, 149
O'Rorke family 189
O'Rourke, Jack 452
Orr, James 259–60, 262
O'Shea, Kitty 295
O'Sheil, James, bishop of Down and
    Connor 137–8
'Oultachs' 192, 226
Our Boys magazine 367
outdoor relief strike (1932) 393
overlords
    curtailing power 117
    England and 86, 88
    and power 40

Paddy's Resource song collection
    232
paganism, Celtic 7, 8, 14–15, 20, 60
Paine, Thomas 239

Pairlement Chloinne Tomáis 97
Paisley, Revd Ian 410–11, 425, 440
    and O'Neill 410–11, 415, 416
Paisleyism 406, 413–15, 434
Pale 25, 29, 31, 34, 43, 85, 119
Papacy
    authority 209
    Catholic loyalty to 164
    dogmatism 351
    and politics 293
    popular devotion to 61
    temporal powers 146, 148, 209,
        270
papist, use of term 136, 141, 182,
    199
parades 223
    and sectarian riots 344–61
parades, Catholic 356, 360
parades, Orange 344–51
    banned (1832) 265, 325, 345,
        349, 352, 354, 356
    in Catholic areas 440–41
    challenged by Catholic youths
        348
    Conservative Government and
        420
    continuing effects 480
    18th-century 225
    as legitimate loyal display 344
    rights 356
    riots and 393–4
Parades Commission 476
paramilitaries, Loyalist 417–18
Parker, Edward 182
Parker, Tony 436
parliamentary elections 385, 397
Parnell, Charles Stewart 292,
    293–4, 295
Parnellism 367–8
parochial development 14
partible inheritance 39–40
partition
    Catholic hierarchy and 297–8,
        300–301
    IRA and 402
    south and 406

partnership leases 195, 197
Passionist order 281
pastoralism, Gaelic 30, 33, 35, 43, 86
Patrick, St 7, 12–14, 16, 21, 26, 64, 76, 457
patriotism, death and 443–4, 449
Patten Commission (1999) 431–2, 476
patterns 153, 286
peace, desire for 434
peace-lines 432
peace process, and meaning of Ulster 481
Pearse, Patrick 11, 299, 443–4, 449, 450
peasants 43, 285–8, 369
Peden, Alexander 249
Peep O'Day Boys 222, 223, 224, 225, 226, 240, 244, 245
penal laws 140, 165–77, 210
  added value 479
  enforcement 177
  evasion 174
  intention behind 173–4
  leases, length 174–5
  Mass legal under 447
  modern reading 164
  and property 167
  repeal 220
  severity 165
  traditional view 163–4, 174, 447, 469
penance, sacrament 201, 202
People's Democracy (PD) 414–15, 416–17
Perrot, Sir John 48
persecution 126, 143, 146–9, 149
  elite and 159
  republicanism and 447–8
personality, Ulster xxxiii
Peter's Hill, Belfast 355
Philbin, William, bishop of Down and Connor 470–71, 474
Phoenix, Eamon 398
Phoenix Park, Dublin 447, 470

physiognomy, and religious affiliation 361–2
Pioneer Total Abstinence Society 285
Pius IX, Pope 282
place, pride of 46, 480–81
Plantation xxxviii, xli, 43, 53, 84–97
  added value 479
  beneficiaries of 89–90, 91
  categories 91
  church lands in 96
  co-operation with 89, 91
  counties 91
  and Cromwellian confiscations 110
  and 'deserving Irish' 48, 73, 90–91
  initial welcome 86
  Irish majority in 92, 97
  land allotment 48, 73
  landlords as trustees 319
  land tenure 38, 41
  as mixed settlement 102
  as religious campaign 83
  and resentment 93–4
  and status 95–7
Plunkett family 188, 193
Plunkett, Oliver, archbishop of Armagh 118, 121, 132, 149, 151–5, 155
  execution 144–5
  and Franciscans 74, 144, 150, 151, 152, 153
  in hiding 150
  and Protestant authorities 151–2
  snobbishness 151
Pococke, Richard, Bishop of Ossory 188, 199–200, 218
poetry
  anti-clerical 203
  anti-English, anti-Scottish 133–5
  Irish 77, 126–7, 195, 274, 342–3
  Jacobitism 213–14
  and James I 77, 78
  proselytisers in 274–5
  religions, attributes in 183

religious 154
settlers insulted 135
Ulster 133, 135
poets
druids as 61
Gaelic 45–8
and preservation of tradition 46,
47–8, 49
role 36
and settlers 96–7
17th-century 133–43
status 96–7, 133
polite society, emergence 163
politics
denominational 294
electoral 294
religious polarisation 291
'poll' 42
Pooler, Revd L. A. 263
Poor Law Unions 308–9
Poor Scholar (Carleton) 197
popery
fear of 269, 271, 434, 435
loyalist view 449–50
penal laws and 168
as political system 168
as threat 352
population decline 30, 86, 306–7,
313
population growth 219, 341
Portadown, Co. Armagh 103, 104,
223, 326, 327, 346
Porter, Revd James 233
Portnaw 103–4
Portnorris 221, 222
potato, reliance on 305
Pound, Belfast 353, 355
poverty
Protestant 318, 323
rural 317, 318
power
clerical 365
overlordship and 40
as Protestant 159, 343, 363, 365
power-sharing 423, 424–6, 427,
428

Powis Commission (1868–70) 281
Poyntz Pass, Co. Armagh 399
PR
see proportional representation
Prehistoric Ulster 3–12
Presbyterianism xxxviii, xxxix
anti-Catholicism 132
evangelism 171
Home Mission 275
introduction in Ireland 256
persecution 126
radicalism 262
suspicion of government 230
varieties of 229
Presbyterians
and Black Oath 99
Catholic perceptions of 156, 228,
233, 263–4
and Catholic rights 238
Catholics, perception of 230–31
increase 131
and Irish language 368
loyalty 226–7
mobility 198
and Orangeism 351
in Orange Order 229
penal laws and 166
stereotype 314
teachers, training 463
and United Irishmen 229, 244
and unjust rule 146
voting pattern 291, 294
Price, Elizabeth 102
pride of place 46, 480–81
priests
see clergy
primary education 461–2
prisoners, republican
and Irish language 453
political status 448–9
prisoners, treatment 66
privilege, Protestant 324
professions
traditional 193–4
property
modern definition 159

prophecies 276
prophecy, ancient 249, 250–51
proportional representation (PR)
   373
   abolition 378, 385, 397
   Northern Ireland Assembly and
      424
proselytism, Protestant 272–7, 278,
   307, 309–11, 458, 460
Protestantism
   anti-popery 479
   Cardinal MacRory and 457–8
   civility and 59
   and clerical marriage 65
   European adoption 69
   and evil 210
   and Gaelic society 69
   as heretical 76
   and land-owning 108–9, 110–11,
      115
   and pagan survivals 21
   perceived materialism 183, 340
   'Second Reformation' 270, 272,
      275–6, 276–7, 282
   as test of loyalty 59
   textual tradition 130
   tithes 69
Protestants
   and Catholic neighbours 126
   Catholic perceptions of 156, 337,
      440, 446
   Catholics, perception of 83, 84,
      146, 170–71, 181–2, 210, 216,
      221, 230–31, 343, 417–18,
      434–5, 436–7
   collusion over penal laws 174
   and demographic change 435
   and early church 13
   evangelism 171–3, 272–7, 278
   in Famine 306, 308
   fear of Catholics 228, 352, 410
   fears for property 167–8, 170
   as foreign usurpers 363–4
   and friars 153
   and fundamentalist preachers
      353–6

Gaelic traditions 130
insecurity 481
and Irish history 479
and Irish language 368
land acquisition xxxviii, xli, 110
majority 131
and mixed marriage 341
nationality 128
and National schools 277
patronising attitude 433–4, 442
persecution 169
political identity 335
population decline 410
and 1641 Rebellion 99, 100–107
self-perception 434, 436–7
sincerity 128
Solemn League and Covenant 297
Special Powers Act invoked
   against 411
status 122
support for Catholics 174–5
unemployment 357, 361, 434
vulnerability 373, 379, 380
Protestant Telegraph 434
provinces 8–9, 17
Provisional IRA 410, 419
   border campaign 435
   British Army mistakes and 419,
      420–21
   Catholic Church and 471–2
   ceasefires 473
   constitutional nationalists and
      442
   damage in nationalist areas 478
   hunger-strikes (1981) 448–50,
      472, 473
   Official IRA, feud with 419
   recruitment 420–21
   and Ulster Workers' Strike 425–6
   war, claim of 448
public service, Catholics and 388
public services, Catholic
   employment in 378, 383, 388,
      389–91, 393, 460
public works, Famine and xl,
   308

Pulleine, James, dean of Dromore
204–5, 206
Pym, John 100

Quakers 312
Queen's Colleges 278–9
Queen's University, Belfast
xxxvii
student protests (1968–9) 413–15
Quigley family 188
Quin family 193
Quinn, Mary 142

radio stations, southern 438–9
Rafroidi, Patrick 11
Randalstown, Co. Antrim 253
Raphoe, Co. Donegal 180
Raphoe diocese 60
rapparees 118–20, 195, 196
rate-in-aid scheme 308–9
Rathcoole estate, Belfast 449
Rathfriland, Co. Down 244,
349–51
Rathlin Island 30, 104, 375, 376
raths 6–7, 14
as fairy forts 290
Reading in the Dark (Deane) 477
Rebellion
1541 (Shane O'Neill's) 43, 51
1595 (Tyrone's) 51
1641 89, 90, 94, 97–107, 132,
156, 164
in popular tradition 83, 101,
103, 106
1798
aftermath 261–7
Catholic clergy in 248, 261
executions 260–61
leadership, middle-class 265
religious dissension within
253–4
rumoured Catholic desertions
256–7, 258, 263
southern rising 262, 263
timing 255
in Ulster 249–61

1803 (Emmet's) 264
recusancy fines 69, 99
Redemptorist order 281
Redmond, John 295, 297, 298
Rees, Merlyn 426
Reformation 13, 52, 61, 68–70,
130
regionalism, intense 135
Reid, Revd Alex 472–3
Reilly, Daniel 187
Reily, Hugh 128–9, 170
religion
admitting to 431
ascertaining 437–8
elite 160
external features 361–2, 437–8
fluidity of affiliation 130–31
physical characterics 361–2, 431
popular 160
transformed into culture 478–9
religious affiliation, ascertaining
361–2, 437–8
religious education 458
religious orders, introduction 281,
283
Reliques of Irish Poetry (Brooke)
232
'Remonstrance' (1661) 147, 148,
149
Remonstrance (Jones) 105
rents 94, 218
Report on the State of Popery
(1731) 180
Republic, Irish
Catholic revisionism 475
declaration (1948) 398
nationalism 479–80
need for involvement 424, 425,
427
and Northern Catholics 399
Protestant population 435
school funding 462
republicanism
clergy and 300
militant 299, 300
rural, Plantation and 84

Restoration (1660) 143
  land settlement 111–14, 147
Ribbonmen 241, 296, 311, 325,
  335, 347, 348, 349–50, 353
Richardson, John 171
Rich Hill, Co. Armagh 226
rights, natural 227
Rights of Man (Paine) 231
ring-forts 6–7
Rinuccini, Giovanni Battista,
  Archbishop 100, 134, 146, 147,
  148, 150
riot, sectarian 218, 324, 325,
  344–51, 353–6, 357–8, 374,
  375, 392, 393–4, 420
Ripley Bogle (Wilson) 478
'Robbery Cut' 177
Rochefort, Jouvin de 155
Roden, Earls of 183, 350
Rodgers, W. R. 439
'Roman' Catholic, use of term 168,
  362
romantic nationalism 367–8, 399,
  443–4, 445, 449
Rome, early Church and 13–14
rosary, devotion to 284, 287, 403,
  451
Rose, Richard 395, 409, 441, 474
Ross, William 329
Rossmore, Henry Robert Westenra,
  3rd baron 364
Route, The, Co. Antrim 29, 87
Royal Belfast Academical Institution
  279
Royal Irish Constabulary (RIC)
  343, 345, 357, 360–61, 374,
  375, 380
Royal Ulster Constabulary (RUC)
  Catholic perception of 380
  Catholics in 376, 380, 381
  demoralisation 418
  disarmed (1970) 419
  Patten Report and 431–2
  proposed reorganisation (1922)
    376–7, 379–80
  reforms 476

sectarianism 375, 377, 415–16
  and student marches (1968–9)
    414, 415
rundale system 317
rural conditions, improvement 317
rural values, as ideal 455
Rushe, D. C. 362
Russell, Revd Matthew 285
Russell, Patrick 114, 187
Russell, Thomas 176, 234, 252, 264
Russell family 27, 86–7, 116
Ryan, John 413

Saintfield, Co. Down 235, 255
St Leger, Anthony, Lord Deputy
  41–2
St Malachy's College, Belfast 328,
  343, 408, 467
St Mary's Christian Brothers School,
  Belfast 460
St Mary's Strawberry Hill,
  Twickenham 463, 464
St Mary's Training College, Belfast
  463
St Matthew's church, Ballymacarrett
  375
St Patrick's Well, Inishowen 286
St Peter's pro-Cathedral, Belfast 284
saints 14–15
  as familial figures 21, 64, 66, 78
  local importance 64, 66, 76, 286
  relics 64, 283, 286
St Vincent de Paul Society 328, 464,
  469
Sands, Bobby 448–9
Sandy Row, Belfast 325, 353, 354,
  355, 357, 452
Saoirse (film) 443
Savage, Hugh 237
Savage, Thomas 237
Savage family 27, 34, 63, 86–7,
  114, 116, 130–31, 187, 188,
  189
Scarman Tribunal (1972) 383
scholars 89, 90–91, 96, 231
schools

see elementary; grammar;
    National; primary; secondary
see also education
Scotland 86, 315–16
Scots settlers xxxix, 28–30, 88, 121,
    128, 129, 131
Scullabogue massacre (1798) 252,
    261
Scullion, Phelix 200
Seceders 229
secondary schools 462–3
'Second Reformation' 270, 272,
    275–6, 276–7, 282
sectarian conflict
    pre-Famine 275–6
    19th-century 338
    1920s 374
    1935 392, 393–4
    1969- 415, 418–19, 420, 421
sectarian polarisation 251
security forces
    in anti-Catholic riots 375
    and Catholics 444, 450
    Protestants and 450
    see also British Army; Royal
        Ulster Constabulary
segregation 432
    in education 459–64
Senchas Már 15
septs 39, 42, 49
settlers 121
    Anglo-Norman xli
    and cultural seepage 131
    English 27
    influx after Plantation 43
    New English 55
    and 1641 Rebellion 101–7
    and resentment 93–4
    and toryism 119
    Tudor 28
    see also Plantation; Scots settlers
Shake Hands with the Devil (film)
    443
Shanaghan, Daniel 244
Shane Fadh's Wedding (Carleton)
    208

Shane's Castle, Randalstown 392
Shankill Rd, Belfast 353, 355, 357,
    358, 404, 418, 420, 452
Shannon valley 8
Shea, Patrick 378, 379, 382, 388,
    389–91, 409, 433
Shewie, Co. Armagh 103
shiring, Ulster (1585) 50
Simms, Katharine 65, 126–7
Simms, Robert 254
Sinn Féin 296, 476
    abstentionism 299–300
    Catholic Church and 466, 474
    Catholic support 427, 450, 457
    elections (1918) 299
    emergence 426
    hunger strikes (1981) 426–7
    and integrated education 459
    and Irish language 453
    and landscape 11–12
    strategy 427
    success 426
    Westminster election (1955) 401
Síogaí Rómhánach, An 133–5, 140,
    215
Sisters of Mercy 281, 464
Six Counties, use of term
    xxxiii–xxxiv
Slieve Gullion, Sinn Féin and 11–12
Small Differences (Akenson) 341
Smaointe beatha Chríost 67
Smith family 86–7
Smithfield, Belfast 324, 325, 326
social class 327–31
Social Democratic and Labour Party
    (SDLP) 422–8, 476
    and consensual unity 423
    as dominant Nationalist party
        424, 427, 428
    in government 424–5
    and Irish Republic 427
    Sinn Féin and 426, 427, 450
    Unionist party and 426
socialism
    Catholicism and 328, 454, 464
    and sectarianism 331

soldiers
  Continental enlistment 92,
    117–18, 192–3
  land settlement 108, 109–10
  recruitment, geography 118
  see also British Army; mercenaries
Solemn League and Covenant 297
'souperism' 273, 309–10, 311, 312
soup kitchens 309–10, 311, 312
South, Sean 405, 444, 451
Spain 59, 193
Spender, Sir Wilfred 390
Spenser, Edmund 34, 39, 43, 46
Sperrin mountains 32, 118, 195,
  305
sport, nationalism in 455
Springfield Rd, Belfast 418
Stanhope St, Belfast 377
state schools 439
station masses 202, 282
status
  declining 37–8, 38–9, 40, 50
  Irish language and 191
  land and 55, 84, 95
  lineage and 39–40, 95
  Plantation and 95–7
  traditional Irish concept 117
stereotypes xxxv–xxxvii, 432–40
  Catholic 228, 231, 238
  Elizabethan 361
  influence on behaviour 432–3
  Irish 456
  1641 Rebellion and 127
  reinforcing 439
  1790s 261
Stewart, Joe 397
Stewartstown, Co. Tyrone 246
Story, George 120
Stormont parliament 399–400
  Catholic chaplain 471
  Catholics employed at 389
  Irish premiers' visits 409, 410
  Nationalist politics and 383,
    396–400
  nationalist politics and 457
  suspended (1972) 422

  as Unionist symbol 400
Story of Ireland (Sullivan) 313
Strabane, Claud Hamilton, Lord
  114
Strabane, Co. Tyrone 86, 181, 315,
  326
Strafford, Thomas Wentworth, earl
  88, 92, 98–9, 101
Strangford Lough 3, 27, 28
Stranmillis College, Belfast 463–4
street-rhymes, sectarian 439
Stuart, James 362
Stuart monarchs 33, 77, 111–14,
  134, 199, 214
subsistence farming 195–7, 317
succession
  disputes 39, 51, 52
  Gaelic 40, 50
  lineal 51
suffering, Catholic tradition of
  468–9
Sullivan, A. M. 313
Sunday school, mixed 181, 277
Sunday Times 417
Sunningdale Agreement (1973) 377,
  424, 426
supernatural, Catholicism and
  286–90
superstition
  Catholicism and 207, 208,
    286–90
  Protestantism and 288
surnames 19
surrender and regrant 40, 50, 51,
  52, 53, 92
Sussex, Lord Deputy (Thomas
  Radcliffe, earl) 66, 69
Swanlinbar, Co. Cavan 329
Sweden 118
Swift, Jonathan 186
Syllabus of Errors (1864) 330
Synge, Edward 166
Synod of Thurles (1850) 279, 282

Taaffe, Revd Lawrence 142
Taaffe family 189

Tagra an dá Theampall (MacCooey) 141, 143
Táin Bó Cuailnge 5, 7, 9–10, 139
Tametsi papal decree 179
Tanderagee, Co. Armagh 223, 346, 347
Tara, Kings of 8
'tate' 42
taxes, collecting 218
Taylor, Lawrence 286, 365
teachers
  Catholic 327, 396
  paid from Dublin 461
  and state 396
  trade unionism among 328
  training 460, 463–4
Teeling, Bartholomew 237, 238, 244, 248, 255
Teeling, Charles 230, 237, 241, 243, 244, 248, 254, 257
Teeling, Luke 189, 236, 237, 265–6
Teeling family 187, 189, 244, 248
Temple, Sir John 105–6, 115, 170
Templepatrick, Co. Antrim 102, 104
tenant-right campaign (1850s) 318–21, 339
tenants
  Catholic 175, 185
  Cromwellian 130–31
  independence 217
  Irish 93–4
  Presbyterian 178, 318
  Protestant 159, 175, 194
  religion 128
  rights 318–21, 339
  security 27, 185
  shortage 121
  status 40
  sub-tenancies 131
tenants-at-will 38–9
Teresa, Mother 466
Termonagurk, Co. Tyrone 44
termon families 152
termon lands 43–5, 96

territory, religion and 195
textile industry 321–3, 394
Thackeray, W. M. 322–3
Thatcher, Margaret 448, 449
Thomas the Rhymer 249
Thompson, James 256
thorn trees 290
Three Tasks, The (Carleton) 181
Tipperary county 109
tithe war (1830–33) 345
Tohill, Revd John 343
Tóibín, Colm 315
tolerance, religious 99, 126
tombstones, survey of 193
Tone, Theobald Wolfe 168, 188, 228–9, 235, 237, 366, 367, 450
Toole, John 189
topography xxxix–xlii
  and Celtic myth 11–12
  and mobility 30, 31
  shaping history 28, 34–5
tories 92, 118–20, 139, 176, 195, 196
tower houses 32
townlands 41, 42
transhumance 35, 36, 86
transitional poets 136
Treaty of Limerick (1691) 165, 169, 175
trees, magical 290
Trew, Revd 326
tricolour, usage 454–5
Tridentine Catholicism 70–71, 75, 149, 151, 199, 202, 203
Trinity College Dublin 91, 105, 129
triumphalism, Catholic 114, 283, 325, 363, 481
Troubles (1969–) 416–22
  Catholic Church and 470–81
  deaths 418, 421–2
  Plantation and 84
Troy, Thomas, archbishop of Dublin 209, 230
tuatha 5–6, 8, 15, 17, 18, 19, 38

Tudor monarchy
  civilising mission 33
  and Gaelic revival 75
  land laws 25
  and overlords 88–9
Tullahoge inauguration site 36, 37,
  41, 51
turncoats 157–9, 273, 309–10, 311
Turner, Samuel 238, 259, 262
Twinbrook estate, Belfast 449
Tynan, Co. Armagh 96
Tyrconnell, Richard Talbot, earl of
  114, 115
Tyrconnell, Ruari O'Donnell, earl of
  54
Tyrconnell earls 51, 53, 74
Tyrone, Conn O'Neill, earl of
  hereditary title 51
  lands, loss 87, 88, 94
  overlordship of Ulster 47
  secrecy 35
Tyrone, Hugh O'Neill, 2nd earl 3
  appeals for return from Pale 43
  and churls 84
  and England 51, 52
  flight abroad (1607) 54, 94
  freehold granted 53
  inauguration 51
  James I and 77
  Jesuits and 71
  lands 40
  lineage expansion 53–4
  O'Cahan's case 54, 55
  in popular tradition 134, 135
  and religion 59, 77
  Tudor support 50
Tyrone county 10
  bog xli
  Boundary Commission and 379
  Church of Ireland 277
  Cromwellian confiscations 109
  dynastic instability 51
  elections 386
  fairies, belief in 289
  Famine 305, 307
  IRA activity 406

local councils 373
lordship 51, 53
O'Neill lands 40
Plantation 91
religious demography xlii
Scots Catholic tenants 128
tories 118
troubles (1790s) 225
United Irishmen 246
Volunteers 221

Uí Echach Cobo 10, 49
Uí Néill 9, 10, 13–14, 16, 17, 18,
  19
Uisliu 5
Uí Thuirtri 18, 26
Ulaid 4–6, 7–10, 14, 15, 16, 18, 47,
  49
Ulidian Tales
  see Ulster Cycle
Ullans 128, 454
Ulster
  boundary 8–9
  east xxxix–xl, 28
  and Leinster, animosity 248
  north-west xli
  pride in 366–7
  as Protestant 121
  south xl, 117
  south-west 118
  topography xxxix–xliii
  use of term xx, 445–6, 481
Ulster Custom 318
Ulster Cycle 4–5, 7–8, 9, 10, 11, 12,
  290
Ulster Examiner 291
Ulster Herald 448
Ulster Irish
  alliances 100
  literacy 130
  Old English and 100, 104
  and settlers 101
  17th-century 117–22
  social leadership 94
Ulster Office 95, 193, 235, 236,
  238

Ulster Protestant Action 410
Ulster Protestant Association 380
Ulster Protestant League 393
Ulster-Scots dialect 128, 454
Ulster Special Constabulary (USC) 373, 380–81, 381–2, 415–16
Ulster Volunteer Force (UVF) 297, 380
Ulster Workers' Strike (1974) 425–6
'Ultach' (J. J. Campbell) 391, 392, 394, 395, 436
Ultach Trust 453
ultramontanism 148, 215, 279
undertakers, Plantation 88, 91
under-tenants 43
unemployment
    industry and 408
    1960s 411
    Protestant 417–18
    religion and 387, 434
Unigenitus (papal bull) 215–16
Union flag 400, 457, 460, 481
Unionist party
    and Boundary Commission 379
    Catholic mistrust 416
    Catholics, perception of 383–4
    Catholic support 409, 416
    and Conservative party 300
    and Council of Ireland 425
    and Home Rule 297, 298
    militant support 381, 384
    Orangeism 352, 384, 389, 391, 393
    patronising attitude 433–4, 442
    and SDLP 426
    splinter groups 425
United Irishmen 106, 184, 225, 342
    aims 231
    and Armagh outrages 226
    assassination committee 247
    Catholic Committee and 190
    Catholics in 229, 246, 248, 254–5, 259, 261
    defections 256–7, 258, 259, 263

    and Defenders 230, 237, 244–9, 253, 254, 265
    and education of public opinion 227, 235
    foundation 213
    leadership 255
    and oath of allegiance 249
    Pearse and 443
    Presbyterians in 254, 256, 258–9, 262–3
    propertied supporters 258, 259
    publications 231–3, 250
    1798 rebellion 249–61
    satire 231, 232–3
    songs 231, 232, 233–4
    tactics, early success 234
United States 425
unity, as aspiration 481
urbanisation
    increasing 284, 321
    18th-century 187
Ussher, James, archbishop of Armagh 76

values, inherited 444–5
Vatican II, Council 467, 469, 471, 476
victimhood
    Catholic 384–5, 480–81
    egoism of 441–2
    IRA and 441–2
    Protestant 363
    traditions of xxxvi–xxxix, 206, 362–3
Vikings 16–17, 75
violence
    ambivalence about 449–50
    Catholic Church and 449, 451, 471, 472–3, 475
    Catholics and 441
    demography of 478
    medieval 40, 55
    republican 481
Volunteers 220–23, 230
vulnerability, Protestant 373, 379, 380

Wales, Edward, Prince of 400
Walker, Brian 318
Walker, Revd George 359
Walker, William 330
'Walking the Dog' (MacLaverty)
    438
Walsh, Peter 148, 149
Ward, Hugh 75, 76
Warden, David Bailie 254, 255,
    256, 258
Waring, William 115, 116
War of the Revolution (1688) 225
Watson, William 328–9
wealth
    modern definition 159
    sectarian division xli
weapons decommissioning 481
wedding customs 182
welfare societies, Catholic 464
welfare state 405, 407, 433, 464,
    465
West, Harry 425
Western Isles 28, 29, 30, 88
Westminster election (1955) 401
Westmorland, Lord (John Fane,
    10th earl) 168
Whigs, and Catholic emancipation
    228–9
whiskey, illicit 218
White, Rowland 115
Whiteboys 174
White City, Belfast xxxv
White/Whyte family 27, 29, 86–7,
    116, 188
Whyte, General 243
Whyte, John 385, 386, 387, 460

Willes, Chief Baron 196
William III, King 137, 138, 144,
    222
Williamite land settlement 115–17
Wilson, Harold 408, 426
Wilson, Paddy 423
Wilson, Robert McLiam 478
Wilson, Robin xliii
Wilson, Sammy 437
witchcraft 289
women
    employment 464
    evangelism 311
    in textile industry 322
woodkerne
    see kerne
work ethic 128, 387
workhouses 308, 309, 311–12
working class
    Catholic 457, 474
    Orangeism 356–7
    Protestant 342, 347, 384, 408,
        422, 433–4
World War I (1914–18) 189, 297
World War II (1939–45) 402,
    403–4
Worrall, Stanley 459
Wright, Frank 258, 308
Wyse, A. N. Bonaparte 391

Yeats, W. B. 11
yeomanry 245, 262, 263, 264, 345
York St, Belfast 358, 394
Young, Arthur 165, 166, 192, 305
Young, Revd Henry 273–4
YP pools 465